How to Use the Maps in *Culture and Values: A Survey of the Humanities, Seventh Edition*

Here are some basic map concepts that will help you to get the most out of the maps in this textbook.

◆ Always look at the scale, which allows you to determine the distance in miles or kilometers between locations on the map.

◆ If the map has a legend, examine it carefully. It explains the colors and symbols used on the map.

◆ Note the locations of mountains, rivers, oceans, and other geographic features, and consider how these would affect such human activities as agriculture, commerce, travel, and warfare.

CULTURE
AND VALUES

CULTURE AND VALUES

A SURVEY OF THE HUMANITIES

SEVENTH EDITION

LAWRENCE S. CUNNINGHAM
John A. O'Brien Professor of Theology
University of Notre Dame

JOHN J. REICH
Syracuse University
Florence, Italy

WADSWORTH
CENGAGE Learning·

Australia • Brazil • Japan • Korea • Mexico • Singapore • Spain • United Kingdom • United States

Culture and Values: A Survey of the Humanities, Seventh Edition
Lawrence S. Cunningham, John J. Reich

Publisher: Clark Baxter

Assistant Editor: Kimberly Apfelbaum

Senior Technology Project Manager: Wendy Constantine

Marketing Manager: Diane Wenckebach

Marketing Assistant: Lorreen Pelletier

Marketing Communications Manager: Heather Baxley

Senior Project Manager, Editorial Production: Lianne Ames

Senior Art Director: Cate Barr

Senior Manufacturing Buyer: Karen Hunt

Permissions Editor: Timothy Sisler

Text Researcher: Elaine Kosta

Production Service: Lachina Publishing Services

Text Designer: Lee Anne Dollison

Photo Manager: Amanda Groszko

Photo Researcher: Abigail Baxter

Cover Designer: Lee Anne Dollison

Cover Image: Mathias Gruenewald (1455-1528), *Allegory of the Nativity*, left side with concert of the angels. From the Isenheim Altarpiece. Ca. 1515. Limewood. Musée d'Unterlinden, Colmar, France. Image © Scala/Art Resource, NY

Compositor: Lachina Publishing Services

For product information and technology assistance, contact us at
Cengage Learning Academic Resource Center, 1-800-423-0563
For permission to use material from this text or product,
submit all requests online at **www.cengage.com/permissions**
Further permissions questions can be emailed to
permissionrequest@cengage.com

Library of Congress Control Number: 2008938413

ISBN-13: 978-0-495-56877-3

ISBN-10: 0-495-56877-5

Wadsworth
25 Thomson Place
Boston, MA 02210-1202
USA

Cengage Learning products are represented in Canada by Nelson Education, Ltd.

For your course and learning solutions, visit **www.cengage.com**

Purchase any of our products at your local college store or at our preferred online store **www.ichapters.com**

Printed in the United States of America
3 4 5 6 7   12 11

CONTENTS

LISTENING CD SELECTIONS

It is now over twenty-five years since we finished the manuscript that would become this textbook. In the various additions, updating, and rewriting that constitute the various editions of *Culture and Values,* we have not modified our earliest convictions about what this book should represent. Our desire is to present, in a chronological fashion, the most crucial landmarks of Western and non-Western cultures with clarity and in such a way that students might react to these traditions and their major accomplishments as enthusiastically as we did when we first encountered them and began to teach about them.

We believe that our own backgrounds have enhanced our appreciation for what we discuss in these pages. Lawrence Cunningham has degrees in philosophy, theology, literature, and humanities, while John Reich is a trained classicist, musician, and field archaeologist. Both of us have lived and lectured for extended periods in Europe. There is very little art or architecture, especially Western art and architecture, in this book that we have not seen firsthand.

In developing the new editions of *Culture and Values,* we have been the beneficiaries of the suggestions and criticisms of classroom teachers who have used the book. The seventh edition incorporates the helpful suggestions of our reviewers, critics, and the many instructors who have noted the increasingly multicultural character of the world in which we live. We have also consulted closely with the editorial team at Cengage Learning. Our own experiences as teachers both here and abroad have also made us sensitive to new needs and refinements as we rework this book.

THE SEVENTH EDITION

In this new edition we have made a number of changes. To help students understand the spirit of each period under discussion, we have added vignettes to open the chapters. We have expanded the discussion of music to address and better integrate into the text discussion each selection included on the LISTENING CD. We have brought the final chapter up to date and have continued to reflect the retrieval of women's voices in the history of Western culture. We have added thumbnails of many significant images to the timelines to help students understand each major period, and we have expanded the Glossary at the back of the book to include pronunciations of key terms, important people, and places. We have replaced many of the images to show new

examples of the art and architecture from Western civilization and around the world.

World Coverage. Newer and ever-expanding information technologies as well as the emergence of a global sociopolitical economy are beginning to render the focus on a purely occidental culture somewhat skewed. Think, for example, of the globalization of popular music. Our aim, however, remains to help students master this sprawling and untidy subject as easily as possible. To that end, our many readers have urged us to retain an organization that covers the West in chronological order and in some detail. These same instructors have, however, expressed an interest in seeing more global coverage of the humanities. Under their guidance and review, three full chapters covering Asian and African cultures appear in the book, and the treatment of Islamic culture remains a full chapter. In each case, the presentation focuses on the unique achievements and traditions of these cultures and their place within the broader human story.

One of the greatest problems we encountered in this new edition was deciding what to leave out. Our aim is to provide some representative examples from each period, hoping that instructors would use their own predilections to fill out where we have been negligent. In that sense, to borrow the zen concept, we are fingers pointing the way—attend to the direction and not to the finger. We refine that direction using input from instructors making those decisions and would like to acknowledge the reviewers of this and our previous editions: Jonathan Austad, Chadron State College; Michael Call, Brigham Young University; Scott Douglass, Chattanooga State Technical Community College; Julie Guidera, Brevard Community College, Titusville; Jason Horn, Gordon College, Barnesville, Ga; Lynne Kogel, Wayne State University; Richard Kortum, East Tennessee State University; John F. Martin, Hanover College; Patricia Matchette, St. Petersburg College; James W. Mock, University Of Central Oklahoma; Andrew Platizky, New Jersey City University; Robert Quist, Ferris State University; Joanna Reed, Sussex County Community College; Gencie S. Rucker, Florida Community College At Jacksonville; Stephanie Satie, California State University, Northridge; Sarah Sattersfield, Central Florida Community College; Mike Sparks, Wallace State Community College; Diana Major Spencer, Snow College; Jennifer Taylor, Valencia Community College East; Trent Tomengo, Seminole Community College; and Joan Monahan Watson, Virginia Polytechnic Institute And State University.

FEATURES

The seventh edition of *Culture and Values* retains many of the features that have made the book so successful.

Enhanced Illustrations. As in prior editions, the text is beautifully illustrated with nearly six hundred images, virtually all of them in color. This new edition includes over three hundred new images. Many of the images previously reproduced in the book have been replaced with higher quality photos that provide either a better view of the original artwork or a truer match to the original's color and overall appearance. A number of the line drawings have also been redrawn for better accuracy of representation and better consistency with similar drawings found in the book. We have expanded the information in many of the captions to help all our readers become better "visual learners."

Music. Expanded discussion of each selection on the LISTENING CD addresses not only the characteristics of the specific musical work but how those characteristics represent the historical period of its creation.

Timelines. Each chapter begins with an illustrated, two-page timeline that organizes the major events and artworks for each era and, where appropriate, for each major category of works discussed in the chapter (that is, general events, literature and philosophy, art, architecture, and music). The timelines provide an instant visual reference that allows students to see the development of each type of art over a given time period.

Boxes. Two types of boxes run throughout the book. VOICES OF THEIR TIMES boxes, taken from letters, journals, and narratives of the time period under discussion, provide students with insight into the concerns of individuals responding to the major events and ideas of the era firsthand. VALUES boxes make explicit the underlying issues or concerns unifying the works of a given era, examining their root causes and their ultimate impact on the type of art produced.

SUPPLEMENTS

LISTENING CD

This audio CD contains twenty-two musical selections discussed in the text and allows students to hear some of history's greatest musical achievements—from Gregorian chants to Mozart to Scott Joplin. The CD can be sold separately or bundled at a discount with any version of the text upon request.

ISBN-10: 0-495-57060-5
ISBN-13: 978-0-495-57060-8

READINGS FOR CULTURE AND VALUES: A SURVEY OF THE HUMANITIES, SEVENTH EDITION

Correlated chapter by chapter with this book, this anthology of readings includes landmark works from philosophy and literature.

ISBN-10: 0-495-57070-2
ISBN-13: 978-0-495-57070-7

THE MUSEUM EXPERIENCE

This practical handbook—one for each geographical region—includes tips on museum etiquette, how to make a museum visit more engaging, how to view the collection, and how to write about a particular work; descriptions of the major museums in your area plus listings including Web sites for all the area museums; and appendices of the major museums in the United States and around the world. It can be sold separately or bundled *free* with new copies of the text.

East *ISBN-10: 0-495-18868-9*
Southeast *ISBN-10: 0-495-18869-7*
Midwest *ISBN-10: 0-495-18867-0*
West *ISBN-10: 0-495-18865-4*
Southwest *ISBN-10: 0-495-18666-2*

ART BASICS: AN ILLUSTRATED GLOSSARY AND TIMELINE

Presented in a beautiful large format with full-color fine art images and quality line art, this brief introduction to the basic terms, styles, and time periods of art history is a handy reference for any beginning student. It can be sold separately or bundled *free* with new copies of the text.

ISBN-10: 0-534-64101-6
ISBN-13: 978-0-534-64101-6

THINKING AND WRITING IN THE HUMANITIES AND A PRACTICAL HANDBOOK FOR WRITING IN THE HUMANITIES

Designed for ease of use, *Thinking and Writing in the Humanities* serves as a quick reference for students planning, drafting, revising, and editing various types of essays, research papers, exhibition reviews—even examinations. The *Practical Handbook* is a concise guide to research, composition, MLA style, and citing sources.

Thinking and Writing ISBN-10: 0-534-62155-4
Practical Handbook ISBN-10: 0-155-05015-X

ONLINE RESOURCES

COMPANION WEBSITE

For the student, quizzes; key terms, people, and places; glossary flash cards with definitions and pronunciations; complete pronunciation glossary; further readings; Web Quests with references to sites that expand upon chapter topics; and a sample final exam.

HUMANITIES RESOURCE CENTER

Free with this book's printed access card or instant access card

Study Guide

Extensive and interactive, the Study Guide gives the student a variety of tools for understanding the material in each chapter. A wide range of study questions—illustrated with thumbnails of pertinent artworks—address the important historical, cultural, and artistic events of each chapter. Additional self-testing reviews range from short fill-in-the-blank quizzes to essay questions.

Pronunciation Glossary Flash Cards

Because we believe that it is difficult to remember or use in class terms one cannot pronounce, these flash cards contain all the key terms, people, and places discussed in the text, with their definitions and pronunciations.

Image Flash cards

Representing all the images in the text, these flash cards help the student identify, remember, and place in their historical periods important works of art and architecture.

Musical Period Flash cards

One-minute audio clips from the LISTENING CD help the student identify, remember, and place in their historical periods all the music discussed in the text.

Video Podcasts in Art History

Correlated by chapter, these topical learning modules contain multimedia mini-lectures that focus on specific artworks, comparisons, mediums, and trends in art history. In addition, nine video clips, under the title IN THE STUDIO, explore the media and techniques of art.

Interactive Resource for Art, Architecture, Music, and Philosophy

Organized by the major fields within the humanities, this feature's readings, documents, interactive timelines, maps, and much more help the student further explore the humanities. Extensive learning modules cover the Basics of Architecture, with comparisons of early modern architecture; the Basics of Art, including identifications of the visual elements and principles of design; and Elements of Musical Styles with audio clips.

THE ARTS: AN INTRODUCTION

One way to see the arts as a whole is to consider a widespread mutual experience: a church or synagogue service or the worship in a Buddhist monastery. Such a gathering is a celebration of written literature done, at least in part, in music in an architectural setting decorated to reflect the religious sensibilities of the community. A church service makes use of visual arts, literature, and music. While the service acts as an integrator of the arts, each art, considered separately, has its own peculiar characteristics that give it shape. The same integration may be seen, of course, in an opera or in a music video.

Music is primarily a temporal art, which is to say that there is music when there is someone to play the instruments and sing the songs. When the performance is over, the music stops.

The visual *arts* and *architecture* are spatial arts that have permanence. When a religious service is over, people may still come into the building to admire its architecture or marvel at its paintings or sculptures or look at the decorative details of the building.

Literature has a permanent quality in that it is recorded in books, although some literature is meant not to be read but to be heard. Shakespeare did not write plays for people to read, but for audiences to see and hear performed. Books nonetheless have permanence in the sense that they can be read not only in a specific context, but also at one's pleasure. Thus, to continue the religious-service example, one can read the psalms for their poetry or for devotion apart from their communal use in worship.

What we have said about the religious service applies equally to anything from a rock concert to grand opera: artworks can be seen as an integrated whole. Likewise, we can consider these arts separately. After all, people paint paintings, compose music, or write poetry to be enjoyed as discrete experiences. At other times, of course, two arts may be joined when there was no original intention to do so, as when a composer sets a poem to music or an artist finds inspiration in a literary text or, to use a more complex example, when a ballet is inspired by a literary text and is danced against the background or sets created by an artist to enhance both the dance and the text that inspired it.

However we view the arts, either separately or as integrated, one thing is clear: they are the product of human invention and human genius. When we speak of *culture*, we are not talking about something strange or "highbrow"; we are talking about something that derives from human invention. A jungle is a product of nature, but a garden is a product of culture: human ingenuity has modified the vegetative world.

In this book we discuss some of the works of human culture that have endured over the centuries. We often refer to these works as *masterpieces*, but what does the term mean? The issue is complicated because tastes and attitudes change over the centuries. Two hundred years ago the medieval cathedral was not appreciated; it was called Gothic because it was considered barbarian. Today we call such a building a masterpiece. Very roughly we can say that a masterpiece of art is any work that carries with it a surplus of meaning.

Having "surplus of meaning" means that a certain work not only reflects technical and imaginative skill, but also that its very existence sums up the best of a certain age, which spills over as a source of inspiration for further ages. As one reads through the history of the Western humanistic achievement it is clear that certain products of human genius are looked to by subsequent generations as a source of inspiration; they have a surplus of meaning. Thus the Roman achievement in architecture with the dome of the Pantheon both symbolized their skill in architecture and became a reference point for every major dome built in the West since. The dome of the Pantheon finds echoes in seventh-century Constantinople (Hagia Sophia); in fifteenth-century Florence (the Duomo); in sixteenth-century Rome (St. Peter's Basilica); and in eighteenth-century Washington, D.C. (the Capitol building).

The notion of surplus of meaning provides us with a clue as to how to study the humanistic tradition and its achievements. Admittedly simplifying, we can say that such a study has two steps that we have tried to synthesize into a whole in this book:

The Work in Itself. At this level we are asking the question of fact and raising the issue of observation: What is the work and how is it achieved? This question includes not only the basic information about, say, what kind of visual art this is (sculpture, painting, mosaic) or what its formal elements are (Is it geometric in style? Bright in color? Very linear? and so on), but also questions of its function: Is this work an homage to politics? For a private patron? For a church? We look at artworks, then, to ask questions about both their form and their function.

This is an important point. We may look at a painting or sculpture in a museum with great pleasure, but that pleasure would be all the more enhanced were we to see that work in its proper setting rather than as an object on display. To ask about form and function, in short, is to ask equally about context. When reading certain literary works (such as the *Iliad* or the *Song of Roland*) we should read them aloud since, in their original form, they were written to be recited, not read silently on a page.

The Work in Relation to History. The human achievements of our common past tell us much about earlier cultures both in their differences and in their similarities. A study of the tragic plays that have survived from ancient Athens gives us a glimpse into Athenians' problems, preoccupations, and aspirations as filtered through the words of Sophocles or Euripides. From such a study we learn both about the culture of Athens and something about how the human spirit has faced the perennial issues of justice, loyalty, and duty. In that sense we are in dialogue with our ancestors across the ages. In the study of ancient culture we see the roots of our own.

To carry out such a project requires willingness to look at art and closely read literature with an eye equally to the aspect of form/function and to the past and the present. Music, however, requires a special treatment because it is the most abstract of arts (How do we speak about that which is meant not to be seen but to be heard?) and the most temporal. For that reason a somewhat more extended guide to music follows.

HOW TO LOOK AT ART

Anyone who thumbs through a standard history of art can be overwhelmed by the complexity of what is discussed. We find everything from paintings on the walls of caves and huge sculptures carved into the faces of mountains to tiny pieces of jewelry or miniature paintings. All of these are art because they were made by the human hand in an attempt to express human ideas and/or emotions. Our response to such objects depends a good deal on our own education and cultural biases. We may find some modern art ugly or stupid or bewildering. We may think of all art as highbrow or elitist despite the fact that we like certain movies (film is an art) enough to see them over and over. At first glance, art from the East may seem odd simply because we do not have the reference points with which we can judge the art good or bad.

Our lives are so bound up with art that we often fail to recognize how much we are shaped by it. We are bombarded with examples of graphic art (television commercials, magazine ads, CD jackets, displays in stores) every day; we use art to make statements about who we are and what we value in the way we decorate our rooms and in the style of our clothing. In all of these ways we manipulate artistic symbols to make statements about what we believe in, what we stand for, and how we want others to see us. The many sites on the Web bombard us with visual clues which attempt to make us stop and find out what is being offered or argued.

The history of art is nothing more than the record of how people have used their minds and imaginations to symbolize who they are and what they value. If a certain age spends enormous amounts of money to build and decorate churches (as in twelfth-century France) and another spends the same kind of money on palaces (like eighteenth-century France), we learn about what each age values the most.

The very complexity of human art makes it difficult to interpret. That difficulty increases when we are looking at art from a much different culture and/or a far different age. We may admire the massiveness of Egyptian architecture, but find it hard to appreciate why such energies were used for the cult of the dead. When confronted with the art of another age (or even our own art, for that matter), a number of questions we can ask of ourselves and of the art may lead us to greater understanding.

For What Purpose Was This Piece of Art Made? This is essentially a question of *context*. Most of the religious paintings in our museums were originally meant to be seen in churches in very specific settings. To imagine them in their original setting helps us to understand that they had a devotional purpose that is lost when they are seen on a museum wall. To ask about the original setting, then, helps us to ask further whether the painting is in fact devotional or meant as a teaching tool or to serve some other purpose.

Setting is crucial. A frescoed wall on a public building is meant to be seen by many people, while a fresco on the wall of an aristocratic home is meant for a much smaller, more elite class of viewer. The calligraphy decorating an Islamic mosque tells us much about the importance of the sacred writings of Islam. A sculpture designed for a wall niche is going to have a shape different from one designed to be seen by walking around it. Similarly, art made under official sponsorship of an authoritarian government must be read in a far different manner than art produced by underground artists who have no standing with the government. Finally, art may be purely decorative or it may have a didactic purpose, but (and here is a paradox) purely decorative art may teach us while didactic art may end up being purely decorative.

What, If Anything, Does This Piece of Art Hope to Communicate? This question is one of *intellectual* or *emotional* context. Funeral sculpture may reflect the grief of the survivors, or a desire to commemorate the achievements of the deceased, or to affirm what the survivors believe about life after death, or a combination of these purposes. If we think of art as a variety of speech we can then inquire of any artwork: What is it saying?

An artist may strive for an ideal ("I want to paint the most beautiful woman in the world," or "I wish my painting to be taken for reality itself," or "I wish to move people to love or hate or sorrow by my sculpture"), illustrate the power of an idea, or (as in the case with most primitive art) "capture" the power of the spirit world for religious and/or magical purposes.

An artist may well produce a work simply to demonstrate inventiveness or to expand the boundaries of what art means. The story is told of Pablo Picasso's reply to a woman who said that her ten-year-old child could paint better than he. Picasso replied, "Congratulations, Madame. Your child is a genius." We know that before he was a teenager Picasso could draw and paint with photographic accuracy. He said that during his long life he tried to learn how to paint with the fresh eye and spontaneous simplicity of a child.

How Was This Piece of Art Made? This question inquires into both the materials and the skills the artist employs to turn materials into art. Throughout this book we will speak of different artistic techniques, like bronze casting or etching or panel painting; here we make a more general point. To learn to appreciate the craft of the artist is a first step toward enjoying art for its worth as art—to developing an "eye" for art. This requires *looking* at the object as a crafted object. Thus, for example, a close examination of Michelangelo's *Pietà* shows the pure smooth beauty of marble, while his *Slaves* demonstrates the roughness of stone and the sculptor's effort to carve meaning from hard material. We might stand back to admire a painting as a whole, but then to look closely at one portion of it teaches us the subtle manipulation of color and line that creates the overall effect.

What Is the Composition of This Artwork? This question addresses how the artist "composes" the work. Much Renaissance painting uses a pyramidal construction so that the most important figure is at the apex of the pyramid and lesser figures form the base. Some paintings presume something happening outside the picture itself (such as an unseen source of light); a cubist painting tries to render simultaneous views of an object. At other times, an artist may enhance the composition by the manipulation of color with a movement from light to dark or a stark contrast between dark and light, as in the *chiaroscuro* of Baroque painting. In all of these cases the artists intend to do something more than merely "depict" a scene; they appeal to our imaginative and intellectual powers as we enter into the picture or engage the sculpture or look at their film.

Composition, obviously, is not restricted to painting. Filmmakers compose with close-ups or tracking shots just as sculptors carve for frontal or side views of an object. Since all of these techniques are designed to make us see in a particular manner, only by thinking about composition do we begin to reflect on what the artist has done. If we do not think about composition, we tend to take an artwork at "face value" and, as a consequence, are not training our "eye." Much contemporary imaging is done by the power of mixing done on the computer.

What Elements Should We Notice about a Work of Art? The answer to this question is a summary of what we have stated above. Without pretending to exclusivity, we should judge art on the basis of the following three aspects:

Formal elements. What kind of artwork is it? What materials are employed? What is its composition in terms of structure? In terms of pure form, how does this particular work look when compared to a similar work of the same or another artist?

Symbolic elements. What is this artwork attempting to "say"? Is its purpose didactic, propagandistic, to give pleasure, or what? How well do the formal elements contribute to the symbolic statement being attempted in the work of art?

Social elements. What is the context of this work of art? Who paid and why? Whose purposes does it serve? At this level, many different philosophies come into play. A Marxist critic might judge a work in terms of its sense of class or economic aspects, while a feminist critic might inquire whether it affirms women or acts as an agent of subjugation or exploitation.

It is possible to restrict oneself to formal criticism of an artwork (Is this well done in terms of craft and composition?), but such an approach does not do full justice to what the artist is trying to do. Conversely, to judge every work purely in terms of social theory excludes the notion of an artistic work and, as a consequence, reduces art to politics or philosophy. For a fuller appreciation of art, then, all of the elements mentioned above need to come into play.

AN EXERCISE IN LOOKING AT ART

Consider Leonardo da Vinci's *Madonna of the Rocks* (Fig.12.26).

SUBJECT MATTER

A representational depiction of the Virgin with the Christ Child and young Saint John the Baptist and angel in a rocky landscape.

COMPOSITION

◆ Foreground: Four figures are seated along a rocky edge of land with very naturalistic plants and grasses. The Virgin is seated in the center and dominates the group. Her right hand reaches around the young Saint John the Baptist who kneels on one knee and looks to the Christ Child seated to her front left-hand side. He is seated in a ¾-profile to the viewer and directly under the Virgin's blessing left hand. To the right is a seated angel who looks out at the viewer while pointing to St. John. The figural group forms a pyramidal or triangular composition with the Madonna at the apex.
◆ *Middleground:* A naturalistic landscape of plants and vegetation among the rocks with a canopy of rock formations suggesting a grotto and plants that encircle the group.
◆ *Background:* A landscape of great depth with rock formations and valleys with light from the setting sun.

© *Scala/Art Resource, NY*

ART ELEMENTS

◆ *Line; shape, volume, and mass; light and value, color; texture; space, time, and motion*

In *Madonna of the Rocks*, light is the most important element and affects all the other elements. The light is very dramatic and its source appears to be from the upper left from off the canvas. The light defines everything; it illuminates and focuses the viewer's attention on the figures. The light affects the colors and creates the warm feeling of flesh against the coldness of the rocky landscape of great depth. This use of light is called *chiaroscuro*, a contrast of very dark to very light values in the brightness of a color. Chiaroscuro creates the atmosphere, the shape and volume of the figures, and the space they occupy, a vast landscape in which real people exist.

HOW TO LISTEN TO MUSIC

The sections of this book devoted to music are designed for readers who have no special training in music theory and practice. Response to significant works of music, after all, should require no more specialized knowledge than the ability to respond to *Oedipus Rex*, say, or a Byzantine mosaic. Indeed, many millions of people buy recorded music in one form or another, or enjoy listening to it on the radio without the slightest knowledge of how the music is constructed or performed.

The gap between the simple pleasure of the listener and the complex skills of composer and performer often prevents the development of a more serious grasp of music history and its relation to the other arts. The aim of this section is to help bridge that gap without trying to provide too much technical information. After a brief survey of music's role in Western culture, we shall look at the "language" used to discuss musical works—both specific terminology, such as *sharp* and *flat*, and more general concepts, such as line and color.

MUSIC IN WESTERN CULTURE

The origins of music are unknown, and neither the excavations of ancient instruments and depictions of performers nor the evidence from modern primitive societies gives any impression of its early stages. Presumably, like the early cave paintings, music served some kind of magical or ritual purpose. This is borne out by the fact that music still forms a vital part of most religious ceremonies today, from the hymns sung in Christian churches or the solo singing of the cantor in an Orthodox Jewish synagogue to the elaborate musical rituals performed in Buddhist or Shinto temples in Japan. The Old Testament makes many references to the power of music, most notably in the famous story of the battle of Jericho, and it is clear that by historical times music played an important role in Jewish life, both sacred and secular.

By the time of the Greeks, the first major Western culture to develop, music had become as much a science as an art. It retained its importance for religious rituals; in fact, according to Greek mythology the gods themselves invented it. At the same time the theoretical relationships between the various musical pitches attracted the attention of philosophers such as Pythagoras (c. 550 BCE), who described the underlying unity of the universe as the "harmony of the spheres." Later fourth-century BCE thinkers like Plato and Aristotle emphasized music's power to affect human feeling and behavior. Thus for the Greeks, music represented a religious, intellectual, and moral force. Once again, music is still used in our own world to affect people's feelings, whether it be the stirring sound of a march, a solemn funeral dirge, or the eroticism of much modern "pop" music (of which Plato would thoroughly have disapproved).

Virtually all of the music—and art, for that matter—that survived from the Middle Ages is religious. Popular secular music certainly existed, but since no real system of notation was invented before the eleventh century, it has disappeared without a trace. The ceremonies of both the Western and the Eastern (Byzantine) church centered around the chanting of a single musical line, a kind of music that is called *monophonic* (from the Greek "single voice"). Around the time musical notation was devised, composers began to become interested in the possibilities of notes sounding simultaneously—what we would think of as harmony. Music involving several separate lines sounding together (as in a modern string quartet or a jazz group) became popular only in the 14th century. This gradual introduction of *polyphony* ("many voices") is perhaps the single most important development in the history of music, since composers began to think not only horizontally (that is, melodically), but also vertically, or harmonically. In the process, the possibilities of musical expression were immeasurably enriched.

THE EXPERIENCE OF LISTENING

"What music expresses is eternal, infinite, and ideal. It does *not* express the passion, love, or longing of this or that individual in this or that situation, but passion, love, or longing in itself; and this it presents in that unlimited variety of motivations which is the exclusive and particular characteristic of music, foreign and inexpressible in any other language" (Richard Wagner). With these words, one of the greatest of all composers described the power of music to express universal emotions. Yet for those unaccustomed to serious listening, it is precisely this breadth of experience with which it is difficult to identify. We can understand a joyful or tragic situation. Joy and tragedy themselves, though, are more difficult to comprehend.

There are a number of ways by which the experience of listening can become more rewarding and more enjoyable. Not all of them will work for everyone, but over the course of time they have proved helpful for many newcomers to the satisfactions of music.

1. *Before listening to the piece you have selected*, ask yourself some questions: What is the historical context of the music? For whom was it composed—for a general or an elite audience?

   Did the composer have a specific assignment? If the work was intended for performance in church, for example, it should sound very different from a set of dances. Sometimes the location of the performance affected the sound of the music: composers of masses to be sung in Gothic cathedrals used the buildings' acoustical properties to emphasize the resonant qualities of their works.

   With what forces was the music to be performed? Do they correspond to those intended by the composer? Performers of medieval music, in particular, often have to reconstruct much that is missing or uncertain. Even in the case of later traditions, the original sounds can sometimes be only approximated. The superstars of the eighteenth-century world of opera were the *castrati*, male singers who had been castrated in their youth and whose soprano voices had therefore never broken; contemporaries described the sounds they produced as incomparably brilliant and flexible. The custom, which seems to us so barbaric, was abandoned in the nineteenth century, and even the most fanatic musicologist must settle for a substitute today. The case is an extreme one, but it proves that even with the best of intentions, modern performers cannot always reproduce the original sounds.

Does the work have a text? If so, read it through before you listen to the music; it is easiest to concentrate on one thing at a time. In the case of a translation, does the version you are using capture the spirit of the original? Translators sometimes take a simple, popular lyric and make it sound archaic and obscure in order to convey the sense of "old" music. If the words do not make much sense to you, they would probably seem equally incomprehensible to the composer. Music, of all the arts, is concerned with direct communication.

Is the piece divided into sections? If so, why? Is the relationship of the sections determined by purely musical considerations—the structure of the piece—or by external factors—the words of a song, for example, or the parts of a Mass?

Finally, given all the above, what do you expect the music to sound like? Your preliminary thinking should have prepared you for the kind of musical experience in store for you. If it has not, go back and reconsider some of the points above.

2. *While you are listening to the music:* Concentrate as completely as you can. It is virtually impossible to gain much from music written in an unfamiliar idiom unless you give it your full attention. Read written information before you begin to listen, as you ask yourself the questions above, not *while* the music is playing. If there is a text, keep an eye on it but do not let it distract you from the music.

Concentrating is not always easy, particularly if you are mainly used to listening to music as a background, but there are some ways in which you can help your own concentration. To avoid visual distraction, fix your eyes on some detail near you—a mark on the wall, a design in someone's dress, the cover of a book. At first this will seem artificial, but after a while your attention should be taken by the music. If you feel your concentration fading, do not pick up a magazine or gaze around; consciously force your attention back to the music and try to analyze what you are hearing. Does it correspond to your expectations? How is the composer trying to achieve an effect? By variety of instrumental color? Are any of the ideas, or tunes, repeated?

Unlike literature or the visual arts, music occurs in the dimension of time. When you are reading, you can turn backward to check a reference or remind yourself of a character's identity. In looking at a painting, you can move from a detail to an overall view as often as you want. In music, the speed of your attention is controlled by the composer. Once you lose the thread of the discourse, you cannot regain it by going back; you must try to pick up

again and follow the music as it continues—and that requires your renewed attention.

On the other hand, in these times of easy access to recordings, the same pieces can be listened to repeatedly. Even the most experienced musicians cannot grasp some works fully without several hearings. Indeed, one of the features that distinguishes "art" music from more "popular" works is its capacity to yield increasing rewards. On a first hearing, therefore, try to grasp the general mood and structure and note features to listen for the next time you hear the piece. Do not be discouraged if the idiom seems strange or remote, and be prepared to become familiar with a few works from each period you are studying.

As you become accustomed to serious listening, you will notice certain patterns used by composers to give form to their works. They vary according to the styles of the day, and throughout this book there are descriptions of each period's musical characteristics. In responding to the general feeling the music expresses, therefore, you should try to note the specific features that identify the time of its composition.

3. *After you have heard the piece,* ask yourself these questions: Which characteristics of the music indicated the period of its composition? Were they due to the forces employed (voices and/or instruments)? How was the piece constructed? Did the composer make use of repetition? Was there a change of mood and, if so, did the original mood return at the end? What kind of melody was used? Was it continuous or did it divide into a series of shorter phrases? If a text was involved, how did the music relate to the words? Were they audible? Did the composer intend them to be? If not, why not?

Were there aspects of the music that reminded you of the literature and visual arts of the same period? In what kind of buildings can you imagine it being performed? What does the music tell you about the society for which it was written?

Finally, ask yourself the most difficult question of all: What did the music express? Richard Wagner described the meaning of music as "foreign and inexpressible in any other language." There is no dictionary of musical meaning, and listeners must interpret for themselves what they hear. We all understand the general significance of words like *contentment* or *despair,* but music can distinguish between a million shades of each.

CONCEPTS IN MUSIC

There is a natural tendency in talking about the arts to use terms from one art form to describe another. Thus most people would know what to expect from a "colorful" story or a painting in "quiet" shades of blue. This metaphorical use of language helps describe characteristics that are otherwise often very difficult to isolate, but some care is required to remain within the general bounds of comprehension.

Line. In music, *line* generally means the progression in time of a series of notes: the melody. A melody in music is a succession of tones related to one another to form a complete musical thought. Melodies vary in length and in shape and may be made up of several smaller parts. They may move quickly or slowly, smoothly or with strongly accented (stressed) notes. Some melodies are carefully balanced and proportional, others are irregular and asymmetrical. A melodic line dictates the basic character of a piece of music, just as lines do in a painting or the plot line does for a story or play.

Texture. The degree to which a piece of music has a thick or thin *texture* depends on the number of voices and/or instruments involved. Thus the monophonic music of the Middle Ages, with its single voice, has the thinnest texture possible. At the opposite extreme is a 19th-century opera, where half a dozen soloists, a chorus, and a large orchestra were sometimes combined. Needless to say, thickness and thinness of texture are neither good nor bad in themselves, merely simple terms of description.

Composers control the shifting texture of their works in several ways. The number of lines heard simultaneously can be increased or reduced—a full orchestral climax followed by a single flute, for example. The most important factor in the texture of the sound, however, is the number of combined independent melodic lines; this playing (or singing) together of two or more separate melodies is called *counterpoint*. Another factor influencing musical texture is the vertical arrangement of the notes: six notes played close together low in the scale will sound thicker than six notes more widely distributed.

Color. The color, or *timbre*, of a piece of music is determined by the instruments or voices employed. Gregorian chant is monochrome, having only one line. The modern symphony orchestra has a vast range to draw upon, from the bright sound of the oboe or the trumpet to the dark, mellow sound of the cello or French horn. Different instruments used in Japanese or Chinese music will result in a quite distinct but very different timbre. Some composers have been more interested than others in exploiting the range of color instrumental combinations can produce; not surprisingly, Romantic music provides some of the most colorful examples.

Medium. The *medium* is the method of performance. Pieces can be written for solo piano, string quartet, sym-

phony orchestra, or any other combination the composer chooses. A prime factor will be the importance of color in the work. Another is the length and seriousness of the musical material. It is difficult, although not impossible, for a piece written for solo violin to sustain the listener's interest for half an hour. Still another is the practicality of performance. Pieces using large or unusual combinations of instruments stand less chance of being frequently programmed. In the nineteenth-century, composers often chose a medium that allowed performance in the home, thus creating a vast piano literature.

Form. Form is the outward, visible (or hearable) shape of a work as opposed to its substance (medium) or color. This structure can be created in a number of ways. Baroque composers worked according to the principle of unity in variety. In most Baroque movements the principal melodic idea continually recurs in the music, and the general texture remains consistent. The formal basis of much classical music is contrast, where two or more melodies of differing character (hard and soft, or brilliant and sentimental) are first laid out separately, then developed and combined, then separated again. The Romantics often pushed the notion of contrasts to extremes, although retaining the basic motions of classical form. Certain types of work dictate their own form. A composer writing a requiem mass is clearly less free to experiment with formal variation than one writing a piece for symphony orchestra. The words of a song strongly suggest the structure of the music, even if they do not impose it. Indeed, so pronounced was the Baroque sense of unity that the sung arias in Baroque operas inevitably conclude with a repetition of the words and music of the beginning, even if the character's mood or emotion has changed.

Thus music, like the other arts, involves the general concepts described above. A firm grasp of them is essential to an understanding of how the various arts have changed and developed over the centuries and how the changes are reflected in similarities—or differences—between art forms. The concept of the humanities implies that the arts did not grow and change in isolation from one another or from around the world. As this book shows, they are integrated among themselves and with the general developments of Western thought and history.

HOW TO READ LITERATURE

"Reading literature" conjures up visions of someone sitting in an armchair with glasses on and nose buried in a thick volume—say, Tolstoy's *War and Peace*. The plain truth is that a fair amount of the literature found in this book was never meant to be read that way at all. Once that fact is recognized, reading becomes an exercise in which different methods can serve as a great aid for both pleasure and understanding. That becomes clear when we consider various literary forms and ask ourselves how their authors originally meant them to be encountered. Let us consider some of the forms that will be studied in this volume to make the point more specifically:

Dramatic Literature. This is the most obvious genre of literature that calls for something more than reading the text quietly. Plays—ancient, medieval, Elizabethan, or modern—are meant to be acted, with living voices interpreting what the playwright wrote in the script. What seems to be strange and stilted language as we first encounter Shakespeare becomes powerful and beautiful when we hear his words spoken by someone who knows and loves language.

A further point: until relatively recent times most dramas were played on stages nearly bare of scenery and, obviously, extremely limited in terms of lighting, theatrical devices, and the like. As a consequence, earlier texts contain a great deal of description that in the modern theater (and, even more, in a film) can be supplied by current technology. Where Shakespeare has a character say "But look, the morn in russet mangle clad/Walks o'er the dew of yon high eastward hill," a modern writer might simply instruct the lighting manager to make the sun come up.

Dramatic literature must be approached with a sense of its oral aspect as well as with awareness that the language reflects the intention of the author to have the words acted out. Dramatic language is meant to be *heard* and *seen*.

Epic. Like drama, epics have a strong oral background. It is commonplace to note that before Homer's *Iliad* took its present form, it was memorized and recited by a professional class of bards. Similarly, the *Song of Roland* was probably heard by many people and read by relatively few in the formative decades of its composition. Even epics that are more consciously literary echo the oral background of the epic; Virgil begins his elegant *Aeneid* with the words "Of Arms and the man I sing" not "Of Arms and the man I write." The Islamic scriptures—the Koran—is most effectively recited.

The practical conclusion to be drawn from this is that these long poetic tales take on a greater power when they are read aloud with sensitivity to their cadence.

Poetry. Under this general heading we have a very complicated subject. To approach poetry with intelligence, we need to inquire about the kind of poetry with which we are dealing. The lyrics of songs are poems, but they are better heard sung than read in a book. On the other hand, certain kinds of poems are so arranged on a page that not to see them in print is to miss a good deal of their power or charm. Furthermore, some poems are meant for the individual reader, while others are public pieces meant for the group. There is, for example, a vast difference between a love sonnet and a biblical psalm. Both are examples of poetry, but the former expresses a private emotion while the latter most likely gets its full energy from use in worship: we can imagine a congregation singing a psalm, but not the same congregation reciting one of Petrarch's sonnets to Laura.

In poetry, then, context is all. Our appreciation of a poem is enhanced once we have discovered where the poem belongs: With music? On a page? With an aristocratic circle of intellectuals? As part of a national or ethnic or religious heritage? As propaganda or protest or to express deep emotions?

At base, however, poetry is the refined use of language. The poet is the maker of words. Our greatest appreciation of a poem comes when we say to ourselves that this could not be said better. An authentic poem cannot be edited or paraphrased or glossed. Poetic language, even in long poems, is economical. One can understand that by simple experiment: take one of Dante's portraits in the *Divine Comedy* and try to do a better job of description in fewer words. The genius of Dante (or Chaucer in the Prologue to *The Canterbury Tales*) is his ability to sketch out a fully formed person in a few stanzas.

Prose. God created humans, the writer Elie Wiesel once remarked, because he loves a good story. Narrative is as old as human history. The stories that stand behind the *Decameron* and *The Canterbury Tales* have been shown to have existed not only for centuries, but in widely different cultural milieus. Stories are told to draw out moral examples or to instruct or warn, but, by and large, stories are told because we enjoy hearing them. We read novels in order to enter into a new world and suspend the workaday world we live in, just as we watch films. The difference between a story and a film is that one can linger over a story; in a film there is no "second look."

Some prose obviously is not fictional. It can be autobiographical like Augustine's *Confessions*, or it may be a philosophical essay like Jean-Paul Sartre's attempt to explain what he means by existentialism. How do we approach that kind of writing? First, with a willingness to listen to what is being said. Second, with a readiness to judge: Does this passage ring true? What objections might I make to it? And so on. Third, with an openness that says, in effect, there is something to be learned here.

A final point has to do with attitude. We live in an age in which much of what we know comes to us in very brief "sound bites" via television, and much of what we read comes to us in the disposable form of newspapers and magazines and inexpensive paperbacks.

To read—*really* to read—requires that we discipline ourselves to cultivate a more leisurely approach to that art. There is merit in speed-reading the morning sports page; there is no merit in doing the same with a poem or a short story. It may take time to learn to slow down and read at a leisurely pace (leisure is the basis of culture, says Aristotle), but if we learn to do so we have taught ourselves a skill that will enrich us throughout our lives. A good thought exercise is to ask whether reading from a computer screen is a different exercise than reading from a book.

HOW TO READ MAPS

Maps may serve various functions. In the ancient world a *mappa mundi* illustrated the imagined size of the known world. In military campaigns maps serve to illustrate the location of the enemy and the physical obstacles ahead of the army's march. Most maps today show political and natural boundaries or, more usefully, the route from one place to another.

The maps in this book have a more restricted purpose. They are meant to illuminate the points made in the text. For example, when the text speaks of the Hellenistic world, the map shows us the extent of that world. When the text speaks of the rapid expansion of Islam after its founding, the map shows the geographical areas and rapidity of its expansion. Students will gain the most benefit from the maps in this book by looking at them with a few pertinent questions in mind:

◆ How does the map relate to the text? Does the information available in the map enhance text discussion? Does the map shed light on discussions in earlier chapters?
◆ How does a map illustrate the power and movement of ideas or artistic styles discussed in this book?
◆ If a map shows the expansion of a certain movement, what can we say about the area shown outside that movement?

Finally, it is very productive to think of each map as another kind of "text" and not merely an "illustration." By that approach we soon learn not to look at maps but to "read" them.

CHAPTER 1

THE BEGINNINGS OF CIVILIZATION

From the dawn of human history, women and their images played a major part in prehistoric religion. Furthermore, women had rights in ancient societies that in many cases they were later to lose. Their position emerges most clearly in the evidence we have about family life. Although most societies were patriarchal, traditional patterns did not exclude the importance of women in the family. Mesopotamians were constantly reminded: "Listen to the word of your mother as to your god; do not anger the heart of your older sister." Similar instructions from an Egyptian father to his son are quoted later in this chapter in *Voices of Their Times.*

Egyptian society as a whole was, perhaps surprisingly, gender-inclusive. Traditionally Egyptian men took only one wife. Even the pharaoh, with his Royal Harem, distinguished between his Great Wife, the senior one, and the others. Egyptian married women retained their own property with the right to inherit it and pass it on. Both men and women could initiate divorce proceedings. Although the majority of women confined most of their time to domestic affairs, some operated businesses, and upper-class women could serve as priestesses. During the New Kingdom, women worked as authors and scribes. One popular Egyptian saying advised husbands to "make your wife's heart glad as long as you live"—advice that would probably have surprised many a male of later ages and cultures.

Similarly Mesopotamian women, although expected to marry and bear children, had considerable legal protection. If unhappily married, a wife could get local authorities to dissolve the marriage. A widow or divorced woman was free to make her own marital arrangements. Among the Assyrians, she could even live with a man without marrying him. If she moved in with her lover, he became the owner of her property. If he moved in with her, however, she became owner of his property. For Mesopotamian women, the worst of fates was not rape, but dying without enjoying sexual pleasure with a man who "loved her like a wife." Clearly we should avoid making superficial generalizations about life in "primitive" societies.

◆ Alabaster statue of an Egyptian woman, 3000–2565 BCE.
(© British Museum, London//Werner Forman/Art Resource, NY)

CIVILIZATION

Around 5000 BCE humans began to lay the bases for the growth of civilization. After millennia of hunting and gathering, the development of agriculture made possible for the first time the formation of settled communities. *Civilization* is so broad a term that it is not easy to define simply. Nonetheless, societies that qualify for the label "civilized" generally possess at least the majority, if not all, of the following characteristics:

1. Some form of urban life involving the construction of permanent settlements—cities, in short.
2. A system of government that regulates political relations.
3. The development of distinct social classes, distinguished from one another by two related factors: wealth and occupation.

4. Tools and specialized skills for the production of goods, leading to the rise of manufacturing and trade.
5. Some form of written communication, making it possible to share and preserve information.
6. A shared system of religious belief, whose officials or priests often play a significant role in community affairs.

It is important to realize at the beginning of our survey of Western civilization that the term *civilized*, when used in this anthropological sense, implies no value judgment as to the merits of a particular society. So-called primitive peoples are capable of producing valuable and lasting works of art and of living full and satisfying lives, whereas, as the twentieth century demonstrated, some of the most civilized societies in history can be responsible for causing indescribable human suffering. Furthermore, at that century's end, advanced industrial civilization seemed increasingly in danger of destroying the environment and making the world uninhabitable for any form of life, human or animal. The pages

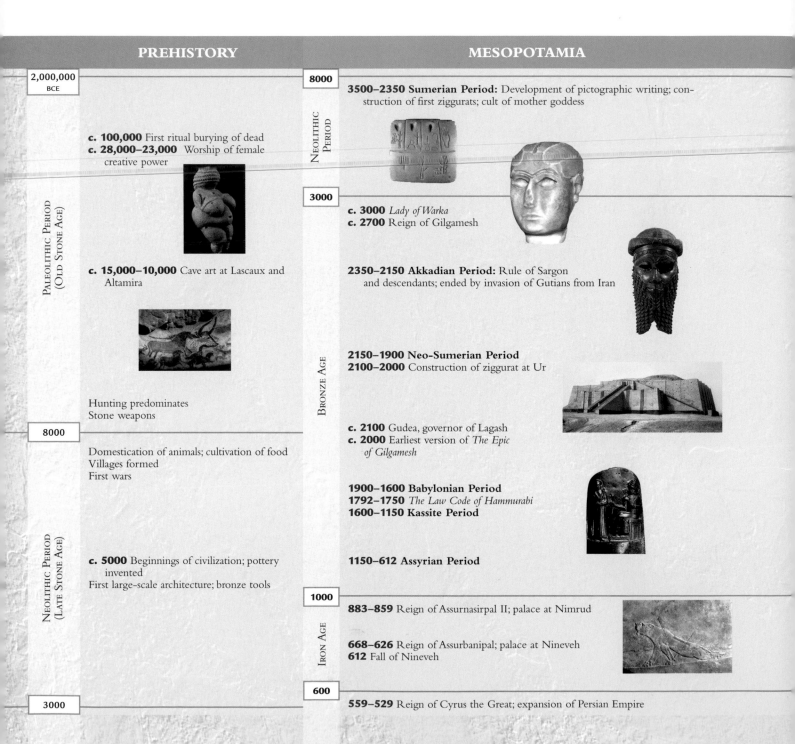

PREHISTORY

MESOPOTAMIA

2,000,000 BCE	8000

NEOLITHIC PERIOD

3500–2350 Sumerian Period: Development of pictographic writing; construction of first ziggurats; cult of mother goddess

c. 100,000 First ritual burying of dead
c. 28,000–23,000 Worship of female creative power

3000

c. 3000 *Lady of Warka*
c. 2700 Reign of Gilgamesh

PALEOLITHIC PERIOD (OLD STONE AGE)

c. 15,000–10,000 Cave art at Lascaux and Altamira

2350–2150 Akkadian Period: Rule of Sargon and descendants; ended by invasion of Gutians from Iran

BRONZE AGE

2150–1900 Neo-Sumerian Period
2100–2000 Construction of ziggurat at Ur

Hunting predominates
Stone weapons

8000

c. 2100 Gudea, governor of Lagash
c. 2000 Earliest version of *The Epic of Gilgamesh*

Domestication of animals; cultivation of food
Villages formed
First wars

1900–1600 Babylonian Period
1792–1750 *The Law Code of Hammurabi*
1600–1150 Kassite Period

NEOLITHIC PERIOD (LATE STONE AGE)

c. 5000 Beginnings of civilization; pottery invented
First large-scale architecture; bronze tools

1150–612 Assyrian Period

1000

IRON AGE

883–859 Reign of Assurnasirpal II; palace at Nimrud

668–626 Reign of Assurbanipal; palace at Nineveh
612 Fall of Nineveh

600

3000

559–529 Reign of Cyrus the Great; expansion of Persian Empire that follow chronicle the high achievements of Western civilization, but the grim background against which many of these appeared should never be forgotten. As the eighteenth-century philosopher Giambattista Vico observed, advanced civilizations can be barbaric in ways far more terrible than preliterate peoples.

The basic advances that made possible the growth of Western civilization were first achieved by the earlier civilizations of the ancient Middle East. These ancient peoples were the first who systematically produced food, mined and processed metals, organized themselves into cities, and devised legal and moral codes of behavior, together with systems of government and religion. In all these areas they had a profound influence on later peoples. At the same time, they produced a major artistic tradition that, quite apart from its high intrinsic interest, was to have many effects on the development of Western art.

To discover the origins of Western civilization, we must therefore look at cultures that at first seem remote in both time and place. Yet these peoples produced the achievements described in this chapter—achievements that form the background to the history of our own culture.

EGYPT	AEGEAN WORLD
3200–2700 Predynastic Period **c. 3100** Development of hieroglyphic writing 	**c. 6000** Introduction of new agricultural techniques from the East
2700–2250 Old Kingdom: Development of mummification ritual; art reflects confidence and certainty **c. 2650** Imhotep constructs first pyramid for King Zoser at Saqqara **2650–2514** Great Pyramids and Sphinx built at Giza 	**2800–2000 Early Minoan Period on Crete:** Growth of Cycladic culture **2000–1600 Middle Minoan Period on Crete:** Construction of palace complexes; development of linear writing
2250–1990 First Intermediate Period **1990–1790 Middle Kingdom:** Art reflects new uncertainty; "Song of the Harper" **c. 1878–1841** Reign of Sesostris III 	**c. 1700** Knossos Palace destroyed by earthquake and rebuilt on grander scale **1600–1400 Late Minoan Period on Crete** **c. 1600** First Mycenaean palace constructed; Royal Grave Circle at Mycenae
1790–1570 Second Intermediate Period **1570–1185 New Kingdom** **1364–1347** Reign of Amenhotep IV (Akhenaton); religious and political reform; worship of single god Aton; capital moved from Thebes to Tel el-Amarna; naturalism in art; Akhenaton, "Hymn to Aton" **1361–1352** Reign of Tutankhamen; return to conservatism **1298–1232** Reign of Ramses II; colossal buildings constructed at Luxor, Karnak, Abu Simbel **1185–500 Late Period:** Egypt's power declines; artists revert to Old Kingdom styles 	**1500** Minoan Frescoes on Thera **1400** Fall of Knossos and decline of Minoan civilization **1400–1200** Mycenaean empire flourishes **1250** Mycenaean war against Troy **1100** Final collapse of Mycenaean power **1100–1000 Dark Age**
	1000–750 Heroic Age **c. 900–700** Evolution of Homeric epics *Iliad* and *Odyssey*
671–663 Assyrian occupation of Egypt	**750–600 Age of Colonization**

THE EARLIEST PEOPLE AND THEIR ART

Even the earliest civilizations appeared relatively late in human history, at the beginning of the period known as the **Neolithic**[1] or Late Stone Age (c. 8000 BCE). The process of human evolution is long and confusing, and many aspects of it remain uncertain. The earliest form of hominid, **Ramapithecus**, is known from fossil fragments dating from eight to eleven million years ago, but our first direct ancestors, **Homo erectus**, probably appeared between a million and half a million years ago in the **Paleolithic** period or Old Stone Age. For most of the succeeding millennia, people were dominated by the physical forces of geography and climate, able to keep themselves alive only by a persistent search for food and shelter. Those who chose the wrong places or the wrong methods did not survive, whereas others were preserved by their instincts or good fortune.

Primitive conditions hardly encouraged the growth of civilization, yet there is some evidence of a kind of intellectual development. Archaeological evidence has shown that about one hundred thousand years ago the ancestors of **Homo sapiens** belonging to the type known as **Neanderthal** people were the first to bury their dead carefully and place funerary offerings in the graves—the earliest indication of the existence of religious beliefs.

Paleolithic Art Toward the end of the Paleolithic period, around 15,000 BCE, a major breakthrough occurred. The human desire for self-expression resulted in the invention of visual art. The cave paintings of Lascaux and Altamira and statuettes like the *Venus of Willendorf* are among the earliest products of the human creative urge. Although the art of this remote age would be valuable for its historical significance alone, many of the paintings and statues stand as masterpieces in their own right.

The lines are concentrated but immensely expressive. In some cases, artists used the surface on which they were painting to create an added sense of realism: a bulge on a cave wall suggested the hump of a bull [**Fig. 1.2**]. The combination of naturalistic observation and abstraction can only be described as sophisticated, and since their discovery in the twentieth century the paintings have served as a powerful inspiration to modern eyes.

The choice of subjects tells us something about the worldview of Paleolithic people. The earliest cave paintings show animals and hunting, which played a vital part in providing food and clothing. More significant, perhaps, is the fact that all of the oldest known statuettes of human figures represent women, who are shown with their sexual characteristics emphasized or enlarged

[**Fig. 1.3**]. The Paleolithic world perhaps viewed woman's practical role—the source of birth and life—as symbolic of a more profound feminine force that underlay the masculine world of the hunt. Worship of female creative power was also to play an important part in the religion of the ancient Middle East and of Bronze Age Greece. Even though the Greeks of a later period emphasized other aspects of human power, reverence for a mother goddess—or Earth Mother—was to live on.

The Neolithic Period The Neolithic period (c. 8000 BCE) represents in all aspects a major break with the past. After a million years of hunting, ways to domesticate animals and cultivate food were discovered. People began to gather together in villages where they could lead a settled existence. The development of improved farming techniques made it possible for a community to accumulate stores of grain and thereby become less dependent for their survival on a good harvest each year. But these stores provided a motive for raids by neighboring communities. Thus war, for the first time in human history, became profitable.

Other more constructive changes followed at a rapid pace. Pottery was invented around 5000 BCE, and not long afterward metal began to replace stone as the principal material for tools and weapons. The first metal used was copper, but it was soon discovered that an alloy of copper and tin would produce a far stronger metal: bronze. The use of bronze became widespread, giving its name to the Bronze Age, which lasted from around 3000 BCE to the introduction of iron around 1000 BCE.

At the beginning of the Bronze Age, large-scale architecture began to appear. The fortified settlements that had been established in Egypt and Mesopotamia were now able to develop those aspects of existence that entitle them to be called the first true civilizations.

Egypt and Mesopotamia have much in common. Their climates are similar and both are dominated by great rivers, Egypt by the Nile and Mesopotamia by the Tigris and Euphrates (see map, "The Ancient World"). Yet each was to develop its own distinct culture and make its own contribution to the history of civilization. Mesopotamia is discussed first in the following account, but both areas developed over the same general time span.

THE CULTURES OF MESOPOTAMIA

The unity that was so characteristic of ancient Egyptian culture has no parallel in the history of ancient Mesopotamia. A succession of different peoples, each with their own language, religion, and customs, produced a wide variety of achievements. This makes it far more difficult to generalize about Mesopotamian culture than about ancient Egyptian culture. The picture is further complicated by the presence of a series of related peoples on the periphery of the Mesopotamian territory. The Hittites,

---

1 Be sure to check the glossary at the back of the book for pronunciations and definitions of key terms.

◆ **1.2** *Hall of the Bulls*, c. 15,000–13,000 BCE. Paintings like these were not intended to be decorations, because they are not in the inhabited parts of the caves, but in the dark inner recesses. They probably had magical significance for their creators, who may have believed that gaining control of an animal in a painting would help to defeat it in the hunt. The variety of styles suggests that more than one artist worked in the cave. Note the detailed depiction of the animals' hair and markings.

Left wall, Lascaux (Dordogne), France. Largest bull c. 11′6″ (3.5 m) long. Image © Caves of Lascaux, Dordogne, France/The Bridgeman Art Library

the Syrians, and the peoples of early Iran all had periods of prosperity and artistic greatness, although in general they were overshadowed by the more powerful nations of Mesopotamia and Egypt. A description of their achievements would be beyond the scope of this book.

Sumer The history of Mesopotamia can be divided into two major periods: the **Sumerian** (c. 3500–2350 BCE) and the Semitic (c. 2350–612 BCE, when Nineveh fell). The Sumerians and Semitic peoples differed in their racial origins and languages; the term **Semitic** is derived from the name of Shem, one of the sons of Noah, and is generally used to refer to people speaking a Semitic language. In the ancient world, these included the Akkadians, Babylonians, Assyrians, and Phoenicians. The most common association of Semitic is with the Jewish people, whose traditional language, Hebrew, falls into the same group; they also originated in the region of Mesopotamia (for a discussion of the early history of the Jews, see Chapter 6). Arabic and certain other Mediterranean languages—including Maltese—are also Semitic.

The earliest Sumerian communities were agricultural settlements on the land between the Tigris and Euphrates rivers, an area known as the Fertile Crescent.

◆ **1.3** *Venus of Willendorf*, c. 28,000–23,000 BCE. This tiny statuette is one of a series of female figurines, known as Venus figures, from the Upper Paleolithic period. The sculptor has emphasized the sexual characteristics, enlarging the breasts and belly (perhaps pregnant), and drawing in the pubic triangle. The upper part of the face, which is featureless, has a hatched design perhaps suggesting hair (or a woven hat?).

From Willendorf, Austria. Limestone, 4¼″ (11 cm) high. Naturhistorisches Museum, Vienna, Austria//© Erich Lessing/Art Resource, NY

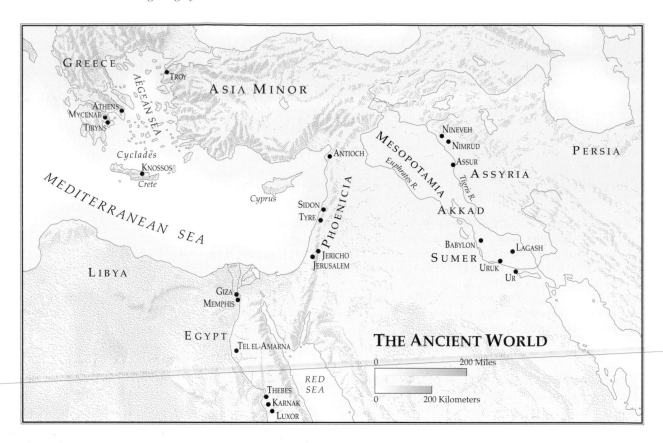

Unlike Upper Egypt, the land here is flat; dikes and canals were therefore needed to prevent flooding during the rainy season and to provide water during the rest of the year. When the early settlers found that they had to undertake these large-scale construction projects in order to improve their agriculture, they began to merge their small villages to form towns.

By far the most important event of this stage in the development of Sumerian culture was the invention of the first system of writing, known as **cuneiform** [**Fig. 1.4**]. The earliest form of writing was developed at Uruk (now Warka in southern Iraq), one of the first Mesopotamian settlements, around the middle of the fourth millennium BCE. It consisted of a series of simplified picture signs (pictographs) that represented the objects they described and, in addition, related ideas. Thus a leg could mean either a leg itself or the concept of walking. The signs were drawn on soft clay tablets, which were then baked hard. These pictorial signs evolved into a series of wedge-shaped marks that were pressed in clay with a split reed. The cuneiform system (*cuneus* is the Latin word for "wedge") had the advantage of being quick and economical, and the inscribed clay tablets were easy to store. The ability to write made it possible to trade and to keep records on a wider scale, and with the increasing economic strength this more highly organized society brought, several powerful cities began to develop.

The central focus of life in these larger communities was the temple, the dwelling place of the particular god who watched over the town. Religion, in fact, played a central part in all aspects of Sumerian culture. The gods were manifest in natural phenomena, sky and earth, sun and moon, lightning and storm. The chief religious holidays were closely linked to the passage of the seasons. The most important annual event was the New Year, the crucial moment when the blazing heat of the previous summer and the cold of winter gave way to the possibility of a fertile spring. The fertility of the earth was symbolized by the Great Mother and the sterility of the winter by the death of her partner, Tammuz. Each year his disappearance was mourned at the beginning of the New Year festival. When his resurrection was celebrated at the end of the festival, hope for the season to come was expressed by the renewal of the sacred marriage of god and goddess.

As in the Paleolithic period, the importance of female creative power is reflected in Sumerian art. Among its finest achievements is the so-called *Lady of Warka* [**Fig. 1.5**], a female head from the city of Uruk. It is not clear whether the head is of a divine or mortal figure. The face shows an altogether exceptional nobility and sensitivity.

The governing power in cities like Uruk was in the hands of the priests, who controlled and administered both religious and economic affairs. The ruler served as the representative on Earth of the god of the city

◆ **1.4** Forms of Early Writing. *Left:* Among the earliest examples of writing, the pictographs on this tablet show a list of slaves' names, with, on the upper right, a hand representing their owner. (Limestone tablet, c. 3200 BCE, from Kish, Iraq, now in the Louvre, Paris, France.) *Center:* This hieroglyphic inscription is dedicated to Amon-Min in his role as god of fertility. Note the "life" sign—the "ankh"—the fourth sign from the right on the top line. (Detail of a limestone bas-relief near the White Chapel, Karnak, Egypt. Middle Kingdom, c. 2065–1785 BCE.) *Right:* The cuneiform writing in this inscription records a bill of sale for a house and field paid for in silver. Note that the cuneiform signs have lost their resemblance to picture writing. (Terracotta tablet, c. 2550 BCE, from Sumer, now in the Louvre, Paris, France.) *(All images © Art Resource, NY, and (left) J. Schorman/Réunion des Musées Nationaux, (center and right) Erich Lessing.)*

but, unlike the pharaoh, was never thought of as divine and never became the center of a cult. His purpose was to watch over his people's interests by building better temples and digging more canals rather than acquiring personal wealth or power. Over the centuries, rulers began to detach themselves increasingly from the control of the priests, but the immense prestige of the temples assured the religious leaders a lasting power.

The Epic of Gilgamesh

The most famous of all Sumerian rulers was **Gilgamesh**, who ruled at Uruk about 2700 BCE. Around his name grew up a series of legends that developed into one of the first great masterpieces of poetic expression. *The Epic of Gilgamesh* begins with the adventures of Gilgamesh and his warrior friend Enkidu. Gilgamesh is courted by the queen of heaven, the goddess Ishtar. He rejects her advances and later kills a bull sent against him as a punishment. In revenge, the gods kill Enkidu; his death marks the turning point of the poem's mood. With the awareness of death's reality even for the bravest, Gilgamesh now sets out to seek the meaning of life. Toward the end of his journey he meets Utnapishtim, the only person to whom the gods have given everlasting life; from him Gilgamesh seeks the secrets of immortality. Utnapishtim, in the course of their conversation, tells him the story of the flood as it was known in Babylonia. By the end of the epic, Gilgamesh fails to achieve immortality and returns home to die.

Originally composed in Sumerian (c. 2000 BCE), the epic was eventually written down on clay tablets by Babylonians, Hittites, and others in their own languages. The poem was widely known. The story of the flood, recorded in tablet eleven, bears a striking resemblance to that of the biblical story in Genesis; both stories have parallel accounts of the building of boats, the coming of torrential rain, and the sending out of birds. The tone is very different, however. The God of the Hebrews acts out of moral disapproval, while the divinities in the epic were disturbed in their sleep by noisy mortals. *The Epic of Gilgamesh* is a profoundly pessimistic work. Unlike the ancient Egyptians, the Mesopotamians saw life as a continual struggle whose only alternative was the bleak darkness of death. Dying Egyptians, if they

◆ **1.5** *Lady of Warka*, c. 3500–3000 BCE. Perhaps an image of Inanna, the Sumerian goddess of love and war, originally, the hair was probably gold leaf and the eyes and eyebrows were colored inlays. The marble has been carved with great delicacy to show the planes of the cheeks and the area around the mouth. Note the small size of the head: marble was a rare material imported into Mesopotamia. The head was looted from the Baghdad Museum in the aftermath of the overthrow of Saddam Hussein in the spring of 2003 and later recovered.

From Uruk, Iraq. Marble, 7⅛″ (20 cm) high. Iraq Museum, Baghdad, Iraq//© Aladin Abdel Naby/Reuters/CORBIS

◆ **1.6** An Akkadian ruler, c. 2200 BCE. Possibly a portrait of King Sargon, the eyes were probably originally precious stones. The artist has taken great care to distinguish between the heavy beard, the finer hair of the mustache, and the even thinner hair on the head, held back by a headband.

From Nineveh (Kuyunjik), Iraq. Bronze, 14¼″ (37 cm) high. Iraq Museum, Baghdad, Iraq//© Scala/Art Resource, NY

◆ **1.7** *Victory Stele of Naram-Sin*, c. 2200 BCE. The king, wearing a horned crown, stands beneath symbols of the gods. The diagonal composition is well suited to the triangular shape of the stele.

From Susa, Iran, Akkadian. Pink sandstone, 6′7″ (2 m) high. Louvre, Paris, France//© Réunion des Musées Nationaux/Art Resource, NY

were righteous, could expect a happy existence in the next life, but for the Mesopotamian there was only the dim prospect of eternal gloom. The story of Gilgamesh rises to a supreme level in the section that describes the last stages of his journey. Then the epic touches on universal questions: Is all human achievement futile in the face of death? Is there a purpose to human existence? If so, how can it be discovered? The quest of Gilgamesh is the basic human search. Only at the end of Gilgamesh's journey do we sense that the purpose of the journey may have been the journey itself and that simply to have asked the questions was important. Weary as he was on his return, he was wiser than when he left, and in leaving us an account of his experiences, "engraved on a stone," he communicates them to us, a dramatic and moving illustration of the power of the written word.

Akkadian and Babylonian Culture In the years from 2350 to 2150 BCE, the whole of Mesopotamia fell under the control of the Semitic king Sargon and his descendants. The art of this Akkadian period (named for Sargon's capital city, Akkad) shows a continuation of the trends of the Sumerian Age, although total submission to the gods is replaced by a more positive attitude to human achievement. A bronze head from Nineveh [**Fig. 1.6**], perhaps a portrait of Sargon, expresses a pride and self-confidence that recur in other works of the period like the famous **Stele** of Naram-Sin (stele: stone slab), showing a later Akkadian king standing on the bodies of his enemies [**Fig. 1.7**].

When Akkadian rule was brought to an abrupt and violent end by the invasion of the Gutians from Iran, the cities of Mesopotamia reverted to earlier ways. As in the early Sumerian period, the chief buildings constructed were large brick platforms with superimposed terraces, known as **ziggurats.** These clearly had religious significance; the one built at Ur around 2100 BCE [**Fig. 1.8**] had huge staircases that led to a shrine at the top. The same return to traditional beliefs is illustrated by the religious inscriptions on the bases of the many surviving statues of Gudea, the governor of the city of Lagash around 2100 BCE, as well as by his humble attitude [**Fig. 1.9**].

The Law Code of Hammurabi By around 1800 BCE, Mesopotamia had once again been unified, this time under the Babylonians. Their most famous king, Hammurabi, was the author of a law code that was one of the earliest attempts to achieve social justice by legislation—a major development in the growth of civilization. The laws were carved on a stele, with Hammurabi shown at the top in the presence of the sun god Shamash [**Fig. 1.10**]. Many of the law code's

◆ **1.8** Ziggurat at Ur, Iraq, c. 2100–2000 BCE. The photograph shows the ziggurat now, partially restored. The drawing shows the probable original appearance. The Akkadian word **ziggurat** means "pinnacle" or "mountaintop"—a place where the gods were thought to reveal themselves. These plains dwellers made artificial mountains surrounded by shrines.

Mudbrick faced with baked brick laid in bitumen. Ur, Iraq//Image © Topham/The Image Works

◆ **1.9** *Seated Statue of Gudea*, c. 2100 BCE. The details of the drapery and headgear contrast with the simplicity of the face, which, like the position of the hands, suggests the humility of this neo-Sumerian ruler.

From Telloh, Iraq. Diorite, 17¼" (43.8 cm) high. Metropolitan Museum of Art, New York, USA//Image copyright © The Metropolitan Museum of Art/Art Resource, NY

◆ **1.10** Stele of Hammurabi (upper part), c. 1780 BCE. The sun god is dictating the law to the king, who is listening reverently. They are shown on a mountain, indicated by the irregular ridges beneath the god's feet. Carved in cuneiform below is *The Law Code of Hammurabi*, a portion of which is visible here.

From Susa, Iran. Basalt, entire stele height 7'4" (2.25 m) high. Louvre, Paris, France//© Réunion des Musées Nationaux/Art Resource, NY

◆ **1.11** *A Dying Lioness,* 668–626 BCE. The hunters' arrows have pierced the animal in several places, and she tries to raise her head as her back legs collapse. The artist's identification with the suffering beast shows greater sympathy than Assyrian depictions of human death in battle scenes.

Detail of relief from the Palace of Assurbanipal, Nineveh, Iraq. © *British Museum, London//Werner Forman/Art Resource, NY*

provisions deal with the relationship between husbands, wives, and other family members, as the following passage from *The Law Code of Hammurabi* shows:

> 131. If a man accuses his wife and she has not been taken in lying with another man, she shall take an oath in the name of god and she shall return to her house.
>
> 142. If a woman hates her husband and says, "Thou shalt not have me," her past shall be inquired into for any deficiency of hers; and if she has been careful and be without past sin and her husband has been going out and greatly belittling her, that woman has no blame. She shall take her dowry and go to her father's house.
>
> 145. If a man takes a wife and she does not present him with children, and he sets his face to take a concubine, that man may take a concubine and bring her into his house. That concubine shall not take precedence over his wife.
>
> 162. If a man takes a wife and she bears him children and that woman dies, her father may not lay claim to her dowry. Her dowry belongs to her children.

From *The Law Code of Hammurabi.* Copyright University of Chicago Press. Reprinted by permission.

The Assyrians By 1550 BCE, Babylon had been taken over by the Kassites, a formerly nomadic people who had occupied Babylonia and settled there, but they too would fall in turn under the domination of the Assyrians, who evolved the last great culture of ancient Mesopotamia. The peak of Assyrian power was between 1000 and 612 BCE, the time when Greek civilization was developing, as described in Chapter 2. But Assyrian achievements are the culmination of the culture of ancient Mesopotamia.

A huge palace constructed at Nimrud during the reign of Assurnasirpal II (883–859 BCE) was decorated with an elaborately carved series of relief slabs. The subjects are often religious, but several slabs that show the king on hunting expeditions have a vigor and freedom that are unusual in Mesopotamian art. The palaces of later Assyrian kings were decorated with similar reliefs. At Nineveh, the palace of Assurbanipal (668–626 BCE) was filled with scenes of war appropriate to an age of increasing turmoil. The representations of dead and dying soldiers on the battlefields are generally conventional, if highly elaborate, but again the hunting scenes are different—they show a genuine and moving identification with the suffering animals [**Fig. 1.11**].

With the fall of Nineveh in 612 BCE, Assyrian domination ended. The Assyrian Empire fell into the hands of two tribes, first the Medes and then the Persians; the great age of Mesopotamia was over. The Persians, like the Medes whom they subsequently conquered and absorbed, were originally a nomadic warrior people. In the century following their victory over the Assyrians, they continued to expand; by the death of the Persian ruler Cyrus the Great (c. 590–529 BCE), their empire stretched from the Mediterranean to the Indus River. After an unsuccessful attempt to conquer Greece (see Chapter 2), the Persians were finally conquered by Alexander the Great around 330 BCE.

Lacking the unifying elements provided in Egypt by the pharaoh and a national religion, the peoples of Mesopotamia perhaps never equaled Egyptian achievements in the arts. However, they formed ordered societies within independent city-states that anticipated the city-states of the Greeks. They also evolved a comparatively enlightened view of human relationships, as shown by *The Code of Hammurabi.*

ANCIENT EGYPT

One major determinant in the development of ancient Egyptian culture was geography. In total area, ancient Egypt was only a little larger than the state of Maryland. At the delta of the Nile was Lower Egypt, broad and flat, within easy reach of neighboring parts of the Mediterranean. Upper Egypt, more isolated from foreign contacts, consisted of a long, narrow strip of fertile soil, hemmed in by high cliffs and desert, running on either side of the Nile for most of its 1250 miles (2000 kilometers).

Because rainfall was sparse along the Nile, agriculture depended on the yearly flooding of the river. The immensely long span of Egyptian history was divided into thirty-one dynasties by an Egyptian priest, Manetho, who wrote a *History of Egypt* in Greek around 280 BCE. Modern scholars still follow his system, putting the dynasties into four groups and calling the period that preceded them the Predynastic. The four main divisions, with their approximate dates, are the Old Kingdom, c. 2700 BCE; the Middle Kingdom, c. 1990 BCE; the New Kingdom, c. 1570 BCE; and the Late Period, c. 1185 BCE until Egypt was absorbed into the Persian Empire around 500 BCE. The periods were separated from one another by intermediate times of disturbances and confusion.

During the final centuries of the Late Period, Egypt was invaded by the Nubians of the upper Nile, a black people whom the Egyptians called Cush. Overrunning first Upper Egypt in 750 BCE and then Lower Egypt around 720 BCE, they and their successors, the Nobatae, helped preserve Egyptian culture through the periods of foreign rule. The role played by these black peoples in the formation of the Western cultural tradition, in particular their influence on the Greeks, has recently become the focus of much scholarly discussion.

Despite its long history, the most striking feature of Egyptian culture is its unity and consistency. Nothing is in stronger contrast to the process of dynamic change initiated by the Greeks and still characteristic of our own culture than the relative absence of change of Egyptian art, religion, language, and political structure over thousands of years. Naturally, even the Egyptians were subject to outside influences, and events at home and abroad affected their worldview. It is possible to trace a mood of increasing pessimism from the vital, life-affirming spirit of the Old Kingdom to the New Kingdom vision of death as an escape from the grim realities of life. Nevertheless, the Egyptians maintained a strong resistance to change. Their art, in particular, remained conservative and rooted in the past.

In a land where regional independence already existed in the natural separation of Upper from Lower Egypt, national unity was maintained by a strong central government firmly controlled by a single ruler, the **pharaoh**. He was regarded as a living god, the equal of any other deity. He had absolute power, although the execution of his orders depended on a large official bureaucracy whose influence tended to increase in time.

EGYPTIAN RELIGION

Beneath the pharaoh were the priests, who saw as their responsibility the preservation of traditional religious beliefs. One of the most fundamental of these beliefs was the concept of divine kingship involving the pharaoh, a belief that reflected the Egyptian view of creation. The first great god of Egyptian religion, the sun god Aton-Ra, had created the world by imposing order on the primeval chaos of the universe; in the same way, the pharaoh ordered and controlled the visible world.

The most striking aspect of Egyptian religious thought, however, is its obsession with immortality and the possibilities of life after death. All Egyptians, not only the ruling class, were offered the hope of survival in the next world as a reward for a good life in a form that was thought of in literal, physical terms. Elaborate funeral rituals at which the dead would be judged and passed as worthy to move on to the afterlife began to develop. The funeral rites, together with their meaning, were described in a series of sacred texts known collectively as the *Book of the Dead*. The god who presided over these ceremonies was Osiris [**Fig. 1.12**]. The

◆ **1.12** *Sethos I*, c. 1290–1279 BCE. Sethos, who was buried in a tomb adjoining the temple decorated with this image, holds the hand of Thoth, the ibis-headed god of wisdom (in particular, writing), who places his hand on Sethos' shoulder.

Painted limestone relief. Image © Valley of the Kings, Thebes, Egypt // Giraudon / The Bridgeman Art Library

worship of Osiris, his wife Isis, and their son, the falcon god Horus, which came in time to symbolize a sense of spiritual afterlife, as opposed to simple material survival, represented the mystical side of Egyptian religion According to the myth, Osiris had been killed and then reborn; he owed his resurrection to the intervention of Isis, the dominant mother goddess of Egyptian religion, protectress of the living and dead. The worship of Isis became one of the most important and durable of Egyptian cults—a temple to her was found among the ruins of Roman Pompeii—while the return to life of Osiris provided a divine parallel to the annual rebirth of the land caused by the flooding Nile.

At the same time the Egyptians worshiped a host of other deities, sub-deities, and nature spirits whose names were often confused and sometimes interchangeable. These gods, responsible for all aspects of existence, inspired mythology and ritual that affected the daily life of every Egyptian. They included Hathor, the goddess of beauty and love, often represented as a cow; Bes, the god of war; and Hapi, the god of the Nile. Several animals, like the jackal and the cat, also had special sacred significance (see **Table 1.1**).

Traditional Egyptian religion involved a bewildering confusion of figures whose rights and privileges were jealously guarded by their priests. One of the ways to worship them was to give them visible form in works

Table 1.1 *Principal Egyptian Deities*

Aton-Ra	Sun God	Creator of Heaven and Earth
Osiris	King of the Underworld	Judge of the Dead
Isis	Sister and Wife of Osiris	Mourner of the Dead
Horus	Son of Isis and Osiris	God of the Morning Sun
Chensu	Moon God	Human-headed with crescent moon
Ptah	Father of the Gods	Created humans
Thoth	Ibis (bird) God	The Scribe of the Gods
Set	Brother of Osiris	Personification of Evil
Anubis	Jackal God	God of the Dead
Hapi	God of the Nile	Fertility God
Hathor	Cow Goddess	Sky Goddess
Seker	Hawk God	God of the Night Sun

of art—a principal function of Egyptian artists. In addition to producing images of deities, artists were required to provide temples and shrines where the deities could be honored. Even the buildings that commemorated the names and deeds of real people served religious purposes.

Thus the same central authority that controlled religion affected the development of the arts. The pharaoh's court laid down the standards applied throughout Egypt. Individual artists had little opportunity to exercise their own ingenuity by deviating from them.

VALUES

Mortality

The first humans to preserve the bodies of their dead were the Neanderthal people. They buried them in shallow graves and left offerings with them, suggesting that they envisioned a future life in which the dead people would use the objects placed with them. Virtually all subsequent cultures either inhumed (buried intact) the bodies of the dead or cremated them, placing the ashes in a container.

The notion of a life beyond the grave became central to the development of religious systems, although it took various forms. For the Egyptians, death brought judgment, and for those who passed the test, survival in the next world. The burial ritual sought to provide the dead person with the means to continue a life that was similar to that of this world. The body was preserved by the process of mummification, and food, servants (in the form of small statuettes known as shawabtis), and other necessities were placed in the tomb.

The Mesopotamian view of the world of the dead was far less comforting: a place of gloom and shadows. Nonetheless, the tombs of the illustrious dead contained treasures and, in the Royal Cemetery at Ur, the bodies of scores of human attendants sacrificed to accompany their dead rulers.

For many cultures, the treatment of a corpse was a major factor in the future life of the dead person. To leave a body unburied was regarded by the Greeks as the most terrible of punishments, because the victim could not complete the journey to the next world. In Sophocles' play Antigone, the heroine buries the body of her brother even though Creon, the king of Thebes, has decreed that he should be left unburied as punishment for his betrayal of his city.

The range of funeral practices over the past ten thousand years or so is vast, but most at least imply a belief in some form of survival—physical or spiritual—after death.

THE OLD AND MIDDLE KINGDOMS

The huge scale of many Egyptian works of art is at least in part the result of the easy availability of stone, the most frequently used material from the early Old King dom to the Late Period. In Dynasty III, the architect Imhotep used stone to construct the earliest **pyramid** as a tomb for his master, the pharaoh Zoser. This began the tradition of building massive funerary monuments that would guarantee immortality for their occupants. At the same time, the practice of mummification developed. The body was embalmed to maintain its physical form, because Egyptian religious belief held that preservation of the body was necessary for the survival of the soul. Imhotep, the first architect known to history, was in later ages regarded as the epitome of wisdom and was deified.

The Age of the Pyramids The great age of the pyramid came in Dynasty IV with the construction of the three colossal pyramids at Giza for the pharaohs Cheops, Chefren, and Mycerinus. In size and abstract simplicity, these structures show Egyptian skill in design and engineering on a massive scale—an achievement probably made possible by slave labor, although some scholars believe that the building of the great monuments was essentially the work of farmers during the off-season. In any case, the pyramids and almost all other Egyptian works of art perpetuate the memories of members of the upper classes and bear witness to a lifestyle that would not have been possible without slaves. We still know little about the slaves or the poor Egyptians who were farm laborers. Many of the slaves were captured prisoners who were forced to labor in the government quarries and on the estates of the tem-ples. Over time, the descendants of slaves could enlist in the army; as professional soldiers they could take their place in Egyptian society.

The construction of the pyramids was an elaborate and complex affair. Stone quarried on the spot formed the core of each structure, but the fine limestone blocks originally used for facing, now eroded away, came from across the Nile. These were quarried in the dry season; then when the floods came, they were ferried across the river, cut into shape, and dragged into place. At the center of each pyramid was a chamber in which was placed the mummified body of the pharaoh, surrounded by the treasures that were to follow him into the next life. The pharaohs planned these massive constructions as their resting places for eternity and as monuments that would perpetuate their names. Their success was partial. Four and a half thousand years later, their names are remembered—their pyramids, still dominating the flat landscape, symbolize the enduring character of ancient Egypt. As shelters for their occupants and their treasures, however, the pyramids were vulnerable. The size of the pyramids drew attention to the riches hidden within them, and robbers were quick to tunnel through and plunder them, sometimes only shortly after the burial chamber had been sealed.

Chefren, who commissioned the second of the three pyramids at Giza, was also responsible for perhaps the most famous of all Egyptian images, the colossal Sphinx [**Fig. 1.13**], a guardian for his tomb. The aloof tranquility of the human face, perhaps a portrait of the pharaoh, set on a lion's body, made an especially strong impression fifteen hundred years later on the Classical Greeks, who saw it as a divine symbol of the mysterious and enigmatic. Greek art frequently uses the sphinx as a motif, and it also appears in Greek mythology, most

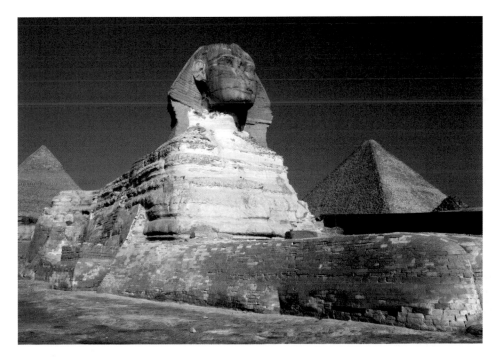

◆ **1.13** The Great Sphinx, c. 2575–2525 BCE. Behind the Great Sphinx on the left is the Pyramid of Chefren, and on the right is the Pyramid of Cheops. The Sphinx is carved out of the natural surface of the rock. It has the body of a lion and a human head (perhaps an idealized portrait of Chefren) and guards the pharaoh's burial chamber at the heart of his pyramid.

At Gizeh, Egypt. Sandstone, c. 65′ (19.8 m) high, 240′ (73.2 m) long. Image © Steve Vidler/SuperStock

◆ **1.14** *Chefren* (right side and front), c. 2575–2525 BCE. The sculptor has shown the drapery and anatomy with great realism, while producing an idealized portrait of the god king. His divine power is represented by Horus, the falcon god of the Morning Sun, perched behind his head.

From Gizeh, Egypt. Dark green diorite, 5′6″ (1.7 m) high. Egyptian Museum, Cairo, Egypt/© The Art Archive/Gianni Dagli Orti

typically in the story of how Oedipus solved its riddle and thereby saved the Greek city of Thebes from disaster.

The appearance of Chefren is preserved for us in several statues that are typical of Old Kingdom art [**Fig. 1.14**]. The sculptor's approach to anatomy and drapery is realistic, and details are shown with great precision, but the features of the pharaoh are idealized; it is a portrait not of an individual but of the concept of divine power, power symbolized by the falcon god Horus perched behind the pharaoh's head. The calmness, even indifference, of the expression is particularly striking.

The art of the Old Kingdom reflects a mood of confidence and certainty that ended abruptly around 2200 BCE with a period of violent disturbance. Divisions between the regions began to strengthen the power of local governors. By the time of the Middle Kingdom, it was no longer possible for pharaoh, priests, or nobles to face the future with complete trust in divine providence. Middle Kingdom art reflects this new uncertainty in two ways: the Old Kingdom came to represent a kind of Golden Age; artists tried to recapture its lofty serenity in their own works. At the same time, the more

troubled spirit of the new period is reflected in the massive weight and somber expressions of some of the official portraits. The furrowed brow and grim look of Sesostris III convey the impression that to be a Middle Kingdom pharaoh was hardly a relaxing occupation [**Fig. 1.15**].

THE NEW KINGDOM

Despite increasing contacts with foreign cultures, New Kingdom artists continued basically to work within age-old traditions. Like virtually all artists in the ancient world, they depicted the idea of what they wanted to show rather than its actual appearance; an eye in a profile carving, for example, would be depicted as if seen from the front. This approach is often called "conceptual," as opposed to the "descriptive" style the Greeks were to develop.

Akhenaton and His Reforms In Dynasty XVIII, however, there was a remarkable change. The pharaoh Amenhotep IV, who ruled from 1379 to 1362 BCE, single-handedly attempted a total reform of Egyptian religious and political life. He replaced the numberless

◆ **1.16** *Akhenaton, Nefertiti, and Three of Their Children,* c. 1370–1350 BCE. The royal family sits beneath the rays of the sun, symbolizing the sun god Aton, whose cult was at the center of Akhenaton's reforms. The extreme ease and naturalism of the style is typical of the period.

From Amarna, Egypt. Limestone relief, 17″ (43 cm) high. Ägyptisches Museum, Staatliche Museen zu Berlin, Berlin, Germany//© Bildarchiv Preussischer Kulturbesitz/Art Resource, NY

◆ **1.15** *Sesostris III*, c. 1878–1841 BCE. Note the strong contrast between the tense pose of this statue, hands gripping his sides, and the relaxed mood of Chefren in Figure 1.14.

From Deir el-Bahri, Egypt. Black granite, 4′10½″ (1.5 m) high. © British Museum, London, UK/The Bridgeman Art Library

deities of traditional religion with a single one, the sun god Aton, and changed his own name to Akhenaton, or "the servant of Aton." The most complete expression of his devotion to Aton survives in the form of a hymn to the god, which movingly expresses his sincerity: "Thou appearest beautifully on the horizon of Heaven, thou living Aton, the beginning of life! When thou art risen on the eastern horizon, thou hast filled every land with thy beauty. . . ." In order to make these revolutionary moves more effective and to escape the influence of the priests at the royal court of Thebes, he transferred the capital to a new location, known today as Tel el-Amarna.

Here a new kind of art developed. The weight and idealism of the traditional conceptual style gave way to a new lightness and naturalism. For the first time, physical characteristics are depicted in detail, and scenes are relaxed and even humorous. A stone relief showing the royal couple and three of their children sitting quietly under the rays of the sun disc is an astonishing departure from the dignified style of the preceding thousand years [**Fig. 1.16**]. Queen Nefertiti is the subject of perhaps the most famous of all Egyptian portraits [**Fig. 1.17**], a sculpture that shows none of the exaggeration to which

◆ **1.17** *Queen Nefertiti,* c. 1355–1335 BCE. Although the portrait is not exaggerated, it is idealized.

From Tel el-Amarna, Egypt. Painted limestone, 20″ (50.8 cm) high. Ägyptisches Museum, Staatliche Museen zu Berlin, Berlin, Germany//© Bildarchiv Preussischer Kulturbesitz/Art Resource, NY

Amarna art is sometimes prone, but a grace and elegance very different from earlier official portraits.

All of these artistic changes were the result of Akhenaton's sweeping and revolutionary religious reforms, but they did not last long. Akhenaton's belief in a single god who ruled the universe was threatening to the priests, who had a vested interest in preserving the old polytheistic traditions. Not surprisingly, Akhenaton's successors branded him a heretic and fanatic and cut out his name from all of the monuments that survived him.

Return to Tradition The reaction against Akhenaton's religious policy and the Amarna style was almost immediate. His successor, Tutankhamen, however, is remembered not for leading the opposition—or for any event in his short life. He owes his fame to the treasures found intact in his undisturbed tomb. These sumptuous gold objects, enriched with ivory and precious stones, still show something of the liveliness of Amarna art, but a return to conservatism is beginning; in fact by Dynasty XIX and XX, Akhenaton had been completely forgotten. In any case, it is not so much for what they reveal about the trends in art that the treasures of Tutankhamen are significant. The discovery of the tomb is important for a different reason. Our knowledge of the cultures of the ancient world is constantly being revised by the work of archaeologists; many of their finds are minor, but some are major and spectacular. In the case of excavations such as the tomb of Tutankhamen, the process of uncovering the past sometimes becomes as exciting and significant as what is discovered. The long search conducted by Howard Carter in the Valley of the Kings that culminated in the opening of the inner chamber of the sealed tomb of Tutankhamen on February 17, 1923, and the discovery of the intact sarcophagus of the king has become part of history [**Figs. 1.18, 1.19**].

The excavations of Knossos and Mycenae, discussed later in this chapter, and the discovery of Pompeii (Chapter 4) are also major turning points in the growth of our knowledge of the past, but sensational finds such as these are exceptions. Understanding the cultural achievements of past civilizations involves a slow and painstaking series of minor discoveries, each of which adds to the knowledge that thus must be constantly revised and reinterpreted.

◆ **1.18** The Treasures of Tutankhamen, 1334–1325 BCE. This is what Howard Carter saw on November 26, 1922, when he opened the doorway of the antechamber of the tomb of Tutankhamen. The objects include three gilt couches in the form of animals and, at the right in back, the pharaoh's golden throne. The tomb was opened three months later.

Antechamber, west side. Valley of the Kings, Thebes, Egypt//Image © François Guenet/Art Resource, NY

◆ **1.19** Death Mask of Tutankhamen, c. 1323 BCE. Note the false beard, symbol of kingship, and the sumptuous use of gold and lapis lazuli.

From Thebes, Egypt. Gold with inlay of semiprecious stones, 1′9¼″ (54 cm) high. Egyptian Museum, Cairo, Egypt//© François Guenet/Art Resource, NY

By the close of the New Kingdom, the taste for monumental building had returned. The temples constructed during the reign of Ramses II (1298–1232 BCE) at Luxor, Karnak, and Abu Simbel are probably the most colossal of all Egyptian constructions [**Fig. 1.20**]. Within a century, however, internal dissensions and foreign events had produced a sharp decline in Egypt's power. Throughout the Late Period, artists reverted again to the styles of earlier periods. Tombs were once again constructed in the shape of pyramids, as they had been in the Old Kingdom, and sculptors tried to recapture the realism and sense of volume of Old and Middle Kingdom art. Even direct contacts with the Assyrians, Persians, and Greeks—during the period between the Assyrian occupation of 671–633 BCE and Alexander's conquest of Egypt in 331 BCE—produced little effect on late Egyptian art. To the end of their history, the Egyptians remained faithful to their three-thousand-year-old tradition. Probably no other culture in human history has ever demonstrated so strong a conservatism and determination to preserve its separate traditions.

◆ **1.20** Temple of Ramses II, c. 1275–1225 BCE. These four huge statues, erected in commemoration of Ramses' military victories, are all of the pharaoh. Between and near their feet are small statues of Ramses' mother, wife, and children. Below are statues of the pharaoh as the god Osiris and the falcon god Horus, to whom the temple was dedicated.

At Abu Simbel (now relocated), Egypt. Colossi c. 65′ (19.8 m) high. Image © Vanni/Art Resource, NY

VOICES OF THEIR TIMES

Love, Marriage, and Divorce in Ancient Egypt

A Young Man's Love Song

Seven days from yesterday I have not seen my
  beloved,
And sickness has crept over me,
And I am become heavy in my limbs
And am unmindful of mine own body.
If the master-physicians come to me,
My heart has no comfort of their remedies,
And the magicians, no resource is in them,
My malady is not diagnosed.
Better for me is my beloved than any remedies,
More important is she for me than the entire
  compendium of medicine.
My salutation is when she enters from without.
When I see her, then am I well;
Opens she her eye, my limbs are young again;
Speaks she, and I am strong;
And when I embrace her, she banishes evil,
And it passes from me for seven days.

From *Life Under the Pharaohs* by Leonard Cottrell, p. 84, 94. Copyright © 1960 by Leonard Cottrell. Reprinted by permission of Henry Holt and Company, LLC.

A Young Girl's Song to Her Beloved

Oh, flower of henna!
My heart stands still in thy presence.
I have made mine eyes brilliant for thee with
  kohl.
When I behold thee, I fly to thee, oh my
  Beloved!
Oh, Lord of my heart, sweet is this hour. An
  hour passed with thee is worth an hour of
  eternity!
Oh, flower of marjoram!
Fain would I be to thee as the garden in which
  are planted flowers and sweet-smelling
shrubs! the garden watered by pleasant
  runlets, and refreshed by the north breeze!
Here let us walk, oh my Beloved, hand in
  hand, our hearts filled with joy!
Better than food, better than drink, is it to
  behold thee.
To behold thee, and to behold thee again!

From *Pharaohs, Fellahs, and Explorers* by Amelia Edwards, p. 225, 1891.

A Father's Advice to His Son

Double the food which thou givest thy mother, carry her as she carried thee. She had a heavy load in thee, but she did not leave it to me. After thou wert borne she was still burdened with thee; her breast was in thy mouth for three years, and though thy filth was disgusting, her heart was not disgusted. When thou takest a wife, remember how thy mother gave birth to thee, and her raising thee as well; do not let thy wife blame thee, nor cause that she raise her hands to the god.

From *Temples, Tombs, and Hieroglyphics* by Barbara Mertz, p. 333, © 1964, 1978.

How a Wife Can Obtain a Divorce

If she shall stand up in the congregation and shall say, "I divorce my husband," the price of divorce shall be on her head; she shall return to the scales and weigh for the husband five shekels, and all which I have delivered into her hand she shall give back, and she shall go away whithersoever she will.

From *Life Under the Pharaohs* by Leonard Cottrell, p. 84, 94. Copyright © 1960 by Leonard Cottrell. Reprinted by permission of Henry Holt and Company, LLC.

AEGEAN CULTURE IN THE BRONZE AGE

Neither the Egyptians of the Old Kingdom nor the Sumerians appear to have demonstrated any interest in their contemporaries living to the west of them, and with good reason. In Greece and the islands of the Aegean Sea, although the arrival of immigrants from farther east in the early Neolithic period (c. 6000 BCE) had brought new agricultural techniques, life in general continued there for the next three thousand years almost completely untouched by the rise of organized cultures elsewhere.

Yet, beginning in the early Bronze Age, there developed in the area around the Aegean Sea a level of civilization as brilliant and sophisticated as any other in Europe or western Asia. (The same period saw the appearance of a similarly urban culture in the Indus Valley on the Indian subcontinent.) Then around 1100 BCE, after almost two thousand years of existence, this Bronze Age Aegean civilization disappeared as dramatically as it had arisen. The rediscovery in the twentieth century of these peoples—the Minoans of Crete and

◆ **1.21** Cycladic vase, c. 2500–2200 BCE. Vase in the shape of a hedgehog drinking from a bowl.

From Syros (Cyclades), Greece. Painted clay, 4¼″ (11 cm) high. National Archaeological Museum, Athens, Greece//© Erich Lessing/Art Resource, NY

◆ **1.22** Cycladic idol, c. 2500 BCE. Like the overwhelming majority of the Cycladic statuettes, this one is of a woman. The form—head back, arms folded—is also standard. Although modern viewers think of them as standing, the figures were probably buried resting on their backs.

From Cyclades, Greece. Marble, 19¼″ (50 cm) high. © British Museum, London/Art Resource, NY

the Mycenaeans of mainland Greece—is perhaps the most splendid achievement in the history of archaeology in the Mediterranean and one that has opened up vast new perspectives in the study of the later Greeks.

What connection is there between Greek culture and the magnificent civilization of the Bronze Age? Did much of later Greek religion, thought, and art have its origins in this earlier period, even though the Greeks seemed to know nothing about it? Or was the culture of the Minoans and Mycenaeans an isolated phenomenon, destroyed utterly near the end of the Bronze Age, lost until it was found again in the twentieth century? The Aegean culture is important not only for the possible light it throws on later times but also because it shows that the ancient world could reach beyond the monumentality and earnestness of the Egyptians and Mesopotamians, that it could attain a way of life that valued grace, beauty, and comfort—a life that could truly be called civilized.

CYCLADIC ART

During most of the Bronze Age, the major centers of Aegean culture were on Crete or the mainland, but in the early phase there were settlements on a group of islands of the central Aegean, the Cyclades. Little is known about these Cycladic people. They used bronze tools. They also produced pottery that, although less finely made than that produced elsewhere in the Aegean

at the time, sometimes shows remarkable imagination and even humor [**Fig. 1.21**]. The chief claim to fame of Cycladic art—a considerable one—lies in the marble statues, or idols, that were produced in large quantities and in many cases buried with the dead. The statues range in height from a few inches to almost life-size; the average is about a foot (30.5 centimeters) high. Most of the figures are female; the most common type shows a naked woman standing or, more probably, lying, with her arms folded and head tilted back [**Fig. 1.22**]. The face is indicated only by a central ridge for the nose. The simplicity of the form and the fine working of the marble—stone of superb quality—often produce an effect of great beauty.

The purpose of the Cycladic idols remains uncertain. The fact that most of them have been found in graves suggests that they had a religious function in the funeral ritual. The overwhelming preponderance of female figures seems to indicate that they were in some way connected with the cult of the mother goddess, which was common in Mesopotamia and which dominated Aegean Bronze Age religion. Whether the figures actually represent goddesses remains uncertain.

THE MINOANS OF CRETE

We now know that the period of the production of the Cycladic idols was one of increasing development on Crete. Yet for the classical Greeks of the fifth century BCE, Crete was chiefly famous as the home of the legendary King Minos, who ruled at Knossos. Here, according to myth, was a Labyrinth that housed the Minotaur, a monstrous creature, half man and half bull, the product of the union of Minos's wife Pasiphae with a bull. Minos exacted from Athens a regular tribute of seven boys and seven girls, who were sent to be devoured by the Minotaur.

According to the myths, after this had been going on for some time, the Athenian hero Theseus volunteered to stop the grisly tribute. He went to Knossos with the new group of intended victims and, with the help of the king's daughter Ariadne (who had fallen in love with him), killed the Minotaur in its lair in the middle of the Labyrinth. He then escaped with Ariadne and the Athenian boys and girls. Theseus later abandoned Ariadne on the island of Naxos, but the god Dionysus discovered her there and comforted her. The story had many more details, and other myths describe other events. The important point is that the later Greeks had a mythological picture of Knossos as a prosperous and thriving community ruled by a powerful and ruthless king from his palace. Knossos was not the only center mentioned in Greek stories of Crete. In the *Odyssey,* Homer even refers to "Crete of a hundred cities."

These were, however, legends. By the time of Classical Greece, no evidence whatsoever for the existence of the Palace of Minos or the other cities could be seen. It is not surprising that the Greeks showed no inclination to try to find any hidden traces. Archaeology, after all, is a relatively modern pursuit, and there is little indication of any serious enthusiasm in classical antiquity for the material remains of the past. Later ages continued to accept the Greeks' own judgment. For many centuries the story of Minos and the Labyrinth was thought to be a good tale with no foundation in fact.

The Excavation of Knossos

By the end of the nineteenth century, however, things had changed. Heinrich Schliemann had proved that the stories of the war against Troy and the Mycenaeans who had waged it were far from mere legends. Was it possible that the mythical palace of King Minos at Knossos also really existed? In 1894 the English archaeologist Arthur Evans first went to Crete to see if he could discover something of its history in the Bronze Age. At Knossos he found evidence of ancient remains, some of them already uncovered by amateur enthusiasts. He returned in 1899 and again in 1900, this time with a permit to excavate. On March 23,

1900, serious work began at Knossos, and within days it became apparent that the finds represented a civilization even older than that of the Mycenaeans. The quantity was staggering: pottery, frescoes, inscribed tablets, and, on April 13, a room with elaborate paintings and a raised seat with high back—the throne room of King Minos [**Fig. 1.23**]. Evans's discoveries at Knossos (and finds later made elsewhere on Crete by other archaeologists) did much to confirm legendary accounts of Cretan prosperity and power. Yet these discoveries did far more than merely give a true historical background to the myth of the Minotaur. Evans had in fact found an entire civilization, which he called Minoan after the legendary king. Evans is said to have once remarked modestly, "Any success as an archaeologist I owe to two things: very short sight, so I look at everything closely, and being slow on the uptake, so I never leap to conclusions."

Actually, the magnitude of his achievement can scarcely be exaggerated. All study of the Minoans has been strongly influenced by his initial classification of the finds, especially the pottery. Evans divided the history of the Bronze Age in Crete into three main periods— Early Minoan, Middle Minoan, and Late Minoan—and further subdivided each of these into three. The precise dates of each period can be disputed, but all of the excavations of the years following Evans have confirmed his initial description of the main sequence of events.

Life and Art in the Minoan Palaces

The Early Minoan period was one of increasing growth. Small towns began to appear in the south and east of Crete, and the first contacts were established with Egypt and Mesopotamia. Around 2000 BCE, however, came the first major development in Minoan civilization, marking the beginning of the Middle Minoan period. The earlier scattered towns were abandoned and large urban centers evolved. These are generally called palaces, although their function was far more than just to provide homes for ruling families.

The best known of these centers is Knossos (other important ones have been excavated at Phaistos, Mallia, and Zakro) [**Fig. 1.24**]. The main palace building, constructed around an open rectangular courtyard, contained rooms for banquets, public receptions, religious ceremonies, and administrative work. In addition, there were living quarters for the royal family and working areas for slaves and craftsmen. Around the palace were the private houses of the aristocrats and chief religious leaders. The technical sophistication of these great centers was remarkable. There were elaborate drainage systems, and the palaces were designed and constructed to remain cool in summer and be heated easily in winter.

Few aspects of the Minoan achievement are more impressive than the development of an architectural style appropriate for these great structures. Unlike the

◆ **1.23** Throne Room, Palace of Minos, Knossos (Crete), Greece, c. 1450 BCE. The room was reconstructed shortly before the final destruction of the palace. The frescoes around the throne show sacred flowers and griffins—mythological beasts with lion bodies and bird heads. *(Image © Vanni/Art Resource, NY)*

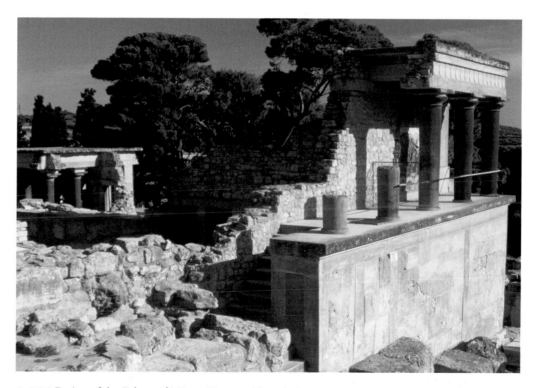

◆ **1.24** Ruins of the Palace of Minos, Knossos (Crete), Greece, c. 1600–1400 BCE. Note the Minoan columns tapering downward and on the wall below, the faint remains of a fresco of a giant, charging bull. This image would have been the first impression of Knossos for many visitors because the walkway led to this main north entrance of the palace. *(© Gail Mooney/CORBIS)*

◆ **1.25** Reconstruction drawing of the Palace of Minos, Knossos (Crete), Greece, c. 1600–1400 bce. Each Cretan palace had a central court oriented north-south, state apartments to the west, and royal living apartments to the east. On the highest of the five levels of the Palace (top left), note the stylized bull's horns, which would have been visible to approaching travelers. *(Private Collection, Paris, France/ © The Art Archive/Gianni Dagli Orti)*

carefully, almost obsessively planned Egyptian building complexes, Minoan palaces seem at first disorganized in plan. In practice, however, the division between the various functions of a palace—official, residential, religious—was achieved by a careful division of space [**Fig. 1.25**]. In the construction of the buildings, rough stonework was hidden behind plaster and frescoes. Minoan columns tapered downward; their narrowest point was at their base, unlike Greek columns, which widen to their base, or Egyptian columns, most of which retain the same width from top to bottom. Minoan architects used these columns to provide impressive entrances and to construct **light-wells** (vertical shafts running down through the buildings to carry light to the lower stories).

Middle Minoan art shows great liveliness and color. The brilliantly painted pottery, superb jewelry such as the famous Wasp Pendant from Mallia [**Fig. 1.26**], and the many exquisitely carved seal stones all attest to the Minoans' love of beauty and artistic skill. Unlike their contemporaries in Egypt and Mesopotamia, the Minoans showed little interest in monumental art. Their greatest works are on a small, even miniature, scale. At the same time, they invented a writing system of hieroglyphic signs that was used in the archives of the palace for administrative purposes.

Toward the end of the Middle Minoan period (c. 1700 bce), the palaces were destroyed, probably by an earthquake, and then rebuilt on an even grander scale. There was further reconstruction about a century later, perhaps because of another earthquake. These palaces of the Late Minoan period represent the high point of Minoan culture. The wall paintings of this period are among the greatest treasures of all. Their spontaneity

◆ **1.26** *Wasp Pendant,* c. 1700 bce. This enlarged view shows the exquisite craftsmanship that made use of the techniques of granulation and wire-working. Two wasps (or perhaps hornets) are curved around a honeycomb.

From Mallia (Crete), Greece. Gold, 1⅞″ (5 cm) wide. Heraklion Museum, Crete, Greece//© The Art Archive/Gianni Dagli Orti

and freedom create a very different mood from Egyptian and Mesopotamian art, and they show a love of nature expressed with brilliant colors and vivid observation. Most of the best examples of these later paintings are from Knossos, but some particularly enchanting scenes have been found in the recent excavation of a Minoan colony on the island of Thera [**Fig. 1.27**].

Although the rulers of the palaces seem to have been male, the central figure of Minoan religion was a mother

◆ **1.27** Landscape with Swallows (Spring Fresco), c. 1650 BCE. A springtime scene—bright flowers and soaring birds— covers three sides of a small room in a Minoan building on the island of Thera.

From Room Delta 2, Akrotiri, (Santorini), Greece. Fresco, 7′6″ (2.3 m) high. National Archaeological Museum, Athens, Greece//© The Art Archive/Gianni Dagli Orti

goddess who was connected with fertility. She seems to have taken on different forms, or rather the function of female divinity was divided among several separate deities. Sometimes when she is shown flanked by animals, as the Mistress of the Beasts, she seems to be the ancestor of the Greek goddess Artemis. Other depictions show goddesses of vegetation. The most famous Minoan figurine is the so-called *Snake Goddess* [**Fig. 1.28**].

Throughout the last great age of the palaces, the influence of Minoan artistic styles began to spread to the mainland, but Minoan political and military power was on the wane, and Knossos seems to have been invaded and occupied by mainlanders around 1450 BCE. Shortly afterward, both at Knossos and elsewhere, there is evidence of widespread destruction.

By 1400 BCE, Minoan culture had ended abruptly. The causes are mysterious and have been much argued; we shall probably never know exactly what happened. The eruption of a volcano on Thera a century earlier, about 1500 BCE, may have played some part in changing the balance of power in the Aegean. In any case, there is no doubt that throughout the last period of the palaces a new power was growing, the Mycenaeans. These people may well have played a part in the destruction of Knossos.

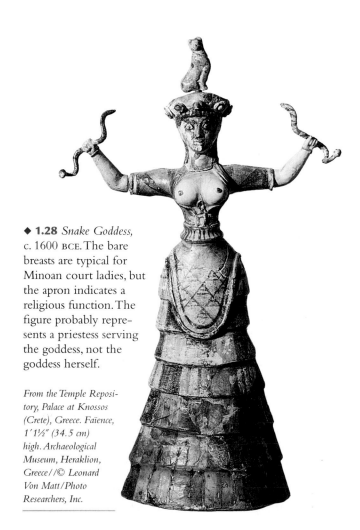

◆ **1.28** *Snake Goddess,* c. 1600 BCE. The bare breasts are typical for Minoan court ladies, but the apron indicates a religious function. The figure probably represents a priestess serving the goddess, not the goddess herself.

From the Temple Repository, Palace at Knossos (Crete), Greece. Faïence, 1′1½″ (34.5 cm) high. Archaeological Museum, Heraklion, Greece//© Leonard Von Matt/Photo Researchers, Inc.

THE DISCOVERY OF MYCENAE AND SCHLIEMANN

The Mycenaeans, the people of mainland Greece in the Bronze Age, are named after the largest of their settlements, Mycenae. Most of the Mycenaean centers were in the southern part of Greece known as the Peloponnesus, although there were also some settlements farther north, of which the two most important were Athens and Thebes. Like the Minoans, the Mycenaeans were familiar from Greek myths long before their material remains were excavated. They were famous in legend mainly for launching an expedition against Troy, across the Aegean Sea. The Trojan War (c. 1250 BCE) and its aftermath provided the material for many later Greek works, most notably the *Iliad* and the *Odyssey,* the two great epic poems of Homer, but for a long time it was believed that the war and even the existence of Troy were myths.

Heinrich Schliemann dedicated his life and work to proving that the legends were founded on reality. Born in Germany in 1822, Schliemann was introduced to the Homeric poems as a child by his father and was overwhelmed by their incomparable vividness. He became determined to discover Homer's Troy and prove the poet right. Excavation has always been expensive, and Schliemann therefore decided to make his fortune in business, retire early, and devote his profits to the pursuit of his goal. By 1863 this remarkable man had accumulated a considerable amount of money from trading in, among other things, tea and was ready to devote himself to his second career. After a period of study and travel, in 1870 he finally began excavations on the site where he had decided the remains of Homer's Troy lay buried beneath the Roman city of Ilium. By 1873 he had found not only walls and the gate of the city but also quantities of gold, silver, and bronze objects.

Inspired by the success of his Trojan campaign, Schliemann moved on to the second part of his task: to discover the Mycenaeans who had made war on Troy. In 1876 he began to excavate within the walls of Mycenae, and there he almost immediately came upon the Royal Grave Circle with its stupendous quantities of gold treasures [**Fig. 1.29**]. Homer had described Mycenae as "rich in gold," and Schliemann was always convinced that the royal family whose graves he had unearthed was that of Agamemnon, leader of the Mycenaean expedition against Troy. We now know that the finds date to an even earlier period, and later excavations both at

◆ **1.29** *Funerary mask,* c. 1600–1500 BCE. This death mask is actually a portrait of a Mycenaean ruler of three centuries earlier than Agamemnon.

From Grave Circle A, Shaft Grave V, Mycenae, Greece. Beaten gold, 10⅛″ (26 cm) high. National Archaeological Museum, Athens, Greece // © Nimatallah / Art Resource, NY

Mycenae and at other mainland sites have provided a much more exact picture of Mycenaean history. This does not diminish Schliemann's achievement. However unscientific his methods, he had proved the existence of a civilization in Bronze Age Greece that surpassed in splendor even the legends; he had opened a new era in the study of the past.

Mycenaean Art and Architecture Like the Minoans, the Mycenaeans centered their lives around great palace complexes. In Mycenae, the palace probably was first built around 1600 BCE, and the graves found by Schliemann date to shortly thereafter. Until the fall of Knossos in 1400 BCE, the Mycenaeans were strongly under the influence of Minoan culture, but with the end of Minoan power they became the natural leaders in the Aegean area. From 1400 to 1200 BCE, Mycenaean traders traveled throughout the Mediterranean, from Egypt and the Near East as far west as Italy. The Mycenaean empire grew in power and prosperity.

Toward the end of this period (around 1250 BCE), the successful expedition was launched against Troy, perhaps for reasons of trade rivalry. A short time later (around 1200 BCE), the Mycenaean empire fell, its major centers destroyed and most of them abandoned. Invasion by enemies, internal strife, and natural causes have all been suggested, but the fall of the Mycenaeans still remains mysterious.

Their collapse is made even more incomprehensible by the massive fortifications that protected most of the palaces. At Mycenae, the walls are 15 feet (4.6 meters) thick and probably were 50 feet (15.3 meters) high. As in the case of other Mycenaean centers, the actual location was chosen for its defensibility [**Fig. 1.30**]. The somber character of these fortress-palaces is reflected in the general tone of Mycenaean civilization.

Unlike the relaxed culture of the Minoans, Mycenaean culture as reflected in its art was preoccupied with death and war. It is no coincidence that many of the richest finds have come from tombs. Like the Minoans, the Mycenaeans decorated their palaces with frescoes, although the Mycenaean paintings are more solemn and dignified than their Minoan counterparts.

The disaster of 1200 BCE violently ended the Mycenaeans' political and economic domination of the Mediterranean, but their culture lingered on for another one hundred years. A few of the palaces were inhabited again, and some Mycenaeans fled eastward, where they settled on the islands of Rhodes and Cyprus. By 1100 BCE, however, renewed violence had extinguished the last traces of Bronze Age culture in Greece. A century later, after a period our lack of information forces us to call the Dark Age, the story of Western culture truly begins with the dawning of the Iron Age.

FROM BRONZE AGE TO IRON AGE

Before leaving the rich achievements of the Bronze Age world, both in Greece and farther afield, it is worth asking how much survived to be handed down to our own

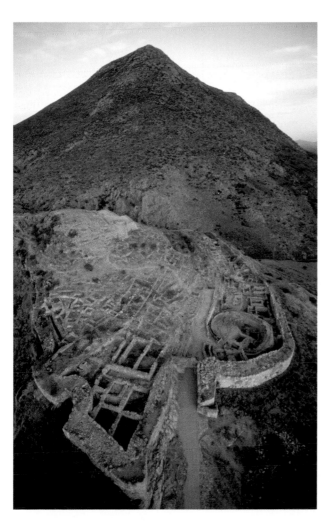

civilization. For the Greeks, the Iron Age brought a new beginning in most material respects. At the same time, however, there are links with the earlier era in less tangible areas. In particular, although Greek religion never placed as strong an emphasis on worship of the mother goddess as did the Bronze Age, she remained a potent force in traditional beliefs. Behind the official reverence for Zeus, father of the gods and mortals, there lay a profound respect for goddesses like Hera, patroness of the family; Artemis, Mistress of the Beasts and goddess of childbirth; and Demeter, the goddess of fertility and agriculture. The continued worship of these goddesses, which was to last under different guises for centuries, represents a reverence for female creative power that is one of the oldest legacies from the period before our culture began—we saw it as far back as the Paleolithic period—and perhaps one of the most significant.

Regarding Egypt and Mesopotamia, their impact on later culture remains the subject of debate. In the course of their growth and development, the Greeks were brought into contact with the black Cushite culture of Egypt, and Greek art and architecture were decisively influenced by it. Although the Greeks retained their artistic independence, the style they developed under the inspiration of Eastern models, including those of Mesopotamia, has conditioned the entire history of Western art. The cultures of ancient Egypt and the Middle East had little firsthand influence on the formation of our civilization, partly because Greek culture had a vitality that was by this time lacking in the older peoples and at least partly because of historical accident. Egypt and Assyria, powerful though they were, fell to the Persians, while Greece managed not only to survive but even to inflict an ignominious defeat on its Persian invaders. Yet even if ancient Egypt and Mesopotamia lie outside the mainstream of our cultural tradition, they continue to exert a powerful influence on the Western imagination, as the Tutankhamen exhibitions and their accompanying "Tut mania" showed in the 1970s. In part, their fascination lies in their exoticism and in the excitement of their rediscovery in our own day. The pharaoh who can curse his excavator from beyond the grave is certainly a dramatic, if fictional, representative of his age. At the same time, the artistic achievements of those distant times need no historical justification. Created in a world remote from our own, they serve as a reminder of the innate human urge to give expression to the eternal problems of existence.

◆ **1.30** Remains of the Citadel of Mycenae, 1600–1200 BCE. Mycenae, Greece. The very thick walls (15'/4.6 m) are visible, as is the Royal Grave Circle to the right, just inside the Lion Gate at the end of the path in the foreground. The rooms of the palace complex have a commanding position at the summit. Behind the Citadel itself, towers a mountain on which the Mycenaeans built a fortress. (*Image © Kevin Fleming/CORBIS*)

SUMMARY

◆ **The Beginnings of Civilization.** The early civilizations of the ancient Middle East laid the basis for the development of Western culture. In Egypt and Mesopotamia, in the period around 3000 BCE, the simple farming communities of the earlier Neolithic (New Stone) Age were replaced by cities, the product of agricultural discoveries that provided the food supply for relatively large numbers of people to live together.

Many of the characteristics of urban life developed during the following centuries: large-scale buildings, trade and commerce, systems of government and religion. The people of the Mesopotamian city of Uruk invented the earliest known writing system in the world.

◆ **The People of Mesopotamia.** Mesopotamian culture lacked the unity of Egyptian life: A series of different peoples had their own languages, religions, and customs. The Sumerians, the earliest, lived in cities dominated by great temples built on artificial platforms. The temple priests administered both religious and economic affairs, sharing their duties with local civic rulers.

Unlike the Egyptian pharaohs who were thought of as gods, Sumerian rulers never became the focus of a cult. They represented their city's god and served the interests of their people by overseeing government projects. Among the earliest of Sumerian kings was Gilgamesh, whose legendary deeds are described in the epic poem that bears his name. Mesopotamia was ruled by the Akkadians, a Semitic people, from 2350 to 2150 BCE. Their kingdom was invaded and destroyed, and in a brief period of Neo-Sumerian revival the principal religious monument at Ur, the Ziggurat, was built. Around 1800 BCE, Mesopotamia was reunified by the Babylonians, whose most famous king, Hammurabi, was the author of an important law code.

The last people to rule Mesopotamia were the Assyrians, the peak of whose power occurred between 1000 BCE and 612 BCE, the year in which their capital Nineveh was sacked by the Persians. Successive royal palaces, first at Nimrud and then at Nineveh, were decorated with massive stone relief carvings that showed aspects of life at court (royal processions, hunting scenes) with considerable realism.

◆ **Ancient Egypt.** Egyptian society was dominated by a strong central monarchy, with the pharaoh (the Egyptian king) presiding over a large bureaucracy that administered the affairs of state. Egyptian religious life was controlled by the priests, who sought to maintain old traditions, and Egyptian art generally reflected the policy of state control. Periods of political uncertainty were reflected in contemporary art. The confidence and stability of Old Kingdom sculpture, for example, disappeared in the unsettled conditions of the Middle Kingdom.

In the reign of the New Kingdom pharaoh Amenhotep IV, better known as Akhenaton (1379–1362 BCE), there was a change: the numberless deities of Egyptian religion were replaced by a single sun god, and Egyptian art became naturalistic for the first time in its history. Akhenaton's successors, however, restored the traditional system of deities and the artistic conventions of former times.

The chief characteristic of Egyptian religious thought was the belief in survival after death for those who had led a good life. Elaborate funeral rituals were devised in which the god Osiris, Judge of the Dead, was invoked. From early in Egyptian history, monumental tombs were constructed for the ruling classes, the most famous of which are the Great Pyramids at Giza.

◆ **The Cultures of Bronze Age Greece.** The first urban culture in the West, known as Minoan, developed on the Mediterranean island of Crete. Around 2000 BCE, large towns were constructed; these served as centers for the ruling families and the chief religious leaders. The largest Minoan community, Knossos, was destroyed several times by earthquakes and each time was rebuilt on a grander scale. Like the other Minoan palaces, Knossos was decorated with vivid wall paintings depicting religious ceremonies and scenes from daily life. Many examples have been found of the elaborate jewelry worn by figures in the paintings; one of the richest is the gold Wasp Pendant from Mallia.

Around 1400 BCE, Knossos was abandoned for reasons that remain mysterious, and power passed to mainland Greece, where a people called the Mycenaeans had appeared by 1600 BCE. Most of our information about the Mycenaeans comes from their tombs. The earliest ones, at Mycenae, were dug into the ground within a circular enclosure; vast quantities of gold treasure—including death masks, jewelry, and weapons—were buried with the bodies of the dead. The Mycenaeans traded widely in the Mediterranean area, and around 1250 BCE they sacked the city of Troy, an economic rival. Shortly after, however, their own cities were destroyed. Within a century Mycenaean culture had vanished, although it was to exert important influence on later Greek civilization.

EXERCISES

1. Compare the religious beliefs of the Egyptians and the Mesopotamians. What do their differences tell us about the cultures involved?
2. How did the development of Egyptian society affect their art? What were the principal subjects depicted by Egyptian artists?

3. What evidence is there for the role of women in the cultures discussed in this chapter?
4. What information do the excavations at the Palace of Knossos provide about Minoan daily life?
5. If you could return in time to visit one of the peoples described in the chapter, which would you choose and why?

Visit the *Culture & Values* Companion website at **www.cengage.com/art/Cunningham/Cultureand Values7E** and the *Humanities Resource Center* for an array of primary source readings, key terms with pronunciations, flash cards, quizzes, and study materials designed especially to help you do well in this course.

CHAPTER 2

EARLY GREECE

Western culture's debt to the ancient Greeks lies principally in the achievements of their city life: art, politics, philosophy, history, and all the other factors described in the following two chapters. Greece itself, however, was basically an agricultural society, and most cities viewed farming and its products as of the highest importance to the whole community. Athenian young men, at the age of eighteen, swore an oath to protect their city's grain, vines, figs, and olives, as well as obey its laws.

Survival depended on healthy eating. On the whole, the average Greek's diet was simple, based chiefly on cereals. Bread was unleavened and often had various herbs and flavorings—thyme, rosemary, olives—mixed in the dough. Sweet loaves contained raisins and dried figs. According to one ancient gourmet, citizens of Athens could choose from seventy-two varieties of bread.

With starch as the basic filler, the Greeks added a wide variety of accompaniments: beans and lentils, olives, onions, and cheese, generally using goat milk for the latter. Poorer Greeks probably lived mainly on this simple diet, along with anchovies and sardines, washing it down with water ("the best drink of all," says the poet Pindar).

Prosperous diners could flavor their food with fine olive oil, for which Athens was famous throughout the Mediterranean, and eat excellent fruit, also an Athenian specialty. Game such as hare and pheasant was popular, but on the whole meat remained a rarity, even for the wealthy. Homer's heroic banquets, at which warriors slaughtered whole oxen and roasted them over coals, represented only a dream for most of his audience. Fish was more common. Both fresh Mediterranean tuna and dried tuna imported from the Black Sea were popular, as were squid and shrimp.

The Greeks always drank their wine diluted with water and often added honey and spices to it. They exported it in jars made waterproof by spreading a layer of pine resin on the inside—the origin of the "Retsina" (resinated wine) still drunk in Greece today.

THE EARLY HISTORY OF GREECE

One of the major turning points of history is the period around 1000 BCE, the change from the Bronze Age to the Iron Age throughout the Mediterranean area. In the following centuries a culture developed in a small corner of southeastern Europe—Greece—which was to form the foundation of Western civilization. By the fifth century BCE, this culture had produced one of the greatest eras of human achievement.

◆ Men harvesting olives, late 6th century BCE, Greece.
(© Bildarchiv Preussischer Kulturbesitz/Art Resource, NY)

In certain basic ways there was some continuity between the Bronze Age and the Iron Age. For example, Athens, which in the fifth century BCE became the intellectual center of Classical Greece, had been a Mycenaean city long before the Iron Age began. In most significant respects, however, the Iron Age Greeks had to discover for themselves almost all the cultural skills associated with civilization—the visual arts, architecture, literature, philosophy, and even the art of writing. The Mycenaeans had known how to write and build and create art. However, their abrupt and violent end around 1100 BCE was followed by a century of disturbance and confusion that cut off the Bronze Age from the new world of the Iron Age. To follow the first attempts of these Iron Age people to develop an artistic style, organize their societies, and question the nature of the universe is to witness the birth of Western culture.

The history of early Greece falls naturally into three periods, each marked by its own distinctive artistic achievement. During the first three hundred years or so of the Iron Age, development was slow and the

		GENERAL EVENTS	ART
BRONZE AGE	**MYCENAEAN PERIOD**	**3,000** BCE		
		c. 1250 Fall of Troy	
		1100	**1100** Collapse of Mycenaean Empire	
	DARK AGE		
		1000		
IRON AGE	**HEROIC AGE**	**1000** Development of Iron Age culture at Athens **800–700** Greeks begin colonizing in East and Italy **776** First Olympic Games **c. 775** First Greek colony in Italy founded at Pithekoussai	**1000–900** Protogeometric pottery decoration: bold circular shapes similar to Mycenaean motifs **900–700** Geometric pottery decoration: linear designs of zig-zags, triangles, diamonds, meanders **8th cent.** Geometric pottery incorporates stylized human figure in painted design; Dipylon amphora
		750		
	AGE OF COLONIZATION	**750–600** Greeks found colonies throughout Mediterranean, from Egypt to Black Sea	**c. 650** Large freestanding sculpture evolves **late 7th cent.** Orientalizing styles in vase painting; Corinthian aryballos
		600		
	ARCHAIC PERIOD	**c. 590** Solon reforms Athenian constitution **546** Rule of Pisistratus begins growth of Athenian power; Persian Empire expands to take over Greek colonies in Asia Minor **510** Restoration of democracy at Athens **490** Start of the Persian Wars; forces of King Darius defeated at Marathon	**c. 600** Athenians develop narrative style in black-figure vase painting; increased naturalism in Greek art **c. 550** *Calf-Bearer* **c. 530** *Anavysos Kouros; Peplos Kore* **c. 525** Exekias, *The Suicide of Ajax*, amphora **late 6th cent.** Red-figure style of vase painting introduced; *Euphronios Vase*, krater **c. 490** *Kritios Boy*; turning point between Archaic and Classical periods
		480		
	CLASSICAL PERIOD	**480** Xerxes leads a second expedition against Greece; wins battle of Thermopylae and sacks Athens; Greeks defeat Persians decisively at Salamis **479** Greek victories at Plataea and Mycale	
		323		

Greeks had only limited contact with other Mediterranean peoples. During this period the first great works of literature were created: the epic poems known as the *Iliad* and the *Odyssey*. Because these works treat heroic themes, the early Iron Age in Greece is sometimes known as the Heroic Age. The visual art of the period used a style known as Geometric.

By the beginning of the eighth century BCE, Greek travelers and merchants had already begun to explore the lands to the east and west. In the next one hundred fifty years (c. 750–600 BCE), called the Age of Coloniza-

tion, many new ideas and artistic styles were brought to Greece. These foreign influences were finally absorbed in the third era of early Greece known as the Archaic period (c. 600–480 BCE). This period, the culmination of the first five hundred years of Greek history, paved the way for the Classical period (discussed in Chapter 3). The Greeks' relationship to the world around them took a decisive turn at the end of the Archaic period with their victory over the Persians in the wars that lasted from 490 to 479 BCE. The events of the Persian Wars thus end this chapter.

ARCHITECTURE	LITERATURE & PHILOSOPHY	MUSIC
	c. 900–700 Evolution of Homeric epics *Iliad* and *Odyssey* **8th cent.** Hesiod, *Works and Days* and *Theogony*	Early music primarily vocal with instrumental accompaniment; use of flute and simple lyre popular
	c. 700 Greeks adapt Phoenician alphabet for their own language **c. 650** Archilochus, earliest Greek lyric poet, active	**7th cent.** Development of aulos (double flute), used to accompany songs **c. 675** Terpander of Lesbos introduces cithara
c. 600 Form of Doric temple fully established, derived from early wooden structures; Temple of Hera at Olympia **c. 550** Basilica at Paestum **c. 540** Temple of Apollo at Corinth **c. 500** Temple of Aphaia, Aegina	**early 6th cent.** Sappho, *Poems* **6th cent.** Development of Presocratic schools of philosophy: Materialists, Pythagoreans, Dualists, Atomists **c. 540–480** Heraclitus of Ephesus teaches his theory of "impermanence" **late 6th cent.** Playwriting competition begins **after 525** First official version of Homeric epics written	**586** Sacadas of Argos composes first known purely instrumental work for performance on aulos at Pythian Games in Delphi **c. 550** Pythagoras discovers numerical relationship of music harmonies and our modern musical scale
5th cent. First widespread use of Ionic order	**c. 475** Parmenides writes on his theory of knowledge **c. 440** Herodotus begins *History of the Persian Wars*	**late 5th cent.** Earliest surviving fragment of Greek music

THRACE

BLACK SEA

BYZANTIUM

PROPONTIS

MACEDON

PELLA

VERGINA

CHALCIDICE

Mt. Olympus ▲

TROY

Helle-pont

PHRYGIA

LEMNOS

ASIA MINOR

THESSALY

AEGEAN SEA

LESBOS

LYDIA

IONIAN SEA

ITHACA

THERMOPYLAE ×

▲ *Artemisium*

SARDIS

CHAERONEA

DELPHI

EUBOEA

BOEOTIA THEBES

LEUCTRA PLATAEA

ACHAEA MEGARA ATTICA

CORINTH MARATHON

MYCENAE ATHENS

ARCADIA ELEUSIS

OLYMPIA ARGOS SALAMIS

PELOPONNESUS ARGOLIS AEGINA

MESSENIA

SPARTA

LACONIA

EPHESUS

Meander R.

SAMOS

MILETUS

CARIA

DELOS

NAXOS

ANCIENT GREECE

0   200 Miles

0   200 Kilometers

RHODES

MEDITERRANEAN SEA

CRETE KNOSSOS

HOMER AND THE HEROIC AGE

During the Mycenaean period most of Greece had been united under a single influence. When the Mycenaeans fell, however, Greece split up into a series of independent regions that corresponded to the geographically separated areas created by the mountain ranges and high hills that crisscross the terrain. Within each of these geographically discrete areas there developed an urban center that controlled the surrounding countryside. Thus Athens became the dominating force in the geographical region known as Attica; Thebes controlled Boeotia; Sparta controlled Laconia; and so on (see map, "Ancient Greece"). A central urban community of this kind was called by the Greeks of a later period a **polis**, a term generally translated as "city-state." The polis served as the focal point for all political, religious, social, and artistic activities within its region. Its citizens felt a loyalty toward their own individual city that was far stronger than any generalized sense of community with their fellow Greeks over the mountains. Each of the leading cities developed its own artistic style, which led to fierce competition and in time to bitter and destructive rivalries. The polis was therefore both the glory and the ruin of Greek civilization, producing on the one hand an unequaled concentration of intellectual and cultural development, and on the other a tendency to internal squabbling at the least provocation.

GREEK RELIGION

The fragmentation of social and cultural life had a marked effect on the development of Greek mythology and religion. Religion played an important part in Greek life, as Greek art and literature demonstrate, but it was highly different from the other systems of belief that influenced our culture, Judaism and Christianity. For one thing, Greek mythology offers no central body of information or teaching corresponding to the Old Testament or New Testament. Often there are varying versions of the same basic story; even when these versions do not actually contradict one another, they are difficult to reconcile. For another thing, the very characters of the Greek gods and goddesses often seem confused and self-contradictory. For example, Zeus, president of the Immortals and father of gods and humans, generally represented the concept of an objective moral code to which both gods and mortals were expected to conform; Zeus imposed justice and supervised the punishment of wrongdoers [**Fig. 2.2**]. Yet this same majestic ruler was also involved in many love affairs and seductions, in the course of which his behavior was often undignified and even comical. How could the Greeks have believed in a champion of morality whose own moral standards were so lax?

The answer lies in the fact that Greek myth and religion of later times consist of a mass of folktales, primitive customs, and traditional rituals that grew up during the Heroic Age and were never developed into a single unified system. Individual cities had their own mythological traditions, some of them going back to the Bronze Age and others gradually developing under the influence of neighboring peoples. Poets and artists felt free to choose the versions that appealed to their own tastes or helped them express their ideas. Later Greeks tried to organize all of these conflicting beliefs into something resembling order. Father Zeus ruled from Mount Olympus, where he was surrounded by the other principal Olympian deities. His wife Hera was the goddess of marriage and morality, as the protectress of the family. His daughter Athena symbolized intelligence and understanding, and was also a warrior goddess. Aphrodite was the goddess of love, Ares, her

◆ **2.2** Zeus, c. 465 BCE. Whether this striding god is Zeus or Poseidon, god of the sea, the combination of majestic dignity and physical strength reflects the Greeks' view of their gods as superior beings with definitely human attributes. This statue, found in the sea off Cape Artemisium, comes from the end of the period covered in this chapter; it may have been intended to commemorate the Greek victory over the Persians.

Bronze, 6′10″ (2.08 m) high. National Archaeological Museum, Athens, Greece//© Nimatallah/Art Resource, NY

lover, the god of war, and so on. But the range and variety of the Greek imagination defied this kind of categorization. The Greeks loved a good story, and so tales that did not fit the ordered scheme continued to circulate.

These contradictions were perfectly apparent to the Greeks, but they used their religion to illuminate their own lives, rather than to give them divine guidance. One of the clearest examples is the contrast that Greek poets drew between the powers of Apollo and Dionysus, two of the most important of their gods. Apollo represented logic and order, the power of the mind; Dionysus was the god of the emotions, whose influence, if excessive, could lead to violence and disorder. By worshiping both of these forces, the Greeks were acknowledging an obvious dual existence in human nature and trying to strike a prudent balance.

The Greek deities served many purposes, therefore, but these purposes were very different from those of the other Western religions. No Greek god, not even Zeus, represents supreme good. At the other end of the moral scale, there is no Greek figure of supreme evil corresponding to the Christian concept of Satan. The Greeks turned to their deities for explanations of both natural phenomena and psychological characteristics they recognized in themselves. At the same time, they used their gods and goddesses as yet another way of enhancing the glory of their individual city-states, as in the case of the cult of Athena at Athens. Problems of human morality required human, rather than divine, solutions. The Greeks turned to art and literature, rather than prayer, as a means of trying to discover the solutions (see **Table 2.1**).

THE HOMERIC EPICS

At the beginning of Greek history stand two epic poems, which even the quarrelsome Greeks saw as national—indeed, universal—in their significance. The *Iliad* and the *Odyssey* have, from that early time, been held in the highest esteem. Homer, their accepted author, is generally regarded as not only the first figure in the Western literary tradition but also one of the greatest.

Table 2.1 *Principal Greek Deities*

Zeus	Father of Gods and Men
Hera	Wife of Zeus, Queen of Heaven
Poseidon	Brother of Zeus, God of the Sea
Hephaestus	Son of Zeus and Hera, God of Fire
Ares	God of War
Apollo	God of Prophecy, Intellect, Music, and Medicine
Artemis	Goddess of Chastity and the Moon
Demeter	Earth Mother, Goddess of Fertility
Aphrodite	Goddess of Beauty, Love, and Marriage
Athena	Goddess of Wisdom
Hermes	Messenger of the Gods, God of Cleverness
Dionysus	God of Wine and the Emotions

Yet even though Homer's genius is beyond doubt, little else about him is clear. In fact, the many problems and theories connected with the Homeric epics and their creator are generally summed up under the label "the Homeric Question."

The ancient Greeks were not sure who had composed the *Iliad* and the *Odyssey*, when and where the author had lived, or even if one person was responsible for both of them. In general, tradition ascribed the epics to a blind poet called Homer; almost every city worthy of the name claimed to be his birthplace. Theories about when he had lived ranged from the time of the Trojan War, around 1250 BCE, to five hundred years later.

The problem of who Homer was, and even whether he existed at all, continues to vex scholars to this day. In any case, most experts would probably now agree that the creation of the *Iliad* and the *Odyssey* was a highly complex affair. Each of the epics consists basically of several shorter folktales that were combined, gradually evolving over a century or more into the works as we now know them.

These epic poems were almost certainly composed and preserved at a time before the introduction of writing in Greece by individuals who passed them down by word of mouth. Professional bards—storytellers—probably learned a host of ready-made components: traditional tales, stock incidents, and a whole catalog of repeated phrases and descriptions. In the absence of any written text the works remained fluid, and individual reciters would bring their own contributions. However, both the Homeric epics show a marked unity of style and structure.

The first crystallization of these popular stories had probably occurred by around 800 BCE, but the poems were still not in their final form for more than a century. The first written official version of each epic was probably not made before the late sixth century BCE. The edition of the poems used by modern scholars was made by a scribe working at Alexandria in the second century BCE.

Where, then, in this long development must we place Homer? He may perhaps have been the man who first began to combine the separate tales into a single whole; or perhaps he was the man who, sometime after 800 BCE, imposed an artistic unity on the mass of remembered folk stories he had inherited. The differences between the *Iliad* and the *Odyssey* have suggested to several commentators that a different "Homer" may have been responsible for the creation or development of each work, but here we enter the realm of speculation. Perhaps after all it would be best to follow the ancient Greeks, contenting ourselves with the belief that at some stage in the evolution of the poems they were filtered through the imagination of the first great genius of the Western literary tradition, without being too specific about which stage it was.

Both works show evidence of their long evolution by word of mouth. All of the chief characters are given standardized descriptive adjectives as "epithets" that are repeated whenever they appear: Achilles is "swiftfooted" and Odysseus "cunning." Phrases, lines, and entire sections are often repeated. There are also minor inconsistencies in the plots.

Furthermore, the heroic world of warfare is made more accessible to the poem's audience by the use of elaborate similes that compare aspects of the story to everyday life in the early Iron Age—the massing of the Greek forces, for example, is likened to a swarm of flies buzzing around pails of milk.

Although the two poems are clearly of a single tradition, they are very different in spirit. The *Iliad* is somber, taut, direct. The concentration of its theme makes it easier to understand, and certainly easier to explain, than the more digressive and lighthearted *Odyssey*. But the *Odyssey* is certainly not a lesser work; if anything, its range and breadth of humanity are even greater, and its design more elaborate.

The *Iliad* The action of the *Iliad* takes place during the final year of the Greeks' siege of Troy, or Ilium. Its subject is only indirectly concerned with the Trojan War, however, and the poem ends before the episode of the wooden horse and the fall of the city. Its principal theme is stated in the opening lines of Book I, which establish the tragic mood of the work. Here the poet invokes the goddess of poetic inspiration: "Sing, goddess, of the anger of Peleus' son Achilles, which disastrously inflicted countless sufferings on the Greeks, sending the strong souls of many heroes to Hades and leaving their bodies to be devoured by dogs and all birds. . . ."

The subject of the *Iliad*, then, is the anger of Achilles and its consequences. Its message is a direct one: we must be prepared to answer for the results of our own actions and realize that when we act wrongly, we will cause suffering both for ourselves and, perhaps more important, for those we love. Although the setting of the *Iliad* is heroic, even mythic, the theme of human responsibility is universal. This relevance to our own experience is underlined by the realism in the scenes of battles and death, which are characteristic of epic literature's interest in heroic warfare. The story of Achilles' disastrous mistake is told in a basically simple and direct narrative. It begins with a quarrel between Agamemnon, commander-in-chief of the Greek forces, and Achilles, his powerful ally, who resents Agamemnon's overbearing assertion of authority. After a public argument, Achilles decides to punish Agamemnon by withdrawing his military support and retiring to his tent, in the hope that without his aid the Greeks will be unable to overcome the Trojans. In the battles that follow he is proved correct; the Trojans inflict a series of defeats on the Greeks, killing many of their leading warriors.

Agamemnon eventually (Book IX) admits that he behaved too highhanded (although no formal apology) and offers Achilles, through intermediaries, generous gifts to return to the fighting and save the Greek cause. Achilles, however, rejects this attempt to make amends and stubbornly nurses his anger as the fighting resumes and Greek casualties mount. Then his dearest friend Patroclus is killed by the Trojan leader Hector, son of their king (Book XVI). Only now does Achilles return to battle, his former anger against Agamemnon now turned against the Trojans in general and Hector in particular.

After killing Hector in single combat (Book XXII), Achilles abuses Hector's corpse in order to relieve his own sense of guilt at having permitted Patroclus's death. Finally, Priam, the old king of Troy, steals into the Greek camp by night to beg for the return of his son's body (Book XXIV). In this encounter with Priam, Achilles at last recognizes and accepts the tragic nature of life and the inevitability of death. His anger melts, and he hands over the body of his dead enemy. The Iliad ends with the funeral rites of Hector, "tamer of horses."

As is clear even from this brief summary, there is a direct relationship between human actions and their consequences. The gods appear in the *Iliad* and frequently play a part in the action, but at no time can divine intervention save Achilles from paying the price for his unreasonable anger. Furthermore, Achilles' crime is committed not against a divine code of ethics but against human standards of behavior. All of his companions, including Patroclus, realize that he is behaving unreasonably.

From its earliest beginnings, therefore, the Greek view of morality is in strong contrast to the Judeo-Christian tradition. At the center of the Homeric universe is not God but human beings, who are at least partly in control of their own destiny. If they cannot choose the time when they die, they can at least choose how they live. The standards by which human life will be judged are those established by one's fellow humans. In the *Iliad* the gods serve as divine "umpires." They watch the action and comment on it and at times enforce the rules, but they do not affect the course of history. Humans do not always, however, fully realize the consequences of their behavior. In fact, they often prefer to believe that things happen "according to the will of the gods" rather than because of their own actions. Yet the gods claim no such power. In a remarkable passage at the beginning of Book 1 of the *Odyssey*, we see the world for a moment through the eyes of Zeus as he sits at dinner on Mount Olympus: "How foolish men are! How unjustly they blame the gods! It is their lot to suffer, but because of their own folly they bring upon themselves sufferings over and above what is fated for them. And then they blame the gods." These are hardly words we can imagine coming from the God of the Old Testament.

VALUES

Destiny

Like most peoples since them, the Greeks had conflicting ideas on how much of human life was preordained by some force in the universe, which they called Fate, or Destiny. In one passage Homer speaks of the three Fates, or Moirai, goddesses who govern the thread of life for each individual person. Clotho spins the thread of life, Lachesis measures it, and Atropos—her name means "she who cannot be turned"—cuts the thread at the moment of death.

Neither Homer nor the later Greeks seemed clear on how the Fates related to the other gods. One author, Hesiod, describes them as the daughters of Zeus and Themis (Righteousness), whereas Plato calls them the daughters of Ananke (Necessity). Sometimes Fate is a force with unlimited power over all humans and deities, and Zeus performs its commands; on other occasions Zeus can change the course of Destiny, and even humans sometimes succeed in reversing their fate.

The Greeks also acknowledged another force operating in their lives, that of pure random chance, which they symbolized by the goddess Tyche, or Fortune. Tyche can award lavish benefits, but she does so at random. Her symbols—wings, a wheel, a revolving ball—convey her variability. With the general decline of traditional religious beliefs in later Greek history, Tyche became revered as one of the most powerful forces in the universe.

Although the Romans adopted the Greek Moirai in the form of the Parcae, they paid far more attention to the notion of luck, worshiped as Fortuna. In art, Fortuna was represented like Tyche, but the Roman goddess appeared in various forms: Fortuna liberum (of children), Fortuna redux (assuring a safe return from a journey), Fortuna privata (of family life), and many more. In the early second century CE, the Roman emperor Trajan founded a special temple in honor of Fortuna as the all-pervading power of the world.

The *Odyssey* The principal theme of the *Odyssey* is the return home of the Greek hero Odysseus from the war against Troy. Odysseus's journey, which takes ten years, is filled with adventures involving one-eyed giants, monsters of various kinds, a seductive enchantress, a romantic young girl, a floating island, a trip to the underworld, and many other fairytale elements. Into this main narrative is woven a description of the wanderings of Odysseus's son, Telemachus, who, searching for his missing father, visits many of the other Greek leaders who have returned safely from Troy.

In the last half of the poem, Odysseus finally returns home in disguise. Without revealing his identity to his ever-faithful wife Penelope, he kills the suitors who have been pestering her for ten years to declare her husband dead and remarry. Homer keeps us waiting almost to the very end for the grand recognition scene between husband and wife. All ends happily, with Penelope, Odysseus, and his aged father Laertes peacefully reunited.

It is worth examining the Homeric world at some length, because the *Iliad* and the *Odyssey* formed the basis of education and culture throughout the Greek and Roman world; children learned the two poems by heart at school. Ideas changed and developed, but reverence for Homer remained constant.

ART AND SOCIETY IN THE HEROIC AGE

GEOMETRIC ART Our impressions of the first three hundred years of Greek art (1000–700 BCE) are based largely on painted pottery, hardly a major art form even in later times, for little else has survived. Of architecture there is almost no trace. Although small bronze and ivory statuettes and relief plaques were being made from the ninth century BCE on, the earliest surviving large stone sculptures date to the mid-seventh century BCE.

Painted vases are therefore our major source of information about artistic developments. It comes as something of a surprise to find that Homer's contemporaries decorated their pots with abstract geometric designs, with no attempt at the qualities most typical of their literature: vividness and realism. This style has given its name to the two subdivisions of the period: the Protogeometric (1000–900 BCE) and the Geometric (900–700 BCE).

For the first hundred years, artists decorated their vases with simple, bold designs consisting mainly of concentric circles and semicircles. In some ways this period represents a transition from the end of the Mycenaean age, but the memory of Mycenaean motifs soon gave way to a new style. If Protogeometric pottery seems a long way from Greek art of later centuries, it does show qualities of clarity and order that reappear later, although in a very different context.

In the Geometric pottery of the following two centuries (900–700 BCE), the use of abstract design continued, but the emphasis changed. Circles and semicircles were replaced by linear designs, zigzags, triangles, diamonds, and above all the **meander** (a maze pattern). There is something strangely obsessive about many of these vessels—a sense of artists searching for a subject, meanwhile

VOICES OF THEIR TIMES

Daily Life in the World of Homer

From the description of scenes on the shield of Achilles.

> Next he showed two beautiful cities full of people. In one of them weddings and banquets were afoot. They were bringing the brides through the streets from their homes, to the loud music of the wedding-hymn and the light of blazing torches. Youths accompanied by flute and lyre were whirling in the dance, and the women had come to the doors of their houses to enjoy the show. But the men had flocked to the meeting place, where a case had come up between two litigants, about the payment of compensation for a man who had been killed. The defendant claimed the right to pay in full and was announcing his intention to

> the people; but the other contested his claim and refused all compensation.
>
> Both parties insisted that the issue should be settled by a referee; and both were cheered by their supporters in the crowd, whom the heralds were attempting to silence. The Elders sat on the sacred bench, a semicircle of polished stone; and each, as he received the speaker's rod from the clear-voiced heralds, came forward in his turn to give his judgment, staff in hand. Two talents of gold were displayed in the center: They were the fee for the Elder whose exposition of the law should prove the best.

Excerpt from Book XVIII of *The Iliad* by Homer, trans. Richard Lattimore. Copyright 1951 University of Chicago Press. Reprinted by permission.

working out over and over the implications of mathematical formulas. Once again we seem a long way from the achievements of later Greek artists, with their emphasis on realism, yet precise mathematical relationships lie behind the design of much of the greatest Greek art.

The Human Form By the eighth century BCE, artists had begun to find their way toward the principal subject of later Greek art: the human form. Thus human and animal figures begin to appear among the meanders and zigzags. This is a moment of such importance in the history of Western art that we should not take it for granted. We have been so conditioned by the art of the ancient Greeks that from the late Geometric period until our own time, Western art has been primarily concerned with the depiction of human beings. Landscapes are a popular subject, and in contemporary times, art has again become abstract. Yet most paintings and sculptures deal with the human form, treated more or less realistically. This realism may seem so obvious as to be hardly worth stating, but it must be remembered that the art of peoples who were not influenced by the Greeks is very different. Islamic art, for example, deals almost exclusively in abstract design. Indian sculptors depicted their gods and heroes in human form, but they certainly did not treat them realistically. The Hindu god Shiva, for example, is often shown with many arms. It is a tribute to the Greeks' overwhelming influence on our culture that, from the Roman period to the beginning of the twenty-first century, artists have accepted the Greeks' decision to make the realistic treatment of the human form the central focus of art, whether the forms were those of mortal people or divine gods and goddesses.

The Greeks did not achieve this naturalism overnight. The first depictions of human beings, which appear on Geometric vases shortly after 800 BCE, are highly stylized. They are painted in silhouette, and a single figure often combines front and side views, the head and legs being shown in profile while the upper half of the body is seen from the front. Some of the vases decorated with stick figures of this kind are of immense size. One of them, the *Dipylon Amphora*, is almost five feet (1.24 meters) tall [**Fig. 2.3**]. These vases were set up over tombs to serve as grave markers; they had holes in their bases so that offerings poured into them could seep down to the dead below. The scenes on them frequently show the funeral ceremony. Others show processions of warriors, both on foot and in chariots.

THE AGE OF COLONIZATION

Throughout the period of Homer and Geometric art, individual city-states were ruled by small groups of

◆ **2.3** Dipylon Amphora, c. 750 BCE. This immense vase was originally a grave marker. The main band, between the handles, shows the lying-in-state of the dead man on whose grave the vase stood; on both sides of the bier are mourners tearing their hair in grief. Note the two bands of animals, deer and running goats, in the upper part of the vase.

Terracotta, 4′11″ (1.24 m) high. National Archaeological Museum, Athens, Greece//© Nimatallah/Art Resource, NY

aristocrats who concentrated wealth and power in their own hands. Presumably, their graves were marked with great amphoras like the *Dipylon* vase. By the eighth century BCE, however, two centuries of peace had allowed the individual city-states to become prosperous. The ruling classes became increasingly concerned with the image of their city-states. They began to function as patrons of the arts as well as military leaders. Great international festivals began to develop at Olympia, Delphi, and other sacred sites, at which athletes and poets—representing their city—would compete against one another.

During the seventh century, as trade with both fellow Greeks and other Near Eastern peoples increased, economic success became a crucial factor in the growth of a polis; individual cities began to mint their own coins shortly before 600 BCE. Yet political power remained in the hands of a small hereditary aristocracy, leaving a growing urban population increasingly frustrated. Both the accumulation of wealth and the problem of overpopulation produced a single result: colonization.

Throughout the eighth and seventh centuries BCE, enterprising Greeks went abroad either to make their fortunes or to increase them. To the west, Italy and Sicily were colonized and Greek cities were established there. Some of these, like Syracuse in Sicily or Sybaris in southern Italy, became even richer and more powerful than the mother cities from which the colonizers had come. Unfortunately if inevitably, the settlers took with them not only the culture of their polis but also their intercity rivalries, often with disastrous results. To the south and east, cities were also established in Egypt and on the Black Sea.

◆ **2.4** Aryballos, c. 600 BCE. The black-figure techniques and the Eastern looking animals are characteristic of the Orientalizing style. Also characteristic are the flowerlike decorations, which are blobs of paint scored with lines. The musculature and features of the animals' bodies are also the result of scoring.

Clay, c. 2⅓″ (6 cm) high, Middle Corinthian. © Benaki Museum, Athens, Greece//The Bridgeman Art Library

◆ **2.5** Ergotimos (potter) and Clitias (vase painter), the "François Vase," c. 575 BCE. This Attic black-figure krater, intended for mixing wine and water, may have been commissioned for a wedding. The upper two and fourth levels show heroic episodes from Greek mythology, including the hunting of the Calydonian boar and a chariot race at the funeral games for Patroclus. The main, third level shows the marriage of Peleus—a mortal—and the goddess Thetis. So rare was such an event (no other example of a divine and human marriage is recorded in Greek mythology) that all of the gods came to the ceremony.

From Chiusi, Italy. Terracotta, 26″ (2.16 m) high. Museo Archeologico, Florence, Italy//© Scala/Art Resource, NY

The most significant wave of colonization was that which moved eastward to the coast of Asia Minor, in some cases back to territory that had been inhabited by the Mycenaeans centuries earlier. From here the colonizers established trade contacts with peoples in the ancient Near East, including the Phoenicians and the Persians. Within Greece the effect on art and life of this expansion to the east was immense. After almost three hundred years of cultural isolation, in a land cut off from its neighbors by mountains and sea, the Greeks were brought face to face with the immensely rich and sophisticated cultures of the ancient Near East. Oriental ideas and artistic styles were seen by the colonizers and carried home by the traders. A growing quantity of Eastern artifacts, ivories, jewelry, and metalwork was sent back to the mother cities and even to the Greek cities of Italy. So great was the impact of Near Eastern art on the Greeks from the late eighth century to around 600 BCE that this period and its style are generally known by the name **Orientalizing**.

THE VISUAL ARTS AT CORINTH AND ATHENS

Different Greek cities reacted to Oriental influences in different ways, although all were strongly influenced. In particular, the growing hostility between the two richest city-states—Athens and Corinth—which two centuries later led to the Peloponnesian War and the fall of Athens, seems already symbolized in the strong differ-

ences between their Orientalizing pottery. The Corinthian artists developed a miniature style that used a wide variety of Eastern motifs—sphinxes, winged human figures, floral designs—all of which were arranged in bands covering almost the entire surface of the vase. White, yellow, and purple were often used to highlight details, producing a bold and striking effect. After the monotony of Geometric pottery, the variety of subject and range of color are a welcome change.

The small size of the pots made them ideal for export. Corinthian vases have in fact been discovered not only throughout Greece but also in Italy, Egypt, and the Near East. Clearly, any self-respecting woman of the seventh century BCE wanted an elegant little Corinthian flask [**Fig. 2.4**] for her perfume, oil, or makeup. The vases are well made, the figures lively, and the style instantly recognizable as Corinthian—an important factor for commercial success. Corinth's notable political and economic strength throughout the seventh and early sixth centuries BCE was, in fact, built on the sale of these little pots and their contents.

In Athens, potters were slower to discard the effects of the Geometric period and less able to develop an all-purpose style like the Corinthian. The vases remain large and the attempts to depict humans and animals are often clumsy. The achievements of later Athenian art are nonetheless clearly foreshadowed in the vitality

◆ *2.6 Kore*, early 6th century BCE. Unlike the kouros to the right, the female figure is completely clothed, although both have the same rigid stance. The figure's right lower arm was probably slotted into the hole at the elbow with the hand extended outwards. Note the careful depiction of the drapery.

From Greek Sicily. Marble. Archaeological Museum, Gela, Sicily//© The Art Archive/Gianni Dagli Orti

◆ *2.7 Kouros*, c. 600 BCE. Note the detailed treatment of the hair, the carefully balanced design of the body, and the absence of a sense of movement: although one foot is forward, there is no displacement of the hips.

From Attic, Greece. Naxian marble, 6′4½″ (1.95 m) high without plinth. The Metropolitan Museum of Art, New York, USA//Image copyright © The Metropolitan Museum of Art/Art Resource, NY

of the figures and the constant desire of the artists to illustrate events from mythology [**Fig. 2.5**] or daily life rather than simply to decorate a surface in the Corinthian manner.

By 600 BCE, the narrative style had become established at Athens. As the Athenians began to take over an increasing share of the market for painted vases and their contents, Corinth's position declined, and the trade rivalry that later had devastating results began to develop.

THE BEGINNINGS OF GREEK SCULPTURE

The influence of Near Eastern and Egyptian models on Greek sculpture and architecture is more consistent and easier to trace than that of pottery. The first Greek set-

tlers in Egypt were given land around the mid-seventh century BCE by the Egyptian pharaoh Psammetichos I. It is surely no coincidence that the earliest Greek stone sculptures, which date from about the same period, markedly resemble Egyptian cult statues and were placed in similarly grandiose temples. (The earliest surviving temple, that of Hera at Olympia, dates at least in part to this period.) These stone figures consist of a few subjects repeated over and over. The most popular were the standing female, or **kore**, clad in drapery [**Fig. 2.6**], and the standing male, or **kouros**, always shown nude [**Fig. 2.7**]. This nudity already marks a break with the Egyptian tradition in which figures wore loincloths and foreshadows the heroic male nudity of Classical Greek art. The stance of the *kouros* figures, however, was firmly based on Egyptian models. One foot (usually the left) is forward, the arms are by the sides, and the hands are clenched. The elaborate wig-like hair is also Egyptian in inspiration.

By 600 BCE, only a few years after the first appearance of these statues, Greek art had reached a critical stage. After the slow and cautious progress of the Geometric period, the entire character of painting and sculpture had changed and, within the century following 700 BCE, Greek artists had abandoned abstract design for increasing realism. At this point in the development of painting and sculpture, the Greek spirit of independence and inquiry asserted itself. Instead of following their Eastern counterparts and repeating the same models and conventions for centuries, Greek painters and sculptors allowed their curiosity to lead them in a new direction, one that changed the history of art. The early stone figures and painted silhouettes had represented human beings, but only in a schematic, stylized form. Beginning in the Archaic period artists used their work to try to answer such questions as, What do human beings really look like? How do perspective and foreshortening work? What in fact is the true nature of appearance? For the first time in history, artists began to reproduce the human form in a way that was true to nature rather than merely to echo the achievements of their predecessors.

SCULPTURE AND PAINTING IN THE ARCHAIC PERIOD

It is tempting to view the works of art and literature of the Archaic period (600–480 BCE) as steps on the road that leads to the artistic and intellectual achievement in the Classical Age of the fifth and fourth centuries BCE rather than to appreciate them for their own qualities. This view would seriously underestimate the vitality of one of the most creative periods in the development of our culture. In some ways, in fact, the spirit of adventure, of striving toward new forms and new ideas, makes the Archaic achievement more exciting, if less perfected, than that of the Classical period. It is better to travel hopefully than to arrive, as Robert Louis Stevenson put it.

The change in Archaic art is a reflection of similar social developments. The hereditary aristocrats were beginning to lose their commanding status. At Athens, Solon (c. 639–559 BCE), the legislator and poet, reformed the legal system in 594 BCE and divided the citizens into four classes; members of all four could take part in the debates of the Assembly and sit in the law courts. In place of the old aristocratic clans, a new class of rich merchant traders, who had made their fortunes in the economic expansion, began to dominate, winning power by playing on the discontent of the oppressed lower classes. These new rulers were called *tyrants*, although the word had none of the unfavorable implications it now has. Many of them were in fact patrons of the arts. The most famous of them all was Pisistratus, who ruled Athens from 546

◆ **2.8** *Kouros*, c. 530 BCE. Note the realism of the muscles and the new sense of power. According to the inscription on the base, this was the funerary monument to a young man, Kroisos, who had died heroically in battle.

From Anavysos, Greece. Marble, 6′4″ (1.93 m) high. National Archaeological Museum, Athens, Greece//© Scala/Art Resource, NY

until 528 BCE. Clearly, revolutions like those that brought Pisistratus and his fellow tyrants to power were likely to produce revolutionary changes in the arts.

Kouroi Astounding progress was made in sculpture from the formalized *kouroi* of the early Archaic period, with their flat planes and rigid stances, to the fully rounded figures of the late sixth century, toward the end

◆ **2.9** *Calf-Bearer*, c. 550 BCE. The archaic smile is softened in this figure. Realism appears in the displacement of the man's hair by the animal's legs and in the expression of the calf.

From the Acropolis, Athens. Marble, 5′5″ (1.65 m) high. Acropolis Museum, Athens, Greece //© Nimatallah/Art Resource, NY

◆ **2.10** *Peplos Kore*, c. 530 BCE. The statue is identified by the woolen *peplos* (mantle) the woman is wearing over her dress. The missing left arm was extended. The Greeks painted important parts of their stone statues; traces of paint show here.

From the Acropolis, Athens. Marble, 4′ (1.21 m) high. Acropolis Museum, Athens, Greece //© Nimatallah/Art Resource, NY

of the period. Statues like the *Anavysos Kouros* [**Fig. 2.8**] show a careful study of the human anatomy. The conventions remain the same, but the statues have a new life and vigor.

Although most of the male figures are shown in the traditional stance, there are a few important exceptions. The finest is perhaps the famous *Calf-Bearer* [**Fig. 2.9**] from the Athenian Acropolis (the hill that dominated the center of ancient Athens). The essential unity between man and beast is conveyed simply but with great feeling by the diagonals formed by the man's hands and the calf's legs and by the alignment of the two heads. The finest female figures of the period

also come from the Acropolis. The Persians broke the figures when they sacked Athens in 480 BCE, and then the Athenians buried the statues when they returned to their city the next year after defeating the Persians. Rediscovered by modern excavators, the statues are among the most impressive of Archaic masterpieces. They show a gradual but sure development from the earliest *korai* (the plural form of *kore*) to the richness and variety of the work of the late sixth century BCE [**Fig. 2.10**].

◆ **2.11** Metope, c. 540 BCE. Perseus is cutting off Medusa's head with the encouragement of Athena, who stands on the left. Medusa, shown in the conventional pose indicating rapid motion, was a gorgon whose look turned anyone to stone. The gorgon's son Pegasus, the winged horse, leaps up at her side.

From Temple C, Selinunte, Sicily, Italy. Limestone, 4′11″ (1.5 m) high. National Museum, Palermo, Italy//© The Art Archive/Gianni Dagli Orti

Relief Sculpture In addition to these freestanding figures, two other kinds of sculpture now appeared: large-scale statues made to decorate temples and carved stone slabs. In both cases, sculptors used the technique of *relief* carving: figures do not stand freely; they are visible from all angles but are carved into a block of stone, part of which is left as background. In **high relief** the figures project from the background so much as to seem almost three-dimensional. In **low relief** the carving preserves the flat surface of the stone. Temple sculpture or, as it is often called, architectural sculpture, was frequently in high relief, as in the depiction of the decapitation of Medusa from Selinus [**Fig. 2.11**]. Individual carved stone slabs are generally in low relief. Most that have survived were used as grave markers. The workmanship is often of a remarkable subtlety, as on the grave stele, or gravestone, of Aristion [**Fig. 2.12**].

The range of Archaic sculpture is great, and the best pieces communicate something of the excitement of their makers in solving new problems. Almost all of them, however, share one feature that often disturbs the modern viewer: the famous "archaic smile." This facial expression, which to our eyes may seem more like a grimace, has been explained in several ways. Some

◆ **2.12** Aristokles, *Stele of Aristion*, c. 510 BCE. This artist was one of the first in history to depict the human body in profile. The leather jacket contrasts with the soft folds of the undershirt. Note the detail of the hair and beard.

Marble, 8′ (2.44 m) high without base. National Archaeological Museum, Athens, Greece//© Scala/Art Resource, NY

◆ **2.14** Exekias, *The Suicide of Ajax*, c. 525 BCE. Ajax buries his sword in the ground so that he can throw himself onto it. The pathos of the warrior's last moments is emphasized by the empty space around him, the weeping tree, and his now useless shield and helmet.

Black-figure vase, 21¼" (54 cm) high. © Musée des Beaux-Arts et D'Archeologie, Boulogne, France//Giraudon/The Bridgeman Art Library

believe that it is merely the result of technical inexperience on the part of the sculptors. Others see it as a reflection of the Archaic Greeks' sense of certainty and optimism in facing a world that they seemed increasingly able to control. Whatever its cause, by the end of the sixth century BCE, and with the increasing threat posed by the Persians, the archaic smile had begun to fade. It was replaced by the more somber expression of works like the *Kritios Boy* [**Fig. 2.13**]. This statue marks a literal turning point between the late Archaic world and the early Classical period. For the first time in ancient art, the figure is no longer looking or walking straight ahead. The head and the upper part of the body turn slightly; as they do so, the weight shifts from one leg to the other and the hips move. Having solved the problem of representing a standing figure realistically, the sculptor has tackled a new and even more complex problem—showing a figure in motion. The consequences of this accomplishment were explored to the full in the Classical period.

Vase Painting By the mid-sixth century BCE, the art of vase painting had also made great progress in a refinement of the earlier Orientalizing technique known as the **black-figure** style. Works like those of Exekias, perhaps the greatest of black-figure painters, combine superb draftsmanship and immense power of expression [**Fig. 2.14**]. For so restricted a medium, vase painting shows a surprising range. If Exekias's style is serious, somber, sometimes even grim, the style of his contemporary, the Amasis painter, is relaxed, humorous, and charming.

◆ **2.13** *Kritios Boy*, c. 490 BCE. The archaic smile has been superseded by a more natural expression, as the turn of the body is shown realistically in the movement of the hips and stomach muscles. Note the extraordinarily fine surface of the stone, which distinguishes between skin, muscle, and bone.

From the Acropolis, Athens. Marble, 2'10" (86 cm) high. Acropolis Museum, Athens, Greece//© Nimatallah/Art Resource, NY

The end of the sixth century BCE marks a major development in vase painting with the introduction of the new **red-figure** style. This showed the figures in the red color of the clay, with details filled in using a brush. The increased subtlety made possible by this style was used to develop new techniques of foreshortening, perspective, and three-dimensionality.

Although some artists continued to produce black-figure works, by the end of the Archaic period, around 525 BCE, almost all had turned to the new style. The last Archaic vase painters are among the greatest red-figure artists. Works such as the *Euphronios Vase* [**Fig. 2.15**] have a solidity and monumentality that altogether transcend the usual limitations of the medium.

ARCHITECTURE: THE DORIC AND IONIC ORDERS

In architecture, the Archaic period was marked by the construction of several major temples in the Doric style or order. As in the case of sculpture, Egyptian models played an important part in the early development of the Greek style. The first architect in history whose name has come down to us was the Egyptian Imhotep. The earliest Egyptian buildings used bundles of papyrus to form posts; from these there soon developed the stone post-and-lintel constructions characteristic of Egyptian architecture. Buildings in this style probably inspired the first Greek temples.

Doric order seems to have been firmly established by 600 BCE, although none of the earlier examples of the evolving style have survived. Important Doric temples include the Temple of Hera at Olympia, the Temple of Apollo at Corinth, and the earliest of the three Doric temples at Paestum, often called the Basilica (meeting hall), but now known to have been dedicated to the goddess Hera [**Fig. 2.16**]. The Ionic style of temple architecture, which was widely used in Classical Greece, did not become fully established until later. In the Archaic period Ionic buildings were constructed at such sites as Samos and Ephesus, but most Ionic temples date to the fifth century BCE and later. For the sake of convenience, both the Doric and Ionic orders [**Fig. 2.17**] are described here. A later order, the Corinthian, is principally of interest for its popularity with Roman architects and is discussed in that context in Chapter 4.

The Doric Order The Doric order is the simpler and the grander of the two styles. Some of its characteristics seem directly derived from construction methods used in earlier wooden buildings, and its dignity is perhaps in part related to the length of its history. Doric columns have no base but rise directly from the floor of a building. They taper toward the top and have twenty flutes, or vertical grooves. The **capital**, which forms the head of each column, consists of two sections, a spread-

◆ **2.15** Euphronios (vase painter), *Crater of Antaeus*, c. 515–510 BCE. This masterpiece of red-figure vase painting shows an episode from the Labors of Herakles: the hero's battle with the giant Antaeus, son of Ge, the Earth Mother goddess. Every time Antaeus touched the ground, he grew stronger, so that Herakles could only kill him by raising him in the air. The hero is shown on the left, kneeling to gain greater leverage. Note the detailed rendering of the giant's anatomy, and the powerful sense of straining muscles.

From Cerveteri, Italy. Red-figure calyx krater, terracotta, 1′7″ (44.8 cm) high, 1′9½″ (55 cm) in diameter. Louvre, Paris, France//© Erich Lessing/Art Resource, NY

ing convex disc (the **echinus**) and, above, a square block (the **abacus**). The upper part of the temple, or **entablature**, is divided into three sections. The lowest, the **architrave**, is a plain band of rectangular blocks, above which is the **frieze**, consisting of alternating **triglyphs** and **metopes**. The triglyphs are divided by grooves into three vertical bands. The metope panels are sometimes plain, sometimes decorated with sculpture or painting. The building is crowned by a cornice, or projecting upper part, consisting of a horizontal section and two slanting sections meeting at a peak. The long extended triangle thus formed is the pediment, often filled with sculptural decoration.

The Ionic Order In contrast, the Ionic order is more graceful and more elaborate in architectural details. Ionic columns rise from a tiered base and have twenty-four flutes. These flutes do not meet at a sharp angle as Doric flutes do but are separated by narrow vertical bands. The capitals consist of a pair of spirals, or **volutes**. The architrave is not flat as in the Doric order but composed of three projecting bands. In place of the Doric triglyphs and metopes is a continuous band often decorated with a running frieze of sculpture.

◆ **2.16** Temple of Hera I ("Basilica"), Paestum, Italy, c. 540–530 BCE. This temple to Hera is one of the earliest surviving Greek temples. The bulging columns and spreading capitals are typical of Doric architecture in the period. The temple probably had sculptural decoration consisting of triglyphs and metopes, but none of these has survived. *(Image © Vanni/Art Resource, NY)*

DORIC ORDER

IONIC ORDER

◆ **2.17** Elevations of the Doric and Ionic orders

The two orders produced different effects. The Doric order suggested simple dignity; the absence of decorative detail drew attention to the weight and massiveness of the Doric temple. Ionic temples, on the other hand, conveyed a sense of lightness and delicacy by means of ornate decorations and fanciful carving. The surface of an Ionic temple is as important as its structural design.

MUSIC AND DANCE IN EARLY GREECE

In comparison to the visual arts, the history of Greek music is highly problematic. The little known evidence is as confusing as it is helpful. Although the frequent references to musical performance make it clear that music played a vital role in all aspects of Greek life, less than a dozen fragments of actual Greek music have survived; the earliest of these dates from the late fifth century BCE. Unfortunately, the problem of understanding the system of notation makes authentic performance of these fragments impossible.

Our inability to re-create even the examples we have is particularly frustrating because from the earliest times music was renowned for its emotional and spiritual power. For the Greeks, music was of divine origin; the gods had invented musical instruments: Hermes or Apollo the lyre, Athena the flute, and so on. Many of the earliest myths told of the powerful effect of music. Orpheus could move trees and rocks and tame wild beasts by his song; the lyre playing of Amphion brought stones to life. Nor was music making reserved for professional performers or women, as so often in later centuries. When, in Book IX of the *Iliad*, Agamemnon's ambassadors arrive at the tent of Achilles, they find the great hero playing a lyre, "clear-sounding, splendid and carefully wrought," and entertaining himself by singing "of men's fame." How one would like to have heard that song!

The Greek belief that music could profoundly affect human behavior meant that it played an important part in both public and private life and was especially important in a religious context. Greek musical theory was later summarized by the two great philosophers of the fourth century BCE, Plato and Aristotle, both of whom discuss the doctrine of **ethos** and give music an important place in their writings. An understanding of doctrines of musical theory was also considered fundamental to a good general education.

Greek music was composed using a series of distinct modes, or scale types, each of which had its own name (see Chapter 3, "Greek Music in the Classical Period"). According to the doctrine of ethos, the characteristic of each mode was so powerful that it gave music written in it the ability to affect human behavior in a specific way. Thus, the **Dorian** mode expressed firm, powerful, even warlike feelings, whereas the **Phrygian** mode produced passionate, sensual emotions. This identification of specific note patterns with individual human reactions seems to reach back to the dawn of Greek music history. The legendary founder of Greek music was Olympus, who was believed by the Greeks to have come from Asia Minor; it is surely no coincidence that two of the modes—the Phrygian and the Lydian—bear names of places in Asia Minor.

The first figure in music about whose existence we can be relatively certain was Terpander, who came from the island of Lesbos. Around 675 BCE, he used the **cithara**, an elaborate seven-string lyre, to accompany vocal music on ceremonial occasions. The simple lyre, relatively small and easy to hold, had a sounding box made of a whole tortoise shell and sides formed of goat horns or curved pieces of wood [**Fig. 2.18**]. The cithara had a much larger sound box made of wood, metal, or even ivory, and broad, hollow sides, to give greater resonance to the sound. The player had to stand while performing on it; the instrument had straps to support it, leaving the player's hands free.

Another musical instrument developed about this time was the **aulos**, a double-reed instrument [**Fig. 2.19**] similar to the modern oboe, which according to the traditional account had first been brought into Greece by Olympus. Like the cithara and lyre, the aulos was generally used by singers to accompany their songs.

The little evidence we have suggests that early Greek music was primarily vocal—the instruments were used mainly to accompany the singers. The breakthrough into purely instrumental music seems to have come at the beginning of the Archaic period. We know that in 586 BCE, Sacadas of Argos composed a work to be played on the aulos for the Pythian Games at Delphi—a piece that remained well-known and popular for centuries. Also, its character confirms the Greek love of narrative, for it described in music Apollo's fight with the dragon that the Pythian Games commemorated. The information is tantalizing, because this first piece of "program music," the remote ancestor of Richard Strauss's *Till Eulenspiegel* and *Don Quixote*, must have been highly effective for its appeal to have lasted so long.

We know little more of the music of the Archaic period than these odd facts. The lyrics of some of the songs have survived, including some of the choral odes performed in honor of various gods. Apollo and his sister Artemis were thanked for delivery from misfortune by the singing of a **paean**, or solemn invocation to the gods, whereas the **dithyramb**, or choral hymn to Dionysus, was sung in his honor at public ceremonies. Also closely tied to music was dance, which also played a significant part in the development of drama. Our knowledge of Greek dance is limited to visual evidence. For example, we have from as early as the late Geometric period actual depictions of dances in progress. One form of dance frequently depicted in the

◆ **2.18** *Young man playing a lyre*, c. 500 BCE. This scene gives a good idea of the Greeks' enthusiasm for music in general and the lyre in particular (the one shown here is the simple form). The young musician is reclining at a banquet and entertaining the guests with his playing. His fingers can clearly be seen plucking the strings.

From Chanias, Greece. Center medallion, terracotta drinking cup. Louvre, Paris, France//© Erich Lessing/Art Resource, NY

◆ **2.19** Douris (vase painter), *Music Lesson*, c. 480 BCE. A teacher demonstrates the technique of playing the *aulos*, while his pupil stands in front of him, observing closely. Note the cithara (a larger form of lyre) hanging on the wall behind, together with other musical instruments.

From Cerveteri, Italy. Detail from a red-figured drinking cup, terracotta, 11″ (28.5 cm) in diameter. Antikensammlung, Staatliche Museen zu Berlin, Berlin, Germany//© Bildarchiv Preussischer Kulturbesitz/Art Resource, NY

Classical period was a war dance, where music and movement would combine to create heightened emotion [**Fig. 2.20**]. In the Late Classical period the function of dance remained religious and social and was rarely described in writing, whereas a vast literature on music theory developed, with philosophical implications that became explicit in the writings of Plato and Aristotle; through this literature some information on early music has been preserved.

What we do know about dancing and individual dances suggests that here, as in music and visual arts, telling a story was important. One famous dance was called the *geranos*, from the word for "crane." The dancers apparently made movements like those of the bird, but the steps of the dance had a more specific meaning. According to tradition, the dance was first performed by Theseus outside the Labyrinth with the boys and girls he had saved by killing the Minotaur. The intricate patterns of the dance were supposed to represent the Labyrinth. Having accomplished two dangerous feats—killing the Minotaur and finding his way out of the Labyrinth—Theseus stayed around long enough to lead a complicated performance. Dancing was obviously of great importance to the Greeks.

◆ **2.20** The Eucharides painter, *War Dance*, early 5th century BCE. A warrior performs a war dance to the accompaniment of music played on an *aulos*. The heroic (if impractical) nudity of the dancer is typical of Greek depictions of warriors.

From Athens, Greece. Center medallion of a red-figured cup. Louvre, Paris, France // © Erich Lessing / Art Resource, NY

EARLY GREEK LITERATURE AND PHILOSOPHY

Our knowledge of literary developments between the time of Homer and the Archaic period is limited. An exception is Hesiod, who probably lived shortly before 700 BCE. He is the author of a poetic account of the origins of the world called the *Theogony* and a rather more down-to-earth long poem, the *Works and Days*, which mainly concerned the disadvantages in being a poor, oppressed (and depressed) farmer in Boeotia, where the climate is "severe in winter, stuffy in summer, good at no time of year." In the Archaic period, however, the same burst of creative energy that revolutionized the visual arts produced a wave of new poets. The medium they chose was lyric verse.

LYRIC POETRY

The emergence of lyric poetry was, like developments in the other arts, a sign of the times. The heroic verse of Homer was intended for the ruling class of an aristocratic society, which had the leisure and the inclination to hear of the great and not-so-great deeds of great men and who were interested in the problems of mighty leaders like Agamemnon and Achilles. Lyric verse is concerned above all else with the poet's own feelings, emotions, and opinions. The writers of the sixth century BCE do not hesitate to tell us how they feel about life, death, love, drinking too much wine, or anything else that crosses their minds. Heroes and the glories of battle are no longer the ideal.

Above all other Greek lyric poets, Sappho has captured the hearts and minds of the following ages. She is the first woman to leave a literary record that reflects her own personal experiences. Her poems have survived only in fragmentary form, and the details of her life remain confused and much disputed. We must be grateful, then, for what we have and not try to over-interpret it.

Sappho was born around 612 BCE on the island of Lesbos, where she spent most of her life. She seems to have been able to combine the roles of wife and mother with those of poet and teacher; within her own lifetime she was widely respected for her works and surrounded by a group of younger women who presumably came to Lesbos to finish their education, in much the same way that Americans used to go to Paris for a final cultural polish.

The affection between Sappho and her pupils was deep and sincere and is constantly reflected in her poems. The nature of this affection has been debated for centuries. The plain fact is that apart from her poetry, we know almost nothing about Sappho. Even her appearance is debatable; she is described by one ancient authority as "beautiful day" and by another as short, dark, and ugly. Her fellow poet Alcaeus calls her "violet-haired, pure, and honey-smiling." Thus, those who read Sappho must decide for themselves what the passion of the poems expresses, for passionate they certainly are. Perhaps Sappho's greatest quality lies in her ability to probe the depths of her own responses and by describing them to understand them. Just as contemporary sculptors and painters sought to understand the workings of their own bodies by depicting them, so Sappho revealed both to herself and to us the workings of her emotions.

THE FIRST PHILOSOPHERS

The century that saw the expression of the intimate self-revelations of lyric poetry was marked by the development of rational philosophy, which challenged the traditional religious ideas of Homer and Hesiod and scoffed at gods who took human form. If horses and cows had hands and could draw, they would draw gods looking like horses and cows, wrote Xenophanes of Colophon in the second half of the sixth century BCE.

The word *philosophy* literally means "love of wisdom," but in the Western tradition it usually refers to inquiries into the nature and ultimate significance of the human experience. Ever since the Archaic period, philosophers have spent some two and a half millennia debating the question: "What is philosophy?" Some of its branches are logic (the study of the structure of valid arguments), metaphysics (investigation into the nature of ultimate reality), epistemology (theory of knowledge), ethics (moral philosophy), aesthetics (the philosophy of the arts and, more generally, taste), and political philosophy.

For the first time in history, the philosophers of the Archaic period turned away from religious teachings; they used the power of human reason to try to discover how the world came into being and how it works, and to understand the place of humans in it. A wide variety of schools of thought developed, which is collectively described by the somewhat confusing label **Presocratics**. The label is accurate in that they all lived and died before the time of Socrates (469–399 BCE) and his pupil Plato (c. 427–347 BCE), who are the greatest names in Greek philosophy. However, these sixth-century philosophers had little in common with one another except the time in which they lived. Thus it is important to remember that the term *Presocratic* does not describe any single philosophical system. Many of the so-called Presocratic philosophers, with their studies into the origins of the world and the workings of nature, were examining questions that we would consider scientific rather than philosophical. The various schools were united principally by their use of logic and theoretical reasoning to solve practical questions about the world and human existence.

The earliest school to develop was that of the *Materialists*, who sought to explain all phenomena in terms of one or more elements. Thales of Miletus (c. 585 BCE), for example, thought that water alone underlay the changing world of nature. He also calculated the height of the pyramids and accurately predicted an eclipse. His notion that the world had evolved naturally, rather than as a result of divine creation, was revolutionary. He also began the Greek tradition of free discussion of ideas in the marketplace and other public areas. Intellectual exchange was no longer limited to an educated elite or a priestly class. In this way, as with his rejection of traditional religion, Thales and his successors created a fundamental breakaway from the traditional values of Homeric society.

Later, Empedocles of Acragas (c. 495 BCE) introduced four elements—fire, earth, air, water. The varying combinations (through love) and separations (through strife and war) of these elements in a cyclical pattern explained how creatures as well as nations were born, grew, decayed, and died. Anaxagoras of Clazomenae (c. 500 BCE) postulated an infinite number of small particles, which, however small they might be, always contained not only a dominant substance (for example, bone or water) but also stray bits of other substances in lesser quantities. Unity in nature, he claimed, came from the force of Reason.

Pythagoras The Presocratic philosopher who had the greatest influence on later times was Pythagoras of Samos (c. 550 BCE). He left his home city for political reasons and settled in southern Italy, where he founded a school of his own. He required his followers to lead pure and devout lives, uniting together to uphold morals and chastity, as well as order and harmony, for the common good. These apparently noble principles did nothing to win him favor from the people among whom he had settled; according to one account, he and three hundred of his followers were murdered.

It is difficult to know which of the principles of **Pythagoreanism** can be directly attributed to Pythagoras and which were later added by his disciples. His chief religious doctrines seem to have been belief in the transmigration of souls and the kinship of all living things— teachings that led to the development of a religious cult that bore his name. In science, his chief contribution was in mathematics. He discovered the numerical relationship of musical harmonics. Our modern musical scale, consisting of an **octave** (a span of eight tones) divided into its constituent parts, derives ultimately from his researches. Inspired by this discovery, Pythagoras went on to claim that mathematical relationships represented the underlying principle of the universe and of morality, the so-called harmony of the spheres. He is chiefly remembered today for a much less cosmic discovery, the geometrical theorem that bears his name.

Dualists In contrast to Pythagoras's belief in universal harmony, the **Dualists** claimed that there existed two separate universes: the world around us, which was subject to constant change, and another ideal world, perfect and unchanging, which could be realized only through the intellect. The chief proponent of this school was Heraclitus of Ephesus (c. 500 BCE), whose cryptic pronouncements won him the label "the Obscure." He summed up the unpredictable, and therefore unknowable, quality of Nature in the well-known saying, "It is not possible to step twice into the same river." Unlike his predecessors, who had tried to understand the fundamental nature of matter, Heraclitus thus drew attention instead to the process whereby matter changed.

Parmenides of Elea (c. 510 BCE), on the other hand, went so far as to claim that true reality can only be apprehended by reason and is all-perfect and unchanging, without time or motion. Our mistaken impressions come from our senses, which are flawed and subject to error. As a result, the world we perceive through them, including the processes of time and change, is a sham and a delusion. His younger pupil, Zeno (c. 490 BCE), presented several difficult paradoxes in support of their doctrines. These paradoxes were later discussed by Plato and Aristotle.

The last and perhaps the greatest school of Presocratic philosophy was that of the **Atomists**, led by Leucippus and Democritus (c. 460 BCE), who believed that the ultimate, unchangeable reality consisted of atoms (small "indivisible" particles not obvious to the naked eye) and the void (nothingness). Atomism survived into Roman times in the later philosophy of Epicureanism and into the nineteenth century in the early Atomic Theory of John Dalton. Even in the recent past, the great physicist Werner Heisenberg (1901–1976), who astonished the world of science with his discoveries in quantum mechanics, derived his initial inspiration from the Greek Atomists.

The various schools of Presocratic philosophers are often complex and difficult to understand because of the kinds of questions they addressed and also the fragmentary nature of the texts in which their ideas have survived. Furthermore, unlike all subsequent philosophers, they had no predecessors on whom to base their ideas or methods. Yet, through the cryptic phrases and often mysterious arguments, there shines a love of knowledge and a passionate search for answers to questions that still perplex humanity. And in their emphasis on the human rather than the divine, they prefigure many of the most important stages in the development of the Western tradition, from Classical Athens to the Renaissance to the eighteenth-century Age of Reason. In the words of Protagoras (c. 485–415 BCE), "Man is the measure of all things, of the existence of those that exist, and of the nonexistence of those that do not."

HERODOTUS: THE FIRST GREEK HISTORIAN

At the beginning of the fifth century BCE, the Greeks had to face the greatest threat in their history. Their success in meeting the challenge precipitated a decisive break with the world of Archaic culture.

In 499 BCE the Greek cities of Asia Minor, with Athenian support, rebelled against their Persian rulers. The Persian king Darius succeeded in checking this revolt; he then resolved to lead a punitive expedition against the mainland Greek cities that had sent help to the eastern cities. In 490 BCE he led a massive army to Greece; to everyone's surprise, the Persians were defeated by the Athenians at the Battle of Marathon. After Darius's death in 486 BCE, his son Xerxes launched an even more grandiose expedition in 480 BCE. Xerxes defeated the Spartans at Thermopylae and then attacked and sacked Athens. While the city was falling, the Athenians took to their ships, obeying an oracle that enjoined them to "trust to their wooden walls." Eventually they inflicted a crushing defeat on the Persian navy at nearby Salamis. In 479 BCE, after being conquered on land and sea, at Plataea and Mycale, the Persians returned home, completely beaten.

The great historian Herodotus (484–420 BCE) has left us, in his nine books of *History of the Persian Wars*, a detailed account of the closing years of the Archaic period. He also, however, has two other claims on our attention. He is the first writer in the Western tradition to devote himself to historical writing rather than epic or lyric poetry, a fact that has earned him the title Father of History. At the same time, he is one of the greatest storytellers, always sustaining the reader's interest in both the mainline of his narrative and the frequent and entertaining digressions. One of these, the tale of Rhampsinitus and the thief, has been described as the first detective story in Western literature.

Herodotus was not a scientific historian in our terms—he had definite weaknesses. He never really understood the finer points of military strategy. He almost always interpreted events in terms of personalities, showing little interest in underlying political or economic causes. His strengths, however, were many. Although his subject involved conflict between Greeks and foreigners, he remained remarkably impartial and free from national prejudice. His natural curiosity about the world around him and about his fellow human beings was buttressed by acute powers of observation. Above all, he recorded as much information as possible, even when versions conflicted. He also tried to provide a reasonable evaluation of the reliability of his sources so later readers could form their own opinions.

Herodotus's analysis of the Greek victory was based on a serious philosophical, indeed theological, belief—that the Persians were defeated because they were morally in the wrong. Their moral fault was **hubris** (excessive ambition); thus the Greeks' victory was at the same time an example of right over might and a demonstration that the gods would guarantee the triumph of justice. In Book VII, Xerxes' uncle, Artabanus, warns him in 480 BCE not to invade Greece: "You know, my lord, that amongst living creatures it is the great ones that Zeus smites with his thunder, out of envy of their pride. It is God's way to bring the lofty low. For He tolerates pride in none but Himself."

Modern readers, however, less influenced by Herodotus's religious beliefs, will be more inclined to draw a political message from the Persian defeat. The Greeks were successful at least partly because for once they had managed to unite in the face of a common enemy. Their victories inaugurated the greatest period in Greek history, the Classical Age.

SUMMARY

◆ **The Dawn of Greek Culture.** Shortly after 1000 BCE, Greek civilization began to develop. From the beginning, the Greek world was divided into separate city-states among which fierce rivalries would grow. For the first two centuries the Greeks had little contact with other peoples, but around 800 BCE, Greek travelers and merchants began to explore throughout the Mediterranean. The visual arts during these early centuries are principally represented by pottery decorated with geometric designs. The period also saw the creation of two of the greatest masterpieces of Western literature: the *Iliad* and the *Odyssey*.

◆ **The Age of Colonization.** During the Age of Colonization (c. 750–600 BCE), the Greeks came in contact with a wide range of foreign peoples. The ancient Near East, in particular, largely influenced the development of Greek art and architecture. The decoration of pottery became Orientalizing in style, while large freestanding sculpture based on Egyptian models began to evolve. Important Greek colonies began to develop in southern Italy and Sicily.

◆ **The Archaic Period.** The period from 600 BCE to 480 BCE, known as the Archaic Age, was marked by political and cultural change. A new literary form, lyric poetry, became popular; one of its leading practitioners was the poetess Sappho. The so-called Presocratics began to develop a wide range of philosophical schools. Sculpture and vase painting both became increasingly naturalistic. The aristocratic rulers of earlier times were supplanted by "tyrants," rich merchant traders who depended on the support of the lower classes. In Athens, Solon's reform of the constitution introduced a form of democracy, which was overthrown by the tyrant Pisistratus in 546 BCE.

◆ **The Persian Wars.** Democratic government was restored at Athens in 510 BCE, and shortly thereafter the Greeks became embroiled with the mighty Persian empire to their east. In 499 BCE the Greek cities of western Asia, established more than a century earlier, rebelled against their Persian rulers; the Athenians sent help. The Persians crushed the revolt and, in 490 BCE, the Persian king Darius led an expedition against the Greeks to punish them for their interference. Against all odds, the Persians were defeated at the Battle of Marathon. Darius, humiliated, was forced to withdraw, but ten years later Xerxes, his son, mounted an even more grandiose campaign to restore Persian honor. In 480 BCE he invaded Greece, defeated Spartan troops at Thermopylae, and sacked Athens. The Athenians took to their ships, however, and destroyed the Persian navy at the Battle of Salamis.

The following year, combined Greek forces defeated Xerxes' army on land, and the Persians returned home in defeat. Faced by the greatest threat in their history, the Greeks had managed to present a united front. Their victories set the scene for the Classical Age of Greek culture. A detailed account of the Greeks' success can be found in the *History of the Persian Wars* written by Herodotus, the first Greek historian and the earliest significant prose writer in Western literature.

EXERCISES

1. What are the main features of the Homeric worldview?
2. What effect do these features have on the style of the Homeric epics?
3. Describe the development of Greek sculpture from the mid-seventh century to the end of the Archaic period.
4. What evidence has survived about the nature of Greek music? What does it tell us about the Greeks' attitude toward music?
5. Discuss the principal schools of Presocratic philosophy.
6. What are the chief differences between the Doric and Ionic orders of architecture?

Visit the *Culture & Values* Companion website at **www.cengage.com/art/Cunningham/Cultureand Values7E** and the *Humanities Resource Center* for an array of primary source readings, key terms with pronunciations, flash cards, quizzes, and study materials designed especially to help you do well in this course.

CHAPTER 3

CLASSICAL GREECE AND THE HELLENISTIC PERIOD

The leading figure in Classical Athens was Pericles, under whose patronage the new building program on the Acropolis was accomplished. His personal life gives us a rare insight into the relations between men and women in his city.

Pericles married early in life, had two sons by his aristocratic wife, and then the couple divorced, apparently by mutual consent. The statesman then devoted all of his time to public life; the Athenians nicknamed him "Zeus," describing his speeches to the Assembly as "divine thunder."

In 445 BCE, at the age of around 50, he began a relationship with a young woman, Aspasia, that provided the Athenians with a never-ending supply of gossip. Aspasia was born around 465 BCE, and earned her living as a "hetaira," a "companion to men." These self-employed prostitutes registered with the state and paid a special tax. The most successful were often educated and cultured women, who could provide a level of intellectual companionship beyond that of most sheltered Athenian housewives. Pericles and

Aspasia openly set up house together. To the amused astonishment of their neighbors, "Pericles would kiss her warmly when he left for work and again when he returned home."

Not all public opinion was so tolerant. Aspasia was accused of influencing Pericles' political decisions. In 432 BCE, as the shadow of the Peloponnesian War began to loom, she was brought to trial for "impiety." Pericles himself appeared in court on her behalf. He broke down and wept, and the jury acquitted her. In 429, a few weeks before the great statesman's death, the Athenian Assembly voted to confer Athenian citizenship on the couple's son, previously regarded as illegitimate. When Pericles died, Aspasia married a democratic politician and continued to live quietly at Athens.

CLASSICAL CIVILIZATION IN ANCIENT GREECE

The victories in the Persian Wars produced a new spirit of optimism and unity in Greece. Divine forces, it appeared, had guaranteed the triumph of right over wrong. There seemed to be no limit to the possibilities of human development. The achievements of the Classical period, which lasted from 479 BCE to the death of Alexander the Great in 323 BCE, do much to justify the Greeks' proud self-confidence. They certainly represent a level of civilization that has rarely, if ever, been reached since—a level that has been a continuing inspiration to our culture.

Classical civilization reached its high point in Athens during the last half of the fifth century BCE, a time of unparalleled richness in artistic and intellectual achievement that is often called the Golden Age of Greece. To

◆ Pericles directing the construction of a wall on the Acropolis, 440–430 BCE, Athens, Greece. (© Réunion des Musées Nationaux/Art Resource, NY)

some extent, the importance of the great figures who dominated this period lies in the fact that they were the first in their fields. There are, in fact, few areas of human thought in which the fifth-century Greeks were not pioneers. In subjects as diverse as drama and historiography, town planning and medicine, painting and sculpture, mathematics and government, they laid the foundations for later achievements. Even more astonishing, often they were not merely the first in their fields but also among the greatest of all time. Greek tragedies, for example, are still read and performed today because

they give experiences that are as intense emotionally and intellectually as anything in the Western dramatic tradition.

With the end of the Peloponnesian War (404 BCE) and the fall of Athenian democracy, both art and political life were to be affected by an atmosphere of considerable confusion. During this Late Classical period (404–323 BCE), artists and writers continued to explore ideas and styles first outlined in the century before, although in different ways. Greek cultural life was no longer dominated by Athens; a single center no longer governed

GENERAL EVENTS	ART
500 BCE	
	c. 490 *Kritios Boy*; turning point between Archaic and Classical Periods
480	
478 Formation of Delian League; beginning of Athenian empire	**480–323** First naturalistic sculpture and painting appear
461 Pericles comes to prominence at Athens	**c. 460** Sculptures at Temple of Zeus, Olympia
454 Treasury of Delian League moved to Athens	
450	
443–429 Pericles in full control of Athens	**c. 450** Myron, *Discus Thrower*
431 Peloponnesian War begins	
429 Pericles dies of plague that devastates Athens	**c. 440** Polykleitos, Treatise *The Canon, Doryphoros*
421 Peace of Nicias	**432** Phidias completes Parthenon sculptures
413 Renewed outbreak of Peloponnesian War	
	late 5th cent. White-ground vase painting and funerary relief sculpture
404	
404 Fall of Athens and victory of Sparta	**c. 350** Scopas, *Pothos*
404–403 Rule of Thirty Tyrants	
387 King's Peace signed	
	c. 350 Frescoes, Royal Cemetery at Vergina
371–362 Ascendancy of Thebes	
359–336 Philip II, king of Macedon	**c. 340** Praxiteles, *Hermes with Infant Dionysus*
338 Macedonians defeat Greeks at Battle of Chaeronaea	**c. 330** Lysippus, *Apoxyomenos 3.22*
336–323 Alexander the Great, king of Macedon	
331 City of Alexandria founded	
323	
323–281 Wars of Alexander's successors	**323–146** Development of realistic portraiture
262 Pergamum becomes independent kingdom	
197–156 Eumenes II, king of Pergamum	
146 Romans sack Corinth; Greece becomes Roman province	**c. 150** *Laocoön*
146	

CLASSICAL PERIOD — GOLDEN AGE — LATE CLASSICAL PERIOD — HELLENISTIC PERIOD artistic developments. This fourth-century period was therefore one of greater variety, with individual artists following their own personal visions. The greatest of all Late Classical contributions to modern cultural tradition was in the field of philosophy. The works of Plato and Aristotle became the basis of Western thought for the next two thousand years.

The accession of Philip in Macedon (359 BCE) changed the balance of power in Greece. The hitherto backward northern kingdom of Macedon began to exert a new unifying influence, despite opposition in Thebes and in Athens, where the great Athenian orator Demosthenes led the resistance. In 338 BCE, at the Battle of Chaeronaea (see map, "Ancient Greece," Chapter 2), Philip defeated Athenian and Theban forces and unified all the cities of Greece, with the exception of Sparta, in an alliance known as the League of Corinth.

Before his assassination in 336 BCE, Philip had developed schemes for enlarging his empire by attacking Persia. His son and successor, Alexander, carried them out. He spent the ten years from 333 BCE until his own death in 323 BCE in an amazing series of campaigns

ARCHITECTURE	LITERATURE & PHILOSOPHY	MUSIC
		c. 500–425 Music serves as accompaniment in dramatic performances
470–456 Libon of Elis, Temple of Zeus at Olympia	**458** Aeschylus, *Oresteia* trilogy wins first prize in drama festival of Dionysus	
449 Pericles commissions work on Acropolis	**440** Sophocles, *Antigone*	
447–438 Ictinus and Callicrates, Parthenon	**c. 429** Sophocles, *Oedipus the King*	
437–431 Mnesikles, Propylaea	**c. 421** Euripides, *The Suppliant Women*	
c. 427–424 Callicrates, Temple of Athena Nike	**c. 420–c. 399** Thucydides, *History of Peloponnesian War*	
421–406 Erechtheum	**414** Aristophanes, *The Birds*	
	411 Aristophanes, *Lysistrata*	
356 Temple of Artemis at Ephesus destroyed by fire and rebuilt	**399** Trial and execution of Socrates	**c. 400** Music dominates dramatic performances
	before 387 Plato, *Republic*	
c. 350 Theater at Epidaurus	**387** Plato founds Academy	**4th cent.** Instrumental music becomes popular
	c. 385 Xenophon chronicles teachings of Socrates	
	c. 347–c. 399 Aristotle, *Poetics, Metaphysics*	
	335 Aristotle founds Lyceum	
323–146 *Tholos* and other new building forms appear		
279 Lighthouse at Alexandria		
c. 180 Eumenes II, Pergamum Altar of Zeus		**late 2nd cent.** Earliest surviving Greek music

across Asia, destroying the Persian Empire and reaching as far as India.

Even after the death of Alexander the Great and the end of the Classical Age, the Hellenistic period that followed was characterized by an artistic vitality that ultimately drew its inspiration from Classical achievements. Only when Greece was conquered by the Romans in the late second century BCE did Greek culture cease to have an independent existence.

THE CLASSICAL IDEAL

Although the Roman conquest of Greece ended the glories of the Classical Age, in a way it also perpetuated them by contributing to the melding of Greek culture into the Western humanistic tradition. It was not the Greeks but their conquerors who spread Greek ideas throughout the ancient world and thus down in time to the present. These conquerors were first the Macedonians and then, above all, the Romans, possessors of practical skills that they used to construct a world sufficiently at peace for ideas to have a place in it. The Greeks did not live in such tranquility; we must always remember that the Athenians of the Golden Age existed not in an environment of calm contemplation but in a world of tension and violence.

Their tragic inability to put into practice their own noble ideals and live in peace with other Greeks—the darker side of their genius—proved fatal to their independence; it led to war with the rest of Greece in 431 BCE and to the fall of Athens in 404 BCE. In this context, the Greek search for order takes on an added significance. The belief that the quest for reason and order could succeed gave a unifying ideal to the immense and varied output of the Classical Age. The central principle of this Classical Ideal was that existence can be ordered and controlled, that human ability can triumph over the apparent chaos of the natural world and create a balanced society. In order to achieve this equilibrium, individual human beings should try to stay within what seem to be reasonable limits, for those who do not are guilty of hubris—the same hubris of which the Persian leader Xerxes was guilty and for which he paid the price. The aim of life should be a perfect balance: everything in due proportion and nothing in excess. "Nothing too much" was one of the most famous Greek proverbs.

The emphasis that the Classical Greeks placed on order affected their spiritual attitudes. Individuals can achieve order, they believed, by understanding why people act as they do and, above all, by understanding the motives for their own actions. Thus confidence in the power of both human reason and human self-knowledge was as important as belief in the gods. The greatest of all Greek temples of the Classical Age, the Parthenon, which crowned the Athenian Acropolis (see Figure 3.13 later in this chapter), was planned not so

much to honor the goddess Athena as to glorify Athens and thus human achievement. Even in their darkest days, the Classical Greeks never lost sight of the magnitude of human capability and, perhaps even more important, human potential—a vision that has returned over the centuries to inspire later generations and has certainly not lost its relevance in our own times.

The political and cultural center of Greece during the first half of the Classical period was Athens. Here, by the end of the Persian Wars in 479 BCE, the Athenians had emerged as the most powerful people in the Greek world. For one thing, their role in the defeat of the Persians had been decisive. For another, their democratic system of government, first established in the late sixth century BCE, was proving to be both effective and stable. All male Athenian citizens were not only entitled but were also required to participate in the running of the state, either as members of the General Assembly, the **ecclesia**, with its directing council, the **boule**, or by holding individual magistracies. They were also eligible to serve on juries.

The Delian League Under Athenian leadership in the years following the wars, a defensive organization of Greek city-states was formed to guard against any future outside attack. The money collected from the participating members was kept in a treasury on the island of Delos, sacred to Apollo and politically neutral. This organization became known as the Delian League.

Within a short time several other important city-states, including Thebes, Sparta, and Athens' old trade rival Corinth, began to suspect that the league was serving not so much to protect all of Greece as to strengthen Athenian power. They believed the Athenians were turning an association of free and independent states into an empire of subject peoples. Their suspicions were confirmed when (in 454 BCE) the funds of the league were transferred from Delos to Athens and some of the money was used to pay for Athenian building projects, including the Parthenon. The spirit of Greek unity was starting to dissolve; the Greek world was beginning to divide into two opposing sides: on the one hand, Athens and her allies (the cities that remained in the league), and on the other, the rest of Greece. Conflict was inevitable. The Spartans were finally persuaded to lead an alliance against Athens to check her "imperialistic designs." This war, called the Peloponnesian War after the homeland of the Spartans and their supporters, began in 431 BCE and dragged on until 404 BCE.

Thucydides Our understanding of the Peloponnesian War and its significance owes much to the account by the great historian Thucydides, who lived through its calamitous events. Born around 460 BCE, Thucydides played an active part in Athenian politics in the years before the war. In 424 BCE he was elected general and put in charge of defending the city of Amphipolis in northern Greece. When the city fell to Spartan troops, Thucydides was condemned in his absence and sentenced to exile. He did not return to Athens until 404 BCE.

Thucydides intended his *History of the Peloponnesian War* to describe the entire course of the war up to 404 BCE, but he died before completing it; the narrative breaks off at the end of 411 BCE. The work is extremely valuable for its detailed description of events, for, although its author was an Athenian, he managed to be both accurate and impartial. At the same time, however, Thucydides tried to write more than simply an account of a local war. The history was an attempt to analyze human motives and reactions so that future generations would understand how and why the conflict occurred and, in turn, understand themselves. The work was not meant to entertain by providing digressions and anecdotes but to search out the truth and use it to demonstrate universal principles of human behavior. This emphasis on reason makes Thucydides' work typical of the Classical period.

The hero of Thucydides' account of the years immediately preceding the war is Pericles, the leader whose name symbolizes the achievements of the Athenian Golden Age [**Fig. 3.2**]. An aristocrat by birth, Pericles began his political career in the aftermath of the transfer of the Delian League's funds to Athens. By 443 BCE, he had unofficially assumed the leadership of the Athenian democracy, although he continued democratically to run for reelection every year. Under his guidance the few remaining years of peace were devoted to making visible the glory of Athens by constructing on the Acropolis—the majestic buildings that still, though in ruins, evoke the grandeur of Periclean Athens (see **Table 3.1**).

Had Pericles continued to lead Athens during the war, the final outcome might have been different, but in 430 BCE the city was ravaged by disease, perhaps bubonic plague, and in 429 BCE Pericles died. No successor could be found who was capable of winning the respect and support of the majority of his fellow citizens. The war continued indecisively until 421 BCE, when an uneasy peace was signed. Shortly thereafter the Athenians made an ill-advised attempt to replenish their treasury by organizing an unprovoked attack on the wealthy Greek cities of Sicily. The expedition proved a total disaster;

thousands of Athenians were killed or taken prisoner. When the war began again (411 BCE), the Athenian forces were fatally weakened.

The end came in 404 BCE. After a siege that left many people dying in the streets, Athens surrendered unconditionally to the Spartans and their allies.

DRAMA AND PHILOSOPHY IN CLASSICAL GREECE

THE DRAMA FESTIVALS OF DIONYSUS

The tumultuous years of the fifth century BCE, passing from the spirit of euphoria that followed the ending of the Persian Wars to the mood of doubt and self-questioning of 404 BCE, may seem unlikely to have

TABLE 3.1 *Athens in the Age of Pericles (ruled 443–429 BCE)*

Area of the city	7 square miles
Population of the city	100,000–125,000
Population of the region (Attica)	200,000–250,000
Political institution	General Assembly, Council of 500, Ten Generals
Economy	Maritime trade; Crafts (textiles, pottery); Farming (olives, grapes, wheat)
Cultural life	History (Thucydides); Drama (Aeschylus, Sophocles, Euripides, Aristophanes); Philosophy (Socrates); Architecture (Ictinus, Callicrates, Mnesicles); Sculpture (Phidias)
Principal buildings	Parthenon, Propylea (the Erechtheum, the other major building on the Athenian Acropolis, was not begun in Pericles' lifetime)

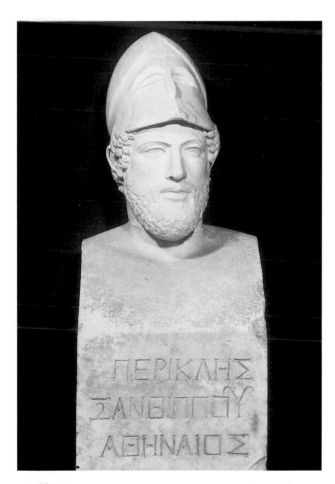

◆ **3.2** Kresilas, *Pericles*. Pericles is wearing a helmet pushed up over his forehead because his official rank, while leader of Athens, was that of general.

Roman copy after a bronze original of 429 BCE. Marble herm, 6′ (1.8m) high. Vatican Museums, Vatican State//© Bildarchiv Preussischer Kulturbesitz/Art Resource, NY

produced the kind of intellectual concentration characteristic of Classical Greek drama. Yet in the plays written specifically for performance in the theater of Dionysus at Athens in these years, Classical literature reached its most elevated heights. The tragedies of the three great masters—Aeschylus, Sophocles, and Euripides—not only illustrate the development of contemporary thought but also contain some of the most memorable scenes in the history of the theater.

Tragic drama was not an invention of the fifth century BCE. It had evolved over the preceding century from choral hymns sung in honor of the god Dionysus, and the religious character of its origins was still present in its fully developed form. The plays that have survived from the Classical period at Athens were all written for performance at one of the two annual festivals sacred to Dionysus before an audience consisting of the entire population of the city. (Like the Egyptian god, Osiris, Dionysus died and was reborn, and the festivals held in his honor may be related to earlier ceremonies developed in Egypt.) To go to the theater was to take part in a religious ritual; the theaters were regarded as sacred ground [**Fig. 3.3**].

Each of the authors of the works given annually normally submitted four plays to be performed consecutively on a single day—three tragedies, or a **trilogy**, and a more lighthearted play called a **satyr play** (a satyr was a mythological figure: a man with an animal's ears and tail). The trilogies sometimes narrated parts of a single story, although often the three works were based on different stories with a common theme. At the end of

each festival, the plays were judged and a prize awarded to the winning author.

The dramas were religious not only in time and place but also in nature. The plots, generally drawn from mythology, often dealt with the relationship between the human and the divine. To achieve an appropriate seriousness, the style of performance was lofty and dignified. The actors, who in a sense served as priests of Dionysus, wore masks, elaborate costumes, and raised shoes.

The **chorus**, whose sacred dithyrambic hymn had been the original starting point in the development of tragedy, retained an important function throughout the fifth century BCE. In some plays (generally the earlier ones) the chorus forms a group centrally involved in the action, as in Aeschylus's *Suppliants* and *Eumenides*. More often, as in Sophocles' *Oedipus the King* or *Antigone*, the chorus represents the point of view of the spectator, rather than that of the characters participating directly in the events on stage; in these plays the chorus reduces to more human terms the intense emotions of the principals and comments on them. Even in the time of Euripides, when dramatic confrontation became more important than extended poetic or philosophical expression, the chorus still retained one important function: that of punctuating the action and dividing it into separate episodes by singing lyric odes, the subjects of which were sometimes only indirectly related to the action of the play.

These aspects of Classical tragedy are a reminder that the surviving texts of the plays represent only a small part of the total experience of the original per-

◆ **3.3** The Ancient Theater at Delphi, Greece, 159 BCE. At the foot of a natural hillside, into which the rows were cut out of the rock face, stood a raised stage on which the actors performed. The chorus, which entered through large doorways at left and right, moved in the circular area between stage and audience. Note that, like most Greek theaters, the one at Delphi commands a magnificent view. The rectangular foundations of the huge Temple to Apollo are also clearly visible behind the stage. *(© Erich Lessing/Art Resource, NY)*

formances. The words—or at least some of them—have survived, but the music to which the words were sung and which accompanied much of the action, the elaborate choreography to which the chorus moved, and the whole grandiose spectacle performed out-of-doors in theaters located in sites of extreme natural beauty before an audience of thousands—all of this can only be recaptured in the imagination. It is perhaps relevant to remember that when, almost two thousand years later, around 1600 CE, a small group of Florentine intellectuals decided to revive the art of Classical drama, they succeeded instead in inventing opera. Similarly, in the nineteenth century, the German composer Richard Wagner was inspired by Greek tragedy to devise his concept of a *Gesamtkunstwerk* (literally "total work of art"), a work of art that combined all the arts into one; he illustrated this concept by writing his dramatic operas.

THE ATHENIAN TRAGIC DRAMATISTS

Even if some elements of the surviving Greek dramas are lost, we do have the words. The differing worldviews of the authors of these works vividly illustrate the changing fate of Athens in the fifth century BCE.

Aeschylus The earliest of the playwrights, Aeschylus (525–456 BCE), died before the lofty aspirations of the early years of the Classical period could be shaken by contemporary events. His work shows a deep awareness of human weakness and the dangers of power (he had fought at the Battle of Marathon in 490 BCE), but he retains an enduring belief that in the end right will triumph. In Aeschylus's plays, the process of being able to recognize what is right is painful. One must suffer to learn one's errors; yet the process is inevitable, controlled by a divine force of justice personified under the name of Zeus.

The essential optimism of Aeschylus's philosophy must be kept in mind because the actual course of the events he describes is often violent and bloody. Perhaps his most impressive plays are the three that form the *Oresteia* trilogy. This trilogy, the only complete one that has survived, won first prize in the festival of 458 BCE at Athens. The subject of the trilogy is nothing less than the growth of civilization, represented by the gradual transition from a primitive law of *vendetta* ("blood for blood") to the rational society of civilized human beings.

The first of the three plays, the *Agamemnon*, presents the first of these systems in operation. King Agamemnon returns to his homeland, Argos, after leading the Greeks to victory at Troy. Ten years earlier, on the way to Troy, he had been forced to choose either to abandon the campaign because of unfavorable tides or to obtain an easy passage by sacrificing his daughter Iphigenia. (The situation may seem contrived, but it clearly symbolizes a conflict between public and personal

VALUES

Civic Pride

Aristotle's comment that "Man is a creature who lives in a city," sometimes translated as "Man is a political animal," summarizes the Greeks' attitude toward their polis (city). The focus of political, religious, and cultural life, and most other aspects as well—sport, entertainment, justice—the polis came to represent the central force in the life of each individual citizen.

The Greeks saw the importance of their city-states as the fundamental difference between their culture and that of the "barbarians," because it enabled them to participate in their community's affairs as responsible individuals. This participation was limited to adult male citizens; female citizens played little significant role in public life, and slaves and resident foreigners were completely excluded.

If the polis was responsible for many of the highest achievements of Greek culture, the notion of civic pride produced in the end a series of destructive rivalries that ended Greek independence. The unity forged in the threat of the Persian invasions soon collapsed in the buildup to the Peloponnesian War. Even in the face of the campaigns of Philip of Macedon, the Greek cities continued to feud among themselves, unable to form a common front in the face of the danger of conquest.

The notion of the individual city as the focus of political and cultural life returned in the Italian Renaissance. Renaissance Florence and Siena, Milan, Venice, and Verona saw themselves as separate city-states, with their own styles of art and society. Even a small community such as Urbino became an independent political and artistic unit, modeled consciously on the city-states of Classical Greece. As in Greek times, civic pride led to strife between rivals and left the Italians helpless in the face of invasions by French forces or those of the Holy Roman Emperor.

responsibilities.) After considerable hesitation and self-doubt, he had chosen to sacrifice his daughter. On his return home at the end of the Trojan War, he pays the price for her death by being murdered by his wife Clytemnestra and her lover Aegisthus. Her ostensible motive is vengeance for Iphigenia's death, but an equally powerful, if less noble, one is her desire to replace Agamemnon both as husband and king by her lover Aegisthus. Thus, Aeschylus shows us that even the "law of the jungle" is not always as simple as it may seem, while the punishment of one crime creates in its turn another crime to be punished. If Agamemnon's murder of his daughter merits vengeance, then so does Clytemnestra's sacrifice of her husband. Violence breeds violence.

The second play, *The Libation Bearers*, shows us the effects of the operation of this principle on Agamemnon and Clytemnestra's son, Orestes. After spending years in exile, Orestes returns to Argos to avenge his father's death by killing his mother [**Fig. 3.4**]. Although a further murder can accomplish nothing except the transfer of blood guilt to Orestes, the primitive law of vendetta requires him to act. With the encouragement of his sister Electra, he kills Clytemnestra. His punishment follows immediately. He is driven mad by the Furies, the implacable goddesses of vengeance, who hound him from his home.

The Furies give their name to the third play, in which they are tactfully called *The Eumenides* ("the kindly ones"). In his resolution of the tragedy of Orestes and his family, Aeschylus makes it clear that violence can only be brought to an end by the power of reason and persuasion. After a period of tormented wandering, Orestes comes finally to Athens, where he stands trial for the murder of his mother before a jury of Athenians, presided over by Athena. The Furies insist on his condemnation on the principle of blood for blood, but Orestes is defended by Apollo, the god of reason, and finally acquitted. His fellow human beings making up the jury brought in a tied verdict, and Athena makes the final decision in Orestes' favor. Thus, the long blood feud is brought to an end, and the apparently inevitable violence and despair of the earlier plays is finally dispelled by the power of persuasion and human reason, which—admittedly with the help of Athena and Apollo—have managed to bring civilization and order out of primeval chaos: from now on, homicide cases were to be tried by the Athenian court system.

Despite all the horror of the earlier plays, therefore, the *Oresteia* ends on a positive note. Aeschylus affirms his belief that progress can be achieved by reason and order. This gradual transition from darkness to light is handled throughout the three plays with unfailing skill. Aeschylus matches the grandeur of his conception with majestic language. His rugged style makes him sometimes difficult to understand, but all the verbal effects are used to dramatic purpose. The piling up of images and complexity of expression produce an emotional tension that has never been surpassed.

◆ **3.4** Orestes Murders Aegisthus. The difference in age between the young Orestes and his mother's lover is indicated by Aegisthus's beard. The young woman on the left fleeing the scene is probably Chrysothemis, daughter of Agamemnon.

From Cerveteri, Italy. Attic red-figured pelike, 500 BCE, clay, 1′2″ (35.6 cm) high. Kunsthistorisches Museum, Vienna, Austria//© Erich Lessing/Art Resource, NY

Sophocles The life of Sophocles (496–406 BCE) spanned both the glories and the disasters of the fifth century BCE. Of the three great tragic poets, Sophocles was the most prosperous and successful; he was a personal friend of Pericles. He is said to have written 123 plays, but only seven have survived, all of which date from the end of his career. They all express a much less positive vision of life than that of Aeschylus. His philosophy is not easy to extract from his work, because he is more concerned with exploring and developing the individual characters in his dramas than with expounding a point of view; in general, Sophocles seems to combine an awareness of the tragic consequences of individual mistakes with a belief in the collective ability and dignity of the human race.

The consequences of human error are vividly depicted in his play *Antigone*, first performed around 440 BCE. Thebes has been attacked by forces under the leadership of Polynices; the attack is beaten off and Polynices killed. In the aftermath Creon, king of Thebes, declares the dead warrior a traitor and forbids anyone to bury him on pain of death. Antigone, Polynices' sister, disobeys, claiming that her religious and family obligations override those to the state. Creon angrily condemns her to death. He subsequently relents, but too late: Antigone, his son (betrothed to Antigone), and his wife have all committed suicide. Creon's stubbornness and bad judgment thus result in tragedy for him as well as for Antigone.

Paradoxically, however, the choice between good and evil is never clear or easy and is sometimes impossible. More than any of his contemporaries, Sophocles emphasizes how much lies outside our own control, in the hands of destiny or the gods. His insistence that we respect and revere the forces that we cannot see or understand makes him the most traditionally religious of the tragedians. These ambiguities appear in his best known play, *Oedipus the King*, which has stood ever since Classical times as a symbol of Greek tragic drama. A century after it was first performed (c. 429 BCE), Aristotle used it as his model when, in the *Poetics*, he discussed the nature of tragedy. Its unities of time, place, and action, the inexorable drive of the story with its inevitable yet profoundly tragic conclusion, the beauty of its poetry—all have made *Oedipus the King* a true classic, in all senses. Its impact has lasted down to the present; it had a notable effect on the ideas of Sigmund Freud. Yet despite the universal admiration the play has excited, its message is far from clear.

The story concerns Oedipus, doomed even before his birth to kill his father and marry his mother, his attempts to avoid fate, and his final discovery that he has failed. If the play seems, in part, to be saying that we cannot avoid our destiny, it leaves unanswered the question of whether we deserve that destiny. Certainly Oedipus does not choose deliberately to kill his father and marry his mother, even though unknowingly everything he does leads to this end. Then why does he deserve to suffer for his actions?

One of the traditional answers to this question can be found in Aristotle's analysis of tragedy in the *Poetics*. Referring particularly to Oedipus, Aristotle makes the point that the downfall of a tragic figure is generally the result of a flaw or an intellectual miscalculation (the Greek word is **hamartia**) in his character. Thus Oedipus's pride and stubbornness in insisting on discovering who he is and the anger he shows in the process bring about the final disastrous revelation. In this way the flaws, or weaknesses, in his character overcome his good points and destroy him. As a description of Oedipus's behavior, this explanation is convincing enough, but it fails to provide a satisfactory account of the original causes of his condition. Perhaps the message of the play is, in fact, that some aspects of existence are beyond our understanding, aspects that operate by principles outside our range of experience. If this is so, and many literary critics would deny it, Sophocles seems to be describing the final helplessness of humanity in the face of forces that we cannot control and warning against too great a belief in self-reliance.

Euripides The significance for the Athenians of Oedipus's fall from greatness emerges in full force in the work of Euripides (c. 484–406 BCE). Although only slightly younger than Sophocles, Euripides expresses all the weariness and disillusion of the war-torn years at the end of the fifth century BCE. Of all the tragedians, Euripides is perhaps the closest to our own time, with his concern for realism and his determination to expose social, political, and religious injustices.

Although Euripides admits the existence of irrational forces in the universe that can be personified in the forms of gods and goddesses, he certainly does not regard them as worthy of respect and worship. This skepticism won him the charge of impiety. His plays show characters frequently pushed to the limits of endurance; their reactions show a new concern for psychological truth. In particular, Euripides exhibits a profound sympathy and understanding for the problems of women who live in a society dominated by men. Characters like Medea and Phaedra challenged many of the basic premises of contemporary Athenian society.

Euripides' deepest hatred is reserved for war and its senseless misery. Like the other dramatists, he draws the subject matter of his plays from traditional myths, but the lines delivered by the actors must have sounded in their hearers' ears with a terrible relevance. *The Suppliant Women* was probably written in 421 BCE, when ten years of indecisive fighting had produced nothing but an uneasy truce. Its subject is the recovery by Theseus, ruler of Athens, of the bodies of seven chiefs killed fighting at Thebes in order to return them to their families for burial. He yields to their mothers—the women of the title—who beg him to recover the corpses. The audience would have little need to be reminded of the grief of wives and mothers or of the kind of political processes that produced years of futile fighting.

If Aeschylus's belief in human progress is more noble, Euripides is certainly more realistic. Although unpopular in his own time, he later became the most widely read of the three tragedians. As a result, more of his plays have been preserved (nineteen in all), works with a wide range of emotional expression. They extend from romantic comedies like *Helen* and *Iphigenia in Taurus* to the profoundly disturbing *Bacchae*, his last completed play, in which Euripides the rationalist explores the inadequacy of reason as the sole approach to life. In this acknowledgment of the power of emotion to overwhelm the order and balance so typical of the Classical ideal, he is most clearly speaking for his time.

ARISTOPHANES AND GREEK COMEDY

Euripides was not the only Athenian to realize the futility of war. The plays of Aristophanes (c. 450–385 BCE), the greatest comic poet of fifth-century-BCE Athens, deal with the same theme. His work combines political satire with a strong vein of fantasy.

In *The Birds*, produced in 414 BCE, two Athenians decide to leave home and find a better place to live. They join forces with the birds and build a new city in midair called Cloudcuckooland, which cuts off contact between gods and humans by blocking the path of the smoke rising from sacrifices. The gods are forced to come to terms with the new city, and Zeus hands over his scepter of authority to the birds.

This is simple escapism, but *Lysistrata*, written a few years later (411 BCE), deals with the problem of how to prevent war in a more practical fashion. In the course of the play, the main protagonist, Lysistrata, persuades her fellow women of Athens to refuse to make love with their husbands until peace is negotiated. At the same time her followers seize the Acropolis. The men, teased and frustrated, finally give in and envoys are summoned from Sparta. The play ends with the Athenians and Spartans dancing together for joy at the new peace.

PHILOSOPHY IN THE LATE CLASSICAL PERIOD

The intellectual and cultural spirit of the new century was foreshadowed in its first year in an event at Athens. In 399 BCE the philosopher Socrates was charged with impiety and leading youth to question authority, found guilty, and executed. Yet the ideas that Socrates represented—concern with the fate of the individual and the questioning of traditional values—could not be killed so easily. They had already begun to spread at the end of the fifth century BCE and came to dominate the culture of the fourth century BCE.

Socrates Socrates is one of the most important figures in Greek history. He is also one of the most difficult to understand clearly. Much of the philosophy of the Greeks and of later ages and cultures has been inspired by his life and teachings. Yet Socrates wrote nothing; most of what we know of him comes from the works of his disciple, Plato. Socrates was born around 469 BCE, the son of a sculptor and a midwife; in later life he claimed to have followed his mother's profession in being a "midwife to ideas." He seems first to have been interested in natural science, but soon turned to the problems of human behavior and morality. Unlike the **sophists** (the professional philosophers of the day), he neither took money for teaching nor did he ever found a school. Instead he went around Athens, to both public places like the markets and the gymnasia and private gatherings, talking and arguing, testing traditional ideas by subjecting them to a barrage of questions—as he put it, "following the argument wherever it led."

Socrates gradually gained a circle of enthusiastic followers, drawn mainly from the young. At the same time he acquired many enemies, disturbed by both his challenge to established morality and the uncompromising persistence with which he interrogated those who upheld it. Socrates was no respecter of the pride or dignity of others, and his search for the truth inevitably exposed the ignorance of his opponents. Among

Socrates' supporters were some who had taken part in an unpopular and tyrannical political coup at Athens immediately following the Peloponnesian War. The rule of the so-called Thirty Tyrants lasted only from 404 to 403 BCE; it ended with the death or expulsion of its leading figures. The return of democracy gave Socrates' enemies a chance to take advantage of the hostility felt toward those who had "collaborated" with the tyrants; thus, in 399 BCE, he was put on trial. It seems probable that to some degree the proceedings were intended for show and that those who voted for the death sentence never seriously thought it would be carried out. Socrates was urged by his friends to escape from prison, and the authorities offered him every opportunity. However, the strength of his own morality and his reverence for the laws of his city prohibited him from doing so. After a final discussion with his friends, he was put to death by the administration of a draught of hemlock.

Many of Socrates' disciples tried to preserve his memory by writing accounts of his life and teachings. The works of only two have survived. One of these is the Greek historian Xenophon, whose *Apology*, *Symposium*, and *Memorabilia* are interesting, if superficial. The other is Plato, who, together with his pupil Aristotle, stands at the forefront of the whole intellectual tradition of Western civilization.

Plato The *Dialogues* of Plato claim to record the teachings of Socrates. In almost all of them Socrates appears, arguing with his opponents and presenting his own ideas. How much of Plato's picture of Socrates is historical truth and how much is Plato's invention, however, is debatable. The Socratic problem has been almost as much discussed as the identity of Homer. In general, modern opinion supports the view that in the early *Dialogues* Plato tried to preserve something of his master's views and methods, whereas in the later ones he used Socrates as the spokesman for his own ideas. There can certainly be no doubt that Plato was deeply impressed by Socrates' life and death. Born in 428 BCE, he was drawn by other members of his aristocratic family into the Socratic circle. Plato was present at the trial of Socrates, whose speech in his own defense Plato records in the *Apology*, one of three works that describe Socrates' last days. In the *Crito*, set in prison, Socrates explains why he refuses to escape. The *Phaedo* gives an account of his last day spent discussing with his friends the immortality of the soul and his death.

After Socrates' death, Plato left Athens, horrified at the society that had sanctioned the execution, and spent several years traveling. He returned in 387 BCE and founded the Academy, the first permanent institution in Western civilization devoted to education and research, and thus the forerunner of all our universities. Its curriculum concentrated on mathematics, law, and political theory. Its purpose was to produce experts for the service of the state. Some twenty years later, in 368 BCE,

Plato was invited to Sicily to put his political theories into practice by turning Syracuse into a model kingdom and its young ruler, Dionysius II, into a philosopher king. Predictably, the attempt was a dismal failure and, by 366 BCE, he was back in Athens. Apart from a second equally unsuccessful visit to Syracuse in 362 BCE, Plato seems to have spent the rest of his life in Athens, teaching and writing. He died there in 347 BCE.

Much of Plato's work deals with political theory and the construction of an ideal society. The belief in an ideal is, in fact, characteristic of most of his thinking. It is most clearly expressed in his *Theory of Forms*, according to which in a higher dimension of existence there are perfect forms, of which all the phenomena we perceive in the world around us represent pale reflections. There can be no doubt that Plato's vision of an ideal society is far too authoritarian for most tastes, involving among other restrictions the careful breeding of children, the censorship of music and poetry, and the abolition of private property. In fairness to Plato, however, it must be remembered that his works are intended not as a set of instructions to be followed literally but as a challenge to think seriously about how our lives should be organized. Furthermore, the disadvantages of democratic government had become all too clear during the last years of the fifth century BCE. If Plato's attempt to redress the balance seems to veer excessively in the other direction, it may in part have been inspired by the continuing chaos of fourth-century Greek politics.

Aristotle Plato's most gifted pupil, Aristotle (384–322 BCE), continued to develop his master's doctrines, at first wholeheartedly and later critically, for at least twenty years. In 335 BCE, Aristotle founded a school in competition with Plato's Academy, the Lyceum, severing fundamental ties with Plato from then on. Aristotle in effect introduced a rival philosophy—one that has attracted thinking minds ever since. In the nineteenth century the English poet Samuel Taylor Coleridge was to comment, with much truth, that one was born either a "Platonist" or an "Aristotelian."

The Lyceum seems to have been organized with typical Aristotelian efficiency. In the morning Aristotle lectured to the full-time students, many of whom came from other parts of Greece to attend his courses and work on the projects he was directing. In the afternoon the students pursued their research in the library, museum, and map collection attached to the Lyceum, while Aristotle gave more general lectures to the public. His custom of strolling along the Lyceum's circular walkways, immersed in profound contemplation or discourse, gained his school the name *Peripatetic* (the "walking" school).

As a philosopher, Aristotle was the greatest systematizer. He wrote on every topic of serious study of the time. Many of his classifications have remained valid to this day, although some of the disciplines, such as psychology and physics, have severed their ties with philosophy and have become important sciences in their own right. The most complex of Aristotle's works is probably the *Metaphysics*, in which he deals with his chief dispute with Plato, which concerned the Theory of Forms. Plato had postulated a higher dimension of existence for the ideal forms and thereby created a split between the apparent reality that we perceive and the genuine reality that we can only know by philosophical contemplation. Moreover, knowledge of these forms depended on a theory of "remembering" them from previous existences.

Aristotle, on the other hand, claimed that the forms were actually present in the objects we see around us, thereby eliminating the split between the two realities. Elsewhere in the *Metaphysics*, Aristotle discusses the nature of God, whom he describes as "thought thinking of itself" and "the Unmoved Mover." The nature of the physical world ruled over by this supreme being is further explored in the *Physics*, which is concerned with the elements that compose the universe and the laws by which they operate.

Other important works by Aristotle include the *Rhetoric*, which prescribes the ideal model of oratory, and the *Poetics*, which does the same for poetry and includes the famous definition of tragedy mentioned earlier. Briefly, Aristotle's formula for tragedy is as follows: The tragic hero, who must be noble, through some undetected "tragic flaw" in character meets with a bad end involving the reversal of fortune and sometimes death. The audience, through various emotional and intellectual relations with this tragic figure, undergoes a "cleansing" or "purgation" of the soul, called **catharsis**. Critics of this analysis sometimes complain that Aristotle was trying to read his own subjective formulas into the Greek tragedies of the time. This is not entirely justified, because Aristotle was probably writing for future tragedians, prescribing what ought to be rather than what was.

Aristotle's influence on later ages was vast, although not continuous. Philip of Macedon employed him to tutor young Alexander, but the effect on the young conqueror was probably minimal. Thereafter Aristotle's works were lost and not recovered until the first century BCE, when they were used by the Roman statesman and thinker Cicero (106–43 BCE). During the Middle Ages, they were translated into Latin and Arabic and became a philosophical basis for Christian theology. Saint Thomas Aquinas's synthesis of Aristotelian philosophy and Christian doctrine still remains the official philosophical position of the Roman Catholic Church. In philosophy, theology, and scientific and intellectual thought as a whole, many of the distinctions first applied by Aristotle were rediscovered in the early Renaissance and are still valid today. No survey such as this can begin to do justice to one described by Dante as "the master of those who know." In the more than two thousand years since his death, only Leonardo da Vinci has come near to equaling his creative range.

GREEK MUSIC IN THE CLASSICAL PERIOD

Both Plato and Aristotle found a place for music in their ideal states; their comments on it provide some information on the status of Greek music in the Classical period. Throughout the fifth century BCE, music played an important part in dramatic performances but was generally subordinated to the poetry. By the end of the Peloponnesian War, however, the musical aspect of tragedy had begun to predominate. It is interesting to note that Euripides was criticized by his contemporaries for the lack of form and symmetry and the over-emotionalism of his music, not of his verse. With its release from the function of mere accompaniment, instrumental music became especially popular in the fourth century BCE.

The belief in the doctrine of ethos, whereby music had the power to influence human behavior, meant that the study of music played a vital part in the education and lifestyle of Classical Greeks. In Plato's view, participation in musical activities molded the character for better or worse—thus the ban on certain kinds of music, those with the "wrong" ethos, in his ideal Republic. At the same time, the musical scale—with its various ratios of pitches—reflected the proportions of the cosmos; music thereby provided a link between the real world and the abstract world of forms. For Aristotle, music held a more practical, less mystical, value in the attainment of virtue. As a mathematician he believed that the numerical relationships, which linked the various pitches, could be used by a musician to compose works that imitated the highest state of reason, and thus virtue. Furthermore, just as individuals could create works with a virtuous, moral ethos, so too the state would be served by "ethical" music.

For all its importance in Greek life and thought, however, the actual sound of Greek music and the principles whereby it was composed are not easy to reconstruct or understand. The numerical relationship of notes to one another established by Pythagoras was used to divide the basic unit of an octave (series of eight notes) into smaller intervals named after their positions in relation to the lowest note in the octave. The interval known as a **fourth**, for example, represents the space between the lowest note and the fourth note up the octave. The intervals were then combined to form a series of scales, or **modes**. Each was given a name and was associated with a particular emotional range. Thus the Dorian mode was serious and warlike, the Phrygian exciting and emotional, and the Mixolydian plaintive and pathetic.

The unit with which Greek music was constructed was the **tetrachord**, a group of four notes, of which the two outer ones are a perfect fourth apart and the inner ones variably spaced. The combination of two tet-

rachords formed a mode. The Dorian mode, for example, consisted of the following two tetrachords:

The Lydian mode was composed of two different tetrachords:

The origin of the modes and their relationship to one another is uncertain; it was disputed even in ancient times. The situation has not been made easier by the fact that medieval church music adopted the same system of mathematical construction and even some of the same names, but applied them to different modes. The word **harmony** is Greek in origin; literally it means a "joining together," and in a musical context the Greeks used it to describe various kinds of scales. There is nevertheless no evidence that Greek music contained any element of harmony in a more modern sense—that is, of groups of notes (chords) sounded simultaneously. Throughout the fifth century BCE, musical rhythm was tied to that of the words or dance steps the music accompanied. Special instruments such as cymbals and tambourines were used to mark the

◆ **3.5** Myron, *Discobolos (Discus Thrower)*. The short, untidy hair and details of the musculature are typical of the Early Classical Period—so is the contrast between the physical tension and the calm facial expression.

Roman copy of bronze original of c. 450 BCE. Marble, 5′1″ (156.5 cm) high. Museo Nazionale Romano, Rome, Italy//© Scala/Art Resource, NY

◆ **3.6** *Warrior*, c. 460-450 BCE. This statue, one of the *Riace Bronzes*, was discovered by chance by a diver on the sea bed a few hundred yards off the southeastern coast of Italy. One possible explanation for its presence there is that it was being shipped to Rome. The captain of the boat, caught in rough seas, may have ordered it thrown overboard to lighten his load. The warrior's head has inlaid eyes, silver teeth and eyelashes, and copper lips.

From the sea off Riace, Italy. Bronze with glass, bone, silver, and copper inlay, 6'6" (2 m) high. Museo Archeologico Nazionale, Reggio Calabria, Italy//© Scala/Art Resource, NY

rhythmical patterns, and Greek writers on music often discussed specific problems presented to composers in terms of the Greek language and its accent system.

Although few traces have survived, a system of musical notation was used to write down compositions; the Greeks probably borrowed it, like their alphabet, from the Phoenicians. Originally used for lyre music, it used symbols to mark the position of fingers on the lyre strings, rather like modern guitar notation (tablature). The system was then adapted for vocal music and for nonstringed instruments such as the *aulos*. The oldest of the few examples to survive dates to around 250 BCE.

THE VISUAL ARTS IN CLASSICAL GREECE

SCULPTURE AND VASE PAINTING IN THE FIFTH CENTURY BCE

Like the writers and thinkers of their time, artists of the mid-fifth century BCE were concerned with ideas of balance and order. Very early Classical works like the *Kritios Boy* (see Figure 2.13) revealed a new interest in realism, and the sculptors who came later began to explore the exciting possibilities of representing the human body in motion. Among the most famous fifth-century-BCE sculptors working at Athens was Myron. Although none of his sculptures have survived, several later copies of one of his most famous pieces, the *Discus Thrower* [**Fig. 3.5**], still exist. The original, made around 450 BCE, is typical of its age in combining realistic treatment of an action with an idealized portrayal of the athlete.

While striving for naturalism, artists like Myron also tried to create a new standard of human beauty by controlling the human form according to principles of proportion, symmetry, and balance. Among the finest examples of mid-fifth-century-BCE sculpture are two bronze statues found off the coast of southeast Italy in the 1980s [**Fig. 3.6**]. Known as the *Riace Bronzes*, they were probably the work of a master sculptor on the Greek mainland. They represent warriors, although their precise subject, together with the reason for their presence in Italian waters, remains a mystery. Around 440 BCE, one of the greatest of Classical sculptors, Polykleitos of

◆ **3.7** Polykleitos, *Doryphoros (Spear-bearer)*. The spiral position of the figure, the downturned gaze, and the dreamy expression of the face are typical of sculpture from the fifth century BCE. In this Roman copy the sculptor has left the right wrist joined to the body with a short support, fearing that the arm might snap off—not a problem in the bronze original.

Marble, 6′11″ (2.11 m) high. Roman copy of Greek original dating from c. 450–440 BCE. Museo Archeologico Nazionale, Naples, Italy//© Scala/ Art Resource, NY

◆ **3.8** Reed Painter, *Warrior Seated at His Tomb,* late 5th century BCE. A youth sits at one side. On the other side stands a young woman who holds the warrior's shield and helmet. The warrior's hopeless expression shows that by the late 5th century—and the last stages of the Peloponnesian War—his profession had lost any glamour or heroism.

White-ground lekythos, 18⅞″ (48 cm) high. National Archaeological Museum, Athens, Greece//© Nimatallah/Art Resource, NY

Argos, devised a mathematical formula for representing the perfect male body, an ideal canon of proportion, and wrote a book about it. The idea behind *The Canon* was that ideal beauty consisted of a precise relationship between the various parts of the body. Polykleitos's book must have set forth the details of his system of proportion. To illustrate his theory, he also produced a bronze statue of a young man holding a spear, the *Doryphoros*. Both book and original statue are lost; only later copies of the *Doryphoros* survive [**Fig. 3.7**].

We do not, therefore, know exactly what Polykleitos's system was. Nevertheless, we have some indication in the writings of a later philosopher, Chrysippus (c. 280–207 BCE), who wrote that "beauty consists of the proportion of the parts; of finger to finger; of all the fingers to the palm and the wrist; of those to the forearm; of the forearm to the upper arm; and of all these parts to one another, as set forth in *The Canon* of Polykleitos." Even if the exact relationships are lost, what was important about Polykleitos's ideal—and what made it so characteristic of the Classical vision as a whole—was that it depended on precisely ordered and balanced interrelationships of the various parts of

◆ **3.10** Reconstruction drawing of the Temple of Zeus, Olympia, Greece, c. 470–456 BCE. The pediment shows Zeus between two contestants before a chariot race. (© *Interfoto Pressebildagentur/Alamy*)

Thus death and mourning became increasingly common subjects. Among the most touching works to survive from the period are several oil flasks used for funerary offerings [**Fig. 3.8**]. They are painted with mourning or graveside scenes on a white rather than red background. The figures are depicted with quiet and calm dignity but with considerable feeling. This personal rather than public response to death is also found on the grave-markers of the end of the fifth century BCE, which show a grief that is perhaps resigned but still intense [**Fig. 3.9**].

ARCHITECTURE IN THE FIFTH CENTURY BCE

In architecture, as in sculpture, designers were concerned with proportion and the interrelationship of the various parts that constitute a complete structure. Nowhere is this more apparent than in the Temple of Zeus at Olympia [**Fig. 3.10**], the first great artistic achievement of the years following the Persian Wars, begun in 470 BCE and finished by 456 BCE. By the time of its completion it was also the largest Doric temple on mainland Greece; it was clearly intended to illustrate the new Classical preoccupation with proportion. The distance from the center of one column to the center of the next was the unit of measurement for the whole temple. Thus the height of each column is equal to two units, and the combined length of a triglyph and a metope equals half a unit. The theme of order, implicit in the architecture of the temple, became explicit in the sculpture that decorated it. At the center of the west pediment, standing calmly amid a fight raging between Lapiths and Centaurs, was the figure of Apollo, the god

◆ **3.9** Grave stele of Crito and Timarista, c. 420 BCE. By the late 5th century, artists had learned to sculpt the body in relief, as seen from the side. Note the contrast between the thin inner drapery and the heavier outer garments, and the way in which the sculptor lets the body show through its covering.

Marble. Archaeological Museum of Rhodes, Greece//© Wolfgang Kaehler/ CORBIS

the human body. Furthermore, the ideal beauty this created was not produced by nature but by the power of the human intellect.

In the late fifth century BCE, as the Greeks became embroiled in the Peloponnesian War, sculpture and vase painting were characterized by a growing concern with the individual rather than a generalized ideal. Artists began to depict the emotional responses of ordinary people to life and death instead of approaching these responses indirectly through the use of myths.

◆ **3.11** Apollo Intervenes in the Battle Between the Lapiths and Centaurs, c. 470–456 BCE. At a wedding party held by the Lapiths (a tribe of Central Greece), the Centaurs (mythical creatures half-human, half-animal) got drunk and tried to abduct the bride. The fight that breaks out is ended only by the intervention of Apollo—at the center here—the god of reason and order.

Sculptures from the west pediment of the Temple of Zeus. Olympia. Archaeological Museum, Olympia, Greece//© Joan Swinnerton/Alamy

◆ **3.12** Model reconstruction of the Acropolis and an aerial view of its present state. Most of the smaller buildings no longer exist, leaving an unobstructed view of the Parthenon that was not possible in ancient times. Note that the Parthenon was not built in the center of the Acropolis, but at its highest point, where it was most visible from below. *(Reconstruction © Agora Museum, Athens, Greece/The Art Archive/Gianni Dagli Orti. Contemporary photo © Yann Arthus-Bertrand/CORBIS)*

of reason, exerting his authority by a single confident gesture [**Fig. 3.11**].

Like the works of Aeschylus, the sculptures from Olympia express a conviction that justice will triumph and that the gods will enforce it. The art of the second half of the fifth century BCE, however, is more concerned with human achievement than with divine will.

The Acropolis Pericles' building program for the Acropolis, or citadel of Athens, represents the supreme expression in visual terms of Classical ideals [**Fig. 3.12**]. This greatest of all Classical artistic achievements has a special grandeur and poignancy. The splendor of its conception and execution has survived the vicissitudes of time; the great temple to Athena, the Par-

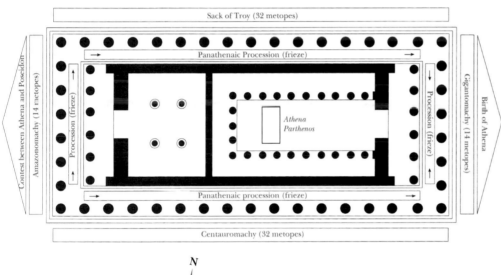

Sack of Troy (32 metopes)

Contest between Athena and Poseidon

Amazononomachy (14 metopes)

Panathenaic Procession (frieze)

Procession (frieze)

*Athena
Parthenos*

Procession (frieze)

Gigantomachy (14 metopes)

Birth of Athena

Panathenaic procession (frieze)

Centauromachy (32 metopes)

N

0 10 20 30 40 50 feet
0   5   10   15 meters

◆ **3.13** Ictinus and Callicrates, The Parthenon, 447–432 BCE. The plan of the temple shows a diagram of the sculptural program. The Parthenon remained almost undamaged until 1687 when Turkish forces occupying Athens had their gunpowder stored inside the building. A cannon ball fired by Venetian besieging troops blew up the gunpowder deposit and, with it, the Parthenon.

Column height 34′ (10.36 m), Acropolis, Athens, Greece. Diagram after Andrew Stewart. Contemporary photo © William Katz / Photo Researchers, Inc.

thenon, remains to this day an incomparable symbol of the Golden Age of Greece. Yet it was built during years of growing division and hostility in the Greek world—the last sculpture was barely in place before the outbreak of the Peloponnesian War in 431 BCE. Pericles died in 429 BCE, but fighting and building both dragged on. The Erechtheum, the final temple to be completed, was not finished until 406 BCE, two years before the end of the war and the fall of Athens. Pericles had intended the entire program to perpetuate the memory of Athens' glorious achievements, but instead it is a reminder of the gulf between Classical high ideals and the realities of political existence in fifth-century-BCE Greece.

Even the funding of the Parthenon symbolizes this gap, because it was paid for at least in part from the treasury of the Delian League. The transfer of the League's funds to Athens in 454 BCE clearly indicated Pericles' imperialist intentions, as did the use to which he put them. In this way the supreme monument of Periclean

Athens was built with money originally intended for a pan-Hellenic League. It is even more ironic that Athens' further high-handed behavior created a spirit of ill feeling and distrust throughout the Greek world that led inevitably to the outbreak of the Peloponnesian War—a war that effectively destroyed the Athenian glory the Parthenon had been intended to symbolize.

The Parthenon The great outcrop of rock that forms the Acropolis was an obvious choice by Pericles for the Parthenon and the other buildings planned with it. The site, which towers above the rest of the city, had served as a center for Athenian life from Mycenaean times, when a fortress was built on it. Throughout the Archaic period, a series of temples had been constructed there, the last of which was destroyed by the Persians in 480 BCE. Work on the Acropolis was begun in 449 BCE under the direction of Phidias, the greatest sculptor of his day and a personal friend of Pericles. The Parthenon [**Fig. 3.13**] was the first

◆ **3.14** Equestrian Group, c. 442–432 BCE. The composition is elaborate but clear. The riders, with their calm, typically Classical expressions, are shown in various positions. Note especially the last figure on the right.

Detail of Parthenon frieze, north face. Pentelic marble, 3′6″ (1.07 cm) high. British Museum, London, UK//© Grant Rooney/Alamy

building to be constructed (the name of the temple comes from the Greek *parthenos* ["virgin"]; that is, the goddess Athena). It was built between 447 and 438 BCE; its sculptural decoration was complete by 432 BCE. Even larger than the Temple of Zeus at Olympia, the building combines the Doric order of its columns (seventeen on the sides and eight on the ends) with some Ionic features, including a continuous running frieze inside the outer colonnade, at the top of the temple wall and inner colonnades.

The design incorporates some refinements intended to prevent any sense of monotony or heaviness and gives the building an air of richness and grace. Like earlier Doric columns, those of the Parthenon are thickest at the point one-third from the base and then taper to the top, a device called **entasis**. In addition, all the columns tilt slightly toward each other (it has been calculated that they would all meet if extended upward for two miles). The columns at the corners are thicker and closer together than the others, and the entablature leans outward. The seemingly flat floor is not flat at all but convex. All of these refinements are extremely subtle and barely visible to the naked eye. The perfection of their execution, requiring incredible precision of

mathematical calculation, is the highest possible tribute to the Classical search for order.

The sculptural decoration of the Parthenon occupied three parts of the building and used three different techniques of carving. The figures in the pediments are freestanding; the frieze is carved in low relief; the metopes are in high relief (see Figures 3.14, 3.15, and 3.16). The Ionic frieze, 520 feet long, is carved in low relief; it depicts a procession that took place every four years on the occasion of the Great Panathenaic Festival. It shows Athenians walking and riding to the Acropolis in a ceremony during which an ancient wooden statue of Athena was presented with a new robe.

The variety of movement, gesture, and rhythm achieved in the relatively limited technique of low relief makes the frieze among the greatest treasures of Greek art [**Fig. 3.14**]. At the beginning of the nineteenth century, most of the frieze, together with other Parthenon sculptures, was removed from the building by the British ambassador to Constantinople, Lord Elgin; these are now in the British Museum. (All the sculptures from the Parthenon that are in the British Museum are generally known as the Elgin Marbles.)

◆ **3.15** Three Goddesses, c. 438–432 BCE. The robes show the sculptor's technical virtuosity in carving drapery. The figures are reacting to the event at the center of the pediment, the birth of Athena. The figure on the left, nearest to the center, is about to rise, the middle figure is beginning to turn, and the right-hand figure is still reclining, unaware of what is happening. Thus the artist uses the group to express the concept of time.

Detail from the east pediment of the Parthenon. Marble, greatest height 4′5″ (1.35 m). © British Museum, London, UK/The Bridgeman Art Library

Equally impressive are the surviving figures from the east and west pediments, which are freestanding. They show, respectively, the birth of Athena and her contest with Poseidon, god of the sea, to decide which of them should be patron deity of the city. They are badly damaged; even so, statues like the group of three goddesses [**Fig. 3.15**], from the east pediment, show a combination of idealism and naturalism that has never been surpassed.

The anatomy of the figures and the drapery, which in some cases covers them, are both treated realistically, even in places where the details of the workmanship would have been barely visible to the spectator below. The realism is combined, however, with a characteristically Classical preoccupation with proportion and balance; the result is sculptures that achieve an almost perfect blend of the two elements of the Classical style: ideal beauty represented in realistic terms. In contrast to the frieze, the technique employed on the metopes is high relief, so high, in fact, that some of the figures seem almost completely detached from their background. These metopes, which illustrate mythological battles, represent a lower level of achievement, although some are more successful than others at reconciling scenes of violence and Classical idealism. The most impressive ones show episodes from the battle between Lapiths and Centaurs [**Fig. 3.16**], the same story we saw on the west pediment at Olympia.

◆ **3.16** Lapith and Centaur, c. 448–442 BCE. The assailed Lapith has dropped to one knee. The theme of the battle between Lapiths and Centaurs, seen also on the Temple of Zeus at Olympia (see Figure 3.11), came to represent the battle between Greeks and Persians a generation earlier, and thus served as a reminder of Greece's moment of triumphant unity.

Metope from the south face of the Parthenon. Pentelic marble, 4′8″ (1.42 m) high. © British Museum, London, UK/The Bridgeman Art Library

The Propylaea The monumental entrance to the Acropolis, the Propylaea [**Fig. 3.17**], was begun in 437 BCE and finished on the eve of the outbreak of war, although probably only by a modification of the architect Mnesikles's original plan. An unusual feature of its design is that both Doric and Ionic columns are used, the Doric ones visible from the front and the back and the Ionic ones lining the passageway through the outer porch.

The Erechtheum The other major building on the Acropolis is the Erechtheum, an Ionic temple of complex design, which was begun in 421 BCE but not completed until 406 BCE. The chief technical problem facing the architect, whose identity is unknown, was the uneven ground level of the site. The problem was solved by creating a building with entrances on different levels. The nature of the building produced other design problems. The Erechtheum had to commemorate a whole series of elaborate religious events and honor several different deities.

One of its four chambers housed the ancient wooden statue of Athena that was at the center of the Great Panathenaic Festival shown on the Parthenon frieze. Elsewhere in the temple were altars to Poseidon and Erechtheus, an early Athenian king; to the legendary Athenian hero Butes; and to Hephaistos, the god of the forge. Furthermore, the design had to incorporate the marks in the ground made by Poseidon's trident during the competition with Athena, as shown on the west pediment of the Parthenon, and the site of the grave of another early and probably legendary Athenian king, Cecrops. The result of all this was a building whose complex plan is still not fully understood. In fact, the exact identification of the inner chambers remains in doubt.

The decoration of the temple is both elaborate and delicate, almost fragile. Its best-known feature is the South Porch, where the roof rests not on columns but on the famous **caryatids**, statues of young women [**Fig. 3.18**]. These graceful figures, which stand gravely upright with one knee slightly bent as if to sustain the weight of the roof, represent the most complete attempt until then to conceal the structural functions of a column behind its form. (One of the caryatids is now in the British Museum; the others have been moved to the Acropolis Museum and have been replaced on the actual building by copies.) In many respects innovations such as these make the Erechtheum as representative of the mood of the late fifth century BCE as the confident Parthenon is of the mood of a generation earlier. The apparent lack of a coherent overall plan and the blurring of traditional distinctions between architecture and sculpture, structure and

◆ **3.17** Mnesikles, *Propylaea* (west front), Acropolis, Athens, Greece, 437–431 BCE. This is the view from the Temple of Athena Nike. (*© Scala/Art Resource, NY*)

decoration, seem to question traditional architectural values in a way that parallels the doubts of Euripides and his contemporaries.

VISUAL ARTS IN THE FOURTH CENTURY BCE

As in the case of literature and philosophy, the confusion of Greek political life in the years following the defeat of Athens (404 BCE) affected the development of the visual arts. In general, the idealism and heroic characters of High Classical art were replaced with a growing interest in realism and emotion. Our knowledge of the visual arts in the fourth century BCE is, however, far from complete. Greek fresco painting of the period has been entirely lost, although recent discoveries in northern Greece at the Royal Cemetery of Vergina suggest that some of it may yet be found [**Fig. 3.19**].

Late Classical Sculpture In sculpture, fortunately, Roman copies of lost original statues enable us to form a fairly good estimation of the main developments. It is clear that Plato's interest in the fate of the individual soul finds its parallel in the sculptural treatment of the human form. Facial expressions become more emotional, often characterized by a mood of dreamy tenderness. Technical skill in depicting drapery and the anatomy beneath are put to the service of a new virtuosity. The two sculptors who dominated the art of the fourth century BCE are Praxiteles and Lysippus.

The influence of Praxiteles on his contemporaries was immense. His particular brand of gentle melancholy

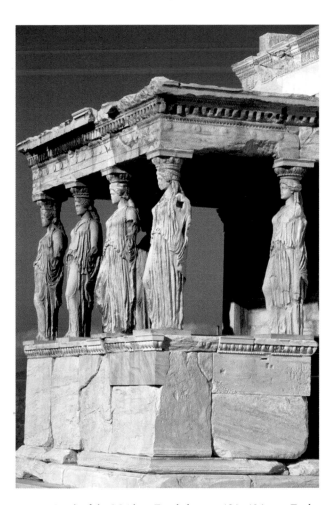

◆ **3.18** *Porch of the Maidens,* Erechtheum, 421–406 BCE. Each figure bends one knee, as if to show how they bear the weight of the building. The originals, replaced by copies, have been removed from the Erechtheum and placed in the Acropolis Museum.

Caryatids 7′7″ (2.31 m) high. Acropolis, Athens, Greece / / © Altrendo / Getty Images

◆ **3.19** *Pluto Seizing Persephone,* mid-4th century BCE. This unique example of Late Classical monumental painting was discovered by the Greek archaeologist Manolis Andronikos in 1977. It shows a remarkable fluency and freedom of technique.

Detail from wall painting 3′3½″ (1 m) high, Royal Tomb I, Vergina, Macedonia, Greece / / © The Bridgeman Art Library

◆ **3.20** Praxiteles, *Hermes with the Infant Dionysus,* c. 340 BCE. Hermes' missing right arm held a bunch of grapes just out of the baby's reach. The small head and elongated proportions are typical of 4th-century sculpture. There has been considerable debate about whether this work is a genuine original or a high-quality later copy. Most experts are inclined to believe the latter.

Marble, 7′1″ (2.16 m) high. Archaeological Museum, Olympia, Greece// © Scala/Art Resource, NY

◆ **3.21** Praxiteles, *Aphrodite of Cyrene,* c. 100 BCE. This copy was found by chance in the Roman baths at Cyrene, North Africa. The statue is also called *Venus Anadyomene,* the Roman name for Aphrodite and a Greek word meaning "rising up from the sea," often used in referring to Aphrodite because she was supposed to have arisen from the sea at her birth. The porpoise is a reminder of the goddess's marine associations.

Marble, 5′ (1.5 m) high. Roman copy of Greek original. Museo Nazionale Romano, Rome, Italy//© Alinari/Art Resource, NY

is well illustrated by the *Hermes* at Olympia [**Fig. 3.20**] that is generally attributed to him. Equally important is his famous statue of Aphrodite nude [**Fig. 3.21**], of which some fifty copies have survived. This represents the discovery of the female body as an object of beauty in itself; it was also one of the first attempts in Western art to introduce the element of sensuality into the portrayal of the female form.

The influence of Lysippus was as much on succeeding periods as on his own time. One of his chief claims

◆ **3.23** Theodoros of Phokaia, the *Tholos* of the Sanctuary of Athena Pronaia, c. 390 BCE. This is one of the first circular designs in Greek architecture. Originally, twenty Doric columns encircled the temple and ten Corinthian columns were set against the wall of the cella within.

Marble and limestone, diameter of cella 28′2⅝″ (8.6 m). Delphi, Greece// © Robert Everts/Getty Images

◆ **3.22** Lysippus, *Apoxyomenos* (*The Scraper*), c. 330 BCE. The young athlete is cleaning off sweat and dirt with a tool called a *strigil*. Note the way in which the right hand and arm thrust toward the viewer.

Marble, 6′9″ (2.06 m) high. Roman copy after bronze original. Vatican Museums, Vatican State (Rome, Italy)//© Canali Photobank, Milan/SuperStock

to fame was as the official portraitist of Alexander the Great. Lysippus's very individual characteristics—a new, more attenuated system of proportion, greater concern for realism, and the large scale of many of his works—had a profound effect later on Hellenistic art [**Fig. 3.22**].

Late Classical Architecture In architecture, as in the arts generally, the Late Classical period was one of innovation. The great sanctuaries at Olympia and Delphi were expanded, and new cities were laid out at Rhodes, Cnidus, and Priene, using Classical principles of town planning. The fourth century BCE was also notable for the invention of building forms new to Greek architecture, including the *tholos*

("circular building") [**Fig. 3.23**]. The most grandiose work of the century was probably the Temple of Artemis at Ephesus, destroyed by fire in 356 BCE and rebuilt on the same massive scale as before. Although the Greeks of the fourth century BCE lacked the certainty and self-confidence of their predecessors, their culture shows no lack of ideas or inspiration. Furthermore, even before Alexander's death, the Macedonian Empire had spread Greek culture throughout the Mediterranean world. If Athens had lost any real political or commercial importance, the ideas of its great innovators began to affect an ever-growing number of people.

When Alexander died in the summer of 323 BCE, the division of his empire into separate independent kingdoms spread Greek culture even more widely. The kingdoms of the Seleucids in Syria and the Ptolemies in Egypt are the true successors to Periclean Athens. Even as far away as India, sculptors and town planners were influenced by ideas developed by Athenians of the fifth and fourth centuries BCE. In due course, the cultural achievement of Classical Greece was absorbed and reborn in Rome, as Chapter 4 will show. Meanwhile, in the period known as the Hellenistic Age, which lasted from the death of Alexander to the Roman conquest of Greece in 146 BCE, that achievement took a new turn.

THE HELLENISTIC PERIOD

Alexander's generals' inability to agree on a single successor after his death made the division of the Macedonian Empire inevitable. The four most important kingdoms that split off—Syria (the kingdom of the Seleucids), Egypt, Pergamum, and Macedonia (see map, "The Hellenistic World")—were soon at loggerheads and remained so until they were finally conquered by Rome. Each of these, however, in its own way continued the spread of Greek culture, as the name of the period implies (it is derived from the verb "to Hellenize," or to spread Greek influence).

The greatest of all centers of Greek learning was in the Egyptian city of Alexandria, where King Ptolemy, Alexander's former personal staff officer and bodyguard, planned a large institute for scholarship known as the Temple of the Muses, or the Museum. The Library at the Museum contained everything of importance ever written in Greek, up to 700,000 separate works, according to contemporary authorities. Its destruction by fire when Julius Caesar besieged the city in 47 BCE must surely be one of the great intellectual disasters in the history of Western culture.

In Asia Minor and farther east in Syria, the Hellenistic rulers of the new kingdoms fostered Greek art and literature as one means of holding foreign influences at bay. Libraries were built at Pergamum and the Syrian capital of Antioch, and philosophers from Greece were encouraged to visit the new centers of learning and lecture there. In this way Greek ideas not only retained their hold but also began to make an impression on more remote peoples even farther east. The first Buddhist monumental sculpture, called **Gandharan** after the Indian province of Gandhara where it developed, used Greek styles and techniques. There is even a classic Buddhist religious work called *The Questions of King Milinda* in which a local Greek ruler, probably called Menandros, is described exchanging ideas with a Buddhist sage, ending with the ruler's conversion to Buddhism—one example of the failure of Greek ideas to convince those exposed to them.

Yet, however much literature and philosophy could do to maintain the importance of Greek culture, Hellenistic rulers turned primarily to the visual arts. In so doing they inaugurated the last great period of Greek art. The most powerful influence on the period immediately following Alexander's death was the memory of his life. The daring and immensity of his conquests, his own heroic personality, the new world he had sought to create—all these conspired to produce a spirit of adventure and experiment. Artists of the Hellenistic period sought not so much to equal or surpass their Classical predecessors in the familiar forms as to discover new subjects and invent new techniques. The development of realistic portraiture dates to this period [**Fig. 3.24**], as

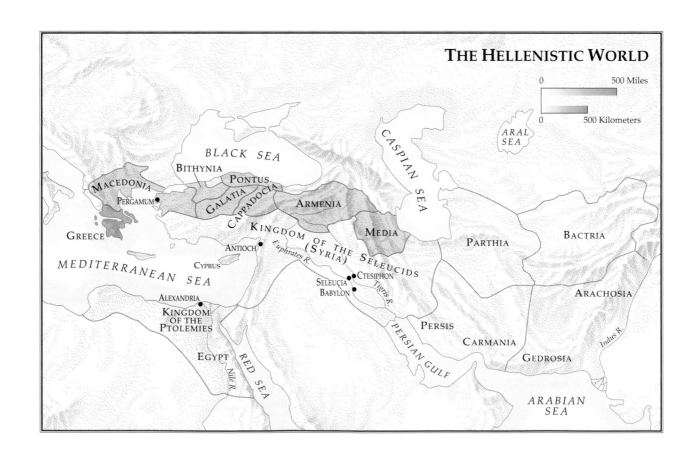

does the construction of buildings such as the Lighthouse at Alexandria [**Fig. 3.25**], in its day the tallest tower ever built and one of the Seven Wonders of the World.

The all-pervading spirit of the Classical Age had been order. Now artists began to discover the delights of freedom. Classical art was calm and restrained, but Hellenistic art was emotional and expressive. Classical artists sought clarity and balance even in showing scenes of violence, but Hellenistic artists allowed themselves to depict riotous confusion involving strong contrasts of light and shade and the appearance of perpetual motion. It is not surprising that the term *baroque*, originally used to describe the extravagant European art of the seventeenth century CE, is often applied to the art of the Hellenistic period. The artists responsible for these innovations created their works for a new kind of patron. Most of the great works of the Classical period had been produced for the state, with the result that the principal themes and inspirations were religious and political.

With the disintegration of the Macedonian Empire and the establishment of prosperous kingdoms at Pergamum, Antioch, and elsewhere, there developed a group of powerful rulers and wealthy businessmen who commissioned works either to provide lavish decoration for their cities or to adorn their private palaces and villas. Artists were no longer responsible to humanity and to the gods, but to whoever paid for the work. Their patrons encouraged them to develop new techniques and surpass the achievements of rivals. At the same time, the change in the artist's social role produced a change in the function of the work. Whereas in the Classical period architects had devoted themselves to the construction of temples and religious sanctuaries, the Hellenistic Age is notable for its marketplaces and theaters, as well as for scientific and technical buildings like the Tower of the Winds at Athens and the Lighthouse at Alexandria (see Figure 3.25). Among the rich cities of Hellenistic Asia, none was wealthier than Pergamum, ruled by a dynasty of kings known as the Attalids. Pergamum was founded in the early third century BCE and reached the high point of its greatness in the reign of Eumenes II (197–159 BCE). The layout of the chief buildings in the city represents a rejection of the Classical concepts of order and

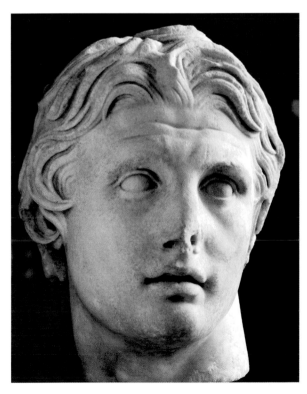

◆ **3.24** Alexander the Great, c. 160 BCE. Note the emotional fire of the eyes and mouth, emphasized by the set of the head, and the untidy hair, tossed back in impatience.

From Pergamum, Turkey. Marble, 1′ (30.48 cm) high. Archaeological Museum, Istanbul, Turkey//© Erich Lessing/Art Resource, NY

◆ **3.25** Reconstruction drawing of the Alexandria Lighthouse, Egypt, 279 BCE. Constructed by Sostratus of Cnidus, for Ptolemy Philadelphus on the island of Pharos, north of the Alexandria harbor, the original height of the lighthouse was 440′ (134.11 m). The beam of light from the lantern atop the lighthouse was intensified by a system of reflectors and could be seen 30 miles (48 km) out at sea. The name of the island, Pharos, became, and still is, another word for lighthouse or beacon. *(© Mary Evans Picture Library/Everett Collection)*

⚜ VOICES OF THEIR TIMES

Kerdo the Cobbler

Herondas was a Greek poet of the third century BCE whose mimes were probably written for public performance. This passage comes from one of them.

KERDO: Step lively: open that drawer of sandals.

Look first at this, Metro; this sole, is it not adjusted like the most perfect of soles? Look, you also, women, at the heel-piece; see how it is held down and how well it is joined to the straps; yet, no part is better than another: all are perfect. And the color!—may the Goddess give you every joy of life!—you could find nothing to equal it. The color! neither saffron nor wax glow like this! Three minæ, for the leather, went to Kandas from Kerdo, who made these. And this other color! it was no cheaper. I swear, by all that is sacred and venerable, women, in truth held and maintained, with no more falsehood than a pair of scales—and, if not, may Kerdo know life and pleasure no more!—this almost drove me bankrupt! For enormous gains no longer satisfy the leathersellers. They do the least of the work, but our works of art depend on them and the cobbler suffers the most terrible misery and distress, night and day. I am glued to my stool even at night, worn out with work, sleepless until the noises of the dawn. And I have not told all: I support thirteen workmen, women, because my own children will not work. Even if Zeus begged them in tears, they would only chant: "What do you bring? What do you bring?" They sit around in comfort somewhere else, warming their legs, like little birds. But, as the saying goes, it is not talk, but money, which pays the bills. If this pair does not please you, Metro, you can see more and still more, until you are sure that Kerdo has not been talking nonsense.

Pistos, bring all those shoes from the shelves. You must go back satisfied to your houses, women. Here are novelties of every sort: of Sykione and Ambrakia, laced slippers, hemp sandals, Ionian sandals, night slippers, high heels, Argian sandals, red ones:—name the ones you like best. (How dogs—and women—devour the substance of the cobbler!)

A WOMAN: And how much do you ask for that pair you have been parading so well? But do not thunder too loud and frighten us away!

KERDO: Value them yourself, and fix their price, if you like; one who leaves it to you will not deceive you. If you wish, woman, a good cobbler's work, you will set a price—yes, by these gray temples where the fox has made his lair which will provide bread for those who handle the tools. (O Hermes! if nothing comes into our net now, I don't know when our saucepan will get another chance as good!)

"Kerdo the Cobbler" by Herondas, from *Greek Literature in Translation*, translated by George Howe and Gustave Adolphus Harrer (NY, Harper, 1924). Reprinted by permission of Marcella Harrer.

balance. Unlike the Periclean buildings on the Athenian Acropolis, the buildings in Pergamum were placed independently of one another with a new and dramatic use of space. The theater, set on a steep slope, seemed to be falling headlong down the hillside [**Fig. 3.26**].

The chief religious shrine of Pergamum was the immense Altar of Zeus erected by Eumenes II (c. 180 BCE) to commemorate the victories of his father, Attalus I, over the Gauls. Its base is decorated with a colossal frieze depicting the battle of the gods and giants. The triumphant figure of Zeus stands presumably as a symbol for the victorious king of Pergamum. The drama and violence of the battle find perfect expression in the tangled, writhing bodies, which leap out of the frieze in high relief, and in the intensity of the gestures and facial expressions [**Fig. 3.27**]. The immense emotional impact of the scenes may prevent us from appreciating the remarkable skill of the artists, some of

◆ **3.26** Reconstruction model of the Upper City, Pergamum, Turkey. The steeply sloping theater is at left; the Altar to Zeus is in the center foreground. It is the small rectangular structure with two open courts, the one on the right larger than that on the left.

Antikensammlung, Staatliche Museen zu Berlin, Berlin, Germany // © Bildarchiv Preussischer Kulturbesitz / Art Resource, NY

◆ **3.27** Athena Slaying the Giant, c. 180 BCE. Athena is grasping the giant Alcyoneus by the hair, the source of his strength, to lift him off the ground. His mother, Ge, the earth goddess, looks on despairingly from below.

Detail of frieze on the Altar to Zeus from Pergamum, Turkey. Marble, 7′6″ (2.03 m) high. Antikensammlung, Staatliche Museen zu Berlin, Berlin, Germany // © Erich Lessing / Art Resource, NY

whom were brought from Athens to work on the project. However, the movement of the figures is far from random, and the surface of the stone has been carefully worked to reproduce the texture of hair, skin, fabric, metal, and so on.

The Altar of Zeus represents the most complete illustration of the principles and practice of Hellenistic art. It is, of course, a work on a grand, even grandiose, scale, intended to impress a wide public. But many of its characteristics occur in freestanding pieces of sculpture

◆ **3.28** Agesander, Athenodorus, and Polydorus of Rhodes, *Laocoön,* early 1st century CE. This statue was unearthed in 1506 in the ruins of Nero's Golden House. Note the similarity between Laocoön's head and the head of the giant Alcyoneus on the Pergamum frieze (see Figure 3.27).

Marble, 7′10½″ (2.4 m) high. Museo Pio Clementino, Vatican Museums, Vatican State//© Scala/Art Resource, NY

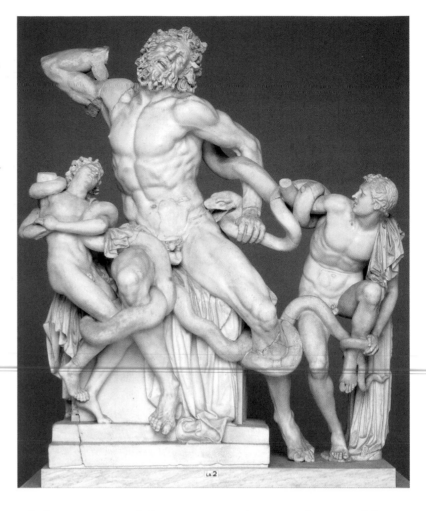

such as the *Laocoön* [**Fig. 3.28**]. This famous work shows the Trojan priest Laocoön, punished by the gods for his attempt to warn his people against bringing into their city the wooden horse left by the Greeks. To silence the priest, Apollo sends two sea serpents to strangle him and his sons. The large piece is superbly composed, with the three figures bound together by the sinuous curves of the serpents; they pull away from one another under the agony of the creatures' coils.

By the end of the Hellenistic period, both artists and public seemed a little weary of so much richness and elaboration, and they returned to some of the principles of Classical art. Simultaneously, the gradual conquest of the Hellenistic kingdoms by Rome and their absorption into the Roman Empire produced a new synthesis in which the achievements of Classical and Hellenistic Greece fused with the native Italian culture and passed on to later ages.

SUMMARY

◆ **The Classical Age.** The period covered in this chapter falls into three parts. The first, the years from 479 to 404 BCE, saw the growth of Athenian power

and the consequent mistrust on the part of the rest of the Greek world of Athens' intentions. The same period was marked by major cultural developments at Athens. Sculptors such as Myron and Phidias created the High Classical blend of realism and idealism. Tragic drama, in which music played an important role, reached its highest achievement in the works of Aeschylus, Sophocles, and Euripides. In 449 BCE, work was begun on the buildings on the Athenian Acropolis planned by Pericles, Athens' ambitious leader. The Parthenon and the Propylaea were completed in an atmosphere made increasingly tense by the deteriorating relations between Athens and the other leading Greek states, particularly Corinth and Sparta.

◆ **The Peloponnesian War.** In 431 BCE the Peloponnesian War erupted, with Athens and her few remaining allies on one side and the remaining Greek world on the other. In 429 BCE Pericles died from a plague that ravaged the city. In the absence of firm leadership the war dragged on and, during a period of truce, the Athenians launched a disastrous campaign against the Greek cities of Sicily. When hostilities resumed, the Athenians were fatally weakened, and in 404 BCE they surrendered to the Spartans and their allies.

◆ **Classical Art and Literature.** The years of fighting profoundly affected cultural developments at Athens.

Both the sculpture and the vase painting of the late fifth century BCE show a new and somber interest in funerary subjects. In the theater, the later plays of Euripides depicted the horrors of war, while the comedies of Aristophanes mocked the political leaders responsible for the turmoil. Thucydides wrote his *History of the Peloponnesian War* to try to analyze the motives and reactions of the participants. Socrates began to question his fellow Athenians about their moral and religious beliefs in a similar spirit of inquiry.

◆ **The Late Classical Period.** The second period, from 404 BCE to 323 BCE, was marked by considerable upheaval. Athens was no longer the dominating force in the Greek world, but there was no successor among her rivals. First Sparta and then Thebes achieved an uneasy control of Greek political life. With the collapse of the optimism of the High Classical period, the Late Classical Age was marked by a new concern with the individual. The dreamy melancholy of Praxiteles's statues is in strong contrast to the idealism of a century earlier, while his figure of Aphrodite naked was one of the first examples in the Western tradition of sensuous female nudity. The most complete demonstration of the new interest in the fate of the individual can be found in the works of Plato, Socrates' disciple, who spent much of his life studying the relationship between individuals and the state. Aristotle, Plato's younger contemporary, also wrote on political theory as well as on a host of other topics.

◆ **The Rise of Macedon.** In 359 BCE the northern kingdom of Macedon passed under the rule of Philip II and began to play an increasing part in Greek affairs. Despite Athenian resistance, led by the orator Demosthenes, Philip succeeded in uniting the cities of Greece in an alliance known as the League of Corinth; the only important city to remain independent was Sparta. When Philip was assassinated in 336 BCE, he was succeeded by his son Alexander, who set out to expand the Macedonian Empire. After defeating the Persians, he set out in an amazing series of campaigns across Asia that brought him to the borders of India. Only the revolt of his weary troops prevented him from going farther. In 323 BCE, in the course of the long journey home, Alexander died of fever.

◆ **The Hellenistic World.** The period from 323 to 146 BCE, marked by the spread of Greek culture throughout the parts of Asia conquered by Alexander, is known as the Hellenistic Age. In the confusion following his death, four kingdoms emerged: Syria, Egypt, Pergamum, and Macedon. Prosperous and aggressive and frequently at war with one another, they combined Greek intellectual ideas and artistic styles with native Eastern ones.

The chief characteristics of Hellenistic art were virtuosity and drama. Works such as the Altar of Zeus at Pergamum were commissioned by Hellenistic rulers to glorify their reigns. Artists were encouraged to develop elaborate new techniques and employ them in complex and dramatic ways. The principal buildings of the age were public works like markets and theaters or scientific constructions such as the Lighthouse at Alexandria.

◆ **The Roman Conquest of Greece.** The inability of the Hellenistic kingdoms to present a united front caused them to fall—one by one—victim to a new force in the eastern Mediterranean: Rome. By the end of the third century BCE, the Romans had secured their position in the western Mediterranean and begun an expansion into Asia that was to bring all of the Hellenistic kingdoms under their control.

In 146 BCE Roman troops captured the city of Corinth, center of the League of Corinth founded by Philip and symbol of Greek independence. Greece was made into a Roman province, and its subsequent history followed that of the Roman Empire. If Greece was under Roman political control, however, Greek art and culture dominated much of Roman cultural life and were passed on by the Romans into the Western tradition.

EXERCISES

1. Explain the chief differences among the three principal Greek tragic dramatists. Illustrate with episodes in particular plays.
2. Discuss the contributions of Plato and Aristotle to the development of philosophy.
3. Describe Greek musical theory in the fifth and fourth centuries BCE.
4. How was sculpture used to decorate the buildings on the Athenian Acropolis? What is the significance of the myths it illustrates?
5. What are the features of a work of art that indicate it is Hellenistic? How does the Hellenistic style contrast with that of the Classical period?

Visit the *Culture & Values* Companion website at **www.cengage.com/art/Cunningham/Cultureand Values7E** and the *Humanities Resource Center* for an array of primary source readings, key terms with pronunciations, flash cards, quizzes, and study materials designed especially to help you do well in this course.

CHAPTER 4

THE ROMAN LEGACY

The chief turning point in the long course of Roman history came in 31 BCE, with the final collapse of the Roman Republic, and its replacement by an Imperial system of government. Augustus, the first emperor, was faced with the task of restoring peace. During his long reign, the spread of economic prosperity produced a hardworking middle class, loyal to the central government.

At the same time his social reforms, aimed chiefly at the upper classes, were intended to return his subjects to traditional family values. Laws provided tax breaks for large families and penalized couples who did not produce children and those who remained unmarried. Adultery became a crime against the state.

Yet despite the success of Augustus's political and economic policies, it is doubtful if his moral reforming zeal met with more than polite attention. His own daughter and granddaughter, both named Julia, were notorious for their scandalous affairs. To make matters worse, one of the lovers of his daughter Julia was a son of the Emperor's old enemy, Mark Antony, whose defeat and suicide in 31 BCE had brought the Republic crashing down. Whatever his personal feelings, duty compelled Augustus to banish Julia to a remote Mediterranean island. A few years later he had to find another distant location for the banishment of his granddaughter. He hushed up the details of both scandals, but there was much gossip.

Augustus himself created a personal image of ancient Roman frugality and morality, although on his death-bed he gave a clue as to his own more complex view of his life. He asked a slave to bring a mirror, so that he could comb his hair. Then, turning to the friends beside him, he asked, "Tell me, have I played well my part in this comedy of life? If so, applaud me and send me on my way."

THE IMPORTANCE OF ROME

If the origins of our intellectual heritage go back to the Greeks and, less directly, to the peoples of Egypt and the Near East, the contribution of Rome to the wider spreading of Western civilization was tremendous. In fields such as language, law, politics, religion, and art Roman culture continues to affect our lives. The road

◆ Young woman putting on perfume, c. 150 BCE, Rome, Italy.
(© Scala/Art Resource, NY)

network of modern Europe is based on one planned and built by the Romans some two thousand years ago; the alphabet we use is the Roman alphabet; and the division of the year into twelve months of unequal length is a modified form of the calendar introduced by Julius Caesar in 45 BCE. Even after the fall of the Roman Empire the city of Rome stood for centuries as the symbol of civilization; later empires deliberately shaped themselves on the Roman model.

The enormous impact of Rome on our culture is partly the result of the industrious and determined character of the Romans, who early in their history saw themselves as the divinely appointed rulers of the world. In the course of fulfilling their mission, they spread Roman culture from the north of England to Africa, from Spain to India (see map, "The Roman World"). This Romanization of the entire known world permitted the Romans to disseminate ideas drawn from other peoples. Greek art and literature were handed down and incorporated into the Western tradition through the Romans, not from the Greeks. The rapid spread of Christianity in the fourth century CE was a result of the decision by the Roman emperors to adopt it as the official religion of the Roman Empire. In these and in other respects, the

		GENERAL EVENTS	ART
ROMAN REPUBLIC	**753 BCE**	**753** Founding of Rome (traditional date)	**c. 650–500** Influence of Greek and Orientalizing styles on Etruscan art
		c. 700 Development of Etruscan culture	
	509	**509** Expulsion of Etruscan kings and foundation of Roman Republic	
	CONQUEST OF ITALY & MEDITERRANEAN	**450** Promulgation of the *Twelve Tables* of laws	
		c. 390 Sack of Rome by Gauls	
		287 Hortensian Law reinforces plebeian power	
		264–241 First Punic War: Roman conquest of Sicily, Sardinia, Corsica	
		218–201 Second Punic War: Roman conquest of Spain	
		146 Destruction of Carthage: Africa becomes Roman province; sack of Corinth: Greece becomes Roman province	
	133	**90–88** Social War	**1st cent.** Realistic portraiture; *Funerary Portrait*
	POLITICAL CRISIS AT ROME	**82–81** Sulla dictator at Rome	
		60 First Triumvirate: Pompey, Caesar, Crassus	
		58–56 Caesar conquers Gaul	
		48 Battle of Pharsalus: war of Caesar and Pompey ends in death of Pompey; Caesar meets Cleopatra in Egypt	**c. 30 BCE–30 CE** Villa of Mysteries frescoes, Pompeii
		46–44 Caesar rules Rome as dictator until assassinated	
		43 Second Triumvirate: Antony, Lepidus, Octavian	
	31	**31** Battle of Actium won by Octavian	**c. 20** *View of a Garden*, fresco from Augustus's villa, Prima Porta
	STABILITY	**30** Death of Antony and Cleopatra	
		27–14 Octavian under name of Augustus rules as first Roman emperor	**13–9** *Ara pacis*
BCE		**BCE c. 6** Birth of Jesus; crucified CE 30	
CE		**CE 14–68** Julio-Claudian emperors: Tiberius, Caligula, Claudius, Nero	
		69–96 Flavian emperors: Vespasian, Titus, Domitian	
		70 Capture of Jerusalem by Titus; destruction of Solomon's Temple	
		79 Destruction of Pompeii and Herculaneum	
		96–138 Adoptive emperors: Nerva, Trajan, Hadrian …	
		138–192 Antonine emperors: Antoninus Pius, Marcus Aurelius …	
ROMAN EMPIRE	**180**	**193–235** Severan emperors: Septimius Severus, Caracalla …	
	DISINTEGRATION	**212** Edict of Caracalla	
	284	**284–305** Reign of Diocletian; return of civil order	Decline of realism
	RECONSTRUCTION & DECLINE	**301** Edict of Diocletian, fixing wages and prices	**324–330** Colossal head from Basilica of Constantine, Rome
		307–337 Reign of Constantine; sole emperor after 324	
		330 Founding of Constantinople	
		381 Paganism officially suppressed; Christianity made state religion	
		409–455 Vandals and Visigoths invade Italy, Spain, Gaul, Africa	
	CE 476	**476** Romulus Augustulus forced to abdicate as last Western Roman emperor	

legacy that Rome was to pass on to Western civilization had been inherited from its predecessors.

The Romans were in fact surprisingly modest about their own cultural achievements, believing that their strengths lay in good government and military prowess rather than in artistic and intellectual attainments. It was their view that Rome should get on with the job of ruling the world and leave luxuries like sculpture and astronomy to others.

Roman Music It is easy but unfair to accept the Romans' estimate of themselves as uncreative without questioning it. True, in some fields the Roman contribution was not impressive. What little we know about Roman music, for example, suggests that its loss is hardly a serious one. It was intended mainly for performance at religious events like weddings and funerals and as a background for social occasions. Musicians were often brought into aristocratic homes to provide after-dinner entertainment at a party, and individual performers, frequently women, would play before small groups in a domestic setting. Small bands of traveling musicians, playing on pipes and such percussion instruments as cymbals and tambourines, provided background music

ARCHITECTURE	LITERATURE & PHILOSOPHY	MUSIC
c. 616–509 Etruscans drain marshes, build temples, construct roads		Extension of Greek trumpet into Roman tuba, used in games, processions, battles
	c. 200–160 Ennius, *Annals*, epic poem; Plautus, *Mostellaria*, Roman comedy; Terence, Roman comedies **2nd cent.** Epicureanism and Stoicism imported to Rome	**c. 2nd cent.** BCE Greek music becomes popular at Rome
1st cent. Discovery of concrete **c. 82** Sulla commissions Sanctuary of Fortuna Primagenia, Praeneste	**c. 65–43** Lucretius, *On the Nature of Things*, Epicurean poem; Cicero, orations and philosophical essays; Catullus, lyric poems; Caesar, *Commentaries*, on Gallic wars	
	c. 27 BCE–**14** CE Horace, *Odes* and *Ars Poetica*; Virgil, *Aeneid, Georgics, Eclogues*; Ovid, *Metamorphoses*, mythological tales; Livy, *Annals of the Roman People*	
1st cent. CE Pont du Gard, Nîmes; atrium-style houses at Pompeii. Use of arch, vault, dome, principles of stress/counter stress **c. 126** Pantheon, Rome	**100–150** Tacitus, *History*; Juvenal, *Satires*; Pliny the Younger, *Letters*; Suetonius, *Lives of the Caesars*; Epictetus, *Enchiridion*, on Stoicism **c. 166–179** Marcus Aurelius, *Meditations*, on Stoicism	
300–305 Diocletian's palace, Split **306–315** Basilica of Constantine, Rome		

THE ROMAN WORLD

◆ **4.2** Roman Mosaic, 2nd–3rd century CE. An organist and a horn player entertain at a gladiatorial contest. The organ is hydraulic (water-operated).

From a Roman villa in Nennig near Trier, Germany. Detail from scenes of gladiatorial combat in the Augusta Treverorum arena. © The Art Archive/ Gianni Dagli Orti

for the acrobats and jugglers who performed in public squares and during gladiatorial contests [**Fig. 4.2**].

Nonetheless, for the Romans music certainly had none of the intellectual and philosophical significance it bore for the Greeks, and when Roman writers mention musical performances, it is often to complain about the noise. The only serious development in Roman music was the extension of the Greek trumpet into a longer and louder bronze instrument known as the **tuba**, which was used on public occasions like games and processions and in battle, when an especially powerful type some four feet (1.2 m) long gave the signals for attack and retreat. The sound was not pleasant.

In general, Roman music lovers contented themselves with Greek music played on Greek instruments. Although serious music began to grow in popularity with the spread of Greek culture, it always remained an aristocratic rather than a popular taste. Emperor Nero's love of music, coupled with his insistence on giving public concerts on the lyre, may have even hastened his downfall.

In areas other than music, the Roman achievement is considerable. There is no doubt that Roman art and literature rarely show the originality of their Greek predecessors, but originality is neither the only artistic virtue nor is its absence always a defect. The Roman genius, in fact, lay precisely in absorbing and assimilating influences from outside and going on to create from them something typically Roman. The lyric poetry of first-century-BCE writers like Catullus was inspired by the works of Sappho, Alcaeus, and other Greek poets of the sixth century BCE, but nothing could be more Roman in spirit than Catullus's poems. In architecture, the Romans achieved a style that is one of the most impressive of all our legacies from the ancient world.

It is useful to emphasize the real value of Roman art and literature because there has been a tendency since the nineteenth century to exalt the Greek cultural achievement at the expense of the Roman. All agree on the superior quality of Roman roads, sewers, and aqueducts; Roman sculpture or drama has in general been less highly rated, mainly because of comparisons to that of the Greeks. Any study of Roman culture inevitably involves examining the influences that went to make it up, and it is always necessary to remember the Roman ability to absorb and combine outside ideas and create something fresh from them.

Rome's history was a long one, beginning with the foundation of the city in the eighth century BCE. For the first two and a half centuries of its existence it was ruled by kings. The rest of the vast span of Roman history is divided into two long periods: Republican Rome (509–31 BCE), during which time democratic government was first developed and then allowed to collapse, and Imperial Rome (31 BCE–476 CE), during which the Roman world was ruled, at least in theory, by one man—the emperor. The date 476 CE marks the deposition of the last Roman emperor in the West; it forms a convenient, if artificial, terminus to the Imperial period.

Shortly after the foundation of the Republic, the Romans began their conquest of neighboring peoples: first in Italy, then throughout Europe, Asia, and North Africa. As their territory grew, Roman civilization developed along with it, assimilating the cultures of the peoples who fell under Roman domination. But long before the Romans conquered Greece or anywhere else, they were conquered by the Etruscans, and the story of Rome's rise to power truly begins with the impact on Roman life made by Etruscan rule there.

THE ETRUSCANS AND THEIR ART

The late eighth century BCE was a time of great activity in Italy. The Greeks had reached the south coast and Sicily. In the valley of the Tiber, farmers and herdsmen of a group of tribes known as the Latins (origin of the name of the language spoken by the Romans) were establishing small village settlements, one of which was to become the future imperial city of Rome. The most flourishing area at the time, however, was to the north of Rome, where in central Italy a new culture—the Etruscan—was appearing.

The Etruscans are among the most intriguing of ancient peoples, and ever since early Roman times scholars have argued about who they were, where they came from, and what language they spoke. Even today, despite the discoveries of modern archaeologists, we still know little about the origins of the Etruscans, and their language has yet to be deciphered. By 700 BCE they had established themselves in the part of Italy named for them, Tuscany, but it is not clear whether they arrived from abroad or whether their culture was a more developed form of an earlier Italian one. The ancient Greeks and Romans believed that the Etruscans had come to Italy from the East, perhaps from Lydia, an ancient kingdom in Asia Minor. Many aspects of their life and much of their art have pronounced Eastern characteristics. In other ways, however, the Etruscans have much in common with their predecessors in central Italy. Even so, no other culture related to the Etruscans' has ever been found. Whatever their origins, they were to have a major effect on Italian life and on the growth of Rome and its culture [**Fig. 4.3**].

Etruscan Art From the beginning of their history, the Etruscans showed an outstanding sophistication and technological ability. The sumptuous gold treasures buried in their tombs are evidence both of their material prosperity and of their superb craftsmanship. The commercial contacts of the Etruscans extended

◆ **4.3** *Capitoline She-Wolf*, c. 500–480 BCE. Although this statue or one very like it became the mascot of Rome, it was probably made by Etruscan craftsmen. The twins Romulus and Remus, legendary founders of the city, were added during the Renaissance.

Bronze, 2′7½″ (80 cm) high, 4′4″ (1.32 m) long. Musei Capitolini, Rome, Italy//© Scala/Art Resource, NY

◆ **4.4** *Apollo of Veii,* c. 510–500 BCE. This Etruscan figure, which was originally painted, strides forward energetically, the body clearly visible beneath the drapery. One of Apollo's roles was as god of music, and a lyre—the symbol of music—stands between his legs.

From the roof of the Portonaccio Temple, Veii, Italy. Painted terracotta, 5'11" (1.78 m) high. Museo Nazionale di Villa Giulia, Rome, Italy//© Araldo de Luca/CORBIS

This gifted people was bound to exert a strong influence on the development of civilization in Italy; Etruscan occupation of Rome (616–510 BCE) marks a turning point in Roman history. According to later tradition, the city of Rome had been founded in 753 BCE and was ruled in its earliest days by kings (in actual fact, Rome was probably not much more than a small country town for most of this period). The later Romans' own grandiose picture of the early days of their city was intended to glamorize its origins, but only with the arrival of the Etruscans did anything like an urban center begin to develop. Etruscan engineers drained a large marshy area, previously uninhabitable, which became the community's center, the future Roman forum. They built temples and shrines and constructed roads. Among other innovations, the Etruscans introduced several things we are accustomed to think of as typically Roman, including public games like chariot racing and even the **toga**, the most characteristic form of Roman dress.

Most important, however, was the fact that under Etruscan domination the Romans found themselves for the first time in contact with the larger world. Instead of being simple villagers living in a small community governed by tribal chiefs, they became part of a large cultural unit with links throughout Italy and abroad. Within a hundred years Rome had learned the lessons of Etruscan technology and culture, driven the Etruscans back to their own territory, and begun her unrelenting climb to power.

The rise of Rome signaled the decline of the Etruscans throughout Italy. In the centuries following their expulsion from Rome in 510 BCE, their cities were conquered and their territory taken over by the Romans. In the first century BCE, they automatically received the right of Roman citizenship and became absorbed into the Roman Empire. The gradual collapse of their world is mirrored in later Etruscan art. The wall paintings in the tombs become increasingly gloomy, suggesting that for an Etruscan of the third century BCE, the misfortunes of this life were followed by the tortures of the next. The old couple from Volterra whose anxious faces are so vividly depicted on the lid of their sarcophagus [**Fig. 4.6**] give us some idea of the troubled spirit of the final days of Etruscan culture.

over most of the western Mediterranean and, in Italy, Etruscan cities like Cerveteri and Tarquinia developed rich artistic traditions. Etruscan art has its own special character, a kind of elemental force almost primitive in spirit, although the craftsmanship and techniques are highly sophisticated. Unlike the Greeks, the Etruscans were less interested in intellectual problems of proportion or understanding how the human body works than in producing an immediate impact on the viewer. The famous statue of Apollo found in 1916 at Veii [**Fig. 4.4**] is unquestionably related to Greek models, but the tension of the god's pose and the sinister quality of his smile produce an effect of great power in a typically Etruscan way. Other Etruscan art is more relaxed, showing a love of nature rarely found in Greek art. The paintings in the Tomb of Hunting and Fishing at Tarquinia [**Fig. 4.5**] convey a marvelous sense of light and air, the hazy blue background evoking the sensations of sea and spray.

REPUBLICAN ROME (509–31 BCE)

With the expulsion of the Etruscans, the Romans began their climb to power, free now to rule themselves. Instead of choosing a new king, Rome constituted itself a Republic, governed by the people somewhat along the lines of the Greek city-states, although less democratically. Two chief magistrates or consuls were elected

◆ **4.5** Etruscan Scene of Fishing and Fowling, c. 520 BCE. Men, fish, and birds are all rendered naturalistically, with acute observation.

From the Tomb of Hunting and Fishing, Tarquinia, Italy. Fresco, detail 5′6″ (1.67 m) high. © SEF/Art Resource, NY

◆ **4.6** Lid of a Funerary Urn, 1st century BCE. Realistic sculptures occupy the top of the urn containing the couple's ashes. Note the detailed depiction of the lines and wrinkles on the two faces, which give them character. The Etruscans invented the idea of realistic portraiture, which the Romans then popularized.

Terracotta, 18″ (47 cm) long. Museo Etrusco Guarnacci, Volterra, Italy//© Scala/Art Resource, NY

◆ **4.7** Ruins of the Roman Forum, Rome, Italy. As the center of the evolving political, economic, and religious life of the Roman world, the Forum's buildings were constructed over a period of more than a thousand years. The small round Temple to Vesta in the bottom left corner dates to shortly after 500 BCE; the columns to the right are part of the Temple of Concord, built in 367 BCE; and the Arch of Titus in the distance dates to around 81 CE. In the background are the remains of the Colosseum (69–79 CE). *(© Richard T. Nowitz/Photo Researchers, Inc.)*

for a one-year term by all the male citizens, but the principal assembly, the Senate, drew most of its members from Roman aristocratic families. From the beginning, therefore, power was concentrated in the hands of the upper class (the **patricians**), although the lower class (the **plebeians**) was permitted to form its own assembly. The leaders elected by the plebeian assembly, the **tribunes**, represented the plebeians' interests and protected them against state officials who treated them unjustly. The meeting place for both the Senate and the assemblies of the people was the **forum**, the large open space at the foot of the Palatine and Capitoline hills that had been drained and made habitable by the Etruscans [**Fig. 4.7**].

From the founding of the Roman Republic to its bloody end in the civil wars following the murder of Julius Caesar (44 BCE), its history was dominated by agitation for political equality. Yet the first major confrontation—the conflict between patricians and plebeians—never seriously endangered political stability in Rome or military campaigns abroad. Both sides showed a flexibility and spirit of compromise that produced a gradual growth in plebeian power while avoiding any split disastrous enough to interrupt Rome's growing domination of the Italian peninsula. The final plebeian victory came in 287 BCE with the passage of the Hortensian Law, which made the decisions of the plebeian assembly binding on the entire Senate and Roman people. By then most of Italy had already fallen under Roman control.

Increasing power brought new problems. In the third and second centuries BCE, Rome began to build its empire abroad. The first major target of Roman aggression was the city of Carthage, founded by the Phoenicians around 800 BCE, and by the third century the independent ruler of territories in North Africa, Spain, and Sicily. In the Punic Wars (called after the Roman name for the Phoenicians, *Poeni*) the Romans decisively defeated the Carthaginians and confiscated their territories. By the first century BCE the entire Hellenistic world had been conquered. From Spain to the Middle East stretched a vast territory consisting of subject provinces, protectorates, and nominally free kingdoms, all of which depended on Roman goodwill and administrative efficiency.

Unfortunately, the Romans had been too busy acquiring their empire to think very hard about how to rule it; the results were frequently chaotic. Provincial administration was incompetent and often corrupt. The long series of wars had hardened the Roman character, leading to insensitivity and, frequently, brutality in the treatment of conquered peoples. This situation was not helped by increasing political instability at home. The old balance of power struck between the patricians and plebeians was being increasingly disturbed by the rise of a middle class, the *equites,* many of whom were plebeians who had made their fortunes in the wars. Against this background were fought bitter struggles that eventually caused the collapse of the Republic.

The End of the Roman Republic By the first century BCE it was apparent that the political system that had been devised for a thriving but small city five hundred years earlier was hopelessly inadequate for a vast empire. Discontent among Rome's Italian allies led to open revolt. Although the Romans were victorious in the Social War of 90–88 BCE, the cost in lives and economic stability was tremendous. The ineffectuality of the Senate and the frustration of the Roman people led to a series of struggles among the leading statesmen for supreme power. The popular leader Marius briefly held power but was replaced by his aristocratic rival, Roman general Sulla, who ruled as dictator for a brief and violent period beginning in 82 BCE, only to resign suddenly three years later, in 79 BCE. There followed a protracted series of political skirmishes between Pompey, the self-appointed defender of the Senate, and Julius Caesar, culminating in Caesar's withdrawal to Gaul and subsequent return to Rome in 49 BCE. After a short but bitter conflict, Caesar defeated Pompey in 48 BCE at the Battle of Pharsalus and returned to Rome as dictator, only to be assassinated in 44 BCE. The civil wars that followed brought the Republic to its unlamented end.

The years of almost uninterrupted violence had a profound effect on the Roman character, and the relief felt when a new era dawned under the first emperor, Augustus, can only be fully appreciated in this light.

LITERARY DEVELOPMENTS DURING THE REPUBLIC

The Romans put most of their energy into political and military affairs, leaving little time for art or literature. By the second century BCE, when most of the Mediterranean was under their control and they could afford to relax, they were overwhelmed intellectually and artistically by the Greeks. Conquest of the Hellenistic kingdoms of the East and of Greece brought the Romans into contact with Hellenistic Greek culture (see Chapter 3, "The Hellenistic Period"). Thus, from the third century BCE, most Roman works of art followed Greek models in form and content. Roman plays were based on Greek originals, Roman temples imitated Greek buildings, and Roman sculpture and painting depicted episodes from Greek mythology.

Greek influence extends to the works of Ennius (239–169 BCE), known to later Romans as the father of Roman poetry. Almost all of his works are lost, but from later accounts Ennius's tragedies appear to have been adapted from Greek models. His major work was the *Annals*, an epic chronicle of the history of Rome, in which for the first time a Greek metrical scheme was used to write Latin verse.

The two comic playwrights—Plautus (c. 254–184 BCE) and Terence (c. 185–159 BCE)—are the first Roman writers whose works have survived in quantity. Their plays are adaptations of Greek comedies; whereas the Greek originals are comic satires, the Roman versions turn human foibles into pure comedy. Plautus, the more boisterous of the two, is fond of comic songs and farcical intrigues. Terence's style is more refined, and his characters show greater realism. It says something about the taste of the Roman public that Plautus was by far the more successful. In later times, however, Terence's

sophisticated style was much admired. His plays were studied and imitated both during the Middle Ages and more recently. Both authors were fond of extremely elaborate plots involving mistaken identities, identical twins, and general confusion, with everything sorted out in the last scene.

In general, however, when educated Romans of the late Republic stopped to think about something other than politics, it was likely to be love. Roman lyric poetry, often on a romantic theme, is one of the most rewarding genres of Latin literature. The first great Roman lyric poet, Catullus (c. 80–54 BCE), is one of the best loved of all Roman authors. Instead of philosophical or historical themes, he returned to a traditional subject from Sappho's time—personal experience—and charted the course of his own love affair with a woman whom he calls Lesbia. Among his works are twenty-five short poems describing the course of that relationship, which range from the ecstasy of its early stages to the disillusionment and despair of the final breakup. The clarity of his style is the perfect counterpart to the direct expression of his emotions. These poems, personal though they are, are not simply an outpouring of feelings. Catullus makes his own experiences universal. However trivial one man's unhappy love affair may seem in the context of the grim world of the late Republic, Lesbia's inconstancy has achieved a timelessness unequaled by many more serious events.

Two of the principal figures who dominated those events also made important contributions to Republican literature. Julius Caesar (100–44 BCE) is perhaps the most famous Roman of them all. Brilliant politician, skilled general, expert administrator and organizer, he was also able to write the history of his own military campaigns in his *Commentaries*, in a simple but gripping style. In the four years during which he ruled Rome, he did much to repair the damage of the previous decades. Caesar's assassination on March 15, 44 BCE, at the hands of a band of devoted republicans, only prolonged Rome's agony for another thirteen years—as well as provided Shakespeare with the plot for one of his best-known plays: *Julius Caesar*.

Perhaps the most endearing figure of the late Republic was Marcus Tullius Cicero (106–43 BCE), who first made his reputation as a lawyer. He is certainly the figure of this period about whom we know the most, for he took part in several important legal cases and embarked on a political career. In 63 BCE he served as consul. A few years later, the severity with which he had put down a plot against the government during his consulship earned him a short period in exile as the result of the scheming of a rival political faction. Cicero returned in triumph, however, and in the struggle between Pompey and Caesar supported Pompey. Although Caesar seems to have forgiven him, Cicero never really trusted Caesar, despite his admiration for the dictator's abilities. His mixed feelings are well expressed in a letter to his friend

Atticus after he had invited Caesar, by then the ruler of the Roman world, to dinner:

> Quite a guest, although I have no regrets and everything went very well indeed.... He was taking medicine for his digestion, so he ate and drank without worrying and seemed perfectly at ease. It was a lavish dinner, excellently served and in addition well prepared and seasoned with good conversation, very agreeable, you know. What can I say? We were human beings together. But he's not the kind of guest to whom you'd say "it's been fun, come again on the way back." Once is enough! We talked about nothing serious, a lot about literature: he seemed to enjoy it and have a good time. So now you know about how I entertained him—or rather had him billeted on me. It was a nuisance, as I said, but not unpleasant.

From letters like these we can derive an incomparably vivid picture of Cicero and his world. Almost nine hundred letters were published, most after his death. If they often reveal Cicero's weaknesses—his vanity, his inability to make a decision, his stubbornness—they confirm his humanity and sensitivity. For his contemporaries and for later ages, his chief fame was nevertheless as an orator. Although the cases and causes that prompted his speeches have ceased to have any but historical interest, the power of a Ciceronian oration can still thrill the responsive reader, especially when it is read aloud.

ROMAN PHILOSOPHY AND LAW

The Romans produced little in the way of original philosophical writing. Their practical nature made them suspicious of professional philosophers and unable to appreciate the rather subtle delights involved in arguing both sides of a complex moral or ethical question. In consequence most of the great Roman philosophical writers devoted their energies to expounding Greek philosophy to a Roman audience. The two principal schools of philosophy to make an impact at Rome—**Epicureanism** and **Stoicism**—were both imported from Greece.

The Philosophy of Epicurus Epicureanism never really gained many followers, despite the efforts of the poet Lucretius (99–55 BCE), who described its doctrines in his brilliant poem *On the Nature of Things (De Rerum Natura)*. A remarkable synthesis of poetry and philosophy, this work alone is probably responsible for whatever admiration the Romans could muster for a system of thought so different from their own traditional virtues of simplicity and seriousness. According to Epicurus (341–271 BCE), the founder of the school (Epicureanism), the correct goal and principle of human actions is pleasure. Although Epicureanism stresses moderation and pru-

VOICES OF THEIR TIMES

A Dinner Party in Imperial Rome

At the end of this course Trimalchio left the table to relieve himself, and so finding ourselves free from the constraint of his overbearing presence, we began to indulge in a little friendly conversation. Accordingly Dama began first, after calling for a cup of wine. "A day! what is a day?" he exclaimed, "before you can turn round, it's night again! So really you can't do better than go straight from bed to board. Fine cold weather we've been having; why! even my bath has hardly warmed me. But truly hot liquor is a good clothier.

I've been drinking bumpers [champagne], and I'm downright fuddled. The wine has got into my head."

Seleucus then struck into the talk: "I don't bathe every day," he said; "your systematic bather's a mere fuller. Water's got teeth, and melts the heart away, a little every day; but there! when I've fortified my belly with a cup of mulled wine, I say 'Go hang!' to the cold. Indeed I couldn't bathe today, for I've been to a funeral. A fine fellow he was too, good old Chrysanthus, but he's given up the ghost now. He was calling me just this moment, only just this moment; I could fancy myself talking to him now.

Alas! alas! what are we but blown bladders on two legs? We're not worth as much as flies; they are some use, but we're no better than bubbles."

"He wasn't careful enough in his diet?"

"I tell you, for five whole days not one drop of water—or one crumb of bread—passed his lips. Nevertheless he has joined the majority. The doctors killed him, or rather his day was come; the very best of doctors is only a satisfaction to the mind.

Anyhow he was handsomely buried, on his own best bed, with good blankets. The wailing was first class—he did a trifle manumission before he died; though no doubt his wife's tears were a bit forced. A pity he always treated her so well. But woman! woman's of the kite kind. No man ought ever to do 'em a good turn; just as well pitch it in the well at once. Old love's an eating sore!"

From Petronius, *The Satyricon*, trans. attributed to Oscar Wilde (privately printed, 1928), p. 81.

dence in the pursuit of pleasure, the Romans insisted on thinking of the philosophy as a typically Greek enthusiasm for self-indulgence and debauchery.

Lucretius tried to correct this impression by emphasizing the profoundly intellectual and rational aspects of Epicureanism. Its principal teaching was that the gods, if they exist, play no part in human affairs or in the phenomena of nature; we can therefore live our lives free from superstitious fear of the unknown and the threat of divine retribution. The Epicurean theory of matter explains the world in purely physical terms. It describes the universe as made up of two elements: small particles of matter, or atoms, and empty space. The atoms are completely solid, possessing the qualities of size, shape, and mass, and can be neither split nor destroyed. Their joining together to form complex structures is entirely caused by their random swerving in space, without interference from the gods. As a result, human life can be lived in complete freedom; we can face the challenges of existence and even natural disasters like earthquakes or plagues with complete serenity, because their occurrence is random and outside our control. According to Epicurus, at death the atoms that make up our body separate and body, mind, and soul are lost. Because no part of us is in any way immortal, we should have no fear of death, which offers no threat of punishment in a future world but rather brings only the complete ending of any sensation.

Stoicism Epicureanism's rejection of a divine force in the world and its campaign against superstition probably appealed to the Romans as little as its claim that the best life was one of pleasure and calm composure. The hardheaded practical moralizing of the Roman mentality found far more appeal in the other school of philosophy imported into Rome from Greece, Stoicism. The Stoics taught that the world was governed by Reason and that Divine Providence watched over the virtuous, never allowing them to suffer evil. The key to becoming virtuous lay in willing or desiring only that which was under one's own control. Thus riches, power, or even physical health—all subject to the whims of Fortune—were excluded as objects of desire. For the Stoic, all that counted was that which was subject to the individual's will.

Although Stoicism had already won a following at Rome by the first century BCE and was discussed by Cicero in his philosophical writings, its chief literary exponents came slightly later. Seneca (8–65 BCE) wrote several essays on Stoic morality. He had an opportunity, and the necessity, to practice the moral fortitude about which he wrote when his former pupil, the emperor Nero, ordered him to commit suicide, since the taking of one's own life was fully sanctioned by Stoic philosophers. Perhaps the most impressive of all Stoic writers is Epictetus (c. 50–134 BCE), a former slave who established a school of philosophy in Rome and then in Greece. In his *Enchiridion* (*Handbook*) he recommends an absolute trust in Divine Providence to be maintained through every misfortune. For Epictetus, the philosopher represented the spokesman of Providence itself "taking the human race for his children."

Epictetus's teachings exerted a profound influence on the last great Stoic, emperor Marcus Aurelius (121–180 CE), who was constantly plagued with the dilemma of being a Stoic and an emperor at the same time. Delicate in health, sentimental, inclined to be disillusioned by the weaknesses of others, Marcus Aurelius struggled hard to maintain the balance between his public duty and his personal convictions. While on military duty he composed his *Meditations*, which are less a philosophical treatise than an account of his own attempt to live the life of a Stoic. As many of his observations make clear, this was no easy task: "Tell yourself every morning 'Today I shall meet the officious, the ungrateful, the bullying, the treacherous, the envious, the selfish. All of them behave like this because they do not know the difference between good and bad.'"

Yet, even though Stoicism continued to attract some Roman intellectuals, most Romans remained immune to the appeal of the philosophical life. In the first century BCE and later, the superstition both Stoicism and Epicureanism sought to combat remained deeply ingrained in the Roman character. Festivals in honor of traditional deities were celebrated until long after the advent of Christianity (see **Table 4.1**). Rituals that tried to read the future by the traditional examination of animals' entrails and other time-honored methods continued to be popular. If the Romans had paused more often to meditate on the nature of existence, they would probably have had less time to civilize the world.

Roman Law Among the most lasting achievements of Julius Caesar's dictatorship and of Roman culture in general was the creation of a single unified code of civil law: the **Ius Civile**. The science of law is one of the few original creations of Roman literature. The earliest legal code of the Republic was the so-called Law of the Twelve Tables of 451–450 BCE. By the time of Caesar, however, most of this law had become either irrelevant or outdated and had been replaced by a mass of later legislation, much of it contradictory and confusing. Caesar's *Ius Civile*, produced with the help of eminent legal experts of the day, served as the model for later

Table 4.1 *Principal Roman Deities and Their Greek Equivalents*

ROMAN	GREEK	ROMAN	GREEK
Jupiter	Zeus	Diana	Artemis
Juno	Hera	Ceres	Demeter
Neptune	Poseidon	Venus	Aphrodite
Vulcan	Hephaestus	Minerva	Athena
Mars	Ares	Mercury	Hermes
Apollo	Apollo	Bacchus	Dionysus

times, receiving its final form in 533 CE, when it was collected, edited, and published by Byzantine Emperor Justinian (527–565 CE).

Justinian's Corpus *Iuris Civilis* remained in use in many parts of Europe for centuries and profoundly influenced the development of modern legal systems. Today, millions of people live in countries whose legal systems derive from that of ancient Rome; one eminent British judge has observed of Roman law that "there is not a problem of jurisprudence which it does not touch: there is scarcely a corner of political science on which its light has not fallen." According to the great Roman lawyer Ulpian (died 228 CE), "Law is the art of the good and the fair." The Romans developed this art over the centuries during which they built up their empire of widely differing peoples. Roman law was international, adapting Roman notions of law and order to local conditions, and changing and developing in the process. Many of the jurists responsible for establishing legal principles had practical administrative experience from serving in the provinces. Legal experts were in great demand at Rome; the state encouraged public service, and problems of home and provincial government frequently occupied the best minds of the day. Many of these jurists acquired widespread reputations for wisdom and integrity. Emperor Augustus gave to some of them the right to issue "authoritative opinions," while a century or so later, Emperor Hadrian formed a judicial council to guide him in matters of law. Their general aim was to equate human law with that of Nature by developing an objective system of natural justice. By using this system, the emperor could fulfill his duty to serve his subjects as benefactor and bring all peoples together under a single government.

Thus, over the centuries, the Romans built up a body of legal opinion that was comprehensive, concerned with absolute and eternal values, and valid for all times and places; at its heart lay the principle of "equity"— equality for all. By the time Justinian produced his codification, he was able to draw on a thousand years of practical wisdom.

REPUBLICAN ART AND ARCHITECTURE

In the visual arts as in literature, the late Republic shows the translation of Greek styles into new Roman forms. The political scene was dominated by individuals such as Cicero and Caesar; their individualism was captured in portrait busts that were both realistic and psychologically revealing. To some extent these realistic sculptures are based on such Etruscan models as the heads of the old couple on the Volterra sarcophagus (see Figure 4.6) rather than on Hellenistic portraits, which idealized their subjects. However, the subtlety and understanding shown in portraits like those of Cicero and Caesar rep-

◆ **4.8** Bust of Cicero, 1st century BCE. This portrait of one of the leading figures of the late Republic suggests the ability of Roman sculptors of the period to capture both likeness and character. Cicero is portrayed as thoughtful and preoccupied.

Uffizi, Florence, Italy//© Alinari/Art Resource, NY

resent a typical Roman combination and amplification of others' styles. In many respects, Roman portraiture represents Roman art at its most creative and sensitive. It certainly opened up new expressive possibilities, as artists discovered how to use physical appearance to convey something about character. Many of the best Roman portraits serve as revealing psychological documents, expressing, for example, Cicero's self-satisfaction as well as his humanity [**Fig. 4.8**]. Realistic details like the lines at the corners of the eyes and mouth, the hollows in the cheeks, or the set of the lips are used to express both outer appearance and inner character. The new skill, as it developed, could of course be put to propaganda use, and statesmen and politicians soon learned that they could project their chosen self-image through their portraits.

The powerful political figures of the period also used the medium of architecture to express their authority. The huge sanctuary constructed by Sulla at Praeneste (modern Palestrina) around 82 BCE [**Fig. 4.9**] has all the qualities of symmetry and grandeur we associate with later Roman imperial architecture, although it took its inspiration from massive Hellenistic building programs such as that at Pergamum. Caesar cleared a large area in the center of Rome for the construction of a forum, to be named after him. In time it was dwarfed by later monumental fora, but it had initiated the construction of public buildings for personal display and glory.

◆ **4.9** Reconstruction Drawing of the Sanctuary of Fortuna Primigenia, Palestrina, Italy, late 2nd century BCE. This vast complex, constructed by Sulla after his destruction of the city in 82 BCE, is a series of six immense terraces crowned by a semicircular structure in front of which stood an altar. *(Artwork by John Burge)*

Table 4.2 *The Principal Roman Emperors*

Augustus	27 BCE–CE 14	
Tiberius	14–37	
Gaius (Caligula)	37–41	Julio-Claudians
Claudius	41–54	
Nero	54–68	
Year of the Four Emperors	69	
Vespasian	69–79	
Titus	79–81	Flavians
Domitian	81–96	
Nerva	96–98	
Trajan	98–117	Adoptive Emperors
Hadrian	117–138	
Antoninus Pius	138–161	
Marcus Aurelius	161–180	Antonines
Commodus	180–193	
Septimius Severus	193–211	
Alexander Severus	222–235	
Decius	249–251	
Diocletian	284–305	
Constantine	306–337	

IMPERIAL ROME (31 BCE–476 CE)

With the assassination of Julius Caesar, a brief respite from civil war was followed by further turmoil. Caesar's lieutenant, Mark Antony, led the campaign to avenge his death and punish the conspirators. He was joined in this endeavor by Caesar's young great-nephew, Octavius, who had been named by Caesar as his heir and who had recently arrived in Rome from the provinces. It soon became apparent that Antony and Octavius (or Octavian, to use the name he then adopted) were unlikely to coexist happily. After the final defeat of the conspirators (42 BCE), a temporary peace was obtained by putting Octavian in charge of the western provinces and sending Antony to the East. A final confrontation could not be long delayed, and Antony's fatal involvement with Cleopatra alienated much of his support in Rome. The end came in 31 BCE at the Battle of Actium. The forces of Antony, reinforced by those of Cleopatra, were routed, and the couple committed suicide. Octavian was left as sole ruler of the Roman world, which was now in ruins. His victory marked the end of the Roman Republic.

When Octavian took supreme control after the Battle of Actium, Rome had been continuously involved in both civil and external wars for the better part of a century. The political and cultural institutions of Roman life were beyond repair, the economy was wrecked, and large areas of Italy were in complete turmoil. By the time of Octavian's death (14 CE), Rome had achieved a peace and prosperity unequaled in its history—before or after. The art and literature created during his reign represents the peak of the Roman cultural achievement. To the Romans of his own time

it seemed that a new Golden Age had dawned, and for centuries afterward his memory was revered. As the first Roman emperor, Octavian inaugurated the second great period in Roman history—the empire, which lasted technically from 27 BCE, when he assumed the title Augustus, until 476 CE, when the last Roman emperor was overthrown. In many ways, however, the period began with the Battle of Actium and continued in the subsequent western and Byzantine empires (see **Table 4.2**).

Augustus's cultural achievement was stupendous, but it could only have been accomplished in a world at peace. In order to achieve this, it was necessary to build a new political order. A republican system of government suitable for a small state had long since proved woefully inadequate for a vast and multiethnic empire. Augustus tactfully, if misleadingly, claimed that he "replaced the State in the hands of the Senate and Roman people." He in fact did the reverse: While maintaining the appearance of a reborn republic, Augustus took all effective power into his and his imperial staff's hands.

From the time of Augustus, the emperor and his bureaucracy controlled virtually all decisions. A huge civil service developed, with various career paths. A typical middle-class Roman might begin with a period of military service, move on to a post as fiscal agent in one of the provinces, then serve in a governmental department back in Rome, and end up as a senior official in the imperial postal service or the police.

Augustus also began the reform of the army, which the central government had been unable to control during the last chaotic decades of the Republic. Its principal function now became to guard the frontiers. It was made up of some 250,000 Roman citizens, and about the same number of local recruits. The commanders of these half a million soldiers looked directly to the emperor as their general-in-chief. The troops did far more than fight. They served as engineers, building roads and bridges. They sowed crops and harvested them. They surveyed the countryside and helped police it. In the process, they won widespread respect and gratitude from Rome's provincial subjects.

Protected by the army, and administered by the civil service, the Empire expanded economically. With freedom of travel and trade, goods circulated with no tariffs or customs duties; traders only had to pay harbor dues. From the time of Augustus, the Roman road system carried increasing numbers of travelers—traders, officials, students, wandering philosophers, the couriers of banks and shipping agencies—between the great urban centers. Cities like Alexandria or Antioch were self-governing to some degree, with municipal charters giving them constitutions based on the Roman model.

Not all later emperors were as diligent or successful as Augustus. Caligula, Nero, and some others have become notorious as monsters of depravity. Yet the imperial system that Augustus founded was to last for almost five hundred years

AUGUSTAN LITERATURE: VIRGIL

Augustus played an active part in supporting and encouraging the writers and artists of his day; many of their works echo the chief themes of Augustan politics: the return of peace, the importance of the land and agriculture, the putting aside of ostentation and luxury in favor of a simple life, and above all the belief in Rome's destiny as world ruler. Some of the greatest works of Roman sculpture commemorate Augustus and his deeds; Horace and Virgil sing his praises in their poems. It is sometimes said that much of this art was propaganda, organized by the emperor to present the most favorable picture possible of his reign. Even the greatest works of the time do relate in some way or other to the Augustan worldview, and it is difficult to imagine a poet whose philosophy differed radically from that of the emperor being able to give voice to it. But we have no reason to doubt the sincerity of the gratitude felt toward Augustus or the strength of what seems to have been an almost universal feeling that at last a new era had dawned. In any case, from the time of Augustus, art at Rome became largely official. Most of Roman architecture and sculpture of

VALUES

Empire

The Romans were certainly not the first people to extend their power by external conquests: from the time of ancient Egypt, ambitious rulers had sought control over weaker states. Neither was the Roman Empire the first multiethnic one. For the Greeks, Persian aggression was the one threat sufficiently strong to drive them to unite, but for many of the peoples who formed part of the Persian Empire, their conquerors' rule was benign—not least for the Jews.

Yet no power before Rome—or since, for that matter—succeeded in ruling so vast and varied an empire for so long. In order to maintain its unity, the Romans had to devise a system of provincial government that guaranteed central control, while allowing for local differences. In the process, they developed many aspects of daily life, which foreshadow the modern world: systems of highways, a postal service, efficient food, and water distribution.

At the same time, the spread of Roman culture became an end in itself. Even in the remotest Roman cities in Europe, Asia, and North Africa, Roman theaters for the performance of Roman plays, Roman

baths, a Roman forum with a temple to Jupiter of the Capitoline at its north end, and Roman schools all reinforced the sense of a dominant imperial power, symbolized in the person of the emperor.

Many later peoples aimed to repeat the Romans' achievements. Constantine built his new capital, which became the center of the Byzantine Empire, as a "New Rome" in the East. The title that Augustus, the first emperor, assumed—Pater Patriae (Father of his native land)—was imitated by many rulers, among them Cosimo de Medici of Renaissance Florence. In nineteenth-century England, the Victorian Age owes its name to the symbolic importance of Queen Victoria, whose crowning glory was to become "Empress of India," while the use of cultural unity to underpin political stability soon became a feature of the growth of the United States. Many of the political characteristics of the young Republic were borrowed by the Founding Fathers from Rome: The U.S. Senate and Congress are based on the Roman Senate and Assembly of the People, while the separation of federal and state government reflects the Romans' distinction between central and provincial rule.

◆ **4.10** View of the Garden, c. 20 BCE. This peaceful scene, with its abundance of fruit and flowers, reflects the interest in country life expressed in Virgil's *Eclogues* and *Georgics*.

From the Villa of Livia and Augustus, Prima Porta, Italy. Fresco detail, 6'7" (2 m) high. Museo Nazionale Romano, Rome, Italy//© Scala/Art Resource, NY

the period was public, commissioned by the state, and served state purposes.

The greater the artist, the more subtle the response to the Augustan vision. Virgil, the greatest of all Roman poets, whose full name was Publius Virgilius Maro (70–19 BCE), devoted the last ten years of his life to the composition of an epic poem intended to honor Rome and, by implication, Augustus. The result was the *Aeneid*, one of the great poems of the world, not completely finished at the poet's death. For much of the Middle Ages, Virgil was held in the highest reverence. A succession of great poets have regarded him as their master: Dante, Tasso, and Milton, among others. Probably no work of literature in the entire tradition of Western culture has been more loved and revered than the *Aeneid*—described by T. S. Eliot as the classic of Western society—yet its significance is complex and by no means universally agreed upon.

The *Aeneid* was not Virgil's first poem. The earliest authentic works that have survived are ten short pastoral poems known as the *Eclogues* (sometimes called the *Bucolics*), which deal with the joys and sorrows of the country and the shepherds and herdsmen who live there. Virgil was the son of a farmer; his deep love of the land emerges also in his next work, the four books of the *Georgics* (29 BCE). Their most obvious purpose is to serve as a practical guide to farming; they offer helpful advice on such subjects as cattle breeding and beekeeping as well as a deep conviction that the strength of Italy lies in its agricultural richness. In a great passage in Book II of the *Georgics*, Virgil hails the "ancient earth, great mother of crops and men." He does not disguise the hardships of the farmer's life, the poverty, hard work, and frequent disappointments, but still feels that only life in the country brings true peace and contentment [**Fig. 4.10**].

Virgil's *Aeneid* The spirit of the *Georgics* clearly matched Augustus's plans for an agricultural revival. The emperor probably commissioned Virgil to write an epic poem that would be to Roman literature what the *Iliad* and *Odyssey* were for Greek literature: a national epic. The task was immense. Virgil had to find a subject that would do appropriate honor to Rome and its past as well as commemorate the achievements of Augustus. The *Aeneid* is not a perfect poem (on his deathbed Virgil ordered his friends to destroy it), but in some ways it surpasses even the high expectations Augustus must have had for it. Virgil succeeded in providing Rome with its national epic and stands as a worthy successor to Homer. At the same time, he created a profoundly moving study of the nature of human destiny and personal responsibility.

The *Aeneid* is divided into twelve books. Its hero is a Trojan prince, Aeneas, who flees from the ruins of burning Troy and sails west to Italy to found a new city, the predecessor of Rome. Virgil's choice was significant: Aeneas's Trojan birth establishes connections with the world of Homer; his arrival in Italy involves the origins of Rome; and the theme of a fresh beginning born, as it were, out of the ashes of the past corresponds perfectly to the Augustan mood of revival. We first meet Aeneas and his followers in the middle of his journey from Troy to Italy, caught in a storm that casts them upon the coast of North Africa. They make their way to the city of Carthage, where they are given shelter by the Carthaginian ruler, Queen Dido. At a dinner in his honor, Aeneas describes the fall of Troy (Book II) and his wanderings from Troy to Carthage (Book III), in the course of which his father Anchises had died.

In Book IV, perhaps the best known, the action resumes where it had broken off at the end of Book I. The tragic love that develops between Dido and Aeneas tempts Aeneas to stay in Carthage and thereby abandon his mission to found a new home in Italy. Mercury, the divine messenger of the gods, is sent to remind Aeneas of his responsibilities. He leaves after an agonizing encounter with Dido, and the distraught queen kills herself.

Book V brings the Trojans to Italy. In Book VI, Aeneas journeys to the underworld to hear from the spirit of his father the destiny of Rome. This tremendous episode provides the turning point of the poem. Before it we see Aeneas, and he sees himself, as a man prone to human weaknesses and subject to personal feelings. After Anchises' revelations, Aeneas's humanity is replaced by a sense of mission, and the weary, suffering Trojan exile becomes transformed into a "man of destiny."

In Books VII and VIII, the Trojans arrive at the river Tiber, and Aeneas visits the future site of Rome while the Italian peoples prepare to resist the Trojan invaders. The last four books describe in detail the war between the Trojans and the Latins, in the course of which there are losses on both sides. The *Aeneid* ends with the death of the great Italian warrior Turnus and the final victory of Aeneas.

It is tempting to see Aeneas as the archetype of Augustus; certainly Virgil must have intended for us to draw some parallels. Other historical analogies can also be found: Dido and Cleopatra, for example, have much in common. The *Aeneid* is, however, far more than an allegorical retelling of the events leading up to the foundation of the Empire. Put briefly, Aeneas undertakes a responsibility for which initially he has no real enthusiasm and which costs him and others considerable suffering. It would have been much easier for him to have stayed in Carthage or settled somewhere else along his way, rather than push forward under difficult circumstances into a foreign land where he and his followers were not welcome.

Once he has accepted his mission, however, Aeneas fulfills it conscientiously and in the process learns to sublimate his own personal desires to a common good. If this is a portrait of Augustus, it represents a far more complex view of his character than we might expect, and Virgil goes further. If greatness can only be acquired by sacrificing human individuals, is it worth the price? Is the future glory of Rome a sufficient excuse for the cruel and unmanly treatment of Dido? Readers will provide their own answers. Virgil's responses might have been that the sacrifices were probably worth it, but barely. Much depends on individual views on the nature and purpose of existence, and for Virgil there is no doubt that life is essentially tragic. The prevailing mood of the poem is one of melancholy regret for the sadness of human lives and the inevitability of human suffering.

AUGUSTAN SCULPTURE

Many of the characteristics of Virgil's poetry can also be found in contemporary sculpture. In a relief from one of the most important works of the period, the *Ara Pacis* (*Altar of Peace*), Aeneas performs a sacrifice on his arrival in Italy before a small shrine that contains two sacred images brought from Troy [**Fig. 4.11**]. More significantly, the *Ara Pacis* depicts the abundance of nature that could flourish again in the peace of the Augustan Age. The altar, begun on Augustus's return to Rome in 13 BCE after a visit to the provinces, was dedicated on January 30, 9 BCE, at a ceremony that is shown in the surrounding reliefs [**Fig. 4.12**]. The procession making its way to the sacrifice is divided into two parts. On the south side, Augustus leads the way, accompanied by priests and followed by the members of his family; the north side shows senators and other dignitaries. The lower part of the walls is decorated with a rich band of fruit and floral motifs, luxuriantly intertwined, amid which swans are placed. The actual entrance to the altar is flanked by two reliefs—on the right, the one showing Aeneas, and on the left, Romulus and Remus.

The *Ara Pacis* is perhaps the single most comprehensive statement of how Augustus wanted his contemporaries and future generations to view his reign. The altar is dedicated neither to Jupiter or Mars nor to Augustus but to the spirit of Peace. Augustus is shown as the first among equals rather than supreme ruler; although he leads the procession, he is marked by no special richness of dress. The presence of Augustus's family indicates that he intends his successor to be drawn from among them and that they have a special role to play in public affairs. The reliefs of Aeneas and of Romulus and Remus relate the entire ceremony to Rome's glorious past. Further scenes at the back showing the Earth Mother and the goddess of war emphasize the abundance of the land and the need for vigilance. The rich vegetation of the lower band is a constant reminder of the rewards of agriculture that can be enjoyed once more in the peace to which the whole altar is dedicated.

Amazingly enough, this detailed political and social message is expressed without pretentiousness and with superb workmanship. The style is deliberately and self-consciously "classical," based on works like the Parthenon frieze. To depict the New Golden Age of Augustus, his artists have chosen the artistic language of the Golden Age of Athens, although with a Roman accent. The figures in the procession, for instance, are portrayed far more realistically than those in the sculpture of fifth-century-BCE Athens.

The elaborate message illustrated by the *Ara Pacis* can also be seen in the best-preserved statue of the emperor, the *Augustus of Prima Porta,* so-called after the spot where an imperial villa containing the sculpture

◆ **4.11** Aeneas Performs a Sacrifice, 13–9 BCE. Aeneas (right) is shown in the manner of a Classical Greek god. The landscape and elaborate relief detail are typical of late Hellenistic art.

Detail from the Ara Pacis Augustae. Marble, 5′3″ (1.6 m) high. © Ara Pacis, Rome, Italy / The Bridgeman Art Library

◆ **4.12** *Ara Pacis Augustae*, 13–9 BCE. The central doorway, through which the altar is just visible, is flanked by reliefs showing Romulus and Remus and Aeneas. On the right side is the procession of the imperial family led by Augustus. The altar originally stood on Rome's ancient Via Flaminia. Fragments were discovered in the 16th century; the remaining pieces were located in 1937 and 1938, and the structure was reconstructed near the mausoleum of Augustus.

Marble, 36′ x 33′ (11 x 10 m). Museum of the Ara Pacis, Rome, Italy // © Scala / Art Resource, NY

◆ **4.13** *Augustus of Prima Porta*, c. 20 BCE. Found in the Imperial Villa of Prima Porta, the statue shows Augustus about to deliver a speech. He wears a mixture of military and civilian dress, and his head and feet are bare. The small Cupid at his feet connects the emperor to the legendary founder of Rome, Aeneas, who, like Cupid, was a child of the goddess Venus.

Marble copy of a bronze original, 6′8″ (2 m) high. Braccio Nuovo, Vatican Museums, Vatican State//© Scala/Art Resource, NY

was excavated [**Fig. 4.13**]. The statue probably dates from about the time of the emperor's death; the face is in the full vigor of life, calm and determined. The stance is one of quiet authority. The ornately carved breastplate recalls one of the chief events of Augustus's reign. In 20 BCE he defeated the Parthians, an eastern tribe, and recaptured from them the Roman standards that had been lost in battle in 53 BCE. On that former occasion, Rome had suffered one of the greatest military defeats in its history, and Augustus's victory played an important part in restoring national pride. The breastplate shows a bearded Parthian handing back the eagle-crowned standard to a Roman soldier. The cupid on a dolphin at Augustus's feet serves two purposes. The symbol of the goddess Venus, it connects Augustus and his family with Aeneas (whose mother was Venus) and thereby with the origins of Rome. At the same time it looks to the future by representing Augustus's grandson Gaius, who was born in the year of the victory over the Parthians and was at one time considered a possible successor to his grandfather.

The choice of his successor was the one problem that Augustus never managed to resolve to his own satisfac-

tion. The death of other candidates forced him to fall back reluctantly on his unpopular stepson Tiberius—the succession was a problem that was to recur throughout the long history of the Empire, because no really effective mechanism was ever devised for guaranteeing a peaceful transfer of power. (As early as the reign of Claudius [41–54 CE], the right to choose a new emperor was seized by the army.) In every other respect, the Augustan age was one of high attainment. In the visual arts, Augustan artists set the styles that dominated succeeding generations, while writers such as the poets Virgil, Horace, Ovid, and Propertius, and the historian Livy established a Golden Age of Latin literature.

THE EVIDENCE OF POMPEII

The first and second centuries CE are probably the best-documented times in the whole of classical antiquity. From the main literary sources and the wealth of art and architecture that has survived, it is possible to reconstruct a detailed picture of life in imperial Rome. Even more complete is our knowledge of a prosperous but unimportant little town some 150 miles (240 km) south of Rome that owes its worldwide fame to the circumstances of its destruction [**Fig. 4.14**]. On August 24 in the year 79 CE, the volcano Vesuvius above the Gulf of Naples erupted and a few small towns were buried, the nearer ones under flowing lava and those some distance away under pumice and ash. By far the most famous is Pompeii, situated some ten miles (16 km) southeast of the erupting peak. Excavation first began there more than two hundred years ago. The finds preserved by the volcanic debris give us a rich and vivid impression of the way of life in a provincial town of the early Empire—from the temples in which the Pompeians worshiped and the baths in which they cleansed themselves to their food on the fatal day [**Figs. 4.15, 4.16, and 4.17**].

An eyewitness report about the eruption comes from two letters written by the Roman politician and literary figure Pliny the Younger (62–before 114 CE)—so-called to distinguish him from his uncle, Pliny the Elder (23–79 CE). The two were in fact together at Misenum on the Bay of Naples on the day of the eruption. Pliny's uncle was much interested in natural phenomena (his chief work was a Natural History in thirty-seven volumes); to investigate for himself the nature of the explosion, he made his way toward Vesuvius, where he was suffocated to death by the fumes. The younger Pliny stayed behind with his mother, and in a letter to the historian Tacitus a little while later described the events of the next few hours.

Pliny the Younger: Letter to Tacitus on the Eruption of Vesuvius

> You say that the letter I wrote at your request about the death of my uncle makes you want to hear about the terrors, and dangers as well, which I endured, having been left behind at Misenum—I had started on that topic but broken off.

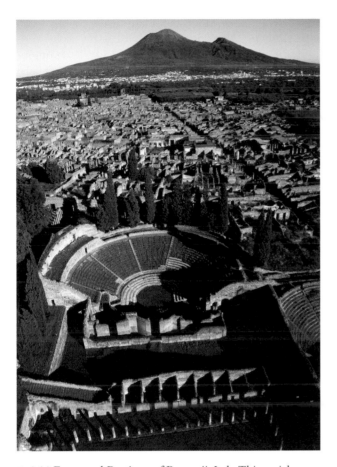

◆ **4.14** Excavated Portions of Pompeii, Italy. This aerial view of Pompeii as it appears today shows the theater in the foreground and Mount Vesuvius's two peaks in the rear; the volcano's crater lies between the peaks. The total area is 166 acres (67.23 ha). Although excavations at Pompeii have been in progress for more than two hundred years, some two-fifths of the city is still buried. (© *O. Louis Mazzatenta/National Geographic/Getty Images*)

◆ **4.16** Victims of Mt. Vesuvius Eruption, Pompeii, Italy, 79 CE. Smothered in volcanic pumice during the eruption, these people were found near a gate in the walls, where they were trying to push their way out of the darkness and blinding waves of hot volcanic dust. In the end they were knocked to the ground, although the man at the back seems to be trying to pull himself up. The technique for recovering and reconstructing human remains found during excavation was first invented in the late 19th century and has been improving ever since. (© *Leonard Von Matt/Photo Researchers, Inc.*)

◆ **4.17** Carbonized Food, Pompeii, Italy, August 24, 79 CE. Most of the foods—like these charred nuts, olives, and a complete cake or loaf of bread—were found preserved under the eruption's ashes on tables set for breakfast the morning of the eruption.

Museo Archeologico Nazionale, Naples, Italy//© Erich Lessing/Art Resource, NY

◆ **4.15** Temple of Apollo, 1st century CE. A statue of Apollo stands on the east side of the temple in the ruins of Pompeii, Italy. (© *G. R. Richardson/Getty Images*)

"Though my mind shudders to remember, I shall begin." After my uncle departed I spent the rest of the day on my studies; it was for that purpose I had stayed. Then I took a bath, ate dinner, and went to bed; but my sleep was restless and brief. For a number of days before this there had been a quivering of the ground, not so fearful because it was common in Campania. On that night, however, it became so violent that everything seemed not so much to move as to be overturned.

My mother came rushing into my bedroom; I was just getting up, intending in my turn to arouse her if she were asleep. We sat down in the rather narrow courtyard of the house lying between the sea and the buildings. I don't know whether I should call it iron nerves or folly—I was only seventeen: I called for a book of Titus Livy and as if at ease I read it and even copied some passages, as I had been doing. Then one of my uncle's friends, who had recently come from Spain to visit him, when he saw my mother and me sitting there, and me actually reading a book, rebuked her apathy and my unconcern. But I was as intent on my book as ever.

It was now the first hour of day, but the light was still faint and doubtful. The adjacent buildings now began to collapse, and there was great, indeed inevitable, danger of being involved in the ruins; for though the place was open, it was narrow. Then at last we decided to leave the town. The dismayed crowd came after us; it preferred following someone else's decision rather than its own; in panic that is practically the same as wisdom. So as we went off we were crowded and shoved along by a huge mob of followers. When we got out beyond the buildings we halted. We saw many strange fearful sights there. For the carriages we had ordered brought for us, though on perfectly level ground, kept rolling back and forth; even when the wheels were checked with stones they would not stand still. Moreover the sea appeared to be sucked back and to be repelled by the vibration of the earth; the shoreline was much farther out than usual, and many specimens of marine life were caught on the dry sands. On the other side a black and frightful cloud, rent by twisting and quivering paths of fire, gaped open in huge patterns of flames; it was like sheet lightning, but far worse. Then indeed that friend from Spain whom I have mentioned spoke to us more sharply and insistently: "If your brother and uncle still lives, he wants you to be saved; if he has died, his wish was that you should survive him; so why do you delay to make your escape?" We replied that we would not allow ourselves to think of our own safety while still uncertain of his. Without waiting any longer he rushed off and left the danger behind at top speed.

Soon thereafter the cloud I have described began to descend to the earth and to cover the sea; it had encircled Capri and hidden it from view, and had blotted out the promontory of Misenum. Then my mother began to plead, urge, and order me to make my escape as best I could, for I could, being young; she, weighed down with years and weakness, would die happy if she had not been the cause of death to me. I replied that I would not find safety except in her company; then I took her hand and made her walk faster. She obeyed with difficulty and scolded herself for slowing me. Now ashes, though thin as yet, began to fall. I looked back; a dense fog was looming up behind us; it poured over the ground like a river as it

followed. "Let us turn aside," said I, "lest, if we should fall on the road, we should be trampled in the darkness by the throng of those going our way." We barely had time to consider the thought, when night was upon us, not such a night as when there is no moon or there are clouds, but such as in a closed place with the lights put out. One could hear the wailing of women, the crying of children, the shouting of men; they called each other, some their parents, others their children, still others their mates, and sought to recognize each other by their voices. Some lamented their own fate, others the fate of their loved ones. There were even those who in fear of death prayed for death. Many raised their hands to the gods; more held that there were nowhere gods any more and that this was that eternal and final night of the universe. Nor were those lacking who exaggerated real dangers with feigned and lying terrors. Men appeared who reported that part of Misenum was buried in ruins, and part of it in flames; it was false, but found credulous listeners.

It lightened a little; this seemed to us not daylight but a sign of approaching fire. But the fire stopped some distance away; darkness came on again, again ashes, thick and heavy. We got up repeatedly to shake these off; otherwise we would have been buried and crushed by the weight. I might boast that not a groan, not a cowardly word, escaped from my lips in the midst of such dangers, were it not that I believed I was perishing along with everything else, and everything else along with me; a wretched and yet a real consolation for having to die. At last the fog dissipated into smoke or mist, and then vanished; soon there was real daylight; the sun even shone, though wanly, as when there is an eclipse. Our still trembling eyes found everything changed, buried in deep ashes as if in snow. We returned to Misenum and attended to our physical needs as best we could; then we spent a night in suspense between hope and fear. Fear was the stronger, for the trembling of the earth continued, and many, crazed by their sufferings, were mocking their own woes and others' by awful predictions. But as for us, though we had suffered dangers and anticipated others, we had not even then any thought of going away until we should have word of my uncle.

You will read this account, far from worthy of history, without any intention of incorporating it; and you must blame yourself, since you insisted on having it, if it shall seem not even worthy of a letter.

With a few exceptions, like the frescoes in the Villa of the Mysteries [**Fig. 4.18**], the works of art unearthed at Pompeii are not masterpieces. Their importance lies precisely in the fact that they show us how the ordinary Pompeian lived, worked, and played. The general picture is impressive. Cool, comfortable houses were decorated with charming frescoes and mosaics and included quiet gardens, remote from the noise of busy streets and watered by fountains [**Fig. 4.19**]. The household silver and other domestic ornaments found in the ruins of houses were often of high quality. Although the population of Pompeii was only twenty thousand, there were no fewer than three sets of public baths, a theater, a concert hall, an amphitheater large enough to seat the entire population, and a more than adequate number of brothels. The forum was closed to traffic, and the major

◆ **4.18** Fresco, Villa of the Mysteries, c. 60 BCE. Probably no ancient work of art has been more argued about than these paintings. They seem to relate to the cult of the Greek god Dionysus and the importance of the cult for girls approaching marriage, but many of the details are difficult to interpret. There is no argument, however, about the high quality of the paintings.

Fresco, frieze 5′4″ (1.6 m) high, Villa of the Mysteries, Pompeii, Italy // © Scala/Art Resource, NY

◆ **4.19** Atrium, House of the Silver Wedding, Pompeii, Italy, 1st century CE. The open plan of substantial houses such as this helped keep the interior cool in summer; the adjoining rooms were closed off by folding doors in winter. (© *Scala/Art Resource, NY*)

public buildings ranged around it include a splendid basilica or large hall that served as both stock exchange and law courts. Life must have been extremely comfortable at Pompeii, even though it was by no means the most prosperous of the towns buried by Vesuvius. Although only a small part of Herculaneum has been excavated, some mansions found there far surpass the houses of Pompeii. In the past few years, work has begun at Oplontis, where a superbly decorated villa has already come to light.

Apart from its historic importance, the excavation of Pompeii in the eighteenth and nineteenth centuries

◆ **4.20** Model Reconstruction of Ancient Rome c. 320 CE. In the lower right is the Pantheon (see Figure 4.23), with the Colosseum in the upper left and the Circus Maximus to its right.

Museo della Civilta Romana, Rome, Italy//© Scala/Art Resource, NY

◆ **4.22** Arch Construction. *Top:* Simple arch composed of wedge-shaped blocks (*voussoirs*) and keystone; the curve of the arch rises from the springers on either side. *Center:* Tunnel (barrel vault) composed of a series of arches. *Bottom:* Dome composed of a series of arches intersecting around a central axis.

◆ **4.21** Arch of Titus, Rome, Italy, 81 CE. Roman arches commemorated victories by successful generals. This arch celebrates the victory of Titus, son of the reigning emperor Vespasian, over the Jews in 70 CE—a victory that saw the destruction of Solomon's Temple when Titus's army captured the city of Jerusalem. While early Imperial arches resembled this one, those built later generally had a large central arch flanked by two smaller ones.

Marble, 47′4″ (14.43 m) high. © Erich Lessing/Art Resource, NY

had a profound effect on contemporary writers and artists. Johann Wolfgang von Goethe visited the site in 1787 and wrote of the buried city that "of all the disasters there have been in this world, few have provided so much delight to posterity." Johann Winckelmann (1717–1768), sometimes called the father of archaeology and art history, used material from the excavations in his *History of Ancient Art*. Artists such as Ingres, David, and Canova were influenced by Pompeian paintings and sculptures; on a more popular level, a style of Wedgwood china was based on Pompeian motifs. Countless poets and novelists of the nineteenth century either set episodes in the excavations at Pompeii or tried to imagine what life there was like in Roman times.

ROMAN IMPERIAL ARCHITECTURE

All the charm and comfort of Pompeii pale before the grandeur of imperial Rome, where both public buildings and private houses were constructed in numbers and on a scale that still remains impressive [**Fig. 4.20**]. The Roman achievement in both architecture and engineering had a lasting effect on the development of later architectural styles. In particular their use of

◆ **4.23** The Pantheon, Rome, Italy, c. 126 CE. The huge concrete dome that crowns the Pantheon is open to the sky at the top. This opening is known as the "oculus" or "eye" and spans 30′ (9.2 m) across. As the sun moves across the sky, its beam moves around the inner wall of the building, making the whole structure a symbol of the world.

Brick, concrete, and marble. Walls c. 20′ (6 m) thick supporting dome weight of 5,000 tons. Portico with 18 Corinthian columns 59′ (18 m) high. Dome © PictureNet/CORBIS. Exterior facade © Scala/Ministero per i Beni e le Attività Culturali/Art Resource, NY

the arch, probably borrowed from the Etruscans, was widely imitated, and pseudo-Roman triumphal arches have sprung up in such unlikely places as the Champs Elysées in Paris and Washington Square in New York. The original triumphal arches commemorated military victories [**Fig. 4.21**]; each was a permanent version of the temporary wooden arch erected to celebrate the return to the capital of a victorious general.

Equally important was the use of internal arches and vaults [**Fig. 4.22**] to provide roofs for structures of increasing size and complexity. Greek and Republican Roman temples had been relatively small, partly because of the difficulties involved in roofing over a large space without supports. With the invention of concrete in the first century BCE and growing understanding of the principles of stress and counter-stress, Roman architects were able to experiment with elaborate new forms, many of which—like the **barrel vault** and the **dome**—were to pass into the Western architectural tradition.

The Greeks rarely built arches, but the Etruscans used them as early as the fifth century BCE, and the Romans may well have borrowed the arch from

them. From the second century BCE on, stone arches were used regularly for bridges and aqueducts. Vaults of small size were often used for domestic buildings, and by the time of Augustus, architects had begun to construct larger-scale barrel vaults, semicylindrical in shape, two or more of which could intersect to roof a large area. The dome, which is really a hemispherical vault, became increasingly popular with the building of the vast public baths of Imperial Rome. Using both bricks and concrete, architects could combine vaults, barrel vaults, and domes to construct elaborate buildings capable of holding thousands of people at a time. The inside and outside surfaces of the buildings were then covered with a marble facing to conceal the elaborate internal support structures.

Much of the work of these architects was destroyed during the Barbarian invasions of the fifth and sixth centuries CE, and more was wrecked in the Renaissance by builders removing bricks or marble. By great good fortune, one of the most superb of all imperial structures has been preserved almost intact. The Pantheon [**Fig. 4.23**] was built around 126 CE, during the reign of Hadrian (117–138 CE) to a design by the

◆ **4.24** Corinthian capital. This elaborate bell-shaped design, decorated with acanthus leaves, first became commonly used in Hellenistic times. It was especially popular with Roman architects who generally preferred it to both the Doric and Ionic styles.

◆ **4.25** The Imperial Fora. Unlike the Republican forum, which served as a public meeting place, the imperial fora were huge complexes constructed as monuments to the emperors who commissioned them. Note the Forum of Trajan (Forum Traiani), one of the largest, in the upper portion.

emperor. An austere and majestic exterior portico is supported on granite columns with Corinthian capitals [**Fig. 4.24**]. It leads into the central rotunda, an astonishing construction approximately 142 feet (43.3 m) high and wide in which a huge concrete dome rests on a wall interrupted by a series of niches. The building's only light source is a huge **oculus** (eye) at the top of the dome, an opening 30 feet (9.2 m) across. The proportions of the building are carefully calculated and contribute to its air of balance. The height of the dome from the ground, for example, is exactly equal to its width.

The Pantheon was dwarfed by the huge complex of buildings that made up the imperial fora. Completed by the beginning of the second century CE, they formed a vast architectural design unsurpassed in antiquity and barely equaled since [**Fig. 4.25**]. Elsewhere in the city, baths, theaters, temples, racetracks, and libraries catered to the needs and fancies of a huge urban population. In many of these structures, builders continued to experiment with new techniques of construction, and architectural principles developed in Rome were applied throughout the Roman Empire. From Spain to the

Middle East, theaters, amphitheaters, and other public buildings were erected according to the same basic designs, leaving a permanent record of construction methods for later generations.

Urban life on such a scale required a constant supply of one of the basic human necessities: water. Their system of aqueducts is one of the most impressive of the Romans' engineering achievements. A vast network of pipes brought millions of gallons of water a day into Rome, distributing it to public fountains and baths and to the private villas of the wealthy. At the same time, a system of covered street drains was built, eliminating the open sewers that had been usual before Roman times. These open drains were to return during the medieval period, when many of the Roman engineering skills were lost.

With the passage of time, most of the aqueducts that supplied ancient Rome have been demolished or have collapsed. Elsewhere in the Roman Empire, however,

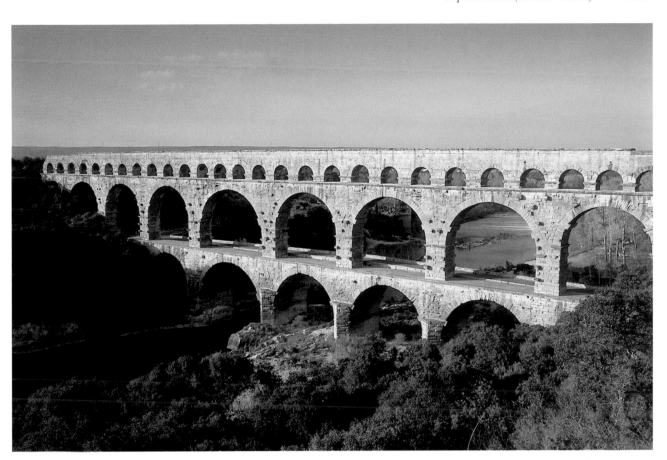

◆ **4.26** Aqueduct Pont du Gard, c. 16 CE. Note the careful positioning of the three rows of arches along the top, which carried the water channel. The entire aqueduct was 25 miles (40 km) long. This section carried the water over the canyon of the Gardon River.

Near Nîmes (ancient Nemausus), France. Stone block, 902′ (274.93 m) long, 161′ (49.07 m) high, each large arch spanning some 82′ (25 m). © DeA Picture Library/Art Resource, NY

examples have survived that give some idea of Roman engineering skill. The famous Pont du Gard [**Fig. 4.26**], which can still be seen in southern France, was probably first constructed during the reign of Augustus. It carried the aqueduct that supplied the Roman city of Nîmes with water—a hundred gallons (387.5 liters) a day—for each inhabitant and was made of uncemented stone. The largest blocks weigh two tons (1.8 MT).

Even with the provision of such facilities, Imperial Rome suffered from overcrowding. The average Roman lived in an apartment block, of which there were some 45,000. Most of these have long since disappeared, although their appearance can be reconstructed from examples excavated at Ostia, Rome's port [**Fig. 4.27**]. The height of the apartment blocks was controlled by law to prevent the construction of unsafe buildings, but it was not unheard of for a building to collapse, and fire was a constant danger. No doubt the grandeur of the public buildings in Rome was intended at least in part to distract the poorer Romans from thoughts of their humble private residences.

◆ **4.27** Model Reconstruction of a Roman Apartment Block, 2nd century CE. Shown here is a reconstruction of an *insula*—a multistory, brick faced, concrete apartment house—in Ostia, the seaport of ancient Rome. As can be seen from the size of the windows, the ground floor, which was intended for shops, was more spacious with higher ceilings. The apartments on the floors above were cramped; few had private toilet facilities.

Museo della Civilta Romana, Rome, Italy//© Scala/Art Resource, NY

◆ **4.28** Ruins of the Basilica of Constantine, 306–315 CE. The last great imperial building in Rome, the basilica was begun in 306 by Maxentius and finished by Constantine after 315. Only the northern side is still standing; the central nave and south aisle collapsed during antiquity. The brickwork visible today was originally hidden behind marble panels, both inside and out. *(Forum Romanum, Rome, Italy//© Scala/Art Resource, NY)*

ROME AS THE OBJECT OF SATIRE

Life in this huge metropolis had many of the problems of big-city living today: noise, traffic jams, dirty streets, and overcrowding were all constant sources of complaint. A particularly bitter protest comes from the Roman satirist Juvenal (c. 60–c. 130 CE). Born in the provinces, he came to Rome, where he served as a magistrate and irritated the then-current emperor, Domitian—not a difficult task. After a period of exile, probably in Egypt, he returned to Rome and lived in considerable poverty. Toward the end of his life, however, his circumstances improved. His sixteen *Satires* make it perfectly clear that Juvenal liked neither Rome nor Romans. He tells us that he writes out of fierce outrage at the corruption and decadence of his day, the depraved aristocracy, the general greed and meanness. "At such a time who could not write satire?" His fiercest loathing is reserved for foreigners, although in the sixth satire he launches a particularly virulent attack against women in one of the archetypal documents of misogyny.

Juvenal does not emerge as a pleasant character, and his obsessive hatred frequently verges on the psy-

chopathic. As a satirical poet, though, he is among the greatest in Western literature, and he strongly influenced many of his successors, including Jonathan Swift. Few other writers can make better or more powerful use of biting sarcasm, irony, and outright invective.

THE END OF THE ROMAN EMPIRE

Few historical subjects have been as much discussed as the fall of the Roman Empire. It is not even possible to agree on when it fell, let alone why. The traditional date—476 CE—marks the deposition of the last Roman emperor, Romulus Augustulus. By that time, however, the political unity of the empire had already disintegrated. Perhaps the beginning of the end was 330 CE, when Emperor Constantine moved the capital from Rome to a new city on the Bosporus, Constantinople, although in another sense the transfer represented a new development as much as a conclusion. It might even be possible to argue that Constantine's successors

◆ **4.29** Head of the Colossal Statue of Constantine, 324–330 CE. The massive and majestic simplicity of this portrait is very different from the detailed observation of earlier, much smaller Roman portraits like that of Cicero (see Figure 4.8), and illustrated the new belief in the emperor as God's regent on earth.

From the Basilica of Constantine. Marble, head alone 8′6″ (2.59 m) high.
Palazzo dei Conservatori, Rome, Italy//© Scala/Art Resource, NY

in the East, the Byzantine emperors, were the successors of Augustus and that a tradition continues from the beginning of the Empire in 31 BCE to the fall of Constantinople in 1453 CE.

Fascinating though the question may be, in a sense it is theoretical rather than practical. The Roman Empire did not fall overnight. Many of the causes for its long decline are obvious, though not always easy to order in importance. One crucial factor was the growing power and changing character of the army. The larger it became, the more necessary it was to recruit troops from the more distant provinces—Germans, Illyrians, and others, the very people the army was supposed to be holding in check. Most of these soldiers had never been anywhere near Rome. They felt no loyalty to the empire, no reason to defend Roman interests. A succession of emperors had to buy their support by raising their pay and promising gifts of lands. At the same time, the army came to play an increasingly prominent part in the choice of a new emperor and, because the army was largely non-

Roman, so were many of the emperors chosen. Rulers of the third and fourth centuries included Africans, Thracians, a Syrian, and an Arab—men unlikely to feel any strong reason to place the interests of Rome over those of themselves and their own men.

Throughout this late period, the empire was increasingly threatened from outside. To the west, barbarian tribes like the Huns, the Goths, and the Alemanni began to penetrate farther and farther into its defenses and even to sack Rome. Meanwhile, in the east, Roman armies were continually involved in resisting the growing power of the Persians. In many parts of the empire it became clear that Rome could provide no help against invaders, and some of the provinces set themselves up as independent states with their own armies.

Problems like these inevitably had a devastating effect on the economy. Taxes increased and the value of money depreciated. The constant threat of invasion or civil war made trade impossible. What funds there were went for the support of the army, and the general standard of living suffered a steady decline. The eastern provinces, the old Hellenistic kingdoms, suffered rather less than the rest of the empire, because they were protected in part by the wealth accumulated over the centuries and by their long tradition of civilization. As a result, Italy sank to the level of a province rather than remaining the center of the imperial administration.

Total collapse was prevented by the efforts of two emperors: Diocletian, who ruled from 284 to 305 CE, and Constantine, who ruled from 306 to 337. Both men were masterly organizers who realized that the only way to save the empire was to impose the most stringent controls on every aspect of life—social, administrative, and economic. In 301 CE, the Edict of Diocletian was passed, establishing fixed maximums for the sale of goods and for wages. A vast bureaucracy was set up to collect taxes and administer the provinces. The emperor became once again the focal point of the empire, but to protect himself from the dangers of coups and assassinations, he never appeared in public. As a result, an elaborate court with complex rituals developed, and the emperor's claim to semi-divine status invested him with a new religious authority.

LATE ROMAN ART AND ARCHITECTURE

Even if the emperor did not show himself to his subjects, he could impress them in other ways, and the reigns of Diocletian and Constantine marked the last great age of Roman architecture. The immense Basilica of Constantine [**Fig. 4.28**], with its central nave rising to a height of 100 feet (30.5 meters), is now in ruins, but in its day this assembly hall must have been a powerful reminder of the emperor's authority. It also contained a 30-foot (9.2 m) statue of the emperor [**Fig. 4.29**]. The palace

◆ **4.30** Reconstruction Drawing of the Palace of Diocletian, Split, Croatia, 300–305 CE. Note the octagonal dome of the emperor's mausoleum, toward the center right. Much of the Palace is still standing and forms the heart of the modern city of Split, Croatia.

◆ **4.31** Constantine Receiving Homage from the Senate, 315 CE. Officials for the emperor (seated in the center) distribute money to the crowds on both sides. The simplified style, in which most of the puppetlike figures are shown frontally, foreshadows Byzantine and medieval art and is certainly very different from the style of earlier reliefs (see Figures 4.11, 4.12).

From the frieze on the Arch of Constantine. Marble relief, 3'4" x 17'6" (1.02 x 5.33 m) long. Rome, Italy//© Alinari/Art Resource, NY

Diocletian built at Split, on the Adriatic coast, is constructed on the plan of a military camp, with enormous central avenues dividing it into four quarters [**Fig. 4.30**]. The decoration uses eastern motifs, and the entire design is far from the Classical style of earlier times.

In sculpture, too, Classical forms and styles were increasingly abandoned. Realistic portraiture and naturalistic drapery were neglected, and sculptors no longer tried to express depth or reality in their relief carving. The lack of perspective and precision in their work foreshadows the art of the early Middle Ages [**Fig. 4.31**]. The general abandonment of Classical ideas these artistic changes indicate went along with a waning of interest in Stoicism and Epicureanism and a new enthusiasm for Eastern religious cults. Traditional Roman religion had always been organized by the state, and from the time of the late Republic, some Romans had sought a more personal religious satisfaction in the worship

of Eastern deities. During the last stages of the empire, strong cults developed around the Phrygian goddess Cybele, the Egyptian Isis, and the sun god Mithras.

The appearance and eventual triumph of Christianity is outside the scope of this account, but its emergence as the official religion of the empire played a final and decisive part in ending the Classical era. Pagan art, pagan literature, and pagan culture as a whole represented forces and ideals that Christianity strongly rejected, and the art of the early Christians is fundamentally different in its inspiration. Yet even the fathers of the early church, implacable opponents of paganism, could not fail to be moved by the end of so great a cultural tradition.

The memory of Rome's greatness lived on through the succeeding ages of turmoil and achievement and the Classical spirit survived, to be reborn triumphantly in the Renaissance.

SUMMARY

◆ **The Monarchy.** The vast extent of ancient Roman history—more than twelve hundred years—can be conveniently divided into three chief periods: the Monarchy (753–510 BCE), the Republic (509–31 BCE), and the Empire (31 BCE–476 CE). The city was founded in the mid-eighth century, around the time the Greeks were setting up colonies in southern Italy and Sicily. Rome's first inhabitants were Latins, an Italian people native to central Italy, after whom the Roman language is named. Traditional accounts of the city's origins claimed that its first rulers were a series of seven kings. The first four were Latin, but in 616 BCE, Rome fell under Etruscan control.

◆ **Rome Under the Etruscans.** The Etruscans had developed in the region of central Italy to the north of Rome, although their origins are uncertain; they may have migrated to Italy from western Asia. Etruscan art was strongly influenced by Greek and Orientalizing styles. Among the most striking works to survive are the tomb paintings at Tarquinia, one of the principal Etruscan cities, and the sculpture from the temple of Apollo at Veii. Although many Etruscan inscriptions can be deciphered, no Etruscan literature has been discovered. For the century during which they ruled Rome, the Etruscans expanded its trade contacts and introduced important technological innovations. In 510 BCE, the Romans drove out the last Etruscan king.

◆ **The Beginnings of the Roman Republic.** In 509 BCE the Roman Republic was declared. The political system of the new state evolved from the need to achieve a balance of political power between the two classes of citizens: the aristocratics (patricians) and the people (plebeians). There gradually developed two political institutions, the Senate and the assembly of the people, while plebeians eventually won the right to run for election to virtually all offices of state. The growth of internal political stability was accompanied by the spread of Roman power throughout Italy. Among those to fall under Roman domination were the Etruscans, their former rulers. Little in the way of art or literature has survived from this early period, and most of what was produced seems to have been inspired by Etruscan or, more generally, Greek models.

◆ **Roman Expansion in the Mediterranean.** In 264 BCE a series of wars (the Punic wars) began between Rome and her chief rival in the western Mediterranean, Carthage. By 201 BCE the Romans had proved victorious, and Roman colonies were established in Spain and North Africa. Throughout the following century Roman power spread eastward. In 146 BCE Greece was absorbed into the Roman Empire, and the Hellenistic kingdom of Pergamum was bequeathed to Rome by its last king, Attalus III, on his death in 133 BCE. The second century BCE also saw the beginnings of the development of an independent Roman culture, although Greek influence remained strong. The Roman poet Ennius composed his epic, the *Annals,* while Plautus and Terence wrote comedies based on Greek originals. Greek music became popular in Rome, and the two chief schools of Greek philosophy, Stoicism and Epicureanism, began to attract Roman adherents.

◆ **The Collapse of the Republic.** With such vast territorial expansion, strains began to appear in Roman political and social life. The growth of a middle class, the *equites,* disturbed the old equilibrium, and the last century of the Republic (133–31 BCE) was beset by continual crisis. A succession of powerful figures—Marius, Sulla, Pompey, Caesar—struggled to assume control of the state. The last of these proved victorious in 48 BCE, only to be assassinated four years later. Amid bitter fighting between Mark Antony, Caesar's lieutenant, and Octavius, the late dictator's nephew and heir, the Republic collapsed.

The political confusion of the Republic's last century was accompanied by important cultural developments. Among the major literary figures of the age were the Epicurean poet Lucretius, the lyric poet Catullus, and the orator and politician Cicero. Caesar combined his political and military career with the writing of accounts of his campaigns. In the visual arts realistic portrait sculpture became common, while the invention of concrete was to have enormous consequences, both for Roman building and for the history of all later architecture in the West. Sulla's great Sanctuary at Praeneste inaugurated the tradition of large-scale public building projects that became common during the empire.

◆ **The Augustan Age.** In 31 BCE Octavius defeated the combined forces of Antony and Cleopatra to emerge as sole ruler of the Roman world; in 27 BCE, under the name Augustus, he became its first emperor. The Augustan Age marked the high point of Roman art and literature, and many of its finest achievements were produced to celebrate the Augustan revolution. Virgil was commissioned to write a Roman national epic: The result was the *Aeneid.* Augustus was portrayed in numerous statues and portraits, including the *Augustus of Prima Porta,* and in the reliefs on the *Ara Pacis.* Important public works included the Pont du Gard near Nîmes, France.

◆ **Life, Art, and Literature in the Early Empire.** From the time of Augustus until 476 CE, the empire was ruled by a series of emperors who depended increasingly on an elaborate state bureaucracy. Augustus and his first four successors were from a single family, but with time emperors either seized power for themselves or were imposed by the army. The empire continued to expand until the reign of Hadrian (117–138 CE), who fixed its borders to achieve stability abroad. Some idea of the character of provincial daily life in the Empire can be gained from the excavations at Pompeii and the other cities around the Bay of Naples that were destroyed by an eruption of the volcano Vesuvius in 79 CE. Writers of the early empire include the historian Tacitus and the satirist Juvenal. Among the most impressive works of architecture of the period is the Pantheon, designed by Hadrian, which makes bold use of concrete.

◆ **The Roman Empire in Decline.** The third century was marked by continual struggles for imperial power. Only Emperor Diocletian (284–305 CE) managed to restore order by massive administrative and economic reform. After Diocletian's retirement to his palace at Split, one of his successors, Constantine (307–337 CE), transferred the imperial capital from Rome to the new city of Constantinople in 330 CE, and the western part of the empire began its final decline. During this last period, Roman art became less realistic as Classical forms and styles were abandoned in favor of simpler, more massive effects. Finally, Rome was shaken by barbarian assaults, and the last western emperor was forced to abdicate in 476 CE.

EXERCISES

1. What are the chief features of Etruscan culture and religion?
2. What light do these features cast on the problem of the Etruscans' origins?
3. "Roman art and culture are late and debased forms of Hellenistic art." Discuss this statement.
4. In what ways does the *Aeneid* fulfill its aim to provide the Romans with a national epic?
5. Compare the *Aeneid* in this respect to the Greek epics, the *Iliad* and *Odyssey*, discussed in Chapter 2.
6. Describe in detail Augustus's use of the visual arts as instruments of propaganda. Are there comparable examples of the arts used for political purposes in recent times?
7. What do the discoveries at Rome and Pompeii tell us about daily life in the Roman Empire? In what significant respects did it differ from life today?

 Visit the *Culture & Values* Companion website at **www.cengage.com/art/Cunningham/Cultureand Values7E** and the *Humanities Resource Center* for an array of primary source readings, key terms with pronunciations, flash cards, quizzes, and study materials designed especially to help you do well in this course.

CHAPTER 5

ANCIENT CIVILIZATIONS OF INDIA AND CHINA

Most lovers of Chinese poetry would agree that Li Po (discussed later in this chapter) is the leading Chinese poet of premodern times. He was famous in his day for his unique rapport with nature and his love of wine. Born in 701, he grew up in Szechuan province. After spending a few years as a hermit, he trained himself in the arts of the "wandering knight," protecting the weak and avenging injustices.

In 742 he was summoned to the emperor's court as a kind of official poet, but his wild lifestyle soon lost him the emperor's favor. He took to wandering, accompanied by a following of singing girls. For a while he became involved with a rival to the imperial throne and was exiled, but then reprieved. He was married four times, but, as a contemporary remarked, "none detained him for very long."

His addiction to wine was legendary, and celebrated in many of his poems, but he was also interested in alchemy and what he called "spiritual journeys." He impressed his admirers by his spontaneous genius and his personal appearance: they called him the "banished immortal." For all the ups and downs of his career, he was not given to bitterness or despair; on the whole his poetry is calm and even sunny. His search for spiritual freedom, and communion with nature (he produced poetic descriptions of most of China's famous mountains and rivers) were united with a deep sensitivity to the beauties of language. Today, the Chinese praise him for his "positive romanticism."

INDIAN CIVILIZATION

THE INDUS VALLEY CIVILIZATION

Three thousand years before the common era (BCE), in present-day Pakistan, a culture existed that had two large centers at Harappa and Mohenjodaro. What we know of these people can be told only by a reading of the archaeological evidence, and that evidence is only imperfectly understood. They possessed a written language based on picture signs, but that language has yet to be deciphered. At

◆ The poet Li Po seated on the branch of a tree. (© *The Art Archive/Gianni Dagli Orti*)

Mohenjodaro, scholars have uncovered a vast assembly hall, a large bath, and other public buildings all made from fired brick. Despite such urban centers, the Indus Valley dwellers were an agriculture-based society. It is believed that they were the first people to cultivate cotton.

From their **seal-stones** and other artworks recovered from excavations, they seem to have been intensely interested (possibly religious) in the figure of the bull, but no direct link between their bull cult and that of the Minoans—who had a similar cult—has been established. Although there is much evidence of a highly developed religious life (based mainly on stone and ceramic remains), there is no clear evidence as to what that reli-

gion entailed [**Fig. 5.2**]. Other archaeological evidence suggests that some centralization existed in their culture because they used standard weights and measures for trading purposes and had communal drainage systems as well as ways of distributing goods (mainly pottery).

Around 1700 BCE the Indus Valley culture, as this complex civilization is known, began to decline as the area was struck by a series of floods and through the exhaustion of the soil as well as the overuse of the woodlands. To these ecological disasters, apparent in the archaeological record, was added a new threat: a series of invasions from the Northwest by a people called the **Aryans**. The decline of the older Indus Valley culture

GENERAL EVENTS	ART & ARCHITECTURE	LITERATURE & PHILOSOPHY
	INDIA	

	GENERAL EVENTS	ART & ARCHITECTURE	LITERATURE & PHILOSOPHY
3000 BCE			
INDUS VALLEY CIVILIZATION	**3000–1700** Sites occupied at Harappa and Mohenjo-daro		Development of written language based on picture signs
		Stone and ceramic remains Public buildings of fired brick Communal drainage system	
1700	**1700–500** Aryan Invasion	Bronze work	First evidence of the Sanskrit language Vedic tradition evolves
1200	**c. 563–483 BCE** Life of Siddartha Gautama, who becomes known as the Buddha		**1000** The *Vedas* committed to writing
500	**326** Invasion of Alexander the Great		*Upanishads* develop
	261 Emperor Ashoka unifies India, making Buddhism the official state religion	Large scale sculpture and architecture begins to appear	*Mahabharata*, including the *Baghavad-Gita*, is written
BCE			
CE			
200	**320–500** Founding of the Gupta Empire Indian development of "Arabic" numerals	Temples of Khajuraho	Kalidasa, *Sakuntala;* Sudraka, *The Little Clay Cart*
400	Use of decimal and zero developed		
	480–500 CE Invasion of the White Huns		
600			
700			
CE 900			

was so complete that archaeologists have failed to find any significant artworks from the period of decline until the later emergence of Buddhist culture.

THE ARYANS

The Aryan people settled in the Indus Valley by around 1500 BCE, but who they were and where they came from is not at all clear. Some scholars point to the Russian steppes, but the picture of their migration into the subcontinent of India is not completely understood. The material evidence mapping the spread of the Aryan peoples is at best spotty. What we do know (mainly by reading back into their history from texts written at a later time) is that they spoke the language we call **Sanskrit**. That language is a branch of the Indo-European language groups, and the ancestor of Indo-Aryan and Romance languages such as Latin. A few examples might help to see how words evolved as Sanskrit words developed in Latin and then were borrowed as English words:

yoga (yoke for an animal; later: discipline)—*jugum* (Latin: yoke)—*yoke* (English)
Agni (God of fire)—*ignis* (Latin: fire)—*ignition* (English)

GENERAL EVENTS	ART & ARCHITECTURE	LITERATURE & PHILOSOPHY
	CHINA	

GENERAL EVENTS	ART & ARCHITECTURE	LITERATURE & PHILOSOPHY
1600–1100 Shang Dynasty System of writing based on picture signs evolves	Bronze works	
1100–221 Chou Dynasty	The Great Wall	*Five Classics* and the *Classic of Songs* circulate **701–762** Li Po, best-known Chinese poet **c. 570** Lao-Tzu **c. 551–479** Life of Confucius
403–221 Period of the Warring States		**c. 3rd century** *Tao te ching* written
221–210 Ch'in Dynasty. Shih Huang-ti ("First Emperor") conquers all rivals in China		
202 BCE–220 CE Han Dynasty. Kao-tsu, the first Han Emperor restores a degree of order after Shih Hung-ti's death	Prancing Horse	Buddhist writings, *Mahayana* and *Hinayana*, circulate
618–906 T'ang Dynasty. Beginning of China's Golden Age	Monumental shrines to Buddha reflect the influence of similar Indian works	

♦ **5.2** Torso of a man from Mohenjo-daro, Pakistan, third millennium BCE. We do not know enough about Indus Valley culture to be able to trace its artistic roots. Indus Valley carved seal-stones were found in graves at the Sumerian site of Ur, but the elegant lines and realistic anatomy of this statue suggest an independent artistic tradition.

Red stone, 3¾″ (9.5 cm) high. National Museum, New Delhi, India//
© *Borromeo/Art Resource, NY*

The Aryans brought with them a culture that made a class distinction between the nobility and the commonality (common people). Over a long period, this distinction developed into a **caste system**, which divided all of society into the castes of the priesthood, the warriors, the laborers, and the serfs. The development of the caste system in India underwent many changes over the millennia, so that today the caste system recognizes the priests, warriors and rulers, merchants, and laborers with a subgroup simply known as **outcasts** (the unclean ones). Within the large groupings there are many subcastes. The caste system was one of the shaping social forces in India, reinforced by many laws concerning marriage, table exclusion (who could eat with whom), laws of ritual purity, and so on.

Aryan culture mixed agricultural and pastoral culture with cattle, serving as a medium of trade, functioning almost like a currency. The horse was also known, but served mainly as an instrument of the warrior caste where the use of the chariot was common. Horses were so important for the warriors that some of the earliest hymns speak of rare but highly important horse rituals including horse sacrifices. Settled agriculture was common enough, but it was not considered as prestigious as cattle raising. The Aryan people also possessed high technical skills, with evidence indicating that they had a keen sense of technology for bronze work. The early Aryans did not found great city centers; they were more tribal in their structure but aggressive in their growth. Over the centuries they would migrate from their strongholds in the Northwest of the subcontinent into the southern reaches of India. The great epic poems of India like the Ramayana and the Mahabharata, written centuries after the events they purport to describe, reflect the warring period when the Aryans subdued the Indus Valley dwellers. These epics—with their complex story lines of gods, heroes, and battles—are central to Indian culture; their dramatization on Indian television has proved to be one of the most popular shows among all classes of people in India.

Most characteristic of Aryan culture was its elaborate religious system that placed enormous emphasis on ritual sacrifice to the pantheon of gods. The fact that the priests had the highest place in the caste system was a result of their responsibility in carrying out the religious ceremonies in honor of the gods. Highly complex in their detail, the rituals had to be carried out exactly according to tradition in order for the ceremonies to attain their goal (for example, the fertility of the soil, the arrival of the rains, and so on). These ceremonies and their companions—hymns and gestures—were passed from one generation of hereditary priests to the next in a fixed oral form. It was only around the year 1000 BCE that these texts were committed to writing in a slow compilation, which is now known as the *Vedas*, with the best known of these compilations called the *Rig Veda*. The *Vedas* represent the oldest strain of Indian religious literature and are still chanted by Hindus at all important moments in Indian religious life: at birth, naming ceremonies, rites of passage to adulthood, in sickness, and at death. They also form the core text of Hindu temple worship. The *Vedas*, in fact, represent one of the oldest bodies of religious writings known to humanity.

Aryan Philosophy Shortly after the composition of the *Rig Veda*, a new kind of literature came into being. The sages of India were interested in the large questions of what we would call philosophical issues, for example: What caused the cosmos to be? How did human beings arise? Why is human life short? Why do people suffer? What is the deep meaning behind the priestly rituals and sacrifices? The responses to these and similar questions are treated in a series of classical Indian texts known as the *Upanishads* (meaning a "session," that is, from a learned person). We possess more than one hundred upanishadic texts, which vary in length and sophistication. Some deal with the allegorical meaning of ritual, whereas others are more philosophical in nature.

The fundamental worldview of the *Upanishads* may be stated briefly. The ultimate reality is an impersonal reality called **Brahman**. Everything else is a manifestation of this underlying reality. Each individual person has within the self Brahman, which, in a person, is called **Atman**. The secret of life is to come to the knowledge that Brahman is the ultimate reality (that is, one's inner self is part of this fundamental reality) and everything else is, in a certain fashion, permeable and "unreal." This fundamental assertion is summed up in a classical Sanskrit expression *Tat tvam asi*: "you (the individual) are that (the eternal essence or Brahman)."

Indian religion, later called the *Hindu* religion (derived from an Arabic word meaning "those who live in the Indus Valley"), combined, then, a highly ritualized worship of the gods of the pantheon (many believe these gods are merely faces or names for the ultimate reality) with a strong speculative tradition that tries to grasp the ultimate meaning of the cosmos and those who live in it. Indian religion, in short, is both a religion of the priest and the temple as well as the religion of solitary meditation and study. Most Indian homes to this day have a small altar for a god or goddess in order for the family to show respect and worship (called **puja**) in the home. The fundamental aim of Indian religion, however, is to find the path that leads one to the correct knowledge of ultimate reality, which, when known, leads one to be liberated from the illusory world of empirical reality and be absorbed into the one true reality, Brahman.

Broadly speaking, three paths have been proposed for attaining such knowledge:

1. The path or discipline (that is, yoga) of asceticism (fasting, nonpossession, bodily discipline, and so on) by which one lives so that the material world becomes accidental and that person becomes enlightened. This is the hardest path of all, which, if at all undertaken, usually comes after one has had a normal life as a householder.
2. The path or discipline of **karma**, in which one does one's duty according to one's caste obligations (for example, priests should sacrifice; warriors fight) and not out of greed or ambition—motives that cloud the mind.
3. The path of devotion, in which all people refer all of their deeds as an act of devotion (**bhakti**) to the gods or to the one god to whom a person has a special devotion. By doing everything out of devotion, one does not fall into the trap of greed or self-centeredness.

BUDDHA

Into this highly complex world of the Indian subcontinent, the person who came to be called *Buddha* (meaning "the enlightened one"; it is a title, not a personal name) was born. Because biographies of Buddha were written several centuries after his death, his story is somewhat clouded by myths. The main lines, however, seem to be reasonably clear. His given name was Siddhartha and his family name was Gautama. He was born around 563 BCE into the family of a king who belonged to the warrior caste in the foothills of the Himalayas in what is present day Nepal. Raised in luxury, he married young and fathered a son. When he was not yet thirty, he traveled outside his palatial quarters and saw enough suffering (beggars, a corpse, a sick person, and a wandering, begging ascetic) to wonder about the inescapability of suffering and death. Leaving his family, he took up a wandering life as an ascetic practitioner of meditation and self-denial. According to Buddhist tradition, he visited learned men, undertook meditation, and practiced fasting and self-deprivation. At age thirty-five, frustrated by his lack of insight, he decided to sit under the shade of a tree until he intuited the truth about existence. At the climax of this long vigil, he received the illumination that caused him to be called the Enlightened One (Buddha). He left his spot and went to the Deer Park at Sarnath near what is present-day Benares (Varanasi) to teach his new doctrine. There he preached his famous first sermon outlining the "Middle Way" between extreme asceticism and self-indulgence. Buddha's doctrine has been called the Fourfold Noble Path:

1. Existence itself is suffering.
2. Suffering comes from craving and attachment.
3. There exists a cessation of suffering, which is called **nirvana**.
4. There is a path to nirvana, which is eightfold.

The eightfold path can be summarized as a "way of life," which derives from the following: right views, right resolve, right speech, right action, right livelihood, right effort, right mindfulness, and right concentration. When these eight basic dispositions are lived correctly, one then might escape the never-ending cycle of rebirth and find nirvana. The specific character of this eightfold disposition would emphasize ethical living; awareness of who one is and what one does; nonviolence (**ahimsa**); temperance in dealing with material realities; erasure of impulses to greed, acquisition, sensual living; and so on. This kind of life leads a person to understand the passing reality in which people are enmeshed and thus find liberation.

Like its parent religion, Buddhism preaches liberation through knowledge. The typical figures that represent Buddha makes the point forcefully: Buddha sits in a meditative position with eyes half closed and a half smile on his face because he has discovered within himself the ultimate truth, which has enlightened him. Buddha does not look up to the heavens to a god or kneel in worship. Truth comes from within.

THE EMPEROR ASHOKA

When Buddha died in 483 BCE, his religious tradition was just one of many that circulated within

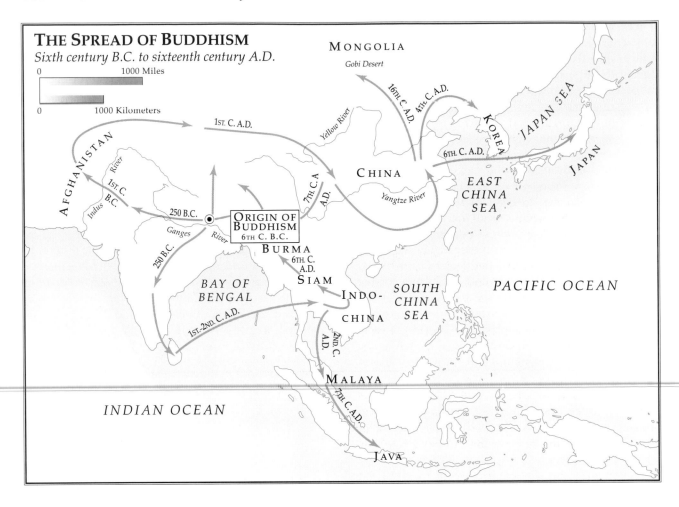

THE SPREAD OF BUDDHISM
Sixth century B.C. to sixteenth century A.D.

VOICES OF THEIR TIMES

War and Religion in the Age of Ashoka

Ashoka's intrinsic tolerance emerges in this extract from his Rock Edict XII:

> His Sacred and Gracious Majesty does reverence to men of all sects, whether ascetics or householders, by gifts and various forms of reverence. His Sacred Majesty, however, cares not so much for gifts or external reverence as that there should be a growth of the essence of matter in all sects. The root of this is restraint of speech; to wit, a man must not do reverence to his own sect by disparaging that of another man without reason. Concord, therefore, is meritorious; to wit, hearkening, and hearkening willingly to the law of piety as accepted by other people. For it is the desire of his Sacred Majesty that adherents of all sects should hear much teaching and hold sound doctrine.

In his Rock Edict XIII, the king describes his attitude to war:

> This pious edict has been written in order that my sons and grandsons, who may be, should not regard it as their duty to conquer a new conquest. If, perchance, they become engaged in a new conquest by arms, they should take pleasure in patience and gentleness, and regard the only true conquest the conquest won by piety. That avails for both this world and the next.

India, even though it had its own growth and the accumulation of a religious tradition based on Buddha's teaching. That situation was to change through the efforts of perhaps the greatest emperor of ancient India: Ashoka. He was a superb and ruthless ruler who unified all of India (including such faraway places as Afghanistan and Baluchistan) around 261 BCE. However, Ashoka was appalled by the suffering and bloodshed he had caused in this enterprise. Out of remorse, he converted from traditional Brahmanism to Buddhism and, out of his Buddhist conviction, began to preach the doctrine of nonviolence in his empire. Although tolerant of all religious traditions, he established Buddhism as the religion of the state. He mitigated the harsh laws of the empire, regulated the slaughter of animals, founded and sustained Buddhist monasteries (called **sanghas**), and erected many **stupas**—those characteristic towers found in Buddhists lands. The stupas may serve as reliquaries for Buddha or as a repository of Buddhist texts, but symbolically they represent the enlightenment of the Buddha. In addition, Ashoka erected pillars and towers with his decrees carved on them, some of which exist to this day. Finally, Ashoka is credited with calling a vast Buddhist convocation to fix the canon of sacred books for Buddhism (that is, the authoritative list of writings that are the measure or canon of Buddhist belief and practice).

Perhaps the most important thing that Ashoka did was to send Buddhist monks as missionaries to all parts of India and to other countries to share Buddhist wisdom. There is evidence that his missionaries went as far as Syria, Egypt, and Greece. One of his most important missions was sending a blood relative (perhaps a son or a brother) to Ceylon (present-day Sri Lanka), where the Buddhist doctrine took root and then spread to other parts of Southeast Asia (see map, "The Spread of Buddhism"). Although Buddhism—like all major religions of the world—has a variety of forms and different cultural expressions, at its core is the code enshrined in the Buddha's Four Noble Truths. It is one of the small ironies of history that Ashoka, the emperor of all of India, spread Buddhism all over the East, while in his native India, Buddhism would shrink in time to a small minority, which is the situation at present.

HINDU AND BUDDHIST ART

There is little evidence for artistic production in the period following the disappearance of the Indus Valley people. Only with the reign of Ashoka does a tradition of large-scale sculpture and architecture begin

◆ **5.3** Lion capital, from a column erected by King Ashoka, 242–232 BCE. One of a series of columns set up during Ashoka's reign, this capital comes from Sarnath, where Buddha preached his first important sermon. The wheel on the base represents the Wheel of the Law, and the four small animals (one is visible here) symbolize the four corners of the earth. The lions crowning the column originally bore a wheel on their backs.

7′ (2.1 m) high. © Archaeological Museum, Sarnath, India//Dinodia/The Bridgeman Art Library

to appear, probably influenced by developments to the west, in Persia. Thus, the earliest monumental Indian sculpture, a column crowned with lions [**Fig. 5.3**], which comes from one of his palaces, resembles similar column decorations found at Persepolis, the capital of Persia.

Both Hindu and Buddhist art are overwhelmingly religious in spirit. The great statues and sculptural reliefs that decorate the temples are narrative, telling the stories of the Hindu deities and the life of Buddha to their worshipers. The difference between the two styles of art reflects the differing characteristics of the two faiths. Much of Hindu art is openly erotic, reflecting the belief of pious Hindus that sexual union

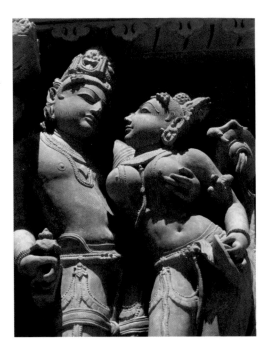

◆ **5.4** Detail from sculptured frieze, Parsvanath Temple, Khajuraho, northern India. The firm, smooth flesh and the openly erotic subject illustrate the close link for Hindu culture between amorous and religious ecstasy. These and similar sculptures were always placed on the outside walls of the temples. (*© Adam Woolfitt/CORBIS*)

◆ **5.6** *Krishna and Radha on a Canopy*. In this scene from the *Mahabharata*, Krishna, who is regarded by the followers of Vishnu as another incarnation of the god, is easily recognizable by the blue color of his skin.

Gouache on paper. Musée des Arts Asiatiques-Guimet, Paris, France//
© Réunion des Musées Nationaux/Art Resource, NY

◆ **5.5** Wooden figures representing the first four *avatars* (incarnations) of the god Vishnu: as the fish Matsya, the tortoise Kuru, the boar Varaha, and the lion Narasima. Vishnu represented the preserving and protecting aspect of the divine. (*© Horniman Museum, London/The Bridgeman Art Library*)

Mahabharata and other great Hindu epics combined the elements of eroticism and naturalism. Figure 5.6 shows Krishna, the hero of the *Mahabharata*'s central section, the *Baghavad-Gita*, in a pleasant setting painted in great detail [**Fig. 5.6**].

By contrast, Buddhist art emphasizes the spiritual, even austere nature of Buddhist doctrines. Buddha and his many saints, the **Bodhisattvas**, are shown as calm, often transcendent images, inviting prayer and meditation [**Fig. 5.7**]. Sometimes the Buddhist command to renounce all worldly pleasures becomes even more powerfully expressed, as in the image of the Fasting Buddha [**Fig. 5.8**].

THE GUPTA EMPIRE AND ITS AFTERMATH

In the years following the death of Ashoka, his empire began to fall apart, and a series of invaders from the north established small kingdoms in the Indus and Ganges valleys. These northerners never penetrated the southern regions, where numbers of small independent states flourished economically by trading with Southeast Asia and, to the west, with the expanding commercial power of the Roman Empire.

represents union with their gods [**Fig. 5.4**]. Other works illustrate the Hindu sense of the unity of all forms of life. Thus, Vishnu—the supreme Hindu spirit—appears in a series of **avatars**, or incarnations, of various animals and humans [**Fig. 5.5**]. Over time, scenes from the

◆ **5.7** Surrounded by devotees, Buddha preaches in a city, 2nd-3rd century CE. The style of the work is known as Gandharan, from the region in northwest India where Greek ideas began to circulate (see Chapter 3). The drapery and hand positions are reminiscent of Greco-Roman art.

Slate, 9″ high x 22″ long (22.8 x 55.9 cm). Museum fuer Asiatisches Kunst, Berlin, Germany//© Bildarchiv Preussischer Kulturbesitz/Art Resource, NY

Only in 320 CE did Chandra Gupta I lay the foundations of a new large-scale kingdom, known as the Gupta Empire, which reached its zenith under his grandson, Chandra Gupta II (ruled c. 380–c. 415 CE). Known as "The Sun of Power," Chandra Gupta's reign was famous for its cultural achievements, economic stability, and religious tolerance. As a Buddhist monk noted, "The people vie with each other in the practice of benevolence and righteousness." Despite this general tolerance, however, the Gupta period saw the rapid decline of Buddhism in India and a return to the traditions of Hinduism.

GUPTA LITERATURE AND SCIENCE

Literary skills assumed vast importance at the Gupta court, where poets competed with one another to win fame. The language they used was ancient Sanskrit, that of the old Hindu *Vedas*, which served as the literary language of the period; it was no longer spoken by the general population. The most famous of all Indian Classical writers was Kalidasa (active c. 400), who wrote plays, epics, and lyric poetry. His best-known work was the play *Sakuntala*, which describes the happy marriage of the beautiful Sakuntala to King Dusyanta, the marriage's collapse as a result of a curse pronounced by an

◆ **5.8** *The Fasting Buddha*, 2nd-3rd century CE. The powerful realism used to depict Buddha's emaciated body is also Gandharan in inspiration. The austerity and renunciation contrast strongly with Hindu images of the joys of the flesh.

From Sikri, Pakistan. Stone, 2′9″ (83.8 cm) high. Lahore Museum, Lahore, Pakistan//© Scala/ Art Resource, NY

irascible holy man, and the couple's eventual triumphant reunion. By contrast to the Classical dramas of the Greek tradition, with their analysis of profound moral dilemmas, Kalidasa's play has the spirit of a fairytale with a happy ending. The work of another author of the same period, Sudraka, is more realistic. Among the characters in his play *The Little Clay Cart* are a nobleman, a penniless Brahmin, a prostitute, and a thief, who at one point offers a vivid description of his technique of housebreaking.

Under the Guptas, many important scientific discoveries were made possible by the foundation of large universities. The most important, at Nalanda, had some five thousand students who came from various parts of Asia. Among the subjects taught were mechanics, medicine, and mathematics. In this latter field, Indian scholars continued to make important advances. The system of so-called Arabic numerals, which only became widespread in Western Europe in the Renaissance (fifteenth and sixteenth centuries), had first been invented in India in the late third century BCE. By the time of the Gupta Empire, Indian mathematicians were using a form of decimal, and the concept of the zero may have been first employed at this time. Among their work in algebra were quadratic equations and the use of the square root of two.

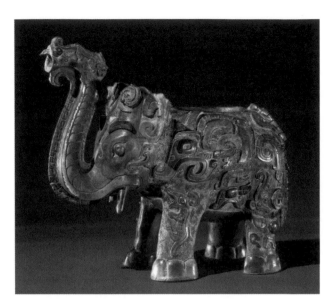

◆ **5.9** Ceremonial container for wine, or *Zun*, in the form of an elephant, c. 1300–1030 BCE. The vessel is covered with decorative motifs that are based on animal forms: birds, snakes, and fish among others. This form of decoration is frequently found on early Chinese bronze vessels.

Bronze. Hunan Provincial Museum, Changsha, China//© The Art Archive/ Laurie Platt Winfrey

THE COLLAPSE OF GUPTA RULE

The decline of the Gupta Empire, which began with the death of Chandra Gupta II, became headlong with a series of invasions around 480–500 CE by the White Huns, a people related to the Huns and other Central Asian tribes. Around the same time, other related tribes moved westward from Central Asia and sacked Rome in 476 CE, thereby effectively ending the Roman Empire. The White Huns never managed to establish a secure power base in India, however, and over the following centuries innumerable local princely states fought both among themselves and against foreign invaders. In part, the difficulty in constructing a central government and a lasting peace was caused by the powerful Hindu priestly class, who were unwilling to surrender conflicting religious interests to an overall secular, political settlement. When a new united Indian Empire did begin to develop in the fifteenth and sixteenth centuries, its rulers were Muslim, not Hindu.

THE ORIGINS OF CIVILIZATION IN CHINA

Although some of the earliest traces in history of human habitation settlements come from Northern China,

urban life seems to have developed in China somewhat later than in Mesopotamia or Egypt. The earliest period for which we have secure evidence is that of the Shang Dynasty (c. 1600–1100 BCE) (see map, "Ancient China"). Under Shang rulers, the Chinese began to work bronze, and many magnificent bronze sacrificial vessels—in a wide variety of shapes—demonstrate their creators' technical skill and artistic imagination [**Fig. 5.9**]. Trade and commerce began to develop and, at the same time, the Chinese devised a system of writing, based—like the Egyptian hieroglyphs—on picture signs representing sounds or ideas.

THE CHOU DYNASTY

Around 1100 BCE, a new dynasty replaced the Shang, known as the Chou Dynasty (c. 1100–c. 221 BCE). The Chou rulers did not provide strong central government, but served as the coordinators of a series of separate kingdoms, each with its own local lord. The relationship of these local rulers with the Chou emperors was often unstable. In times of trouble they could supply the Chou with military aid, but they frequently feuded with both the central authority and each other. Over time, Chou influence began to diminish, and the last period of their dynasty is known as the Period of the Warring States (403–221 BCE). During these centuries

◆ **5.10** Portrait of Confucius, c. 3rd century BCE. This image of Confucius is stylized rather than realistic. The wise old sage with a long beard and hands peacefully folded symbolizes the nature of Confucian teaching. There is no evidence of realistic portraiture from this period. (© *Mary Evans Picture Library/Alamy*)

of increasing crisis, the foundations of Chinese thought and culture were laid.

CONFUCIANISM AND TAOISM

Confucius (c. 551–479 BCE) and Lao-tzu (active c. 570 BCE) founded the two chief schools of Chinese philosophy. Born in humble circumstances in central China at a time when local wars were raging, Confucius's chief aim was to restore the peace of earlier times by encouraging the wise and virtuous to enter government service. A state run by a wise ruling class, he believed, would produce similar characteristics in its people. To achieve this he traveled throughout China in search of pupils [**Fig. 5.10**].

According to the central dogma of Confucianism, the morally superior person should possess five inner virtues and acquire another two external ones. The five with which each virtuous person is born are righteousness, inner integrity, love of humanity, altruism, and loyalty. Those with these natural gifts should also acquire culture (education) and a sense of decorum, or ritual. If individuals with these qualities served their rulers in government, they would be loyal and unconcerned with material rewards, yet fearlessly critical of their masters.

Traditional religion played no part in Confucius's teachings. He refused to speculate about the gods or the possibility of life after death; he is said to have commented, "Not yet understanding life, how can we understand death?" Confucius was a revolutionary figure in that he defended the rights of the people and believed that the state existed for the benefit of the people, rather than the reverse. At the same time, however, he strongly endorsed strict authority and discipline, both within the state and the individual family—devotion to parents, worship of ancestors, respect for elders, and loyalty to rulers were all crucial to the Confucian system. In the centuries following his death, many totalitarian regimes in China abused the innate conservatism of Confucius's teaching, using it to justify their assaults on the freedom of individuals.

If the central principle of Confucianism is the possibility of creating a new, virtuous social order, Taoism emphasized the limitations of human perceptions and encouraged withdrawal and passivity. Its central concept is that of "the Way" (**tao**). According to this principle, one should follow one's own nature, not distinguishing between good and bad, but accepting both as part of the Way. The traditional founder of this school of philosophy, Lao-tzu, an obscure, even legendary figure, is said to have lived around the time of Confucius. Many modern scholars, however, believe that the book that sets out Lao-tzu's teachings, *The Classic of the Way and Its Power (Tao te ching)*, was written two or more centuries after the death of Confucius, at some point in the third century BCE.

The followers of Taoism often expressed their ideas in obscure and frequently contradictory language. Their overriding concept is perhaps best illustrated by one of the central images of Taoist art: water. As it flows, water gives way to the rocks in its path, yet over time "the soft yield of water cleaves the obstinate stone." Humans should, in the same way, avoid participating in society or culture or seeking actively to change them. Far from sharing Confucius's mission to reform the world, the Taoists preached passivity and resignation. Worst of all was war, for "every victory celebration is a funeral rite."

Both Confucianism and Taoism can be seen as reactions—albeit opposing ones—to the increasingly chaotic struggles of the later Chou period. They were to remain powerful sources of inspiration over the succeeding centuries, and the tension between them played a large part in the evolution of Chinese civilization.

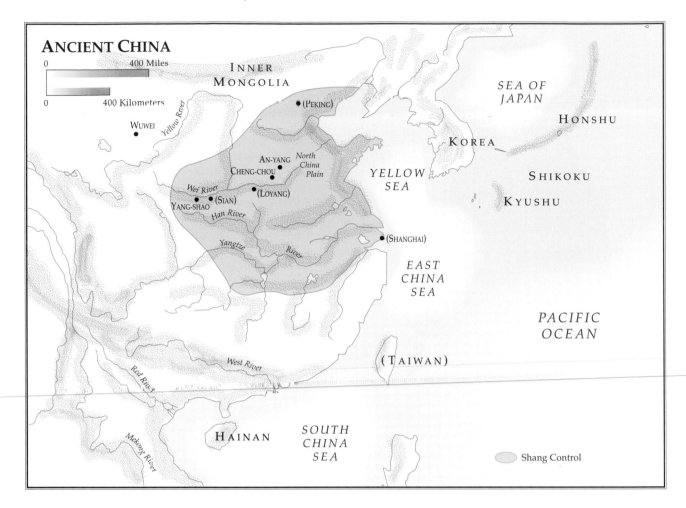

ANCIENT CHINA

THE UNIFICATION OF CHINA: THE CH'IN, HAN, AND T'ANG DYNASTIES

The Ch'in Dynasty

In the struggle for power in the last years of the Chou period, one state emerged victorious. In 221 BCE the king of the state of Ch'in succeeded in conquering all of his rivals and ruling them by means of a centralized government, thereby establishing the Ch'in Dynasty. He took the name of Shih Huang-ti ("First Emperor") and was remembered by later generations for the brutality of his conquests as much as for the brilliant organizational skill with which he organized his new empire.

He ordered the building of a magnificent capital city, Hsien-yang (near modern Sian), and instructed the leading noble families from the former independent kingdoms to move there, where they would be under his direct control, and thus unable to lead revolts. No private citizen was allowed to possess weapons, and it was left to the imperial army to maintain order. The emperor divided his territory into thirty-six provinces, imposed a single writing system, and unified weights and measures throughout them. In order to check criti-

cism, he ordered the destruction of all philosophical writings, the so-called Burning of the Books—including, of course, the works of Confucius—an action that his successors bitterly condemned.

To defend his empire from outside invaders, Shih Huang-ti connected a series of preexisting defensive walls to make the Great Wall, some fourteen hundred miles long (about 2,200 km) [**Fig. 5.11**]. Peasants and prisoners of war were forced into construction gangs. In the extreme climates of north and south, it was said that each single stone cost the life of one of the workers. The Great Wall has remained continuously visible to this day; it is one of the few human constructions on earth that can be seen from the moon. The emperor's other great building project, the massive tomb he designed for himself, barely survived his death and was only rediscovered in 1974. Ever since, archaeologists have been exploring its riches [**Fig. 5.12**].

Shih Huang-ti believed that he was creating an empire to last forever, but his ruthless methods ensured that his rule barely survived his death. One contemporary described him as "a monster who had the heart of a tiger and a wolf. He killed men as though he thought he could never finish, he punished men as though he were afraid he would never get round to them all." When Shih Huang-ti died in 210 BCE, the empire plunged into chaos as nobles and peasants alike ran riot.

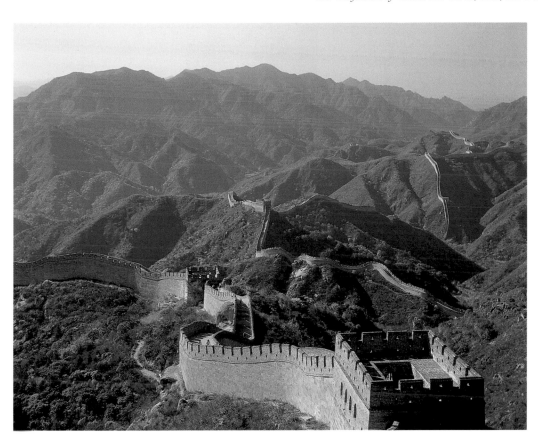

◆ **5.11** The Great Wall of China. Ch'in Dynasty. Wide enough for horsemen to ride along it, the wall has been extended, repaired, and rebuilt many times since its first construction in the late 3rd century BCE.

Roughly 4000 miles (c. 6400 km) long from Shanhaiguan in the east to Lop Nur in the west; averaging c. 16–20′ (5–6 m) wide, 16–26′ (5–8 m) high, plus c. 13′ (4 m) at the watchtowers.
© *Steve Vidler/SuperStock*

THE HAN DYNASTY

By 202 BCE a new dynasty had established itself—the Han Dynasty—which was to rule China for the next four centuries. The first Han emperor, Kao-tsu (256–195 BCE), returned a degree of power to the local rulers but maintained the Ch'in system of provinces, with governors appointed by the central authority. In order to strengthen the imperial administration, Kao-tsu and his successors created an elaborate central bureaucracy. To reinforce their authority, the early Han emperors lifted the ban on philosophical works and encouraged scholars to reconstruct the writings of Confucius and others either from the few surviving texts or from memory. With the emperor's encouragement, many of

◆ **5.12** The Army of Shih Huang-ti (First Emperor) in pits next to his burial mound. Ch'in dynasty, c. 210 BCE. There are more than 8000 life-size clay warriors and horses, as well as bronze chariots and horses in the excavation. The parts of the bodies (arms, torsos, legs) were made from a limited number of molds, but they were put together in many different combinations, with the result that no two figures are identical. The Emperor's burial chamber has been located but remains unexcavated: Chinese archaeologists do not want to disturb it until they have developed more sophisticated archaeological techniques.

Painted terracotta, average figure 5′10″ high. Xian, Shaanxi Province, China//
© *Gavin Hellier/Getty Images*

these reconstructions emphasized the need for loyalty to the emperor and a central bureaucracy, and omitted Confucius's emphasis on constructive criticism by virtuous observers.

THE T'ANG DYNASTY

By the second century CE, the central government gradually lost its control over the provinces. The great aristocratic families began to take control, as successive emperors became paralyzed by internal feuding and plotting. In the ensuing civil war, the last Han emperor finally abdicated in 220 CE, only to plunge China into another extended period of confusion. Finally, in the early seventh century, the T'ang Dynasty (618–906 CE) managed to reunite China. The political and economic stability they created made possible a period of cultural achievement known as China's Golden Age.

THE ARTS IN CLASSICAL CHINA

With the notable exception of the period of Ch'in rule, literature played an important part in Chinese culture. As early as the Chou period, standard texts, known as the *Five Classics*, circulated widely—Confucius may have been partly responsible for editing them. They included history, political documents such as speeches, and descriptions of ceremonies. The *Classic of Songs* contained more than three hundred poems dealing with private life (love, the family) and public affairs. Because the Chinese language uses pitch and stress (inflections; the meanings of words and/or phrases change according to the way they are pronounced), poetry became especially popular, and any educated Chinese person was expected to memorize and recite Classical verse.

Later generations drew inspiration from these Classical texts, developing their themes and expressing new ideas based on familiar concepts. The introduction of Buddhism into China during the Han Dynasty provided a new subject for philosophical writing; during the years of chaos following the fall of the Han rulers, Buddhist texts provided consolation for the suffering by offering eventual release from pain. The two main strains of Buddhism were **Mahayana**, the "Great Vehicle," and **Hinayana**, the "Lesser Vehicle." The first of these was less ascetic and more worldly than the second, and thus appealed more to those influenced by Confucianism. It also met with more favor in the eyes of the ruling class, although, when the Buddhist monasteries began to grow in wealth and influence, the central authorities started to limit the number of monasteries permitted and to control the ordination of monks and priests. For this reason, Buddhist writings

◆ **5.13** Pendant in the form of a dragon. Late Chou (Warring States) period (403–221 BCE), China. Jade, an extremely hard stone, was commonly used for objects to be buried with the dead. The perforated dragon, seen here in a characteristic spiral pose, was doubly symbolic. The ancient Chinese believed that dragons flew between earth and sky, bringing rain. They thus represented fertility, and at the same time, the power of Chinese rulers to influence the weather.

Green jade, 5″ x 2½″ high (18.5 x 9 cm). Musée des Arts Asiatiques-Guimet, Paris, France//© Réunion des Musées Nationaux/Art Resource, NY.

never acquired the status that religious texts have in the Christian world.

During the T'ang Dynasty, a new literary form developed: the short story. Unlike the works inspired by Classical models, these tales often provide a vivid picture of contemporary life. The best known of all Chinese poets, Li Po (701–762 CE), lived in the early years of T'ang rule. Appointed court poet in 742, after a couple of years his unruly temperament and wild behavior (many of his poems describe his addiction to wine) drove him to a life of wandering. Inspired by Taoism, Li Po preferred simple language and ignored the rules of the Classical style. Impressing his contemporaries as much by his charisma and personal appearance as by his writings, he could produce poems of all kinds and lengths, and his unconventional lifestyle provided him with unlimited subject matter. Many of his best-loved poems describe scenes from nature, often involving rivers or waterfalls—images central to Taoist thought.

The visual arts continued to use traditional styles while introducing new ones. A jade pendant from the end of the Chou Dynasty [**Fig. 5.13**] depicting a dragon is reminiscent of the Shang bronzes of centuries earlier, whereas a bronze horse from a little later shows much greater realism [**Fig. 5.14**]. Other works offer a more direct impression of daily life, whether in the form of a stone carving illustrating a peasant plowing [**Fig. 5.15**] or a painting of T'ang ladies at a feast [**Fig. 5.16**]. With the coming of Buddhism, Chinese devotees began to construct shrines and decorate them with monumental carvings. Many of these show the influence of similar

◆ **5.14** *Prancing Horse*, Han Dynasty, 2nd century CE. The only horses native to China were small and slow animals. The Han emperors, learning that the peoples of Central Asia used much faster animals as warhorses, sent a series of missions to try to import Central Asian horses into China. So great was the delight that the Chinese took in their new warhorses, one of which is shown here with one leg resting on a swallow, that they called them "heavenly" horses.

From Wu-Wai, Kansu, China. Bronze, 17'8¾" x 13'7" high (45 x 34 cm). Gansu Provincial Museum, Lanzhou, People's Republic of China//© Lauros-Giraudon, Paris/SuperStock

◆ **5.15** Scene of a man with an ox-drawn plow, Han Dynasty, 200 BCE–200 CE.

Brick tomb relief, Szechuan, China//© Werner Forman Archive/Topham/The Image Works

◆ **5.16** *A Palace Concert,* 10th century. The T'ang Dynasty is often known as the Golden Age of Chinese figure painting. This typical example, show-ing elegant ladies of the Tang imperial court enjoying a feast and music, has no background setting but convincingly places the figures in space. The forms of the bodies are visible beneath the simple, dignified lines of the drapery, and the faces portray the individual feelings of these court ladies with considerable subtlety. Note the dog, a house-hold pet, beneath the table.

Hanging scroll, ink and colors on silk, 19.2" x 27.4" (48.7 x 69.5 cm). National Palace Museum, Taipei, Taiwan//© Werner Forman/Art Resource, NY

◆ **5.17** Fengxian Temple, Longmen Grottoes, Luoyang, China. The Buddhist sculptures were begun in the sixth century CE, and greatly extended around 690, when Luoyang became the new T'ang capital. The central figure of the Vairocana Buddha (the Buddha of Illumination) is 56′3″ (17.4 m) high; to either side stand monks, Bodhisattvas, and guardian figures. The simplicity of the folds of Buddha's robe adds to the grandeur of the figure.

Limestone grotto, c. 136′ long (41 m), 118′ deep (36 m). Henan Province, China//© Liu Xiaoyang/Alamy

relief sculptures in India, particularly in the treatment of drapery [**Fig. 5.17**].

In all the art of the Classical period, great emphasis went into craftsmanship. From the smallest carved jade or ivory to the huge stone statues, precision and clarity of design were the mark of the supreme artist. One of the effects of this emphasis on beauty of line was that writing became an art; examples of fine handwriting—calligraphy—were as prized as a work made of precious material [**Fig. 5.18**].

SUMMARY

◆ **The Indus Valley People.** The earliest culture to develop in the subcontinent of India appeared in the Indus Valley around 3000 BCE. Its people supported themselves by farming, growing grain and rice, and cotton. The two main centers were Harappa and Mohenjo-daro, which became large urban settlements with imposing public buildings and elaborate drainage systems. They mass-produced pottery and

invented a hieroglyphic script (still undeciphered), which they carved on seal-stones. Around 1700 BCE, their civilization went into decline, in part as the result of the arrival of a new people, the Aryans.

◆ **The Aryans.** The founders of the culture we think of as Indian were the Aryans, a people whose origin is uncertain and who brought to India two of its most vital aspects: religion (Hinduism) and language (Sanskrit). The Hindu religion, as it developed, acquired a mass of deities and legends, but its basis remained, and remains to this day, the sacred texts of the Vedas, which were first written down around 1000 BCE. Over time, Hinduism evolved into a complex philosophical vision of life, which aims to distinguish between the illusions of everyday life and the ultimate reality. One way to achieve this reality is by yoga, a renunciation of worldly pleasures. Another is by fulfilling the requirements of one's caste, or destiny, and living according to one's duty (karma). Aryan society was divided into castes (social classes), of which the priestly caste was the highest.

◆ **Buddha.** At the end of the sixth century BCE, the figure known to posterity as Buddha inspired a new

◆ **5.18** A Confucian text, *The Eulogy of Ni Kuan*, written by the early T'ang minister Chu Suilang. The writing of each character separately, rather than continuously, is known as the "Official Style." A contemporary of the minister described his writing as having "the grace and delicacy of a beautiful woman."

National Palace Museum, Taipei, Taiwan//© Werner Forman/Art Resource, NY

approach to life that emphasized the more austere aspects of Hinduism. Buddhism claimed that human suffering came from indulgence in superficial pleasures. Whereas Hinduism taught that life consisted of an endless series of deaths and reincarnations, according to the Buddha this cycle could be broken by renouncing all worldly ambitions and satisfactions. In this way it was possible to achieve nirvana, the ultimate freedom and release from the ego. The truth came not from external ritual or ceremony, but as a result of personal internal meditation. Thus, while Hinduism encouraged its followers to enjoy the pleasures of life permitted to them by their caste, Buddhism viewed life pessimistically and emphasized the rejection of the world in favor of spiritual redemption.

◆ **King Ashoka.** The spread of Buddhism owed much to Ashoka, the third-century BCE Indian ruler, who abandoned his early military campaigns, supposedly horrified at the human suffering they caused, gave up traditional Hindu beliefs, and converted to Buddhism. Under his rule, Buddhism became the predominant religion in India, although, like Buddha, Ashoka encouraged religious tolerance. Ashoka's reign strengthened the influence of Buddhism in two important ways: (1) He established a standard edition of Buddhist texts—the Canon—and (2) he encouraged Buddhist missionaries to spread the master's teachings outside India. As a result, Buddhism became widespread throughout southeast Asia, most notably in China.

◆ **Hindu and Buddhist Art.** Most Indian art of the period of Ashoka and his successors was religious in inspiration. Hindu artists depicted their gods, in their various incarnations, as representative of all aspects of life, and Hindu myths often stressed sensual ele-

ments: sexual union served as a symbol of union with the divine. By contrast, Buddhist art aimed to inspire spiritual meditation and a rejection of worldly values.

◆ **The Gupta Empire.** After the collapse of Ashoka's empire, India split into a series of local states until it became united again in 320 CE under the rule of Gupta emperors. Hinduism regained its position as the dominating religion in India, and art, literature, and science flourished. The Gupta court became a center of learning and culture, and commerce developed with China and other parts of southeast Asia. Shortly before 500 CE, the invasion of the White Huns from Central Asia caused the collapse of Gupta power, however, and India once again fragmented into separate local kingdoms. Only with the arrival of Muslim rule—almost a thousand years later—did India reunite under a central authority.

◆ **Early China: The Shang Dynasty (c. 1600–1100 BCE).** The first organized urban society in China came under the rule of the Shang Dynasty. Trade and commerce began to develop, a system of writing was invented, and craftsmen achieved a high standard of workmanship in bronze.

◆ **The Chou Dynasty (c. 1100–221 BCE).** The Chou rulers, who replaced the Shang Dynasty around 1100 BCE, served as the coordinators of a series of regional kingdoms rather than as a central governing authority. In a system that somewhat resembles the feudal system of Medieval Europe, the Chou ruler relied on the support and military resources of the nobles who ruled the local kingdoms. Over time this support fluctuated and eventually collapsed: the end of Chou rule is known as the Period of the Warring States (403–221 BCE).

◆ **Confucianism and Taoism.** The two schools of philosophy that have influenced Chinese culture for much of the past 2500 years developed around 500 BCE, toward the end of the Chou Dynasty. Confucianism, an essentially optimistic system of belief, argued that those who were naturally virtuous should, while behaving with loyalty and respect, help govern their country by maintaining their independence and criticizing their rulers if necessary: the government served its citizens, rather than the reverse. Taoism, by contrast, taught that humans should withdraw from culture and society, devoting themselves to meditation and, like water, adapt themselves to natural forces.

◆ **The Ch'in, Han, and T'ang Dynasties.** The disorder of the latter part of Chou rule led finally to the brief Ch'in Dynasty (221–202 BCE). Shih Huang-ti, the Ch'in leader, forcibly united the warring kingdoms; removed from power the regional noble rulers; and created a centralized state with an imperial army, unified writing system, and standardized weights and measures. By a policy known as the Burning of the Books, he eliminated philosophical writings he viewed as dangerous (including Confucian texts). So cruel was his reign that it barely survived his own death in 210 BCE.

The succeeding dynasty, that of the Han emperors (202 BCE–221 CE), sought to establish a compromise between central government and local independence. During the first two centuries of the emperors' reign, China prospered, the arts flourished, and the philosophical teachings that had been banned under the Ch'in returned to circulation. As the emperors' authority began to wane, however, under challenge by the regional states, China once again fell into chaos. Order was only restored under the T'ang Dynasty (618–906 CE), which saw an artistic and cultural revival often known as China's Golden Age.

◆ **The Arts in Classical China.** Under the Han and T'ang dynasties China enjoyed a cultural revival. A standard body of literature, the *Five Classics*, circulated widely. Among the new subjects to inspire writers, painters, and sculptors was Buddhism, which spread throughout China following its introduction in the first century CE. The most important poet of the T'ang Dynasty—and one of the best-loved of all China's writers—was Li Po.

tion about the Indus Valley people could they hope to learn? Are there any other ancient cultures whose writing we have but cannot understand?

2. What are the chief features of Buddhism? How do they differ from traditional Hindu beliefs, and why did they induce many Indians to convert?

3. Both Buddhism and Hinduism have many followers today. What gives these religions their continuing appeal? More particularly, why does Buddhism continue to attract increasing numbers in the United States and other Western countries?

4. Indian art and literature was based in large measure on the great epic poems, the *Mahabharata* and the *Ramayana*. What are the characteristics of their heroes? Illustrate them by describing two or three episodes.

5. Buddhism never acquired the same importance in China that Hinduism has always had in India. What effect has this had on the history of the two countries, both in ancient times and today?

6. What light do Chinese painting and sculpture of the Han and T'ang dynasties cast on daily life in those times?

EXERCISES

1. The early civilization of the Indus Valley had many of the marks of a sophisticated culture, including a writing system. This is still, however, undeciphered. If scholars one day decipher it, what new informa-

 Visit the *Culture & Values* Companion website at **www.cengage.com/art/Cunningham/Cultureand Values7E** and the *Humanities Resource Center* for an array of primary source readings, key terms with pronunciations, flash cards, quizzes, and study materials designed especially to help you do well in this course.

CHAPTER 6

THE RISE OF THE BIBLICAL TRADITION

Abraham is considered not only the father of the Jewish people but Christianity and Islam also invoke his name with great reverence. The three great monotheistic religions of Judaism, Christianity, and Islam are often called "Abrahamic Religions" because they look back on this ancient patriarch as their common ancestor.

The story of Abraham begins in the twelfth chapter of the biblical Book of Genesis when God tells him and his tribal family to leave Ur of the Chaldees (present day Iraq), and promises him: "I will make of you a great nation and I will bless you and make your name great." The next thirteen chapters of Genesis tell Abraham's story.

Jesus himself calls God the "God of Abraham." In the very important chapter eleven of the Epistle to the Hebrews, the author praises Abraham as a model of faith: "By faith, Abraham obeyed when he was called to set out for a place that he was to receive as an inheritance; and he set out. By faith he stayed a long time in the land he had been promised as in a foreign land, living in tents, as did Isaac and Jacob, who were heirs with him of the same promise . . . Therefore from one person . . . descendants were born, as many as the stars of heaven and the innumerable grains by the seashore" (Heb 11:8–12).

Muslims count themselves among those descendants of Abraham (*Ibrahim* in Arabic) and call him the Father of the Arabs. Abraham is honored as one of the authentic prophets and bears the title of *hanif*—a revealer of belief in one God. Pious Muslims believe that Abraham built the Muslim shrine, the *Ka'aba* (see Chapter 8), and when they make the pilgrimage to Mecca (the *haj*), they consider themselves to be following in the footsteps of Abraham, Hagar (one of the wives of Abraham), and Ishmael. Within the *Ka'aba* is thought to be an actual footprint of Abraham impressed into stone.

◆ Mosaic of the Prophet Abraham *(© Cameraphoto Arte/Art Resource, NY)*

JUDAISM AND EARLY CHRISTIANITY

One of the interesting ironies of history is the fact that, more than three thousand years ago in the Middle East, a small tribe-turned-nation became one of the central sources for the development of Western civilization. The fact is incontestable: the marriage of the biblical tradition and Graeco-Roman culture has produced, for better or worse, the West as we know it today.

The irony is all the more telling because these ancient biblical people did not give the world great art, significant music, philosophy, or science. Their language did not have a word for *science*. Their religion discouraged the plastic arts. We have the texts of their hymns, canticles, and psalms, but we can only speculate how they were sung and how they were accompanied instrumentally. What these people did give us was a book; more precisely, a collection of many different books we now call the Bible.

These people called themselves the Children of Israel or Israelites; at a later time they became known as the Jews (from the area around Jerusalem known as Judaea). In the Bible they are called Hebrews (most often by their neighbors), the name now most commonly used to describe these biblical people.

		GENERAL EVENTS	ART
BRONZE AGE	**BEFORE 1200 BCE** 3000 BCE	**1800–1600** Age of Hebrew Patriarchs: Abraham, Isaac, Jacob **1600** Israelite tribes in Egypt **1280** Exodus of Israelites from Egypt under leadership of Moses	
	1260 **PERIOD OF THE JUDGES**	**1260** Israelites begin to penetrate land of Canaan	
	1040	**1040–1000** Reign of Saul, first king of Israel	
	1000 **AGE OF THE MONARCHY**	**1000–961** Reign of King David **961–922** Reign of Solomon; height of ancient Israel's cultural power: achievements form basis of Judaic, Christian, and Islamic religions Use of iron-tipped plow and iron war chariots	Depiction of divinity in art prohibited in Jewish religion
	922 **AGE OF THE TWO KINGDOMS**	**922** Civil War after death of Solomon splits Northern Kingdom (Israel) and Southern Kingdom (Judah); classical prophetic period begins **721** Northern Kingdom destroyed by Assyria	
IRON AGE	587 **AGE OF EXILE, RETURN, & OCCUPATIONS**	**587** Southern Kingdom defeated; Jews driven into captivity in Babylonia **539** Cyrus the Persian permits Jews to return to Jerusalem **516** Dedication of Second Temple in Jerusalem **332** Conquest of Jerusalem by Alexander the Great **2nd cent.** Cult of Mithra in Rome	
	63 BCE CE **ROMAN PERIOD** CE 381	**63** Conquest of Jerusalem by Romans under Pompey **37 BCE–CE 4** Reign of Herod the Great under Roman tutelage **c. 6 BCE** Birth of Jesus **c. 30 CE** Death of Jesus; beginnings of Christianity in Palestine **45–49** First missionary journeys of Saint Paul **66–70** Jewish rebellions against Romans **c. 70** Titus destroys Jerusalem and razes the Temple; Jews sent into exile **3rd cent.** Roman & Jewish religions coexist in Dura Europos (Syria) **307–327** Reign of Constantine **313** Edict of Milan gives Christians freedom of religion **330** Founding of Constantinople **381** Paganism officially suppressed; Christianity made state religion	**c. 250** Frescoes embellish Christian cemeteries (catacombs) **c. 300** Appearance of Christian sculpture **4th cent.** Inscriptions, particularly *Chi-Rho*, decorate Christian tombs

BIBLICAL HISTORY

The history of the Hebrew people is long and complex, but the stages of their growth can be outlined as follows:

◆ *The Period of the Patriarchs*. According to the Bible, the Hebrew people had their origin in Abraham, the father (patriarch) of a tribe who took his people from ancient Mesopotamia to the land of Canaan on the east coast of the Mediterranean about 2000 BCE. After settling in this land, divided into twelve tribal areas, they eventually went to Egypt at the behest of

Joseph, who had risen to high office in Egypt after his enslavement there.

◆ *The Period of the Exodus*. The Egyptians eventually enslaved the Hebrews (perhaps around 1750 BCE), but they were led out of Egypt under the leadership of Moses. This "going out" (**exodus**) is one of the central themes of the Bible; this great event also gives its name to one of the books of the Bible.

◆ *The Period of the Conquest*. The biblical books of Joshua and Judges relate the struggles of the Hebrews to conquer the land of Canaan as they fought against the native peoples of that area and the competing

ARCHITECTURE	LITERATURE & PHILOSOPHY	MUSIC
	c. 1000 Formation of the Scriptures in written form	
	c. 950 Book of Psalms	
	10th–9th cent. Book of Kings	
c. 961–922 Building of the Temple of Solomon		Music often accompanied the Psalms; musical instruments in use: drums, reed instruments, lyre, harp, horns
	8th–6th cent. Old Testament books of Isaiah, Jeremiah, and Ezekiel	
	8th cent. Book of Amos	
587 Solomon's Temple destroyed by Babylonians	**after 5th cent.** Book of Job	
	end of 2nd cent. Apocryphal Book of Judith	
19 Herod the Great begins rebuilding Third Temple of Solomon		
70 Herod's Temple destroyed by the armies of Titus under Emperor Vespasian	**c. 70** "Sermon on the Mount" in Gospel of Saint Matthew, New Testament	
c. 333 Old Saint Peters, Rome, built	**c. 150** Justin Martyr, *Apology*	
c. 326–345 Church of the Holy Sepulchre, Jerusalem, built	**c. 203** Vibia Perpetua, narrative	

◆ **6.2** Reconstruction drawing of Solomon's Temple, Jerusalem, Israel. The description in the Bible of this destroyed temple was an inspiration for sacred architecture well into the Middle Ages. The two bronze columns in front may have represented the columns of fire and smoke that guided the Israelites while they were in the desert.

"Sea People" (the Philistines) who came down from the north.

◆ *The United Monarchy.* The high point of the Hebrew political power came with the consolidation of Canaan and the rise of a monarchy. There were three kings: Saul, David, and Solomon. An ambitious flurry of building during the reign of Solomon (c. 961–922 BCE) culminated in the construction of the great temple in Jerusalem [**Fig. 6.2**].

◆ *Divided Kingdom and Exile.* After the death of Solomon, a rift over the succession resulted in the separation of the Northern Kingdom and the Southern Kingdom, the center of which was Jerusalem. Both were vulnerable to pressure from the surrounding great powers. The Northern Kingdom was destroyed by the Assyrians in the eighth century BCE, and its inhabitants (the so-called Lost Tribes of Israel) were swept away by death or exile. In 587 BCE the Babylonians conquered the Southern Kingdom, destroyed Solomon's temple in Jerusalem, and carried the Hebrew people into an exile known to history as the Babylonian Captivity.

◆ *The Return.* The Hebrews returned from exile about 520 BCE to rebuild their shattered temple and to resume their religious life. Their subsequent history was marked by a series of foreign (Greek, Egyptian, and Syrian) rulers, one brief period of political independence (c. 165 BCE), and, finally, rule by Rome after the conquest of 63 BCE. In 70 CE, after a Jewish revolt, the Romans destroyed Jerusalem and razed the rebuilt temple [**Fig. 6.3**]. One small band of Jewish rebels that held off the Romans for two years at a mountain fortress called Masada was defeated in 73 CE. Except for pockets of Jews who lived there over the centuries, not until 1948, when the state of Israel was established, would Jews hold political power in their ancestral home.

◆ **6.3** The Spoils of Jerusalem, c. 81 CE. Roman soldiers carry the seven-branched candelabrum (a menorah) as part of the booty from their sack of Jerusalem.

Passageway relief from the Arch of Titus, Rome, Italy //
© Werner Forman / Art Resource, NY

THE HEBREW BIBLE AND ITS MESSAGE

The English word *bible* comes from the Greek name for the ancient city of Byblos, from which the papyrus reed used to make books was exported. As already noted, the Bible is a collection of books that took its present shape over a long period.

The ancient Hebrews divided the books of their Bible into three large groupings: the Law, the Prophets, and the Writings. The Law referred specifically to the first five books of the Bible, called the **Torah** (from the Hebrew word for "instruction" or "teaching"). The Prophets consists of writings attributed to the great moral teachers of the Hebrews, who were called prophets because they spoke with the authority of God (**prophet** derives from a Greek word for "one who speaks for another"). The Writings contain the wisdom literature of the Bible, prose or poetry (like the Book of Psalms) or a mixture of the two, as in the Book of Job (see **Table 6.1**).

The list of books contained in the modern Bible was not established until 90 CE, when an assembly of rabbis drew up such a list or **canon** even though its main outline had been known for centuries. The Christians in turn accepted this canon and added the twenty-seven books that make up what we know as the Christian Scriptures of the New Testament. (Roman Catholics and Orthodox Christians also accept as canonical some books of the Old Testament that are not in the Hebrew canon but are found in an ancient Greek version of the Hebrew Scriptures known as the **Septuagint**, a version of the Bible widely used in the ancient world.) (See **Table 6.2**.)

One fundamental issue about the Bible must be emphasized: Both ancient Israel, subsequent Jewish history, and the Christian world have made the Bible *the* central document not only for worship and the rule of faith but also as a moral guide and anchor for ethical and religious stability. The Bible, directly and indirectly, has shaped our law, literature, language, ethics, and social outlook. It permeates our culture. To cite one single example: At Solomon's temple the people sang hymns of praise (psalms) to God, just as they are sung in Jewish synagogues today. Those same psalms were sung by Jesus and his followers in their time, just as they are sung and recited in Christian churches in every part of the world. That ancient formulation is, in a deep sense, part of our common religious culture.

The Bible is not a philosophical treatise; it is a sacred book. It is, nonetheless, a book that contains ideas; those ideas have enormously influenced the way we think and the way we look at the world. Some of the basic motifs of the Bible have been so influential in our culture that they should be considered in some detail. We will examine four such motifs that run like strands throughout the Hebrew Scriptures.

Table 6.1 *Books of the Old and New Testaments*

OLD	NEW
Genesis	*The Gospels:*
Exodus	Matthew
Leviticus	Mark
Numbers	Luke
Deuteronomy	John
Joshua	*The Acts of the Apostles*
Judges	*The Letters of Paul:*
Ruth	Romans
I and II Samuel	I Corinthians
I and II Kings	II Corinthians
I and II Chronicles	Galatians
Ezra	Ephesians
Nehemiah	Philippians
Esther	Colossians
Job	I Thessalonians
Psalms	II Thessalonians
Proverbs	I Timothy
Ecclesiastes	II Timothy
Song of Solomon	Titus
Isaiah	Philemon
Jeremiah	Hebrews
Lamentations	*The Letters of:*
Ezekiel	James
Daniel	I Peter
Hosea	II Peter
Joel	I John
Amos	II John
Obadiah	III John
Jonah	Jude
Micah	*The Book of Revelation*
Nahum	(also called *The Apocalypse*)
Habakkuk	
Zephaniah	
Haggai	
Zechariah	
Malachi	

Table 6.2 *The Deuterocanonical Books of the Bible*

Roman Catholicism and Orthodoxy accept in their canon books some additional books that were accepted as canonical in the Greek Old Testament known as the Septuagint version. These books are called the **deuterocanonical** books. The Roman Catholics accept the following:

Tobit
Judith
Wisdom of Solomon
Ecclesiasticus (also known as *The Wisdom of Ben Sira*)
Baruch (containing the *Letter of Jeremiah*)
I and II Maccabees
Some additional chapters of *Esther* and *Daniel*

In addition to the above books, the Orthodox Churches also include:
First Esdras
The Prayer of Manasseh
Psalm 151
III Maccabees (*with* IV Maccabees *in an appendix*).

Biblical Monotheism A central conviction of biblical religion is that there is one God, that this God is good, and (most crucially) that this God is involved in the arena of human history. This God is conceived of as a person and not as some impersonal force in the world of nature. **Monotheism** (the belief in one god) can thus be distinguished both from *henotheism* (the belief that there may be other gods, although only one is singled out for worship) and **polytheism** (the belief that there are many gods).

The opening pages of the Bible set out a creation story (see Genesis 1:1–2:4a) that, properly understood, provides us with a rather complete vision of what the Bible believes about God. The creation story of Genesis makes three basic assertions about God. First, God exists before the world and called it into existence by the simple act of utterance. God, unlike the gods and goddesses of the Hebrews' ancient neighbors, is not born out of the chaos that existed before the world. God is not to be confused with the world, and neither did God have to struggle with the forces of chaos to create. Second, God pronounces each part of creation and creation as a whole as "good." Thus, the Book of Genesis does not present the material universe as evil or, as certain Eastern religions teach, an illusory world that conceals the true nature of reality. Finally, God creates human beings as the apex and crown of creation. The material world is a gift from God, and human beings are obliged to care for it and be grateful for it. A basic motif of biblical prayer is gratitude to God for the gift of creation.

Biblical monotheism must not be thought of as a theory that simply sees God as the starting point or originator of all things after the fashion of a craftsperson who makes a chair and then forgets about it. The precise character of biblical monotheism is its conviction that God creates and sustains the world in general and chose a particular people to be both vehicle and sign of divine presence in the world. The precise character of that relationship can be found in the biblical notion of covenant.

Covenant Covenant is the crucial concept for setting out the relationship between God and the Hebrew people. The covenant can be summed up in the simple biblical phrase "I will be your God; you will be my people." In Hebrew history, the Bible insists, God has always been faithful to that covenant that was made with the people of Israel while the people must learn and relearn how to be faithful to it. Scholars have pointed out that the biblical covenant may be based on the language of ancient marriage covenants (for example, "I will be your husband; you will be my wife"); if that is true, it gives us an even deeper understanding of the term: the relationship of God and Israel is as close as the relationship of husband and wife.

This strong portrait of a single, deeply involved God who is beyond image or portrayal has had a profound impact on the shape of the Judeo-Christian worldview. The notion of covenant religion not only gave form to Hebrew religion, the idea of a renewed covenant became the central claim of Christianity. (Remember that another word for covenant is *testament*; hence the popular Old/New Testament split Christianity insists upon.) The idea has even spilled over from synagogues and churches into our national civil religion, where we affirm a belief in "One nation under God" and "In God we trust"—both sentiments rooted in the idea of a covenant.

Ethics The Bible is not primarily an ethical treatise; it is a theological one even though it does set out a moral code of behavior both for individuals and society. The Bible has many rules for worship and ritual, but its fundamental ethical worldview lies in the idea that humans are created in "the image and likeness of God" (Genesis 1:26). The more detailed formulation of that link between God and individual and social relationships is contained in the Ten Commandments, which the Bible depicts as being given by God to Moses after the latter brings the people out of the bondage of Egypt and before they reach the Promised Land (see Exodus 20). These commandments, consisting of both prohibitions (against murder, theft, idolatry, and so on) and positive commands (for worship, honoring of parents, and so on), are part of the larger ethical commands of all civilizations. The peculiarly monotheistic parts of the code appear in the first cluster, with the positive command to worship God alone and the prohibition of graven images and their worship.

Ancient Israel's ethics take on a more specific character in the writings of the prophets. The prophet (Hebrew *nabi*) speaks with God's authority. In Hebrew religion the prophet was not primarily concerned with the future (prophet and seer are thus not the same thing), even though the prophets do speak of a coming of peace and justice in the age of the **messiah** (the Hebrew word meaning "anointed one"). The main prophetic task was to call people back to the observance of the covenant and to warn them about the ways in which they failed that covenant. The great eighth-century prophets who flourished in both the north and the south after the period of the monarchy left a great literature. They insisted that worship of God, for example, in the worship of the temple, was insufficient if that worship did not come from the heart and include love and compassion for others. The prophets were radical critics of social injustice and defenders of the poor. They linked worship with a deep concern for ethics. They envisioned God as a God of all people and insisted on the connection between worship of God and righteous living.

Prophets were not a hereditary caste in ancient Israel, as were the priests. Prophets were "called" to preach. In many instances they even resisted that call and expressed reluctance to undertake the prophetic task. The fact that they had an unpopular message explains both why many of them suffered a violent end and why some were reluctant to undertake the task of preaching.

The prophetic element in religion was one of Israel's most enduring contributions to the religious sensibility of the world. The idea that certain people are called directly by God to preach peace and justice in the context of religious faith would continue beyond the biblical period in Judaism and Christianity. It is not accidental, to cite one modern example, that the great civil rights leader Martin Luther King Jr. (1929–1968) often cited the biblical prophets as exemplars for his own struggle in behalf of African Americans. That King died a violent death by assassination in 1968 is an all-too-ready example of how disquieting the prophetic message can be.

Models and Types Until modern times, relatively few Jews or Christians actually read the Bible on an individual basis. Literacy was rare, books expensive, and leisure at a premium. Bibles were read to people most frequently in public gatherings of worship in synagogues or churches. The one time that the New Testament reports Jesus as reading is from a copy of the prophet Isaiah kept in a synagogue (Luke 4:16). The biblical stories were read over the centuries in a familial setting (as at the Jewish Passover) or in formal worship on the Sabbath. The basic point, however, is that for more than three thousand years, the stories and (equally important) the people in these stories have been etched in the Western imagination. The faith of Abraham, the guidance of Moses, the wisdom of Solomon, the sufferings of Job, and the fidelity of Ruth have become proverbial in our culture.

These events and stories from the Bible are models of instruction and illumination; they have taken on a meaning far beyond their original significance. The events described in the Book of Exodus, for example, are often invoked to justify a desire for freedom from oppression and slavery. It is not accidental that Benjamin Franklin suggested depicting the crossing of the Reed Sea (not the Red Sea as is often said) by the Children of Israel as the centerpiece of the Great Seal of the United States.

Long before Franklin's day, the Pilgrims saw themselves as the new Children of Israel who had fled the oppression of Europe (read: Egypt) to find freedom in the land "flowing with milk and honey" that was America. At a later period in history, slaves in this country saw themselves as the oppressed Israelites in bondage. The desire of African Americans for freedom was couched in the language of the Bible as they sang "Go down, Moses.... Tell old Pharaoh: Let my people go!"

No humanities student can ignore the impact of the biblical tradition on our common culture. Our literature echoes it; our art is saturated in it; our social institutions are shaped by it. Writers in the Middle Ages said that all knowledge came from God in the form of two great books: the book of nature and the book called the Bible. We have enlarged that understanding today but, nonetheless, have absorbed much of the Hebrew Scriptures into the texture of our culture.

THE BEGINNINGS OF CHRISTIANITY

The fundamental fact to remember when studying the life of Jesus is that he was a Jew, born during the reign of Roman Emperor Augustus in the Roman-occupied land of Judaea (see map, "Israel at the Time of Jesus"). What we know about Him, apart from a few glancing references in pagan and Jewish literature, comes from the four Gospels (*gospel* derives from the Anglo-Saxon

 VALUES

Revelation

One deep theme that runs through the Bible is the concept of revelation. Revelation means a disclosure or "making plain" (literally: "pulling back the veils"). The Bible has the strong conviction that God reveals Himself in the act of creation but, more important, through the process of human history. The Old Testament makes clear the Hebrew conviction that God actually chose a people, exercised His care for them (providence), prompted prophets to speak, and inspired people to write. Christians accepted this divine intervention and expanded it with the conviction that God's final revelation to humanity came in the person of Jesus of Nazareth.

Several consequences derive from the doctrine of revelation. First is the idea that God gives shape to history and is most deeply revealed through history. Second, biblical religion conceived of God not as a distant figure separated from people but One who guided, encouraged, and finally shaped the destiny of a particular people (the Jews) and eventually the whole human race. The concept of revelation is intimately connected to the idea of covenant, which we discuss in the text.

It should also be noted that Islam, in continuity with biblical religion, also focuses on the idea of revelation. Islam teaches respect for the Hebrew patriarchs, prophets, and the person of Jesus but insists that Muhammad receives the final unveiling of God's purposes for the human race.

ISRAEL AT THE TIME OF JESUS

This area coincides more or less with the kingdom known in the time of King David.

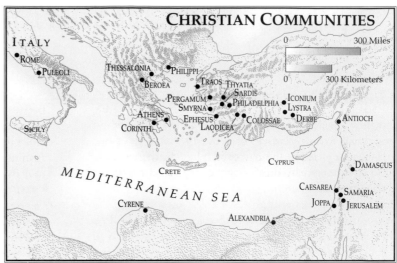

CHRISTIAN COMMUNITIES

word meaning "good news") attributed to Matthew, Mark, Luke, and John. These Gospels began to appear more than a generation after the death of Jesus, which probably occurred in 30 CE. The Gospels are religious documents, not biographies, but they contain historical data about Jesus as well as theological reflections about the meaning of His life and the significance of His deeds.

Jesus must also be understood in the light of the Jewish prophetical tradition discussed previously. He preached the coming of God's kingdom, which would be a reign of justice and mercy. Israel's enemies would be overcome. Until that kingdom arrived, Jesus insisted on a life of repentance; an abandonment of earthly concerns; love of God and neighbor; compassion for the poor, downcast, and marginalized; and set forth His own life as an example. His identification with the poor and powerless antagonized his enemies—who included the leaders of His own religion and the governing authorities of the ruling Romans. Perhaps the most characteristic expression of the teachings of Jesus is to be found in His parables and in the moral code He expressed in what is variously called the Beatitudes or the Sermon on the Mount.

All of the teachings of Jesus reflect a profound grasp of the piety and wisdom of the Jewish traditions, but the Gospels make a further claim for Jesus, depicting Him as the **Christ** (a Greek translation of the Hebrew messiah, "anointed one")—the Savior promised by the

ancient biblical prophets who would bring about God's kingdom. His tragic death by crucifixion (a punishment so degrading that it could not be inflicted on Roman citizens) would seem to have ended the public career of Jesus. The early Christian church, however, insisted that Jesus overcame death by rising from the tomb three days after His death. This belief in the resurrection became a centerpiece of Christian faith and preaching and the basis on which early Christianity proclaimed Jesus as the Christ.

CHRISTIANITY SPREADS

The slow growth of the Christian movement was given an early boost by the conversion of a Jewish zealot, Saul of Tarsus, around the year 35 CE near Damascus, Syria. Paul (his post-conversion name) won a crucial battle in the early Christian church, insisting that non-Jewish converts to the movement would not have to adhere to all Jewish religious customs, especially male circumcision. Paul's victory was to change Christianity from a religious movement within Judaism to a religious tradition that could embrace the nonJewish world of the Roman Empire. One dramatic example of Paul's approach to this pagan world was a public sermon he gave in the city of Athens in which he used the language of Greek culture to speak to the Athenians with the message of the Christian movement (see Acts 17:16–34).

Paul was a tireless missionary. He made at least three long journeys through the cities on the northern shore of the Mediterranean (and may once have gotten as far as Spain). On his final journey he reached Rome, where he met his death at the hands of a Roman executioner around the year 62 CE. In many of the cities he visited he left small communities of believers. Some of his letters (to the Romans, Galatians, Corinthians, and so on)

VOICES OF THEIR TIMES

Vibia Perpetua

Excerpt from the narrative of Vibia Perpetua, who was martyred in Carthage in 203 CE, when she was twenty-two years old. The last line of her narrative, written the day before her death, says simply, "If anyone wishes to write of my outcome, let him do so."

> Another day, while we were dining at noonday, we were summoned away to a hearing at the forum. At once, rumors swept the neighborhoods and a huge crowd assembled. We mounted the tribune. The others, when questioned, confessed. Then it was my turn. My father arrived with my infant son and pulled me down saying, "Sacrifice! Have mercy on your child!" The governor Hilarianus, who held judicial power in place of the proconsul Minucius Timianus, chimed in: "Pity your father's old age! Have mercy on your infant child!

> "Perform the imperial rituals for the well-being of the emperor." And I answered, "I will not perform it." Hilarianus: "You are a Christian?" And I answered, "I am a Christian." And as my father still stood by trying to change my mind, Hilarianus ordered him expelled from his sight; he was struck with a rod. I wept for my father's misfortune as if I had been hit myself; I grieved for his old age.

> Then the governor read out the sentence: condemned to the beasts of the arena.

> Cheerfully, we returned to prison.

> Since my child was an infant and accustomed to breastfeeding in prison, I sent the deacon Pomponius to my father imploring that my child be returned to me. But my father refused to give the child up. Somehow, through the will of God, the child no longer required the breast nor did my breasts become sore. I was neither tortured with grief over the child nor with pain in my breasts.

are addressed to believers in these places and provide details of his theological and pastoral concerns.

Early Martyrs By the end of the first century, communities of Christian believers existed in most of the cities of the vast Roman Empire (see map, "Christian Communities"). Their numbers were sufficient enough that, by 64 CE, Emperor Nero could make Christians scapegoats for a fire that destroyed the city of Rome (probably set by the emperor's own agents). The Roman writer Tacitus provides a vivid description of the terrible tortures meted out against the Christians:

> Nero charged, and viciously punished, people called Christians who were despised on account of their wicked practices. The founder of the sect, Christus, was executed by the procurator Pontius Pilate during the reign of Tiberius. The evil superstition was suppressed for a time but soon broke out afresh not only in Judea where it started but also in Rome where every filthy outrage arrives and prospers. First, those who confessed were seized and then, on their witness, a huge number was convicted, less for arson than for their hatred of the human race.

> In their death they were mocked. Some were sewn in animal skins and worried to death by dogs; others were crucified or burned so that, when daylight was over, they could serve as torches in the evening. Nero provided his own gardens for this show and made it into a circus. He mingled with the crowd dressed as a charioteer or posed in his chariot. As a result, the sufferers guilty and worthy of punishment although they were, did arouse the pity of the mob who saw their suffering resulted from the viciousness of one man and not because of some need for the common good.

> [*Annals* XV]

The Successful Spread of Christianity Two questions arise at this point: Why were the Christians successful in spreading their religion? Why did they become the object of persecution at the hands of the Romans?

Several social factors aided the growth of Christianity: There was peace in the Roman Empire; a good system of safe roads made travel easy; there was a common language in the empire (a form of common Greek called *koine*: the language of the New Testament); and Christianity was first preached in a network of Jewish centers. Scholars have also offered some religious reasons: the growing interest of pagans in monotheism; the strong Christian emphasis on salvation and freedom from sin; the Christian custom of offering mutual aid and charity for its members; and its relative freedom

◆ **6.4** Christ Teaching the Apostles, c. 300 CE. The beardless Christ and the use of the Roman toga, characteristic of frescoes during this period, were borrowed by the artist from contemporary pagan Roman art. Partially destroyed; the original setting was meant to depict a eucharistic banquet.

Wall painting. 1′3″ x 4′3″ (.38 x 1.3 m). Catacombs of Domitilla, Rome, Italy//Photo © Held Collection/The Bridgeman Art Library

from class distinctions. Paul wrote that in this faith there was "neither Jew nor Gentile; male nor female; slave nor free person."

This new religion met a good deal of resistance. The first martyrs died before the movement spread outside Jerusalem because of the resistance of the Jewish establishment. Very quickly, too, the Christians earned the enmity of the Romans. Even before Nero's persecution in 64 CE, the Christians had been expelled from the city of Rome by Emperor Claudius. From those early days until the third century, there were sporadic outbreaks of persecutions. In 250 CE, under Emperor Decius, there was an empire-wide persecution, with two others coming in 257 (under Emperor Valerian) and in 303 (under Emperor Diocletian). Finally, in 312 CE, Emperor Constantine issued a decree in Milan allowing Christianity toleration as a religion.

What was the basis for this long history of persecution? The reasons are complex. Ordinarily, Rome had little interest in the religious beliefs of its subjects so long as these beliefs did not threaten public order. The Christian communities seemed secretive; they had their own network of communication in the empire; they kept away from active life in the political realm; most telling of all, they refused to pay homage to the state gods and goddesses. A common charge made against them was that they were atheists: they denied the existence of the Roman gods. Romans conceived of their society as bound together in a seamless web of *pietás*, a virtue that meant a combination of love and reverential fear. The Romans felt that one should express *pietás* to the parents of a family, the family should express that *pietás* toward the state, and the state in turn owed *pietás* to the gods. That brought everything into harmony, and the state would flourish. The Christian refusal to express *pietás* to the gods seemed to the Romans to strike at the heart of civic order. The Christians, in short, were traitors to the state.

Apologists Christian writers of the second century tried to answer these charges by insisting that the Christians wished to be good citizens and, in fact, could be. These writers (called *apologists*) wrote about the moral code of Christianity, about their beliefs and the reasons they could not worship the Roman deities. Their radical monotheism, inherited from Judaism, forbade such worship. Furthermore, they protested their roles as ready scapegoats for every ill—real and imagined—in society. The acid-tongued North African Christian writer Tertullian (c. 160–225 CE) provided a sharp statement concerning the Christian grievance about such treatment: "If the Tiber floods its banks or the Nile doesn't flood; if the heavens stand still or the earth shakes, if there is hunger or drought, quickly the cry goes up, 'Christians to the lions!'"

One of the most important of the early Christian apologists was Justin Martyr. Born around 100 CE in Palestine, he converted to Christianity and taught, first, at Ephesus, and later in Rome. While in Rome he wrote two lengthy apologies to the emperors asking for toleration and attempting, at the same time, to explain the Christian religion. These early writings are extremely important because they provide a window onto early Christian life and Christian attitudes toward both Roman and Jewish culture. Justin's writings did not, however, receive the audience for which he had hoped. In 165 CE he was scourged and beheaded in Rome under the anti-Christian laws.

EARLY CHRISTIAN ART

Little significant Christian art or architecture dates from before the fourth century because of the illegal status of the Christian church and the clandestine life it was forced to lead. We do have art from the cemeteries of Rome and some other cities that were maintained by the Christian communities. These cemeteries (known as **catacombs** from the name of one of them, the *coemeterium ad catacumbas*) were the burial places of thousands of Christians. Contrary to romantic notions, these underground galleries, hewn from the soft rock known as *tufa*, were never hiding places for Christians during the times of persecution, neither were they secret places for worship. Such ideas derive not from fact but from nineteenth-century novels. Similarly, only a minuscule number of the tombs contained the bodies of martyrs; none do today, because the martyrs were reburied inside the walls of the city of Rome in the early Middle Ages.

These underground cemeteries are important, however, because they provide us with some visual evidence about early Christian beliefs and customs. This artistic material falls into the following categories.

◆ **6.5** Virgin and Child, c. 250 CE. Above an eroded portion of the fresco, Mary sits with the infant Jesus on her lap. Beside her stands a figure, perhaps the prophet Isaiah, who, pointing to the star above her head with one hand and to the infant Jesus with the other, indicates the fulfillment of prophecy. Behind them, and added at a later date, are a sheep (top left) and a tree bearing red fruits or flowers.

Wall painting. Catacomb of Priscilla, Rome, Italy//© Scala/Art Resource, NY

FRESCOES

Frescoes (wall paintings done on wet plaster) are found frequently in the catacombs. Most depict biblical subjects that reflect the Christian hope of salvation and eternal life. Thus, for example, common themes like the story of Jonah or the raising of Lazarus from the dead allude to the Christian belief that everyone would be raised at the end of time. Another common motif is the communion meal of Jesus at the Last Supper as an anticipation of the heavenly banquet that awaited all believers in the next life [**Fig. 6.4**]. These frescoes herald the beginnings of artistic themes that would continue down through the centuries. In the catacombs of Priscilla in Rome, for example, we find the first known depiction of the Virgin and Child, a subject that would in time become commonplace [**Fig. 6.5**].

◆ **6.6** *The Good Shepherd,* c. 300 CE. This depiction of Christ, borrowed from Greaco-Roman models, is common in early Christian art, although sculptural examples are rather rare.

Marble. 3′3″ (99 cm) high. Museo Pio Cristiano, Vatican Museums, Vatican State//© Scala/Art Resource, NY

GLASS AND SCULPTURE

Although sculpture is rare before the fourth century, a statue of Christ as Good Shepherd [**Fig. 6.6**], beardless and with clearly classical borrowings, may be dated from this period. The figure repeats a common theme in the catacomb fresco art of the period. More common are the glass disks with gold paper cutouts pressed in them that are found in both Jewish and Christian catacombs as a decorative motif on individual tomb slots. After the period of Constantine, carved sarcophagi also became both common and elaborate [**Fig. 6.7**].

INSCRIPTIONS

Each tomb was covered by a slab of marble that was cemented in place. On those slabs would be carved the name and death date of the buried person. Quite frequently, there was also a decorative symbol such as an anchor (for hope) or a dove with an olive branch (peace). At times they used the first two letters of the Greek word for Christ: *Chi Rho* [**Fig. 6.8**]. One of the most common symbols was a fish. The Greek letters that spell out the word *fish* were considered an anagram for the phrase "Jesus Christ, Son of God and Savior," so that the fish symbol became a shorthand way of making that brief confession of faith [**Fig. 6.9**].

DURA-EUROPOS

Despite the persecutions of the Christians and the hostility of the Romans to the Jews, the religions managed to coexist and, to a certain extent, to thrive in the Roman Empire. One small indication of this fact can be seen in the spectacular archaeological finds made in the 1930s at a small town in present-day Syria called Dura-

◆ **6.7** Jonah Sarcophagus, 4th century CE. In addition to the Jonah cycle, there are other biblical scenes: at the top left, the raising of Lazarus; to the right of the sail at top, Moses striking the rock; at the far top right, a shepherd with a sheep.

Limestone. Museo Lateranense, Vatican Museums, Vatican State//© Alinari/Art Resource, NY

Europos. This small Roman garrison town, destroyed by Persian armies in 256 CE, was covered by desert sands for nearly seventeen hundred years. The scholars who excavated it found a street that ran roughly north and south along the city wall (they called it Wall Street) and contained a Christian house church with some intact frescoes, a temple to a Semitic god called Aphlad, a temple to the god Zeus (Roman Jupiter), a meet-

ing place for the worshipers of the cult of Mithra, and a Jewish synagogue with more than twenty well-preserved fresco paintings of scenes from the Hebrew Scriptures [**Fig. 6.10**].

The Dura-Europos discoveries both revealed the mingling of many religious cultures and demonstrated

◆ **6.9** Anchor with entwined fish, 4th century CE. A symbol of Christ and his followers, the anchor motif was a hidden reference to the cross, which was rarely depicted before the fourth century.

Mosaic from the Catacombs of Hermes, Sousse, Tunisia//© The Art Archive/Archaeological Museum, Sousse, Tunisia/Gianni Dagli Orti

◆ **6.8** *Chi Rho* Monogram, 4th century CE. The area bears a monogram formed by the Greek letters *chi* and *rho*, the first two letters of Christ's name, together with the Greek letters *alpha* and *omega*, the first and last letters of the Greek alphabet, another symbol of Christ drawn from the New Testament Book of Revelations.

From a wall painting in a Roman villa, Lullingstone, Kent, England. © British Museum, London/HIP/Art Resource, NY

◆ **6.10** *The Crossing of the Red Sea*, c. 239 CE. This extraordinary scene shows Moses (staff in hand), Aaron, and the Israelites pursued by the Egyptian armies on their right and the drowning Egyptian armies on their left. Found in a synagogue at Dura-Europos (Syria), this scene is part of a huge wall mural depicting events from the Hebrew Scriptures. (© *Princeton University Press/Art Resource, NY*)

◆ **6.11** Old Saint Peter's Basilica, Rome, Italy, begun c. 319 CE. Restored cutaway view (*top*) and plan (*bottom*). (1) nave, (2) aisle, (3) apse, (4) transept, (5) narthex, (6) atrium. This kind of basilica floor plan would be common in the west until the rise of the Romanesque period.

Length of grand axis 835′ (254.5 m), width of transept 295′ (86.87 m). Artwork by John Burge.

that the usual Jewish resistance to the visual arts was not total. Furthermore, the evidence of a building for Christian worship (part of a papyrus of the four Gospels harmonized into one whole was found at the site) in place sixty years before Constantine's Edict of Toleration and in use during a time when there were empire-wide persecutions of Christians is a significant discovery. Scholars see in the art of Dura-Europos the mingling of both Eastern and Roman styles that might be the source for the art that would emerge more fully in the Byzantine world. Most significantly, the finds at Dura-Europos demonstrate how complex the religious

situation of the time really was and how the neat generalizations of historians do not always correspond to the complicated realities of actual life.

EARLY CHRISTIAN ARCHITECTURE

Two of the most famous churches in Christendom are associated with the reign of Emperor Constantine

◆ **6.12** Church of the Holy Sepulchre, Jerusalem, Israel, c. 345 CE. In this drawing, we see the round, domed building that covered the burial place of Christ and the detached basilica behind it. The present church exhibits no separation between the domed area and the basilica. *(Artwork by Cecilia Cunningham)*

(306–337 CE). The present Saint Peter's Basilica in the Vatican rests on the remains of a **basilica** built by Constantine and dedicated in 326 CE [**Fig. 6.11**]. We do not have a fully articulated plan of that church, but its main outlines are clear. The faithful would enter into a courtyard called an ***atrium***, around which was a colonnaded arcade, and from there through a vestibule called the **narthex** into the church proper. The basilica, modeled after secular counterparts in Rome, featured a long central *nave* with two parallel side aisles. The nave was intersected at one end by a ***transept***, the roof of which was pitched with wooden trusses and supported by the outer walls and the columned interiors. High up on the walls above the arches and below the roof was the so-called ***clerestory*** (windows that provided most of the interior illumination). This basilica-type church became a model from which many of the features of later church architecture evolved.

The other famous church built in the Constantinian period is the Church of the Holy Sepulchre in Jerusalem [**Fig. 6.12**]. This church was also built in the basilica style, its atrium in front of the basilica hall, but with a significant addition: Behind the basilica was a domed structure that covered—it was believed—the rocky place where the body of Christ had been buried for three days. The domelike structure was utilized in Christian architecture as an adaptation of existing domed structures in pagan Rome, most notably the Pantheon and some of the vast baths.

EARLY CHRISTIAN MUSIC

If the visual arts of early Christianity turned to Graeco-Roman models for inspiration, the music of the early church drew on Jewish sources. The tradition of singing (or, rather, chanting) sacred texts at religious services was an ancient Jewish custom that appears to go back to Mesopotamian sources. What little we know of Jewish

◆ **6.13** *The Blind Harper*, c. 1340–1330 BCE. It is quite possible that the stringed instrument depicted here is similar to those mentioned in the book of Psalms. The word "psalm" comes from a Greek word meaning "to pluck a lyre."

From the tomb of Paatenemmheb, Saqqara, Egypt. Limestone basalt relief, detail, 11½" (29 cm) high. Rijksmuseum van Oudheden, Leiden, Netherlands // © Erich Lessing/Art Resource, NY

music, in fact, suggests that it was influenced strongly by the various peoples with whom the Jews came into contact. The lyre used by Jewish musicians was a common Mesopotamian instrument, whereas the harp for which King David was famous came to the Jews from Assyria by way of Egypt [**Fig. 6.13**].

By early Christian times, Jewish religious services consisted of a standardized series of prayers and scriptural readings organized to create a cycle that fit the Jewish calendar. Many of these readings were taken over by early Christian congregations, particularly those where the number of converted Jews was high. In chanting the Psalms, the style of execution often depended on how well they were known by the congregation. Where the Jewish component of the congregation was strong, the congregation would join in the chant. Increasingly, however, the singing was left to trained choruses, with the other congregants joining in only for the standard response of "Amen" or "Alleluia." As the music fell more into the hands of professionals, it became increasingly complex.

This professionalization proved unpopular with church authorities, who feared that the choirs were concerned more with performance than with worship. In 361 CE a provincial council of the Christian church in Laodicea ordered that there should be only one paid performer (**cantor**) for each congregation. In Rome the authorities discouraged poetic elaboration on the liturgical texts, a practice common among the Jews and the Christians of the East.

Part of the early Christian suspicion of music, in the West at least, was a reaction against the Greek doctrine of ethos in music, which claimed that music could have a profound effect on human behavior. That music might induce moods of passion or violence or might even be an agreeable sensation in itself was not likely to appeal to a church that required the ethos of its music to express religious truth alone. For this reason instrumental music was rejected as unsuitable for the Christian liturgy. Such instrumentation was, in the minds of many Christians, too reminiscent of pagan customs.

By the fourth century, then, the standard form of music in Christian churches was either **responsorial** singing, with a cantor intoning lines from the Psalms and the congregation responding with a simple repeated refrain, or **antiphonal** singing, with parts of the congregation (or the cantor and the congregation) alternating verses of a psalm in a simple chant tone. By the beginning of the fifth century, there is evidence of nonscriptural hymns being composed. Apart from some rare fragments, we have no illustration of music texts with notation before the ninth century.

SUMMARY

This chapter traces a long history from the beginnings of the biblical tradition to the emergence of Christianity as a state religion in the Roman Empire, a history so complex that one hesitates to generalize about its shape and significance. Nonetheless, certain points deserve to be highlighted both because they are instructive in their own right and because of their continuing impact on the shape of Western culture.

◆ **Monotheism.** The biblical tradition reflects the emergence of monotheism (a belief in one God) as a leading idea in Western culture. Judaism held the ideal of the uniqueness of God against the polytheistic cultures of Babylonia, Assyria, and Egypt. That idea carried over into Christianity and became a point of conflict with Roman culture. The Roman charge that Christians were atheists meant not that they denied the existence of God but that they rejected the Roman gods.

◆ **Belief in Ethics.** The entire biblical tradition had a strong ethical emphasis. The prophets never ceased to argue that the external practice of religion was worthless unless there was a "pure heart." Jesus preached essentially the same thing in his famous criticisms of those who would pray publicly but secretly, in his words, "devour the substance of widows" (Luke 20:47).

This ethic was rooted in the biblical notion of *prophetism*—the belief that people could be called by God to denounce injustice in the face of hostility either from their own religious establishment or from equally hostile civil governments. Such prophetic protest, inspired by the biblical message, was always a factor in subsequent Judaism and Christianity.

◆ **A Covenant with God.** Both Judaism and Christianity insisted on a personal God who was actively involved with the world of humanity to the degree that there was a *covenant* between God and people and that the world was created and sustained by God as a gift for humans. This was a powerful doctrine that flew in the face of the ancient belief in impersonal fate controlling the destiny of people or a pessimism about the goodness or reliability of the world as we have it and live in it.

The biblical belief in the providence of God would have an enormous impact on later Western culture in everything from shaping its philosophy of history (that history moves in a linear fashion and has a direction to it) to an optimism about the human capacity to understand the world and make its secrets known for the benefit of people. Western culture never accepted, at least as a majority opinion, that the physical world was sacred or an illusion; rather it was a gift to be explored and at times exploited.

◆ **The Bible's Influence.** Finally, the Jewish and Christian tradition produced a work of literature: the Bible. The significance of that production can best be understood in the subsequent chapters of this book. It will soon become clear that a good deal of what the humanistic tradition of art, literature, and music produced until well into the modern period is unintelligible if not seen as an ongoing attempt to interpret that text in various artistic media according to the needs of the age.

EXERCISES

1. Hebrew religion begins in a patriarchal culture (a tribe headed by a "father"), and much of its language derives from that fact. What are the common titles for God that reflect that masculine dominance? Do some feminists have a case in their criticism of the overly patriarchal nature of biblical religion?

2. Biblical religion insists that God has no name and cannot be depicted in art. What do you believe were the reasons behind that attitude (almost unique in the ancient world), and what were its cultural consequences?

3. The biblical covenant is summed up in "I will be your God; you will be my people." Can you suggest a short phrase to sum up a marriage covenant? a covenant between citizens and the state? What are the essential characteristics of a covenant?

4. Reread the Ten Commandments (Exodus 20). Which of them make sense only to religious believers? Which have general applications? Could you suggest other commandments for inclusion in a modern version?

5. How would you characterize Jesus as a cultural type: teacher? philosopher? prophet? hero? martyr? other? Explain.

6. It is said that the Beatitudes are at the heart of the teaching of Jesus. Paraphrase those Beatitudes in contemporary language. Which of them sound strangest to our ears?

7. Do you see any lessons about religious tolerance today from the history of the persecution of the Christians in the Roman Empire?

8. Constantine extended the aid of the state to Christians. What are the benefits of state support for religion? the problems?

9. In his famous praise of the virtue of love (I Cor.13), Paul the Apostle says that love outlives both faith and hope. What kind of love is he talking about? How does love outlive both hope and faith?

 Visit the *Culture & Values* Companion website at **www.cengage.com/art/Cunningham/Cultureand Values7E** and the *Humanities Resource Center* for an array of primary source readings, key terms with pronunciations, flash cards, quizzes, and study materials designed especially to help you do well in this course.

CHAPTER 7

BYZANTIUM

Television has made us aware of sports fans who riot at athletic events, but one of the worst instances of fans run amok happened in sixth-century Constantinople. The *Nika revolt* was a strange episode in which sports, religion, and political unrest created a "perfect storm" of chaos, destruction, and revolt.

Christian pressures in Constantinople had forced a ban on the ancient gladiatorial games and people flocked instead to the chariot races held at the city's *hippodrome*, the centerpiece of urban athletics, complete with a box for the emperor. The passion for these races was such that around the year 500, the fans organized themselves into opposing factions called the Greens and the Blues, each supporting different teams of charioteers and horses, and effectively dividing the city. Each faction dressed in ways that asserted its allegiance—the Blues, for example, shaved their heads in the front and let their hair grow long in back in imitation of the Barbarian Asiatic Huns. More strangely, each faction also claimed allegiance to a different position on the divinity of Christ. The Blues believed that Christ had two natures (human and divine) in one person, while the Greens held that Christ had only one nature.

These rivalries came to a head in January, 532, when the Nika revolt (named for the Greek word *nike* meaning "victory" and used as a battle cry by the participants) broke out in the hippodrome and soon spilled out into the city. According to the contemporary historian Procopius, what started as a riot soon became a bloodbath in an open revolt against the emperor Justinian's attempts to suppress the traditional rights of the factions. In the end both Blues and Greens merged into an anti-imperial movement. Justinian almost fled the city until his wife, the formidable Theodora, rallied Belisarius, the emperor's head of the military, to lead the imperial army against the dissidents. At the revolt's bloody conclusion were left burned-out shells of buildings and, by some reckoning, thirty- to thirty-five-thousand dead. The races were stopped for a period of five years to be resumed in 537 with the factions more orderly and less polarized.

THE DECLINE OF ROME

By the early fourth century, the Roman Empire already had severe economic, political, and social problems. In 330, Emperor Constantine dedicated a Greek trading town on the Bosporus as his eastern capital, changing its name from Byzantium to Constantinople. It was to be a "new" Rome.

Constantinople had some obvious advantages for a major city. It straddled the most prominent land route between Asia and Europe. It had a deepwater port with natural shelter. It guarded the passage between the Mediterranean and the Black Sea. The surrounding countryside was rich in forests and water. The neighboring areas of both Europe (Thrace) and Asia (Bithynia) were rich agricultural areas that could supply the city's food needs.

♦ A chariot race in the amphitheatre at Pompeii, 1st century *(© Werner Forman/Art Resource, NY)*

Because of the tumultuous conditions, the emperors spent less time in Rome. By the beginning of the fifth century (in 402), Emperor Honorius moved the capital of the Western empire to the northern Italian city of Ravenna on the Adriatic coast. Seventy-four years later, in 476, the last Roman emperor in the West would die there. Goths would occupy Ravenna only to be defeated in turn by the imperial forces from Constantinople in 540 (see map, "The Byzantine World").

In the waning decades of the fourth and fifth centuries, Christianity continued to grow and expand in influence. During that period, in far different places,

two writers would live who saw the decline of the West: Augustine in Roman North Africa and Boethius in the city of Ravenna. Their writings were to have an enormous impact on the culture of Europe. Each deserves consideration.

LITERATURE AND PHILOSOPHY

Augustine of Hippo The greatest writer of the Christian Latin West, Augustine of Hippo, was a witness to the decline of Roman power. Born in 354 in North Africa (then part of the Roman provinces), Augustine

GENERAL EVENTS	ART

64 CE

EARLY CHRISTIAN ERA

PERIOD OF PERSECUTION

250 Persecution of Christians under Decius
286 Diocletian divides Roman Empire into East and West parts ruled by himself and Maximian
305 Abdication of Diocletian and Maximian; Constantius and Galerius rule as joint emperors
307–327 Reign of Constantine

313

PERIOD OF RECOGNITION

313 Edict of Milan gives Christians freedom of religion
324 Constantine convenes Council of Nicaea
330 Constantine dedicates new capital of Roman Empire on site of Byzantium, naming it Constantinople
337 Constantine is baptized a Christian on his deathbed

383 Ostrogoths accept Christianity

c. 390 Obelisk of Theodosius erected in Hippodrome at Constantinople

395

BYZANTINE ERA

GROWTH OF EMPIRE

395 Division of Roman Empire begun by Diocletian becomes total separation

4th–5th cent. Decline of Western Roman Empire
410 Visigoths sack Rome
455 Vandals sack Rome

476 Romulus Augustulus forced to abdicate as last Western Roman emperor; Ostrogoths rule Italy
493–526 Theodoric the Ostrogoth reigns in Italy
527–565 Reign of Justinian as Eastern Roman emperor in Constantinople
532 Nika revolt; civil disorders in Constantinople
c. 533 Justinian codifies Roman Law

540 Belisarius conquers Ostrogoths in Italy for Justinian; Ravenna comes under Byzantine rule

c. 415 Theodosius II moves gilded horses and chariot from Rome to Hippodrome
c. 425 Mosaics at Mausoleum of Galla Placidia, Ravenna
c. 450 Dome mosaic in Orthodox Baptistery, Ravenna
6th cent. Art tied to theological doctrine and liturgical practice of Orthodox Church
c. 500–530 Christ Pantocrater, icon
c. 546–556 Ivory throne of Archbishop Maximian given to the Church of San Vitale by Justinian
c. 550 Mosaics at Sant' Apollinare Nuovo and San Vitale, Ravenna

565

DECLINE AND FALL

570 Muhammad born; dies 632

730–843 Iconoclastic controversy: ban on religious imagery

988–989 Russians accept Christianity

730–843 Ban on religious imagery; most earlier pictographic art destroyed

1453 Constantinople falls to Ottoman Turks, ending Byzantine Empire; Church of Hagia Sophia becomes a mosque

1453

received a thorough Classical education in Africa and in Rome. He was converted to Christianity in Milan and soon afterward returned to his native country, where he was named Bishop of Hippo in 390. When the Visigoths sacked Rome in 410, the pagan world was aghast, and many blamed the rise of Christianity for this event. Partially as a response to this charge, Augustine wrote *The City of God* in an attempt to demonstrate that history had a direction willed by God and that "in the end" all would be made right as the city of man gave way to the city of God. Augustine's huge work, packed with reflections on scripture, philosophy, and pagan wisdom, is often cited as one of the most influential philosophies of history written in the Western world.

Augustine of Hippo's intellectual impact on the subsequent cultural history of the West is difficult to overestimate. His influence within Christianity is without parallel. Until Thomas Aquinas in the thirteenth century, all Christian theologians in the West started from explicitly Augustinian premises. Even Thomas did not shake off his debt to Augustine, although he replaced Augustine's strong Platonic orientation with a more empirical Aristotelian one. Augustine emphasized the

ARCHITECTURE	LITERATURE & PHILOSOPHY	MUSIC
	c. 67 Apostle Paul, bearer of Christian message throughout Mediterranean, martyred at Rome	
c. 324 Constantine enlarges stadium in Constantinople to form Hippodrome **c. 326-345** Holy Sepulchre, Jerusalem	**c. 350** *Codex Sinaiticus*, earliest extant Greek codex of New Testament **c. 374–404** Saint John Chrysostom active as writer and preacher	**after 350** Beginnings of Byzantine music, based probably on Syriac and Hebrew music
c. 333 Old Saint Peter's Basilica, Vatican; use of basilica plan and central plan with dome	**c. 386** Saint Jerome translates Bible into Latin	**386** Saint Ambrose of Milan begins use of vernacular hymns in church
c. 450 Mausoleum of Galla Placidia, Ravenna **c. 493–526** Church of Sant' Apollinare Nuovo, Ravenna **527–565** Monastery of Saint Catherine, Mount Sinai, Egypt **c. 530–548** San Vitale, Ravenna **532–537** Church of Hagia Sophia, Constantinople, combines basilica plan and central plan with dome	**397** Augustine of Hippo, *Confessions* **412–426** Augustine of Hippo, *The City of God* **c. 522–524** Boethius, *The Consolation of Philosophy*, allegorical treatise; translation of Aristotle's writings **524** Execution of Boethius by Theodoric the Ostrogoth **c. 562** Procopius, *History of the Wars, The Buildings, Secret History*	
	c. 620 Qur'an develops	**590–602** Gregorian Chant established at Rome during papacy of Gregory the Great **7th cent.** Golden Age of Byzantine hymnody

absolute majesty of God, the immutability of God's will, and the flawed state of the human condition (notions derived from Saint Paul). These tenets received a powerful reformulation in the Protestant Reformation by Martin Luther (who as a Catholic friar had lived under the rule of Saint Augustine) and by John Calvin, a profound student of Augustine's theological writings.

The City of God Augustine also made a notable impact beyond theology. *The City of God*, begun about 412, was an attempt to formulate a coherent and all-embracing philosophy of history, the first such attempt in the West. For Augustine, history moves on a straight line in a direction from its origin in God until it ends, again in God, at the consummation of history in the Last Judgment. Augustine rejected the older pagan notion that history repeats itself in endless cycles. His reading of the Bible convinced him that humanity had an origin, played out its story, and would terminate. The city of man would be judged and the city of God would be saved. Subsequent philosophers of history have secularized this view but, with few exceptions (Vico, a seventeenth-century Italian philosopher, for example), have maintained the outlines of Augustine's framework to some extent. "A bright future," "an atomic wasteland of the future," and "classless society" are all statements about the end of history, all statements that echo, however dimly, the worldview of Augustine.

The Confessions Augustine also invented the genre of self-reflective writing in the West. "I would know myself that I might know Thee," Augustine writes of God in the *Confessions*. Before Augustine's time, memoirs related a life in terms of social, political, or military affairs (as did, for example, Caesar's *Gallic Wars*), but Augustine's intimate self-scrutiny and inquiry into the significance of life were new in Western culture. There would be no other work like the *Confessions* until Petrarch, an indefatigable student of Augustine, wrote his *Letter to Posterity* in the mid-fourteenth century. The Renaissance writers, an extremely self-conscious generation, were devoted students of Augustine's stately Latin prose; even the great later autobiographies of our inherited culture—those of Gibbon, Mill, Newman—are literary and spiritual descendants of Augustine.

Augustine's *Confessions* is a compelling analysis of his spiritual and intellectual development from his youth until the time of his conversion to Christianity and readiness to return to his native Africa. The title must be understood in a triple sense—a confession of sin, an act of faith in God, and a confession of praise—so it is appropriate that Augustine began his book as a prayer directed to God.

Although strongly autobiographical, the *Confessions* is actually a long meditation by Augustine on the hidden grace of God as his life is shaped toward its appointed end. Augustine "confesses" to God (and the reader) how

his early drive for fame as a teacher of rhetoric, his flirtation with the Manichean sect and its belief in gods of evil and good, his liaison with a woman that resulted in the birth of a son, and his restless movement from North Africa to Rome and Milan were all part of a seamless web of circumstance that made up an individual life. Interspersed in the narrative line of his early life are Augustine's reflections on the most basic philosophical and theological questions of the day, always linked to his own experience.

If the *Confessions* can be said to be the beginning of autobiography, beyond that historic importance it is classic and singular in its balance of immense learning, searching speculation, and intense self-scrutiny. It is a work concerned first of all with meaning at the deepest philosophical level, and its full power is evident only to the reader who will take the time to enter Augustine's line of argument.

BOETHIUS

In the twilight period in Ravenna, between the death of the last Roman emperor and the arrival of Justinian's troops, an important figure who bridged the gap between Classical paganism and Christianity lived and died. Anicius Manlius Severinus Boethius was a highly educated Roman who entered the service of the Goth king Theodoric in 522. Imprisoned in the city of Pavia for reasons that are not clear, Boethius wrote a treatise called *The Consolation of Philosophy* while awaiting execution. Cast as a dialogue between Lady Philosophy and the author on the philosophical and religious basis for human freedom, the work blends the spirit of the biblical Book of Job with Roman stoicism. Attempting to console him for his sad state of disgrace and imprisonment, Lady Philosophy demands that the author avoid self-pity, that he face his troubles with serenity and hope. Insisting that a provident God overcomes all evil, Philosophy insists that blind fate has no control over humanity. She explains that human freedom exists along with an all-knowing God and that good will triumph. Although Christian themes permeate the work, there is no explicit mention of Christian doctrine. What one does sense is the recasting of Roman thought into Christian patterns. In a way, *The Consolation of Philosophy* is one of the last works of the late Roman period. It reflects the elegance of Roman expression, the burgeoning hope of Christianity, and the terrible sadness that must have afflicted any sensitive Roman living in this period.

The Consolation of Philosophy was one of the most widely read and influential works of the Middle Ages (Chaucer made an English translation of it from an already-existing French version). Its message of hope and faith was quoted liberally by every major medieval thinker from Thomas Aquinas to Dante Alighieri.

Boethius sets out a basic problem and provides an answer that would become normative Christian thought

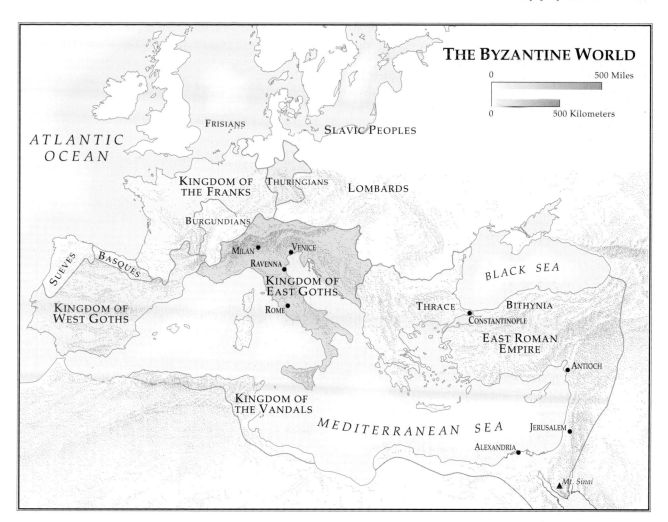

THE BYZANTINE WORLD

for subsequent centuries. In *The Consolation*, Boethius asks how one can reconcile human freedom with the notion of an all-knowing God. Put another way: if God knows what we do before we do it, how can we be said to be free agents who must accept responsibility for personal acts? The answer, Boethius insists through Lady Philosophy, is to look at the problem from the point of view of God, not from the human vantage point. God lives in eternity. Eternity does not mean a "long time" with a past and a future. Eternity means "no time": God lives in an eternal moment that for Him is a "now." In that sense, God does not "foresee" the future. There is no future for God. God sees everything in one simple moment that is only past, present, and future from the human point of view. Boethius says that God does not exercise *praevidentia* (seeing things before they happen) but *providence* (seeing all things in the simultaneity of their happening). Thus God, in a single eternal, ineffable moment, grasps all activity, which exists for us as a long sequence of events. More specifically, in that moment, God sees our choices, the events that follow from them, and the ultimate consequences of those choices.

The consolation of Boethius, as Lady Philosophy explains it, rests in the fact that people do act with freedom, that they are not in the hands of an indifferent fate, and that the ultimate meaning of life rests with the all-seeing presence of a God, not a blind force. Lady Philosophy sums up her discussion with Boethius by offering him this "consolation." It is her assurance that his life, even while awaiting execution in a prison cell, was not the product of a blind fate or an uncaring force in the universe.

The language of Boethius, with its discussion of time, eternity, free will, and the nature of God, echoes the great philosophical tradition of Plato and Aristotle (Boethius had translated the latter's works), as well as the stoicism of Cicero and the theological reflections of Augustine. It is a fitting end to the intellectual tradition of the late Roman Empire in the West.

THE ASCENDANCY OF BYZANTIUM

CONSTANTINOPLE

The city of Constantinople in Turkey became the center of imperial life in the early fifth century and reached its highest expression of power in the early sixth century with the ascension to the throne of Justinian in 527 (see map, "Justinian's Empire"). His stated intention was to restore the empire to a state of grandeur. In this project he was aided by his wife Theodora. A former dancer and prostitute, Theodora was a tough-minded and capable woman who added strength and resolve to the grandiose plans of the emperor. She was Justinian's equal, and perhaps more.

The reign of Justinian and Theodora was impressive, if profligate, by any standard. The emperor encouraged Persian monks residing in China to bring back silkworms for the introduction of the silk industry into the West. Because the silk industry of China was a fiercely guarded monopoly, the monks accomplished this rather dangerous mission by smuggling silkworm eggs out of the country in hollow tubes and, within a decade, the silk industry in the Western world rivaled that of China.

Justinian also revised and codified Roman law, a gigantic undertaking of scholarship and research. Roman law had evolved over a thousand-year period and, by Justinian's time, was a vast jumble of disorganized and often contradictory decisions, decrees, statutes, opinions, and legal codes. Under the aegis of the emperor, a legal scholar named Tribonian produced order out of this chaos. First a *Code* that summarized all imperial decrees from the time of Hadrian (in the second century) to the time of Justinian was published. The *Code* was followed by the *Pandects* ("digest"), which synthesized a vast quantity of legal opinion and

scholarship from the past. Finally came the *Institutes*, a legal collection broken down into four categories by which the laws concerning persons, things, actions, and personal wrongs (in other words, criminal law) were set forth. The body of this legal revision became the basis for the law courts of the empire and, in later centuries, the basis for the use of Roman law in the West.

Justinian and Theodora were fiercely partisan Christians who took a keen interest in theology and ecclesiastical governance. Justinian's fanatical devotion prompted him to shut down the last surviving Platonic academy in the world on the grounds that its paganism was inimical to the true religion. His own personal life—despite evidences of cruelty and capriciousness—was austere and abstemious, influenced by the presence of so many monks in the city of Constantinople. His generosity to the church was great, with his largess shown most clearly in openhanded patronage of church building. Hagia Sophia, his most famous project, has become legendary for the beauty and opulence of its decoration.

CHURCH OF HAGIA SOPHIA: MONUMENT AND SYMBOL

Hagia Sophia (Greek for "Holy Wisdom") was the principal church of Constantinople. It had been destroyed twice, once by fire and—during Justinian's reign—during the terrible civil disorders of the Nika revolt in 532 that devastated most of the European side of the city. Soon afterward, Justinian decided to rebuild the church using the plans of two architects: Anthemius of Tralles and Isidore of Miletus. Work began in 532, and the new edifice was solemnly dedicated five years later in the presence of Justinian and Theodora.

The Church of Hagia Sophia was a stunning architectural achievement that combined the longitudinal shape of the Roman basilica with a domed central plan. Two centuries earlier Constantine had used both the dome and basilica shapes in the Church of the Holy Sepulcher in Jerusalem, as we have seen, but he had not joined them into a unity. In still earlier domed buildings in the Roman world, such as the Pantheon and Santa Costanza, the dome rested on a circular drum. This gave the dome solidity but limited its height and expansiveness. Anthemius and Isidore solved this problem by the use of *pendentives* [**Fig. 7.2**], triangular masonry devices that carried the weight of the dome on massive piers rather than straight down from the drum.

In the Church of Hagia Sophia, the central dome was abutted by two half-domes so that a person looking down at the building from above might see a nave in the form of an oval instead of a quadrangle [**Fig. 7.3**].

◆ **7.2** Dome construction: 1. Pendentive; 2. Drum; 3. Cupola; 4. Lantern.

◆ **7.3** Church of Hagia Sophia, Constantinople (Istanbul), Turkey, 532–537. Exterior view from the southeast. The towers, of Turkish origin, are a later addition.

Architects, Anthemius of Tralles and Isidore of Miletus. Image © Alan Oddie/PhotoEdit

VOICES OF THEIR TIMES

Procopius of Caesarea

Procopius was in the service of Emperor Justinian. His *Secret History* was a bitterly critical portrait of the emperor and the empress.

The whole ceiling is overlaid with pure gold . . . yet the light reflecting from the stones [of the mosaics] prevails, shining out of rivalry with the gold. There are two colonnades, one on each side, not separated in any way from the church itself. . . . They have vaulted ceilings and are decorated with gold. One of these is designated for men-worshipers and the other for women but they have nothing to distinguish them nor do they differ in any way. Their very equality serves to beautify the church and their similarity to adorn it.

Who can recount the beauty of the columns and the stones with which the church is decorated? One might imagine that he had come upon a meadow with its flowers in full bloom. For he would surely marvel at the purple of some, the green tint of others, and at those from which the white flashes, and again, at those which Nature, like some painter, varies with contrasting colors.

And whenever anyone enters this church to pray . . . his mind is lifted up toward God and is exalted, feeling that He cannot be very far away, but must especially love to dwell in this place which He has favored. And this does not happen only to one who sees the church for the first time, but the same experience comes to him on each successive occasion, as though the sight were new each time. Of this spectacle no one ever has a surfeit, but when present in the church people rejoice in what they see, and when they depart they take enormous delight in talking about it.

Reprinted by permission of the publishers and the Trustees of the Loeb Classical Library from *Procopius*: Volume I, Loeb Classical Library®, Volume 48, translated by H. B. Dewing, Cambridge, Mass: Harvard University Press, 1914. The Loeb Classical Library® is a registered trademark of the President and Fellows of Harvard College.

The church—184 feet (55.2 m) high, 41 feet (12.3 m) higher than the Pantheon—retained a hint of the old basilica style as a result of the columned side aisles and the gallery for female worshipers in the triforium space above the arches of the aisles, but the overwhelming visual impression came from the massive dome. Because the pendentives reduced the weight of the dome, the area between drum and dome could be pierced by forty windows that made the dome seem to hang in space. Light streamed into the church from the windows and refracted off the rich mosaics and colored marbles that covered the interior [**Fig. 7.4**].

Light, in fact, was a key theoretical element behind the entire conception of Hagia Sophia. Light is the symbol of divine wisdom in the philosophy of Plato and in the New Testament. A common metaphor in pagan and biblical wisdom had the sun and its rays represent the eternity of God and His illumination of mortals. The suffusion of light was an element in the Hagia Sophia that went far beyond the functional need to illuminate the interior of the church. Light refracting in the church created a spiritual ambience analogous to that of heaven, where the faithful would be bathed in the actual light of God.

Worship in Hagia Sophia The sequence of the various parts of the worship service at Constantinople—the **liturgy**—was developed from the inspiration of Saint John Chrysostom (345–407), patriarch of the city in the century before Justinian. The official liturgy of Byzantine Christianity is still the Divine Liturgy of Saint John Chrysostom, modified and added to over the centuries. In that liturgy, the worshiping community visualized itself as standing in the forecourt of heaven when it worshiped in the church. Amid the swirling incense, the glittering light, and the stately chants of the clergy and people comes a sense of participation with the household of heaven standing before God. A fragment from the liturgy—added during the reign of Justinian's successor Justin II (565–578)—underscores the point dramatically. Note the characteristic cry of *Wisdom!* and the description of the congregation as mystically present in heaven:

PRIEST Wisdom! That ever being guarded by Thy power, we may give glory to Thee, Father, Son, and Holy Spirit, now and forevermore.

◆ **7.4** Interior of the Church of Hagia Sophia. Looking toward the apse, this view shows how the windows between drum and dome give an impression of floating lightness that continues down to the floor. Note the hanging shields with Arabic quotations from the Qur'an. (*© Robert Harding/Getty Images*)

CONGREGATION Amen. Let us here who represent the mystic Cherubim in singing the thrice holy hymn to the life-giving Trinity now lay aside every earthly care so that we may welcome the King of the universe who comes escorted by invisible armies of angels. Alleluia. Alleluia. Alleluia.

Hagia Sophia was enriched by subsequent emperors, and after repairs were made to the dome (in 989), new mosaics were added to the church. After the fall of Constantinople (1453), the Turks turned the church into a mosque; the mosaics were whitewashed or plastered over because the Qur'an (also called Koran) prohibited the use of images. When the mosque was converted to a museum by the modern Turkish state, some of the mosaics were uncovered, so today we can get some sense of the splendor of the original interior.

Other Churches in Constantinople Other monuments bear the mark of Justinian's creative efforts. His Church of the Holy Apostles, built on the site of an

◆ **7.5** The Mausoleum of Galla Placidia, Ravenna, Italy, early 5th century. This building has sunk more than a meter (3¼′) into the marshy soil, thus making it rather squat in appearance. (*Image © Scala/Art Resource, NY*)

earlier church of the same name destroyed by an earthquake, did not survive the fall of the city in 1453 but did serve as a model for the Church of Saint Mark in Venice. Near the Church of Hagia Sophia is the Church of Hagia Eirene ("Holy Peace"), now a mosque, whose architecture also shows the combination of basilica and dome. The church, dedicated to the martyr saints Sergius and Bacchus and begun in 527, was a preliminary study for the later Hagia Sophia. In all, Justinian built more than twenty-five churches and convents in Constantinople. His program of secular architecture included an impressive water conduit system that still exists.

RAVENNA: ART AND ARCHITECTURE

Ravenna, Italy, is a repository of monuments that reflect its late Roman, barbarian Gothic, and Byzantine history. The Mausoleum ("burial chapel") of Galla Placidia (who reigned as regent from 430 to 450) was built at the end of the Roman period of Ravenna's history [**Fig. 7.5**]. Once thought to be the tomb of the empress (hence its name), it is more likely a **votive chapel** to Saint Lawrence originally attached to the nearby Church of the Holy Cross. The huge **sarcophagi** in the building are probably medieval. This small chapel in the shape of a cross, very plain on the outside, shows the architectural tendency to combine the basilica-style nave with the structure of a dome (it even uses a modified pendentive form) used later in monumental structures like Hagia Sophia.

Mosaics The importance of Galla Placidia rests in the complete and breathtakingly beautiful mosaics that decorate the walls and ceiling. The north niche,

◆ **7.6** *Christ as the Good Shepherd*, 5th century. Symbolizing the heavens, the motif of gold, stylized sunbursts and stars set in a deep blue ground can be seen in the vault. Note the beardless Christ dressed in a Roman toga.

Lunette mosaic, Mausoleum of Galla Placidia, Ravenna, Italy. Image © Scala/Art Resource, NY

just above the entrance, has a *lunette* (small arched space) mosaic depicting Christ as the Good Shepherd [**Fig. 7.6**]. Clothed in royal purple and with a gold staff in his hand, the figure of Christ has a courtly, almost languid elegance that refines the more rustic depictions of the Good Shepherd theme in earlier Roman Christian art. The vaulting of both the *apse* (the altar end of the church) and the dome is covered with a deep blue mosaic interspersed with stylized sunbursts and stars in gold. This "Persian rug" motif symbolized the heavens, the dwelling place of God. Because the *tesserae* (the small cubes that make up the mosaic) are not set fully flush in the wall, the surfaces of the mosaic are irregular. These surfaces thus refract and break up the light in the chapel, especially from flickering lamps and candles.

Opposite the lunette of the Good Shepherd is another lunette that depicts the deacon martyr of the Roman Church, Saint Lawrence, who stands next to the gridiron that was the instrument of his death. Beyond the gridiron is an open cabinet containing codices of the four gospels [**Fig. 7.7**]. The spaces above these mosaics are filled with figures of the apostles. Between these are symbols of the search for religious understanding: deer, doves, fountains. In the arches, more spectacular and often overlooked, are the abstract interlocking designs

with their brightness and *trompe l'œil* ("trick-the-eye") quality.

Baptisteries The two baptisteries of Ravenna represent a major religious division of the time between the **Orthodox** Christians, who accepted the divinity of Christ, and the **Arian** Christians, who did not. The Neonian Baptistery, built by Orthodox Christians in the early fifth century next to the ancient cathedral of the city, is octagonal, as were most baptisteries, because of their derivation from Roman bathhouses. The ceiling mosaic, directly over the baptismal pool, is particularly striking. The lower register of the mosaic, above the windows, shows floral designs based on common Roman decorative motifs. Just above is a circle of empty thrones interspersed with altars with biblical codices open on them [**Fig. 7.8**]. In the band above are the apostles, who seem to be walking in a stately procession around the circle of the dome. In the central disc is a mosaic of the baptism of Christ by John the Baptist in the river Jordan. The spirit of the river is depicted as Neptune.

The mosaic ensemble in the ceiling was designed to reflect the beliefs of the participants in the ceremonies below. The circling apostles reminded the candidates for baptism that the church was founded on the apostles;

◆ **7.7** *The Martyrdom of Saint Lawrence*, 5th century. Saint Lawrence stands to the right of the gridiron on which, legend says, he was roasted. The window, a modern addition, is made of alabaster.

Mosaic, Mausoleum of Galla Placidia, Ravenna, Italy//© Scala/Art Resource, NY

◆ **7.8** Baptisteries of the Orthodox and Arians, Ravenna, Italy. On the left is the mosaic of the Baptistery of the Orthodox (middle of the 5th century) and on the right, the mosaic of the Baptistery of the Arians (end of the 5th century). In the central disks of both ceiling mosaics, John the Baptist baptizes Christ in the river Jordan (symbolized by a seated Neptune) while the apostles encircle them in an outer disk. Notice the more severe style of the Arians mosaic.

Cupola mosaics, Ravenna, Italy//Both images © Scala/Art Resource, NY

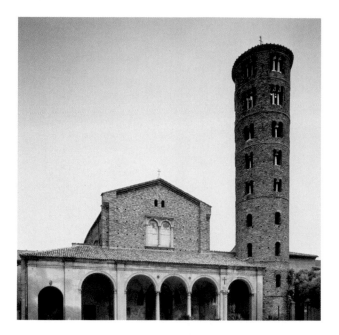

◆ **7.9** Church of Sant'Apollinare Nuovo, Ravenna, Italy, c. 493–526. The clear outlines of the basilica style can be seen in the photograph. (The tower is a medieval addition.) Bishop Apollinaris, a second-century apologist for Christianity, defended his faith in a treatise addressed to Emperor Marcus Aurelius. (*Image © Scala/Art Resource, NY*)

the convert's baptism was a promise that one day he or she would dwell with the apostles in heaven. Finally, the codices on the altars taught of the sources of their belief, whereas the empty thrones promised the new Christians a place in the heavenly Jerusalem. The art, then, was not merely decorative but, in the words of a modern Orthodox thinker, "theology in color."

The Arian Baptistery, built by the Goths toward the end of the fifth century, is far more severely decorated. Again the traditional scene of Christ's baptism is in the central disc of the ceiling mosaic. Here the figure of the river Jordan has lobster-like claws sprouting from his head—a curiously pagan marine touch. The Twelve Apostles in the lower register are divided into two groups: one led by Peter and the other by Paul. These two groups converge at a throne bearing a jeweled cross (the crucifix with the body of Christ on the cross is uncommon in this period) that represents in a single symbol the passion and the resurrection of Christ.

Sant' Apollinare Nuovo Theodoric, the emperor of the Goths who had executed Boethius and reigned from 493 to 526, was buried in a massive mausoleum that may still be seen on the outskirts of Ravenna. The cap of the mausoleum is a huge stone that measures 36′ x 10′ (11 x 3 m). Aside from this mausoleum, the most famous

◆ **7.10** South wall mosaic, Sant'Apollinare Nuovo, Ravenna, Italy, early 6th century. The procession of male saints is in the lower register. The prophets and apostles are placed between the windows. Scenes from the Gospels are in the upper register. Theodoric's palace appears in the lower right. The mosaic curtains cover older representations of Arian saints. Note the hands from the original portraits on some of the columns. (*Image © Leonard Von Matt/Photo Researchers, Inc.*)

◆ **7.11** North wall mosaic, Sant'Apollinare Nuovo, Ravenna, Italy, early 6th century. Note the procession of female saints oriented behind the Three Magi, who all approach the enthroned Madonna. Details appear in Figure 7.12 and Figure 7.13. *(Image © Leonard Von Matt/Photo Researchers, Inc.)*

extant monument of Theodoric's reign is the Church of Sant'Apollinare Nuovo, originally called the Church of the Redeemer, the palace church of Theodoric [**Fig. 7.9**]. This church is constructed in the severe basilica style: a wide nave with two side aisles partitioned off from the nave by double columns of marble. The apse decorations have been destroyed, but the walls of the basilica, richly ornamented with mosaics, can be seen.

The mosaics, however, are of two different dates and reflect in one building both the Roman and Byzantine styles of art. On each side of the aisles, in the spaces just above the aisle arches, are processions of male and female saints, each procession facing toward the apse and main altar [**Fig. 7.10 7.11**]. They move to an enthroned Christ on one side and toward a Madonna and Child on the other. These mosaics were added to the church when the building passed from the Goths into Byzantine hands in the reign of Justinian. The depiction of Theodoric's palace in the lower register of the south wall mosaic (see Figure 7.10) still in fact shows evidence of Orthodox censorship. In the arched spaces one can still see traces of halos of now-excised Arian saints (or perhaps members of Theodoric's court) and on several columns can be seen the hands of figures replaced by decorative twisted draperies. The next register above has a line of prophetic figures. At the level of the clerestory windows are scenes from the New Testament—the miracles of Christ on one side [**Fig. 7.12**] and scenes from his passion on the

◆ **7.12** Jesus calls the apostles Peter and Andrew. Note the Christ figure in the royal purple toga and his beardless appearance.

Detail, upper-register mosaic, north wall, Sant'Apollinare Nuovo, Ravenna, Italy//Image © Scala/Art Resource, NY

other. These mosaics are very different in style from the procession of sainted martyrs on the lower level. The Gospel sequence is more Roman in inspiration: severe and simple. Certain themes of earlier Roman Christian iconography are evident. The procession of saints, most

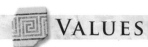

VALUES

Autocracy

The Byzantine Empire was characterized by its acceptance of the belief that the emperor was God's representative on earth who was the sole ruler of the empire and from whom all of the social and political goods for the empire flowed. This view of the political order is called autocracy, which means, in essence, that the imperial power is unlimited, and whatever power others may have (for example, in the military or in the state bureaucracy), that power flows from the unlimited power of the emperor, who has it by divine right. In this view, the emperor is both the highest civil and religious leader of the empire.

In the actual political order, emperors were overthrown or manipulated by political intrigue, but officially autocracy was accepted as the divinely ordered nature of things. Symbolic reinforcement of the autocratic power of the emperor (visually represented in the Ravenna mosaics of Justinian and Theodora) came through various symbolic means. The emperor alone dressed in the purple and gold once reserved for the semidivine pagan emperors. He lived in a palace with a rigid protocol of ceremony. When participating in the public worship of the church (the liturgy), he was given a special place and special recognition within that liturgy. Public insignia and other artifacts like coins recognized his authority as coming from God. It was commonplace in the literature of the time to see the emperor as the regent of God on earth, with his role compared to the sun, which brings light and warmth to his subjects.

Many autocracies (from the Egyptian pharaohs to the French kings just before the Revolution) claimed such a relationship to the divine. The Byzantine Empire not only built itself on this idea but also maintained an intimate bond between the human and the divine in the person of the emperor. This concept would last almost a millennium in Constantinople and be replicated in Russia with the tsar until modern times.

◆ **7.13** The Magi bearing gifts. Christian legend had already named these figures Balthasar, Melchior, and Caspar, which can be seen inscribed on the mosaic.

Detail, lower-register mosaic, north wall, Sant' Apollinare Nuovo, Ravenna, Italy//Image © Scala/Art Resource, NY

◆ **7.14** Church of San Vitale, Ravenna, Italy, c. 530–548. This complex building, the inspiration for Charlemagne's church at Aachen (see Figure 9.9), gives little exterior evidence that it is constructed in the basilica style. *(Image © Angelo Hornak/CORBIS)*

likely erected by artists from a Constantinople studio, is much more lush, reverent, and static in tone. The Orientalizing element is especially noteworthy in the depiction of the Three Magi (with their Phrygian caps) [**Fig. 7.13**] who offer gifts to the Christ Child.

San Vitale The Church of San Vitale most clearly testifies to the presence of Justinian in Ravenna [**Fig. 7.14**]. Dedicated by Bishop Maximian in 547, it had been begun by Bishop Ecclesius in 526, the year Justinian came to the throne, while the Goths still ruled Ravenna. The Church of San Vitale is octagonal, with

◆ **7.15** Christ enthroned, with Saint Vitalis and Bishop Ecclesius, c. 530. At the extreme right, the bishop holds a model of the church while Christ hands the crown of martyrdom to the saint on the left.

Ceiling mosaic, San Vitale, Ravenna, Italy // Image © Scala / Art Resource, NY

◆ **7.16** Emperor Justinian and courtiers, c. 547. The church authorities stand at the emperor's left; the civil authorities at the right. Note the *Chi Rho* on the shield of the soldier.

Mosaic, north wall of the apse, Church of San Vitale, Ravenna, Italy // Image © Cameraphoto Arte, Venice / Art Resource, NY

only the barest hint of basilica length. The octagon has another octagon within it. This interior octagon, supported by columned arches and containing a second-story women's gallery, is the structural basis for the dome. The dome is supported on the octagonal walls by small vaults called *squinches* that cut across the angles of each part of the octagon.

The most arresting characteristic of San Vitale, apart from its intricate and not fully understood architectural design, is its stunning program of mosaics. In the apse is a great mosaic of Christ the Pantocrator, the one who sustains all things in his hands [**Fig. 7.15**]. Christ is portrayed as a beardless young man, clothed in royal purple. He holds in his left hand a book with seven seals (a reference to the Book of Revelation) and offers the crown

of martyrdom to Saint Vitalis with his right. Flanked by the two archangels, Christ is offered a model of the church by Bishop Ecclesius, who laid its foundations. Above the figures are symbolic representations of the four rivers of paradise.

Mosaics to the left and right of the apse mosaic represent the royal couple as regents of Christ on earth. On the left wall of the sanctuary is a mosaic depicting Justinian and his attendants [**Fig. 7.16**]. It is no mere accident or exercise of simple piety that the soldiers carry a shield with *Chi Rho* (the first Greek letters in the name of Christ) or that there are twelve attendants or that the figure of the emperor divides clergy and laity. The emperor considered himself the regent of Christ, an attitude summed up in the iconographic, or

◆ **7.17** Empress Theodora and retinue, c. 547. Note the Three Magi on the hem of the empress's gown.

Mosaic, south wall of the apse, Church of San Vitale, Ravenna, Italy//Image © Cameraphoto Arte, Venice/Art Resource, NY

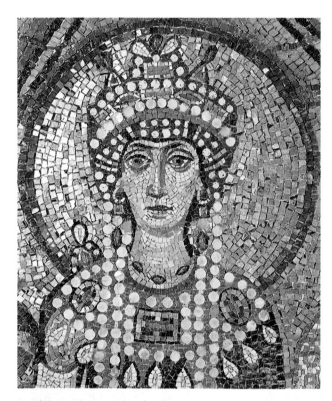

◆ **7.18** Empress Theodora, c. 547. Note the mosaic's uneven surface that refracts and reflects the flickering light of candles and lamps and is created by setting the tesserae (the small cubes that make up the mosaic) less than fully flush with the wall.

Detail of apse south wall mosaic, Church of San Vitale, Ravenna, Italy//Image © Leonard Von Matt/Photo Researchers, Inc.

◆ **7.19** Bishop's *cathedra* ("throne") of Maximian, c. 546–556. Bishop Maximian (Maximianus) is portrayed in the Justinian mosaic (Figure 7.16).

Ivory panels on wood frame, 22" (.6 m) wide x 4'11" (1.5 m) high. Museo Arcivescovile, Ravenna, Italy//© Scala/Art Resource, NY

◆ **7.20** Aerial view of the fortress Monastery of Saint Catherine, Sinai Desert, Egypt, 6th century. Constructed by order of the Emperor Justinian between 527 and 565 at the foot of Mount Moses, the fortress surrounds the monastery and its church, which was built over what is thought to be Moses' Burning Bush. The church (called the *Katholikon* from Justinian's time) can be seen flanked by a bell tower in the lower center of the walled enclosure. The formal name of the monastery is the Monastery of the Transfiguration. *(Image © H. Le Floc/Explorer/Photo Researchers, Inc.)*

symbolic, program: Justinian represents Christ on earth, and his power balances both church and state. The only figure identified in the mosaic is Bishop (later Archbishop) Maximian flanked by his clergy, who include a deacon with a jeweled gospel and a subdeacon with a chained incense pot.

Opposite the emperor's retinue, Empress Theodora and her attendants look across at the imperial group [**Fig. 7.17 and 7.18**]. Theodora holds a chalice to complement the *paten* ("bread basket") held by the emperor. At the hem of Theodora's gown is a small scene of the Magi bringing gifts to the Christ Child. Scholars disagree whether the two mosaics represent the royal couple bringing the eucharistic gifts for the celebration of the liturgy or the donation of the sacred vessels for the church. It was customary for rulers to give such gifts to the more important churches of their realm. The fact that the empress seems to be leaving her palace (two male functionaries of the court are ushering her out) makes the latter interpretation more probable. The women at Theodora's left are striking; those to the extreme left are stereotyped, but the two closest to the empress appear more individualized, leading some art historians to suggest that they are idealized portraits of two of Theodora's closest friends: the wife and daughter of the conqueror of Ravenna, Belisarius.

Maximian's Throne The royal generosity extended not only to the building and decoration of the Church of San Vitale. An ivory throne, now preserved in the episcopal museum of Ravenna, was a gift from the emperor to Bishop Maximian, the ecclesiastical ruler of Ravenna when San Vitale was dedicated [**Fig. 7.19**]. A close stylistic analysis of the carving on the throne has led scholars to see the work of at least four different artists on the panels, all probably from Constantinople. The front of the throne bears portraits of John the Baptist

and the four evangelists, while the back has scenes from the New Testament with sides showing episodes from the Old Testament of the life of Joseph. The purely decorative elements of trailing vines and animals show the style of a different hand, probably Syrian. The bishop's throne (*cathedra* in Latin; a cathedral is a church where a bishop presides) bears a small monogram: "Maximian, Bishop." The entire ensemble of San Vitale, with its pierced capitals typical of the Byzantine style, its elaborate mosaic portraits of saints and prophets, its lunette mosaics of Old Testament prefigurations of the Eucharist, and monumental mosaic scenes, is a living testimony to the rich fusion of imperial, Christian, and Middle Eastern cultural impulses. San Vitale is a microcosm of the sociopolitical vision of Byzantium fused with the religious worldview of early Christianity.

SAINT CATHERINE'S MONASTERY AT MOUNT SINAI, EGYPT

Justinian is remembered not only in Constantinople and Ravenna but also in the Near East, where he founded a monastery that is still in use some fifteen hundred years later—a living link back to the Byzantine world.

In her *Peregrinatio*, that wonderfully tireless traveler of the fourth century, Etheria, describes a visit to the forbidding desert of the Sinai to pray at the site where God appeared to Moses in a burning bush (that, Etheria assures us, "is still alive to this day and throws out shoots") and to climb the mountain where the Law was given to Moses. She says that there was a church at the spot of the burning bush, with some hermits living nearby to tend it and see to the needs of pilgrim visitors. More than a century later, Emperor Justinian built a monastery fortress at the foot of Mount Sinai and some pilgrimage chapels on the slopes of the mountain [**Fig. 7.20**]. An Arabic inscription over one of the gates tells the story:

The pious king Justinian, of the Greek Church, in the expectation of divine assistance and in the hope of divine promises, built the monastery of Mount Sinai and the Church of the Colloquy [a church over the spot where Moses spoke to God in the burning bush] to his eternal memory and that of his wife, Theodora, so that all the earth and all its inhabitants should become the heritage of God; for the Lord is the best of masters. The building was finished in the thirtieth year of his reign and he gave the monastery a superior named Dukhas. This took place in the 6021st year after Adam, the 527th year [by the calendar] of the era of Christ the Savior.

Because of several factors—most important its extreme isolation and the very dry weather—the monastery is an immense repository of ancient Byzantine art and culture. It preserves some of Justinian's architecture and also some of the oldest icons in Christianity. The monastery is also famous as the site of the rediscovery of the earliest Greek **codex** of the New Testament hitherto found. Called the *Codex Sinaiticus*, it was discovered in the monastery by the German scholar Konstantin von Tischendorf in the nineteenth century. The codex, from the middle of the fourth century, was given by the monks to the Tsar of Russia. In 1933 the Soviet government sold it to the British Museum for £100,000, where it remains today, a precious document.

The monastery is surrounded by heavy, fortified walls, the main part of which date from before Justinian's time. Within those walls are some modern buildings, including a fireproof structure that houses the monastery's library and icon collections. The monastic church, the *Katholikon*, dates from the time of Justinian, as recently discovered inscriptions carved into the wooden trusses in the ceiling of the church prove. Even the name of the architect, Stephanos, was uncovered. This church thus is unique: signed sixth-century ecclesiastical architecture.

Icons One of the more spectacular holdings of the monastery is its vast collections of religious icons. Because of the **iconoclastic** controversies of the eighth and ninth centuries in the Byzantine Empire, almost no pictorial art remains from the period before the eighth century. Sinai survived the purges of the iconoclasts that engulfed the rest of the Byzantine world because of its extreme isolation. At Sinai, a range of icons (the Greek word *icon* means "image") that date from Justinian's time to the modern period can be seen. In a real sense, the icons of the monastery of Saint Catherine show the entire evolution of icon painting.

In the Byzantine Christian tradition, icon refers to a painting of a religious figure or a religious scene that is used in the public worship (the liturgy) of the church. Icons are not primarily decorative, and they are didactic only in a secondary sense: For the Orthodox Christian faithful, the icon is a window into the world of the sacred. Just as Jesus Christ was in the flesh but

imaged God in eternity, so the icon is a "thing," but it permits a glimpse into the timeless world of religious mystery. One stands before the icon and speaks through its image to the reality beyond it. This explains why the figures in an icon are usually portrayed full-front with no shadow or sense of three-dimensionality. The figures "speak" directly and frontally to the viewer against a hieratic background of gold.

This iconic style becomes clear by an examination of an icon of Christ that may well have been sent to his new monastery by Justinian himself [**Fig. 7.21**]. The icon is done using the *encaustic* method of painting (a technique common in the Roman world for funerary portraits): painting with molten wax that has been colored by pigments. Christ, looking directly at the viewer, is robed in royal purple; in his left hand he holds a jeweled codex, and with his right hand he blesses the viewer.

This icon is an example from a large number found at Sinai that can be dated from before the tenth century. The entire corpus represents a continuous tradition of

◆ **7.21** *Christ Pantocrater*, c. 500–530. The book is a complex symbol of the Bible, Christ as the Word of God, and the record of human secrets that will be opened on the Last Day.

Encaustic on wood panel. 32" x 27" (84 x 46 cm). Monastery of Saint Catherine, Sinai, Egypt//Image © The Art Archive/Gianni Dagli Orti

Byzantine art and piety. Mount Sinai is unique in its great tradition of historical continuity. Despite the rise of Islam, the harshness of the atmosphere, the vicissitudes of history, and the changing culture of the modern world, the monastery fortress at Sinai is living testimony to a style of life and a religiosity with an unbroken history to the time of Justinian's building program.

THE PERSISTENCE OF BYZANTINE CULTURE

It is simplistic to describe Byzantine art as unchanging—it underwent regional, intellectual, social, and iconographic changes—but a person who visits a modern Greek or Russian Orthodox church is struck more by the similarities than by the dissimilarities with the art of early medieval Constantinople. Furthermore, the immediately recognizable Byzantine style can be found in the history of art in areas as geographically diverse as Sicily in southern Italy and the far-eastern reaches of Russia. What explains this basic persistence of style and outlook?

RUSSIA

First of all, until it fell to the Turks in 1453, Constantinople exerted an extraordinary cultural influence over the rest of the Eastern Christian world. Russian emissaries sent to Constantinople in the late tenth century to inquire about religion brought back to Russia both favorable reports about Byzantine Christianity and a taste for the Byzantine style of religious art. The impact of services in Hagia Sophia most impressed the delegates of Prince Vladimir, the first Christian ruler in Russia. Although art in Christian Russia was to develop its own regional variations, it was still closely tied to the art of Constantinople; Russian "onion-dome" churches, for example, are native adaptations of the central-dome churches of Byzantium.

Russia, in fact, accepted Christianity about one hundred fifty years after the ban on icons was lifted in Constantinople in 843. By this time the second "golden age" of Byzantine art was well under way. By the eleventh century, Byzantine artists were not only working in Russia but had also established schools of icon painting in such centers as Kiev. By the end of the century, these schools had passed into the hands of Russian monks, but their stylistic roots remained the artistic ideas of Byzantium. Even after the Mongol invasions of Russia in 1240, Russian religious art continued to have close ties to the Greek world, although less with Constantinople than with the monastic centers of Mount Athos and Salonica in Greece.

ITALY

Byzantine influence was also strong in Italy. We have already seen the influence of Justinian's court on Ravenna. Although northern Italy fell to Lombard rule in the eighth century, Byzantine influence continued in the south of Italy for the next five hundred years. During the iconoclastic controversy in the East, many Greek artisans went into exile in Italy, where their work is still to be seen. Even while the Kingdom of Sicily was under Norman rule in the twelfth century, Byzantine artisans were still active, as the great mosaics of Monreale, Cefalù, and Palermo testify. In northern Italy, especially in Venice, the trade routes to the East and the effects of the Crusades permitted a strong presence of Byzantine art, as the mosaics of the Church of Saint Mark (as well as Byzantine art looted when the crusaders entered Constantinople in 1204) and the cathedral on the nearby island of Torcello attest. We shall see in later chapters the impact of this artistic presence on panel painting in Italy. Until the revolutionary changes by Cimabue and Giotto at the end of the thirteenth century, the pervasive influence of this style was so great that Italian painting up to that time is often characterized as Italo–Byzantine.

BYZANTINE ART

There is another reason that Byzantine aesthetics seem so changeless over the centuries. From the time of Justinian (and even more so after controversies of the eighth and ninth centuries), Byzantine art was intimately tied to the theology and liturgical practices of the Orthodox Church. The use of icons, for example, is not merely a pious practice but a deep-rooted part of the faith. Each year the Orthodox Church celebrated a feast commemorating the triumph of the Icon party called the Feast of the Triumph of Orthodoxy.

Art, then, is tied to theological doctrine and liturgical practice. Because of the innate conservatism of the theological tradition, innovation either in theology or in art was discouraged. The ideal of the artists was not to try something new but to infuse their work with a spirit of deep spirituality and unwavering reverence. This art, while extremely conservative, was never stagnant. The artists strove for fidelity to the past as their aesthetic criterion. As art historian André Grabar has noted, "Their role can be compared to that of musical performers in our day, who do not feel that their importance is diminished by the fact that they limit their talent to the interpretation of other people's work, since each interpretation contains original nuances."

This attitude of theological conservatism and aesthetic stability helps explain why, for example, the art of icon painting is considered a holy occupation in the Eastern Orthodox Church. Today, when a new Orthodox church is built, the congregation may commission from a monk or icon painter the necessary icons for the interior of the church. The expeditions of scholars who went to Saint Catherine's monastery to study the treasures there recall the sadness they felt at the funeral of a monk, Father Demetrios, in 1958. The last icon painter in the monastery, he marked the end of a tradition that stretched back nearly fifteen hundred years.

Travelers to Mount Athos in Greece can visit (with some difficulty) the small monastic communities (*sketes*) on the south of the peninsula, where monastic icon painters still work at their art. In our century there has been a renaissance of the appreciation of this style of painting. In Greece there has been a modern attempt to purge icon painting of Western influences (especially those of the Renaissance and the Baroque periods) in order to recover a more authentic link with the great Byzantine tradition of the past. In Russia there has been a surge of interest in the treasures of past religious art. This has resulted in careful conservation of the icons in Russia, exhibits of the art in the museums of Russia and abroad, and an intense scholarly study of this heritage as well as a revival of interest in the Orthodox Church.

BYZANTINE CULTURE

Byzantine culture was not confined to artistic concerns. We have already seen that Justinian made an important contribution to legal studies. Constantinople also had a literary, philosophical, and theological culture. Although Justinian closed the pagan academies, later Byzantine emperors encouraged humanistic and theological studies. Even though the links between Constantinople and the West were strained over the centuries, those links did remain intact. At first a good deal of Greek learning came into the West (after having been lost in the early Middle Ages) through the agency of Arabic sources. The philosophical writings of Aristotle became available to Westerners in the late twelfth and early thirteenth centuries in the form of Latin translations or Arabic translations of the Greek: Aristotle came to the University of Paris from the Muslim centers of learning in Spain and northern Africa. Not until the fifteenth century did Greek become a widely known language in the West; in the fourteenth century Petrarch and Boccaccio had a difficult time finding anyone to teach them the language. By the fifteenth century this situation had changed. One factor contributing to the Renaissance love for the classics was the presence in Italy of Greek-speaking scholars from Constantinople.

The importance of this reinfusion of Greek culture can be seen easily enough by looking at the great libraries of fifteenth-century Italy. Of the nearly four thousand books in the Vatican library listed in a catalog of 1484, a thousand were in Greek, most of which were from Constantinople. The core of the great library of Saint Mark's in Venice was Cardinal Bessarion's collection of Greek books, brought from the East when he went to the Council of Ferrara–Florence to discuss the union of the Greek and Latin churches in 1438. Bessarion brought with him, in addition to his books, a noted Platonic scholar, Genistos Plethon, who lectured on Platonic philosophy for the delighted Florentines. This event prompted Cosimo de' Medici to subsidize the collection, translation, and study of Plato's philosophy under the direction of Marsilio Ficino. Ficino's Platonic Academy, supported by Medici money, became a rallying point for the study of philosophical ideas.

The fall of Constantinople to the Turks in 1453 brought a flood of émigré Greek scholars to the West, in particular to Italy. The presence of these scholars enhanced the already considerable interest in Greek studies. Greek refugee scholars soon held chairs at the various **studia** ("schools") of the leading Italian cities. These scholars taught language, edited texts, wrote commentaries, and fostered an interest not only in Greek pagan learning but also in the literature of the Greek Fathers of the church. By the end of the fifteenth century, the famous Aldine press in Venice was publishing a whole series of Greek classics to meet the great demand for such works. This new source of learning and scholarship spread rapidly throughout Western Europe, so that by the early sixteenth century the study of Greek was an ordinary but central part of both humanistic and theological education.

The cultural worldview of Justinian's Constantinople is preserved directly in the conservative traditionalism of Orthodox religious art and indirectly by Constantinople's gift of Greek learning to Europe during the Renaissance. The great social and political power of the Byzantine Empire ended in the fifteenth century, although it had been in decline since the end of the twelfth century. Only the great monuments remain to remind us of a splendid and opulent culture now gone but once active and vigorous for nearly a thousand years.

SUMMARY

This chapter traces briefly the slow waning of Roman power in the West by focusing on two late Roman writers who are both Christians: Boethius, who wrote in provincial Ravenna, and Augustine, who lived in Roman North Africa.

◆ **The Ascendancy of Byzantine Culture.** As the wheel of fortune turned downward for Rome, Byzantium began its ascent as the center of culture. Our focus was on the great builder and patron of Byzantine culture, Emperor Justinian and his consort, Theodora. The central feature of their reign is its blending of their political power with the Christian Church so that church and state became a seamless whole. Christianity, which had been a despised and persecuted sect, now became the official religion of the state.

Byzantine Christianity had a readily recognizable look to it, which was most apparent in its art and architecture. It was an art that was otherworldly, formal, and profoundly sacred. A contemporary Orthodox theologian has said that the proper attitude of a Byzantine worshiper is *gazing*. The mosaics and icons of this tradition were meant to be seen as windows through which the devout might view the eternal mysteries of religion. No conscious attempt was made to be innovative in this art. The emphasis was always on deepening the experience of sacred mystery.

◆ **The Influence of Byzantine Culture.** The influence of this art was far-reaching. Italo–Byzantine styles of art persisted in the West up to the beginnings of the Italian Renaissance. These same styles entered Russia at the end of the tenth century and still persist. Today, students can visit Greek or Russian churches and see these art forms alive as part of traditional Christian Orthodox worship and practice.

Because Byzantium (centered in the city of Constantinople) was Greek-speaking, the culture of ancient Greece was kept alive in that center until the middle of the fifteenth century, when the city fell to the Ottoman Turks. The removal of much of that culture to the West was a strong influence on the development of the Renaissance, as we shall see in subsequent chapters.

EXERCISES

1. Augustine understood the word *confessions* to mean both an admission of sin and a statement of belief. Why is that term so useful and correct for an autobiography? Do most modern autobiographies constitute a confession in Augustine's sense of the term?

2. In *The City of God*, Augustine defines peace as "the tranquillity of order." What does he mean? Is that definition a good one?

3. The outstanding art of the Byzantine period is the mosaic. What made mosaic such a desirable art form for the period? What do you see as its limitations?

4. Take a long look at the Ravenna mosaics of Justinian and Theodora and their court. Taken as a whole, what political and social values show through in the composition of the scenes?

5. Look carefully at the various depictions of Christ found in Byzantine mosaics and icons. Which religious values are underscored in those depictions? Which values are neglected?

6. Define the word *icon*, and be sure you understand its function in Orthodox Christianity. Is there anything comparable in contemporary art in terms of function?

7. Byzantine art prided itself not on changing its style but on preserving and perfecting it. Is there something to be said for continuity rather than change in artistic styles? What are the more apparent objections to such a philosophy?

Visit the *Culture & Values* Companion website at **www.cengage.com/art/Cunningham/Cultureand Values7E** and the *Humanities Resource Center* for an array of primary source readings, key terms with pronunciations, flash cards, quizzes, and study materials designed especially to help you do well in this course.

CHAPTER 8

ISLAM

arun al-Rashid (786–809) was the fifth and most famous caliph (ruler) of the so-called Abbasid Period. Famous for encouraging music, poetry, art, and science at his court in Baghdad, and the inspiration for the Arabic tales *A Thousand and One Nights* (which had little foundation in fact), al-Rashid achieved mythic stature. A military leader as well, he waged intermittent war on the Byzantine empire. But in 798, with his army encamped around Constantinople, he negotiated with the Empress Irene to accept an annual tribute of seventy thousand pieces of gold in lieu of certain victory. Not until 1453 would Constantinople fall to Islam.

During a reign that marked the highpoint of the Abbasid dynasty's social and political power, Harun al-Rashid maintained diplomatic ties with countries as far away as China in the East. In the West he conducted a diplomatic correspondence with Charlemagne (see Chapter 9). Charlemagne's biographers describe negotiations over Christian access to the Holy Places in Jerusalem. These negotiations were critical to Charlemagne

◆ Portrait of caliph Harun al-Rashid as a young man
(© Snark/Art Resource, NY)

because the Christian West bitterly regretted the loss of Jerusalem in 638—a bitterness that would erupt into the crusades several centuries later.

As was customary, Charlemagne sent his delegates with gifts for the caliph. Because Harun al-Rashid was a keen equestrian, Charlemagne sent Spanish horses and hunting dogs, as well as Frisian woven cloth. In 802 Harun reciprocated, sending among silks, candelabra, perfumes, ivory chessmen, and slaves, evidence of the technological inventiveness of the Muslim world—a water clock with twelve bronze balls that marked the hour by falling on a cymbal as twelve mechanical knights paraded out of small windows. Implausibly, Harun al-Rashid also sent Charlemagne an elephant named Abul-Abbas. Somehow, the elephant traveled from Baghdad (present-day Iraq) to Aachen (present-day Germany) where it fascinated the populace until 811, when it succumbed to the northern cold.

MUHAMMAD AND THE BIRTH OF ISLAM

Muhammad, the founder of Islam, was born in 570 in the Arabian city of Mecca. Orphaned as a child and reared in poverty, while still young he married a rich widow who would bear him a daughter, Fatima. Fatima would later marry the first Imam (authoritative religious leader) of the Shiites. As an ancestor of all followers of Islam, Fatima is highly venerated by all Muslims as a model of piety and purity. Muhammad's deep religious nature led him to ponder the reasons for his good fortune, and he began to retreat into caves in the neighboring mountains to meditate. At about the age of forty, he began receiving revelations from God through the agency of the angel Gabriel. When he began to speak publicly about his ideas of religious reform, Muhammad soon encountered severe opposition from the citizens of Mecca, who had little patience with his sermons against the city's prevalent idolatry and his insistence on the worship of one God. The antagonism was so adamant that he had to flee the city in 622, a year the Muslims now mark as the beginning of their calendar: the *hegira.*

In Medina, his city of refuge, Muhammad soon attracted a community of supporters. He achieved such success in this endeavor that he was able, less than ten years later, to return to Mecca and make its once pagan shrine called the Ka'aba (Arabic for "cube") the focal point of his new religion. It did not take him long to consolidate his hold over that city. By the time Muhammed reached Mecca, the rough outlines of the basis for his religious faith were already in place.

THE FIVE PILLARS

The fundamental principle of the faith was a bedrock **monotheism** (the word *Islam* means "submission [to God]"). This belief was a conscious rejection of the Christian doctrine of the Trinity of persons in God. The prophet began to articulate the so-called five pillars of Islam:

1. The recitation of the Muslim act of faith that there is one God and that Muhammad is God's messenger.
2. The obligation to pray five times a day in a direction that points to the Ka'aba in Mecca. Soon there was

GENERAL EVENTS	ART
500	
570–632 Life of Muhammad	
600	
610–733 Spread of Islam to Arabia, Egypt, Syria, Iraq, and parts of northern Africa	
622 Muhammad flees to Mecca; this year now marks the beginning of the Muslim calendar	
638 Muslims capture Jerusalem	
700	
700 Islam spreads to all of northern Africa and to southern Spain	**730–843** Muslim belief that God's divinity defies representation leads to a blend of intricate geometric design and sacred script in Muslim art and architecture
732 Charles Martel holds off Muslim northern expansion at Tours	
786–809 Harun al-Rashid, fifth caliph of Abbasid Period	
794 First paper factory established in Baghdad	
800	
1000	
1099 Crusading Christians capture Jerusalem	
1100	
1200	
1258 Mongols sack Baghdad	
1281 Ottoman Empire founded	
1400	
1453 Constantinople falls to Ottoman Turks, ending Byzantine Empire; Church of Hagia Sophia becomes a mosque	
1492 Muslims driven from Spain in the "Reconquista"	
1500	
1600	

added the obligation to participate in Friday prayers as a community and hear a sermon.

3. To donate a portion of the surplus of one's wealth to charity.
4. To fast during the holy month of **Ramadan**—a total abstinence of all food and drink from sunrise to sunset.
5. To make a pilgrimage to Mecca (called the *Haj*) at least once in a lifetime.

That latter obligation was performed by Muhammad around the purified and restored Ka'aba in 632, which was the same year he died in the arms of his wife. The pilgrimage to Mecca today draws millions of faithful [**Fig. 8.2**].

In addition to these core practices there are other characteristic practices of Islam: like Jews, Muslims do not eat pork products. Unlike Judaism and Christianity, Islam forbids the consumption of alcoholic beverages. Muslim males are circumcised. Polygamy is permitted under Islamic law but not practiced universally. The taking of interest on loans or lending for interest (usury) is forbidden by Islamic law. Over the course of time, a cycle of feast days and observances developed (for example, the birthday of the Prophet).

ARCHITECTURE	LITERATURE & PHILOSOPHY
	c. 530–850 Development of Kufic script; Qur'an develops and with it the tradition of *Hadith*, religious commentary
	Development of *Shari'a*, the Islamic legal code
	651 Publication of Qur'an
687–692 Dome of the Rock	
706–715 Great Mosque of Damascus built by Al Walid	
c. 790 Great Mosque of Córdoba begun	
	801 Death of Rabia, Sufi saint and poet
	833 House of Wisdom established in Baghdad; draws Muslim scholars who translate and preserve Greek texts
	780–850 Al-Khwarizmi, inventor of algebra, develops use of zero as a number
c. 980 Al-Hakam enhances existing structure	
	980–1037 Avicenna, philosopher-scientist
	1126–1198 Averröes, philosopher, astronomer, writer on jurisprudence, medicine, and mathematics
	1135–1204 Maimonides, great Jewish thinker, physician, Talmudist
1200–1300 The Alhambra	**1207–1273** Life of Rumi, perhaps the best-known Sufi mystic-poet
1532 Cathedral begun inside the Great Mosque of Córdoba	

◆ **8.2** The Sanctuary at Mecca, Saudi Arabia. This is the central focus of the Islamic pilgrimage to Mecca. Pious pilgrims circle the draped, black stone (*Ka'aba*)—seen in the upper center of the crowd—upon which, it is believed, one can see the footprints of Abraham. To the left and front of the *Ka'aba* is the tomb of Ishmael, from whom Muslims trace their descent. According to the Saudi Hajj ministry, each year about two million Muslim pilgrims from around the world arrive at Mecca to perform *Al-Hajj* or *Bilgirame*. (© *Abid Katib/Getty Images*)

 # VALUES

Pure Monotheism

Islam, considered as a culture, is a highly complex reality that contains various religious, philosophical, artistic, and theoretical currents. One thing, however, that is fundamental in Islam is its unbending teaching about the oneness of God; the Islamic statement of faith begins, "There is but One God, Allah. . . ." To grasp this belief in radical monotheism is to understand a whole variety of issues connected to Islam that are touched on in our brief survey. The word Islam means "submission" to God. Because God is almighty, his divinity is hidden from humanity; as a consequence Allah may not be depicted in artistic form. Because the revelation of Allah is final and definitive, Islam sees the reality of God beyond the revelation of the God of the Jewish Scriptures and is explicitly resistant to the Trinitarian faith of Christianity. Jesus is honored as a prophet, but the idea of Jesus as divine is denied in the pages of the Qur'an. The Qur'an insists that the revelation to Muhammad brought the pure monotheism of Moses back to its original meaning. Whether God's power is such that it controls all human activity has been a subject of discussion among Islamic thinkers since the early medieval period, who divide into the "free will" and "predestination" schools relative to human activity.

The fundamental monotheism of Islam also helps explain why Islam has a tradition of missionary expansion. The omnipotent will of God is for all humanity to submit to God; if people are not aware of that fact, they are not living according to the will of God. Hence, the devout are encouraged to teach people this fundamental truth.

ISLAMIC EXPANSION

- ☐ Islam in 632
- ☐ Expansion to 661
- ☐ Expansion to 750

THE GROWTH OF ISLAM

The simplicity of the original Islamic teaching—its emphasis on submission to the will of the one God, its insistence on daily prayer, its appeal for charity, and a demand for some asceticism in life—all help explain the phenomenal and rapid spread of this new religion coming out of the deserts of Arabia. In less than ten years after the death of the Prophet, Islam had spread to all of Arabia, Egypt, Syria, Iraq, and parts of North Africa (see map, "Islamic Expansion"). A generation after the Prophet's death, the first Muslim attack (unsuccessful) on Constantinople was launched; within two generations Muslims constituted a forceful majority in the holy city of Jerusalem. By the eighth century, Islam had spread to all of North Africa (modern-day Libya, Morocco, Tunisia, and Algeria) and had crossed the Mediterranean near Gibraltar to create a kingdom in southern Spain.

THE QUR'AN

Evidently, many of the revelations received by the Prophet during his life at both Mecca and Medina were maintained orally, but soon after his death followers began to write down the revelations as they had received them from him. Within a generation, a serious attempt was made to collate the various oral revelations with a view of producing a uniform edition of the revelations received both at Medina and Mecca. The net result of these long editorial efforts resulted in a cen-

tral sacred text of Islam called the Qur'an (sometimes spelled Koran; the word is Arabic for "recitation").

The Qur'an is roughly as long as the Christian New Testament. The book is divided into one hundred fourteen chapters (called *sûras*). There is an opening chapter in the form of a short prayer invoking the name of God followed by one hundred thirteen chapters arranged in terms of their length, with chapter two being the longest and the final chapter only a line or two long. Muslims have devised ways of dividing these chapters—for example, into thirty parts of near equal length so that one could complete reciting the entire book during the thirty days of the sacred month of Ramadan, which is a time of intense devotion accompanying the annual fast.

The language of the Qur'an is Arabic. Like all Semitic languages (for example, Hebrew and Syriac), the text is written and read from right to left. Because Muslims believe that the Qur'an came as a result of divine dictation, it cannot be translated into other languages. Although many vernacular versions of the Qur'an exist, they are considered to be paraphrases or glosses. The result of this conviction is that no matter where Muslims live, they will hear the Qur'an recited only in Arabic. Although Arabs (contrary to popular belief) make up a relatively small proportion of the total Muslim population of the world (the largest Muslim population resides in Indonesia), the Qur'an serves as a source of unification for all Muslims. Reverence for the Qur'an, further, means that it is literally God's word to people and as such is held in the highest respect. Committing the entire Qur'an to memory is a sign of devotion, and

◆ **8.3** Page from the Qur'an, 9th–10th century. The highly stylized calligraphy is known as *Kufic* script; it is one of the earliest and most beautiful of Arabic calligraphy styles. Arabic, like Hebrew, is written from right to left.

From Iraq or Syria. 8″ x 13″ (21.6 x 32.5 cm). Museum fuer Islamische Kunst (Inv. I. 2211), Staatliche Museen zu Berlin, Berlin, Germany//© Bildarchiv Preussischer Kulturbesitz/Art Resource, NY

the capacity to chant it aloud is a much-admired gift because the beauty and care of such recitation is deemed an act of religious piety in its own right. Today public competitions of recitations of the Qur'an are a regular feature on radio and television in Muslim countries. In cities having a Muslim majority, it is not uncommon to find radio stations that feature a reading of the Qur'an twenty-four hours a day.

The Qur'an is the central text of Islam, but another authoritative tradition has also shaped Islamic religion and culture. Authoritative commentators on the Qur'an and the explication of certain oral traditions about the Prophet and the early Islamic community constitute a body of literature called *Hadith*. From this living stream of sacred text and tradition, Islamic sages and jurists have developed a complex legal code called **Shari'a** ("law"). When Muslim countries are described as adopting Islamic law for their governance, *Shari'a* is being referred to. Like all legal codes *Shari'a* is both traditional and conservative yet adaptable to the needs and circumstances of time.

CALLIGRAPHY

In order to render adequate honor to the written text of the Qur'an, the skill of calligraphy was developed. *Calligraphy* comes from two Greek words that mean "beautiful writing." The evolution of Arabic script is a long and highly complex study in its own right, but certain standard forms of writing were developed. One of the most characteristic forms of this writing, although it also admits of many variations, is called *Kufic* [**Fig. 8.3**].

Calligraphy and Art in Mosques Such calligraphic skills were brought to bear not only on the text of the Qur'an but also as a decorative feature of public buildings—especially the great halls erected for assemblies of the faithful for Friday prayers and the sermons preached at the end of those prayers. These buildings are called *mosques* (from the Arabic word *masjid*, meaning "a place for ritual prostration"). Perhaps nothing is so familiar to people than pious Muslim men kneeling in prayer, touching their heads to the ground, in the great mosques of the world. This act of prostration can be read as a gesture touching the heart of the religion: to prostrate is to show submission to God (in Arabic, *Allah*).

The exterior and interior decoration of the great classical mosques are always done in an art form that emphasizes the abstract and the geometric, because Muslims believe that one cannot depict divinity since Allah is beyond all imagining. It is therefore commonplace to see an intricate blend of abstract geometric designs entwined with exquisitely rendered sacred texts from the Qur'an. Some of the decoration found on the exterior of mosques—like that found decorating the great seventeenth-century Friday Mosque of Isfahan in Iran—uses blue tiling to set forth intricate patterns of **arabesques** and highly stylized bands of calligraphic renderings of lines from the Qur'an [**Fig. 8.4**].

Although Islamic decoration is usually abstract, it is not exclusively so. Some mosques do in fact have representational scenes in the interior. These usually depict nonhuman images of plants and flowers executed mainly in mosaic—especially when the skills of Byzantine mosaic artists were available to do such work. One does not find narrative scenes in such art because little of the Qur'an has a narrative quality.

◆ **8.4** Detail of wall mosaic from the portal of the Friday Mosque, Isfahan, Iran (1611–1666). Decorative, blue, white, and gold mosaic tile work combine with Islamic script to decorate a long pier of the portal (entrance). The interplay of calligraphy and abstract design is typical of mosque decoration in various periods. *(Image © CORBIS)*

◆ **8.5** The Dome of the Rock, Jerusalem, Israel, late 7th century. The blue decoration in the upper registers is made of tile. The tile work replaces earlier mosaic work that probably was done by Byzantine craftsmen who were acknowledged experts in that art. *(Image © Yoram Lehmann/Photo Researchers, Inc.)*

ISLAMIC ARCHITECTURE

Islam has a fifteen-hundred-year history. Its communities are found in every part of the world. In that long history it has built its buildings suitable to the circumstances in which it finds itself, even though the basic needs of the mosque remain fairly constant: a large covered space for the faithful to pray, especially when the community gathers for Friday prayers. Typically the gathering area is covered with rugs; except for the steps leading up to a *minbar* (the "pulpit"), there is no furniture in a mosque. A niche in the wall called a *mihrab* indicates the direction of Mecca so that the faithful at prayer are accurately oriented east. In traditional Friday mosques, there is also usually some type of fountain so that the devout may ritually cleanse their hands, feet, and mouth before prayer. Adjacent to the mosque is a tower or minaret so that the *Muezzin* may call the faithful to prayer five times a day. Visitors to Muslim countries soon become accustomed to the Muezzin's predawn call, "Wake up! Wake up! It is better to pray than to sleep . . ."

Although primarily designed to shelter the faithful at prayer, the mosque serves a larger community function in Islam. It is a community gathering center; it is a place where scholars meet to study and debate; courtroom proceedings could be held there; leisurely con-versations could be held in its courtyards, and people could escape the heat of the sun in its covered areas. As scholars have noted, the mosque is to Islamic countries what the Roman forum or the precincts of the medieval cathedral or the town square were to other cultures: a gathering place for the community to express itself. The simple requirements for the mosque leave much for the ingenuity and genius of the individual architect to develop. As a result, the history of Islamic architecture provides extraordinary examples of art.

The Dome of the Rock The Dome of the Rock in Jerusalem is the earliest and one of the most spectacular achievements of Islamic architecture [**Fig. 8.5**], built toward the end of the seventh century by Caliph Abd al Malik of Damascus on the Temple Mount in Jerusalem. The Temple Mount is an elevated space that was once the site of the Jewish temple destroyed by the Romans in 70 CE. The Dome of the Rock is an octagonal building capped by a golden dome, which sits on a heavy drum supported by four immense piers and twelve columns. The interior is decorated lavishly with mosaics, as was the outside of the building until, in the late Middle Ages, the mosaics were replaced by tiles. The building owes a clear debt to Roman and Byzantine architecture, but its Qur'anic verses on the inside make it clear that it was to serve an Islamic function.

What was that function? Was its original purpose to be a mosque? a mausoleum? It may well have been erected to serve as a counterpoint to the Church of the Holy Sepulcher in Jerusalem, acting as a rebuff in stone to Christianity, making the artistic argument (as the Qur'an itself does) that Islam is a worthy successor to both Judaism and Christianity. Built around a still visible rock outcropping, it is not totally clear what the original purpose of the building was. Scholars still do not agree on the building's original purpose (some have even argued that it was built as a rival to the *Qa'aba* in Mecca), but all are unanimous that it is a splendid example of Islamic architecture. A ninth-century story speaks of it commemorating the spot of the night journey of the Prophet from Jerusalem to heaven, whereas other traditions speak of it as being the place where Abraham (regarded by Muslims as the first great prophet) sacrificed his son (whom the Muslims believe was Ishmael) or the place where Adam died and was buried. Apart from the tiling of the exterior in more modern times, the building stands pretty much as it did when first built two generations after Muhammad's death.

The Great Mosque of Damascus The great Mosque of Damascus, built by Abd al Malik's son, al Walid (died 715), on the site of what had been a Roman temple turned into a Byzantine church, used the massive walls surrounding the church complex as the walls of the mosque [**Fig. 8.6**]. The building within the walls had its façade facing the inside of the walls (mosques tend to be inward looking). The interior prayer hall had three spaces each separated by heavy columns. Like the Dome of the Rock, the interior was decorated lavishly, with the lower walls paneled in marble and the upper registers decorated (by Byzantine craftsmen) with mosaics, including a depiction of heaven resplendent with palaces and flowing waters [**Fig. 8.7**]. The caliph's palace (now gone) was next to the mosque so that the ruler could pass easily from his home to the mosque.

The Mosque at Cordoba One final mosque showing the relationship of Islamic architecture and Byzantine decoration is the great mosque in Córdoba (Spain). Muslims arrived in Spain in the eighth century and made Córdoba their capital. Construction began on a mosque in the late eighth century with additions both to the courtyard and the prayer hall executed in the ninth and tenth century. In the late tenth century, Al-Hakam, the ruler of the city, decided to enhance his mosque to make it a rival of the great mosque in Damascus. The interior of the mosque seems to be a vast tangle of columns supporting Roman arches [**Fig. 8.8**]. To enhance the interior, Al-Hakam sent

◆ **8.6** Main courtyard of the Great Mosque, Damascus, Syria, with the ablutions fountain (left) and Dome of the Hours (right), c. 715. Worshippers at Friday prayers would spill over from the mosque to gather in the courtyard. The mosque incorporates a former Christian church, details of which (for example, the façade, laterals, and dome) can be detected in the present-day architecture. The faithful use the domed fountain in the courtyard to refresh themselves and to bathe their hands and feet before prayers. *(Image © The Art Archive/Manuel Cohen)*

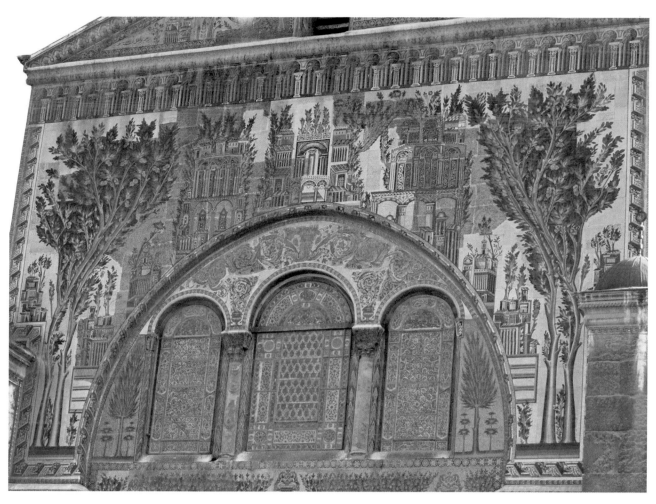

◆ **8.7** Mosaic decoration on the façade of the Great Mosque, Damascus, Syria, early 8th century. Even though trees and houses are easily detectable in the mosaic, the absence of any human figure is striking. This absence reflects early Islamic resistance to depicting the human figure. *(Image © Ivan Vdovin/Alamy)*

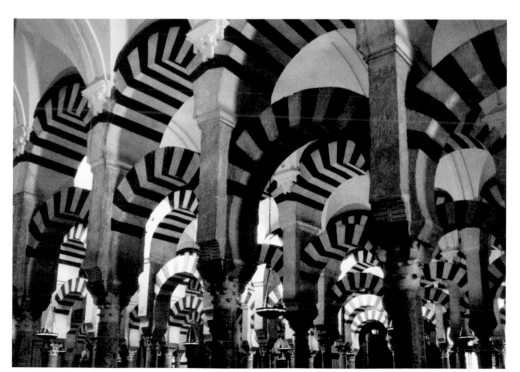

◆ **8.8** Maqsura screen of the Córdoba Mosque, Spain, 8th–10th centuries. The elaborate stone work columns cordoned off the *maqsura*, the space reserved for the ruler and his elite company to worship in the mosque. The red bands are made of brick and the white are made of stone. *(© Glen Allison/Getty Images)*

◆ **8.9** Central Dome of the Mosque of Córdoba, Spain, mid-10th century. The decoration of the mosque, done a century after its construction, is elaborate. Contemporary records show that the ruler of Córdoba imported 30,000 mosaic tesserae as well as workmen from Constantinople to execute the lavish decoration. This dome covers the *mihrab*, which points toward the *Ka'aba* in Mecca. *(Image © age fotostock/SuperStock)*

emissaries to the emperor in Constantinople with a request for workmen. Contemporary sources state that the emperor complied not only with workmen but also sent roughly seventeen tons of **tesserae**. The master mosaic artist, who enjoyed the hospitality of the caliph, decorated the interior of the mosque lavishly, finishing his work, according to an inscription, in 965 [**Fig. 8.9**]. The mosque managed to survive the destruction of Islamic building when the Christians drove the Muslims out of Spain in 1492—the period known as the *Reconquista*. Within the confines of the mosque, an undistinguished cathedral was begun in 1532, and much of its original interior still remains today.

The Alhambra One other notable Islamic building in Spain that escaped the destruction of Muslim architecture during the Reconquista was the palace complex in Granada known as the Alhambra. Its beauty was so renowned that an inscription of a poet's line on one of its exterior towers urging donations for the blind beggars of the city bears witness:

> Give him alms, good woman,
> For in life there is nothing like the heartache
> Of being blind in Granada.

The exterior of the Alhambra, with its complex of towers and walls, provides no hint of the beauty of its interior. Built largely in the thirteenth and fourteenth

◆ **8.10** Court of the Lions in the Alhambra, Granada, Spain, c. 1391. This final, great piece of Islamic architecture is characterized by the delicacy of its interior. Note the slender double columns, the waterways, and fountains at the level of the floor. The court takes its name from the lions that support the great fountain basin in the center. *(Image © Bildarchiv Steffens/The Bridgeman Art Library)*

VOICES OF THEIR TIMES

Al-Ghazali on the Mystic Path

Al-Ghazali (1058–1111) reflects on his discovery of the Sufi path during his lifetime of philosophical study and research. Some see his quest for truth to be not unlike that of the Christian writer, Saint Augustine of Hippo.

> Lastly, I turned to the way of the mystics. I knew that in their path there has to be both knowledge and activity and that the object of the latter is to purify the self from vices and faults of character. Knowledge was easier for me than activity so I began by reading their books. . . . Then I realized that what is most distinctive of them can be attained only by personal experience, ecstasy, and change of character. I saw clearly that the mystics were people of personal experience not of words, and that I had gone as far as possible by way of study and intellectual application, so that only personal experience and walking in the mystic way was left. . . .

centuries, the Alhambra actually consists of two adjacent palaces: the Palace of the Myrtles (so-called because of the myrtle plants in the gardens) and the Court of the Lions [**Fig. 8.10**]. Both palaces have central courtyards with covered walkways or porches. The Palace of the Myrtles was evidently used for public occasions; the Palace of the Lions was designed as a private home. A recent scholar has argued that the whole complex was meant to be for study, teaching, and research—a kind of Islamic university. The interiors were decorated lavishly with colored tiles and intricate woodwork. The most cunning aspect of this complex is the use of water, which runs through small interior streams springing up into fountains. The quiet murmur of the water is evident in all parts of the palaces, so that one gains a sense of both interior space connected to the outside by the sound of water. The mid-fourteenth-century Court of the Lions is perhaps the most representative example of the opulence within the Alhambra: slender columns; careful wooden ceiling work; molded plaster decoration; delicate tracery providing a frame for the fountain in the center held up by lions; and the water trough running to a simple, circular bubbling fountain set in the tiled floor.

SUFISM

Like all of the world's religions, Islam has various traditions within it. About 85 percent of all Muslims belong to what is called the *Sunni* ("well trod") tradition. A significant minority (the majority in Iran) are members of the *Shi'a* (meaning "party" or "tradition") branch of Islam. Within those two large branches are various minor branches and traditions. From the perspective of Muslim literature, one of the most influential of these traditions is *Sufism*. The name *Sufi* most likely derives from the Arabic word for unbleached wool—the simple clothing many Sufis adopted.

Sufism is a word that describes an ancient and complex movement of communities or small groups of teachers of immense religious authority called *sheiks* and their disciples that emphasized practices and disciplines that would lead a person to come to some direct experience of God in this life. In other words, Sufism represents the mystical dimension of Islam. Like most mystical movements in a religious tradition, Sufism was sometimes embraced with enthusiasm by religious and civil authorities, whereas during other periods its practices and followers were looked at with suspicion or downright hostility. In its earliest manifestations, Sufi mystics tended to live a life of retirement in poverty, preaching to people about piety and repentance.

There are many forms of Sufism in Islamic history, but it has been a significant thread in Muslim life to the present. Sufi *tariqas* ("communities") are to be found in various Muslim lands with a significant presence in North Africa and Egypt. Westerners have expressed a keen interest in Sufi practices with most large bookstores stocking translations of Sufi texts.

The Writer Saint Rabia Two representative Sufi writers might provide us with some sense of the range of Sufi thought and expression. The Sufi woman Saint Rabia, known as the flute player (died 801), regarded a highly developed sense of the love of God as the key to union with God. Kidnapped and sold into slavery as a child, after receiving a grant of freedom from her master she became convinced that she was one of God's chosen ones. Rabia expressed her convictions in a series of aphorisms, poems, and meditations. Her intuition about love derived from her conviction that the Qur'an is filled with verses speaking about the concern that Allah has for His people and the corresponding love that we should have for Allah. Like many mystics (and others concerned with the issue of love), Rabia enunciated her sayings most frequently in the form of poetry. Her focus on the love of God was highly central, so she taught that when one loved God centrally in one's life,

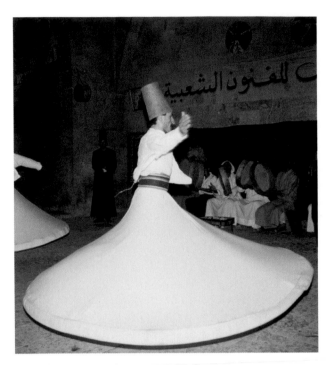

◆ **8.11** Dancing Dervishes. As part of their religious devotions, many Sufi Orders perform ecstatic dancing to the accompaniment of musical instruments. The practice, not universally admired by Muslims, may represent the souls of the Just whirling toward paradise. *(Image © K. M. Westermann/CORBIS)*

such a focus would exclude any fear of damnation as well as any hope for paradise. Love would be its own concern. "The best thing in the whole world," she once wrote, "is to possess nothing in this world or the next world except Allah."

The Poet Rumi Perhaps the most famous of the Sufi mystic poets was the thirteenth-century writer known as Rumi (1207–1273). Born in what is now Afghanistan, Rumi moved with his family to what is present-day Turkey. A prolific writer of religious verse in a form that used rhyming **couplets** developed by earlier Sufis, Rumi, writing in the Persian language, composed more than three thousand poems while also leaving behind seventy long discourses on mystical experience. His poetic corpus is extensive and so powerfully expressed that some have called his body of work the "Qur'an" in Persian. He was most admired for his capacity to take almost any observable ordinary thing and turn his observance of it into a poem of religious praise.

One feature of Rumi's poetry was his practice of reciting his poems while dancing in a formal but ecstatic fashion. Rumi believed that the combination of recitation and movement would focus the devotee's total attention on Allah. Rumi founded a community of these ecstatic dancers (dervishes), whose practitioners continue ecstatic dancing to this day [**Fig. 8.11**].

THE CULTURE OF ISLAM AND THE WEST

One of the high points of Islamic culture in its earlier history was centered in the city of Baghdad (present day Iraq) under the Abbasid Dynasty, which flourished in the eighth and ninth centuries. It was there that papermaking was learned from a Chinese prisoner who had learned the process in China, where papermaking had long been commonplace. Baghdad opened its first papermaking factory in 794. It would be some centuries before this process would pass to the West.

THE HOUSE OF WISDOM

Caliph Al-Mamun built a library and study center, completed in 833, which was known as the *Bait alhikma* (the "House of Wisdom"). Scholars flocked to that center from all over the Muslim world. A crucial part of the scholarly labors at the House of Wisdom was the translation of texts into Arabic. We owe to this center the preservation of the works of Aristotle, which were translated into Arabic by a team of Greek-speaking Christians who were in the center's employ. It is estimated that every text of Aristotle we know today (except *Politics*) was translated in the House of Wisdom. Additionally, these scholars translated several Platonic texts, the medical texts of Galen, and many treatises of the Neo-Platonic authors. When scholars (like Saint Thomas Aquinas) read Aristotle in Paris in the thirteenth century, they did so in Latin versions translated from Arabic manuscripts—the work of the scholars of Baghdad.

Al-Khwarizmi and Mathematics The greatest single scholar at the House of Wisdom was the polymath researcher Al-Khwarizmi (780–850), who made revolutionary discoveries. He led three expeditions to India and Byzantium in order to gather manuscripts and meet other scholars. As a consequence, Al-Khwarizmi had at his disposal much learning from both Indian and Byzantine (Greek) sources. He invented algebra (the word *algebra* derives from the Arabic title of one of his books). Medieval Europeans who knew his writings in Latin gave us another important mathematical term, which is a corruption of his name: *algorithm*.

The most important contribution made by Al-Khwarizmi was his adaptation of Hindu notations for numbers that used nine symbols and a placeholder. This simplified numerical system replaced the clumsy Greek and Latin notational system, as any person who has tried to multiply CLXII by LIV instead of 162 x 54 will testify. The Hindu placeholder called *sunya* in Sanskrit and *cifra* ("cipher") in Arabic came to be called *zero* in the West, was now regarded not merely as a placeholder, but as a number. One further advance, made in the next century by an otherwise obscure Syrian Muslim named

Al-Uqlidisi, was the development of decimal fractions, which then permitted, for example, the computation of a solar year at 365.242199 days.

Although these profound mathematical advances developed rapidly in the Islamic world, their development in the West would be slow. It would take nearly one hundred fifty years before these ideas entered the Christian West via translations in those places that had the closest connection to the Muslim world, namely, Sicily (not a distant voyage from North Africa) and especially through that part of Spain that was Muslim.

Science and Medicine Mathematics was not the only area where Islamic scholarship advanced. The Egyptian scientist Al-Hazen (died 1038) did crucial work in optics and on the technology of the grinding and making of lenses. Three other scholars in the Muslim world who had had contact with Greek medicine and other sources shaped the future of medicine. Rhazes (died 932), head of the hospital in Baghdad, excelled in clinical observation, giving the world for the first time a clear description of smallpox and measles, demonstrating that they were two distinct diseases. It was from the observations of Rhazes that other scientists began to understand the nature of infection and the spread of infectious diseases. In the following two centuries influential writers like Avicenna (died 1037) and Averröes (died 1198), in addition to their important work in philosophy, wrote influential treatises in medicine. The important Jewish thinker Moses Maimonides (died 1204) was trained first as a physician. He stressed the need for personal hygiene as a way of avoiding disease (a concept not common in his day) and had done influential work on the nature of poisons. Maimonides was so renowned as a physician that he was called from his native Spain to serve as personal doctor to the sultan of Baghdad, Saladin. The high reputation of Jewish doctors trained in Arabic medicine was such that the popes consulted Jewish physicians who lived in the Jewish quarter across from the Vatican right through the Renaissance period.

Other Contributions from the Islamic World Despite the antagonism between the Christian West and the Islamic world in the centuries between the Abassid Dynasty in Baghdad and the flourishing culture of North Africa and Muslim Spain, the two cultures developed a common exchange of ideas and goods. The results were widespread. The West learned how to make windmills from the Muslims. The sword makers of both Damascus (Syria) and Toledo (Spain) were legendary for their quality. The woven silk of Damascus still lingers in our word *damask*. Among the earlier gifts of the Muslim world is coffee. The plants, native to tropical Africa, became a common hot beverage when Muslim traders in Ethiopia began to pulverize the beans to brew the drink. So popular was the result that in a short time one could find in Mecca, Damascus, and even in Constantinople, an institution popular to this day: the coffeehouse.

VOCABULARY FROM THE ISLAMIC WORLD

The exchanges between the Western World and the Islamic World have enriched the Western vocabulary with many new words. Arabic has given us *algebra, amber, almanac, alchemy, azimuth, caliph, cotton, elixir, hazard, lute, mattress, mosque, saffron, sheriff,* and *syrup*. From Persian (via Iran) we have gained the words *azure, mummy, scarlet, taffetta;* as well as the word *chess* and two words from that game: *rook* and *checkmate*.

Finally, as emphasized in other chapters, Muslim scholars provided not only a great body of Greek philosophical writing but also a vast commentary on it in the High Middle Ages. When Al-Ghazali (died 1111) attacked Greek philosophy in a book called *The Incoherence of the Philosophers*, he was answered by Averröes, who wrote a treatise showing how Islam could be reconciled with Greek philosophy. Averröes called his book *The Incoherence of Incoherence*. Dante regarded Muhammad and Islam with disdain, but a century after the death of Averröes, Dante would salute him in the *Divine Comedy* by calling him "He of the Great Commentary."

SUMMARY

◆ **The Birth of Islam.** Muhammad always thought of the new revelation he had received from God as a new religion that could unify the whole human race under one God and bring with it amity among nations. Islam regards itself as the final perfection of God's revelation first announced to the Jews and later to the Christians. For that reason, Muhammad's religion was an unapologetic missionary faith. Within two hundred years, Islam had spread from the desert world of Arabia throughout the present-day Middle East and along the southern coast of the Mediterranean Sea and the Iberian peninsula of present-day southern Spain; much of this dispersion came via military conquest.

◆ **Islamic Expansion.** Islam's rise coincided with a period of stagnation in what was the Christian West. The old Roman Empire was in a state of decline, having been hammered by successive waves of Barbarian invasions. The Byzantine Empire with its capital at Constantinople controlled only the city and its adjacent territories. It was an essentially inward looking, conservative, and noninnovative culture. Islam, by contrast, was a vigorous young religious culture, and at its apex—when the Abassids ruled from its center in Baghdad and later in Damascus and Córdoba—was innovative and forward-looking.

◆ **Cultural Exchange.** Although Islamic incursions were halted in the West in the generations before Charlemagne, and Muslims would not take possession of Constantinople until the fifteenth century, there were constant exchanges between the two cultures even though they warred against each other with ferocity (that is, the Crusades). This hostility shows up clearly in the West. The Muslims, in Christian eyes, were simply the Infidel, and their wickedness is a theme in *The Song of Roland*, where their beliefs and their practices were criticized and twisted into parody. The Christian Crusades had the express aim to wrest the Christian holy places from these Infidels. It should not surprise us that Dante comes to describe the walls of the city of hell as crenellated walls with domes of "fiery mosques."

◆ **Cultural Resistance.** The antagonism between the Christian West and the world of Islam has a long and bitter history. It is an antagonism that reflects itself today in the stereotyping of Muslims as backward, fundamentalist terrorists out to ruin the world. The irony is, of course, that we read such things on paper—an innovation that the House of Wisdom in Baghdad gave to the West in the medieval period. The truth is that Islam is a highly complex and deeply rich culture in which religion is so central that it cannot be disentangled from political and social culture. Islam has a long tradition of learning and the arts with a worldview that attempts to explain the place of people in the social order under the watchful eye of an all-powerful God who is adored under the name of Allah.

EXERCISES

1. Contrast the interior space of a mosque and a Christian basilica. What similarities can be noted? differences?
2. Is the Muslim concept of Allah compatible with the biblical view of God? Explain why or why not.
3. Look at a map to see where the closest points of contact were in the eighth century between Islamic countries and the Christian West.
4. How does the Muslims' gesture of kneeling and profoundly bowing at prayer symbolize their basic belief in God? Be attentive in future chapters to the attitude of the Christian West to the rise of Islam.

Visit the *Culture & Values* Companion website at **www.cengage.com/art/Cunningham/Cultureand Values7E** and the *Humanities Resource Center* for an array of primary source readings, key terms with pronunciations, flash cards, quizzes, and study materials designed especially to help you do well in this course.

CHAPTER 9

CHARLEMAGNE AND THE RISE OF MEDIEVAL CULTURE

Feudal society was rigidly organized with the serfs bound to the land at the lowest rung of society. Only slaves ranked lower on the social scale. It is estimated that the majority of serfs almost never traveled more than ten miles from where they were born. They worked in the fields or as craftsmen in the small villages wholly owned by the manorial lords. A third of what they produced belonged to the manor; the rest sustained them with precious little left over. If lands worked by serfs were sold, the serfs went with the new owner because they were understood to be "part" of the land.

One serf who managed to escape this form of bondage was beautifully described by the Venerable Bede (672–735) in his *Ecclesiastical History of the English People*. According to Bede, the formidable abbess Hilda of Whitby spotted a swineherd singing. Enchanted by the quality of his voice, and presiding over both a men's and women's monastery, she had him brought to the monks to be educated. In Bede's words: "So Caedmon stored up in his memory all that he learned and like one of the clean animals chewing the cud, turned it into such melodious verse that his delightful renderings turned his instructors into listeners" (IV.24).

Only one of his poems has survived, known as "Caedmon's Hymn," a nine-line piece that begins, "Now [we] must honour the guardian of heaven, the might of the architect." The importance of "Caedmon's Hymn" lies in the fact that it is the oldest example we have of a composition in Old English. Caedmon died in 680, but his hymn has immortalized this one-time serf as the pioneer figure in the history of English poetry.

CHARLEMAGNE AS RULER AND DIPLOMAT

Charles the Great (742?–814)—known to subsequent history as Charlemagne—was crowned emperor of the Roman Empire in Saint Peter's Basilica in Rome on Christmas Day 800 by Pope Leo III, in the first imperial coronation in the West since the late sixth century. The papal coronation was rebellion in the eyes of the Byzantine court, and the emperor in Constantinople considered Charlemagne a usurper, but this act marked the revival of the Roman Empire in the West.

Charlemagne was an able administrator of lands brought under his subjugation. He modified and adapted the classic Roman administrative machinery to fit the

◆ The Venerable Bede at his desk. *(© British Library/The Art Archive)*

needs of his own kingdom. Charlemagne's rule was essentially **feudal**—structured in a hierarchical fashion, with lesser rulers bound by acts of fealty to higher ones. Lesser rulers were generally large landowners who derived their right to own and rule their land from their tie to the emperor. Charlemagne also maintained several vassal dependents at his court who acted as counselors at home and as legates to execute and oversee the imperial will abroad. From his palace the emperor regularly issued legal decrees modeled on old Imperial Rome decrees. These decrees were detailed sets of instructions that touched on a wide variety of secular and religious issues. Those that have survived give us some sense of what life was like in the early medieval period. The legates of the emperor carried the decrees to the various regions of the empire and reported back on their acceptance and implementation. This burgeoning bureaucratic system required a class of civil servants with a reasonable level of literacy, an important factor in the cultivation of letters that was so much a part of the so-called Carolingian Renaissance.

The popular view of the early Middle Ages—often referred to as the Dark Ages—is that of a period of isolated and ignorant peoples with little contact outside

		GENERAL EVENTS	ART	ARCHITECTURE
EARLY MIDDLE AGES	**RISE OF THE FRANKS**	**711** Muslims invade Spain **714–741** Charles Martel, grandfather of Charlemagne, reigns as first ruler of Frankish kingdom **732** Charles Martel defeats Muslims at Battle of Poitiers **741–768** Reign of Pepin the Short, father of Charlemagne	**8th–9th cent.** Irish *Book of Kells*	Monastic complexes become important centers in rural life
	CAROLINGIAN PERIOD	**768** Charlemagne (742-814) ascends Frankish throne **772–778** Charlemagne's military campaigns against Muslim Emirates **778** Battle of Roncesvalles **c. 790** Charlemagne settles his court at Aachen (Aix-la-Chapelle) **800** Charlemagne crowned Holy Roman emperor at Rome by Pope Leo III **910** Founding of Monastery at Cluny **987–996** Reign of Hugh Capet in France ends Carolingian line of succession	Illuminated manuscripts and carved ivories prevalent **c. 775** Dagulf Psalter **early 9th cent.** *Crucifixion Ivory* **c. 820–840** *Utrecht Psalter*	**c. 795** Palace and chapel of Charlemagne at Aachen **c. 820** Plan for Abbey of Saint Gall, the "ideal" monastery
	ROMANESQUE PERIOD	**11th cent.** Pilgrimages become very popular **1066** Norman invasion of England by William the Conqueror **1096–1099** First Crusade; capture of Jerusalem by Christians	**1100–1125** Sculptures at Abbey Church of Saint-Pierre, Moissac **1120–1132** Sculptures at Abbey Church of La Madeleine, Vézelay	Use of massive walls and piers, rounded arches, and minimal windows **c. 1080–1120** Church of Saint Sernin, Toulouse, pilgrimage center **1096–1120** Abbey Church of La Madeleine, Vézelay
GOTHIC PERIOD		**1187** Sultan Saladin conquers Jerusalem **1202–1204** Fourth Crusade; sack of Constantinople by crusaders **1291** Fall of Acre, last Christian stronghold in Holy Land	**c. 1140** Portal sculptures at Priory Church, Saint-Gilles-du-Gard	

Timeline markers: 650, 768, 1000, 1140, 1400

the confines of their own immediate surroundings, and at times that was indeed the general condition of life. Nonetheless, it is important to note that in the late eighth and early ninth centuries, Charlemagne not only ruled over an immense kingdom (all of modern-day France, Germany, the Low Countries, and Italy as far south as Calabria) but also had extensive diplomatic contact outside that kingdom (see map, "The Carolingian World"). Charlemagne maintained regular, if somewhat testy, diplomatic relations with the emperor in Constantinople (at one point he tried to negotiate a marriage between himself and Byzantine Empress Irene in order to consolidate the two empires). Envoys from Constantinople were received regularly in his palace at Aachen, and Charlemagne learned Greek well enough to understand the envoys speaking their native tongue.

CHARLEMAGNE AND ISLAM

Charlemagne's relationship with the rulers of Islamic kingdoms is interesting. Islam had spread all along the southern Mediterranean coast in the preceding century. Arabs were in complete command of all the Middle East, North Africa, and most of the Iberian Peninsula.

LITERATURE & PHILOSOPHY	MUSIC
680 Death of the poet Caedmon	
735 Death of Venerable Bede, author of *Ecclesiastical History of the English People* and other religious writings	
after 780 Carolingian minuscule form of lettering developed **781** Charlemagne opens palace school, importing such scholars as Theodulf of Orléans and Alcuin of York **785** Alcuin, *Sacramentary*	**c. 800** Monasteries become centers for encouragement of sacred music; theoretical study of music at Charlemagne's palace school
	9th cent. Use of semi-dramatic trope in liturgical music; *Quem Quaeritis* trope introduced into Easter Mass
after 814 Carolingian monasteries adopt *Rule* of Saint Benedict of Nursia (480–547?) **821** Einhard, *Vita Caroli* (*Life of Charlemagne*) **after 950** Hroswitha's *Thais*	**c. 810** Gregorian plain chant *(cantus planus)* obligatory in Charlemagne's churches **822** Earliest documented church organ
1098–1179 Hildegard of Bingen **c. 1098** *Song of Roland, chanson de geste* inspired by the Battle of Roncesvalles (778), written down after 300 years of oral tradition **12th cent.** Development of liturgical drama **c. 1125** Saint Bernard of Clairvaux denounces extravagances of Romanesque decoration	**11th–12th cent.** Gregorian chant codified
4th–15th cent. Play cycles performed outside the church; *Everyman* (15th cent.), morality play	

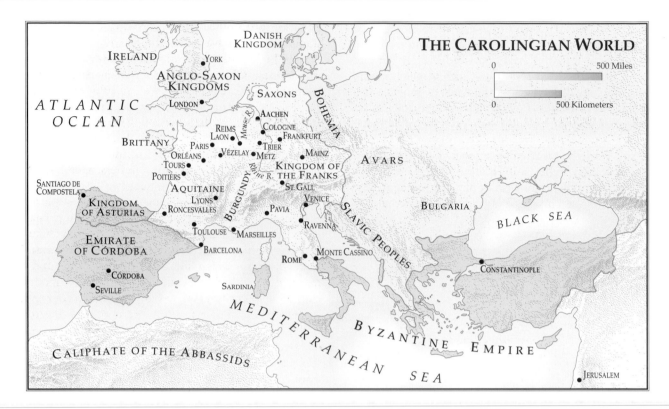

Charlemagne's grandfather Charles Martel (Charles the Hammer) had defeated the Muslims decisively at the Battle of Poitiers in 732, thus halting an Islamic challenge from Spain to the rest of Europe. Charlemagne had fought the Muslims of the Córdoba caliphate on the Franco–Spanish borders; the Battle of Roncesvalles (778) was the historical basis for the later epic poem the *Song of Roland* discussed later in this chapter.

Despite his warlike relationship with Muslims in the West, Charlemagne had close diplomatic ties with the great Harun al-Rashid, the caliph of Baghdad. In 787 Charlemagne sent an embassy to the caliph to beg protection for the holy places of the Christians in Muslim-held Palestine. The caliph (of *A Thousand and One Nights* fame) received and welcomed the Frankish legates and their gifts (mainly bolts of the much-prized Frisian cloth) and sent an elephant back to the emperor as a gesture of friendship. This gift arrived at Aachen and lived there for a few years before succumbing to the harsh winter climate. Charlemagne's negotiations were successful. From a pair of Palestinian monks he received the keys to the church of the Holy Sepulchre and other major Christian shrines, an important symbolic act that made the emperor the official guardian of the holiest shrines in Christendom.

CHARLEMAGNE AND ECONOMICS

Charlemagne's reign was also conspicuous for its economic developments. He stabilized the currency system

of his kingdom. The silver *denier*, struck at the royal mint in Frankfurt after 804, became the standard coin of the time; its presence in archaeological finds from Russia to England testifies to its widespread use and the faith traders had in it [**Fig. 9.2**].

Trade and commerce were vigorous. Charlemagne welcomed Jewish immigrants to his kingdom to provide a merchant class for commerce. There were annual **trade fairs** at Saint Denis near Paris, at which English merchants could buy foodstuffs, honey, and wine from the Carolingian estates. A similar fair was held each year at Pavia, an important town of the old Lombard kingdom of northern Italy. Port cities such as Marseilles provided mercantile contracts with the Muslims of Spain and North Africa. Jewish merchants operated as middlemen in France for markets throughout the Near East. The chief of Charlemagne's mission to Harun al-Rashid's court was a Jew named Isaac who had the linguistic ability and geographic background to make the trip to Baghdad and back—with an elephant—at a time when travel was a risky enterprise. Rivers such as the Rhine and the Moselle were utilized as important trade routes. One of the most sought-after articles from the Frankish kingdom was the iron broadsword produced at forges in and around the city of Cologne and sold to Arabs in the Middle East through Jewish merchants at the port cities. Vivid testimony to these swords' value can be read in the repeated embargoes (imposed under penalty of death) decreed by Charlemagne against their export to the land of the Vikings, who too often put them to effective use

◆ **9.2** Silver denier, after 800. This kind of coin, with Charlemagne wearing the Roman laurel wreath and military cloak, has been found in many archaeological sites, a testament to the reach of Charlemagne's influence. The Latin inscription reads, "Karolus" meaning Charles, "Imp(erator)" meaning emperor, "Avg(ustus)" meaning political heir to the Roman Empire of Augustus.

1.71 grams; ¾″ (20 mm) diameter. Muenzkabinett, Staatliche Museen zu Berlin, Berlin, Germany//© Bildarchiv Preussischer Kulturbesitz/Art Resource, NY

against their Frankish manufacturers in coastal raids on North Sea towns and trading posts.

LEARNING IN THE TIME OF CHARLEMAGNE

At Aachen, Charlemagne opened his famous palace school—an institution that was a prime factor in initiating what has been called the Carolingian Renaissance. Literacy in Western Europe before the time of Charlemagne was rather spotty; it existed, but hardly thrived, in certain monastic centers that kept alive the old tradition of humanistic learning taken from ancient Rome. Original scholarship was rare, although monastic copyists did preserve the tradition of literary conservation. Charlemagne could not write.

The scholars and teachers Charlemagne brought to Aachen provide some clues about the various locales in which early medieval learning had survived. Peter of Pisa and Paul the Deacon (from Lombardy) came to teach grammar and rhetoric at his school because they had had contact with the surviving liberal arts curriculum in Italy. Theodulf of Orleans was a theologian and

poet. He had studied in the surviving Christian kingdom of Spain and was an heir to the encyclopedic tradition of Isadore of Seville and his followers. Finally and importantly, Charlemagne brought an Anglo-Saxon, Alcuin of York, to Aachen after meeting him in Italy in 781. Alcuin had been trained in the English intellectual tradition of the Venerable Bede (died 735), the most prominent intellectual of his day, a monk who had welded together the study of humane letters and biblical scholarship. These scholar–teachers were hired by Charlemagne for several purposes.

First, Charlemagne wished to establish a system of education for the young of his kingdom. The primary purpose of these schools was to develop literacy; Alcuin of York developed a curriculum for them. He insisted that humane learning should consist of those studies that developed logic and science. From this distinction, later medieval pedagogues developed the two courses of studies for all schooling before the university: the *trivium* (grammar, rhetoric, and dialectic) and the *quadrivium* (arithmetic, geometry, music, and astronomy). These subjects remained at the heart of the school curriculum from the medieval period until modern times. The *trivium* and *quadrivium* made up the **Seven Liberal Arts**, which for centuries constituted classical education.

CAROLINGIAN CULTURE

Few books were available, and writing was done on slates or waxed tablets because parchment was expensive. In grammar, some of the texts of the Latin grammarian Priscian might be studied and then applied to passages from Latin prose writers. In rhetoric, the work of Cicero was studied, or Quintilian's *Institutio Oratoria*, if it was available. For dialectic, some of the work of Aristotle might be read in the Latin translation of Boethius. In arithmetic, multiplication and division were learned, and perhaps there was some practice on the abacus, because the Latin numerals were clumsy to compute with pen and paper. Arithmetic also included some practice in chronology as students were taught to compute the variable dates of Easter. They would finish with a study of the allegorical meaning of numbers. Geometry was based on the study of Euclid. Astronomy was derived from the Roman writer Pliny, with some attention to Bede's work. Music was the theoretical study of scale, proportion, the harmony of the universe, and the "music of the spheres." Music in this period was distinguished from *cantus*, which was the practical knowledge of chants and hymns for church use. In general, all study was based largely on rote mastery of the texts.

Beyond the foundation of schools, Charlemagne needed scholars to reform existing texts and to halt their terrible corruption, especially those used in church worship. Literary revival was closely connected with liturgical revival. Part of Charlemagne's educational reform envisioned people who would read aloud and sing in church from decent, reliable texts. Literacy was conceived as a necessary prerequisite for worship.

Alcuin of York mainly worked at the task of revising the liturgical books. Alcuin published a book of Old and New Testament passages in Latin for public reading during Mass. He sent for books from Rome in order to publish a *sacramentary*, a book of prayers and rites for the administration of the sacraments of the church. Alcuin's sacramentary was made obligatory for the churches of the Frankish kingdom in 785. Charlemagne made the Roman chant (called **Gregorian** after Pope Gregory the Great, who was said to have initiated such chants at the end of the sixth century) obligatory in all churches of his realm. Alcuin also attempted to correct scribal errors in the **Vulgate Bible** (the Latin version of Saint Jerome) by a comparative reading of manuscripts—a gigantic task he never completed.

Beyond the practical need for literacy, there was a further aim of education in this period. It was generally believed that all learning would lead to a better grasp of revealed truth—the Bible. The study of profane letters (by and large the literature of Rome) was a necessary first step toward the full study of the Bible. The study of grammar would set out the rules of writing, while dialectic would help distinguish true from false propositions. Models for such study were sought in the works of Cicero, Statius, Ovid, Lucan, and Virgil. These principles of correct writing and argumentation could then be applied to the study of the Bible in order to get closer to its truth. The pursuit of analysis, definition, and verbal clarity are the roots from which the scholastic form of philosophy would spring in the High Middle Ages. Scholasticism, which dominated European intellectual life until the eve of the Renaissance, had its first beginnings in the educational methodology established by Alcuin and his companions.

These educational enterprises were not centered exclusively at the palace school at Aachen. Under Charlemagne's direction, Alcuin developed a system of schools throughout the Frankish Empire—schools centered in both monasteries and towns. Attempts were also made to attach them to parish churches in the rural areas. The monastic school at Metz became a center for singing and liturgical study; schools at Lyons, Orleans, Mainz, Tours, and Laon had centers for teaching children rudimentary literary skills and offered some opportunity for further study in the liberal arts and the study of scripture. The establishment of these schools was accomplished by a steady stream of decrees and **capitularies** emanating from the Aachen palace. A circular letter, written most likely by Alcuin, called *On the Cultivation of Learning*, encouraged monks to study the Bible and to teach the young to do the same. A decree of 798 insisted that prelates and country clergy alike start schools for children.

This program of renewal in educational matters was an ideal set forth at a time when education was at a low ebb in Europe. Charlemagne tried to reverse that trend and in so doing encouraged real hope for an educated class in his time. His efforts were not entirely successful; many of his reforms came to naught in following generations when Europe slipped back into violence and ignorance.

Most of those who were educated were young men, although there is some evidence of learning among the aristocratic women of Charlemagne's court. The only book written in Charlemagne's time by a Frankish woman who was not a nun was a sort of manual for Christian living written by Dhouda for the instruction of her own son. We do, however, know that there had to be a certain level of literacy for nuns, and some evidence also suggests that illuminated **manuscripts** that have come to us were done by women in such convents.

MONASTICISM

Monasticism—from the Greek *monos* ("alone")—was an integral part of Christianity from the third century on. Monasticism came into the West from the great Eastern tradition of asceticism (self-denial) and eremitism (the solitary life). Its development in the West was complex, and we cannot speak of any one form of monasticism as predominant before the time of Charlemagne.

Celtic monasticism in Ireland was characterized both by austere living and by a rather lively intellectual tradition. Monasticism in Italy was far more simple and rude. Some of the monasteries on the continent were lax, and Europe was full of wandering monks. No rule of life predominated in the sixth and seventh centuries. Monastic lifestyles varied not only from country to country but also from monastery to monastery.

THE RULE OF SAINT BENEDICT

One strain of European monasticism derived from a rule of life written in Italy by Benedict of Nursia (480–547?) in the early sixth century. Although it borrowed from earlier monastic rules and was applied only to a small proportion of monasteries for a century after its publication, the Rule of Saint Benedict eventually became the Magna Carta of monasticism in the West. Charlemagne had Alcuin of York bring the rule to his kingdom and impose it on the monasteries of the Frankish kingdom to reform them and impose on them some sense of regular observance. In fact, the earliest copy of the Rule of Saint Benedict we possess today (a ninth-century manuscript preserved in the Swiss monastery of Saint Gall) is a copy of a copy Charlemagne had made in 814 from Saint Benedict's autographed

VOICES OF THEIR TIMES

An Abbot, an Irish Scholar, and Charlemagne's Biographer

A ninth-century monk-copyist describes labor in the scriptorium.

> Even as the sailor, fatigued with his labors, rejoices when he sights the familiar shore toward which he has long aspired, so does the scribe rejoice who sees the long-desired end of the book which has so overcome him with weariness. The man who does not know how to write makes light of the scribes' pains, but those who have done it know how hard is this work.

An Irish scholar and his cat.

> I love, better than all glory, to sit in diligent study over my little book. Pangur Ben has no envy of me, for he finds a mouse in his snares while only a difficult argument falls into mine. He bumps against the wall and I against the rigors of science. . . . He rejoices when he has a mouse in his paw as I rejoice when I have understood a difficult question. . . . Each of us loves our art.

Einhard in his biography of Charlemagne.

> He paid the greatest attention to the liberal arts. He had great respect for men who taught them, bestowing high honors on them. When he was learning the rules of grammar he received tuition from Peter the Deacon of Pisa who, by then, was an old man. For all other subjects he was taught by Alcuin, surnamed Albinus, a man of the Saxon race who came from Britain and was the most learned man anywhere to be found. Under him, the emperor spent much time and effort in studying rhetoric, dialectic, and especially astrology. He applied himself to mathematics and traced the course of the stars with great attention and care. He also tried to learn to write. With this end in view he used to keep writing tablets and notebooks under the pillows of his bed, so that he could try his hand at forming letters during his leisure moments; but, although he tried very hard, he had begun late in life and he made very little progress.

copy then preserved at the abbey of Monte Cassino in Italy (now lost).

The Rule of Saint Benedict consists of a prologue and seventy-three chapters (some only a few sentences long), which set out the ideal of monastic life. Monks (the brethren) were to live a family life in community under the direction of a freely elected father (the abbot) for the purpose of being schooled in religious perfection. They were to possess nothing of their own (poverty); they were to live in one monastery and not wander (stability); their life was to be one of obedience to the abbot; and they were to remain unmarried (chastity). Their daily life was to be a balance of common prayer, work, and study. Their prayer life centered on duly appointed hours of liturgical praise of God that were to mark the intervals of the day. Called the "Divine Office," this consisted of the public recitation of psalms, hymns, and prayers with readings from the Holy Scriptures. The offices were interspersed throughout the day and were central to the monks' lives. The periods of public liturgical prayer set off the times for reading, study, and the manual labor that was performed for the good of the community and its sustenance. The lifestyle of Benedictine monasticism can be summed up in its motto: "Pray and work." The rule is observed by both men and women.

The Regulated Day in the Monastery The daily life of the monk was determined by sunrise and sunset (as it was for most people in those days). Here is a typical day—called the *horarium*—in an early medieval monastery. The italicized words designate the names for the liturgical hours of the day:

Horarium Monasticum

2:00 A.M.	Rise
2:10–3:30	*Nocturns* (later called *Matins*; the longest office of the day)
3:30–5:00	Private reading and study
5:00–5:45	*Lauds* (the second office; also called "morning prayer")
5:45–8:15	Private reading and *Prime* (the first of the short offices of the day); at times, there was communal Mass at this time and, in some places, a light breakfast, depending on the season
8:15–2:30	Work punctuated by short offices of *Tierce*, *Sext*, and *None* (literally the third, sixth, and ninth hours)
2:30–3:15	Dinner
3:15–4:15	Reading and private religious exercises
4:15–4:45	*Vespers*—break—*Compline* (night prayers)
5:15–6:00	To bed for the night

This daily regimen changed on feast days (less work and more prayer) and during the summer (earlier rising, work later in the day when the sun was down a bit, more food, and so on). Although the schedule now seems harsh, it would not have surprised a person of the time. Benedict would have found it absurd for people to sleep while the sun was shining and then stay up under the glare of artificial light. When we look at the horarium closely, we see a day in which prayer and reading get four hours each, while there are about six hours of work. The rest of the day was devoted to personal chores, eating, and the like.

The triumph of the Benedictine monastic style of life (the early Middle Ages has been called the Benedictine centuries by some historians) is to be found in its sensible balance between the extreme asceticism of Eastern monastic practices and the unstructured life of Western monasticism before the Benedictine reforms. There was an even balance of prayer, manual labor, and intellectual life.

WOMEN AND THE MONASTIC LIFE

We tend to think of monasticism as a masculine enterprise, but it should be remembered that the vowed religious life was open to both men and women. The entire early history of Christianity records a flourishing monastic life for women. In the late Roman period, groups of religious women flourished all over the Roman Empire. Saint Benedict's own sister, Scholastica (died c. 543), was head of a monastery not far from her brother's establishment at Monte Cassino. Her contemporary, Brigid of Ireland (died c. 525), was such a powerful figure in the Irish church that legends grew up about her prowess as a miracle worker and teacher. Her reputation as a saint was such that churches dedicated to her dotted Ireland, England, and places on the continent where Irish monasticism took root. In England in the seventh century, Hilda, abbess of Whitby (614–680), not only ruled over a prominent monastery that was a center of learning (many Anglo-Saxon bishops were educated there), but she also held a famous episcopal gathering (synod) to determine church policy. Hilda also encouraged lay learning. She fostered the talents of the cowherd poet Caedmon, who produced vernacular poetry concerned with Christian themes.

Hildegard of Bingen Because monasticism presumed a certain degree of literacy, it was possible for women to exercise their talents in a way that was not possible within the confines of the more restricted life of the court or the family. The Benedictine tradition produced great figures such as that of Hildegard of Bingen (1098–1179), who wrote treatises on prayer,

philosophy, medicine, and devotion. She was also a painter, illustrator, musician, critic, and a preacher. Among her most important works are included a vast visionary work called *Scivias* (*The Way to Knowledge*); the medical treatises *Physica* and *Causae et Curae* (*Causes and Cures*); as well as a song sequence called the *Symphonia* and a morality play set in music called the *Ordo Virtutum*; music from these latter works has been performed recently and recorded with a wonderful contemporary response. Hildegard commissioned illustrations for her *Scivias* but, alas, the originals were destroyed during the bombing of Dresden in World War II, and we now know them only in copies [**Fig. 9.3**].

From this great tradition of monastic women, we possess several edifying lives written by the contemporaries of these women, which laud their decision to give up marriage in order to serve God. These lives of the saints were extremely popular because they served

◆ **9.3** Hildegard of Bingen, the First Vision of Book 3, *Scivias*, 12th century. Above a blue sphere representing the fear of God, God is enthroned on man's faith.

Tafel 19, Codex Rupertsberg, Benediktinerinnenabtei St. Hildegard, Rüdesheim am Rhein, Germany// © Erich Lessing / Art Resource, NY

as exemplars of holy living. They were read publicly in churches (hence they were called *legends*—things read aloud) and for private devotion.

MUSIC AND MONASTICISM— GREGORIAN CHANT

The main occupation of the monk was the *Opus Dei* (work of God)—the liturgical common prayer of the *monasteric horarium*—and life revolved around the monastic church, where the monks gathered seven times a day for prayer. The centrality of the liturgy also explains why copying, correcting, and illuminating manuscripts were such an important part of monastic life. Texts were needed for religious services as well as for spiritual reading. The monks were encouraged to study the scriptures as a lifelong occupation. For monks this study was *lectio divina* (divine reading) and was central to their development as a monk. This monastic imperative encouraged the study of the Bible and such ancillary disciplines (grammar, criticism, and the like) as necessary for the study of scripture. From the seventh century on, monastic scriptoria were busily engaged in copying a wealth of material, both sacred and profane.

The monasteries were also centers for the development of sacred music. We have already seen that Charlemagne was interested in church music. His biographer Einhard tells us that the emperor "made careful reforms in the way in which the psalms were chanted and the lessons read. He was himself an expert at both of these exercises but he never read the lesson in public and he would sing only with the rest of the congregation and then in a low voice." Charlemagne's keen interest in music explains why certain monasteries of his reign—notably those at Metz and Trier—became centers for church music.

Charlemagne brought monks from Rome to stabilize and reform church music in his kingdom as part of his overall plan of liturgical renovation. In the earlier period of Christianity's growth, diverse traditions of ecclesiastical music developed in various parts of the West. Roman music represented one tradition—later called *Gregorian chant* after Pope Gregory the Great (540–604), who was believed to have codified the music in the late sixth century. Milan had its own musical tradition, known as *Ambrosian* music—in honor of Saint Ambrose, who had been a noted hymn writer, as Saint Augustine attests in the *Confessions*. There was a peculiar regional style of music in Spain known as *Mozarabic* chant, while the Franks also had their own peculiar style of chant. All of these styles derive from earlier models of music that have their roots in Hebrew, Greco–Roman, and Byzantine styles. Lack of documentation permits only an educated reconstruction of this early music and its original development.

CD Track 1
Anonymous, "Victimae paschali Laudes"

This listening selection is an early example of Gregorian Chant in which every syllable has its own note and the only extended phrases come at the end of each line. Even the final Alleluia is simple and unelaborated.

Note that of the three elements that characterize most Western music—melody, harmony, and rhythm—only the first is present. The melody is based entirely on the words of the text. No accompanying line provides harmony and no repeated rhythm provides musical form: the text dominates the musical structure. The only element of musical variety is the contrast between a single voice and massed voices. Although we cannot be certain that this was typical of the original performances, we can know that all the voices were male, as was appropriate to the original monastic context. We might say, in summary, that the musical content of the listening selection is intended to heighten the significance of the text, rather than add any extra element of its own.

Gregorian chant, as we know it today, was not codified until the eleventh and twelfth centuries, so it is rather difficult to reconstruct precisely the music of Charlemagne's court. It was probably a mixture of Roman and Frankish styles of singing. It was **monophonic** (one or many voices singing a single melodic line) and, ordinarily, would be sung **a capella** (without musical accompaniment) in the monastic churches. Scholars believe that most music consisted of simple chants for the recitation of the psalms at the Divine Office; more elaborate forms were used for the hymns of the office and the Mass chants. The music was simply called **cantus planus** (plainsong or plainchant).

Gregorian Style As the printed example shows, the written form of the music does not correspond to the modern style, which would not be invented until around 1000 by Guido D'Arezzo. In its elementary form the chant consisted of a single note for each syllable of a word. The basic symbols used to notate Gregorian chant were called *neums*. Using the Gregorian notational system with its four-line staff and the opening line of Psalm 109, *Dixit Dominus Domino Meo, sede a dextris meis* (The Lord said to my Lord: sit on my right hand), a line of syllabic chant would look like this:

1. Di-xit Dóminus Dómino mé- o : * Séde a déxtris mé- is.

Even in the earliest form of chants, a **cadence** (sense of completion or ending) was created by emphasizing the final word of a phrase with the addition of one or two extra notes, as seen in the preceding example. Later, more notes were added to the final words or syllables for elaboration and variation.

The simplicity of syllabic chant should not be regarded as useful only for the monotonous chanting of psalm verses. Very simple yet hauntingly melodic Gregorian compositions still exist that do not use elaborate cadences but rely on simple syllabic notes.

Certain phrases, especially words of acclamation (like *Alleluia*) or the word at the end of a line, were musically elaborated beyond the one-to-one correlation between note and syllable in the simple chant. This extensive addition of a chain of intricate notes sung on the vowel sound of a final syllable (or any syllable) was called a **melisma**. Thus for example, a melisma might elaborate the final *a* (ah) of *Alleluia* or the *i-e* (ee-ay) of *Kyrie* in the *Kyrie Eleison* (the Greek "Lord, have mercy on us" retained in the Latin Mass).

LITURGICAL MUSIC AND THE RISE OF DRAMA

THE LITURGICAL TROPE

Because books were scarce in the Carolingian period, monks memorized a great deal of liturgical chant. To aid memorization and add variety in the chant, words would be added to the long melismas. These words, **tropes**, were verbal elaborations of, or comments on, the text. Thus, for example, the melismatic *Kyrie Eleison* might take on such tropes as *sanctus* (holy) and *dominus* (lord), which were sung to the tune of the melisma. The use of tropes grew rapidly and became standard in liturgical music until they were removed from the liturgy at the time of the Counter-Reformation in the sixteenth century.

Scholars have pointed to the introduction of tropes into liturgical music as the origin of drama in the Western world. There had been drama in the Classical and Byzantine worlds, but drama in Europe developed from the liturgy of the medieval church after it had largely been lost (or suppressed) in the very early Middle Ages.

A ninth-century manuscript (preserved at the monastery of Saint Gall) preserves an early trope that was added to the music of the Easter entrance hymn (the *Introit*) for Mass. It is in the form of a short dialogue and seems to have been sung by either two different singers or two choirs. It is called the *Quem Quæritis* trope from its opening lines:

The *Quem Quæritis* Trope

De Resurrectione Domini	Of the Lord's Resurrection
Int[errogatio]:	Question [of the angels]:
Quem quæritis in sepulchro, {o}Christicolæ?	*Whom seek ye in the sepulcher, O followers of Christ?*
R[esponsio]:	Answer [of the Marys]:
Jesum Nazarenum crucifixum, o cœlicolæ.	*Jesus of Nazareth, which was crucified, O celestial ones.*
[Angeli:]	[The angels:]
Non est hic; surrexit, sicut, prædixerat. Ite, nuntiate quia surrexit de sepulchro.	*He is not here; he is risen, just as he foretold. Go, announce that he is risen from the sepulchre.*

Very shortly after the introduction of this trope into the Easter Mass, the short interrogation began to be acted, not at Mass but at the end of the night services preceding Easter dawn. The dialogue of the *Quem Quæritis* was not greatly enlarged, but the directions for its singing were elaborated into the form of a short play. By the eleventh and twelfth centuries, the dialogue was elaborated beyond the words of the Bible and more people were added. By the twelfth century, the stories took on greater complexity.

It was a logical step to remove these plays from the church and perform them in the public square. By the fourteenth century, sizable cycles of plays were performed in conjunction with various feast days and underwritten by the craft or merchants' guilds. Some of these cycles acted out the major stories of the Bible, from Adam to the Last Judgment. The repertory also began to include plays about the lives of the saints and allegorical plays about the combats of virtue and vice, such as the fifteenth-century work *Everyman*. These plays were a staple of public life well into the sixteenth century. William Shakespeare, for example, may well have seen such plays in his youth.

THE MORALITY PLAY: *EVERYMAN*

Everyman is a fifteenth-century play that may well be a translation from a much earlier Dutch play. The subject is no longer a redoing of a biblical theme but rather the personification of abstractions representing a theme dear to the medieval heart: the struggle for the soul. The unprepared reader of *Everyman* will note the heavy-handed allegorizing and moralizing (complete with a "Doctor" who makes a final appearance to point up the moral of the play) with some sense of estrangement, but with a closer reading, students will also note the stark dignity of the play, the earnestness with which it is constructed, and the economy of its structure. Written in rather spare rhyming couplets, *Everyman* is a good example of the transitional play that forms a link between the earlier liturgical drama and the more secular drama that was to come at the end of the English medieval period.

The plot of *Everyman* is simplicity itself; it is quickly summarized by the messenger who opens the play. Everyman must face God in final judgment after death. None of the aids and friends of this life will support Everyman, as the speeches of the allegorical figures of Fellowship and others make clear. The strengths for Everyman come from the aiding virtues of Confession, Good Deeds, and Knowledge. The story, however, is not the central core of this play; the themes that run through the entire play are what should engage our attention. First is the common medieval notion of life as a pilgrimage, which surfaces repeatedly. It is embedded not only in the medieval penchant for pilgrimage but also in the use of that term (as one sees, for example, in Chaucer) as a metaphor. Second, the notion of the inevitability of death as the defining action of human life is omnipresent in medieval culture. *Everyman* has an extremely intense *memento mori* ("Keep death before your eyes!") motif. Finally, medieval theology places great emphasis on the will of the human being in the attainment of salvation. It is not faith (this virtue is presumed) that will save Everyman; his or her willingness to learn (Knowledge), act (Good Deeds), and convert (Confession) will make the difference between salvation and damnation.

The Messenger says that *Everyman* is "By figure a moral play." It is meant not merely to instruct on the content of religion (as does a mystery play) but to instruct for the purposes of moral conversion. The earlier mystery plays usually point out a moral at the end of the performance. The morality play uses its resources to moralize throughout the play.

The one lingering element from the liturgy in a play like *Everyman* is its pageant quality: The dramatic force of the presentation is enhanced by the solemn wearing of gowns, the stately pace of the speeches, and the seriousness of the message. The play depends less on props and place. Morality plays did not evolve directly out of liturgical drama (they may owe something to the study of earlier plays based on the classics studied in schools), but the liturgical overtones are not totally absent.

THE NONLITURGICAL DRAMA OF HROSWITHA

At the end of the early Middle Ages we also have evidence of plays that did not depend on liturgical worship. Thus, a German nun–poet named Hroswitha (or Roswitha; the name is spelled variously), who lived at the aristocratic court of Gandersheim and died around the year 1000, has left us both a collection of legends written in Latin and six plays modeled on the work of the Roman dramatist Terence. What is interesting about this well-educated woman is the broad range of her learning and her mastery of classical Latin in an age that did not put a high premium on the education of females. Scholars also point out that her prose legend called *Theophilus* is the first known instance in German literature of the Faust theme—the selling of one's soul to the devil for material gain and public glory.

Hroswitha's plays were probably meant to be read aloud by a small circle of literate people, but some internal evidence suggests that they may also have been acted out in some rudimentary fashion. They are heavily moralistic (typically involving a religious conversion or steadfastness in faith during a time of persecution) and didactic. In the play *The Conversion of the Harlot Thaïs*, for example, the holy man Pafnutius begins with a long conversation with his disciples on a liberal education and the rules of musical proportion and harmony. Such a discussion would seem a wild digression to us today, but for Hroswitha's audience it would be a way not only of learning about the liberal arts but also a reminder that their study inevitably leads to a consideration of God. That her plays do not have a finished dramatic quality underscores the fact that she was the *first* dramatist writing in Germany (as well as Germany's first female poet). Her model was the ancient drama of Rome as far as style was concerned, but her intention was to use that style to educate and convert. She was a direct heir of the humane learning that developed in the Carolingian and Ottonian periods.

THE LEGEND OF CHARLEMAGNE

Charlemagne's kingdom did not long survive intact after the death of the emperor. By the tenth century, the Frankish kingdom was fractured and Europe reduced to a state worthy of the name Dark Ages. Anarchy, famine, ignorance, war, and factionalism were constants in tenth-century Europe; Charlemagne's era was looked back to as a long-vanished Golden Age. By the twelfth century, Charlemagne's reputation was such that he was canonized (in Aachen on December 29, 1165) by Emperor Frederick Barbarossa. Charlemagne's cult was immensely popular throughout France—especially at the royal abbey of Saint Denis in Paris, which made many claims of earlier links with the legendary emperor.

A fifteenth-century oil painting in Aachen depicts an idealized Charlemagne as saint, wearing the crown of the Holy Roman Emperor and carrying a model of the

◆ **9.4** Reliquary of Charlemagne, c. 1349. Reliquaries of this type are containers for a relic of the person depicted by the statue, in this case the crown of Charlemagne's skull.

Gold, silver, gems, enamel, 33.9″ (86 cm) high. Crown, before 1349; bust, after 1349. Cathedral Treasury, Palatine Chapel, Cathedral, Aachen, Germany// © Art Resource, NY

church he had built at Aachen. Frederick Barbarossa commemorated the canonization by commissioning a great wrought-bronze candelabrum to hang in the Aachen cathedral. He also ordered a gold reliquary (now in the Louvre in Paris) to house the bones of one of his saintly predecessor's arms; another reliquary, in the form of a portrait bust that contains fragments of Charlemagne's skull, is in the cathedral treasury at Aachen [**Fig. 9.4**].

Epic Poetry—The *Song* of *Roland*

The memory of Charlemagne and his epoch was kept more vividly alive, however, in cycles of epic poems and in tales and memoirs developed, embroidered, and disseminated by poets and singers throughout Europe from shortly after Charlemagne's time until the late Middle

Ages. These are the famous *chansons de geste* ("songs of deeds") or, as some were called, *chansons d'histoire* ("songs of history"). Of these songs, the oldest extant—as well as the best and most famous—is the *Song of Roland*.

The *Song of Roland* was written sometime late in the eleventh century, but behind it lay some three hundred years of oral tradition and earlier poems celebrating a battle between Charlemagne's army and a Muslim force at the Spanish border. Charlemagne did campaign against the emirate of Spain in 777 and 778 without conclusive result. In August 778 Charlemagne's rear guard was ambushed by the Basques while making its way through the Pyrenees after the invasion of Spain. The real extent of that battle (later placed, on not too much evidence, at the town of Roncesvalles) is unclear. Some experts maintain that it was a minor skirmish, remembered in the area in local legends later told and retold (and considerably embroidered in the process) by monks of the monasteries and sanctuaries on the pilgrimage routes to the great shrine of Saint James at Santiago de Compostela in Spain. Other historians insist that the battle was a horrendous bloodbath for the army of Charlemagne and that the tale was carried back to the Frankish cities, the legend was transformed as it was repeated by the descendants of the few survivors.

In any event, by the eleventh century the tale was widely known in Europe. Excerpts from the *Song of Roland* were sung to inspire the Norman army before the Battle of Hastings in 1066, and in 1096 Pope Urban II cited it in an appeal to French patriotism when he attempted to raise armies for a crusade to free the Holy Land. Medieval translations of the poem into German, Norse, and Italo–French attest to its widespread popularity outside the French-speaking area.

The *Song of Roland* is an epic poem; its unknown writer or writers had little interest in historical accuracy or geographic niceties. Its subject matter is the glory of the military campaign, the chivalric nature of the true knight, the constant possibility of human deviousness, and the clash of good and evil. The poem, although set in the eighth century, reflects the military values and chivalric code of the eleventh century.

The story is simple: Muslims attack the retreating rear portion of Charlemagne's army (through an act of betrayal) while it is under the command of Roland, a favorite nephew of the emperor. Roland's army is defeated, but not before he sounds his ivory horn to alert the emperor to the peril. The emperor in turn raises a huge army from throughout Christendom while the Muslims also raise a great force. An epic battle follows; Charlemagne, with divine aid, is victorious.

The *Song of Roland* is some four thousand lines long; it is divided into stanzas, and each line contains ten syllables. It is impossible to reproduce the rhyme in English, because each stanza ends with an assonance, so the poem is best read in blank verse translation—although that sacrifices the recitative quality of the original.

This poem was meant to be heard, not read. It was recited by wandering minstrels—*jongleurs*—to largely illiterate audiences. This fact explains the verse style, the immediacy of the adjectives describing the characters and the situations, and the somewhat repetitive language. The still-unexplained AOI at the end of many stanzas may have something to do with the expected reaction of the *jongleur* as he uttered that particular sound to give emphasis to a stanza. (Some sense of the immediacy of the original may be gained by a reader today who declaims some of these stanzas with gestures and appropriate pauses.)

Certain details of the poem merit particular attention. A portion of the poem recounts Charlemagne's arrival on the scene and his victory over the Saracens who are beleaguering the forces commanded by Roland. Most striking is the mixture of military and religious ideals, not an uncommon motif in the medieval period. This mixture is reflected not only in the imagery and in the plot (Charlemagne's prayer keeps the sun from setting in order to allow time for victory, an echo of the biblical siege of Jericho by Joshua) but also in the bellicose Archbishop Turpin. Christian valor is contrasted with Saracen wickedness and treachery; the anti-Muslim bias of the poem is clear. The Muslim Saracens are pagans and idolaters—an odd way to describe the rigidly monotheistic followers of Islam. The *Song of Roland*, like much of the epic tradition from which it springs, is nevertheless devoted to the martial virtues of courage and strength, the comradeship of the battlefield, and the power of great men as well as the venality of evil ones.

The *Song of Roland* was immensely popular in its own time. It spawned several other compositions like the *Pseudo-Turpin* and the *Song of Aspremont* in order to continue the story or elaborate portions of it. At a much later time in Italy, the story was redone in the telling of the exploits of Orlando (Roland). To this day, children in Sicily visit the traditional puppet shows in which the exploits of brave Roland and his mates are acted out with great clatter and verve. Spectators at those shows witness stories that go back to the beginnings of the medieval period.

THE VISUAL ARTS

THE ILLUMINATED BOOK

Given Charlemagne's preoccupation with literary culture, it should not be surprising that a great deal of artistic effort was expended on the production and illumination of manuscripts. Carolingian manuscripts were made of parchment (treated animal skins, mainly from cows and sheep) because papyrus was unavailable and the process of papermaking was unknown during this period. For very fine books, the parchment was dyed

purple and the letters were painted on with silver and gold pigments.

Although a good deal of decoration of Carolingian manuscripts shows the influence of Irish models, the illustrations often show other influences. This is strikingly apparent in the illustrations of the *Gospel Book of Charlemagne* (800–810), where it is clear that the artists were conscious of the Roman style [**Fig. 9.5**]. The page showing the four evangelists with their symbolic emblems is strikingly classical: the four evangelists are toga-clad like ancient Roman consuls. Some evidence shows that the artists attempted some experiments in three-dimensionality. The wooded background in the receding part of the upper two illustrations tends to bring the evangelists forward and thus diminish the flatness we associate with both Byzantine and Celtic illustrations.

The *Utrecht Psalter* The *Utrecht Psalter* (so-called because its present home is the University of Utrecht in Holland) has been called the masterpiece of the

◆ **9.5** The four evangelists and their symbols, Palatine School at Aachen, early 9th century. Over the four evangelists are their symbols (clockwise from top left): Matthew (angel), John (eagle), Luke (ox), and Mark (lion). The symbols derive from the Book of Ezekiel.

Manuscript illustration from the Gospel Book of Charlemagne, *Treasury Gospels (fol. 14v), Cathedral Treasury, Palatine Chapel, Cathedral, Aachen, Germany//© D.Y./Art Resource, NY*

QUIABEHEPLACITUMEST   ADEACIENDAMUINDICIA   EIUS

◆ **9.6** Illustration for Psalm 150, *Utrecht Psalter*, c. 820–840. This page is typical of the quick, nervous style of the unknown illustrator who did similar symbolic drawings for the entire Psalter of 150 psalms. Note the variety of musical instruments representing those mentioned in Psalm 150: *Praise the LORD. . . . with the sound of the trumpet, . . . with the psalter and harp, . . . with timbourine and dance, . . . with stringed instruments and organs, . . . upon the loud cymbals . . .*

From Hautvilliers (near Reims), France. 12⅞″ x 10″ (32.5 x 25.4 cm). University Library, Utrecht, Netherlands//Image © New York Public Library, New York, USA/Art Resource, NY

◆ **9.7** *Crucifixion*, 9th century. The crowded scene refers to the saving power of the cross. The figure to the left captures blood from the dying Christ, an allusion to the Eucharist (mass) of the Body and Blood of Christ. Such ivories were often used as covers for Gospel books and other liturgical works and were frequently produced as gifts for special occasions.

From Metz, France. Ivory plaque, 4¾″ x 8¼″ (12 x 21 cm) high. Image © Victoria and Albert Museum, London, UK/Art Resource, NY

Carolingian Renaissance. Executed at Rheims sometime around 820 to 840, it contains the whole psalter, with wonderfully free and playful pen drawings around the text of the psalms. The figures are free from any hieratic stiffness; they are mobile and show a nervous energy. The illustration for Psalm 150, for example, has a scene at the bottom of the page showing various figures "praising God with horn and cymbals" [**Fig. 9.6**]. There are two other interesting aspects of the same illustration. One is that the figures are in the act of praising Christ, who stands at the apex of the illustration with the symbols of his resurrection (the staff-like cross in his hand). Although the psalms speak of the praise of God, for the medieval Christian the "hidden" or true meaning of the scriptures was that they speak in a prefigurative way of Christ. Thus the psalmist who praises God is a "shadow" of the church that praises Christ. A second thing to note in this illustration is the bottom-center scene of an organ with two men working the bellows to supply the air for the organ pipes.

◆ **9.8** Cover panels, *Dagulf Psalter*, late 8th century. In the left panel, top, King David orders the psalms to be written down, and on the bottom, accompanied by musicians, sings them. In the top right panel, Saint Jerome receives the Pope's orders to edit the psalms and, on the bottom, corrects the psalter, which reflects the common work in the monasteries of the Carolingian period.

Made for Pope Hadrian in the palace workshops of Emperor Charlemagne at Aachen, Germany. Ivory, 3⅛" x 6½" (9.4 x 16.6 cm) high. Louvre, Paris, France//© Réunion des Musées Nationaux /Art Resource, NY

The style of the *Utrecht Psalter* has much in common with early Christian illustration. The lavish purple and silver manuscripts show a conscious imitation of Byzantine taste. We have also noted the influence of Celtic illustration. Carolingian manuscript art thus had a certain international flavor, and the various styles and borrowings offer ample testimony to the cosmopolitan character of Charlemagne's culture. This universality diminished in the next century; not until the period of the so-called International Style in the fourteenth century would such a broad eclecticism again be seen in Europe.

Ivory Carving One other art form that developed from the Carolingian love for the book is ivory carving. This technique was not unique to Charlemagne's

time; it was known in the ancient world and highly valued in Byzantium. The ivories that have survived from Charlemagne's time were used for book covers. One beautiful example of the ivory carver's art is a crucifixion panel made at the palace workshop at Aachen sometime in the early ninth century [**Fig. 9.7**]. Note the crowded scenes that surround the crucifixion event. The entire ivory is framed with acanthus leaf floral designs. The composition indicates that the carver had seen some examples of Christian carving, whereas the bearded Christ and the flow of the drapery indicate familiarity with Byzantine art.

The ivory covers of the *Dagulf Psalter* have been preserved and are now in the Louvre [**Fig. 9.8**]. Rather than the usual crowded scenes of most of these covers, the ivories from the *Dagulf Psalter* are composed of two scenes on each of the panels; the scenes refer to both the psalter and the papal connection. The top-left panel shows David and his court; in the scene below, David is shown singing one of his psalms to the accompaniment of his lyre. The top-right panel depicts Saint Jerome receiving a letter from Pope Damasus instructing him to correct the psalter; the scene below depicts Jerome in the act of working on the psalter while a grateful clergy looks on.

Calligraphy One other advance in manuscript production during the Carolingian period was in the area of fine handwriting or, as it is more technically known, calligraphy. Handwriting before the Carolingian period was cluttered, unformed, and cramped. It was difficult to read because of its erratic flourishes and lack of symmetry. After 780 scribes in Carolingian scriptoria began to develop a precise and rounded form of lettering that became known as the Carolingian *minuscule*, as opposed to the *majuscule* or capital letter. This form of lettering was so crisp and legible that it soon became a standard form of manuscript writing. Even in the fifteenth century the Florentine humanists preferred the minuscule calligraphy for their manuscripts. When printing became popular in the early sixteenth century, printers soon designed type fonts to conform to Carolingian minuscule. It superseded Gothic type in popularity and is the ancestor of modern standard lettering systems.

CAROLINGIAN AND ROMANESQUE ARCHITECTURE

CHARLEMAGNE'S PALACE AT AACHEN

Beyond his immediate commercial, military, and political goals, Charlemagne had an overwhelming desire to model his kingdom on that of ancient Rome. His coronation in Rome symbolized the fusion of the ancient imperial ideal with the notion of Christian destiny. It was not accidental that Charlemagne's favorite book—he had it read to him frequently at meals—was Augustine's *The City of God*. One highly visible way of making this ideal concrete was to build a capital.

At Aachen (in French it is called Aix-la-Chapelle) Charlemagne built his palace and royal chapel [**Fig. 9.9**]. Except for the chapel (incorporated into the pres-

ent cathedral), all the buildings of Charlemagne's palace have been destroyed, and the Aachen city hall (built in the fourteenth century) covers the palace site. The palace proper was a long one-story building; its main room was the large royal hall, which measured roughly 140′ x 60′. So richly decorated that even the fastidious and sophisticated Byzantine legates were favorably impressed, the room had as its focal point at the western end the emperor's throne. In front of the palace was an open courtyard around which were outbuildings and apartments for the imperial retinue. Around the year 800, the courtyard held a great bronze statue of Theodoric, once king of the Ravenna Ostrogoths, that Charlemagne had brought back from Ravenna to adorn his palace.

The royal hall was joined to Charlemagne's chapel by a long wooden gallery. This royal chapel was probably built around 795. With sixteen exterior walls, the chapel was a central-plan church based on an octagon [**Fig. 9.10**]; its model undoubtedly was the Church of San Vitale in Ravenna, which Charlemagne had visited and admired. The octagon formed the main nave of the church, which was surrounded by **cloisters**; the building was two-storied. At the eastern end of the chapel was an altar dedicated to the Savior, with a chapel dedicated to the Virgin directly below it. The central space was crowned with an octagonal cupola, the lower part of which was pierced by windows—the main source of light in the church. The outside of the church was austere; the inside was richly ornamented with marbles brought to Aachen from Ravenna and Rome. The interior of the cupola was decorated with a rich mosaic depicting Christ and the twenty-four elders of the Apocalypse (now destroyed; the present mosaics in the chapel are modern copies) while the other planes of the interior were covered with frescoes (now also destroyed). The railing of the upper gallery was made from bronze screens that are still in place, wrought in geometrical forms.

The chapel included two objects that emphasized its royal status: the most important relic of the kingdom, Saint Martin of Tours' cape, and a throne. Charlemagne's throne was on the second floor, opposite the Savior chapel. From this vantage point, the emperor could observe the liturgical services being conducted in the Savior chapel and at the same time view the Virgin chapel with its rich collection of relics.

Charlemagne's throne, with its curved back and armrests, was mounted by six stone steps. This arrangement was obviously taken from King Solomon's throne as described in the Bible (I Kings 10:18–19). Charlemagne was to be thought of as the "new Solomon" who, like his ancient prototype, was an ambitious builder, a sagacious lawgiver, and the symbol of national unity. That this analogy was not an idle fancy is proved by

◆ **9.9** Reconstruction of Charlemagne's palace, Aachen, Germany. The royal hall with its long gallery is in the background. Compare the octagonal royal chapel in the foreground to the Church of San Vitale in Ravenna, Italy (Figure 7.14).

Watercolor on paper. Image © Archives Larousse, Paris, France//Lauros/ Giraudon/The Bridgeman Art Library

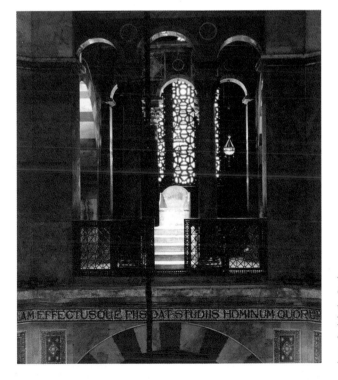

◆ **9.10** Palatine Chapel interior, Charlemagne's palace, Aachen, Germany. This view, toward the east, shows the emperor's throne in the second story (center) from which he would follow the religious services celebrated on the first floor of the chapel. The inscriptions below the throne are modern additions. *(Image © Erich Lessing/Art Resource, NY)*

◆ **9.11** Plan for an ideal monastery, St. Gall, Switzerland, c. 820. The monastery site would have been 480′ x 640′ (146 x 195 m) and would have housed 120 monks and 170 serfs. Over the centuries, the St. Gall plan for future monasteries exerted considerable influence on monastery construction. The areas colored green highlight the gardens within the monastery complex.

Reconstruction © by Cecilia Cunningham based on original plan (3′8″ across, drawn to scale on vellum) in the Library of the Monastery of Saint Gall, Switzerland.

a letter to the emperor from Alcuin, Charlemagne's friend and tutor, in anticipation of his return to Aachen: "May I soon be allowed to come with palms, accompanied with children singing psalms, to meet your triumphant glory, and to see once more your beloved face in the Jerusalem of our most dear fatherland, wherein is the temple set up to God by this most wise Solomon."

THE CAROLINGIAN MONASTERY

In the period between Saint Benedict and Charlemagne, the Benedictine monastery underwent a complex evolution. Originally the monasteries were made up of small communities with fewer than fifteen members who led a life of prayer and work in a rather simple setting. With the decline of city life and the disorders brought on by the repeated invasions of the Barbarians after the fifth century, the monastery became increasingly a center of life for rural populations. Monaster-

ies not only kept learning alive and worship intact but were also called on to serve as shelters for the traveler, rudimentary hospitals for the sick, places of refuge in time of invasion, granaries for the farmer, centers of law for both religious and civil courts, and places that could provide agricultural services such as milling and brewing.

This expansion of services, making the monastery into what has been called a "miniature civic center," inevitably changed the physical character of the monastery compound. By Charlemagne's time the monastery was an intricate complex of buildings suitable for the many tasks it was called on to perform (see **Table 9.1**). One vivid example of the complexity of the Carolingian monastery can be gained by a study of a plan for an ideal monastery developed about 820 at the Benedictine abbey of Saint Gall in present-day Switzerland [**Fig. 9.11**].

In the Saint Gall plan the monastic church dominated the area. Set off with its two round towers, it was

Table 9.1 *The Major Parts of the Monastery*

The Monastic Church	Site of the major religious services
The Chapter House	Ordinary meeting room of the monastic community; the name comes from the custom of reading a chapter of the Rule of Saint Benedict aloud each day to the community
The Cloister	Technically, the enclosed part of the monastery; more commonly, the enclosed garden and walkway in the interior of the monastery
The Scriptorium	Library and copying area of the monastery
The Refectory	Monks' dining hall
The Novitiate	Quarters for aspirant monks not yet vowed in the community
The Dormitory	Sleeping area for the monks
The Infirmary	For sick, retired, and elderly monks
The Guest House	For visitors, retreatants, and travelers
The Outbuildings	Buildings for the farms and crafts of the monastery. Small buildings far from the main monastery that housed farmer monks were called *granges*

a basilica-style church with numerous entrances for the use of the monks. To the south of the church was a rectangular garden space surrounded by a covered walkway (the *cloister*), from which radiated the monk's dormitory, dining hall (*refectory*), and kitchens. To the north of the church were a copying room (**scriptorium**), a separate house for the abbot, a school for youths and young novices, and a guest house. To the extreme south of the church were ranged workshops, barns, and other utilitarian outbuildings. To the east beyond the church were an infirmary and a separate house for aspirant monks (the *novitiate*), gardens, poultry houses, and the community cemetery.

THE ROMANESQUE STYLE

The plan of Saint Gall was never realized in stone, but the Benedictines did participate in ambitious architectural works after the Carolingian period. In the eleventh century, after a long period of desolation and warfare, Europe began to stir with new life. Pilgrimages became popular as travel became safe. Pilgrimage routes—in particular to sites in Spain, England, and Italy—crisscrossed Europe. Crusades were mounted to free the holy places of the Middle East from the Muslims so that pilgrims could journey in peace to the most desired goal of the pilgrim: Jerusalem. During this period monks built and maintained pilgrimage churches and hostels on the major routes of the pilgrims.

The building style of this period (roughly from 1000 to 1200) is called *Romanesque* because the architecture was larger and more Roman-looking than the work done in the earlier medieval centuries. The two most striking characteristics of this architecture were the use of heavy stone arches and generous exterior decoration, mainly sculpture. The Romanesque style had two obvi-

0	50	100 feet
0	10	20	30 meters

1 nave	5 transept
2 choir	6 aisles
3 ambulatory	7 apse
4 chapels	8 narthex

◆ **9.12** Floor plan, Church of Saint Sernin, Toulouse, France. Note the ample aisles for easy passage of pilgrim groups around the entire church. The radiating chapels around the ambulatory permitted many priests to celebrate Mass simultaneously.

ous advantages. First was that the use of heavy stone and masonry walls permitted larger and more spacious interiors. Second, the heavy walls could support stone arches (mainly the Roman barrel arch), at least in France and Spain, which in turn permitted fireproof stone and masonry roofs. Long experience had shown that basilica-style churches, with their wooden trusses and wooden roofs, were notoriously susceptible to destruction by fire.

Romanesque architecture sprouted all over Europe, and while it showed great regional variation, its main lines are distinct. The Benedictine pilgrimage Church of Saint Sernin in Toulouse was designed to accommodate the large number of pilgrims as they made their way to the famous shrine of Santiago de Compostela in Spain. A glimpse at the floor plan [**Fig. 9.12**] and the interior

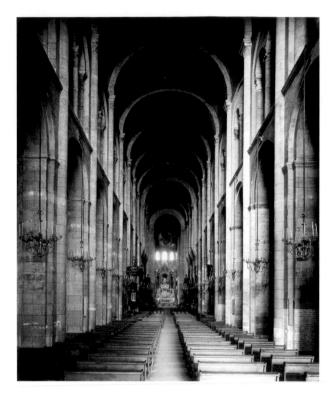

◆ **9.13** Nave, Church of Saint Sernin, Toulouse, France, c. 1080–1120. The massive ceiling vaults are called *barrel* or *tunnel* vaults. The heavy stonework required heavy walls to support the weight of the vaults. The galleries, with their own vaults, also helped support the cut-stone ceiling vaults. The pulpit to the left is a much later addition to the church. *(Image © Scala/Art Resource, NY)*

◆ **9.14** North jamb, central portal, Monastery of Saint Gilles, Saint Gilles du Gard, France, c. 1140. Notice the echoes of classical column capitals and low-relief carving on the jambs. *(Image © Bildarchiv Monheim GmbH (Schütze/Rodemann)/Alamy)*

[**Fig. 9.13**] shows clearly that the generous interior space was articulated in a manner such that large numbers of people besides the monastic community could move freely through the building. For example, the floor plan allows for an aisle parallel to the nave to go completely around the church. In that fashion the monastic choir, which extended out into the nave, was circumvented by the faithful—who could make a complete circle of the church without disturbing the monks.

ROMANESQUE SCULPTURE

Exterior church decoration was almost unknown in the Carolingian period, but during the Romanesque period there was a veritable explosion of exterior sculpture. The lack of interior light (precluded by the thick, solid walls needed for roof vaulting) in a sense drove the artist outside. A favorite area of decoration was the *portal* or doorway, because the crowds would pass through the doors to enter the church and receive edifying instruction in the process. The artist might decorate a door jamb [**Fig. 9.14**], a capital [**Fig. 9.15**], or the central supporting post of a portal, the *trumeau* [**Fig. 9.16**].

The fullest iconographic program of the Romanesque sculptor can usually be found in the half-moon shaped space called the *tympanum* over the portal; Romanesque churches in France offer many splendid examples of this elaborated art. The sculptural program over the inner west door of the Benedictine abbey Church of Sainte Madeleine at Vézelay is representative of the elaborated art in stone [**Fig. 9.17**].

The Vézelay tympanum depicts Christ, ascending into heaven, giving his church the mission to preach the gospel to the entire world. Christ, in the center almond shape called the *mandorla*, sends the power of the Holy Spirit into the apostles, who cluster on either side and just below with copies of the Gospel in their hands. Below the apostles the lintel stone depicts the peoples of the world, including fanciful races known to the sculptor only through the legendary travel books and encyclopedias that circulated in Europe. The theme of the exotic peoples to be healed by the Gospel is repeated in the eight arching compartments above the central scene, which depict strange peoples, lepers, cripples, and others who need to hear the Gospel.

◆ **9.15** Capital relief sculpture, nave, Abbey Church of La Madeleine, Vézelay, France, c. 1130. Here, avarice (greed) and calumny (destruction of another's good name) are punished. This kind of extravagant figure would later be criticized by monastic reformers of the 12th century. *(Image © Ray Roberts/Alamy)*

◆ **9.16** The Prophet Jeremiah, trumeau, south portal, Abbey Church of St. Pierre, Moissac, France, early 12th century. The life-size, serpentine figure of the prophet (may also be Isaiah) leans toward the church as he holds the scroll of his biblical book. The lions probably reflect the influence of Islamic art from Spain. *(Image © Bildarchiv Monheim GmbH (Florian Monheim)/Alamy)*

◆ **9.17** *Pentecost*, tympanum, Abbey Church of La Madeleine, Vézelay, c. 1120–1132. The lowest band of figures represents all of the peoples of the earth called to salvation by the central figure of Christ, framed in a mandorla. *(Image © The Art Archive/Gianni Dagli Orti)*

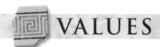

Feudalism

The social organization of late Carolingian society was based on feudalism, a form of government that had its primary focus on the holding of land. Theoretically, the monarch held all land with nobles, who swore allegiance to the monarch, possessing land as a gift from the monarch. Under the nobles were people, again pledging allegiance to their noble superiors, who held a smaller piece of land (for example, a manor). The agricultural peasants (serfs) had the use of the land in exchange for fees and for cultivating a certain percentage for the lord above them. The clergy also had the legal right to certain tithes on the production of goods and services. This highly stratified system also affected the system of warfare. Each knight (a small landholder) pledged loyalty to a higher noble, who in turn pledged loyalty to the crown. Armies could be raised when, for instance, a monarch would call up the nobles pledged to him, and they in turn would call up the knights who had sworn loyalty to them.

Feudal society existed only so long as a country remained rural and without large towns. Italy, with its long history of town life, never had as strong a feudal society as did the Frankish lands of what are today France and Germany. Feudalism was a highly static, hierarchical, and basically agricultural way of organizing life. It would undergo vast changes with the slow emergence of city life and the increased mobility brought on by vigorous trade and such military movements as the Crusades.

The outer arches, or *archivolts*, depict the signs of the zodiac and the symbolic seasons of the year, a reminder that the Gospel depicted in the central scene is to be preached "in season and out"; these symbolic medallions are interspersed with mythical and fantastic beasts. The outer archivolts are purely decorative, derived perhaps from Islamic sources known to the artists through the Muslim architecture of Spain.

Romanesque style was a European phenomenon—its variant forms in Italy, Germany, and England give ample testimony—and a summing-up of much of European culture between the end of the Carolingian period and the rise of city life and the Gothic style in the late twelfth century. The roots of the Romanesque were in the Benedictine tradition of service, scholarship, and solidity. Churches like Vézelay also manifest the period's concern with travel, expansion, and the attendant knowledge that comes from such mobility. When reaction came against the more extravagant forms of Romanesque decoration, it came from Bernard of Clairvaux (1090–1153), who was primarily a monastic reformer. Bernard was horrified by the fantastic nature of Romanesque sculpture because he felt so many "and so marvelous are the varieties of diverse shapes that we are more tempted to read in the marbles than in the Book and to spend our whole day wondering at these things rather than meditating on the Law of God." Even Bernard's strictures testify to the close relationship between the Benedictines and the Romanesque (especially the French Romanesque), which is another reason the period after Charlemagne and before the primacy of the city can be called simply the Benedictine Age.

SUMMARY

◆ **Carolingian Renaissance.** Our attention in this chapter shifted from Byzantium to the West and, more specifically, to the rise of the kingdom of the Franks under Charlemagne. The so-called Carolingian Renaissance rekindled the life of culture after the dark period following the fall of the last Roman emperor in the West in the late fifth century and the rise of the so-called Barbarian tribes.

◆ **Cultural Revival.** Charlemagne's reign saw the standardization of monasticism, worship, music, and education in the church. Those reforms would give general shape to Western Catholicism that in some ways endured into the modern period. Equally important was Charlemagne's assumption of the title of Holy Roman Emperor. This act would establish a political office that would exist in Europe until the end of World War I in the twentieth century. It also became a cause for friction between Rome and Constantinople because the Byzantine emperors saw Charlemagne's act as an intrusion on their legitimate claim to be the successors of the old Roman Empire.

◆ **Social Structure.** The Carolingian world was essentially rural and feudal. Society was based on a rather rigid hierarchy with the emperor at the top, the nobles and higher clergy below him, and the vast sea of peasants bound to the land at the bottom. There was little in the way of city life on any scale. The outpost of rural Europe was the miniature town known as the monastery or the stronghold of the nobles. The rise of the city and increased social mobility would eventually destroy the largely agricultural and feudal society as the High Middle Ages emerged in the eleventh century.

◆ **Charlemagne as a Mythic Ideal.** Finally, there was Charlemagne as a mythic figure who eventually would be drawn larger than life in the *Song of Roland*. The growth of such myths always occurs because they have some deep desires behind them. In the case of Charlemagne, the desire was to describe the ideal warrior who could perform two fundamental tasks for Europe: vanquish the Islamic powers that threatened Christian Europe and provide a model for a unified empire (the Holy Roman Empire) that would be both a perfect feudal society and one strong enough to accomplish the first task of destroying Islam. Not without reason was the *Song of Roland* a central poem for the first crusaders who turned their faces to the East.

from what we understand them to be today. How were they understood and how do we understand them?

3. One feature of the Carolingian period was the central place of monasticism. Why was monasticism exceptionally suited to a time when there was little urban life?

4. Many scholars have argued that monasticism is the living out of a utopian ideal. How is monasticism a "utopian" behavior, and to what degree is it also a form of countercultural living?

5. Why is plainchant (Gregorian chant) ideally suited for congregational singing, especially for the unaccompanied voice?

6. Contrast the place of books in early medieval culture and in our own beyond the obvious issue of our better production technologies.

7. Drama evolved out of worship in the early medieval period just as Greek tragedy evolved out of worship in its time. Speculate on why there should be this connection between worship and drama.

8. Byzantine churches tended to lavish their decorative efforts on the insides of churches whereas Romanesque churches tended to decorate the outsides, more especially the façades. Suggest reasons for this widely observable fact.

EXERCISES

1. The "seven liberal arts" are divided into the trivium and the quadrivium. How much of the trivium lingers in primary education today? What has been added to those "trivial" subjects?

2. Two subjects studied in the quadrivium were music and astronomy. Those subjects were quite different

Visit the *Culture & Values* Companion website at **www.cengage.com/art/Cunningham/Cultureand Values7E** and the *Humanities Resource Center* for an array of primary source readings, key terms with pronunciations, flash cards, quizzes, and study materials designed especially to help you do well in this course.

CHAPTER 10

HIGH MIDDLE AGES: THE SEARCH FOR SYNTHESIS

No person is so typical of the medieval period as the figure of the knight. Chaucer praises him as "gentil and perfaite" in the prologue of the *Canterbury Tales*. The knight, splendid in armor and mounted on a horse, is commonly depicted in the art and literature of the period. In fact, since the knight had to pay for both armor and mount, knighthood was associated with the upper classes. In many modern languages the knight, because he was mounted, is associated with the horse: *Chevalier* (derived from the French word for horse, *cheval*) *Caballero* (Spanish), and *Cavagliere* (Italian). The fact that the knight was to obey a code of honor has given rise to our modern English word "chivalry" coming directly from the French word for knight. Typically, he was attended by a young squire who was his shield and armor bearer.

Knights swore allegiance to lords of the manors who, in obedience to a king, raised the armies necessary for war. When not otherwise employed by a given lord, some knights sought employment with whatever group had a need for military men. They were known as "Knights Errant," that is, "Wandering Knights." During the period of the Crusades, the Church even encouraged religious orders of knights who combined the monastic life with the task of protecting Christian sites and pilgrims in the Holy Land from Muslim incursions.

A medieval army was typically made up of ranks of foot soldiers who carried various weapons ranging from swords, pikes, and staves to bowmen who were expert with the arrow. Keeping them in control were foot soldiers who were known as "sergeants" deriving from the Latin word for servant (*servus*). Below those ranks were hordes of others collectively known as "camp followers," suppliers of food, drink, gambling, and prostitution, as well as some wives and families, who followed armies as they traveled during the season of warfare.

The class distinction between the knight and the foot soldier has lingered in the present day classification of the officer class and the class of enlisted men.

◆ Foot soldier and knight in battle. *(© The Art Archive/Gianni Dagli Orti)*

THE SIGNIFICANCE OF PARIS

From about 1150 to 1300, Paris could well claim to be the center of Western civilization. Beyond its position as a royal seat, it was a strong mercantile center. Its annual trade fair was famous. In addition, Paris gave birth to Gothic architecture, the philosophical and theological traditions known as scholasticism, and the educational community that in time became known as the university (see map, "The Ile de France"). These three creations have their own distinct history but sprang from a common intellectual impulse: the desire to articulate all knowledge systematically.

The culture of the Middle Ages derives from the twin sources of all Western high culture: (1) the humane learning inherited from the culture of Greece and Rome and (2) the accepted faith of the West, which has its origin in the worldview of the Judeo–Christian scriptures and religious worldview.

The flowering of a distinct expression of culture in and around medieval Paris was made possible by many factors. There was a renewed interest in learning, fueled largely by the discovery of hitherto lost texts from the Classical world—especially the writings of Aristotle—which came to the West via the Muslim world. The often ill-fated Crusades begun in the eleventh century to recover the Holy Land, and the increasing vogue for pilgrimages created a certain cosmopolitanism that in turn weakened the static feudal society. Religious reforms initiated by new religious orders like that of the Cistercians in the twelfth century and the begging friars in the thirteenth breathed new life into the church.

GENERAL EVENTS	ART

EARLY MIDDLE AGES

ROMANESQUE PERIOD

768

987 Paris made center of feudal kingdom of Hugh Capet

1000

11th cent. Capetian kings consolidate power and expand French kingdom

1096–1099 First Crusade; capture of Jerusalem by Christians

12th cent. *Notre Dame de Belle Verrière*, stained glass window at Chartres Cathedral

1140

EARLY GOTHIC PERIOD

1141 Saint Bernard of Clairvaux leads condemnation of Abelard at Council of Sens

c. 1145–1170 Tympanum of right door, Royal Portal, Chartres Cathedral

c. 1150 Universities of Paris and Bologna founded

c. 1163 Oxford University founded

1180 Philip Augustus assumes throne of France; promotes Paris as capital

1194

HIGH MIDDLE AGES

MATURE GOTHIC PERIOD

1202–1204 Fourth Crusade; crusaders sack Constantinople on way to Holy Land

c. 1215 *Christ Blessing*, trumeau, south porch, Chartres

c. 1209 Cambridge University founded

1215 Magna Carta, limiting powers of king, signed in England

c. 1215–c. 1250 Guild windows at Chartres Cathedral

c. 1220 Growth begins of mendicant friars: Franciscans, Dominicans

1258 Robert de Sorbon founds Paris hospice for scholars, forerunner of Sorbonne

1270 Eighth Crusade; death of Saint Louis of France

1235 *Saint Francis of Assisi* altarpiece, San Francesco

c. 1271–1293 Marco Polo travels to China and India

c. 1365 *The Triumph of Saint Thomas Aquinas*, Santa Maria Novella

1291 Fall of Acre, last Christian stronghold in Holy Land

1465 *Dante and His Poem*, Cathedral of Florence, Italy

1348–1367 Universities based on Paris model founded in Prague, Vienna, Cracow, Pecs

c. 1480–1465 Botticelli's portrait of *Dante*

1400

Beyond these more generalized currents, one can also point to individuals of genius who were crucial in the humanistic renaissance of the time. The University of Paris is inextricably linked with the name of Peter Abelard just as scholasticism is associated with the name of Thomas Aquinas. The Gothic style, unlike most art movements, can be pinpointed to a specific time at a particular place and with a single individual. Gothic architecture began near Paris at the Abbey of Saint Denis in the first half of the twelfth century under the sponsorship of the head of the abbey, Abbot Suger (1080–1151).

THE GOTHIC STYLE

SUGER'S BUILDING PROGRAM FOR SAINT DENIS

The Benedictine Abbey of Saint Denis, over which Abbot Suger presided from 1122 until his death nearly twenty-nine years later, was the focal point for French patriotism. The abbey church—built in Carolingian times—housed the relics of Saint Denis, a fifth-century martyr who had evangelized the area of Paris before

ARCHITECTURE	LITERATURE & PHILOSOPHY	MUSIC
		10th cent. *Organum* develops
		11th cent. Guido of Arezzo invents musical notation used today
	12th cent. Golden Age of University of Paris under scholastic masters	
	1113 Abelard begins teaching in Paris; meets Heloise	
c. 1130 Halt of construction at Great Third Abbey Church of Cluny	**1121** Abelard, *Sic et Non*; birth of Scholasticism	**12th cent.** Notre Dame School of Paris is center of music study and composition
1140 Abbot Suger, Abbey Church of Saint Denis; Gothic style derives	**after 1150** Recovery of lost texts by Aristotle and others via Arabic translations	**12th–13th cent.** French troubadours and trouvères flourish
c. 1163–1250 Cathedral of Notre Dame, Paris		**1160** Léonin of Paris, *Magnus Liber Organi*
c. 1180 Philip Augustus commissions Louvre as royal residence and treasury	**c. 1190** Maimonides, *Guide for the Perplexed* **13th cent.** Era of secular poems; Goliardic verse	**1181** Pérotin, director of Notre Dame School of Paris
1194 Chartres cathedral destroyed by fire; rebuilding begins (ends 1260)	**c. 1224–1226** Saint Francis of Assisi, "Canticle of Brother Sun"	**13th cent.** German minnesingers flourish
1220–1269 Cathedral of Amiens **c. 1235** Honnecourt, practical geometry	**c. 1267–1273** Aquinas, *Summa Theologica*	**c. 1250** Polyphonic motets are principal form of composition
1243–1248 Sainte Chapelle, Paris	**1300** Dante exiled from Florence **c. 1303–1321** Dante, *Divine Comedy*	
1247–1568 Cathedral of Beauvais; Cathedral of Strasbourg **1399–1439** Spire of Strasbourg cathedral erected	**c. 1385–1400** Chaucer, *The Canterbury Tales*	

his martyrdom. The crypt of the church served as the burial place for Frankish kings and nobles from before the reign of Charlemagne, although it lacked the tomb of Charlemagne. One concrete link between the Abbey of Saint Denis and Charlemagne came through a series of literary works. The fictitious *Pélerinage de Charlemagne* claimed that the relics of the Passion housed at the abbey had been brought there personally by Charlemagne when he returned from a pilgrimage–crusade to the Holy Land.

Another work, the *Pseudo-Turpin*, has Charlemagne returning to the Abbey of Saint Denis after his Spanish campaign and proclaiming all France to be under the protection and tutelage of the saint. These two legends were widely believed in the Middle Ages; there is fair evidence that Suger accepted their authenticity. The main themes of the legends—pilgrimages, crusades, and the mythical presence of Charlemagne—created a story about the abbey that made it a major Christian shrine as well as one worthy of the royal city of Paris.

Pilgrims and visitors came to Paris to visit Saint Denis either because of the fame of the abbey's relics or because of the annual *Lendit* (the trade fair held near the precincts of the abbey). Accordingly, in 1124 Suger decided to build a new church to accommodate those who flocked to the popular pilgrimage center. This rebuilding program took the better part of fifteen years and never saw completion. Suger mentions as models two sacred buildings that by his time already had archetypal significance for Christianity. He wanted his church to be as lavish and brilliant as Hagia Sophia in Constantinople, which he knew only by reputation, and as loyal to the will of God as the Temple of Solomon as it was described in the Bible.

The first phase of Suger's project was basically a demolition and repair job; he had to tear down the more deteriorated parts of the old church and replace them. He reconstructed the western façade of the church and added two towers. In order to better handle the pilgrimage crowds and the increasingly elaborate processions called for in the medieval liturgy, the entrance was given three portals. The *narthex*, the part of the church one enters first (before the nave), was rebuilt and the old nave was to be extended by about 40 feet (12.2 m). In about 1140 Suger abruptly ceased work on the narthex to commence work at the opposite end— the *choir*, the area of the church where the monks sang the office. By his own reckoning, he spent three years and three months on this new construction. The finished choir made a revolutionary change in architecture in the West.

Suger's choir was surrounded by a double *ambulatory*, an aisle around the apse and behind the high altar. The outer ambulatory had seven radiating chapels to accommodate the increasing number of monks who were priests and thus said Mass on a daily basis. Two tall windows pierced the walls of each chapel so that there was little external masonry wall in relation to the amount of space covered by windows. The chapels were shallow enough to permit the light from the windows to fall on the inner ambulatory [**Fig. 10.2**].

The Cathedrals of Senlis and Noyon

Although Suger's nave was never completed, some evidence suggests that it would have had characteristics similar to that of the choir: crossed rib vaults with an abundance of stained-glass windows to permit the flooding of light into the church. We can get some idea of what that nave

0 50 100 feet
0 10 20 30 meters

1. choir; 2. ambulatory; 3. radiating chapels; 4. narthex

◆ **10.2** The Abbey Church of Saint Denis, St. Denis, France, built around 1140, floor plan and contemporary photograph. Parts of the existing church (shaded black in the plan) were rebuilt by Abbot Suger. The photograph shows how the ribbed vault and pointed arches give scope for the passage of light through the lancet windows. Behind the altar, the lower windows light the ambulatory. *(Image © Scala/Art Resource, NY)*

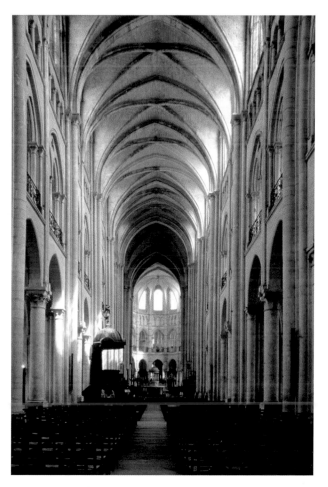

◆ **10.3** Interior of Noyon Cathedral, Noyon, France. The nave was finished between 1285 and 1330. A fine example of the older style of Gothic architecture. The walls have four rather than the typical three levels: the nave arcade at floor level; a triforium; the clerestory with its windows. The rather thick walls of the triforium level would give way in other Gothic churches to thinner walls and more pointed arches. The pulpit and organ are much later additions. *(Image © Anthony Scibilia/Art Resource, NY)*

might have looked like by looking at churches directly inspired by Saint Denis: the cathedrals of Senlis and Noyon [**Fig. 10.3**] (their bishops were both at the consecration of Saint Denis in 1144), begun respectively in 1153 and 1157, as well as the Cathedral of Notre Dame in Paris, the first stone of which was laid in 1163. This quick emulation of the style of Saint Denis blossomed by the end of the century into a veritable explosion of cathedral building in the cities and towns radiating out from Paris, the so-called Île de France. The Gothic impulse so touched other countries as well that, by the end of the thirteenth century, there were fine examples of Gothic architecture in England, Germany, and Italy.

Characteristics of the Gothic Style The term *Gothic* merits a word of explanation. It was used first in the seventeenth century as a pejorative term meaning "barbarous" or "rude" to distinguish buildings that did not follow the Classical models of Greece and Rome, a use still current in the mid-eighteenth century. It was

◆ **10.4** The Cathedral of Notre Dame, Paris, France, transverse half-sectional drawing. Notice the very steep pitched roof, the pointed arches, the flying buttresses, and the placement of gargoyles. The flying buttresses absorb the outward thrust of the massive roof and ceiling by means of flying arches and transfer that thrust to other parts of the building. The pointed arch has less lateral thrust than a round arch and can be easily adapted to openings of different heights and widths. The pinnacles are small narrow towers serving two purposes: to cap flying buttresses and to thrust weight straight downward. Thus they act as free-standing means of support.

Height approximately 140′ (42.7 m). Artwork by Cecilia Cunningham (after Bannister Fletcher).

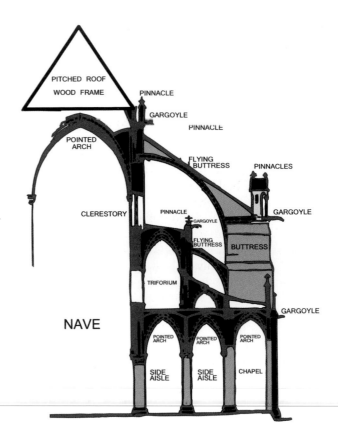

◆ **10.5** Nave elevations of four French Gothic cathedrals at the same scale. Gothic nave designs evolved from the Early Gothic four-story elevation to the High Gothic three-story elevation (arcade, triforium, and clerestory). The height of the vault also increased from 80 to 144 feet (24 to 44 m). *(Elevation drawings after Louis Grodecki)*

| a Laon | b Paris | c Chartres | d Amiens |

only as a result of the reappraisal of the medieval period in the late nineteenth century that the word lost its negative meaning.

It is tempting to say that the common characteristic of these cathedrals was the desire for verticality. We tend to identify the Gothic style with pointed arches, pinnacles and columns, and increasingly higher walls buttressed from the outside by **flying buttresses** to accommodate the weight of a pitched roof and the sheer size of the ascending walls [**Fig. 10.4**]. It is a truism that medieval builders seemed to engage in contests to build higher and higher almost as a matter of civic pride [**Fig. 10.5**]: Chartres (begun in 1194) reached a height of 122 feet (37.2 m); almost as a response, the builders of Amiens (begun 1220) stretched that height to 140 feet (42.7 m), while Beauvais (begun 1247) pushed verticality almost to the limit with a height of 157 feet (47.9 m) from the cathedral pavement to the roof arch; Beauvais had a serious collapse of the roof when the building was barely completed.

That verticality typified Gothic architecture is indisputable, yet Romanesque architects only a generation before Suger had attempted the same verticality, as is evident in such churches as the proposed third abbey church of Cluny or the **pilgrimage church** at Santiago de Compostela in Spain. What prevented the Romanesque architect from attaining greater verticality was not lack of desire but insufficient technical means. The pointed arch was known in Romanesque architecture but not fully understood. It distributed weight more thoroughly in a downward direction and lessened the need for the massive interior piers of the typical Romanesque church. The size of the piers was further reduced by using buttresses outside the building to prop the interior piers and absorb some of the downward thrust. Furthermore, the downward thrust of the exterior buttresses could be increased by the addition of heavy decorative devices such as spires.

The net result of these technical innovations was to lessen the thickness, weight, and mass of the walls of the Gothic cathedral. This reduction provided an opportunity for greater height with less bulk to absorb the weight of the vaulted roof. Such a reduction made the walls more available as framing devices for the windows that are so characteristic of the period. It has been said, perhaps with some exaggeration, that walls in Gothic cathedrals were replaced by masonry skeletal scaffolding for windows [**Fig. 10.6**]. In any case, the basic characteristic of Gothic architecture is not verticality but luminosity. The Gothic may be described as transparent—diaphanous—architecture.

THE MYSTICISM OF LIGHT

Abbot Suger wrote two short booklets about his stewardship of the abbey and his ideas about the building and decorating program he initiated for the abbey church—

◆ **10.6** Interior upper chapel, La Sainte Chapelle, Paris, France, 1243–1248. Built to house relics of Christ's Passion, this is an exquisite example of Gothic luminosity. Restored heavily, the overall effect is nonetheless maintained of skeletal architecture used to frame the windows. *(Image © Réunion des Musées Nationaux/Art Resource, NY)*

extremely important sources for our understanding of the thought that stood behind the actual work of the builder and artist. Underlying Suger's description of the abbey's art treasures and architectural improvements was a theory or (perhaps better) a theology of beauty. Suger was heavily indebted to his reading of certain mystical treatises written by Dionysius the Areopagite (whom Suger and many of his contemporaries wrongly assumed was the Saint Denis for whom the abbey was named), a fifth-century Syrian monk whose works on mystical theology were strongly influenced by Neo-Platonic philosophers as well as by Christian doctrine. In the doctrine of the Pseudo-Dionysius (as later generations have called him), every created thing partakes, however imperfectly, of the essence of God. There is an ascending hierarchy of existence that ranges from inert mineral matter to the purity of light, which is God. The Pseudo-Dionysius described all of creation under the category of light: Every created thing is a small light that illumines the mind a bit. Ultimately, as light becomes more pure (as one ascends the hierarchy) one gets closer to pure light, which is God.

Stained Glass The high point of this light mysticism is expressed in the stained-glass window. Suger believed that when he finished his nave with its glass windows (never completed in fact) to complement his already finished choir, he would have a total structure that would make a single statement: "Bright is that which is brightly coupled with the bright, and bright is the noble edifice which is pervaded by the new light [*lux nova*]." The *lux nova* is an allusion to the biblical description of God as the God of light. Suger did not invent stained glass, but he fully exploited its possibilities both by encouraging an architecture that could put it to its most advantageous employment and at the same time providing a theory to justify and enhance its use.

No discussion of light and glass in this period can overlook the famous windows of the Cathedral of Chartres, a small but important commercial town southwest of Paris. When the cathedral was rebuilt after a disastrous fire in 1194 (which destroyed everything except the west façade of the church), the new building gave wide scope to the glazier's art.

When the walls were rebuilt, more than one hundred seventy-three windows were installed covering an area of about two thousand square yards (1672 sq. m) of surface. It is important to note that, except for some fine details like facial contours, the glass is not painted. The glaziers produced the colors (the blues and reds of Chartres are famous and the tones were never again reproduced exactly) by adding metallic salts to molten glass. Individual pieces were fitted together like a jigsaw puzzle and fixed by leading the pieces together. Individual pieces were rarely larger than 8 feet (2.4 m) square, but 30 feet (9.2 m) sections could be bonded together safely in the leading process. The sections were set into stone frames (**mullions**) and reinforced in place by the use of iron retaining rods. Windows as large as 60 feet (18.3 m) high could be created in this fashion.

It would be useful at this point to compare the aesthetics of the stained-glass window to the mosaics discussed in Chapter 7 (Figures 7.16–7.18). There was a strong element of light mysticism in the art of Byzantine mosaic decoration, derived from some of the same sources later utilized by Abbot Suger: Neo-Platonism and the allegorical reading of the Bible. The actual perception of light in the two art forms, however, was radically different. The mosaic refracted light off an opaque surface. The "sacred" aura of the light in a Byzantine church comes from the oddly mysterious breaking up of light as it strikes the irregular surface of the mosaic tesserae. The stained-glass window was the medium through which the light was seen directly, even if it was subtly muted into diverse colors and combinations of colors.

You can only read the meaning of the window by looking at it from the inside with an exterior light

◆ **10.7** *Notre Dame de Belle Verrière* ("Our Lady of the Beautiful Window"), stained-glass window, Chartres Cathedral, France, early 13th century. The heavy vertical and horizontal lines are iron reinforcing rods to hold the window in place. The thinner lines are the leading. Details such as the Virgin's eyes, nose, and mouth are painted in enamels and metallic oxides, which are then fused by heat to the glass surface. The red is a distinctive characteristic of the Chartres stained-glass workshops. *(Image © Giraudon/Art Resource, NY)*

source—the sun—illuminating it. (*Read* is not a rhetorical verb in this context. It was a commonplace of the period to refer to the stained-glass windows as the "Bible of the Poor" because the illiterate could read the biblical stories in their illustrated form in the cathedral.) It was a more perfectly Platonic analogy of God's relationship to the world and its creatures. The viewer sees an object (the illustrated window) but "through it" is conscious of a distant unseen source (the sun—God) that illumines it and gives it its intelligibility.

◆ **10.8** Tympanum, right door royal portal, west façade, Chartres Cathedral, France. Carved 1145–1170. The central panel shows the Virgin and Child framed by adoring angels within an interior arch, while the outer arch depicts the Seven Liberal Arts. At the lower left is Aristotle dipping his pen in ink with the female figure of Dialectic above him. Under the central figure of the Virgin the lintel shows scenes from the life of Mary and the young Christ; on the upper level, the Presentation in the Temple, and on the lower level (l. to r.), representations of the Annunciation, the Visitation, the Nativity, and the Adoration of the Shepherds. *(Image © Erich Lessing/Art Resource, NY)*

Our Lady of the Beautiful Window A close examination of one window at Chartres will illustrate the complexity of this idea. The *Notre Dame de Belle Verrière* ("Our Lady of the Beautiful Window") [**Fig. 10.7**], one of the most famous works in the cathedral, is a twelfth-century work saved from the rubble of the fire of 1194 and reinstalled in the south choir. The window, with its characteristic pointed arch frame, depicts the Virgin enthroned with the Christ Child surrounded by worshiping angels bearing candles and censers (incense vessels). Directly above her is the dove that represents the Holy Spirit and at the very top a stylized church building representing the cathedral built in her honor.

To a simple viewer, the window honored the Virgin to whom one prayed in time of need and to whom the church was dedicated. A person of some theological sophistication would further recognize the particular scene of the Virgin enthroned as the symbol of Mary as the Seat of Wisdom, an ancient motif in religious art.

The window also has a conceptual link with the exterior sculptural program. In the tympanum of the portal is an enthroned Madonna and Christ Child with two censer-bearing angels. This scene is surrounded by sculptured arches, called *archivolts*, in which there are symbolic representations of the Seven Liberal Arts [**Fig. 10.8**], which together constitute a shorthand version of the window.

The Blessed Virgin depicted as the Seat of Wisdom would be an especially attractive motif for the town of Chartres. The cathedral school was a flourishing center of literary and philosophical studies—studies that emphasized that human learning became wisdom only when it led to the source of wisdom: God. The fact that Mary was depicted here in glass would also call to mind an oft-repeated *exemplum* ("moral example") used in medieval preaching and theology: Christ was born of a virgin. He passed through her body as light passes through a window, completely intact without changing the glass. The Christ/light–Mary/glass analogy is an apt and deepened metaphor to be seen in the Belle Verrière of Chartres.

That kind of interpretation can be applied profitably to many aspects of Gothic art and architecture. Builders and theologians worked together closely while a cathedral was under construction. Church authorities felt it a primary duty not only to build a place suitable for divine worship but also to utilize every opportunity to teach and edify participating worshipers. The famous Gothic **gargoyles** [**Fig. 10.9**] are a good example of this blend of functionality and didacticism. These carved beasts served the practical purpose of funneling rainwater off the roofs while, in their extended and jutting positions on the roofs and buttresses, signifying that evil flees the sacred precincts of the church. At a far more ambitious level, the whole decorative scheme of a cathedral was an attempt to tell an integrated story about the history of salvation—a story alluded to in both profane and divine learning. The modern visitor may be overwhelmed by what appears a chaotic jumble of sculptures depicting biblical scenes, allegorical figures, symbols of the labors of the month, signs of the Zodiac, representatives of pagan learning, and panoramic views of Last Judgments; for the medieval viewer the variegated scenes represented a patterned whole. The decoration of the cathedral was, as it were, the common vocabulary of sermons, folk wisdom, and school learning fleshed out in stone.

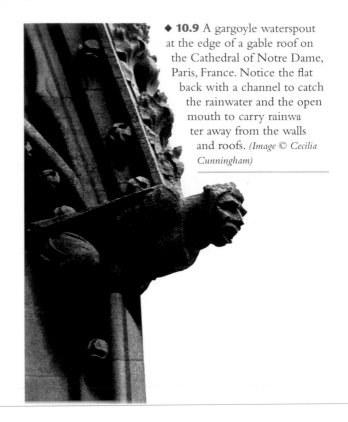

◆ **10.9** A gargoyle waterspout at the edge of a gable roof on the Cathedral of Notre Dame, Paris, France. Notice the flat back with a channel to catch the rainwater and the open mouth to carry rainwater away from the walls and roofs. *(Image © Cecilia Cunningham)*

THE MANY MEANINGS OF THE GOTHIC CATHEDRAL

Some theological and philosophical background is crucial for an appreciation of the significance of the Gothic cathedral, but it is a serious oversimplification to view the cathedral only in the light of its intellectual milieu. The cathedral was, after all, the preeminent building in the episcopal towns of the Île de France, as a view of any of the towns shows. The cathedral overwhelms the town either by crowning a hilly site, as at Laon, or rising up above the town plain, as at Amiens. The cathedrals were *town* buildings (Saint Denis, a monastic church, is a conspicuous exception), and one might well inquire into their functional place in the life of the town. It is simplistic to think that their presence in the town reflected a credulous faith on the part of the populace or the egomania of the civil and religious builders. In fact, the cathedral served vital social and economic functions in medieval society.

A modern analogy illustrates the social function of architecture and building. Many a small town in America, especially in rural areas of the South and the Northeast, centers its civic and commercial life in a town square. The courthouse symbolically emanates social control (justice), social structures (registration of births, weddings, and deaths), power (the workplace of the sheriff, commissioners or aldermen, and the mayor), and—to a degree—culture, with its adjacent park and

military or civic monuments to the founders and war dead. The better stores, the "uptown" churches, and the other appurtenances of respectability—banks, lawyers' and physicians' offices—cluster about the square. (The urbanization and suburbanization of America have steadily destroyed this basic symmetry, replacing it with a far more diffuse city or suburban pattern where the concept of "center" is less easily identified.) The cathedral square of the typical European or Latin American town is the ancestor of the courthouse square. The difference is that the medieval cathedral exercised a degree of social control and integration more comprehensive than that of the courthouse.

The cathedral and its power were a serious force that shaped both individual and social life in the town. The individual was baptized in, made a communicant of, married in, and buried from, the cathedral. Schooling was obtained from the cathedral school and social services (hospitals, poor relief, orphanages, and so on) directed by the decisions of the cathedral staff (the *chapter*). The daily and yearly round of life was regulated by the **horarium** of the cathedral. People rose and ate and went to bed in rhythm with the tolling of the cathedral bell just as they worked or played in line with the feast days of the liturgical calendar of the church year. Citizens could sue and be sued in the church courts, and those same courts dispensed justice on a par with the civil courts; the scenes of the Last Judgment over the central portals of medieval cathedrals referred to more than divine justice.

◆ **10.10** Chartres Cathedral, Chartres, France, as rebuilt after 1194. Aerial view from the southeast. The cathedral rises above the entire town and countryside and can be seen from far away. Notice the elaborate south porch with its rose window (center forefront) and the flying buttresses (right) on the apsidal section and nave walls. *(Image © Marc Garanger/CORBIS)*

The Cathedral and Economics Far more significant than the social interaction of town and cathedral was the economic impact of the cathedral on the town. The building of a cathedral was an extremely expensive enterprise. When the people of Chartres decided to rebuild their cathedral in 1194 [**Fig. 10.10**], the bishop pledged all of the diocesan revenues for three years (three to five million dollars!) simply to initiate the project. It should be remembered that a town like Chartres was very small in the late twelfth century, with no more than ten to fifteen thousand residents in the town proper. Some economic historians have attempted to show that the combination of civic pride and religious enthusiasm that motivated the town to build a cathedral was economically ruinous in the long run. Most scholars, however, insist that economic gain

was the significant factor in construction. This was surely the case with Chartres.

From the late ninth century, Chartres had been a major pilgrimage site. The cathedral possessed a relic of the Virgin (the tunic she wore when Jesus was born) given in 877 by Charles the Bald, the great-grandson of Charlemagne. **Relics** were popular throughout the Middle Ages, and this particular one was especially important to the pilgrims of the time. The relic had not been destroyed by the fire of 1194, a sure sign in the eyes of the populace that the Virgin wished the church rebuilt. Furthermore, the four great feasts of the Blessed Virgin in the liturgical year (the Purification of Mary on February 2, the Annunciation on March 25, the Assumption on August 15, and the Nativity of the Virgin on September 8) were celebrated in Chartres in

◆ **10.11** Vintner's window, glass roundel, Chartres Cathedral, Chartres, France, c. 1215. This panel from a window donated by the winemakers of the area shows a wine merchant transporting a cask of wine.

Detail, stained glass window "Scenes from the Life of Saint Lubin." © *Chartres Cathedral, Chartres, France / The Bridgeman Art Library*

conjunction with large trade fairs that drew merchants and customers from all over Europe.

These fairs were held in the shadow of the cathedral and their conduct was protected by legislation issued by the cathedral chapter. Regulations from the chapter, for example, stated that the prized textiles of the area were to be sold near the north portal while the purveyors of fuel, vegetables, fruit, and wine were to be located by the south portal. There were also sellers of images, medals, and other religious objects (forerunners of the modern souvenir) to the pilgrims, who came both for the fair and for reasons of devotion. The church, then, was as much a magnet for outsiders as it was a symbol for the townspeople.

The Guilds The patrons who donated the windows of Chartres Cathedral also give some indication of the economics of the place. It was only natural that some of the large windows—like a rose window—would be the gift of a royal family or that a tall, pointed *lancet* window like those in the choir would be given by the nobility or the higher clergy. Many of the windows, however, were donated by the members of the various craft and commercial guilds in the town; their "signature frames" can be found at the bottoms of the windows. The fact that the five large windows in honor of the Virgin in the *chevet*, the east end of the cathedral, were donated by merchants—principally the bakers, butchers, and vintners—indicates the significant power of the guilds [**Fig. 10.11**].

The guild, a fraternal society of craftsmen or merchants, was a cross between a modern-day union and a fraternal organization like the Elks or the Knights of Columbus. Members of the guilds put themselves under the patronage of a saint, promised to perform certain charitable works, and acted as a mutual-aid society. Many of the economic guilds appear to have developed out of earlier, more purely religious confraternities. One had to belong to a guild to work at any level beyond day labor. The guild accepted and instructed apprentices; certified master craftsmen; regulated prices, wages, and working conditions; and maintained funds for the care of older members and the burial of their dead. The guilds were a crucial part of town life and would remain so well into the modern period. As we shall see, the university developed from the guild idea in the twelfth century.

The Builders The motivation for the building of a medieval cathedral, then, came from the theological vision, religious devotion, civic pride, and socioeconomic interest. The actual construction depended on many people. The cathedral chapter decided to construct a building, raised the money, and hired the master builder–architect. He in turn was responsible for hiring the various master craftsmen, designing the building, and creating the decorative scheme from ideas generated and approved by the theologians or church officials of the chapter. A great workshop was set up near the proposed site, with each master (mason, stonecutter, glazier) hiring his crew, obtaining his material, and setting up work quarters. Manual and occasional labor was recruited from the local population, but the construction crews were usually migratory groups who traveled from job to job.

The names of several master builders, including the builder of Chartres, have been lost, but others have survived in funerary inscriptions, commemorative plaques, and building records. Notes intended for students of buildings written by Villard de Honnecourt (about 1235), an architect from northern France, preserved in a unique copy at the Bibliothèque Nationale in Paris, provide us a rare glimpse into the skills of a medieval cathedral builder. Villard says in his book that he could teach a willing apprentice a wide variety of skills ranging from carpentry and masonry to the more demanding skills of practical geometry [**Fig. 10.12**] and plan drafting. The notebook also has random sketches and ideas jotted down for his own personal use; they include religious figures to serve as models for stone carvers; animals and buildings that caught his eye; a perpetual motion machine (which didn't work); the first example of clockwork in the West; and a self-operating saw for cutting huge timbers for buttressing and roofing, among others. He visited Rheims and made sketches of the cathedral. He tells of traveling as far as Hungary to get work. Although not as complete and wide-ranging as the Renaissance notebooks of Leonardo da Vinci (with which they have often been compared), Villard's notebook reveals a highly skilled, persistently inquisitive, and inventive man.

A look through Villard's notebook forcefully reminds us that because our tendency is to emphasize the religious and social significance of a cathedral (as that is what first strikes us about it), we easily overlook the basic fact that a cathedral is a stunning technological achievement. A prime example of the technological virtuosity of such buildings is the elegant spire of Strasbourg Cathedral. Finished in 1439, the spire is 466 feet (142.1 m) high from pavement to tip—as high as a forty-story building. This stone structure remained the tallest in Europe until the mid-1960s, when the London Post Office Tower was completed.

The Gothic cathedral is an almost perfect artifact for the study of the humanistic enterprise because it may be approached from so many angles and at so many levels. It was first an architectural and technological

◆ **10.12** Villard de Honnecourt, practical geometry for the construction of buildings, c. 1275. *Top row:* Measuring the diameter of a partially visible column; finding the middle of a circle; cutting the mold of an arch; arching a vault with an outer covering; making an apse with twelve windows; cutting the spring stone of an arch. *Second row:* Bringing together two stones; cutting a voussoir (a wedge-shaped brick for constructing arches) for a round building; cutting an oblique voussoir. *Third row:* Bridging a stream with timbers; laying out a cloister without plumb line or level; measuring the width of a river without crossing it; measuring the width of a distant window.

Pen and ink on parchment, The Portfolio of Villard de Honnecourt. © Bibliothèque Nationale, Paris, France//Giraudon/The Bridgeman Art Library

achievement. Its ensemble of walls, windows, sculpture, and decoration demonstrated a peculiar way of combining human knowledge and religious faith that provides a basic aesthetic experience to the viewer. It had a fundamental economic and social significance for the community in which it was located. Finally, it was, for those who entered it in faith, a transcendental religious experience of passing from the profane to the sacred world. Henry Adams, in his wonderfully eccentric book *Mont-Saint-Michel and Chartres,* says that only a person coming to Chartres as a pilgrim could understand the building. The pilgrim is a central metaphor for the period whether one speaks of the actual pilgrim on the road to Santiago de Compostela or Canterbury or life itself as a pilgrimage toward God. Pilgrims to Chartres or the other cathedrals were pilgrims in both senses: They traveled to visit a real monument and, at the same time, hoped to find rest and salvation through the act

◆ **10.13** *Le Beau Dieu* ("Beautiful Lord"), Chartres Cathedral, Chartres, France, c. 1215. Showing Christ in the act of blessing, this figure symbolically blesses all pilgrims who pass through the door, the "Gate of Heaven," of Chartres Cathedral. Represented on the jambs (the vertical posts that form the sides of the portal) are the twelve apostles.

Marble sculpture on trumeau (the central column supporting the tympanum), south portal, Chartres Cathedral, Chartres, France. © Giraudon/Art Resource, NY

[**Fig. 10.13**]. It is no wonder Abbot Suger should have called Saint Denis the "Gate of Heaven." That is exactly what it was meant to be.

MUSIC OF THE SCHOOL OF NOTRE DAME

It should not be surprising that in an age of artistic and architectural development such as the Gothic, the austere music of the early church should also undergo change. From the time Charlemagne introduced Gregorian chant into the church life of the Frankish kingdom, there had been further developments of that musical form. In the eleventh century, Guido di Arezzo had worked out a system of musical notation that provided the basis for the development of the musical notation used today. Church musicians from the tenth century on also experimented with a single melodic line of plainchant by adding parallel voices at different musical intervals above the line of chant. This first step toward *polyphony*, a musical term for "many voices," is called *organum*. Outside the church, the knightly classes also composed and performed secular music. Some of the melodies of the *troubadours* and *trouvères* have survived, giving us an idea of secular music in the twelfth and thirteenth centuries. The German *minnesingers* (*minne* means "love") of the thirteenth century used traditional church modes and melodies to create secular and sacred songs.

The school of Notre Dame in Paris was the center of systematic musical study and composition in the twelfth century. Léonin's *Magnus Liber Organi* (c. 1160) is an important source for our knowledge of music in the period of the Gothic cathedral. Léonin's book was a collection of organum compositions for use during the liturgical services throughout the church year. Léonin's work was carried on by the other great composer of the century, Pérotin, who assumed the directorship of the music school of Notre Dame sometime around 1181.

CD Track 2
Léonin, "Viderunt omnes fines terre" from *Magnus Liber Organi*

As in the earlier listening selection of Gregorian Chant, a clear pronunciation of the text remains the music's main feature. But as opposed to the earlier monophony, here, Léonin introduces a new musical element by using additional voices or "lines" to provide interest. Most of the time, particularly in the opening, the additional lower voice simply serves as a bass background, but as the piece develops, parallel voices enter to accompany the principal line. This early form of polyphony, known as *organum*, was to become increasingly important in the development of Western music. It must be added that many modern scholars believe that Léonin did not so much compose the music (in the modern sense) as encourage his singers to improvise. The form in which we have his work was not written down until over a century after his death. The music is still purely vocal, although secular music of the same period may well have made use of musical instruments.

In Pérotin's music, the Notre Dame organum utilized the basic melodic line of the traditional chant (the *cantus firmus*) while a second melodic line (the *duplum*), a third (*triplum*), and in some cases a fourth (*quadruplum*) voice were added above the melody. These added lines mirrored the rhythmic flow of the *cantus firmus*. It was soon learned, however, that pleasing and intricate compositions could be created by having the duplum and triplum move in opposition to the cantus firmus. This *counterpoint* (from *contrapunctum*, "against the note") meant, at its most basic level, that a descending series of notes in the cantus firmus would have an ascending series of notes in the melodic lines above it.

One development in the Gothic period deriving from the polyphony of organum was the motet. The *motet* usually had three voices (in some cases four). The tenor—from the Latin *tenere* ("to hold"), another term for *cantus firmus*—maintained the traditional line, usually derived from an older ecclesiastical chant. Because some of the manuscripts from the period show no words for this tenor position, it has been thought that for many motets the tenor line was the musical accompaniment. Above the tenor were two voices who sang interweaving melodies. In the early thirteenth century, these melodies were invariably in Latin and exclusively religious in content. In the late thirteenth century, it was not uncommon to sing the duplum in Latin and the triplum in French. The two upper voices could be singing quite distinct songs: a hymn in Latin with a love lyric in French with a tenor voice (or instrument) maintaining an elaborated melody based on the melismas of Gregorian chant.

This increasingly sophisticated music, built on a monastic basis but with a new freedom of its own, is indicative of many of the intellectual currents of the period. It is a technically complex music rooted in the distant past but open to daring innovation, a blend of the traditional and the vernacular—all held together in a complicated balance of competing elements. Gothic music was an aural expression of the dynamism inherent in the medieval Gothic cathedral.

SCHOLASTICISM

THE RISE OF THE UNIVERSITIES

Several contemporary institutions have their roots in the Middle Ages. Trial by jury is one, constitutional monarchy another. By far the best-known and most widely diffused cultural institution that dates from the Middle Ages is the **university**. In fact, some of the most prestigious centers of European learning today stand where they were founded eight hundred years ago: Oxford and Cambridge in England; the University of Paris in France; the University of Bologna in Italy (see map, "The University"). There is also a remarkable continuity between the organization and purposes of the medieval university and our own, except that we have coeducation. The medieval student would be puzzled, to be sure, by the idea of football games, coeducation, degrees in business or agriculture, and well manicured campuses, were he to visit an American university.

Such a student would find himself at home with the idea of a liberal arts curriculum, the degrees from the baccalaureate through the master's to the doctorate, and the high cost of textbooks. At a less serious level, he would be well acquainted with drinking parties, fraternities, and friction between town and gown (the phrase itself has a medieval ring). The literature that has come down to us from the period is full of complaints about poor housing, high rents, terrible food, and lack of jobs after graduation. Letters from the Middle Ages between students and parents have an almost uncanny contemporaneity about them except for the fact that women did not study in the medieval universities.

European universities developed in the late twelfth and early thirteenth centuries along with the emergence of city life. In the earlier medieval period, schools were most often associated with the monasteries, which were perforce situated in rural areas. As cities grew in importance, schools also developed at urban monasteries or, increasingly, under the aegis of bishops whose cathedrals were in the towns. The episcopal or cathedral school was a direct offshoot of the increasing importance of towns and the increasing power of bishops, the spiritual leaders of town life. In Italy, where town life had been relatively strong throughout the early Middle Ages and where feudalism never took hold, there was also a tradition of schools controlled by the laity. The center of medical studies in Salerno and the law faculty of Bologna had been in secular hands since the tenth century.

Several factors help explain the rapid rise of formal education institutions in the twelfth century. First, the increasing complexity of urban life created a demand for an educated class who could join the ranks of administrators and bureaucrats. Urban schools were not simply interested in providing basic literacy. They were designed to produce an educated class who could give support to the socioeconomic structures of society. Those who completed the arts curriculum of a twelfth-century cathedral school (like the one at Chartres) could find ready employment in either the civil or the ecclesiastical bureaucracy as lawyers, clerks, or administrators.

There were also intellectual and cultural reasons for the rise of the universities. In the period from 1150 to 1250 came a wholesale discovery and publication of texts from the ancient world. Principal among these were lost books by Aristotle that came to the West through Muslim sources in Spain. Aristotle's writings covered a vast range of subjects ranging from meteorology and physics to logic and philosophy. Furthermore, with a closer relationship between Christian and Arabic scholars, a large amount of scientific and mathematical material was coming into Europe [**Fig. 10.14**]. There was also a renaissance of legal studies centered primarily at Bologna, the one intellectual center that could nearly rival Paris. Finally, a new tool was being refined by such scholars as Peter Abelard and Peter Lombard: dialectics. Theologians and

philosophers began to apply the principles of logic to the study of philosophy and theology. Abelard's book *Sic et Non* (1121) combined conflicting opinions concerning theological matters with contradictory passages from the Bible and the Church Fathers and then attempted to mediate and reconcile the apparent divergences. This method was later refined and stylized into the method that was to become *scholasticism*, so-called because it was the philosophical method of the schools, the communities of scholars at the nascent universities.

The University of Paris The most famous and representative university to emerge in the Middle Ages was the University of Paris. The eminence of Paris rested mainly on the fame of the teachers who came there to instruct. At this stage of educational development, the teacher was the school. Students in the twelfth century flocked from all over Europe to frequent the lectures of teachers like William of Champeaux (1070–1121) and, later, his former student and vehement critic, Peter Abelard (1079–1142). Besides these famous individual teachers, Paris also had some established centers of learning that enjoyed a vast reputation. There was a school attached to the Cathedral of Notre Dame, a theological center associated with the canons of the

VALUES

Dialectics

In ancient Greece the word dialectics originally meant the "art of conversation." By the fifth century, dialectics took on the meaning of techniques used to come to logical conclusions based on a rigorous style of reasoning. Plato singled out dialectic in *The Republic* as a mark of the philosopher–king, whereas Aristotle saw it containing the "path to the principles of all inquiries."

The rediscovery of dialectic (which was the common medieval term for "logic") coincided with the rise of the university. The study of theology and philosophy were increasingly cast into terms that could be expressed in logic modes like that of the deductive syllogism. University professors of theology, for example, had three duties: to explain the text of scripture; to preach; and to dispute—that is, to set out Christian doctrines in some logical form. What was true of these Christian scholars was also true of both contemporary Islamic and Jewish thinkers who had inherited the same tradition of Aristotle's logic. Modern scholars have pointed out that this form of dialectical reasoning, with its focus on resolving problems, had ramifications for both literature and architecture.

The greatest weakness of this emphasis was the temptation to turn the logical process into an end in itself: forgetting the search for truth in a desire to dazzle people with the sheer technique of logic. Dante would open Canto XI of the *Paradiso* with a critique of such mental pyrotechnics as he complained of those who were useless in their "reasoning" (literally: their "syllogisms") that make the wings of the mind bend "in downward flight."

◆ **10.14** Laurencius de Voltolina, *The Classroom of Henricus de Allemania at the University of Bologna*, mid to late 1300s. The professor delivers his lecture, expounding his text from the professorial chair (*cathedra*). Note the sleeping student at the lower right.

Manuscript illumination from Lecture of Henricus de Alemania. *Kupferstichkabinett, Staatliche Museen zu Berlin, Germany//*
© *Bildarchiv Preussischer Kulturbesitz, Berlin, Germany/Art Resource, NY*

Church of Saint Victor, and a school of arts maintained at the ancient monastery of Sainte Geneviève.

Although assigning precise dates is difficult, it is safe to say that the university at Paris developed in the final quarter of the twelfth and early part of the thirteenth centuries. Its development began with the *magistri* ("masters"; "teachers") of the city forming a corporation after the manner of the guilds. At this time the word **universitas** simply meant a guild or corporation.

The masters formed the *universitas* in Paris in order to monitor the quality of the teaching and the performance of the students entrusted to their care. At Bologna, the reverse was true. The students formed the *universitas* in order to hire the teachers with the best qualifications and according to the most advantageous financial terms.

The *universitas* soon acquired a certain status in law with a corporate right to borrow money, to sue (and be sued), and to issue official documents. As a legal body it could issue stipulations for the conduct of both masters and students. When a student completed the course of studies and passed examinations, the *universitas* would grant him a teaching certificate that enabled him to enter the ranks of the masters: he was a master of arts (our modern degree has its origin in that designation). After graduation, a student could go on to specialized training in law, theology, or medicine. The completion of this specialized training entitled one to be called *doctor*

(from the Latin *doctus*, "learned") in his particular field. The modern notion that a professional person (doctor, lawyer, and the like) should be university-trained is an idea derived directly from medieval university usage.

Since the Carolingian period—indeed, earlier—the core of education was the arts curriculum. In the late twelfth century in Paris, the arts began to be looked on as a prelude to the study of theology. This inevitably caused a degree of tension between the arts faculty and the theology masters. In 1210 this tension resulted in a split, with the masters and students of arts moving their faculty to the Left Bank of the Seine, where they settled in the area intersected by the rue du Fouarre ("Straw Street"—so named because the students sat on straw during lectures). That part of the Left Bank has traditionally been a student haunt. The name Latin Quarter reminds us of the old language that was once the only tongue used at the university.

Student Life By the end of the twelfth century, Paris was the intellectual center of Europe. Students came from all over Europe to study there. We do not have reliable statistics about their number, but an estimate of five to eight thousand students would not be far from the mark for the early thirteenth century. The students were organized into *nations* by their place of national origin. By 1294 there were four recognized *nationes* in Paris: the French, the Picard, the Norman,

VOICES OF THEIR TIMES

The Medieval Parent and the Medieval Student

Parent to a son at the university in Orleans, fourteenth century.

I have recently discovered that you live dissolutely and slothfully, preferring license to restraint and play to work and strumming a guitar while the others are at their studies, whence it happens that you have read but one volume of law while more industrious companions have read several. I have decided to exhort you herewith to repent utterly of your dissolute and careless ways that you may no longer be called a waster and that your shame may be turned to good repute.

Scholar to his father, Orleans, fourteenth century.

We occupy a good and comely dwelling, next door but one from the schools and market-

place, so that we can go to school each day without wetting our feet. We have good companions in the house with us, well advanced in their studies, and of excellent habits—an advantage which we appreciate for, as the psalmist says "with an upright man thou wilt show thyself upright." Wherefore, lest production should cease for lack of material, we beg your paternity to send us by the bearer money for the purchase of parchment, ink, a desk, and the other things which we need, in sufficient amount that we may suffer no want on your account (God forbid!) but finish our studies and return home with honor. The bearer will also take charge of the shoes and stockings which you will send us, and any news at all.

and the Anglo-German. Student support came from families, pious benefactors, church stipends, or civic grants to underwrite an education. Certain generous patrons provided funds for hospices for scholars, the most famous of which was that underwritten by Robert de Sorbon in 1258 for graduate students in theology; his hospice was the forerunner of the Sorbonne in Paris.

By our standards, student life in the thirteenth century was harsh. Food and lodging were primitive, heating scarce, artificial lighting nonexistent, and income sporadic. The daily schedule was rigorous, made more so by the shortage of books and writing material. An "ideal" student's day, as sketched out in a late medieval pamphlet for student use, now seems rather grim:

A Student's Day at the University of Paris

4:00 A.M.	Rise
5:00–6:00	Arts lectures
6:00	Mass and breakfast
8:00–10:00	Lectures
11:00–12:00	Disputations before the noon meal
1:00–3:00 P.M.	"Repetitions"—study of morning lectures with tutors
3:00–5:00	Cursory lectures (generalized lectures on special topics) or disputations
6:00	Supper
7:00–9:00	Study and repetitions
9:00	Bed

The masters' lectures consisted of detailed commentaries on certain books the master intended to cover in a given term. Because books were expensive, emphasis was put on note taking and copying so that the student might build up his own collection of books. Examinations were oral, before a panel of masters. Students were also expected to participate in formal debates (called disputations) as part of their training.

Geoffrey Chaucer provides us an unforgettable, albeit idealized, portrait of the medieval student (the clerk or cleric—many of the students were members of the minor clerical orders of the church) in his Prologue to the *Canterbury Tales*:

> A clerk from Oxford was with us also,
> Who'd turned to getting knowledge, long ago.
> As meagre was his horse as is a rake,
> Nor he himself too fat, I'll undertake,
> But he looked hollow and went soberly.
> Right threadbare was his overcoat; for he
> Had got him yet no churchly benefice,
> Nor was so worldly as to gain office.
> For he would rather have at his bed's head
> Some twenty books, all bound in black and red,
> Of Aristotle and his philosophy
> Than rich robes, fiddle, or gay psaltery.
> Yet, and for all he was philosopher,
> He had but little gold within his coffer;
> But all that he might borrow from a friend

> On books and learning he would swiftly spend,
> And then he'd pray right busily for the souls
> Of those who gave him wherewithal for schools.
> Of study took he utmost care and heed.
> Not one word spoke he more than was his need;
> And that was said in fullest reverence
> And short and quick and full of high good sense.
> Pregnant of moral virtue was his speech;
> And gladly would he learn and gladly teach.

Chaucer's portrait of the lean, pious, poor, zealous student was highly idealized to create a type. We probably get a far more realistic picture of what students were actually thinking and doing from the considerable amount of popular poetry that comes from the student culture of the medieval period. This poetry depicts a student life we are all familiar with: a poetry of wine, women, song, sharp satires at the expense of pompous professors or poor accommodations, and the occasional episodes of cruelty that most individuals are capable of only when banded into groups.

Carmina Burana The student subculture had also invented a mythical Saint Golias, who was the patron saint of wandering scholars. Verses (called **Goliardic verse**) were written in honor of the "saint." The poems that have come down to us are a far cry from the sober commentaries on Aristotle's *Metaphysics* that we usually associate with the medieval scholar.

One of the more interesting collections of these medieval lyrics was discovered in a Bavarian monastery in the early nineteenth century. The songs in this collection were written in Latin, Old French, and German and seem to date from the late twelfth and thirteenth centuries. Their subject range was wide but, given the nature of such songs, predictable. There were drinking songs, laments over the loss of love or the trials of fate, hymns in honor of nature, salutes to the end of winter and the coming of spring, and cheerfully obscene songs of exuberant sexuality. The lyrics reveal a shift of emotions ranging from the happiness of love to the despair of disappointment just as the allusions range from classical learning to medieval piety. One famous song, for example, praises the beautiful powerful virgin in language that echoes the piety of the church. The last line reveals, however, that the poem salutes not Mary but generous Venus.

In 1935 and 1936, German composer Carl Orff set some of these poems to music under the title *Carmina Burana*. His brilliant, lively blending of heavy percussion, snatches of ecclesiastical chant, strong choral voices, and vibrant rhythms have made this work a modern concert favorite. The listener gets a good sense of the vibrancy of these medieval lyrics by the use of the modern setting. Because the precise character of student music has not come down to us, Orff's new setting of these lyrics is a fine beginning for learning about the musicality of this popular poetry from the medieval university.

Did women study at the university? By and large they did not. Medieval customs sheltered women in a manner we find difficult to imagine. Women were educated either privately (Heloise was tutored by her uncle in Paris where she met Abelard) or within the cloister of the convent. Furthermore, most of university life was tied to the church. The masters were clerics (except at Bologna), and most students depended on ecclesiastical *benefices* ("pensions") to support them. There are exceptions to this rule. There seem to have been women in universities in both Italy and Germany. At Salerno, famous for its faculty of medicine, there may have been women physicians who were attached to the faculty. We do know that by the fourteenth century the university was licensing women physicians. There is also a tradition that Bologna had a woman professor of law who, according to the story, was so beautiful that she lectured from behind a screen so as not to dazzle her students! It is well to remember that the universities were conservative and traditional institutions. It was not until the twentieth century, for example, that provisions were made for women's colleges at Oxford that enjoyed the full privileges of university life. The discrimination against women at the university level was something, for example, that moved the bitter complaints of the English novelist, Virginia Woolf, as late as the 1920s.

THOMAS AQUINAS

The Golden Age of the University of Paris was the thirteenth century, since in that period Paris could lay fair claim to being the intellectual center of the Western world. It is a mark of the international character of medieval university life that some of its most distinguished professors did not come from France: Albert the Great (a German), Alexander of Hales (English), Bonaventure and Thomas Aquinas (Italian).

Thomas Aquinas (1225?–1274) was the most famous and influential of the Parisian masters of the thirteenth century [**Fig. 10.15**]. His intellectual influence went far beyond the lecture halls of Paris and is felt to the present. Born of noble parentage in southern Italy, Thomas Aquinas joined the Preaching Friars of Saint Dominic (the Dominicans) in 1243. From 1245 to 1248, he studied with Albert the Great at both Paris and Cologne. He was made a *magister* of theology in 1258 after completing his doctoral studies. During this same period (roughly 1256 to 1259), Thomas Aquinas lectured on theology in Paris. From 1259 to 1268, he was back in Italy where he lectured and wrote at Orvieto (the papal court for a time), Rome, and Naples. From 1268 to 1272, he again held a chair of theology, when he returned to Naples to teach there. He died two years later on his way to a church council at Lyons in France.

Thomas Aquinas's life ended before he was fifty, but in that span he produced a vast corpus of writings (they fill forty folio volumes) on theology, philosophy, and biblical studies. It is a mark of his mobility that his masterpiece—the *Summa Theologica*—was composed at Rome, Viterbo, Paris, and Naples, although it was unfinished at his death. Although his writings touched on a wide variety of subjects, at root Thomas Aquinas was interested in and made a lifetime study of a basic problem: How does one harmonize those things that are part of human learning (reason) with those supernatural truths revealed by God in the Bible and through the teaching of the church (revelation)? Aquinas's approach was to steer a middle path through two diametrically opposed opinions, both of which had avid supporters in the Middle Ages: the position of *fideism*, which held that religious faith as an absolute is indifferent to the efforts of human reason (*credo quia absurdum est*, "I believe because it is absurd") and *rationalism*, which insists that everything, revelation included, must meet the test of rational human scrutiny. Aquinas wanted to demonstrate what the Gothic cathedral illustrated: that the liberal arts, the things and seasons of the world, and the mysteries revealed by God could be brought into some kind of intellectual harmony based on a single criterion of truth.

For Aquinas, reason finds truth when it sees evidence of truth. The mind judges something true when it has observed a sufficient number of facts to compel it to make that judgment. The mind gives assent to truth on the basis of evidence. Aquinas was convinced that there was a sufficient amount of observable evidence in the world to conclude the existence of God. He proposed five arguments in support of such a position. Still he recognized that such argumentation only yields a limited understanding of God. Aquinas did not believe that the naked use of reason could ever discover or prove the mysteries about God revealed in the Bible: that God became a man in Jesus Christ or that there was a Trinity of persons in God. God had to tell us that. Our assent to it is not based on evidence, but on the authority of God who reveals it to us. If we could prove the mysteries of faith, there would have been no need for revelation and no need of faith.

Thus, for Aquinas there is an organic relationship between reason and revelation. Philosophy perfects the human capacity to know and revelation perfects one beyond self by offering salvation and eternal life. Aquinas stated this relationship between reason and revelation at the beginning of his great work of theology, the *Summa Theologica*.

◆ **10.15** Andrea di Buonaiuto, *The Triumph of St. Thomas Aquinas*, c. 1365. The saint is enthroned between figures of the Old and New Testaments with the personification of the Virtues, Sciences, and Liberal Arts below. This Florentine church had a school of studies attended by Dante Alighieri in his youth.

Fresco, Church of Santa Maria Novella, Florence, Italy//Image © Scala/Art Resource, NY

When we read Aquinas today, we get some sense of his stark and rigorous attempt to think things through. For one thing, he offers no stylistic adornment to relieve his philosophical and rational discourse. For another, he makes clear that philosophical and theological reasoning is difficult; it is not a pastime for the incompetent or the intellectually lazy. Yet Aquinas was not a mere machine for logic. He had the temperament of a mystic. Some months before he died he simply put down his pen; when his secretary asked him why he had stopped writing, Aquinas simply said that in prayer and quiet he had had a vision and that what he had written "seemed as straw." Aquinas was a rare combination of intellectual and mystic.

The intellectual tradition Aquinas used in his writing was that of the Greek philosopher Aristotle. He first knew Aristotle's work in Latin translations based on Arabic texts done by Muslim scholars in the south of Spain and North Africa. Later Aquinas was able to use texts translated directly out of Greek by a Flemish friar and sometime companion, William of Moerbeke. Aquinas's use of Aristotle was certainly not a novelty in the Mid-

dle Ages. Such Arabic scholars as Avicenna (980–1036) and Averröes of Córdoba (1126–1198) commented on Aristotle's philosophy and its relationship to the faith of Islam. Jewish thinkers like the famous Moses Maimonides (born in Córdoba in 1135, died in Egypt in 1204) made similar attempts to bridge Greek thought and their own religious faith. Maimonides wrote his famous *Guide for the Perplexed* to demonstrate the essential compatibility of the Hebrew scriptures with the thought of Aristotle. Maimonides was determined that essentials of the biblical message not be compromised, but he likewise felt that in nonessentials there was room for human reflection. In this task of distinguishing the place of intellect and faith, Maimonides anticipated the work of Thomas Aquinas by two generations.

Two other characteristics of the thought of Aquinas should be noted. First, his worldview was strongly hierarchical. Everything has its place in the universe, and that place is determined in relation to God. A rock is good because it *is* (to Aquinas existence was a gift), but an animal is more nearly perfect because it has life and thus shares more divine attributes. In turn, men and

◆ **10.16** *Saint Francis of Assisi.* This may be the earliest portrait of Saint Francis (1181–1226); some scholars believe that it was executed during the saint's lifetime. The scroll in his left hand reads "Peace to this house."

Fresco, Sacro Specchio (the Holy Cave), Subiaco, Italy. Image © Scala/Art Resource, NY

person would speak on psychology, physics, politics, theology, and philosophy with equal authority would strike us as presumptuous, just as any building decorated with symbols from the classics, astrology, the Bible, and scenes from everyday life would now be considered a hodgepodge. Such was not the case in the thirteenth century, because it was assumed that everything ultimately pointed to God.

Although Thomas is often thought of as a philosopher, he understood himself to be a commentator on the Bible—"Master of the Sacred Page." Like all such lecturers he was charged by the university with the three tasks: "reading" (of the Bible), "disputing" (using logic and argument to solve theological problems), and preaching. While attention is often given to his great "summas," it is well to remember that he also wrote long commentaries on specific books of the Bible as well as compiling anthologies of early commentators on biblical material. In addition, he also composed hymns, which are still sung today.

FRANCIS OF ASSISI

In Italy, at the end of the twelfth century, a young man would be born who would reshape medieval religious and cultural life. Giovanni Bernadone, born in 1181 in the Umbrian hill town of Assisi, was renamed "Francesco" ("Little Frenchman") by his merchant father. The son of wealthy parents, Francis grew up as a popular, somewhat spendthrift, and undisciplined youth. He joined the volunteer militia as a youth to do battle against the neighboring city of Perugia only to be captured and put into solitary confinement until a ransom could be found.

That incident seems to have marked a turning point in his life. He dropped out of society and began to lead a life of prayer and self-denial. Eventually he concluded that the life of perfect freedom demanded a life of total poverty. He gave away all of his goods and began a life of itinerant preaching that took him as far away as the Middle East. His simple lifestyle attracted followers who wished to live in imitation of his life. By 1218 there were over three thousand "Little Brothers" (as he called them) who owed their religious allegiance to him. Francis died in 1226 when the movement he started was already a powerful religious order in the church [**Fig. 10.16**].

If we know Francis of Assisi today, it is because of garden shop statues of him with a bird on his shoulder. That he preached to the birds is a fact [**Fig. 10.17**], but to think of him only as a medieval Doctor Doolittle speaking to animals is to trivialize a man who altered medieval culture profoundly. First, his notion of a *mendicant* ("begging") brotherhood that would be mobile and capable of preaching in the newly emerging cities of

women are better still because they possess mind and will. Angels are closer yet to God because they, like God, are pure spirit.

This hierarchical worldview explains other characteristics of Aquinas's thought in particular and medieval thought in general: It is wide-ranging, it is encyclopedic, and in interrelating everything it is synthetic. Everything fits and has its place, meaning, and truth. That a

◆ **10.17** Bonaventura Berlinghieri, *Saint Francis Preaching to the Birds*, 1235. This detail from the Berlinghieri Altarpiece (Figure 10.18) shows an incident taken from early legends of the saint's life.

San Francesco, Pescia, Italy. Image © Scala/Art Resource, NY

◆ **10.18** Bonaventura Berlinghieri, *Scenes from the Life of St. Francis*, Altarpiece panel, 1235. Note that Francis looks forward to the viewer so that one could "speak directly to the saint."

Tempera on wood, 5′ x 3′ x 6′ (1.5 x .9 x 1.8 m), predella panel of altarpiece, San Francesco, Pescia, Italy. Image © Scala/Art Resource, NY

Europe was a worthy substitute for the more rural, land-bound monasteries of the past. Second, Francis believed that the Gospels could be followed literally, and this led him to identify closely with the humanity of Christ. It is said that in 1224, he had so meditated on the Passion of Christ that his own body bore the crucifixion marks of Christ (*stigmata*). This emphasis on Christ's humanity would have a powerful impact in making religious art more realistic and vivid. Finally, Francis's attitude toward religious faith was powerfully affirmative. He praised the goodness of God's creation; he loved the created world; he preached concern for the poorest of the poor; he felt that all creation was a gift and that everything in creation praised God in its own way. Some scholars have argued that the impact of the Franciscan vision on the imagination of European culture was a remote cause of the Renaissance preoccupation with the natural world and the close observation of nature.

The Berlinghieri altarpiece, one of the earliest depictions of the saint, in the Franciscan church at Pescia has a central panel depicting the saint with scenes from his life on both sides [**Fig. 10.18**]. Such altarpieces were not only tributes to the saint but also ways of reminding viewers of incidents of the saint's life, which would have been read out to congregations to reinforce stories about the saint. These early sacred biographies were known as **legends** because they were "read aloud" (from the Latin *legere* meaning "to read"). Such altarpieces served

the double purpose of teaching about the saint's life as well as devotional aids for the people.

The early part of the thirteenth century, in fact, saw that rise of two complementary impulses that would energize late medieval culture: the intellectualism of the schools epitomized in someone like Thomas Aquinas (discussed in the preceding section) and the affective and emotional religion of a Francis of Assisi. Those two impulses were best synthesized in the masterpiece that summed up high medieval culture: the *Commedia* of Dante Alighieri.

DANTE'S *DIVINE COMEDY*

In any discussion of the culture of the High Middle Ages, two descriptive adjectives come immediately to mind: hierarchical and synthetic. It is commonplace, for example, to compare the Gothic cathedral and the

◆ **10.19** Sandro Botticelli, *Dante*, c. 1480–1485. Like most portraits of Dante, Botticelli's depicts him wearing the traditional laurel wreath of the poet.

Oil on canvas, 24½" x 18½" (54 x 47 cm). Image © Private Collection / The Bridgeman Art Library

Table 10.1 *The Structure of Dante's Comedy*

Hell

The Anteroom of the Neutrals
Circle 1:	The Virtuous Pagans (Limbo)
Circle 2:	The Lascivious
Circle 3:	The Gluttonous
Circle 4:	The Greedy and the Wasteful
Circle 5:	The Wrathful
Circle 6:	The Heretics
Circle 7:	The Violent against Others, Self, God/Nature/and Art
Circle 8:	The Fraudulent (subdivided into ten classes, each of which dwells in a separate ditch)
Circle 9:	The Lake of the Treacherous against kindred, country, guests, lords and benefactors. Satan is imprisoned at the center of this frozen lake.

Purgatory

Ante-Purgatory: The Excommunicated/The Lazy/ The Unabsolved/Negligent Rulers
The Terraces of the Mount of Purgatory

1. The Proud
2. The Envious
3. The Wrathful
4. The Slothful
5. The Avaricious
6. The Gluttonous
7. The Lascivious

The Earthly Paradise

Paradise

1. The Moon: The Faithful who were inconstant
2. Mercury: Service marred by ambition
3. Venus: Love marred by lust
4. The Sun: Wisdom; the theologians
5. Mars: Courage; the just warriors
6. Jupiter: Justice; the great rulers
7. Saturn: Temperance; the contemplatives and mystics
8. The Fixed Stars: The Church Triumphant
9. The Primum Mobile: The Order of Angels
10. The Empyrean Heavens: Angels, Saints, the Virgin, and the Holy Trinity

systematic treatises on philosophy and theology like the *Summa Theologica* of Saint Thomas Aquinas. On close inspection such comparisons may be facile, but they point to the following truths about this period that are relatively secure: Both the Gothic cathedral and the theology of Aquinas, for example, started from the tangible and sensual ("Nothing comes to the mind except through the senses" is a basic axiom for Aquinas) in order to mount in a hierarchical manner to the light that is God. Again, both writer and architect felt it possible to be universal in their desire to synthesize all human knowledge as prelude and pointer to the full revelation of God. Finally, they both constructed their edifices by the juxtaposition of tensions and syntheses.

If the Gothic cathedral and the *Summa Theologica* represent two masterpieces of the hierarchical and synthetic religious humanism of the Middle Ages, the *Divine Comedy* of Dante Alighieri (1265–1321) represents the same masterly achievement in literature. Dante [**Fig. 10.19**] was a Florentine. He was nonetheless deeply influenced by the intellectual currents that emanated from the Paris of his time. As a comfortably fixed young man he devoted himself to a rigorous program of philosophical and theological study in order to enhance his already burgeoning literary talent. His published work gives evidence of a profound culture and a deep love for study. He wrote on the origin and development of language (*De Vulgari Eloquentia*), political theory (*De Monarchia*), and generalized knowledge (*Convivio*) as well as his own poetic aspirations (*Vita Nuova*). His masterpiece is the *Divine Comedy*.

Dante was exiled from Florence for political reasons in 1300. In his bitter wanderings in the north of Italy he worked on—and finally brought to conclusion—a long poem to which he gave a bitingly ironical title: *The Comedy of Dante Alighieri, A Florentine by Birth but Not in Behavior*. Dante called his poem a comedy because, as he noted, it had a happy ending and was written in the popular language of the people. The adjective *divine* was added later; some say by Boccaccio, who in the next generation lectured on the poem in Florence and wrote one of the first biographies of the great poet.

The *Divine Comedy* relates a symbolic journey that the poet begins on Good Friday, 1300, through hell, purgatory, and heaven (see **Table 10.1**). In the first two parts

QVI COELVM CECINIT MEDIVMQVE IMVMQVE TRIBVNAL⋅ LVSTRAVIT QVE ANIMO CVNCTA POETA SVO⋅ DOCTVS ADEST DANTES SVA QVEM FLORENTIA SAEPE⋅ SENSIT CONSILIIS AC PIETATE PATREM⋅ NIL POTVIT TANTO MORS SAEVA NOCERE POETAE⋅ QVEM VIVVM VIRTVS CARMEN IMAGO FACIT⋅

◆ **10.20** Domenico di Michelino, *Dante and His Poem*, 1465. Dante, with an open copy of the *Comedy*, points to Hell with his right hand. The Mount of Purgatory with its seven terraces is behind him. Florence's cathedral (with its newly finished dome) represents Paradise on the poet's left.

Fresco, Cathedral of Santa Maria del Fiore (Duomo), Florence, Italy. Image © Scala/Art Resource, NY

of his journey, Dante is guided by the ancient Roman poet Virgil, whose *Aeneid* was such an inspiration to him and from which he borrowed (especially from Book VI, which tells of Aeneas's own journey to the Underworld). From the border at the top of the Mount of Purgatory to the pinnacle of heaven where Dante glimpses the "still point of light" that is God, Dante's guide is Beatrice, a young woman Dante had loved passionately if platonically in his youth [**Fig. 10.20**].

Every significant commentator on the *Comedy* has noted its careful organization. The poem is made up of one hundred **cantos**. The first canto of the *Inferno* serves as an introduction to the whole poem. There are then thirty-three cantos for each of the three major sections (*Inferno, Purgatorio,* and *Paradiso*). The entire poem is written in a rhyme scheme called *terza rima* (*aba, bcb, cdc,* and so on) that is almost impossible to duplicate in English because of the shortage of rhyming words in our language. The number three and its multiples, symbols of the Trinity, occur over and over. The *Inferno* is divided into nine regions plus a vestibule, and the same number is found in the *Purgatorio*. Dante's *Paradiso* is constituted by the nine heavens of the Ptolemaic system plus the Empyrean, the highest heaven. This scheme mirrors the whole poem of ninety-nine cantos plus one. The sinners in the *Inferno* are arranged according to whether they sinned by incontinence, violence, or fraud (a division Dante derived from Aristotle's *Ethics*), while the yearning souls of purgatory are divided in three ways according to how they acted or failed to act in relation to love. The saved souls in the *Paradiso* are divided into the lay folk, the active, and the contemplative. Nearest the throne of God, but reflected in the circles of heaven, are the nine categories of angels.

Dante's interest in the symbolic goes beyond his elaborate manipulation of numbers. In the *Inferno* sinners suffer punishments that have symbolic value; their sufferings both punish and instruct. The gluttonous live on heaps of garbage under driving storms of cold rain, while the flatterers are immersed in pools of sewage and the sexually perverse walk burning stretches of sand in an environment as sterile as their attempts at love. Conversely, in the *Paradiso*, the blessed dwell in the circles most symbolic of their virtue. The theologians are in the circle of the sun because they provided such enlightenment to the world, and the holy warriors dwell in the sphere of Mars.

We can better appreciate the density and complexity of Dante's symbolism by looking at a single example. Our common image of Satan is that of a sly tempter (in popular art he is often in formal dress whispering blandishments in a willing ear with just a whiff of sulfur about him) after the manner of Milton's proud, perversely tragic, heroic Satan in *Paradise Lost*. For Dante, Satan is a huge, stupid beast, frozen in a lake of ice in the pit of hell. He beats six bat-like wings (a demonic leftover from his angelic existence; see Isaiah 6:1–5) in an ineffectual attempt to escape the frozen pond that is watered by the four rivers of hell. He is grotesquely three-headed (a parody of the Trinity), and his slavering mouths remorselessly chew the bodies of three infamous traitors from sacred and secular history (Judas, Cassius, and Brutus).

Why does Dante portray Satan so grotesquely? It is clear that Dante borrowed some of the picture of Satan from Byzantine mosaics with which he would have been familiar in the baptistery of Florence [**Fig. 10.21**]. Beyond that, the whole complex of Satan is heavily weighted with symbolic significance. Satan lies in frozen darkness at a point in the universe farthest from the warmth and light of God. He is the fallen angel of light (Lucifer means "light-bearer"), now encased in a pit in the center of the earth excavated by the force of his own fall from heaven. Satan is immobile, in contrast to God, who is the mover of all things in the universe. He is totally inarticulate and stupid because he represents, par excellence, all of the souls of hell who have lost what Dante calls "the good of intellect." Satan, and all the souls in hell, will remain totally unfulfilled as created rational beings because they are cut off from the final source of rational understanding and fulfillment: God. Intellectual estrangement from God is for Dante, as it was for Thomas Aquinas, the essence of damnation. This estrangement is most evident in the case of Satan, who symbolizes in his very being the loss of rationality and all that derives from that fact.

Dante, following a line of thought already developed by Suger and Aquinas, conceived the human journey as a slow ascent to the purity of God by means of the created things of this world. To settle for

◆ **10.21** *Hell*, 13th century. As a young man Dante would have seen this mosaic on the ceiling over the high altar of the Baptistery of St John ("My beautiful San Giovanni," he calls it in his poem) in his native city of Florence.

Detail from the Last Judgment *segment of mosaic ceiling vault, Battistero di San Giovanni, Forence, Italy. Image © Scala/Art Resource, NY*

less than God was, in essence, to fail to return to the natural source of life, God. This explains why light is such a crucial motif in the *Divine Comedy* as it had been in the theories of Abbot Suger. Neither light nor the sources of light (the sun) is ever mentioned in the *Inferno*. The overwhelming visual impression of the *Inferno* is darkness—a darkness that begins when Dante is lost in the "dark wood" of Canto I and continues until he climbs from hell and sees above his head the stars (the word *stars* ends each of the three major parts of the poem) of the Southern Hemisphere. In the ascent of the mountain of purgatory, daylight and sunset are controlling motifs to symbolize the reception and rejection of divine light. In the *Paradiso*, the blessed are bathed in the reflected light that comes from God. At the climax of the *Paradiso*, the poet has a momentary glimpse of God as a point of light and rather obscurely understands that God, the source of all intelligibility, is the power that also moves the "sun and the other stars." Within the broad reaches of Dante's philosophical and theological preoccupations, the poet still has the concentrated power to sketch unforgettable portraits: the doomed lovers Paolo and Francesca—each of the **tercets** that tell their story starts with the word *amore* ("love"); the haughty political leader Farinata degli Umberti; the pitiable suicide Pier delle Vigne; or the caricatures of gluttons like Ciacco the Hog. Damned, penitent, or saved, the characters are by turns both symbols and persons. Saint Peter represents the church in the *Paradiso* but also explodes with ferociously human anger at its abuses. Brunetto Latini in the *Inferno* with "his brownbaked features" is a condemned sodomite but still anxious that posterity at least remember his literary accomplishments.

It has been said that a mastery of the *Divine Comedy* would be a mastery of all that was significant about the intellectual culture of the Middle Ages. It is certainly true that the poem, encyclopedic and complex as it is, would provide a primer for any reader interested in the science, political theory, philosophy, literary criticism, and theology of the thirteenth century as well as a detailed acquaintance with the burning questions of Dante's time. The comprehensiveness of the poem has often been its major obstacle for the modern reader. Beyond that hurdle is the strangeness of the Dantean world, so at variance with our own: earth-centered, manageably small, sure of its ideas of right and wrong, orthodox in its theology, prescientific in its outlook, Aristotelian in its philosophy. For all that, Dante is not only to be read for his store of medieval lore but because he is, as T. S. Eliot once wrote, the most universal of poets. He had a deeply sympathetic appreciation of human aspiration, love and hate, the destiny of humanity, and the meaning of nature and history.

class," which stood on the social ladder between the rural peasant/city worker and the landed royalty or hereditary aristocracy.

◆ **Intellectual and Technical Expansion.** The twelfth and thirteenth centuries were times of intense intellectual ferment and advance. New sources of knowledge came through Arabic sources either as original contributions (for example, in medicine and science) or in the form of lost works of the Classical past (the writings of Aristotle) to fuel the work of scholars. Advances in technology evolving from the ambitious plans of both Romanesque and Gothic architects had their impact. The increase of a money economy over a barter economy aided the growth of artistic and musical culture.

◆ **Hierarchical Synthesis.** One conspicuous characteristic of medieval culture was its belief that everything knowable could be expressed in a manageable and rational whole. Whether it appeared in stone (Chartres) or technical prose (Thomas Aquinas) or in poetry (Dante), the medieval mind saw hierarchy, order, intelligibility, and, above all, God in all of observable creation. This hierarchy expressed itself in its emphasis on advancing steps of understanding. The sculptural program of Chartres, for example, is a revelation of the Old Testament figures who point us to their proper fulfillment in the New. In the theology of Aquinas we move from the plane of natural reason to a fuller truth taught by revelation. In Dante we progress from an awareness of our sinful nature to an intuition into the nature of God. In all of these cases the emphasis is on harmony and gradation and a final purpose of all knowledge, which is to become aware of God. In that sense, at least, much of medieval culture could be said to be oriented in an otherworldly manner.

SUMMARY

◆ **The Rise of Cities and Universities.** The High Middle Ages saw the growth of several institutions that stood in sharp contrast to those of the Carolingian period. Foremost was the rise of the city. Urbanization brought with it a lessening of the importance of monastic life as a cultural center and the emergence of the influence of the bishop and the cathedral school. The increased need for a "knowledge class" triggered an expansion in education that would eventually lead to the university of scholars. Urbanization also warred against the old feudal values; it fostered trade and commerce; it made possible the growth of what we today call a "middle

EXERCISES

1. Is it possible to think of a building or complex of buildings serving as an organizing metaphor for a contemporary city in the way a cathedral served in the Middle Ages?
2. What positive and/or negative outcomes do you see deriving from the medieval cult of the Virgin?
3. Compare the use and role of light in the atmosphere of Hagia Sophia and the Cathedral of Chartres.
4. Describe some of the technological problems medieval builders had to solve in an age with limited power sources, no tempered metals, no computers or slide rules for calculations, and so on.
5. The medieval university was organized around the body of scholars who made up the faculty. To what

degree does that model hold up today? What is the organizing principle of the modern college or university?

6. A good deal of medieval education utilized *dialectics*. What does that word mean? Where do dialectics, broadly understood, find their usefulness today?

7. Thomas Aquinas had no doubt that all knowledge was both interrelated and capable of being synthesized into a whole. Everything from science and philosophy to theology would fit into that synthesis. Would that view find many supporters today? If not, why not?

8. If you were to organize a contemporary hell for the great villains of our day, would you use Dante's classification or would you construct another schema? On what basis would it be organized?

9. Dante looks back to Virgil as the model for his great work of poetry. If we were to write a work today to celebrate our culture and destiny, would we feel the need to invoke a past model to do so? If so, who might it be? If not, why not?

 Visit the *Culture & Values* Companion website at **www.cengage.com/art/Cunningham/Cultureand Values7E** and the *Humanities Resource Center* for an array of primary source readings, key terms with pronunciations, flash cards, quizzes, and study materials designed especially to help you do well in this course.

CHAPTER 11

THE FOURTEENTH CENTURY: A TIME OF TRANSITION

Overshadowing all the achievements described in this chapter lay the terrible pandemic of infectious disease we know as the Black Death. The plague first appeared in central Asia, and in 1347 a fleet of ships from the Crimea carrying infected rats and their fleas, brought it to the port of Messina, Sicily. By 1348 the plague had begun its journey throughout most of Europe.

There seem to have been two basic forms. Bubonic plague was the result of a flea bite that transmitted a bacterium. The pneumonic variety, caused by airborne bacteria that attacked the lungs, was probably the deadliest form for most Europeans in the fourteenth century. Medieval doctors had no idea how the plague spread, although they understood that it was infectious. The cities were worst affected, families often fleeing from infected relatives. Wealthier citizens took refuge in the countryside, as Boccaccio's work, the *Decameron* describes.

We shall never know in detail how many people died. The Italian city-states, which had the best public health systems of the time, lost about 2 million people. Many physicians refused to treat victims, and the cemeteries soon ran out of space. The effects were often equally devastating psychologically and culturally.

In practical terms, the huge decline in population disrupted the economy and interrupted the production of goods (cloth, construction materials) and agriculture. Labor shortages led to higher wages for those who could (or would) work, and therefore higher prices. Social unrest spread, and from 1350 to 1450 there were waves of peasant and worker uprisings against employers. To many, the events triggered by the Black Death seemed to prefigure the end of the world. As one observer commented, "It was as if the voice of existence in the world had called out for oblivion, and the world responded to its call."

CALAMITY, DECAY, AND VIOLENCE

The fourteenth century (often called the **Trecento**, Italian for "three hundred") is usually described by historians as the age that marks the end of the medieval

◆ The Black Death personified strangles a victim of the plague, Prague, 1376. *(Image © Werner Forman/Art Resource, NY)*

period and the beginning of the Renaissance in Western Europe. If we accept this rather neat description of the period, we should expect to see strong elements of the medieval sensibility as well as some stirrings of the "new birth" (*Renaissance*) of culture that was the hallmark of fifteenth-century European life. We must, however, be cautious about expecting the break between "medieval" and "Renaissance" to be clean and dramatic. History does not usually work with the precision employed by the historians. Neither should we expect to see cultural history moving upward in a straight line toward greater modernity or greater perfection. In fact, the fourteenth century was a period of unparalleled natural calamity, institutional decay, and cruel violence.

THE BLACK DEATH

Midway through the century, in 1348, bubonic plague swept through Europe in a virulent epidemic that killed untold numbers of people and upset trade, culture, and daily life in ways difficult for us to imagine. It has been estimated that some cities in Italy lost as many as two-thirds of their population in that year alone (see map, "The Black Death").

GENERAL EVENTS	ART
1200	**13th cent.** Dependence on Byzantine models in Italian painting
	c. 1240–1302 Cimabue, *Madonna Enthroned*; *Crucifixion*
	c. 1300 New naturalism in Italian painting appears with work of Giotto
1299 Ottoman Turk dynasty founded	**1305–1306** Giotto, Arena Chapel frescoes
1300 Pope Boniface VIII proclaims first Jubilee Year ("Holy Year")	**c. 1308–1311** Duccio, *Maestà* altarpiece, Siena
1303 Philip the Fair of France humiliates Pope Boniface VIII	
1309 "Babylonian Captivity" of the papacy at Avignon begins	**c. 1310** G. Pisano completes Pisa Cathedral pulpit
1326 Earliest known use of cannon	**1333** Martini, *The Annunciation*
1337–1453 "Hundred Years' War" between France and England	
1346–1378 Reign of Charles IV, Holy Roman emperor	**1338–1339** A. Lorenzetti, *Allegory of Good Government* fresco, Siena
1346 English defeat French at Crécy	
1348 Bubonic plague depopulates Europe	
1356 English defeat French at Poitiers	
1358 Revolt of lower classes (*Jacquerie*) in France	
1363–1404 Reign of Philip the Bold, duke of Burgundy	**c. 1347–1360** Prague, as residence of Charles IV, becomes major art center
1376 Popes return to Rome from Avignon	**c. 1363** Court of dukes of Burgundy at Dijon becomes important center of International Style
1377	
1377–1399 Reign of Richard II in England	**c. 1395** *Wilton Diptych*
1378 "Great Schism" in Catholic Church begins	
1381 Peasant riots ("Wat Tyler Rebellion") in England	
1399–1413 Reign of Henry IV in England	**1395–1406** Sluter, *The Well of Moses*
1413 English defeat French at Agincourt	
1417 Council of Constance ends "Great Schism" with election of Pope Martin V	
1417	**1413–1416** Limbourg Brothers, illustrations for *Très Riches Heures du Duc de Berry*

Side heading (rotated): LATE MIDDLE AGES/PROTO-RENAISSANCE — "BABYLONIAN CAPTIVITY" OF THE PAPACY — THE GREAT SCHISM

One prominent figure who lived through that devastation was the Italian writer Giovanni Boccaccio (1313–1375). His great collection of stories, the *Decameron*, has a plague setting. A group of young men and women flees Florence to avoid the plague; during their two-week sojourn in the country, they amuse each other by telling stories. Each of the ten young people tells a story on each of the week days (*Decameron* is Greek for "ten days"). The resulting one hundred stories constitute a brilliant collection of folktales, **fabliaux** ("ribald fables"), **exempla** ("moral stories"), and romances Boccaccio culled from the oral and written traditions of Europe. Because of their romantic elements, earthiness, and somewhat shocking bawdiness, the *Decameron* has often been called the "Human Comedy" to contrast it with the lofty moral tone of Dante's epic work of an earlier generation.

However delightful and pleasing these stories are to read, they stand in sharp contrast to the horrific picture Boccaccio draws of the plague in his introduction to the *Decameron*. Boccaccio's account has the ring of authenticity. He had been an eyewitness to the events he describes. His vivid prose gives some small sense of what the plague must have been like for a people who

ARCHITECTURE	LITERATURE & PHILOSOPHY	MUSIC
1288–1309 Palazzo Pubblico, Siena		
1295 Santa Croce, Florence, begun		
1296 Florence Cathedral (Duomo) begun		
1298 Palazzo Vecchio, Florence, begun	**c. 1303–1321** Dante, *Divine Comedy*	
1332–1357 Gloucester Cathedral choir ("Perpendicular" style)	**1348–1352** Boccaccio, *Decameron*, collection of tales	**14th cent.** Secular music flourishes **1325** Vitry, *Ars Nova Musicae*, treatise describing new system of musical notation
	after 1350 Petrarch compiles *Canzoniere*, collection of poems	
	c. 1370 Saint Catherine of Siena urges end of "Babylonian Captivity"	**after 1337** Machaut, *Messe de Notre Dame*, polyphonic composition
c. 1345–1438 Doge's Palace, Venice	**1373** Petrarch, *Letter to Posterity*, autobiography	**c. 1350** Landini famous in Florence as performer and composer of madrigals and ballads
	c. 1377 Wycliffe active in English church reform; translates Bible into English	
1386 Duomo of Milan begun	**c. 1385–1400** Chaucer, *The Canterbury Tales*, collection of tales	
	c. after 1389 Christine de Pisan, *The Book of the City of Ladies*	

THE BLACK DEATH

- Cities and regions struck by plague
- Extent of plague at specific date
- Cities and regions partially spared by plague

0 — 300 Miles
0 — 300 Kilometers

December 31, 1349
June 30, 1349
December 31, 1348

December 31, 1348
June 30, 1348
December 31, 1347

DROGHEDA DUBLIN KILKENNY PRESTON CHESTER NOTTINGHAM LEICESTER NORTHAMPTON OXFORD BRISTOL WEYMOUTH SOUTHAMPTON DURHAM LANCASTER YORK LINCOLN NORWICH YARMOUTH CAMBRIDGE LONDON CANTERBURY CALAIS AMIENS PARIS ANGERS STRASBOURG COLMAR BASEL LUCERNE ZÜRICH ST GALL BORDEAUX TOULOUSE AVIGON BÉZIERS BEARN NARBONNE HUESCA MARSEILLES SARAGOSSA LERIDA PERPIGNAN BARCELONA TERUEL VALENCIA SEVILLE ALMERIA LÜBECK ROSTOCK HAMBURG WISMAR BREMEN OSNABRÜCK MAGDEBURG FRANKFURT A. ODER COLOGNE ERFURT WÜRZBURG FRANKFURT NUREMBERG VIENNA MÜHLDORF MILAN VERONA VENICE GENOA FERRARA BOLOGNA FLORENCE PISA ANCONA SEBENICO SIENA PERUGIA RAGUSA ROME NAPLES MESSINA CATANIA AGRIGENTO SYRACUSE

possessed only the most rudimentary knowledge of medicine and no knowledge at all about the source of illness and disease.

THE GREAT SCHISM

Nature was not the only scourge to affect the stability of Europe. The medieval Christian church, that most powerful and permanent large institution in medieval life, underwent convulsive changes in the fourteenth century—changes that issued distant warning signals of the Reformation to come at the beginning of the sixteenth century.

A quick look at some dates indicates clearly the nature of these changes. In 1300 Pope Boniface VIII

celebrated the great jubilee year at Rome that brought pilgrims and visitors from all over the Christian West to pay homage to the papacy and the church it represented and headed. This event was one of the final symbolic moments of papal supremacy over European life and culture. Within the next three years, Philip the Fair of France imprisoned and abused the same pope at the papal palace of Anagni. The pope died as a result of his humiliating encounters with royal power; even Dante's implacable hatred of Boniface could not restrain his outrage at the humiliation of the office of the pope. By 1309 the papacy, under severe pressure from the French, had been removed to Avignon in Southern France, where it was to remain for nearly seventy years. In 1378 the papacy was further weakened by the **Great Schism**, which saw European Christianity divided into

VALUES

Natural Disaster and Human Response

All of the chapters in this book single out a particular value expressed in the culture of the period under discussion. In this chapter, however, we raise another kind of issue affecting human values: How do people respond to catastrophic events in their lives? One historian has called the Plague Years of 1347–1351 the "greatest natural disaster ever to have struck Europe." Although firm figures are difficult to come by, it is safely assumed that Europe lost 30 percent of its population in that period, with mortality rates in some areas as high as 60 percent.

Boccaccio, in his *Decameron*, said that the Florentines responded either with an orgy of entertainment, on the presumption that on the morrow they might all be dead, or by turning to religion for solace, while many, like the ten young people of the *Decameron*, fled to what they thought would be an area of safety.

We have abundant documentation to show that other (not surprising) reactions were common. One was to find a scapegoat on whom blame for the plague could be laid. The most conspicuous fourteenth-century scapegoat was the Jewish population, who became the object of expulsion orders, riots, and massacres by unruly mobs with the compliance of

the Christian authorities, particularly in Northern Europe.

Another common reaction was the outbreak of religious mania. During the plague years, itinerant bands of men and women marched through villages and towns, scourging themselves, crying out for penance, and describing the plague as God's judgment. These flagellants (as they were called) came mainly from the lay ranks, who were infected with a hysteria over a catastrophe they could not understand.

With the slow passing of the plague, its long-range effects began to take hold: famine caused by the shortage of manpower in agriculture, and the breakdown of social authority, which, within a generation, would result in the uprisings of the lower classes in places as different as Italy, France, and England.

The most poignant of the Plague Chronicles was written by an Irish friar in 1349 who says that he left some unused parchment attached to his story in case anyone "of Adam's race" would survive to continue his story. Another hand wrote in that blank space: "Here it seems that the author died."

hostile camps, each of whom pledged allegiance to a rival claimant to the papacy. Not until 1417 was this breach in church unity healed; a church council had to depose three papal pretenders to accomplish the reunification of the church.

The general disarray of the church in this period spawned ever more insistent demands for church reforms. Popular literature (as both Boccaccio and, in England, Geoffrey Chaucer, clearly demonstrate) unmercifully satirized the decadence of the church. Great saints like the mystic Catherine of Siena (1347–1380) wrote impassioned letters to the popes at Avignon in their "Babylonian Captivity" demanding that they return to Rome free from the political ties of the French monarchy. In England, John Wycliffe's cries against the immorality of the higher clergy and the corruption of the church fueled indignation at all levels. The famous Peasant Revolt of 1381 was greatly aided by the activism of people aroused by the ideas of Wycliffe and his followers.

The 1381 revolt in England was only the last in a series of lower-class revolutions that occurred in the

fourteenth century. The frequency and magnitude of these revolts (like that of the French peasants beginning in 1356) highlight the profound dissatisfactions with the church and the nobility in the period. It is not accidental that the story of Robin Hood, with its theme of violence toward the wealthy and care for the poor, began in the fourteenth century.

THE HUNDRED YEARS' WAR

The terrible violence of the fourteenth century was caused not only by the alienation of the peasants but also by the Hundred Years' War between France and England. While the famous battles of the period—Poitiers, Crécy, Agincourt—now seem romantic and distant, it is undeniable that they brought unrelieved misery to France for long periods. Between battles, roaming bands of mercenaries pillaged the landscape to make up for their lack of pay. The various battles were terrible in themselves. One example must suffice. According to Jean Froissart's *Chronicles*, the English

King Edward III sent a group of his men to examine the battlefield after the Battle of Crécy (1346), in which the English longbowmen slaughtered the more traditionally armed French and mercenary armies: "They passed the whole day upon the field and made a careful report of all they saw. According to their report it appeared that eighty banners, the bodies of eleven princes, twelve hundred knights, and thirty thousand common men were found dead on the field." It is no wonder that Barbara Tuchman's splendid history of life in fourteenth-century France, *A Distant Mirror* (1978), should have been subtitled "The Calamitous Fourteenth Century."

LITERATURE IN ITALY, ENGLAND, AND FRANCE

Amid the natural and institutional disasters of the fourteenth century, there were signs of intense human creativity in all the arts, especially in literature. In Italy, Dante's literary ominence was secure at the time of his death (1321), and the reputation of Italian letters was further enhanced by two other outstanding Tuscan writers: the poet Francesco Petrarch and Giovanni Boccaccio, famed for the *Decameron*. In England, one of the greatest authors in the history of English letters was active: Geoffrey Chaucer. His life spanned the second half of the fourteenth century; he died, almost symbolically, in 1400.

PETRARCH

It is appropriate to begin a discussion of fourteenth-century culture with Petrarch. His life spanned the better part of the century (1304–1374), and in that life we can see the conflict between the medieval and early Renaissance ideals being played out.

Petrarch (Petrarca in Italian) was born in Arezzo, a small town in Tuscany, south of Florence. As a young man, in obedience to parental wishes, he studied law for a year in France and for three years at the law faculty in Bologna. He abandoned his legal studies immediately after his father's death to pursue a literary career. To support himself he accepted some minor church offices but was never ordained to the priesthood.

Petrarch made his home at Avignon (and later at a much more isolated spot near that papal city, Vaucluse), but for the greater part of his life he wandered from place to place. He could never settle down; his restlessness prevented him from accepting lucrative positions that would have made him a permanent resident of any one place. He received invitations to serve as secretary to various popes in Avignon and, through the intercession of his close friend Boccaccio, was offered a professorship in Florence. He accepted none of these positions.

Petrarch was insatiably curious. He fed his love for the ancient classics by searching out and copying ancient manuscripts that had remained hidden and unread in the various monasteries of Europe. It is said that at his death he had one of the finest private libraries in Europe. He wrote volumes of poetry and prose, carried on a vast correspondence, advised the rulers of the age, took a keen interest in horticulture, and kept a wide circle of literary and artistic friends. We know that at his death he possessed pictures by both Simone Martini and Giotto, two of the most influential artists of the time. In 1348 Petrarch was crowned poet laureate of Rome, the first artist so honored since the ancient days of Rome.

One true mark of the Renaissance sensibility was a keen interest in the self and an increased thirst for personal glory and fame. Petrarch surely is a fourteenth-century harbinger of that spirit. Dante's *Divine Comedy* is totally oriented to the next life; the apex of Dante's vision is that of the soul rapt in the vision of God in eternity. Petrarch, profoundly religious, never denied that such a vision was the ultimate goal of life. At the same time, his work exhibits a tension between that goal and his thirst for earthly success and fame. In his famous prose work *Secretum* (*My Secret*), written in 1343, the artist imagines himself in conversation with Saint Augustine. In a dialogue extraordinary for its sense of self-confession and self-scrutiny, Petrarch discusses his moral and intellectual failings, his besetting sins, and his tendency to fall into fits of depression. He agrees with his great hero Augustine that he should be less concerned with his intellectual labors and the fame that derives from them and more with salvation and the spiritual perfection of his life. However, Petrarch's argument has a note of ambivalence: "I will be true to myself as far as it is possible. I will pull myself together and collect my scattered wits, and make a great endeavor to possess my soul in patience. But even while we speak, a crowd of important affairs, though only of this world, is waiting for my attention."

The inspiration for the *Secretum* was Augustine's *Confessions*, a book Petrarch loved so much that he carried it with him everywhere. It may well have been the model for Petrarch's *Letter to Posterity*, one of the few examples of autobiography we possess after the time of Augustine. That Petrarch would have written an autobiography is testimony to his strong interest in himself as a person. The *Letter* was probably composed in 1373, a year before his death. Petrarch reviews his life up until 1351, where the text breaks off abruptly. The unfinished work is clear testimony to Petrarch's thirst for learning, fame, and self-awareness. At the same time it is noteworthy for omitting any mention of the Black Death of 1348, which carried off the woman he loved. The letter is an important primary document of the sensibility of the fourteenth-century "proto-Renaissance."

Petrarch regarded as his most important works the Latin writings over which he labored with devotion and in conscious imitation of his most admired Classical masters: Ovid, Cicero, and Virgil. Today, however, only a literary specialist or an antiquarian is likely to read his long epic poem in Latin called *Africa* (written in imitation of Virgil's *Aeneid*) or his prose work in praise of the past masters of the world (*De Viris Illustris*) or his meditations on the benefits of the contemplative life (*De Vita Solitaria*). What has assured the literary reputation of Petrarch is his incomparable vernacular poetry, which he considered somewhat trifling but collected carefully into his **Canzoniere** (*Songbook*). The *Canzoniere* contains more than three hundred **sonnets** and forty-nine **canzoni** (songs) written in Italian during the span of his adult career.

The subject of a great deal of Petrarch's poetry is his love for Laura, a woman with whom he fell immediately in love in 1327 after seeing her at church in Avignon. Laura died in the plague of 1348. The poems in her honor are divided into those written during her lifetime and those mourning her untimely death. Petrarch poured out his love for Laura in more than three hundred sonnets (fourteen-line poems) he typically broke into an octave and a sestet. Although they were never actually lovers (Petrarch says in the *Secretum* that this was due more to her honor than to his; Laura was a married woman), his Laura was no mere literary abstraction. She was a flesh-and-blood woman whom Petrarch genuinely loved. One of the characteristics of his poetry, in fact, is the palpable reality of Laura as a person; she never becomes (as Beatrice does for Dante) a symbol without earthly reality.

The interest in Petrarch's sonnets did not end with his death. Petrarchism, by which is meant the Petrarchan form of the sonnet and particularly the poet's attitude toward his subject matter—praise of a woman as the perfection of human beauty and the object of the highest expression of love—was introduced into other parts of Europe before the century was over. In England, Petrarch's sonnets were first imitated in form and subject by Sir Thomas Wyatt in the early sixteenth century. Although the Elizabethan poets eventually developed their own English form of the sonnet, the English Renaissance tradition of poetry owes a particularly large debt to Petrarch, as the poetry of Sir Philip Sidney (1554–1586), Edmund Spenser (1552–1599), and William Shakespeare (1564–1616) shows. Their sonnet sequences follow the example of Petrarch in linking together a series of sonnets in such a way as to indicate a development in the relationship of the poet to his love.

Petrarch's Sonnet 15

Backwards at every weary step and slow
These limbs I turn which with great pain I bear;
Then take I comfort from the fragrant air
That breathes from thee, and sighing onward go.
But when I think how joy is turned to woe,
Remembering my short life and whence I fare,
I stay my feet for anguish and despair,
And cast my tearful eyes on earth below.
At times amid the storm of misery
This doubt assails me: how frail limbs and poor   10
Can severed from their spirit hope to live.
Then answers Love: Hast thou no memory
How I to lovers this great guerdon give,
Free from all human bondage to endure?
(John Addington Symonds, trans.)

CHAUCER

While it is possible to see the beginning of the Renaissance spirit in Petrarch and other Italian writers of the fourteenth century, the greatest English writer of the century, Geoffrey Chaucer (1340–1400), still reflects the culture of his immediate past. The new spirit of individualism discernible in Petrarch is missing in Chaucer. He is still very much a medieval man. Only in the later part of the fifteenth century, largely under the influence of Italian models, can we speak of the Renaissance in England. This underscores the valuable lesson about history that movements do not necessarily happen immediately and everywhere.

Scholars have been able to reconstruct Chaucer's life with only partial success. We know that his family had been fairly prosperous wine merchants and vintners and that he entered royal service early in his life, eventually becoming a squire to King Edward III. After 1373 he undertook various diplomatic tasks for the king, including at least two trips to Italy to negotiate commercial contracts. During these Italian journeys, Chaucer came into contact with the writings of Dante, Petrarch, and Boccaccio. There has been some speculation that he actually met Petrarch, but the evidence is tenuous. Toward the end of his life Chaucer served as the customs agent for the port of London on the river Thames. He was thus never a leisured "man of letters"; his writing had to be done amid the hectic round of public affairs that engaged his attention as a highly placed civil servant.

Like many other successful writers of the late medieval period, Chaucer could claim a widespread acquaintance with the learning and culture of his time. This was still an age when it was possible to read most of the available books. Chaucer spoke and wrote French fluently, and his poems show the influence of many French allegories and "dream visions." That he also knew Italian literature is clear from his borrowings from Dante and Petrarch and from his use of stories and tales in Boccaccio's *Decameron* (although it is not clear that he knew that work directly). Chaucer also had a deep knowledge of Latin literature, both classical and ecclesiastical. Furthermore, his literary output was not limited to the composition of original works of poetry. He made a translation from Latin (with an eye on an earlier French version) of Boethius's *Consolation of Philosophy* as well as a translation from French of the thirteenth-century allegorical erotic fantasy *Romance of the Rose*. He also composed a short treatise on the astrolabe and its relationship to the study of astronomy and astrology (two disciplines not clearly distinguished at that time).

The impressive range of Chaucer's learning pales in comparison to his most memorable and noteworthy talents: his profound feeling for the role of the English language as a vehicle for literature, his efforts to extend the range of the language (the richness of Chaucer's vocabulary was not exceeded until Shakespeare), and his incomparable skill in the art of human observation. Chaucer's characters are so finely realized that they have become standard types in English literature: his pardoner is an unforgettable villain, his knight the essence of courtesy, his wife of Bath a paradigm of rollicking bawdiness.

These characters, and others, are from Chaucer's masterpiece, *The Canterbury Tales*, begun sometime after 1385. To unify this vast work, a collection of miscellaneous tales, Chaucer used a typical literary device: a narrative frame, in this case a journey during which people tell each other tales. As noted, Boccaccio had used a similar device in the *Decameron*.

Chaucer's plan was to have a group of thirty pilgrims travel from London to the shrine of Saint Thomas à Becket at Canterbury and back. After a general introduction, each pilgrim would tell two tales on the way and two on the return trip in order to pass the long hours of travel more pleasantly. Between tales they might engage in perfunctory conversation or prologues of their own to cement the tales further into a unified whole.

Chaucer never finished this ambitious project; he died before half of it was complete. The version we possess has a General Prologue in which the narrator, Geoffrey Chaucer, describes the individual pilgrims, his meeting with them at the Tabard Inn in London, and the start of the journey. Only twenty-three of the thirty pilgrims tell their tales (none tells two tales) and the group has not yet reached Canterbury. There is even some internal evidence that the material we possess was not meant for publication in its present form.

Although *The Canterbury Tales* is only a draft of what was intended to be Chaucer's masterwork, it is of incomparable literary and social value. A close reading of the General Prologue, for instance—with its representative, although limited, cross section of medieval society (no person lower in rank than a plowman or higher in rank than a knight appears)—affords an effortless entry into the complex world of late medieval England. With quick, deft strokes Chaucer not only creates verbal portraits of people who at the same time seem both typical and uniquely real but also introduces us to a world of slowly dying knightly values; a world filled with such contrasts as clerical foibles, the desire for knowledge, the ribald taste of the lower social classes, and an appetite for philosophical conversation.

After the General Prologue, the various members of the pilgrim company begin to introduce themselves and proceed to tell their tales. Between the tales they engage in small talk or indulge in lengthy prologues of their own. In the tales that he completed, we see that Chaucer drew on the vast treasury of literature—both written and oral—that was the common patrimony of medieval culture. The Knight's Tale is a courtly romance; the miller and reeve tell stories that spring from the ribald *fabliaux* tradition of the time; the pardoner tells an *exemplum* such as any medieval preacher might employ; the prioress draws from the legends of the saints; the nun's priest uses an animal fable, while the parson characteristically enough provides a somewhat tedious example of a medieval prose sermon.

At places, as in the prologue to the tale of the Wife of Bath, we get from Chaucer a long meditation on some of the problems of the age. The Wife of Bath introduces her tale, for instance, with a discourse explaining why the persistent tradition against women (misogyny) is unjust and contrary to authentic Christian theology. She also makes a passionate plea for seeing sexual relations as a good given by God. This may strike us as unnecessary, but in an age that prized the unmarried state (for example, for monks, nuns, priests) it was a necessary corrective.

CHRISTINE DE PISAN

Christine de Pisan (1365–1428?) is an extraordinary figure in late medieval literature if for no other reason than her pioneering role as one of Europe's first women professional writers to make her living with the power of her pen.

Born in Venice, Christine accompanied her father Thomas de Pizzano to the French court of Charles V when she was still a small child. Thomas was the king's physician, astrologer, and close adviser. He evidently gave his daughter a thorough education: she was able to write in both Italian and French and probably knew Latin well enough to read it. At fifteen she married Eugene of Castel, a young nobleman from Picardy. That same year (1380) the king died and the

❖ VOICES OF THEIR TIMES

John Ball

Sermon of the priest John Ball, a leader in the English Peasant Revolt of 1381, recorded in *The Chronicles of Froissart*.

Good people: things cannot go right in England and never will, until goods are held in common and there are no more villeins ["peasants"] and gentlefolk. . . . In what way are those whom we call lords greater masters than ourselves? How have they deserved it? If we all spring from a common mother and father, Adam and Eve, how can they claim or prove that they are lords more than us except by making us produce and grow the wealth which they spend?

They are clad in velvet and camlet lined with squirrel and ermine, while we go dressed in course cloth.

They have the wines, the spices, and the good bread; we have the rye, the husks, and the straw and we drink water.

They have shelters and ease in their fine manors and we have hardship and toil, the winds and the rains in the fields.

And from us must come, from our labor, the things which keep them in luxury.

We are called serfs and beaten if we are slow in service to them, yet we have no sovereign lord we can complain to; none to hear us and do us justice.

Let us go to the king—he is young—and show him how we are oppressed and tell him how we want things changed or else we will change them ourselves. If we go in good earnest and all together, very many people who are called serfs and are held in subjection will follow us to get their freedom.

When the king hears us he will remedy the evil, willingly or otherwise!

---

family fell on hard times with the loss of royal patronage. Five years later her father and her husband were both dead, leaving Christine the sole supporter of her mother, niece, and three young children. To maintain this large family, Christine hit on an almost unheard of solution for a woman of the time: she turned to writing and the patronage such writing could bring to earn a living.

Between 1399 and 1415, Christine composed fifteen books, which, as one of her translators has noted, is a staggering record in an age that had neither typewriters nor word processors. In 1399 she entered a famous literary debate about the *Romance of the Rose*. The *Romance*, a long and rather tedious poem, had been written in the preceding century and was immensely popular (Chaucer did an incomplete English translation of it). In 1275 Jean de Meung had written an addition to it that was violently critical of women. Christine attacked this misogynistic addition in a treatise called *A Letter to the God of Love*. In 1404 she wrote her final word on this debate in a long work titled *The Book of the City of Ladies*.

The Book of the City of Ladies is indebted in its structure to Augustine's *The City of God*, and for its sources, a Latin treatise by Boccaccio titled *De Claris Mulieribus*. Through use of stories of famous women (*clarae mulieres*), Christine demonstrates that they possessed virtues precisely opposite to those vices imputed to women by Jean de Meung.

The following year (1405) Christine wrote *The Treasure of the City of Ladies*, a book of etiquette and advice to help women survive in society. What is extraordinarily interesting about this book (one of the few available in English translation) is its final section, in which Christine pens advice for every class of women—from young brides and wives of shopkeepers to prostitutes and peasant women.

Around 1418, Christine retired to a convent in which her daughter was a nun, where she continued to write. Besides a treatise on arms and chivalry and a lament about the horrors of civil war, she also composed prayers and seven allegorical psalms. Of more enduring interest was *The Book of Peace*, a handbook of instruction for the Dauphin who was to become Charles VII and a short hymn in honor of the great Joan of Arc. Whether Christine lived to see the bitter end of Joan is uncertain, but her hymn is one of the few extant works written while Joan was alive.

Immensely popular in her own time (the Duc de Berry owned copies of every book she wrote), her reputation waned in the course of time, to be revived only in the last decade or so as scholars have tried to do justice to the forgotten heroines of our common history.

ART IN ITALY

Giorgio Vasari's *Lives of the Artists* (1550), the earliest account of the rebirth of Italian art in the Renaissance, treats first of all the great Florentine painter Giotto da Bondone (1266 or 1267–1337). In his *Life of Giotto*, Vasari pays tribute to Giotto's work and also gives him credit for setting painting once again on the right path, from which it had strayed.

Later generations have accepted Vasari's assessment and have seen Giotto as a revolutionary figure not for the fourteenth century alone but for the entire history of European art, marking a major break with the art of the Middle Ages. Like all revolutionary figures, Giotto was more intimately linked with his past than his contemporaries and immediate successors realized, and to understand the magnitude of his achievements we must first see something of their context.

THE ITALO-BYZANTINE BACKGROUND

Throughout the later Middle Ages, art in Italy showed little of the richness and inventiveness of the great centers of northern Europe. Not only in France, where the University of Paris formed the intellectual capital of the Western world, but also in England and Germany, con- struction of the great Gothic cathedrals provided opportunities for artists to refine and develop their techniques. Sculptured decorations like *The Death of the Virgin* from Strasbourg Cathedral [**Fig. 11.2**] are stylistically far more advanced than contemporary work in Italy. One of the reasons for this is that northern Gothic artists were beginning to return for inspiration not to their immediate predecessors but to Classical art, with its realistic portrayal of the body and drapery. In Italy, however, artists were still rooted in the Byzantine tradition. Italian churches were generally decorated not with lifelike sculptural groups like the one from Strasbourg, but with solemn and stylized frescoes and mosaics, a style called Italo–Byzantine.

Sculpture of Pisano, Father and Son There are notable exceptions to the generally conservative character of Italian art in the thirteenth century. Nicola Pisano (1220/1225–1284?) and his son Giovanni (1245/1250–1314) have been described as the creators of modern sculpture. Nicola's first major work was a marble pulpit for the baptistery in Pisa completed in 1260, clearly influenced by the Roman sarcophagi the sculptor could see around him in Pisa. By crowding in his figures and filling the scene with lively detail, Nicola recaptured much of the vitality and realism of late Roman art while retaining the expressive qualities of Gothic sculpture. The work of his son Giovanni was less influenced by Classical models than by his contemporaries in north-

◆ **11.2** *The Death of the Virgin*, c. 1220. The expressive faces and elaborate drapery show the influence of Classical sculpture. Note Christ holding Mary's soul in the form of a small doll-like figure.

Tympanum, south transept portal, Strasbourg Cathedral, France. Image © Bildarchiv Monheim GmbH (Achim Bednorz)/Alamy ern Europe—so much so that some scholars believe he must have spent some time in France. In his pulpit for the cathedral at Pisa, finished in 1310, the figures are more elegant and less crowded than those of his father and show an intensity of feeling typical of northern late Gothic art [**Fig. 11.3**, **Fig. 11.4**]. Both of these great sculptors foreshadowed major characteristics in the art of the Renaissance, Nicola by his emphasis on Classical models and Giovanni by the naturalism and emotionalism of his figures and by his use of space.

While some Italian sculptors were responding to influences from outside, painting in Italy remained firmly grounded in the Byzantine tradition. Byzantine art was originally derived from Classical art. Although its static and solemn characteristics seem a long way away from Greek or Roman styles, Byzantine painters and mosaicists inherited the late Hellenistic and Roman artists' ability to give their figures a three-dimensional quality and to represent foreshortening. With these techniques available to him, Giotto was better able to break away from the stereotypical forms of Italo-Byzantine art and bring to painting the same naturalism and emotional power that appear in Giovanni Pisano's sculptures.

Cimabue Giotto's predecessor as the leading painter in Florence, and perhaps also his teacher, was Cimabue (1240?–1302?). Not enough of his work has survived for us to have a clear impression of how much Giotto owed to Cimabue's influence, but the crucifix Cimabue painted for the Church of San Domenico in Arezzo

◆ **11.3** Nicola Pisano, *Annunciation and Nativity*, 1259–1260. By crowding his figures together, Nicola was able to combine the scene of the Nativity with the Annunciation and the shepherds in the fields.

Marble relief, 2'10" x 3'9" (85 x 114 cm). Pulpit detail, Baptistery, Pisa, Italy. Image © Alinari Archives/CORBIS

◆ **11.4** Giovanni Pisano, *Nativity and Annunciation to the Shepherds*, 1302–1310. The slender figures and sense of space create an effect very different from that of the work of the artist's father. Note the more realistic landscape and animals.

Marble relief, 2'10" x 3'4" (85 x 101 cm). Pulpit detail, Pisa Cathedral, Pisa, Italy. Image © Scala/Art Resource, NY

◆ **11.5** Cimabue, *Crucifixion*, c. 1287–1288. The anatomy of Christ's body is molded with a new sense of realism, particularly the muscular structure of the legs. At the same time, the weight of the body causes it to hang to one side.

Panel, 14′8″ x 12′10″ (448 x 390 cm), San Domenico, Arezzo, Italy. Image © Scala/Art Resource, NY

◆ **11.6** Cimabue, *Madonna Enthroned with Angels and Prophets*, 1280–1290. Although much of the detail is Byzantine in inspiration, the scale of this painting has no Byzantine counterpart; the sense of space within which Cimabue sets his Madonna is a sign of the new stylistic development.

From Santa Trinità, Florence, Italy. Tempera and gold leaf on wood on panel, 12′7″ x 7′4″ (3.81 x 2.24 m). Galleria degli Uffizi, Florence, Italy// © Scala/Art Resource, NY

shows a remarkable realism and sophistication in the depiction of Christ's body [**Fig. 11.5**]. Cimabue shows a genuine if incomplete understanding of the anatomy of the figure and, more important, uses it to enhance the emotional impact of his painting by emphasizing the sense of strain and weight. At the same time the draped loincloth is not merely painted as a decorative design but as naturalistically soft folds through which the limbs beneath are visible. If, in other works, like the immense Santa Trinità *Madonna* [**Fig. 11.6**], Cimabue is more directly in the Italo–Byzantine tradition, here at least he seems to prefigure the impact of Giotto's art.

Duccio di Buoninsegna The works of Cimabue's contemporary Duccio di Buoninsegna (1255–60 to 1318–19) are more clearly Byzantine in inspiration, but here too the new spirit of the times can be felt (see **Table 11.1**). His greatest achievement was the huge *Maestà*, painted between 1308 and 1311, for the high altar of Siena Cathedral in his native city. The majestic Madonna who gives the work its name faced the congregation [**Fig. 11.7**], while both the front and back of the altarpiece were covered with small compartments filled with scenes from the lives of Christ and the Virgin. The episodes are familiar from earlier painters, but the range of emotional expression is new and astonishing, as Duccio reveals to us not only the physical appear-

Table 11.1 *Siena in the Age of Duccio (1255–1260 to 1318–1319)*

Population	20,000
Political Institutions	Council of the Nine, rotating Consistory (Magistracy)
Economy	Banking, wool manufacture, jewelry, and gold work
Cultural Life	Painting (Duccio, Martini); Sculpture (della Quercia); Laudi, or sacred songs (Bianco da Siena); Theology (Saint Catherine)
Principal Buildings	Cathedral, Palazzo Pubblico (Town Hall)
Divine Protectress	The Virgin Mary, Queen of Siena

ance of each of his subjects but their emotional states as well. In some of the scenes the action takes place within an architectural setting that conveys a greater sense of space than we find in any earlier paintings, including those from the ancient world [**Fig. 11.8**].

◆ **11.7** Duccio, *Madonna Enthroned with Saints*, c. 1308–1311. In this principal panel of the *Maestà* altarpiece, note the greater gentleness of the faces and the softer, flowing robe of the Virgin compared with Cimabue's painting (Figure 11.6).

Principal panel of the Maestà altarpiece from Siena Cathedral, Siena, Italy. Tempera and gold leaf on wood, 7′ x 13′ (2.13 x 3.96 m). Museo dell'Opera Metropolitana del Duomo, Siena, Italy//© Scala/Art Resource, NY

◆ **11.8** Duccio, *The Annunciation of the Death of the Virgin*, c. 1308–1311. This scene from the *Maestà* altarpiece demonstrates Duccio's ability to create a convincing architectural space around his figures.

Front, crowning panel of the Maestà altarpiece, from Siena Cathedral, Siena, Italy. Tempera on wood, ca. 16″ x 21″ (41.5 x 54 cm). Museo dell'Opera Metropolitana del Duomo, Siena, Italy//© Scala/Art Resource, NY

◆ **11.9** Giotto, *Madonna Enthroned with Child, Angels, and Saints*, c. 1310. Although contemporary with Duccio's Madonna from the Maestà altarpiece, Giotto's painting has a much greater sense of weight and volume, as the solid throne contrasts with the flat background. Furthermore, we see the Virgin's form beneath her drapery.

From the Church of Ognissanti, Florence, Italy. Tempera and gold leaf on wood, 10'8" x 6'8" (3.25 x 2.03 m). Galleria degli Uffizi, Florence, Italy// © Scala/Art Resource, NY

GIOTTO'S BREAK WITH THE PAST

Great as Duccio's contribution was to the development of painting, it was achieved without any decisive break with the tradition in which he worked. Even if we can now see in the works of Cimabue the roots of some of Giotto's achievements, the boldness of his vision, and the certainty with which he communicates it to us, represent one of the supreme achievements of Western art.

Giotto's preeminent characteristic was his realism. The Byzantine style had aimed for a rich, glowing surface, with elaborate linear designs. Now for the first time, figures were painted with a sense of depth, their volume represented by a careful use of light and dark, so that they took on the same strength and presence as works of sculpture. Instead of being confronted with an image, spectators saw the living and breathing figures before them. In his great altarpiece, *Madonna Enthroned*, painted in 1310, Giotto brings us into the presence of the Virgin [**Fig. 11.9**]. We see the majestic solidity of her form, an impression enhanced by the realistic throne on which she sits. This is achieved not only by the three-

◆ **11.10** Giotto, *The Meeting of Joachim and Anna*, c. 1305. Joachim and Anna has each separately received a divine revelation that Anna is to have a child. As they meet and embrace, the bridge and arch where they stand seem to symbolize the sense of unity of the couple.

Fresco, 6½' x 6' (200 x 185 cm), Cappella Scrovegni (Arena Chapel), Padua, Italy. Image © Alinari/Art Resource, NY

dimensional modeling of the figures but also by the sense of space that surrounds the Virgin and child and separates them from the worshiping angels.

But Giotto's greatness lay not so much in his ability to create realistic images—to "imitate Nature," as his contemporaries called it—as in using these images for dramatic effect. Rather than confining himself to single subjects in individual panel paintings, like that of the Madonna enthroned, he preferred to work on a more complex and monumental scale. His chief claim to fame is the great cycle of frescoes that fills the walls of the Arena Chapel in Padua. In these panels illustrating the lives of the Virgin and of Christ, Giotto used the new naturalistic style he had developed to express an almost inexhaustible range of emotions and dramatic situations. In the scene depicting the meeting of Joachim and Anna, the parents of the Virgin, the couple's deep affection is communicated to us with simplicity and humanity [**Fig. 11.10**]. The quiet restraint of this episode is in strong contrast to the cosmic drama of the lamentation over the dead body of Christ [**Fig. 11.11**]. Angels wheel overhead, screaming in grief, while below Mary supports her dead son and stares fiercely into his face. Around her are the other mourners, each a fully characterized individual. If the disciple John is the most passionate in the expression of his sorrow, as he flings his arms out, no less moving are the silent hunched figures in the foreground.

The Franciscans also engaged the talents of Giotto to pay honor to their patron, Francis of Assisi. Although there is no scholarly consensus that Giotto painted the great cycle on the life of Francis once attributed to him in the upper basilica at Assisi (most scholars now attribute those works to an unknown artist called the "Mas-

◆ **11.11** Giotto, *The Lamentation over the Dead Christ*, 1305. The entire force of movement in the scene draws the viewer's eyes down to the dead Christ: the angels swooping toward the earth, the lines of drapery worn by all the figures. The bleakness is emphasized by the withered tree in the top right-hand corner.

Fresco, 7'7" x 7'9" (2.31 x 2.36 m), Cappella Scrovegni (Arena Chapel), Padua, Italy. Image © Scala/Art Resource, NY

◆ **11.12** Giotto, *Saint Francis Renounces His Worldly Goods*, 1290–1304. Note Giotto's use of an architectural background and his portrayal of the figures in the scene as individuals, from the angry father to the restless children.

Fresco, 9' x 15' (2.8 x 4.5 m) Bardi Chapel, Church of Santa Croce, Florence, Italy. Image © Scala/Art Resource, NY

ter of the St. Francis Cycle"), there is no doubt that in the second decade of the fourteenth century, he did the fresco cycle in the Bardi Chapel in the Church of Santa Croce in Florence.

Giotto interpreted the deeds of Francis based on the life of the saint written by Saint Bonaventure (died 1274), who had been a contemporary of Thomas Aquinas. The narratives are not as simple as they first seem. The scene depicting Francis renouncing all of his earthly goods [**Fig. 11.12**] shows a dramatic confrontation set before the palace of the local bishop. On the left is Pietro Bernadone holding the clothes of the saint

◆ **11.13** Simone Martini, *The Annunciation with Saints Ansano and Margaret*, 1333. The courtly elegance of the figures is in strong contrast to the massive realism of Giotto's Madonna (Figure 11.9). Speaking to the Virgin, the Angel Gabriel proclaims, "Ave gratia plena dominus tecum" (Hail thou that are full of grace, the Lord is with you).

From Siena Cathedral, Siena, Italy. Frame reconstructed in the 19th century. Tempera and gold leaf on wood with four medallions (l. to r.) Prophets Jeremiah, Ezechiel, Isaiah, and Daniel. Center panel 10′1″ x 8′8½″ (3.05 x 2.54 m). Galleria degli Uffizi, Florence, Italy//© Erich Lessing/Art Resource, NY

who had stripped himself nude as a sign of renunciation. To the viewer's right is Bishop Guido, covering the nakedness of the saint with his episcopal cape (symbolizing his entry into the life of the church) while Francis assumes an attitude of prayer. Bonaventure's *Life* says that on that occasion Francis said, "Once I was called the son of Pietro Bernadone; now I say 'Our Father, who art in heaven'." Giotto frames this dramatic scene with children placed at opposite ends of the line of figures, reacting to the confrontation of father and son.

THE INTERNATIONAL STYLE IN SIENA, ITALY

Simone Martini Giotto's appeal was direct and immediate, and at Florence his pupils and followers continued to work under his influence for most of the remainder of the fourteenth century, content to explore the implications of the master's ideas rather than devise new styles. As a result, the scene of the most interesting new developments in the generation after Giotto was Siena, where Duccio's influence (although considerable) was much less overpowering. Among Duccio's pupils was Simone Martini (c. 1285–1344), a close friend of Petrarch, who worked for a time at Naples for the French king Robert of Anjou and spent the last years of his life at the papal court of Avignon. In Martini's work we find the first signs of the last great development of Gothic art, the so-called International Style. The elegant courts of France and the French kingdoms of Italy had developed a taste for magnificent colors, fashionable costumes, and rich designs. Although Martini's Sienese background preserved him from the more extreme effects, his *Annunciation* has an insubstantial grace and sophistication that are in strong contrast to the solid realism of Giotto [**Fig. 11.13**]. The resplendent robe and mantle of the angel Gabriel and the deep-blue dress of the Virgin, edged in gold, produce an impression of great splendor, while their willowy figures approach the ideal of courtly elegance.

◆ **11.14** Ambrogio Lorenzetti, the city, detail from *The Good City* (also called *The Effects of Good Government on the City and the Country*,) 1338–1339. Note the skillful use of perspective. The scene is that of Siena: the striped tower of the cathedral is visible in the top left-hand corner. The three buildings in the foreground show typical urban activities. To the left is a shoe shop, in the middle a school lesson is in progress, and to the right is a tavern selling wine.

Detail c. 23′ of fresco, 46′ (14.04 m) long, east wall, Hall of the Nine (Sala dei Nove), Palazzo Pubblico, Siena, Italy. Image © Scala/Art Resource, NY

◆ **11.15** Ambrogio Lorenzetti, countryside, detail from *The Good City*, (also called *The Effects of Good Government on the City and the Country*), 1338–1339. The figure in the top left-hand corner is Securitas, who promises that all may walk in peace, and holds out a gallows with a hanged man as a warning to those thinking of disturbing that peace.

Detail c. 23′ of fresco, 46′ (14.04 m) long, east wall, Hall of the Nine (Sala dei Nove), Palazzo Pubblico, Siena, Italy. Image © Scala/Art Resource, NY

Pietro and Ambrogio Lorenzetti If Simone Martini was willing to sacrifice naturalism to surface brilliance, two of his contemporaries in Siena were more interested in applying Giotto's discoveries to their own work. Pietro Lorenzetti was born around 1280, his brother Ambrogio around 1285; both probably died in 1348, the year of the Black Death. The younger brother's best-known work is a huge fresco that decorates an entire wall in Siena's city hall, the Palazzo Pubblico; it was painted between 1338 and 1339 and illustrates the effects of good government on the city of Siena and the surrounding countryside. The streets and buildings, filled with scenes of daily life, are painted with elaborate perspective [**Fig. 11.14**]. Richly dressed merchants with their wives, craftsmen at work, and graceful girls who dance in the street preserve for us a vivid picture of a lifestyle that was to be abruptly ended by the Black Death. The scenes in the country, on the other hand, show a world that survives even today in rural Tuscany: peasants at work on farms and in orchards and vineyards [**Fig. 11.15**].

◆ **11.16** French School, *Richard II Presented to the Virgin and Child by His Patron Saints (Wilton Diptych)*, c. 1395. The detailed painting of the fabrics is accentuated by the strong color contrast between the two panels: the overwhelming blue of the right-hand panel emphasizes the golden tones on the left.

Oak panels, each 18″ x 11½″ (46 x 29 cm). National Gallery, London, UK//© Erich Lessing/Art Resource, NY.

ART IN NORTHERN EUROPE

By the middle of the fourteenth century, the gulf between artists in Italy and those north of the Alps had been reduced considerably. Painters like Simone Martini, who carried the latest developments in Sienese art to France, were in turn influenced by styles they found there, and subsequently brought them back to Italy. The growing tendency toward a unity of artistic language throughout Western Europe was further increased by political developments. When, for example, in 1347 the city of Prague became the residence of Emperor Charles IV, it became a major art center rivaling even Paris in importance.

The *Wilton Diptych* By the end of the century it was no longer possible to identify an artist's origins from the work. The *Wilton Diptych* was painted in England sometime after 1377 [**Fig. 11.16**]. One of the two panels (hence the word ***diptych***) shows the

young King Richard II accompanied by his patron saints, while on the other the Virgin and child appear before the praying king, accompanied by eleven angels. They probably commemorate Richard's coronation in 1377, since he was eleven years old at the time. The wonderfully delicate yet rich colors and the careful use of shading have no parallel in English art of the period. The artist seems to have been familiar with the work of painters like Duccio and Simone Martini, but the elegance of the paintings and technique are neither simply Italian nor French. The painter of the *Wilton Diptych* was working in a style that can only be called International.

Claus Sluter One of the first great centers of the International Style was the court of the Duke of Burgundy at Dijon, where sculptors like the Dutchman Claus Sluter and painters like the Flemish Melchior Broederlam served Duke Philip the Bold, who ruled there from 1364 to 1404, and his brother John, Duc de Berry. Sluter (active about 1380–1406) was commissioned to provide sculpture for a monastery, the

◆ **11.17** Claus Sluter, *The Well of Moses*, 1395–1406. The horns represent rays of light (a usage based on a Bible mistranslation). Note the movement outward of the figures, with a scroll falling forward over Moses's shoulder.

Limestone with traces of paint, Moses 6′ (1.8 m) high. Chartreuse de Champmol, Dijon, France. Image © Erich Lessing/Art Resource, NY

◆ **11.18** Limbourg Brothers, February, page from *Très Riches Heures du Duc de Berry*, 1416. The chart above the painting represents the signs of the zodiac for the month of February. Note the details of the figures sitting before the fireplace and the bleak choice of colors to express the wintry scene.

Manuscript illumination, 8½″ x 5⅜″ (22 x 14 cm). © Musée Condé, Chantilly, France//Giraudon/The Bridgeman Art Library

Chartreuse de Champmol, founded near Dijon by Duke Philip. His most impressive work there is the so-called *Well of Moses*, designed for the monastery's cloister [**Fig. 11.17**]. Not really a well at all, it consists of an elaborate base surrounded by statues of Moses and five other Old Testament prophets on which originally stood a crucifixion, now missing. At first glance, the style of the figures is reminiscent of earlier Gothic statues, like those at Strasbourg, but a more careful look shows a host of carefully depicted details. In the figure of Moses the textures of the heavy drapery, the soft beard, and the wrinkled face are differentiated skillfully, and the expression has the vividness of a portrait. Equally realistic is the sense of weight and mass of the body beneath the drapery.

The Limbourg Brothers But for the most attractive details in all of late Gothic art, we must turn to the *Trés Riches Heures du Duc de Berry*, an illustrated prayer book commissioned by Philip the Bold's brother and completed in 1416. It was painted by the Limbourg brothers—Pol, Hennequin, and Herman. They were Flemish in origin, may have spent some time in Italy,

and finally settled in France. Twelve illuminated pages are included in the book; these illustrate the twelve months of the year. These paintings are filled with an almost inexhaustible range of details that combine to depict the changing seasons of the year with poetry and humanity. On the page representing February, the farm workers warming themselves inside the cottage, and the sheep huddling together outside, attract our attention immediately, but the whole scene is filled with marvelously painted details, from the steamy breath of the girl on the far right, stumbling back through the snow toward a warm fireside, to the snow-laden roofs of the frozen village in the far distance [**Fig. 11.18**]. In May we move from the world of peasants to that of the aristocracy as a gorgeously dressed procession of lords and ladies rides out in the midst of the fresh greenery of springtime with the roof and turrets of a great castle

◆ **11.19** Limbourg Brothers, May, page from *Très Riches Heures du Duc de Berry*, 1416. The hunters blow their horns, but the courtiers are more interested in the ladies. By contrast with the February page (Figure 11.18), note the brilliant colors of the costumes and the fresh green of spring.

Manuscript illumination, 8½″ x 5⅜″ (22 x 14 cm). © Musée Condé, Chantilly, France// Giraudon/The Bridgeman Art Library

in the background [**Fig. 11.19**]. The sense of idleness and the delightful conceits of chivalry seem to evoke the world of Chaucer, while stylistically the sense of perspective and elegance of the figures is still another reminder of the influence of Sienese art.

LATE GOTHIC ARCHITECTURE

ITALY

As in the case of painting and sculpture, the generally unified style of northern Gothic architecture never really crossed the Alps into Italy. Although some of the most important Italian buildings of the fourteenth century are generally labeled Gothic, their style is very different from that of their northern counterparts. Two of the centu-

ry's greatest churches illustrate this point, both begun in Florence at the end of the thirteenth century—Santa Croce around 1295 and the cathedral (better known by the Italian word for cathedral, **duomo**) in 1296. Neither has buttresses and in both most of the wall surface is solid rather than pierced with the typical Gothic windows. The duomo's most outstanding feature does not even date to the fourteenth century: its magnificent dome was built by the great early Renaissance architect Filippo Brunelleschi between 1420 and 1436 [**Fig. 11.20**].

More self-consciously Gothic is the duomo in Milan, begun in 1386, which perhaps makes one feel relieved that Italian architects in general avoided the chief features of northern Gothic style. The immensely elaborate façade, bristling with spires, and the crowded piers of the sides seem to be stuck on rather than integrated into the design. The presence of Classical elements in the decorations is a reminder that by the time the Milan Duomo was completed, the Renaissance had dawned [**Fig. 11.21**].

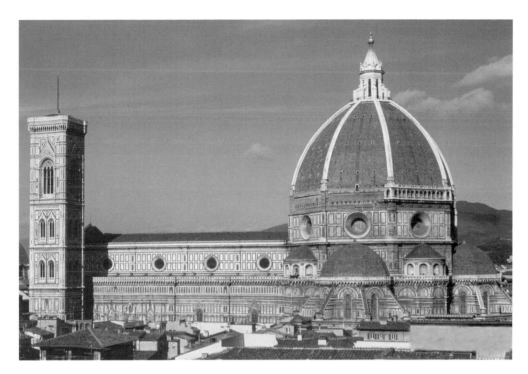

◆ **11.20** Florence Cathedral, Florence, Italy, 1296–1436 (view from the south). Brunelleschi's dome consists of an inner and outer shell, and a skeleton of 24 ribs: the eight main ones are visible on the outside. The bell-tower, designed by Giotto, stands apart from the cathedral, as was the custom in Italy. *(Image © Scala/Art Resource, NY)*

◆ **11.21** Milan Cathedral (Duomo), Milan, Italy, begun 1386. The Classical moldings over the windows and doorways of the façade contrast with the Gothic spires and are a reminder that the duomo was not completed until the Renaissance. *(Image © age fotostock/SuperStock)*

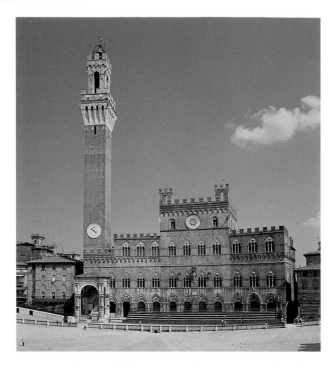

◆ **11.22** Palazzo Pubblico, Siena, Italy, 1288–1309. The slits around the base of the gallery at the top of the tower were used for firing through on attackers below. The building forms a backdrop for the famous **Palio,** a horserace that takes place in Siena twice a year. *(Image © Scala/Art Resource, NY)*

Far more attractive are the secular public buildings of the age. The town halls of Florence and Siena, the Palazzo Vecchio (begun 1298) and the Palazzo Pubblico (begun 1288), respectively, convey the sense of strong government and civic pride that characterized life in these cities during the Trecento [**Fig. 11.22**]. The towers served the double purpose of providing a lookout over the city and surrounding countryside while they expressed the determination of the city rulers to resist attack. The most beautiful of all government centers is probably the Doge's Palace in Venice, a city where more than anywhere else Gothic architecture took on an almost magical quality of lightness and delicacy. The Doge's Palace (begun about 1345) is composed of a heavy upper story that seems to float on two arcades, the lower a short and sturdy colonnade and the upper composed of tall, slender columns. The effect is enhanced by the way in which the entire building seems suspended in space between sky and sea [**Fig. 11.23**].

ENGLAND

For a final look at late Gothic architecture at its most typical we must turn to England, where the style of this period is generally known as **Perpendicular**. The choir of Gloucester Cathedral, built between 1332 and 1357, illustrates the reason for the label [**Fig. 11.24**]. The vertical line is emphasized, and our eyes are carried up to the roof,

◆ **11.23** Doge's Palace, Venice, Italy, 1345–1438. Unlike the heavily fortified Palazzo Pubblico at Siena, this palace of the rulers of Venice, with its light, open arches, reflects the stability and security of the Venetian Republic. As in the case of Florence (Figure 11.20), note the bell tower standing independently. *(© David Clapp/OSF/Photolibrary)*

where a complex web of ribs decorate the vault. Unlike the ribs in earlier buildings, these serve no structural purpose but have become purely decorative. Their delicacy seems an apt reflection in stone of the graceful precision of the *Wilton Diptych* and the *Très Riches Heures*.

A NEW MUSICAL STYLE—*ARS NOVA*

While Giotto was laying the foundations for a new naturalistic style of painting, and writers like Petrarch and Chaucer were breathing fresh life into literary forms, composers in France and Italy were changing the style of music. To some extent this was the result of social changes. Musicians had begun to break away from their traditional role as servants of the church and to establish themselves as independent creative figures; most of the music that survives from the fourteenth century is secular. Much of it was written for singers and instrumentalists to perform at home for their own pleasure [**Fig. 11.25**] or for the entertainment of aristocratic audiences like those depicted in the *Très Riches Heures*. The texts composers set to music were increas-

◆ **11.24** Choir, Gloucester Cathedral, Gloucester, England, 1332–1357. The strong vertical lines show why the style of such buildings is called Perpendicular. *(Image © Scala/Art Resource, NY)*

◆ **11.25** A knight playing and singing to a lady. The romantic interlude is enhanced by the idyllic surroundings: a walled garden with a fountain playing.

Flemish school, manuscript illumination of the lover and Dame Oyeuse in a garden, from Romance of the Rose. *14" x 10" (35.6 x 25.4 cm). © British Library, London, UK//Art Resource, NY* ingly varied: ballads, love songs, even descriptions of contemporary events, in contrast to the religious settings of the preceding century.

As the number of people who enjoyed listening to music and performing it began to grow, so did the range of musical expression. The term generally used to describe the sophisticated musical style of the fourteenth century is **ars nova**, derived from the title of a treatise written by the French composer Philippe de Vitry (1291–1361) around 1325. The work was written in Latin and called *Ars Nova Musicae (The New Art of Music)*. Although it is really concerned with only one aspect of composition and describes a new system of rhythmic notation, ars nova has taken on a wider use and is applied to the new musical style that began to develop in France in the early fourteenth century and soon spread to Italy.

Its chief characteristic is a much greater richness and complexity of sound than before. This was partly achieved by the use of richer harmonies; thirds and sixths were increasingly employed and the austere sounds of parallel fifths, unisons, and octaves were generally avoided. Elaborate rhythmic devices were also introduced, including the method of construction called **isorhythm** (from the Greek word *isos*, which means "equal"). Isorhythm consisted of allotting to one of the voices in a **polyphonic** composition a repeated single melody. The voice was also assigned a repeating rhythmical pattern. Because the rhythmical pattern was of a different length from the melody, different notes would be stressed on each repetition. The purpose of this device was twofold: it created a richness and variety of texture, and it imparted an element of unity to the piece.

GUILLAUME DE MACHAUT

The most famous French composer of this period was Guillaume de Machaut (1304?–1377), whose career spanned the worlds of traditional music and of the *Ars Nova*. He was trained as a priest and took holy orders, but much of his time was spent traveling throughout Europe in the service of the kings of Bohemia, Navarre, and France. Toward the end of his life he retired to Rheims, where he spent his last years as a canon. His most famous composition, and the most famous piece of music from the fourteenth century, is the *Messe de Notre Dame*. A four-part setting of the Ordinary of the Mass (discussed below), it is remarkable chiefly for the way in which Machaut gives unity to the five sections that make up the work by creating a similarity of mood and even using a single musical motif that recurs throughout.

Machaut's *Messe de Notre Dame* is the first great example of the entire Ordinary of the Mass set to polyphonic music by a single composer. The Ordinary of the Mass refers to those parts of the Roman Catholic liturgy that do not change from day to day, in contrast to the Prop-

ers (the readings from the Gospel or Epistles), which do change daily. The parts of the Ordinary are as follows:

1. The *Kyrie Eleison*: the repeated Greek phrases that mean "Lord have mercy on us!" and "Christ have mercy on us!"
2. The *Gloria*: a hymn of praise sung at all masses except funerals and masses during Lent and Advent.
3. The *Credo*: the Profession of Faith sung after the Gospel.
4. The *Sanctus* and *Benedictus*: a short hymn based on the angelic praise found in Isaiah 6, sung at the beginning of the eucharistic prayer.
5. The *Agnus Dei*: the prayer that begins "Lamb of God," sung before Communion.

CD Track 3
Guillaume de Machaut, The Credo (excerpt) from the *Messe de Notre Dame*

With the music of Machaut, we begin to approach the main characteristics of Western music. After a single voice has intoned the opening words of the Credo, the other voices enter to provide the elements absent from Gregorian Chant and to a lesser extent, Léonin's organum: **harmony** (*the sounding together of several lines or voices*) and a recognizable rhythmic structure. The rhythm is varied and uses melodic motifs as its basis. Although rooted in the principles laid out in Philipe de Vitry's *Ars Nova Musicae*, the free flow of the Credo is truly novel.

The four voices move simultaneously so that it is easy for the listener to follow the words, which remain clear but are given a new vigor by the freedom of their treatment. In his rhythmical inventiveness and sense of the structural importance of harmony (note the satisfying way in which the listening selection comes to rest at its conclusion), Machaut points the way to the next stage in the development of Western music.

Machaut's *Messe de Notre Dame* stands at the head of a long tradition of musical composition in which composers use the Ordinary of the Mass to express the timeless words of the liturgy in their own cultural idiom. In that sense Machaut's Mass is the ancestor of the Renaissance compositions of Palestrina in the sixteenth century, the Baroque masses of Johann Sebastian Bach in the eighteenth century, and the frenetically eclectic modern *Mass* of Leonard Bernstein.

Machaut is also one of the earliest musicians to leave a substantial body of secular music, contributing to another great musical tradition, that of secular song. With the increasing use of polyphony, composers began to turn their attention to the old troubadour songs and write new settings that combined several different voices. Machaut's polyphonic secular songs took several forms. His **ballades** were written for two or three voices, the top voice carrying the melody while

◆ **11.26** Music and musicians, 14th century. Some of the instruments of the time are shown. The goddess Music is at the center, playing a small organ. Grouped around her are musicians with stringed instruments, percussion, and wind instruments. The inset shows David, founder of church music, plucking a psaltery.

Manuscript illumination from De Musica I. *Biblioteca Nationale, Naples, Italy//© Scala/Art Resource, NY*

the others provided the accompaniment. These lower voices were probably sometimes played on instruments rather than sung. As in the ballades of earlier times the poems consisted of three stanzas, each of seven or eight lines, the last one or two lines being identical in all the stanzas to provide a refrain.

Many of these secular songs, both by Machaut and by other composers, deal with amorous topics and are often addressed to the singer's beloved. The themes are predictable—the sorrow of parting, as in Machaut's *Au dè partir de vous*, reproaches for infidelity, protestations of love, and so on—but the freshness of the melodies and Machaut's constant inventiveness prevent them from seeming artificial.

FRANCESCO LANDINI

The other important composer of the fourteenth century was the Italian Francesco Landini (1325–1397),

who lived and worked in Florence. Blinded in his youth by smallpox, he was famous in his day as a virtuoso performer on the organ, lute, and flute. Among his surviving works are several **madrigals**, a form of word setting involving two or three verses set to the same music and separated by a refrain set to different music. In addition, he wrote a large number of *ballate* ("ballads"), including many for solo voice and two accompanying instruments. The vocal lines are often elaborate, and Landini uses rich, sonorous harmonies. But in the case of these and other works of the period, there is no specification of the instruments intended or of the general performance style Landini would have expected [**Fig. 11.26**]. We know from contemporary accounts that in some cases performers would have changed the written notes by sharpening or flattening them, following the convention of the day. This practice of making sounds other than those on the page was called ***musica ficta*** ("fictitious music"), but no systematic description of the rules followed has been handed down to us. As a result, modern editors and performers often have only their own historical research and instincts to guide them. Although the *Ars Nova* of the fourteenth century marks a major development in the history of music, our knowledge of it is far from complete.

The fourteenth century was a time of stark contrast between the horrors of natural and social disasters and the flowering of artistic and cultural movements that were the harbingers of the fifteenth-century Renaissance in Italy. Chaucer, as noted, died in 1400, the year that may be taken as the close of the medieval period. By that time, some of the prime figures of the Italian Renaissance—Donatello, Fra Angelico, and Ghiberti—were already in their teens. The great outburst of cultural activity that was to mark Florence in the fifteenth century was near, even though it would not make a definite impact on England until the end of the century. The calamitous fourteenth century was a costly seedbed for rebirth and human renewal.

SUMMARY

◆ **The Transition from Medieval Culture to the Renaissance.** The fourteenth century marks the painful transition from the medieval period to the world of the Renaissance. Its beginning saw the construction of several major buildings in Italy, including Florence's duomo and Siena's Palazzo Pubblico, seat of city government. Music flourished throughout the century, especially in France, where Machaut was the leading composer of his day. In the years shortly after 1300, the new naturalistic style of Giotto revolutionized the art of painting, whereas the works of the Pisano family proved equally important for the history of sculpture. Yet the age was fraught with disaster and racked by war: the Hundred Years' War between France and England (1337–1453) was barely under way when in 1348 Europe was devastated by bubonic plague—the Black Death. Among the works of literature to reflect the effects of the terrible plague is Boccaccio's *Decameron*.

◆ **The Papacy in Avignon and Petrarch.** As the century began, the church appeared to be at the height of its influence. In 1300 Pope Boniface VIII proclaimed the first holy year, and pilgrims flocked to Rome. Yet within a few years the French had forced the transfer of the papacy to Avignon in Southern France. Among those who accompanied the papal court was the poet Petrarch, many of whose sonnets deal with his love for Laura, who was killed by the Black Death. The Babylonian Captivity lasted from 1309 to 1376, and the pope's return to Rome was embittered by the Great Schism, which saw the Western powers locked in a struggle to impose rival claimants.

◆ **The International Style.** One of the artistic consequences of the papal move from Rome was that Italian styles were carried north of the Alps. The resulting blend of Italian and Northern elements is called the International Style, which quickly spread throughout Europe; two of its main centers were at Prague and at Dijon. The more cosmopolitan spirit of the age is also illustrated by the career of the greatest English writer of the time, Chaucer, who traveled to Italy and to France and may have actually met Petrarch.

◆ **Social Protests.** In an age of such foment, the pressure for reform intensified. In England, John Wycliffe's charges of church corruption heightened dissatisfaction among the lower classes, leading to the peasant riots of 1381. Similar popular protests against both the church and the aristocracy occurred in France in 1356, while in 1378 the poor woolen workers of Florence revolted against the city authorities. These manifestations of general discontent brought no immediate radical changes in government, but they did prepare the way for the social mobility of the Renaissance.

◆ **The Hundred Years' War.** The greatest struggle of the century, the Hundred Years' War, was supposedly fought over the right of succession to the French throne. In fact, its underlying cause was the commercial rivalry between France and England and the attempts of both countries to gain control of the wool-manufacturing region of Flanders. The war's early stages were marked by a series of English victories, culminating in the Battle of Poitiers (1356). By 1380 the French had reversed the tide, and the last years of the century saw inconclusive skirmishes, with both sides resigned to a stalemate.

Thus, a century in which political, economic, and religious strife and revolutionary artistic developments were accompanied by the disaster of plague produced deep changes in the fabric of European society and made possible the renewal of the Renaissance.

EXERCISES

1. Compare the literary achievements of Boccaccio and Petrarch. What light does their work throw on the history of their times?
2. How does Chaucer characterize the participants in *The Canterbury Tales*? Select two and describe their chief features.

3. Describe Giotto's contribution to the history of painting and compare him to his predecessors.
4. What are the principal characteristics of Northern European art in the fourteenth century? How does it differ from Italian art?
5. How did musical styles change in the fourteenth century? Discuss the contribution of Guillaume Machaut.

Visit the *Culture & Values* Companion website at **www.cengage.com/art/Cunningham/Cultureand Values7E** and the *Humanities Resource Center* for an array of primary source readings, key terms with pronunciations, flash cards, quizzes, and study materials designed especially to help you do well in this course.

CHAPTER 12

THE EARLY RENAISSANCE

When Johannes Gutenberg published the first printed Bible in 1455 in Mainz, Germany, the event marked a revolution in human communications. It is worthwhile to recall the effort that went into that enterprise. Gutenberg produced about 150 copies of the Latin Vulgate Bible on paper and another thirty copies on the much more expensive parchment made of animal skin. Each page had forty-two lines of print. Not all the work was done by his workshop. Gutenberg printed the pages; another workshop colored in the initial letters and made the illuminations, and a third workshop did the binding. His Bibles appeared in two volumes and, by modern standards, were enormous. Those printed on paper weigh about thirty pounds while the vellum or parchment Bibles weigh close to fifty pounds. Scholars have estimated that each vellum Bible must have needed the skins of roughly 160 animals, meaning that Gutenberg's first printing required close to 4800 skins.

Only about fifty copies of that original printing have survived, although many more single pages are still extant. Those Bibles were not meant for private use. They were "pulpit Bibles" meant to be read from a lectern (reading desk) either during church services or in religious houses of monks or nuns. Some were bought for the private collections of the nobility.

Gutenberg's invention of moveable type coincided with the emerging technology of papermaking. Muslims had learned papermaking from their contacts with China where paper had been invented. The first European paper mill was founded in the early twelfth century near Valencia in Spain, and by around 1400 papermaking became common in parts of Italy and Germany. Paper made woodblock prints possible, but later in the fifteenth century Gutenberg took advantage of its availability for the printing of books. As that technology improved, reading became democratized as the production of books, pamphlets, and broadsheets came within the economic reach of vast numbers of people.

TOWARD THE RENAISSANCE

The fourteenth century was a period of great social strife and turmoil as well as a time in which new stirrings were abroad in Europe.

◆ Gutenberg's printing press, c. 1455. (© SSPL/The Image Works)

It was the century of Dante, Petrarch, Boccaccio, and Chaucer. The entrenched scholastic approach to learning was being tempered by renewed interest in Classical literature. The long-cherished Byzantine art style was being challenged by the new realism of such Italian artists as Cimabue and Giotto in Florence, Simone Martini, and the Lorenzetti brothers, among others. Renewed interest in the world of nature was fueled by the enormous impact of Saint Francis of Assisi (1181–1226), who taught Europeans to see God in the beauty of the world and its creatures.

In the fifteenth century, Europe was slowly recovering from the fearful plague that had struck around 1348, a rebirth aided by political changes across Europe (see **Table 12.1**) and a new growth in economics and trade. Wealth was being created by an emerging class whose claim to eminence was based less on noble blood than on ability to make money.

The center of this new vitality was Florence in Italy (see map, "Renaissance Italy"). No city its size has in its day exerted more influence on culture at large than this focus of banking and commerce. From roughly the 1420s until the end of the century, a collaborative effort of thinkers, artists, and wealthy patrons enriched the city, and, in the process, made it a magnet for all Europe.

	GENERAL EVENTS	ART
1400	**15th cent.** Florence center of European banking system Age of Exploration begins **1417** Council of Constance ends Great Schism	**1401** Ghiberti wins competition for North Doors of Florence Baptistery **1403** Ghiberti begins Baptistry doors; Brunelleschi, Donatello study Roman ruins **c. 1415–1417** Donatello, *Saint George* **1423** Gentile, *Adoration of the Magi*, International Style altarpiece **c. 1427** Masaccio, *The Tribute Money* **c. 1428** Use of linear perspective to create three-dimensional space; naturalistic rendering of figures; return to classical ideals of beauty and proportion: Masaccio, *The Holy Trinity*
	1432 Florentines defeat Sienese at San Romano	**c. 1428–1432** Donatello, *David,* first free-standing nude since antiquity
1434	**1434** Cosimo de' Medici becomes de facto ruler of Florence	**1434** Jan Van Eyck, *Giovanni Arnolfini and His Bride* **1435** Ghiberti sculpts panels for East Doors of Florence Baptistery
	1453 Fall of Constantinople to Turks; scholarly refugees bring Greek manuscripts to Italy	**1445–1450** Fra Angelico, *Annunciation*
	1464 Piero de' Medici takes power in Florence after death of Cosimo	**1455** Uccello, *Battle of San Romano*
	1469 Lorenzo de' Medici rules city after death of Piero	**c. 1459** Gozzoli, *The Journey of the Magi* **1478–c. 1482** Botticelli, *La Primavera, The Birth of Venus*
	1478 Pazzi conspiracy against the Medici fails	**1483** Leonardo da Vinci, *Madonna of the Rocks*
	1489 Savonarola begins sermons against Florentine immorality	**c. 1489–1492** Michelangelo begins studies in Lorenzo's sculpture garden; *Madonna of the Stairs*
	1492 Death of Lorenzo de' Medici	**late 15th–early 16th cent.** Leonardo, *Notebooks*
1494	**1494** Medici faction in exile; Savonarola becomes de facto ruler of Florence; Charles VIII of France invades Italy, beginning foreign invasions **1498** Savonarola burned at stake by order of Pope	**c. 1495–1498** Leonardo da Vinci, *The Last Supper* **c. 1496** Botticelli burns some of his work in response to Savonarola's sermons **1498–1499** Michelangelo, *Pietá* **1501–1504** Michelangelo, *David*
1503		
	1512 Medici power restored in Florence; Machiavelli exiled	**c. 1503–1505** Leonardo da Vinci, *Mona Lisa*
1520		

Left margin labels: FLORENTINE RENAISSANCE — ROMAN RENAISSANCE; THE FIRST PHASE; THE MEDICI ERA

Table 12.1 *Major Events of the Fifteenth Century*

1439—Council of Florence attempts to reconcile Catholic and Orthodox churches
1453—End of the Hundred Years' War
1453—Constantinople (Byzantium) falls to the Turks
1469—Spain united under Ferdinand and Isabella
1485—Henry VII begins reign as first Tudor King of England
1486—First European voyage around Cape of Good Hope
1492—Columbus discovers America
1492—Last Islamic city in Spain (Granada) falls to Ferdinand and Isabella
1494—Spain and Portugal divide spheres of influence in the New World
1497—Vasco da Gama begins first voyage to India
1498—Savonarola executed in Florence

FLORENCE AND THE RENAISSANCE

At the beginning of the fifteenth century, Florence had every reason to be a proud city. It stood on the main road connecting Rome with the north. Its language—known at the time as the Tuscan dialect or the Tuscan idiom—was the strongest and most developed of the Italian dialects; its linguistic power had been demonstrated more than a century earlier by Dante Alighieri and his literary successors, Petrarch and Boccaccio. The twelve great *Arti* ("trade guilds") of Florence

ARCHITECTURE	LITERATURE & PHILOSOPHY	MUSIC
1417–1420 Brunelleschi designs and begins construction of Florence Cathedral dome (completed 1436)		**c 1400–1474** Guillaume Dufay, teacher and composer, secularized motet, chanson masses
1419–1426 Brunelleschi, Foundling Hospital		
1430–1433 Brunelleschi, Pazzi Chapel—Use of classical order and proportion to achieve rational harmony of elements		
1437–1459 Michelozzo, Convent of San Marco & Palazzo Medici-Riccardi, Florence	**1446–1450** Gutenberg invents movable printing type
1455–1456 *Gutenberg Bible* printed at Mainz
1462 Cosimo de' Medici founds Platonic Academy in Florence
1465 First Italian printing press, at Subiaco
1470–1499 Laura Cetera's humanist writings
1470–1527 Height of humanist learning
1475 *Recuyell of the Historyes of Troye*, first book printed in English by William Caxton
c. 1476–1477 Lorenzo de' Medici begins *Comento ad Alcuni Sonetti*
1482 Ficino, *Theologia Platonica*
1486 Pico della Mirandola, *Oration on the Dignity of Man*
1490 Lorenzo de' Medici, *The Song of Bacchus*
1491 Lorenzo de' Medici, *Laudi* | **c. 1450–1500** Johannes Ockeghem, *Missa pro Defunctis*, earliest known polyphonic requiem mass

1479–1492 Heinrich Isaac, court composer to Medici family and organist and choirmaster at Florence Cathedral, sets Lorenzo's poems to music |
| | **c. 1494** Aldus Manutius establishes Aldine Press in Venice
1496 Book-burning inspired by Savonarola | |
| | **1502** Erasmus, *Enchiridion militis Christiani*
1506 Erasmus travels to Italy
1509 Erasmus, *The Praise of Folly*
1513 Machiavelli, *The Prince*
1516 Erasmus, *Greek New Testament* | |

RENAISSANCE ITALY

were commercially important for the city; in addition, representatives of the seven senior **guilds** formed the body of magistrates that ruled the city from the fortress like town hall, the Palazzo Vecchio. This "representative" government, limited though it was to the prosperous guilds, preserved Florence from the rise of the terrible city tyrants who plagued so many other Italian cities.

Florence had been one of the centers of the wool trade since the late Middle Ages. In the fifteenth century it was also the center of the European banking system. In fact, our modern banks (the word *bank* is from the Italian *banco,* which means "counter" or "table"— the place where money is exchanged) and their systems of handling money are based largely on practices developed by the Florentines. They devised advanced accounting methods, letters of credit, and a system of checks; they were the first to emphasize the importance of a stable monetary system. The gold florin minted in Florence was the standard coin in European commerce for centuries.

Great Florentine banking families made and lost fortunes in trading and banking. These families—the Strozzi, Bardi, Tornabuoni, Pazzi, and Medici—were justly famous in their own time. They, in turn, were justly proud of their wealth and their city. A visitor to Florence today walks on streets named for these families and past palaces built for them. They combined a steady sense of business conservatism with an adventuresome pursuit of wealth and fame. No great Florentine banker would have thought it odd that one of this group began his will with the words "In the name of God and profit. Amen."

For all their renown and wealth, it was not the bankers who really gave Florence its lasting fame. By some mysterious stroke of good fortune, Florence and its immediate surroundings produced, in the fifteenth century, a group of artists who revolutionized Western art to such an extent that later historians refer to the period as a time of *renaissance* ("rebirth") in the arts.

Gentile da Fabriano The character of this revolutionary change in art is not easy to define, but we

◆ **12.2** Gentile da Fabriano, *Adoration of the Magi*, 1423. This painting reflects the flat two-dimensional quality of most Byzantine and medieval painting. Note the crowded composition and the highly ornate frame of the whole.

Altarpiece from Santa Trinita, Florence. Tempera on wood, approx. 9′11″ x 9′3″ (3.02 x 2.81 m). Galleria degli Uffizi, Florence, Italy//© Erich Lessing/Art Resource, NY

◆ **12.3** Masaccio, *The Holy Trinity*, c. 1428. The donors of the panel kneel at bottom left and right. The Trinity, with the Holy Spirit symbolized as a dove, is set in a Classical Roman architectural frame. At the foot of the architectural frame a skeleton in an open sarcophagus represents death.

Fresco, 21′10½″ x 10′5″ (6.66 x 3.19 m). Santa Maria Novella, Florence, Italy//© Erich Lessing/Art Resource, NY

can develop a partial definition by comparing two early fifteenth-century Florentine paintings. Sometime before 1423 a wealthy Florentine banker, Palla Strozzi, commissioned Gentile da Fabriano (c. 1385–1427) to paint an altarpiece for the Florentine Church of Santa Trinitá. The *Adoration of the Magi*, completed in 1423, is ornately framed in the style of Gothic art, with evidence of influences from the miniature painting of Northern Europe and from the older painting tradition of Italy [**Fig. 12.2**]. The altarpiece is in the style called "International" because it spread far beyond the area of its origins in France. This style reflects the old-fashioned tendency to fill up the spaces of the panel, to employ the brightest colors on the palette, to use gold lavishly for halos and in the framing, and to ignore any strict proportion between the characters and the space they occupy. Gentile's altarpiece is, in fact, a strikingly beautiful painting that testifies to the lush possibilities of the conservative International Gothic style.

Masaccio Only about five years later, Tommaso Guidi (1401–1428), known as Masaccio, the precocious genius of Florentine painting, painted a **fresco** for the Dominican Church of Santa Maria Novella in Florence, *The Holy Trinity* [**Fig. 12.3**], that is strikingly different from the kind of painting by Gentile. The most apparent difference is in the utilization of space. In *The Holy Trinity* the central figures of God the Father, the Holy Spirit, and the crucified Christ seem to stand in the foreground of deep three-dimensional space created by painting the illusion of an architectural framing of the

◆ **12.4** Masaccio, *The Tribute Money*, c. 1427. Three moments of the story (found in Matthew 17:24–27) are seen simultaneously. *Center:* Jesus instructs Peter to find the coin of tribute. *Left:* Peter finds it in the mouth of a fish. *Right:* Peter pays the tribute money.

Fresco, 8′1″ x 19′7″ (2.54 x 5.9 m). Brancacci Chapel, Santa Maria del Carmine, Florence, Italy//© Scala/Art Resource, NY

Trinity. The character of the architecture is Roman, its barrel vaulting and coffering sustained by Corinthian columns and pilasters. At the sides, and slightly lower, Mary looks out at the viewer, while Saint John looks at Mary. At the edge of the scene, members of the donor family kneel in profile. The entire scene has an intense geometrical clarity based on the pyramid, with God as the apex of the triangle formed with the line of donors and saints at the ends of the baseline.

In this single fresco appear many of the characteristics of Florentine Renaissance painting that separate it from earlier painting styles: clarity of line, a concern for mathematically precise perspective, close observation of real people, concern for psychological states, and an uncluttered arrangement that rejects the earlier tendency in painting to produce crowded scenes to fill up all the available space.

Masaccio's earlier frescoes in the Brancacci Chapel of the Church of Santa Maria del Carmine in Florence also show his revolutionizing style. His fresco called *The Tribute Money*, c. 1427 [**Fig. 12.4**], reflects his concern with realistic depiction of human beings. The central scene portrays Christ telling Peter that he can find the tax money for the temple in the mouth of a fish; at the left Peter recovers the coin of tribute; at the right he makes the tribute payment (Matthew 17:24–27). The clusters of figures surrounding Christ reflect a faithfulness to observed humanity that must have been startling to Masaccio's contemporaries, who had never seen anything quite like it. The figures are in a space made believable by the receding lines of the buildings to the right. The fresco of the *Expulsion of Adam and Eve from Eden* [**Fig. 12.5**] in the same chapel shows not only realism in the figures, but also a profound sense of human emotions: the shame and dismay of the first human beings as they are driven from the Garden of Paradise.

The revolutionary character of Masaccio's work was recognized in his own time. His influence on any number of Florentine painters who worked later in the century is clear. Two generations after Masaccio's death the young Michelangelo often crossed the river Arno to sketch the frescoes in the Brancacci chapel. In the next century, Giorgio Vasari (1511–1574) in his *Lives of the Artists* would judge Masaccio's influence as basic and crucial: "The superb Masaccio . . . adopted a new manner for his heads, his draperies, buildings, and nudes, his colors, and foreshortening. He thus brought into existence the modern style which, beginning during his period, has been employed by all of our artists down to the present day."

The Baptistery Competition The innovative character of fifteenth-century art was not limited to painting. Significant changes were occurring in sculpture and architecture as well. A famous competition was announced in 1401 for the right to decorate the doors of the Florence Baptistery, dedicated to Saint John the Baptist and a focal point of Florentine life. The baptistery is an ancient octagonal Romanesque building which, in the fifteenth century, had such a reputation for antiquity that some thought it had originally been a Roman temple. Vasari tells us that an eminent group of artists including Lorenzo Ghiberti (1378–1455) and Filippo Brunelleschi (1377–1466) were among the competitors. Ghiberti won.

A comparison of the Brunelleschi and Ghiberti panels shows the differences between the two and allows us to infer the criteria used to judge the winner. The assigned subject for the competition was Abraham's sacrifice of

◆ **12.5** Masaccio, *Expulsion of Adam and Eve from Eden*, c. 1425. The artist manages to convey a sense of movement as well as the expelled couple's deep psychological distress and shame.

Fresco, 7′¼″ x 2′11″ (2.14 x .90 m). Brancacci Chapel, Santa Maria del Carmine, Florence, Italy//© Erich Lessing Art Resource, NY

◆ **12.6** Filippo Brunelleschi, *The Sacrifice of Isaac*, 1401–1402. Competition panel for the North Doors of the Baptistery of Florence. Note the figures spilling over the bottom part of the frame.

Gilt bronze relief, 21″ x 17½″ (53 x 44 cm). Museo Nazionale del Bargello, Florence, Italy//© Scala/Art Resource, NY

◆ **12.7** Lorenzo Ghiberti, *The Sacrifice of Isaac*, 1401–1402. The winning panel in the competition for the North Doors of the Baptistery of Florence.

Gilt bronze relief, 21″ x 17½″ (53 x 44 cm). Museo Nazionale del Bargello, Florence, Italy//© Alinari/Art Resource, NY

Isaac (Genesis 22:1–14). Brunelleschi's version [**Fig. 12.6**] has a certain vigor, but it is a busy and crowded composition. The figures of the servants spill out of the four-leaf or quatrefoil frame, whereas the major figures (the ram, the angel, and the two principals) are in flattened two-dimensional profile with little background space.

By contrast, Ghiberti's panel on the same subject [**Fig. 12.7**] is divided dramatically by a slashing diagonal line separating the two sets of actors into clearly designated planes of action. The drastically foreshortened angel appears to be flying into the scene from deep space. Furthermore, as a close examination of the cast shows, Ghiberti's panel is a technical tour de force. Except for the figure of Isaac and Abraham's left foot (and part of the rock it rests on), the entire scene was cast as a single unit. Demonstrating his strong background as a goldsmith, Ghiberti finely modeled and skillfully finished his panel. It is a piece of fierce sentiment, mathematical perspective, and exquisite work.

Ghiberti worked for almost a quarter of a century on the North Doors, completing twenty panels. Just as he was finishing, the cathedral authorities commissioned him (in 1425) to execute another set of panels for the East Doors, those facing the cathedral. This commission occupied the next quarter of a century (from roughly 1425 to 1452 or 1453), and the results of these labors were so striking that Michelangelo later in the century said Ghiberti's East Doors were not unworthy to be called the "Gates of Paradise," and they are so-called to this day.

The panels of the East Doors [**Fig. 12.8**] differed radically in style and composition from the North Door panels. The Gothic style quatrefoils were replaced by more classically severe rectangular frames. The complete set of panels was framed, in turn, by a series of portrait busts of prophets and sibyls.

Although Brunelleschi lost to Ghiberti in the sculpture competition of 1401, he made a major contribution to this early developmental phase of Renaissance art in another area: architecture. During his stay in Rome, where he had gone with the sculptor Donatello after the competition, he studied Roman architectural monuments. In fact, Vasari records that Brunelleschi and Donatello were reputed to be treasure hunters because of their incessant prowling amid the ruins of the Roman Forum. These intensive studies, together with his own intuitive genius, gave Brunelleschi an idea for solving a problem then thought insoluble: how to construct the dome for the still unfinished Cathedral of Saint Mary of the Flower (Santa Maria del Fiore) in Florence.

The Florence Cathedral The Cathedral of Florence had been built by Arnolfo di Cambio in the previous century over the remains of the older Church of Santa Reparata. In the early fifteenth century, however, the church was still unfinished, although the nave was already complete [**Fig. 12.9**]. No one had quite figured out how to span the great area without immense buttresses on the outside and supporting armatures on the inside. Brunelleschi worked on this problem between 1417 and 1420, trying, simultaneously, to solve the technical aspects of doming the building and convincing the skeptical cathedral overseers that it could be done. He won the day eventually, but work on the dome was not completed until 1436.

◆ **12.8** Lorenzo Ghiberti, East Doors ("Gates of Paradise") of the Baptistery of the Cathedral of Florence, 1425–1452.

Gilt bronze relief, 17′ (5.18 m) high. Modern copy, c. 1980. Original panels in Museo del Opera del Duomo, Florence, Italy//© Alinari/Art Resource, NY

His solution, briefly, was to combine the buttressing methods of the Gothic cathedral and classical vaulting techniques that he had mastered by his careful study of the Roman Pantheon and other buildings from antiquity. By putting a smaller dome within the larger dome to support the greater weight of the outside dome, he could not only cover the great *tambour* ("drum") [**Fig. 12.10**] but also free the inside of the dome from any need for elaborate armatures or supporting structures. This dome was strong enough to support the lantern that eventually crowned the whole construction. It was a breathtaking technical achievement, as well as an aesthetic success, as any person viewing Florence from the surrounding hills can testify. Years later, writing about his own work on the dome of Saint Peter's in the Vatican, Michelangelo had Brunelleschi's dome in mind when he said, "I will create your sister; bigger but no more beautiful."

The technical brilliance of Brunelleschi's dome cannot be over praised, but his real architectural achievement lies in his building designs that break with older forms of architecture. His Foundling Hospital [**Fig. 12.11**], with its open-columned **loggias** and their

◆ **12.9** Cathedral of Florence in 1390. An artist's reconstruction of the cathedral as Brunelleschi would have found it when he began his work. (1) Façade and side wall. (2) Gallery. (3) Circular windows. (4) Armature under construction. (5) Vaulting under construction. (6) Sacristy piers. (7) Excavations for buttresses.

◆ **12.10** Cathedral of Florence in 1418. (1) Buttressing. (2) Completed drum (tambour). (3) Side tribunes under construction. (4) Armature under construction. (5) Vaulting under construction. (6) Sacristy piers.

◆ **12.11** Filippo Brunelleschi, Foundling Hospital (Ospedale degli Innocenti), Florence, Italy, 1419–1426. The glazed terracotta medallions of the swaddled children are from the della Robbia workshop in Florence.
(Image © Scala/Art Resource, NY)

graceful Corinthian pillars, arches, and **entablature**, is, despite its seeming simplicity, a highly intricate work, its proportions calculated with mathematical rigor. The building is an open departure from the heaviness of the Romanesque so common in the area of Tuscany as well as a rejection of the overly elaborate Gothic exteriors.

This same concern with Classical order, proportion, and serenity can be seen in Brunelleschi's finest work, the chapel he designed for the Pazzi family next to the Franciscan Church of Santa Croce in Florence [**Fig. 12.12**]. Its exterior evokes Roman austerity with its delicate columns, severe façade, and small dome reminiscent of the lines of Rome's Pantheon.

In this brief look at three different art forms and artists in the early fifteenth century, certain recurring words and themes give a rough descriptive outline of what the Florentine Renaissance style reflects: a concern with, and the technical ability to handle, space and volume in a believable way; a studious approach to models of art from ancient Rome; a departure from the more ethereal mode of medieval otherworldliness to a greater concern for human realism. The Florentine artistic temperament leaped over its medieval heritage (although not completely) in order to reaffirm what it considered the Classical ideal of ancient Rome and Greece.

◆ **12.12** Filippo Brunelleschi, Pazzi Chapel, Florence, Italy, 1430–1433. Part of the Franciscan Church of Santa Croce can be seen in the left background. *(Image © Nicolas Sapieha/Art Resource, NY)*

THE MEDICI ERA

The Florentine Republic was governed by representatives of the major trade guilds. This control by a select group of people who represented commercial power and wealth inevitably led to domination by the most wealthy of the group. From 1434 until 1492, Florence was under the control of one family: the Medici.

The Medici family had old, though until then undistinguished, roots in the countryside around Florence. Their prosperity in the fifteenth century rested mainly on their immense banking fortune. By the middle of that century, Medici branch banks existed in London, Naples, Cologne, Geneva, Lyons, Basel, Avignon, Bruges, Antwerp, Lübeck, Bologna, Rome, Pisa, and Venice. The great Flemish painting by Jan van Eyck, *Giovanni Arnolfini and His Bride* [**Fig. 12.13**], in fact, commemorates van Eyck's witnessing of the marriage in 1434 of this Florentine representative of the Medici bank in Bruges. Although it is more usual to look at the painting because of its exquisite technique, its rich symbolism, and its almost microscopic concern for detail, it is also profitable to view it sociologically as a testimony to how far the influence of the Medici extended.

COSIMO DE' MEDICI

Cosimo de' Medici (de facto ruler of Florence from 1434 to 1464) was an astute banker and a highly cultivated man of letters. His closest friends were professional humanists, collectors of books, and patrons of the arts. Cosimo spent vast sums on collecting and copying ancient manuscripts. He had his copyists work in a neat cursive hand that would later be the model for the form of letters we call *italic*. His collection of books (together with those added by later members of his family) formed the core of the great humanist collection housed today in the Laurentian Library in Florence.

Although Cosimo never mastered Greek to any degree, he was intensely interested in Greek philosophy and literature. He financed the chair of Greek at the ***Studium* of Florence**. When Greek prelates visited Florence during the ecumenical council held in 1439 (the council sought a union between the Greek and Latin churches), Cosimo took the opportunity to seek out scholars from Constantinople in the retinue of the prelates. He was particularly struck with the brilliance of Genisthos Plethon (c. 1355–1452), who lectured on Plato. Cosimo persuaded Plethon to remain in the city to continue his lectures.

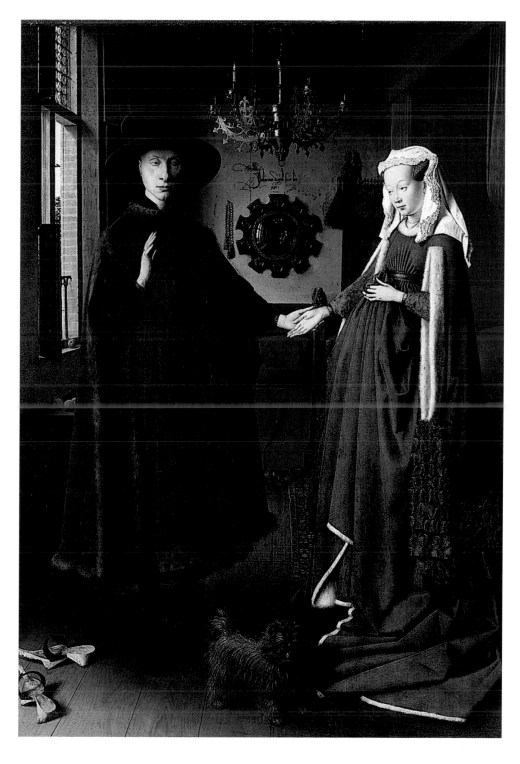

◆ **12.13** Jan van Eyck, *Giovanni Arnolfini and His Bride*, 1434. The artist, reflected in the mirror on the back wall, stands in the doorway. The Latin words on the wall read "Jan van Eyck was here." The pair of sandals at the lower left symbolizes a sacred event; the dog is a symbol of fidelity and domestic peace.

Tempera and oil on wood, approx. 32″ x 23″ (81.3 x 59.7 cm). National Gallery, London, UK// © Erich Lessing/Art Resource, NY

The Platonic Academy Cosimo's most significant contribution to the advancement of Greek studies was the foundation and endowment of an academy for the study of Plato. For years Cosimo and his heirs supported a priest, Marsilio Ficino, in order to allow him to translate and comment on the works of Plato. In the course of his long life (he died in 1499), Ficino translated into Latin all of Plato, Plotinus, and other Platonic thinkers. He wrote his own compendium of Platonism called the *Theologia Platonica*. These translations and commentaries had an immense influence on art and intellectual life in Italy and beyond the Alps.

Cosimo often joined his friends at a suburban villa to discuss Plato under the tutelage of Ficino. This elite group embraced Plato's ideas of striving for the ideal good and persistently searching for truth and beauty.

This idealism became an important strain in Florentine culture. Ficino managed to combine his study of Plato with his own understanding of Christianity. Ficino coined the term "Platonic love"—the spiritual bond between two persons who were joined together in the contemplative search for the true, the good, and the beautiful. Cosimo, a pious man in his own right, found great consolation in this Christian Platonism of Ficino. "Come and join me as soon as you possibly can and be sure to bring with you Plato's treatise *On the Sovereign Good*," Cosimo once wrote his protégé: "There is no pursuit to which I would devote myself more zealously than the pursuit of truth. Come then and bring with you the lyre of Orpheus."

A fiercely patriotic Florentine known to his contemporaries as *Pater Patriae* ("Father of the Homeland"), Cosimo lavished his funds on art projects to enhance the beauty of the city, at the same time glorifying his family name and atoning for his sins, especially usury (taking interest on money), by acts of generous charity. He befriended and supported many artists. He was an intimate friend and financial supporter of the greatest Florentine sculptor of the first half of the fifteenth century, Donato di Niccolò di Betto Bardi (1386–1466), known as Donatello. Donatello was an eccentric genius who cared for little besides his work; it was said that he left his fees in a basket in his studio for the free use of his apprentices or whoever else might be in need.

Donatello Even today a leisurely stroll around the historic center of Florence can, in a short time, give an idea of the tremendous range of Donatello's imaginative and artistic versatility. One need only compare his early *Saint George* [**Fig. 12.14**], fiercely tense and classically severe, to the later bronze *David* [**Fig. 12.15**]. The *Saint George* is a niche sculpture originally executed for the Church of Or San Michele, whereas the *David* is meant to be seen from all sides. The *David*, a near life-size figure, is the first freestanding statue of a nude figure sculpted since Roman antiquity. It also marks a definite step in Renaissance taste: despite its subject, it is more clearly "pagan" than biblical in spirit. The sculptor obviously wanted to show the beauty of form of this adolescent male clothed only in carefully fashioned military leg armor and a Tuscan shepherd's hat. The figure was most likely made for a garden. Some scholars have speculated that the commission was from Cosimo, although clear documentary proof is lacking.

Donatello's larger-than-life-sized wooden figure of Mary Magdalene [**Fig. 12.16**] seems light years away from the spirit of *David*. Carved around 1455, it shows the Magdalene as an ancient penitent, ravaged by time and her own life of penance. The viewer is asked to mentally compare this older woman with the younger

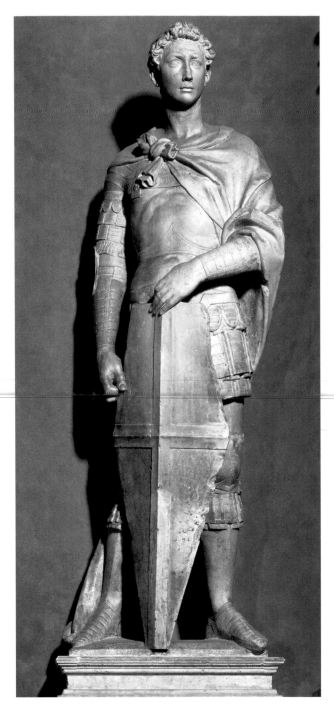

◆ **12.14** Donatello, *Saint George*, 1415–1417. Originally, the saint grasped a spear in his right hand.

From Or San Michele. Marble (replaced by a bronze copy), 6′10″ (2.08 m) high. Museo Nazionale del Bargello, Florence, Italy//© Scala/Art Resource, NY

woman described in the Bible. The statue, then, is a profound meditation on the vanity of life, a theme lingering in Florentine culture from its medieval past and, at the same time, a hymn to the penitential spirit that made Magdalene a saint in the popular imagination.

◆ **12.15** Donatello, *David*, c. 1428–1432. The biblical episode of David killing Goliath is shown at three stages in this book. Michelangelo's *David* is shown as he sees his foe (Figure 12.29). Bernini's *David* is shown in the exertion of his attack (Figure 15.8). Here, Donatello's *David* reposes after the attack as he leans on the sword of the giant and rests his other foot on Goliath's severed head.

Bronze, 5′2½″ (1.58 m) high. Museo Nazionale del Bargello, Florence, Italy//© Erich Lessing/Art Resource, NY

◆ **12.16** Donatello, *Saint Mary Magdalene*, c. 1454–1455. Cleaned and restored after flood damage in 1966, this statue now reveals some traces of the original **polychrome**.

From the Baptistery of the Florence Cathedral. Polychromed and gilded wood, 6′2″ (1.88 m) high. Museo Dell'Opera del Duomo, Florence, Italy//© Scala/Art Resource, NY

Fra Angelico Cosimo de' Medici had a particular fondness for the Dominican Convent of San Marco in Florence. In 1437 he asked Michelozzo (1396–1472), the architect who designed the Medici palace in Florence, to rebuild the convent for the friars. One of the Dominicans who lived there was a painter of estab-

lished reputation, Fra Angelico (1387–1455). When Michelozzo's renovations were done, Fra Angelico decorated many of the convent walls and most of the cells of the friars with paintings, executing many of these works under the watchful eye of Cosimo, who stayed regularly at the convent. Fra Angelico's famous

◆ **12.17** Fra Angelico, *Annunciation*, 1445–1450. Note how the architecture frames the two principal figures in the scene. Botanists can identify the flowers in the garden to the left.

Fresco, 7′6″ x 10′5″ (2.29 x 3.18 m). Museo di San Marco, Florence, Italy//© Scala/Art Resource, NY

Annunciation fresco [**Fig. 12.17**] shows his indebtedness to the artistic tradition of Masaccio: the use of architecture to frame space, a sense of realism and drama, and a close observation of the actual world.

Paolo Uccello Another painter who enjoyed the Medici largesse was Paolo Uccello (1397–1475), who created a series of three paintings for the Medici palace commemorating the earlier Battle of San Romano (1432) in which the Florentines defeated the Sienese. The paintings (now dispersed to museums in London, Florence, and Paris) show Uccello's intense fascination with perspective [**Fig. 12.18**]. The scenes are marked by slashing lines, foreshortened animals, receding backgrounds, and seemingly cluttered landscapes filled with figures of differing proportion. When the three paintings were together as a unit, they gave a panoramic sweep of the battle running across thirty-four feet (10.3 m) of the wall space.

Cosimo's last years were racked with chronic illness and depression brought on by the premature deaths of his son Giovanni and a favorite grandson, as well as the physical weakness of his other son, Piero. Toward the end of his life, Cosimo's wife once found him in his study with his eyes closed. She asked him why he sat in that fashion. "To get them accustomed to it," he replied. Cosimo de'

Medici died on August 1, 1464. His position as head of the family and as first citizen of the city was assumed by his son Piero, called "the Gouty" in reference to the affliction of gout from which he suffered all his life.

PIERO DE' MEDICI

Piero's control over the city lasted only five years. It was a time beset by much political turmoil as well as continued artistic activity. Piero continued to support his father's old friend Donatello and maintained his patronage of Ficino's Platonic labors and his generous support of both religious and civic art and architecture.

Botticelli One new painter who came under the care of Piero was Alessandro di Mariano dei Filipepi (1444–1510), known more familiarly as Sandro Botticelli. Botticelli earlier had been an apprentice of the painter Fra Filippo Lippi (c. 1406–1469), but Piero and his aristocratic wife Lucrezia Tornabuoni (a highly cultivated woman who was a religious poet) took Botticelli into their home and treated him as a family member. Botticelli stayed closely allied with the Medici for decades.

One tribute to the Medici was Botticelli's painting *Adoration of the Magi* [**Fig. 12.19**], a work commissioned for the Florentine Church of Santa Maria Novella. The

◆ **12.18** Paolo Uccello, *The Battle of San Romano*, 1455. The upraised spears and javelins give the picture a sense of frantic complexity.

Tempera on wood, 6′10″ x 10′7″ (1.83 x 3.22 m). Galleria degli Uffizi, Florence, Italy//© Erich Lessing/Art Resource, NY

◆ **12.19** Sandro Botticelli, *Adoration of the Magi*, 1475. Cosimo de' Medici kneels in front of the Virgin; Lorenzo is in the left foreground; Giuliano is at the right against the wall. The figure in the right foreground looking out toward the viewer is thought to be the artist.

Tempera on wood, 3′7½″ x 4′4¾″ (1.1 x 1.34 m). Galleria degli Uffizi, Florence, Italy//© Scala/Art Resource, NY

Magi are shown as three generations of the Medici family; there are also portraits of Lorenzo and Giuliano, the sons of Piero. The painting was paid for by a friend of the Medici family. Many scholars believe it was a votive offering to the church in thanksgiving for the safety of the family during the political turmoil of 1466.

The theme of the Magi was a favorite of the Medici. They regularly took part in the pageants in the streets of Florence celebrating the three kings on the Feast of the Epiphany (January 6). It is for that reason, one assumes, that Piero commissioned a fresco of that scene for the chapel of his own palace. The painter was Benozzo Gozzoli (1420–1495), once an apprentice of Fra Angelico. Gozzoli produced an opulent scene filled with personages of Oriental splendor modeled on the Greek scholars who had come to Florence during the ecumenical council and who stayed on to teach Greek. The fresco also included some contemporary portraits, including a self-portrait of the artist himself [**Fig. 12.20**].

LORENZO DE' MEDICI ("THE MAGNIFICENT")

Piero de' Medici died in 1469. The mantle of power settled on the shoulders of his son Lorenzo, who accepted the responsibility with pragmatic resignation, saying, "It bodes ill for any wealthy man in Florence who doesn't control political power." Lorenzo, a rather ugly man with a high raspy voice, became the most illustrious of the family; in his own day he was known as Lorenzo il Magnifico ("the magnificent"). His accomplishments were so many and varied that the last half of the fifteenth century in Florence is often called the Laurentian Era.

◆ **12.20** Benozzo Gozzoli, *The Journey of the Magi*, c. 1459. The horseman, representing one of the Magi, is thought to be an idealized portrait of Byzantine Emperor John VII Paleologus, who visited Florence at the invitation of Cosimo de' Medici for a church council in 1439.

Detail from fresco. Entire work, 12′4½″ (3.77 m). Chapel, Palazzo Medici Riccardi, Florence, Italy//© Erich Lessing/Art Resource, NY

VALUES

Intellectual Synthesis

It would be a bit misleading to see the Renaissance as a naïve recovery of the Classical past. What actually occurred was a desire for *synthesis*, which is to say, a recovery of the inherited past of Greece and Rome in order to use that recovery for the needs and aspirations of the time. The first step in this synthesis required a study of the past. It is worthwhile noting how extensive that study was. It ranged from the careful observation and measurement of ancient buildings to the close study of archaeological remains from Rome like coins, carved gems, and sculpture to the humanistic work of editing texts, translating them, and providing those aids (like dictionaries, etc.) that would permit this work to go on. The synthesis came when people took what they had recovered from the past (a process called in French *ressourcement*—"going back to the sources") and transformed what they discovered to meet the needs of their own contemporary situation.

That process of synthesis needs emphasis if one is to understand what happened in, say, fifteenth-century Florence. Brunelleschi did not study Rome's Pantheon to rebuild it but as an exercise in order to better create church architecture. Ficino loved Plato but he thought that in Plato he could explain the Christian faith better than the schoolmen of an earlier period. Machiavelli and Erasmus—radically different types that we have noted in the text—loved the classics for their own sakes, but they also saw in them pragmatic clues that would help them understand contemporary problems ranging from how politics ought to be ordered to how church reform might be effected.

If one is to understand the Renaissance, it is crucial to see that the Classical past was not merely ancient history but a source for new and innovative ideas and concepts that addressed real and pertinent issues.

Lorenzo continued the family tradition of art patronage by supporting various projects and by adding to the Medici collection of ancient gems, other antiquities, and books. He was also more directly involved in the arts. Lorenzo was an accomplished poet, but his reputation as a political and social leader has made us forget that he was an important contributor to the development of vernacular Italian poetry. He continued the sonnet tradition begun by Petrarch. One of his most ambitious projects—done in conscious imitation of Dante's *Vita Nuova*—was a long work that alternated his own sonnets with extended prose commentaries; this was the *Comento ad alcuni sonetti* (*A Commentary on Some Sonnets*, begun c. 1476–1477). In addition to this ambitious work, Lorenzo wrote hunting songs, poems for the carnival season, religious poetry, and occasional burlesque poems with a cheerfully bawdy tone.

The poem for which Lorenzo is best known is "The Song of Bacchus." Written in 1490, its opening stanzas echo the old Roman dictum of living for the present because life is short and the future is uncertain.

The Song of Bacchus
How beautiful is youth,
That flees so fleetingly by.
Let him be who chases joy
For tomorrow there is no certainty.

Look at Bacchus and Ariadne
So beautiful and much in love.
Since deceitful time flees
They are always happy.

Joyful little satyrs of the nymphs enamored,
In every cave and glade
Have set traps by the hundred;
Now, by Bacchus intoxicated,
Dance and leap without end.

Let him be who chases joy
For tomorrow there is no certainty.

Lorenzo's interests in learning were deep. He had been tutored as a youth by Ficino and as an adult continued the habit of spending evenings with an elite group of friends and Ficino. He often took with him his friend Botticelli and a young sculptor who worked in a Medici-sponsored sculpture garden, Michelangelo Buonarroti.

The Laurentian patronage of learning was extensive. Lorenzo contributed the funds necessary to rebuild the University of Pisa and designated it the principal university of Tuscany (Galileo taught there in the next century). He continued to underwrite the study of Greek at the *Studium* of Florence.

The Greek faculty at Florence attracted students from all over Europe. This center was a principal

◆ **12.21** Sandro Botticelli, *La Primavera (Springtime)*, c. 1478. This work and *The Birth of Venus* (Figure 12.22) are the best examples of Botticelli's fusion of pagan symbolism, Neo-Platonic idealism, and the quest for the ideal female.

Tempera on canvas, 6'8" x 10'4" (2.03 x 3.14 m). Galleria degli Uffizi, Florence, Italy//© Scala/Art Resource, NY

means by which Greek learning was exported to the rest of Europe, especially to countries beyond the Alps. English scholars such as Thomas Linacre, John Colet, and William Grocyn came to Florence to study Greek and other Classical disciplines. Linacre was later to gain fame as a physician and founder of England's Royal College of Physicians. Grocyn returned to England to found the chair of Greek at Oxford. Colet used his training to become a biblical scholar and a founder of Saint Paul's School in London. The two greatest French humanists of the sixteenth century had, as young men, come under the influence of Greek learning from Italy.

Guillaume Budé (died 1540) founded, under the patronage of the French kings, a library at Fontainebleau that was the beginning of the Bibliothèque Nationale of Paris. He also founded the Collège de France, still the most prestigious center of higher learning in France. Jacques Lefèvre d'Étaples had also studied in Florence and became the greatest intellectual church reformer of sixteenth-century France.

Lorenzo was less interested in painting than either his father Piero or his grandfather Cosimo. Neverthe-

less, some of the paintings created during his lifetime have come to epitomize the spirit of the age because of their close familial and philosophical links to Lorenzo's family. This is especially true of the work of Botticelli and, more specifically, his paintings *La Primavera* and *The Birth of Venus*.

Botticelli Botticelli painted *La Primavera* (*Springtime*) [**Fig. 12.21**] for a cousin of Lorenzo named Lorenzo di' Pierfrancesco. One of the most popular paintings in Western art, *La Primavera* is an elaborate mythological **allegory** of the burgeoning fertility of the world. The allegory has never been fully explicated, but the main characters are clearly discernible: at the extreme right the wind god Zephyr pursues a nymph who is transformed into the goddess Flora (next figure), who scatters her flowers; at the left are the god Mercury and three dancing Graces. Over the Graces and the central female figure (who represents Spring) is blind Cupid ready to launch an arrow that will bring love to the one he hits. The rich carpeting of springtime flowers and the background of the orange grove provide luxuriant surroundings.

◆ **12.22** Sandro Botticelli, *The Birth of Venus*, c. 1482. Scholars have expended great effort to unlock the full meaning of this highly allegorical work and *La Primavera*. A comparison of the two shows some close similarity in the figures.

Tempera on canvas, approx. 5′8″ x 9′1″ (1.72 x 2.77 m). Galleria degli Uffizi, Florence, Italy//© Scala/ Art Resource, NY

In the sixteenth century, Vasari saw *La Primavera* in Lorenzo di' Pierfrancesco's villa together with another painting by Botticelli, *The Birth of Venus* (c. 1482). A gentle, almost fragile work of idealized beauty, *The Birth of Venus* [**Fig. 12.22**] shows the wind gods gently stirring the sea breezes as Venus emerges from the sea and an attendant waits for her with a billowing cape. The Venus figure is inspired by the *Venus pudica* (the "Modest" Venus) figures of antiquity. The most significant aspect of the painting (and of *La Primavera*) is the impulse, motivated by Platonism, to idealize the figures. Botticelli is trying to depict not a particular woman but the essential ideal of female beauty. The Venus of this painting reflects a complex synthesis of Platonic idealism, Christian mysticism relating to the Virgin, and the Classical ideal of the female figure of Venus.

Leonardo da Vinci Leonardo da Vinci (1452–1519) came from a small Tuscan town near Florence called Vinci. He lived in Florence until the 1480s, when he left for Milan; from there he moved restlessly from place to place until his death in France. Leonardo has been called *the* genius of the Renaissance not so much for what he left in the way of art—although his *Mona Lisa* [**Fig. 12.23**] is surely among the more famous art pieces of all time—as for the things that he dreamed of doing, the problems he set himself to solve, and the phenomena he observed and set down in his *Notebooks*.

If we had nothing but the *Notebooks*, we would still say that Leonardo had one of humanity's most fertile minds. He left sketches for flying machines, submarines, turbines, elevators, ideal cities, and machines of almost every

◆ **12.23** Leonardo da Vinci, *Mona Lisa*, c. 1503–1505.

Oil on wood, approx. 30″ x 21″ (76.2 x 53.3 cm). Musée du Louvre, Paris, France//© Réunion des Musées Nationaux/Art Resource, NY

◆ **12.24** Leonardo da Vinci, *Helicopter or Aerial Screw*, c. 1485–1490. Leonardo's code writing is decipherable only when held up to a mirror.

Bibliothèque de l'Institut de France, Paris, France//© Réunion des Musées Nationaux/Art Resource, NY

◆ **12.26** Leonardo da Vinci, *Madonna of the Rocks*, begun 1483. Another version of this painting hangs in London's National Gallery, but this one is thought to be entirely from the hand of Leonardo. Never completed, it was intended to be part of a large altarpiece honoring the Virgin.

Panel painting transferred to canvas, 78″ x 48″ (198.1 x 121.9 cm). Musée du Louvre, Paris, France//© Scala/Art Resource, NY

◆ **12.25** Leonardo da Vinci, *The Last Supper*, 1495–1498. Below the figure of Christ one can still see the doorway cut into the wall during the Napoleonic period by soldiers who used the monastery as a military headquarters.

Fresco, post-restoration, 14′5″ x 28′¼″. Refectory, Santa Maria delle Grazie, Milan, Italy. Image © The Gallery Collection/CORBIS description [**Fig. 12.24**]. His knowledge of anatomy was unsurpassed (he came close to discovering the circulation path of blood), and his interest in the natural worlds of geology and botany was keen. The *Notebooks*, in short, reflect a restlessly searching mind that sought to understand the world and its constituent parts. Its chosen fields of inquiry are dominated by many of the characteristics common to the period: a concern with mathematics, a deep respect for the natural world, and a love for beauty.

Leonardo's *The Last Supper* [**Fig. 12.25**] is a good example of these characteristics. Leonardo chooses the moment when Jesus announces that someone at the table will betray him. The apostles are arranged in four distinct groups. The central figure of Christ is highlighted by the apostles, who either look at him or gesture toward him. Christ is haloed by the central window space behind him, with the lines of the room all converging toward that point. The painting has great emotional power even though it is mathematically one of the most perfect paintings ever executed.

Leonardo's expressive power as a painter is ably illustrated in his striking *Madonna of the Rocks* [**Fig. 12.26**], begun shortly after his arrival in Milan in 1483, a decade before he painted *The Last Supper*. The Virgin drapes her right arm over the figure of the infant Saint John the Baptist while her hand hovers in protective blessing over the Christ child. An exquisitely rendered angel points to the scene. The cavern-like space in the background would remind the perceptive viewer both of the cave at Bethlehem where Christ was born and the cave in which he would be buried. Leonardo's rendering of the jagged rocks stands in sharper relief because of the misty light in the extreme background. The particular beauty of the painting derives at least partially from the juxtaposition of the beautifully rendered persons in all their humanity with the wildly mysterious natural frame in which they are set.

Michelangelo The other great genius of the late fifteenth century is Michelangelo Buonarroti (1476–1564). After his early days in the sculpture garden of Lorenzo, he produced many of his greatest works in Rome (discussed in Chapter 13). However, even a few examples of his early work show both the great promise of Michelangelo's talent and some of the influences he absorbed in Florence under the Medici. The *Madonna of the Stairs* [**Fig. 12.27**], an early marble relief, reflects his study of ancient relief or **cameo carving** (which he may well have seen in Lorenzo's collection). By 1498 his style had matured enough for him to carve, for a French cardinal in Rome, the universally admired *Pietá* [**Fig. 12.28**], which combines his deep sensitivity

◆ **12.27** Michelangelo, *Madonna of the Stairs*, 1489–1492. A fine example of low-relief (bas-relief) carving, with its figures nearly flush to the marble surface.

Marble, 21¾″ x 15¾″ (55 x 40 cm). Casa Buonarroti, Florence, Italy // © Scala/Art Resource, NY

◆ **12.28** Michangelo, *Pietá*, 1498–1499. One of the most finished of Michelangelo's sculptures, its high sheen is the result of intense polishing of the marble.

Marble, 5′9″ (1.75 m) high. Saint Peter's, Rome, Vatican State // © Scala/Art Resource, NY

◆ **12.29** Michelangelo, *David*, 1501–1504. Much of the weight of this figure is borne by David's right leg (with the stylized tree trunk in the rear) in a position called *contraposto* in Italian.

Marble, 18′ (5.49 m) high. Accademia di Belle Arti, Florence, Italy//© Erich Lessing/Art Resource, NY

with an idealism in the beauty of the Madonna's face that is reminiscent of Botticelli.

Finally, this early period of Michelangelo's work includes a sculpture that has become almost synonymous with Florence: the *David* [**Fig. 12.29**], carved in 1501–1504 from a massive piece of Carrara marble that had lain behind the cathedral in Florence since the middle of the preceding century. The sculpture's great size and its almost photographically realistic musculature combine to make it one of Michelangelo's clearest

statements of idealized beauty. The statue was intended to be seen from below with the left arm (the one touching the shoulder) facing the viewer and the right side turned back toward the cathedral. In fact, it was placed outside the Palazzo Vecchio as a symbol of the civic power of the city, where it remained until weathering and damage required its removal to a museum in the nineteenth century.

It has been said that Botticelli's paintings, the *David* of both Donatello and Michelangelo, and the general skepticism of a mind like Leonardo's are all symptoms of the general pagan tone of Laurentian Florence—that Athens and Rome, in short, seemed far more important to fifteenth-century Florence than did Jerusalem. There is no doubt that the Classical revival was central to Florentine culture. Neither is there any doubt that the times had little patience with, or admiration for, medieval culture.

Savonarola Nonetheless, the notion that the Renaissance spirit marked a clean break with medieval ideals must take into account the life and career of the Dominican preacher and reformer Fra Savonarola (1452–1498). Savonarola lived at the Convent of San Marco in Florence from 1490 until his execution in 1498. His urgent preaching against the vanities of Florence in general and the degeneracy of its art and culture in particular had an electric effect on the populace. His influence was not limited to the credulous masses or workers in the city. Lorenzo called him to his own deathbed in 1492 to receive the last sacraments, even though Savonarola had been a bitter and open enemy of Medici control over the city. Savonarola, in fact, wanted a restored Republic with a strong ethical and theocratic base. Botticelli was so impressed by Savonarola that he burned some of his more worldly paintings, and scholars see in his last works a more profound religiosity derived from the contact with the reforming friar. Michelangelo, when an old man in Rome, told a friend that he could still hear the words of Savonarola ringing in his ears. Pico della Mirandola (1463–1494), one of the most brilliant humanists of the period, turned from his polyglot studies of Greek, Hebrew, Aramaic, and Latin to a devout life under the direction of the friar; only his early death prevented him from joining Savonarola as a friar at San Marco.

Savonarola's hold over the Florentine political order (for a brief time he was the de facto ruler of the city) ended in 1498 when he defied papal excommunication and was then strangled and burned in the public square before the Palazzo Vecchio. By that time Lorenzo had been dead for six years, and the Medici family had lost power in Florence. They were to return in the next century, but the Golden Age of Lorenzo had ended with a spasm of medieval piety. The influence of the city and its ideals had, however, already spread far beyond its boundaries.

THE CHARACTER OF RENAISSANCE HUMANISM

Jules Michelet, a nineteenth-century French historian, first coined the word *Renaissance* specifically to describe the cultural period of fifteenth-century Florence. The broad outline of this rebirth is described by the Swiss historian Jakob Burckhardt in his massive *The Civilization of the Renaissance in Italy*, published in 1860, a book that is the beginning point for any discussion of the topic. Burckhardt's thesis is simple and persuasive. European culture, he argued, was reborn in the fifteenth century after a long dormant period that extended from the fall of the Roman Empire until the beginning of the fourteenth century.

The characteristics of this new birth, Burckhardt said, were first noticeable in Italy and were the foundation blocks of the modern world. It was in late fourteenth- and fifteenth-century Italy that new ideas about the nature of the political order developed, of which the Republican government of Florence is an example, as well as the consciousness of the artist as an individual seeking personal fame. This pursuit of glory and fame was in sharp contrast to the self-effacing and world-denying attitude of the Middle Ages. Burckhardt also saw the thirst for Classical learning, the desire to construct a humanism from that learning, and an emphasis on the good life as an intellectual repudiation of medieval religion and ethics.

Burckhardt's ideas have provoked strong reactions from historians and scholars, many of whom reject his theory as simplistic. Charles Homer Haskins, an American scholar, attacked Burckhardt's ideas in 1927 in a book the title of which gives away his line of argument: *The Renaissance of the Twelfth Century*. Haskins pointed out that everything Burckhardt said about Florentine life in the fifteenth century could be said with equal justification about Paris in the twelfth century. Furthermore (as noted in Chapter 10), scholars have also spoken of a Carolingian Renaissance identified with the court of Emperor Charlemagne.

What is the truth? Was there a genuine Renaissance in fifteenth-century Italy? Many scholars today try to mediate a position between Burckhardt and his detractors. They admit that something new was happening in the intellectual and cultural life of fifteenth-century Italy and that contemporaries were conscious of it. "May every thoughtful spirit thank God that it has been given to him to be born in this new age, so filled with hope and promise, which already enjoys a greater array of gifted persons than the world has seen in the past thousand years," wrote Matteo Palmieri, a Florentine businessman, in 1436. Yet this "new age" of which Palmieri spoke did not spring up overnight. The roots must be traced to Italy's long tradition of lay learning, the Franciscan movement of the thirteenth century, the relative absence of feudalism in Italy, and the long maintenance of Italian city life. In short, something new was happening precisely because Italy's long historical antecedents permitted it.

The question remains, however: what was new in the Renaissance? The Renaissance was surely more than a change in artistic taste or an advance in technological artistic skill. We need to go deeper. What motivated the shift in artistic taste? What fueled the personal energy that produced artistic innovation? What caused flocks of foreign scholars to cross the Alps to study in Florence and in other centers where they could absorb the "new learning"?

The answer to these questions, briefly, is this: There arose in Italy, as early as the time of Petrarch (1304–1372), but clearly in the fifteenth century, a strong conviction that humanist learning would not only ennoble and perfect the individual but could also serve as a powerful instrument for social and religious reform. Very few Renaissance humanists denied the need for God's grace, but all felt that human intellectual effort should be the first concern of anyone who wished truly to advance the good of self or society. The career of Pico della Mirandola, one of the most brilliant and gifted Florentine humanist scholars, illustrates this humanist belief.

Pico della Mirandola Pico della Mirandola (1463–1494) was an intimate friend of Lorenzo de' Medici and a companion of the Platonic scholar Marsilio Ficino. Precociously brilliant, Pico once bragged, not totally implausibly, that he had read every book in Italy. He was deeply involved with the intellectual life of his day.

Pico was convinced that all human learning could be synthesized in a way such as to yield basic and elementary truths. To demonstrate this, he set out to master all the systems of knowledge that then existed. He thoroughly mastered the Latin and Greek classics. He studied medieval Aristotelianism at the University of Paris and learned Arabic and the Islamic tradition. He was the first Christian in his day to take an active interest in Hebrew culture; he learned Hebrew and Aramaic and studied the **Talmud** with Jewish scholars. At the age of twenty, Pico proposed to defend at Rome his nine hundred *theses* ("intellectual propositions"), which he claimed summed up all current learning and speculation. Church leaders attacked some of his propositions as unorthodox; Pico left Rome and the debate was never held.

The preface to these theses, called the *Oration on the Dignity of Man*, has often been cited as the first and most important document of Renaissance humanism. Its central thesis is that humanity stands at the apex of creation in a way such as to create the link between the world of God and that of the creation. Pico brings

VOICES OF THEIR TIMES

Fra Savonarola

From a sermon by Fra Savonarola to a congregation in the Cathedral of Florence.

Creatures are beautiful insofar as they share in and approach the beauty of the soul. Take two women of like bodily beauty, and if one is holy and the other is evil, you will notice that the holy one is more loved by everyone than the evil one, so all eyes will rest on her.

The same is true of men. A holy man, however deformed bodily, pleases everyone because, no matter how ugly he may be, his holiness shows itself and makes everything he does gracious.

Think how beautiful the Virgin was, who was so holy. She shines forth in all she does. Saint Thomas [Aquinas] says that no one who saw her ever looked on her with evil desire, so evident was her sanctity.

But now think of the saints as they are painted in the churches of the city. Young men go about saying "This is the Magdalen and that is Saint John," and only because the paintings in the church are modeled on them. This is a terrible thing because the things of God are undervalued.

You fill the churches with your own vanity.

Do you think that the Virgin Mary went about dressed as she is shown in paintings? I tell you she went about dressed like a poor person with simplicity and her face so covered that it was hardly seen. The same is true of Saint Elizabeth.

You would do well to destroy pictures so unsuitably conceived. You make the Virgin Mary look like a whore. How the worship of God is mocked!

---

his wide learning to bear on this fundamental proposition: humanity is a great miracle. He not only calls on the traditional biblical and Classical sources but also cites, from his immense reading, the opinions of the great writers of the Jewish, Arabic, and Neo-Platonic traditions. The enthusiasm of the youthful Pico for his subject is as apparent as his desire to display his learning.

Scholars disagree on Pico's originality as a thinker. Many argue that his writings are a hodgepodge of knowledge without any genuine synthesis. There is no disagreement, however, about Pico's immense ability as a student of languages and culture to open new fields of study and, in that way, contribute much to the enthusiasm for learning in his own day. His reputation attracted students to him. The most influential of these was a German named Johann Reuchlin (1455–1522), who came to Florence to study Hebrew with Pico. After mastering that language and Greek as well, Reuchlin went back to Germany to pursue his studies and to apply them to biblical scholarship. In the early sixteenth century he came under the influence of Martin Luther (see Chapter 14) but never joined the Reformation. Reuchlin passionately defended the legitimacy of biblical studies oriented to the original languages. When his approach was attacked in one of those periodic outbursts of anti-Semitism so characteristic of European culture of the time, Reuchlin, true to his humanist impulses, not only defended his studies as

a true instrument of religious reform but also made an impassioned plea for toleration that was not characteristic of his time.

Printing Technology and the Spread of Humanism The export of humanist learning was not restricted to the exchange of scholars between Italy and the countries to the north. Printing had been invented in the early fifteenth century, so books were becoming more accessible to the educated classes. The most famous humanist printer and publisher of the fifteenth century was Aldus Manutius (1449–1515), whose Aldine Press was in Venice, his native city. Aldus was a scholar in his own right; he learned Greek from refugee scholars who settled in Venice after the fall of Constantinople in 1453. Recognizing the need for competent and reliable editions of the Classical authors, he employed professional humanists to collate and correct manuscripts. Erasmus, the greatest of the northern humanists, was, for a time, in his employ.

Aldus was also a technical innovator. He designed Greek **typefaces**, created italic type fonts (modeled after the scribal hand used for copying Florentine manuscripts), developed new inks, and obtained new paper from the nearby town of Fabriano, still a source of fine papers for artists and printmakers. His books were near pocket-size, easily portable, and inexpensive.

The scope of the press's activities was huge: after 1494, Aldus (and later his son) published, in about twenty years, the complete works of Aristotle and the works of Plato, Pindar, Herodotus, Sophocles, Aristophanes, Xenophon, and Demosthenes. Aldus reissued the Latin classics in better editions and published vernacular writers like Dante and Petrarch as well as contemporary poets like Poliziano, the Florentine friend of Lorenzo.

The Aldine Press was not an isolated phenomenon. Germany, where Western printing really started, already had an active printing and publishing tradition. Johann Gutenberg (c. 1395–1468) originated the method of printing from movable type that continued to be used with virtually no change until the late nineteenth century. Gutenberg finished printing a Bible at Mainz in 1455–1456. The first book printed in English, *The Recuyell* (collection) of the *Historyes of Troye,* was published by William Caxton in 1475. Historians have estimated that before 1500, European presses produced between six and nine million books in thirteen thousand different editions. Nearly fifty thousand of these books survive in libraries throughout the world.

This conjunction of pride in humanist learning and technology of printing had profound consequences for European culture. It permitted the wide diffusion of ideas to large numbers of people in a relatively short time. There is no doubt that vigorous intellectual movements—one thinks immediately of the Protestant Reformation—benefited immensely from printing. This communications revolution was as important for the Renaissance period as radio, film, television, and the Internet have been for our own.

Women and the Renaissance

Recent scholars have asked: did women have an intellectual/artistic rebirth? It is clear that women, as the idealization of certain images and ideas, were central to the Renaissance conception of beauty (think of Botticelli's *Primavera* or *Venus*), but it is equally true that little provision was made for women to participate in the new learning that constituted the heart of humanism. A recent generation of scholars, however, has recovered for us voices that have been hitherto silent. When women did receive a humanist education, it was either because they came from aristocratic families that allowed them the leisure and means to get an education or they were children of families who prized learning highly and saw nothing amiss to educate women as well as men.

A further element that helped women get an education was the rise of printing. After the popularization of the printed work, books took on a certain "mobility" that permitted women—especially those who came from wealthy or aristocratic families—to possess both books and the leisure to study them. Examples of humanistic writing coming from women in the fifteenth century almost uniformly reflect an upper-class culture.

A recently published anthology of texts by women humanists in Italy demonstrates that most came from the more illustrious families of the time. Thus Ippolita Sforza (of the Milan Sforzas) actually delivered an oration before the Renaissance humanist and Pope Pius II in 1459. Others, like Isotta Nogarola, had to swim against the tide and choose a life of letters while resisting both marriage and pressure to enter a convent. Others, like Cecilia Gonzaga, entered into convent life for the precise reason of finding the shelter and leisure to advance their studies in the new learning.

It is instructive that a determined humanist named Laura Cereta (died 1499) from Brescia continued her scholarly life throughout her mature years against a tide of criticism from both men who were her peers and from women. Out of those struggles came two letters that were penned to answer both critics: a defense of learning aimed at male humanists and a defense of her vocation directed toward her female critics. Those two documents testify to the difficulty of her life apart from the roles expected of her in society.

TWO STYLES OF HUMANISM

In the generation after the death of Lorenzo de' Medici, the new learning made its way north, where it was most often used in attempts to reform the religious life of the area; in Italy, however, learning remained tied to more worldly matters. The double usage of humanist learning for secular and spiritual reform can be better appreciated by a brief consideration of the work of the two most important writers of the period after the golden period of the Medicean Renaissance: Niccolò Machiavelli and Desiderius Erasmus.

MACHIAVELLI

Niccolò Machiavelli (1469–1527), trained as a humanist and active as a diplomat in Florence, was exiled from the city when the Medici reassumed power in 1512. In his exile, a few miles from the city that he had served for many years, Machiavelli wrote a political treatise on politics called *The Prince* that was published posthumously.

The Prince is often considered the first purely secular study of political theory in the West. Machiavelli's inspiration is the government of Republican Rome (509–31 BCE). He sees Christianity's role in politics as a disaster that destroys the power of the state to govern. For that reason, Machiavelli asserts, the state needs to restrict the power of the church, allowing it to exercise its office only in the spiritual realm. The prince, as ruler of the state, must understand that the key to success in governing is in the exercise of power. Power is to be used with wisdom and ruthlessness. The prince, in a favorite illustration of Machiavelli, must be as sly as the fox and as brutal as the lion. Above all, the prince must not be deterred from his tasks by any consideration of morality beyond that of power and its ends. In this sense, cruelty or hypocrisy is permissible; judicious cruelty consolidates power and discourages revolution. Senseless cruelty is, however, counterproductive.

The basic theme of *The Prince* is the pragmatic use of power for state management. Previously the tradition of political theory had always invoked the transcendent authority of God to ensure the stability and legitimacy of the state. For Machiavelli it was power, not the moral law of God, that provided the state with its ultimate sanction. The final test of the successful ruler was the willingness to exercise power judiciously and freedom from the constraints of moral suasion. "A prince must not keep faith when by doing so it would be against his self-interest," Machiavelli says in one of the most famous passages from his book. His justification is "If all men were good this precept would not be a good one but as they are bad and would not observe their faith with you, so you are not bound to keep faith with them." This bold pragmatism explains why the Catholic Church put *The Prince* on its *Index of Prohibited Books* and why the adjective *Machiavellian* means, in English, "devious or unscrupulous in political dealings." Machiavelli had such a bad reputation that many sixteenth-century English plays had a stock evil character—an Italian called "Old Nick." The English phrase "to be filled with the Old Nick," meaning to be devilish, derives from Machiavelli's reputation as an immoral man. But Machiavelli's realistic pragmatism also explains why Catherine the Great of Russia and Napoleon read him with great care.

In the final analysis, however, the figure of the prince best defines a view of politics that looks to a leader who understands that power is what keeps a political person as a strong ruler. Such a leader uses a simple rule of thumb: how does one exercise power in order to retain power? Such a ruler does not appeal to eternal rules but to simple calculations: Will the exercise of power in this or that particular fashion guarantee the stability of the state? If ruthlessness or violence is needed, let there be ruthlessness or violence (or terror!). Machiavelli did not want to create a monster, and he certainly did not want violence for its own sake. He did favor, however, whatever means it took to keep the state intact and powerful. That is the deepest meaning of the adjective *Machiavellian*.

ERASMUS

Desiderius Erasmus (1466–1536) has been called the most important Christian humanist in Europe [Fig. 12.30]. Educated in Holland and at the University of Paris, Erasmus was a monk and priest who soon tired of his official church life. He became aware of humanist learning through his visits to England, where he met men like John Colet and Thomas More. Fired by their

◆ **12.30** Albrecht Dürer, *Erasmus of Rotterdam*, 1526. The Latin inscription says that the artist drew the portrait from life; the Greek epigram praises the written word. The stylized letters *AD* are the signature of the artist and appear in all his engravings and prints.

Detail, writing stand and monogram, from intaglio print, 9¾″ x 7½″ (25 x 19 cm). Image © Foto Marburg/Art Resource, NY

enthusiasm for the new learning, Erasmus traveled to Italy in 1506, with lengthy stays in both Rome and Venice. Thereafter he led the life of a wandering scholar, gaining immense fame as both scholar and author.

Erasmus's many books were attempts to combine Classical learning and a simple interiorized approach to Christian living. In the *Enchiridion Militis Christiani* (1502), he attempted to spell out this Christian humanism in practical terms. The title has a typical Erasmus-style pun; the word *enchiridion* can mean either "handbook" or "short sword"; thus the title can mean the handbook or the short sword of the Christian knight. His *Greek New Testament* (1516) was the first attempt to edit the Greek text of the New Testament by a comparison of extant manuscripts. Because Erasmus used only three manuscripts, his version is not technically perfect, but it was a noteworthy attempt and a clear indication of how a humanist felt he could contribute to ecclesiastical work.

The most famous book written by Erasmus, *The Praise of Folly* (1509), was dashed off almost as a joke while he was a houseguest of Sir Thomas More in England. Again, the title is a pun; *Encomium Moriae* can mean either "praise of folly" or "praise of More"—Thomas More, his host. *The Praise of Folly* is a humorous work, but beneath its seemingly lighthearted spoof of the foibles of the day there are strong denunciations of corruption, evil, ignorance, and prejudice in society. Erasmus flailed away at the makers of war (he had a strong pacifist streak), venal lawyers, and fraudulent doctors, but, above all, he bitterly attacked religious corruption: the sterility of religious scholarship and the superstitions in religious practice. Reading *The Praise of Folly* makes one wonder why Luther never won Erasmus over to the Reformation (Erasmus debated Luther, in fact). Erasmus remained in the old church, but as a bitter critic of its follies and an indefatigable proponent of its reform. Some have said that Erasmus laid the egg that Luther hatched.

This sweeping social criticism struck an obvious nerve. The book delighted not only the great Sir Thomas More (who was concerned enough about religious convictions to die for them later in the century) but also many sensitive people of the time. *The Praise of Folly* went through twenty-seven editions in the lifetime of Erasmus and outsold every other book except the Bible in the sixteenth century.

Comparing Machiavelli and Erasmus is a bit like comparing apples and potatoes, but a few points of contact can be noted that help us generalize about the meaning of the Renaissance. Both men were heavily indebted to the new learning coming out of fifteenth century Italy. Both looked back to the great Classical heritage of the past for their models of inspiration. Both were elegant Latinists who avoided the style and thought patterns of the medieval world. Machiavelli's devotion to the Roman past was total. He saw the historic development of Christianity as a threat and stumbling block to the fine workings of the state. Erasmus, by contrast, felt that learning from the past could be wedded to the Christian tradition to create an instrument for social reform. His ideal was a Christian humanism based on this formula. It was a formula potent enough to influence thinking throughout the sixteenth century.

The tug of war between Classicism and Christianity may be one key to understanding the Renaissance. It may even help us understand something about the character of almost everything we have discussed in this chapter. The culture of the fifteenth century often was, in fact, a dialectical struggle: At times Classical ideals clashed with biblical ideals; at other times, the two managed to live either in harmony or in a temporary marriage of convenience. The strains of Classicism and Christianity interacted in complex and subtle ways. This important fact helps us understand a culture that produced, in a generation, an elegant scholar like Ficino and a firebrand like Savonarola, a pious artist like Fra Angelico and a titanic genius like Michelangelo—and a Machiavelli and an Erasmus.

MUSIC IN THE FIFTEENTH CENTURY

By the early fifteenth century, the force of the Italian *ars nova* movement in music had spent itself. The principal composers of the early Renaissance were from the North. Strong commercial links between Florence and the North ensured the exchange of ideas, and a new musical idiom that had been developed to please the ear of the prosperous merchant families of the North soon found its way to Italy.

GUILLAUME DUFAY

Guillaume Dufay (c. 1400–1474), the most famous composer of the century, perfectly exemplifies the tendency of music to cross national boundaries. As a young man, Dufay spent several years in Italy studying music and singing in the papal choir at Rome. He later served as music teacher in the French (Burgundian) court of Charles the Good. The works he composed there included masses and motets; he was one of the first composers after Machaut to write complete settings of the Mass. His secular works include several charming *chansons* ("songs") that are free in form and expressive in nature.

Among the changes introduced into music by Dufay and his Burgundian followers (many of whom went to Italy for employment) was the secularization of the motet, a choral work that had previously used a religious text. Motets were now written for special occasions like coronations or noble marriages and the conclusions of peace treaties. Composers who could supply such motets on short notice found welcome in the courts of Renaissance Italian city-states.

Dufay was also one of the first composers to introduce a familiar folk tune into the music of the Mass, the best-known example being his use of the French folk tune *L'homme armé* (*The Man in Armor*) in a mass that is now named for it. Other composers followed suit, and the so-called *chanson masses* were composed throughout the fifteenth and sixteenth centuries. The *L'homme armé* alone was used for more than thirty different masses, including ones by such composers as Josquin and Palestrina. The intermingling of secular with religious elements is thoroughly in accordance with Renaissance ideals.

Among Dufay's most prominent pupils was the Flemish composer Johannes Ockeghem (c. 1430–1495), whose music was characterized by a smooth-flowing but complex web of contrapuntal lines generally written in a free style (the lines do not imitate one another). The resulting mood of the music is more serious than Dufay's, partly because of the intellectual complexity of the counterpoint and partly because Ockeghem sought a greater emotional expression. The combination of intellect and feeling is characteristic of the Renaissance striving for Classical balance. Ockeghem's Requiem Mass is the oldest of the genre to survive (Dufay wrote one, but it has not survived).

MUSIC IN MEDICI FLORENCE

The fact that Italian composers were overshadowed by their northern contemporaries did not in any way stifle Italian interest in music. Lorenzo de' Medici founded a school of harmony that attracted musicians from many parts of Europe, and he had some skill as a lute player. Musical accompaniment enlivened the festivals and public processions of Florence. Popular dance tunes for the *saltarello* and the *pavana* have survived in lute transcriptions.

We know that the Platonist writer Marsilio Ficino played the lyre before admiring audiences, although he had intentions more serious than mere entertainment. Unlike the visual artists, who had models from Classical antiquity for inspiration, students of music had no Classical models to follow: no Greek or Roman music had survived in any significant form. Still, the ideas about music expressed by Plato and other writers fascinated Ficino and others. Greek music had been patterned after the meter of verse and its character carefully controlled by the mode in which it was composed. The Greek doctrine of ethos is still not fully understood today, but Ficino and his friends realized that Plato and Aristotle regarded music as of the highest moral (and hence political) significance. The closest they could come to imitating ancient music was to write settings of Greek and Roman texts in which they tried to follow the meter as closely as possible. Among the most popular works was Virgil's *Aeneid*: The lament of Dido was set to music by no fewer than fourteen composers in the fifteenth and sixteenth centuries.

A more popular music form was the *frottola*, probably first developed in Florence, although the earliest surviving examples come from the Renaissance court of Mantua. The *frottola* was a setting of a humorous or amorous poem for three or four parts consisting of a singer and two or three instrumentalists. Written to be performed in aristocratic circles, the *frottola* often had a simple folk quality. The gradual diffusion of *frottole* throughout Europe gave Italy a reputation for good simple melody and clear vigorous expression.

The *canto carnascialesco* ("carnival song") was a specifically Florentine form of the *frottola*. Written to be sung during the carnival season preceding Lent, such songs were very popular. Even the great Flemish composer Heinrich Issac wrote some during his stay with Lorenzo de' Medici around 1480. With the coming of the Dominican reformer Savonarola, however, the carnivals were abolished because of their alleged licentiousness. The songs also disappeared. After the death of

Savonarola, the songs were reintroduced but died out again in the sixteenth century.

SUMMARY

The main focus of this chapter is on the city of Florence in the fifteenth century. There are two basic reasons for this attention, one rooted in economics and the other in something far more difficult to define.

◆ **Economic and Political Foundations of the Florentine Renaissance.** Florence was not a feudal city governed by a hereditary prince; it had a species of limited participatory government that was in the hands of its landed and monied individuals. It was the center of European banking in the fifteenth century and the hub of international wool and cloth trade. The vast monies in Florentine hands combined with a great sense of civic pride to give the city unparalleled opportunities for expansion and public works. The results can be seen in the explosion of building, art, sculpture, and learning that stretched throughout the century. The great banking families of Florence built and supported art to enhance their reputations, that of their cities, and partly as a form of expiation for the sin of taking interest on money (**usury**)—a practice forbidden by the church. We tend to view Florence today from the perspective of their generosity.

Other forces were also at work. The urban workers were exploited; they had rioted during the end of the fourteenth century and were ready for further protest. An undercurrent of medieval religiosity in the city manifested itself most conspicuously in the rise of Savonarola, who not only appealed to the common people but who also had a reputation for sanctity that could touch the lives of an educated man like Pico della Mirandola and a powerful one like Lorenzo "The Magnificent." Every Florentine could visit the Duomo or see the art in the city's churches, but not everyone was equally touched by the great renaissance in ideas and art that bubbled up in Florence.

◆ **Artistic Foundations of the Renaissance.** Most puzzling about Florence in this period is the sheer enormity of artistic talent it produced. Florence was not a huge city; it often portrayed itself as a David in comparison to a Roman or Milanese Goliath. Yet this relatively small city produced a tradition of art that spanned the century: in sculpture Donatello and Michelangelo bridged the generations, as did Masaccio and Botticelli in painting. Part of the explanation was native talent, but part of it also lies in the character of a city that supported the arts, nurtured artists, and enhanced civic life with beauty and learning.

EXERCISES

1. Choose one of the major paintings of this period and analyze it closely in terms of composition, gradations of color, and use of perspective.

2. List the chief problems of construction involved in raising the dome of the Florence Cathedral in an age that did not have today's building technologies.

3. To what artistic and cultural enterprises would wealthy people most likely contribute today if they had the resources and the power of a Medici family in a contemporary city?

4. What does the word *humanism* mean today, and how does that meaning differ from its use in the fifteenth century? Why do some people think that the term *humanism* is a pejorative term today?

5. If Erasmus were writing today, what would be his most likely targets of satire? What are the great follies of our age?

6. What advice would a contemporary Machiavelli give a contemporary "prince" (powerful political leader)? Why do political philosophers continue to study Machiavelli?

7. Many say that computers are changing learning as radically as did printing in its age. How are computer technologies changing learning?

 Visit the *Culture & Values* Companion website at **www.cengage.com/art/Cunningham/Cultureand Values7E** and the *Humanities Resource Center* for an array of primary source readings, key terms with pronunciations, flash cards, quizzes, and study materials designed especially to help you do well in this course.

CHAPTER 13
THE HIGH RENAISSANCE IN ITALY

The Renaissance in the arts coincided with the Age of Exploration, which in turn prompted a renaissance in Europe's kitchens. The tomato, for example, arrived in Europe from the explorers in the New World who sent back seeds to Spain and Portugal. Mentioned for the first time in Italy around 1550, the yellowish hue of the earliest tomato strains led the Italians to call tomatoes *pomi d'oro* (apples of gold) while the French called them *pommes d'amour* (love apples) because they were thought to have aphrodisiac qualities. In fact, the leaves and stems are somewhat toxic because the tomato belongs to the unpalatable nightshade family of plants. Consequently, although initially cultivated as ornamental, once the fear of eating the tomato was overcome, this fruit became the base of much cooking, especially in the Mediterranean world where the climate made it easy to grow.

The tomato was not the only member of the nightshade family that found its way to Europe from Latin America. Spanish explorers brought the potato back from Peru in the fifteenth century, and its cultivation spread throughout Europe and then back to North America with colonizers. The potato became much more central to diet in Northern Europe because it could be cultivated in cool, damp climates. It is said that the Irish found potato plants amid the wreckage of the Spanish ships of the Armada in the late sixteenth century. As a result, the potato became the staple of Irish peasant food.

POPES AND PATRONAGE

Artists must work where their art is appreciated and their labors rewarded. Florence in the fifteenth century, shaped by the generous and refined **patronage** of the Medici and others, was an

◆ *The Fruit Vendor* (detail), Vincenzo Campi, 1580. *(Image © Scala/Art Resource, NY)*

◆ **295**

extremely congenial place for the talented artist. But when the political power of the Medici declined in the last decade of that century, many major artists inevitably migrated or were summoned to other centers of wealth and stability. The papal court at the Vatican in Rome was preeminently such a center.

In the fifteenth century (and even earlier), artists found rewarding work at the Vatican (see **Table 13.1**). Pope Sixtus IV (reigned 1471–1484) commissioned many artists who were famous in Florence—among them Ghirlandaio, Botticelli, and Perugino—to fresco

the side walls of the Sistine Chapel, named for himself, as well as work on other projects that caught his artistic fancy. Not the least of these projects was the enlargement and systematization of the Vatican Library.

The period known as the High Renaissance really began, however, in 1503, when a nephew of Sixtus IV became Pope Julius II (died 1513); both were members of the della Rovere family. Pope Julius was a fiery man who did not hesitate to don full military armor over his vestments and lead his papal troops into battle. Thanks to the influence of his papal uncle, he appreciated the

	GENERAL EVENTS	ART
1400	**1471–1484** Reign of Pope Sixtus IV (della Rovere)	**1471–1484** Perugino, Botticelli, and others decorate Sistine Chapel side walls
FLORENTINE RENAISSANCE	**1492** Columbus discovers America	**1493–1506** Ancient frescoes and statues uncovered in Rome; *Laocoön* found 1506 **c. 1494** Decline of Medici power in Florence causes artists to migrate to Rome
	1494 Foreign invasions of Italy begin	**1494–1495** Dürer's first trip to Venice
		c. 1500–1505 Giorgione, *Enthroned Madonna with Saints*
1503	**1503–1513** Reign of Pope Julius II (della Rovere)	**1505** Michelangelo called to Rome by Julius II to begin Pope's tomb
		1505–1508 Raphael works in Florence
	c. 1510 Decline of Venetian trade as a result of new geographic discoveries	**1508** Raphael begins frescoes for rooms in Vatican Palace
		1508–1511 Michelangelo, Sistine Chapel ceiling
		c. 1510 Giorgione, *Le Concert Champêtre*
	1513–1521 Reign of Pope Leo X (de Medici)	**1515–1547** Francis I lures Leonardo and other Italian artists to France
		Painting in Venice emphasizes brilliant color and light; less linear than in Rome and Florence
	1517 Reformation begins in Germany with Luther's 95 Theses challenging the practice of indulgences	
		1519 Death of Leonardo **1519–1534** Michelangelo works on Medici Chapel sculptures
1520	**1523–1534** Reign of Pope Clement VII (de Medici)	**1520** Death of Raphael **c. 1520** Mannerism emerges as artistic style **c. 1528** Pontormo, *Deposition*
	1527 Sack of Rome by Emperor Charles V	**1534–1541** Michelangelo, *The Last Judgment* fresco, Sistine Chapel **c. 1535** Parmigianino, *Madonna of the Long Neck*
	1534 Churches of Rome and England separate	**1538** Titian, *Venus of Urbino*
	1545 Council to reform Catholic Church begins at Trent	**1554** Cellini casts bronze *Perseus* in Florence **1555** Anguissola, *A Game of Chess* **1564** Death of Michelangelo **1576** Titian dies of plague **1581** Fontana, *Noli Me Tangere*
1603		

fine arts, indulging his artistic tastes with the same single-mindedness that characterized his military campaigns. It was Pope Julius—called by his contemporaries *il papa terribile* ("the awesome pope")—who summoned both Raphael Sanzio and Michelangelo Buonarroti to Rome.

RAPHAEL

Raphael Sanzio (1483–1520) was born in Urbino, a center of humanist learning east of Florence domi-

nated by the court of the Duke of Urbino. His precocious talent was first nurtured by his father, a painter, whose death in 1494 cut short the youth's education. The young Raphael then went to Perugia as an apprentice to the painter Perugino. Here his talents were quickly recognized. In 1505, at the age of twenty-two, he moved on to Florence, where he worked for three years.

During his stay in Florence, Raphael painted many Madonnas in a style that has become almost synonymous with his name. The *Madonna of the Meadow*

ARCHITECTURE	LITERATURE & PHILOSOPHY	MUSIC
1473–1480 Sistine Chapel built for Pope Sixtus IV		**1473** Sixtus IV establishes Sistine Choir
	c. 1494 Aldine Press established in Venice	**1486–1494** Josquin des Prez intermittently in service of Sistine Choir as composer of masses and motets
1506 Pope Julius II commissions Bramante to rebuild Saint Peter's Basilica		
Palladio—Andrea di Pietro (1508–1580)—reintroduces Classical forms		**1512** Julius II establishes Julian Choir for Saint Peter's Basilica
1514–1547 Death of Bramante; Raphael, Sangallo, and others continue work on Saint Peter's		
1519–1534 Michelangelo, Medici Chapel, Church of San Lorenzo, Florence		
1524–1559 Michelangelo, Laurentian Library	**c. 1524–1534** Strozzi, poem on Michelangelo's *Night*	**1527** Adrian Willaert becomes choirmaster of Saint Mark's, Venice; multiple choirs and addition of instrumental music are Venetian innovations to liturgical music
	1527 Luther translates Bible into German	
	1528 Castiglione, *The Courtier*, dialogue on ideal courtly life	**1567** Palestrina, *Missa Papae Marcelli*
1547 Michelangelo appointed architect of Saint Peter's	**1550** Vasari, *Lives of the Painters*	**1571–1594** Palestrina, choirmaster of Sistine Choir, in charge of musical reform for Vatican
1590 Michelangelo's dome for Saint Peter's finished by Giacomo della Porta	**1558–1566** Cellini, *Autobiography of Benvenuto Cellini*	
	1561 *The Courtier* translated into English by Sir Thomas Hoby	**1603** Vittoria, *Requiem Mass for the Empress Maria*

Table 13.1 *Some Renaissance Popes of the Sixteenth Century*

Julius II (1503–1513). Of the della Rovere family; Patron of Raphael and Michelangelo.

Leo X (1513–1521). Son of Lorenzo the Magnificent; patronized Michelangelo. Excommunicated Martin Luther.

Hadrian VI (1522–1523). Born in the Netherlands; a ferocious reformer and the last non-Italian pope until the 1970s.

Clement VII (1523–1534). Bastard grandson of Lorenzo de' Medici; commissioned the Medici tombs in Florence. Excommunicated Henry VIII. Commissioned *The Last Judgment* for the Sistine Chapel just before his death.

Paul III (1534–1549). Commissioned Michelangelo to build the Farnese Palace in Rome. Called the reform Council of Trent, which first met in 1545.

Julius III (1550–1555). Patron of the composer Palestrina. Confirmed the constitutions of the Jesuits in 1550. Appointed Michelangelo as chief architect of St. Peter's.

Marcellus II (1555). Reigned as pope twenty-two days. Palestrina composed the *Missa Papae Marcelli* in his honor.

Paul IV (1555–1559). Began the papal reaction against the Renaissance spirit. A fanatical reformer; encouraged the Inquisition and instituted the *Index of Forbidden Books* in 1557.

◆ **13.2** Raphael, *Madonna of the Meadow*, 1508. The infant John the Baptist kneels at the left of the picture in homage to the Christ child, who stands before his mother.

Oil on panel, 44½″ x 34¼″ (113 x 87 cm). Kunsthistorisches Museum, Vienna, Austria//© Erich Lessing/Art Resource, NY

[**Fig. 13.2**] is typical. In this painting Raphael arranged his figures in a **pyramidal configuration** to create a believable and balanced space. This geometrical device, which had already been popularized by Leonardo da Vinci, was congenial to the Renaissance preoccupation with rationally ordered composition. More important than the arrangement of shapes, however, is the beautiful modeling of the human forms, especially the figures of the two children, and the genuine sweetness and warmth conveyed by the faces. The head of the Madonna is peaceful and luminous, while the infant Christ and Saint John convey a somewhat more playful mood. The human quality of the divine figure is Raphael's trademark.

Raphael left Florence for Rome in 1508. By the following year, Pope Julius, whom Raphael later captured in an unforgettably fine portrait, had him working in the Vatican on various projects. The pope, who genuinely loved Raphael, commissioned him to decorate various rooms of his palace. Raphael spent the rest of his brief life working on these projects and filling assorted administrative posts for the papacy, including, at one time, the office of architect of Saint Peter's Basilica and at another time superintendent of the Vatican's collection of antiquities.

One of Raphael's most outstanding works—and certainly one of the most important for defining the meaning of the sixteenth-century Renaissance in Rome—is a large fresco executed in 1509–1511 on the wall of the Stanza della Segnatura, an office in the Vatican Palace where documents requiring the pope's signature were prepared. Called now the *School of Athens* [**Fig. 13.3**], the fresco is a highly symbolic homage

to philosophy that complements Raphael's similar frescoes in the same room that symbolize poetry, law, and theology.

The *School of Athens* sets the great philosophers of antiquity in an immense illusionistic architectural framework that must have been at least partially inspired by the impressive ruins of Roman baths and basilicas, and perhaps by the new Saint Peter's, then under construction. Raphael's fresco depicts Roman barrel vaulting, coffered ceilings, and broad expanses not unlike the still existing baths of ancient Rome. Occupying the center of the fresco, in places of honor framed by the receding lines of the architecture as a device to focus the viewer's eye, are the two greatest ancient Greek philosophers: Plato and Aristotle. Plato holds a copy of the *Timaeus* in one hand and with the other points to the heavens, the realm of ideal forms. Aristotle holds a copy of his *Ethics* and points to the earth, where his science of empirical observation must begin. Clustered about the two philosophers in varying poses and at various distances are other great figures of antiquity. Diogenes sprawls in front of the philosophers, while Pythagoras calculates on a slate and Ptolemy holds a globe. At the right, the idealized figure of Euclid with his compass is actually a portrait of Raphael's Roman protector, the architect Bramante. Raphael himself, in a self-portrait, looks out

◆ **13.3** Raphael, *Philosophy (School of Athens)*, 1509–1511. The central figures represent Plato and Aristotle. The figure in the forefront is Michelangelo resting his head on his left fist.

Fresco, 26′ x 18′ (7.92 x 5.48 m). Stanza della Segnatura, Stanze di Raffaello, Vatican Palace, Vatican State//© Erich Lessing/Art Resource, NY

◆ **13.4** Raphael, *The Transfiguration*, 1517. Note how the gesturing hands frame the figure of Christ.

Tempera panel, 15′11½″ x 9′1½″ (4.6 x 2.8 m). Pinacoteca, Vatican Museums, Vatican State//© Scala/Art Resource, NY

at the viewer at the extreme lower-right corner of the fresco.

Raphael's *School of Athens* reflects a high degree of sensitivity to ordered space, a complete ease with Classical thought, obvious inspiration from the Roman architectural past, a brilliant sense of color and form, and a love for intellectual clarity—characteristics that could sum up the Renaissance ideal. That such a fresco should adorn a room in the Vatican, the center of Christian authority, is not difficult to explain. The papal court of Julius II shared the humanist conviction that philosophy is the servant of theology and that beauty, even if derived from a pagan civilization, is a gift from God and not to be despised. To underscore this point, Raphael's homage to theology across the room, his fresco called the *Disputà*, shows in a panoramic form similar to the *School of Athens* the efforts of theologians to penetrate Divine mystery.

The Transfiguration was Raphael's last work, left unfinished at his death [**Fig. 13.4**]. A great scene, evenly

◆ **13.5** Michelangelo, *Moses*, 1513–1515. The horns on the head of Moses represent rays of light; the use of horns instead of rays is based on a mistranslation in the Latin Vulgate Bible.

Marble, 8′4″ (2.54 m) high. San Pietro in Vincoli, Rome, Italy//© Scala/Art Resource, NY

◆ **13.6** Michelangelo, Atlas Slave (one of the *Boboli Captives*), mid 1500s. Note the chisel marks in the marble.

Marble sculpture, unfinished, 7′6½″ (2.3 m) high. Accademia di Belle Arti, Florence, Italy//© Nimatallah/Art Resource, NY

divided between the airy transcendence of the transfigured Christ, flanked by Old Testament figures, and overpoweringly blinded apostles and the rest of the world on the darker level of the earth is still held together with a great sense of balanced activity. This painting is usually considered as one of the great moments of the Roman High Renaissance.

MICHELANGELO

In the lower center of Raphael's *School of Athens* is a lone figure leaning one elbow on a block of marble and scribbling, taking no notice of the exalted scene about him. Strangely isolated in his stonecutter's smock, the figure has recently been identified, at least tentatively, as Michelangelo. If this identification is correct, this is the younger artist's act of homage to the solitary genius who was working just a few yards away from him in the Sistine Chapel.

Michelangelo Buonarroti (1475–1564) was called to Rome in 1505 by Pope Julius II to create for him a monumental tomb. We have no clear sense of what the

◆ **13.7** Drawing of tomb of Julius II, after Michelangelo by his pupil Giacomo Rocchetti. This is only one of many projected plans for the tomb of Julius. Note the slaves/captives at the bottom level and Moses on the right at the second level. The semi-recumbent figure of the deceased pope is supported by angelic figures, with an allegorical figure of Victory overhead in the center.

Pen and brown ink, color wash, 22½″ x 15¼″ (57 x 39 cm). Kupferstichkabinett, Staatliche Museen zu Berlin, Berlin, Germany//© Bildarchiv Preussischer Kulturbesitz/Art Resource, NY

The tomb of Pope Julius II was never finished. Michelangelo was interrupted in his long labors by both Pope Julius and, after the pope's death, the popes of the Medici family, who were more concerned with projects glorifying their own family. What was completed of the tomb represents a twenty-year span of frustrating delays and revised schemes. Even those finished pieces provide no sense of the whole, but they do represent some of the highest achievements of world art.

One of the finished pieces is the *Moses* [**Fig. 13.5**], begun after the death of Julius in 1513. We easily sense both the bulky physicality of Moses and the carefully modeled particulars of musculature, drapery, and hair. The fiercely inspired look on the face of Moses is appropriate for one who has just come down from Mount Sinai after seeing God. The face radiates both divine fury and divine light. It is often said of Michelangelo that his work can overwhelm the viewer with a sense of awesomeness; Italians speak of his *terribilità*. If any single statue has this awesomeness, it is the *Moses*.

The highly finished quality of the *Moses* should be compared to the roughness of the *Boboli Captives* [**Fig. 13.6**], the four figures Michelangelo worked on for the tomb of Julius in Florence in 1527–1528. There is no evidence that Michelangelo intended to leave these figures in so crude a state. Nevertheless, these magnificent works give a visual demonstration of the sculptor's methods. Michelangelo sometimes said that a living figure was concealed in a block of marble and that only the excess needed to be carved away to reveal it. The truth of the Neo-Platonic notion that ideal form struggles to be freed from the confines of gross matter can almost be seen in these figures. A close examination reveals the bite marks of the sculptor's chisel as he worked to reveal each living figure by removing hard marble. Seldom do we have a chance, as we do here, to see the work of a great artist still unfolding.

It is not clear where the *Captives* fit into the overall plan of the tomb of Julius. Most likely they were meant to serve as corner supports for the bottom level of the tomb, writhing under the weight of the whole [**Fig. 13.7**]. Whatever the ultimate plan was for these figures, they are a stunning testament to the monumentally creative impulse of Michelangelo the sculptor.

Michelangelo had hardly begun work on the pope's tomb when Julius commanded him to fresco the ceiling of the Sistine Chapel to complete the work done in the previous century under Sixtus IV. But Michelangelo resisted the project (he actually fled Rome and had to be ordered back by papal edict). He considered himself a sculptor, and there were technical problems presented by the shape of the ceiling. Nevertheless, he gave in and in three years (1508–1511) finished the

tomb was to look like, because over the years it went through at least five conceptual revisions. Certain features, however, at least in the initial stages, are definite. It was to have three levels; the bottom level was to have sculpted figures representing Victory and bound slaves. The second level was to have statues of Moses and Saint Paul as well as symbolic figures of the active and contemplative life—representative of the human striving for, and reception of, knowledge. The third level, it is assumed, was to have an effigy of the deceased pope.

◆ **13.8** Michelangelo, Ceiling of the Sistine Chapel, 1508–1511.

Fresco, 44' x 128' (13.44 x 39.01 m), Sistine Chapel, Vatican Palace, Vatican State. Image © Erich Lessing/Art Resource, NY

◆ **13.9** Schematic drawing of the iconographic plan of the Sistine Ceiling. The corner triangles are called the *vele* ("sails").

ceiling [**Fig. 13.8**]. He signed it "Michelangelo, Sculptor" to remind Julius of his reluctance and his own true vocation.

The ceiling is as difficult to describe as it is to observe when standing in the Sistine Chapel. The overall organization consists of four large triangles at the corners; a series of eight triangular spaces on the outer border; an intermediate series of figures; and nine central panels (four larger than the other five), all bound together with architectural motifs and nude male figures. The corner triangles depict heroic action in the Old Testament (Judith beheading Holofernes, David slaying Goli-

ath, Haman punished for his crimes, the rod of Moses changing into a serpent), whereas the other eight triangles depict the biblical ancestors of Jesus Christ. The ten major intermediate figures are alternating portraits of pagan sibyls (prophetesses) and Old Testament prophets. The central panels are scenes from the Book of Genesis. The one closest to the altar shows God dividing darkness from light, and the one at the other end shows the drunkenness of Noah (Genesis 9:20–27). This bare outline oversimplifies what is actually a complex, intricate design [**Fig. 13.9**].

Michelangelo conceived and executed this huge work as a single unit. Its overall meaning is a problem. The issue has engaged historians of art for generations without satisfactory resolution. Any attempt to formulate an authoritative statement must include the following elements:

VOICES OF THEIR TIMES

Donna Vittoria and Michelangelo

An exchange between Michelangelo and his friend and spiritual adviser, Donna Vittoria Colonna. She was the recipient of a number of his poems and, according to Vasari, he made several small sculptures and drawings for her.

Donna Vittoria Colonna to Michelangelo:

> Most honored Master Michelangelo, your art has brought you such fame that you would perhaps never have believed that this fame could fade with time or through any other cause. But the heavenly light has shone into your heart and shown you that, however long earthly glory may last, it is doomed to suffer the second death.

Michelangelo's poem on this theme:

> I know full well that it was a fantasy
> That made me think that art could be made into
> An idol or a king. Though all men do
> This, they do it half-unwillingly.
> The loving thoughts, so happy and so vain,
> Are finished now. A double death comes near—
> The one is sure, the other is a threat.

◆ **13.10** Michelangelo, *Creation of Adam*, 1508–1512. Compare the figure of Adam to the figure of David (see Figure 12.29) to get a sense of Michelangelo's concept of musculature.

Ceiling fresco, detail, c. 8′ x 9′2″ (2.44 x 2.8 m), Sistine Chapel, Vatican Palace, Vatican State. Image © Erich Lessing/Art Resource, NY

1. Michelangelo's interest in the **Neo-Platonism** he had studied as a youth in Florence. Many writers have noted the Neo-Platonic roots of his interest in the manipulation of darkness and light (the progression of darkness to light from the outer borders to the center panels; the panel of God creating light itself), the liberation of spirit from matter (the souls represented by nudes; the drunkenness of Noah, symbolic of humanity trapped by gross matter and thereby degraded); and the numerous geometrical allusions done in triads, a triple division being much loved in Neo-Platonic number symbolism.

2. The Christian understanding of the Old Testament as a work pointing to the coming of Christ, combined with the notion that even pagan prophets were dimly prophetic figures of Christ.

3. The complex tree symbolism in seven of the nine central panels, which refer to the symbolism of the tree in the Bible (the tree of good and evil in the Genesis story, the tree of the Cross, and so forth), as well as being allusions to the pope's family name, which happened to be della Rovere ("of the oak tree").

4. The traditional theories of the relationship of the world of human wisdom (represented by the sibyls) and God's revelation (represented by the prophets).

In the panel depicting the *Creation of Adam* [**Fig. 13.10**], to cite one specific example, many of these elements

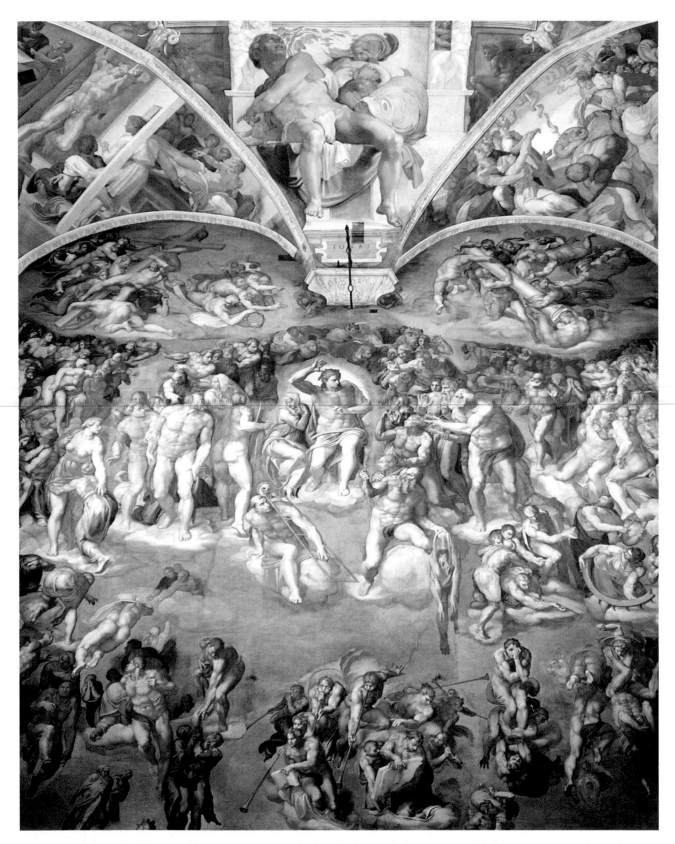

◆ **13.11** Michelangelo, *The Last Judgment*, 1534–1541. The loincloths on the figures were added later to appease the puritan sensibilities of post-Reformation Catholicism. The figure in the flayed skin of Saint Bartholomew below and to the right of Christ is a self-portrait of the painter.

Fresco (restored) on the altar wall, 48′ x 44′ (14.63 x 13.41 m), Sistine Chapel, Vatican Palace, Vatican State. Image © age fotostock/SuperStock

◆ **13.12** Michelangelo, Medici Chapel, 1519–1534. Church of San Lorenzo, Florence, Italy. Inside of the New Sacristy, showing the tomb of Lorenzo and altar. *(Image © Scala/Art Resource, NY)*

come together. A majestically muscular Adam rises, as if from sleep, from the bare earth as God stretches forth His creative finger to call Adam into being. God's left arm circles a woman and child who represent simultaneously Eve and her children and, by extension, the New Eve, who is the Blessed Virgin. Adam is a prefiguration of Christ. Below Adam a youth holding a cornucopia spilling forth leaves and acorns (symbols of the della Rovere family) stands just above the Persian sibyl. Stylistically, the fresco demonstrates Michelangelo's intense involvement with masculine anatomy seen as muscular monumentality. His ability to combine great physical bulk with linear grace and a powerful display of emotion fairly well defines the adjective *Michelangelesque*, applied to many later artists who were influenced by his style.

The full force of that Michelangelesque style can be seen in the artist's second contribution to the Sistine Chapel: *The Last Judgment*, which he painted on the wall behind the main altar between the years 1534 and 1541 [**Fig. 13.11**]. A huge fresco marking the end of the world when Christ comes back as judge, *The Last Judgment* shows the Divine Judge standing in the upper center of the scene, with the world being divided into the Dantean damned at the bottom and those who are called to glory above. Into that great scene Michelangelo poured both his own intense religious vision and a reflection of the troubled days during which he lived. It was, after all, a Rome that had already been sacked in 1527 and a church that had been riven by the Protestant Reformation in the North.

Under the patronage of popes Leo X and Clement VII—both from the Medici family—Michelangelo worked on another project, the Medici Chapel in the Florentine Church of San Lorenzo. This **chapel** is particularly interesting because Michelangelo designed and executed both the sculptures and the chapel in which they were to be placed. Although Michelangelo first conceived the project in 1519, he worked on it only in fits and starts from 1521 to 1534. He never completely finished the chapel. In 1545 some of Michelangelo's students set the statues in place.

The interior of the Medici Chapel [**Fig. 13.12**] echoes Brunelleschi's Pazzi Chapel with its dome, its use of a light grayish stone called *pietra serena (serena*

◆ **13.13** Michelangelo, *Night*, 1519–1534. The owl and the mask under the recumbent figure are emblems of night and dreams.

Marble, 6′4½″ (1.94 m) long. Detail of the tomb of Giuliano de' Medici, Church of San Lorenzo, Florence, Italy. Image © Erich Lessing/Art Resource, NY

stone), its Classical decoration, and its chaste and severe style. The plan envisioned an altar at one end of the chapel and opposite it, at the other end, statues of the Madonna and child with saints Cosmas and Damian. The saints were the patrons of physicians, an allusion to the name *Medici,* which means "the doctor's family." At the base of these statues are buried in utter simplicity the bodies of Lorenzo the Magnificent and his brother Giuliano. On opposite walls are niches with idealized seated figures of relatives of Lorenzo the Magnificent, the dukes Lorenzo and Giuliano de' Medici in Roman armor. Beneath each are two symbolic figures resting on a **sarcophagus**, *Night* and *Day* and *Dawn* and *Dusk.*

This great complex, unfinished like many of Michelangelo's projects, is a brooding meditation on the shortness of life, the inevitability of death, and the Christian hope for resurrection. Both the stark decoration of the chapel and the positioning of the statues (Duke Lorenzo seems always turned to the dark with his head in shadow, whereas Duke Giuliano seems more readily to accept the light) form a mute testament to the rather pessimistic and brooding nature of their creator. When Michelangelo had finished the figure of *Night* [**Fig. 13.13**], a Florentine poet named Strozzi wrote a poem in honor of the statue, with a pun on the name Michelangelo:

The Night you see sleeping in sweet repose
Was carved in stone by an angel.
Because she sleeps, she has life.
If you do not believe this, touch her and
She will speak.

Michelangelo, an accomplished poet in his own right, answered Strozzi's lines with a pessimistic rejoinder:

Sleep is precious; more precious to be stone
When evil and shame are abroad;
It is a blessing not to see, not to hear.
Pray, do not disturb me. Speak softly!

THE NEW SAINT PETER'S

In 1506 Pope Julius II, in a gesture typical of his imperious nature, commissioned the architect Donato Bramante (1444–1514) to rebuild Saint Peter's Basilica in the Vatican. Old Saint Peter's had stood on Vatican Hill since it was first constructed more than a thousand years earlier, during the time of Roman Emperor Constantine. By the early sixteenth century it had suffered repeatedly from roof fires, structural stresses, and the simple ravages of time. In the minds of the Renaissance "moderns" it was a shaky anachronism.

◆ **13.14** Floor plans for the new Saint Peter's Basilica, Rome, Italy, 1506–1666. (I) Bramante's plan, 1506–1514, showed a compact plan of a Greek cross with arms or transepts (b) of equal length meeting at a central altar (a) set under a dome, each arm ending in a semicircular apse (e) opening to a portal or entrance (c), and including several chapels (d) for smaller services. (II) Antonio da San Gallo's plan, 1516–1546, imposed a Latin cross, adding Raphael's choir (f) to surround the altar on three sides, closing the portals in favor of a formal entrance (c), and forming a nave (g) from the arm proceeding from a huge vestibule or narthex (h). (III) Michelangelo's plan, 1547–1564, rejected San Gallo's design and returned to a centralized domed Greek cross inscribed within a square but retained the vestibule (c) now fronted by a portico with giant columns. (IV) Carlo Maderna's plan, 1606–1615, returned to a Latin cross with elongated nave (g), narthex (h), portico (c), and Baroque façade. This plan also shows Gianlorenzo Bernini's piazza (j) with colonnades, 1656–1667 (see Figure 15.2). Maderna's final additions, especially the elongated nave, narthex, and large façade, obscured Michelangelo's original design. *(Artwork by Cecilia Cunningham)*

Bramante's Plan Bramante's design envisioned a central domed church with a floor plan in the shape of a Greek cross with four equal arms [**Fig. 13.14**]. The dome would have been set on a columned arcade with an exterior colonnaded arcade, called a *peristyle*, on the outer perimeter of the building. Any of the four main doors was to be directly across from a *portal* ("door") on the opposite side. This central plan was not executed in Bramante's lifetime, but a small chapel he built in 1502 next to the Church of San Pietro in Montorio, Rome, may give us a clue to what Bramante had in mind. This *tempietto* ("little temple") is believed to have been done in a style similar to what Bramante wanted later for Saint Peter's.

Michelangelo's Plan After Bramante's death, other architects—including Raphael and Sangallo—worked on the massive project. Both of these architects added a nave and aisles. In 1547 Michelangelo was appointed architect, because the plans previously drawn up seemed unworkable. Michelangelo returned to Bramante's plan for a central domed Greek cross church but envisioned a ribbed, arched dome somewhat after the manner of the cathedral in Florence but on a far larger scale.

The present Saint Peter's seen from the front gives us no clear sense of what Michelangelo had in mind when he drew up his plans. Michelangelo's church had a long nave and a façade added by Carlo Maderna in the early seventeenth century. The colonnaded piazza was

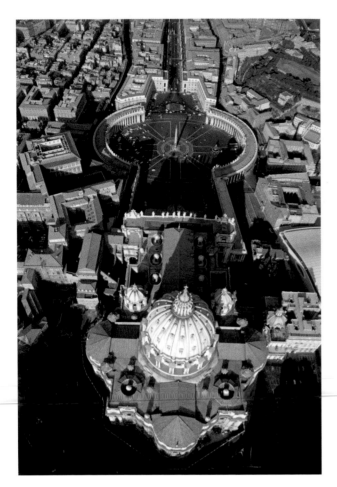

◆ **13.15** Michelangelo, Saint Peter's Basilica, Vatican City, Vatican State (Italy), 1546–1564. Dome completed 1590 by Giacomo della Porta. The Vatican Gardens are behind the basilica, visible at the lower center of this aerial photograph.

View from the southwest. Length of church, 693.8' (211.5 m); diameter of dome, 137.7' (42 m); height of nave, 151.5' (46.2 m); height from nave floor to summit of cross on dome, 434.7' (132. m). Image © Georg Gerster/Photo Researchers, Inc.

completed under the direction of Gian Lorenzo Bernini in 1663, almost a century after Michelangelo's death. Michelangelo lived to see the completion of the **drum** that was to support his dome, which was raised some thirty years after his death by Giacomo della Porta. The best way to understand what Michelangelo intended is to view Saint Peter's from behind, from the Vatican Gardens, where one can see the great dome looming up over the arms of the Greek cross design [**Fig. 13.15**].

THE HIGH RENAISSANCE IN VENICE

The brilliant and dramatic outbreak of artistic activity in sixteenth-century Rome and Florence does not diminish the equally creative art being done in the Republic of Venice to the north. While Rome excelled in fresco, sculpture, and architecture, Venice (and its territory) was famous for its revival of Classical architecture and for its tradition of easel painting. Venice's impressive cosmopolitanism derived from its position as a maritime port and its trading tradition.

ARCHITECTURE: ANDREA PALLADIO

The leading architect of the whole of northern Italy in the High Renaissance, the only one to rival the achievements of Tuscan architects of the caliber of Alberti and Michelangelo, was Andrea di Pietro (1508–1580)—better known by his nickname, Palladio. Coined by his first patron, Giangiorgio Trissino of Vicenza, the name derived from that of the ancient Greek goddess Pallas Athene and indicates the main source of Palladio's inspiration: the architecture of Classical Greece as he saw it reflected in the buildings of ancient Rome. The young Palladio and his patron made several visits to Rome, studying both High Renaissance buildings and the ruins of the ancient city. His designs for villas, churches, and palaces stressed the harmonic proportions and Classical symmetry that the Romans had inherited from the Greeks. His Four Books of Architecture (1570) helped to spread his style throughout Europe. The Palladio style became particularly popular in eighteenth-century England and in due course was exported to America, where it inspired much of the "Greek Revival" architecture of the American south (for an example of this see Figure 16.18).

Whether Palladio was born in Padua or Vicenza is uncertain, but it is the latter city that contains the largest number of his buildings, both public and private. As a result Vicenza is one of the most beautiful and architecturally interesting cities of Renaissance Venetian territory, and indeed, of Italy as a whole. One of the finest of his works there is the Palazzo Chiericati [**Fig. 13.16**]. The building is set on a large piazza, and Palladio took advantage of this to create one of his most imaginative facades.

Using strictly Classical forms, the architect managed to add his own contribution. The facade is divided into two parts horizontally: the lower open loggia has Doric columns, while the upper level is supported by Ionic columns (note the difference in the capitals at the top of the columns). By adding a wall to the central part of the upper story, however, Palladio has created three vertical divisions. He emphasizes this by having this central section stand out from the rest of the building on both levels, with columns bunched at each end. Thus it seems to float above the columns below.

Other Classical features include the Triglyphs (three-grooved slabs) above the lower level of columns, which are placed in a strict rhythmic pattern—one over each column and two over the gaps between columns. The windows of the second level have triangular and semicircular pediments in strict alternation.

◆ **13.16** Palladio, Palazzo Chiericati, Vicenza, Italy, begun 1550s. In this brick structure faced with stucco, note Palladio's imaginative use of roof decorations consisting of Classical-style statues alternating with fantastical architectural forms called "balusters." *(© Cameraphoto Arte, Venice/Art Resource, NY)*

The result is a building that combines the elegance and clarity of Classical architecture with Palladio's own imaginative ideas. The sense of harmony and balance of proportion is a perfect example of the Renaissance revival of Classical ideals.

PAINTING IN VENICE

Because of the damp atmosphere of their watery city, Venetian painters quickly adopted oil painting, which had first been popularized in the north. Oil painting gave the artist unparalleled opportunities to enrich and deepen color by the application of many layers of paint. Oil painting in general, and Venetian painting in particular, placed great emphasis on the brilliance of its color and the subtlety of its light. The sunny environment of Venice, with light reflecting off the ever-present waterways, further inspired the Venetian feel for color and light. Although the generalization is subject to refinement, there is truth in the observation that Venetian painters emphasized color, whereas painters in the south were preoccupied with line. Venetian painters, like their counterparts in Northern Europe, had an eye for close detail and a love for landscape (an ironic interest, since Venice had so little land).

Giorgione The most celebrated and enigmatic painter in early sixteenth-century Venice was Giorgio di Castelfranco (c. 1477–1510), more commonly known as Giorgione. His large altarpiece, *Enthroned Madonna with Saints Liberalis and Francis of Assisi* [**Fig. 13.17**],

◆ **13.17** Giorgione, *Enthroned Madonna with Saints Liberalis and Francis of Assisi*, c. 1500–1505. Saint Francis on the right shows the *stigmata* of Christ that he bore on his body.

Oil on panel, 6′6¾″ x 5′ (1.99 x 1.52 m), Cathedral (Duomo), Castelfranco Veneto, Italy. Image © Scala/Art Resource, NY

VALUES

Patronage

We have noted in several places in these chapters about art patronage in the Renaissance period. The question is, to what end did people and/or organizations give lavish funds to sustain the various arts? The answer to that question helps us understand the social value of art.

In the earlier Renaissance, many wealthy laypersons patronized the arts to "pay back" monies earned from interest-taking, which was considered a sinful practice. A more common motive was a combination of a desire to memorialize the family name (a common custom even today), to promote civic pride, and to solidify one's standing in the community. Wealthy cities like Venice underwrote lavish art projects as a projection of civic pride and as a demonstration of power and wealth. The enormous papal expenditures in the fifteenth and sixteenth centuries reversed an earlier trend.

In the past, laypersons endowed the churches with their monies. The Renaissance popes, by contrast, used church monies to reflect the power of the papacy; to enhance the Roman claim to be the center of the church; to promote a visible form of piety; and, incidentally, to glorify the reign of the pope and his family. Visitors to the Vatican can still see the coats of arms of the families from which the popes came.

The patronage impulses of the past are not all that different from our own (although the church is hardly a central source of artistic patronage today) except that the monies that make art patronage possible come from different sources. This patronage is also the source of much social debate as our contemporaries argue the merits of state and national funding for the arts.

◆ **13.18** Giorgione, *Le Concert Champêtre*, c. 1510. Giorgione's robust nude figures would be much imitated by later baroque painters like Peter Paul Rubens. Giorgione died before he could finish the painting. It was completed by Titian.

Oil on canvas, c. 3'7¼" x 4'6⅛" (1.05 x 1.38 m). Musée du Louvre, Paris, France//© Réunion des Musées Nationaux/Art Resource, NY idiosyncratic characteristics—the luminous quality of the armor of Saint Liberalis and the minutely rendered landscape. This landscape, with its two soldiers in the bend of the road and the receding horizon, echoes painters from the north like Jan van Eyck.

Far more typical of Giorgione's work are his paintings without religious content or recognizable story line or narrative quality. Typical of these is *Le Concert Champêtre* [**Fig. 13.18**], done in the final year of the painter's life. The two voluptuous nudes frame two young men who are shadowed but also glowing in their richly rendered costumes. The sky behind threatens a storm, but Giorgione counterposes the storm to a serene pastoral scene that includes a distant farmhouse and shepherds with their flock. What does the painting hope to convey? Why does one woman pour water into the well? Is the lute in the hand of one man or the recorder in the hand of the other woman a clue? We do not know. It may be an elaborate allegory on music or poetry. What is clear is that the painting is a frankly secular homage to the profane joy of life rendered with the richness and lushness of concept and color.

Titian If Giorgione's life was short, that of his one-time apprentice Tiziano Vecelli (c. 1488–1576), known as Titian, was long. Titian brought the Venetian love for striking color to its most beautiful fulfillment. His work had an impact not only on his contemporaries but also on later baroque painters in other countries, such as Peter Paul Rubens in Antwerp and Diego Velázquez in Spain.

Titian's artistic output during seventy years of activity was huge. His reputation was such that he was lionized by popes and princes. He was a particular favorite of Holy Roman Emperor Charles V, who granted him noble rank after having summoned him on several occasions to work at the royal court. From this tremendous body of work two representative paintings, emblematic of the wide range of his abilities, provide a focus.

The huge panel painting in the Venetian Church of the Frari called *Assumption of the Virgin* [**Fig. 13.19**] shows Titian at his monumental best. The swirling color in subtly different shadings and the dramatic gestures of the principals, all of which converge on the person of the Madonna, give a feeling of vibrant upward movement; color and composition define the subject of the assumption of Mary into heaven. The energy in the panel, however, should not distract the viewer from its meticulous spatial relationships. The use of a triangular composition, the subtle shift from dark to light, the lines converging on the Madonna from both above and below are all part of carefully wrought ideas that give the work its final coherence.

◆ **13.19** Titian, *Assumption of the Virgin*, 1516–1518. Note the three distinct levels in the composition of the painting: the apostles on the ground; Mary and angels; God and angels.

Oil on canvas, 22′6″ x 11′8″ (6.86 x 3.56 m). Santa Maria Gloriosa dei Frari, Venice, Italy//© Erich Lessing/Art Resource, NY

painted for the cathedral of his hometown of Castelfranco, illustrates many of the characteristics of the Venetian Renaissance style. It is a highly geometric work (using the now conventional form of the triangle with the Madonna at the apex) typical of Renaissance aesthetics of form. At the same time it shows some

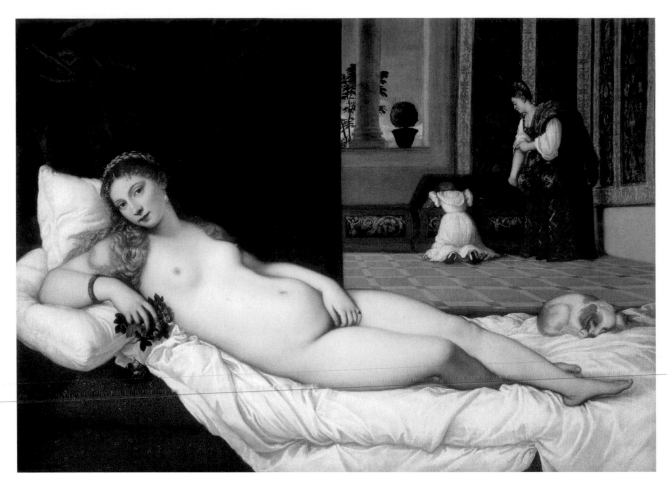

◆ **13.20** Titian, *Venus of Urbino*, 1538.

Oil on canvas, c. 3′11″ x 5′5″ (1.19 x 1.62 m). Galleria degli Uffizi, Florence, Italy//© Scala/Art Resource, NY

Contrast this *Assumption* with Titian's work of twenty years later, the *Venus of Urbino* [**Fig. 13.20**]. The religious intensity of the *Assumption* gives way to the sensual delight of the *Venus* done in homage to feminine beauty from a purely human perspective. The architectural background, evenly divided between light and dark coloration, replaces Giorgione's natural landscapes. The lushness of the nude figure is enhanced by the richness of the brocade, the small bouquet of flowers, the little pet dog, and the circumspect maids at their tasks around a rich clothes chest in the background. The *Venus of Urbino* reflects a frank love of the human body, which is presented in a lavish artistic vocabulary. Titian obviously painted this work for an aristocratic and wealthy patron.

Tintoretto The last of the Venetian giants was Jacopo Robusti (1518–1594), known more familiarly as Tintoretto ("little Dyer"—named for his father's occupation). After a short apprenticeship with Titian, Tintoretto

worked in his own studio in Venice, a city from which he rarely strayed. It was said that over his studio door he wrote the words "The drawing of Michelangelo and the color of Titian." His most famous work was a huge cycle of frescoes done for the *Scuola* ("Confraternity") of San Rocco in Venice. He began work on the frescoes in 1564 and in 1577 was named the Scuola's official painter. The oil painting depicting *The Last Supper* [**Fig. 13.21**], done for the Church of San Giorgio Maggiore in the final years of his life, is a good example of Tintoretto's energetic and dramatic style as well as providing an opportunity for contrasting Tintoretto's work to that of Leonardo. After 1577, Tintoretto was called to decorate the ducal palace in Venice as part of a restoration project following a terrible fire. Besides allegorical work celebrating the grandeur of the city, Tintoretto and his son Domenico worked on the frescoes of the great hall of the palace contributing a huge oil painting of paradise, which is more famous for its size (it covered an eighty-foot wall) than for its beauty.

◆ **13.21** Tintoretto, *The Last Supper*, 1592–1594. Note the dramatic use of light and the brilliant asymmetrical composition.

Oil on canvas, 12′ x 18′8″ (3.66 x 5.69 m). Chancel, San Giorgio Maggiore, Venice, Italy//© Scala/Art Resource, NY

MANNERISM

There is general agreement that at the end of the second decade of the sixteenth century, High Renaissance art in Italy—under severe intellectual, psychological, and cultural pressure—gave way to an art style that seemed to be an exaggeration of Renaissance form and a loosening of Renaissance intellectuality. It is not so much that a new school of artists arose but that a mood touched some artists at some point in their careers and captivated others totally. An earlier generation of art historians saw this tendency, called *Mannerism*, as a sign of decadence and decay. Scholarly opinion is less harsh today, viewing Mannerism as a distinct aesthetic to be judged on its own terms.

Mannerism is difficult to define, and the term is often used without any precise sense. The schema once proposed by art historian Frederick Hartt might serve in place of a strict definition:

High Renaissance

Content:	Normal, supernormal, or ideal; appeals to universal
Narrative:	Direct, compact, comprehensible
Space:	Controlled, measured, harmonious, ideal
Composition:	Harmonious, integrated, often centralized
Proportions:	Normative, idealized
Figure:	Easily posed, with possibility of motion to new position
Color:	Balanced, controlled, harmonious
Substance:	Natural

Mannerism

Content:	Abnormal or anormal; exploits strangeness of subject uncontrolled emotion, or withdrawal
Narrative:	Elaborate, involved, abstruse
Space:	Disjointed, spasmodic, often limited to foreground plane
Composition:	Conflicting, acentral, seeks frame
Proportions:	Uncanonical, usually attenuated
Figure:	Tensely posed; confined or overextended
Color:	Contrasting, surprising
Substance:	Artificial

Using Hartt's schema we can detect Mannerist tendencies in some of Michelangelo's later work. The figures of *Night, Day, Dawn,* and *Dusk* seem to reflect the

◆ **13.22** Michelangelo, vestibule stairway of the Laurentian Library, San Lorenzo, Florence, Italy, begun 1524, completed 1559. Note the contrast between the rounded steps in the center and the straight line steps at the sides. This library today contains many of the books and manuscripts collected by the Medici family. *(Image © Scala/Art Resource, NY)*

exaggerations of the Mannerist style Hartt describes. The entrance to the Laurentian Library [**Fig. 13.22**] in Florence, begun by Michelangelo in 1524 to rehouse the Medici book collection, shows some of these characteristics. Its windows are not windows, its columns support nothing, its staircases with their rounded steps seem agitated and in motion, its dominant lines break up space in odd and seemingly unresolved ways.

Mannerist characteristics show up in only some of Michelangelo's works (*The Last Judgment* fresco in the Sistine Chapel might also be analyzed in this fashion), but some of his contemporaries clearly broke with the intellectual unity of the High Renaissance. Two in particular deserve some attention because they so clearly illustrate the Mannerist imagination.

Pontormo Jacopo Carucci da Pontormo (1494–1557) was an eccentric and reclusive painter who had studied with Leonardo da Vinci in his youth. Pontormo's greatest painting is the *Deposition* [**Fig. 13.23**], painted

around 1528 for the Church of Santa Felicità in Florence. The most striking feature of this work is its shocking colors: pinks, apple-greens, washed-out blues. It is hard to think of any other Renaissance painting to which this stunningly original and exotic work can be compared.

Parmigianino An even more dramatic example of the Mannerist aesthetic is by Francesco Mazzola (1503–1540), called Parmigianino. He painted the *Madonna of the Long Neck* [**Fig. 13.24**] for a church in Bologna. The gigantic proportions in the picture space are made all the more exaggerated by forcing the eye to move from the tiny prophetic figure in the background to the single column and then to the overwhelmingly large Madonna. The infant almost looks dead; in fact, his hanging left arm is reminiscent of the dead Christ in Michelangelo's *Pietá*. The Virgin's figure is rendered in a strangely elongated, almost serpentine, fashion. There is something oddly erotic and exotic about her

◆ **13.23** Jacopo Carucci da Pontormo, *Deposition*, c. 1528. The twisted figures seem suspended in an airy space of no definite location. Note the odd palette the painter used to emphasize the horror and strangeness of the facial expression.

Oil on wood, c. 11' x 6'6" (3.5 x 1.98 m). Capponi Chapel, Church of Santa Felicità, Florence, Italy. Image © Scala/Art Resource, NY

◆ **13.24** Parmigianino, *Madonna of the Long Neck*, c. 1535. Note the odd prophetic figure in the middle ground of the lower right-hand corner and the elongated row of columns in the background.

Oil on wood, c. 7'1" x 4'4" (2.15 x 1.32 m). Galleria degli Uffizi, Florence, Italy//© Scala/Art Resource, NY

because of the shape of her body, the long fingers, and the great curving S of her neck. The implied eroticism is reinforced by the partially clad figures clustered at her side.

How and under what circumstances Mannerism grew and matured is the subject of much debate. Some elements of that debate must include the intellectual and social upheavals of the time (everything from wars to the Protestant Reformation) and the human desire and need to innovate once the problems and potential of a given art style have been fully worked out. In a sense, Mannerism is a testament to the inventiveness and restlessness of the human spirit.

Lavinia Fontana Daughter of an accomplished painter in Bologna, Lavinia Fontana (1552–1614) was accomplished enough that she went to Rome, where she managed to gain patronage even at the level of the papal court. Like her father she adopted the Mannerist style of painting. She had a successful career, mainly as a portrait painter, both in Bologna and later in Rome. Her work shows not only the technical skill gained in her father's studio but also in her own careful study of the works of Raphael, Michelangelo, and Parmigianino. Her prolific career was aided by her husband, Giano Paolo Zappi, who gave up his own career after they married in 1577 to aid and manage her career.

◆ **13.25** Lavinia Fontana, *Noli Me Tangere (Do Not Touch Me)*, 1581. The painting depicts Mary Magdalene suddenly realizing that the gardener is actually the Risen Christ. Replicating a story found in the Gospel of St. John (20:11–18), the painting takes on a narrative quality by showing in the background the three Marys at the tomb.

Oil on canvas 31½″ x 25¼″ (80 x 65.5 cm). Galleria degli Uffizi, Florence, Italy//© Scala/Art Resource, NY

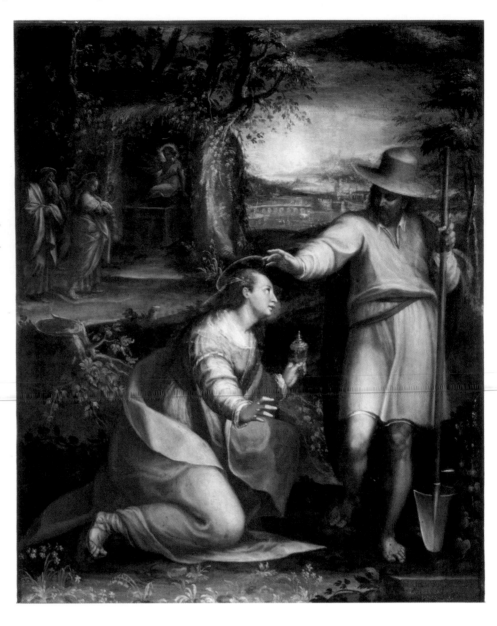

Fontana's painting of the *Noli Me Tangere* (*Do Not Touch Me*) [**Fig. 13.25**] depicts Mary Magdalene as she suddenly realizes that the gardener was in reality, the Risen Christ. Fontana rather boldly has Christ dressed as a gardener. The painting replicates the story found in the Gospel of John (20:11–18).

Sofonisba Anguissola In 1556 Giorgio Vasari traveled to Cremona to see the "marvels" of six sisters, children of the Anguissola family, who were "excellent in painting, music, and *belles artes.*" The beneficiary of a humanist education at home, the most famous of these sisters was Sofonisba, who enjoyed a great degree of fame in her own lifetime. Born in 1532(?), she studied art with a minor master in Cremona. As a young woman she traveled with her father to Rome, where she most likely met Michelangelo. Sofonisba also spent time in Milan until, in 1560, she traveled to Spain as a court painter; there she met a Sicilian noble in the service of the Spanish monarch. The couple lived in Sicily, but after her husband's death she returned to Cremona. After a remarriage, she moved to Genoa (where she probably met Caravaggio) but finally went back to Palermo, Sicily, where she died in 1624 after the famous Antony Van Dyck had painted her portrait.

Sofonisba produced an enormous amount of work, which is now represented in museums around the world. Her mature work indicates how much she learned not only from the Renaissance masters but also from the *chiaroscuro* techniques of painters like Caravaggio (discussed in Chapter 15). *A Game of Chess* [**Fig. 13.26**] painted in 1555 when the artist was only twenty-three, is a group portrait of a servant and the artist's three sisters playing chess set against a richly detailed background.

◆ **13.26** Sofonisba Anguissola, *A Game of Chess*, 1555. From offstage (far right), a servant observes the young women, the painter's three sisters, while the oldest sister looks directly at the viewer.

Oil on canvas, 28⅓" x 38⅓" (72 x 97 cm). Muzeum Nardowe, Poznan, Poland// © Erich Lessing/Art Resource, NY

MUSIC IN THE SIXTEENTH CENTURY

MUSIC AT THE PAPAL COURT

The emphasis in this chapter on painting, sculpture, and architecture makes it easy to forget that many of these artistic creations were intended for the service of Roman Catholic worship. It should be no surprise that fine music was subsidized and nurtured in Rome at the papal court. In fact, the active patronage of the popes for both the creation and the performance of music dates back to the earliest centuries of the papacy. Gregorian chant, after all, is considered a product of the interest of Pope Gregory and the school of Roman chant. In 1473 Pope Sixtus IV established a permanent choir for his private chapel, which came to be the most important center of Roman music. Sixtus's nephew Julius II endowed the choir for Saint Peter's, the Julian Choir.

The Sistine Choir used only male voices. Preadolescent boys sang the soprano parts, while older men—chosen by competition—sang the alto, tenor, and bass parts. The number of voices varied then from sixteen to twenty-four (the choir eventually became, and still is, much larger). The Sistine Choir sang *a cappella* (without accompaniment), although we know that the popes enjoyed instrumental music outside the confines of the church. Cellini, for example, mentions that he played instrumental motets for Pope Clement VII.

Josquin des Prez While Botticelli and Perugino were decorating the walls of the Sistine Chapel, the greatest composer of the age, Josquin des Prez (c. 1440–1521), was in the service of the Sistine Choir, composing and directing music for its members from 1486 to 1494. From his music we can get some sense of the quality and style of the music of the time.

Josquin, who was Flemish, spent only those eight years in Rome, but his influence was widely felt in musical circles. He has been called the bridge figure between the music of the Middle Ages and the Renaissance. Although he wrote madrigals and many masses in his career, it was in the motet for four voices—a form not held to traditional usage in the way masses were—that he showed his true genius for creative musical composition. Josquin has been most praised for homogeneous musical structure, a sense of balance and order, a feel for the quality of the lyrics. These are all characteristics common to the aspirations of the sixteenth-century Italian humanists. In that sense, Josquin combined the considerable musical tradition of Northern Europe with the new intellectual currents of the Italian south.

The Renaissance motet uses a sacred text sung by four voices in polyphony. Josquin divided his texts into clear divisions but disguised them by using overlapping voices so that one does not sense any break in his music. He also took considerable pains to marry his music to the obvious grammatical sense of the words while still expressing their emotional import by the use of the musical phrase.

Palestrina The sixteenth-century composer most identified with Rome and the Vatican is Giovanni Pierluigi da Palestrina (1525–1594). He came from the Roman hill town of Palestrina as a youth and spent the rest of his life in the capital city. At various times in his career, he was the choirmaster of the choir of Saint Peter's (the *cappella Giulia*), a singer in the Sistine Choir, and choirmaster of two other Roman basilicas (Saint John Lateran and Saint Mary Major). Finally, from 1571 until his death, he directed all music for the Vatican.

Palestrina flourished during the rather reactionary period in which the Catholic Church, in response to the Protestant Reformation, tried to reform itself by returning to the simpler ways of the past. It should not surprise us, then, that the more than one hundred masses he wrote were conservative. His polyphony, while a model of order, proportion, and clarity, is closely tied to the musical tradition of the ecclesiastical past. Rarely does Palestrina move from the Gregorian roots of church music. For example, amid the polyphony of his *Missa Papae Marcelli* (*Mass in Honor of Pope Marcellus*) one can detect the traditional melodies of the Gregorian *Kyrie*, *Agnus Dei*, and so on. Despite that conservatism, he was an extremely influential composer whose work is still regularly heard in the Roman basilicas. His music was consciously imitated by the Spanish composer Vittoria (or Victoria, c. 1548–1611), whose motet *O Vos Omnes* is almost traditional at Holy Week Services in Rome, and by William Byrd (c. 1543–1623), who brought Palestrina's style to England.

CD Track 4
Palestrina, Credo (excerpt) from *Missa Papae Marcelli*

In this listening selection, we hear Palestrain's successful return to earlier traditions of church music, a return that satisfies the Counter-Reformation requirement of keeping the text clearly audible. Indeed, he may have composed the mass to illustrate the need for musical seriousness and textual intelligibility laid down as requirements by the Council of Trent.

Nevertheless, for all Palestrina's conservatism, his work is clearly more complex and advanced than that of Machaut (see Chapter 11). The richness of harmony and the perfect balance of the voices produce a smoothness of texture and beauty and a variety of line that break new ground in the history of Western music. Note the entrance of one voice immediately after another and the decorative ornamentation of many of the phrases that by the addition of shorter notes add musical interest without blurring the text.

In the purity of his style, his return to the ideal values of the past, and the inventiveness of his own musical contributions, Palestrina is a perfect example of a Renaissance artist. His music has remained widely admired, and a twentieth-century composer, Hans Pfitzner (1869–1949), wrote the opera *Palestrina* to pay homage to the inner certainties of artistic genius.

VENETIAN MUSIC

The essentially conservative character of Palestrina's music can be contrasted to the far more adventuresome situation in Venice, a city less touched by the ecclesiastical powers of Rome. In 1527 a Dutchman—Adrian Willaert—became choirmaster of the Church of Saint Mark. He in turn trained Andrea Gabrieli and his more famous nephew, Giovanni Gabrieli, who became the most renowned Venetian composer of the sixteenth century.

The Venetians pioneered the use of multiple choirs for their church services. Saint Mark's regularly used two choirs, called split choirs, which permitted greater variation of musical composition in that the choirs could sing to and against each other in increasingly complex patterns. The Venetians were also more inclined to add instrumental music to their liturgical repertoire. They pioneered the use of the organ for liturgical music. The independent possibilities of the organ gave rise to innovative compositions that highlighted the organ. These innovations in time became standard organ pieces: the prelude, the music played before the services began (called in Italy the *intonazione*), and the virtuoso prelude called the toccata (from the Italian *toccare*, "to touch"). The toccata was designed to feature the range of the instrument and the dexterity of the performer.

Both Roman and Venetian music were deeply influenced by the musical tradition of the North. Josquin des Prez and Adrian Willaert were, after all, both from the Low Countries. In Italy their music came in contact with the intellectual tradition of Italian humanism. Without pushing the analogy too far, it could be said that Rome gave the musician the same Renaissance sensibility that it gave the painter: a sense of proportion, classicism, and balance. The Venetian composers, much like Venetian painters of the time, were interested in color and emotion.

CONTRASTING RENAISSANCE VOICES

Early sixteenth-century Renaissance culture was a study in contrasts. The period not only marked a time when some of the most refined artistic accomplishments were achieved, but it was also a period of great social upheaval. The lives of both Raphael and Leonardo ended at precisely the time Luther was struggling with the papacy. In 1527 Rome was sacked by Emperor Charles V's soldiers in an orgy of rape and violence the city had not seen since the days of the Vandals in the

◆ **13.27** Raphael, *Baldassare Castiglione*, c. 1514. Raphael would have known the famous humanist through family connections in his native Urbino.

Oil on panel, transferred to canvas, 29½" x 25½" (75 x 65 cm). Museé du Louvre, Paris, France//© Réunion des Musées Nationaux/Art Resource, NY

fifth century. It would be simplistic to reduce the period of the High Renaissance to a contrast between cool intellectual sophistication and intensely violent passion; nevertheless, it is true that two of the most interesting Italian writers of the period reflect precisely these opposing tendencies.

CASTIGLIONE

Baldassare Castiglione (1478–1529) served in the diplomatic corps of Milan, Mantua, and Urbino. He was a versatile man—a person of profound learning, equipped with physical and martial skills, and possessed of a noble and refined demeanor. Raphael's famous portrait of Castiglione [**Fig. 13.27**] faithfully reflects both Castiglione's aristocratic and intellectual qualities.

While serving at the court of Urbino from 1504 to 1516, Castiglione decided to write *The Courtier*, a task that occupied him for the next dozen years. It was finally published by the Aldine Press in Venice in 1528, a year before the author's death. In *The Courtier*, cast in the form of an extended dialogue and borrowing heavily from the style and thought of ancient writers from Plato to Cicero, Castiglione has his learned friends discuss a range of topics: the ideals of chivalry, classical virtues, the character of the true courtier, the ideals of

Platonic love. Posterity remembers Castiglione's insistent plea that the true **courtier** should be a person of humanist learning, impeccable ethics, refined courtesy, physical and martial skills, and fascinating conversation. He should not possess any of these qualities to the detriment of any other.

The *uomo universale* ("well-rounded person") should do all things with what Castiglione calls *sprezzatura*. *Sprezzatura*, which is almost impossible to translate into a single English word, means something like "effortless mastery." The courtier, unlike the pedant, wears learning lightly, while his mastery of sword and horse has none of the fierce clumsiness of the common soldier in the ranks. The courtier does everything equally well but with an air of unhurried and graceful effortlessness.

Castiglione's work was translated into English by Sir Thomas Hoby in 1561. It exercised an immense influence on what the English upper classes thought the educated gentleman should be. We can detect echoes of Castiglione in some of the plays of Ben Jonson as well as in the drama of William Shakespeare. When in *Hamlet* (III, I), for example, Ophelia cries out in horror at the lunatic behavior of Hamlet (at his loss of *sprezzatura*?), the influence of Castiglione is clear:

> Oh, what a noble mind is here o'erthrown!
> The courtier's, soldier's, scholar's eye, tongue, sword:
> The expectancy and rose of the fair state,
> The glass of fashion and the mould of form,
> The observed of all observers . . .

The most common criticism of Castiglione's courtier is that he reflects a world that is overly refined, too aesthetically sensitive, and excessively preoccupied with the niceties of decorum and decoration. The courtier's world, in short, is the world of the wealthy, the aristocratic, and the most select of the elite. If the reader shares that criticism when reading Castiglione, the *Autobiography of Benvenuto Cellini* should prove a bracing antidote to the niceties of Castiglione.

CELLINI

Benvenuto Cellini (1500–1571) was a talented Florentine goldsmith and sculptor whose life, frankly chronicled, was a seemingly never-ending panorama of violence, intrigue, quarrel, sexual excess, egotism, and political machination. His *Autobiography*, much of it dictated to a young apprentice who wrote while Cellini worked, is a vast and rambling narrative of Cellini's life from his birth to the year 1562. We read vignettes about popes and commoners, artists and soldiers, cardinals and prostitutes, assassins and artists, as well as a gallery of other characters from the Renaissance demimonde of Medicean Florence and papal Rome.

Above all, we meet Benvenuto Cellini, who makes no bones about his talent, his love of life, or his taste

◆ **13.28** Benvenuto Cellini, *Perseus Holding the Head of Medusa*, 1545–1554. Earlier models of this statue, including a first effort in wax, are preserved in the Bargello Museum in Florence.

Bronze, 18′ (5.48 m) high, post restoration. Loggia dei Lanzi, Florence, Italy//© Scala/Art Resource, NY

for violence. Cellini is not one of Castiglione's courtiers. Cellini fathered eight legitimate and illegitimate children; he was banished from Florence for sodomy; imprisoned for assault; fled Rome after murdering a man; and fought on the walls of the Castel Sant' Angelo in Rome during the siege of 1527 in defense of the Medici Pope Clement VII. Anyone who thinks of the Renaissance artist solely in terms of proportion, love

of the Classics, Neo-Platonic philosophy, and genteel humanism is in for a shock when encountering Cellini's *Autobiography*.

One particular part of Cellini's book is interesting not for its characteristic bravado or swagger, but for its insight into the working methods of an artist. In a somewhat melodramatic account, Cellini describes the process of casting the bronze statue of Perseus that actually turned out to be his most famous work [**Fig. 13.28**]. It now stands in the Loggia dei Lanzi next to the Palazzo Vecchio in Florence.

Cellini does not belong to the first rank of sculptors, although no one has denied his skill as a craftsman. The *Perseus*, finished in 1554 for Duke Cosimo I de' Medici, is a highly refined work made more interesting because of Cellini's record of its genesis.

SUMMARY

Art follows patronage, as we have noted. The "high" Renaissance is summed up in the lives and works of three artists: Michelangelo, Raphael, and Leonardo da Vinci. The first two did their most famous work in the Vatican in the sixteenth century, whereas Leonardo, true to his restless spirit, sojourned there only for a time before he began his wanderings through the courts of Europe. These artists' work gives full meaning to the summation of Renaissance ideals.

- **Renaissance and Reformation.** When we look at the work of Raphael and Michelangelo under the patronage of the popes, we should not forget that this explosion of art and culture was taking place while a new and formidable revolution was in the making: the Protestant Reformation. Although it would be overly simplistic to believe that the Renaissance caused the Reformation, it must certainly be seen as a contributing factor—as we will see in the next chapter. Even so, there is a marked shift in the atmosphere in which Michelangelo worked in Rome before 1521 and afterward, when the full force of the Protestant revolt in the North was making itself felt in Rome.

- **Rome and Venice.** The artistic work in Rome can be contrasted profitably with that which took place in Venice during roughly the same period. The Roman Renaissance was under the patronage of the church. Venetian art and music enjoyed the same patronage source as did Florence in the preceding century: commerce and trade. Venice made its fortune from the sea: the shipping of its busy port looked to both Europe and the Middle East. It was fiercely protective of its independence (including its independence from papal Rome) and proud of its ancient traditions. Even the religious art of Venice possessed a certain freedom from the kind of art being produced in Rome in the same century because Venice had less contact with the seething ideas current in the century.

◆ **The Role of the Duchies.** Renaissance ideas had also penetrated other areas of Italy. Florence still had its artistic life (although somewhat diminished from its great days in the fifteenth century), but provincial cities like Parma and Mantua were not without their notables. Much of this artistic activity rested in the courts of the nobility, who supplied the kind of life and leisure that made possible the courtier and the court lifestyle immortalized in the book by Castiglione. The insufficiencies of this court culture would become clear when the religious wars of the sixteenth century broke out and humanism had to confront the new realities coming from the increasingly Protestant North.

EXERCISES

1. If you were to transpose Raphael's *School of Athens* into a contemporary setting, what kind of architecture would you use to frame the scene and whom would you include among the personages in the picture?

2. Critics use the adjective *Michelangeloesque*. Now that you have studied his work, what does that adjective mean to you? Give an all-inclusive definition of the term.

3. Michelangelo's Medici Chapel represents the artist's best attempt to express a permanent tribute to the dead. How does it differ in spirit from such monuments today? (You might begin by comparing it to the Vietnam Memorial in Washington, DC, or some other such public monument.)

4. Castiglione's concept of *sprezzatura* was an attempt to summarize the ideal of the educated courtier. Is there a word or phrase that would best sum up the character of the well-rounded person today? Do we have a similar ideal? If so, how would you characterize it? If not, why not?

5. Mannerism as an art style contains an element of exaggeration. Can you think of any art form with which we are familiar that uses exaggeration to make its point?

6. Art patronage in the sixteenth century came mainly from the church and from the wealthy. Are they equally sources of patronage today? If not, what has replaced the church as a source of art patronage today? What does that say about our culture?

Visit the *Culture & Values* Companion website at **www.cengage.com/art/Cunningham/Cultureand Values7E** and the *Humanities Resource Center* for an array of primary source readings, key terms with pronunciations, flash cards, quizzes, and study materials designed especially to help you do well in this course.

CHAPTER 14

THE RENAISSANCE IN THE NORTH

One of the greatest centers of cultural achievement in Northern Renaissance times was England. Its high point is often known as the Elizabethan Age, after the queen who ruled her country for almost half a century from 1558 to 1603. Her parents were Henry VIII and Anne Boleyn whom the king divorced and beheaded when Elizabeth was barely two and a half years old. Thus she grew up illegitimate until Henry's will declared her to be in line for the throne.

Tall, red-haired, and temperamental, she was to become every inch a queen, dominating and unpredictable, using both royal anger and gentleness. Her single guiding principle seems to have been an utter devotion to her country and its interests. Her predecessor, Mary Tudor, had sought to take England back into the Catholic faith with which Henry VIII had broken. Elizabeth restored Protestantism by a series of compromises. The secret of her success was that she herself was motivated more by practical results than religious fervor.

The question of a potential marriage was a problem that seemed to have no satisfactory solution. Had she married an English nobleman, she would have disturbed the delicate balance of power that kept England's leading aristocratic families loyal to her. Marriage to a foreign ruler would have reduced England's status as a leading European power, just at the moment when she was intent on strengthening it. Elizabeth avoided the dilemma by choosing to remain the "Virgin Queen," although both during her reign and ever since gossips questioned the accuracy of her title.

Toward the end of her life, a long war with Spain weakened England's economy, and a series of bad harvests badly affected its agriculture. For a while the queen's authority seemed to falter, but by the end of her reign she had regained the love of her people. As she herself said in 1601, "Though God hath raised me high, yet this I count the glory of my crown, that I have reigned with your love, and you never shall have any on this throne who will love you better."

THE SPREAD OF HUMANISM

The ideas and artistic styles that developed in Italy during the fifteenth and sixteenth centuries produced immense

◆ *Elizabeth I of England*, Nicholas Hilliard, 1585. (© *Hatfield House, London, UK/SuperStock*)

changes in the cultural life of England, France, Germany, and the Netherlands. As the Renaissance spread beyond the Alps, the new humanism it carried roused Northern Europe from its conservative intellectual patterns and offered an alternative to traditional religious doctrines. The infusion of Italian ideas produced a new breadth of vision that was responsible for some of the greatest northern painting and for important developments in music. By the end of the sixteenth century, under the influence of humanism, a brilliant cultural life had developed in Elizabethan England, where

Renaissance English drama achieved its greatest glory in the work of William Shakespeare.

This was not the first time Northern Europe and Italy had come into contact. During the fourteenth century, a style of late-Gothic painting reflecting the grace and elegance of courtly life on both sides of the Alps had developed. Known as the International Style, it was popular in both Italy and Northern Europe. Furthermore, as early as the beginning of that century, German scholars who had traveled to Italy to study returned home with a new enthusiasm for classical

GENERAL EVENTS	ART
1494	
1498 Vasco da Gama lands in India	
1500	
1515–1547 Francis I reigns in France **1517** Luther's 95 Theses trigger the 　　Reformation in Germany **1519–1556** Charles V reigns as Holy 　　Roman Emperor **1521** Excommunication of Luther by Pope Leo X	**1500** Dürer, *Self-Portrait* **early 16th cent.** Italian Renaissance art and 　　thought spread northward **c. 1505–1510** Bosch, *Garden of Earthly 　　Delights* **1513** Dürer, *Knight, Death, and the Devil*
Genesis of the Reformation	
1524–1525 Peasants' War in Germany	**1515** Grünewald, Isenheim Altarpiece
1525	
1525 Charles V defeats Francis I at Pavia	**1525** Altdorfer, *Landscape*
1527 Charles V sacks Rome	**c. 1530** Clouet, Portrait of *Francis I* **c. 1530–1550** Sacred art denounced 　　as idolatry by reforming iconoclasts **c. 1533–1540** Decorations by Rosso 　　Fiorentino for Palace at Fontainebleau
1534 Henry VIII founds Anglican Church in England	
1539 Saint Ignatius of Loyola founds Society of Jesus (Jesuits)	**1539–1540** Holbein, *Portrait of Henry VIII* **1540–1543** Cellini, *The Saltcellar*
Spread of Protestantism	
1545–1564 Council of Trent initiates Counter-Reformation 　　under Jesuit guidance	
1550	
1550–1555 Lutheran and Catholic wars in Germany end with 　　Peace of Augsburg **1556** Charles V retires **1556–1598** Philip II reigns in Spain and Netherlands **1558–1603** Elizabeth I reigns 　　in England **1572** Saint Bartholomew's Day 　　Massacre in France	**c. 1562–1567** Bruegel the Elder, major works
Growth of Counter-Reformation	
1575	
1581 United Provinces of 　　Netherlands declare 　　independence from Spain **1585** England sends troops to support Netherlands against Spain **1588** Philip's Spanish Armada defeated by English	**c. 1590** Hilliard, Portrait of a Youth
Religious and Nationalistic Unrest	
1598 Edict of Nantes establishes religious toleration in France **1600** British found East India Tea Company **1602** Dueling banned in France **1607** English found colony of Virginia in New World **1609** Independence of Netherlands recognized by Spain	**c. 1600** Patronage for sacred art wanes in 　　Reformation countries, flourishes in 　　Counter-Reformation countries
1620	

antiquity. Nor was the northern Renaissance merely based on Italian ideas, the wholesale adoption by Northern European artists of foreign ways and styles. Northern artists drew on a rich native past and were able to incorporate exciting new ideas from Italy into their own vision of the world. One of the chief characteristics of northern Renaissance art, in fact, was its emphasis on individualism; painters like Albrecht Dürer and Albrecht Altdorfer are as different from each other as they are from the Italian artists who initially influenced them.

The spread of Italian Renaissance ideas to the north was in many respects political rather than cultural. Throughout most of the sixteenth century, the great monarchs of Northern Europe vied with one another for political and military control over the states of Italy. In the process, they came in contact with the latest developments in Italian artistic and intellectual life and often based their own courts on Italian models. Francis I, who ruled France from 1515 to 1547, made a deliberate attempt to expose French culture to Italian influences by doing everything he could to attract Ital-

ARCHITECTURE	LITERATURE & PHILOSOPHY	MUSIC
1506 Rebuilding begins of Saint Peter's Basilica, Rome	**1506–1532** Ariosto active in Italy	Vernacular hymns stressed by Reformers Musical elements in Protestant services simplified by Luther to increase comprehension
1519 Château de Chambord built by Francis I	**1516** Thomas More, *Utopia*	**c. 1510** Isaac and Sendl active in Northern Europe
	1524 Erasmus, *De Libero Arbitrio* (*On Free Will*)	**c. 1520** Marot and Janequin compose chansons
	1525 Luther, *De Servo Arbitrio* (*On the Bondage of the Will*)	**c. 1525–1530** Luther, "A Mighty Fortress Is Our God"
	1530 Budé persuades Francis I to found Collège de France as center for humanism	
1546 Lescot and Goujon, Square Court of Louvre, begun	**1534** Luther publishes his German translation of Bible	
	16th cent. Humanism spreads, along with interest in scientific inquiry; availability of books increases literacy	**1544** First English-language litany based on Gregorian chant
	1543 Copernicus, *On the Revolution of Celestial Bodies*; Vesalius, *Seven Books on the Structure of the Human Body*	**1549** Merbecke, *The Boke of Common Praier Noted*
c. 1550 Reformation ends building of elaborate churches in Protestant countries	**1559** Pope Paul IV publishes first *Index of Prohibited Books*	**c. 1570** Tallis, *Lamentations of Jeremiah*
	1580 Montaigne's first *Essays*	**1588** English translation of *Musica Transalpina*
	c. 1587 Marlowe, *Tamburlaine*	
	1590 Sidney, *Arcadia*	
	1590–1596 Spenser, *The Faerie Queene*	
	1590–1610 Shakespeare's plays	**1591** Byrd, *My Ladye Nevells Booke*
	1593 Marlowe, *Dr. Faustus*	
	late 16th–early 17th cent. Cervantes active in Spain, Jonson in England, Tasso in Italy	**Late 16th–early 17th cent.** English madrigals by Byrd, Morley, and Weelkes follow Italian models; ayres by Dowland
	1611 *Authorized Version* of Bible	
	1620 Francis Bacon, *Novum Organum*	

◆ **14.2** Benvenuto Cellini, *The Saltcellar of Francis I*, 1540–1543. The male figure is Sea; the female is Land; the salt bowl (called a saltcellar) is in the background. "Both figures were seated with their legs interlaced, just as the arms of the sea run into the land," said Cellini. The sculptor had fled to the French court after the sack of Rome in 1527.

Gold, niello work, and ebony base, 10¼" x 13⅛" (26 x 33 cm). Kunsthistorisches Museum, Vienna, Austria//© Erich Lessing/Art Resource, NY

◆ **14.3** Leone Leoni, *Bust of Emperor Charles V*, 1533–1555. The sculptor deliberately portrayed the German ruler as a Roman emperor, thus associating Charles with both Italy and Classical antiquity. Note the eagle at the base, symbol of imperial rule since Roman times.

Bronze, 44" (112 cm) high. Museo del Prado, Madrid, Spain//© Erich Lessing/Art Resource, NY

ian artists to the French court; among those who came were Leonardo da Vinci, Andrea del Sarto (1486–1530), and Benvenuto Cellini [**Fig. 14.2**]. Francis and his successors also esteemed literature and scholarship highly. Francis's sister, Marguerite of Navarre, a writer of considerable gifts, became the center of an intellectual circle that included many of the finest minds of the age.

The history of Germany is intimately bound up with that of the Hapsburg family. In the first half of the sixteenth century, the same Hapsburg king who ruled Germany (under the old name of the Holy Roman Empire) with the title of Charles V ruled Spain under the title of Charles I. Charles was the principal competitor of Francis I for political domination of Italy, and although his interest in the arts was less cultivated than that of his rival, his conquests brought Italian culture to both Spain and the north [**Fig. 14.3**]. On his abdication (1556) he divided his vast territories between his brother Ferdinand and his son Philip. The Austrian and Spanish branches of the Hapsburg family remained the principal powers in Europe until the 1650s.

For most of the Renaissance, England remained under the dominion of a single family—the Tudors—whose last representative was Elizabeth I. Like her fellow rulers, in the course of her long reign (1558–1603) Elizabeth established her court as a center of art and learning. Although the influence of Italian models on the visual arts was less marked in England than elsewhere, revived interest in Classical antiquity and the new humanism it inspired is reflected in the works of Shakespeare and other Elizabethan writers.

Although the art of the great northern centers drew heavily on Italy for inspiration, another factor was equally important. The sixteenth century was a period

◆ **14.4** Lucas Cranach, *Portrait of Martin Luther*, c. 1526. Around the time this portrait was painted, Luther—seen here wearing austere black—married Katharina von Bora, a former nun; they had six children.

Oil on panel, 15″ x 9″ (38 x 24 cm). Galleria degli Uffizi, Florence, Italy // © *Scala/Art Resource, NY*

of almost unparalleled intellectual tumult in which traditional ideas on religion and the nature of the universe were shaken and often permanently changed. Many of the revolutionary movements of the age were in fact northern in origin, and not surprisingly they had a profound effect on the art, music, and literature being produced in the same place and time. While northern artists were being influenced by the styles of their fellow artists south of the Alps, their cultural world was being equally shaped by theologians and scientists closer to home. The intellectual developments of this world form a necessary background to its artistic achievements.

THE REFORMATION

On the eve of All Saints' Day in 1517, a German Augustinian friar, Martin Luther (1483–1546), tacked on the door of the collegiate Church of Wittenberg a parchment containing ninety-five **theses** (academic propositions) written in Latin—the usual procedure for advertising an academic debate [**Fig. 14.4**]. Luther's theses constituted an attack on the Roman Catholic doctrine of **indulgences** (forgiveness of punishment for sins, usually obtained either through good works or prayers along with the payment of an appropriate sum of money); this was a timely topic because an indulgence was currently being preached near Wittenberg to help raise funds for the rebuilding of Saint Peter's in Rome.

Luther's act touched off a controversy that went far beyond academic debate. For the next few years there were arguments among theologians, while Luther received emissaries and directives from the Vatican as well as official warnings from the pope. Luther did not waver in his criticisms. On June 15, 1520, Pope Leo X (Giovanni de' Medici, son of Lorenzo the Magnificent) condemned Luther's teaching as heretical and, on January 3, 1521, excommunicated him from the Catholic Church. The Protestant Reformation had been born.

Luther's reformation principles began to be applied in churches throughout Germany, and a rapid and widespread outbreak of other reforming movements was touched off by Luther's example. By 1523, radical reformers far more iconoclastic than Luther began to agitate for a purer Christianity free from any trace of "popery." These radical reformers are often called **Anabaptists** ("baptized again") because of their insistence on adult baptism even if baptism had been performed in infancy. Many of these Anabaptist groups had radical social and political ideas, including pacifism and the refusal to take oaths or participate in civil government, which appealed to the discontent of the lower classes. One outcome was the Peasants' War in Germany, which was put down with ferocious bloodshed in 1525.

The Reformation was not confined to Germany. In 1523 Zurich, Switzerland, accepted the reformation ideal for its churches. Under the leadership of Ulrich Zwingli (1484–1531), Zurich, and later Berne and Basel, adopted Luther's reforms, including the abolition of statues and images and the right of the clergy to marry (abolishing celibacy). In addition, the list of sacraments was greatly reduced and modified to include only baptism and the Lord's Supper (communion). In Geneva, John Calvin (1509–1564) preached a brand of Protestantism even more extreme than that of either Luther or Zwingli. Calvin's doctrines soon spread north to the British Isles, especially Scotland, under the Calvinist John Knox, and west to the Low Countries, especially Holland. In England, King Henry VIII (born 1491, reigned 1509–1547), formerly a stout opponent of Lutheranism, broke with Rome in 1534 because the pope refused to grant him an annulment from his first

Katherine Zell

Many of the Reformation's most active figures were women. Katherine Zell (1497–1562) was the wife of Matthew Zell, one of the first priests to demonstrate his break from the church by marrying. When he died, Katherine continued his teaching and pastoral work. She wrote this letter in 1558 to an old friend who was suffering from leprosy.

My dear Lord Felix, since we have known each other for a full thirty years I am moved to visit you in your long and frightful illness. I have not been able to come as often as I would like, because of the load here for the poor and the sick, but you have been ever in my thoughts. We have often talked of how you have been stricken, cut off from rank, office, from your wife and friends, from all dealings with the world which recoils from your loathsome dis-

ease and leaves you in utter loneliness. At first you were bitter and utterly cast down till God gave you strength and patience, and now you are able to thank him that out of love he has taught you to bear the cross. Because I know that your illness weighs upon you daily and may easily cause you again to fall into despair and rebelliousness, I have gathered some passages which may make your yoke light in the spirit, though not in the flesh. I have written meditations on the 51st Psalm: "Have mercy upon me, O God, according to thy loving-kindness," and the 130th, "Out of the depths have I cried unto thee, O Lord." And then on the Lord's Prayer and the Creed.

Letter by Katherine Zell, reprinted from *Women of the Reformation in Germany and Italy* by Roland H. Bainton, © 1971 Augsburg Fortress Press.

◆ **14.5** Hans Holbein the Younger, *Henry VIII in Wedding Dress*, 1540. Weddings were not uncommon events in Henry's life. This wedding to his fourth wife, Anne of Cleves (see Figure 14.26), took place in his forty-ninth year (as the inscription reads) and was annulled within the year.

Oil on panel, 32½″ x 29″ (83 x 74 cm). Galleria Nazionale d'Arte Antica, Rome, Italy//© Scala/Art Resource, NY

wife, Katherine of Aragon [**Fig. 14.5**]. In that same year (1534), Henry issued the Act of Supremacy, declaring the English sovereign head of the church in England.

By the middle of the sixteenth century, Europe—for centuries solidly under the authority of the Church of Rome—was divided in a way that has remained essentially unaltered. Spain and Portugal, Italy, most of France, southern Germany, Austria, parts of Eastern Europe (Poland, Hungary, and parts of the Balkans), and Ireland remained Catholic, whereas most of Switzerland, the British Isles, all of Scandinavia, northern and eastern Germany, and other parts of Eastern Europe gradually switched to Protestantism (see map, "Religious Divisions in Europe c. 1600").

CAUSES OF THE REFORMATION

What conditions permitted this rapid and revolutionary upheaval in Europe? The standard answer is that the medieval church was so riddled with corruption and incompetence that it was like a house of cards waiting to be toppled. This answer, while containing some truth, is not totally satisfactory because it does not explain why the Reformation did not occur a century earlier, when similar or worse conditions prevailed. Why had the Reformation not taken place during the fourteenth century, when there were such additional factors as plague, schisms, and wars as well as incipient reformers clamoring for change? The exact conditions that permitted the Reformation to happen are difficult

RELIGIOUS DIVISIONS IN EUROPE C. 1600

☐ Catholicism   ☐ Anglicanism

▨ Orthodox Christianity   ☐ Calvinism

☐ Lutheranism

(Religious minorities are not represented)

to pinpoint, but any explanation must take into account several elements that were clearly emerging in the sixteenth century.

First, there was a rising sense of nationalism in Europe combined with increasing resentment at the economic and political demands made by the papacy, many of which ignored the rights of individual countries. Thus Luther's insistence that the German rulers reform the church because the church was impotent to do so appealed to both economic and nationalistic self-interests.

Second, the idea of reform in the church had actually been maturing for centuries, with outcries against abuses and pleas for change. Some of the great humanists who were contemporaries of Luther—including Erasmus of Rotterdam, Thomas More in England, and Jacques Lefèvre d'Étaples in France—had also

pilloried the excesses of the church. These men, and many of their followers and devoted readers, yearned for a deeper, more interior piety, free from the excessive pomp and ceremony that characterized so much of popular medieval religion. Luther's emphasis on personal conversion and his rejection of much of the ecclesiastical superstructure of Catholicism appealed to the sensibilities of many people. That the reformers to the left of Luther demanded even more rejection of Catholic practices shows how widespread was the desire for change.

Third, several other factors clustered around the two already mentioned. The low moral and intellectual condition of much of the clergy was a scandal; the wealth and lands of the monastic and episcopal lords were envied. In short, many related economic and political factors fed the impulses of the Reformation.

RENAISSANCE HUMANISM
AND THE REFORMATION

The relationship between Renaissance humanism and the Protestant Reformation is significant if complex. With the single exception of John Calvin, none of the major church reformers were professional humanists, although all came into contact with the movement. Luther had no early contact with the "new learning," even though he utilized its fruits. Nevertheless, humanism as far back as the time of Petrarch shared many intellectual and cultural sentiments with the Reformation. We should note these similarities before treating the wide differences between the two movements.

The reformers and the humanists shared several religious aversions. They were both fiercely critical of monasticism, the decadent character of popular devotion to the saints, the low intellectual preparation of the clergy, and the general venality and corruption of the higher clergy, especially the papal **curia**—the body of tribunals and assemblies through which the pope governed the church.

Both the humanists and the reformers felt that the scholastic theology of the universities had degenerated into quibbling arguments, meaningless discussions, and dry academic exercises bereft of any intellectual or spiritual significance. In a common reaction, both rejected the scholastics of the medieval universities in favor of Christian writers of an earlier age. John Calvin's reverence in the sixteenth century for the writings of the early Christian church father and philosopher Augustine (354–430) echoed the equal devotion of Petrarch in the fourteenth century.

Humanists and reformers alike spearheaded a move toward a better understanding of the Bible based not on the authority of theological interpretation but on close, critical scrutiny of the text, preferably in the original Hebrew and Greek. Mastery of the three biblical languages (Latin, Greek, and Hebrew) was considered so important in the sixteenth century that schools were founded especially for the specific purpose of instruction in them. Some famous academic institutions, including Corpus Christi College, Oxford; the University of Alcalá, Spain; and the Collège de France in Paris, were founded for that purpose. Luther's own University of Wittenberg had three chairs for the study of biblical languages.

We can see the connection between humanist learning and the Reformation more clearly by noting some aspects of Luther's great translation of the Bible into German. Although there had been many earlier vernacular translations into German, Luther's, which he began in 1521, was the first produced entirely from the original languages, and the texts he used illuminate the contribution of humanist learning. For the New Testament, he used the critical Greek edition prepared by Erasmus. For the Book of Psalms, he used a text published in Hebrew by the humanist printer Froben at Basel in

1516. The other Hebrew texts were rendered from a Hebrew version published by Italian Jewish scholars who worked in the Italian cities of Soncino and Brescia. His translations of the Apocrypha (books not found in the Hebrew canon) utilized the Greek edition of the Apocrypha printed in 1518 by Aldus Manutius at his press in Venice. As an aid for his labors, Luther made abundant use of grammars and glossaries published by the humanist scholar Johann Reuchlin.

In short, Luther's great achievement was possible only because much of the groundwork had already been laid by a generation of humanist philologists. This scholarly tradition endured. In 1611, when the translators of the famous English King James Version wrote their preface to the Bible, they noted that they had consulted commentaries and translations as well as translations or versions in Chaldee, Hebrew, Syriac, Greek, Latin, Spanish, French, Italian, and Dutch.

Although there were similarities and mutual influences between humanists and reformers, there were also vast differences. Two are of particular importance. The first relates to concepts of the nature of humanity. The humanist program was rooted in the notion of human perfectibility. This was as true of the Florentine humanists with their strong Platonic bias as it was of northern humanists like Erasmus. The humanists placed great emphasis on the profoundly Greek (or, more accurately, Socratic) notion that education can produce a moral person. Both humanist learning and humanist education had a strong ethical bias: learning improves and ennobles. The reformers, by contrast, felt that humanity was hopelessly mired in sin and could only be raised from that condition by the freely offered grace of God. For the reformers, the humanists' position that education could perfect a person undercut the notion of a sinful humanity in need of redemption.

Luther and Erasmus The contrast between these two points of view is most clearly evident in a polemical debate between Luther and Erasmus on the nature of the human will. In a 1524 treatise called *De Libero Arbitrio (On Free Will)*, Erasmus defended the notion that human effort cooperates in the process of sanctification and salvation. Luther answered in 1525 with a famous tract titled *De Servo Arbitrio (On the Bondage of the Will)*. The titles of the two pamphlets provide a shorthand description of the severe tension existing between the two viewpoints. A second difference between the humanists and the reformers begins with the humanist notion that behind all religious systems lies a universal truth that can be detected by a careful study of religious texts. Pico della Mirandola, for example, believed that the essential truth of Christianity could be detected in Talmudic, Platonic, Greek, and Latin authors. He felt that a sort of universal religion could be constructed from a close application of humanist scholarship to all areas of religion. The reformers, on the other hand, held

VALUES

Reform

It is almost too obvious, but one would have to say that the predominant value that energized Western Europe in the first half of the sixteenth century was the desire for religious reform. This impulse manifested in different ways, but the acting out of the reform impulse would have great sociopolitical effects in Europe and in the newly discovered lands of the New World.

This desire for reform was an explicit motivating impulse in the work of the northern humanists who believed that their scholarly labors of biblical translation and the recovery of early Christian classics would be a vehicle by which the Christian life of Europe would be invigorated. The humanists of the North believed in reform by scholarship.

The great Protestant reformers did not set out to start new churches. Their goal was to get back to an earlier, less corrupt, kind of Christianity that would reform Christian life. The close contact between Calvin's reform of Geneva and the city's political life was an attempt not only to reinvigorate religious faith but also to provide a different model of governance in civil affairs.

The Catholic response to Protestantism is often called a "counterreformation" but, in fact, it was a genuinely internal reformation clarifying both its own beliefs and triggering new religious impulses within. The various reactive strategies of Catholicism to the rise of the Protestant world all derived from a deep sense that the church needed a thorough reformation.

The reforming impulses early in the century eventually solidified into discrete church bodies: the Anglicans in England; Presbyterians in Scotland; Calvinists in parts of Switzerland and Holland; Catholicism in the Mediterranean countries; and Lutheranism in parts of Germany and Scandinavia. Like all reforming movements, that of the sixteenth century eventually formed institutions ready and waiting for a time when new reforming impulses would be required.

Already evident in this period was a new spirit in scientific investigation, which would sweep away the older authority-based approach to scientific questions in favor of an empirical, investigative mode that would not only revolutionize science but also create the need for new reformations in church life. In the rise of the experimental sciences we can see, in the deepest meaning of the word, a reformation of intellectual life coming alive in the culture of the time, a reformation that would show itself to be, in time, antagonistic to the religious reforms of the first part of the century.

---

to a simple yet unshakable dictum: *Scriptura sola* ("the Bible alone"). While the reformers were ready to use humanist methods to investigate the sacred text, they were adamant in their conviction that only the Bible held God's revelation to humanity.

As a result of the translation of the Bible into the vernacular language of millions of Northern Europeans, Reformation theologians were able to stress the Scriptures as the foundation of their teachings. Luther and Calvin further encouraged lay education, urging their followers to read the Bible themselves and find there—and only there—Christian truth. In interpreting what they read, individuals were to be guided by no official religious authority but were to make their own judgment following their own consciences. This doctrine is known as "universal priesthood," because it denies a special authority to the clergy. All of these teachings, although primarily theological, were to have profound and long-range cultural impacts.

We can see that there was an intense positive and negative interaction between humanism and the Reformation—a movement energized by books in general and the Bible in particular. The intensely literary preoccupations of fourteenth- and fifteenth-century humanism provided a background and impetus for the sixteenth-century Reformation. As a philosophical and cultural system, however, humanism was in general too optimistic and ecumenical for the more orthodox reformers. In the latter sixteenth century, humanism as a worldview found a congenial outlook in the Christian humanism of Cervantes and the gentle skepticism of Montaigne, but in Reformation circles it was used only as an intellectual instrument for other ends.

CULTURAL SIGNIFICANCE OF THE REFORMATION

Cultural historians have attributed a great deal of significance to the Reformation. Some have argued, for example, that with its strong emphasis on individuals and their religious rights, the Reformation was a harbinger of the modern political world. However, with equal plausibility one could make the case that with

◆ **14.6** Portion of a page from the Gutenberg Bible, 1456. The first edition of this Bible printed at Mainz a year earlier probably consisted of no more than 150 copies. Gutenberg was the first in Europe to set up his pages with movable type, although printing with individual characters that could be combined and reused had occurred in China by the 11th century. *(Image © Classic Image/Alamy)*

its strong emphasis on social discipline and its biblical authoritarianism, the Reformation was the last great spasm of the medieval world. Likewise, in a famous **thesis** developed in the early twentieth century by the German sociologist Max Weber, Calvinism was seen as the seedbed and moving force of modern capitalism. Weber's proposition has lingered in our vocabulary in phrases like "work ethic" or "Puritan ethic," although most scholars now see it as more provocative than provable. Regardless of the scholarly debates about these large questions, there are other, more clearly defined ways in which the Protestant Reformation changed the course of Western culture.

First, the Reformation gave a definite impetus to the already growing use of books in Europe. The strong emphasis on the reading and study of the Bible produced inevitable concern for increased literacy. Luther, for example, wanted education to be provided free to children from all classes in Germany. The central place of the Bible in religious life made an immense impact on the literary culture of the time. Luther's Bible in Germany and the King James Version in England exercised an inestimable influence on the very shape of the language spoken by their readers. In other countries touched by the Reformation the literary influence of the translated Bible was absolutely fundamental. In the Scandinavian countries, vernacular literature really began with translations of the Bible. In Finland, a more extreme example, Finnish was used as a written language for the first time in translating the Bible.

The Bible was not the only book to see widespread diffusion in this period. Books, pamphlets, and treatises crisscrossed Europe as the often intricate theological battles were waged for one or another theological position. It is not accidental that the Council of Trent (1545–1564), a prime instrument of the Catholic counter reform, stringently legislated the manner in which copies of the Bible were to be translated and distributed. The fact that the infamous *Index* (a list of forbidden books) was instituted by the Catholic Church at this time is evidence that the clerical leadership recognized the immense power of books. The number of books circulating during this period is staggering. Between 1517 and 1520 (even before his break with Rome) Luther's various writings sold about three hundred thousand copies in Europe.

None of this would, of course, have been possible before the Reformation for the simple reason that printing did not exist in Europe. The invention of the printing press and movable type revolutionized Renaissance culture north and south of the Alps in the same way that films, radio, television, and the Internet changed the twentieth century [**Fig. 14.6**]. There were two important side effects. The early availability of "book learning" undermined the dominance of universities, which had acted as the traditional guardians and spreaders of knowledge. Also, Latin began to lose its position as the only language for scholarship, because many of the new readers could not read or write it. Luther grasped the implications of the spread of literacy fully, and his use of it to advance his cause was imitated countless times in the centuries that followed.

A second cultural fact about the Reformation, closely allied to the first, is also noteworthy. The reformers placed great emphasis on the Word. Besides reading and listening there was also singing, and the reformers—especially Luther—stressed vernacular hymns. Hymns were seen as both a means of praise and an instrument of instruction. Luther was a hymn writer of note. The famous *Ein' Feste Burg Ist Unser' Gott* ("A Mighty Fortress Is Our God"), one of the best-loved hymns in Christianity, is generally attributed to him [**Fig. 14.7**]. The German musical tradition, which ultimately led to Johann Sebastian Bach in the seventeenth century, was very much the product of the Lutheran tradition of hymnody.

On the other hand, the sixteenth-century reformers had little need or sympathy for painting and sculpture. They were in fact militantly iconoclastic. One of the hallmarks of the first reformers was their denunciation of paintings, statues, and other visual representations as forms of papist idolatry. The net result of this iconoclastic spirit was that, by the beginning of the seventeenth century, patronage for the sacred visual arts had virtually died out in countries where the Reformation was strong. With the single exception of Rembrandt (and this exception is gigantic), it is difficult to name any first-rate painter or sculptor who worked from a Refor-

◆ **14.7** German Hymn Book, 1540s. The book is open at Luther's hymn *Ein' Feste Burg, Ist Unser' Gott* ("A Mighty Fortress Is Our God"), taken from one of the psalms and printed in German. Using the language people actually spoke (as opposed to Latin) was an important factor in Luther's Reformation.

Forschungsbibliotek, Gotha, Germany//© James L. Amos/CORBIS

mation religious perspective after the sixteenth century, although much secular art was produced.

The attitude of the sixteenth-century reformers toward the older tradition of the visual arts may best be summed up by the Church of Saint Peter in Geneva, Switzerland. Formerly a Romanesque Catholic cathedral of the twelfth century, Saint Peter's became Calvin's own church. The stained glass was removed, the walls whitewashed, the statues and crucifixes taken away, and a pulpit placed where the high altar once stood. The Church of Saint Peter is a thoroughly reformed church, a building for hearing the Word of God preached and read. Gone is the older notion (represented, for example, by the Cathedral of Chartres) of the church reflecting the otherworldly vision of heaven in the richness of its art. Reformation culture was in short an *aural*, not a *visual*, culture.

INTELLECTUAL DEVELOPMENTS

MONTAIGNE'S ESSAYS

Michel Eyquem de Montaigne (1533–1593) came from a wealthy Bordeaux family. His father, who had been in Italy and was heavily influenced by Renaissance ideas, provided his son with a fine early education. Montaigne spoke nothing but Latin with his tutor when he was a child so that when he went to school at age six, he spoke Latin not only fluently but with a certain elegance. His later education (he studied law for a time) was a keen

disappointment to him because of its pedantic narrowness. After a few years of public service, in 1571 Montaigne retired with his family to a rural estate to write and study. He remained there, with the exception of a few years traveling and some further time of public service, until his death.

The times were not happy. France was split over the religious issue, as was Montaigne's own family. He remained a Catholic, but his mother and sisters became Protestants. Only a year after his retirement came the terrible Saint Bartholomew's Day Massacre (August 24, 1572), in which thousands of French Protestants were slaughtered in a bloodbath unequaled in France since the days of the Hundred Years' War. In the face of this violence and religious bigotry, Montaigne returned to a study of the classics and wrote out his ideas for consolation.

Montaigne's method was to write on a widely variegated list of topics gleaned either from his readings or from his own experiences. He called these short meditations **essays**. Our modern form of the essay is rooted in Montaigne's first use of the genre in Europe. The large numbers of short essays Montaigne wrote share certain qualities characteristic of a mind wearied by the violence and religious bigotry of the time: a sense of stoic calmness (derived from his study of Cicero and Seneca), a tendency to moralize (in the best sense of that abused word) from his experiences, a generous nondogmatism, a vague sense of world-weariness.

THE GROWTH OF SCIENCE

The sixteenth century was not merely a turning point in the history of religions, it was also a decisive age in

◆ **14.8** *The Alchemist*, artist unknown, 14th century. Alchemists, whose tradition goes back to Hellenistic Egypt (c. 300 BCE), sought to turn base metals into gold. By the late medieval period, alchemists were trying to combine various chemicals (nitric and sulfuric acid, ethanol, and others) in search of the "philosopher's stone," a magical elixir that could produce the required effect. The figure seen here is feeding a brew of this sort into an oven, in the (impossible) hope that he could bake it into gold.

© *Palazzo della Ragione, Padua, Italy/SuperStock*

◆ **14.9** Hans Holbein the Younger, *Nikolaus Kratzer*, 1528. The new scientists are represented here by Kratzer, official astronomer to the court of Henry VIII and a friend of Dürer. The tools used in the calculation he is making are devised for maximum precision, and the room in which Kratzer is working is equipped as a library.

Tempera on panel, 32" x 26" (83 x 67 cm). Musée du Louvre, Paris, France//© Réunion des Musées Nationaux/Art Resource, NY

the history of science. In earlier times a scientist was likely enough to be an ingenious tinkerer with elaborate inventions who dabbled in alchemy, astrology, and magic [**Fig. 14.8**]. The new Renaissance scientist, a person of wide learning with a special interest in mathematics and philosophy, would develop bold and revolutionary ideas but always subject them to the test of practical experience [**Fig. 14.9**].

The age produced many advances in science. In England alone William Gilbert (1540–1603) discovered that the earth was a large magnet the pole of which points approximately north; Sir William Harvey (1578–1657) solved the problem of how the blood could "circulate"—get from the arteries to the veins and return to the heart—by postulating the existence of the then-undiscovered channels we now call "capillaries"; John Napier (1550–1615) discovered the practical mathematical tool called the **logarithm**, which greatly reduced the time and effort needed to solve difficult equations.

Elsewhere in Europe, the German Paracelsus (1493–1541) laid the foundations of modern medicine by his decisive rejection of traditional practices. Although his own theories were soon rejected, his insistence on observation and inquiry had important consequences, one of which can be seen in the work of Andreas Vesa-

lius (1514–1564), who was born in Brussels and studied in Padua. Vesalius's *De humani corporis fabrica (Seven Books on the Structure of the Human Body)*, published in 1543, comprise a complete anatomical treatise, illustrating in minute detail and with impressive accuracy the human form [**Fig. 14.10**].

The philosophical representative of the "new science" was Francis Bacon (1561–1626), who combined an active and somewhat disreputable political career with the writing of works intended to demolish traditional scientific views. The chief of these books was the *Novum Organum (New Organon*, 1620), which aimed to free science from the two-thousand-year-old grasp of Aristotle while at the same time warning against the unrestrained use of untested hypotheses. Science and religion came into direct conflict in the work of the Polish astronomer Nicholaus Copernicus (1473–1543), who studied at the universities of Cracow and Bologna. In 1543, the same year Vesalius's work appeared, Copernicus published *De Revolutionibus orbium coelestium (On the Revolutions of Celestial Bodies)*, a treatise in which he denied that the sun and the planets revolve around the

◆ **14.10** Andreas Vesalius, "Third Musculature Table," 1543. Although the work was chiefly intended to have a scientific value, Vesalius has set his figure into a scene showing a landscape and, in the distance, evidence of human construction. By placing the human in the foreground, towering over the rest of the scene, Vesalius emphasizes the Humanists' view of the central importance of humanity.

From De humani corporis fabrica, published in Basel, Switzerland. Image courtesy of the National Library of Medicine, Bethesda, Maryland, USA

Table 14.1 *Principal Discoveries and Inventions in the Sixteenth Century*

1486	Diaz rounds Cape of Good Hope
1492	Columbus discovers America
1493–1541	Paracelsus pioneers the use of chemicals to treat disease
1513	Balboa sights the Pacific Ocean
1516	Portuguese ships reach China
1520–1522	First circumnavigation of globe by Magellan
1530–1543	Copernicus refutes geocentric view of universe
1533	Gemma Frisius invents principle of triangulation in surveying
1542	Leonhart Fuchs publishes herbal guide to medicine
1543	Vesalius publishes anatomical treatise
1546	Agricola publishes guide to metallurgy
1569	Mercator devises system of mapmaking
1572	Tycho Brahe observes first supernova and produces first modern star catalogue
1582	Pope Gregory XIII reforms the calendar
c. 1600	First refracting telescope constructed in Holland
1600	William Gilbert publishes treatise on magnetism

earth, that appearance is a "given" in nature, not to be questioned. Copernicus questioned the assumption, claiming that it was equally plausible to take the earth's mobility as a given, because everything that had been explainable in the old way was fully explainable in the new (see **Table 14.1**). Copernicus's position on scientific matters was thus the equivalent of Luther's stand on the fallibility of the church.

THE VISUAL ARTS IN NORTHERN EUROPE

PAINTING IN GERMANY

The conflict between Italian humanism, with its belief in human perfectibility, and the Reformation, which emphasized sin and the need for prayer, is reflected in the art of the greatest German painters of the early sixteenth century. It might even be said that the intellectual and religious battles of the times stimulated German art to its highest achievements, for both Albrecht Dürer (1471–1528) and Matthias Grünewald (c. 1470–1528) are, in very different ways, towering figures in the development of European painting. Despite his sympathy with Luther's beliefs, Dürer was strongly influenced by Italian artistic styles and, through Italian models, by Classical ideas. Grünewald, on the other hand, rejected almost all Renaissance innovations and turned instead to traditional northern religious themes, treating them with new passion and emotion. Other artists, meanwhile, chose not to wrestle with the problems of the times. Some, including Albrecht Altdorfer (1480–1538), preferred to stand back and create a worldview of their own.

earth, and reverted instead to a long-dead Greek theory that the earth and planets orbit the sun. Catholic and Protestant theologians for once found themselves united in their refusal to accept an explanation of the universe that seemed to contradict the teaching of the Bible, but Copernicus's work, though not a complete break with the past, provided stimulus for Galileo's astronomical discoveries in the following century.

Additionally, the general principle behind Copernicus's method had important repercussions for the entire history of science. Up to his time, scientists had taken the position that, with certain exceptions, reality is as it appears to be. If the sun appears to revolve about the

◆ **14.11** Albrecht Dürer, *Self-Portrait*, 1500. The frontal pose and solemn gaze convey Dürer's belief in the seriousness of his calling. The artist's characteristic signature stands to the upper left, with the date, 1500, above it.

Panel, 25⅛″ x 18⅛″ (64 x 48 cm). Alte Pinakothek, Munich, Germany//
© Giraudon/Art Resource, NY

◆ **14.12** Albrecht Dürer, "Saint Michael Fighting the Dragon," from the *Apocalypse* series, 1498. Note the contrast between the violence of Saint Michael's struggle in the upper part and the tranquil scene below, with the calm waters of its harbor.

Woodcut, 15½″ x 11⅛″ (39 x 28 cm). © SuperStock

Albrecht Dürer Dürer was born in Nuremberg, the son of a goldsmith. Even as a child he showed remarkable skill in drawing. His father apprenticed him to a wood engraver, and in 1494 to 1495—after finishing his training—Dürer made the first of two visits to Italy. There he saw for the first time the new technique of **linear perspective** (where all parallel lines converge at a single vanishing point) and came into contact with the growing interest in human anatomy. Quite as important as these technical discoveries, however, was his perception of a new function for the artist. The traditional German—indeed, medieval—view of the artist was as an artisan whose task was humbly, if expertly, to reproduce God's creations.

Dürer adopted Renaissance humanism's concept of the artist as an inspired genius, creating a unique personal world. It is not by chance that a first glance at his *Self-Portrait* of 1500 [**Fig. 14.11**] suggests a Christ-like figure rather than a prosperous German painter of the turn of the century. The effect is intentional. The lofty gaze of the eyes underlines the solemn, almost religious

nature of the artist's vision, while the prominent hand draws attention to his use of the pen and the brush to communicate it to us.

In his paintings, Dürer shows a fondness for precise and complex line drawing rather than the softer use of mass and color typical of Italian art. In fact, much of his greatest work appears in the more linear **woodcuts** and **engravings**. In 1498, Dürer published a series of fifteen woodcuts illustrating the Revelation of Saint John, known as the Apocalypse series. Woodcut engravings are produced by drawing a design on a block of soft wood, then cutting away the surrounding wood to leave the lines of the drawing standing in relief. The blocks of wood can then be coated with ink and used to print an impression on paper.

In the hands of Dürer this relatively simple technique was raised to new heights of expressiveness, as in his depiction of Saint Michael's fight against the dragon from the Apocalypse series [**Fig. 14.12**]. In the upper part of the scene, Michael and other angels—all with long hair curiously like Dürer's own—do battle with a

◆ **14.13** Albrecht Dürer, *Knight, Death, and the Devil*, 1513. The knight's calm determination reflects Dürer's confidence in the ability of the devout Christian to resist temptation. This engraving may have been inspired by Erasmus's *Handbook of the Christian Knight*.

Engraving, 9⅝″ x 7⅜″ (24 x 18 cm). Image © British Museum, London, UK//HIP/Art Resource, NY

gruesome horde of fiends, while the peaceful German landscape below seems untouched by the cosmic fight in progress. Dürer's vision of an apocalyptic struggle between good and evil reflected the spirit of the time, and copies of the Apocalypse series sold in large quantities. Growing discontent with the church was, as we have seen, one of the causes of Luther's Reformation; the general sense of forthcoming trouble and upheaval gave Dürer's woodcuts a particular aptness.

The medium of *line engraving* was also one to which Dürer brought an unsurpassed subtlety and expressiveness. Unlike a woodblock, where the artist can complete the drawing before cutting away any material, the copper plate from which a line engraving is printed has to be incised directly with the lines of the design by means of a sharp-pointed steel instrument called a **burin**. The richness of effect Dürer achieved in this extremely difficult medium is almost incredible.

For most of the remainder of his life he devoted himself to engraving and to writing theoretical works on art. Between 1513 and 1515, Dürer produced his three greatest engravings. The earliest of these, *Knight,*

Death, and the Devil [**Fig. 14.13**], again reflects contemporary religious preoccupation with its symbolic use of the Christian knight accompanied by a dog who represents untiring devotion, and beset by the temptations of the devil (in a particularly untempting guise, it must be admitted). Neither this fearsome creature nor the appearance of Death, armed with an hourglass, can shake the knight's steadfast gaze.

By the end of his life, Dürer was acknowledged as one of the great figures of his time. Like Luther, he used the new possibilities of the printing press to disseminate his ideas. At the time of his death, Dürer was working on *Libri IV De Humani Corporis Proportionibus (Four Books on Human Proportions)*. This work (in Latin), aimed to accomplish for art what Vesalius's did for medicine. It was inspired by two of the great intellectual concerns of the Renaissance: a return to Classical ideals of beauty and proportion, and a new quest for knowledge and scientific precision.

Matthias Grünewald Although the work of Grünewald represents the other high point in German Renaissance art, little is known about his life. Only in the twentieth century did we discover his real name, Mathis Gothart Neithart; the date of his birth and the early years of his career are still a mystery. Grünewald seems to have worked for a while at the court of the Cardinal Archbishop of Mainz, but in the 1525 Peasants' War he sided with the German peasants in their revolt against the injustices of their rulers, after which his enthusiasm for Luther's new ideas kept him from returning to the cardinal's service. He retired to Halle, where he died in 1528.

What we know about his political and religious sympathies—his support for the oppressed and for the ideals of the Reformation—is borne out by the characteristics of his paintings. Unlike Dürer, Grünewald never visited Italy and showed no interest in the new styles developed there. The Renaissance concept of ideal beauty and the humanist interest in Classical antiquity left him unmoved. Instead, he turned repeatedly to the traditional religious themes of German medieval art, bringing to them a passionate, almost violent intensity that must at least in part reflect the religious heart-searching of the times. Yet it would be a mistake to view Grünewald's unforgettable images as merely another product of the spirit of the age, for an artist capable of so unique and personal a vision is in the last analysis inspired by factors that cannot be explained in historical terms. All that can safely be said is that no artist, before or since, has depicted the Crucifixion as a more searing tragedy or Christ's Resurrection as more radiantly triumphant.

Both of these scenes occur in Grünewald's greatest work, the Isenheim Altarpiece (completed in 1515), which was commissioned for the church of a hospital run by members of the Order of Saint Anthony.

◆ **14.14** Matthias Grünewald, *Crucifixion*, c. 1515. Behind Mary Magdalene, who kneels in grief, stand Mary and John; on the other side, John the Baptist points to Christ's sacrifice. Beside him, in Latin, are inscribed the words, "He must increase, but I must decrease." Above Christ are the initial letters of the Latin words meaning "Jesus of Nazareth, King of the Jews."

Panel (with framing) 9′9½″ x 10′9″ (2.98 x 3.28 m) from the Isenheim Altarpiece (exterior). Image © Musée d'Unterlinden, Colmar, France/The Bridgeman Art Library

The folding panels are painted with scenes and figures appropriate to its location, including saints associated with the curing of disease and events in the life of Saint Anthony. In particular, the patients who contemplated the altarpiece were expected to meditate on Christ's Crucifixion and Resurrection and derive from them comfort for their own sufferings.

In his painting of Christ in the *Crucifixion* panel [**Fig. 14.14**], Grünewald uses numerous details to depict the intensity of Christ's anguish—from his straining hands frozen in the agony of death, to the thorns stuck in his festering body, to the huge iron spike that pins his feet to the cross.

It is difficult to imagine anything further from the Italian Renaissance and its concepts of ideal beauty than this tortured image. Grünewald reveals an equal lack of interest in Renaissance or Classical theories of proportion or perspective. The figure of Christ, for example, is not related in size to the other figures—it dominates the panel—as a glance at the comparative size of the hands will show. Yet the sheer horror of this scene only throws into greater relief the triumph of the Resurrection [**Fig. 14.15**]. Christ seems almost to have exploded out of the tomb in a great burst of light that dazzles the viewers as well as the soldiers stumbling below. No greater contrast can be imagined than that between the

◆ **14.16** Albrecht Altdorfer, *Danube Landscape Near Regensburg*, c. 1522–1525. The only traces of human existence here are the road and the distant castle to which it leads.

Panel, 11″ x 8⅝″ (28 x 22 cm). Alte Pinakothek, Munich, Germany // © Scala/Art Resource, NY

◆ **14.15** Matthias Grünewald, *Resurrection*, c. 1515. Note the absence of any natural setting and the confused perspective, which give the scene an otherworldly quality. The artist contrasts the soaring figure of Christ with the soldiers tumbling down in shock at the vision.

Panel, 8′2½″ x 3′½″ (2.45 x .93 m) from the Isenheim Altarpiece (first opening). © Musée d'Unterlinden, Colmar, France / The Bridgeman Art Library

drooping body on the cross and this soaring, weightless image that suggests a hope of similar resurrection to the sufferers in the hospital.

Albrecht Altdorfer The drama of Grünewald's spiritual images is in strong contrast to the quiet, poetic calm of the work of Albrecht Altdorfer. Although closer in style to Grünewald than to Dürer, Altdorfer found his favorite subject not in religious themes but in landscapes. *Danube Landscape Near Regensburg* [**Fig. 14.16**], probably dating from around 1525, is one of the first examples in the Western tradition of a painting without a single human figure. From the time of the Greeks, art had served to tell a story—sacred or secular—or to illustrate some aspect of human behavior. Now for the

first time the contemplation of the beauties of nature was in itself deemed a worthy subject for an artist. In this painting, Altdorfer depicts a kind of ideal beauty. Part of his inspiration may have come from the landscapes that can be seen in the background of paintings by Venetian artists like Giorgione, although there is no evidence that Altdorfer ever visited Italy. Even if he had, his sympathy with the forces of nature, its light and scale and sense of life, seems more directly inspired by actual contact.

PAINTING IN THE NETHERLANDS

The two greatest Netherland painters of the Renaissance, Hieronymus Bosch (c. 1450–1516) and Pieter Bruegel (1525–1569), are linked both by their pessimistic view of human nature and by their use of satire to express it. Bosch furthermore drew on an apparently inexhaustible imagination to create a fantasy world that alternately fascinates and repels as the eye wanders from one bizarre scene to another. Although modern observers have

◆ **14.17** Hieronymus Bosch, *Garden of Earthly Delights*, c. 1505–1510. Perhaps surprisingly, this catalog of the sins of the flesh was among the favorite works of the gloomy King Philip II of Spain.

Panel center 7′2⅝″ x 6′4¼″ (2.2 x 1.95 m), each wing 7′2⅝″ x 3′2¼″ (2.2 x .97 m). © Museo del Prado, Madrid, Spain/SuperStock

◆ **14.18** Hieronymus Bosch, "Hell," detail from *Garden of Earthly Delights*, c. 1505–1510. Note the violence of the imagery in Bosch's hell. A lute and harp, symbols of heavenly music, are used as instruments of torture, while below a gambler is pinned to his table. Meanwhile, in the background, the fires of hell blaze.

Right panel, 7′2⅝″ x 3′2¼″ (2.2 x .97 m). © Museo del Prado, Madrid, Spain/Peter Willi/SuperStock

interpreted Bosch's work in various ways, it is generally agreed that, contrary to appearances, he was in fact a deeply religious painter. His chief subject is human folly in its innumerable forms, his theme that the inevitable punishment of sin is Hell. Salvation is possible through Christ, but few, according to Bosch, have the sense to look for it. His paintings show us the consequences.

Hieronymus Bosch Almost nothing is known of Bosch's life, so his body of work must speak for itself. The most elaborate in its fantasy is a **triptych** (a three-paneled painting) known as the *Garden of Earthly Delights* [**Fig. 14.17, 14.18**], which was probably finished around 1510. Into it are crowded hundreds of nude figures engaged in activities that range from the unimaginable to the indescribable, all in pursuit of erotic pleasure. The movement from the apparently innocent scene of the creation of Eve on the left to the fires of hell on the right illustrates Bosch's belief that the pleasures of the body lead to damnation along a road of increasing depravity. Even in the Garden of Eden we sense what is to come, as Adam sits up with excited enthusiasm on being presented with the naked Eve, while God seems to eye him nervously.

The bright world of the middle panel, in which the pallid, rubbery figures seem to arrange themselves (and one another) in every conceivable position and permutation, gives way on the right to a hallucinatory vision of eternal damnation. Bosch's symbolism is too complex

◆ **14.19** Pieter Bruegel the Elder, *The Triumph of Death*, c. 1562–1564. Note the huge coffin on the right into which the dead are being piled, guarded by rows of skeleton-soldiers. Nobody is spared, not even the king in the lower left-hand corner.

Oil on panel, 3′ 10″ x 5′ 3¼″ (1.17 x 1.62 m). Museo del Prado, Madrid, Spain//© Erich Lessing/Art Resource, NY

and too private to permit a detailed understanding of the scene, yet his general message is clear enough: Hell is not terrifying so much as it is sordid and pathetic. The frantic scenes of activity are as senseless and futile as those of worldly existence, but in hell their monstrous nature becomes fully apparent.

The sources of Bosch's inspiration in this and his other work are unknown. Many of his demons and fantastic animals seem related to similar manifestations of evil depicted in medieval art, but no medieval artist ever devised a vision such as this or possessed the technique to execute it. To modern eyes some of Bosch's creations, like the human-headed monster on the right-hand panel turning both face and rear toward us, seem to prefigure the surrealist art of the twentieth century. There is a danger, however, in applying labels from the art of later times to that of an earlier period. Bosch must be allowed to stand on his own as one of the great originals in the history of painting.

Pieter Bruegel Pieter Bruegel, often called the Elder to distinguish him from his son of the same name, represents the culmination of Renaissance art in the Netherlands. Like Bosch, his work is often fantastic, and his crowded canvases are frequently filled with scenes of grotesque activity. Some of his paintings suggest that he shared Bosch's view of the apparent futility of human existence and the prevalence of sin. In many of his pictures, however, the scenic backgrounds reveal a love and understanding of nature very different from Bosch's weird worldview and represent one of the keys

to understanding his work. For Bruegel, the full range of human activity formed part of a world in which there existed an underlying order. The beauty of nature forms the background not only to his pictures but actually to the lives of us all, he seems to say; by seeing ourselves as part of the natural cycle of existence we can avoid the folly of sin. If this interpretation of his work is correct, it places Bruegel with the humanists who believed in the possibilities for human good, and some evidence suggests that his friends did include members of a group of humanist philosophers active at Antwerp.

Although Bruegel's best-known paintings are scenes of peasant life, it is a mistake to think of him as unsophisticated. On the contrary, during the final years of his life, which he spent in Brussels, he was familiar with many of the leading scholars of the day and seems to have been a man of considerable culture. He certainly traveled to Italy, where he was apparently unaffected by the art but deeply impressed by the beauty of the landscape. Back home, he may well have supported the move to free the Netherlands from Spanish rule; some of his paintings seem to contain allusions to Spanish cruelties.

Bruegel's vision is so rich and understanding of the range of human experience that it almost rivals that of Shakespeare, who was born in 1564, five years before Bruegel's death. In his great painting *The Triumph of Death* [**Fig. 14.19**], Bruegel looks with uncompromising honesty at the universal phenomenon of death, which comes eventually to all: rich and powerful or poor and hopeless. Unlike Bosch, who reminds us that the righteous (if there are any) will be saved, Bruegel

◆ **14.20** Pieter Bruegel the Elder, *Peasant Wedding Feast*, 1566–1567. The composition of this painting is based on the diagonal line of the receding table that leads the eye past the bride and the bagpiper to the back of the room. The small boy in the foreground, licking his fingers, is a typical example of Breugel's ability to make his scenes come to life.

Oil on panel, 3′8⅛″ x 5′4⅛″ (1.14 x 1.63 m). Kunsthistorisches Museum, Vienna, Austria//© Erich Lessing/Art Resource, NY

◆ **14.21** Pieter Bruegel the Elder, *Hunters in the Snow*, 1565. Note Bruegel's careful use of color to suggest a cold, clear, sunless day. From his first crossing of the Alps in the 1530s, Bruegel was inspired by mountain scenery, and it reappeared throughout his work. In this painting, the panoramic sweep from the foreground to the lofty peaks behind makes the scene appear a microcosm of human existence. Thus Bruegel's "world landscapes" or *Weltlandss-chaften* are both literal depictions of scenes from nature and symbolic representations of the relationship between human beings and the world around them.

Oil on wood, c. 46′ x 64′ (116.8 x 162.6 cm). Kunsthistorisches Museum, Vienna, Austria//© Erich Lessing/Art Resource, NY

◆ **14.22** Jean Clouet, *Francis I*, c. 1525–1530. This famous work is now thought to be by an unknown artist rather than by Clouet, but its style is similar to that of his many official portraits of the king. For all the apparent relaxation of the king's pose, his hand is on the handle of his dagger, ready for use.

Tempera and oil on wood, c. 38″ x 29″ (96 x 74 cm). Musée du Louvre, Paris, France.//© Réunion des Musées Nationaux/Art Resource, NY

seems to offer no hope. Yet the same artist painted the *Peasant Wedding Feast* [**Fig. 14.20**], a scene of cheerful celebration. True, Bruegel's peasants find pleasure in simple rather than sophisticated delights, in this case chiefly food and drink, but he reminds us that some are luckier than others. The little boy in the foreground, so completely engrossed in licking up every last delicious morsel of food, is counterbalanced by the bagpiper who looks wistfully and wanly over his shoulder at the tray of pies nearby. Nor should we be too hasty to view Bruegel's peasants as unthinking creatures, content with a brutish existence. The bride certainly does not seem either bright or beautiful, but she radiates happiness, and the general air of merriment is attractive.

Bruegel's most profound statements are perhaps to be found in a cycle of paintings intended to illustrate the months of the year, rather like the *Très Riches Heures* of the Limbourg brothers a century earlier (see Chapter 11, Figures 11.18 and 11.19). Bruegel completed only five, including the magnificent *Hunters in the Snow* (1565) [**Fig. 14.21**]. In the background tower lofty peaks representing Bruegel's memory of the Alps, seen on his trip to Italy. From the weary hunters in the foreground, a line of barren trees leads the eye to fields of snow where peasants are hard at work. The scene can hardly be called a happy one, but neither is it unhappy. There is an inevi-

tability in the way humans, animals, birds, and nature are all bound together into a unity, expressive of a sense of order and purpose. The lesson of Italian humanism has been translated into a very different language, spoken with a highly individual accent, but Bruegel's northern scene seems in its own way inspired by a similar regard for human dignity.

ART AND ARCHITECTURE IN FRANCE

France of the sixteenth century bears little resemblance to the artistic achievements of Germany and the Netherlands. The influence of Italian art on France was so strong, due in great part to the actual presence at the French court of Italian artists, that French painting was almost completely overwhelmed. The only native artist of note was Jean Clouet (c. 1485–1541), who was retained by Francis I chiefly to serve as his official portrait painter. Among the many portraits of the king attributed to Clouet is one of around 1530 [**Fig. 14.22**] that does full justice to the sensual but calculating character of his master.

◆ **14.23** Château de Chambord, France, begun 1519. The turrets and pinnacles are reminiscent of French medieval architecture: compare the background on the May page of the *Tres Riches Heures* (Figure 11.19). The central block, though, and much of the decorative detail suggest Italian Renaissance models. *(© Scala/Art Resource, NY)*

More interesting than French painting during the sixteenth century is French architecture. The series of luxurious châteaux that Francis I had built along the valley of the river Loire combined the airiness of the earlier French Gothic style with decorative motifs imported from Italian Renaissance architecture. The result was buildings like the beautiful Château de Chambord [**Fig. 14.23**].

The love of decoration shown by the builders of Chambord emerges even more strongly as a feature of French architectural style in the design of the Square Court of the Louvre [**Fig. 14.24**]. This structure was begun in 1546 by the architect Pierre Lescot (1510–1578) and the sculptor Jean Goujon (c. 1510–1568), working for once without Italian guidance. The façade of the court is a compendium of Classical forms, from the window moldings to the Corinthian columns to the decorative motifs. The total effect, however, is very different from Italian buildings using the same features. Instead of being grand or awe-inspiring, the building seems graceful and harmonious, perhaps even a little fussy, and the emphasis on decoration became a prominent characteristic of French art in the following two centuries.

ART IN ELIZABETHAN ENGLAND

Throughout the sixteenth century, English political and cultural life followed a path notably different from that of continental Europe, as it did so often in its previous history. The social unrest that had marked the latter Middle Ages in England was finally ended in 1485 by the accession of Henry VII, the first king of the Tudor Dynasty. For the entire sixteenth century, England enjoyed a new stability and commercial prosperity on the basis of which it began to play an increasingly active role in international politics. Henry VIII's final break with the Catholic Church in 1534 led to the later development of ties between England and the other countries of the Reformation, particularly the Netherlands. When years of tension between the Netherlanders and their Spanish rulers finally broke out into open rebellion, England (then ruled by Queen Elizabeth I) supplied help secretly. Relations between Elizabeth and Spanish King Philip II were already strained, and English interference in the Spanish Netherlands was unlikely to help. In 1585 a new Spanish campaign of repression in the

Art in Elizabethan England ♦ **345**

♦ **14.24** Façade of the Square Court of the Louvre, Paris, begun 1546, Pierre Lescot (architect) and Jean Goujon (sculptor). The architectural and sculptural decoration is Italian in origin but used here as typically French elaborate ornamentation. On the first floor, the use of arches is reminiscent of ancient Roman architecture. *(© Erich Lessing/Art Resource, NY)*

Netherlands, coupled with the threat of a Spanish invasion of England, drove the queen to resort to more open action—she sent six thousand troops to fight alongside the Netherlanders. Their presence proved decisive.

Philip's anger at his defeat and at the progress of the campaign for an independent Netherlands was turned in fury against England. The massive Spanish Armada—the largest fleet the world had ever seen—was ready early in 1588 and sailed majestically north, only to be met by a fleet of lighter, faster English ships commanded by Sir Francis Drake. The rest is part history, part legend. Even before the expedition sailed, Drake had "singed the beard of the King of Spain" by sailing into Cadiz harbor and setting fire to some of the Spanish galleons anchored there. What was left of the Armada reached the English Channel, where it was destroyed, partly by superior English tactics and partly by a huge storm promptly dubbed (by the victors, at least) the "Protestant Wind." The subsequent tales told of English valor and daring brought a new luster to the closing years of the Elizabethan Age [**Fig. 14.25**].

In view of England's self-appointed position as bulwark of Protestantism against the Catholic Church in general and Spain in particular, it is hardly surprising that Renaissance ideas developed south of the Alps took some time to affect English culture. Few Italian artists were tempted to work at the English court or, for that matter, were likely to be invited. Furthermore, England's geographic position inevitably cut it off from intellectual developments in continental Europe and produced a kind of psychological insularity that was bolstered in the

♦ **14.25** Nicholas Hilliard, *Ermine Portrait of Queen Elizabeth I*, 1585. The ermine on the queen's sleeve is a symbol of virginity. The portrait as a whole is a symbol of her majesty, not intended to show her actual appearance.

Oil on canvas, 41¾" x 35" (106 x 89 cm). © Hatfield House, London, UK/SuperStock

late sixteenth century by a wave of national pride. The finest expression of this is probably to be found in the lines William Shakespeare put into the mouth of John of Gaunt in Act II, scene I of *Richard II*, a play written some six years after the defeat of the Spanish Armada:

> This royal throne of kings, this sceptered isle,
> This earth of majesty, this seat of Mars,
> This other Eden, demi-Paradise,
> This fortress built by Nature for herself
> Against infection and the hand of war,
> This happy breed of men, this little world,
> This precious stone set in the silver sea,
> Which serves it in the office of a wall
> Or as a moat defensive to a house
> Against the envy of less happier lands—
> This blessed plot, this earth, this realm,
> this England. . . .

On the other hand, the same spirit of nationalism was bound to produce a somewhat narrow-minded rejection of new ideas from outside. English sculpture and painting suffered as a result. The only foreign painter to work in England was a northerner, Hans Holbein the Younger (1497/98–1543), whose portrait of Henry VIII appears earlier in this chapter (see Figure 14.5). A magnificent portraitist, Holbein was sent by Henry to paint prospective brides so that the king could make his choice with at least some idea of their appearance—an effective if rather tedious method before photography. It must be added that the artist seems to have done his work rather too well, since his picture of *Anne of Cleves* [**Fig. 14.26**] inspired Henry to marry the princess only to divorce her within six months, contemptuously dismissing her as his "Flanders Mare."

Apart from Holbein, English artists were virtually cut off from the new ideas current elsewhere. The only English painter of note during the sixteenth century was Nicholas Hilliard (1547–1619), best known for his miniatures, small portraits often painted in watercolor. The finest is of an unidentified young man who has something of the poetic melancholy of a Shakespearean lover [**Fig. 14.27**]. When Hilliard turned to larger works, specifically to portraits of Queen Elizabeth, he was inevitably inhibited by his monarch's demand for a painting that would look regal and imposing rather than realistic. The result, *Ermine Portrait of Queen Elizabeth I* (see Figure 14.25), is a symbolic representation of majesty rather than a mere portrait.

MUSIC OF THE NORTHERN RENAISSANCE

As in the visual arts, the Renaissance produced major stylistic changes in the development of music, but,

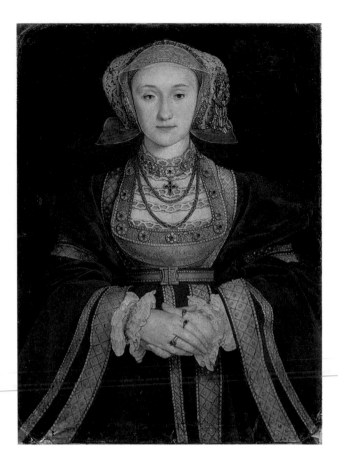

◆ **14.26** Hans Holbein the Younger, *Anne of Cleves*, c. 1539–1540. After viewing this portrait, Henry VIII sent for Anne of Cleves and made her his fourth queen. Note the formal pose and suitably modest downturned gaze.

Vellum applied to canvas, 25⅝″ x 18⅞″ (65 x 48 cm). Musée du Louvre, Paris, France//© Réunion des Musées Nationaux/Art Resource, NY

in general, musical development in the Renaissance was marked by a less severe break with medieval custom than was the case with the visual arts. Although sixteenth-century European composers began to increase the complexity of their style, frequently using polyphony, they continued to use forms developed in the High Middle Ages and the early Renaissance. In religious music, the motet remained popular, set to a religious text. Composers also continued to write *madrigals* (songs for three or more solo voices based generally on secular poems). For the most part these were intended for performance at home, and elaborate, interweaving polyphonic lines often tested the skill of the singers. The difficulty of the parts often made it necessary for the singers to be accompanied instrumentally. This increasing complexity produced a significant change in the character of madrigals, which were especially popular in Elizabethan England. Nonetheless, sixteenth-century musicians were recognizably the heirs of their thirteenth- and fourteenth-century predecessors.

◆ **14.27** Nicholas Hilliard, *Portrait of a Youth*, c. 1590. The thorns of the wild rose growing in the foreground may represent friendship in adversity. (The miniature is shown here at almost its actual size.)

Parchment, 5⅜″ x 2¾″ (14 x 7 cm). © Victoria & Albert Museum, London, UK/Art Resource, NY

MUSIC IN FRANCE AND GERMANY

The madrigal form was originally devised in Italy for the entertainment of courtly circles. By the early sixteenth century, French composers, inspired by such lyric poets as Clement Marot (1496–1544), were writing more popular songs known as **chansons**. The best known composer of chansons was Clement Janequin (c. 1485–c. 1560), who was famous for building his works around a narrative program. In "La Guerre" ("The War") the music imitates the sound of shouting soldiers, fanfares, and rattling guns; other songs feature street cries and birdsong. Frequently repeated notes and

the use of nonsense syllables help give Janequin's music great rhythmic vitality, although it lacks the harmonic richness of Italian madrigals.

The same tendency to appeal to a general public characterized German and Flemish songs of the period with texts that were romantic, military, or sometimes even political in character. Among the great masters of the period was the Flemish composer Heinrich Isaac (c. 1450–1517), who composed songs in Italian and French as well as in German. His style ranges from simple chord-like settings to elaborately interweaving lines that imitate one another. Isaac's pupil, the German Ludwig Sendl (c. 1486–c. 1542), was, if anything, more prolific than his teacher; his music is generally less complex and graceful—almost wistful—in mood.

ELIZABETHAN MUSIC

English music suffered far less than the visual arts from the cultural isolationism of Elizabethan England; the Elizabethan Age, in fact, marks one of the high points in its history. Almost two hundred years earlier, the English musician John Dunstable (c. 1385–1453) had been one of the leading composers in Europe. By bringing English music into the mainstream of continental developments, Dunstable helped prepare the way for his Elizabethan successors. Several other factors were also responsible for the flourishing state of English music.

To begin with, in England there had always been a greater interest in music than in the visual arts. Also, the self-imposed ban on the importation of foreign artworks and styles did not extend to printed music, with the result that by the early years of the reign of Elizabeth, Italian secular music began to circulate in English musical circles. A volume of Italian songs in translation was published in 1588 under the title *Musica Transalpina (Music from Across the Alps)*.

As for sacred music, when Henry VIII broke away from the pope he was not at all ready to convert wholeheartedly to Lutheranism or Calvinism and discard those parts of the liturgy that were sung. The services, psalms, and hymns the new Anglican Church had to devise generally (although by no means invariably) used English rather than Latin texts, echoing Luther's use of the vernacular, but continued for the most part to follow Catholic models. Thus, when the first official version of the English Litany was issued in 1544 by Archbishop of Canterbury Thomas Cranmer, it used the traditional Gregorian chant, simplified so that only one note was allocated to each syllable of the text. This innovation preserved the flavor of the original music, while making it easier for a listener to follow the meaning of the words and thereby participate more directly in the worship. In more elaborate music, the effects of the Reformation were even less evident. Most of the professional composers of the day had after all been brought up in a Catholic musical tradition, and while the split with Rome affected religious dogma (and permitted Henry to marry and divorce at will), it did not alter their freedom to compose religious music as they wished. They continued to write pieces that alternated and combined the two chief styles of the day: blocks of chords in which every voice moved at the same time and the elaborate interweaving of voices known as **counterpoint**.

The musical forms also remained unchanged except in name. Among the most popular compositions throughout Europe were motets, the words of which were often in Latin. English composers continued to write works of this kind but used English texts and called them **anthems**. A piece that used the full choir throughout was called a *full anthem* and one containing passages for solo voice or voices a *verse anthem*. English musicians nevertheless did not entirely abandon the use of Latin. Some of the greatest figures of the period continued to write settings of Latin texts as well as ones in the vernacular.

Thomas Tallis The dual nature of Elizabethan music is well illustrated by the career of Thomas Tallis (c. 1505–1585), who spent more than forty years of his life as organist of the Chapel Royal at the English court. Although his official duties required him to compose works for formal Protestant occasions, he also wrote Latin motets and Catholic masses. Tallis was above all a master of counterpoint, bringing the technique of combining and interweaving several vocal lines to a new height of complexity in one of his motets, *Spem in Alium (Hope in Another)*, written for no less than forty voices, each moving independently. In his anthems, however, he adopted a simpler style with a greater use of chord passages so that the listener could follow at least part of the English text. His last works combine both techniques to achieve a highly expressive, even emotional effect, as in his setting of the *Lamentations of Jeremiah*.

William Byrd Among Tallis's many pupils was William Byrd (c.1543–1623), the most versatile of Elizabethan composers and one of the greatest in the history of English music. Like Tallis, he produced both Protestant and Catholic church music, writing three Latin masses and four English services, including the so-called Great Service for five voices. Byrd also composed secular vocal and instrumental music, including a particularly beautiful elegy for voice and strings, *Ye Sacred Muses*, inspired by the death of Tallis.

Much of Byrd's instrumental music was written for the **virginal**, an early keyboard instrument in the form of an oblong box small enough to be placed on a table or held in the player's lap. It was once believed that the instrument was so-called because of its popularity at the

◆ **14.28** Thomas Morley, score page from *The First Booke of Canzonets* (Short Songs) [for] *Two Voices*. Published in London in 1595 by Thomas Este. This single page could easily have been held and read by two music lovers singing in the privacy of their own home. *(© Lebrecht Music & Arts/The Image Works)*

court of Elizabeth, the self-styled Virgin Queen, but references have been found to the name before her time, and its true origin is unknown. Forty-two pieces written for the virginal by Byrd were copied down in 1591 in an album known as *My Ladye Nevells Booke*. They include dances, variations, and fantasias and form a rich compendium of Byrd's range of style.

Byrd also wrote madrigals. The madrigal began in Italy, where the words were as important as the music, and Italian composers often chose poems that reflected the Renaissance interest in Classical antiquity. The English madrigal was not intended for an elite audience but for domestic performance by an increasingly prosperous middle class [**Fig. 14.28**]. Less concerned with Renaissance ideas of refinement than with the expression of emotional extremes, some English madrigals were quite serious, even mournful. "Noel, Adieu" by Thomas Weelkes (c. 1575–1623) is striking for its use of extreme dissonance to express grief.

Many of the madrigals of Thomas Morley (1557–1602), on the other hand, are lighthearted in tone and fast moving, using refrains such as "Fa-la-la." Among his best known are such settings of popular verses as

"Sing We and Chaunt It" and "Now Is the Month of Maying."

CD Track 5
Thomas Morley, "Now Is the Month of Maying"

Morley's madrigal for five voices is typical of his light-hearted music, the aim of which was to please both listeners and performers. Written for amateur singers who chose to make music for their own pleasure, it demanded little technical skill. The setting is divided into three parallel verses, and the words, punctuated by non-verbal refrains, are simple and repetitive.

One reason that Morley's music became so popular was, of course, the new technique of printing, which not only made written music available but allowed it to circulate widely into private homes. At the same time, the exuberance and grace of his madrigals, together with their sheer energy, won them a wide—and continuing—audience. "Now is the Month of Maying" was first printed in 1595 and reprinted several times during the following century.

Morley's work is the perfect illustration of one of the chief aspects of Renaissance music, especially that aimed at domestic consumption. As expressed by a contemporary writer, "as for music, the principal thing we seek in it is to delight the ear."

John Dowland The most melancholy works of all Elizabethan music are the **ayres** (simple songs for one voice accompanied by either other voices or instruments) of John Dowland (1562–1626)—the rare example of an Elizabethan musician who traveled widely. Irish by birth, Dowland visited France, Germany, and Italy and even worked for a while at the court of King Christian IV of Denmark; ultimately, he settled in England.

Dowland was the greatest virtuoso of his day on the lute (a plucked string instrument that is a relative of the guitar), and he used it to accompany his ayres. Dowland's gloomy temperament was given full expression both in the ayres and in his solo pieces for lute, most of which are as obsessively depressed and woeful as Morley's madrigals are determinedly cheerful. Popular in his own day, in more recent times Dowland's music has undergone something of a revival with the growth of interest in the guitar and other similar instruments.

ENGLISH LITERATURE: SHAKESPEARE

English literature in the sixteenth century, unlike the visual arts and to a greater extent even than music, was strongly affected by new currents of Renaissance

thought. One reason for this is purely practical. Soon after the invention of printing in Germany (see Figure 14.6), William Caxton (c. 1421–1491) introduced the printing press into England and, during the first half of the sixteenth century, books became increasingly plentiful and cheap. With the spread of literature an increased literacy developed, and the new readers were anxious to keep in touch with all the latest ideas of their day. The development of humanism in England undoubtedly influenced Erasmus of Rotterdam, who was brought into contact with humanist ideas during his visits there. In addition to teaching at Cambridge, Erasmus formed a warm personal friendship with the English statesman Sir Thomas More (1478–1535), who became Lord Chancellor in 1529.

More's *Utopia*, a philosophical romance in Latin describing an ideal world resembling that of Plato's *Republic*, was written under Erasmus's influence and was firmly based on humanistic ideals. Once introduced, these ideas caught on, and so did the use of Classical or Italian models to express them. Sir Philip Sidney (1554–1586), the dashing youth who has been described as Castiglione's courtier come to life, wrote a series of sonnets in imitation of Petrarch, and a romance, *Arcadia*, of the kind made popular in Italy by Lodovico Ariosto (1474–1533). Edmund Spenser (1552–1599), the greatest nondramatic poet of Elizabethan England, was also influenced by Ariosto and by Torquato Tasso (1544–1595), Ariosto's Italian successor in the production of massive epic poems. In *The Faerie Queene*, Spenser combined the romance of Ariosto and the Christian allegory of Tasso to create an immensely complex epic. Its chivalrous hero, the Knight of the Red Cross, represents both Christianity and, through his resemblance to Saint George, England. At the same time, the tests he undergoes make him a Renaissance version of the medieval figure of Everyman. The epic takes place in the imaginary land of Faerie, where the knight's path is frequently blocked by dragons, witches, wizards, and other magical creatures. All of this mythological paraphernalia not only advances the plot but also provides a series of allegorical observations on moral and political questions of the day. The result has, in general, been more admired than read.

Drama in Elizabethan England The greatest of all English achievements in the Renaissance were in drama. The Classical models of English drama were the Latin tragedies of Seneca and the comedies of Plautus and Terence, which, with the introduction of printing, became more frequently read and performed. These ancient Roman plays created a taste for the theater that English dramatists began to satisfy in increasing quantities. At the same time, the increasing prosperity and leisure that created a demand for new madrigals produced a growing audience for drama. To satisfy this

◆ **14.29** A model of the Globe Playhouse, London, as it probably appeared in the 16th century. Part of the wall has been cut away to show the seats arranged in tiers inside. (© *Guildhall Art Gallery, London, UK//HIP/Art Resource, NY*)

audience, traveling groups of actors began to form, often attaching themselves to the household of a noble who acted as their patron. These companies gave performances in public places, especially the courtyards of inns. When the first permanent theater buildings were constructed, their architects imitated the form of the inn courtyards, with roofs open to the sky and galleries around the sides. The stage generally consisted of a large platform jutting out into the center of the open area known as the **pit** or **ground** [**Fig. 14.29**].

The design of these theaters allowed—indeed encouraged—people of all classes to attend performances regularly because the price of admission varied for different parts of the theater. The more prosperous spectators sat in the galleries, where they had a clear view of the stage, while the poorer spectators stood on the ground around the stage. Dramatists and actors soon learned to please these so-called **groundlings** by appealing to their taste for noise and spectacle.

Not all performances were given in public before so democratic an audience. The most successful companies were invited to entertain Queen Elizabeth and her court. The plays written for these state occasions were generally more sophisticated in both content and style than those written for the general public. The works written for the court of James I, Elizabeth's successor, are among the most elaborate of all. In general, English drama developed from a relatively popular entertainment in the mid-sixteenth century to a more formal artificial one in the early seventeenth century. It is probably no coincidence that the greatest of all Elizabethan dramatists, Shakespeare and Mar-

lowe, wrote their best works at about the midpoint in this development, from about 1590 to 1610. Their plays reflect the increasing appreciation and demand for real poetry and high intellectual content without losing the "common touch" that has given their work its continual appeal.

Christopher Marlowe Born two months before Shakespeare, had Christopher Marlowe (1564–1593) not been killed in a fight over a tavern bill at age twenty-nine, he might well have equaled Shakespeare's mighty achievements. It is certainly true that by the same age Shakespeare had written relatively little of importance, whereas Marlowe's works include the monumental two-part *Tamburlaine*, a vast tragic drama that explores the limits of human power; exuberant erotic verse like his *Hero and Leander*; and his greatest masterpiece, *Dr. Faustus*. Marlowe's use of blank verse for dramatic expression was imitated by virtually every other Elizabethan playwright, including Shakespeare. It consists of non-rhyming iambic pentameter lines of five metrical feet in which each foot has two syllables, and the second foot generally bears the rhythmic stress. In style, Marlowe's work reflects the passion and violence of his own life, with heroes striving to achieve the unachievable by overcoming all limits, only to be defeated by destiny.

William Shakespeare Regret at the loss of what Marlowe might have written had he lived longer is balanced by gratitude for the many works William Shakespeare (1564–1616) left us. Shakespeare [**Fig. 14.30**] is universally acknowledged as the greatest writer in the English language and one of the greatest in any tongue. His position is best summarized in the words of his leading contemporary and rival playwright Ben Jonson (1572–1637): "He was not of an age, but for all time!"

Surprisingly little is known about Shakespeare's life. He was born at Stratford-upon-Avon; his early years and education seem to have been typical of provincial England, although no details are known. In 1582 he married Anne Hathaway, and over the following three years the couple had three children. By 1592 Shakespeare was established in London as an actor and playwright. Exactly how he became involved in the theater and what he did from 1585 to 1592 remain a mystery. From the beginning of his time in London, Shakespeare was associated with the leading theatrical company of the day—the Lord Chamberlain's Men—which changed its name to the King's Men at the accession of James I in 1603.

Shakespeare's earliest plays followed the example of Classical models in being carefully constructed, although their plots sometimes seem unnecessarily overcompli-

◆ **14.30** Droeshout, *William Shakespeare*, 1609, engraving after an oil painting. So little is known of Shakespeare's life and appearance that it is difficult to judge the accuracy of this image, but it probably served as the basis for the engraving of Shakespeare that appeared on the title page of the *First Folio.* This first collected edition of Shakespeare's works was prepared by two of the playwright's fellow actors and published in London in 1623. *(© Lebrecht Music & Arts/The Image Works)*

cated. In *The Comedy of Errors* (1592–1593), for example, Shakespeare combined two plays by the Roman comic writer Plautus (c. 254–184 BCE) to create a series of situations replete with mistaken identities and general confusion. The careful manipulation of plot in the early plays is achieved at the expense of characterization, and the poetry tends to use artificial literary devices. Even Shakespeare's first great tragedy, *Romeo and Juliet* (1595), is not altogether free from an excessive use of puns and plays on words, although the psychological depiction of the young lovers is convincing and the play contains some magnificent passages.

The comedies of the next few years, including both *The Merchant of Venice* (c. 1596) and *Twelfth Night* (c. 1600), are more lyrical. The brilliant wit of the earlier plays is often replaced by a kind of wistful melancholy. *Twelfth Night* is, in fact, often regarded as Shakespeare's supreme achievement in the field of comedy. Although the plot hinges on a series of well-worn comic

devices—mistaken identities, separated twins, and so on—the characters are as vivid and individual as in any of his plays. Furthermore, the work's principal subject, romantic love, is shown from an almost infinite number of viewpoints. Yet at the same time Shakespeare was attracted to historical subjects, generally drawn from English history, as in *Henry IV*, Parts I and II (1597–1598), but also from Roman history, as in *Julius Caesar*.

Julius Caesar (1599) is notable for several reasons. It shows that Shakespeare shared the renewed interest of his contemporaries in Classical antiquity. It is, in fact, based directly on the *Lives* of Caesar, Brutus, and Marc Antony by the Greek historian Plutarch (c. 46–127 CE), which had appeared in a new translation by Sir Thomas North in 1579. *Julius Caesar* also illustrates Shakespeare's growing interest in psychological motivation rather than simple sequencing of events.

The playwright tells us not so much what his characters do as why they do it, using the **soliloquy** (a kind of speech in which characters utter their thoughts aloud, without addressing them to anyone else), and thereby revealing to the audience the inner workings of the characters' minds. The use of this device becomes increasingly common in Shakespeare's supreme achievements, the series of tragedies he wrote between 1600 and 1605: *Hamlet* (c. 1600), *Othello* (c. 1604), *King Lear* (c. 1605), and *Macbeth* (c. 1605). In dramatic truth, poetic beauty, and profundity of meaning, these four plays achieve an artistic perfection equaled only by the tragic dramas of Classical Greece. Through his protagonists, Shakespeare explores the great problems of human existence—the many forms of love, the possibilities and consequences of human error, the mystery of death—with a subtlety and yet a directness that remain miraculous through countless readings or performances and continue to provide inspiration to artists and writers.

Shakespeare's later plays explore new directions. *Antony and Cleopatra* (c. 1607–1608) returns to Plutarch and to ancient Rome but with a new richness and magnificence of language. The conciseness of his great tragedies is replaced by a delight in the sound of words, and the play contains some of the most musical of all Shakespearean verse. His last works examine the borderline between tragedy and comedy with a sophistication that was perhaps intended to satisfy the new aristocratic audience of the court of King James I. *The Tempest* (1611), set on an enchanted island, blends high romance and low comedy to create a world of fantasy unlike that of any of his other plays.

In the year he wrote *The Tempest*, Shakespeare left London and retired to Stratford to live out the remaining years of his life in comparative prosperity. Although he continued to write, it is tempting to see in the lines he gave to Prospero toward the end of *The Tempest*

(IV, I, 148–158) his own farewell to the theater and to the world he created for it:

> Our revels now are ended. These our actors,
> As I foretold you, were all spirits, and
> Are melted into air, into thin air.
> And, like the baseless fabric of this vision,
> The cloud-capped towers, the gorgeous palaces,
> The solemn temples, the great globe itself—
> Yea, all which it inherit—shall dissolve
> And, like this insubstantial pageant faded,
> Leave not a rack behind. We are such stuff
> As dreams are made of, and our little life
> Is rounded with a sleep.

SUMMARY

◆ **The Cultural Consequences of the Reformation.** The political and cultural life of Northern Europe was profoundly changed by the Reformation. After centuries of domination by the Church of Rome, many northern countries gradually switched to one of the various forms of Protestantism, whose ideas and teachings were rapidly spread by the use of the newly invented printing press. The consequences of this division did much to shape modern Europe, while the success of the Reformation movement directly stimulated the Counter-Reformation of the seventeenth century.

◆ **Printing and Literature.** The growth of literacy both north and south of the Alps made possible by the easy availability of books produced a vast new reading public. Among the new literary forms to be introduced was that of the essay, first used by Montaigne. Epic poems were also popular; the works of Lodovico Ariosto and Torquato Tasso circulated widely and were imitated by many writers, including Edmund Spenser. The revival of interest in Classical drama produced a new and enthusiastic audience for plays; those written by Elizabethan dramatists like Christopher Marlowe combined high poetic and intellectual quality with popular appeal. The supreme achievement in English literature of the time and perhaps of all time may be found in the works of William Shakespeare. Furthermore, in an age when the importance of education was emphasized, many advances in science were made and important scientific publications appeared. These included Vesalius's work on anatomy and Copernicus's revolutionary astronomical theories.

◆ **Painting in Germany: Dürer and Grünewald.** In the visual arts the sixteenth century saw the spread of Italian Renaissance ideas northward. In some cases they were carried by Italian artists like Benvenuto Cellini, who went to work in France. Some major northern artists, like Albrecht Dürer, actually traveled to Italy. Dürer's art was strongly influenced by Italian theories of perspective, proportion, and color, although he retained a strong interest in line typical of northern art. But not all of his contemporaries showed the same interest in Italian styles. Matthias Grünewald's paintings do not show Renaissance concerns for humanism and ideal beauty; instead, they draw on traditional medieval German art to project the artist's own passionate religious beliefs, formed against the background of the bitter conflict of the Peasants' War.

◆ **Painting in the Netherlands: Bosch and Bruegel.** The two leading Netherlands artists of the century, Hieronymus Bosch and Pieter Bruegel the Elder, were also influenced by contemporary religious ideas. Their work has other characteristics in common: a pessimistic attitude toward human nature and the use of satire—yet the final effect is very different. Bosch's paintings are complex and bizarre; Bruegel shows a broader range of interest in human activities, together with a love of nature.

Elsewhere in Northern Europe artistic inspiration was more fitful. The only English painter of note was the miniaturist Nicholas Hilliard, while in France the principal achievements were in the field of architecture. Even in Germany and the Netherlands, by the end of the century the Reformation movement's unsympathetic attitude toward the visual arts had produced a virtual end to official patronage for religious art.

◆ **Musical Developments in Reformation Europe.** Music was central to Reformation practice: Luther was a hymn writer of note. In England, after Henry VIII broke with Rome to form the Anglican Church, the hymns devised by the new church generally followed Reformation practice by using texts in the vernacular rather than in Latin. The music, however, retained the complexity of the Italian style; as a result, the religious works of musicians like Tallis and Byrd are among the finest of northern Renaissance compositions.

Secular music also had a wide following throughout Northern Europe, particularly as the printing of music became increasingly common. The form of the madrigal, originally devised in Italy, spread to France, Germany, the Netherlands, and England. Many of the works of the leading composers of the day, including the French Clement Janequin and the Flemish Heinrich Isaac, were intended for a popular audience and dealt with romantic or military themes.

Thus the combination of new Renaissance artistic ideas and new Reformation religious teachings roused Northern Europe from its conservative traditions and stimulated a series of vital cultural developments.

EXERCISES

1. Discuss the career of Albrecht Dürer, and compare his work to that of his contemporaries in Germany and Italy.
2. What were the principal causes of the Reformation? What was its impact on the development of the arts?
3. Describe the effect of the spread of humanism in Northern Europe. What part was played by the invention of printing?
4. What are the main features of musical development during the sixteenth century? Discuss the relationship between sacred and secular music.
5. Describe Shakespeare's development as a dramatist, and analyze the plot of one of his plays.

Visit the *Culture & Values* Companion website at **www.cengage.com/art/Cunningham/Cultureand Values7E** and the *Humanities Resource Center* for an array of primary source readings, key terms with pronunciations, flash cards, quizzes, and study materials designed especially to help you do well in this course.

CHAPTER 15

THE BAROQUE WORLD

One of the many consequences of an increasingly prosperous middle-class population in Renaissance and Baroque Europe was the use of personal dress to express their prosperity. For the growing merchant classes, clothing was an essential symbol of social status. Around 1600, the Venetian ambassador to France noted that a man was only considered well-to-do if he owned some thirty suits and changed them daily. Forms of personal adornment became popular among the middle and upper classes. Men grew facial hair, and women used increasing quantities of makeup. Both sexes began to wear artificial hairpieces as a sign of social distinction.

Peasants usually wore simple garments of coarse, homespun fabric often mixing hemp and wool, and generally dyed them black or some other dark color. Their clothing had to be durable and provide protection against the cold. The standard form of dress for males was a loose-fitting shirt and tight trousers. Most peasants went barefoot, and underwear did not become customary until the fourteenth century. Neither rich nor poor generally wore nightclothes to bed.

The style of dress among the wealthy reflected the political and cultural realities of the age. In the late 1500s, when the chief centers of power were France and England, French and English fashions were popular. Noble (or would-be noble) ladies wore dresses of cotton, velvet, and silk, decorated with gold thread and jewels. By the height of the baroque period, with the rise to power of Spain and the Hapsburg Empire, Spanish-style dress became common: dark and severe, with padded stockings and high collars. Toward the end of the seventeenth century, as Spanish influence began to decline, the bright colors of French fashion once again became popular.

THE COUNTER-REFORMATION SPIRIT

By about 1600 the intellectual and artistic movements of the Renaissance and Reformation had taken a new turn. Although the cultural activity of the following hundred and fifty years was the natural outgrowth of earlier developments, the difference in spirit—already signaled by the middle of the sixteenth century—was striking.

The chief agent of this new spirit was the Roman Catholic Church. After its initial shock at the success of Protestantism, the Catholic Church decided that the best defense was a well-planned

◆ *A Woman and Five Children*, Le Nain, 1642.
(© Erich Lessing/Art Resource, NY)

attack. Switching to the offensive, the church relied in great measure on new religious orders like the Jesuits to lead the movement known as the Counter-Reformation. Putting behind them the anxieties of the past, the chief representatives of the Counter-Reformation gave voice to a renewed spirit of confidence in the universality of the church and the authority of its teachings.

The official position of the church was newly stated at the Council of Trent, which met sporadically from 1545 to 1563. Under the leadership of Pope Paul III, the council redefined Catholic doctrines and reaffirmed those dogmas that Protestantism had challenged. Transubstantiation, the apostolic succession of the priesthood,

the belief in purgatory, and the rule of celibacy for the clergy were all confirmed as essential to the Catholic system of faith. The pope remained as monarchical ruler of the church. At the same time, the council tried to eliminate abuses by the clergy and to tighten discipline. Bishops and priests could no longer hold more than one benefice, and theological seminaries were set up in every diocese to improve the educational level of the priesthood.

One of the key instruments in the campaign to reestablish the authority of the church was the Society of Jesus, an order of priests and brothers dedicated to the defense of the faith. The order was founded in 1534 by

GENERAL EVENTS	ART
1560	
DECLINE OF SPANISH POWER	
1603–1625 James I reigns in England **1609** Holland and Flanders achieve virtual independence in truce with Spain **1610–1643** Louis XIII reigns in France initially under regency of his mother, Marie de' Medici	**1581–1584** El Greco, *Martyrdom of Saint Maurice and the Theban Legion* Work of French painter Nicolas Poussin (c. 1594–1665) protests excesses of the baroque **1597–1600** Annibale Carracci, Palazzo Farnese Galleria completed
	c. 1600–1602 Caravaggio, *The Calling of Saint Matthew* **1616** Hals, *Banquet of the Officers of the Civil Guard of Saint George*
1618	
THIRTY YEARS' WAR	
1618–1648 Thirty Years' War; ends with Peace of Westphalia	**c. 1618** Rubens, *The Rape of the Daughters of Leucippus*
1620 English Pilgrims land at Plymouth (Massachusetts colony)	**c. 1620** Artemisia Gentileschi, *Judith and Holofernes* **1622–1625** Rubens paints cycle of 24 paintings glorifying Marie de' Medici **1623** Bernini, *David*
1621–1665 Philip IV reigns in Spain	**1623** Van Dyck, *Portrait of the Marchesa Cataneo* **c. 1639** Ribera, *The Martyrdom of Saint Bartholomew*
1643 Five-year-old Louis XIV ascends throne of France under regency	**1642** Rembrandt, *The Night Watch* **1645–1652** Bernini, *Saint Teresa in Ecstasy*
1649	
PURITAN RULE	
1649 Execution of Charles I of England; Cromwell rules 1649–1658	**1656** Velázquez, *Las Meninas*
1660	
AGE OF LOUIS XIV AND XV	
1660 Restoration of monarchy in England under Charles II **1661** Louis XIV assumes full control of France **1682** Louis XIV moves court to newly remodeled Versailles **1688** Parliamentary enemies of James II invite William of Orange to invade England	**1662–1664** Vermeer, *Woman Reading a Letter* **1701** Rigaud, *Louis XIV*
1689 Declaration of Rights establishes English constitutional government; William and Mary rule **1715** Louis XIV dies after 72-year reign; Louis XV ascends throne	
1774	

Ignatius Loyola (1491–1556), a Spanish nobleman. After spending the first part of his career as a soldier, Loyola converted to the religious life after suffering a serious wound. His *Spiritual Exercises* (begun 1522–1523) express a mystical, even morbid spirit of introspection, inspired by visions of Satan, Jesus, and the Trinity. A similarly heightened spiritual sense and attempt to describe mystical experiences occurs in the writings of other Spanish Catholics of the Counter-Reformation, most notably Saint Teresa of Avila (1515–1582) and Saint John of the Cross (1542–1591); the latter wrote powerfully of the soul's emergence from the "dark night" to attain union with God.

The order that Loyola founded soon became the most militant of the various religious movements to appear during the sixteenth century. Its members, the Jesuits, fought not with swords or guns, but with eloquence and the power of persuasion. The Jesuits were organized on the model of a military company, led by a general as their chief commander, and required to exercise iron discipline. Their duty was simple: to promote the teachings of the church unquestioningly—Loyola taught that if the church ruled that black was white, its followers were obliged to believe it. They reinforced this position by their vigorous missionary work throughout Europe, the Americas, and the Far East,

ARCHITECTURE	LITERATURE & PHILOSOPHY	MUSIC
	1565 Teresa of Avila, *Autobiography* **1572–1631** John Donne, metaphysical poet **1582–1584** John of the Cross, *The Dark Night* **1605–1615** Cervantes, *Don Quixote* **1611** Publication of King James *Authorized Version* of Bible	**late 16th cent.** Birth of opera in Florence, development of monody **1594–1595** Peri, *Dafne*, first play set to music, performed in Florence **1600** Peri, *Euridice* Opera, concerto grosso, oratorio, cantata, and sonata established as musical forms. Virtuoso tradition begins **1607** Monteverdi, *L'Orfeo*
Retention of classical vocabulary of Renaissance but on grandiose scale; civic planning and private-house construction also prevalent because of rise of middle classes	**1637** Descartes publishes *Discourse on Method* **1638** Galileo, *Dialogue Concerning the Two Chief World Systems* **1640–1643** Corneille, *Horace, Polyeucte* **1641** Descartes, *Meditations* **1646** Crashaw, *Steps to the Temple*	**1619** Schütz, *Psalms of David* **1632** Monteverdi, *scherzi musicali* (musical jokes) **1634** Frescobaldi active at Rome
	c. 1650 philosophers Locke active in England, Pascal in France, Spinoza in Holland **1651** Hobbes, *Leviathan* **c. 1659–1699** Poet and dramatist John Dryden active in England	
1663 Bernini, piazza and colonnades for Saint Peter's, Rome **1665–1667** Borromini, façade added Church of San Carlo alle Quattro Fontane, Rome **1669–1685** Le Vau and Hardouin-Mansart, Garden façade Versailles **1678** Le Brun and Hardouin-Mansart begin Hall of Mirrors, Palace of Versailles	**1664** Molière, *Tartuffe* **1667** Milton, *Paradise Lost* **1677** Racine, *Phèdre* **1690** Locke, *Concerning Human Understanding*	**1668** Buxtehude becomes organist at Lübeck **1674** Lully's *Alceste* first performed at Versailles **1685** Births of Bach, Handel, Scarlatti **c. 1720** Vivaldi, *The Four Seasons*, violin concertos **1721** J. S. Bach, Brandenburg Concertos **1729** J. S. Bach, *St. Matthew Passion* **c. 1735** Rameau, *Les Indes Galantes* **1742** Handel's *Messiah* first performed

◆ **15.2** Aerial view of Saint Peter's, Rome, Italy. The nave and façade were finished by Carlo Maderna (1556–1629) between 1606 and 1612, and the colonnades around the square were built between 1656 and 1663 to Bernini's design. The completion of Saint Peter's was one of the first great achievements of baroque architecture.

Façade 147′ high x 374′ long (44.8 x 114 m). St. Peter's Square with Basilica and Vatican Palaces, Vatican State. Image © Alinari/Art Resource, NY

while improving educational institutions throughout Catholic Europe.

At the same time, the Council of Trent called on artists to remind Catholics of the power and splendor of their religion by commissioning a massive quantity of works of art dedicated to underlining the chief principles of Counter-Reformation teachings. Now it was the task of religious leaders and, under their guidance, of the artists to make this position known to the faithful.

New emphasis was placed on clarity and directness. The impression of the church's triumphant resurgence was further reinforced by a new emphasis on material splendor and glory. In Rome, the construction of lavish churches was crowned by the completion at last of Saint Peter's and the addition of Bernini's spectacular **piazza** ("square") in front of it [**Fig. 15.2**], while throughout Catholic Europe there developed a rich and ornate art that could do justice to the new demands for expressive power and spectacle.

The term used to describe the new style, at first in derision but since the nineteenth century simply as a convenient label, is *baroque*. The word's origins are obscure. It may be related to the Portuguese *barroco* ("an irregularly shaped pearl") or perhaps to *baroco* (an Italian term used to describe a complicated problem in medieval logic). In any case, baroque came to be applied in general to anything elaborate and fanciful, in particular to the artistic style of the seventeenth and early eighteenth centuries.

Although strictly speaking *baroque* is a term applied only to the visual arts, it is frequently used to describe the entire cultural achievement of the age. To extend its use to literature, music, and even intellectual developments of the same period inevitably implies that all the arts of the baroque period had certain characteristics in common. In fact, a close comparison between the visual arts, music, and literature of the seventeenth and early eighteenth centuries does reveal some shared ideas and attitudes. It is important to remember from the outset, however, that this artistic unity is by no means obvious. A first glance at the cultural range of the period actually reveals an astonishing variety of styles, developing individually in widely separated places and subject to very different political and social pressures.

In this respect the baroque period marks a significant break with the Renaissance, when Italy had been the center of virtually all artistic development. Despite the impact of the Counter-Reformation, the Reformation had begun an irreversible process of decentralization. By the beginning of the seventeenth century, although Rome was still the artistic capital of Europe, important cultural changes were taking place elsewhere. The economic growth of countries like Holland and England, and the increasing power of France, produced a series of artistic styles that developed locally rather than being imported wholesale from south of the Alps. Throughout Northern Europe the rise of the middle class continued to create a new public for the arts, which in turn affected the development of painting, architecture, and music. For the first time European culture began to spread across the Atlantic, carried to the Americas by Counter-Reformation missionaries.

The much greater geographic spread of artistic achievement was accompanied by the creation of new artistic forms in response to new religious and social pressures. In music, for instance, the seventeenth century saw the birth of **opera** and of new kinds of instrumental music, including works for orchestra like the **concerto grosso**. Painters continued to depict scenes from the Bible and from Classical mythology, but they turned increasingly to other subjects including portraits, landscapes, and scenes from everyday life. Architects constructed private townhouses and started to take an interest in civic planning instead of devoting themselves exclusively to churches and palaces.

A similar richness and variety can be found in the philosophical and scientific thought of the period, which managed temporarily to reconcile its own pursuit of scientific truth with traditional theological and political attitudes. By the end of the seventeenth century, however, the practical discoveries of science had begun to undermine long-accepted ideas and to lay the basis for the new skepticism that came to dominate the eighteenth century.

It would be unwise to look for broad general principles operating in an age of such dynamic and varied change. Nonetheless, to understand and appreciate the baroque spirit as it appears in the individual arts, it is helpful to bear in mind the chief assumptions and preoccupations shared by most baroque artists. Whatever the medium in which they worked, baroque artists were united in their commitment to strong emotional statements, psychological exploration, and the invention of new and daring techniques.

Perhaps the most striking of these is the expression of intense emotions. During the Renaissance, artists had generally tried to achieve the calm balance and order they thought of as typically Classical. During the baroque period, artists were attracted by extremes of feeling—sometimes these strong emotions were personal. Painters and poets alike tried to look into their own souls and reveal by color or word the depths of their own psychic and spiritual experience. More often artists tried to convey intense religious emotions. In each case, far from avoiding painful or extremely emotional states as subjects, their works sought out and explored them.

This concern with emotion produced in its turn an interest in what came to be called *psychology*. Baroque artists attempted to explain how and why their subjects felt as strongly as they did by representing their emotional states as vividly and analytically as possible. This is particularly evident in seventeenth-century opera and drama, where music in the one case and words in the other were used to depict the precise state of mind of the characters.

Table 15.1 *Characteristics and Examples of Baroque Art*

CHARACTERISTIC	EXAMPLE
Emotionalism	Caravaggio, *The Martyrdom of Saint Matthew* [15.4]
	Rubens, *The Rape of the Daughters of Leucippus* [15.23]
Illusionism	Bernini, *David* [15.8]
	Rembrandt, *The Night Watch* [15.28]
Splendor	Bernini, Saint Peter's Square [15.2]
	Palace of Versailles [15.17–18]
	Carracci, *The Triumph of Bacchus and Ariadne* [15.7]
Light and Shade	Caravaggio, *The Calling of Saint Matthew* [15.3]
	de La Tour, *The Lamentation over Saint Sebastian* [15.12]
	Velázquez, *Las Meninas* [15.22]
	Vermeer, *Woman Reading a Letter* [15.27]
Movement	Borromini, Façade for San Carlo alle Quattro [15.11]
	El Greco, *Burial of Count Orgaz* [15.20]
Religious Fervor	El Greco, *Martyrdom of Saint Maurice and the Theban Legion* [15.19]
	Ribera, *The Martyrdom of Saint Bartholomew* [15.21]
Domestic Intimacy	Caravaggio, *Madonna of Loreto* [15.5]
	Rubens, Hélène *Fourment and Her Children* [15.1]
	Rembrandt, *Jacob Blessing the Sons of Joseph* [15.29]

The desire to express the inexpressible required the invention of new techniques. As a result, baroque art placed great emphasis on virtuosity. Sculptors and painters achieved astonishing realism in the way in which they handled their media. Stone was carved in a way such as to give the effect of thin, flowing drapery, while seventeenth-century painters found ways to reproduce complex effects of light and shade (see **Table 15.1**). Baroque writers often used elaborate imagery and complicated grammatical structure to express intense emotional states. In music, both composers and performers began to develop new virtuoso skills; composers in their ability to write works of greater and greater complexity, and performers in their ability to sing or play music in the new style. In fact some pieces, like **toccatas** (free-form rhapsodies for keyboard), were principally intended to allow instrumentalists to demonstrate their technique, thus inaugurating the tradition of the virtuoso performer that reached a climax in the nineteenth century.

THE VISUAL ARTS IN THE BAROQUE PERIOD

PAINTING IN ROME: CARAVAGGIO AND THE CARRACCI

The foundations of baroque style, which was to dominate much of European painting for one hundred and fifty years, were laid in Rome around 1600 by two artists

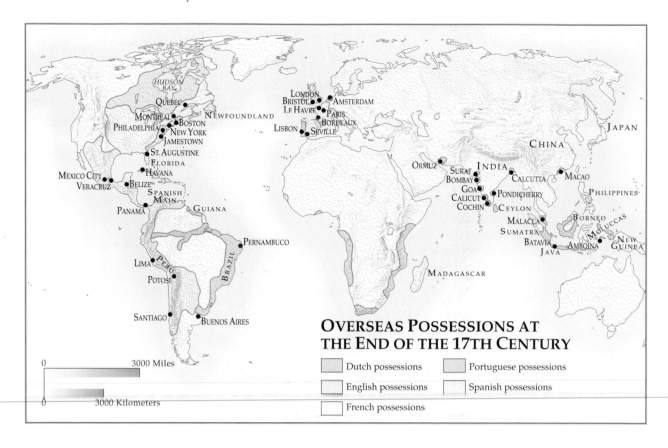

OVERSEAS POSSESSIONS AT THE END OF THE 17TH CENTURY

Dutch possessions

English possessions

French possessions

Portuguese possessions

Spanish possessions

whose works at first glance seem to have little in common. Michelangelo Merisi (1573–1610), better known as Caravaggio, the name of his hometown in northern Italy, explored the darker aspects of life and death in some of the most naturalistic and dramatic pictures ever painted. Annibale Carracci (1560–1609) preferred to paint light and elegant depictions of the loves of gods and goddesses and charming landscapes. That both artists exerted an immense influence on their successors says something for the extreme range of baroque painting. Of the two painters, Caravaggio was certainly the more controversial in his day. His own lifestyle did little to recommend him to the aristocratic and ecclesiastical patrons on whom he depended. From his first arrival in Rome (around 1590), Caravaggio seems to have lived an unconventional and violent life, in continual trouble with the police, and alienating potential friends by his savage temper.

Any chances Caravaggio had for establishing himself successfully in Rome were brought to an abrupt end in 1606 when he quarreled violently with an opponent in a tennis match and stabbed him to death. He avoided punishment only by fleeing to Naples and then to Malta, where he was thrown into prison for attacking a police officer. Escaping, he made his way to Sicily and then back to Naples, where he yet again got involved in a violent quarrel, this time in a sleazy inn. Seriously wounded, he heard of the possibility of a pardon if he were to return to Rome, but on the journey back he died of a fever (brought on, it was said,

by a final attack of rage at some sailors he mistakenly thought had robbed him). The pardon from the pope arrived a few days later. The spirit of rebellion that governed Caravaggio's life can be seen in his art. In his depiction of religious scenes he refused to accept either the traditional idealizing versions of earlier artists or the Counter-Reformation demands for magnificent display. Furthermore, instead of placing his figures in an elaborate setting in accordance with Counter-Reformation principles, Caravaggio surrounded them with shadows, a device that emphasizes the drama of the scene and the poverty of the participants.

Caravaggio's preference for **chiaroscuro** (extreme contrasts between light and dark) was one of the aspects of his style most imitated by later painters. When not handled by a master, the use of heavy shadows surrounding brightly lit figures in the foreground tends to become artificial and over theatrical, but in Caravaggio's work it always serves a true dramatic purpose.

In his painting *The Calling of Saint Matthew* [**Fig. 15.3**], one of three pictures painted between 1597 and 1603 for the Contarelli Chapel in the Church of San Luigi dei Francesi at Rome—Caravaggio's first important Roman commission—the stern hand of Jesus summoning the future apostle is emphasized by the beam of light that reveals the card players at the table; Matthew, awed and fearful, tries to shrink back into the darkness.

In his painting of *The Martyrdom of Saint Matthew* [**Fig. 15.4**], Caravaggio used his own experience of

◆ **15.3** Caravaggio, *The Calling of Saint Matthew*, c. 1600–1602. A bright light emanates from Jesus, half-hidden on the right and pointing at Matthew. The artist produces a strong dramatic effect by directing the light at Matthew's head, who draws back from the glare in fear.

Oil on canvas, 11'1" x 11'5" (3.38 x 1.48 m). Contarini Chapel, Church of San Luigi dei Francesi, Rome, Italy//© Scala/ Art Resource, NY

◆ **15.4** Caravaggio, *The Martyrdom of Saint Matthew*, c. 1602. The violent contrast of light focuses the eye on the executioner and fallen saint. The deeply moved onlooker at the very back of the scene is, according to one tradition, a self-portrait of the artist.

Oil on canvas, 10'9" x 11'6" (3.3 x 3.5 m). Contarini Chapel, Church of San Luigi dei Francesi, Rome, Italy//© Scala/ Art Resource, NY

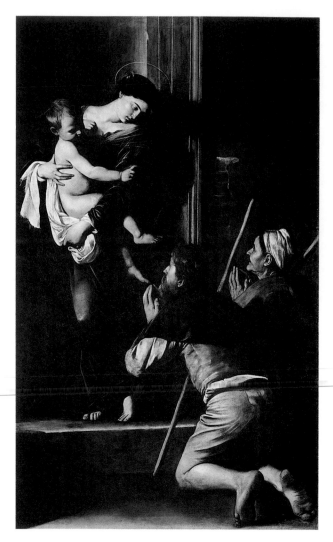

◆ **15.5** Caravaggio, *Madonna of Loreto*, 1604. The shabby clothes show the poverty of the two pilgrims. The light that illuminates their faces seems to shine directly from the Madonna and Child.

Oil on canvas, 8′6½″ x 4′10½″(2.6 x 1.5 m). Cavaletti Chapel, Church of San Agostino, Rome, Italy//© Scala/Art Resource, NY

suffering to portray the scene with painful realism; the painting tells us as much about the reactions of the onlookers as about Matthew. They range from the sadistic violence of the executioner to the apparent indifference of the figures in shadow on the left; only the angel swooping down with the palm of martyrdom relieves the brutality and pessimism of the scene.

It would be a mistake to think of Caravaggio's work as lacking tenderness. In the *Madonna of Loreto* [**Fig. 15.5**], he shows us not the remote grace of a Botticelli Virgin or the sweet, calm beauty of a Raphael Madonna but a simple Roman mother. As she stands gravely on the doorstep of her backstreet house where the plaster is falling away from the walls, two humble pilgrims fall to their knees in confident prayer. They raise their loving faces to the Virgin and Christ child

while turning toward us their muddy, travel-stained feet. It is perhaps not surprising that some of Caravaggio's contemporaries, brought up on the elegant and well-nourished Madonnas and worshipers of the Renaissance and surrounded by the splendor of Counter-Reformation art, should have found pictures like these disrespectful and lacking in devotion. It should be equally unsurprising that once the initial shock wore off, the honesty and truth of Caravaggio's vision made a profound impact on both artists and the public.

Artemisia Gentileschi Among the painters working in Rome who fell under the spell of Caravaggio's works was Orazio Gentileschi (1563–1639), who was born in Pisa and studied in Florence. Much impressed by Caravaggio's dramatic naturalism and concern for psychological truth, Gentileschi based his own style on that of his younger contemporary. Since he spent the last eighteen years of his life traveling and living in Northern Europe, first in France and then in England, he played an important part in spreading a knowledge of Caravaggio's style outside Italy. At the same time, he handed on his enthusiasm to a painter nearer home—his own daughter Artemisia (1592–c. 1652).

Artemisia Gentileschi has been described as the first woman in the history of the Western world to make a significant contribution to the art of her time. The question of why so few women achieved eminence in the visual arts before recent times is a complicated one, and the chief answers are principally social and economic rather than aesthetic. Certainly, Artemisia was typical of the few women painters of the Renaissance and baroque periods who did become famous in that she was the daughter of a painter and therefore at home in the world of art and artists.

Gentileschi's most famous painting is *Judith and Holofernes* [**Fig. 15.6**]. Done in chiaroscuro, the painting conveys a tremendous sense of violence as Judith and her maid loom over the drastically foreshortened body of Holofernes. There is a stark contrast between the realistic violence of the beheading and the sensual richness of the silken bed, jewelry, and cunning drapery. It is not inconceivable that the painter, a rape victim in her youth, poured her own passionate protest into this painting of a woman taking retribution against a would-be defiler. This work depicts a scene from the biblical story of the Jewish heroine Judith, who used her charms to save her people from an invading Assyrian army; she won the confidence of its general, Holofernes, and then beheaded him in the privacy of his tent.

The Carracci It is a far cry from the dark, emotional world of Caravaggio and his followers to the brilliant, idealized world of Annibale Carracci, his brother Agostino, and his cousin Ludovico, all often spoken of collectively as the Carracci. The most gifted member of this Bolognese family was Annibale, whose earliest important work in Rome—the decoration of the **galleria** (formal reception hall) of the Palazzo Farnese—was painted between 1597 and 1604, precisely the years when Caravaggio was working on the Contarelli Chapel. The many scenes in the galleria constitute a fresco cycle based on Greek and Roman mythology, depicting the loves of the gods, including *The Triumph of Bacchus and Ariadne* [**Fig. 15.7**]. The sense of exuberant life and movement and the mood of unrestrained sensual celebration seem farthest removed from Caravaggio's somber paintings, yet both artists share the baroque love of extreme emotion, and both show the same concern for realism of detail.

ROMAN BAROQUE SCULPTURE AND ARCHITECTURE

The most influential of all Italian baroque artists of the Counter-Reformation was a sculptor and architect, not a painter. The sculptural achievement of Gian Lorenzo Bernini (1598–1680), of seemingly unlimited range of expression and unbelievable technical virtuosity, continued to influence sculptors until the nineteenth century; as the chief architect of Counter-Reformation Rome, he permanently changed the face of that venerable city.

Gian Lorenzo Bernini Born the son of a Florentine sculptor in Naples, Bernini showed signs of his extraordinary abilities at an early age. One of

◆ **15.6** Artemisia Gentileschi, *Judith and Holofernes*, c. 1620. Gentileschi has chosen to show the moment when the sword slices into Holofernes's neck and blood spurts from the wound. The blow requires the combined force of Judith and her attendant. Note the influence of Caravaggio in the dark background and dramatic effect of light on the three figures.

Oil on canvas, 78⅓" x 64" (199 x 162.5 cm). Galleria degli Uffizi, Florence, Italy//© Scala/Art Resource, NY

◆ **15.7** Annibale Carracci, *The Triumph of Bacchus and Ariadne*, 1597–1600. The god's chariot, drawn by tigers, is accompanied by a wild procession of cupids, nymphs, and satyrs. The sense of movement is created by the distorted poses of many of the figures.

Ceiling fresco, Palazzo Farnese, Rome, Italy. Image © Scala/Art Resource, NY

◆ **15.8** Gian Lorenzo Bernini, *David*, 1623. It is said that Bernini carved the face while looking at his own in a mirror. The expression reinforces the tension of the pose with straining leg and foot muscles.

Marble, life size, 5′6¼″ (1.7 m) high. Galleria Borghese, Rome, Italy//© Scala/Art Resource, NY

◆ **15.9** Gian Lorenzo Bernini, *Cardinal Scipione Borghese*, 1632. Breaking with the tradition of Renaissance portraiture, which showed the subject in repose, Bernini portrays the cardinal, his first patron, with a sense of lively movement. Note the rippling effect of the drapery, which hides the fact that it is carved from stone.

Marble, 30¾″ (78 cm) high. Galleria Borghese, Rome, Italy//© Scala/Art Resource, NY

his first important works, a statue of *David* [**Fig. 15.8**], seems to have been deliberately intended to evoke comparison with works by his illustrious predecessors. Unlike the *David* of Donatello (see Figure 12.15) or Michelangelo (see Figure 12.29), which show the subject in repose, Bernini's figure is definitely in the midst of action. From the bitten lips to the muscular tension of the arms to the final detail of the clenched toes of the right foot, this David seems to personify energy, almost exploding through space. Bernini gives the figure additional expressive power by his deep cuts in the stone, producing a strong contrast between light and dark. In its expression of violent emotion, its communication of the psychological state of its subject, and its virtuoso technique, this David is a truly baroque figure.

Some of Bernini's sculptures depict his aristocratic patrons with the same mastery he applied to spectacular subjects. The bust of Cardinal Scipione Borghese [**Fig. 15.9**], with its quizzical expression and almost uncanny sense of movement, conveys the personality of the sitter with sympathy and subtlety. Most of his finest masterpieces, however, deal with religious themes and draw their inspiration from Counter-Reformation teachings.

The most spectacular of these is *Saint Teresa in Ecstasy*, which uses a combination of architecture, sculpture, and natural light to convey the saint's ecstatic vision of an angel [**Fig. 15.10**]. Gilded bronze shafts of light are further illuminated by light from a concealed window, as Saint Teresa, torn by violent emotion, awaits the blow of the angel, about to pierce her to the heart.

Works such as these would have been more than sufficient to guarantee Bernini's immortality, but his architectural achievements are equally impressive. The physical appearance of baroque Rome was enriched by numerous Bernini fountains, Bernini palaces, and Bernini churches. Most important of all was his work on Saint Peter's, where he created in front of the basilica a vast piazza with its oval colonnade, central obelisk, and fountains—an ensemble (see Figure 15.2) that rivals in grandeur even the fora of Imperial Rome.

Francesco Borromini Bernini's expansive personality and his success in obtaining important commissions brought him tragically if inevitably into conflict with the other great architect of baroque Rome: Francesco Borromini (1599–1667). Brooding and melancholy much of the time, Borromini spent most of his career in constant competition with his brilliant rival and finally committed suicide (see Voices of Their Times, this chapter).

◆ **15.10** Gian Lorenzo Bernini, *Saint Teresa in Ecstasy*, 1645–1652. One of the supreme masterpieces of baroque art, this famous work shows Bernini's virtuoso skill in the expression of heightened religious emotion. Note the contrast between the light texture of the angel's robe and the heavier weight of the saint's costume, as she seems to swoon before our eyes.

Marble group, 11′6″ (3.5 m) high. Cornaro Chapel, Santa Maria della Vittoria, Rome, Italy//© Scala/Art Resource, NY

◆ **15.11** Francesco Borromini, Façade of San Carlo alle Quattro Fontane, begun 1638, façade finished 1667. The curves and counter curves of the façade, together with the rich, almost cluttered, decoration, mark a deliberate rejection of the Classical style.

Exterior façade, 38′ (11.58 m) wide, Church of San Carlo alle Quattro Fontane, Rome, Italy. Image © Nimatallah/Art Resource, NY

Whereas Bernini was concerned with the broad sweep of a design and grandiose effects, Borromini concentrated on elaborate details and highly complex structures.

Borromini's greatest and most influential achievement was the church of San Carlo alle Quattro Fontane. The inside, designed between 1638 and 1641, was his first important work; the façade, which he added in 1665–1667, was his last [**Fig. 15.11**]. On a relatively small exterior wall space, Borromini has placed a wide range of decorative elements—columns, niches, arches, statues—while the façade flows in sinuous curves. The almost obsessive elaboration of design is in strong contrast to the clarity of many of Bernini's buildings, but its ornateness represents another baroque approach to architecture, one that was to have a continual appeal.

BAROQUE ART IN FRANCE AND SPAIN

FRANCE

In general, the more extravagant aspects of Italian baroque art never appealed greatly to French taste,

which preferred elegance to display and restraint to emotion. The conservative nature of French art found expression before the end of the century in the foundation of the Académie des Beaux-Arts (Academy of the Fine Arts). The first of the special exhibitions organized by the academy took place in 1667 under the patronage of Louis XIV. Both then and through the succeeding centuries, academy members saw their function as the defense of traditional standards and values rather than the encouragement of revolutionary new developments. Their innate conservatism affected both the works selected for exhibition and those awarded prizes. The tension between these self-appointed guardians of tradition and those artists who revolted against established ideas lasted well into the nineteenth century.

The closest parallel in French baroque painting to the intensity of Caravaggio is found in the strangely moving paintings of Georges de La Tour (1590–1652), whose candlelit scenes and humbly dressed figures are reminiscent of some aspects of the Italian's work. Yet the mood of such paintings as *The Lamentation over Saint*

Giambattista Passeri

In this passage the seventeenth–century painter and biographer Giambattista Passeri describes the suicide of Francesco Borromini. In the summer of 1667, tormented by Bernini's triumphant successes, Borromini

. . . was assailed again with even greater violence by hypochondria which reduced him within a few days to such a state that nobody recognized him any more for Borromini, so haggard had his body become, and so frightening his face. He twisted his mouth in a thousand horrid ways, rolled his eyes from time to time in a fearful manner, and sometimes would roar and tremble like an irate lion. His nephew [Bernardo] consulted doctors, heard the advice of friends, and had him visited several times by priests. All agreed that he should never be left alone, nor be allowed any occasion for working, and that one should try to make him sleep at all costs, so that his spirit might calm down. This was the precise order which the servants received from his nephew and which they carried out. But instead of improving, his illness grew worse. Finding that he was never obeyed, as all he asked for was refused him; he imagined that this was done in order to annoy him rather than for his good, so that his restlessness increased and as time passed his hypochondria changed into pains in his chest,

asthma, and a sort of intermittent frenzy. One evening, during the height of summer, he had at last thrown himself into his bed, but after barely an hour's sleep he woke up again, called the servant on duty, and asked for a light and writing material.

Told by the servant that these had been forbidden him by the doctors and his nephew, he went back to bed and tried to sleep. But unable to do so in those hot and sultry hours, he started to toss agitatedly about as usual, until he was heard to exclaim "When will you stop afflicting me, O dismal thoughts? When will my mind cease being agitated? When will all these woes leave me? . . . What am I still doing in this cruel and execrable life?" He rose in a fury and ran to a sword which, unhappily for him and through carelessness of those who served him, had been on a table, and letting himself barbarously fall on the point was pierced from front to back. The servant rushed in at the noise and seeing the terrible spectacle called others for help, and so, half-dead and covered in blood, he was put back to bed. Knowing then that he had really reached the end of his life, he called for the confessor and made his will.

By Giambattista Passeri, translated by Rudolf and Margot Wittkower, and included in their book *Born Under Saturn*, © 1963 by Rudolf and Margot Wittkower, renewed 1991 by Margot Wittkower. Used by permission of Random House Inc.

Sebastian [**Fig. 15.12**] is far more restrained—the emotions are not stressed.

Nicolas Poussin The greatest French painter of the seventeenth century, Nicolas Poussin (c. 1594–1665), echoed this French preference for restraint when he decisively rejected the innovations of Caravaggio, whose works he claimed to detest. He saw his own work as a kind of protest against the excesses of the baroque; a strong dislike of his Roman contemporaries did not, however, prevent Poussin from spending most of his life in Rome. It may seem strange that so French an artist should have chosen to live in Italy, but what drew him there was the art of ancient, not baroque, Rome. Poussin's only real and enduring enthusiasm was for the world of Classical antiquity. His friends in Rome included the leading antiquarians of the day, and his paintings often express a nostalgic yearning for a long-vanished past.

Among Poussin's most poignant early works is *Et in Arcadia Ego* [**Fig. 15.13**], in which four country dwellers

gather at a large stone tomb in an idyllic landscape. The inscription they struggle intently to decipher says *Et in Arcadia Ego* ("I am also in Arcadia"), a reminder that death exists even in the midst of such beauty and apparent simple charm. (Arcadia, although an actual region in Greece, was also used to refer to an imaginary land of perfect peace and beauty.) That charm is not altogether so simple, however. Poussin's rustic shepherds and casually dressed shepherdess seem to have stepped directly from some actual antique scene, such as Poussin often incorporated into his paintings, while the rich landscape is reminiscent of Venetian painting. The entire work therefore represents not so much the authentic representation of an actual past as the imaginative creation of a world that never really existed.

As his career developed, Poussin's style changed. The poetry of his earlier work was replaced by a grandeur that sometimes verges on stiffness. The *Abduction of the Sabine Women* [**Fig. 15.14**] is conceived on a massive scale and deals with a highly dramatic subject, yet the

◆ **15.12** Georges de La Tour, *The Lamentation over Saint Sebastian*, 1645. The influence of Caravaggio is obvious in the contrasting play of light. Nevertheless, the simplification of details and the distaste for violence (there is no blood around the arrow) are typical of the restraint of de La Tour's paintings.

Oil on canvas, c. 5′3″ x 4′3″ (1.6 x 1.3 m). Musée du Louvre, Paris, France//© Erich Lessing/Art Resource, NY

◆ **15.13** Nicolas Poussin, *Et in Arcadia Ego*, c. 1627. Although influenced by Classical sources, this early version of the subject has a poetical character that owes much to the art of Titian.

Oil on canvas, c. 40″ x 32″ (102 x 81 cm). Collection Duke of Devonshire, Chatsworth, Devonshire, UK//© Erich Lessing/Art Resource, NY

◆ **15.14** Nicolas Poussin, *Abduction of the Sabine Women*, c. 1634. At the time of this painting, Poussin was strongly influenced by the ancient sculptures he had studied in Rome, most notably the careful depiction of the musculature of the figures.

Oil on canvas, 60⅞″ x 82⅝″ (154.6 x 209.9 cm). Metropolitan Museum of Art, New York, USA//Image © The Metropolitan Museum of Art/Art Resource, NY

◆ **15.15** Nicolas Poussin, *Et in Arcadia Ego*, c. 1638–1640. When compared to Figure 15.13, an earlier version, this treatment is found to be calmer and less dramatic. The group is seen from the front rather than diagonally, and both faces and poses are deliberately unemotional.

Oil on canvas, 33½" x 47⅝" (85 x 121 cm). Musée du Louvre, Paris, France//© Réunion des Musées Nationaux/Art Resource, NY

desperate women and violent Roman soldiers seem almost frozen in motion. Every figure is depicted clearly and precisely, as in Carracci's *The Triumph of Bacchus and Ariadne* (see Figure 15.7), yet with none of the exuberance of the earlier artist. The artificial, contrived air is deliberate.

By the end of his life, Poussin had returned to the simplicity of his earlier style, but it was drained of any trace of emotion. Another version of the subject of *Et in Arcadia Ego* [**Fig. 15.15**], painted some ten years later, provides a revealing contrast. The same four figures study the same tomb, but in a mood of deep stillness. Gone is the urgency of the earlier painting and much of the poetry. In its place, Poussin creates a mood of philosophical calm and tries to recapture the lofty spirit of antiquity, most notably in the noble brow and solemn stance of the shepherdess. Compensating for the loss of warmth is the transcendent beauty of the image.

Even had Poussin been prepared to leave Rome and return to the French court, the austere nature of his art would hardly have served to glorify that most autocratic and magnificent of monarchs, Louis XIV (born 1638, reigned 1643–1715). For the most part, the king had only second-rate artists available to him at court.

Hyacinthe Rigaud Although most official court painters achieved only mediocre respectability, an exception must be made for Hyacinthe Rigaud (1659–1743), whose stunning portrait of Louis XIV [**Fig. 15.16**] epit-

omizes baroque grandeur. It would be difficult to claim the intellectual vigor of Poussin or the emotional honesty of Caravaggio for this frankly flattering image of majesty. The stilted pose and gorgeous robes may even suggest an element of exaggeration, almost of parody; yet a glance at the king's sagging face and stony gaze immediately puts such an idea to rest. Rigaud has captured his patron's outward splendor while not hiding his increasing weakness, due in great part to his decadent lifestyle. The signs of physical collapse are visible—*Et in Versailles Ego*.

The Palace of Versailles Louis XIV's most lasting artistic achievement was a new center for the court—the Palace of Versailles—built a few miles outside Paris [**Fig. 15.17**]. The history of its construction is long and complicated, and the final result betrays some of the uncertainties that went into its planning.

Louis XIV, an acute politician and astute judge of human psychology, was well aware of the fact that the aristocratic courtiers who surrounded him were likely to turn on him if he showed the faintest sign of weakness or hesitation. By constructing an elaborate setting at Versailles in which he could consciously act out the role of Grand Monarch, Louis conveyed the image of himself as supreme ruler and thereby retained his mastery over the aristocracy.

The Hall of Mirrors The Palace of Versailles was therefore conceived by the king in political terms. The architects' task, both inside and out, was to create

◆ **15.16** Hyacinthe Rigaud, *Louis XIV*, 1701. Louis was sixty-three when this portrait was painted. The swirling ermine-lined robes are a mark of the king's swagger. The ballet pose of his feet is a reminder of the popularity of dancing at the French court.

Oil on canvas, 9 7/8" x 6'4" (2.77 x 1.94 m). Musée du Louvre, Paris, France // © Réunion des Musées Nationaux / Art Resource, NY

◆ **15.17** Aerial view, Palace of Versailles, begun 1669, and a small portion of the surrounding park. The chief architects for the last stage of construction at Versailles were Louis le Vau (1612–1670) and Jules Hardouin-Mansart (1646–1708). Although the external decoration of the palace is Classical in style, the massive scale (1935' or 590 m wide) is characteristic of baroque architecture.

Chateaux de Versailles et de Trianon, Versailles, France. Image © Réunion des Musées Nationaux / Art Resource, NY

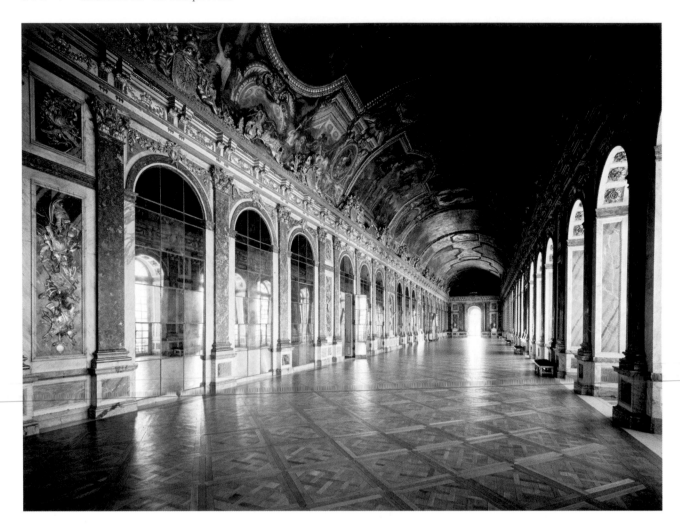

◆ **15.18** Hall of Mirrors (Galerie des Glaces), begun 1676, Palace of Versailles. Jules Hardouin-Mansart was the architect and Charles Le Brun (1619–1690) designed the interior. Le Brun borrowed the idea of a ceiling frescoed with mythological scenes from Carracci's painted ceiling in the Farnese Palace (see Figure 15.7).

Hall of Mirrors, 240′ (73.15 m) long, 34′ (10.36 m) wide, 43′ (13.11 m) high. Chateaux de Versailles et de Trianon, Versailles, France. Image © Scala/Art Resource, NY

a building that would illustrate Louis XIV's symbolic concept of himself as the Sun King. Thus, each morning the king would rise from his bed, make his way past the assembled court through the Hall of Mirrors [Fig. 15.18], where the seventeen huge mirrors reflected both the daylight and his own splendor, and enter the gardens along the main wing of the palace—laid out in an east-west axis to follow the path of the sun. At the same time both the palace and its gardens, which extend behind it for some two miles, were required to provide an appropriate setting for the balls, feasts, and fireworks displays organized there.

Given the grandiose symbolism of the ground plan and interior decorations, the actual appearance of the outside of the Palace of Versailles, with its rows of Ionic columns, is surprisingly modest. The simplicity of design and decoration is another demonstration of the French ability to combine the extremes of baroque art with a more Classical spirit.

SPAIN

El Greco The Spanish reaction to the baroque was very different. Strong religious emotion had always been a characteristic of Spanish Catholicism, and the new possibilities presented by baroque painting were foreshadowed in the work of the greatest painter active in Spain in the late sixteenth century, El Greco "the Greek" (1541–1614). Domenikos Theotokopoulos (El Greco's birth name) was born on the Greek island of Crete, which at the time was under Venetian rule. He apparently traveled to Venice, where he was influenced

◆ **15.19** El Greco, *Martyrdom of Saint Maurice and the Theban Legion*, 1581–1584. Pointing up toward the heavenly vision he sees, the saint faces forward. The elongated figures and bright colors are reminiscent of Italian Mannerists like Pontormo (see Figure 13.23), but El Greco's arrangement of his figures is much more irregular.

Oil on canvas, 14′6″ x 9′10″ (4.42 x 3 m). Escorial Palace, Madrid, Spain//© Scala/Art Resource, NY

◆ **15.20** El Greco, *Burial of Count Orgaz*, 1586. Note the elongated proportions of the figures in the heavens and the color contrasts between the upper and lower sections of the painting. This division is accentuated by the relatively straightforward composition of the burial scene, with the figures arranged in a row, in strong contrast to the swirling scene in Heaven.

Oil on canvas, 16′ x 11′10″ (4.88 x 3.61 m). San Tomé, Toledo, Spain//© Scala/Art Resource, NY

by Titian, and to Rome. It is not known why he went to Spain, but El Greco is recorded as having lived in Toledo from 1577 until his death.

Although he tried to obtain court patronage, the violence of contrasts in his work—clashes of color, scale, and emotion—did not appeal to official taste: his first royal commission, the *Martyrdom of Saint Maurice and the Theban Legion* [**Fig. 15.19**], was his last. The painting illustrates the theme of moral responsibility and choice. The Roman soldier Maurice, faced with a conflict between the demands of Roman law and of his Christian faith, chooses the latter, together with his fellow Theban and Christian legionnaires. The hallucinatory brightness of the colors is probably derived from Italian Mannerist painting of earlier in the sixteenth century,

as are the elongated proportions, but the effect—underlined by the asymmetrical composition—is incomparably more fierce and disturbing.

In the absence of court patronage, El Greco produced many of his works for Toledo, his city of residence. Among the most spectacular is the *Burial of Count Orgaz* [**Fig. 15.20**], a local benefactor who was rewarded for his generosity by the appearance of Saint Augustine and Saint Stephen at his funeral in 1323. They can be seen in the lower center of the painting, burying the count while his soul rises; the small boy dressed in black in the left-hand corner is the artist's eight-year-old son, identified by an inscription. The rich, heavy robes of the saints are balanced by the swirling drapery of the heavenly figures above, while the material and spiritual worlds are clearly separated by a row of grave, brooding local dignitaries.

José de Ribera   The same religious fervor appears in the work of José de Ribera (1591–1652) but is expressed in a far more naturalistic style. Like Caravaggio, Ribera used peasants in his religious scenes, which were painted with strong contrasts of light and dark. In his *The Martyrdom of Saint Bartholomew* [**Fig. 15.21**], Ribera spares us nothing in the way of realism as the saint is hauled into position to be flayed. The muscular brutality of his executioners and the sense of impending physical agony are almost masochistic in their vividness. Only in the compassionate faces of some onlookers do we find any relief from the torment of the scene.

Although paintings like Ribera's are representative of much of Spanish baroque art, the work of Diego Velázquez (1599–1660), the greatest Spanish painter of the baroque period, is very different in spirit. Velázquez used his superlative technique to depict scenes brimming with life, preferring the court of Philip IV (where he spent much of his career) and the lives of ordinary people to religious or mythological subjects.

The finest and most complex work of Velázquez is *Las Meninas (The Maids of Honor)* [**Fig. 15.22**]. Unlike Louis XIV, the Spanish king was fortunate enough to have one of the greatest painters in history to preserve the memory of his court. It is to Philip IV's credit that he treated Velázquez with respect and honor. In return, Velázquez produced several superb portraits of the monarch and his family. *Las Meninas* is an evocation of life in the royal palace. The scene is Velázquez's own studio; there the five-year-old Princess Margarita has come with her two maids to visit the painter at work on a huge painting that must surely be *Las Meninas* itself. Despite the size of the picture, the mood is quiet, even intimate: two figures in casual conversation, a sleepy dog, a passing court official who raises a curtain at the back to peer into the room. Yet so subtle is Velázquez's use of color that we feel the presence of the room as a three-dimensional space filled with light—now bright, now shadowy. The reality of details like the little princess's hair or dress never distracts from the overall unity of color and composition. That Velázquez was justifiably proud of his abilities is shown by the two distinguished visitors whose presence is felt rather than seen, reflected as they are in the mirror hanging on the back wall: the king and queen come to honor the artist by visiting him in his own studio.

BAROQUE ART IN NORTHERN EUROPE

Most baroque art produced in Northern Europe was intended for a middle-class rather than an aristocratic audience, as in Italy, France, and Spain. Before examining the effects of this, however, we must look at two

◆ **15.21** José de Ribera, *The Martyrdom of Saint Bartholomew*, c. 1639. Unlike La Tour (Figure 15.12), Ribera refuses to soften the subject by idealizing his figures. Nor is there any sign of heavenly intervention, as there is in Caravaggio's *Martyrdom of St. Matthew* (Figure 15.4).

Oil on canvas, 92″ x 92″ (2.34 x 2.34 m). Museo del Prado, Madrid, Spain//© Erich Lessing/Art Resource, NY

notable exceptions, Peter Paul Rubens (1577–1640) and his assistant and later rival, Anthony van Dyck (1599–1641), both Flemish by birth.

Peter Paul Rubens Rubens is often called the most universal of painters because he produced with apparent ease an almost inexhaustible stream of work of all kinds—religious subjects, portraits, landscapes, mythological scenes—all on the grandest of scales. He must certainly have been among the most active artists in history: in addition to running the workshop used for the production of his commissions, he pursued a career in diplomacy, which involved considerable traveling throughout Europe, and still had time for academic study. He is said to have spoken and written six modern languages and to have read Latin fluently. He was also versed in theology. Furthermore, in contrast to solitary and gloomy figures like Caravaggio and Borromini, Rubens seems to have been contented in his personal life. After the death of his first wife he remarried at age fifty-three, a girl of sixteen, Hélène Fourment, with whom he spent an ecstatically happy ten years before his death.

For the most part, however, intimacy is not the quality most characteristic of Rubens' art. Generally his pictures convey something of the restless energy of his life. In *The Rape of the Daughters of Leucippus* [**Fig. 15.23**],

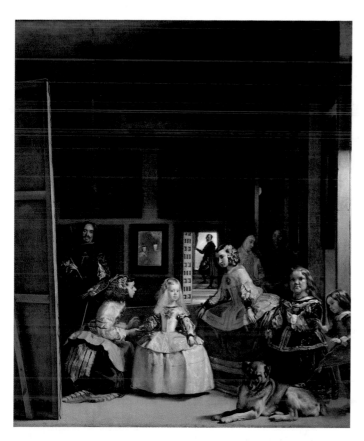

◆ **15.22** Diego Velázquez, *Las Meninas (The Maids of Honor)*, 1656. The red cross on the artist's breast, symbol of the noble Order of Santiago, was painted there by the king's command after Velázquez's death. Velázquez regarded his nomination to the order in 1658 as recognition of both his own nobility and that of his art. He thus became one of the first victors in the war that artists had waged ever since the Renaissance for a social status equal to that of their patrons. Throughout the 16th and 17th centuries, their aristocratic and ecclesiastical employers regarded them as little better than servants; only by the end of the 18th century were artists and musicians able to assert their social and political independence.

Oil on canvas, 10′5″ x 9′ (3.18 x 2.74 m). Museo del Prado, Madrid, Spain//© Scala/Art Resource, NY

◆ **15.23** Peter Paul Rubens, *The Rape of the Daughters of Leucippus*, c. 1618. According to the Greek legend, Castor and Pollux, twin sons of Zeus, carried off King Leucippus' two daughters, who had been betrothed to their cousins. The myth here becomes symbolic of physical passion. Note the ample forms of the two women; this physique has come to be called "Rubensesque."

Oil on canvas, 7′3″ x 6′10″ (2.21 x 2.08 m). Alte Pinakothek, Munich, Germany//© Scala/ Art Resource, NY

◆ **15.24** Peter Paul Rubens, *The Journey of Marie de' Medici*, 1622–1625. This painting focuses on the triumphant figure of the queen. As in many of his large works, Rubens probably painted the important portions and left other sections to his assistants.

Oil on canvas, 14′11″ x 9′6″ (3.94 x 2.95 m). Musée du Louvre, Paris, France//© Giraudon/The Bridgeman Art Library

◆ **15.25** Anthony van Dyck, *Marchesa Elena Grimaldi, Wife of Marchese Nicola Cataneo*, c. 1623. Painted fairly early in van Dyck's career during a stay in Genoa, the portrait emphasizes the aristocratic bearing of its subject by somber colors and an artificial setting that accentuates her grandeur.

Oil on canvas, 97′ x 68′ (2.46 x 1.72 m). National Gallery of Art, Washington, DC, USA//© The Art Archive/National Gallery of Art

every part of the painting is filled with movement as the mortal women, divine riders, and even the horses are drawn into a single pulsating spiral. The sense of action, so characteristic of Rubens' paintings, is in strong contrast to the frozen movement of Poussin's depiction of a similar episode (see Figure 15.14). Equally typical of the artist is his frank delight in the women's sensuous nudity and ample proportions—the slender grace of other artists' nudes was not at all to Rubens' taste.

Perhaps the most extraordinary achievement of Rubens' remarkable career was his fulfillment of a commission from Marie de' Medici, widow of Henry IV and mother of Louis XIII, to decorate an entire gallery with paintings illustrating her life. In a mere three years, from 1622 to 1625, he created twenty-four enormous paintings commemorating the chief events in which she played a part, with greater flattery than truth. The splendid *Journey of Marie de' Medici* [**Fig. 15.24**] shows the magnificently attired queen on horseback at the Battle of Ponts-de-Cé, accompanied by the spirit of Power, while Fame and Glory flutter around her head.

It hardly matters that the queen's forces were ignominiously defeated in the battle, so convincingly triumphant does her image appear.

Anthony van Dyck Paintings on this scale required the help of assistants, and there is no doubt that in Rubens' workshop much of the preliminary work was done by his staff. One of the many artists employed for this purpose eventually became as much in demand for portraits of the aristocracy as his former master. Anthony van Dyck spent two years (1618–1620) with Rubens before beginning his career as an independent

◆ **15.26** Frans Hals, *Banquet of the Officers of the Civic Guard of Saint George at Haarlem*, 1616. The diagonal lines of the curtains, banner, and sashes help bind the painting together and make it at the same time both a series of individual portraits and a single unified composition.

Oil on canvas, 5′8¼″ x 10′6⅜″ (1.75 x 3.24 m). Frans Halsmuseum, Haarlem, The Netherlands//© Erich Lessing/Art Resource, NY

artist. Although from time to time he painted religious subjects, his fame rests on his formal portraits, many of which were produced during the years he spent in Italy and England.

Van Dyck's refined taste equipped him for satisfying the demands of his noble patrons that they be shown as they thought they looked rather than as they actually were. It is certainly difficult to believe that any real-life figure could have had quite the haughty bearing and lofty dignity of the Marchesa Cataneo [**Fig. 15.25**] in van Dyck's portrait of her, although the Genoese nobility of which she was a member was known for its arrogance.

International celebrities like Rubens and van Dyck, at home at the courts of all Europe, were far from typical of northern artists. Painters in the Netherlands in particular found themselves in a very different situation from their colleagues elsewhere. The two most lucrative sources of commissions—the church and the aristocracy—were unavailable to them because the Dutch Calvinist Church followed the post-Reformation practice of forbidding the use of images in church and because Holland had never had its own powerful hereditary nobility. Painters therefore depended on the tastes and demands of the open market.

Frans Hals One highly profitable source of income for Dutch artists in the seventeenth century was the group portrait, in particular that of a militia or civic guard company. These bands of soldiers had originally served a practical purpose in the defense of their country, but their regular reunions tended to be social gatherings, chiefly for the purpose of eating and drinking. A group of war veterans today would hire a photographer to commemorate their annual reunion; the militia companies engaged the services of a portrait painter. If they were lucky or rich enough, they might even get Frans Hals (c. 1580–1666) whose group portraits capture the individuality of each of the participants while conveying the general convivial spirit of the occasion as in *Banquet of the Officers of the Civic Guard of Saint George at Haarlem* [**Fig. 15.26**]. Hals was certainly not the most imaginative or inventive of artists, but his sheer ability to paint, using broad dynamic brush strokes and cleverly organized compositions, makes his work some of the most attractive of that period.

Jan Vermeer Very different in spirit was Jan Vermeer (1632–1675), who worked almost unknown in the city of Delft and whose art was virtually forgotten after his death. Rediscovered in the nineteenth century, it is now regarded as second only to Rembrandt's for depth of feeling. At first sight this may seem surprising because Vermeer's subjects are rather limited in scope. A woman reading a letter

[**Fig. 15.27**], girls sewing or playing music—through such intimate scenes Vermeer reveals qualities of inner contemplation and repose that are virtually unique in the entire history of art. Unlike Hals, with his loose style, Vermeer built up his forms by applying the paint in the form of tiny dots of color and then rendering the details with careful precision. Like Velázquez's *Las Meninas* (see Figure 15.22), his paintings are dominated by light so palpable as to seem to surround the figures with its presence. However, where Velázquez's canvas is suffused with a warm, Mediterranean glow, Vermeer's paintings capture the coolness and clarity of northern light. The perfection of his compositions creates a mood of stillness so complete that mundane activities take on a totally unexpected concentration and become endowed with a heightened sense of importance.

Rembrandt

Rembrandt Rembrandt van Rijn (1606–1669) is one of the most deeply loved of all painters. No summary of his achievements can begin to do them justice. Born in Leiden in the Netherlands, he spent a short time at the university there before beginning his stud-

◆ **15.27** Jan Vermeer, *Woman Reading a Letter*, 1662–1664. Much of the sense of balance and repose that Vermeer conveys is achieved by his careful color contrasts between blue and yellow and the repetition of rectangular surfaces such as the table, chair backs, and the map of the Netherlands on the wall.

Oil on canvas, 18⅛″ x 15¼″ (46 x 39 cm). © Rijksmuseum, Amsterdam, The Netherlands / The Bridgeman Art Library

ies as a painter. The early part of his career was spent in Amsterdam, where he moved in 1631 and soon became known as a fashionable portrait painter. His life was that of any successful man of the time: happily married, living in his own fine house.

Rembrandt's interest in spiritual matters and the eternal problems of existence, however, coupled with his researches into new artistic techniques, seem to have prevented his settling down for long to a bourgeois existence of this kind. The artistic turning point of his career came in 1642, the year of the death of his wife, when he finished the painting known as *The Night Watch* [**Fig. 15.28**]. Although ostensibly the same kind of group portrait as Hals' *Banquet of the Officers of the Civic Guard* (see Figure 15.26), *The Night Watch* is composed with much greater complexity and subtlety. The arrangement of the figures and the sense of depth show how far Rembrandt was outdistancing his contemporaries.

The price Rembrandt paid for his genius was growing neglect, which by 1656 had brought bankruptcy. The less his work appealed to the public of his day, the more Rembrandt retreated into his own spiritual world. About 1645 he set up house with Hendrickje Stoffels, although he never married her, and his unconventional behavior succeeded in alienating him still further from his contemporaries. The faithful Hendrickje, however, together with Titus, Rembrandt's son by his first marriage, helped put his financial affairs in some sort of order. Her death in 1663 left him desolate.

Rembrandt used contrast between light and darkness to achieve dramatic and emotional effect in all his work. Light also served to build composition and to create depth in his paintings and etchings. In the paintings, he often built up layers of paint to create a richness of color and sense of texture unmatched by any of his contemporaries. In his etchings and engravings, he developed ways of varying the lines to produce a similarly elaborate surface. A supremely baroque artist, Rembrandt always used his mastery of composition and texture to deepen and enhance the emotional power of the image.

In the final years of his life, Rembrandt turned increasingly to biblical subjects, always using them to explore some aspect of human feelings. In *Jacob Blessing the Sons of Joseph* [**Fig. 15.29**] all the tenderness of family affection is expressed in the juxtaposition of the heads of the old man and his son, whose expression of love is surpassed only by that of his wife as she gazes almost unseeingly at her sons. The depth of emotion and the dark shadows mark that school of baroque painting initiated by Caravaggio, yet it seems almost an impertinence to categorize so universal a statement. Through this painting Rembrandt seems to offer us a deep spiritual comfort for the tragic nature of human destiny revealed by the self-portraits.

◆ **15.28** Rembrandt, *The Sortie of Captain Frans Banning Cocq's Company of the Civic Guard* (*The Night Watch*), 1642. Recent cleaning has revealed that the painting's popular name, though conveniently brief, is inaccurate. Far from being submerged in darkness, the principal figures were originally bathed in light and painted in glowing colors.

Oil on canvas, 11′9½″ x 14′2½″ (3.63 x 4.37 m). © Rijksmuseum, Amsterdam, The Netherlands/SuperStock

◆ **15.29** Rembrandt, *Jacob Blessing the Sons of Joseph*, 1656. This very personal version of the biblical story, which must at least in part have come from Rembrandt's lifelong meditation on the Scriptures, was painted the year of his financial collapse. Rembrandt includes Asenath, Joseph's wife, although she is not mentioned in the text, and her presence here emphasizes the family nature of the occasion.

Oil on canvas, 5′8¼″ x 6′9″ (1.75 x 2.1 m). Gemaeldegalerie, Staatliche Museen, Kassel, Germany//© Erich Lessing/Art Resource, NY

◆ **15.30** Pieter de Hooch, *Portrait of a Family Playing Music*, 1683. This group portrait of a prosperous Dutch family seems to symbolize the harmonious nature of family as the mother and father lead their children in a musical performance.

Oil on canvas, 39′ x 47′ (99 x 119 cm). Cleveland Museum of Art, Cleveland, OH, USA//© Francis G. Mayer/CORBIS

BAROQUE MUSIC

Although the history of music is as long as that of the other arts, the earliest music with which most modern music lovers are on familiar ground is that of the baroque period. It is safe to say that many thousands of listeners have tapped their feet to the rhythm of a baroque concerto without knowing or caring anything about its historical context, and with good reason: baroque music, with its strong emphasis on rhythmic vitality and attractive melody, is easy to respond to with pleasure. Furthermore, in the person of Johann Sebastian Bach, the baroque period produced one of the greatest geniuses in the history of music, one who shared Rembrandt's ability to communicate profound experience on the broadest level.

The qualities that make baroque music popular today were responsible for its original success. Composers of the baroque period were the first since Classical antiquity to write large quantities of music intended for the pleasure of listeners as well as the glory of God. The polyphonic music of the Middle Ages and the Renaissance, with its interweaving of many musical lines, had enabled composers like Machaut or Palestrina to praise the Lord on the highest level of intellectual achievement, but the result was a musical style far above the heads of most of their contemporary listeners. The Council of Trent, in accordance with Counter-Reformation principles, had even considered prohibiting polyphony in religious works in order to make church music more accessible to the average congregation before finally deciding that this would be too extreme a measure. For once, the objectives of Reformation and Counter-Reformation coincided, for Luther had already simplified the musical elements in Protestant services for the same reason (see Chapter 14).

The time was therefore ripe for a general move toward sacred music with a wider and more universal appeal. Since at the same time the demand for secular music was growing, it is not surprising that composers soon developed a style sufficiently attractive and flexible not only for the creation of masses and other liturgical works, but also of instrumental and vocal music that could be played and listened to at home [Fig. 15.30].

THE BIRTH OF OPERA

Perhaps the major artistic innovation of the seventeenth century was a new form of musical entertainment that appeared at the beginning of the baroque period: opera. This consisted of a play in which the text was sung rather than spoken. Throughout the seventeenth century the taste for opera and operatic music swept Europe, attracting aristocratic and middle-class listeners alike. In the process, the public appetite for music with which it could identify grew even greater. Small wonder that twentieth-century listeners have found pleasure and delight in music written to provide our baroque predecessors with precisely these satisfactions.

Like much else of beauty, opera was born in Florence. Ironically enough, an art form that was to become so popular in so short a time was originally conceived of in lofty intellectual terms. Toward the end of the sixteenth century, a group of thinkers, poets, and musicians began to meet regularly at the house of a wealthy Florentine noble, Count Giovanni Bardi. This group, known as the Florentine *Camerata*, objected strongly to the way in which the polyphonic style in vocal music reduced the text to incomprehensible nonsense. They looked back nostalgically to the time of the Greeks, when almost every word of Greek tragedy was both sung and accompanied by instruments, yet remained perfectly understandable to the spectators. Greek music was lost forever, but at least the group could revive what they considered its essence.

The result was the introduction of a musical form known as **monody**, or **recitative**, which consisted of the free declamation of a single vocal line with a simple instrumental accompaniment for support. Thus listeners could follow the text with ease. The addition of music also gave an emotional intensity not present in simple spoken verse, thus satisfying the baroque interest in heightened emotion.

Although in theory monody could be used for either sacred or secular works, its dramatic potential was obvious. In the winter of 1594–1595 the first play set to music, Jacopo Peri's *Dafne*, was performed in Florence. Its subject was drawn from Classical mythology and dealt with Apollo's pursuit of the mortal girl Daphne, who turned into a laurel tree to elude him. In the words of a spectator, "The pleasure and amazement of those present were beyond expression." *Dafne* is now lost, but another of Peri's works, *Euridice*, has survived to become the earliest extant opera. It too was based on a Greek myth, that of Orpheus and Eurydice. The first performance took place in 1600, again in Florence, at the wedding of Henry IV of France to the same Marie de' Medici whom Rubens was to portray a generation later (see Figure 15.24).

It is no coincidence that both of Peri's works as well as many that followed were written on Classical subjects, because the Camerata had taken its initial inspiration from Greek drama. The story of Orpheus and Eurydice, furthermore, had a special appeal for composers, because it told how the musician Orpheus was able to soften the heart of the King of the Underworld by his music and thereby win back his wife Eurydice from the dead. The theme was treated many times in the music of the following four hundred years, yet no subsequent version is more moving or psychologically convincing than that of Claudio Monteverdi (1567–1643), the first great genius in the history of opera.

Claudio Monteverdi Monteverdi's *L'Orfeo* was first performed in 1607. Its composer brought to the new form not only a complete understanding of the possibilities of monody but in addition an impressive mastery of traditional polyphonic forms such as the madrigal. Equally important for the success of his work was Monteverdi's remarkable dramatic instinct and his ability to transform emotion into musical terms. The contrast between the pastoral gaiety of the first act of *L'Orfeo*, depicting the happy couple's love, and the scene in the second act in which Orpheus is brought the news of his wife's death is achieved with marvelous expressive power.

In his first opera, Monteverdi was able to breathe real life into the academic principles of the Florentine Camerata, but *L'Orfeo* was written for his noble employer, the Duke of Mantua, and intended for a limited aristocratic public. Monteverdi lived long enough to see the new dramatic form achieve widespread popularity at all levels of society throughout Europe. A taste for Italian opera spread to Germany and Austria and then to England where, by the end of the century, Italian singers dominated the London stage. The French showed their usual unwillingness to adopt a foreign invention wholesale; nonetheless, the leading composer at the court of Louis XIV was a Florentine who tactfully changed his name from Giovanni Battista Lulli to Jean Baptiste Lully (1632–1687). His stately tragedies, which were performed throughout Europe, incorporated long sections of ballet, a custom continued by his most illustrious successor, Jean Philippe Rameau (1683–1764).

Opera won its largest public in Italy proper. In Venice alone, where Monteverdi spent the last thirty years of his life, at least sixteen theaters were built between 1637—when the first public opera house was opened—and the end of the century. As in the Elizabethan theater (see Figure 14.29), the design of these opera houses separated the upper ranks of society, who sat in the boxes, from the ordinary citizens—the groundlings.

There is a notable similarity, too, between Elizabethan drama and opera in the way they responded to growing popularity. Just as the groundlings of Shakespeare's day demanded ever more sensational and melodramatic entertainment, so the increasingly demanding and vociferous opera public required new ways of being satisfied. The two chief means by which these desires were met became a feature of most operas written during the following century. The first was the provision of lavish stage spectacles involving mechanical cloud machines that descended from above and disgorged singers and dancers, complex lighting effects that gave the illusion that the stage was being engulfed by fire, apparently magical transformations, and so on—baroque extravagance at its most extreme. The second was a move away from the declamatory recitative of the earliest operas to self-contained musical pieces known as **arias**. (In the case of both opera and many other musical forms, we continue to use technical terms like aria in their Italian form—a demonstration of the crucial role played by Italy, and in particular Florence, in the history of music.) The function of music as servant of the drama was beginning to change. Beauty of melody and the technical virtuosity of the singers became the glory of baroque opera, although at the expense of dramatic truth.

CD Track 6
Claudio Monteverdi, "Quel Sguardo Sdegnosetto"

In addition to his operas, Monteverdi wrote religious works, madrigals, and—as here—songs. "Quel Sguardo Sdegnosetto" was one of three *scherzi musicali* (musical jokes) composed in 1632 and shows a characteristically baroque love of virtuosity and emotion. Unlike Morley's madrigal (Chapter 14), it is certainly not written for an amateur performer: the soloist is required to perform feats of brilliant singing (involving considerable breath control), while conveying the feeling behind a somewhat conventional anonymous baroque poem.

The words deal with the joys and dangers of physical love (a new and typically baroque subject: compare Bernini's *Saint Teresa in Ecstasy*, Figure 15.10). Note the change of mood in the central section of the song's three parts. Much of the effect of the song comes from the way in which Monteverdi constructs a solid bass line, above which the singer seems to weave her line at random (although, of course, everything is carefully calculated).

Thus, in miniature, Monteverdi constructs a subtle and varied picture of erotic delights. The middle verse contains the words: "Bombard my heart with a shower of sparks, but let not your lips be slow to revive me when I die." The singer here is Emma Kirkby, the purity of whose voice (musicians would describe it as "without vibrato") is regarded as highly appropriate for baroque vocal music.

BAROQUE INSTRUMENTAL AND VOCAL MUSIC

The development of opera permitted the dramatic retelling of mythological or historical tales. Sacred texts as stories derived from the Bible were set to music in a form known as the **oratorio**, which had begun to appear toward the end of the sixteenth century. One of the baroque masters of the oratorio was the Italian Giacomo Carissimi (1605–1674), whose works, based on well-known biblical episodes, include *The Judgment of Solomon* and *Job*. By the dramatic use of the chorus, simple textures, and driving rhythms, Carissimi created an effect of strength and power that late-twentieth century listeners have begun to rediscover.

Heinrich Schütz The concept of the public performance of religious works, rather than secular operas, appealed especially to Protestant Germans. Heinrich Schütz (1585–1672) wrote a wide variety of oratorios and other sacred works. In his early *Psalms of David* (1619), Schütz combined the choral technique of Renaissance composers like Gabrieli with the vividness and drama of the madrigal. His setting of *The Seven Last Words of Christ* (1645–1646) uses soloists, chorus, and instruments to create a complex sequence of narrative sections (recitatives), vocal ensembles, and choruses. Among his last works are three settings of the Passion, the events of the last days of the life of Jesus, in the accounts given by Matthew, Luke, and John. Written in 1666, these works revert to the style of a century earlier, with none of the instrumental coloring generally typical of baroque music, both sacred and secular.

Schütz is, in fact, one of the few great baroque composers who, so far as is known, never wrote any purely instrumental music. The fact is all the more striking because the baroque period was notable for the emergence of independent instrumental compositions unrelated to texts of any kind. Girolamo Frescobaldi (1583–1643), the greatest organ virtuoso of his day—he was organist at Saint Peter's in Rome—wrote a series of rhapsodic fantasies known as toccatas that combined extreme technical complexity with emotional and dramatic expression. His slightly earlier Dutch contemporary Jan Pieterszoon Sweelinck (1562–1621), organist at Amsterdam, built sets of variations out of different settings of a chorale melody or hymn tune. The writing of **chorale variations**, as this type of piece became known, became popular throughout the baroque period.

Dietrich Buxtehude The Danish Dietrich Buxtehude (1637–1707), who spent most of his career in Germany, combined the brilliance of the toccata form with the use of a chorale theme in his chorale fantasies. Starting with a simple hymn melody, he composed free-form rhapsodies that are almost improvisational in style. His suites for **harpsichord** (the keyboard instrument that was a primary forerunner of the modern piano) include movements in variation form, various dances, slow lyric pieces, and other forms; like other composers of his day, Buxtehude used the keyboard suite as a kind of compendium of musical forms.

Domenico Scarlatti One of the greatest composers of the late baroque period was Domenico Scarlatti (1685–1757). The greatest virtuoso of his day on the harpsichord, Scarlatti wrote hundreds of **sonatas** (short instrumental pieces) for it and laid the foundation for modern keyboard techniques.

Georg Frideric Handel Scarlatti's contemporary Georg Frideric Handel (1685–1759) was born in Halle,

Germany, christened with the name he later changed to George Frederick Handel when he settled in England and became a naturalized citizen. London was to prove the scene of his greatest successes, among them *Messiah*, first performed in Dublin in 1742. This oratorio is among the most familiar of all baroque musical masterpieces, and its most famous section is the Hallelujah Chorus.

CD Track 7
Georg Frideric Handel, "Hallelujah Chorus" from *Messiah*

From the time of its first performance, Handel's Hallelujah Chorus, which ends the second part of his oratorio *Messiah*, has been recognized as one of the great masterpieces of baroque splendor and fervor. With its hammering drums and triumphant trumpets soaring, it epitomizes the grandeur and religious conviction of the baroque era.

It uses the typical baroque device of light and shade to achieve its effect, with the music changing volume in order to dramatize the text. The chorus begins vigorously and fervently, repeating the word *hallelujah* with increasing emphasis and volume. Then the music suddenly drops to a lower level as the chorus sings, "For the Lord God omnipotent reigneth." The music becomes even quieter with the next section, beginning "The Kingdom of this world . . . ," as if the sound were about to fade away.

But Handel has a final punch up his sleeve. As the singers launch at top volume into the final section, "And He shall reign for ever and ever," the voices pile up into a massive and increasingly complex texture, urged on by trumpets and drums, until they reach their triumphant climax. Thus the Hallelujah Chorus combines the emotionalism, spirituality, light and shade, and religious fervor that are all typical of baroque art (see Table 15.1).

Handel also wrote operas, including a series of masterpieces in Italian for performance in England. Among their greatest glories are the arias, which are permeated by Handel's rich melodic sense; one of the most famous is "Ombra mai fu" from *Xerxes*, often called the "Largo." His best-known orchestral works are probably *The Water Music* and *The Music for the Royal Fireworks*, both originally designed for outdoor performance. Written for numerous instruments, they were later rearranged for regular concerts.

JOHANN SEBASTIAN BACH

In the year that saw the births of both Scarlatti and Handel, Johann Sebastian Bach (1685–1750) was born in Eisenach, Germany, into a family that had already been producing musicians for more than a century. With the exception of opera, which, as a devout Lutheran, did not interest him, Bach mastered every musical form of the time, pouring forth some of the most intellectually rigorous and spiritually profound music ever created.

It is among the more remarkable achievements in the history of the arts that most of Bach's music was produced under conditions of grinding toil as organist and choir director in relatively provincial German towns. Even Leipzig—where Bach spent twenty-seven years (from 1723 to his death) as **kantor** ("music director") at the school attached to Saint Thomas's Church—was far removed from the glittering centers of European culture where most artistic developments were taking place. As a result, Bach was little known as a composer during his lifetime and virtually forgotten after his death; only in the nineteenth century did his body of work become known and published. He has since taken his place at the head of the Western musical tradition as the figure who raised the art of polyphony to its highest level.

If the sheer quantity of music Bach wrote is stupefying, so is the complexity of his musical thought. Among the styles he preferred was the **fugue** (derived from the Latin word for "flight"). In the course of a fugue a single theme is passed from voice to voice or instrument to instrument (generally four in number), each imitating the principal theme in turn. The theme thus becomes combined with itself and, in the process, the composer creates a seamless web of sound in which each musical part is equally important; this technique is called *counterpoint (contrapunctum)*. Bach's ability to endow this highly intellectual technique with emotional power is little short of miraculous. The range of emotions Bach's fugues cover can best be appreciated by sampling his two books of twenty-four preludes and fugues each, known collectively as *The Well-Tempered Clavier*. Each of the forty-eight preludes and fugues creates its own mood while remaining logically organized according to contrapuntal technique.

Many of Bach's important works are permeated by a single concern: the expression of his deep religious faith. A significant number were written in his capacity as director of music at Saint Thomas's for performance in the church throughout the year. Organ music, masses, oratorios, motets; in all of these he could use music to glorify God and to explore the deeper mysteries of Christianity. His **chorale preludes** consist of variations on chorales and use familiar and well-loved songs as the basis for a kind of musical improvisation. He wrote some two hundred **cantatas** (short oratorios) made up of sections of declamatory recitative and lyrical arias, which contain an almost inexhaustible range of religious emotions, from joyful celebrations of life to profound meditations on death. Most overwhelming of all is his setting of the *Saint Matthew Passion* the story of the trial and crucifixion of Jesus as recorded in the Gospel of Matthew. In this immense work, Bach asserted his Lutheranism by using the German rather than the Latin translation of the Gospel and by incorporating Lutheran chorales. The use of self-contained arias is Italian, though, and the spirit of deep religious commitment and dramatic fervor can only be described as universal.

It would be a mistake to think of Bach as somehow unworldly and touched only by religious emotions. Certainly his personal life had its share of domestic happiness and tragedy. His parents died when he was ten, leaving him to be brought up by an elder brother who treated him with less than complete kindness. At the age of fifteen, Bach jumped at the chance to leave home and become a choirboy in the little town of Luneberg. He spent the next few years moving from place to place, perfecting his skills as organist, violinist, and composer.

In 1707 Bach married his cousin, Maria Barbara Bach, who bore him seven children, of whom four died in infancy. Bach was always devoted to his family, and the loss of these children, followed by the death of his wife in 1720, made a deep impression on him. It may have been to provide a mother for his three surviving sons that he remarried in 1721. At any event, his new wife, Anna Magdalena, proved a loving companion, bearing him thirteen more children and helping him with the preparation and copying of his music. One of the shortest but most touching of Bach's works is the little song, "Bist du bei mir," which has survived, copied out in her notebook. The words are "As long as you are with me I could face my death and eternal rest with joy. How peaceful would my end be if your beautiful hands could close my faithful eyes." (Some scholars now believe that the song may have originally been written by G. H. Stölzel, a contemporary musician whom Bach much admired.)

The move to Leipzig in 1723 was dictated at least in part by the need to provide suitable schooling for his children, although it also offered the stability and security Bach seems to have required. The subsequent years of continual work took their toll, however. Bach's sight had never been good, and the incessant copying of manuscripts produced a continual deterioration. In 1749 Bach was persuaded to undergo two disastrous operations, which left him totally blind. A few months later his sight was suddenly restored, but within ten days he died of apoplexy (stroke).

Although most of Bach's works are on religious themes, the best known of all, the six *Brandenburg Concertos*, were written for the private entertainment of a minor prince, the Margrave of Brandenburg. Their form follows the Italian *concerto grosso*, an orchestral composition in three **movements** (sections): fast (allegro)-slow (adagio or largo)-fast (allegro). The form had been pioneered by the Venetian composer Antonio Vivaldi (c. 1676–1741), who delighted in strong contrasts between the orchestra, generally made up of string instruments and a solo instrument, often a violin, but sometimes a flute, bassoon, or other wind instrument. Vivaldi's most often performed work is a set of four violin concertos known as *The Four Seasons*, which illustrate in sound a set of four poems describing the characteristics of the annual cycle of the seasons. The one for spring, for example, describes the happy songs and dances with which the season is celebrated.

CD Track 8
Antonio Vivaldi, First Movement from "Spring" (*La Primavera*, Concerto No. 1 in E major), *Four Seasons*

Written according to typical baroque practice, each movement of Vivaldi's concertos is based on a single, strongly rhythmic theme, heard right at the beginning of the section. The fast tempo of first movement of the "Spring" concerto indicates in the work a delight at the return of the season of flowers. Two further baroque devices help Vivaldi characterize the specific season: virtuosity (on the part of the solo violinist) and illusionism. Shortly after the opening, the violin imitates the trilling of the birds who have returned, and the music suddenly becomes quiet, as all the instruments imitate the sound of the gentle spring breezes.

A sudden plunge announces the arrival of a spring storm, with upward leaps portraying lightning. The solo violin expresses the violence of the abrupt gusts of wind, while the lower strings seem to hint at not-so-distant thunder. Then the storm passes, the birdsong is heard again, and all ends with the joyful music of the opening.

In a matter of a few minutes, and with only a handful of instruments, Vivaldi has used baroque techniques to illustrate human emotions evoked by natural events.

Bach's *Brandenburg Concertos* Four of Bach's six *Brandenburg Concertos* use a group of solo instruments, although the group differs from work to work. The whole set forms a kind of compendium of the possibilities of instrumental color, a true virtuoso achievement requiring equal virtuosity in performance. The musical mood is light, as befits works written primarily for entertainment, but Bach was incapable of writing music without depth, and the slow movements in particular are strikingly beautiful.

The second *Brandenburg Concerto* is written for solo trumpet, recorder, oboe, and violin accompanied by a string orchestra. The first movement combines all of these to produce a brilliant rhythmic effect as the solo instruments now emerge from the orchestra, now rejoin it. The melodic line avoids short themes. Instead, as in much baroque music, the melodies are long, elaborate patterns that seem to spread and evolve, having much of the ornateness of baroque art. The opening theme forms an unbroken line of sound, rising and falling and doubling back as it luxuriantly spreads itself out.

The slow second movement forms a tranquil and meditative interlude. The brilliant tone of the trumpet would be inappropriate here, and Bach therefore omits it, leaving the recorder, oboe, and violin quietly to intertwine in a delicate web of sound. After its enforced silence, the trumpet seems to burst out irrepressibly at the beginning of the third movement, claiming the right to set the mood of limitless energy that carries the work to its conclusion.

CD Track 9
Johann Sebastian Bach, Third Movement, Allegro Assai, from Brandenburg Concerto No. 2 in F major

Whereas Vivaldi's baroque virtuosity is reserved for the solo violinist in his *Four Seasons*, Bach expects every one of his performers to be capable of extraordinary feats of virtuosity and movement. Listen to the opening trumpet solo with its difficult trills: the player barely has time to breathe. And the oboist who picks up the tune has an even longer passage before the solo violin breaks in. With the entry of the flute, the texture becomes more complex but always remains crystal clear, as the four principal instruments play with fragments of the opening theme, breaking them up and putting them back together with the typical sense of baroque unity in variety. The arrival of the other instruments provides a background for the continuous display of virtuosity, as the trumpet seems to reach ever higher.

Other works of Bach illustrate a broader range of baroque characteristics: religious fervor, illusionism, emotionalism. We hear this last feature in this work, where his music seems to express boundless joy. In two other respects the work is typical of the baroque period. It is written for a group of performers playing together—a technique that was to develop into the Classical orchestra—and, more importantly perhaps, the music's purpose is to give pleasure to performers and listeners alike—music as entertainment.

PHILOSOPHY AND SCIENCE IN THE BAROQUE PERIOD

Throughout the seventeenth century, philosophy—like the visual arts—continued to extend and intensify ideas first developed in the Renaissance by pushing them to new extremes. With the spread of humanism, the sixteenth century had seen a growing spirit of philosophical and scientific inquiry. In the baroque period, that fresh approach to the world and its phenomena was expressed in clear and consistent terms for the first time since the Greeks. It might be said, in fact, that

if the Renaissance marked the birth of modern philosophy, the seventeenth century signaled its coming of age.

Briefly stated, the chief difference between the intellectual attitudes of the medieval period and those inaugurated by the Renaissance was a turning away from the contemplation of the absolute and eternal to a study of the particular and the perceivable. Philosophy ceased to be the preserve of the theologians and instead became an independent discipline, no longer prepared to accept a supernatural or divine explanation for the world and human existence.

For better or worse, we are still living with the consequences of this momentous change. The importance of objective truth, objectively demonstrated, lies at the heart of all scientific method and most modern philosophy. Yet great thinkers before the Renaissance, such as Thomas Aquinas (1225–1274), had also asked questions in an attempt to understand the world and its workings. How did seventeenth-century scientists and philosophers differ from their predecessors in dealing with age-old problems?

The basic difference lay in their approach. When, for example, Aquinas was concerned with the theory of motion, he discussed it in abstract, metaphysical terms. Armed with his copy of Aristotle, he claimed that "motion exists because things which are in a state of potentiality seek to actualize themselves." When Galileo wanted to study motion and learn how bodies move in time and space, he climbed to the top of the Leaning Tower of Pisa and dropped weights to watch them fall. It would be difficult to imagine a more dramatic rejection of abstract generalization in favor of objective demonstration (see **Table 15.2**).

GALILEO GALILEI

The life and work of Galileo Galilei (1564–1642) are typical both of the progress made by science in the seventeenth century and of the problems it encountered. Galileo changed the scientific world in two ways: first, as the stargazer who claimed that his observations through the telescope proved Copernicus right, for which

Table 15.2 *Principal Scientific Discoveries of the Seventeenth Century*

1609	Kepler announces his first two laws of planetary motion
1614	Napier invents logarithms
1632	Galileo publishes *Dialogue Concerning the Two Chief World Systems*
1643	Torricelli invents the barometer
1660	Boyle formulates his law of gas pressure
1675	Royal Observatory founded at Greenwich, England
1687	Isaac Newton publishes his account of the principle of gravity
1710	Leibnitz invents new notations of calculus
1717	Fahrenheit invents system of measuring temperature

statement he was tried and condemned by the Inquisition; and second, as the founder of modern physics. Although he is probably better known for his work in astronomy, from the scientific point of view his contribution to physics is more important.

Born in Pisa, Galileo inherited from his father Vincenzo, who had been one of the original members of the Florentine Camerata, a lively prose style and a fondness for music. As a student at the University of Padua from 1581 to 1592, he began to study medicine but soon changed to mathematics. After a few months back in Pisa, he took a position at the University of Padua as professor of mathematics, remaining there from 1592 to 1600.

In Padua, Galileo designed and built his own telescopes [**Fig. 15.31**] and saw for the first time the craters of the moon, sunspots, the phases of Venus, and other phenomena that showed that the universe is in a constant state of change, as Copernicus had claimed. From the time of Aristotle, however, it had been a firm belief that the heavens were unalterable, representing perfection of form and movement. Galileo's discoveries thus disproved what had been a basic philosophical principle for 2000 years and so outraged a professor of philosophy at Padua that he refused to shake his own prejudices by having a look through a telescope for himself.

The more triumphantly Galileo proclaimed his findings, the more he found himself involved in something beyond mere scientific controversy. His real opponent was the church, which had officially adopted the Ptolemaic view of the universe: that the earth formed the center of the universe around which the sun, moon, and planets circled. This theory accorded well with the Bible, which seemed to suggest that the sun moves rather than the earth; for the church, the Bible naturally took precedence over any reasoning or speculation independent of theology. Galileo, however, considered ecclesiastical officials incompetent to evaluate scientific matters and refused to give way. When he began to claim publicly that his discoveries had proved what Copernicus had theorized but could not validate, the church initiated a case against him on the grounds of heresy.

Galileo had meanwhile returned to his beloved Pisa, where he found himself in considerable danger from the Inquisition. In 1615 he left for Rome to defend his position in the presence of Pope Paul V. He failed and, as a result, was censured and prohibited from spreading the Copernican theory either by teaching or publication.

In 1632 Galileo returned to the attack when a former friend was elected pope. He submitted to Pope Urban VIII a *Dialogue Concerning the Two Chief World Systems*, having carefully chosen the dialogue form so that he could put ideas into the mouths of other characters and thereby claim that they were not his own. Once more, under pressure from the Jesuits, Galileo

◆ **15.31** Telescope and lens of Galileo, 1609. After his death near Florence in 1642, many of Galileo's instruments, including this telescope, were collected and preserved. The Museum of Science (Museo della Scienza) in Florence, Italy, where they can now be seen, was one of the earliest museums to be devoted to scientific rather than artistic works. *(© Scala/Art Resource, NY)*

was summoned to Rome. In 1633 he was put on trial after spending several months in prison. His pleas of old age and poor health won no sympathy from the tribunal. He was made to recant and humiliate himself publicly and was sentenced to prison for the rest of his life. (It might well have appealed to Galileo's sense of bitter irony that three hundred forty-seven years later, in 1980, Pope John Paul II, a fellow countryman of the Polish Copernicus, ordered the case to be reopened so that belated justice might be done.)

Influential friends managed to secure Galileo a relatively comfortable house arrest in his villa just outside Florence, and he retired there to work on physics. His last and most important scientific work, *Dialogues Concerning Two New Sciences*, was published in 1638. In it he examined many long-standing problems, including that of motion, always basing his conclusions on practical experiment and observation. In the process he established the outlines of many areas of modern physics.

◆ **15.32** Frans Hals, *René Descartes*, 1649. The great French philosopher, Descartes, spent many years in Holland, where his ideas found a receptive audience and where he sat for this portrait.

Oil on panel, 29½″ x 27″ (75 x 68.5 cm). Musée du Louvre, Paris, France//© Erich Lessing/Art Resource, NY

In all his work Galileo set forth a new way of approaching scientific problems. Instead of trying to understand the final cause or cosmic purpose of natural events and phenomena, he tried to explain their character and the manner in which they came about. He changed the question from why? to what? and how?

René Descartes

Scientific investigation could not solve every problem of human existence. While it could try to explain and interpret objective phenomena, there remained other more subjective areas of experience involving ethical and spiritual questions. The Counter-Reformation on the one hand and the Protestant churches on the other claimed to have discovered the answers. The debates nevertheless continued, most notably in the writings of the French philosopher René Descartes (1596–1650), often called the Father of Modern Philosophy [**Fig. 15.32**].

In many ways Descartes' philosophical position was symptomatic of his age. He was educated at a Jesuit school but found traditional theological teaching unsatisfactory. Turning to science and mathematics, he began a lifelong search for reliable evidence in his quest to distinguish truth from falsehood. Attacking philosophi-

cal problems, his prime concern was to establish criteria for defining reality. His chief published works, the *Discourse on Method* (1637) and the *Meditations* (1641), contain a step-by-step account of how he arrived at his conclusions.

According to Descartes, the first essential in the search for truth was to make a fresh start by refusing to believe anything that could not be decisively proved to be true. This required that he doubt all of his previously held beliefs, including the evidence of his own senses. By stripping away all uncertainties he reached a basis of indubitable certainty on which he could build: that he existed. The very act of doubting proved that he was a thinking being. As he put it in a famous phrase in his second *Meditation*, *"Cogito, ergo sum"* ("I think, therefore I am").

From this foundation Descartes proceeded to reconstruct the world he had taken to pieces by considering the nature of material objects. He was guided by the principle that whatever is clearly and distinctly perceived must exist. He was aware at the same time that our perceptions of the exact nature of these objects are extremely likely to be incorrect and misleading. When, for example, we look at the sun, we see it as a very small disk, although the sun is really an immense globe. We must be careful, therefore, not to assume that our perceptions are bound to be accurate. All that they demonstrate is the simple existence of the object in question.

If the idea of the sun comes from the perception, however inaccurate, of something that actually exists, what of God? Is the idea of a divine being imagined or based on truth? Descartes concluded that the very fact that we who are imperfect and doubting can conceive of a perfect God proves that our conception is based on a reality. In other words, who could ever have imagined God unless God existed? At the center of the Cartesian philosophical system, therefore, lay the belief in a perfect being—not necessarily to be identified with the God of the Old and New Testaments—who had created a world permeated by perfect (that is, mathematical) principles.

At first, this may seem inconsistent with Descartes' position as the founder of modern rational thought. It may seem even stranger that, just at the time when scientific investigators like Galileo were explaining natural phenomena without recourse to divine intervention, Descartes succeeded in proving to his own satisfaction the undeniable existence of a divine being. Yet a more careful look at Descartes' method reveals that both he and Galileo shared the same fundamental confidence in the rational powers of human beings.

Thomas Hobbes

Although Galileo and Descartes represent the major trends in seventeenth-century thought, other important figures made their own individual contributions. Descartes' fellow countryman Blaise Pascal (1623–1662), for example, launched a strong attack on the Jesuits while providing his own somewhat eccentric defense of Christianity. A more mystical approach to religion was that of the Dutch philosopher Baruch Spinoza (1632–1677), whose concept of the ideal unity of nature later made a strong appeal to nineteenth-century Romantics.

The English philosopher Thomas Hobbes (1588–1679), however, had little in common with any of his contemporaries—as he was frequently at pains to make plain. For Hobbes, truth lay only in material things: "All that is real is material, and what is not material is not real." Hobbes is thus one of the first modern proponents of **materialism** and, like many of his materialist successors, was interested in solving political rather than philosophical problems. Born in the year of the Spanish Armada, Hobbes lived through the turbulent English Civil War, a period marked by constant instability and political confusion. Perhaps in consequence, he developed an enthusiasm for the authority of the law, as represented by the king, that verges on totalitarianism.

Hobbes' political philosophy finds its fullest statement in his book *Leviathan*, first published in 1651. The theory of society that he describes there totally denies the existence in the universe of any divinely established morality. (Hobbes never denied the existence of God, not wishing to outrage public and ecclesiastical opinion unnecessarily, although he might as well have.) According to Hobbes, all laws are created by humans to protect themselves from one another—a necessary precaution in view of human greed and violence. Organized society in consequence is arrived at when individuals give up their personal liberty in order to achieve security. As a result, the ideal state is that in which there is the greatest security, specifically one ruled by an absolute ruler.

From its first appearance *Leviathan* created a scandal; it has been subjected to continual attack ever since. Hobbes managed to offend both of the chief participants in the intellectual debates of the day: the theologians, by telling them that their doctrines were irrelevant and their terminology "insignificant sound"; and the rationalists, by claiming that human beings, far from being capable of the highest intellectual achievements, are dangerous and aggressive creatures who need to be saved from themselves. Hobbes' pessimism and the extreme nature of his position have won him few wholehearted supporters in the centuries since his death. Yet many modern readers, like others in the time since *Leviathan* first appeared, must reluctantly admit that there is at least a grain of truth in his picture of society, which can be attested to by personal experience and observation. At the very least, his political philosophy is valuable as a diagnosis and a warning of some aspects of human potential virtually all of his contemporaries and many of his successors have preferred to ignore.

JOHN LOCKE

The leading English thinker of the generation following Hobbes was John Locke (1632–1704), whose work helped pave the way for the European Enlightenment. The son of a country attorney, his education followed traditional Classical lines, but the young Locke was more interested in medicine and the new experimental sciences. In 1666 he became physician and secretary to the future Earl of Shaftesbury, who encouraged Locke's interest in political philosophy.

In his first works, Locke explored the subjects of property and trade and the role of the monarch in a modern state. He then turned to more general questions: What is the nature of ideas? How do we get them? and What are the limitations of human knowledge? His most influential work, *An Essay Concerning Human Understanding*, appeared in 1690. In it he argued against a theory of innate ideas, proposing instead that our ideas derive from our perceptions. Thus, our notions and characters are based on our own individual sense impressions and on our reflections on them, not on inherited values. Rejecting traditional metaphors and metaphysics, Locke advocated an antimonarchical, property-oriented political philosophy in which ideas served as a kind of personal property.

For his successors in the eighteenth century, Locke seemed to have set human nature free from the control of divine authority. Humans were no longer perceived as the victims of innate original sin or the accidents of birth, but instead derived their ideas and personalities from their experiences. Like many of the spokesmen of the Enlightenment, Voltaire acknowledged the importance of Locke's ideas, while few modern students of education or theory of knowledge have failed to be influenced by him.

LITERATURE IN THE SEVENTEENTH CENTURY

FRENCH BAROQUE COMEDY AND TRAGEDY

It is hardly surprising that the baroque age, which put so high a premium on the expression of dramatic emotion, should have been an important period in the development of the theater. In France in particular, three of the greatest names in the history of drama were active simultaneously, all of them benefiting at one point or another from the patronage of Louis XIV.

Molière was the stage name of Jean Baptiste Poquelin (1622–1673), who was the creator of a new theatri-

VALUES

Scientific Truth

Many factors contributed to the growth of science in the seventeenth century. Among them were the spread of education, the discovery of the Americas, explorations in Asia and Africa, and the development of urban life. Perhaps the most important of all was a growing skepticism in traditional religious beliefs, induced by the violent wars of religion provoked by the Reformation and Counter-Reformation.

One of the leading figures in the scientific revolution, Francis Bacon (1561–1626), wrote that scientists should follow the example of Columbus and think all things possible until all things could be tested. This emphasis on the "empirical faculty"—learning based on experience—is a method of drawing general conclusions from particular observations. Medieval thinkers, relying on the examples of Aristotle and Ptolemy, had devised general theories and then looked for specific examples to confirm them. Scientific truth sought to reason in the opposite way: start from the specific and use it to establish a general theory, a process known as **induction**. Above all, the new scientists took nothing for granted and regarded no opinion as "settled and immovable."

The search for objective, scientific truth required the invention of new instruments. Galileo's telescope allowed him to study the sky and revolutionize astronomy. Other researchers used another form of optical instrument—the microscope—to analyze blood and describe bacteria. The invention of the thermometer and barometer made it possible to perform atmospheric experiments.

With the increasing circulation of knowledge, scientists could spread and test their ideas. An international scientific community began to develop, stimulated by the formation of academies and learned societies. The most influential were the Royal Society for Improving Natural Knowledge, founded in London in 1662, and the French Académie des Sciences, founded in 1666. By means of published accounts and private correspondence, scientists were able to see how their own discoveries related to other fields.

Although the study of natural science does not involve questions of theology or philosophy, the growing interest in finding rational explanations for natural phenomena led to a change in views of religion. Most early scientists continued to believe in God but abandoned the medieval view of the deity as incomprehensible Creator and Judge. Rather, they saw God as the builder of a world-machine, which He then put into motion. Humans could come to understand how the machine worked, but only if they used their powers of reason to establish scientific truth.

---

cal form, French baroque comedy. Having first made his reputation as an actor, he turned to the writing of drama as a means of deflating pretense and pomposity. In his best works, the deceptions or delusions of the principal characters are revealed for what they are with good humor and considerable understanding of human foibles, but dramatic truth is never sacrificed to mere comic effect. Unlike so many comic creations, Molière's characters remain believable. Jourdain, the good-natured social climber of *Le Bourgeois Gentilhomme*, and Harpagon, the absurd miser of *L'Avare*, are by no means mere symbols of their respective vices but victims of those vices, albeit willing ones. Even the unpleasant Tartuffe in the play of that name is a living character with his own brand of hypocrisy.

Classical motifs play a strong part in the works of the two greatest tragic dramatists of the age: Pierre Corneille (1606–1684) and Jean Racine (1639–1699). Corneille created, as counterpart to Molière's comedy, French baroque tragedy. Most of his plays take as their theme an event in Classical history or mythology, which is often used to express eternal truths about human behavior. The themes of patriotism, as in *Horace*, or martyrdom, as in *Polyeucte*, are certainly as relevant today as they were in seventeenth-century France or in ancient Greece or Rome. However, most people's response to Corneille's treatment of subjects such as these is probably conditioned by the degree to which they enjoy the cut and thrust of rhetorical debate.

Racine may well provide for many modern readers an easier entry into the world of French baroque tragedy. Although for the most part he followed the dramatic form and framework established by Corneille, he used it to explore different areas of human experience. His recurrent theme is self-destruction: the inability to control one's own jealousy, passion, or ambition and the resulting inability, as tragic as it is inevitable, to survive its effects. Furthermore, in plays like *Phèdre*, he explored the psychological state of mind of his principal characters, probing for the same kind of understanding of motivation that Monteverdi tried to achieve in music.

CERVANTES AND THE SPANISH NOVEL

By the middle of the sixteenth century, the writing of fiction in Spain had begun to take a characteristic form that was to influence future European fiction. The **picaresque novel** (in Spanish *pícaro* means "rogue" or "knave") was a Spanish invention; books of this genre tell a story that revolves around a rogue or adventurer. The earliest example is *Lazarillo de Tormes*, which appeared anonymously in 1554. Its hero, Lazarillo, is brought up among beggars and thieves, and many of the episodes serve as an excuse to satirize priests and church officials—so much so, in fact, that the Inquisition ordered parts omitted in later printings. Unlike prose being written elsewhere at the time, the style is colloquial, even racy, and heavy with irony.

Although *Don Quixote*, by general agreement the greatest novel in the Spanish language, has picaresque elements, its style and subject are both far more subtle and complex. Miguel de Cervantes Saavedra (1547–1616), its author, set out to satirize medieval tales of chivalry and romance by inventing a character—Don Quixote—who is an amiable elderly gentleman looking for the chivalry of storybooks in real life. This apparently simple idea takes on almost infinite levels of meaning, as Don Quixote pursues his ideals, in general without much success, in a world with little time for romance or honor. In his adventures, which bring him into contact with all levels of Spanish society, he is accompanied by his squire Sancho Panza, whose shrewd practicality serves as a foil for his own unworldliness.

The structure of the novel is as leisurely and seemingly as rambling as the Don's wanderings. Yet the various episodes are linked by the constant confrontation between reality and illusion, the real world and that of the imagination. Thus at one level the book becomes a meditation on the relationship between art and life. By the end of his life, Don Quixote has learned painfully that his noble aspirations cannot be reconciled with the realities of the world, and he dies disillusioned. In the last part of the book, where the humor of the hero's mishaps does not conceal their pathos, Cervantes reaches that rare height of artistry where comedy and tragedy are indistinguishable.

THE ENGLISH METAPHYSICAL POETS

In England, the pinnacle of dramatic expression had been reached by the turn of the century in the works of Shakespeare, and nothing remotely comparable was to follow. The literary form that proved most productive during the seventeenth century was that of lyric poetry, probably because of its ability to express personal emotions, although the single greatest English work of the age was John Milton's epic poem *Paradise Lost*.

The King James Bible It may well be argued that the most important of all literary achievements of the seventeenth century was not an original artistic creation but a translation. It is difficult to know precisely how to categorize the *Authorized Version* of the Bible, commissioned by King James I and first published in 1611, often called the only great work of literature ever produced by a committee. The fifty-four scholars and translators who worked on the task deliberately tried to create a "biblical" style that would transcend the tone of English as it was then generally used. Their success can be measured by the immense influence the King James Bible has had on speakers and writers of English ever since (see Chapter 14). It remained the *Authorized Version* for English-speaking people until the late nineteenth century, when it was revised in light of the new developments in biblical studies.

John Donne Of all seventeenth-century literary figures, the group known as the metaphysical poets, whose poetry sought to give intellectual expression to emotional experience, make a particular appeal to modern readers. As is often pointed out, the label **metaphysical** is misleading for two reasons. In the first place, it suggests an organized group of poets consciously following a common style. While it is true that the earliest poet to write in the metaphysical style, John Donne (1572–1631), exerted a strong influence on a whole generation of younger poets, a unified group or school never existed. (Some scholars would, in fact, classify Donne's style as *Mannerist*.)

Second, *metaphysical* seems to imply that the principal subject of their poetry was philosophical speculation on the nature of reality. While it is certainly true that the metaphysical poets were interested in ideas and that they used complex forms of expression and a rich vocabulary to express them, the chief subject of their poems was not philosophy, but themselves—particularly their own emotions.

Yet this concern with self-analysis should not suggest a limitation of vision. Some critics have ranked Donne as second only to the Shakespeare of the Sonnets in range and depth of expression. Donne's intellectual brilliance and his love of paradox and ambiguity make his poetry sometimes difficult to follow. Donne always avoided the conventional, either in word or thought, while the swift changes of mood within a single short poem from light banter to the utmost seriousness can confuse the careless reader. Although it sometimes takes patience to unravel his full meaning, the effort is more than amply rewarded by contact with one of the most daring and honest of poets.

Donne's poems took on widely differing areas of human experience, ranging from some of the most passionate and frank discussions of sexual love ever penned to profound meditations on human mortality and the nature of the soul. Born a Catholic, he traveled widely as a young man and seems to have led a hectic and exciting life. He abandoned Catholicism, perhaps in part to improve his chances of success in Protestant England and, in 1601, on the threshold of a successful career in public life, entered Parliament. The same year, however, he secretly married his patron's sixteen-year old niece, Anne More. Her father had him dismissed and even imprisoned for a few days, and Donne's career never recovered from the disgrace.

Although Donne's marriage proved a happy one, its early years were clouded by debt, ill health, and frustration. In 1615, at the urging of friends, he finally joined the Anglican Church and entered the ministry. As a preacher he soon became known as among the greatest of his day. By 1621, Donne was appointed to one of the most prestigious positions in London: Dean of Saint Paul's. During his last years he became increasingly obsessed with death. After a serious illness in the spring of 1631, he preached his own funeral sermon and died within a few weeks.

Thus the successful worldliness of the early years gave way to the growing somberness of his later career. We might expect a similar progression from light to darkness in his work, yet throughout his life the two forces of physical passion and religious intensity seem to have been equally dominant, with the result that in much of his poetry each is sometimes used to express the other.

Richard Crashaw The poems of Donne's younger contemporary, Richard Crashaw (1613–1649), blend extreme emotion and religious fervor in a way that is completely typical of much baroque art. Yet Crashaw serves as a reminder of the danger of combining groups of artists under a single label, because although he shares many points in common with the other metaphysical poets, his work as a whole strikes a unique note.

There can be little doubt that Crashaw's obsessive preoccupation with pain and suffering has more than a touch of masochism and that his religious fervor is extreme even by baroque standards. Some of the intensity is doubtless a result of his violent rejection of his father's Puritanism and his own enthusiastic conversion to Catholicism. Stylistically Crashaw owed much to the influence of the flamboyant Italian baroque poet Giambattista Marino (1569–1625), whose virtuoso literary devices he imitated. Yet the eroticism that so often tinges his spiritual fervor gives a highly individual air to his work.

JOHN MILTON'S HEROIC VISION

While the past hundred years have seen a growing appreciation for Donne and his followers, the reputation of John Milton has undergone some notable ups and downs. Revered in the centuries following his death, Milton's work came under fire in the early years of the twentieth century from major poets such as T. S. Eliot and Ezra Pound, who claimed that his influence on his successors had been pernicious and led much of subsequent English poetry astray. Now that the dust of these attacks has settled, Milton has resumed his place as one of the greatest of English poets. The power of his spiritual vision, coupled with his heroic attempt to wrestle with the great problems of human existence, seems in fact to speak directly to the uncertainties of our own time.

Milton's life was fraught with controversy. An outstanding student with astonishing facility in languages, he spent his early years traveling widely in Europe and in the composition of relatively lightweight verse—lightweight, that is, when compared to what was to come. Among his most entertaining early works are the companion poems "L'Allegro" and "Il Penseroso," which compare the cheerful and the contemplative character, to appropriate scenery. They were probably written in 1632, following his graduation from Cambridge.

By 1640, however, he had become involved in the tricky issues raised by the English Civil War and the related problems of church government. He launched into the fray with a series of radical pamphlets that advocated, among other things, divorce on the grounds of incompatibility. (It is presumably no coincidence that his own wife had left him six weeks after their marriage.) His growing support for Oliver Cromwell and the Puritan cause won him an influential position at home but considerable enmity in continental Europe, where he was seen as the defender of those who had ordered the execution of King Charles I in 1649. The strain of his secretarial and diplomatic duties during the following years destroyed his eyesight, but although completely blind, he continued to work with the help of assistants.

When Charles II was restored to power (in 1660), Milton lost his position and was fortunate not to lose his life or liberty. Retired to private life, he spent his remaining years in the composition of three massive works: *Paradise Lost* (1667), *Paradise Regained* (1671), and *Samson Agonistes* (1671).

By almost universal agreement, Milton's most important, if not most accessible, work is *Paradise Lost*, composed in the early 1660s and published in 1667. It was intended as an account of the fall of Adam and Eve, and its avowed purpose was to "justify the ways of God to man." The epic is in twelve books (originally ten, but Milton later revised the divisions), written in blank verse.

Milton's language and imagery present an almost inexhaustible combination of biblical and Classical reference. From the very first lines of Book I, where the poet calls on a Classical Muse to help him tell the tale of The Fall, the two great Western cultural traditions are inextricably linked. Like Bach, Milton represents the summation of these traditions. In his work, Renaissance and Reformation meet and blend to create the most complete statement in English of Christian humanism, the philosophical reconciliation of humanist principles with Christian doctrine. To the Renaissance Milton owed his grounding in the Classics. In composing *Paradise Lost*, an epic poem that touches on the whole range of human experience, he was deliberately inviting comparison to Homer and Virgil. His language is also classical in its inspiration, with its long, grammatically complex sentences and preference for abstract terms. Yet his deeply felt Christianity and his emphasis on human guilt and repentance mark him as a product of the Reformation. Furthermore, although he may have tried to transcend the limitations of his own age, he was as much a child of his time as any of the other artists discussed in this chapter. The dramatic fervor of Bernini, the spiritual certainty of Bach, the psychological insight of Monteverdi, the humanity of Rembrandt—all have their place in Milton's work and mark him, too, as an essentially baroque figure.

SUMMARY

◆ **The Counter-Reformation.** If the history and culture of the sixteenth century were profoundly affected by the Reformation, the prime element to influence those of the seventeenth century was the Counter-Reformation, the Catholic Church's campaign to regain its authority and influence. By clarifying and forcefully asserting their teaching, backed up with a vigorous program of missionary work, church leaders aimed to present a positive and optimistic appearance that would eliminate past discords.

◆ **Counter-Reformation Art.** Among the resources used by Counter-Reformation reformers were the arts. Imposing architectural complexes like Saint Peter's Square in Rome, paintings and sculptures, music and verse could all reinforce the glory of the church. In some cases, works were commissioned officially; in others, artists responded individually to the spirit of the times. Bernini's *Saint Teresa in Ecstasy*, a statue that reflects the artist's own devout faith, was commissioned for the church in Rome in which it still stands. Richard Crashaw's poetry represents a more personal response to the religious ideas of his day.

◆ **The Rise of Science.** For all the importance of religion, the seventeenth century was also marked by significant developments in philosophy and science. Galileo, the father of modern physics, revolution

ized astronomy by proving Copernicus's claims of the previous century correct. Thinkers like Descartes and Hobbes, instead of accepting official church teachings, tried to examine the problems of human existence by their own intellectual approaches. Descartes was the founder of modern rational thought (although a believer in a supreme being); Hobbes was the first modern materialist.

◆ **The Arts in the Baroque Period.** The principal artistic style of the seventeenth century was the *baroque*, a term originally used for the visual arts but also applied by extension to the other arts of the period. Although the baroque style was created in Italy, it spread quickly throughout Europe and was even carried to the New World by missionaries. Baroque art is marked by a wide range of achievements, but there are several common features. Artists in the seventeenth century were concerned with expressing strong emotions, either religious or personal. This in turn led to an interest in exploring human behavior from a psychological point of view. With the new subjects came new techniques, many of which emphasized the virtuosity of the artist. These in turn led to the invention of new forms: for example, in music that of opera, and in painting that of landscape scenes.

◆ **Baroque Painting.** Two artists created the chief characteristics of baroque painting in Rome around 1600. Caravaggio's work is emotional and dominated by strong contrasts of light and darkness. Annibale Carracci painted scenes of movement and splendor, many on Classical themes. Both strongly influenced their contemporaries and successors.

Caravaggio's use of light was the forerunner of the work of artists as diverse as the Spaniard Velázquez and the Dutchman Vermeer, while Carracci's choice of Classical subjects was followed by the French Poussin. The two greatest painters of Northern Europe— Rembrandt and Rubens—were also influenced by the ideas of their day. Rembrandt used strong contrasts of light and dark to paint deeply felt religious scenes as well as the self-portraits that explore his own inner emotions. Rubens, one of the most versatile of artists, ranged from mythological subjects to historical paintings like the Marie de' Medici cycle to intimate personal portraits.

◆ **Baroque Architecture.** Although the seventeenth century saw architects increasingly employed in designing private houses, most of the principal building projects were public. At Rome the leading architect was Bernini, also one of the greatest sculptors of the age, whose churches, fountains, and piazzas changed the face of the city. In his sculpture, Bernini drew on virtually all the themes of Counter-Reformation art, including mythological and reli gious works and vividly characterized portraits. The other great building project of the century was the palace built for Louis XIV at Versailles, where the splendor of the Sun King was reflected in the grandiose decoration scheme.

◆ **Music in the Counter-Reformation.** In music, as in the visual arts, the baroque period was one of experimentation and high achievement. Counter-Reformation policy required that music for church use should be easily understood and appreciated, as was already the case in the Protestant countries of Northern Europe. At the same time, there was a growing demand for secular music for performance both in public and at home.

◆ **The Birth of Opera.** One of the most important innovations of the seventeenth century was opera. The first opera was performed just before 1600 in Florence, and by the middle of the century, opera houses were being built throughout Europe to house the new art form. The first great composer of operas was the Italian Monteverdi, whose *L'Orfeo* is the earliest opera still performed. Among later musicians of the period to write works for the theater was the German Georg Frideric Handel, many of whose operas were composed to Italian texts for performance in England.

◆ **Bach and Handel.** Handel also wrote oratorios (sacred dramas performed without any staging); the most famous of all oratorios is his *Messiah*. The oratorio was a form with a special appeal for Protestant Germans; among its leading exponents was Heinrich Schütz. The greatest of all Lutheran composers, Johann Sebastian Bach, wrote masterpieces in just about every musical form other than opera. Like many of the leading artists of the age, Bach produced works inspired by deep religious faith as well as pieces like the *Brandenburg Concertos* composed for private entertainment.

◆ **Baroque Literature.** The baroque interest in emotion and drama, exemplified by the invention of opera, led to important developments in writing for the theater as well as in the style of poetic composition and the invention of new literary forms. In France, the comedies of Molière and the tragedies of Corneille and Racine, written in part under the patronage of Louis XIV, illustrate the dramatic range of the period. The religious fervor of the English

metaphysical poets is yet another sign of baroque artists' concern with questions of faith and belief. The more practical problems involved in reconciling ideals with the realities of life are described in *Don Quixote*, one of the first great novels in Western literature. The most monumental of all literary works of the seventeenth century, Milton's *Paradise Lost*, aimed to combine the principles of Renaissance humanism with Christian teaching. Its drama, spirituality, and psychological insight mark it as a truly baroque masterpiece.

For all the immense range of baroque art and culture, its principal lines were drawn by reactions to the Counter-Reformation. Furthermore, paradoxically enough, by the end of the seventeenth century, a movement that had been inspired by opposition to the Reformation had accomplished many of the aims of the earlier reformers. Through art, music, and literature both artists and their audiences were made more familiar with questions of religious faith and more sensitive to aspects of human experience.

EXERCISES

1. What characteristics are common to all the arts in the baroque period? Give examples.
2. Compare the paintings of Caravaggio and Rembrandt with regard to subject matter and use of contrasts in light.
3. Describe the birth and early development of opera.
4. What were the principal scientific and philosophical movements of the seventeenth century? To what extent were they the result of external historical factors?
5. Discuss the treatment of religious subjects by baroque artists, writers, and musicians. How does it contrast with that of the Renaissance?

Visit the *Culture & Values* Companion website at **www.cengage.com/art/Cunningham/Cultureand Values7E** and the *Humanities Resource Center* for an array of primary source readings, key terms with pronunciations, flash cards, quizzes, and study materials designed especially to help you do well in this course.

CHAPTER 16

THE EIGHTEENTH CENTURY: FROM ROCOCO TO REVOLUTION

Ideas developed by figures such as Montesquieu and Voltaire during the eighteenth-century Age of Enlightenment had an effect on Western society that far transcended their impact on the humanities. Two fields that would benefit from the new ideas in circulation were the treatment of criminals and the relatively new discipline of economics.

One of Montesquieu's most ardent followers was the Italian Cesare Beccaria (1738–1794), who was influenced by the older man's social and political views. In 1764 at the age of 26, Beccaria published *On Crimes and Punishments,* the first work to provide a rational study of criminal punishment. An instant success, the book was widely translated and led to criminal reform in many European countries. Beccaria's main thesis was that harsh punishment, consisting of long prison sentences or even the death penalty, for relatively minor crimes was wrongly based on the notion that criminals were hopelessly evil. As a child of the Enlightenment, Beccaria believed that all humans were capable of improvement. Prisons should be for rehabilitation, rather than as places for pointless and vindictive punishment. He also argued strongly against torture and the death penalty.

His contemporary, the Scotsman Adam Smith (1723–1790), visited Voltaire and made the acquaintance of a group of French economists, the *physiocrats,* whose main principle was *laissez faire*—"let it be." They believed that the natural laws of economics required only noninterference to produce a successful economy. Based on this doctrine, Smith wrote his famous work, *The Wealth of Nations* (1776), which claimed that if market forces were allowed to operate without state intervention, an "invisible hand" would guide self-interest for the benefit of all—another example of Enlightenment optimism. He was in favor of open competition and against price rings (the modern cartels).

AGE OF DIVERSITY

Even the most determined cultural historians, fully armed with neat labels for successive stages of Western cultural development, acknowledge serious difficulty in categorizing the eighteenth century. Although it has often been called the Age of Enlightenment or the Age of Reason, these labels—which do in fact describe some of its aspects—fail to encompass the full spirit of the age.

From one perspective, the eighteenth century was an age of optimism. It had trust in science and in the power of human reason, belief in a natural order, and an overriding faith in the theory of progress that the world was better than it had ever been and was bound to get better still. Looked at from another perspective, however, the eighteenth century was marked by pervasive resentment and dissatisfaction with established society—especially in the population centers (see map,

◆ Scottish copper penny from 1797 saluting Adam Smith's *The Wealth of Nations* and showing the symbols of 1700s industry: trading ships, spinning wheel, and plow. (© *The Art Archive/British Museum, London, UK*)

"Eighteenth-Century Europe"). By its end, criticism and the press for reform had actually grown into a desire for violent change, producing the American and then the French revolutions. Furthermore, even these two apparently contradictory views—of unqualified optimism and extreme discontent—do not cover all aspects of eighteenth-century culture. For example, one of the most popular artistic styles of the period, the rococo, was characterized by frivolity and lightheartedness. Rococo artists deliberately aimed to create a fantasy world of pleasure into which their patrons could escape from the problems around them.

The eighteenth century, then, presents an immense variety of artistic and intellectual ideas, seemingly contradictory yet in fact coexistent. Each style or idea seems far easier to grasp and categorize by itself than as part of an overall pattern of cultural development. Nevertheless, it is possible to discern at least one characteristic that links some of the diverse artistic achievements of the century: a conscious engagement with social issues. An

GENERAL EVENTS	ART

1700

DAWN OF THE ENLIGHTENMENT

1710–c. 1795 Rise of Prussia and Russia

1715 Death of Louis XIV

1715–1774 Reign of Louis XV in France

c. 1715 Rococo style emerges in France
1717 Watteau, *Return from Cythera*

c. 1730 Carriera, *Anna Sofia d'Este, Princess of Modena*

1740

AGE OF ENLIGHTENED DESPOTS

1740–1786 Reign of Frederick the Great in Prussia

1773–1814 Jesuits disbanded

1774–1792 Reign of Louis XVI and Marie Antoinette in France

1776 American Declaration of Independence

1778–1783 American War of Independence

1788 Collapse of French economy; riots in Paris

1740 Boucher, *Pastoral Scene*

1743–1745 Hogarth paints satirical series, *Marriage à la Mode*
1748 Excavations begin at Pompeii; interest in ancient classical styles increases
1748 Sculpture more virtuosic than profound; Queirolo, *Deception Unmasked* (after 1752)

c. 1765 Gainsborough, *Mary, Countess Howe*
1769 Tiepolo, *The Immaculate Conception*, rococo style applied to religious subject
1771 Houdon, *Diderot*
1773 Fragonard, *Love Letters*
1773 Reynolds, *Three Ladies Adorning a Term of Hymen*, influenced by classical and Renaissance models
c. 1776 Vanvitelli, *The Great Cascade*, fountains at castle of Caserta near Naples
1784–1785 David, *Oath of the Horatii*, establishes official style of revolutionary art

1789

REVOLUTIONARY AND NAPOLEONIC WARS

1789 French Revolution begins; new American Constitution

1793 Execution of Louis XVI
1793–1795 Reign of Terror in France
1799–1804 Napoleon rules France as consul

1804–1814 Napoleon rules France as emperor

c. 1790 Houdon, *George Washington*, statue

1800 David, *Napoleon Crossing the Alps*

1808 Canova, *Pauline Bonaparte Borghese as Venus Victorious*

1815

opera such as Wolfgang Amadeus Mozart's *The Marriage of Figaro*, a series of satiric paintings of daily life such as William Hogarth's *Marriage à la Mode*, a mock epic poem such as Alexander Pope's *The Rape of the Lock*, and evolutionary ideas such as those of Jean-Jacques Rousseau are all examples of ways in which artists and thinkers joined with political leaders to effect social change.

Meanwhile, artists who supported the establishment and resisted change were equally engaged in social issues. They too used their art to express and defend their position. François Boucher's portraits of his wealthy aristocratic patrons, for example, often show them in the guises of Greek gods and goddesses, thus imparting a sense of glamour and importance to an aristocracy that was soon to be fighting for its survival.

The contrast between revolutionaries and conservatives lasted right to the eve of the French Revolution. Jacques-Louis David's famous painting *Oath of*

ARCHITECTURE	LITERATURE & PHILOSOPHY	MUSIC
	1711 Pope, *Essay on Criticism*	**c. 1700–1730** Couperin leading composer of *style galant* music at French court
1732 Boffrand begins Hôtel de Soubise, Paris; rococo style applied to room decoration	**1713–1720** Pope's translation *Iliad*, 1725–1726, *Odyssey*	
	1726 Swift, *Gulliver's Travels*; Voltaire exiled from France (returns 1729)	
	1729 Swift, *A Modest Proposal*	
	1733–1734 Pope, *Essay on Man*	
	1734 Voltaire, *Lettres philosophiques*	
	1739 Hume, *Treatise of Human Nature*	
1743–1772 Neumann, Vierzehnheiligen Pilgrim Church near Bamberg, Germany	**1750–1753** Voltaire at court of Frederick the Great in Potsdam	**1750** Death of J. S. Bach
	1751–1772 Diderot's *Encyclopédie* includes writings by Montesquieu and J. J. Rousseau	**c. 1750** C. P. E. Bach chief representative of emotional *empfindsamkeit* at court of Frederick the Great
1755–1792 Soufflot converts church of Sainte Geneviève into the Pantheon, neoclassical memorial for dead of French Revolution	**1758–1778** Voltaire sets up own court in Ferney	**1750–1800** Development of classical style and symphonic form
	1759 Voltaire, *Candide*	**1752** J. J. Rousseau, *Le Devin du Village*, opera
	1762 J. J. Rousseau, *The Social Contract*, *Emile*	**1759** Death of Handel
	1764 Beccaria publishes *On Crimes and Punishments*	**1761** Haydn ("Father of the Symphony") begins 30-year service with Esterhazys
	1776 Adam Smith publishes *The Wealth of Nations*	**1786** First performance of Mozart's *The Marriage of Figaro*, opera based on Beaumarchais play
	1776 Paine publishes *Common Sense*, series of pamphlets, in Philadelphia	
1785–1796 Jefferson's state capitol, Richmond, Virginia, modeled on ancient Roman Maison Carrée at Nimes	**1776–1788** Gibbon, *History of the Decline and Fall of the Roman Empire*	**1788** Mozart, Symphony No. 40 in G Minor
	1792 Paine, *The Rights of Man*	**1791** Mozart, Piano Concerto 27 in B Flat; opera *The Magic Flute*
		1791–1795 Haydn composes 12 symphonies during visits to London

◆ **16.2** Jacques-Louis David, *Oath of the Horatii*, 1784–1785. The story of the Horatii, three brothers who swore an oath to defend Rome even at the cost of their lives, is used here to extol patriotism. Painted only five years before the French Revolution, David's work established the official style of revolutionary art.

Oil on canvas, 10′10″ x 14′ (3.3 x 4.25 m). Musée du Louvre, Paris, France//© Réunion des Musées Nationaux/Art Resource, NY

◆ **16.3** François Boucher, *Pastoral Scene*, 1740. These charming and elegant peasants, neither of whom looks exactly ravaged by hard work in the fields, represent the artificial world of rococo art. Note the plentiful supply of fruit piled up in the right-hand corner (obviously the result of an exceptional harvest), and the wine carafe in the hand of the shepherdess, who has filled her own glass.

Oil on canvas, 45″ x 34″ (1.15 x .88 m). State Hermitage Museum, St. Petersburg, Russia//© Alexander Burkatovski/CORBIS

the Horatii (1784–1785) [**Fig. 16.2**], a clarion call to action and resolve, was painted around the same time as François Boucher's idealized picture of a *Pastoral Scene* [**Fig. 16.3**]. The former, in keeping with the spirit of the times, prefigures the mood of revolution. The latter turns its back on reality, evoking a nostalgic vision of love among the haystacks. In so doing it reinforces the aristocracy's refusal to see the working classes as real people with serious problems of their own. The same

contrast occurs in the literature of the age; the conservative stance of Pope or Swift is very different from the views of Enlightenment figures such as Voltaire or Rousseau.

The eighteenth century opened with Louis XIV still strutting down the Hall of Mirrors at the Palace of Versailles, but his death in 1715 marked the beginning of the end of absolute monarchy. Although most of Europe continued to be ruled by hereditary kings,

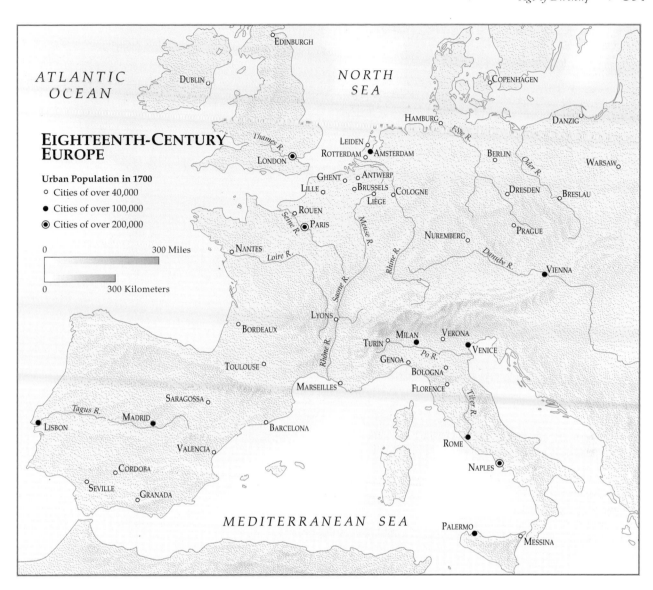

EIGHTEENTH-CENTURY EUROPE

Urban Population in 1700
- ○ Cities of over 40,000
- ● Cities of over 100,000
- ◉ Cities of over 200,000

0 ———— 300 Miles

0 ———— 300 Kilometers

the former emphasis on splendor and privilege was leavened with a new concern for the welfare of the ordinary citizen. Rulers such as Frederick the Great of Prussia (ruled 1740–1786) were no less determined than their predecessors to retain all power in their own hands, but they no longer thought of their kingdoms as private possessions to be manipulated for personal pleasure. Instead, they regarded them as trusts, which required them to show a sense of duty and responsibility. They built new roads, drained marshes, and reorganized legal and bureaucratic systems along rational lines (see **Table 16.1**).

Because of their greater concern for the welfare of their people, these new, more liberal kings, often known as enlightened despots, undoubtedly postponed for a while the growing demand for change. Inevitably, however, by drawing attention to the injustices of the past, they stimulated an appetite for reform that they were in no position to satisfy. Furthermore, for all their claims—Frederick the Great, for example, described himself as

Table 16.1 *European Rulers in the Eighteenth Century*

Enlightened Despots	
Frederick II of Prussia	1740–1786[a]
Catherine the Great of Russia	1762–1796
Gustavus III of Sweden	1771–1792
Charles III of Spain	1759–1788
Joseph II of Austria	1780–1790

Rulers Bound by Parliamentary Government[b]	
George I of England	1714–1727
George II of England	1727–1760
George III of England	1760–1820

Aristocratic Rulers	
Louis XV of France	1715–1774
Louis XVI of France	1774–1792

[a] All dates are those of reigns.
[b] English political life was dominated not by the kings but by two powerful prime ministers: Robert Walpole and William Pitt.

◆ **16.4** Jean Antoine Watteau, *Return from Cythera*, 1717. One ancient Greek tradition claimed the isle of Cythera as the birthplace of Venus, goddess of love. Thus, the island became symbolic of ideal, tender love. Note that the mood of nostalgia and farewell is conveyed not only by the autumnal colors but also by the late-afternoon light that washes over the scene.

Oil on canvas, 4′3″ x 6′4½″ (1.3 x 1.94 m). Musée du Louvre, Paris, France//© Scala/Art Resource, NY

"first servant of the state"—their regimes remained essentially autocratic.

THE VISUAL ARTS IN THE EIGHTEENTH CENTURY

THE ROCOCO STYLE

Despite the changing social climate of the time, most eighteenth-century artists still depended on the aristocracy for commissions. The baroque style had partially evolved to satisfy just these patrons, and throughout the early part of the eighteenth century, many artists continued to produce works following baroque precedents. Yet, despite the continued fondness for the baroque characteristics of richness and elaboration, there was a significant change of emphasis. The new enlightened despots and their courts had less time for pomposity or excessive grandeur. They wanted not so much to be glorified as entertained. In France, too, the death of Louis XIV served as an excuse to escape the oppressive

ceremony of life at the Palace of Versailles; the French court moved back to Paris to live in elegant comfort.

The artistic style that developed to meet these new, less grandiose needs first reached its maturity in France. It is generally called *rococo*, a word derived from the French word *rocaille*, which means a kind of elaborate decoration of rocks and shells that often adorned the grottoes of baroque gardens. Rococo art was conceived of as antibaroque, a contrast to the weighty grandeur of seventeenth-century art. It makes plentiful use of shell motifs, along with other decorative elements such as scrolls and ribbons, to produce an overall impression of lightness and gaiety. The subject matter is rarely serious, often frivolous, with strong emphasis on romantic dalliance and the pursuit of pleasure.

The style is graceful and harmonious, in contrast to the flamboyant, dramatic effects of much baroque art. It might be said that whereas baroque artists preached or declaimed to their public, rococo art was the equivalent of polite, civilized conversation. The eighteenth century was an age of polite society: a time of letter writing, chamber music, dancing. Clearly, such pastimes only represented one aspect of eighteenth-century life, and the revolutions

◆ **16.5** François Boucher, *Diana Leaving the Bath,* 1742. Diana is seen in a relaxed and thoughtful mood as she and her attendant unselfconsciously show off their naked limbs. The erotic nature of the scene is reinforced by the artist's reminder that Diana is also the goddess of the hunt, as can be seen by the arrows and hunting dog on the left and the game already hunted down and killed on the right.

Oil on canvas, 29″ x 22″ (57 x 73 cm). Musée du Louvre Museum, Paris, France//© Peter Willi/SuperStock

that shook Europe and the European colonies of North America at the end of the century called on a very different artistic style, the Neo-Classical, discussed in the following section. Neo-Classical artists rejected baroque extravagance and rococo charm in favor of dignity and austerity.

Critics have often said that the only purpose of rococo art was to provide pleasure, but this is a somewhat incomplete view of its social role. The rococo style was for the most part aimed at an aristocratic audience; its grace and charm served the important purpose of shielding this class from the growing problems of the real world. The elegant picnics, the graceful lovers, the Venuses triumphant represent an almost frighteningly unrealistic view of life, and one that met with disapproval from Enlightenment thinkers who were anxious to promote social change. Yet even the sternest moralist can hardly fail to respond to the enticing fantasy existence that the best of rococo art presents. In a sense, the knowledge that the whole rococo world was to be so completely swept away imparts an added (and, it must be admitted, unintentional) poignancy to its art. The existence of all those fragile ladies and their refined suitors was to be cut short by the guillotine.

ROCOCO PAINTING

Watteau The first and probably the greatest French rococo painter, Jean Antoine Watteau (1684–1721), seems to have felt instinctively the transitory and impermanent world he depicted. Watteau is best known for his paintings of *fetes galantes* (elegant outdoor festivals attended by courtly figures dressed in the height of fashion). Yet the charming scenes are always touched with a mood of nostalgia that often verges on melancholy. In *Pilgrimage to Cythera* [**Fig. 16.4**], for instance, the handsome young couples are returning home (despite the traditional title of the painting) from a visit to Cythera, the island sacred to Venus and to love. As they leave, a few of them gaze wistfully over their shoulders at the idyllic life they must leave behind, symbolized by the statue of Venus. Watteau thus emphasizes the moment of renunciation, underscoring the sense of departure and farewell by the autumnal colors of the landscape.

Boucher François Boucher (1703–1770), the other leading French rococo painter, was also influenced by Rubens. Lacking the restraint or poetry of Watteau, Boucher's paintings carry Rubens' theme of voluptuous beauty to an extreme. His canvases often seem to consist of little beyond mounds of pink flesh, as in *Diana Leaving the Bath* [**Fig. 16.5**]. It would certainly be difficult to find profundity of intellectual content in most of his work, the purpose of which is to depict only one aspect of human existence. His visions of erotic delights are frankly intended to arouse other than aesthetic feelings (see also Figure 16.3).

Fragonard Among Boucher's pupils was Jean Honoré Fragonard (1732–1806), the last of the great French rococo painters, who lived long enough to see all demand for rococo art disappear with the coming of the French Revolution. Although his figures are generally more clothed than those of Boucher, they are no less erotic. Even more than his master, Fragonard was able to use

◆ **16.6** Jean Honoré Fragonard, *Love Letters*, 1773. Fragonard's style is far more free and less precise than Boucher's. Compare the hazy, atmospheric landscape of this painting to the background of *Diana Leaving the Bath* (Figure 16.5). The statue on the pedestal to the right is, appropriately, of Venus and Cupid.

Oil on canvas, 10′5″ x 7′1″ (3.17 x 2.17 m). The Frick Collection, New York, USA//© Geoffrey Clements/CORBIS

◆ **16.7** Rosalba Carriera, *Anna Sofia d'Este, Princess of Modena*, c. 1730. The pale elegance of the subject is typical of most of Carriera's aristocratic sitters, as is the charming untidiness of her dress. Note how the delicate colors of the pastels convincingly reproduce the tones of the sitter's skin.

Pastel. Galleria degli Uffizi, Florence, Italy//© Finsiel/Alinari/Art Resource, NY

landscape to accentuate the mood of romance. In *Love Letters* [Fig. 16.6], for example, the couple flirting in the foreground is surrounded by a jungle of trees and bushes that seems to impart a heady, humid air to the apparently innocent confrontation. The end of Fragonard's career is a reminder of how much eighteenth-century artists were affected by contemporary historical developments. When his aristocratic patrons either died or fled France during the Revolution, he was reduced to complete poverty. It was perhaps because Fragonard supported the ideals of the Revolution, despite its disastrous effect on his personal life, that Jacques-Louis David, one of the Revolution's chief artistic arbiters, found him a job in the Museums Service. The last representative of the rococo tradition died poor and in obscurity as a minor official in the new French Republic.

Carriera Taken together, the three leading representatives of rococo painting provide a picture of the

fantasy life of eighteenth-century aristocratic society. The work of other rococo artists, however, gives us a clearer impression of what life was really like in that aristocratic world. The Venetian artist Rosalba Carriera (1675–1757) traveled widely throughout Europe producing large numbers of portraits in the rather unusual medium of pastel—dry sticks of color that leave a soft, powdery hue when rubbed on paper. The medium is delicate, but so, unfortunately, are the works executed in it, because the powder smudges easily and tends to drop off if the paper is shaken. It is unlikely that Carriera was concerned with conveying psychological depths. Her chief aim was to provide her subjects flattering likenesses that reinforced their own favorable visions of themselves. Works like her portrait of *Anna Sofia d'Este, Princess of Modena* [Fig. 16.7] emphasize the delicacy, charm, and sensuality of eighteenth-century society beauties.

Gainsborough English art in the eighteenth century was also notable for its aristocratic portraits. The

◆ **16.8** Thomas Gainsborough, *Mary, Countess Howe*, c. 1765. The wild background and threatening sky set off the subject, but their artificiality is shown by her shoes—hardly appropriate for a walk in the country. Gainsborough was famous for his ability to paint fabric: note the contrast between the heavy silk dress and the lacy sleeves.

Oil on canvas, 8′ x 5′ (2.59 x 1.52 m). Image © The Iveagh Bequest, Kenwood House, London, UK/The Bridgeman Art Library

◆ **16.9** Giovanni Battista Tiepolo, *The Immaculate Conception*, 1769. The sense of weightlessness and the wonderful cloud effects are both typical of Tiepolo's style.

Oil on canvas, 9′2″ x 5′ (2.79 x 1.52 m). Museo del Prado, Madrid, Spain//© Erich Lessing/Art Resource, NY

more extreme elements of rococo eroticism had little appeal to the English nobility, but the artists who were commissioned to paint their portraits could hardly help being influenced by the style of their day. Thomas Gainsborough (1727–1788), who together with Sir Joshua Reynolds (1723–1792) dominated the English art of the time, even studied for a while with a pupil of Boucher, although he went on to develop his own unique style, especially in his conversation pieces. Gainsborough's chief reputation, however, was made by his landscapes and portraits. Most of the portraits are set against a landscape background, as in the case of *Mary, Countess Howe* [**Fig. 16.8**]. In this painting, setting and costume are reminiscent of Watteau, but the dignified pose and cool gaze of the subject suggest that she had other than romantic thoughts in mind. There is no lack of poetry in the scene, though,

and the resplendent shimmer of the countess's dress is set off perfectly by the more somber tones of the background.

Tiepolo Portraits and landscapes lend themselves naturally to rococo treatment, but what of religious art? One of the few painters who tried to apply rococo principles to religious subjects was the Venetian painter Giovanni Battista Tiepolo (1696–1770). Many of Tiepolo's most ambitious and best-known works are decorations for the ceilings of churches and palaces, for which projects he was helped by assistants. A more personal work is his painting *The Immaculate Conception* [**Fig. 16.9**]. The light colors and chubby cherubs of

◆ **16.10** Francesco Queirolo, *Deception Unmasked*, after 1752. The figure is a Christian sinner freeing himself, with the help of an angel, from the net of deception. Both figure and net are carved from a single piece of stone.

Marble, c. 5'8" (1.75 m) high. Cappella Sansevero, Santa Maria della Pietá del Sangro, Naples, Italy//© Araldo de Luca/CORBIS

Boucher and the haughty assurance of Gainsborough's society ladies are here applied to the life of the Virgin Mary.

ROCOCO SCULPTURE AND ARCHITECTURE

For the most part, Rococo sculptors were more concerned with displaying their virtuosity in works aimed at a brilliant effect than with exploring finer shades of meaning. For instance, the figure of *Deception Unmasked* [**Fig. 16.10**] by the Genoese sculptor Francesco Queirolo (1704–1762) theoretically has serious religious significance; in practice its principal purpose is to dazzle us with the sculptor's skill at rendering such details as the elaborate net in which Deception hides.

Rococo architecture likewise was principally concerned with delighting the eye rather than inspiring

noble sentiments. It is most successful in decorative interiors like those of the Hôtel de Soubise in Paris [**Fig. 16.11**], where the encrustation of ornament flows from the ceiling down onto the walls, concealing the break between them.

Neumann One region of Europe in which the rococo style did exert a powerful influence on religious architecture was southern Germany and Austria. Throughout the seventeenth century, a series of wars in that area had discouraged the construction of new churches or public buildings; with the return of relatively stable conditions in the German states, new building again became possible. By one of those fortunate chances in the history of the arts, the fantasy and complexity of the rococo style provided a perfect complement to the new mood of exuberance. The result is a series of churches that is among the happiest of all rococo achievements.

The leading architect of the day was Balthazar Neumann (1687–1753), who had begun his career as an engineer and artillery officer. Among the many palaces and churches he designed, none is more spectacular than the Vierzehnheiligen ("fourteen saints") near Bamberg, Germany. The relative simplicity of the exterior deliberately leaves the visitor unprepared for the spaciousness and elaborate decoration of the interior [**Fig. 16.12**], with its rows of windows and irregularly placed columns. As in the Hôtel de Soubise, the joint between the ceiling and walls is hidden by a fresco that, together with its border, spills downward in a series of gracious curves. It is not difficult to imagine what John Calvin would have said of such an interior, but if a church can be allowed to be a place of light and joy, Neumann's design succeeds admirably.

NEO-CLASSICAL ART

For all its importance, the rococo style was not the only style to influence eighteenth-century artists. The other principal artistic movement of the age was Neo-Classicism, which increased in popularity as the appeal of the rococo declined.

There were good historical reasons for the rise of Neo-Classicism. The excavation of the buried cities of Herculaneum and Pompeii, beginning in 1711 and 1748, respectively, evoked immense interest in the art of classical antiquity in general and that of Rome in particular. The wall paintings from Pompeian villas of the first century ce were copied by countless visitors to the excavations, and reports of the finds were published throughout Europe. The German scholar Johannes Winckelmann (1717–1768), who is sometimes called the Father of Archaeology, played a major part in creating a new awareness of the importance of classical art; in many of his writings he encouraged his contemporaries

◆ **16.11** Salon de la Princesse, Hôtel de Soubise, Paris, France, c. 1737–1740, architect, Germain Boffrand. The decoration is typical of the rococo style. The shape of the room, the sculptures by J. B. Lemoine, the paintings by Natoire that flow from ceiling to walls, and the reflections in the mirrors all create an impression of light and grace.

Oval room, 33' x 26' (10 x 7.9 m). Image © Scala/Art Resource, NY

◆ **16.12** Balthazar Neumann, architect, Vierzehnheiligen Pilgrim Church, near Bamberg, Germany, 1743–1772. This interior view shows the high altar at the back of the nave (back left) and the oval altar in the middle of the church (center). The oval altar, the *Gnadenaltar* ("Mercy Altar"), the work of J. M. Feichtmayer and J. G. Uebelherr dates to 1763; its central location is characteristic of the pilgrimage churches of southern Germany and Austria, while its shape is echoed in the oval ceiling paintings. Neumann deliberately rejected the soaring straight lines of Gothic architecture and the symmetrical balance of the Renaissance style in favor of an intricate interweaving of surfaces, solid volumes, and empty spaces. *(Image © Erich Lessing/Art Resource, NY)*

Table 16.2 *The Rediscovery of Classical Antiquity in the Eighteenth Century*

1711	First excavations at Herculaneum
1734	Society of Dilettanti formed in London to encourage exploration
1748	First excavations at Pompeii
1753	Robert Wood and James Dawkins publish *The Ruins of Palmyra*
1757	Wood and Dawkins publish *The Ruins of Baalbec*
1762	James Stuart and Nicholas Revett publish the first volume of *The Antiquities of Athens*
1764	Robert Adam publishes *The Ruins of the Palace of Diocletian at Spalato*; Johannes Winckelmann publishes *History of Ancient Art*
1769	Richard Chandler and William Pars publish the first volume of *The Antiquities of Ionia*
1772	The Hamilton collection of Greek vases purchased by the British Museum
1785	Richard Colt Hoare explores Etruscan sites in Tuscany
1801	Lord Elgin receives Turkish permission to work on the Parthenon in Athens

◆ **16.13** Jacques-Louis David, *Napoleon Crossing the Alps*, 1800. After he took his army across the Alps, Napoleon surprised and defeated an Austrian army. His calm, controlled figure guiding a wildly rearing horse is symbolic of his own vision of himself as bringing order to postrevolutionary France.

Oil on canvas, 8′10″ x 7′7″ (2.44 x 2.31 m). Chateau de Versailles, Versailles, France//© Giraudon/The Bridgeman Art Library

not only to admire ancient masterpieces but to imitate them (see **Table 16.2**).

David Furthermore, the aims and ideals of the Roman Republic—freedom, opposition to tyranny, valor—held a special appeal for eighteenth-century republican politicians, and the evocation of Classical models became a characteristic of the art of the French Revolution. The painter who best represents the official revolutionary style is Jacques-Louis David (1748–1825). His *Oath of the Horatii* (see Figure 16.2) draws not only on a story of ancient Roman civic virtue but also on a knowledge of ancient dress and armor derived from excavations of Pompeii and elsewhere. The simplicity of its message—the importance of united opposition to tyranny—is expressed by the simple austerity of its style and composition, a far cry from the lush, effete world of Fragonard. David used the same lofty grandeur to depict Napoleon soon after his accession to power [**Fig. 16.13**], although there is considerable if unintentional irony in the use of the revolutionary style to represent the military dictator.

Reynolds The austere poses and orderly decorations of ancient art came as a refreshing change for those artists who, regardless of politics, were tired of the excesses of the baroque and rococo styles. One of the most notable painters to introduce a Neo-Classical sense of statuesque calmness into his works was Sir Joshua Reynolds, Gainsborough's chief rival in England. *Three Ladies Adorning a Term of Hymen* [**Fig. 16.14**] shows three fashionable ladies-about-town in the guise of figures from Greek mythology. Their static poses seem derived from actual ancient statues. The Classical bust and antique vessel on the right are evidence of a careful attempt to imitate ancient models. Even the stool at center is based on examples found at Pompeii.

Hogarth Although the rococo and Neo-Classical styles dominated most of eighteenth-century paint-

ing, a few important artists avoided both the escapism of the one and the idealism of the other to provide a more truthful picture of the age. The work of William Hogarth, for example, presents its own individual view of aristocratic society in the eighteenth century.

As a master of line, color, and composition, Hogarth was in no way inferior to such contemporaries as Fragonard or Gainsborough, but he used his skills to paint a series of "moral subjects" that satirized the same patrons his colleagues aimed to entertain and to flatter. In his series of paintings called *Marriage à la Mode*, Hogarth illustrated the consequences of a loveless marriage between an impoverished earl and the daughter of a wealthy city merchant who wants to improve his social position. By the second scene in the series, *Shortly After the Marriage* [**Fig. 16.15**], matters have already begun to deteriorate.

Canova The principal Neo-Classical sculptors—the Italian Antonio Canova (1757–1822) and the Frenchman Jean Antoine Houdon (1741–1829)—succeeded in using Classical models with real imagination and creativity (see Figures 16.22 and 16.24). Canova's portrait, *Pauline Bonaparte Borghese as Venus Victorious*

◆ **16.14** Sir Joshua Reynolds, *Three Ladies Adorning a Term of Hymen*, 1773. A term is a pillar topped with a bust, in this case of Hymen, god of marriage. Reynolds introduced a marriage theme because the fiancé of one of the ladies, who were daughters of Sir William Montgomery, commissioned the painting. The Neo-Classical composition was deliberately chosen by the artist because it gave him "an opportunity of introducing a variety of graceful historical attitudes."

Oil on canvas, 7′8″ x 10′4½″ (2.34 x 2.9 m). Image © Tate Gallery, London, UK/Art Resource, NY

◆ **16.15** William Hogarth, "Shortly After the Marriage," from *Marriage à la Mode*, c. 1745. Although he achieved his effects through laughter, Hogarth attacked the corruption and hypocrisy of his day with serious moral purpose. The young husband, exhausted from his night out, shows his empty trouser pockets, while the small dog sniffs suspiciously at the woman's cap hanging from his coat pocket.

Oil on canvas, 28″ x 36″ (68 x 89 cm). National Gallery, London, UK//© Erich Lessing/Art Resource, NY

◆ **16.16** Antonio Canova, *Pauline Bonaparte Borghese as Venus Victorious*, 1808. Canova's blend of simplicity and grace was widely imitated by European and American sculptors throughout the 19th century. The apple that Venus holds in her left hand is the apple of discord, inscribed "to the fairest." According to legend, the goddesses Aphrodite (Venus), Hera, and Athena each offered a tempting bribe to the Trojan Paris, who was to award the apple to one of them. Paris chose Venus, who had promised him the most beautiful of women. The result was the Trojan War, which began when Paris abducted his prize, Helen, wife of a Greek king.

Marble, life size, 6′6″ (1.98 m) long. Image © The Art Archive/Galleria Borghese, Rome, Italy/Gianni Dagli Orti

[**Fig. 16.16**], depicts Napoleon's sister with an idealized Classical beauty as she reclines on a couch modeled on one found at Pompeii. The cool worldly elegance of the figure, however, is Canova's own contribution.

For serious projects such as major public buildings, architects tended to follow Classical models, as in the portico of the Pantheon in Paris [**Fig. 16.17**], the design of which uses Classical proportions. As might have been expected, the architects of the American Revolution also turned to classical precedents when they constructed their new public buildings. Thomas Jefferson's State Capitol at Richmond [**Fig. 16.18**], for example, shows a conscious rejection of the rococo and all it stood for in favor of the austere world (as it seemed to him) of ancient Rome.

CLASSICAL MUSIC

For the most part, music in the eighteenth century followed the example of literature in retaining a serious purpose, and was relatively untouched by the mood of the rococo style. At the French court, however, there was a demand for elegant, lighthearted music to serve as entertainment. The leading composer in this *style gallant* was François Couperin (1668–1733), whose many compositions for keyboard emphasize grace and delicacy at the expense of the rhythmic drive and intellectual rigor of the best of baroque music. Elsewhere in Europe, listeners continued to prefer music that expressed emotion. At the court of Frederick the Great (an accomplished performer and composer), for example, a musical style known as *empfindsamkeit* ("sensitiveness") developed.

The chief exponent of this expressive style was Carl Philipp Emanuel (hereafter referred to as C. P. E.) Bach (1714–1788), a son of Johann Sebastian Bach. His works have considerable emotional range and depth; their rich harmonies and contrasting moods opened up new musical possibilities. Like all his contemporaries, C. P. E. Bach was searching for a formal structure with which to organize them. A single piece or movement from a baroque work had first established a single mood and then explored it fully, whether it be joyful, meditative, or tragic. Now composers were developing a musical organization that would allow them to place different emotions side-by-side, contrast these, and thereby achieve expressive variety.

By the middle of the eighteenth century, a musical style developed that made possible this new range of expression. It is usually called *classical*, although the term is also used in a more general sense, which can

◆ **16.17** Pantheon (Sainte Geneviève), Paris, 1755–1792, architect, Germain Soufflot. Originally built as the Church of Sainte Geneviève, the building was converted into a memorial to the illustrious dead at the time of the French Revolution. The architect studied in Rome for a time; the columns and pediment were inspired by ancient Roman temples. *(Image © age fotostock/SuperStock)*

◆ **16.18** State Capitol, Richmond, Virginia, 1785–1796, architect, Thomas Jefferson. Like the Pantheon, Jefferson's building was modeled on a Roman temple, the Maison Carrée at Nîmes, but the austere spirit of the American Revolution prompted Jefferson to replace the elaborate Corinthian capitals of the original with simpler Ionic ones. *(Image © Mark Gibson/Index Stock/Photolibrary)*

be confusing. It would be as well to begin by carefully distinguishing between these two usages.

In its general sense, the term *classical* is frequently used to distinguish so-called serious music from popular, so that all music likely to be met with in a concert hall or opera house, no matter what its age, is labeled "classical." One reason this distinction is confusing is that for many composers before our own time, there was essentially no difference between serious and popular music. They used the same musical style and techniques for a formal composition to be listened to attentively by an audience of music lovers, as for a religious work to be performed in church, or for dance music or background music for a party or festive occasion. Furthermore, used in this sense, classical tells us nothing significant about the music itself or its period or form. It does not even describe its mood, because many pieces of "classical" or "serious" music were in fact deliberately written to provide light entertainment.

The more precise and technical meaning of "classical" as it relates to music denotes a musical style that was in use from the second half of the eighteenth century and reached its fulfillment in the works of Franz Joseph Haydn (1732–1809) and Wolfgang Amadeus Mozart (1756–1791). It evolved in answer to new musical needs the baroque style could not satisfy and lasted until the early years of the nineteenth century, when it in turn gave way to the romantic style. The figure chiefly responsible for the change from classical to romantic music was Ludwig van Beethoven (1770–1827). Although his musical roots were firmly in the classical style, he is

more appropriately seen as a representative of the new romantic age and will be discussed in Chapter 17.

It is no coincidence that the classical style in music developed at much the same time as painters, architects, and poets were turning to Greek and Roman models, because the aims of classical music and Neo-Classical art and literature were similar. After the almost obsessive exuberance and display of the Baroque period, the characteristic qualities of ancient art—balance, clarity, intellectual weight—seemed especially appealing. The eighteenth-century composer, however, faced a problem that differed from that of the artist or writer. Unlike literature or the visual arts, ancient music has disappeared almost without trace. As a result, the classical style in music had to be newly invented to express ancient concepts of balance and order. In addition, it had to combine these intellectual principles with the no-less-important ability to express a wide range of emotion. Haydn and Mozart were the two supreme masters of the classical style because of their complete command of the possibilities of the new idiom within which they wrote.

THE CLASSICAL SYMPHONY

The most popular medium in the classical period was instrumental music. In extended orchestral works, symphonies, divided into several self-contained sections called *movements*, composers were most completely able to express classical principles.

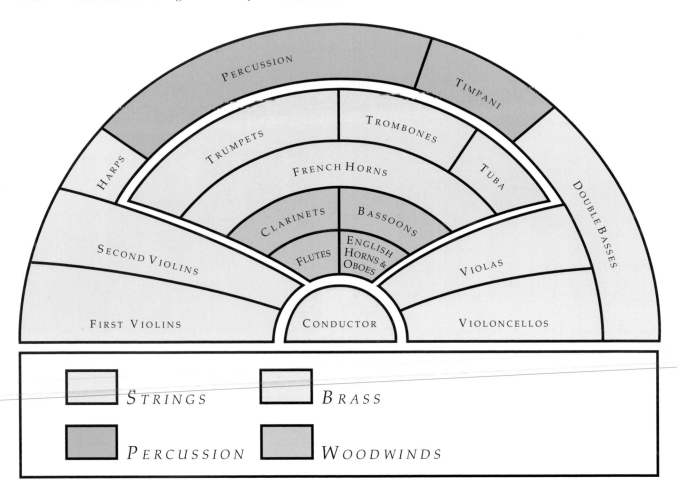

◆ **16.19** Plan of the layout of a modern symphony orchestra.

The Orchestra One reason for this was the new standardization of instrumental combinations. In the Baroque period, composers such as Bach had felt free to combine instruments into unusual groups that varied from composition to composition. Each of Bach's Brandenburg Concertos was written for a different set of solo instruments. By about 1750, however, most instrumental music was written for a standard orchestra [**Fig. 16.19**], the nucleus of which was formed by the string instruments: violins (generally divided into two groups known as first and second), violas, cellos, and double basses. To the strings were added wind instruments, almost always the oboe and bassoon and fairly frequently the flute; the clarinet began to be introduced gradually and, by about 1780, had become a regular member of the orchestra. The only brass instrument commonly included was the French horn. Trumpets, along with the timpani or kettle drums, were reserved for reinforcing volume or rhythm. Trombones were never used in classical symphonies until Beethoven did so.

Orchestras made up of these instruments were capable of rich and varied sound combinations ideally suited to the new classical form of the symphony. In general, the classical symphony has four movements (as opposed to the baroque concerto's three): a first, relatively fast one, usually the most complex in form; then a slow, lyrical movement, often songlike; a third movement in the form of a minuet (a stately dance); and a final movement, which brings the entire work to a spirited and usually cheerful conclusion. As time went on, the length and complexity of the movements grew, and many of Haydn's later symphonies last for nearly half an hour. In most cases, however, the most elaborate musical "argument" was always reserved for the first movement, presumably because during it the listeners were freshest and most able to concentrate.

Sonata Form The structure almost invariably chosen for the first movement of a classical symphony was that called sonata form. Because sonata form was not only one of the chief features of classical style but also a principle of musical organization that remained popular throughout the nineteenth century, it merits our attention in some detail. The term is actually rather confusing, because the word *sonata* is used to describe a work in several movements (like a symphony) but written for one or two instruments rather than for an orchestra. Thus, a piano sonata is a piece for solo piano, a violin sonata is a piece for violin and an accompanying instrument, almost always a piano, and so on. A symphony is, in fact, a sonata for orchestra.

The term "sonata form," however, does not, as might be reasonably expected, describe the form of a sonata but a particular kind of organizing principle frequently found in the first movement of both symphonies and sonatas as well as other instrumental combinations like string quartets (two violins, viola, and cello). Because first movements are generally played at a fast tempo ("speed"), the term sonata allegro form is also sometimes used. (The Italian word *allegro* means "fast"; Italian terms are traditionally used in music, as we have seen.)

Unlike baroque music, with its unity based on the use of a single continually expanding theme, sonata form is dominated by the idea of contrasts. The first of the three main sections of a sonata form movement is called the exposition, because it sets out, or "exposes," the musical material. This consists of at least two themes, or groups of themes, that differ from one another in melody, rhythm, and key. They represent, so to speak, the two principal characters in the drama. If the first theme is lively, the second may be thoughtful or melancholy; or a strong march-like first theme may be followed by a gentle, romantic second one. During the exposition, the first of these themes (or "subjects," as they are often called) is stated, followed by a linking passage leading to the second subject and a conclusion that rounds off the exposition.

During the course of the movement, it is of the utmost importance that listeners be able to remember these themes and identify them when they reappear. To help make this task easier, classical composers replaced the long, flowing lines of baroque melodies with much shorter tunes, often consisting of only a few notes, comparatively easy to recognize when they recur. Just in case their listeners were still not perfectly familiar with the basic material of a movement, composers reinforced it by repeating the entire exposition note for note.

In the second section of a sonata form movement, the development, the themes stated in the exposition are changed and varied in whatever way the composer's imagination suggests. One part of the first subject is often detached and treated on its own, passing up and down the orchestra, now loud, now soft, as happens in the first movement of Mozart's Symphony No. 40. Sometimes different themes will be combined and played simultaneously. In almost all cases the music passes through a wide variety of keys and moods. In the process the composer sheds new light on what have by now become familiar ideas.

At the end of the development, the original themes return to their original form for the third section of the movement, the recapitulation ("repeated" theme). The first section is recapitulated with both first and second subjects now in the same key. In this way the conflict implicit in the development section is resolved. A final coda (or "tailpiece"; coda is the Italian word for "tail") is sometimes added to bring the movement to a suitably firm conclusion.

Sonata form embodies many of the classical principles of balance, order, and control. The recapitulation, which carefully balances the exposition, and the breaking down of the material in the development and its subsequent reassembling both emphasize the sense of structure behind a sonata form movement. Both the first and last movements of Mozart's Symphony No. 40 demonstrate how the sonata form can be used to create music of extreme dramatic power.

HAYDN

The long and immensely productive career of Franz Joseph Haydn spanned a period of great change in both artistic and social terms. Born in Rohrau on the Austro-Hungarian border, he sang as a child in the choir of Saint Stephen's Cathedral in Vienna. After scraping together a living for a few precarious years, in 1761 he entered the service of a wealthy nobleman, Prince Esterhazy.

Haydn began work for the prince on the same terms as any carpenter, cook, or artisan in his master's employ. That he was a creative artist was irrelevant, because social distinctions were made on grounds of wealth or birth, not talent. By the time he left the Esterhazy family almost thirty years later, the aristocracy was competing for the privilege of entertaining him! The world was changing; in the course of two visits to London, Haydn found himself feted and honored, and during his last years in Vienna he was among the most famous figures in Europe. Thus Haydn was one of the first musicians to attain a high social position solely on the strength of his genius. His success signaled the new relationship between the artist and society that was to characterize the nineteenth century.

In personal terms, Haydn seems to have been little affected by his fame. During the long years of service to Prince Esterhazy and his descendants, Haydn used the enforced isolation of the palace where he lived to experiment with all of the musical forms available to him. In addition to operas, string quartets, piano sonatas, and hundreds of other pieces, Haydn wrote more than one hundred symphonies that exploit almost every conceivable variation on sonata and other classical forms, winning him the nickname "Father of the Symphony." During his visits to London (in 1791–1792 and 1794–1795), he wrote his last twelve symphonies, which are often known as the "London" Symphonies. Although less obviously experimental than his earlier works, they contain perhaps the finest of all his orchestral music; the slow movements in particular manage to express the greatest seriousness and profundity without tragedy or gloom.

MOZART

In 1781, in his fiftieth year and at the height of his powers, Haydn met a young man about whom he was to say a little while later to the young man's father: "Before God and as an honest man, I tell you that your son is

◆ **16.20** Joseph Lange, *Mozart at the Pianoforte*, 1789. This unfinished portrait shows the composer for once without the wig that was customarily worn at the time. Mozart must have liked the painting because he had a copy made and sent to his father.

Oil on canvas, 13½" x 11½" (35 x 30 cm). Mozarteum, Salzburg, Austria// © Alinari/Art Resource, NY

the greatest composer known to me either in person or by name." Many of us, for whom the music of Wolfgang Amadeus Mozart (1756–1791) represents a continual source of inspiration and joy and a comforting reminder of the heights the human spirit can attain, would see no reason to revise Haydn's judgment [**Fig. 16.20**].

Although Mozart's life, in contrast to Haydn's, was to prove one of growing disappointments and setbacks, his early years were comparatively happy. During his childhood he showed extraordinary musical ability. By age six he could already play the violin and piano and had begun to compose. His father Leopold, a professional musician in the service of the Archbishop of Salzburg, where the family lived, took Wolfgang on a seemingly never-ending series of trips throughout Europe to exhibit his son's musical prowess. The effect of constant travel on the boy's health and temperament can be imagined, but during these trips he became exposed to the most sophisticated and varied musical ideas of the day; the universality of his own musical style must in part be the result of the wide range of influences he was able to assimilate, from the style galant of the rococo to the Renaissance polyphonies he heard in Rome. From time to time father and son would return to Salzburg, where by this time they both held appointments at the court of the archbishop.

In 1772 the old archbishop died. His successor, Hieronymus Colloredo, was far less willing to allow his two leading musicians to come and go as they pleased. Artistic independence of the kind Haydn was to achieve was still in the future, and the following ten years were marked by continued quarreling between Mozart and his aristocratic employer. Finally, in 1781, when Mozart could take no more and asked the archbishop for his freedom, he was literally kicked out the palace door. Mozart spent the last years of his life (from 1781 to 1791) in Vienna, trying in vain to find a permanent position while writing some of the most sublime masterpieces in the history of music. When he died at age thirty-five, he was buried in a pauper's grave.

The relationship between an artist's life and work is always fascinating. In Mozart's case it raises particular problems. We might expect that continual frustration, poverty, and depression would have left its mark on his music, yet it is a grave mistake to look for autobiographical self-expression in the work of an artist who devoted his life to achieving perfection in his art. In general, Mozart's music reflects only the highest and noblest of human aspirations. Perhaps more than any other artist in any medium, Mozart combines ease and grace with profound learning in his art to come as near to ideal beauty as anything can. Nevertheless, his music remains profoundly human. We are reminded many times not of Mozart's own suffering but of the tragic nature of life itself.

A year before his death, Mozart wrote the last of his great series of concertos for solo piano and orchestra, the Piano Concerto No. 27 in B Flat, K. 595 (Mozart's works are generally listed according to the catalog first made by Köchel; hence the letter *K* that precedes the catalogue numbers). The wonderful slow movement of this work expresses, with a profundity no less moving for its utter simplicity, the resignation of one for whom the beauty of life is perpetually tinged with sadness. We can only marvel at so direct a statement of so universal a truth.

Mozart's Last Three Symphonies In the summer of 1788, living in Vienna and with no regular work or source of income, Mozart wrote his last three symphonies, Nos. 39, 40, and 41. He composed without a commission or even the possibility of hearing his own works; he may have died without ever hearing any of them performed.

The range of the three symphonies discourages us from making any easy connection between the composer's outward misery (some begging letters to friends from the same period have survived) and the spirit of his music. No. 39 is a serene and genial work. Some details—the major key, the writing for woodwind instruments, and some phrases in the first movement—suggest a Masonic connection in their sense of fellowship and kindness (Mozart himself was a Freemason and a firm believer in their ideas). The minuet forming

◆ **16.21** *The Marriage of Figaro*, Act I, Metropolitan Opera, New York, 1994. In this scene from Mozart's opera, Figaro (sung by Bryn Terfel) has learned of the Count's amorous intentions toward Susanna (Dawn Upshaw), whom Figaro is soon to marry. To outwit the Count, Figaro has not only arranged for a peasants' chorus (in the background) to praise the Count for renouncing his *droit de seigneur* but has asked him to perform an immediate civil ceremony. The Count (sung by Dwayne Croft and seated center left) evades and postpones, trying to figure out how to work his aristocratic will, while Susanna and Figaro, on the right, urgently confer. *(Image © Beatriz Schiller//Time Life Pictures/Getty Images)*

CD Track 10
Wolfgang Amadeus Mozart, Symphony No. 40, 4th Movement

The final movement, far from bringing us any light, is, from its very opening, the culmination of the tragedy. A short string passage leads upwards, only to be beaten down again no less than four times. Two powerful chords from the whole orchestra discourage the strings when they try to repeat their escape. From then on, the music hurtles to the end of the exposition, with only a brief, wan attempt to lighten the mood. The development section is brusque and in places violent, and when the opening returns, it does so with no resolution of the tension. While all of this emotion is subject to clear, classical forms, the movement—and the symphony—storm to a close offering no grounds for optimism or hope.

There is no real parallel in the Classical period for the almost unrelieved gloom of Mozart's Symphony No. 40. It would be easy to read it as the emotional expression of a desperate man. And yet it is flanked by the serenity and fellowship of No. 39 and the magisterial grandeur of No. 41. All three were written between June 26 and August 10, 1788.

The need to earn a living, coupled with the inexhaustibility of his inspiration, drew from Mozart works in almost every conceivable category. Symphonies, concertos, masses, sonatas, and string quartets are only some of the forms he enriched. Many admirers of Mozart would choose his operas, however, if faced with a decision as to what to save if all else were to be lost. Furthermore, his operas provide the clearest picture of his historical position.

Mozart and Opera Mozart's opera *The Marriage of Figaro* is based on a play of the same name by the French dramatist Pierre-Augustin Beaumarchais (1732–1799). Although a comedy, the play, which was first performed in 1784, contains serious overtones. The plot is too complicated to permit even a brief summary, but among the characters are a lecherous and deceitful, though charming, Count; his deceived wife, the Countess; her maid, Susanna, who puts up a determined resistance against the Count's advances; and Susanna's husband-to-be, Figaro, who finally manages to outwit and embarrass the would-be seducer, who is also his own employer [**Fig. 16.21**]. In other words, the heroes of the play are the servants and the villain their master. Written as it was on the eve of the French Revolution, Beaumarchais's play was interpreted rightly as an attack on the morals of the ruling classes and a warning that the lower classes would

the third movement is even festive in character, and the finale positively cheerful.

Symphony No. 41, generally known as the "Jupiter" symphony, is Mozart at his most Classical, combining elegance of ideas with a powerfully intellectual treatment. In the last movement, he builds excitement by combining themes into a massive but elegant texture of sound. Nothing could be more triumphant than the splendor and power of the overwhelming structure he builds, leaving us stunned by his brilliance and exhilarated by the music's drive. This is surely one of the high points of musical genius.

If we are to look for a darker side to the composer's state of mind, however, it can be found in Symphony No. 40, a work almost entirely written in a minor key. The first movement opens with an inexorable drive. Even a brief moment of relief is soon cut short, and the movement ends with the hopelessness of its beginning. The slow movement has a tentative melancholy that breaks into occasional outbursts of passion. The minuet, normally an occasion for relaxation, is stern and forceful, with only its wistful trio section to bring some relief.

fight back. Beaumarchais was firmly associated with the moves toward social and political change; he was an early supporter of the American Revolution and helped organize French support for the insurgent colonists.

Mozart's opera was first performed in 1786. It retains the spirit of protest in the original but adds a sense of humanity and subtlety perhaps only music can bring. No one suffered more than Mozart from the highhandedness of the aristocracy, yet when *The Marriage of Figaro* gives voice to the growing mood of revolution, it does so as a protest against the abuse of human rights rather than in a spirit of personal resentment. In the first act, Figaro's aria "Se vuol' ballare" expresses the pent-up frustration of generations of men and women who had endured injustices and who could take no more. The musical form and expression is still restrained, indeed classical, but Mozart pours into it the feelings of the age.

Mozart's ability to create characters who seem real, with whose feelings we can identify, reaches its height in the Countess. Ignored and duped by her husband, the laughingstock of those around her, she expresses the conflicting emotions of a woman torn between resentment and deep attachment. Her aria in the third act, "Dove sono," begins with a recitative in which she vents her bitterness. Gradually it melts into a slow and meditative section in which she asks herself what went wrong: "Where are those happy moments of sweetness and pleasure, where did they go, those vows of a deceiving tongue?" The poignant theme to which these words are set returns toward the end of the slow section to provide one of the most affective moments in all opera. Mozart's gift for expressing human behavior at its most noble is conveyed in the aria's final section, where the Countess decides, despite everything, to try to win back her husband's love. Thus, in seven or eight minutes, we have been carried from despair to hope, and Mozart has combined his revelation of a human heart with music that by itself is of extraordinary beauty.

The opera as a whole is far richer than discussion of these two arias can suggest. For instance, among the other characters is one of the composer's most memorable creations, the pageboy Cherubino, whose aria "Non so più" epitomizes the breathless, agonizing joy of adolescent love. An accomplishment of another kind is exemplified by the *ensembles* (scenes in which a large number of characters are involved). Here Mozart combines clarity of musical and dramatic action while advancing the plot at a breakneck pace.

The Marriage of Figaro expresses at the same time the spirit of its age and the universality of human nature, a truly classical achievement. Equally impressively, it illuminates the personal emotions of individual people, and through them teaches us about our own reactions to life and its problems. As one distinguished writer has put it, in this work Mozart has added to the world's understanding of people—of human nature.

LITERATURE IN THE EIGHTEENTH CENTURY

INTELLECTUAL DEVELOPMENTS

While painters, poets, and musicians were reflecting the changing moods of the eighteenth century in their art, social and political philosophers were examining the problems of contemporary society more systematically. Individual thinkers frequently alternated between optimism and despair, because awareness of the greatness of which human beings were capable was always qualified by the perception of the sorry state of the world. The broad range of diagnosis and/or proposed solutions makes it difficult to generalize on the nature of eighteenth-century intellectual life, but two contrasting trends can be discerned. A few writers, notably Jonathan Swift, reacted to the problems of the age with deep pessimism, bitterly opposing the view that human nature is basically good. Others, convinced that progress was possible, sought to devise new systems of intellectual, social, or political organization. Rational humanists like Diderot and political philosophers like Rousseau based their arguments on an optimistic view of human nature. However, Voltaire, the best known of all eighteenth-century thinkers, fitted into neither of these two categories—rather, he moved from one to the other. The answer he finally proposed to the problems of existence is as applicable to the world of today as it was to that of the eighteenth century, although perhaps no more welcome.

The renewed interest in Classical culture, visible in the portraits by Sir Joshua Reynolds and buildings like the Pantheon, also made a strong impression on literature. French writers like Racine had already based works on Classical models, and the fables of Jean de La Fontaine (1621–1695) drew freely on Aesop and other Greek and Roman sources. Elsewhere in Europe throughout the eighteenth century, poets continued to produce works on Classical themes, from the plays of Pietro Metastasio (1698–1782) in Italy to the lyric poetry of Friedrich von Schiller (1759–1805) in Germany.

The appeal of Neo-Classical literature was particularly strong in England, where major Greek and Roman works like Homer's *Iliad* and *Odyssey* or Virgil's *Aeneid* had long been widely read and admired. In the seventeenth century, Milton's *Paradise Lost* had represented a deliberate attempt to create an equally monumental epic poem in English. Before the eighteenth century, however, several important works, including the tragedies of Aeschylus, had never been translated into English.

The upsurge of enthusiasm for Classical literature that characterized the eighteenth-century English literary scene had two chief effects: poets and scholars began to translate or retranslate the most important Classical authors; and creative writers began to produce original

VOICES OF THEIR TIMES

A Visit to the Court of Louis XV

The English writer and connoisseur Horace Walpole (1717–1797) was presented to the king and queen of France and described the encounter to a friend.

> You perceive that I have been presented. The Queen took great notice of me; none of the rest said a syllable.
>
> You are let into the king's bedchamber just as he has put on his shirt; he dresses and talks good-humoredly to a few, glares at strangers, goes to mass, to dinner, and a-hunting. The good old Queen, who is like Lady Primrose in the face, and Queen Caroline in the immensity of her cap, is at her dressing-table, attended by two or three old ladies, who are languishing to be in Abraham's bosom, as the only man's bosom to whom they can hope for admittance. Thence you go to the Dauphin, for all is done in an hour. He scarce stays a minute; indeed, poor creature; he is a ghost, and cannot possibly last three months. The Dauphiness is in her bedchamber, but dressed and standing; looks cross, is not civil, and has the true Westphalian grace and accents.
>
> The four Mesdames, who are clumsy, plump old wenches, with a bad likeness to their father, stand in a bedchamber in a row, with black cloaks and knitting-bags, looking good-humored, not knowing what to say, and wriggling as if they wanted to make water. This ceremony too is very short; then you are carried to the Dauphin's three boys, who you may be sure only bow and stare. The Duke of Berry looks weak and weak-eyed: the Count de Provence is a fine boy; the Count d'Artois well enough. The whole concludes with seeing the Dauphin's little girl dine, who is as round and as fat as a pudding.

From *The Letters of Horace Walpole*, P. Cunningham, ed. London, 1892.

---

works in Classical forms, deal with Classical themes, and include Classical references. The general reading public was by now expected to understand and appreciate both the ancient masterpieces and modern works inspired by them.

The Augustans The principal English writers formed a group calling themselves Augustans. The name reveals the degree to which these writers admired and modeled themselves on the Augustan poets of ancient Rome. In 27 CE the victory of the first Roman emperor Augustus ended the chaos of civil war in Rome and brought peace and stability to the Roman world. The principal poets of Rome's Augustan Age, writers like Virgil and Horace, had subsequently commemorated Augustus's achievement in works intended for a sophisticated public. In the same way in England, the restoration to power of King Charles II (in 1660) seemed to some of his contemporaries a return to order and civilization after the tumultuous English Civil War. The founders of the English Augustan movement, writers like John Dryden (1631–1700), explored not only the historical parallel by glorifying English achievement under the monarchy but also the literary one by imitating the highly polished style of the Roman Augustan poets in works intended for an aristocratic audience. He also translated the works of Virgil, Juvenal, and other Roman poets into English.

Pope's Rococo Satires Alexander Pope (1688–1744), the greatest English poet of the eighteenth century, was one of the Augustans, yet the lightness and elegance of his wit reflect the rococo spirit of the age. His genius lay precisely in his awareness that the dry bones of Classical learning needed to have life breathed into them. The spirit that would awaken art in his own time, as it had done for the ancient writers, was that of Nature—not in the sense of the natural world but in the sense of that which is universal and unchanging in human experience. Pope's conception of the vastness and truth of human experience given form and meaning by rules first devised in the ancient past represents eighteenth-century thought at its most constructive.

Like Watteau, Pope suffered throughout his life from ill health. At age twelve an attack of spinal tuberculosis left him permanently crippled. Perhaps in compensation he soon developed the passion for reading and for the beauty of the world around him that shines through his work. A Catholic in a Protestant country, he was unable to establish a career in public life or obtain public patronage for his literary work. As a result he was forced to support himself entirely by writing and translating. Pope's literary reputation was first made by the *Essay on Criticism*, but he won economic independence by producing highly successful translations of Homer's *Iliad* (1713–1720) and *Odyssey* (1725–1726) and an edition of the works of Shakespeare (1725). With the money he earned from these endeavors, he abandoned commercial publishing and confined himself, for the most part, to his house on the river Thames at Twickenham, where he spent the rest of his life writing, entertaining friends, and indulging his fondness for gardening.

Pope's range as a poet was considerable, but his greatest achievements were in the characteristically rococo medium of satire. Like his fellow countryman Hogarth, Pope's awareness of the heights to which humans can rise was coupled with an acute sense of the frequency of their failure to do so. In the long poem *Essay on Man* (1733–1734), for example, Pope combines Christian and humanist teaching in a characteristically eighteenth-century manner to express his philosophical position with regard to the preeminent place occupied by human beings in the divine scheme of life. He is at his best, however, when applying his principles to practical situations and uncovering human folly. Pope's reverence for order and reason made him the implacable foe of those who in his eyes were responsible for the declining political morality and artistic standards of the day. It is sometimes said that Pope's satire is tinged with personal hostility. In fact, a series of literary and social squabbles marked his life, suggesting that he was not always motivated by the highest ideals; nonetheless, in his poetry he nearly always based his moral judgments on what he described as "the strong antipathy of good to bad," a standard he applied with courage and wit.

Swift's Savage Indignation

Perhaps the darkest of all visions of human nature in the eighteenth century was that of Jonathan Swift (1667–1745). In a letter to Alexander Pope he made it clear that, whatever his affection for individuals, he hated the human race as a whole. According to Swift, human beings were not to be defined automatically as rational animals, as so many eighteenth-century thinkers believed, but as animals capable of reason. It was precisely because so many of them failed to live up to their capabilities that Swift turned his "savage indignation" against them into bitter satire, never more so than when the misuse of reason served "to aggravate man's natural corruptions" and provide him with new ones.

Swift was in a position to observe at close quarters the political and social struggles of the times. Born in Dublin, for much of his life he played an active part in supporting Irish resistance to English rule. After studying at Trinity College, Dublin, he went to England and (in 1694) was ordained a priest in the Anglican Church. For the next few years he moved back and forth between England and Ireland, taking a leading role in the political controversies of the day by publishing articles and pamphlets that in general, were strongly conservative.

A fervent supporter of the monarchy and of the Anglican Church, Swift had good reason to hope that his advocacy of their cause would win him a position of high rank. In 1713 this hope was partially realized with his appointment as Dean of Saint Patrick's Cathedral in Dublin. Any chances he had of receiving an English bishopric were destroyed in 1714 by the death of Queen Anne and the subsequent dismissal of his political friends from power.

Swift spent the remainder of his life in Ireland, cut off from the mainstream of political and cultural life. Here he increasingly emerged as a publicist for the Irish cause. During his final years his mind began to fail, but not before he had composed the epitaph under which he lies buried in Saint Patrick's Cathedral: *Ubi saeva indignatio ulterius cor lacerare nequit* ("He has gone where savage indignation can tear his heart no more").

During his years in Ireland, Swift wrote his best-known work, *Gulliver's Travels*, first published in 1726. In a sense *Gulliver's Travels* has been a victim of its own popularity, because its surprising success as a work for young readers has distracted attention from the author's real purpose: to satirize human behavior. (It says much for the eighteenth century's richness that it could produce two writers working in the same genre—the satirists Swift and Pope—with such differing results.) The first two of Gulliver's four voyages, to the miniature land of Lilliput and to Brobdingnag, the land of giants, are the best known. In these sections the harshness of Swift's satire is to some extent masked by the charm and wit of the narrative. In the voyage to the land of the Houyhnhnms, however, Swift draws a bitter contrast between the Houyhnhnms, a race of horses whose behavior is governed by reason, and their slaves the Yahoos, human in form but bestial in behavior. As expressed by the Yahoos, Swift's vision of the depths to which human beings can sink is profoundly pessimistic. His insistence on their deep moral and intellectual flaws is in strong contrast to the rational humanism of many of his contemporaries, who believed in the innate dignity and worth of human beings.

Yet even the Yahoos do not represent Swift's most bitter satire. It took his experience of the direct consequences of "man's inhumanity to man" to draw from his pen a short pamphlet, *A Modest Proposal for Preventing the Children of Poor People in Ireland from Being a Burden to Their Parents or Country, and for Making Them Beneficial to the Public*, the title of which is generally abbreviated to *A Modest Proposal*. First published in 1729, this brilliant and shocking work was inspired by the poverty and suffering of a large sector of Ireland's population. Even today the nature of the supposedly benevolent author's "modest proposal" can take the reader's breath away, both by the calmness with which it is offered and by the devastatingly quiet logic with which its implications are explained. All the irony of which this master satirist was capable is here used to express anger and disgust at injustice and the apparent inevitability of human suffering. Although Swift was writing in response to a particular historical situation, the deep compassion for the poor and oppressed that

◆ **16.22** Jean Antoine Houdon, *Denis Diderot*, 1771. Unlike most official portraiture of the 18th century, Houdon's work aims to reveal the character of his sitters. Here he vividly conveys Diderot's humanity and quizzical humor.

Terra cotta, 16' (41 cm) high. Musée du Louvre, Paris, France//© Réunion des Musées Nationaux/Art Resource, NY

inspired him transcends its time. Our own world has certainly not lost the need for it.

RATIONAL HUMANISM: THE ENCYCLOPEDISTS

Diderot Belief in the essential goodness of human nature and the possibility of progress, which had first been expressed by the humanists of the Renaissance, continued to find supporters throughout the eighteenth century. The enormous scientific and technical achievements of the two centuries since the time of Erasmus tended to confirm the opinions of those who took a positive view of human capabilities. It was in order to provide a rational basis for this positive humanism that the French thinker and writer Denis Diderot (1713–1784) [**Fig. 16.22**] conceived the project of preparing a vast encyclopedia that would describe the state of contemporary science, technology, and thought and provide a system for the classification of knowledge.

Work on the *Encyclopédie*, as it is generally called, began in 1751; the last of its seventeen volumes appeared in 1772. By its conclusion, what had begun as a com-

pendium of information had become the statement of a philosophical position: that the extent of human powers and achievements conclusively demonstrates that humans are rational beings. The implication of this position is that any political or religious system seeking to control the minds of individuals is to be condemned. It is hardly surprising, therefore, that some years before the conclusion of the project, the *Encyclopédie* had been banned by decree of Louis XV; the last volumes were published clandestinely.

Montesquieu In religious terms, the *Encyclopédie* took a position of considerable skepticism, advocating freedom of conscience and belief. Politically, however, its position was less extreme and less consistent. One of the most distinguished philosophers to contribute political articles was Charles-Louis Montesquieu (1689–1755), whose own aristocratic origins may have helped mold his relatively conservative views. Both in the *Encyclopédie* and in his own writings, Montesquieu advocated the retention of a monarchy, with powers divided between the king and a series of "intermediate bodies" that included parliament, aristocratic organizations, the middle class, and even the church. By distributing power in this way, Montesquieu hoped to achieve a workable system of "checks and balances," thereby eliminating the possibility of a central dictatorial government. His ideas proved particularly interesting to the authors of the Constitution of the United States.

Rousseau A very different point of view was espoused by another contributor to the *Encyclopédie*, Jean Jacques Rousseau (1712–1778), whose own quarrelsome and neurotic character played a considerable part in influencing his political philosophy. Diderot had originally commissioned Rousseau to produce some articles on music, since the latter was an accomplished composer (his opera *Le Devin du Village* is still performed occasionally). After violently quarreling with Diderot and others, however, Rousseau spent much of an unhappy and restless life writing philosophical treatises and novels that expressed his political convictions. Briefly stated, Rousseau believed that the natural goodness of the human race had been corrupted by the growth of civilization and that the freedom of the individual had been destroyed by the growth of society. For Rousseau, humans were good and society was bad.

Rousseau's praise of the simple virtues like unselfishness and kindness and his high regard for natural human feelings have identified his philosophy with a belief in the "noble savage," but this phrase is misleading. Far from advocating a return to primitive existence in some nonexistent Garden of Eden, Rousseau passionately strove to create a new social order. In *The Social Contract* (1762), he tried to describe the basis of his ideal state in terms of the General Will of the people, which would delegate authority to individual organs of government, although neither most of his readers nor Rousseau seemed clear on how this General Will should operate.

Although Rousseau's writings express a complex political philosophy, most of his readers were more interested in his emphasis on spontaneous feeling than in his political theories. His contempt for the superficial and the artificial, and his praise for simple and direct relationships between individuals, did a great deal to help demolish the principles of aristocracy and continue to inspire believers in human equality.

VOLTAIRE'S PHILOSOPHICAL CYNICISM: *CANDIDE*

It may seem extravagant to claim that the life and work of François Marie-Arouet (1694–1778), best known to us as Voltaire (one of his pen names), can summarize the events of a period as complex as the eighteenth century. That the claim can be not only advanced but also supported is some measure of the breadth of his genius. A writer of poems, plays, novels, and history; a student of science, philosophy, and politics; a man who spent time at the courts of Louis XV and Frederick the Great but also served a prison sentence; a defender of religious and political freedom who simultaneously supported enlightened despotism, Voltaire was above all a man *engagé*—one committed to the concerns of his age [**Fig. 16.23**].

After being educated by the Jesuits, he began to publish writings in the satirical style he was to use throughout his life. His belief that the aristocratic society of the times was unjust must have received strong confirmation when his critical position earned him first a year in jail and then, in 1726, exile from France. Voltaire chose to go to England, where he found a system of government that seemed to him far more liberal and just than that of the French. On his return home in 1729 he discussed the advantages of English political life in his *Lettres philosophiques*, published in 1734, and escaped from the scandal and possibility of arrest that his work created by spending the next ten years in the country.

In 1744 Voltaire was finally tempted back to the French court but found little in its formal and artificial life to stimulate him. He discovered a more congenial atmosphere at the court of Frederick the Great at Potsdam, where he spent the years from 1750 to 1753. Frederick's warm welcome and considerable intellectual stature must have come as an agreeable change from the sterile ceremony of the French court, and the two men soon established a close friendship. It seems, however, that Potsdam was not big enough to contain two such powerful intellects and temperaments. After a couple of years, Voltaire quarreled with his patron and once again abandoned sophisticated life for that of the country.

◆ **16.23** Jean Baptiste Pigalle, *Voltaire*, 1770–1776. This most unusual statue of the great philosopher places a powerful head on the torso of an old man. The head was modeled from life when Voltaire was seventy-six; the body is based on that of a Roman statue. The statue seems to represent the triumph of the spirit over the frailty of the body.

Marble, 4′9⅛″ (1.47 m) high. Musée du Louvre, Paris, France//© Giraudon/ Art Resource, NY

In 1758 Voltaire finally settled in the village of Ferney, where he set up his own court. Here the greatest names in Europe—intellectuals, artists, politicians—made the pilgrimage to talk and, above all, listen to the sage of Ferney, while he published work after work, each of which was distributed throughout Europe. Only in 1778, the year of his death, did Voltaire return to Paris, where the excitement brought on by a hero's welcome proved too much for his failing strength.

It is difficult to summarize the philosophy of a man who touched on so many subjects. Nevertheless, one theme recurs continually in Voltaire's writings: the

VALUES

Revolution

The eighteenth century saw a series of vast upheavals in patterns of European life that had remained constant since late medieval times. The Renaissance and the subsequent Reformation and Counter-Reformation had laid the intellectual bases for the change. The eighteenth century was marked by their consequences. One revolution was in economic affairs. As a result of exploration and colonization, international trade and commerce increased, which enriched ever-growing numbers of middle-class citizens and their families. On the other hand, the endless wars of the seventeenth century left national governments deeply in debt. In England, the state introduced paper money for the first time in an attempt to restore financial stability. The transfer of wealth from the public sector to private hands encouraged speculation. Spectacular financial collapses of private companies—the most notorious was that of the South Sea Company—produced panic and revolutionary changes in banking systems.

Another revolution, perhaps in the long run the most important of all, was the development of industry. The Industrial Revolution, which reached its climax in the mid-nineteenth century, had its origins a century earlier. The invention of new machines, particularly in the textile industry, led to the establishment of factories, which in turn produced the growth of urban life. New mining techniques turned coal into big business. New technologies revolutionized

modes of travel that had been virtually unchanged since Roman times.

At the same time, the complex structure of international diplomatic relations that had existed for centuries began to collapse. Although France remained the leading European power, its economy and internal stability were undermined by the refusal of its ruling class to admit change, and Britain became the richest country in the world. The dominant powers of Renaissance Europe and the Age of Exploration—Spain, Portugal, the city-states of Italy—were in decline, while important new players appeared on the scene: Prussia under the Hohenzollerns, the Russia of Peter the Great.

Impatience with the ways of the Old Regime, together with the desire for revolutionary political and social change, found expression in the writings of Enlightenment figures such as Voltaire. By the end of the eighteenth century, many people throughout Europe were increasingly frustrated by living in continual political and social deprivation. As a result, they took to the streets in direct physical action.

The American Revolution undermined the power of the monarchy in Britain, and speeded up the collapse of the Old Regime in France. The French Revolution petered out in the years of Napoleonic rule but marked a watershed in Western history and culture: ever since the late eighteenth century, governments have had to reckon with intellectual protest and direct political action by their citizens.

importance of freedom of thought. Voltaire's greatest hatred was reserved for intolerance and bigotry; in letter after letter he ended with the phrase he made famous, *Écrasez l'infâme* ("Crush the infamous thing"). The "infamous thing" is superstition, which breeds fanaticism and persecution. Those Voltaire judged chiefly responsible for superstition were the Christians—Catholic and Protestant alike.

Voltaire vehemently attacked the traditional view of the Bible as the inspired word of God. He claimed that it contained a mass of anecdotes and contradictions totally irrelevant to the modern world and that the disputes arising from it, which had divided Christians for centuries, were absurd and pointless. Yet Voltaire was far from being an atheist. He was a firm believer in a God who had created the world, but whose worship could not be tied directly to one religion or another: "The only book that needs to be read is the great book of

nature." Only natural religion and morality would end prejudice and ignorance.

Voltaire's negative criticisms of human absurdity are more convincing than his positive views on a universal natural morality. It is difficult not to feel at times that even Voltaire had only the vaguest ideas of what natural morality really meant. In fact, in *Candide* (1759), his best-known work, he reaches a much less optimistic conclusion. *Candide* was written with the avowed purpose of ridiculing the optimism of the German philosopher Gottfried von Leibnitz (1646–1716) who believed that "everything is for the best in the best of all possible worlds." Because both intellect and experience teach that this is far from the case, Voltaire chose to demonstrate the folly of unreasonable optimism, as well as the cruelty and stupidity of the human race, by subjecting his hero Candide to a barrage of disasters and suffering.

THE LATE EIGHTEENTH CENTURY: TIME OF REVOLUTION

Throughout the eighteenth century, Europe continued to prosper economically. The growth of trade and industry, particularly in Britain, France, and Holland, led to several significant changes in the lifestyles of increasing numbers of people. Technological improvements in coal mining and iron casting began to lay the foundations for the Industrial Revolution of the nineteenth century. The circulation of more books and newspapers increased general awareness of the issues of the day. As states began to accumulate more revenue, they increased both the size of their armies and the number of those in government employ. The Baroque period had seen the exploitation of imported goods and spices from Asia and gold from Latin America; the eighteenth century was marked by the development of trade with North America and the Caribbean.

Amid such vast changes, it was hardly possible that the systems of government should remain unaffected. Thinkers like Rousseau and Voltaire began to question the hitherto unquestioned right of the wealthy aristocracy to rule throughout Europe. In Britain, both at home and in the colonies, power was gradually transferred from the king to Parliament. Prussia, Austria, and Russia were ruled by so-called enlightened despots, as we have seen.

The French Revolution In France, however, the center of much of the intellectual pressure for change, the despots were not even enlightened. Louis XV, who ruled from 1715 to 1774, showed little interest in the affairs of his subjects or the details of government. The remark often attributed to him, *Après moi le déluge* ("After me the flood"), suggests that he was fully aware of the consequences of his indifference. Subsequent events fully justified his prediction, yet throughout his long reign he remained either unwilling or unable to follow the example of his fellow European sovereigns and impose some order on government. By the time his grandson Louis XVI succeeded him in 1774, the damage was done. Furthermore, the new king's continued reliance on the traditional aristocratic class, into whose hands he put wealth and political power, offended both the rising middle class and the peasants.

When in 1788 the collapse of the French economy was accompanied by a disastrous harvest and consequent steep rise in the cost of food in the first phase of the revolution, riots broke out in Paris and in rural districts. In reaction to the ensuing violence "The Declaration of the Rights of Man and Citizen," which asserted the universal right to "liberty, property, security, and resistance to oppression," was passed on August 26, 1789. Its opening section clearly shows the influence of the American Declaration of Independence.

from **The Declaration of the Rights of Man**

The representatives of the French people, organized in National Assembly, considering that ignorance, forgetfulness, or contempt of the rights of man are the sole causes of public misfortunes and of the corruption of governments, have resolved to set forth in a solemn declaration the natural, inalienable, and sacred rights of man, in order that such declaration, continually before all members of the social body, may be a perpetual reminder of their rights and duties; in order that the acts of the legislative power and those of the executive power may constantly be compared to the aim of every political institution and may accordingly be more respected; in order that the demands of the citizens, founded henceforth upon simple and incontestable principles, may always be directed toward the maintenance of the Constitution and the welfare of all.

Accordingly, the National Assembly recognizes and proclaims, in the presence and under the auspices of the Supreme Being, the following rights of man and citizen.

1. Men are born and remain free and equal in rights; social distinctions may be based only on general usefulness.
2. The aim of every political association is the preservation of the natural and inalienable rights of man; these rights are liberty, property, security, and resistance to oppression.
3. The source of all sovereignty resides essentially in the nation; no group, no individual may exercise authority not emanating expressly therefrom.
4. Liberty consists of the power to do whatever is not injurious to others; thus the enjoyment of the natural rights of every man has for its limits only those that assure other members of society the enjoyment of those same rights; such limits may be determined only by law.
5. The law has the right to forbid only actions which are injurious to society. Whatever is not forbidden by law may not be prevented, and no one may be constrained to do what it does not prescribe.
6. Law is the expression of the general will; all citizens have the right to concur personally, or through their representatives, in its formation; it must be the same for all, whether it protects or punishes. All citizens, being equal before it, are equally admissible to all public offices, positions, and employments, according to their capacity, and without other distinction than that of virtues and talents.

Declarations alone hardly sufficed, however; after two and a half years of continual political bickering and unrest, the revolution entered its second phase. On September 20, 1792, the National Convention was assembled. One of its first tasks was to try Louis XVI, now deposed and imprisoned for treason. After unanimously finding him guilty, the convention was divided on whether to execute him. He was finally condemned to the guillotine by a vote of 361 to 360 and beheaded forthwith. The resulting Reign of Terror lasted until 1795. During it, utopian theories of a republic based on liberty, equality, and fraternity were ruthlessly put into practice. The revolutionary leaders cold-bloodedly eliminated all opponents, real or potential, and created massive upheaval throughout all levels of French society.

The principal political group in the convention, the Jacobins, was at first led by Maximilien Robespierre (1758–1794). One of the most controversial figures of the revolution, Robespierre is viewed by some as a demagogue and bloodthirsty fanatic, by others as a fiery idealist and ardent democrat; his vigorous commitment to revolutionary change is disputed by no one. Following Rousseau's belief in the virtues of natural human feelings, Robespierre aimed to establish a "republic of virtue," made up democratically of honest citizens.

In order to implement these goals, revolutionary courts were established, which tried and generally sentenced to death those perceived as the enemies of the revolution. The impression that the Reign of Terror was aimed principally at the old aristocracy is incorrect. Only nobles suspected of political agitation were arrested, and the vast majority of the guillotine's victims—some 70 percent—were rebellious peasants and workers. Neither were revolutionary leaders immune. Georges-Jacques Danton (1759–1794), one of the earliest spokesmen of the revolution and one of Robespierre's principal political rivals, was executed in March 1794 along with some of his followers.

Throughout the rest of Europe, events in France were followed with horrified attention. Austria and Prussia were joined by England, Spain, and several smaller states in a war against the revolutionary government. After suffering initial defeat, the French enlarged and reorganized their army and succeeded in driving back the allied troops at the Battle of Fleurus in June 1794. Paradoxically, the military victory, far from reinforcing Robespierre's authority, provided his opponents the strength to eliminate him; he was declared an outlaw on July 27, 1794, and guillotined the next day.

By the spring of the following year, the country was in economic chaos and Paris was torn by street rioting. Many of those who had originally been in favor of revolutionary change, including businessmen and landowning peasants, realized that whatever the virtues of democracy, constitutional government was essential. In reply to these pressures the convention produced a new constitution, known as the Directory. This first formally established French republic lasted only until 1799, when political stability returned to France with the military dictatorship of Napoleon Bonaparte.

Revolution in America Although the French Revolution was an obvious consequence of extreme historical pressures, many of its leaders were additionally inspired by the successful outcome of another revolution: that of the Americans against their British rulers. More specifically, the Americans had rebelled against not the British king but the British parliament. In eighteenth-century England the king was given little chance to be enlightened or otherwise, because supreme power was concentrated in the legislative assembly, which ruled

◆ **16.24** Jean Antoine Houdon, *George Washington*, 1790. The sculptor has emphasized the dignity and lofty calm of the first president.

Marble, 6′8″ (2.03 m) high. © State Capitol of Virginia, Richmond / David Corson / SuperStock

both England and, by its appointees, British territories abroad. A series of economic measures enacted by Parliament succeeded in thoroughly rousing American resentment. The story of what followed the Declaration of Independence of July 4, 1776, is too involved to be summarized here. Its result was the signing of a peace treaty in 1783 with Britain that acknowledged the independent sovereignty of the new nation, the United States of America, and the inauguration of the new American Constitution in 1789.

Although the Declaration of Independence was certainly not intended as a work of literature, its author, generally assumed to be Thomas Jefferson, was as successful as any of the literary figures of the eighteenth century in expressing the more optimistic views of the age. The principles enshrined in the document assume that human beings are capable of achieving political and social freedom. Positive belief in equality and justice is expressed in universal terms like *man* and *nature*—universal for their day, that is—typical of eighteenth century enlightened thought [**Fig. 16.24**].

from **The Declaration of Independence**

When in the Course of human events, it becomes necessary for one people to dissolve the political bonds which have connected them with another, and to assume among the Powers of the earth, the separate and equal station to which the Laws of Nature and of Nature's God entitle them, a decent respect to the opinions of mankind requires that they should declare the causes which impel them to the separation.

We hold these truths to be self-evident, that all men are created equal, that they are endowed by their Creator with certain unalienable Rights, that among these are Life, Liberty and the pursuit of Happiness. That to secure these rights, Governments are instituted among Men, deriving their just powers from the consent of the governed. That whenever any Form of Government becomes destructive of these ends, it is the Right of the People to alter or to abolish it, and to institute new Government, laying its foundation on such principles and organizing its powers in such form, as to them shall seem most likely to effect their Safety and Happiness. Prudence, indeed, will dictate that Governments long established should not be changed for light and transient causes; and accordingly all experience hath shown, that mankind are more disposed to suffer, while evils are sufferable, than to right themselves by abolishing the forms to which they are accustomed. But when a long train of abuses and usurpations, pursuing invariably the same Object, evinces a design to reduce them under absolute Despotism, it is their right, it is their duty, to throw off such Government, and to provide new Guards for their future security. Such has been the patient sufferance of these Colonies; and such is now the necessity which constrains them to alter their former Systems of Government. The history of the present King of Great Britain is a history of repeated injuries and usurpations, all having in direct object the establishment of an absolute Tyranny over these States.

SUMMARY

◆ **Monarchy in the Eighteenth Century.** The eighteenth century marked the passage in European life from the old aristocratic order to the beginnings of modern society. When the age began, Louis XIV was still firmly entrenched; before the century ended, Louis XVI and his wife had been executed by the National Convention of the French Revolution—itself inspired, in theory at least, by the American Revolution of a few years earlier.

Elsewhere in Europe enlightened despots like Frederick the Great of Prussia responded to the growing restlessness of their subjects by reorganizing government and improving living conditions. Frederick's court even became one of the leading cultural and intellectual centers of the time; C. P. E. Bach directed the music there, and Voltaire spent two years as Frederick's guest.

◆ **Rococo Art.** In the visual arts the principal style to emerge from the baroque splendors of the previous century was the rococo. Lighter and less grandiose, it was wonderfully suited to the civilized amenities of aristocratic life. The chief rococo painters were French and Italian—appropriately enough, because rulers both in France and in the kingdoms of Italy made few concessions to the growing demands for reform. In architecture, the builders of Parisian private houses such as the Hôtel de Soubise indulged their taste for fanciful decoration, while the rococo churches of southern Germany and Austria represent some of the happiest of all eighteenth-century achievements.

◆ **The Neo-Classical Style.** The other important artistic style of the period was the Neo-Classical. Inspired by the increasing quantities of ancient art being excavated at Pompeii and elsewhere, artists began to turn to the style and subjects of Classical antiquity, which provided a refreshing contrast to the theatricality of baroque and the artificiality of rococo. Furthermore, in the history of the Roman Republic (at least as they perceived it) revolutionary artists of the later eighteenth century found a vehicle for expressing their battle for freedom. In many cases painters incorporated into their works discoveries from the various excavations in progress: the French Jacques-Louis David in his paintings for the revolution as well as the English Joshua Reynolds in his portraits of society women.

Ancient sculpture provided a stimulus to some of the leading artists of the day, most notably the Italian Antonio Canova and the French Jean Antoine Houdon. Both of them worked principally during and after the revolutions; Houdon even produced a Neo-Classical statue of George Washington. Washington and the other leaders of the American Revolution turned naturally to classical architecture for their public buildings. Among the finest examples is Thomas Jefferson's State Capitol at Richmond.

◆ **Music in the Eighteenth Century: Haydn and Mozart.** In music the emotional style of baroque composers began to give way to a new way of organizing musical forms. By the mid-eighteenth century, the classical style was beginning to evolve, and the two greatest composers of the age—Franz Joseph Haydn and Wolfgang Amadeus Mozart (both Austrian)—used it to write their symphonies, concertos, and sonatas. Most of these works employed sonata form, a system of musical composition involving contrasts rather than the unity of baroque music. Haydn's hundred or so symphonies show an almost infinitely endless exploration of the possibilities offered by sonata form while also reflecting the evolution of the modern symphony orchestra. His own personal career furthermore illustrates the changing status of the artist: after years of serving in the household of an aristocratic family, he became transformed by his compositions into one of the most famous men in Europe.

Mozart's relations with his noble employers were far less happy. His music, however, transcends the difficulties of his life and achieves the supreme blend of eighteenth-century art's two chief concerns: beauty and learning. Like Haydn, he explored the possibilities of sonata form and also wrote several operas that remain among the best-loved of all musical works for the stage. *The Marriage of Figaro* illustrates Mozart's genius for expressing universal human emotions in music, while in its story it reflects the revolutionary mood of the times.

◆ **Eighteenth-Century Literature: History and Satire.** Like music, the literature of the eighteenth century was generally serious. Many writers avoided the lightness of the rococo, preferring to produce works based on Classical models or themes. They included the Italian dramatist Metastasio. An exception is provided by the satirical writings of Alexander Pope, which poke fun at the pretensions of eighteenth-century society, although many of Pope's other works are Neo-Classical in style. Other writers used satire, in itself a characteristically rococo medium, as a bitter weapon against human folly. Jonathan Swift's writings present an indictment of his fellow humans that offers little hope for their improvement.

◆ **The Encyclopedists.** The French Encyclopedists offered a more optimistic point of view. Denis Diderot and most of his colleagues believed in the essential goodness of human nature and the possibility of progress, and their *Encyclopédie* was intended to exalt the power of reason. Not all of the contributors agreed on this goal, however. Jean Jacques Rousseau claimed that society was an evil that corrupted essential human goodness and called for a new social

order. Yet all of the leading intellectuals of the day, including the greatest of them all, Voltaire, were united in urging the need for radical social change. In novels, pamphlets, plays, and countless other publications, Voltaire attacked traditional religion and urged the importance of freedom of thought.

By the end of the century, the battle for freedom had plunged France into chaos and demonstrated to the whole of Europe that the old social order had come to an end. The following century was to see the struggle to forge a new society.

EXERCISES

1. Compare and contrast the rococo and Neo-Classical styles in the visual arts, illustrating your answer with reference to specific works of art.

2. Describe the principles of sonata form and compare it to musical form in the Baroque period.

3. What were the main schools of philosophical thought in eighteenth-century France? How are these expressed in the writings of Voltaire?

4. Describe the use of satire in the works of Pope and Swift. What are the authors' aims, and how successful are they?

5. How were the social and political developments that led to the French Revolution reflected in the arts?

 Visit the *Culture & Values* Companion website at **www.cengage.com/art/Cunningham/Cultureand Values7E** and the *Humanities Resource Center* for an array of primary source readings, key terms with pronunciations, flash cards, quizzes, and study materials designed especially to help you do well in this course.

CHAPTER 17
THE ROMANTIC ERA

The Romantic Era saw an ever larger public interest in the arts. Novels circulated widely, and the popular press drew increasing numbers of readers. Even poetry, particularly that of Lord Byron, created enthusiasm. Paintings became the subjects of general discussion (see Figure 17:15) and opera flourished. All of this arose out of a society transformed by the rapid growth of industrial cities in the nineteenth century. By the 1870s, approximately one-third of all Western Europeans, regardless of class or income, lived in cities.

Crowds of provincials flocked to the cities to enjoy metropolitan life. One visitor to Paris described it as "a glass beehive, a treat to the student of humanity." Great cities like London, Paris, and Vienna provided public gardens, fireworks, and dance halls to the growing working class. For the rich there was the glittering life of parties and balls characterized in Verdi's opera *La Traviata*, which was based on the real life of the Parisian courtesan, Marie Duplessis. Described by one admirer as "a young woman of exquisite distinction, a pure and delicate type of beauty," Marie, like Verdi's Violetta, died at twenty-three of tuberculosis, a disease in large measure spread by the overcrowded and unsanitary conditions that were common in the sudden growth of large cities in the nineteenth century.

So vast a change in the lives of millions outstripped society's ability to keep pace, and the need for urban planning became urgent. With the arrival of the railways and, in London and Paris, subways, cities reoriented around station terminals. As industries, heavy and light, spread throughout the cities, overcrowding and squalor followed. Public hygiene required the laying of underground sewers and water pipes for the first time since the Roman Empire. Many who arrived from declining farms in search of their fortunes drifted into marginal jobs, rag-picking, collecting human excrement, and public welfare programs sprang up to address poverty. Others migrants turned to crime. In 1829, Sir Robert Peel established the first British police force whose members became known as "bobbies," after their founder.

Against this background of extremes—a society that one migrant to London called a "wilderness of human beings"—many Romantic artists led the social and political movements of their times.

◆ *The Iron Works of Colebrook Dale*, William Pickett, 1805, from *The Romantic and Picturesque Scenery of England and Wales* (Image © British Library, London/HIP/Art Resource, NY)

THE CONCERNS OF ROMANTICISM

The tide of revolution that swept away much of the old political order in Europe and America in the last quarter of the eighteenth century had momentous consequences for the arts. Both the American and the French revolutions had in fact used art as a means of expressing their spiritual rejection of the aristocratic society against which they were physically rebelling, and both had adopted the Neo-Classical style to do so. Jacques-

Louis David's images of stern Roman virtue (see Figure 16.2) and Jefferson's evocation of the simple grandeur of Classical architecture (see Figure 16.18) represented, as it were, the revolutionaries' view of themselves and their accomplishments. Neo-Classicism, however, barely survived into the beginning of the nineteenth century. The movement that replaced it, Romanticism, eventually dominated virtually every aspect of nineteenth-century artistic achievement.

The essence of Romanticism is particularly difficult to describe because it is far more concerned with broad general attitudes than with specific stylistic fea-

GENERAL EVENTS	ART
1765	**1765** Copley, *Samuel Quincey* **1784–1785** David, *Oath of the Horatii*
1789	
REVOLUTIONARY AND NAPOLEONIC WARS **1789** French Revolution begins **1793–1795** Reign of Terror in France **1799–1804** Napoleon rules France as consul **1804–1814** Napoleon rules France as emperor **1812** Failure of Napoleon's Russian campaign **1814** Stephenson's first locomotive **1814–1815** Congress of Vienna	**1799** Goya becomes court painter to Charles IV of Spain; *The Family of Charles IV* (1800) **19th cent.** Romantic emphasis on emotion, nature, exotic images, faraway lands **1808** Girodet-Trioson, *The Entombment of Atala*, inspired by Chateaubriand's romantic novel **1809** Friedrich, *Abbey in an Oak Forest* **1811** Ingres, *Jupiter and Thetis* **1814** Goya, *May 3, 1808*, a retreat from idealism in art
1815	
GROWTH OF INDUSTRIALIZATION **1815** Napoleon escapes Elba; defeated at Battle of Waterloo **1815–1850** Industrialization of England **1816** Wreck of French vessel *Medusa* **1821–1829** Greek War of Independence against Turks **1830–1860** Industrialization of France and Belgium **1837–1901** Reign of Queen Victoria in England **1840–1870** Industrialization of Germany	**1818–1819** Géricault, *Raft of the Medusa*, first exhibited 1819 **1820–1822** Goya paints nightmare scenes on walls of his house; *Saturn Devouring One of His Sons* **1821** Constable, *Hay Wain* **1824** Delacroix, *Massacre at Chios* **1826** Delacroix, *The Death of Sardanapalus* **c. 1830** Social realism follows romanticism; Daumier, *The Legislative Belly* (1834) **c. 1830s** Development of national styles. American artists influenced by Transcendentalism; Cole, *The Ox Bow* (1836) **1844** Turner, *Rain, Steam, and Speed*
1848	
AGE OF NATIONALISM **1848** Revolutionary uprisings throughout Europe **1860–1870** Unification of Italy **1861–1865** American Civil War **1866–1871** Unified Germany **1867** Canada granted dominion status; British Factory Act gives workers Saturday afternoons off **1869** First transcontinental railroad completed in United States	**1855** Courbet, *The Studio: A Real Allegory of the Last Seven Years of My Life* **c. 1860** American luminist painting develops; Heade, *Newburyport Meadows* (1876)
1870	
1876 Bell patents the telephone **1888** Pasteur Institute founded in Paris	**1870** Homer, *Eaglehead, Manchester, Massachusetts* **1870** Corot, *Ville d'Avray* **c. 1880** Eakins searches for realism, *The Swimming Hole* (1885)
1900	

tures. Painters, writers, and musicians in the nineteenth century shared several concerns in their approach to their art. First was the important emphasis they placed on personal feelings and their expression. Ironically enough, the revolutionary movements that had encouraged artists to rebel against the conventional styles of the early eighteenth century had proved too restricting and conventional.

Second, emphasis on emotion rather than intellect led to the expression of subjective rather than objective visions; after all, the emotions known best are those we have experienced. The Romantics used art to explore and dissect their own personal hopes and fears (more often the latter) rather than as a means to arrive at some general truth. This in turn produced a third attitude of Romanticism—its love of the fantastic and the exotic—which made it possible to probe more deeply into an individual's creative imagination. Dreams, for example, were a way of releasing the mind from the constraints of everyday experience and bringing to the surface those dark visions reason had submerged, as the Spanish artist Francisco Goya shows us unforgettably in a famous etching [**Fig. 17.2**]. Artists felt free to invent their own dream worlds. Some chose to reconstruct such ages

ARCHITECTURE	LITERATURE & PHILOSOPHY	MUSIC
1785–1796 Jefferson, State Capitol, Richmond, Virginia	**1773** Goethe leads *Sturm und Drang* movement against Neo-Classicism **1774** Goethe, *The Sorrows of Young Werther*	**1788** Mozart composes last three symphonies
	1790 Kant, *Critique of Judgment*, expounding Transcendental Idealism **1794** Blake, "London" **1798** Wordsworth, "Tintern Abbey" **1807–1830** Philosophy of Hegel published in Germany **1808** Goethe's *Faust*, Part I	**1795** Debut of Beethoven as pianist Development from classical to romantic music most evident in work of Beethoven; "Pathétique" Sonata (1799) **1804** First performance of Beethoven's "Eroica" Symphony, originally meant to honor Napoleon **1804–1808** Beethoven's Symphony No. 5, first performed 1808 **1814** Beethoven's opera *Fidelio* performed
19th cent. Sequence of revival styles affected by growth of industry and technology **1836** Barry and Pugin, neo-Gothic Houses of Parliament, London	**1819** Schopenhauer, *The World as Will and Idea*; Keats, *Ode to a Nightingale* **1820** Shelley, *Prometheus Unbound* **1821** Byron, *Don Juan* **1824** Byron dies in Greece **1829–1847** Balzac, *The Human Comedy*, 90 realistic novels **1832** Goethe, *Faust*, Part II **1836–1860** Transcendentalist movement in New England, United States **1837–1838** Dickens, *Oliver Twist* **1840** Poe, *Tales of the Grotesque* **1846** Sand, *Lucrezia Floriani* **1847** E. Brontë, *Wuthering Heights*	**c. 1815–1828** Schubert creates genre of art song *(lied)*, setting to music poetry of Goethe, Schiller, others **1822** Schubert, "Unfinished" Symphony **1824** First performance of Beethoven's Symphony No. 9 with choral version of Schiller's "Ode to Joy" as finale **1830** Berlioz, *Symphonie fantastique* **1831** Bellini's *bel canto* opera *Norma* performed **1835** Donizetti, *Lucia di Lammermoor* **c. 1835–c. 1845** Virtuoso performance at peak; brilliant composer-performers create works of immense technical difficulty **1839** Chopin completes Twenty-Four Preludes, Op. 28 **1842** Verdi's *Nabucco* symbolic of Italians' suffering under Austrian rule **1846** Berlioz, *The Damnation of Faust*
1861–1875 Garnier, neo-Baroque Opéra, Paris **1865** Reynaud, Gare du Nord, Paris	**1848** Marx, *Communist Manifesto* **1851** Melville, *Moby Dick* **1854** Thoreau, *Walden* **1855** Whitman, *Leaves of Grass* **1856–1857** Flaubert, *Madame Bovary* **1859** Darwin publishes theory of evolution, *On the Origin of Species by Means of Natural Selection* **1862** Hugo, *Les Misérables* **1863–1869** Tolstoy, *War and Peace*	**1851–1874** Wagner, *The Ring of the Nibelung*; first staged at new Bayreuth opera house 1876 **1853** First performances of Verdi's *La Traviata* and *Il Trovatore* **1865** Wagner experiments with harmony in *Tristan and Isolde*
	1873–1877 Tolstoy, *Anna Karenina* **1890** Dickinson's poems first published, four years after her death	**1874** First production of Moussorgsky's opera *Boris Godunov* in St. Petersburg **1876** Brahms, Symphony No. 1 in C Minor **1882** Wagner, *Parsifal* **1887** Verdi, *Otello*; Bruckner begins Symphony No. 8 in C Minor

◆ **17.2** Francisco Goya, *The Sleep of Reason Produces Monsters* (*El sueño de la razón produce monstruos*), 1797–1798. The precise meaning of the work is not clear, but it evidently represents the inability of reason to banish monstrous thoughts. Its title is written on the desk below the student, who sleeps with his head on his textbooks.

Plate 43 from Los Caprichos. Etching and aquatint, 8″ x 6″ (203 x 152 mm). Image © Victoria and Albert Museum, London, UK/Art Resource, NY

Table 17.1 *Principal Characteristics of the Romantic Movement*

The Expression of Personal Feelings

Chopin, *Preludes*
Goya, *The Family of Charles IV* [17.12]
Goethe, *The Sorrows of Young Werther*

Self-Analysis

Berlioz, *Symphonie fantastique*
Poetry of Keats
Whitman, *Leaves of Grass*

Love of the Fantastic and Exotic

Music and performances of Paganini
Girodet-Trioson, *The Entombment of Atala* [17.14]
Delacroix, *The Death of Sardanapalus* [17.17]

Interest in Nature

Beethoven, *Pastoral Symphony*
Constable, *Hay Wain* [17.24]
Wordsworth, poetry
Emerson, *The American Scholar*

Nationalism and Political Commitment

Verdi, *Nabucco*
Smetana, *My Fatherland*
Goya, *The Third of May, 1808* [17.11]
Byron's support of the Greeks

Erotic Love and the Eternal Feminine

Goethe, *Faust*, Part II
Wagner, *Tristan and Isolde*

long past as the medieval, a period that was particularly popular. The design of Britain's Houses of Parliament [**Fig. 17.3**], begun in 1836, reflected the Gothic style of six centuries earlier. Others preferred to imagine remote and exotic lands and dreamed of life in the mysterious Orient or on a primitive desert island. Still others simply trusted to the powers of their imagination and invented a fantasy world of their own.

A fourth characteristic of much Romantic art is a mystical attachment to the world of nature that was also the result of the search for new sensations. Painters turned increasingly to landscape, composers sought to evoke the rustling of leaves in a forest or the noise of a storm, and poets tried to express their sense of union with the natural world. Most eighteenth-century artists had turned to nature in search of order and reason. In the nineteenth century, the wild unpredictability of nature would be emphasized, depicted neither objec-

tively nor realistically but as a mirror of the artist's individual emotions. At the same time, the romantic communion with nature expressed a rejection of the Classical notion of a world centered on human activity.

These attitudes, and the new imaginative and creative power they unleashed, had two different but equally important effects on the relationship between the artist and society. On the one hand, many creative artists became increasingly alienated from their public. Whereas they had once filled a precise role in providing entertainment or satisfying political and religious demands, now their self-expressive works met no particular needs except their own.

On the other hand, an increasing number of artists sought to express the national characteristics of their people via art. Abandoning the common artistic language of earlier periods and instead developing local styles that used traditional folk elements, artists were able to stimulate (and in some cases to initiate) the growth of national consciousness and the demand for national independence (see map, "Europe in 1848"). This was particularly effective in the Russian and Austrian empires (which incorporated many nationalities) and even in America, which had always been only on the fringe of the European cultural tradition, but it also became an increasingly strong tendency in the art of France and Italy, countries that had hitherto shared the same general culture. Thus while some artists were retreating into a private world of their own creation, others were in the forefront of the social and political movements of their own age (see **Table 17.1**).

◆ **17.3** Houses of Parliament, London, 1836–1860, architects, Sir Charles Barry and Augustus Welby Pugin. The relative symmetry of the façade (940 feet; 287 meters long) is broken only by the placement of the towers—Gothic in style, as is the decorative detail. *(Image © Vanni/Art Resource, NY)*

THE INTELLECTUAL BACKGROUND

It might be expected that a movement like Romanticism, which placed a high value on the feelings of the moment at the expense of conscious reason, would remain relatively unaffected by intellectual principles. Notwithstanding, several Romantic artists did in fact draw inspiration from contemporary philosophy. A rapid survey of the chief intellectual developments of the nineteenth century therefore provides a background to the artistic ones.

Kant The ideas that proved most attractive to the Romantic imagination had developed in Germany at the end of the eighteenth century. Their chief spokesman was Immanuel Kant (1724–1804), whose *Critique of Judgment* (1790) defined the pleasure we derive from art as "disinterested satisfaction." Kant conceived of art as uniting opposite principles. It unites the general with the particular, for example, and reason with the imagination. For Kant, the only analogy for the way in which art is at the same time useless and yet useful was to be found in the world of nature.

Hegel Even more influential than Kant was Georg Wilhelm Friedrich Hegel (1770–1831), whose ideas continued to affect attitudes toward art and artistic criticism into the twentieth century. Like Kant, Hegel stressed art's ability to reconcile and make sense of opposites, and to provide a **synthesis** of the two opposing components of human existence, called **thesis** (pure, infinite being) and **antithesis** (the world of nature). This process, he held, applied to the workings of the mind and also to the workings of world history, through the development and realization of what he called the "World Spirit." Hegel's influence on his successors lay less in the details of his philosophical system than in his acceptance of divergences and his attempt to reconcile them. The search for a way to combine differences, to permit the widest variety of experience, is still the basis of much contemporary thinking about the arts.

Both Kant and Hegel developed their ideas in the relatively optimistic intellectual climate of the late eighteenth and early nineteenth centuries, and their approach both to art and to existence is basically positive. A different position was that of Arthur Schopenhauer (1788–1860), whose major work, *The World as Will and Idea* (1819), expresses the belief that the dominating will, or power, in the world is evil. At the time of its appearance, Schopenhauer's work made little impression, largely because of the popularity of Kant's and Hegel's idealism. Schopenhauer did not help matters by launching a bitter personal attack on Hegel. But the failure of the nationalist uprisings of 1848 in many parts of Europe produced a growing mood of pessimism and gloom, against which background Schopenhauer's vision of a world condemned perpetually to be ravaged by strife and misery seemed more convincing. Thus, his philosophy, if it did not mold the Romantic movement, came to reflect its growing despondency.

Marx It must be admitted that many of the major developments in nineteenth-century thought had little direct impact on the contemporary arts. The most influential of all nineteenth-century philosophers was probably Karl Marx (1818–1883), whose belief in the inherent evil of capitalism and in the historical inevitability of a proletarian revolution was powerfully expressed in his *Communist Manifesto* (1848).

Marx's belief that revolution was both unavoidable and necessary was based at least in part on his own observation of working conditions in industrial England, where his friend and fellow communist Friedrich Engels (1820–1895) had inherited a textile factory. Marx and Engels both believed that the factory workers,

EUROPE IN 1848
— Boundaries of German Confederation
● Centers of Revolution

although creating wealth for the middle classes, derived no personal benefit. Living in overcrowded, unsanitary conditions, the workers were deprived of any effective political power and only kept quiet by the drug of religion, which offered them the false hope of rewards in a future life. The plight of the working classes seemed to Marx to transcend all national boundaries and create a universal proletariat who could only achieve freedom through revolution: "Workers of the world, unite! You have nothing to lose but your chains!" The drive to political action was underpinned by Marx's economic philosophy, with its emphasis on the value of labor and, more generally, on the supreme importance of economic and social conditions as the true moving forces behind historical events. This so-called materialist concept of history was to have worldwide repercussions in the century that followed Marx's death. More contemporary writers such as Bertolt Brecht (1898–1956) have embraced Marxist principles, and Marxist critics have

developed a school of aesthetic criticism that applies standards based on Marxist doctrines. During the nineteenth and early twentieth centuries, however, Marx's influence was exclusively social and political.

Marx clearly laid out his views on the arts. Art has the ability to contribute to important social and political changes, and is thus a determining factor in history. Neither is artistic output limited to the upper or more prosperous social classes; according to the "principle of uneven development," a higher social order does not necessarily produce a correspondingly high artistic achievement. Capitalism is, in fact, hostile to artistic development because of its obsession with money and profit. As for styles, the only one appropriate for the class struggle and the new state is realism, which would be understood by the widest audience. Lenin inherited and developed this doctrine further when he ordered that art should be a specific "reflection" of reality, and used the party to enforce the official cultural policy.

※◇ VOICES OF THEIR TIMES

Isabella Bird Meets a Mountain Man

Isabella Bird (1831–1904), the English travel writer, was a tireless traveler throughout America, Asia, and Australia. When Isabella finally settled down for a while and married, her husband observed that he "had only one formidable rival in Isabella's heart, and that is the high Table Land of Central Asia." In 1873, she met Rocky Mountain Jim in Colorado—"a man who any woman might love, but who no sane woman would marry."

Roused by the growling of the dog, his owner came out, a broad, thickset man, about the middle height, with an old cap on his head, and wearing a gray hunting-suit much the worse for wear (almost falling to pieces, in fact), a digger's scarf knotted round his waist, a knife in his belt, and a bosom friend, a revolver, sticking out of the breast pocket of his coat; his feet, which were very small, were bare, except for some dilapidated moccasins made of horse hide. The marvel was how his clothes hung together, and on him. The scarf round his waist must have had something to do with it. His face was remarkable. He is a man about 45, and must have been strikingly handsome. He has large gray-blue eyes, deeply set, with well-marked eyebrows, a handsome aquiline nose, and a very handsome mouth. His face was smooth shaven except for a dense moustache and imperial [a pointed beard]. Tawny hair, in thin uncared for curls, fell from under his hunter's cap and over his collar. One eye was entirely gone, and the loss made one side of the face repulsive, while the other might have been modeled in marble. "Desperado" was written in large letters all over him. I almost repented of having sought his acquaintance.

His first impulse was to swear at the dog, but on seeing a lady he contented himself with kicking him, and coming up to me he raised his cap, showing as he did so a magnificently formed brow and head, and in a cultured tone of voice asked if there were anything he could do for me? I asked for some water, and he brought some in a battered tin, gracefully apologizing for not having anything more presentable. We entered into conversation, and as he spoke I forgot both his reputation and appearance, for his manner was that of a chivalrous gentleman, his accent refined, and his language easy and elegant. I inquired about some beavers' paws which were drying, and in a moment they hung on the horn of my saddle. Apropos of the wild animals of the region, he told me that the loss of his eye was owing to a recent encounter with a grizzly bear, which after giving him a death hug, tearing him all over, breaking his arm and scratching out his eye, had left him for dead.

From *A Lady's Life in the Rocky Mountains* (London, 1879); reprinted by Virago Press (London, 1982).

Industry The nineteenth century saw vast changes in the lives of millions of people, as industrial development and scientific progress overthrew centuries-old ways. The railroad, using engines powered by steam, first appeared in 1825 between Stockton and Darlington in England. By 1850, there were 6000 miles of track in Britain, 3000 in Germany, 2000 in France, and the beginnings of a rail system in Austria, Italy, and Russia. The economic impact was overwhelming. The railroad represented a new industry that fulfilled a universal need; it provided jobs and offered opportunities for capital investment. At the same time, it increased the demand for coal and iron.

Industry soon overtook agriculture as the source of national wealth. With the growth of mass production in factories, the cities connected by rail became vast urban centers, attracting wholesale migration from the countryside. The number of persons living in cities rose dramatically. The population of Turin, in northern Italy, was 86,000 in 1800, 137,000 by 1850, and more than 200,000 by 1860. Half of Britain's inhabitants lived in cities by 1850, the first time in history that this was true for any large society. The results were by no means always pleasant; one Londoner described his city in the 1820s as "a wilderness of human beings."

In science, constant research brought a host of new discoveries. Experiments in magnetism and electricity advanced physics. Using new chemical elements, the French chemist Louis Pasteur (1822–1895) explored the process of fermentation and invented "pasteurization"—a discovery that helped improve the safety of food. Equally beneficial was Pasteur's demonstration that disease is spread by living but invisible (to the naked eye, at least) germs, which can be combated by vaccination and the sterilization of medical equipment.

Darwin No single book affected nineteenth-century readers more powerfully than *On the Origin of Species by Means of Natural Selection* by Charles Robert Darwin (1809–1882), which appeared in 1859. As a student at Cambridge, in 1831 Darwin was offered the post of naturalist aboard the H.M.S. *Beagle*, a ship ready to embark on a surveying expedition around the world. In the course of the voyage, Darwin studied geological formations, fossils, and the distribution of plant and animal types. On examining his material, Darwin became convinced that species were not fixed categories, as had always been held, but were instead capable of variation. Drawing on the population theories of Malthus, and the geological studies of Sir Charles Lyell, Darwin developed his theory of evolution as an attempt to explain the changes, disappearances, and new appearances of various species.

According to Darwin, animals and plants evolve by a process of **natural selection** (he chose the term to contrast it with the "artificial selection" used by animal breeders). Over time, some variations of each species survive while others die out. Those likely to survive are those best suited to prevailing environmental conditions—a process called by one of Darwin's followers "the survival of the fittest." Changes in the environment would lead to adjustments within the species. The first publication of this theory appeared in 1858, in the form of a short scientific paper; *On the Origin of Species* appeared a year later. In 1871 Darwin published *The Descent of Man*, in which he claimed that the human race is descended from an animal of the anthropoid group.

The impact of both books was spectacular. Their author quietly continued his research and tried to avoid the popular controversy surrounding his work. Church leaders thundered their denunciations of a theory that utterly contradicted the notion that humans, along with everything else, had been created by God in accordance with a divine plan. Scientists and freethinkers stoutly defended Darwin, often enlarging his claims. Others held that the development of modern capitalism and industrial society represented a clear demonstration of the "survival of the fittest," although Darwin never endorsed this "Social Darwinism" (see **Table 17.2**).

Achievements in science and technology are reflected to a certain extent in Romantic art, although chiefly from a negative point of view. The growing industrialization of life in the great cities, and the effect of inventions like the railway train on urban architecture stimulated a "back-to-nature" movement, as Romanticism provided an escape from the grim realities of urbanization and industrialization. Furthermore, at a time when many people felt submerged and depersonalized in overcrowded cities, the Romantic emphasis on the individual and on self-analysis found an appreciative audience. Many artists contrasted the growing problems of urban life with an idyllic (and highly imaginative) picture of rustic bliss.

Table 17.2 *Nineteenth-Century Scientific and Technological Developments*

1814	Stephenson builds first locomotive
1821	Faraday discovers principle of electric dynamo
1825	Erie Canal opened in the United States
	First railway completed (England)
1839	Daguerre introduces his process of photography
1844	Morse perfects the telegraph
1853	First International Exhibition of Industry (New York)
1858	Transatlantic cable begun (completed 1866)
1859	Darwin publishes *On the Origin of Species*
	First oil well drilled (in Pennsylvania)
1867	Nobel invents dynamite
1869	Transcontinental railway completed in the United States
	Suez Canal opened
1876	Bell patents the telephone
1879	Edison invents the electric light
1885	First internal combustion engines using gasoline

Scientific ideas had something of the same negative effect on nineteenth-century artists. The English Victorian writers (so-called after Queen Victoria, who reigned from 1837 to 1901) responded to the growing scientific materialism of the age. Although few were, strictly speaking, Romantics, much of their resistance to progress in science and industry and their portrayal of its evil effects has its roots in the Romantic tradition.

MUSIC IN THE ROMANTIC ERA

BEETHOVEN

For many of the Romantics, music was the supreme art. Free from the intellectual concepts involved in language and the physical limits inherent in the visual arts, it was capable of the most wholehearted and intuitive expression of emotion. Ludwig van Beethoven (1770–1827), widely regarded as the pioneer of musical Romanticism, also manifested many characteristically Romantic attitudes—love of nature, a passionate belief in the freedom of the individual, and a fiery temperament—so it is not surprising that he has come to be regarded as the prototype of the Romantic artist [**Fig. 17.4**]. When Beethoven wrote proudly to one of his most loyal aristocratic supporters, "There will always be thousands of princes, but there is only one Beethoven," he spoke for a new generation of creators. When he used the last movement of his Symphony No. 9 to preach the doctrine of universal brotherhood, he inspired countless ordinary listeners by his fervor. Even today familiarity with Beethoven's music has not dulled its ability to give dramatic expression to the noblest of human sentiments.

Although Beethoven's music served as the springboard for the Romantic movement in music, his own roots were deep in the classical tradition. He pushed classicism to the limits through use of the sonata allegro form. In spirit, furthermore, his work is representative of the Age of Enlightenment and the revolutionary mood

◆ **17.4** Ferdinand Georg Waldmuller, *Ludwig van Beethoven*, 1823. Painted a year before the first performance of Beethoven's Symphony No. 9 in D Minor, the portrait emphasizes the composer's stubborn independence by both the set of the mouth and the casual, even untidy, dress and hair. Beethoven, who became irascible in his later years, allowed the artist only one sitting for his portrait commissioned by one of his music publishers.

Canvas, 28″ x 31″ (72 x 78 cm). Breitkopf und Haertel, Leipzig, Germany// © *Erich Lessing/Art Resource, NY*

of the turn of the century, as seen in the words and music of his opera *Fidelio*. A complex and many-sided genius, Beethoven transcended the achievements of the age in which he was born and set the musical tone for the nineteenth century.

Beethoven was born in Bonn, Germany, where he received his musical training from his father, an alcoholic. Beethoven's father saw the possibility of producing a musical prodigy in his son and forced him to practice hours at the keyboard, often locking him in his room and beating him on his return from drinking bouts. All possibilities of a happy family life were brought to an end in 1787 when Beethoven's mother died and his father descended into advanced alcoholism. Beethoven sought compensation in the home of the von Breuning family, where he acted as private tutor. It was there that he met other musicians and artists and developed a lifelong love of literature. He also struck up a friendship with a local minor aristocrat, Count Waldstein, who remained his devoted admirer until the composer's death.

In 1792 Waldstein was one of the aristocrats who helped Beethoven go to Vienna to study with Haydn, who was then regarded as the greatest composer of his day; but although Haydn agreed to give him lessons, the young Beethoven's impatience and suspicion, and Haydn's deficiencies as a teacher, did not make for a happy relationship. Nevertheless, many of the works Beethoven wrote during his first years in Vienna are essentially classical in both form and spirit; only by the end of the century had he begun to extend the emotional range of his music.

CD Track 11
Ludwig van Beethoven, "Pathétique" Piano Sonata No. 8 in C Minor, Finale

One of the first pieces to express the characteristically Beethovenian spirit is his Piano Sonata No. 8 in C Minor, Op. 13, generally known as the "Pathétique." Beethoven's sonata is characteristic of Romantic music in its strong expression of personal feelings. Its three movements, of which we hear the last, tell a continuous story in which the hero (the composer) fights an increasingly desperate battle against what seems his certain destiny. Unlike the tragic resignation of Mozart's Symphony No. 40 (see Chapter 16), which accepts its suffering with Classical resignation, Beethoven's Romantic spirit drives him to fight.

After a first movement, in which grim resistance gives way to forceful, turbulent struggle, and a second movement with a serene vision of beauty that offers hope of relief, Beethoven returns to the battle. The final movement appears to arrive at a synthesis between the drama of the opening and the hushed beauty of the slow movement. The music opens in a fragile, reflective mood. The composer has not yet recovered from the solemn beauty of the slow movement, and we hear his changes of mood echoed in the music, as if he hesitates to prepare himself for further combat. His repeated instruction to the performer is "tranquillo" ("peacefully"). Yet the mood darkens and the music is marked "agitato" ("with agitation"). The strife-ridden mood of earlier sweeps away the sense of resignation. There are brief moments of respite, and, just before the very end, the opening theme returns quietly and "with simplicity." Yet the conclusion is both decisive and sudden. The piano hurtles down a violent scale, and a final brutal chord puts an end to the piece, with its alternating moods of faint hope and despair.

Before the Romantics, no one had used music for such frank expression of the most fluctuating emotions, and Beethoven's use of abrupt changes of volume, his hesitations, and his sense of self-revelation are all typical of the new musical era.

It is important to understand precisely how Beethoven used music in a new and revolutionary way. Other composers had written music to express emotion long before Beethoven's time, from Bach's outpouring of religious fervor to Mozart's evocation of human joy and sorrow. What is different about Beethoven is that his emotion is autobiographical. His music tells us how he feels, what his succession of moods is, and what conclusion he reaches. It does other things at the same time, and at this early stage in his career for the most part it self-consciously follows classical principles of construction, but the vivid communication of personal emotions is its prime concern. That Beethoven's range was not limited to anger and frustration is immediately demonstrated by the beautiful and consoling middle slow movement of the "Pathétique" with its lyrical main theme, but the final movement returns to turbulent passion.

Parallels for the turbulent style of the "Pathétique" can be found in other contemporary arts, especially literature, but although to some extent Beethoven was responding to the climate of the times, there can be no doubt that he was also expressing a personal reaction to the terrible tragedy that had begun to afflict him as early as 1796. In that year the first symptoms of his deafness began to appear; by 1798, his hearing had grown very weak; and by 1802, he was virtually totally deaf.

Nonetheless, although obviously affected by his condition, Beethoven's music was not exclusively concerned with his own fate. The same heroic attitude with which he faced his personal problems was also given universal expression, never more stupendously than in the Symphony No. 3 in E Flat, Op. 55, subtitled the "Eroica" or "Heroic" Symphony. As early as 1799, the French ambassador to Vienna had suggested that Beethoven write a symphony in honor of Napoleon Bonaparte. At the time Napoleon was widely regarded as a popular hero who had triumphed over his humble origins to rise to power as a champion of liberty and democracy. Beethoven's own democratic temperament made him one of Napoleon's many admirers. The symphony was duly begun, but in 1804—the year of its completion—Napoleon had himself crowned emperor. When Beethoven heard the news, he angrily crossed out Napoleon's name on the title page. The first printed edition, which appeared in 1806, bore only the dedication "to celebrate the memory of a great man."

It would be a mistake to view the "Eroica" as merely a portrait of Napoleon. Rather, inspired by what he saw as the heroic stature of the French leader, Beethoven created his own heroic world in sound, in a work of vast dimensions. The first movement alone lasts for almost as long as many a classical symphony. Its complicated structure requires considerable concentration on the part of the listener. The form is basically the classical sonata allegro form (see Chapter 16) but on a much grander scale and with a wealth of musical ideas. Yet the principal theme of the movement, which the cellos announce at the beginning after two hammering, impatient chords demand our attention, is of a rocklike sturdiness and simplicity.

Beethoven's genius emerges as he uses this and other similarly straightforward ideas to build his mighty structure. Throughout the first movement his use of harmony and, in particular, discord, adds to the emotional impact, especially in the middle of the development section, where slashing dissonances seem to tear apart the orchestra. His classical grounding emerges in the recapitulation, where the infinite variety of the development section gives way to a restored sense of unity; the movement ends triumphantly with a long and thrilling coda. The formal structure is recognizably classical, but the intensity of expression, depth of personal commitment, and heroic defiance are all totally Romantic.

The second movement of the "Eroica" is a worthy successor to the first. A funeral march on the same massive scale, it alternates a mood of epic tragedy—which has been compared, in terms of impact, with the works of the Greek playwright Aeschylus—with rays of consolation that at times achieve a transcendental exaltation. Although the many subtleties of construction deserve the closest attention, even a first hearing will reveal the grandeur of Beethoven's conception.

The third and fourth movements relax the tension. For the third, Beethoven replaces the stately minuet of the classical symphony with a **scherzo**—the word literally means "joke" and is used to describe a fast moving, generally lighthearted piece of music. Beethoven's introduction of this kind of music, which in his hands often has something of the crude flavor of a peasant dance, is another illustration of his "democratization" of the symphony. The last movement is a brilliant and energetic series of variations on a theme Beethoven had composed a few years earlier for a ballet he had written on the subject (from Classic mythology) of Prometheus, who defied the ancient gods by giving mortals the gift of fire, for which he was punished by Zeus—a final reference to the heroic mood of the entire work.

Many of the ideas and ideals that permeate the "Eroica" reappear throughout Beethoven's work. His love of liberty and hatred of oppression are expressed in his only opera, *Fidelio*, which describes how a faithful wife rescues her husband who has been unjustly imprisoned for his political views. A good performance of *Fidelio* is still one of the most uplifting and exalting experiences music has to offer.

CD Track 12
Ludwig van Beethoven, Symphony No. 5 in C Minor, First Movement

This is probably the most famous opening of the most famous symphony ever composed. Nothing could be further from the Classical balance of Haydn and Mozart than Beethoven's Romantic drive and passion. The mood of pathos and agitation is present from the opening hammering motive that permeates the entire movement, and eventually drives it to its fatal conclusion.

The careful listener will hear that Beethoven constructs his torrent of sound according to the principles of traditional sonata form (this performance does not repeat the opening, "exposition," section). The first section ends with a pause, and the middle "development" section concentrates almost exclusively on the opening motive, which is passed around the orchestra. We then hurtle into the "recapitulation" which repeats the opening section with one important addition: a pathetic, almost weeping solo passage for the oboe, which plays alone while the rest of the orchestra remains silent. Then, as the recapitulation comes to its stormy end, Beethoven plunges into an extended "coda" (conclusion), which builds up to new heights of tension and violence, before its abrupt conclusion.

Never before in the history of music had any composer maintained such emotional intensity and concentration throughout a symphonic movement. It is difficult for us today to realize the revolutionary impact of his music on Beethoven's contemporaries as an expression of personal feelings. When the French composer Hector Berlioz (the creator of the next selection on this CD, and himself much influenced by Beethoven) took his old teacher of composition to the first Paris performance of the Fifth Symphony, the old man was so bewildered that, on leaving, he couldn't put on his hat because, Berlioz tells us, he couldn't find his head.

Beethoven's Symphony No. 6, Op. 68, called the "Pastoral," consists of a Romantic evocation of nature and the emotions it arouses, while his Symphony No. 9, Op. 125, is perhaps the most complete statement of the human striving to conquer all obstacles and win through to universal peace and joy. In it Beethoven introduced a chorus and soloists to give voice to the "Ode to Joy" by his compatriot Friedrich von Schiller (1759–1805). The symphony represents the most complete artistic vindication of Kant's Transcendental Idealism. It is also one of the most influential works of the entire Romantic movement.

INSTRUMENTAL MUSIC AFTER BEETHOVEN

Berlioz After Beethoven, music could never again return to its former mood of classical objectivity. Although Beethoven's music may remain unsurpassed for its universalization of individual emotion, his successors tried—and in large measure succeeded—to find new ways to express their own feelings. Among the first to follow Beethoven was Hector Berlioz (1803–1869), the most distinguished French Romantic composer who produced, among other typically Romantic works, *The Damnation of Faust*, a setting of Part One of Goethe's work, and the *Symphonie fantastique* ("Fantastic Symphony"), which describes the hallucinations of an opium-induced dream. In both of these, Berlioz used the full Romantic apparatus of dreams, witches, demons, and the grotesque to lay bare the artist's innermost feelings.

In 1830 (three years after the death of Beethoven) Berlioz presented to an astonished Parisian public his "Fantastic Symphony," subtitled "Episode in the Life of an Artist." Clearly this was self-confessed expression of personal feelings and self-analysis at its most Romantic.

Berlioz himself provides the background. A young musician of extraordinary sensibility, in the depths of despair because of hopeless love has poisoned himself with opium. The drug is too feeble to kill him, but plunges him into a heavy sleep accompanied by weird visions. His sensations, emotions, and memories become transformed into musical images and ideas. The Beloved herself becomes a melody—what Berlioz calls his *idée fixe* ("fixed idea")—that recurs throughout all five movements of the work. The writing for the orchestra introduces new sound colors and combinations, in order to render the horror of the scene, in particular, Berlioz' highly unusual use of the woodwinds.

The last movement, from which we hear the opening section, depicts the funeral of the dreamer, who has seen his own execution in the preceding movement. The scene is that of a "Witches' Sabbath," and the music begins with a series of muffled groans and cries that convey a gradual assembly of cackling old witches. The theme that earlier represented the dreamer's lover, the Beloved, appears in a horribly distorted form played by the woodwinds, and at the climax of the tumult, the brass instruments hurl out the old Gregorian Chant theme of the **dies irae** ("day of wrath"), which forms part of the traditional Requiem Mass for the Dead. The brass blare combines with the witches' dance to form what the composer calls a "diabolical orgy."

It only remains for the historian to add that the "Beloved" in question was the Irish actress Harriet Smithson, whom Berlioz married in 1833, and from whom he separated in 1842.

Schubert A highly intimate and poetic form of Romantic self-revelation is the music of Franz Schubert (1797–1828), who explored in the few years before his premature death the new possibilities opened up by Beethoven in a wide range of musical forms. In general, Schubert was happiest when working on a small scale, as evidenced by his more than six hundred **Lieder** ("songs"), which are an inexhaustible store of musical and emotional expression.

On the whole, the more rhetorical nature of the symphonic form appealed to Schubert less, although the wonderful Symphony No. 8 in B Minor, called the "Unfinished" because he only completed two movements, combines great poetic feeling with a genuine sense of drama. His finest instrumental music was written for small groups of instruments. The two trios for piano, violin, and cello are rich in the heavenly melodies that seemed to come to him so easily; the second, slow movement of the Trio in E flat, Op. 100, touches profound depths of romantic expression. Like the slow movement of Mozart's Piano Concerto No. 27 in B Flat

CD Track 13
Hector Berlioz, *Symphonie fantastique*, Fifth Movement, "Dream of a Witches' Sabbath," opening section

◆ **17.5** Eugène Delacroix, *Frédéric Chopin*, 1838. Delacroix's portrait of his friend captures Chopin's Romantic introspection. Delacroix was a great lover of music, although perhaps surprisingly the great Romantic painter preferred the Classical Mozart to Beethoven.

Oil on canvas, 18″ x 15″ (45 x 38 cm). Musée du Louvre, Paris, France //
© Réunion des Musées Nationaux / Art Resource, NY

(see Chapter 16), its extreme beauty is tinged with an unutterable sorrow. But whereas Mozart seems to speak for humanity at large, Schubert moves us most deeply by communicating his own personal feelings.

Brahms Most nineteenth-century composers followed Beethoven in using the symphony as the vehicle for their most serious musical ideas. Robert Schumann (1810–1856) and his student Johannes Brahms (1833–1897) regarded the symphonic form as the most lofty means of musical expression, and each as a result wrote only four symphonies. Brahms did not even dare to write a symphony until he was forty-four and is said to have felt the presence of Beethoven's works "like the tramp of a giant" behind him. When it finally appeared, Brahms' Symphony No. 1 in C Minor, Op. 68, was inevitably compared to Beethoven's symphonies. Although Brahms' strong sense of form and conservative style won him the hostility of the arch-Romantics of the day, other critics hailed him as the true successor to Beethoven.

Both responses were, of course, extreme. Brahms' music certainly is Romantic with its emphasis on warm melody and a passion no less present for being held tightly in rein—but far from echoing the heaven-storming mood of many of the symphonies of his great predecessor, Brahms was really more at home in a relaxed vein. Although the Symphony No. 1 begins with a gesture of defiant grandeur akin to Beethoven's, the first movement ends by fading dreamily into a glowing tranquility. The lovely slow movement is followed not by a scherzo but by a quiet and graceful **intermezzo** ("interlude"), and only in the last movement are we returned to the mood of the opening.

Bruckner Closer to the more cosmic mood of the Beethoven symphonies are the nine symphonies of Anton Bruckner (1824–1896). A deeply religious man imbued with a romantic attachment to the beauties of nature, Bruckner combined his devout Catholicism and mystical vision in music of epic grandeur. It has often been remarked that Bruckner's music requires time and patience on the listener's part. His pace is leisurely and he creates huge structures in sound that demand our full concentration if we are to appreciate their "architecture." There is no lack of incidental beauty, however, and the rewards are immense. No other composer has been able to convey quite the tone of mystical exaltation that Bruckner achieves, above all in the slow movements of his last three symphonies. The **adagio** movement from the Symphony No. 8 in C Minor, for instance, moves from the desolate Romanticism of its opening theme to a mighty, blazing climax as thrilling and stirring as anything in nineteenth-century music.

THE AGE OF THE VIRTUOSOS

Beethoven's emphasis on the primacy of the artist inspired another series of Romantic composers to move in a different direction from that of the symphony. Beethoven had first made his reputation as a brilliant pianist, and much of his music—both for piano and for other instruments—was of considerable technical difficulty. As composers began to demand greater and greater feats of virtuosity from their performers, performing artists came to attract more attention. Singers had already, in the eighteenth century, commanded high fees and attracted crowds of fanatical admirers, and they continued to do so. Now, however, they were joined by instrumental virtuosos, some of whom were also highly successful composers.

Chopin The life of Frédéric Chopin (1810–1849) seems almost too Romantic to be true [**Fig. 17.5**]. Both in his piano performances and in the music he composed, he united the aristocratic fire of his native Poland with the elegance and sophistication of Paris, where he spent much of his life. His concerts created a sensation throughout Europe, while his piano works exploited (if they did not always create) new musical forms like the **nocturne**—a short piano piece in which an expressive, if often melancholy, melody floats over a murmuring

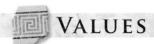

VALUES

Nationalism

One of the consequences of the rise of the cities and growing political consciousness was the development of nationalism: the identification of individuals with a nation-state, with its own culture and history. In the past, the units of which people felt a part were either smaller (a local region) or larger (a religious organization or a social class). In many cases, the nations with which people began to identify were either broken up into separate small states, as in the case of the future Germany and Italy, or formed part of a larger state: Hungary, Austria, and Serbia were all under the rule of the Hapsburg Empire, with Austria dominating the rest.

The period from 1848 to 1914 was one in which the struggle for national independence marked political and social life and left a strong impact on European culture. The arts, in fact, became one of the chief ways in which nationalists sought to stimulate a sense of peoples' awareness of their national roots. One of the basic factors that distinguished the Hungarians or the Czechs from their Austrian rulers was their language, and patriotic leaders fought for the right to use their own language in schools, government, and legal proceedings. In Hungary, the result was the creation by Austria of the Dual Monarchy in 1867, which allowed Hungarian speakers to have their own systems of education and public life. A year later, the Hapsburgs granted a similar independence to minorities living there: Poles, Czechs, Slovaks, Romanians, and others.

In Germany and Italy, the reverse process operated. Although most Italians spoke a dialect of the same language, they had been ruled for centuries by a bewildering array of outside powers. In Sicily alone, Arabs, French, Spaniards, and English were only some of the occupiers who had succeeded one another. The architects of Italian unity used the existence of a common language, which went back to the poet Dante, to forge a sense of national identity.

The arts also played their part. Nationalist composers used folk tunes, sometimes real and sometimes invented, to underscore a sense of national consciousness. In the visual arts, painters illustrated historical events, and sculptors portrayed patriotic leaders. While the newly formed nations aimed to create an independent national culture, the great powers reinforced their own identities. Russian composers turned away from Western models to underline their Slavic roots, while in Britain the artists and writers of the Victorian Age depicted the glories (and, in some cases, the horrors) of their nation.

The consequences of the rise of national consciousness dominated the twentieth century and are still with us today. The age of world war was inaugurated by competition between nation-states, and the last half of the twentieth century saw the collapse and regrouping of many of the countries created in the first half. Among the casualties are the former Czechoslovakia and Yugoslavia. The struggle of minorities to win their own nationhood remains a cause of bloodshed. The Basques of northern Spain and the Corsican separatists are just two examples. In both cases, language and the arts continue to serve as weapons in the struggle.

accompaniment. Chopin is characteristically Romantic in his use of music to express his own personal emotions. The structure of works like the twenty-four **Preludes**, Op. 28, is dictated not by formal considerations but by the feeling of the moment. Thus the first three take us from excited agitation to brooding melancholy to bubbling high spirits in just over three minutes.

In private, Chopin's life was dominated by a much-talked-about liaison with the leading French woman author of the day, George Sand (1804–1876). His early death from tuberculosis put the final Romantic touch to the life of a composer who has been described as the soul of the piano.

Liszt Franz Liszt (1811–1886) shared Chopin's brilliant skill at the keyboard and joined to it his own more robust temperament. A natural Romantic, Liszt ran the gamut of Romantic themes and experiences. After beginning his career as a handsome, impetuous young rebel, the idol of the salons of Paris, he conducted several well-publicized affairs and ended up by turning to the consolations of religion. His vast musical output includes some of the most difficult of all piano works (many of them inspired by the beauties of nature), two symphonies on the characteristically Romantic subjects of Faust and Dante (with special emphasis, in the latter case, on the *Inferno*), and a host of pieces that use the folk tunes of his native Hungary.

Paganini Assessment of Liszt's true musical stature is difficult. He was probably a better composer than his present reputation suggests, although not so great a one as his contemporaries (and he) thought. As a virtuoso performer even *he* takes second place to Nicolò

Paganini (1782–1840), the greatest violinist of the age, if not of all time.

Like Chopin and Liszt, Paganini also composed, but his public performances won him his amazing reputation. So apparently impossible were the technical feats he so casually executed that rumor spread that, like Faust, he had sold his soul to the devil. This typically Romantic exaggeration was, of course, assiduously encouraged by Paganini, who cultivated a suitably ghoulish appearance to enhance his public image. Nothing more clearly illustrates the nineteenth century's obsession with music as emotional expression (in this case, diabolical) than the fact that Paganini's concerts earned him both honors throughout Europe and a considerable fortune.

MUSICAL NATIONALISM

Both Chopin and Liszt introduced the music of their native lands into their works, Chopin in his **mazurkas** and **polonaises** (traditional Polish dances) and Liszt in his *Hungarian Rhapsodies*. For the most part, however, they adapted their musical styles to the prevailing international fashions of the day.

Other composers placed greater emphasis on their native musical traditions. In Russia, a group of five composers (Moussorgsky, Balakirev, Borodin, Cui, and Rimsky-Korsakov) consciously set out to exploit their rich musical heritage. The greatest of the five was Modest Moussorgsky (1839–1881), whose opera *Boris Godunov* (1874) is based on an episode in Russian history. It makes full use of Russian folksongs and religious music in telling the story of Tsar Boris Godunov, who rises to power by killing the true heir to the throne. Although Boris is the opera's single most important character, the work is really dominated by the chorus, which represents the Russian people. Moussorgsky powerfully depicts their changing emotions, from bewilderment to awe to fear to rage, and in so doing gives voice to the feelings of his nation.

Elsewhere in Eastern Europe composers were finding similar inspiration in national themes and folk music. The Czech composer Bedrich Smetana (1824–1884), who aligned himself with his native Bohemia in the uprising against Austrian rule in 1848, composed a set of seven pieces for orchestra under the collective title of *Má Vlast* (*My Fatherland*). The best known, *Vltava* (*The Moldau*), depicts the course of the river Vltava as it flows from its source through the countryside to the capital city of Prague. His fellow countryman Antonin Dvořák (1841–1904) also drew on the rich tradition of folk music in works like his *Slavonic Dances*, colorful settings of Czech folk tunes.

OPERA

Throughout the nineteenth century, opera achieved new heights of popularity in Europe, and "opera mania" began to spread to America, where opera houses opened in New

◆ **17.6** Maria Callas as Norma in Bellini's opera of the same title. The Greek-American Maria Callas (1923–1977), one of the great sopranos of the twentieth century, made her professional debut in Verona, Italy, in 1947. Her first appearances at La Scala in Milan (1950), Covent Garden in London (1952), and, as shown here, the Metropolitan Opera in New York followed in 1956. *(Image © Gordon Parks//Time Life Pictures/Getty Images)*

York (1854) and Chicago (1865). Early in the century, the Italian opera-going public was interested in beautiful and brilliant singing rather than realism of plot or action.

***Bel Canto* Opera** This love of what is often called *bel canto* ("beautiful singing") should not be misunderstood. Composers like Gaetano Donizetti (1797–1848) and Vincenzo Bellini (1801–1835) used their music to express sincere and deep emotions and even drama, but the emotional expression was achieved primarily by means of song and not by a convincing dramatic situation. The plots of their operas serve only as an excuse for the music; thus characters in *bel canto* operas are frequently given to fits of madness in order to give musical expression to deep emotion. Within the necessary framework provided by the plot, a great singer, inspired by great music, could use the magic of the human voice to communicate a dramatic emotion that transcended the time and place of the action.

The revival and subsequent popularity of much early-nineteenth-century opera is largely the result of the performances and recordings of Maria Callas [**Fig. 17.6**],

◆ **17.7** Scene from Verdi's opera *La Traviata* showing the first encounter between the heroine Violetta (here played by Teresa Stratas) and her future lover Alfredo (Placido Domingo).

Still from Franco Zeffirelli's film La Traviata, 1982. Image © Tony Frank/Sygma/CORBIS

whose enormous talent showed how a superb interpreter could bring such works to life. Following her example, other singers turned to *bel canto* opera, with the result that performances of Bellini's *Norma* and of Donizetti's best-known opera, *Lucia di Lammermoor* (1835), have become a regular feature of modern operatic life, while lesser-known works are revived in increasing numbers.

Under the inspiration of Verdi and Wagner, however, opera began to move in a different direction. The subjects composers chose remained larger than life, but dramatic credibility became increasingly important. On both sides of the Atlantic, opera house stages are still dominated by the works of the two nineteenth century giants: the Italian Giuseppe Verdi and the German Richard Wagner.

Verdi Perhaps the best-loved of all opera composers, Giuseppe Verdi (1813–1901) showed a new concern for dramatic and psychological truth. Even in his early operas like *Nabucco* (1842) or *Luisa Miller* (1849), Verdi was able to give convincing expression to human relationships. At the same time, his music became associated with the growing nationalist movement in Italy. *Nabucco*, for example, deals ostensibly with the captivity of the Jews in Babylon and their oppression by Nebuchadnezzar, but the plight of the Jews became symbolic of the Italians' suffering under Austrian rule. The chorus the captives sing as they think of happier days, "Va, pensiero . . ." ("Fly, thought, on golden wings, go settle on the slopes and hills where the soft breezes of our native land smell gentle and mild"), became a kind of theme song for the Italian nationalist movement, the Risorgimento, largely because of the inspiring yet nostalgic quality of Verdi's tune.

Verdi's musical and dramatic powers reached their first great climax in three major masterpieces—*Rigoletto* (1851), *Il Trovatore* (1853), and *La Traviata* (1853)—which remain among the most popular of all operas. They are very different in subject and atmosphere. *Il Trovatore* is perhaps the most traditional in approach, with its gory and involved plot revolving around the troubadour Manrico and its abundance of superb melodies. In *Rigoletto*, Verdi achieved one of his most convincing character portrayals in the hunchback court jester Rigoletto, who is forced to suppress his human feelings and play the fool to his vicious and lecherous master, the Duke of Mantua.

With *La Traviata*, based on Dumas' play *La dame aux camélias* (*The Lady of the Camellias*), Verdi broke new ground in the history of opera by dealing with contemporary life rather than a historical or mythological subject. The principal character of *La Traviata* is Violetta, a popular courtesan (high-class prostitute) in Paris, and modeled on an actual individual, Marie Duplessis (1824–1847), who died from tuberculosis at the age of twenty-three. Living at the center of a rich and decadent social whirl, Duplessis earned enough in her short career to leave such quantities of jewelry, silver, porcelain, and other goods that the sale of her estate took four days and raised some 100,000 francs.

CD Track 14
Giuseppe Verdi, Violetta's Aria "Ah, fors' è lui," Act I, *La Traviata*

Act I of *La Traviata* takes place at a party given by Violetta. She is used to being admired and flattered, but during the course of the party a naïve young man from the provinces, Alfredo Germont, confesses that he feels a real and sincere love for her [**Fig. 17.7**]. Violetta

◆ **17.8** Wilhelm Bekmann, *Richard Wagner at His Home in Bayreuth*, 1880. Characteristically, Wagner is holding forth to his wife and friends, in this case Liszt in his garb as Abbot (with white hair) and the author Hans von Wolzogen. At lower left are some stage designs for Wagner's final work, *Parsifal*.

Oil on canvas, 4'¾" x 5'1⅝" (1.25 x 1.58 m). Richard Wagner Museum, Bayreuth, Germany/© The Art Archive/ Alfredo Dagli Orti

is amused but moved, and when the guests have gone and she finds herself alone, she sings the aria "Ah fors' è lui." Perhaps this is the man who can offer her the joy of loving and being loved, a joy she has never known but for which she yearns. In typical Romantic fashion she explores and analyzes her own feelings, repeating the phrase "croce e delizia" (torment and delight).

Her conflicting emotions are expressed by a melody that at first is broken and unsure, but as her confidence grows, it breaks out into glowing, soaring phrases. Note that at the end, the unaccompanied vocal line serves not to display the excellent technique of the singer (although it certainly requires that) but the innermost personal feelings of the singer—another Romantic characteristic. Equally Romantic is the way in which her fluctuating emotions reflect the illness which proves fatal at the end of the opera.

As the opera progresses, Violetta falls in love with Alfredo and decides to give up her sophisticated life in the capital for country bliss. Her reputation follows her, however, in the form of Alfredo's father. In a long and emotional encounter, he persuades her to abandon his son and put an end to the disgrace she is bringing on his family. Violetta, who is aware of her fatal illness, returns alone to the cruel glitter of her life in Paris. By the end of the opera, her money gone, she lies dying in poverty and solitude. At this tragic moment Verdi gives her one of his most moving arias, "Addio del passato" ("Goodbye bright dreams of the past"). Alfredo, learning of the sacrifice she has made for his sake, rushes to find her, only to arrive for a final farewell—Violetta dies in his arms.

Throughout the latter part of his career, Verdi's powers continued to develop and enrich, until in 1887 he produced in *Otello*, a version of Shakespeare's tragedy of the same name, perhaps the supreme work in the entire Italian operatic tradition. From the first shattering chord that opens the first act to Otello's heartbreaking death at the end of the last, Verdi rose to the Shakespearean challenge with music of unsurpassed eloquence. In a work that is so consistently inspired, it seems invidious to pick out highlights, but the ecstatic love duet of Act I between Otello and Desdemona deserves mention as one of the noblest and most moving of all depictions of romantic passion.

Wagner The impact of Richard Wagner (1813–1883) on his times went far beyond the opera house. Not only did his works change the course of the history of music, but many of his ideas also had a profound effect on writers and painters [**Fig. 17.8**]. This truly revolutionary figure even became actively involved with the revolutionary uprisings of 1848 and spent several years in exile in Switzerland.

It is difficult to summarize the variety of Wagner's ideas, which ranged from art to politics to vegetarianism and are not noted for their tolerance. Behind many of his writings on opera and drama lay the concept that the most powerful form of artistic expression was one that united all the arts—music, painting, poetry, movement—in a single work of art, the **Gesamtkunstwerk** ("complete artwork"). To illustrate this theory, Wagner wrote both the words and music of what he called "music dramas" and even designed and built a special

◆ **17.9** Scene from *The Valkyrie*, the second work in Wagner's *Ring of the Nibelung*. Following the famous "Ride of the Valkyries," the warrior maidens surround their fellow Valkyrie, Brünnhilde (played here by Eva Johannson), center stage. The woman dressed in white, lying prostrate, is Sieglinde, who is destined to give birth to Siegfried, the cycle's eventual hero.

Performance Grand Theatre de Provence, Aix-en-Provence, France, June 24, 2007. Image © Anne-Christine Poujoulat/AFP/Getty Images

theater for their performance at Bayreuth, where they are still performed every year at the Bayreuth Festival.

Several characteristics link all of Wagner's mature works. First, he abolished the old separation between *recitatives* (in which the action was advanced) and arias, duets, or other individual musical numbers (which held up the action). Wagner's music flowed continuously from the beginning to the end of each act with no pauses. Second, he eliminated the vocal display and virtuosity that had been traditional in opera. Wagner roles are certainly not easy to sing, but their difficulties are always for dramatic reasons and not to show off a singer's skill. Third, he put a new emphasis on the orchestra, which not only accompanied the singers but also provided a rich musical argument of its own. This was enhanced by his fourth contribution, the famous device of the **leitmotiv** ("leading motif"), which consisted of giving each of the principal characters, ideas, and even objects an individual theme of his, her, or its own. By recalling these themes and by combining them or changing them, Wagner achieved highly complex dramatic and psychological effects.

Wagner generally drew his subjects from German mythology. By peopling his stage with heroes, gods, giants, magic swans, and the like, he aimed to create universal dramas that would express universal emotions. In his most monumental achievement, *The Ring of the Nibelung*, written between 1851 and 1874, he even represented the end of the world. *The Ring* consists of four separate music dramas: *The Rhinegold*, *The Valkyrie*, *Siegfried*, and *The Twilight of the Gods*, the plot of which defies summary [**Fig. 17.9**]. In music of incredible richness, Wagner depicted not only the actions and reactions of his characters but also the wonders of nature. In *Siegfried*, for example, we hear the rustling of the forest and the songs of wood birds, while throughout *The Ring* and especially in the well-known "Rhine Journey" from *The Twilight of the Gods*, the mighty river Rhine sounds throughout the score. At the same time, *The Ring* has several philosophical and political messages, many of which are derived from Schopenhauer. One of its main themes is that power corrupts, while Wagner also adopted Goethe's idea of redemption by a woman in the final resolution of the drama.

CD Track 15
Richard Wagner, "The Ride of the Valkyries," Act III, *The Valkyrie*

The second opera of Wagner's Ring cycle, *The Valkyrie*, introduces us to the work's heroine, Brünnhilde, who is one of the nine Valkyries, warrior daughters of Wotan, father of the gods. Their task is to roam the battlefields and carry the bodies of dead heroes to Valhalla (the home of the gods).

At the beginning of the third act *The Valkyrie*, Brünnhilde's sisters gather on a mountaintop, and Wagner's stormy music describes their ride through the clouds. Note how the composer sets the scene by his use of the orchestra. The woodwinds begin with a series of wild trills, the strings play scales that rush up and down, and then the heavy brass enter with the rhythmic motive of the Valkyries (a theme that returns many times during the rest of the Ring cycle). As each warrior maid arrives with her fallen hero, the music subsides, only to rise again to ever greater peaks of excitement as another rides in.

The version heard on the CD is orchestral, prepared for performance in the concert hall rather than in the opera house, so that no voices are heard. In the original we hear the Valkyries calling to one another. The ending of the selection is also modified for concert performance; in the opera, the scene continues unbroken.

◆ **17.10** Jacques-Louis David, *The Sabine Women Halting the Battle between Romans and Sabines*, 1799. David may have intended this depiction of feminine virtue as a tribute to his wife, who left him when he voted for the execution of Louis XVI but returned to him when he was imprisoned for a time.

Oil on canvas, 12′5″ x 16′9″ (3.8 x 5.1 m). Musée du Louvre, Paris, France//© Réunion des Musées Nationaux/Art Resource, NY

The wild and exotic nature of the music is typical of fully developed Romanticism, as is the extended development of the plot of the *Ring*, with its emphasis on erotic love and the role of Wotan as eventual redeemer at the very end of the cycle, while the use of Norse and Germanic mythology (rather than biblical or Classical background) illustrates the Romantics' love of Nationalism.

No brief discussion can begin to do justice to so stupendous a work as *The Ring*. It is probably easier to see Wagner's genius in operation by looking at a work on small scale, a single self-contained music drama—albeit one of some four hours' duration. *Tristan and Isolde* was first performed in 1865, and its first notes opened a new musical era. Its subject is the overwhelming love of the English knight Tristan and the Irish princess Isolde, so great that the pair betray his dearest friend and lord and her husband, King Mark of Cornwall, and so overpowering that it can achieve its complete fulfillment only in death.

Wagner's typically Romantic preoccupation with love and death may seem morbid and far-fetched, but under the sway of his intoxicating music it is difficult to resist. The sense of passion awakened but unfulfilled is expressed in the famous opening bars of the Prelude. The music imparts no sense of settled harmony or clear direction. This lack of **tonality**, used here for dramatic purpose, was to have a considerable influence on modern music.

The core of *Tristan and Isolde* is the long love scene at the heart of the second act, where the music reaches heights of erotic ecstasy too potent for some listeners. Whereas Verdi's love duet in *Otello* presents two noble spirits responding to one another with deep feeling but

with dignity, Wagner's characters are racked by passions they cannot begin to control. If ever music expressed what neither words nor images could depict, it is in the overwhelming physical emotion of this scene. The pulsating orchestra and surging voices of the lovers build up an almost unbearable tension that Wagner suddenly breaks with the arrival of King Mark. Once again, as in the Prelude, fulfillment is denied both to the lovers and to us.

That fulfillment is reached only at the end of the work in Isolde's "Liebestod" ("Love Death"). Tristan has died, and over his body Isolde begins to sing a kind of incantation. She imagines she sees the spirit of her beloved, and in obscure, broken words describes the bliss of union in death before sinking lifeless upon him. Although the "Liebestod" does make its full effect when heard at the end of the entire work, even out of context the emotional power of the music as it rises to its climax can hardly fail to affect the sensitive listener.

ROMANTIC ART

PAINTING AT THE TURN OF THE CENTURY

Just as Beethoven and his Romantic successors rejected the idealizing and universal qualities of classical music to achieve a more intense and personal communication, painters also began to abandon the lofty, remote world of Neo-Classical art for more vivid images. In the case of painting, however, the question of style was far more related to political developments. We have already seen

◆ **17.11** Francisco Goya, *The Third of May, 1808*, 1814. The painting shows the execution of a group of citizens, the Madrileños, of Madrid who had demonstrated against the French occupation by Napoleon's troops. The Spanish government commissioned the painting after the expulsion of the French army.

Oil on canvas, 8'8¾" x 11'3¾" (2.66 x 3.45 m). Museo del Prado, Madrid, Spain//© Erich Lessing/ Art Resource, NY

in Chapter 16 that Neo-Classicism had become, as it were, the official artistic dress of the French Revolution, so it was not easy for a painter working in France, which was still the center of artistic life, to suddenly abandon the revolutionary style. The problem is particularly visible in the works of Jacques-Louis David (1748–1825), whose *Oath of the Horatii* (see Figure 16.2) had been inspired by the pre-Revolutionary longing for austere Republican virtue.

David By the end of the revolution, David had come to appreciate the advantages of peace; his painting *The Sabine Women Halt the Battle of the Romans and the Sabines* [**Fig. 17.10**] expresses his desire for an end to violence and bloodshed. The subject is drawn from Roman mythology and focuses on that moment when Hersilia, wife of the Roman leader Romulus, interrupts the battle between Romans and Sabines and begs for an end to war. Its significance is precisely the reverse of the *Oath of the Horatii*. In place of a masculine call to arms and sacrifice, David shows his heroine making an impassioned plea for peace. The style, however, remains firmly Neo-Classical, not only in the choice of subject but also in its execution. For all the weapons and armor, there is no sign of actual physical violence. The two opponents, with their heroic figures and noble brows, are idealized along typical Neo-Classical lines. The emotional gestures of Hersilia and others are also stylized and frozen. The painting is powerful, but it depicts a concept rather than individual human feelings.

Goya The contrast between the Neo-Classical representation of the horrors of war and a Romantic treat-

ment of the same theme can be seen by comparing David's painting to *The Third of May, 1808* [**Fig. 17.11**] by Francisco Goya (1746–1828). In Goya's painting, nothing is idealized. The horror and the terror of the victims, their faceless executioners, and the blood streaming in the dust all combine to create an almost unbearable image of protest against human cruelty. Goya's painting is Romantic because it conveys to us his own personal emotions at the thought of the executions and because, great artist that he was, his emotions become our own.

As Beethoven by his own passionate commitment convinces us of the necessity to struggle against the injustices of human beings and of fate, so Goya by his intensity urges us to condemn the atrocities of war. Furthermore, both Beethoven and Goya shared a common sympathy with the oppressed and a hatred of tyranny. The soldiers firing their bayoneted guns in Goya's painting were serving in the army of Napoleon; the event shown took place some four years after Beethoven had seen the danger Napoleon presented to the cause of liberty and had erased his name from the "Eroica."

It was easier for an artist outside France to abandon the artistic language of Neo-Classicism for more direct ways of communication. Although from 1824 to his death Goya lived in France, he was born in Spain and spent most of his working life there. Removed from the mainstream of artistic life, he seems never to have been attracted by the Neo-Classical style. Some of his first paintings were influenced by the rococo style of Tiepolo (see Figure 16.9), who was in Spain from 1762 until 1770, but his own introspective nature and the strength of his feelings seem to have driven Goya to find

◆ **17.12** Francisco Goya, *The Family of Charles IV*, 1800. In this scathing portrayal of the Spanish royal family, the artist depicts himself working quietly at the far left. The French writer Alphonse Daudet said the painting showed "the grocer and his family who have just won top prize in the lottery."

Oil on canvas, 9′2″ x 11′ (2.79 x 3.35 m). Museo del Prado, Madrid, Spain//© Scala/Art Resource, NY

◆ **17.13** Francisco Goya, *Saturn Devouring One of His Sons*, 1819–1823. The painting originally decorated a wall in Goya's country house, La Quinta del Sordo ("Deaf Man's Villa").

Detail of a detached fresco on canvas, full size c. 57′ x 32′ (146 x 83 cm). Museo del Prado, Madrid, Spain//© Scala/Art Resource, NY

more direct means of expression. Personal suffering may have played a part also, because Goya, like Beethoven, became totally deaf.

In 1799 Goya became official painter to King Charles IV of Spain and was commissioned to produce a series of formal court portraits. The most famous of these, *The Family of Charles IV* [**Fig. 17.12**], was deliberately modeled on Velázquez's *Las Meninas* (see Figure 15.22). Goya shows us the royal family—king, queen, children, and grandchildren—in the artist's studio, where they have come to visit. The comparison he intends us to make between his own painting and that of his distinguished predecessor is devastating. At first glance, Goya's painting may seem just another official portrait, but it does not take a viewer long to realize that something is wrong at the court of Spain. Instead of grace and elegance, Goya's patrons radiate arrogance, vanity, and stupidity. The king and queen, in particular, are especially unappealing.

The effect of Goya's painting is not so much one of realism as of personal comment, although there is every reason to believe that the queen was in fact as ugly as she appears here. The artist is communicating his own feelings of disgust at the emptiness—indeed the evil— of court life. That he does so through the medium of

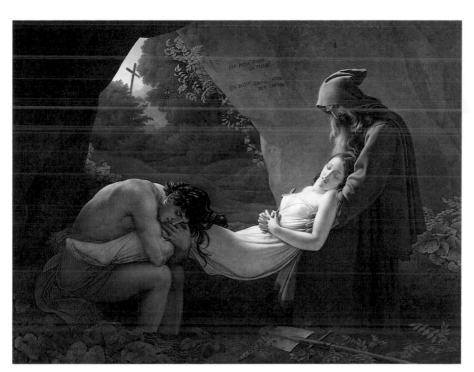

◆ **17.14** Anne Louis Girodet-Trioson, *The Entombment of Atala*, 1808. The anti-Classical nature of the subject is emphasized by the Christian symbolism of the two crosses, one leaning on the cave wall behind Atala and the other rather improbably placed high in the jungle outside the cave.

Oil on canvas, 6′11″ x 8′9″ (2.07 x 2.67 m). Musée du Louvre, Paris, France // © Réunion des Musées Nationaux / Art Resource, NY

an official court portrait that is itself a parody of one of the most famous of all court portraits is an intentional irony.

Even at the time of his official court paintings, Goya was obsessed by the darker side of life. His engraving *The Sleep of Reason Produces Monsters* (see Figure 17.2) foreshadowed the work of his last years. Between 1820 and 1822, Goya covered the walls of his own house with paintings that depict a nightmare world of horror and despair. *Saturn Devouring One of His Sons* [**Fig. 17.13**] uses a Classical myth to portray the god of time in the act of destroying humanity, but the treatment owes nothing to Neo-Classicism. No simple stylistic label seems adequate to describe so personal a vision. The intensity of expression, the fantastic nature of the subject, and the mood of introspection are all typically Romantic, yet the totality transcends its components. No one but Goya has ever expressed a vision of human existence in quite these terms.

PAINTING AND ARCHITECTURE IN FRANCE: ROMANTICISM AND REALISM

Girodet-Trioson Although the events of the French Revolution and Napoleon's subsequent dictatorship had an immediate impact on artists, writers, and musicians outside France, their effect on French artists was more complex. As we have seen earlier in this chapter, David was never able to throw off the influence of Neo-Classicism, and his immediate successors had a hard time finding a style that could do justice to romantic themes while remaining within Neo-Classical limits. One solution was offered by Anne Louis Girodet-

Trioson (1767–1824), whose painting *The Entombment of Atala* [**Fig. 17.14**] depicts a highly Romantic subject acted out, as it were, by Classical figures.

The subject is from a popular novel by the French Romantic novelist René de Chateaubriand (1768–1848) and depicts the burial of its heroine, Atala, in the American wilderness where the book is set. The other figures are her Indian lover, Choctas, and a priest from a nearby mission in the Florida swamps. The story of the painting therefore contains just about every conceivable element of Romanticism: an exotic location, emphasis on personal emotion, the theme of unfulfilled love. Girodet provides for his characters a Romantic setting, with its dramatic light and mysterious jungle background, but the figures are idealized in a thoroughly Classical way. Atala's wan beauty and elegant drapery and the muscular nudity of her lover are obviously reminiscent of Classical models. Only the mysterious figure of the old priest provides a hint of Romantic gloom.

Géricault It took a real-life disaster and a major national scandal to inspire the first genuinely romantic French painting. In 1816, a French government vessel, the *Medusa*, bound for Africa with an incompetent political appointee as captain, was wrecked in a storm. The one hundred forty-nine passengers and crewmembers were crowded onto a hastily improvised raft that drifted for days under the equatorial sun. Hunger, thirst, madness, and even, it was rumored, cannibalism had reduced the survivors to fifteen by the time the raft was finally sighted.

The young French painter Jean Louis André Théodore Géricault (1791–1824), whose original enthusiasm for Napoleon had been replaced by adherence to the liberal cause, depicted the moment of the sighting of

◆ **17.15** Jean Louis André Théodore Géricault, *Raft of the Medusa*, 1818. Note the careful composition of this huge work, built around a line that leads from the bottom-left corner to the top right, where a survivor desperately waves his shirt.

Oil on canvas, 16′1¼″ x 23′6″ (4.91 x 7.16 m). Musée du Louvre, Paris, France//© Réunion des Musées Nationaux/Art Resource, NY

◆ **17.16** Eugéne Delacroix, *Massacre at Chios*, 1824. Rather than depict a single scene, the painter chose to combine several episodes, contrasting the static misery of the figures on the left with a swirl of activity on the right.

Oil on canvas, 13′7″ x 11′10″ (4.19 x 3.54 m). Musée du Louvre, Paris, France//© Réunion des Musées Nationaux/Art Resource, NY

the raft in his painting *Raft of the Medusa* [**Fig. 17.15**]. Horror at the suffering of the victims and anger at the corruption and incompetence of the ship's officers (and their political supporters) inspired a work that, from its first exhibition in 1819, created a sensation in artistic circles. Even the general public flocked to see a painting that illustrated contemporary events so dramatically. In the process they became exposed to the principles of Romantic painting. Géricault's work deliberately rejects the ideal beauty of Classical models. The agonizing torment of the survivors is powerfully rendered, and the dramatic use of lighting underlines the intense emotions of the scene.

Delacroix When Géricault died following a fall from a horse, the cause of Romanticism was taken up by his young friend and admirer, Ferdinand Victor Eugéne Delacroix (1798–1863), whose name has become synonymous with Romantic painting. Although the subjects of many of his paintings involve violent emotions, Delacroix seems to have been aloof and reserved. He never married or for that matter formed any lasting relationship. His *Journal* reveals him as a man constantly stimulated by ideas and experience, but he preferred to live his life through his art—a true Romantic. Among

his few close friends was Chopin; his portrait of the composer (see Figure 17.5) seems to symbolize the introspective creative vision of the romantic artist.

Like his mentor Géricault, Delacroix supported the liberal movements of the day. His painting *Massacre at Chios* [**Fig. 17.16**] depicted a particularly brutal event in the Greek War of Independence. In 1824, the year in which Lord Byron died while supporting the Greek

◆ **17.17** Eugéne Delacroix, *The Death of Sardanapalus*, 1826. This painting makes no attempt to achieve historical accuracy but instead concentrates on exploiting the violence and cruelty of the story. Delacroix called this work *Massacre No. 2*, a reference to his earlier painting, the *Massacre at Chios* (Figure 17.16). Although this suggests a certain detachment on the artist's part, there is no lack of energy or commitment in the free, almost violent, brush strokes.

Oil on canvas, 12'1" x 16'3" (3.68 x 4.95 m). Musée du Louvre, Paris, France/© Giraudon/The Bridgeman Art Library

cause, the Turks massacred some 90 percent of the population of the Greek island of Chios, and Delacroix's painting on the subject was intended to rouse popular indignation. It certainly roused the indignation of the traditional artists of the day, one of whom dubbed it "the massacre of painting," principally because of its revolutionary use of color. Whereas David and other Neo-Classical painters had drawn their forms and then filled them in with color, Delacroix used color to create form. The result is a much more fluid use of paint.

Lord Byron figures again in another of Delacroix's best-known paintings, because it was on one of the poet's works that the artist based *The Death of Sardanapalus* [**Fig. 17.17**]. The Assyrian king, faced with the destruction of his palace by the Medes, decided to prevent his enemies from enjoying his possessions after his death by ordering that his wives, horses, and dogs be killed and their bodies piled up, together with his treasures, at the foot of the funeral pyre he intended for himself. The opulent, violent theme is treated with appropriate drama; the savage brutality of the foreground contrasts with the lonely, brooding figure of the king reclining on his couch above. Over the entire scene, however, hovers an air of unreality, even of fantasy, as if Delacroix is trying to convey not so much the sufferings of the victims as the intensity of his own imagination.

Ingres Although with Delacroix's advocacy Romanticism acquired a vast popular following, not all French artists joined the Romantic cause. A fierce and bitter rearguard action was fought by the leading Neo-Classical proponents, headed by Jean Auguste Dominique Ingres (1780–1867), who was, in his own different way, as great a painter as Delacroix. The self-appointed defender of

◆ **17.18** Jean Auguste Dominique Ingres, *Jupiter and Thetis*, 1811. The figure of Jupiter, with his youthful face surrounded by a vast wreath of beard and hair, is highly unconventional. Thetis's arms and throat are purposely distorted to emphasize her supplication.

Oil on canvas, 10'10" x 8'5" (3.3 x 2.57 m). Musée Granet, Aix-en-Provence, France//© Erich Lessing/Art Resource, NY

◆ **17.19** Jean Auguste Dominique Ingres, *La Comtesse d'Haussonville*, 1845. The artist seems to have been more interested in his subject's dress, which is marvelously painted, than in her personality. The reflection in the mirror reinforces the highly polished air of the painting.

Oil on canvas, 4'5" x 3'1/4" (1.36 x .92 m). The Frick Collection, New York, USA//© Geoffrey Clements/CORBIS

Classicism, Ingres once said of Delacroix that "his art is the complete expression of an incomplete intelligence." Characteristically, his war against Romantic painting was waged vindictively and on the most personal terms.

Now that the dust has settled, however, it becomes clear that Ingres, far from religiously adhering to Classical doctrines, was unable to suppress a Romantic streak. His extraordinary painting *Jupiter and Thetis* [**Fig. 17.18**] deals with an event from Homer's *Iliad* and shows Thetis, the mother of Achilles, begging the father of gods and mortals to avenge an insult by the Greek commander Agamemnon to her son by allowing the Trojans to be victorious. The subject may be Classical, but Ingres's treatment of it is strikingly personal, even bizarre.

Sensuality blends with an almost hallucinatory sharpness of detail to create a memorable if curiously disturbing image. Even in his more conventional portraits [**Fig. 17.19**], Ingres's stupendous technique endows subject and setting with an effect that is the reverse of academic. The style that in the end succeeded in replacing the full-blown romanticism of Delacroix and his followers was not that of the Neo-Classical school, with its emphasis on idealism, but a style that stressed precisely the reverse qualities.

Daumier The greatest French painters of the second half of the nineteenth century were Realists, who used the everyday events of the world around them to express their views of life. One of the first Realist artists was Honoré Daumier (1808–1879), who followed the example of Goya in using his work to criticize the evils of society in general and government in particular. In *Le Ventre Legislatif* (*The Legislative Belly*) [**Fig. 17.20**], Daumier produced a powerful image of the greed and corruption of political opportunists that has lost neither its bitterness nor, unfortunately, its relevance.

Courbet Equally political was the realism of Gustave Courbet (1819–1877), a fervent champion of the work-

◆ **17.20** Honoré Daumier, *Le Ventre Législatif* (*The Legislative Belly*), 1834. Although obviously caricatures, the politicians arranged in tiers were recognizable as individual members of the legislative assembly of the time.

Lithograph, 11¹⁄₁₆″ x 17¹⁄₁₆″ (28.1 x 43.3 cm). Image © Bibliothèque Nationale, Paris, France / The Bridgeman Art Library

◆ **17.21** Gustave Courbet, *The Artist's Studio: A Real Allegory of the Last Seven Years of My Life*, 1855. Although most of the figures can be convincingly identified as symbols of real people, no one has ever satisfactorily explained the small boy admiring Courbet's work or the cat at his feet.

Oil on canvas, 11′9¾″ x 19′6″ (3.6 x 5.96 m). Musée d'Orsay, Paris, France//© Scala/Art Resource, NY

ing class, whose ability to identify with ordinary people won him the label of Socialist. Courbet tried to correct this political impression of his artistic and philosophical position in a vast and not entirely successful allegorical work, *The Artist's Studio: A Real Allegory of the Last*

Seven Years of My Life [**Fig. 17.21**]. Like Goya's royal portrait (see Figure 17.12), the painting deliberately evokes memories of Velázquez's *Las Meninas* (see Figure 15.22), although the artist is now placed firmly in the center of the picture, hard at work on a landscape, inspired by a

◆ **17.22** Charles Garnier, Paris Opera House, 1861–1875. The incredibly rich and complex ornamentation has earned this style of architecture the label Neo-Baroque. *(Image © Erich Lessing/Art Resource, NY)*

nude model who may represent Realism or Truth. The various other figures symbolize the forces that made up Courbet's world. There is some doubt as to the precise identification of many of them, and it is not even clear that Courbet had any single allegory in mind. The total effect of the confusion, unintentional though it may be, is to underline the essentially Romantic origins of Courbet's egocentric vision.

French Architecture and Garnier Neither Romanticism nor its realistic vision made much impression on architectural styles in nineteenth-century France. French architects retained a fondness for classical forms and abandoned them only to revive the styles of the Renaissance. In some of the public buildings designed to meet the needs of the age, however, the elaborate decoration uses Classical elements to achieve an ornateness of effect that is not very far from the opulent splendor of Delacroix's *Death of Sardanapalus* (see Figure 17.17).

The most ornate of all nineteenth-century French buildings was the Paris Opera House **[Fig. 17.22]** of Charles Garnier (1824–1898). The new opera house

◆ **17.23** Caspar David Friedrich, *Abbey in an Oak Forest*, 1809–1810. The vast bare trees in the foreground and the ruined Gothic abbey emphasize the bleakness of the scene.

Oil on canvas, 3'7" x 5'7" (110.4 x 171 cm). Nationalgalerie, Staatliche Museen zu Berlin, Berlin, Germany//© Bildarchiv Preussischer Kulturbesitz/Art Resource, NY

had to be sufficiently large to accommodate the growing public for opera and sufficiently ostentatious to satisfy its taste. Garnier's building, designed in 1861 and finally opened in 1875, uses Classical ornamentation like Corinthian columns and huge winged Victories, but the total effect is highly un-Classical, a riot of confusion that would surely have appalled Classical and Renaissance architects alike.

PAINTING IN GERMANY AND ENGLAND

Friedrich Unlike their French counterparts, Romantic artists in both Germany and England were particularly attracted by the possibilities offered by landscape painting. The emotional range of their work illustrates once again the versatility of the Romantic style. The German painter Caspar David Friedrich (1774–1840) seems to have drawn some of his Gothic gloom from a tradition that had been strong in Germany since the Middle Ages, although he uses it to Romantic effect. His *Abbey in an Oak Forest* [**Fig. 17.23**], in fact, illustrates several Romantic preoccupations, with its ruined medieval architecture and melancholy dreamlike atmosphere.

Constable The English painter John Constable (1776–1837), on the other hand, shared the deep and warm love of nature expressed by Wordsworth. His paintings convey not only the physical beauties of the landscape but also a sense of the less tangible aspects of the natural world. In *Hay Wain* [**Fig. 17.24**], for example, we not only see the peaceful rustic scene, with its squat, comforting house on the left, but we also can even sense that light and quality of atmosphere, prompted by the billowing clouds that, responsible for the fertility of the countryside, seem about to release their moisture.

Turner Constable's use of color pales besides that of his contemporary, Joseph Mallord William Turner

◆ **17.24** John Constable, *Hay Wain*, 1821. Note Constable's bold use of color, which impressed Delacroix.

Oil on canvas, 4′3″ x 6′1″ (1.28 x 1.85 m). The National Gallery, London, UK//© Art Resource, NY

◆ **17.25** Joseph Mallord William Turner, *The Slave Ship*, 1840. The title of this painting is an abbreviation of the longer *Slavers Throwing Overboard the Dead and Dying; Typhoon Coming On*. At the lower center, Turner includes the horrifying detail of the chains that still bind the slaves whose desperate hands show above the water. Note the extreme contrast between Turner's interpretation of color and light and that of the American luminists as shown in Heade's painting (Figure 17.31).

Oil on canvas, 35¾″ x 48¼″ (90.8 x 122.6 cm). Image © Museum of Fine Arts, Boston, MA, USA///The Bridgeman Art Library

(1775–1851). In a sense, the precise subjects of Turner's paintings are irrelevant. All his mature works use light, color, and movement to represent a cosmic union of the elements in which earth, sky, fire, and water dissolve into one another and every trace of the material world disappears. His technique is seen at its most characteristic in *The Slave Ship* [**Fig. 17.25**].

Like Géricault's *Raft of the Medusa* (see Figure 17.15), Turner's *Slave Ship* deals with a social disgrace of the time; in this case, the horrifyingly common habit of the captains of slave ships to jettison their entire human cargo if an epidemic broke out. Turner only incidentally illustrates his specific subject—the detail of drowning figures in the lower-right corner seems to have been added as an afterthought—and concentrates instead on conveying his vision of the grandeur and mystery of the universe.

LITERATURE IN THE NINETEENTH CENTURY
GOETHE

The towering figure of Johann Wolfgang von Goethe (1749–1832) spans the transition from Neo-Classicism to Romanticism in literature like a colossus. So great was the range of his genius that in the course of a long and immensely productive life he wrote in a bewildering variety of disciplines. One of the first writers to rebel against the principles of Neo-Classicism, Goethe used both poetry and prose to express the most turbulent emotions; yet he continued to produce work written according to Neo-Classical principles of clarity and balance until his final years, when he expressed in his writing a profound if abstruse symbolism.

◆ **17.26** Illustration for Goethe's *The Sorrows of Young Werther*. The hero has just declared his hopeless passion for Charlotte, who violently rejecting his love (she is, of, course, happily married), declares, "This is the last time, Werther, you will never see me again!"

Engraving, Jean Baptiste Simonet (1742–1813) after Jean Michel Moreau, the Younger. Bibliothèque Nationale, Paris, France//© Lauros/Giraudon/The Bridgeman Art Library

Although the vein of Romanticism is only one of many that runs through Goethe's work, it is an important one. As a young man Goethe studied law, first at Leipzig and then at Strassburg, where by 1770 he was already writing lyric poetry of astonishing directness and spontaneity. By 1773, he was acknowledged as the leader of the literary movement known as **Sturm und Drang** ("Storm and Stress"). This German manifestation of Romanticism rebelled against the formal structure and order of Neo-Classicism, replacing it with an emphasis on originality, imagination, and feelings. Its chief subjects were nature, primitive emotions, and protest against established authority. Although the Sturm und Drang movement was originally confined to literature, its precepts were felt elsewhere. For instance, it was partly under the inspiration of this movement that Beethoven developed his fiery style.

The climax of this period in Goethe's life is represented by his novel *The Sorrows of Young Werther* (1774), which describes how an idealistic young man comes to feel increasingly disillusioned and frustrated by life, develops a hopeless passion for a happily married woman, and ends his agony by putting a bullet through his head. All of these events but the last were autobiographical. Instead of committing suicide, Goethe left

town and turned his life experiences into the novel that won him international fame. Not surprisingly it became a key work of the Romantic movement. Young men began to dress in the blue jacket and yellow trousers Werther is described as wearing, and some, disappointed in love, even committed suicide with copies of the book in their pockets—a dramatic if regrettable illustration of Goethe's ability to communicate his own emotions to others [**Fig. 17.26**].

The years around the turn of the century found Goethe extending the range of his output. Along with such plays as the Classical drama *Iphigenia in Tauris*, which expressed his belief in purity and sincere humanity, were stormy works like *Egmont*, inspired by the idea that human life is controlled by demonic forces. The work for which Goethe is probably best known, *Faust*, was begun at about the turn of the century, although its composition took many years. Part One was published in 1808, and Part Two was only finished in 1832, shortly before his death.

The subject of Dr. Faustus and his pact with the devil had been treated before in literature, notably in the play by Christopher Marlowe. The theme was guaranteed to appeal to Romantic sensibilities with its elements of the mysterious and fantastic and, in Part One, Goethe put additional stress on the human emotions involved. The chief victim of Faust's lust for experience and power is the pure and innocent Gretchen, whom he callously seduces and then abandons. She becomes deranged as a result. At the end of Part One of *Faust*, Gretchen is accused of the murder of her illegitimate child, condemned to death, and executed. Moving from irony to wit to profound compassion, the rich tapestry of Part One shows Goethe, like Beethoven and Goya, on the side of suffering humanity.

Part Two of *Faust* is very different. Its theme, expressed symbolically through Faust's pact with the devil, is nothing less than the destiny of Western culture. Our civilization's unceasing activity and thirst for new experiences inevitably produces error and suffering; at the same time, it is the result of the divine spark within us and will, in the end, guarantee our salvation. In his choice of the agent of this salvation, Goethe established one of the other great themes of Romanticism, the Eternal Feminine. Faust is finally redeemed by the divine love of Gretchen, who leads him upward to salvation.

ROMANTIC POETRY

English Romantic poetry of the first half of the nineteenth century represents a peak in the history of English literature. Its chief writers, generally known as the Romantic poets, touched on several themes characteristic of the age. William Wordsworth's deep love of the country led him to explore the relationship between human beings and the world of nature; Percy Bysshe

◆ **17.27** Thomas Phillips, *Lord Byron in Albanian Costume*, 1814. Byron is shown during his first visit to Greece, dressed for the role of Romantic sympathizer with exotic lands and peoples.

Oil on canvas, 29½″ x 24½″ (75 x 62 cm). Image © National Portrait Gallery, London, UK//SuperStock

Shelley and George Gordon, Lord Byron (hereafter called Lord Byron), probed the more passionate, even demonic aspects of existence; and John Keats expressed his own sensitive responses to the eternal problems of art, life, and death.

Wordsworth William Wordsworth (1770–1850), often called the founder of the Romantic movement in English poetry, clearly described his aims and ideals in his critical writings. For Wordsworth, the poet was a person with special gifts, "endowed with more lively sensibility, more enthusiasm and tenderness, who has a greater knowledge of human nature, and a more comprehensive soul" than ordinary people.

Rejecting artificiality and stylization, Wordsworth aimed to make his poetry communicate directly in easily comprehensible terms. His principal theme was the relation between human beings and nature, which he explored by thinking back calmly on experiences that had earlier produced a violent emotional reaction: his famous "emotion recollected in tranquility."

Byron Wordsworth's emotion recollected in tranquility is in strong contrast to the poetry of Lord Byron (1788–1824), who filled both his life and work with the same moody, passionate frenzy of activity [**Fig. 17.27**]. Much of his time was spent wandering throughout Europe, where he became a living symbol of the unconventional, homeless, tormented Romantic hero who has come to be called Byronic after him. Much of his flamboyant behavior was no doubt calculated to produce the effect it did, but his personality must have been striking for no less a figure than Goethe to describe him as "a personality of such eminence as has never been before and is not likely to come again." Byron's sincere commitment to struggles for liberty—like the Greek war of independence against the Turks—can be judged by the fact that he died while on military duty in Greece.

Shelley Percy Bysshe Shelley (1792–1822), who like Byron spent many of his most creative years in Italy, lived a life of continual turmoil. After being expelled from Oxford for publishing his atheistic views, he espoused the cause of anarchy and eloped with the daughter of one of its chief philosophical advocates. The consequent public scandal, coupled with ill health and critical hostility toward his work, gave him a sense of bitterness and pessimism that lasted until his death by drowning.

Shelley's brilliant mind and restless temperament produced poetry that united extremes of feeling, veering from the highest pitch of exultant joy to the most extreme despondency. His belief in the possibility of human perfection is expressed in his greatest work, *Prometheus Unbound* (1820), where the means of salvation is love—the love of human beings for one another expressed in the last movement of Beethoven's Ninth Symphony—rather than the redeeming female love of Goethe and Wagner. His most accessible works, however, are probably the short lyrics in which he seized a fleeting moment of human emotion and captured it by his poetic imagination.

Keats Even Shelley's sensitivity to the poetic beauty of language was surpassed by that of John Keats (1795–1821), whose life, clouded by unhappy love and the tuberculosis that killed him so tragically young, inspired poetry of rare poignance and sensitivity. In his *Odes* (lyric poems of strong feeling), in particular, Keats conveys both the glory and the tragedy of human existence and dwells almost longingly on the peace of death. In the wonderful "Ode to a Nightingale," the song of a bird comes to represent a permanent beauty beyond human grasp. The sensuous images, the intensity of emotion, and the flowing rhythm join to produce a magical effect.

THE NOVEL

Although great novels have been written in our own time, the nineteenth century probably marked the high point in the creation of fiction. Increases in literacy and a rise in the general level of education resulted in a public that was eager for entertainment and instruction, and the success of such writers as Charles Dickens and Leo Tolstoy was largely the result of their ability to combine the two. The best of nineteenth-century novels were those rare phenomena: great works of art that achieved popularity in their own day. Many of these are still able to enthrall modern readers with their humanity and insight.

Most of the leading novelists of the mid-nineteenth century wrote within a tradition of Realism that came gradually to replace the more self-centered vision of Romanticism. Instead of describing an imaginary world of their own creation, they looked outward to find inspiration in the day-to-day events of real life. The increasing social problems produced by industrial and urban development produced not merely a lament for the spirit of the times but also a passionate desire for the power to change them as well.

Hugo In some cases, writers were able to combine the Romantic style with a social conscience, as in the case of the French novelist Victor Hugo (1802–1885), whose *Les Misérables* (1862) describes the plight of the miserable victims of society's injustices. The hero of the novel, Jean Valjean, is an ex-convict who is rehabilitated through the agency of human sympathy and pity. Hugo provides graphic descriptions of the squalor and suffering of the poor, but his high-flown rhetorical style is essentially Romantic.

Flaubert Increasingly, however, writers found that they could best do justice to the problems of existence by adopting a more naturalistic style and describing their characters' lives in realistic terms. One of the most subtle attacks on contemporary values is *Madame Bovary* (1856–1857) by Gustave Flaubert (1821–1880). Flaubert's contempt for bourgeois society finds expression in his portrait of Emma Bovary, who tries to discover in her own provincial life the romantic love she reads about in novels. Her shoddy affairs and increasing debts lead to an inevitably dramatic conclusion. Flaubert is at his best when portraying the banality of Emma's everyday existence.

Balzac Honoré de Balzac (1779–1850) was the most versatile of all French novelists. He created a series of some ninety novels and stories, under the general title of *The Human Comedy*, in which many of the same characters appear more than once. Above all a Realist, Balzac depicted the social and political currents of his time while imposing on them a sense of artistic unity. His novels are immensely addictive. The reader who finds in one of them a reference to characters or events described in another novel hastens there to be led on to a third, and so on. Balzac thus succeeds in creating a fictional world that seems, by a characteristically Romantic paradox, more real than historical reality.

Sand Among the leading literary figures of Balzac's Paris, and a personal friend of Balzac, was the remarkable Aurore Dupin (1804–1876), better known by her pseudonym George Sand. This redoubtable defender of women's rights and attacker of male privilege used her novels to wage war on many of the accepted conventions of society. In her first novel, *Lélia* (1833), she attacked, among other institutions, the church, marriage, the laws of property, and the double standard of morality whereby women were condemned for doing what was condoned for men.

Unconventional in her own life, Sand became the lover of Chopin, with whom she lived from 1838 to 1847. Her autobiographical novel *Lucrezia Floriani* (1846) chronicles as thinly disguised fiction the remarkable course of this relationship, albeit very much from its author's point of view.

Tolstoy If France was one of the great centers of nineteenth-century fiction, another was Russia, where Leo Tolstoy (1828–1910) produced, among other works, two huge novels of international stature: *War and Peace* (1863–1869) and *Anna Karenina* (1873–1877). The first is mainly set against the background of Napoleon's invasion of Russia in 1812. Among the vast array of characters is the Rostov family, aristocratic but far from wealthy, who, together with their acquaintances, have their lives permanently altered by the great historical events through which they live. Tolstoy even emphasizes the way in which the course of the war affects his characters by combining figures he created for the novel with real historical personages, including Napoleon, and allowing them to meet.

At the heart of the novel is the young and impressionable Natasha Rostov, whose own confused love life seems to reflect the confusion of the times. Yet its philosophy is profoundly optimistic, despite the tragedies of Natasha's own life and the horrors of war that surround her. Her final survival and triumph represent the glorification of the irrational forces of life, which she symbolizes as the "natural person," over sophisticated and rational civilization. Tolstoy's high regard for irrationality and contempt for reason link him with other nineteenth-century Romantics, and his ability to analyze character through the presentation of emotionally significant detail and to sweep the reader up in the panorama of historical events make *War and Peace* the most important work of Russian Realistic fiction.

Toward the end of his life, Tolstoy gave up his successful career and happy family life to undertake a mystical search for the secret of universal love. Renouncing his property, he began to wear peasant dress and went to work in the fields, although at the time of his death he was still searching in vain for peace. Russia's other great novelist, Fyodor Dostoyevsky (1821–1881), although he died before Tolstoy, had far more in common with the late nineteenth century than with the

Romantic movement, and he is accordingly discussed in Chapter 18.

The English Novel The riches of the English nineteenth-century novel are almost unlimited. They range from the profoundly intellectual and absorbing works of George Eliot, the pen name of Mary Ann Evans (1819–1880), to *Wuthering Heights* (1847), the only novel by Emily Brontë (1818–1848) and one of the most dramatic and passionate pieces of fiction ever written. The book's brilliant evocation of atmosphere and violent emotion produces a shattering effect. Like the two already mentioned, many of the leading novelists of the time were women, and the variety of their works soon puts to flight any facile notions about the feminine approach to literature. Elizabeth Gaskell (1810–1865), for example, was one of the leading social critics of the day; her novels study the effects of industrialization on the poor.

Dickens If one figure stands out in the field of the English novel, it is Charles Dickens (1812–1870), who was immensely popular during his lifetime and has been widely read ever since. It is regrettable that one of Dickens' best-known novels, *A Tale of Two Cities* (1859), is one of his least characteristic, because its melodramatic and not totally successful historical reconstruction of the French Revolution may have deterred potential readers from exploring the wealth of humor, emotion, and imagination in his more successful books. Each of Dickens' novels and short stories creates its own world, peopled by an incredible array of characters individualized by their tics and quirks of personality. Dickens' ability to move us from laughter to tears and back again gives his work a continual human appeal, although it has won him the censure of some of the more severe critics.

Throughout his life, Dickens was an active campaigner against social injustices and used his books to focus on individual institutions and their evil effects. *Oliver Twist* (1837–1838) attacked the treatment of the poor in workhouses and revealed Dickens' view of crime as the manifestation of a general failing in society [**Fig. 17.28**]. In *Hard Times* (1854) he turned, like Gaskell, to the evils of industrialization and pointed out some of the harm that misguided attempts at education can do.

THE ROMANTIC ERA IN AMERICA

The early history of the arts in America was intimately linked to developments in Europe. England, in particular, by virtue of its common tongue and political

◆ **17.28** George Cruikshank, illustration for Dickens' *Oliver Twist*, 1837–1838, captioned "The Artful Dodger picking a pocket to the amazement of Oliver Twist." When Oliver leaves the workhouse, he finds himself among a gang of youthful thieves. Their leader, known as "The Artful Dodger," here shows Oliver how easy it is to pick someone's pocket. Oliver, on the right, reels back in a mixture of astonishment and horror. Cruikshank (1792–1878) was a famed illustrator and caricaturist who frequently worked with Dickens. *(Private Collection//© Image Select/Art Resource, NY)*

connections, exerted an influence on literature and painting that even the War of Independence did not end. American writers sought publishers and readers there and modeled their style on that of English writers. American painters went to London to study, sometimes with less than happy results. John Singleton Copley (1738–1815), for example, produced a series of portraits in a simple, direct style of his own [**Fig. 17.29**] before leaving Boston for England, where he fell victim to Sir Joshua Reynolds' grand manner (see Figure 16.14). Of American music we cannot say much, because the earliest American composers confined their attention to settings of hymns and patriotic songs. A recognizably American musical tradition of composition did not develop before the end of the nineteenth century, although much earlier European performers found a vast and enthusiastic musical public in the course of their American tours.

In the case of literature and the visual arts, the French Revolution provided a change of direction, for revolutionary ties inevitably resulted in the importation

AMERICAN LITERATURE

In a land where daily existence was lived so close to the wildness and beauty of nature, the Romantic attachment to the natural world was bound to make a special appeal. The Romantic concept of the transcendental unity of humans and nature was quickly taken up in the early nineteenth century by a group of American writers who even called themselves the **Transcendentalists**. Borrowing ideas from Kant and from his English followers such as Coleridge and Wordsworth, they developed notions of an order of truth that transcends what we can perceive by our physical senses and that unites the entire world.

Emerson One of the leading Transcendentalist representatives, Ralph Waldo Emerson (1803–1882), underlined the particular importance of the natural world for American writers in his essay "The American Scholar," first published in 1837. In calling for the development of a national literature, Emerson laid down as a necessary condition for its success that his compatriots should draw their inspiration from the wonders of their own country. A few years later he was to write: "America is a poem in our eyes; its ample geography dazzles the imagination, and it will not wait long for metres."

Emerson always tried to make his own work "smell of pines and resound with the hum of insects," but although his ideas have exerted a profound effect on the development of American culture, Emerson was a better thinker than creative artist. Far more successful as a literary practitioner of Transcendentalist principles was Henry David Thoreau (1817–1862), whose masterpiece *Walden* (1854) uses his day-to-day experiences as he lived in solitude on the shore of Walden Pond to draw general conclusions about the nature of existence. Thoreau's passionate support of the freedom of the individual led him to be active in the antislavery movement and, by the end of his life, he had moved from belief in passive resistance to open advocacy of violence against slavery.

Whitman Ideas of freedom, tolerance, and spiritual unity reached their most complete poetic expression in the works of America's first great poet, Walt Whitman (1819–1892). His first important collection of poems was published in 1855 under the title *Leaves of Grass*. From then until his death he produced edition after edition, retaining the same title but gradually adding many new poems and revising the old ones. Whitman was defiantly, even aggressively, an American poet, yet the central theme of most of his work was the importance of the individual. The contradiction this involves serves as a reminder of the essentially Romantic character of Whitman's mission since, by describing the details of his own feelings and reactions, he hoped to

◆ **17.29** John Singleton Copley, *Samuel Quincey*, 1765. In this portrait of a member of a distinguished Bostonian family, Copley avoids technical tricks. The result is an attractive simplicity of style that still allows him to reveal something of the subject's personality.

Oil on canvas, 35" x 58" (90.49 x 147.64 cm). Image © Museum of Fine Arts, Boston, MA, USA//The Bridgeman Art Library

of Neo-Classicism into America. With the dawning of the Romantic era, however, American artists began to develop for the first time an authentic voice of their own. In many cases they still owed much to European examples. The tradition of the expatriate American artist who left home to study in Europe and remained there had been firmly established by the eighteenth century. Throughout the nineteenth century, writers like Washington Irving (1783–1859) and painters like Thomas Eakins (1844–1916) continued to bring back to America themes and styles they had acquired during their European travels. Something about the nature of Romanticism, however, with its emphasis on the individual, seemed to fire the American imagination. The Romantic love of the remote and mysterious reached a peak in the macabre stories of Edgar Allan Poe (1809–1849). For the first time, in the Romantic era American artists began to produce work that was both a genuine product of their native land and at the same time of international stature.

◆ **17.30** Thomas Cole, *View from Mount Holyoke, Northampton, Massachusetts, after a Thunderstorm: The Ox Bow*, 1836. This shows a meticulous care for detail that is never allowed to detract from the broad sweep of the view. Note the shape of the river, its characteristic turns known as the Ox Bow.

Oil on canvas, 51½″ x 76″ (130.8 x 193 cm). Metropolitan Museum of Art, New York, USA//Image copyright © The Metropolitan Museum of Art/Art Resource, NY

communicate a sense of the essential oneness of the human condition. Much of the time the sheer vitality and flow of his language helps make his experiences our own, although many of his earlier readers were horrified at the explicit sexual descriptions in some of his poems. Above all, Whitman was a fiery defender of freedom and democracy. His vision of the human race united with itself and with the universe had a special significance for the late twentieth century that continues.

Dickinson Emily Dickinson (1830–1881) was as private in her life and work as Whitman was public in his. Only seven of her poems appeared in print during her lifetime, and the first complete edition was published as late as 1958. Yet, today, few American poets are better known or better loved. Her work tries to create a balance between passion and the prompting of

reason, while her interest in psychological experience appeals to modern readers. Many, too, are attracted by her desire for a secure religious faith, equaled only by her stubborn skepticism.

Novelists The essential optimism of the Transcendentalists, especially as interpreted by Whitman, is absent from the work of the two great American novelists of the nineteenth century: Nathaniel Hawthorne (1804–1864) and Herman Melville (1819–1891).

Hawthorne in particular was deeply concerned with the apparently ineradicable evil in a society dedicated to progress. In *The Scarlet Letter* (1850), his first major success, and in many of his short stories, he explored the conflicts between traditional values and the drive for change.

Melville imitated Hawthorne's example in combining realism with allegory and in dealing with profound

◆ **17.31** Martin Johnson Heade, *Newburyport Meadows*, 1876–1881. Note the smooth surface of the painting, which reveals no trace of the artist's brush strokes. The variations in light as storm clouds move in to obscure the sun are rendered with such extreme precision that they imbue the photographic effect with an innate sense of drama.

Oil on canvas, 10½" x 22" (26.7 x 55.9 cm). Metropolitan Museum of Art, New York, USA//Image copyright © The Metropolitan Museum of Art/Art Resource, NY

moral issues. His subjects and style are both very different, however. *Moby Dick* (1851), his masterpiece, is often hailed as the greatest of all American works of fiction. It shares with Goethe's *Faust* the theme of the search for truth and self-discovery, which Melville works out by using the metaphor of the New England whaling industry. Both Melville and Hawthorne were at their greatest when using uniquely American settings and characters to shed light on universal human experience.

AMERICAN PAINTING

Under the influence of the Transcendentalists, landscape painting in America took on a new significance. Emerson reminded the artist who set out to paint a natural scene that "landscape has a beauty for his eye because it expresses a thought which to him is good, and this because the same power which sees through his eyes is seen in that spectacle." Natural beauty, in other words, is moral beauty, and both demonstrate the Transcendental unity of the universe.

Cole The earliest painters of landscapes intended to glorify the wonders of nature are known collectively as the Hudson River School. The foundations of their style were laid by Thomas Cole (1801–1848), born in England, whose later paintings combine grandeur of effect with accurate observation of details. His *View*

from Mount Holyoke after a Thunderstorm: The Ox Bow [**Fig. 17.30**] is particularly successful in capturing a sense of atmosphere and presence.

By mid-century, a new approach to landscape painting had developed. Generally called **luminism**, it aimed to provide the sense of artistic anonymity Emerson and other Transcendentalists demanded. In a way this is the exact antithesis of Romanticism. Instead of sharing with the viewer their own reactions, the luminists tried by realism to eliminate their own presence and let nothing stand between the viewer and the scenes. Yet the results, far from achieving only a photographic realism, have an utterly characteristic and haunting beauty that has no real parallel in European art of the time. The painting *Newbury Meadows* [**Fig. 17.31**] by Martin J. Heade (1819–1904), one of the leading luminists, seems to combine a realistic depiction of the scene with the emotion it inspires.

Homer The two great American painters of the latter nineteenth century—Winslow Homer (1836–1910) and Thomas Eakins (1844–1916)—both used the luminist approach to realism as a basis for their own individual styles. In the case of Homer, the realism of his early paintings was largely the result of his work as a documentary artist, recording the events of the Civil War. His style underwent a notable change as he became exposed to contemporary French Impressionist

◆ **17.32** Winslow Homer, *Eagle Head, Manchester, Massachusetts*, 1870. This painting, produced after Homer's visit to France, shows a new, more Impressionistic approach to light and sea.

Oil on canvas, 26" x 38" (66 x 96.5 cm). Metropolitan Museum of Art, New York, USA//Image copyright © The Metropolitan Museum of Art/Art Resource, NY

◆ **17.33** Thomas Eakins, *The Swimming Hole*, 1885. Eakins painted figures directly from models placed in poses from Greek sculpture in order to try to see nature as the Greeks saw it, but without the Greeks' idealization. The figure swimming in the bottom right-hand corner is Eakins.

Oil on canvas, 27⅛" x 36⅛" (69.5 x 92.4 cm). Amon Carter Museum, Fort Worth, Texas, USA// Digital image © Superstock

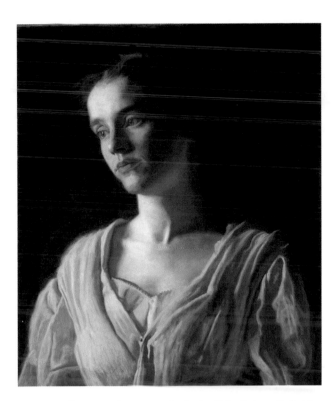

◆ **17.34** Thomas Eakins, *Maude Cooke (Mrs. Robert C. Reid)*, 1895. Note how, in contrast to the portraits by Ingres (Figure 17.19) and Copley (Figure 17.29), Eakins achieves deep feeling and sensitivity by the angle of his subject's head and her pose.

Oil on canvas, 24½″ x 20¹⁄₁₆″ (62.2 x 51 cm). Yale University Art Gallery, New Haven, CT, USA//Image © Yale University Art Gallery/Art Resource, NY

painting (discussed in Chapter 18). His mysterious *Eagle Head* [**Fig. 17.32**] is certainly far more than a naturalistic depiction of three women and a dog on a beach. By the way in which he has positioned the figures, Homer suggests rather than spells out greater emotional depths than initially meet the eye. The sense of restrained drama occurs elsewhere in his work, while the sea became a growing obsession with him and provided virtually the only subject of his last works.

Eakins Thomas Eakins used Realism as a means of achieving objective truth. His pursuit of scientific accuracy led him to make a particular study of the possibilities of photography. Animals and, more particularly, humans in motion continually fascinated him. This trait can be observed in *The Swimming Hole* [**Fig. 17.33**], where the variety of poses and actions produces a series of individual anatomical studies rather than a unified picture.

In his own day Eakins' blunt insistence on accuracy of perception did not endear him to a public that demanded more glamorous art. Yet if many of his works

seem essentially anti-Romantic in spirit, foreshadowing as they do the age of mechanical precision, in his portraits he returns to the Romantic tradition of expressing emotions by depicting them. The subject in *Maude Cook (Mrs. Robert C. Reid)* [**Fig. 17.34**], as in most of his portraits, turns her eyes away from us, rapt in profound inner contemplation. The artist's own emotional response to the mood of his subject is made visible in his painting.

Painters such as Homer and Eakins, like Whitman and other writers discussed here, are important in the history of American culture not only for the value of their individual works. Their achievements demonstrated that American society could at last produce creative figures capable of absorbing the European cultural experience without losing their individuality.

SUMMARY

◆ **The Rise of Nationalism.** The revolutionary changes that ushered in the nineteenth century, and that were to continue throughout it, profoundly affected society and culture. The industrialization of Europe produced vast changes in the lifestyles of millions of people. The Greek struggle for independence, the unification of Italy and of Germany, and the nationalist revolutionary uprisings of 1848 in many parts of Europe all radically changed the balance of power and the nature of society. The same period further saw the gradual assertion of the United States, tested and tried by its own civil war, as one of the leading Western nations. By the end of the nineteenth century, America had not only established itself as a world power, but it had also produced artists, writers, and musicians who created works with an authentically American spirit.

◆ **Intellectual Ferment: Darwin and Marx.** A period of such widespread change was naturally also one of major intellectual ferment. The political philosophy of Karl Marx and the scientific speculations of Charles Darwin, influential in their day, remain powerful and controversial in the present. The optimism of Immanuel Kant and Friedrich Hegel and the pessimism of Arthur Schopenhauer were reflected in numerous works of art.

◆ **Romanticism in the Arts.** The artistic movement that developed alongside these ideas was Romanticism. The Romantics, for all their divergences, shared several common concerns. They sought to express their personal feelings in their works rather than search for some kind of abstract philosophical or religious "truth." They were attracted by the fantastic and the exotic and by worlds remote in time (the Middle Ages) or in place (the mysterious Orient). Many of them felt a special regard for nature, in the context of which human achievement seemed so reduced. For some, on the other hand, the new age of industry and technology was exotic and exciting. Many Romantic artists identified with the nationalist movements of the times and either supported their own country's fight for freedom (as in the case of Verdi) or championed the cause of others (as did Lord Byron).

◆ **Beethoven and His Successors.** In music the transition from the Classical to the Romantic style can be heard in the works of Ludwig van Beethoven. With roots deep in the Classical tradition, Beethoven used music to express emotion in a revolutionary way, pushing traditional forms like the sonata to their limits. Typical of the age is his concern with freedom, which appears in *Fidelio* (his only opera), and human unity, as expressed in the last movement of the Ninth Symphony.

Many of Beethoven's successors in the field of instrumental music continued to use symphonic forms for their major works. Among the leading symphonists of the century were Hector Berlioz, Johannes Brahms, and Anton Bruckner. Other composers—Franz Schubert and Robert Schumann—although they wrote symphonies, were more at home in the intimate world of songs and chamber music. The Romantic emphasis on personal feelings and the display of emotion encouraged the development of another characteristic of nineteenth-century music: the virtuoso composer-performer.

Frédéric Chopin, Franz Liszt, and Niccolò Paganini all won international fame performing their own works. The nationalist spirit of the times was especially appealing to musicians who could draw on a rich tradition of folk music. The Russian Modest Moussorgsky and the Czech Bedrich Smetana both wrote works using national themes and folk tunes.

◆ **Wagner and Verdi.** The world of opera was dominated by two giants: Giuseppe Verdi and Richard Wagner. The former took the forms of early nineteenth-century opera and used them to create powerful and dramatic masterpieces. An enthusiastic supporter of Italy's nationalist movement, Verdi never abandoned the basic elements of the Italian operatic tradition—expressive melody and vital rhythm—but he infused these with new dramatic truth. Wagner's quest for "music drama" led him in a different direction. His work breaks with the operatic tradition of individual musical numbers; the music, in which the orchestra plays an important part, runs continuously from the beginning to the end of each act. In addition, the use of leading motifs to represent characters or ideas makes possible complex dramatic effects. Wagner's works revolutionized the development of both operatic and non-operatic music, and his theoretical writings on music and much else made him one of the nineteenth century's leading cultural figures.

◆ **Romanticism and Realism in Nineteenth-Century Painting.** Just as Beethoven spanned the transition from Classical to Romantic in music, so Francisco Goya, some of whose early works were painted in the rococo style, produced some of the most powerful of Romantic paintings. His concern with justice and liberty, as illustrated in *The Third of May, 1808*, and with the world of dreams, as in *The Sleep of Reason Produces Monsters*, was prototypical of much Romantic art.

In France, painters were divided into two camps. The fully committed Romantics included Théodore Géricault, also concerned to point out injustice, and Eugéne Delacroix, whose work touched on virtually every aspect of romanticism: nationalism, exoticism, eroticism. The other school was that of the Realists. Honoré Daumier's way of combating the corruption of his day was to portray it as graphically as possible. In the meantime, Ingres waged his campaign against both progressive movements by continuing to paint in the academic Neo-Classical style of the preceding century—or at least his version of it.

◆ **The World of Nature.** Painters in England and Germany were particularly attracted by the Romantic love of nature. Caspar David Friedrich used the grandeur of the natural world to underline the transitory nature of human achievement, while in John Constable's landscapes there is greater harmony between people and their surroundings. Joseph M. W. Turner, Constable's contemporary, falls into a category by himself. Although many of his subjects were Romantic, his use of form and color make light and movement the real themes of his paintings.

◆ **From Neo-Classicism to Romanticism in Literature: Goethe.** In literature no figure dominated his time more than Johann Wolfgang von Goethe, the German poet, dramatist, and novelist. One of the first writers to break the fetters of Neo-Classicism, he nonetheless continued to produce Neo-Classical works as well as more Romantic ones. The scale of his writings runs from the most intimate love lyrics to the monumental two parts of his *Faust* drama.

◆ **The Romantic Poets and the Novel.** The work of the English Romantic poets William Wordsworth, Percy Bysshe Shelley, John Keats, and Lord Byron touched on all the principal Romantic themes. Other English writers used the novel as a means of expressing their concern with social issues, as in the case of Charles Dickens, or their absorption with strong emotion, as did Emily Brontë. Indeed, the nineteenth century was the great age of the novel, with Honoré de Balzac and Gustave Flaubert writing in France and above all Leo Tolstoy in Russia.

◆ **The Nineteenth Century in America.** The Romantic Era was the first period in which American artists created their own original styles rather than borrow them from Europe. Love of nature inspired writers like Henry David Thoreau and painters like Thomas Cole. The description of strong emotions, often personal ones, characterizes the poetry of Walt Whitman and many of the paintings of Winslow Homer. Thomas Eakins, with his interest in Realism, used a nineteenth-century invention that had an enormous impact on the visual arts: photography.

By the end of the century the audience for art of all kinds had expanded immeasurably. No longer commissioned by the church or the aristocracy, artworks expressed the hopes and fears of individual artists and of humanity at large. Furthermore, as the revolutionaries of the eighteenth century had dreamed, they had helped bring about social change.

EXERCISES

1. Analyze the elements of the Romantic style and compare its effect on the various arts.

2. Discuss the career of Beethoven and assess his influence on the development of music in the nineteenth century.

3. What were the principal schools of French Romantic painting? Who were their leaders? What kinds of subjects did they choose? Explain why.

4. Which factors—historical, cultural, social—favored the popularity of the novel in the nineteenth century? How do they compare to present conditions? What is the current status of the novel?

5. Discuss the American contribution to the Romantic movement.

Visit the *Culture & Values* Companion website at **www.cengage.com/art/Cunningham/Cultureand Values7E** and the *Humanities Resource Center* for an array of primary source readings, key terms with pronunciations, flash cards, quizzes, and study materials designed especially to help you do well in this course.

CHAPTER 18

TOWARD THE MODERN ERA: 1870-1914

The rise of new political movements during the nineteenth century, of which socialism was perhaps the most prominent, drew upon a section of society new to political activism: women. Indeed the first use of the term *feminism* dates to this period. Women campaigned for a wide variety of causes—divorce reform, property ownership—but the issue that united most women across barriers of class or nationality was suffrage: the right to vote.

British women could vote in local elections from 1868, and they could vote in local governments in Finland and Sweden in the 1870s. In the 1890s some American states granted women the vote, but this was limited to single women who were property owners. By the eve of World War I, with the exception of Finland, no Western country (including the United States) allowed women to vote in national elections.

In France, feminists began to organize protest groups, refusing to pay taxes and overturning voting urns. The best known British group was the Women's Social and Political Union, founded in 1903 by Emmeline Pankhurst. Pankhurst and her daughters believed that only direct, violent action would secure women the vote. Her organization campaigned against political candidates who were opposed to women's suffrage. When leading politicians, including the British Prime Minister Herbert Asquith and his minister David Lloyd George, refused to back women's right to vote, her supporters smashed the windows of London's most exclusive shops, assaulted leading politicians, and chained themselves to the railings of official buildings. When sent to prison, they staged hunger strikes (only to be gruesomely force-fed). One of their activists, Emily Wildind Davison, threw herself in front of the King's horse on Derby day, 1913, and was trampled to death. Only after World War I, in 1918, did the suffragettes in Britain win the right to vote. American women voted for the first time in 1920.

THE SPIRIT OF THE AGE

Distance lends perspective in human experience. The more intimately we are affected by events, the more difficult it is to evaluate them objectively. Looking back, we can see that the world in which we live—with

◆ Suffragette Emmeline Pankhurst arrested at a demonstration outside Buckingham Palace, London, 1914.
(*© Jimmy Sime/Getty Images*)

its great hopes and even greater fears—began to take its present shape in the early years of the twentieth century. World War I (1914–1918) marked an end to almost three thousand years of European political and cultural supremacy as well as the beginning of a world in which events in any corner of the globe could—and still do—have immense consequences for good or ill for the entire human race. The effects on the humanities of so vast a change in direction will be the subject of Chapters 21 and 22. Here, we will consider some of the causes and early symptoms of the change.

Although the period in which the modern world was formed is the historical era that directly affects our

daily lives, our cultural traditions go back to ancient Greece and Rome. Yet even if the cataclysmic events of the twentieth century did not destroy the value of centuries of accumulated experience, we naturally feel more intimately linked to the generation of our parents and grandparents than to the more distant generations of ancestors of which we are also the product. Nevertheless, our parents and grandparents are the people whose nearness to us in time and emotional impact makes them and their world more difficult to understand objectively.

Our own responses to the increasing complexity of historical forces during the formative stages of modern

GENERAL EVENTS	ART

1860

Growth of Big Business

1876 Speech first transmitted through telephone by Alexander Graham Bell
1880–1914 Height of European colonialism
1886 Dedication of Statue of Liberty, presented by France to America

1889 International League of Socialist Parties founded

1863 Manet exhibits *Le Déjeuner sur l'Herbe* to public outrage

1874 Impressionism emerges when Monet and others exhibit at Café Guerbois, Paris; *Impression: Sunrise* (1872)
1875 Monet, *Argenteuil*
1876 Renoir, *Le Moulin de la Galette*

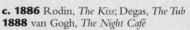

c. 1880 Postimpressionists reject impressionism
1882 Manet, *A Bar at the Folies-Bergère*
1884–1886 Seurat, *A Sunday on La Grande Jatte*
c. 1885 Protocubist experiments of Cézanne; *Still Life with Commode*

c. 1886 Rodin, *The Kiss*; Degas, *The Tub*
1888 van Gogh, *The Night Café*

1889 van Gogh, *The Starry Night*

1890

Height of European Colonialism

1890–1914 Industrialization of Russia

1891 Gauguin, *Ia Orana Maria*
Mary Cassatt's first solo exhibition in Paris

1893 Munch, *The Scream*; Rodin begins *Monument to Balzac*
1894–1898 Kollwitz, *March of the Weavers*, etching based on Hauptmann play

1899–1902 Boer War

1900

Rise of German Military Power

1901 Death of Queen Victoria of England; reign of Edward VII begins; first message sent over Marconi's transatlantic wireless telegraph
1903 Wright brothers make first airplane flight; Emmeline Pankhurst founds Women's Social and Political Union
1904 Russo–Japanese War
1905 First Revolution breaks out in Russia; Einstein formulates theory of relativity; first motion-picture theater opens in Pittsburgh
1908 Model T touring car introduced by Ford
1911 Revolution in China establishes republic
1914 World War I begins

c. 1904–1906 Cézanne paints last series of landscapes depicting *Mont Sainte-Victoire*

1903–1913 German expressionist movement *Die Brücke*
1905 First Fauve exhibition in Paris; Matisse, *The Joy of Life* (1905–1906)
1907–1914 Picasso and Braque develop cubism in Paris
1909 Nolde, *Pentecost*; Rodin, *Portrait of Mahler*
1911 Matisse, *The Red Studio*; German expressionist group *Der Blaue Reiter* formed
1912 Heckel, *Two Painters at the Table (To Dostoyevsky)*

1914

culture are still so confused that it is helpful to turn to the reactions of individual artists and thinkers who lived through the times and can to some extent interpret them to us. Furthermore, within the relatively limited sphere of artistic creativity we can observe at work forces that also operated on a much larger scale. As so often in the history of Western civilization, the arts provide a direct and powerful, if incomplete, expression of the spirit of an age. It may even be that the enduring importance of the humanities as a reflection of the human condition is one of the few aspects of Western civilization to survive a century of global turmoil and help us now in the twenty-first century.

THE GROWING UNREST

By the last quarter of the nineteenth century there was a widespread if unfocused feeling in Europe that life could not continue as before. Social and political revolutions had replaced the old monarchies with more nearly equitable forms of government. Scientific and technological developments had affected millions of ordinary people, bringing them improved standards of living and a more congenial existence. As a result, a new mood of cheerfulness began to make itself felt in the great cities of Europe; in Paris, for example, the period became known as the **belle époque** ("beautiful age").

ARCHITECTURE	LITERATURE & PHILOSOPHY	MUSIC
	1866 Dostoyevsky, *Crime and Punishment*	**mid-19th cent.** Liszt's symphonic poems precursors of *program music*
	1870–1914 New areas explored in writing: impact of subconscious on human behavior, the role of women	
	1879 First performance of Ibsen's realistic drama, *A Doll's House*	
	1881 Death of Dostoyevsky	
1883 Birth of Gropius		**1886** R. Strauss begins tone poem *Don Juan*
	1883–1892 Nietzsche, *Thus Spoke Zarathustra*	
1890–1891 Sullivan, Wainwright Building, St. Louis, first skyscraper	**1891** Shaw, drama critic for *Saturday Review*, champions Ibsen	**1890** Debussy, musical Impressionist, composes *Claire de Lune*
	1893 Wilde, *Salome*	**1893** Tchaikovsky, *Pathétique* Symphony, precedes composer's suicide. Mahler's Symphony No. 1 in D marks transition from romantic to modern music
		1894 Debussy, *Prélude à l'après-midi d'un faune*
		1895 R. Strauss, *Till Eulenspiegel*
		1896 Puccini champions verismo in Italian opera; *La Bohème*
	1899 Kate Chopin, *The Awakening*	**1899** R. Strauss, *A Hero's Life*
1905–1907 Gaudí, Casa Milá, Barcelona	**1900** Freud, *Interpretation of Dreams*	**1900–1904** Puccini, *Tosca, Madama Butterfly*
	1904 Death of Chekhov	**1905** First performance of R. Strauss' opera *Salome*, based on Wilde's play
		1908 Schönberg, Three Piano Pieces, Op. 11, first major atonal work
		1909–1910 Mahler, Symphony No. 9
		1910–1912 Stravinsky composes *The Firebird* and *Petrouchka*, for Diaghilev's Ballet Russe in Paris
1909 Robie House, Chicago, Frank Lloyd Wright's first big success		**1911–1915** R. Strauss, *An Alpine Symphony*
		1912 Schönberg, *Pierrot Lunaire*
	1913 Publication of *Swann's Way*, first volume of Proust's *Remembrance of Things Past*; final volume published posthumously (1927)	**1912–1913** *Rite of Spring*
		1913 Ravel composes *Daphnis and Chloe* for Diaghilev

◆ **18.2** Ludwig Meidner, *Apocalyptic Landscape*, 1912–1913. The distorted forms and violent, heaving composition reflect the spirit of a world on the point of collapse. The work was painted in the years when the coming of war seemed increasingly inevitable.

Oil on canvas, 31½″ x 45⅝″ (80 x 116 cm). Nationalgalerie, Staatliche Museen zu Berlin, Berlin, Germany. © Ludwig Meidner-Archiv, Juedisches Museum der Stadt, Frankfurt am Main//Bildarchiv Preussischer Kulturbesitz/Art Resource, NY

But the apparent gaiety was only superficial. The price of the immense changes that made it possible had been unrest and violence, and the forces that had been built to achieve them remained in existence. Thus, in a period of nominal peace, most of the leading countries in Europe were maintaining huge armies and introducing compulsory military service. Long before 1914, a growing mood of frustration led many people to assume that sooner or later war would break out—a belief that certainly did not help to avert it [**Fig. 18.2**].

The many historical causes of this mood are beyond the scope of this book, but some of the more important underlying factors are easy enough to perceive. First, the growth of democratic systems of government had taught increasing numbers of people that they had a right to share in the material benefits made possible by the Industrial Revolution. Discontent grew on all sides. In the richest countries in Europe—France, England, and Germany—the poor compared their lot to that of the more affluent. Simultaneously, in the poorer European countries, including Ireland, Spain, Portugal, and all of Eastern Europe, everyone looked with envy toward their wealthier neighbors. Even more significantly, those vast continents that the empire-building European powers were introducing to European civilization for the first time, including parts of Africa, Asia, and South America, began increasingly to resent European domination.

Second, the scientific progress that made possible improvements in people's lives created problems of its own. New medical advances reduced the rate of infant mortality, cured hitherto fatal diseases, and prolonged life expectancy. As a result, populations in most of Europe soared to record levels, creating food and housing shortages. New forms of transport and industrial processes brought vast numbers of workers to the cities. Consequently, the lives of many people were uprooted, and their daily existence became anonymous and impersonal.

Third, the growth of a world financial market, primarily dependent on the value of gold, gave new power to the forces of big business. In turn, the rise of capitalism, fiercely opposed by the growing forces of socialism [**Fig. 18.3**], provoked the development of trade unions to protect the workers' interests.

Finally, at a time when so many political and social forces were pitted against one another, there seemed to be no certainty on which to fall back. Religion had lost its hold over intellectual circles by the eighteenth century and, by the end of the nineteenth century, strong religious faith and its manifestation in church attendance began to fall drastically at all levels of society. The newly developing fields of anthropology and psychology, far from replacing religion, provided fresh controversy with their radically different explanations of human life and behavior.

VALUES

Imperialism

The transition from the world of the late Middle Ages to the dawn of the modern era was largely the result of European expansion overseas and the economic developments that it brought. By the mid-nineteenth century, the European search for new territories to engage in trade had solidified into a competitive drive to conquer and colonize them. Imperialism became one of the chief motivating forces in nineteenth-century politics and culture.

Imperialism arose in response to economic, political, and psychological goals. Economically, conquests of overseas territories and peoples provided sources of raw materials and abundant cheap labor. As the capitalist system grew, the colonies became centers for investment and thereby absorbed accumulating surplus capital—a point made by Lenin, one of the fiercest opponents of both capitalism and imperialism.

Politically, imperialism provided a means whereby the leading European powers could continue their rivalries outside Europe. At the beginning of the nineteenth century, the delegates at the Congress of Vienna in 1815 had created a political balance of power under which no European nation was able to dominate the others. By conquering more and richer territory in Africa and Asia, however, Western European colonizers could try to surpass one another.

No less important were the psychological factors inherent in nationalism. National pride became a powerful factor in determining political and military decisions. As European possessions abroad began to accumulate, the conquest of a well-located port or island could open up new territories, allow nations to hold on to territories, or effectively block a rival nation. At the patriot's level, heroic achievement abroad, particularly military prowess, brought personal glory and offered avenues of advancement to the less advantaged.

At least some of the drive for imperialism also rested on the claim—expressed by many imperialists and surely believed by some—that colonizers were spreading civilization, in its European form at least. Missionaries accompanied most colonial expeditions, and colonial governments tried to outlaw those local customs that appalled their administrators: cannibalism, child marriage, nakedness. While, in some cases, the physical conditions and education of the local populations improved, colonizers nevertheless resisted calls for self-government.

The eventual result was that the colonized peoples slowly began to fight for their own independence. In the course of the twentieth century, struggles for independence have reversed colonialism. In the process, European dominance has given way to a global culture that links the destinies of all parts of the world. Technological changes, weapons of mass destruction, and rapid progress in electronic communication have all helped build a global environment in which imperialism is now seen as arrogant and self-serving.

◆ **18.3** Käthe Kollwitz, "March of the Weavers" from *The Weavers Cycle*, 1897. This print is based on a play, *The Weavers*, by the German playwright Gerhart Hauptmann (1862–1946), dealing with the misery and helplessness of both workers and owners in the industrial age. The axes and mattocks in the workers' hands point to the coming violence.

Etching, 8⅜″ x 11⅝″ (21 x 29 cm). University of Michigan Museum of Art, Ann Arbor, USA// © Bettmann/CORBIS

Nietzsche In a state of such potential explosiveness it is hardly surprising that a major collapse of the fabric of European civilization seemed inevitable. Only in America, where hundreds of thousands of Europeans emigrated in the hope of making a new start, did optimism seem possible [**Fig. 18.4**]. Events were moving at so fast a pace that few thinkers were able to detach themselves from their times and develop a philosophical basis for dealing with them. One of the few who did was Friedrich Wilhelm Nietzsche (1844–1900), whose ominous diagnosis of the state of Western civilization in *Thus Spoke Zarathustra* (1883–1892) and other works led him to propose drastic remedies.

For Nietzsche, Christianity was a slave religion, extolling feeble virtues such as compassion and self-sacrifice, the greatest curse of Western civilization. He viewed democracy as little better, calling it the rule of the mediocre masses. The only valid life force, according to Nietzsche, is the "will to power"—that energy that casts off all moral restraints in its pursuit of independence. Anything that contributes to power is good. Society can only improve if strong and bold individuals who can survive the loss of illusions, by the free assertion of the will, establish new values of nobility and goodness. Nietzsche called this superior individual an **Übermensch** (literally "overperson"). Like Schopenhauer in the early nineteenth century (see Chapter 17), Nietzsche is valuable principally for the way in which he anticipated future ideas rather than because he was the leader of a movement. Unfortunately, his concepts were later taken up and distorted by many would-be world rulers of the twentieth century, most notoriously the leaders of Nazi Germany.

Cut adrift from the security of religion or philosophy, the arts responded to the restless mood of the times by searching for new subjects and styles, which often challenged principles that had been accepted for centuries. In music, traditional concepts of harmony and rhythm were first radically extended and then, by some composers at least, completely discarded. In literature, new areas of experience were explored, including the impact of the subconscious on human behavior, and traditional attitudes like the role of women were examined afresh. In the visual arts, the Impressionists found a totally new way of looking at the world, which in turn opened up other exciting new fields of artistic expression. Whatever their defects, the formative years of the modern world were certainly not dull with respect to the arts.

NEW MOVEMENTS IN THE VISUAL ARTS

Something of the feverish activity in the visual arts during this period can be gauged by the sheer number of movements and styles that followed one another

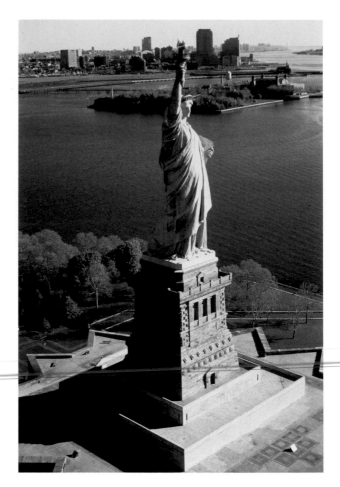

◆ **18.4** Frédéric-Auguste Bartholdi, *Statue of Liberty (Liberty Enlightening the World)*, 1876–1884. This famous monument, which still dominates New York's harbor, became the symbol to European immigrants in the late 19th century of the welcome they would find in the New World. Designed by the French sculptor Frédéric-Auguste Bartholdi (1834–1904), the colossal statue was a gift from France to the United States. Its supporting framework was created by the French engineer Gustave Eiffel (1832–1923), known mainly for his Eiffel Tower (1889) in Paris, France. Behind the statue lies Ellis Island where millions of immigrants disembarked.

Hammered copper sheets over iron trusswork and armature, figure 151′ (46 m) high, the head alone 13′6″ (4.4 m) high; total height including pedestal, 306′ (93 m) above sea level. Constructed and erected in Paris, 1876–1884; disassembled, shipped to New York, re-erected in the New York City harbor, dedicated 1886. Image © A. & L. Sinibaldi/Getty Images

in rapid succession: Impressionism, post-Impressionism, Fauvism, and Expressionism, culminating in the birth of Cubism around the time of World War I. Cubism is discussed in Chapter 21 because of its effects on the whole of twentieth-century art, but all of the other movements form important stages in the transition from traditional artistic styles to present-day art, much of which rejects any attempt at Realism in favor of abstract values of line, shape, and color. An understanding of their significance is thus a necessary prerequisite for a full appreciation of modern abstract art. Quite apart from their historical interest, however, the artistic movements of the late

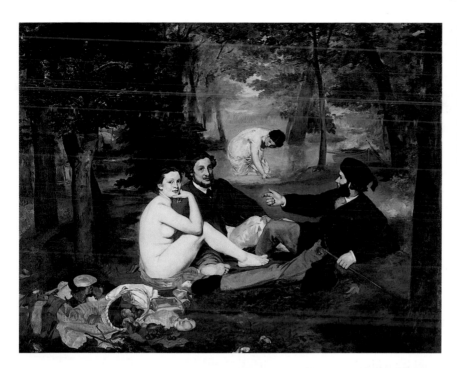

◆ **18.5** Édouard Manet, *Le Déjeuner sur l'Herbe*, 1863. Manet probably based the landscape on sketches made outdoors but painted the figures from models in his studio, something a careful scrutiny of the painting seems to confirm.

*Oil on canvas, 7'3⅛" x 8'10⅛" (2.15 x 2.7 m).
© Musée d'Orsay, Paris, France//Giraudon/The Bridgeman Art Library*

◆ **18.6** Édouard Manet, *A Bar at the Folies-Bergère*, 1882. Note the Impressionistic way in which Manet painted the girl's top-hatted customer, reflected in the mirror at right.

*Oil on canvas, c. 37" x 51" (.95 x 1.3 m).
© Courtauld Institute and Galleries, London, UK/SuperStock*

nineteenth and twentieth centuries have much visual pleasure to offer.

Manet As so often in the past, the center of artistic activity was Paris, where Édouard Manet (1832–1883) created a sensation in 1863 with his painting *Le Déjeuner sur l'Herbe* (*Luncheon on the Grass*) [**Fig. 18.5**]. Public outcry was directed against the subject of the painting: a female nude among two fully clothed young men and another clothed female figure. Other artists had combined nude females and clothed males before in a single picture, but Manet's scene has a particular air of reality; the way the unclad young woman stares out from the canvas and the two smartly dressed young

men appear nonchalantly indifferent to her condition can still take the spectator by surprise. The true break with tradition, however, lay not in the picture's subject but its style. The artist is much less interested in telling us what his characters are doing than in showing us how he sees them and their surroundings. Instead of representing them as rounded, three-dimensional forms, he has painted them as a series of broad, flat areas in which the brilliance of color is unmuted. In creating this style, Manet laid the philosophical foundations that made Impressionism possible.

The massive, almost monumental human form reappears in one of Manet's last paintings, *A Bar at the Folies-Bergère* of 1882 [**Fig. 18.6**], where the barmaid amid her

◆ **18.7** Claude Monet, *Impression, Sunrise*, 1872. Although this was the painting after which the Impressionist movement was named, its use of Impressionistic techniques is relatively undeveloped compared to Figure 18.8 and Figure 18.9.

Oil on canvas, 19½″ x 14½″ (50 x 62 cm). © Musée Marmottan, Paris, France//Giraudon/The Bridgeman Art Library

◆ **18.8** Claude Monet, *Argenteuil*, 1875. Painted the year after the first Impressionist exhibition in Paris, this work shows Monet's characteristic way of combining separate colors to reproduce the effect of light.

Oil on canvas, 22″ x 26⅛″ (56 x 67 cm). Musée de l'Orangerie, Paris, France// © Réunion des Musées Nationaux/Art Resource, NY

bottles and dishes presents the same solid appearance as the nude in *Déjeuner*. If we glance over her shoulder, however, and look into the mirror as it reflects her back and the crowded scene of which we have temporarily become a part, the style changes. The sharp outlines and fully defined forms of the foreground are replaced by a blur of shapes and colors that conveys the general impression of a crowded theater without reproducing specific details. A comparison between the backgrounds of the two pictures makes it clear that between 1863 and 1881, something drastic had occurred in the way painters looked at scenes and then reproduced them.

IMPRESSIONISM

Monet In 1874, a group of young artists organized an exhibition of their work during conversations at the Café Guerbois in Paris. Their unconventional approach to art and their contempt for traditional methods meant that normal avenues of publicity were closed to them; they hoped that the exhibition would succeed in bringing their work to public attention. It certainly did! One of the paintings, *Impression: Sunrise* [**Fig. 18.7**] by Claude Monet (1840–1926), particularly scandalized the more conventional critics, some of whom derisively borrowed its title and nicknamed the whole group Impressionists. Within a few years the Impressionists had revolutionized European painting.

Although Impressionism seemed at the time to represent a radical break with the past, it first developed out of yet another attempt to achieve greater realism, a tradition that had begun at the dawn of the Renaissance with Giotto. The Impressionists concentrated, however, on realism of light and color rather than realism of form and sought to reproduce—with utmost fidelity—the literal impression an object made on their eyes. If, for example, we look at a house or a human face from a distance, we automatically interpret it on the basis of our mental knowledge, and "see" details that are not truly visible. Impressionist painters tried to banish all such interpretations from their art and to paint with an "innocent eye." In *Argenteuil* [**Fig. 18.8**], Monet recorded all of the colors he saw in the water and the reflections of the boats without trying to blend them together conventionally (or intellectually). The result

is not a painting of boats at anchor but a representation of the instantaneous impact on the eye of the lights and colors of those boats; that is, what the artist saw rather than what he knew.

Throughout his long career, Monet retained a total fidelity to visual perception. His fellow painter Paul Cézanne (1839–1906) is said to have called him "only an eye, but my God what an eye!" Monet's preoccupation with the effects of light and color reached its most complete expression in his numerous paintings of water lilies in his garden. In version after version he tried to capture in paint the effect of the shimmering, ever-changing appearance of water, leaves, and blossoms. The result, as in the *Water Lilies* of 1920–1921 [**Fig. 18.9**], reproduces not so much the actual appearance of Monet's lily pond as an abstract symphony of glowing colors and reflecting lights. Paradoxically, the most complete devotion to naturalism was to pave the way for abstraction and for what we know as "modern art."

Renoir Monet's art represents Impressionism in its purest form. Other painters, while preserving its general principles, devised variants on it. Pierre Auguste Renoir (1841–1919) shared Monet's interest in reproducing the effects of light in patches of color, but he brought to his subjects a human interest that derived from his own joy in life. It is a refreshing change, in fact, to find an artist whose work consistently explored the beauty of the world around him rather than the great problems of human existence. Neither was Renoir's interest limited, as was Monet's, to the wonders of nature. His most enduring love was for women as symbols of life; in his paintings, they radiate an immense warmth and charm. His painting of *Le Moulin de la Galette* [**Fig. 18.10**], a popular Parisian restaurant and dance hall, captures the spirit of the crowd by means of the same fragmentary patches of color Manet used in the background of *A Bar at the Folies-Bergère* (see Figure 18.6), but Renoir

adds his own sense of happy activity. The group in the foreground is particularly touching, with its sympathetic depiction of adolescent love. The boy leans impetuously forward, while the girl who has attracted his attention leans back and looks gravely yet seductively into his face, restrained by the protective arm of an older companion. Although the encounter may be commonplace, Renoir endows it with a significance and a humanity far different from Monet's more austere, if more literal, vision of the world by setting it against the warmth and movement of the background.

Unlike many other Impressionists, Renoir traveled widely throughout Europe in order to see the paintings of the great Renaissance and Baroque masters. The influence of artists like Raphael, Velázquez, and Rubens is visible in his work. This combination of an Impressionistic approach to color with a more traditional attitude toward form and composition emerges in *Two Girls at the Piano* [**Fig. 18.11**], where the girls' arms have a genuine sense of roundness and weight. This painting is no mere visual exercise—Renoir endows his figures

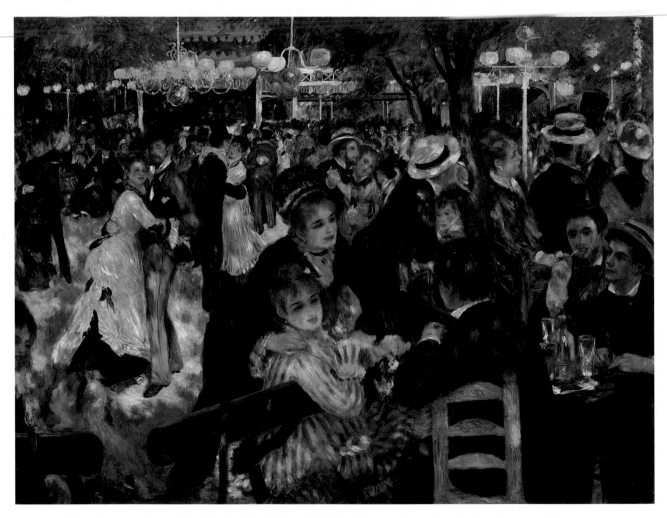

◆ **18.10** (Pierre) Auguste Renoir, *Le Moulin de la Galette*, 1876. By using small patches of color, Renoir achieves the impression of dappled sunlight filtering through the trees. The general mood of pleasure tinged with a certain wistful nostalgia is typical of the *belle époque*.

Oil on canvas, c. 51″ x 68″ (129. 5 x 172. 7 cm). Musée d'Orsay, Paris, France//© Réunion des Musées Nationaux/Art Resource, NY

with a sense of self-assurance that only emphasizes their vulnerability.

Degas The artist Edgar Hilaire Germain Degas (1834–1917) shared Renoir's interest in people, but unlike Renoir (who emphasized the positive side of life) he simply reported what he saw, stressing neither the good nor the bad. By showing us intimate moments in other people's lives, revealed by a momentary gesture or expression, his frankness, far from being heartless as some of his critics have claimed, conveys the universality of human experience. Although Degas exhibited with the Impressionists and, like them, chose to paint scenes from the everyday events of life, his psychological penetration distinguishes his art from their more literal approach to painting. Even the Impressionist principle of capturing a scene spontaneously, in action, becomes in Degas's hands a powerful means of expression. One of the themes he turned to again and again was ballet, perhaps because of the range of movement it involved, although he also often underlined the gulf between the Romantic façade of ballet and its down-to-earth reality. In *The Rehearsal* [**Fig. 18.12**] we are left in no doubt that neither ballet nor ballet dancers are entirely glamorous. Degas's point of view is emphasized by the unusual vantage point from which the stage is shown: close to and from a position high up on the side. Far from coldly observing and reproducing the scene, Degas creates an instant bond between us and the hard-worked dancers, based on our perception of them as human beings.

Degas's honesty won him the reputation of being a misogynist because many of his representations of female nudes lack the idealizing qualities of Renoir's

◆ **18.11** (Pierre) Auguste Renoir, *Two Girls at the Piano*, 1892. The position of the two girls, one leaning forward and resting her arm on the back of a chair, is very similar to the position of the woman and the girl in the center of Figure 18.10; this position seems to have appealed to Renoir as a gesture of affection.

Oil on canvas, 45½″ x 34½″ (116 x 90 cm). Musée d'Orsay, Paris, France//© Réunion des Musées Nationaux/Art Resource, NY

◆ **18.12** Edgar Degas, *The Rehearsal*, 1874. Degas's careful observation extends even to the director of the ballet troupe at the right-hand edge of the stage, hat almost over his eyes, holding the back of his chair.

Oil on canvas, 26″ x 32¼″ (65 x 81 cm). Musée d'Orsay, Paris, France//© Réunion des Musées Nationaux/Art Resource, NY

◆ **18.13** Edgar Degas, *The Tub (bathing woman)*, c. 1886. The beautiful simplicity of Degas' drawing gives an impression of action glimpsed momentarily, as if by one passing by. As in *The Rehearsal*, Degas chooses to visualize the scene from an unusual angle. Here, we view from above the crouching figure and still life of toilet articles on a shelf.

Pastel on card, 23½″ x 32½″ (60 x 83 cm). Musée, d'Orsay, Paris, France// © Erich Lessing/Art Resource, NY

◆ **18.14** Mary Cassatt, *Mother Combing Sara's Hair.* By turning the mother's face away, the artist concentrates attention on the child, an effect enhanced by the vague background.

Private Collection//Photo © Christie's Images/The Bridgeman Art Library

◆ **18.15** Berthe Morisot, *View of Paris from the Trocadero*, 1872. The separation between the various planes of the view produces an effect of breadth and tranquility. Note the depictions of human activity—the boat on the river, the horse and carriage—which help bring the scene to life.

Oil on canvas, 18⅛″ x 32¹⁄₁₆″ (46.3 x 81.3 cm). © Museum of Art, Santa Barbara, CA, USA/The Bridgeman Art Library

◆ **18.16** Auguste Rodin, *Monument to Balzac*, 1897–1898. Unlike most sculptors who worked in bronze, Rodin avoided a smooth surface by roughening and gouging the metal.

Bronze, 9′3″ x 48¼″ x 41″ (282 x 122.5 x 104.2 cm). © Musée Rodin, Paris, France/Peter Willi/SuperStock

and other painters' works. In a series of pastels he shows women caught unawares in simple, natural poses. *The Tub* [**Fig. 18.13**], with its unusual angle of vision, shows why these were sometimes called "key-hole visions." Far from posing, his subjects seem to be spied on while they are engrossed in the most intimate and natural activities.

Cassatt One of Degas's closest friends was the American artist Mary Cassatt (1844–1926), who, after overcoming strong opposition from her father, settled in Europe to pursue an artistic career. Like Degas, Cassatt painted spontaneous scenes from daily life, particularly situations involving mothers and children. *Mother Combing*

Sara's Hair [**Fig. 18.14**] shows the mother turned away from us and a child who is saved from sentimentality by her complete unawareness of our presence. Cassatt never married, but there is no reason to think that her paintings of children were created out of frustration. She seems to have had a rich and happy life, and her championship of the Impressionist cause among her American friends led to many of them buying and taking home Impressionist works. Cassatt's artist friends had much to thank her for and so do the curators of many American museums and galleries, which have inherited collections of Impressionist paintings.

Morisot Another member of the same circle was Berthe Morisot (1841–1895). In 1868, Morisot met Manet and they became warm friends; a few years later she married his younger brother. An active member of the Impressionist group, she exhibited works in almost all their shows.

Morisot's work has often been labeled "feminine," both by her contemporaries and by more recent critics. Like Cassatt, a close friend, she often painted women and children. Yet she also produced works of considerable breadth. *View of Paris from the Trocadero* [**Fig. 18.15**] presents a panoramic view of the city. The sense of light and atmosphere is conveyed by loose, fluid brushstrokes. The figures in the foreground do not seem part of any story or incident but help focus the scale of the view, which is seen as if from a height.

Rodin The impact of Impressionism on sculptors was inevitably limited, because many of its principles depended on color and light and could only be applied in paint. Nevertheless, the greatest sculptor of the age (according to many, the greatest since Bernini), Auguste François René Rodin (1840–1917), reproduced in bronze something of the Impressionist love of shifting forms and light and shadow. His remarkable figure of Balzac [**Fig. 18.16**] demonstrates the irregularity of surface by which Rodin converted two-dimensional Impressionist effects to a three-dimensional format. It also reveals one of the ways in which he differed from his Impressionist contemporaries, because his themes are generally massive and dramatic rather than drawn from everyday life. The statue of Balzac shows the great novelist possessed by creative inspiration, rather than his actual physical appearance. The subject of this sculpture is really the violent force of genius, a concept also illustrated in Rodin's portrayal of the composer Gustav Mahler (see Figure 18.32), and Rodin conveys it with almost elemental power. It should perhaps not be surprising that critics of the day were unprepared for such burning intensity. One of them dubbed the statue a "toad in a sack," but in retrospect, Rodin

◆ **18.17** Auguste Rodin, *The Kiss*, 1886. As in his Balzac statue, Rodin uses the texture of the material to enhance the appearance of his work, but in contrast to the rough surface of the bronze, here, the smooth, slightly blurred surface of the marble produces a glowing effect.

Marble, 6′2″ (1.9 m) high. Musée Rodin, Paris, France//© Erich Lessing/Art Resource, NY

breathed new life into sculpture. The "primitive" grandeur of his images formed a powerful attraction for future sculptors.

In general, Rodin's works in marble are less Impressionistic than those in bronze, but his famous *The Kiss* [**Fig. 18.17**] achieves something of Renoir's blurred sensuality by the soft texture of the stone and the smooth transitions between the forms of the figures. Yet even though Rodin at times seems to strive for an Impressionistic surface effect, the drama and full-blooded commitment of many of his works show the inadequacy of stylistic labels. We can only describe Rodin as a sculptor who used the Impressionist style in works that foreshadow modern developments; that is, as a great original.

POST-IMPRESSIONISM

As a stylistic category, **post-Impressionism** is one of the least helpful or descriptive terms in art history. The artists who are generally grouped together under it have as their only real common characteristic a rejection of Impressionism for new approaches to painting. All of them arrived at their own individual styles. Their grouping together is therefore more a matter of historical convenience than critical judgment. The scientific precision of Georges Pierre Seurat (1859–1891), for example, whose paintings, based on the geometric relationship of forms in space, are made up of thousands of tiny dots of paint applied according to strict theories of color [**Fig. 18.18**], has little in common with the flamboyant and exotic art of (Eugéne Henri) Paul Gauguin (1848–1903). Particularly in his last paintings, based on his experiences in Tahiti, Gauguin attacked primitive subjects in a highly sophisticated manner, producing results like *Ia Orana Maria* [**Fig. 18.19**], which may attract or repel viewers but rarely leave them indifferent.

Cézanne The greatest post-Impressionist painter was Paul Cézanne. It would be difficult to overestimate the revolutionary quality of Cézanne's art, which has been compared to that of the proto-Renaissance Florentine painter Giotto as an influence on Western art. Cézanne's innovations ended the six-hundred-year attempt since Giotto's time to reproduce nature in painting. In place of nature Cézanne looked for order; or rather he tried to impose order on nature, without worrying if the results were realistic. It is not easy to comprehend or express in intellectual terms the character of Cézanne's vision, although, as so often in the arts, the works speak for themselves. He claimed that he wanted to "make of Impressionism something solid and durable," and many of his paintings have a monumental air; they convey the mass and weight, in terms of both shape and color of his subject matter, rather than its literal physical appearance. His *Still Life with Commode* [**Fig. 18.20**] does not try to show how the fruit, vase, and cloth really look or reproduce their actual relationship to one another. On the contrary, the painter has deliberately distorted the surface of the table and oversimplified the shapes of the objects to achieve a totally satisfying composition. Abstract considerations, in other words, take precedence over fidelity to nature. Cézanne believed that all forms in nature are based on the cone, the sphere, and the cylinder; and he shapes and balances the forms to make them conform to this notion using vigorous, rhythmical brush strokes. In the process, a simple plate of fruit takes on a quality that can only be called massive.

The miracle of Cézanne's paintings is that for all their concern with ideal order, they are still vibrantly alive.

◆ **18.18** Georges Seurat, *A Sunday on La Grande Jatte*, 1884–1886. For all the casual activity in this scene of strollers in a park on an island in the river Seine, Seurat's remarkable sense of form endows it with an air of formality. Both shape and color (applied in minute dots) are rigorously ordered.

Oil on canvas, 6'9" x 10'3⁄8" (207.5 x 308 cm). Image © Art Institute of Chicago, IL, USA/The Bridgeman Art Library

◆ **18.19** Paul Gauguin, *Ia Orana Maria* ("We hail thee, Mary"), 1891. The painting shows a Tahitian Madonna and child being worshiped by two women with an angel standing behind them. The whole scene presents a fusion of Western spiritual values and the simple beauty of primitive Polynesian life.

Oil on canvas, 44¾ " x 34½" (113.7 x 87.7 cm). The Metropolitan Museum of Art, New York, USA//Image copyright © The Metropolitan Museum of Art/Art Resource, NY

◆ **18.20** Paul Cézanne, *Still Life with Commode*, c. 1887–1888. So painstakingly did the artist work on the precise arrangement and representation of the objects in his still life the fruit usually rotted long before a painting was complete.

Oil on canvas, 25½" x 31¾" (65.1 x 80.8 cm). Image © Fogg Art Museum, Harvard University Art Museums, USA/The Bridgeman Art Library

◆ **18.21** Paul Cézanne, *Mont Sainte-Victoire*, 1904–1906. The reduction of the elements in the landscape to flat planes and the avoidance of the effect of perspective give the painting a sense of concentrated intensity.

Oil on canvas, 28⅞″ x 36¼″ (73 x 92 cm). Image © The Philadelphia Museum of Art, Philadelphia, PA, USA/Art Resource, NY

◆ **18.22** Vincent van Gogh, *The Starry Night*, 1889. The impression of irresistible movement is the result of the artist's careful use of line and shape. The scene is dominated by vertical spirals formed by the cypress trees and horizontal spirals in the sky, which create a sense of rushing speed.

Oil on canvas, 29″ x 36¼″ (73.7 x 92.1 cm). The Museum of Modern Art, New York, USA/Digital Image © The Museum of Modern Art/Licensed by Scala/Art Resource, NY

◆ **18.23** Vincent van Gogh, *The Night Café*, 1888. Compare the lack of perspective in Cézanne's *Mont Sainte-Victoire* (Figure 18.21) to the highly exaggerated perspective used by van Gogh here to achieve a sense of violent intensity.

Oil on canvas, 28½" x 36¼" (72 x 92 cm). Yale University Art Gallery, New Haven, CT, USA//© Yale University Art Gallery/Art Resource, NY

Mont Sainte-Victoire [**Fig. 18.21**] is one of several versions Cézanne painted of the same scene, visible from his studio window. Perhaps the contrast between the peaceful countryside and the grandeur of the mountain beyond partially explains the scene's appeal to him. He produced the transition from foreground to background and up to the sky by the wonderful manipulation of planes of pure color. It illustrates his claim that he tried to give the style of Impressionism a more solid appearance by giving his shapes a more continuous surface, an effect produced by broad brushstrokes. Yet the painting equally conveys the vivid colors of a Mediterranean landscape, with particular details refined away to leave behind the pure essence of all its beauty.

van Gogh Nothing could be in greater contrast to Cézanne's ordered world than the tormented vision of Vincent van Gogh (1853–1890), the tragedy of whose life found its expression in his work. The autobiographical nature of van Gogh's painting, together with its passionate feelings, has a special appeal to modern sensibilities. In fairness to van Gogh, however, we should remember that by giving expression to his desperate emotions the artist was, however briefly, triumphing over them. Furthermore, in a way that only the arts make possible, the suffering of a grim, even bizarre life became transformed into a profound if admittedly partial statement on the human condition. Desperate ecstasy and passionate frenzy are not emotions common to most people, yet *The Starry Night* [**Fig. 18.22**] communicates them immediately and unforgettably.

The momentum of swirling, flickering forms in *The Starry Night* is intoxicating, but for the most part van Gogh's vision of the world was profoundly pessimistic. *The Night Café* [**Fig. 18.23**] was described by the artist as "one of the ugliest I have done," but the ugliness was deliberate. Van Gogh's subject was "the terrible passions of humanity," expressed by the harsh contrasts between red, green, and yellow, which were intended to convey the idea that "the café is a place where one can ruin oneself, go mad, or commit a crime."

Much of van Gogh's pessimism was undoubtedly the result of the unhappy circumstances of his own life, but it is tempting to place it in the wider context of his times and see it also as a terrifying manifestation of the growing social and spiritual alienation of society in the late nineteenth century. That van Gogh was actually aware of this is shown by a remark he made about his *Portrait of Dr. Gachet* [**Fig. 18.24**], the physician who treated him in his last illness. He had painted the doctor, he said, with the "heartbroken expression of our times."

FAUVISM AND EXPRESSIONISM

By the early years of the twentieth century, the violent mood of the times had intensified still further, and artists continued to express this in their art. The impact of post-Impressionists like van Gogh inspired several new movements—the most important of which was **Fauvism**. This developed in France, and **Expressionism**, which reached its high point in the same period, developed in Germany (see **Table 18.1**).

The origin of the term *fauvism* reveals much of its character. In 1905 a group of artists exhibited paintings that broke so violently with tradition in their use of color and form that a critic described the painters as "*les fauves*" ("the wild beasts"). These painters had little in common apart from their desire to discard all traditional values; not surprisingly, the group broke up after a short while, but one of their number, Henri Matisse (1869–1954), became a major force in twentieth-century art.

Matisse Henri Matisse was the leading spirit of the Fauves. His works are filled with the bold accents and brilliant color typical of Fauvist art. Yet the flowing images of Matisse's paintings strike an individual note, expressing a mood of optimism and festivity curiously at odds with the times. One of his first important paintings, *The Joy of Life* [**Fig. 18.25**], shows fields and trees in bright sunlight, where men and women are sleeping, dancing, and making music and love. It is difficult to think of any work of art further removed from the anguish of the years immediately preceding World War I than this image of innocent joy painted between 1905 and 1906.

Matisse was saved from the gloom of his contemporaries by his sheer pleasure in seeing and painting; his work communicates the delight of visual sensation eloquently. His still-life paintings, like those of Cézanne, sacrifice Realism in effective and satisfying design, but his use of color and the distortion of the natural relationships of the objects he paints are even greater than Cézanne's. In *The Red Studio* [**Fig. 18.26**], every form is clearly recognizable but touched by the painter's unique vision. It is as if Matisse compels us to look through his eyes and see familiar objects suddenly take on new, vibrant life.

◆ **18.24** Vincent van Gogh, *Portrait of Dr. Gachet*, 1890. Gachet was an amateur artist and friend of van Gogh who often provided medical treatment for his painter acquaintances without taking any fee. Mentally ill and in despair, van Gogh committed suicide while staying with Gachet.

Oil on canvas, 26¼" x 22½" (67 x 57 cm). Musée d'Orsay, Paris, France// © Réunion des Musées Nationaux/Art Resource, NY

Table 18.1 *Principal Characteristics of Fauvism and Expressionism*

Fauvism

Violent, startling color contrasts
Paintings reflect the effect of visual contact on the psyche
Nature interpreted and subjected to the spirit of the artists
Composition: a decorative arrangement of elements to express the artist's feelings
Technique deliberately crude to disturb the form of objects
No effect of light or depth
Art for art's sake

Expressionism

Brilliant, clashing colors
Paintings reflect mysticism, self-examination, speculation on the infinite
Nature used to interpret the universe
Composition: distorted forms in a controlled space, derived from late Gothic woodcut tradition
Technique influenced by medieval art and the primitivistic art of Africa and Oceania
No use of traditional perspective
Art to convey emotional or psychological truth

The Expressionists Matisse's sunny view of the world was very unusual, however. In northern Europe, particularly, increasing social and political tensions inspired a group of artists generally known as Expressionists to produce works that are at best gloomy and foreboding, sometimes chilling.

◆ **18.25** Henri Matisse, *The Joy of Life*, 1905–1906. By varying the sizes of the figures without regard to the relationship of one group to another, the artist accentuates the sense of dreamlike unreality. Note Matisse's characteristically simple, flowing lines.

Oil on canvas, 5′8″ x 7′9¾″ (1.74 x 2.38 cm). Copyright © 2009 Succession H. Matisse, Paris/Artists Rights Society (ARS), New York//Digital image © The Barnes Foundation, Merion, Pennsylvania, USA/The Bridgeman Art Library

◆ **18.26** Henri Matisse, *The Red Studio*, Issy-les-Molineaux, 1911. The paintings and small sculptures in the studio are actual works by Matisse; they show the brilliant colors typical of Fauve art.

Oil on canvas, 5′11¼″ x 7′2¼″ (1.81 x 2.19 m), The Museum of Modern Art, New York, NY, USA. © 2009 Succession H. Matisse, Paris/Artists Rights Society (ARS), New York//Digital Image © The Museum of Modern Art/Licensed by Scala/Art Resource, NY

◆ **18.27** Edvard Munch, *The Scream*, 1893. Munch once said, "I hear the scream in nature," and in this painting the anguish of the human figure seems to be echoed by the surrounding world. Munch painted several versions of the subject. The one illustrated here was stolen several years ago and subsequently recovered. Another version was stolen in 2004 and is still missing.

Tempera and pastels on cardboard, 35½" x 28¾" (91 x 73.5 cm), National Gallery, Oslo, Norway. Copyright © 2009 The Munch Museum/The Munch-Ellingsen Group/Artists Rights Society (ARS), New York//Digital Image © Scala/Art Resource, NY

Munch The forerunner of Expressionist art was the Norwegian painter Edvard Munch (1863–1944), whose influence on German painting was comparable to that of Cézanne's on French. The morbid insecurity that characterized Munch's own temperament emerges with horrifying force in his best-known work, *The Scream* [**Fig. 18.27**], from which the lonely figure's cry seems to reverberate visibly through space. This painting is more than autobiographical, however, because it reflects a tendency on the part of Norwegian and other Scandinavian artists and writers to explore social and psychological problems. Elsewhere in Europe the Spanish architect Antonio Gaudí (1852–1926) applied the same artistic principles to his buildings, with often startling results. His Casa Milá [**Fig. 18.28**], an apartment house in Barcelona, like *The Scream*, uses restless, waving lines that seem to undulate as we look. The sense of disturbance is continued by the spiraling chimneys, although Gaudí's intention was neither to upset nor necessarily to protest.

By 1905, Expressionist artists in Germany were using the bold, undisguised brushstrokes and vivid colors of Fauvism to paint subjects with more than a touch of Munch's torment. The German Expressionists, many of them grouped in "schools" with such names as *Die Brücke* ("*The Bridge*") and *Der Blaue Reiter* ("*The Blue Rider*"), were relatively untouched by the intellectual and technical explorations of their contemporaries elsewhere. Instead, they were concerned with the emotional impact that a work could produce on the viewer. They were fascinated by the power of color to express mood, ideas, and emotion. They wanted their art to affect not only the eye but also the viewer's inner sense. When they succeeded, as they often did, their works aroused strong emotions. One of their principal themes was alienation and loneliness, so it is not surprising that they often turned to the writings of Dostoyevsky for inspiration. *Two Painters at the Table* [**Fig. 18.29**], by Erich Heckel (1883–1970), is in fact subtitled *To Dostoyevsky*.

◆ **18.28** Antonio Gaudí, Casa Milá, Barcelona, 1907. Note the rough surface of the stone and the absence of any straight lines. *(Image © Stephanie Colasanti/CORBIS)*

◆ **18.30** Emil Nolde, *Pentecost*, 1909. The broad, simplified faces and the powerful gestures of Christ in the center and two apostles clasping hands impart to the scene a concentration of emotional intensity.

Oil on canvas, 2′8″ x 3′6″ (87 x 107 cm). © Nolde-Stiftung Seebuell, Neukirchen, Germany//Private Collection/The Bridgeman Art Library

◆ **18.29** Erich Heckel, *Two Painters at the Table, To Dostoyevsky*, 1912. The two figures seem separated from one another by doubt and distrust, each wrapped up in his own isolation. Behind them is a distorted image of the crucified Christ.

Oil on canvas, 38⅛″ x 48⅛″ (97 x 120 cm), Hamburger Kunsthalle, Hamburg, Germany. © 2009 Artists Rights Society (ARS), New York/VG Bild-Kunst, Bonn//Digital Image © Bildarchiv Preussischer Kulturbesitz/Art Resource, NY

Nolde Emil Nolde (1867–1956), who identified himself with Die Brücke after 1906, was one of the few Expressionists to paint biblical scenes. To these he brought his own ecstatic, barbaric intensity. *Pentecost* [Fig. 18.30] shows the apostles seated around the table literally burning with inspiration; the tongues of flame

of the biblical account are visible above their heads. Their faces have a mask-like simplicity, but the huge eyes and heavy eyebrows convey frighteningly intense emotion. The image is far more disturbing than inspiring. Even in a religious context, Expressionist art touches chords of alarm, and hysteria, unhappily appropriate to the times.

NEW STYLES IN MUSIC

Impressionism had forced both artists and public to think afresh about painting and seeing; by the early years of the twentieth century, musicians and music lovers were also to have many of their preconceptions challenged. Not only were traditional forms like the symphony either discarded or handled in a radical new way, but even the basic ingredients of musical expression, *melody*, *harmony*, and *rhythm*, were subject to startling new developments. Few periods in the history of music are in fact more packed with change than those between 1870 and 1914, which saw a fresh approach to symphonic form, the rise of a musical version of Impressionism, and the revolutionary innovations of the two giants of modern music: Schönberg and Stravinsky.

ORCHESTRAL MUSIC AT THE TURN OF THE NINETEENTH CENTURY

Although many extended orchestral works written in the last years of the nineteenth century and the early twentieth century were called symphonies by their composers, they would hardly have been recognizable as such to Haydn or Beethoven. The custom of varying the traditional number and content of symphonic movements had already begun during the Romantic period; Berlioz had written his *Fantastic Symphony* as early as 1829 (see Chapter 17). Nonetheless, by the turn of the century, so-called symphonies were being written that had little in common with one another, much less the Classic symphonic tradition.

The driving force behind many of these works was the urge to communicate something beyond purely musical values. From the time of the ancient Greeks, many composers attempted to write instrumental music that told a story or described some event, including Vivaldi in his *Four Seasons* and Beethoven in his curious work known as the *Battle Symphony*. By the mid-nineteenth century, however, composers had begun to devise elaborate *programs* (plots), which their music would then describe. Music of this kind is generally known as **program music**, the first great exponent of which was Liszt (see Chapter 17), who wrote works with titles such as *Hamlet*, *Orpheus*, and *The Battle of the Huns*, for which he invented the generic description **symphonic poem**.

The principle behind program music is no better or worse than many another. The success of any individual piece depends naturally on the degree to which narrative and musical interest can be combined. There are, to be sure, some cases where a composer has been carried away by eagerness for realism. Ottorino Respighi (1879–1936), for example, incorporated the sound of a nightingale by including a record player and a recording of live birdsong for *Pines of Rome* (1924).

Strauss No one was more successful at writing convincing program symphonies and symphonic poems (**tone poems**, as he called them) than the German composer Richard Strauss (1864–1949). One of his first successful tone poems, *Don Juan*, begun in 1886, deals with the familiar story of the compulsive Spanish lover from a characteristically late-nineteenth-century point of view. Instead of the unrepentant Don Giovanni of Mozart or Byron's amused (and amusing) Don Juan, Strauss presents a man striving to overcome the bonds of human nature, only to be driven by failure and despair to suicide. The music, gorgeously orchestrated for a vast array of instruments, moves in bursts of passion, from the surging splendor of its opening to a bleak and shuddering conclusion.

Strauss was not limited to grand and tragic subjects. *Till Eulenspiegel* tells the story of a notorious practical joker and swindler and is one of the most successful examples of humor in music. Even when Till goes too far in his pranks and ends up on the gallows (vividly depicted by Strauss's orchestration), the music returns to a cheerful conclusion.

One of Strauss's most remarkable works, and one that clearly demonstrates the new attitude toward symphonic form, is his *An Alpine Symphony*, written between 1911 and 1915. In one huge movement lasting some fifty minutes it describes a mountain-climbing expedition, detailing the adventures on the way (with waterfalls, cowbells, glaciers all in the music) and, at its climax, the arrival on the summit. The final section depicts the descent, during which a violent storm breaks out, and the music finally sinks to rest in the peace with which it opened. All this may sound more like a movie's soundtrack than a serious piece of music, but skeptical listeners should try the *Alpine Symphony* for themselves. It is as far from conventional notions of a symphony as Cézanne's painting of *Mont Sainte-Victoire* (see Figure 18.21) is from a conventional landscape, but genius makes its own rules. Strauss's work should be taken on its own terms.

Not surprisingly, a composer capable of such exuberant imagination was also fully at home in the opera house. Several of Strauss's operas are among the greatest of all twentieth-century contributions to the repertoire. In some, he was clearly influenced by the prevailingly gloomy and morbid mood of German Expressionist art. His first big success, for example, was a setting of the English writer Oscar Wilde's play *Salome*, based on the biblical story, first performed to a horrified audience in 1905. After one performance (in 1907) at the Metropolitan Opera House in New York, it was banned in the United States for almost thirty years. The final scene provides a frightening yet curiously moving depiction of erotic depravity, as Salome kisses the lips of the severed head of John the Baptist. This subject had been gruesomely represented by the German Expressionist painter Lovis Corinth (1858–1925) in 1899 [**Fig. 18.31**].

Works like *Don Juan* and *An Alpine Symphony* deal with stories we know or describe events with which we are familiar. In other cases, Strauss took as his subject his own life, and a few of his pieces, including the *Domestic Symphony* and the somewhat immodestly titled *Ein Heldenleben (A Hero's Life)*, are frankly autobiographical. In this he was following a custom that had become increasingly popular in the late nineteenth century—the composition of music concerned with the detailed revelation of its composer's inner emotional life.

Tchaikovsky One of the first musicians to make his personal emotions the basis for a symphony was the late-Romantic composer Peter Ilych Tchaikovsky (1840–1893), whose Symphony No. 6 in B Minor, Op. 74, known as the *Pathétique*, was written in the year of his death. An early draft outline of its "story" was found among his papers, describing its "impulsive passion, confidence, eagerness for activity," followed by love and disappointments, and finally collapse and death. It is now believed that the Russian composer's

◆ **18.31** Lovis Corinth, *Salome and the Head of Saint John the Baptist*, 1899. Note the strikingly modern look of Salome, with her heavy eye makeup and lipstick, here representing the degeneracy of the artist's own times.

Oil on canvas, 50″ x 58″ (127 x 147 cm). Museum der Bildenden Kunstarten, Leipzig, Germany//© Erich Lessing/Art Resource, NY

death from cholera was not, as used to be thought, accidental, but deliberate suicide. The reasons are still not clear, but they perhaps related to a potentially scandalous love affair in high places with which Tchaikovsky had become involved. In the light of this information, the *Pathétique* takes on new poignancy. Its last movement sinks mournfully into silence after a series of climaxes that seem to protest bitterly if vainly against the injustices of life.

Mahler The revelation of a composer's life and emotions through his music reached its most complete expression in the works of Gustav Mahler (1860–1911). Until around 1960, the centenary of his birth in Bohemia, Mahler's music was almost unknown, and he

was generally derided as unoriginal and overambitious. Now that he has become one of the most frequently performed and recorded of composers, we can begin to appreciate his true worth and learn the danger of hasty judgments.

The world of Mahler's symphonies is filled with his own anxieties, triumphs, hopes, and fears, but it also illuminates our own problem-ridden age. It may well be that Mahler speaks so convincingly and so movingly to a growing number of ordinary music lovers because his music touches on areas of human experience that were unexplored before his time and increasingly significant to ours. In purely musical terms, however, Mahler can now be seen as a profoundly original genius. Like Rodin, who produced a marvelous portrait of him

◆ **18.32** (Pierre) Auguste Rodin, *Gustav Mahler*, 1909. As in his *Monument to Balzac* (Figure 18.16), Rodin deliberately roughened the surface of the bronze for dramatic effect. In this case Mahler's hollow cheeks and intense gaze are powerfully suggested.

Bronze, 13⅝″ x 9⅝″ x 9¾″ (34.6 x 24.5 x 24.7 cm). Vienna State Opera, Vienna, Austria//© Erich Lessing/Art Resource, NY

[**Fig. 18.32**], Mahler stands as both the last major figure of the nineteenth century in his field and a pioneer in the modern world. Mahler's innovations won him the scorn of earlier listeners: his deliberate use of popular, banal tunes, for example, and the abrupt changes of mood in his music. A symphony, he once said, should be like the world; it should contain everything. His own nine completed symphonies (he left a tenth unfinished), and *Das Lied von der Erde (The Song of the Earth)*, a symphony for two singers and orchestra, certainly contain just about every human emotion.

As early as the Symphony No. 1 in D, we can hear the highly individual characteristics of Mahler's music. The third movement of the symphony is a funeral march, but its wry, ironic tone is totally unlike any other in the history of music. The movement opens with the mournful sound of a solo double bass playing the old round "Frère Jacques," which is then taken up by the rest of the orchestra. There are sudden bursts of trite nostalgia and violent aggression until the mood gradually changes to one of genuine tenderness. After a gentle middle section, the movement returns to the bizarre and unsettling spirit of the opening.

By the end of his life, Mahler was writing far less optimistic music than his Symphony No. 1, which—despite its third-movement funeral march—concludes with a long finale ending in a blaze of triumphant glory. Mahler's last completed works, *The Song of the Earth* and Symphony No. 9, composed under the shadow of fatal heart disease and impending death, express all of the beauty of the world together with the sorrow and ultimate resignation of one who has to leave it. The final movement of the Symphony No. 9, in particular, is a uniquely eloquent statement of courage in the face of human dissolution. Opening with a long, slow theme of great passion and nobility, the movement gradually fades away as the music dissolves into fragments and finally sinks into silence. Like all of Mahler's music, and like the paintings of van Gogh or Munch, the Symphony No. 9 does not turn its back on the ugliness and tragedy of life, but Mahler, unlike many of his contemporaries, was able to see beyond these realities and express something of the painful joy of human existence. Perhaps this is why his music has become so revered today.

IMPRESSIONISM IN MUSIC

Debussy At about the same time painters in France were developing the style we call Impressionist, Claude Debussy (1862–1918), a young French composer, began to break new musical ground. Abandoning the concept of the development of themes in a systematic musical argument, which lies behind classical sonata form and Romantic symphonic structure, he aimed for a constantly changing flow of sound. Instead of dealing with human emotions, Debussy's music evoked the atmosphere of nature: the wind and rain and the sea. The emphasis on shifting tone colors led inevitably to comparisons to Impressionist painting. Like Monet or Renoir, he avoided grand, dramatic subjects in favor of ephemeral, intangible sensations and replaced Romantic opulence with refinement.

These comparisons should nevertheless not be exaggerated. Debussy and the Impressionists shared a strong reaction against tradition in general and the Romantic tradition in particular, in response to which they created a radically new approach to their respective arts, but Impressionism permanently changed the history of painting, while the only really successful Impressionist composer was Debussy. Later musicians borrowed some of Debussy's musical devices, including his highly fluid harmony and frequent dissonances, but Debussy never really founded a school. The chief developments in twentieth-century music after Debussy took a different

VOICES OF THEIR TIMES

Gustav Mahler

A letter from Mahler to his wife Alma, reporting on a meeting with Richard Strauss. Mahler had heard *Salome* and was impressed. The *she* in the second sentence is Pauline, Strauss's wife.

Berlin, January 190-

My dear, good Almschili;

Yesterday afternoon I went to see Strauss. She met me at the door with pst! pst! Richard is sleeping, pulled me into her (very slovenly) boudoir, where her old mama was sitting over some mess (not coffee) and filled me full of nonsensical chatter about various financial and sexual occurrences of the last two years, in the meantime asking hastily about a thousand and one things without waiting for a reply, would not let me go under any circumstances, told me that yesterday morning Richard had had a very exhausting rehearsal in Leipzig, then returned to Berlin and conducted *Götterdämmerung* in the evening, and this afternoon, worn to a frazzle, he had gone to sleep, and she was carefully guarding his sleep. I was dumbfounded.

Suddenly she burst out: "Now we have to wake up the rascal!" Without my being able to prevent it, she pulled me with both her fists into his room and yelled at him in a very loud voice: "Get up, Gustav is here!" (For an hour I was Gustav—then suddenly Herr Direktor again.) Strauss got up, smiled patiently, and then we went back to a very animated discussion of all that sheer bilge. Later we had tea and they brought me back to my hotel in their automobile, after arranging for me to take lunch with them at noon Saturday.

There I found two tickets for parquet seats in the first row for *Salome* and I took Berliner along. The performance was excellent in every respect—orchestrally, vocally, and scenically it was pure Kitsch and Stoll, and again it made an extraordinary impression on me. It is an extremely clever, very powerful piece, which certainly belongs among the most significant of our time! Beneath a heap of rubbish an infernal fire lives and burns in it—not just fireworks.

That's the way it is with Strauss's whole personality and it's difficult to separate the wheat from the chaff. But I had felt tremendous respect for the whole manifestation and this was confirmed again. I was tremendously pleased. I go the whole hog on that. Yesterday Blech conducted—excellently. Saturday Strauss is conducting and I am going again. Destinn was magnificent; the Jochanaan [Berger] very fine. The others, so-so. The orchestra really superb.

Letter of Gustav Mahler to his wife from *Letters of Composers* by G. Norman and M. L. Shrifte.

---

direction, were summed up rather unsympathetically by the French poet Jean Cocteau (1891–1963): "After music with the silk brush, music with the axe." These developments represent a more determined break with tradition than the refined style of Debussy. With the passing of time, Debussy's musical style appears increasingly to represent the last gasp of Romanticism rather than the dawn of a new era.

Whatever his historical position, Debussy was without doubt one of the great creative musical figures of his time. He is at his best and most Impressionist in orchestral works like *La Mer* (*The Sea*), which Debussy called symphonic sketches—a rather curious term that shows the composer for once willing to accept a traditional label. This marine counterpart of Strauss's *Alpine Symphony* is in three movements, the titles of which ("From Dawn to Noon on the Sea," "Play of the Waves," and "Dialogue of the Wind and the Sea") describe the general atmosphere that concerned Debussy rather than literal sounds. There are no birdcalls or thunderclaps in the music; instead the continual ebb and flow of the music suggest the mood of a seascape. The second movement, for example, depicts the sparkling sunlight on the waves by means of delicate, flashing violin scales punctuated by bright flecks of sound color from the wind instruments. It is scarcely possible to resist a comparison with the shimmering colors of Monet's *Water Lilies* (see Figure 18.9).

Elsewhere, Debussy's music is less explicitly descriptive. His piano music, among his finest compositions, shows an incredible sensitivity to the range of sound effects that instrument can achieve. Many of his pieces have descriptive titles—"Footsteps in the Snow," "The Girl with the Flaxen Hair," and so on—but these were often added after their composition as the obligatory touch of musical Impressionism. Sometimes they were even suggested by Debussy's friends as their own personal reactions to his music. His *Claire de Lune* (*Moonlight*) is a case in point. The tranquil calm of the music might well convey to some listeners the beauty of a moonlit night, but equally, the piece can be enjoyed as a musical experience in its own right.

CD Track 16
Claude Debussy, *Claire de Lune* (Moonlight)

Claire de Lune is one of Debussy's earliest piano works, written in 1890, at a time when he was closer to Impressionist art than he was to become as his style developed. Thus the peaceful descending scale that begins the piece might very well be intended to depict a calm, glowing night. Throughout the piece, interest is centered on the right hand and the higher, "celestial" notes of the piano. The music intensifies, although remaining within the limits of its placid opening.

Debussy's interest in French keyboard music of the rococo period may be responsible for the slightly "antique" air of the piece. Like most of his music it creates its own form, following neither Classical nor Romantic principles of organization, and remaining the expression of a mood rather than a personal outpouring of feeling. Whether that mood is related to a peaceful scene under moonlight or is more generalized is up to the individual listener to decide. It is interesting to speculate on what our reactions to the piece would have been if we did not know its title.

Ravel The only composer to make wholehearted use of Debussy's Impressionistic style was his fellow countryman Maurice Joseph Ravel (1875–1937), who, however, added a highly individual quality of his own. Ravel was far more concerned with classical form and balance than Debussy. His musical god was Mozart, and something of the limpid clarity of Mozart's music can be heard in many of his pieces, although certainly not in the all-too-familiar *Bolero*. His lovely Piano Concerto in G alternates a Mozartian delicacy and grace with an exuberance born of Ravel's encounters with jazz. Even in his most overtly Impressionistic moments, like the scene in his ballet *Daphnis and Chloe* that describes dawn rising, he retains an elegance and verve that differs distinctly from the veiled and muted tones of Debussy.

THE SEARCH FOR A NEW MUSICAL LANGUAGE

In 1908 the Austrian composer Arnold Schönberg (1874–1951) wrote his Three Piano Pieces, Op. 11, in which he was "conscious of having broken all restrictions" of past musical traditions. After the first performance one critic described the pieces as "pointless ugliness" and "perversion." In 1913 the first performance of *The Rite of Spring*, a ballet by the Russian-born composer Igor Fyodorovich Stravinsky (1882–1971), was given in Paris, where he was then living. It was greeted with hissing, stamping, and yelling, and Stravin-

sky was accused of the "destruction of music as an art." Stravinsky and Schönberg are today justly hailed as the founders of modern music, but we can agree with their opponents in at least one respect: their revolutionary innovations permanently changed the course of musical development.

It is a measure of their achievement that today listeners find *The Rite of Spring* exciting, even explosive, but perfectly approachable. If Stravinsky's ballet score has lost its power to shock and horrify, it is principally because we have become accustomed to music written in its shadow. *The Rite of Spring* has created its own musical tradition, one without which present-day music at all levels of popularity would be unthinkable. Schönberg's effect has been less widespread and subtler; nonetheless, no serious composer writing since his time has been able to ignore his music. It is significant that Stravinsky, who originally seemed to be taking music down a radically different "path to destruction," eventually adopted principles of composition based on Schönberg's methods.

As is true of all apparently revolutionary breaks with the past, Stravinsky and Schönberg were really only pushing to extreme conclusions developments that had been under way for some time. Traditional harmony had been collapsing since the time of Wagner, and Schönberg only dealt it a deathblow by his innovations. Wagner's *Tristan and Isolde* had opened with a series of chords that were not firmly rooted in any key and had no particular sense of direction (see Chapter 17), a device Wagner used to express the poetic concept of restless yearning. Other composers followed him in rejecting the concept of a fixed harmonic center from which the music might stray so long as it returned there, replacing it with a much more fluid use of harmony. (Debussy, in his attempts to go beyond the bounds of conventional harmony, often combined chords and constructed themes to avoid the sense of a tonal center; the result can be heard in the wandering, unsettled quality of much of his music.)

Schönberg Arnold Schönberg believed that the time had come to abandon a harmonic (or tonal) system that had served music well for more than three hundred years but had simply become worn out. He therefore began to write **atonal** music, which deliberately avoided traditional chords and harmonies. Thus Schönberg's **atonality** was a natural consequence of earlier musical developments. At the same time, it was fully in accordance with the spirit of the times. The sense of a growing rejection of traditional values, culminating in a decisive and violent break with the past, can be felt not only in the arts but also in the political and social life of Europe; Schönberg's drastic abandonment of centuries of musical tradition prefigured by only a few years the far more drastic abandonment of centuries of tradition brought about by World War I.

There is another sense in which Schönberg's innovations correspond to contemporary developments. One of the principal effects of atonality is a mood of instability—even disturbance—which lends itself to the same kind of morbid themes that attracted Expressionist painters. In fact, many of Schönberg's early atonal works deal with such themes. Schönberg was a painter of some ability and generally worked in an Expressionist style.

One of Schönberg's most extraordinary pieces is *Pierrot Lunaire*, finished in 1912, a setting of twenty-one poems for a woman's voice and small instrumental group. The poems describe the bizarre experiences of their hero, Pierrot, who is an Expressionist version of the eternal clown, and their mood is grotesque and at times demonic. The eighth poem, for example, describes a crowd of gigantic black moths flying down to block out the sunlight, while in the eleventh, titled "Red Mass," Pierrot holds his own heart in his bloodstained fingers to use as a "horrible red sacrificial wafer." Schönberg's music clothes these verses in appropriately fantastic and macabre music. The effect is enhanced by the fact that the singer is instructed to speak the words at specific pitches. This device of **Sprechstimme** ("voiced speech"), invented by Schönberg for *Pierrot Lunaire*, is difficult to execute, but when it is done properly by a skilled performer, it imparts a wistfully dreamlike quality to the music.

CD Track 17
Arnold Schönberg, "Mondestrunken," No. 1, *Pierrot Lunaire*

In this first poem of Schönberg's *Pierrot Lunaire*, "Mondestrunken" (literally Moondrunk), the poet, his eyes drunk with wine and moonlight, seeks inspiration in the beauty of the night. The piece begins with brief piano scales before the voice enters, accompanied by the flute, later the violin and cello. Indeed, the flute dominates the setting, soaring and trilling, as if to express the ecstasy of the moment. The piece reaches a brief climax, with the flute in its highest register, and then fades away.

This first poem sets the tone for the whole cycle. Schönberg uses a group of eight solo instruments to accompany his "reciter," varying the combination from piece to piece. The moon as a topic returns in several of the later pieces, most notably No. 7, "The Sick Moon."

Of all the tracks on the Listening CD, none is likely to seem more perplexing to the first-time listener, or further from most people's musical experience. It may help the listener to know that in an earlier work, his String Quartet No. 2, Schönberg includes a setting of a poem by the German Symbolist poet Stefan George, which includes the line: "I feel the breath of another planet." Schönberg was indeed seeking to break with the long history of musical development and open up new worlds.

The freedom atonality permitted the composer became something of a liability, and by the 1920s Schönberg replaced it with a system of composition as rigid as any earlier method in the history of music. His famous **twelve-tone technique** uses the twelve notes of the chromatic scale (on the piano, all of the black and white notes in a single octave), which are carefully arranged in a **row** or **series**, the latter term having given rise to the name **serialism** to describe the technique. The basic row, together with variant forms, then serves as the basis for a movement or even an entire work, with the order of the notes remaining always the same.

Just as with program music, the only fair way to judge the twelve-tone technique is by its results. Not all works written using it are masterpieces, but we can hardly expect them to be. It is not a system that appeals to all composers or brings out the best in them, but few systems ever have universal application. Some of Schönberg's own twelve-tone works, including his unfinished opera *Moses and Aaron* and the Violin Concerto of 1934, demonstrate that serial music can be both beautiful and moving. The twenty-first century will decide whether the system has permanent and enduring value.

Stravinsky Like *Pierrot Lunaire*, Igor Stravinsky's *The Rite of Spring* deals with a violent theme. It is subtitled *Pictures from Pagan Russia* and describes a springtime ritual culminating in the sacrifice of a chosen human victim. Whereas Schönberg jettisoned traditional harmony, Stravinsky used a new approach to rhythm as the basis of his piece. Constantly changing, immensely complex, and frequently violent, his rhythmic patterns convey a sense of barbaric frenzy that is enhanced by the weight of sound obtained from the use of a vast orchestra. There are some peaceful moments, notably the nostalgic opening section, but in general the impression is of intense exhilaration.

CD Track 18
Igor Stravinsky, "Dance of the Adolescents," *The Rite of Spring*

The Rite of Spring opens quietly, with no hint of the violence to come. The first outbreak occurs in this dance, with the strings hammering out a repeated dissonant chord, while wind instruments can be heard in the background, playing fragments of themes. Stravinsky creates a sense of excitement by repeating the same rhythm obsessively, while violently stressing some of the notes. When the heavy brass instruments enter, they bring an ominous tone, but soon we return to the hammering string chords. The mood grows quieter for a while, but as Stravinsky increases the tension the Dance moves to a frenzied climax, with rhythm and melodic fragments reaching a fever-pitch, before plunging into the next dance.

It is difficult to imagine a more complete break with the Romantic movement. Subject and style, the violence

◆ **18.33** Vaslav Nijinsky, 1911. One of the greatest dancers of all time, the Russian Nijinsky (1890–1950) appears here as the puppet Petrouchka in the Ballets Russes performance of Igor Stravinsky's ballet of that name in Paris, 1911. The ballet was choreographed by Fokine (1880–1942), also a Russian, who broke new ground in ballet just as the Impressionists did in art and music.

Photograph by Mishkin, 6" x 8" mounted on board 14" x 20". Performing Arts Dance Division, The New York Public Library at Lincoln Center, New York, NY, USA//© The New York Public Library/Art Resource, NY

of contrasts, the sheer brute power of the music, all took his contemporaries by storm, and many accounts have survived of the scandalous scenes of protest that broke out at the ballet's first performance. In a way, *The Rite of Spring* marks both a beginning and an end: Stravinsky never returned to the work's style. Yet as an illustration of the collapse of traditional values on the eve of World War I (the ballet was first performed in 1913), Stravinsky's musical revolution, like Picasso's in the visual arts, was indeed prophetic of the troubled twentieth century.

The Rite of Spring was the last of three ballets (the others were *The Firebird* and *Petrouchka*) that Stravinsky based on Russian folk subjects [**Fig. 18.33**]. In the years following World War I, he wrote music in a wide variety

of styles, absorbing influences as varied as Bach, Tchaikovsky, and jazz. Yet a characteristically Stravinskian flavor pervades all of his best works, with the result that his music is almost always instantly recognizable. Short, expressive melodies and unceasing rhythmic vitality, both evident in *The Rite of Spring*, recur in works like the Symphony in Three Movements in 1945. Even when, in the 1950s, he finally adopted the technique of serialism, he retained his own unique musical personality. Stravinsky is a peculiarly twentieth-century cultural phenomenon, an artist uprooted from his homeland, cut off (by choice) from his cultural heritage, and exposed to a barrage of influences and counterinfluences. That he never lost his sense of personal identity or his belief in the enduring value of art made him a twentieth-century hero.

NEW SUBJECTS FOR LITERATURE

PSYCHOLOGICAL INSIGHTS IN LITERATURE AND DRAMA

At the end of the nineteenth century, many writers were still as concerned with exploring the nature of their own individual existences as they had been when the century began. In fact, the first years of the twentieth century saw an increasing interest in the effect of the subconscious on human behavior, a result largely of the work of the Austrian psychoanalyst Sigmund Freud (1856–1939); the general conclusions Freud reached are discussed in Chapter 21. In many ways his interest in the part played by individual frustrations, repressions, and neuroses (particularly sexual) in creating personality was prefigured in the writing of two of the greatest novelists of the late nineteenth century: Fyodor Dostoyevsky (1821–1881) and Marcel Proust (1871–1922).

Dostoyevsky Self-knowledge played a major part in Dostoyevsky's work, and his concern for psychological truth led him into a profound study of his characters' subconscious motives. His empathy for human suffering derived in part from his identification with Russian Orthodox Christianity, with its emphasis on suffering as a means to salvation. Although well aware of social injustices, he was more concerned with their effect on the individual soul than on society as a whole. His books present a vivid picture of the Russia of his day, with characters at all levels of society brought brilliantly to life. Nevertheless, he was able to combine realism of perception with a deep psychological understanding of the workings of the human heart. Few artists have presented so convincing a picture of individuals struggling between good and evil.

The temptation to evil forms a principal theme of one of his most powerful works, *Crime and Punishment*. In it Dostoyevsky tells the story of a poor student, Raskolnikov, whose growing feeling of alienation from his fellow human beings leads to a belief that he is superior to society and above conventional morality. To prove this to himself, Raskolnikov decides to commit an act of defiance: the murder of a defenseless old woman, not for gain but as a demonstration of his own power.

He murders the old woman and also her younger sister, who catches him in the act. Crime is followed immediately, however, not by the punishment of the law but by the punishment of his own conscience. Guilt and remorse cut him off even farther from human contact until finally, in utter despair and on the verge of madness, he goes to the police and confesses to the murder. Here and in his other works, Dostoyevsky underlines the terrible dangers of intellectual arrogance. The world he portrays is essentially cruel, one in which simplicity and self-awareness are the only weapons against human evil, and suffering is a necessary price paid for victory.

Chekhov If Dostoyevsky used violence to depict his worldview, his contemporary and fellow Russian Anton Pavlovich Chekhov (1860–1904) used irony and satire to show the passivity and emptiness of his characters. In plays and short stories, Chekhov paints a provincial world whose residents dream of escape, filled with a frustrated longing for action. The three sisters who are the chief characters in the play of that name never manage to achieve their ambition to go "To Moscow, to Moscow!" In stories such as "The Lady with the Dog," Chekhov uses apparent triviality to express profound understanding, whereas in "The Bet" he ironically challenges most of our basic values.

Proust One of the most influential of all modern writers was the French novelist Marcel Proust. Proust's youth was spent in the fashionable world of Parisian high society, where he entertained lavishly and mixed with the leading figures of the day while writing elegant if superficial poems and stories. The death of his father in 1903 and of his mother in 1905 brought about a complete change. He retired to his house in Paris and rarely left his soundproofed bedroom, where he wrote the vast work for which he is famous, *Remembrance of Things Past*. The first volume appeared in 1913; the eighth and last volume was not published until 1927, five years after his death.

It is difficult to do justice to this amazing work. The lengthy story is told in the first person by a narrator who, though never named, obviously has much in common with Proust. The story's entire concern is to recall the narrator's past life—from earliest childhood to middle age—by bringing to mind the people, places, things, and events that have affected him. In the course of the narrator's journey back into his past, he realizes that all of it lies hidden inside him and that the tiniest circumstance—a scent, a taste, the appearance of someone's hair—can trigger a whole chain of memory associations. By the end of the final volume the narrator has decided to preserve the recollection of his past life by making it permanent in the form of a book—the book the reader has just finished.

Proust's awareness of the importance of the subconscious and his illustration of the way in which it can be unlocked have had a great appeal to modern writers, as has his **stream of consciousness** style, which appears to reproduce his thought processes as they actually occur rather than as edited by a writer for logical connections and development. Furthermore, as we follow Proust's (or the narrator's) careful and painstaking resurrection of his past, it is important to remember that his purpose is far more than a mere intellectual exercise. By recalling the past we bring it back to life in a literal sense. Memory is our most powerful weapon against death.

THE ROLE OF WOMEN

Not all writers in the late nineteenth and early twentieth centuries devoted themselves to the kind of psychological investigation found in the works of Dostoyevsky and Proust. The larger question of the nature of society continued to attract the attention of more socially conscious writers who explored the widening range of problems created by industrial life as well as a whole new series of social issues (see **Table 18.2**).

One of the most significant aspects of the development of the modern world has been the changing role of women in family life and in society at large. The

Table 18.2 *Social and Intellectual Developments: 1870–1914*

1875	German Social Democratic party founded
1879	Edison invents electric light bulb
1881	Pasteur and Koch prove "germ theory" of disease
1883	Social insurance initiated by Bismarck in Germany
1888	Brazil abolishes slavery, the last nation to do so
1889	International League of Socialist Parties founded, the so-called Second International
1894–1906	Dreyfus affair in France reveals widespread anti-Semitism and leads to separation of church and state
1895	Roentgen discovers x-rays; Marconi invents wireless telegraphy
1900	Freud publishes *The Interpretation of Dreams*
1903	Wright brothers make first flight with power-driven plane
1905	Einstein formulates theory of relativity; Revolution in Russia fails to produce significant social change
1906–1911	Social insurance and parliamentary reform enacted in Britain
1909	Ford produces assembly-line-made automobiles
1911	Revolution in China establishes republic; Rutherford formulates theory of positively charged atomic nucleus

issue of women's right to vote was bitterly fought in the early years of the twentieth century, and not until 1918 in Great Britain and 1920 in the United States were women permitted to participate in the electoral process. On a more personal basis, the growing availability and frequency of divorce began to cause many women (and men) to rethink the nature of the marriage tie. The pace of women's emancipation from the stock role assigned to them over centuries was extremely slow, and the process is far from complete. A beginning had to be made somewhere, however, and it is only fitting that a period characterized by cultural and political change should also be marked by social change in this most fundamental of areas.

In the same way Dickens had led the drive against industrial oppression and exploitation in the mid-nineteenth century, writers of the late nineteenth and early twentieth centuries not only reflected feminist concerns but actively promoted them as well. They tackled a range of problems so vast that we can do no more than look at just one area, marriage, through the eyes of two writers of the late nineteenth century. One of them, Henrik Ibsen (1828–1906), was the most famous playwright of his day and a figure of international renown. The other, Kate Chopin (1851–1904), was ignored in her own lifetime even in her native America.

Ibsen Ibsen was born in Norway, although he spent much of his time in Italy. Most of his mature plays deal with the conventions of society and their consequences, generally tragic. Although many are technically set in Norway, their significance was intended to be universal. The problems Ibsen explored were frequently ones regarded as taboo, including venereal disease, incest, and insanity. The realistic format of the plays brought issues like these home to his audience with shocking force. At first derided, Ibsen eventually became a key figure in the development of drama, particularly in the English-speaking world, where his work was championed by George Bernard Shaw (1856–1950), who later inherited Ibsen's mantle as a progressive social critic.

In one of his first important plays, *A Doll's House* (1879), Ibsen dealt with the issue of women's rights. The principal characters, Torvald Helmer and his wife Nora, have been married for eight years, apparently happily enough. Early in their marriage, however, before Helmer had become a prosperous lawyer, Nora had secretly borrowed some money from Krogstad, a friend, to pay for her husband's medical treatment; she had told Torvald that the money came from her father because Helmer was too proud to borrow. As the play opens, Krogstad, to whom Nora is still in debt, threatens to blackmail her if she does not persuade Helmer to find him a job. When she refuses to do so, Krogstad duly writes a letter to Helmer revealing the truth. Helmer recoils in horror at his wife's deception. The mat-

ter of the money is eventually settled by other means and Helmer eventually forgives Nora, but not before the experience has given her a new and unforgettable insight into her relationship with her husband. In the final scene, she walks out the door, slams it, and leaves him forever.

Nora decides to abandon her husband on two grounds. In the first place, she realizes how small a part she plays in her husband's real life. As she says, "Ever since the first day we met, we have never exchanged so much as one serious word about serious things." The superficiality of their relationship horrifies her. In the second place, Helmer's inability to rise to the challenge presented by the discovery of his wife's deception and prove his love for her by claiming that it was he who had borrowed and failed to repay the debt diminishes him in Nora's eyes. Ibsen tries to express what he sees as an essential difference between men and women when, in reply to Helmer's statement "One doesn't sacrifice one's honor for love's sake," Nora replies, "Millions of women have done so." Nora's decision not to be her husband's childish plaything—to leave the doll's house in which she was the doll—was so contrary to accepted social behavior that one noted critic remarked, "That slammed door reverberated across the roof of the world."

Kate Chopin In comparison to the towering figure of Ibsen, the American writer Kate Chopin found few readers in her own lifetime; even today she is not widely known. Only recently have critics begun to do justice to the fine construction and rich psychological insight of her novel *The Awakening*, denounced as immoral and banned when first published in 1899. Its principal theme is the oppressive role women are forced to play in family life. Edna, its heroine, like Nora in *A Doll's House*, resents the meaninglessness of her relationship with her husband and the tedium of her daily existence. Her only escape is to yield to her sexual drives and find freedom not in slamming the door behind her but by throwing herself into a passionate if unloving affair.

In her short stories, Chopin dealt with the same kind of problem, but with greater delicacy and often with a wry humor. Frequently on the smallest of scales, these stories examine the prison that marriage seems so often to represent. In the course of a couple of pages, Chopin exposes an all-too-common area of human experience and, like Ibsen, touches a chord that rings as true now as it did at the turn of the century.

SUMMARY

◆ **The Coming of World War.** The last years of the nineteenth century saw the threat of war gathering with increasing speed over Europe. The gap between the prosperous and the poor, the growth of the forces of big business, and overcrowding and food shortages in the cities all tended to create a climate of unease that the rivalries of the major European powers exacerbated. Many emigrated to America in search of a new start. For the philosopher Friedrich Nietzsche, only drastic remedies could prevent the collapse of Western civilization.

◆ **Impressionist Painting.** In each of the arts, the years leading up to World War I were marked by far-reaching changes. In the case of painting, the Impressionist school developed in Paris. Foreshadowed in the work of Édouard Manet, Impressionist art represented a new way of looking at the world. Painters like Claude Monet, Auguste Renoir, and Berthe Morisot reproduced what they saw rather than visually interpreted their subjects. The depiction of light and atmosphere became increasingly important. The figure studies of Edgar Degas and Mary Cassatt avoided the careful poses of earlier times in favor of natural, intimate scenes.

◆ **The Post-Impressionists.** The various schools that developed out of Impressionism are collectively known as post-Impressionist, although they have little in common with one another. Among the leading artists were Paul Gauguin, with his love of exotic subjects, and Vincent van Gogh, whose deeply moving images have made him perhaps the best known of all nineteenth-century painters. In historical terms, the most important figure was probably Paul Cézanne: his works are the first since the dawn of the Renaissance to eliminate perspective and impose order on nature rather than try to reproduce it.

◆ **Expressionism and the Fauves.** In the early years of the twentieth century, two movements began to emerge: Fauvism and Expressionism—the former in France and the latter in Germany and Scandinavia. Both emphasized bright colors and violent emotions, and the works of Edvard Munch and other Expressionists are generally tormented in spirit. Henri Matisse, the leading Fauve artist, however, produced joyous and optimistic works; he was to become a major force in twentieth-century painting.

◆ **Orchestral Music at the Turn of the Nineteenth Century.** Composers of orchestral music in the late nineteenth and early twentieth centuries turned increasingly to the rich language of post-Wagnerian harmony and instrumentation to express either extramusical "programs" or to compose "autobiographical" works. The leading figures of the period included Richard Strauss and Gustav Mahler. Many of Strauss's operas have held the stage since their first performances, while his tone poems use a vast orchestra either to tell a story (as in *Don Juan*) or to describe his own life (*Domestic Symphony*). Mahler's

symphonies, neglected in the composer's lifetime, have come to represent some of the highest achievements of the symphonic tradition. Openly autobiographical, they reflect at the same time the universal human problems of loss and anxiety.

In France, the music of Claude Debussy and, to a lesser extent, Maurice Ravel, set out to achieve the musical equivalent of Impressionism. In works like *La Mer*, Debussy used new harmonic combinations to render the atmosphere of a seascape.

◆ **New Approaches to Music: Schönberg and Stravinsky.** The experiments of composers like Mahler and Debussy at least retained many of the traditional musical forms and modes of expression, although they vastly extended them. In the early years of the twentieth century, Arnold Schönberg and Igor Stravinsky wrote works that represented a significant break with the past. Schönberg's atonal and, later, serial music sought to replace the traditional harmonic structure of Western musical style with a new freedom, albeit one limited by the serial system. In *The Rite of Spring* and other works, Stravinsky revealed a new approach to rhythm. Both composers profoundly influenced the development of twentieth-century music.

◆ **Literature and the Subconscious.** Like other arts, literature also underwent revolutionary change in the latter decades of the nineteenth century. In the hands of Fyodor Dostoyevsky and Marcel Proust, the novel became a vehicle to reveal the effects of the subconscious on human behavior. In Dostoyevsky's books, self-knowledge and psychological truth are combined to explore the nature of human suffering. Proust's massive exploration of the past not only seeks to uncover his own memories, but it also deals with the nature of time. Both writers, along with many of their contemporaries, joined painters and musicians in pushing their art to its limits in order to extend its range of expression.

◆ **Writers and the Changing Role of Women.** A more traditional aim of literature was to effect social change. At a time when society was becoming aware of the changing role of women in the modern world, writers aimed to explore the implications for marriage and the family of the gradual emancipation of women and the increasing availability of divorce. The plays of Henrik Ibsen not only described the issues of his day, including feminist ones, but they were also intended to open up discussion of topics—venereal disease, incest—that his middle-class audience would have preferred to ignore.

With the outbreak of war in 1914, the arts were wrenched from their traditional lines of development to express the anxieties of the age. Nothing—in art, culture, politics, or society—was ever to return to its former state.

EXERCISES

1. Assess the impact of political and philosophical developments on the arts in the late nineteenth century.

2. Describe the goals and achievements of the Impressionist movement in painting. How do you account for the enormous popularity of Impressionist art ever since?

3. How did Arnold Schönberg's music break with the past? How does his serial system function? What is its purpose?

4. In what ways is the changing role of women reflected in art and literature at the turn of the century?

5. Compare the fiction of Dostoyevsky and Proust. How does it differ from earlier nineteenth-century novels discussed in Chapter 17?

 Visit the *Culture & Values* Companion website at **www.cengage.com/art/Cunningham/Cultureand Values7E** and the *Humanities Resource Center* for an array of primary source readings, key terms with pronunciations, flash cards, quizzes, and study materials designed especially to help you do well in this course.

CHAPTER 19

INDIA, CHINA, AND JAPAN: FROM THE MEDIEVAL TO THE MODERN WORLD

By the end of the nineteenth century, all the civilizations described in this chapter had begun to adjust to their place in a world dominated by the Western powers. Japan's transition was the least painful, as the Emperor Mitsuhito introduced Western systems of government and industrialization. China endured decades of internal revolution, reflected in Chinese art, while India struggled against Britain, the colonial power that had controlled its economy and then its government since 1600. The fight for Indian independence was led by one of the twentieth century's most original and admired figures, Mohandas Gandhi, known to his followers and his enemies alike as the Mahatma (the saintly one). His policy of nonviolent civil disobedience inspired (and inspires) liberation movements throughout the world.

Gandhi was born into a wealthy Hindu family and studied law in London. He began his legal career in South Africa where he found brutal discrimination against Indian workers imported by British employers. To draw attention to these injustices, he devised his strategy of peaceful protest marches and nonviolent resistance to police actions.

Returning to India, he soon acquired supporters both among sophisticated nationalist leaders and also among the Hindu rural masses, who respected his austere way of life. In 1919, after hundreds of peaceful nationalist demonstrators had been gunned down by British-controlled forces at Amritsar, Gandhi, as leader of the Indian National Congress Party, campaigned for noncooperation and nonviolent civil disobedience. He encouraged the boycott of British products, urged the friendship of Hindus and Muslims, and spoke out against the terrible conditions of the untouchables. During his numerous prison sentences between 1922 and 1942, he regularly went on hunger strikes.

Shortly after the end of World War II, in 1947, India was declared an independent Republic, and Gandhi reluctantly agreed to the partition that created the separate state of Pakistan for India's Muslim minority. In 1948 he was assassinated by a young Hindu fanatic on the grounds of his sympathy with Muslims.

At the same time that the medieval era in Western Europe was nearing its end, two principal regions in southeast Asia—India and China—underwent lasting changes as a result of outside invaders. The third, Japan, maintained its cultural isolation from the rest of the world until the nineteenth century. All three regions eventually came into contact with Western culture.

◆ Indian nationalist leader, Mohandas "Mahatma" Gandhi (1869–1948). *(© Dinodia/The Bridgeman Art Library)*

INDIA: FROM MUGHAL CONQUEST TO BRITISH RULE

With the decline of Buddhism and the fall of the Gupta Empire, India separated into a series of kingdoms, many of which were ruled by **rajputs**. For the most part, these local rulers were descendants of warriors from Central Asia who had converted to Hinduism and claimed membership in the warrior caste. (For general developments in Asia during this period, see the "Map of Asia.")

Their constant feuding prevented the formation of a thriving economy or stable government and left India vulnerable to conquest by an outside force—that of the Muslims.

The first major seat of Muslim power was at Delhi, where Turkish forces established a *sultanate* (a Muslim kingdom ruled by a sultan) in 1192. Although it fell to successive waves of invaders, the Sultanate of Delhi established Islam as a new force in the subcontinent; it was strongest in the northwest—the Indus Valley—a region that centuries later broke away from India to become the Islamic Republic of Pakistan after World War II.

GENERAL EVENTS	ART & ARCHITECTURE	LITERATURE & PHILOSOPHY
INDIA		
1100		
1192 Sultanate of Delhi establishes first major seat of Muslim power in India		
1200		
1300		
1400		
1500		
1500–1700 The Mughal Empire in India **1526** Afghanistan chieftain Babur (1483–1530) wins control of northern India **1542–1605** Akbar, Babur's grandson, extends Muslim rule to most of India	Under the Mughal emperors, secular art forms show realistic portraits and historical events	Akbar commissions a new language, Urdu, to establish a common language for the empire
1600		
	Taj Mahal built by Shah Jehan (1632–1649)	Hindu poet Tulsi Das (1532?–1623) writes the Sanskrit epic "The Holy Lake of the Acts of Rama"
1618–1707 Aurangzeb, last significant Mughal emperor, orders systematic destruction of Hindu works		
1700		
1764 India falls under the virtual control of the British East India		Prem Cand (1880–1936) Indian novelist and short-story writer
1800		
1800 British control of India made official **1885** Founding of India's National Congress party		
1900		
1914–1917 World War I **1917** Mohandas Gandhi (1869–1948) leads postwar campaign for Indian independence, espousing "Satyagraha" or nonviolent civil disobedience **1939–1945** World War II **1948** Gandhi assassinated by Hindu extremist **1950** End of British rule		In *The Apu Trilogy*, and other works, Indian filmmaker Satyajit Ray (1921–1992) tells the stories of ordinary people, using the details of everyday life to convey their culture
2000		

THE MUGHAL EMPIRE

In 1526 Babur (1483–1530), an Afghanistan chieftain, led his troops into India and in a short time won control over most of northern India. His grandson, Akbar (1542–1605), further extended Muslim rule to cover most of India and Afghanistan. Akbar's kingdom was called the **Mughal** (the Persian word for "Mongol") Empire and lasted until the British took control of India in the eighteenth century (see map, "The Mughal Empire in India").

Unlike earlier raiders bent on plunder, both Akbar and his grandfather intended from the outset that the land they conquered should become a center for civilization. Akbar was famous not only for his courage and military prowess, but also as a book collector and patron of the arts. Unlike Muslim rulers elsewhere, Akbar made no attempt to impose the Islamic faith on his subjects. He married a Hindu princess and allowed Hindu women at his court to practice their religion openly. In order to provide a common language for all his subjects, Akbar commissioned scholars to create a blend of Hindi (hitherto the most widely spoken language in India) with Arabic and Persian. The new language, called **Urdu**, is, together with Hindi and English, one of India's three official languages today.

GENERAL EVENTS	ART & ARCHITECTURE	LITERATURE & PHILOSOPHY
	CHINA	
1279 Mongols invade China, seizing Beijing	**1200s** Construction of imperial capital Beijing, including the Forbidden City, follows conservative plan	
1368–1644 Ming Dynasty Confucianism with its emphasis on obedience and loyalty to authorities develops under the Ming Dynasty	Ming Dynasty produces vases of exceptional quality	Confucianism results in both a rigid conservatism in existing forms and an explosion of experimentation in new artistic forms
	1400 Landscape provides a new subject for painters	
		1500s First collections of "Hua-Pen," works based on the oral traditions of traveling storytellers appear *Chin P'ing Mei,* one of the first novels to focus on daily life rather than the fantastic or epic stories of tradition *Monkey,* by Wu Ch'eng-en (c. 1501–1580), relates the legendary travels of Tripitaka, an actual Buddhist priest
1644–1911 Qing Dynasty **1654–1722** Kang establishes the Grand Council to solidify his power with local bureaucratic structures **1669** Ferdinand Verbiest (1623–1688), a westerner, becomes head of the Beijing Astronomical Bureau **1689** Treaty with Peter the Great limits Russian expansion into China British East India Company arrives in China		Painter Shitao introduces a more vigorous line in landscape painting
1800 Chinese independence threatened by traders importing opium **1839–1842** Opium War results when China resists western efforts to import opium **1851–1864** Tai Ping Rebellion		
1900–1901 Boxer Rebellion results in full western control of China **1911** Sun Yat-sen (1866–1925) and the Republican army defeat the monarchy **1928** Chiang Kai-shek (1887–1975) leads the Kuomintang before retreating to Taiwan **1949** Mao Tse-tung (1893–1976) Chinese communist party leader assumes power	Despite rigid control by the Communist Party, filmmakers like Zhang Yimou (b. 1951) made such films as *Raise the Red Lantern* (1951) and *The Story of Qiu Ju* (1992) that highlighted China's social system and paid special attention to hardships faced by women	After World War II virtually all art either glorifies communism or vilifies previous regimes

Under Akbar's successors, the Mughal Empire expanded further to include all but the extreme southern tip of the subcontinent. During the first half of the seventeenth century, patronage of the arts reached new heights, as Mughal architects and painters devised a new style that, like the Urdu language, combined aspects of the Hindu tradition with Persian and other Muslim elements.

MUGHAL ART

The most visible remains of Mughal rule in India were left by Mughal architects. Mosques, palaces, walled cities, and forts all show traditional Indian techniques combined with new innovations from Arabic architecture. Among the most important of these innovations are the dome, pointed arch, and **minaret** ("tower"); this last feature formed a vital element in the construction of mosques, Islam's most important religious architectural form. The most famous of Mughal buildings—and one of the best known anywhere in the world—is the Taj Mahal at Agra, built by order of Shah Jehan (1592–1666) during the years 1632–1649 [**Fig. 19.2**]. The shah commissioned the Taj Mahal as a tomb and monument for his beloved wife Banu Begam, the mother of fourteen of his children, a woman as renowned for her charity as for

	GENERAL EVENTS	ART & ARCHITECTURE	LITERATURE & PHILOSOPHY
		JAPAN	
200	Agricultural communities based on tribal chiefs develop in Japan		
780	**780** Heian, present-day Kyoto, becomes new capital and stable center of government		Japanese develop their own system of writing *Noh* plays develop, combining ritual and slapstick elements to tell traditional stories
THE HEIAN PERIOD	Fujiwara Michinaga (966–1027) serves as regent to the royal family		Lady Murasaki Shikibu (c. 980–1030) writes *The Tale of Genji*, based on her experiences at the Heian court; it becomes the most famous literary work of its day The "pillow-book" or diaries of Sei Shonagon (c. 1000) also survive from this era
1185	**1185** The Period of Feudal Rule The city of Kakamura becomes a more aggressive rival to the capital at Kyoto, marking the beginning of feudal rule under a new warrior class of *samurai* serving under the military command of the *shogun* **1274, 1281** Successive waves of Mongol invasion		
1450	**1467–1568** Age of the Warring States **1590** Hideyoshi (1537–1598) reunites Japan		
1603	Tokugawa (1543–1616) creates a new capital at Edo, the modern Tokyo	Japanese artists continue to develop traditional Chinese models for landscape painting	Basho (1644–1694), a great poet of the age, develops the *haiku* Ihara Saikaku (1642–1693) becomes famous for his novels, including *Life of an Amorous Woman* In *The Love Suicide at Amijima* and other works, Chikamatsu Monzaemon (1653–1725) contributes to the new dramatic form *kabuki*, which draws on real life for material
THE EDO PERIOD	**1853** Commodore Matthew Perry arrives, intent on opening Japan to American trade	Hokusai Katsushika (1760–1849) explores the popular new medium of woodblock	
1868	**1868** The Meiji Japan begins a vast program of modernization under the Meji emperors		
1900	By 1905 Japan has industrialized successfully enough to defeat the Russians in the Russo–Japanese War **1914–1917** World War I **1939–1945** World War II		
1950	**1952** End of American occupation of Japan	1950s, acclaimed Japanese film director Akira Kurosawa (1910–1998) directs *Rashomon* and *Seven Samurai*; his career continues well into the 1980s with *Kagemusha* and *Ran*, reflecting the influence of such classic American filmmakers as John Ford	
2000			

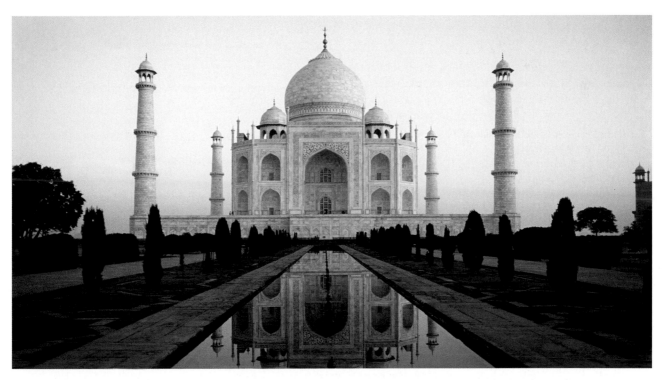

◆ **19.2** The Taj Mahal, Agra, India. Built 1632–1649, at the command of Shah Jehan, as the tomb for his favorite wife, it eventually served as the Shah's own tomb. Much of the building's visual effect comes from its proportions: the height of the central structure is equal to its width, and the dome and central façade on which it sits are the same height. (*© Brian A. Vikander/CORBIS*)

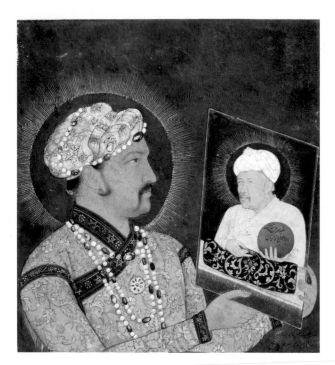

◆ **19.3** *Portrait of Jahangir,* c. 1614. Mughal emperor from 1605 to 1627. Jahangir is holding a portrait of Akbar, his father and political predecessor. Jahangir's reign was notable for the contacts he established with Europe and the acquisition of many objects, among them, prints and portraits.

Mughal miniature, School of Jahangir (Abu'l Hassan and Hashin), watercolor, gouache, heightened with gold on paper, 4¾″ x 3¼″ (12.0 x 8.3 cm). Musée des Arts Asiatiques-Guimet, Paris, France//© Réunion des Musées Nationaux/Art Resource, NY

◆ **19.4** Basawan and Chatar Muni, *Akbar and the Elephant Hawai.* The painting depicts an actual event that took place when Akbar was 19. An elephant he rode charged after another elephant and broke a bridge resting on boats. The emperor is shown successfully maintaining control over his beast—a symbol of his success in governing the state.

Folio 22 from the Akbarnama (History of Akbar) by Abul Fazl, c. 1590. Opaque watercolor on paper, 1′1⅛″ x 8¾″ (32.5 by 22 cm.). Victoria and Albert Museum, London, UK//Image © Victoria & Albert Museum, London/Art Resource, NY

her beauty. The dome, towers, and landscaping—in particular the use of water—are all typical Mughal features. Together with the elaborate decorations, or arabesques, they make the Taj Mahal seem an eternal symbol of the queen, "radiant in her youthful beauty, who still lingers on the riverbanks, at early morn, in the glowing midday sun, or in the silver moonlight."

Virtually all Mughal painting is in the form of book illustrations or miniature paintings that were collected in portfolios. Unlike earlier Hindu and Buddhist art, Mughal painting is secular. It shows scenes of courtly life, including—for the first time in Indian art—realistic portraits [**Fig. 19.3**], and often depicts historical events [**Fig. 19.4**]. As in the case of Mughal architecture, the overwhelming influence comes from Persian art of the period. A new art form in India also drew inspiration from Persian models, that of **calligraphy**, which was often combined with miniature paintings. Very few earlier Sanskrit or Hindu texts contained illustrations. By contrast, Mughal artists made full use of the decorative possibilities of Arabic or Persian script [**Fig. 19.5**].

Literature and the production of fine books was highly esteemed by Mughal aristocrats. Babur, the founder of Mughal rule, wrote his autobiography, the

Babur-nama, in Eastern Turkish. It is still regarded as one of the finest examples of Turkish prose literature. His successor, Homayun (ruled 1530–1540; 1555–1556), was so devoted to books that when he rode into battle he took with him part of his library, carried on camelback. Homayun also wrote poetry, using the Persian, rather than Turkish language. Mughal tolerance allowed Hindu writers to continue to write works in their own language and on traditional themes. The poet Tulsi Das (1532?–1623), drawing on the Sanskrit epic, the *Ramayana,* produced *Ramcaritmanas (The Holy Lake of the Acts of Rama),* a work that combines monotheism with traditional Hindu polytheism and is still widely read.

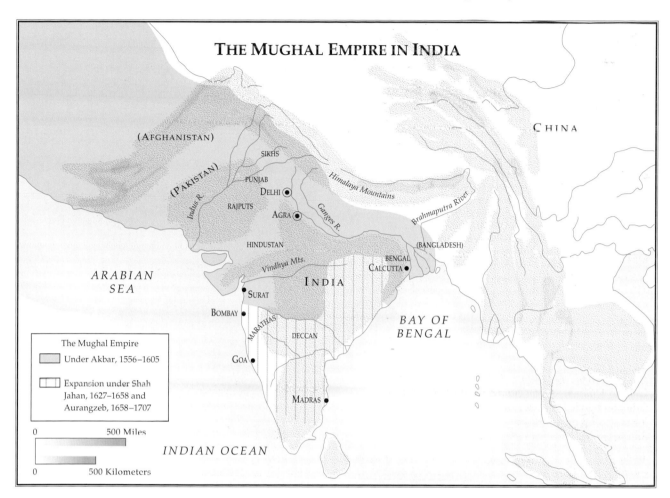

THE MUGHAL EMPIRE IN INDIA

The Mughal Empire
Under Akbar, 1556–1605

Expansion under Shah
Jahan, 1627–1658 and
Aurangzeb, 1658–1707

◆ **19.5** *Rudaba letting down her hair to assist Zal climbing to her balcony*, Iran. c. mid 16th century. In this illustration of an episode from the *Shahnama*, note the written text that accompanies the image.

Ink, watercolor, and gold on paper, 7¾" x 11½" (195 x 300 mm). Image © British Library, London, UK/The Art Archive

THE END OF MUGHAL RULE AND THE ARRIVAL OF THE BRITISH

The religious tolerance of the early Mughal rulers eroded over time. The last significant Mughal emperor, Aurangzeb (1618–1707), destroyed Hindu temples and increased his Hindu subjects' taxes. For the first time, Hindus serving in the imperial bureaucracy had to convert to Islam. Another factor contributing to the collapse of Mughal power was the rise of a new religion, related to Hinduism, but with no caste system: Sikhism. The Sikhs combined Hindu rituals with a highly activist approach, forming a military brotherhood that succeeded in setting up an independent state of their own, which lasted until 1849. In that same year, British forces had won control over the rest of India.

Throughout the eighteenth century, the British and French had fought their battle for colonial supremacy on Indian soil. The British East India Trading Company began its operations as early as 1600, and the superiority of British naval forces assured them victory over other European rivals—first Portugal, then France. By 1764, although India was theoretically made up of separate kingdoms, including a Sikh state and a much reduced Mughal Empire, in practice government was in British hands, first under the East India Company and then, by 1800, directly under the British government. For the next century and a half, India was the "Jewel in the Crown" of the British Empire.

THE RISE OF NATIONALISM

Throughout the early years of the twentieth century, many of those colonized by the chief European powers began to strive for self-rule. In India, the battle began in 1885 with the founding of India's National Congress party. During World War I, three million Indian soldiers fought in British armies. This brought about further impetus, and a postwar campaign for India's independence was led by Mohandas Gandhi (1869–1948). First in South Africa, and then—after 1915 in India—Gandhi developed the principle of **Satyagraha** ("nonviolent civil disobedience"). Born a Brahmin (the highest Hindu caste), Gandhi opposed the caste system, to the delight of the poor and India's Muslims, while maintaining Hindu backing by praising religious tradition. Pressure for independence grew during the 1930s and, by the end of World War II, Britain had no choice but to withdraw. Despite Gandhi's efforts to unite Hindus and Muslims—a policy that led to his assassination in 1948 by a Hindu extremist—Britain had played its own part in encouraging Hindu-Muslim tension, and the subcontinent split into the Republic of India (predominantly Hindu) and the Republic of Pakistan (mostly Muslim).

One of the effects of the struggle for self-rule was to create a generation of Indian authors who, writing in both their own languages and in English, sought to draw attention to their country's plight. They include the novelist and short-story writer Prem Cand (1880–1936) and, most famously, Rabindranath Tagore (1861–1941). In 1913 Tagore won the Nobel Prize for literature; he also painted and composed music, including India's first national anthem, and founded a school and a university. Tagore's writing and teaching stressed that national freedom was meaningless without personal freedom and that true authority comes only from basic humanity. The tradition of Indian writers using English for their works continued throughout the twentieth century, and at the beginning of the twenty-first century many of the leading novelists of the day who write in English—Salman Rushdie, Vikram Seth, and many others—are Indian.

◆ **19.6** The Belgian Jesuit missionary, R. P. Verbiest, China, 17th century. Note that the missionary is dressed in traditional Chinese costume and, for the Chinese, is associated not with religious teaching, but with science and mathematics. He holds a telescope, while a globe and a compass rest on the table beside him, and other instruments stand on the ground.

Watercolor. Bibliothèque Nationale, Paris, France//© Giraudon/Art Resource, NY

CHINA: IMPERIAL RULE OF THE MING AND QING DYNASTIES

China retained a central government for most of its history. For the period from 1368 to the Republican Revolution of 1911, two dynasties controlled Chinese political and cultural life: the Ming (1368–1644) and the Qing (1644–1911). As in India, European traders established operations in China—the British East India Company arrived in 1689. Portuguese Jesuit missionaries had been established in the preceding century, using Macao (leased by the emperor to Portugal) as their base [**Fig. 19.6**]. Unlike the Indian experience, however, where the European colonial powers fought out their wars on Indian soil, China remained virtu-

THE MING EMPIRE
Fourteenth to seventeenth centuries

ally untouched by the West, and Macao remained the only port of entry for non-Chinese until the nineteenth century. Thus the central government was able to maintain tight control over the arrival of both people and ideas. This encouraged the stability of the state bureaucracy and the social structure but did little to encourage trade or manufacturing. As a result, the rapid increase in population between 1600 and 1800—from around one hundred fifty million to some three hundred million—led inevitably to widespread poverty and political unrest, conditions that Western colonial powers were quick to exploit during the nineteenth century, culminating in the Republican Revolution of 1911.

THE ARTS UNDER THE MING DYNASTY

In 1279, the urban society created in China under the T'ang and Sung dynasties fell under the control of Mongol invaders from Central Asia. It took almost a century for resentment of foreign occupation, coupled with a series of disastrous floods, to provoke a widespread peasants' revolt. One of the rebels' leaders seized the Mongol capital, Beijing, and in 1368 declared himself the first emperor of the Ming Dynasty (see map, "The Ming Empire").

Confucianism Under the Ming emperors, China enjoyed an extended period of political and economic stability and cultural enrichment. The basis for all aspects of life was Confucianism in its most traditional form. The importance of obedience and loyalty to the authorities became paramount, both within the individual family, headed by the father, and in the state as a whole, headed by the emperor, the Son of Heaven, who ruled as the "father" of his country. The effect of this conservatism on the arts was twofold. Those fields that had been cultivated in the past remained little changed; one Ming writer observed that since the early writers on Confucius had discovered everything worth knowing, it was unnecessary to write any more scholarly works. Furthermore, writers and painters tackling traditional themes tended to imitate past models. As a result the Ming period saw the invention of new artistic forms in which creative artists felt free to experiment.

Literature The most popular new literary genres were the novel and the short story. The latter, known as **Hua-Pen**, were often based on the oral tales of professional traveling storytellers, or at any rate aimed to give that impression. They included verses inserted into the prose narrative, audience reaction, and the use of the speech of the streets. Traditional Buddhist subjects were combined with scenes from everyday life. The earliest collections of Hua-Pen date to the sixteenth century, although many of these had probably circulated for more than a century.

One of the first novels to focus on daily life rather than extraordinary events is the anonymous *Chin P'ing Mei*. This story chronicles the lurid career of the licentious Hsi-men. The society it describes is driven mainly by lust, greed, and vanity, although its author makes no attempt to moralize. The book owed its immediate and continuing popularity to its openly erotic episodes. Another novel to achieve a large readership, particularly among children, is *Monkey*, written by Wu Ch'eng-en (c. 1501–1580). Describing the journey to India of a Buddhist priest, Tripitaka, it uses centuries-old tales and legends. Tripitaka is a historical figure who actually made a pilgrimage to India in the seventh century. By the tenth century, his travels had already inspired an entire cycle of fantastic tales, which by the beginning of the Ming Dynasty were the subject of stage plays. Wu Ch'eng-en thus had a mass of material to draw on for his long fairy tale. The real hero of the story is not Tripitaka but his assistant, Monkey, whose magical powers and craftiness enable the two travelers to overcome all obstacles—both natural and supernatural—and complete their journey. The story combines fantasy, folklore, and history, together with strong elements of satire. The absurd bureaucratic behavior of the gods is clearly intended to poke fun at the complexity of the Chinese state bureaucracy. Tripitaka represents a kind of Chinese "Everyman," blundering along through the various problems he has to face, whereas Monkey represents the ingenuity of human intelligence. One of Tripitaka's other fellow pilgrims, Pigsy, personifies human physical desires and brute strength. None of these layers of meaning are allowed to interfere with the narrative drive and the richness of the various adventures encountered by the pilgrims.

◆ **19.7** Shen Zhou, *Invitation to Reclusion at Chaisang,* Ming Dynasty, China. One of the leading painters of the Ming Dynasty, Shen Zhou came from a family of painters and scholars. In this early Ming Dynasty painting, a couple poles to a secluded island across a broad sweep of the river. Note the careful depiction of the vegetation.

Handscroll, ink and color on paper, c. 9¾″ x 430¼″ (24.8 x 1094.1 cm). © Indianapolis Museum of Art, USA/The Bridgeman Art Library

◆ **19.8** Shen Zhou, *Figure on a Riverbank*, Ming Dynasty, China. As opposed to Figure 19.7, here Zhou takes even further the sense of human insignificance in the vastness of the natural world. The tiny figure seated on the bank is suspended between the river and the mountains.

Painting, ink on paper, c. 15″ x 25¾″ (37.9 x 65.3 cm). From an Album of Eight Landscapes and Eight Poems, *Museum of Fine Arts, Boston, USA//Image © Burstein Collection/CORBIS*

Ming Painting and the Decorative Arts In the visual arts, landscape provided a new subject for painters. Early Ming Dynasty works take traditional human subjects—a group of diners seated at a table, for example, gazing at the moon—and place them in a natural setting [**Fig. 19.7**]. As the century progressed, the human subject is barely visible, overwhelmed by the grandeur of the river and mountain scenery [**Fig. 19.8**]. Like many other individuals of the period, Shen Zhou (1427–1509) was a gentleman-scholar rather than a

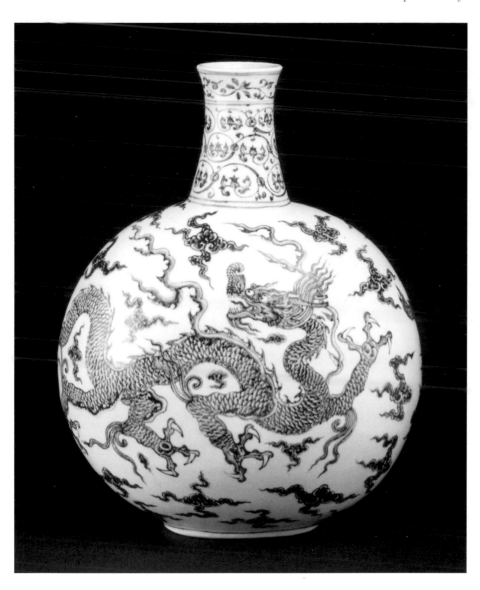

◆ **19.9** Vase in the shape of a flask, China, c. early 15th century Ming Dynasty. The blue on white is typical of much Ming ware. The motif of a running dragon (another one appears on the reverse side of the flask) is commonly found throughout Chinese art, and dragons (or rather humans dressed as dragons) still form an important part of popular festivals and processions today.

Porcelain with underglaze blue decoration. Victoria and Albert Museum, London, UK//Image © Victoria & Albert Museum, London/Art Resource, NY

professional artist. One of the differences between art in China and in the West was that the Chinese paid no particular respect to professional artists, who mainly worked on decorative projects. Ideas such as the Renaissance notion of the inspired genius who produces a masterpiece did not form part of the Chinese aesthetic. Amateurs, who considered themselves above "mere" technique, were the most admired of painters.

Another way in which the arts in China differed from those in the West was that the Chinese did not distinguish between the major art forms—painting, sculpture, architecture—and the so-called decorative arts: painted pottery and calligraphy, for example. The same gentleman-scholar who could produce a landscape would also pride himself on his elegant handwriting. The paintings illustrated in Figure 19.6 and Figure 19.8 include examples of calligraphy, a practice unimaginable in Western art of the same period. Chinese connoisseurs had always prized and collected painted ceramic ware, and potters of the Ming Dynasty produced vases of exceptional

quality [**Fig. 19.9**]. Pieces of decorated porcelain began increasingly to circulate in the West, taken there by traders and missionaries. These transported pieces added a new word to the English language for high-quality pottery: **china**.

Ming Architecture: The Forbidden City

While artists working in the fields of literature and painting could experiment and invent new forms, architects were tied far more closely to the traditions of Confucianism, particularly if they were working on official projects. Nowhere is this more clearly visible than in the construction of Beijing as Imperial capital. It was originally laid out in a rectangular plan during the thirteenth century, by order of the Mongol King Kublai Khan (c. 1216–1294). We have a description of how it then looked from perhaps the most famous travel writer of all time, Marco Polo (c. 1254–1324), who arrived in China in 1275 and spent time there as an envoy of Kublai Khan. When the Chinese succeeded in

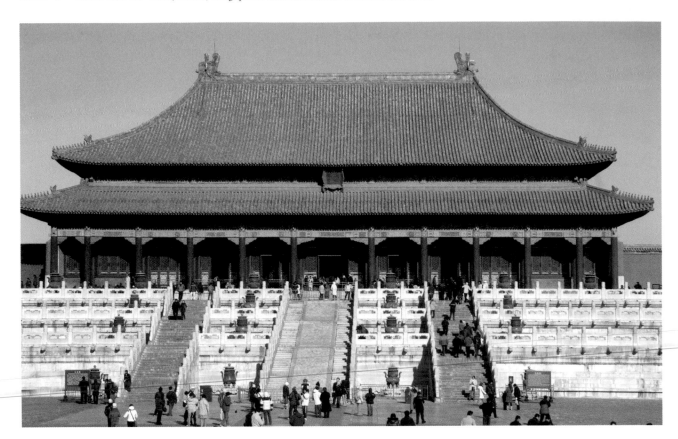

◆ **19.10** Hall of Supreme Harmony in The Forbidden City, Beijing, China. The Forbidden City served both as private residence for the emperor and as the setting for his official appearances. The Hall of Supreme Harmony served as the throne room, set as it is on a high platform with marble staircases. The throne, inside, was set on another high dais. *(Image © age fotostock/SuperStock)*

driving out the Mongols, they retained Beijing as Imperial capital; the city was reconstructed early in the Ming Dynasty, at the beginning of the fifteenth century.

The chief buildings, including the emperor's residence—known as the Forbidden City—and the main government offices, or Imperial City, were laid out on a grid plan with a north-south axis, to the north of the rest of the city. All of these buildings faced south, with their backs to the direction that symbolized evil: the Mongol invasion. This was just one more example to the Chinese of the fact that north represented misfortune. The Forbidden City stood to the extreme north of the complex, so that the emperor, like the northerly Pole star, could overlook his subjects [**Fig. 19.10**]. A series of gateways and courtyards led from the main entrance, the southern Gate of Heavenly Peace (which now gives its name to the vast square in front of the buildings, "Tiananmen") to the heart of the palace, the Hall of Supreme Harmony, where the emperor held audiences and performed special rituals. Thus the entire complex represented traditional symbolic values.

The general attitude toward cultural development during the Ming Dynasty can be summed up in a phrase frequently used by Ming-period scholars:

"change within tradition." The result was to produce a culture—and also a society—that was stable but that lacked dynamic development. The preeminence of gentleman-scholars, artists, and bureaucrats, rather than professionals, inevitably led to economic decline. By the early seventeenth century, as the bureaucracy became increasingly corrupt and the emperors began to lose control, rebellions and banditry became rampant and, in 1628, a popular uprising drove the last Ming emperor to hang himself. The resulting confusion attracted invaders from the south, who soon established a new dynasty, the Qing, the last royal house to rule China.

THE QING DYNASTY: CHINA AND THE WESTERN POWERS

The new Qing rulers, who came from Manchuria, were foreigners in the eyes of most Chinese. Although they maintained their own army, they had to rely on the established bureaucracy for the day-to-day running of the empire. One of the early Qing emperors, Kang Hsi (1654–1722), set up a grand council to supervise the bureaucrats, and succeeded in interweaving local and

VOICES OF THEIR TIMES

The Emperor of China Studies Western Mathematics

Chinese Emperor Kang Hsi Muses on His Contacts with Western Ideas.

I realized, too, that Western Mathematics has its uses. I first grew interested in this subject shortly after I came to the throne, during the confrontations between the Jesuit Adam Schall and his Chinese critic, Yang Kuanghsien, when the two men argued the merits of their respective techniques by the Wumen gate, and none of the great officials there knew what was going on.

Schall died in prison, but after I had learned something about astronomy I pardoned his friend Verbiest in 1669 and gave him an official position, promoting him in 1682. In 1687, I let the newly arrived Jesuit Fontaney and the others come to Beijing, although they had come to China illegally on a Chinese merchant vessel and the Board of

Rites had recommended their deportation; and throughout the 1680s I discussed Western skills in Manchu with Verbiest, and I made Grimaldi and Pereira learn the language as well, so they could converse with me.

After the treaty of Nerchinsk had been signed with the Russians, I ordered the Jesuits Thomas, Gerbillon, and Bouvet to study Manchu also, and to compose treatises in that language on Western arithmetic and the geometry of Euclid. In the early 1690s, I often worked several hours a day with them. With Verbiest I had examined each stage of the forging of cannons, and made him build a water fountain that operated in conjunction with an organ, and erect a windmill in the court.

From *Emperor of China* by Jonathan D. Spence, copyright © 1974 by Jonathan D. Spence. Used by permission of Alfred A. Knopf, a division of Random House, Inc.

central administration. These measures strengthened the power of the emperor. Simultaneously, Kang Hsi began to make tentative contacts abroad. In 1689 he signed a treaty with Peter the Great of Russia, to set limits on the expanding Russian Empire, and encouraged the introduction—carefully controlled—of Western arts and education. The Jesuit missionary Matteo Ricci (1552–1610) had already studied Chinese in order to familiarize some of those at court with Western mathematics, geography, and astronomy. Kang Hsi employed other Jesuits as mapmakers and took Jesuit physicians with him on his travels. Some Westerners even received appointments at court. The Flemish missionary and astronomer Ferdinand Verbiest (1623–1688) became head of Beijing's Astronomical Bureau in 1669 and played a part in helping to determine the Chinese-Russian border. When, however, the pope sent an ambassador to ask if a permanent papal legation could be set up in Beijing (in part, probably, to keep an eye on the Jesuits), the emperor refused permission and required all resident Jesuits to sign a declaration stating that they understood and accepted the definition of Confucianism and ancestral rituals as formulated by Kang Hsi.

In cultural terms, however, China remained stagnant. Technological methods remained basic [**Fig. 19.11**]. Artistic works followed old formulas, often on a more lavish scale, with the studied elegance of earlier Ming

◆ **19.11** A Chinese papermaker producing paper for export, c. 1790. The process consisted of dipping a bamboo frame into pulp, which was then spread thinly across the frame to dry. The Chinese had been the first to develop the technique of printing on paper: the earliest known manufacture of individual characters that could be combined and stamped on paper occurred in China as early as the 11th century. As this illustration shows, however, at a time when Western Europe was undergoing the Industrial Revolution, the Chinese continued to use traditional methods.

Watercolor, Victoria and Albert Museum, London, UK//© Victoria & Albert Museum, London/Art Resource, NY

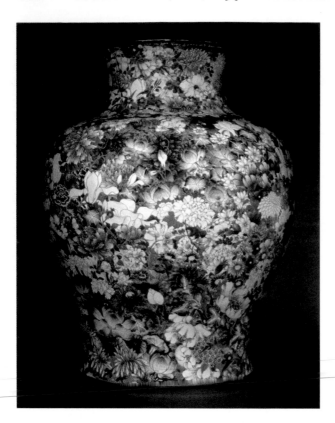

◆ **19.12** Thousand Flowers vase, China, Qianlong Period (1736–1795), Qing Dynasty. For all the brilliance of the colors, the piece lacks the elegance of ceramic design from the Ming period (see Figure 19.9).

Color enamels, 18⅞″ (48 cm) high. Musée des Arts Asiatiques Guimet, Paris, France//© Réunion des Musées Nationaux/Art Resource, NY

◆ **19.13** Shitao, *Jinting Mountains and Waterfall in the Autumn*, China, 1671. The painter Shitao became a Buddhist monk at the age of 20. By contrast with earlier landscape artists (compare with Figure 19.8), the natural world he paints is less a passive, lofty setting and more a place of action: note the spiky trees and the rushing water.

Detail from hanging scroll, black China ink on paper, c. 34″ x 16″ (86.0 x 41.7 cm). Musée des Arts Asiatiques Guimet, Paris, France//© Réunion des Musées Nationaux/Art Resource, NY

ware replaced by the use of multicolored techniques [**Fig. 19.12**]. A few painters tried to reestablish the vigor of former days. The painter Shitao (1641–1707) stressed the vitality of line, as can be seen in his landscape scene showing a hut in the mountains [**Fig. 19.13**], which is far more vigorous than the landscapes of the Ming period.

By 1800 Chinese independence was beginning to come under threat. As Western traders established themselves in India and other parts of Asia, they recognized the potential for profit at home as demand rose for Chinese tea, fine vases, silks, and exotic works of art. Trade, however, depended on exchange, and foreign merchants could find little in the way of Western products to interest the Chinese. Silver and gold would have been acceptable, but the British, who were the chief traders, had no intention of damaging their balance of trade by incurring trade deficits. British merchants, therefore, began importing large quantities of opium from India into China. The Chinese, well aware of the harmful effects of the drug, made little use of it. The Chinese government, therefore, attempted to prevent its importation; the emperor even addressed a personal appeal to Queen Victoria, which she ignored.

When (in 1839) the Chinese tried to block the introduction of opium, the result was outright war. The Opium War of 1839–1842, in which the British used their vastly superior naval power to blockade the entire coast, forced the Chinese to open up a string of ports along their coast, including Canton and Shanghai, thereby ending their isolation. Quite apart from their bitter resentment at the introduction of a drug that soon became widely used (importation rose from six thousand cases in 1820 to one hundred thousand in 1880), the Chinese also had to face the arrival of other Westerners—France and the United States, among others. One of the results of all this turmoil was a series of internal rebellions, which the Chinese authorities could only put down by humiliatingly having to ask the invading foreigners for help. During the Tai Ping Rebellion (1851–1864), a Franco-British force occupied Beijing, drove out the emperor, and burned down the Summer Palace.

THE COLLAPSE OF CHINESE IMPERIAL RULE

When the central government grew increasingly ineffectual, the foreign trading powers benefited from a

◆ **19.14** The North Church, Beijing, China, late 19th century. With complete disregard for the culture surrounding them, the foreign community built a church that makes no pretense to fit into its context. Note the contrast between the neo-Gothic style of the windows and doorways of the church and the Chinese pavilion to the right, and the very Chinese lion in the foreground. *(Image © Panorama Media (Beijing/Chai Zhirong) Ltd./Alamy)*

妇女能顶半边天　管教山河换新颜

◆ **19.15** *Women Hold up Half of Heaven* and, *Cutting through Mountains and Rivers, Change to a New Attitude*, a propaganda poster from the Chinese Cultural Revolution of 1970. One of Mao's chief aims was to bring China's industrial strength to the level of Western powers, and to accomplish this women were needed in the workforce. There is little evidence, however, that the Revolution or Mao's methods brought any real change to traditional gender attitudes. *(Image © Private Collection/The Bridgeman Art Library)*

weak central authority that depended on them for the little influence it possessed. The utter unconcern of these foreign traders and settlers for the culture they were invading is evidenced by the design of a Western church built in Beijing in the late nineteenth century [**Fig. 19.14**]. With the suppression of the bloody Boxer Rebellion of 1900–1901, the Western powers took virtual control, constructing railways and opening up river traffic to all parts of the interior.

In 1911 republicans led by Sun Yat-sen (1866–1925) finally brought down the monarchy, but the collapse of centuries-old institutions created decades of chaos, complicated by two world wars. Two chief movements struggled for power in China. The Kuomintang, led by Chiang Kai-shek (1887–1975), offered authoritarian rule, which was supposed to evolve into a form of democracy. The other group, the Chinese Communist Party, aimed to follow the example of Russia's Bolshevik movement and was led by Mao Tse-tung (1893–1976). The communists came to power in 1949. Virtually all of the art produced under communist rule exhorts the party (under Mao especially) and the virtues of hard work—most notably in the posters produced at the time of the Cultural Revolution of 1970 [**Fig. 19.15**].

THE ART AND CULTURE OF JAPAN

EARLY JAPANESE HISTORY AND CULTURE

Archaeological evidence suggests that although early settlers in Japan had developed agricultural communities by 200 CE, these were based on tribal chiefs; each tribal group had its own god, thought of as an ancestor. Around 400, one of these communities was sufficiently sophisticated to bring in scribes from Korea to keep records, because no system of writing as yet existed in Japan. The original chief city had been Nara, laid out in 706 in imitation of Chinese urban design. Less than

◆ **19.17** Scene from *Tale of Genji*, Japan, late Heian period, early 12th century. The elaborate setting in which Prince Genji visits his wife gives an idea of the nature of Japanese court life during the Heian period, at a time when Kyoto was Japan's capital.

Painting attributed to Tusa Tokayoshi. © Private Collection, Paris, France//The Art Archive/Gianni Dagli Orti.

◆ **19.16** Portrait of an actor in a Japanese *noh* play. The pinned hairstyle suggests the actor is playing a female role. All of the performers in *noh* plays were male; as here, they used traditional wooden masks. They combined speech, singing, dance, and mime. *(Image © Scala/Art Resource, NY)*

a century later, however, the various settlements, now much expanded, came together in a new capital, Kyoto (then known as Heian), which remained a center of stable government and economic growth until 1185.

Although early Japanese religious thought owed much to the influences of Buddhism and Confucianism, the native Japanese religion was **Shintoism**. This involved not only worship of the spirits of nature—including the all-important rice god—and a complex series of rituals, but also the imperial cult; that is, the ruling emperor and his ancestors were worshiped as divine. The tension between Shintoism and the influence of Chinese Buddhism always remained an important factor in Japanese religious life. The move from Nara to Kyoto was in part to escape from the domination of Nara's Buddhist priests.

During this period, the Japanese developed their own writing system, partly based on the Chinese system. Poetry was popular, and as urban centers grew, various forms of theater became common. Perhaps the best known is the *noh* play, in which dancers enact dramatic stories combined with ritual and slapstick [**Fig. 19.16**]. The most famous literary work of the age was *The Tale of Genji*, written by Lady Murasaki Shikibu (c. 980–1030). Murasaki lived during the so-called Fujiwara period, one dominated by members of that family; the

most important, Fujiwara Michinaga, ruled as regent from 966 to 1027.

Murasaki's father held a minor position at court. She married and had children, but when her husband died and her father was transferred to the provinces, Murasaki took a position in the service of Empress Akiko. The diary she wrote during her years at court gives precious insight into life there. Basically serious minded, Murasaki had little time for the frivolity of many of her contemporaries. By a remarkable chance, another diary of the same period has also survived, kept by Sei Shonagon (active c. 1000). Sei Shonagon's work takes the form of a **pillow-book**—a collection of her notes and observations on the day's events that are often malicious and sometimes indelicate, forming an interesting contrast with the more straitlaced Murasaki.

Murasaki's enduring fame is based on her novel, *The Tale of Genji*. One of the great achievements of Japanese literature, the book describes the amorous adventures of Prince Genji, set against a court background very similar to that in which Murasaki herself moved. She writes with great delicacy and an underlying melancholy, often underlined by descriptions of nature. The autumnal winds, swift-flowing rivers, snow in winter—all serve as background to the book's more poignant scenes. One of the unintentional effects of Murasaki's psychological subtlety is to reveal the gulf between the aesthetic sensibilities of the aristocratic elite at court and the lives of the peasants, the overwhelming majority of the population. It seems that life at court consisted of music and love affairs, poetry recitations, and apt quotations from the classics. The art of the same period shares this otherworldly quality. A scene illustrating an episode from *The Tale of Genji* shows the hero visiting his wife. Note the ornate setting and rich fabrics [**Fig. 19.17**].

THE PERIOD OF FEUDAL RULE

As the increasingly remote court life of Kyoto led to internal rivalry, in 1185 a new, more aggressive center developed at Kakamura. The emperor now combined legal and administrative duties with military command, creating a new office—**samurai-dokoro**—which gave him control of all of Japan's warriors (*samurai* is the Japanese name for a professional warrior). His title was Seiitaishogun ("barbarian-suppressing commander-in-chief"), later shortened to **shogun**. This newly enhanced warrior class dominated Japanese culture sufficiently enough to defeat two waves of Mongol invaders (in 1274 and 1281). Bands of warriors followed their aristocratic leader, who was in turn bound to the emperor—a system not unlike the feudal system developing independently in Western Europe around the same period.

Over time, the local **daimyo** ("warlords") began to assert their own authority against that of the shogun, and the years 1467 to 1568 are known as the Age of the Warring States. With the introduction of firearms first

obtained from Portuguese traders, and then manufactured in Japan, individual daimyo began to build their own fortified centers, and the authority of the central government grew ever weaker. The Portuguese guns may have increased the influence of individual warriors, but they undercut the traditional samurai fighting style and raised the problem of outside influence in a society that had been virtually closed to the outside world for centuries. Fighting between the various warlords was finally ended under two powerful leaders, Hideyoshi (1537–1598), who once more united Japan by 1590, and Tokugawa (1543–1616), who created a new capital in 1603 at Edo (present-day Tokyo). Members of the Tokugawa family ruled there until 1868.

THE EDO PERIOD

Artists in the Edo period produced a wide variety of work, catering to the needs of an increasingly urban and sophisticated population. The landscape scenes of Chinese gentleman-scholars (see Figure 19.7 and Figure 19.8) proved a popular influence, but the Japanese versions used gentler colors. Both vegetation and background mountains are more abstract, giving a dreamlike quality to the view [**Fig. 19.18**]. Other artists aimed

◆ **19.19** Maruyama Okyo, *Tiger Screen*, Japan, Edo period, 1781. The vividness with which the artist depicts the tiger's pose and stare was probably influenced by Western models.

Ink, color, and gold on paper, c. 66" x 74" (168 x188 cm). © Detroit Institute of Arts, Detroit, MI, USA / The Bridgeman Art Library

to combine the richness of color of traditional Japanese art with the precision in description of Western artists, as in the dramatic *Tiger Screen* [**Fig. 19.19**]. Woodblock, a popular new medium, made possible the making of multiple copies for a growing number of collectors. The most famous artist in this field was Hokusai Katsushika (1760–1849), whose image of a wave crashing in the foreground, while a diminutive but enduring Mount Fuji appears at the center of the background, is one of the most familiar of all Japanese works of art [**Fig. 19.20**].

Japanese writers of the Edo period made major contributions in poetry, fiction, and dramatic writing. The greatest poet of the age was Basho (1644–1694), who developed one of the most important Japanese verse forms, the **haiku** (originally called hokku). This consists of three lines of five, seven, and five syllables, respectively. Haiku typically uses an image, often drawn from nature, to evoke or suggest a feeling or mood. Basho spent most of his life either in retreat or on solitary journeys, writing poems that evoke entire landscapes by the telling selection of the crucial details. In this way, he aimed to provide a poetic equivalent of the flash of enlightenment that a meditating Buddhist hoped to achieve. Basho was a devout Buddhist, with a special interest in Zen Buddhism. (Zen, which avoided images, rituals, and sacred texts, and stressed contemplation and meditation, had a great influence on Japanese culture.)

Basho's contemporary, Ihara Saikaku (1642–1693), also wrote poetry but was chiefly famous for his novels. Many of these follow the various adventures of their heroes and heroines rather in the manner of *The Tale of Genji* to which they form a middle-class equivalent. *Life of an Amorous Woman*, for example, is narrated by an old woman as she looks back over her life from the Buddhist retreat to which she has retired. Beginning as a high-class prostitute, she gradually declined to a mere streetwalker and eventually scraped a living from the few occupations open to women. The overt eroticism is in strong contrast with Lady Murasaki's delicacy and emerges in Saikaku's other writings, which include a collection of tales about male homosexual love. Similar themes of love among the bourgeois merchant classes inspire the plays of Chikamatsu Monzaemon (1653–1725). One of the most famous is *The Love Suicide at Amijima*, which describes the life and eventual death of a paper merchant, ruined by his hopeless love for a prostitute. The earlier *noh* dramas had enacted traditional stories, passed down from generation to generation. This new form of drama, based on real-life incidents, is called **kabuki**, and grew increasingly popular despite government opposition.

At the end of the Edo period, Japan was thrust into contact with the Western powers. In 1853 the famous American naval expedition of Commodore Matthew Calbraith Perry arrived in Edo Bay and insisted, under threat of bombardment, that Americans be allowed to trade. Britain, Russia, and Holland soon followed. The ensuing contest between conservatives and reformers was soon won by the latter, when a new emperor ascended to the throne in 1867.

◆ **19.20** Hokusai Katsushika, *The Great Wave off Kanagawa*, Japan, Togukawa period, c. 1831. This is one of a series of woodblocks called *Thirty-Six Views of Mount Fuji*; the mountain can be seen in the distance. Note the two boats, whose crews are trying to negotiate the perilous sea.

Polychrome woodblock print, 9⅜″ x 14⅝″ (25.5 x 37.1 cm): Private collection/© Art Resource, NY

MODERN JAPAN: THE MEIJI

The new Emperor Mitsuhito's reign (1817–1912), known as the **Meiji** ("enlightened government"), introduced a radical program of reform, abolished feudalism, and quickly built a strong central government. A new army, modeled on the German system, was formed. A parliament, consisting of an upper and a lower house, served under the emperor. Banks, railways, and a merchant marine all permitted Japan to industrialize at a speed that far outstripped India or China and, by 1905, Japan could claim military victory over a European opponent in the Russo-Japanese War.

Although the tumultuous events of the twentieth century brought ever-increasing globalization of culture and economies, Japanese artists have continued to work in ways inherited from the past. As in China, high-quality ceramic manufacture has always been a feature of artistic production, and the tradition continues with contemporary artists adapting new styles and techniques to old art forms [**Fig. 19.21**].

ASIAN FILM

One of the most direct and enjoyable means of access to an unknown culture is by way of its films. In the case of the cultures of Southeast Asia, movies made since World War II provide an especially rich source of information. In China, government censorship meant that for much of the postwar period, filmmakers had little choice but to echo the official party line. But in recent years, independent directors have been able to create works that reflect their own vision. Perhaps the best-known of Chinese directors is Zhang Yimou, whose films include *Raise the Red Lantern* and *The Story of Qiu Ju*, both of which give

◆ **19.21** Hamada Shoji, square bottle, Japan, 1965. The Japanese have retained their love for traditional ceramics. This bottle is made of stoneware, rather than the finer porcelain of Chinese pottery, and its simple, apparently casual decoration emphasizes its relationship to folk art and craft.

Stoneware, 9¼″ x 4″ (23.5 x 10 cm). Mingei International Museum, San Diego, California, USA//© Mingei International Museum/Art Resource, NY

a vivid impression of the social system existing in China, with special attention to the hardships of women.

In the case of India and Japan, two directors in particular—the Indian Satyajit Ray (1921–1992) and the Japanese Akira Kurosawa (1910–1998)—have made films that many movie critics consider as among the greatest ever produced, and they are already classics of the medium.

Ray was born into a prosperous Bengali family and studied art as a young man. His films aim to show the lives of ordinary people and use the details of their everyday existence to give a more general impression of the culture of which they form a part. His best-known work is probably *The Apu Trilogy*, three films that tell the story of a young Bengali boy growing to maturity: *The Song of the Road (Pather Panchali)* of 1955, *The Unvanquished (Aparajito)* of 1957, and *The World of Apu* of 1958. Taken together, the three movies, with specially composed background music played by Ravi Shankar, provide an unforgettably moving impression of coming of age in both rural and urban India and point out the similarities between a culture that at first seems so remote from life in the West in the twenty-first century. A later Ray film, *The Home and the World* (1984), sets a romantic love triangle against the background of the early years of the twentieth century, with its scheming and treacherous British rulers.

The greatest Japanese filmmaker—Kurosawa—is, if anything, even more highly esteemed. Influenced by American movies, in particular those of John Ford, Kurosawa brought his own insights to bear on a wide range of human situations and historical periods. The first of his films to catch international attention was *Rashomon* (1950), a study in human perception and memory. This was followed by *Seven Samurai* (1954), which brilliantly re-creates the lives—and deaths—of Japanese feudal warriors and has been listed as one of the ten greatest films of all time. This film was later remade as an American film, *The Magnificent Seven*. A later historical epic, set in the sixteenth century, is *Kagemusha* (1980), which explores the notion of identity: a petty thief, who resembles the dying warlord of a powerful clan, takes over as leader and gradually assumes the character of the man he is pretending to be. One critic writing of Kurosawa referred to the "Shakespearean cast of his genius"; two of his most dramatic films are based on works by Shakespeare: *Throne of Blood* (1957), based on *Macbeth*, and *Ran* (1985), Kurosawa's version of *King Lear*. The latter is a movie of immense power, profoundly pessimistic in tone.

SUMMARY

◆ **The Mughal Empire.** Muslim forces had arrived in northwest India in the thirteenth century, but with the conquest of large parts of the subcontinent by the Mughal general Babur in 1526, most of India came under the rule of the Mughals for the following two and a half centuries. The Mughal Empire, both under Babur and his grandson Akbar, established an organized system of administration, which devoted considerable effort to cultural achievement and aimed to promote unity. The emperors did not impose the Islamic religion on their Hindu subjects and introduced a new language, Urdu, which combined elements of Arabic and Persian with the Hindi language spoken most commonly in India before their arrival.

◆ **Mughal Art.** The art of the Mughal period similarly aimed to combine elements of preexisting Indian styles with Arabic and, above all, Persian characteristics. Buildings such as the Taj Mahal introduced forms of dome, arch, and tower that were commonly used in Islamic architecture. Mughal painters depicted scenes from real life and portraits, rather than restricting themselves to religious subjects, as earlier Hindu and Buddhist artists had done. The emperors highly valued literature, both collecting books and writing their own works. At the same time, Hindu writers continued to produce religious texts in their own language.

◆ **The End of Mughal Rule and the Arrival of the British.** Toward the end of the Mughal period, later emperors proved less tolerant, and local resistance led to the collapse of the empire. At the same time, European traders began to assert ever greater influence. The leaders in this were the British, who defeated European rivals and during the eighteenth century won virtual political and economic control over the separate states into which India had once again fallen.

◆ **The Rise of Nationalism.** With the formation of the Indian National Congress Party toward the end of the nineteenth century, India was one of the first colonized nations to begin the struggle for independence. Throughout the 1920s and 1930s, Mohandas Gandhi played a major role in leading this cause, with his policy of nonviolent civil disobedience. Many leading Indian writers of the day used English to introduce India's problems to a wider audience. Finally, following World War II, British rule ended, although one of the consequences was the partition of the subcontinent into mainly Hindu India and the new Muslim state of Pakistan. The mass population transfers that accompanied partition involved millions of deaths on both sides.

◆ **Chinese Culture Under Imperial Rule.** Following the centuries of confusion caused by the Mongol invasions, China once again came under central rule. The two dynasties to govern China from the fourteenth century to modern times were the Ming (1368–1644) and the Qing (1644–1911).

◆ **The Arts Under Ming Rule.** With the restoration of imperial rule came a return to traditional Confucian values and familiar artistic forms. One of the effects was to encourage artists in search of new ideas to invent or develop new artistic forms. Writers turned to the short story, based on everyday life, or to the novel. In some cases, as in the novel *Monkey*, the author could use what seemed pure fantasy to satirize aspects of contemporary political life. Painters, many of whom were gentleman-scholars rather than professionals, depicted landscapes in which individual humans were dwarfed by the grandeur of nature. The major building project of the age was the construction of the Imperial palace—the Forbidden City—at Beijing; the Mongols had made Beijing their capital, and the Ming emperors retained it as such.

◆ **The Qing Dynasty: China and the West.** When the Ming Dynasty finally collapsed, invaders from northeast China, Manchuria, set up the Qing Dynasty, the last to rule China before modern times. Early Qing rulers succeeded in limiting contacts with Western traders, although Jesuit missionaries succeeded in establishing limited contacts, not the least of which was at the Imperial court, where they managed to introduce some Western technology and culture. In general, however, the Qing period saw growing stagnation, with artists continuing to repeat familiar subjects.

By the nineteenth century, China was under growing pressure to allow trade with outside powers. The Opium War of 1839–1842, in which the British compelled the Chinese to accept increasing quantities of a drug whose harmful effects were well known to both sides, led to the opening of Chinese markets to other Western nations, including France and the United States. As internal revolutionaries fought against the collapse of traditional ways in China—first in the Taiping Rebellion of 1851–1864 and then in the Boxer Rebellion of 1900–1901—the last Qing rulers were forced to turn to the outside powers who were the cause of the revolts to help crush them. By 1911 mass dissatisfaction led to the end of millennia of Imperial rule. The republic that followed saw its own share of bloody conflict before the establishment of the Communist Chinese Peoples' Republic in 1949.

◆ **The Arts and Culture of Japan: Early Japanese History and Culture.** The early history of Japan seems to have been mainly agricultural, but over time settlements grew in size, and the first Japanese capital was founded at Nara (c. 700). Although Buddhism played an important role in influencing Japanese culture throughout its history, the religion native to Japan was Shintoism, essentially a form of nature worship. Shintoism differs from other Asian religions, however, in its belief in the divine nature of the emperor, descended from the sun goddess. In the early ninth century, Japan's capital moved to Kyoto, where a rich and elaborate court life developed, with much emphasis on elegance and formal ritual. One of the most revealing sources of information about the artificiality and ceremony of the court is the novel by Lady Murasaki, *The Tale of Genji*.

◆ **The Period of Feudal Rule.** In an attempt to counteract what was seen as the weakness of Imperial rule at Kyoto, a new administrative center was set up (in 1185) at Kakamura. Japanese soldiers were formed into a new warrior class of samurai, under the military command of the shogun. Individual warrior bands owed their loyalty to their own warlords, who in turn were subject to the emperor. Over time, this system degenerated into fighting between rival groups—a period of violence exacerbated by the importation of firearms from the Portuguese.

◆ **The Edo Period.** Peace was only restored by a strong leadership that transferred the capital once again, this time to Tokyo (Edo). With renewed central government, Japan began to develop an increasingly sophisticated urban culture, and the Edo period was one in which the arts flourished. Painters produced works inspired by a host of outside styles, from traditional Chinese landscape scenes to Western realistic depictions of people and animals. Novelists and storytellers drew on contemporary everyday life, rather than the artificial world of the Imperial court. Poets, of whom the most popular was Basho, invented a new form of short poem, the haiku, derived in part from the inspiration of Zen Buddhism, which aimed to provide the enlightenment of sudden insight derived from the world of nature.

◆ **Modern Japan: The Meiji.** Beginning in 1868, under the Meiji emperors, Japan began a hasty program of modernization. Catapulted into the modern world by the arrival of Commodore Matthew Perry's American fleet in 1853, Japan soon began to acquire the infrastructure of an industrial economy. These changes, together with reforms in education, politics, and communications, allowed Japan, in its first hostile encounter with a European power in the Russo-Japanese War of 1905–1906, to prove victorious. By the end of the twentieth century, of all the cultures of Asia, Japan was the one best capable of competing with the West on equal terms.

EXERCISES

1. What effects did contact with Western civilization have on the cultures of India, China, and Japan? In each case, how did the effects differ?

2. What were the lasting results of the Mughal conquest of India for the history of the subcontinent?

3. Urdu is just one of many attempts to construct a new language. What others have been tried? Why did Urdu succeed? Why did others fail?

4. What are the outstanding features of Marco Polo's account of his travels? Which other travelers left descriptions of their travels in Asia before modern times?

5. Why has Zen Buddhism become popular in the West in modern times? What are its chief characteristics?

6. Lady Murasaki is a rare example of a woman artist before the nineteenth century, either in Western or Asian culture. Why have there been so few? Why did such a high proportion of those few write rather than paint or compose music?

Visit the *Culture & Values* Companion website at **www.cengage.com/art/Cunningham/Cultureand Values7E** and the *Humanities Resource Center* for an array of primary source readings, key terms with pronunciations, flash cards, quizzes, and study materials designed especially to help you do well in this course.

CHAPTER 20

THE PEOPLES AND CULTURES OF AFRICA

The central role of family life in Africa has often led to the creation of patriarchal societies in which women's rights are limited. Yet one of the most influential figures in Africa today is the Kenyan female environmentalist Wangari Muta Maathai, sometimes nicknamed the "Forest Queen." She was the first Kenyan woman to earn a doctorate, to become a professor, and to serve as a university department chair.

In 1977 she began the Greenbelt Movement, the most successful environmental movement in Africa.

It involves (and thereby empowers) rural women who plant millions of indigenous trees—fig, blue gum, acacia—that were destroyed during the colonial period. So far over twenty million trees have been planted. Kenya is thus one of the few African countries to deal with the problem of deforestation.

Her husband, a businessman and politician, was ridiculed for having such a highly educated and influential wife who was "beyond his control." The social pressure led to his divorcing her, leading Dr. Maathai to unite women's issues with environmental ones. Yet she does not advocate extending men's rights to women. She concedes that many women in Africa lead miserable lives, but "we forget that these miserable women are married to miserable men. They are oppressed together." The oppressors are the African elite, who are "no better than the world which colonized us."

The political elite have hit back; the government has restricted her travel and the police have beaten and teargassed her. Nonetheless, her environmental work has won her national and international acclaim. Al Gore highly praised her achievements in his book *Earth in the Balance*, and in 2002 she was elected to Kenya's parliament, serving as Assistant Minister for the environment and wildlife. In 2004 she was awarded the Nobel Peace Prize.

A study of the humanities as they developed in Africa requires a special approach. In the first place, the sheer size of Africa—three times as big as the continental United States and Alaska—and the variety of climates and landforms prevented the formation of a single unified culture (see map, "The African Environment"). Unlike China or India, the content's separate cultures never

◆ Wangari Muta Maathai, Kenya, 2007. In 2004 she became the first African woman to win the Nobel Peace Prize. *(© Raveendran/AFP/Getty Images)*

united under a single government. The geographical and political states of modern Africa are the result, for the most part, of Western colonization, and their borders do not conform to original settlement patterns (see "Map of Africa"). Because technology and the ability to write developed more slowly than in Europe and Asia, we have no consistent written records before the nineteenth century. Further confusion was created by the arrival of Muslim and European traders in the sixteenth century and the subsequent centuries of generally brutal colonization. To reconstruct the earliest civilizations on African soil, we must rely on archaeological remains and written accounts by the first outsiders to visit the early African kingdoms. The general picture is that of a series of powerful and highly developed states.

RELIGION AND SOCIETY IN EARLY AFRICA

At first sight, African life seems to have been divided by its size into a wide variety of differing peoples and cultures. It is often observed that today more than one thousand languages are spoken in sub-Saharan Africa.

GENERAL EVENTS	ART
Stone Age / **BCE** First occupation of site of Great Zimbabwe	
CE / **300**	
300–1075 Kingdom of Ghana Ghana emerges as a trading center between Africa and the Mediterranean, exporting gold and other goods	
1000	
Height of Ghana's success; at this time it is the world's largest gold producer Introduction of new food crops in Nigeria **1075** Defeat of Ghana by Muslim Berbers Shona-speaking people occupy site of Great Zimbabwe	More sophisticated metal-working tools make larger communities possible **1200–1400** People of Great Zimbabwe create soapstone carvings
1300	
1300–1500 Kingdom of Benin (Nigeria) Benin Kingdom (Nigeria) flourishes under the hereditary rule of the Oba, trading in pepper and ivory Great Zimbabwe serves as base for a trading empire extending from the Near East, Persia, and China	Benin artists (Nigeria) create sculptures honoring their rulers and ancestors Yoruba culture creates ceremonial costumes for masquerade honoring Egungun (collective spirit of ancestors)
1500	
Beginning of European colonization and the slave trade	
1700	
Legendary King Shaka (South Africa, 1787?–1828) unites Zulu warriors as a formidable fighting force Dogon people, fleeing Islamic enslavement and conversion, locate in Mali near the Niger River.	Dogon people (Mali) create masks to be worn in ceremony and dance
1800	
Mass deportation of male Benin population by Arab and European slave traders **1895** Ghana falls under French rule	
1900	
1960 Nigeria receives independence from the British **1967** Igbo people of eastern Nigeria secede to form the Republic of Biafra; Chinua Achebe becomes Minister of Information in the new state	As African artworks begin to circulate among Western collectors, African artistic styles begin to influence the work of Western artists like Pablo Picasso
1970 to Present **1970** Igbo breakaway crushed by the Nigerian government; Achebe stays under a general amnesty for rebels **1984** Desmond Mpilo Tutu (South Africa) wins Nobel Peace Prize **1993** Nelson Mandela (South Africa) and Frederik Willem de Klerk (South Africa) share Nobel Peace Prize **2001** Kofi Annan (Ghana) shares Nobel Peace Prize with the United Nations **2004** Wangari Muta Maathai (Kenya) wins the Nobel Peace Prize	Contemporary African art continues to examine the conflict between traditional cultures and the West. Traditional art forms and rituals involving masks and headdresses continue to play a crucial role in African communities

Yet most of these are related to four or five basic tongues, suggesting that beneath the apparent diversity there lies a common cultural inheritance. Other factors bear this out. One important characteristic many Africans share is their attitude toward their environment and living creatures. Although a single common African religion never existed, most African peoples developed a variety of animist beliefs. These took forms specific to individual regions, but all basically aimed to understand the world and human life through the workings of nature, using rituals and ceremonies to deal with illness, death, and natural disasters. For many groups, the focus of their specific cult was a particular animal—which became sacred—and could not therefore be killed by members of the group. Because, in the absence of written texts, the accumulation of religious practices and beliefs had to be memorized and passed on by word of mouth, the elderly became revered, and a tradition of ancestor worship developed. This in turn laid emphasis on the family and, more broadly, the village community. Within the community certain extended families, or kinship groups, served specific functions: hunters, farmers, traders, and so on. Thus, religion and social structure reinforced one another and allowed for the slow evolution of increasingly powerful kingdoms.

ARCHITECTURE

1000–1300 Bantu-speaking ancestors of the Shona erect Great Zimbabwe, huge stone buildings surrounded by massive walls

LITERATURE & PHILOSOPHY

Before the 20th century, most African storytelling was done by word-of-mouth
1500 Religious verse brought by Muslim traders is paraphrased in Swahili; over time, the Swahili-Arabic script becomes a new poetic tradition

Oral poet Raage Ugaas (Somalia) becomes popular for his wisdom and piety
Saiyid Abdallah (Somalia, c. 1720–1810) writes *Self-examination*, a long poem using the decline of great Arab trading cities on the East African coast as a symbol of the inevitability of death

c. 1805 Qamaan Bulhan (Somalia) becomes well-known for his philosophical and reflective verses, which in some cases have now become proverbial expressions

1906 Thomas Mofolo (Lesotho, 1875?–1948) writes *Traveler of the East* in his native Sesotho language, becoming the first African novelist
1912 Mofolo (Lesotho) writes *Chaka*, his most celebrated book, but the missionary-run press that published his previous works refuses to publish it
1925 *Chaka* becomes an instant best seller and is widely translated
1929 Poet Leopold Senghor (Senegal, 1906–1989), writing in French, creates a literary movement known as "negritude," which celebrates the unique traditions of African art
1958 Africa's most acclaimed 20th-century writer Chinua Achebe (Nigeria) writes his first novel, *Things Fall Apart*, in English
1960 Wole Soyinka (Nigerian writer) becomes president of Senegal, retiring voluntarily in 1980
Achebe publishes *No Longer at Ease*

1986 Wole Soyinka (Nigeria) becomes the first African to receive a Nobel Prize for Literature

THE AFRICAN ENVIRONMENT

0   600 Miles

0   600 Kilometers

SPAIN

TURKEY

MEDITERRANEAN SEA

PERSIA

Atlas Mts.

LIBYAN DESERT

EGYPT

Tropic of Cancer

HOGGAR
SAHARA DESERT

23 N

TIBESTI

ARABIA

NUBIA RED SEA

Nile River

Senegal River

Niger River

L Chad

THE SUDAN

MEROE

SOMALI PENINSULA

GOLD COAST

IVORY COAST

SLAVE COAST

ETHIOPIAN HIGHLANDS

ADAMAWA HIGHLANDS

GULF OF GUINEA

L Rudolf

Equator

CONGO BASIN

0

Congo River

L Victoria

ATLANTIC OCEAN

ZANZIBAR

L Tanganyika

INDIAN OCEAN

L Malawi

Zambezi River

Tropic of Capricorn

MADAGASCAR

23 S

KALAHARI DESERT

THE VELDT

Drakensburg Mts.

CAPE OF
GOOD HOPE

◤ Probable routes of the spread of Ironworking
☐ Mediterranean type conditions
☐ Desert and Semi-desert
☐ Tropical Grassland and Savannah
☐ Temperate Grassland
☐ Hot Humid Rainforest

THREE EARLY AFRICAN KINGDOMS: GHANA, BENIN, AND ZIMBABWE

All three kingdoms flourished long before the Europeans entered Africa's interior. From the sixteenth century, with the beginning of the age of European colonization and the slave trade that accompanied it, Europeans began to settle in coastal regions, which served as bases for exploring and exploiting Africa's extraordinary natu-

ral resources. Islamic missionaries had carried their religion southward across the Sahara desert centuries earlier. The arrival of the Europeans brought Christianity and, under the influence of both religions, traditional patterns of ritual and ancestor worship began to die out.

THE KINGDOM OF GHANA

One of the earliest states to develop was Ghana, in West Africa. Caravan routes crossing the Sahara linked the region to Mediterranean cities, first by horse and oxen and then, after 300 CE, by camel. Shortly after, the city

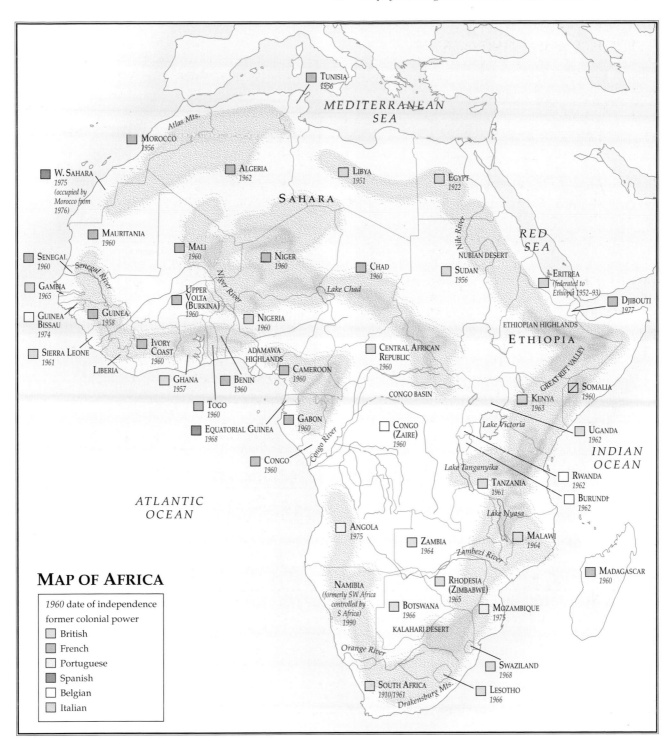

MAP OF AFRICA

1960 date of independence
former colonial power

- British
- French
- Portuguese
- Spanish
- Belgian
- Italian

of Ghana, on the upper river Niger, began to export gold, animal hides, pepper, ivory, and slaves in exchange for salt, cloth, pottery, and other manufactured goods. Ghana grew increasingly wealthy and, at the height of its success (around 1000), was probably the world's largest gold producer. According to an Arab traveler who visited Ghana in 1065, the army numbered two hundred thousand, of whom forty thousand were armed with bows and arrows. This formidable fighting force was defeated a decade later by a nomadic army of Muslim Berbers. The Berbers moved north after a few years to attack Morocco, but Ghana never fully recovered (in part because the gold mines were beginning to peter out), and by 1300, the great kingdom was only a memory.

THE KINGDOM OF BENIN

During the time of Ghana's slow decline, the kingdom of Benin was beginning to grow in what is now modern-day Nigeria (ancient Benin should not be confused with the modern African state of Benin). The

◆ **20.2** Frieze showing an Oba (ruler) with his warriors, Kingdom of Benin (Nigeria), 15th–16th century. By means of a complex method of casting bronze, the artist has made the figure of the Oba stand out virtually in the round, while the two kneeling soldiers recede in the background, which is decorated with further details.

Bronze, 18½″ x 14½″. British Museum, London, UK//© British Museum/ The Bridgeman Art Library

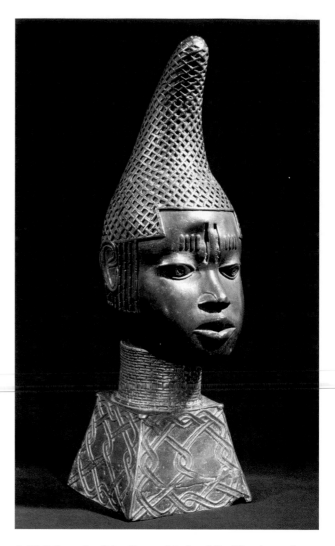

◆ **20.3** Portrait of the Queen Mother Idia, Kingdom of Benin (Nigeria), 16th century. Note the elegant contrast between decoration (on the Queen's headdress and on the stand supporting the head) and realism (the very precise rendering of her cheeks and lips), suggesting a sophisticated artistic tradition.

From the palace complex at Benin, Nigeria. Brass, 20½″ (52 cm) high. National Museum, Lagos, Nigeria//Photo © Held Collection/The Bridgeman Art Library

period around 1000 saw the introduction of new food crops from East Asia and more sophisticated methods of metalworking, making larger communities possible. The kingdom of Benin flourished between the fourteenth and sixteenth centuries, trading widely in pepper and ivory. Its eventual decline was caused by the massive deportation of its male population in the nineteenth century by Arab and European slave traders. The kingdom was ruled by a hereditary male absolute monarch with the title of Oba, who had at his disposal a powerful army and an effective central government.

Benin Culture The Oba's central palace was adorned with a series of bronze plaques, showing the life of the court and military exploits. On one of these, we see an Oba flanked by the royal bodyguard. The Oba wears a high crown and a ceremonial cape, and is brandishing a spear. The soldiers, smaller in stature to indicate their lesser importance, kneel quietly by his side [**Fig. 20.2**]. Among the sculptures discovered in the complex is a

small portrait of a royal woman with tribal markings and a conical headdress, which offers insight into life at the Benin court. She is the Queen Mother Idia, to whose mystical powers her son, the Oba Esigie, attributed his success in warfare. In gratitude, he allowed her to have her own palace and sacred altars, and this head was made to decorate one of the altars. At the same time, the beauty of line and balance between decoration and naturalism give some idea of how much we have lost with the disappearance of so much African art [**Fig. 20.3**].

Another bronze from Benin throws light on religious practices at court. It comes on an *ikegobo*, or

◆ **20.4** Altar to the Hand and Arm, Kingdom of Benin (Nigeria), c. 17th–18th century. Note the large size of the Oba's head, both on the main body of the altar and on the lid: one of the standard terms used to praise the ruler was "great head," symbol of his power.

Bronze, 1′5½″ (19 cm) high. British Museum, London, UK//© British Museum/The Bridgeman Art Library

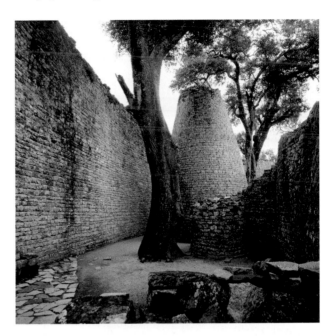

◆ **20.5** The ancient walls and one of the conical towers showing the inner passage of the Great Enclosure at Great Zimbabwe, 15th century, Zimbabwe. Built of granite during the African Iron Age, the surrounding walls probably enclosed a royal residence with private living quarters and an open area for ceremonial assemblies. Some of the larger towers may have been used to store grain. *(Image © SuperStock, Inc./SuperStock)*

royal shrine, at which the Oba would have offered up sacrifices either for favors received from the gods or in the hope of receiving future ones. The Oba appears both on the side and on the lid, again dominating the accompanying attendants. On the lid, two meek leopards crouch humbly at his feet. Even the creatures of the wild acknowledge the supreme power of their master, while other animals range around the base [**Fig. 20.4**].

THE KINGDOM OF ZIMBABWE

The greatest ancient kingdom in South Africa was Zimbabwe. Bushmen paintings and tools show that the earliest people to occupy the site settled there in the Stone Age. Around 1300, its rulers ordered the erection of huge stone buildings surrounded by massive walls; the complex is now known as Great Zimbabwe [**Fig. 20.5**]. Finds in the ruins include beads and pottery from the Near East, Persia, and even China, suggesting

that the complex served as the base for a trading empire that must have been active well before the arrival of the Europeans, some two centuries later.

Attempts to understand the function of Great Zimbabwe's constructions are largely based on accounts of Portuguese traders who visited the site after its original inhabitants had abandoned it. The main building seems to have been a royal residence, with other structures perhaps for nobles, and a great open ceremonial court. It has been calculated that at the height of its power, the complex may have served as the center for a population of some eighteen thousand persons, with the ruling class living inside and the remainder in less permanent structures on the surrounding land.

Portuguese documents describe Great Zimbabwe as "the capital of the god-kings called Monomotapa." In the sixteenth century, Europeans used this name for two Shona rulers: Mutota and Matope. The original inhabitants may well have been ancestors of the Shona people, who are now among the groups living in modern Zimbabwe. Part of Shona beliefs is the idea that ancestral spirits take the form of birds, often eagles. In one of the enclosed structures, perhaps an ancestral shrine, archaeologists discovered a soapstone carving of an eagle, which may represent one of these ancestral

◆ **20.6** Sculpture of a bird, Great Zimbabwe (Zimbabwe), 1200–1400. Thought to represent a mythical eagle that carries messages from man to the gods, the piece is remarkable for its elegant simplicity of form and beauty of line.

Soapstone (steatite) carving. Private Collection, New York, USA//© Werner Forman/Art Resource, NY

spirits, which were believed to carry messages between the human and divine worlds [**Fig. 20.6**].

AFRICAN LITERATURE

Although very little written African literature existed before the twentieth century, there was a rich tradition of storytelling, often in verse. Much of this was passed down by word of mouth, in the same way as the earliest works of Western literature—Homer's *Iliad* and *Odyssey*—and a little has been preserved, written down by later generations using either the Arabic or Western alphabet. Somalia had a rich poetic tradition. Raage Ugaas (eighteenth century), of the Somali Ogaden clan, was popular for his wisdom and piety, whereas another Somali oral poet, Qamaan Bulhan (probably mid-nineteenth century), was well-known for his philosophical and reflective verses, some of which have become proverbial expressions.

One area that did develop an earlier written tradition was the coastal region of East Africa, where Swahili (an African language strongly influenced by Arabic) was and still is spoken. Beginning in the sixteenth century, Muslim traders brought with them to the coastal trading centers didactic and religious verse that was paraphrased in Swahili, with the Swahili version written between the lines of the Arabic text. Over time, poets used this Swahili-Arabic script to compose their own works, either recording traditional songs or creating new ones. Saiyid Abdallah (c. 1720–1810) was born on the island of Lamu, now part of present-day Kenya. In his long poem *Self-examination*, he uses the decline of the great Arab trading cities on the East African coast, increasingly overshadowed during Abdallah's time by the new European colonial centers, as a symbol of the inevitability of death.

LEOPOLD SENGHOR AND *NEGRITUDE*

Over time, as African writers began to use the Western alphabet, they also adopted Western languages, normally the one spoken by their colonial occupiers. The modern state of Senegal, which once formed part of the eleventh-century kingdom of Ghana, fell under French rule in 1895. As a young boy, Leopold Senghor (1906–1989) was sent to a Catholic mission school where he learned French and Latin. In due course he won a scholarship to study in Paris, where Senghor became part of a group of talented black writers, some African, some West Indian, and some, including Langston Hughes, American. Overwhelmed by the squalor of the city of Paris and the arrogance of its people—the conquerors of his country—Senghor found strength in his "blackness." He later talked of discovering Africa in France and feeling his "pagan sap which prances and dances."

Together with his fellow black African exiles, he created a literary movement known as negritude. Senghor defined *negritude* as "the sum total of the civilization of the African world. It is not racialism, it is culture." Negritude's contribution to universal civilization, he believed, lay in Africa's uniqueness: the song styles and rhythms of its oral literature and poetry, but also its social values of traditionalism, earthiness, and the importance of community. In his own poems, Senghor often used woman as a symbol for Mother Africa,

VOICES OF THEIR TIMES

An Arab and a European Visit Africa

The Arab geographer al-Bakri (1014–1094) gives this account of the kingdom of Ghana's capital (probably Kumbi Saleh).

Ghana consists of two towns lying in a plain. One of these towns is inhabited by Muslims. It is large and possesses twelve mosques. . . . The town in which the king lives is six miles from the Muslim one and bears the name Al Gaba. The land between the two towns is covered with houses. The houses of the inhabitants are made of stone and acacia wood. The king has a palace and a number of dome-shaped dwellings, the whole surrounded by an enclosure like the defensive wall of a city. . . . The king adorns himself like a woman, wearing necklaces and bracelets, and when he sits before the people he puts on a high cap decorated with gold and wrapped in turbans of fine cotton.

Cited in E. Jefferson Murphy, *History of African Civilization* (New York: Crowell, 1972), p. 110.

A Dutch trader, writing in the late 1600s, long after the kingdom of Benin's heyday, gives this description of the capital.

The town is enclosed on one side by a wall ten feet high, made of a double palisade of trees, with stakes in between interlaced in the form of a cross, thickly lined with earth. On the other side a marsh, fringed with bushes, which stretches from one end of the wall to the other, serves as a natural rampart to the town. There are several gates, eight or nine feet high, and five feet wide. . . . The king's palace . . . is a collection of buildings which occupy as much space as the town of Haarlem [Netherlands], and which is enclosed within walls. There are numerous apartments for the king's ministers and fine galleries most of which are as big as those on the Exchange at Amsterdam.

Cited in Murphy, op. cit., p. 172.

---

his version of Mother Earth. Not all African writers were convinced by Senghor's philosophy. One Senegalese contemporary described it as "mystification" that ignored the class struggle, elitist, and out of touch with the masses. Many younger African critics have attacked negritude as a compromise with Neo-Colonialism, a refusal to complete the decolonization of the African mind. The Nigerian writer Wole Soyinka (who in 1986 was the first African to receive the Nobel Prize for literature) has dismissed negritude by observing that "tigers do not contemplate their 'tigritude' but just act naturally by pouncing." Senghor went on to a career in politics, building on negritude to form a variety of African socialism, neither capitalist nor Marxist. Becoming president of Senegal in 1960, he retired in 1980, the first African president to do so by his own choice. Whatever the lasting value of his aesthetic theories, his influence on twentieth-century African history is undeniable. One of his fellow countrymen called him "the myth that is endlessly discussed."

AFRICAN NOVELISTS

Mofolo Other important African writers used their own language, rather than that of the colonizers. The first African novelist, Thomas Mofolo (1875?–1948), was born in Lesotho, a landlocked kingdom in the middle of South Africa, upon which it has always depended economically. While he was teaching in South Africa and Lesotho, Mofolo's passion for storytelling encouraged friends to urge him to begin writing. In 1906 he published *Traveler of the East*, writing in the Sesotho language. The book is generally considered both the first novel by an African and the first written in an African language. In his early work, Mofolo sought to combine Christian elements with traditional tales and poems.

By the time he came to write his most important and successful novel, *Chaka* (1912), Mofolo used African religion as the overriding influence in his characters' lives. The book describes the career of Zulu King Shaka (1787?–1828), an actual historical figure who organized the hitherto weak Zulu warriors into a formidable fighting force. The real king was notorious for his cruelty and paranoia. In Mofolo's story, however, Chaka begins as genuinely heroic and courageous. The tragic hero then declines into tyranny and eventual insanity when, in an African version of Faust's pact with the devil, he sells his soul into sorcery. The missionary press, which had published Mofolo's earlier books, refused to publish it, and it did not appear in print until

1925. *Chaka* became an instant best-seller and has been widely translated.

Achebe The most widely read and acclaimed African novelist of the twentieth century is probably Chinua Achebe, born in Nigeria in 1930; his family belonged to the Igbo people of eastern Nigeria. When Nigeria became independent in 1960, the country (an artificial creation of the British) began to divide. In 1967 the Igbo seceded to form the Republic of Biafra, and Achebe, a passionate supporter of the Igbo, became Minister of Information in the new state. The Igbo breakaway was crushed in 1970, and the central Nigerian government seized control again. Achebe, overwhelmed by the death of many of his closest friends and the defeat of his people, chose to remain in Nigeria under the terms of the general amnesty for the rebels, and the war became a constantly recurring subject in much of his poetry.

The central theme of Achebe's work is the conflict between two worlds: Western technology and values, and traditional African society. In most of his novels, the chief character is torn by these opposing forces and is often destroyed in the process. His first book, *Things Fall Apart* (1958), forewarns us by its title (a quotation from W. B. Yeats's poem, "The Second Coming") that its story is tragic. When the British arrive in a traditional Igbo society, they undermine the values that have sustained it, and one of the community's most respected leaders is driven to suicide, as "things fall apart." Although the disaster is implicit from the beginning, Achebe's cool, laconic prose style distances the storyteller from his tale.

In his next novel, *No Longer at Ease* (1960), conflict becomes internalized. Its chief character, Obi Okonkwo, has been sent by his community to England for his education, and on his return takes an uneasy position among the corrupt minor British bureaucrats governing local affairs. As the story unfolds, Achebe paints a bitter, if ironic, picture of the colonial ruling classes, the bewilderment of the Africans, and the disastrous effect of both forces on the innocent young man in the middle. Obi's plight is made even more poignant by the impact on him of two powerful aspects of Western culture: Christianity and romantic love.

Achebe wrote his novels in English and, as in the case of Senghor, many of his fellow African writers have reproached him for writing in a colonial language. Achebe has always argued, however, that only Western languages can carry the message to those who most need to hear it. Furthermore, by using European languages, Africans can prove that their work can stand alongside Western literature with honor. Above all, throughout his long career, Achebe has always believed that the retelling of the African experience is crucial. In one of his novels, an elder says, "It is the story that saves our progeny from blundering like blind beggars into

◆ **20.7** Headdress, Igbo culture (Nigeria), 1900s. Worn by a dancer in a ritual, this headdress shows a slave trader, wearing a European hat, with his captive woman.

Wood carving. American Museum of Natural History, New York, NY, USA // © *Werner Forman / Art Resource, NY*

the spikes of the cactus fence. The story is our escort; without it, we are blind."

TRADITIONAL AFRICAN ART IN THE MODERN PERIOD

In order to appreciate traditional African art, it is necessary to bear in mind its cultural context. Unlike most modern Western artists, African artists generally have not produced works as aesthetic objects to be viewed for pleasure, but rather to fulfill a precise function in society and religion. Until the commercialization of recent times, the notion of a museum or gallery was alien to African art. Also, far from following Western ideas of "inspiration" or progress, African art is firmly rooted in tradition. The identity of the individual creator is far less important than the authenticity of the object and, as a result, we know very few names of African artists. Whether it exalts the secular power of rul-

◆ **20.8** Two ritual dance masks, one representing a monkey, the other a buffalo, Dogon culture, Mali, c. 1975–1995.
(Images © Charles & Josette Lenars/CORBIS)

ers or the spiritual force of the spirit world—and often the two overlap—the sculpture or mask must evoke age-old memories and associations. At the same time, African artists are as open to the influences of changing times and the world around them as are Western or Asian artists.

The conflict between Achebe's Igbo tradition and the newly arrived Western forces, which leads to tragedy in his novels, is made visible in a pair of wooden figures produced by an Igbo artist to crown a dancer's headdress [**Fig. 20.7**]. The male figure, who wears a European-style hat, is a slave-trader, while the woman, bound to him with rope, is his captive.

The same conflict of influences can be seen in the customs of the Dogon people of the modern state of Mali. The coming of Islam to Africa produced a conflict between the strict Islamic ban on music, dancing, and the carving of realistic images, whether of humans or animals, and traditional African art, music, and

dance. The Dogons reject the principles of Islam, and dance continues to play a central role in their culture, marking religious events, honoring ancestors, welcoming the rainy season, and, most importantly, accompanying funerals. On all these occasions, masks play an important role in the ceremonies. As the Dogon philosopher Ogotemmeli has said, "Masked dancers are the world, and when they dance in a public place, they are dancing the process of the world and the world order." At funerals the dancers wear masks representing animals, as they usher the dead from village life back to the bush, thereby restoring that natural world order [**Fig. 20.8**].

Many traditional African works of art are used in customs that celebrate the transitions of life and rites of passage. When a young man of the Maasai tribe undergoes circumcision, he and his friends construct a special bird headdress to mark the occasion. They hunt down a variety of birds—kingfishers, orioles, lovebirds, and

◆ **20.10** Ceremonial costume for the Egungun masquerade ritual, Yoruba culture (Republic of Benin), 1900s. Representing the collective spirit of ancestors, the Egungun costume uses velvet, cotton, and wool, decorated with a mixture of sequins, beads, metallic threads and cowrie shells.

Indianapolis Museum of Art, Indianapolis, IN, USA//Image © Indianapolis Museum of Art/The Bridgeman Art Library

◆ **20.9** The bird headdress of a young Maasai warrior, Tanzania, 2006. Note the tribal designs painted on his face as well the multicolored headdress that marks his recent rite of passage. *(Image © Wendy Stone/CORBIS)*

others—clean them out, and stuff them with a mixture of ashes and dried grass. The birds, which may be as many as forty in number, are then attached to a large horseshoe-shaped crown, which the young man proudly wears at ceremonies and public occasions until the healing process is completed [**Fig. 20.9**].

Other rituals require different forms of ceremonial dress. The Yoruba Egungun masquerade ceremony is performed in long elaborate costumes that cover the performer from head to foot. They often involve a variety of fabrics, which are then decorated with sequins, beads, and other materials, using traditional tribal patterns [**Fig. 20.10**].

Masks, headdresses, and costumes all serve as important elements in perhaps the most important of all artistic manifestations in Africa: the performance art of dance. Often religious or ceremonial, African dance is an integral part of cultural life, used to mark all important occasions [**Fig. 20.11**].

THE IMPACT OF AFRICAN CULTURE ON THE WEST

Throughout the nineteenth century as Western nations continued to colonize Africa, a growing number of African artworks began to circulate among Western collectors. One result was to create increasing interest in the study of anthropology as scholars began to try to understand and distinguish among the various cultures. By the turn of the century, however, African artistic styles were directly influencing Western art. Pablo Picasso, one of the towering figures of twentieth century art, returned throughout his long career to the African masks he had seen at a Paris exhibition and which he began to collect. One of the first of his works to show the effect of masks on his painting is illustrated at the beginning of the next chapter (see Figure 21.4), the painting known as *Les Demoiselles d'Avignon*. Sixty years later, commissioned to produce a monumental sculpture for the city of Chicago, Picasso had a huge copy made of one of his small cubist sculptures from that period, a work inspired by the same source [**Fig. 20.12**].

◆ **20.12** Pablo Picasso, Sculpture (untitled), Chicago, 1967. Notice that the mask has the same prominent nose as the standing figure to the right in Picasso's *Les Demoiselles d'Avignon* (Figure 21.4).

Welded steel, 65′9″ (20.9 m) high. Civic Center Plaza, Chicago, USA. Copyright © 2009 Estate of Pablo Picasso/Artists Rights Society (ARS), New York/Digital image © Art Resource, NY

◆ **20.11** Tribal dancer on stilts, Zimbabwe, January 1, 2000. The dance commemorates the dawn of the third millennium. *(© Torleif Svensson/CORBIS)*

Perhaps an even more direct link between African culture and modern Western culture is in music. As Chapter 21 describes in detail, jazz derives ultimately from the music of the African ancestors of African Americans. Yet jazz only partially represents Africa's musical legacy, as the growing interest in world music continues to show.

SUMMARY

The development of culture in Africa was largely conditioned by climate and the varieties of environment. The absence before modern times of a consistent written record means that our picture of early societies there is based largely on archaeological evidence and the historical accounts of the first Muslim and Western travelers.

◆ **Religion and Society in Early Africa.** Although African culture was never unified, certain characteristics were shared by many early African societies. Religious beliefs were generally animist, using the world of nature to explain to individuals their own lives. Successive generations passed on traditional beliefs by word of mouth, and the elders in a family or group therefore acquired a special status. Within each society, particular families or kin groups undertook specific tasks.

◆ **Three Early Kingdoms: Ghana, Benin, Zimbabwe.** Of the many powerful and sophisticated kingdoms that developed in Africa before the age of colonization, Ghana was outstanding for its wealth and exported large quantities of gold. Its period of greatest richness occurred around 1000. Both Benin (in West Africa) and Zimbabwe (in South Africa) began to grow around 1300. We can document life in Benin by means of the bronze plaques used to decorate the royal buildings. They reveal a society ruled by a hereditary king and a religion that emphasized the cult of ancestor worship. Zimbabwe was chiefly notable for its massive stone buildings and for its trade with Asia long before the Europeans established trade links there.

◆ **African Literature.** The earliest literary tradition in Africa was oral, although some of the Muslim traders in East Africa introduced Arabic script. One of the results was the development of Swahili, an African language influenced by Arabic. In the early twentieth century, African writers were faced with the choice of whether to write in their own language or that of their colonizers. Leopold Senghor (of Senegal) wrote in French but was a leading influence in the literary movement known as "negritude," which emphasized the specifically African contribution to world culture. The first African novelist, Thomas Mofolo, wrote in the language of his birthplace: Lesotho. The Nigerian Chinua Achebe writes in English; his books explore the impact of Western colonialism on African culture and lifestyles.

◆ **Traditional African Arts in the Modern Period.** The same contrast between Western culture and traditional African artistic styles recurs in the visual arts. Most African artists created works for secular rulers or ritual purposes. Recurrent symbols included animals and natural phenomena. Masks played an important role as a means of transforming or concealing identity.

◆ **The Impact of African Culture on the West.** The discovery of African art by Western artists in the late nineteenth century and the development of jazz in the early twentieth century are two important illustrations of African influence on Western culture.

EXERCISES

1. Which aspects of their culture did African slaves bring with them to the United States? How have these transplanted forms been changed or modified?

2. Compare the effects of Islam and Christianity on African art and religion.

3. The question of which language to write in has been a major issue for twentieth-century African writers. What are the arguments for and against the use of Western languages?

4. Masks play an important role in African art and ritual. How does their use compare to that in Western culture? How have other cultures used masks?

5. For most of their history, African poets and storytellers depended on transmission of their compositions by word of mouth. What other cultures have used similar methods?

 Visit the *Culture & Values* Companion website at **www.cengage.com/art/Cunningham/Cultureand Values7E** and the *Humanities Resource Center* for an array of primary source readings, key terms with pronunciations, flash cards, quizzes, and study materials designed especially to help you do well in this course.

CHAPTER 21

BETWEEN THE WORLD WARS

The young Scottish doctor, Alexander Fleming, served as a physician for the British forces during World War I. He was appalled by the number of soldiers who died as a result of infection and blood poisoning (septicemia) resulting from wounds. Apart from basic disinfectants, medicine had nothing in its armory to treat such infections. After the war, working as a researcher in bacteriology in London, Fleming discovered quite by chance that the secretions of certain molds destroyed the bacteria that caused certain infections. For centuries folk medicine had used moldy bread as a way of healing infections arising from simple cuts or tooth extractions, but no one had set this practice in the context of scientific research. Focusing on the secretions—which he named an antibiotic—of one form of mold, *penicillium notatum*, he developed the antibiotic penicillin in 1928. Further research in the early years of World War II made it possible to synthesize this new drug and bring it to common use in the treatment of bacterial infection. For that discovery Fleming won the Nobel Prize in 1945. He died in 1955.

Some medical historians have postulated that as many as two hundred million lives were saved as a result of Fleming's pioneering labors and have ranked penicillin as the most important discovery of the twentieth century. The discovery of penicillin opened up a new field of research that has led to the variety of antibiotics we know today.

Remembering Fleming's discovery also reminds us of the primitive nature of medical practice well into the modern period. The old picture of a family doctor sitting by a patient's bedside and monitoring a fever brought on by pneumonia was not only a nostalgic picture of a sympathetic family doctor but a gentle reminder that until such discoveries as Fleming's were made, there was very little that doctors could do but wait, watch, and hope for the best.

◆ *Penicillium notatum* (center), a common mold with a secretion—the "antibiotic"—that destroys colonies of the bacterium staphylococcus (note the red to pink disintegration of the bacterium cells closest to the mold). (© *Biophoto Associates/Photo Researchers, Inc.*)

THE GREAT WAR (WORLD WAR I) AND ITS SIGNIFICANCE

The armed conflict that raged throughout Europe from 1914 until 1918 put to rest forever the notion that war was a heroic rite of passage conferring nobility and glory. The use of technology—especially poison gas, tanks, and planes—made possible slaughter on a scale hitherto only imagined by storytellers. The sheer numbers of soldiers killed in the major battles of World War I continue to stagger the imagination. By the end of the war, the Germans had lost three and a half million men and the Allies five million (see map, "Europe After World War I").

The sociopolitical consequences of the Great War were monumental. The geopolitical face of Europe was considerably altered. The October Revolution of 1917 led by V. I. Lenin toppled the tsarist regime and produced a communist government in Russia; it was a direct result of Russia's humiliation in the war. The punitive attitude of the Allies and the stricken state of Germany's postwar economy provided the seedbed from which Hitler's National Socialist movement (Nazism) sprang. Postwar turmoil led to Mussolini's ascendancy in Italy. England had lost many of its best young men in the war; those who survived leaned toward either frivolity or pacifism.

Culturally, World War I sounded the death knell for the world of settled values. The battle carnage and the senseless destruction—in no small part the result of callous and incompetent military leadership—made a

GENERAL EVENTS	ART
1901	
Edwardian Age in England	
1900–1905 Einstein researches the theory of relativity	**1907** African sculpture fascinates artists in Paris: Picasso, *Les Demoiselles d'Avignon*
	Picasso and Braque begin cubist experiments
	1909–1915 Italian futurists glorify technological progress
1910	
The Calm and the "Great War"	
1910 Death of Edward VII of England	**1910** Roger Fry's First Post-Impressionist Exhibition scandalizes London
1914 World War I begins; European colonialism wanes	**c. 1911** German expressionism flourishes
1917 October Revolution ends tsarist rule in Russia	**1913** New York Armory Show brings avant-garde art to attention of American public
	1913–1914 Mondrian, *Color Planes in Oval*
	1915–1916 Dada artists begin assault on traditional concepts of art
1918	
Between the World Wars	
1918 World War I ends; women granted right to vote in Great Britain	**1918** Chagall, *The Green Violinist*
1920 Women granted right to vote in United States	**1919** Duchamp, *L.H.O.O.Q.*
1922 Fascists come to power in Italy after Mussolini's march on Rome	**1921** Picasso, *Three Musicians*
1925 Eisenstein, *Potemkin*, about Russian Revolution	**1924** Surrealism begins
	1926 Klee, *Around the Fish*
1927 Lindbergh's solo flight across Atlantic	Kandinsky, *Pink accent*
1928 First sound movie produced	
1928 Dr. Alexander Fleming discovers penicillin; awarded Nobel Prize in 1945	**1928** Magritte, *Man with a Newspaper*
1929 Great Depression begins in Europe and America	
1929–1930 Buñuel and Dalí collaborate on surrealist films *Un Chien Andalou, L'Âge d'Or*	**1931** Dalí, *The Persistence of Memory*
1933 Nazis come to power in Germany under Hitler; first refugees leave country	
1936 Riefenstahl, *Triumph of the Will*, film glorifying Nazis	
1936–1939 Spanish Civil War; Guernica bombed (1937)	**1937** Picasso paints *Guernica* in protest against war
	1935–1940 WPA photographers active
1939	
1939 Germany invades Poland; World War II begins	**1940** Kahlo, *Self Portrait with a Monkey*
1939 First commercial TV; death of Freud	**1941** Tamayo, *Women with Guitar*
1941 United States enters war	
1945 World War II ends	
1945	

mockery of patriotic slogans, appeals to class, and the metaphysical unity of nations. One result of this disillusionment was a spirit of frivolity, but another was bitterness and cynicism about anything connected with military glory. A whole school of poets, many of whom did not survive the war, vented their hatred and disgust with this first modern war. English poets like Rupert Brooke (1887–1915) and Wilfred Owen (1893–1918) both died in the war, but not before penning powerful poems about the stupidity, the carnage, and the waste of the battles.

New Technology The political upheavals and cultural tremors of the immediate postwar period coincided with a technological revolution in transportation and communications. After World War I, radio came into its own. It is difficult to comprehend what this information linkup meant for people who were previously isolated by lack of access to the larger world of information and culture. Similarly, the mass production of the automobile, made possible by the assembly-line techniques of Henry Ford in the United States, provided mobility to many who a generation before

ARCHITECTURE	LITERATURE & PHILOSOPHY	MUSIC
	1900–1905 Freud formulates basic ideas of psychoanalysis; *The Interpretation of Dreams* (1900) **1908–1915** Marinetti publishes futurist manifestos	**c. 1900** Roots of jazz originate among black musicians in New Orleans
	1910 Death of Tolstoy **1910–1941** British Bloomsbury Group rejects Edwardian mentality **1913** Carl Jung breaks with Freud **1915–1916** Dada movement founded Café Voltaire in Zurich	**c. 1910** Peak and decline of ragtime music; jazz becomes fully developed **1913** Stravinsky's *The Rite of Spring* first performed in Paris **1916** Scott Joplin records his *Maple Leaf Rag* **1917** Diaghilev's Ballet Russe performs *Parade* with book by Cocteau, music by Satie, and sets by Picasso Avant-garde compositions draw on jazz and ragtime
1919 Walter Gropius founds Bauhaus design school at Weimar; Bauhaus ideas find wide acclaim in architecture and industry **1925–1926** Bauhaus forced to move to Dessau, Germany; forced to close in 1933 **late 1930s** Bauhaus architects Gropius and van der Rohe flee Nazi Germany for United States	**1919** Yeats, "The Second Coming" **1922** Postwar literature expresses alienation and cultural despair: T. S. Eliot, *The Waste Land*; Joyce, *Ulysses*, Sinclair Lewis, *Babbitt* **1924** Freudian theory and Dadaism foster surrealism in art and literature **c. 1925** Black cultural regeneration, "Harlem Renaissance," in Northern U.S. cities **1925** Eliot, *The Hollow Men*; Kafka, *The Trial* **1929** V. Woolf, *A Room of One's Own* **1930** Freud, *Civilization and Its Discontents* **1932** Huxley, *Brave New World*, warns against unrestrained technology	**c. 1920** With the presence of "King" Oliver and Louis Armstrong, Chicago becomes jazz center **1923** Schoenberg perfects twelve-tone technique (serialism) **1925** Josephine Baker and other American performers bring jazz and blues to Paris **1924** Gershwin, *Rhapsody in Blue* **1927** The Duke Ellington Orchestra becomes house band at Harlem's Cotton Club **1928** First recording of Armstrong's *West End Blues* **1928** Weill, *The Threepenny Opera*, text by Bertolt Brecht **1935** Gershwin's *Porgy and Bess*, first widely successful American opera
		1943 Duke Ellington's symphonic suite *Black, Brown, and Beige* premieres at Carnegie Hall
	1945 Orwell, *Animal Farm*	**1945** Stravinsky, *Symphony in Three Movements*

were confined to an urban neighborhood or a rural village. The widespread popularity of the cinema gave new forms of entertainment and instruction to those who were already accustomed to the voices of the radio coming into their homes each evening.

LITERARY MODERNISM

EUROPEAN WRITERS

Yeats At the end of World War I, the Irish poet William Butler Yeats (1865–1939), profoundly moved by unrest in his own country (particularly the Easter Rebellion of 1916) and the rising militarism on the Continent, wrote one of the most extraordinarily beautiful and prophetic poems of modern times, "The Second Coming." The title of the poem is deeply ironic because it refers not to the glorious promised return of the Savior but to an event the poet only hints at in an ominous manner. A line from that poem with its prescient look into the future is as strikingly relevant for our times as it was for Yeats.

> Things fall apart; the centre cannot hold;
> Mere anarchy is loosed upon the world,
> The blood-dimmed tide is loosed, and everywhere
> The ceremony of innocence is drowned;
> The best lack all conviction, while the worst
> Are full of passionate intensity.

Source: Reprinted with permission of Scribner, a division of Simon & Schuster Adult Publishing Group, from *The Collected Poems of W. B. Yeats, Volume 1, The Poems,* Revised, edited by Richard J. Finneran. Copyright © 1924 by Macmillan Publishing Company, copyright renewed © 1952 by Bertha Georgie Yeats.

Eliot The year 1922 was a turning point for literary modernism. In that year T. S. Eliot (1888–1965), an **expatriate** American living in England, published his poem *The Waste Land*, and James Joyce (1882–1941), an expatriate Irish writer living on the Continent, published his novel *Ulysses*. In their respective works, Eliot and Joyce reflect some of the primary characteristics of what is called the *modernist temper* in literature. There is fragmentation of line and image, the abandonment of traditional forms, an overwhelming sense of alienation and human homelessness (both authors were self-imposed exiles), an ambivalence about the traditional culture, an intense desire to find some anchor in a past that seems to be escaping, a blurring of the distinction between reality "out there" and the world of subjective experience, and, finally, a straining and pushing of language to provide new meanings for a world they see as exhausted.

Both Eliot and Joyce reflect the conviction that, in Yeats's phrase, "the centre cannot hold." For Joyce, only

art would give people a new worldview that would provide meaning. Eliot felt that if culture was to survive, one had to recover a sense of cultural continuity through a linkage of the artistic and religious tradition of the past. That perceived need for past cultural links helps explain why Eliot's poems are filled with allusions to works of art and literature as well as fragments from Christian rituals.

The gradual shift from cultural despair in *The Waste Land* can be traced in Eliot's later poems beginning with "The Hollow Men" (1925) and "Ash Wednesday" (1930) and culminating in *Four Quartets*, which were completed in the early forties. The *Quartets* were Eliot's mature affirmation of his Christian faith as a bulwark against the ravages of modernist culture. To read *The Waste Land* and the *Four Quartets* in tandem is to see one way in which a sensitive mind moved from chaos to stability in the period between the wars.

Joyce Before World War I, Joyce had already published his collection of short stories under the title *Dubliners* (1912) and his *Portrait of the Artist as a Young Man* (1916). The former was a series of linked short stories in which people come to some spiritual insight (which Joyce called an **epiphany**), while the latter was a thinly disguised autobiographical memoir of his own youth before he left for the Continent in self-imposed exile after his graduation from college. With the 1922 publication of *Ulysses*, Joyce was recognized as a powerful innovator in literature. In 1939, two years before his death, Joyce published the dauntingly difficult *Finnegans Wake*. Joyce once said that *Ulysses* was a book of the day (the action takes place in one day) while *Finnegans Wake* was a haunting dream book of the night.

Joyce's blend of myth and personal story, his many-layered puns and linguistic allusions, his fascination with stream of consciousness, his sense of the artist alienated from his roots, and his credo of the artist as maker of the world have all made him one of the watershed influences on literature in the twentieth century.

Kafka Perhaps the quintessential modernist in literature is the Czech writer Franz Kafka (1883–1924). A German-speaking Jew born and raised in Prague, Kafka was by heritage alienated from both the majority language of his city and its predominant religion. An obscure clerk for a major insurance company in Prague, he published virtually nothing during his lifetime. He ordered that his works be destroyed after his death, but a friend did not accede to his wish. What we have from Kafka's pen is so unique that it has contributed the adjective *Kafkaesque* to our language. A Kafkaesque experience is one in which a person feels trapped by forces that seem simultaneously ridiculous, threatening, incomprehensible, and dangerous.

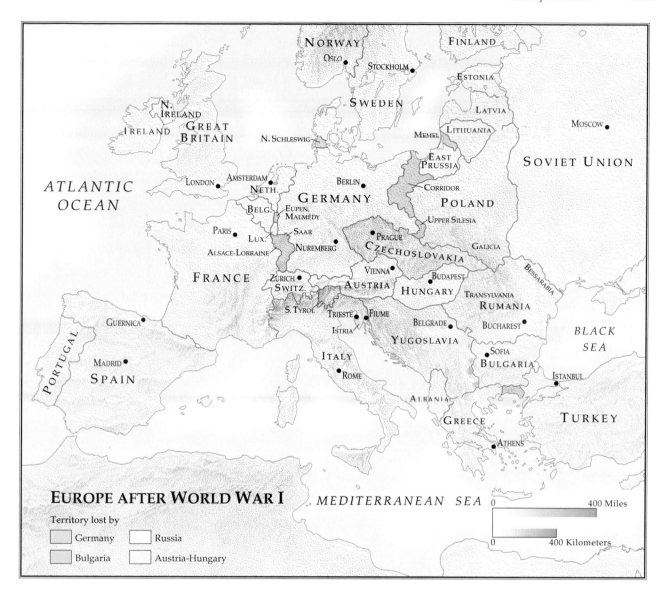

EUROPE AFTER WORLD WAR I

Territory lost by
- Germany
- Bulgaria
- Russia
- Austria-Hungary

This is precisely the tone of Kafka's fiction. In Kafka's *The Trial* (1925), Joseph K. (note the near-anonymity of the name) is arrested for a crime that is never named by a court authority that is not part of the usual system of justice. At the end of the novel, the hero (if he can be called that) is executed in a vacant lot by two seedy functionaries of the court. In *The Castle* (1926), a land surveyor known merely as K., hired by the lord of a castle overlooking a remote village, attempts in vain to approach the castle, to communicate with its lord, to learn of his duties. In time, he would be satisfied just to know if there actually is a lord who has hired him.

No critic has successfully uncovered the meaning of these novels—if in fact they should be called novels. Kafka's work might better be called extended parables that suggest, but do not explicate, a terrible sense of human guilt, a feeling of loss, and an air of oppression and muted violence.

Woolf Virginia Woolf (1882–1941) is one of the most important writers in the period of literary modernism. Novels like *Mrs. Dalloway* (1925), *To the Lighthouse* (1927), and *The Waves* (1931) have been justly praised for their keen sense of narrative, sophisticated awareness of time shifts, and profound feeling for the textures of modern life.

Woolf's reputation would be secure if she had been known only for her novels, but she was also an accomplished critic, a founder (with her husband Leonard Woolf) of the esteemed Hogarth Press, and a member of an intellectual circle in London known as the Bloomsbury Group. That informal circle of friends was at the cutting edge of some of the most important cultural activities of the period. Lytton Strachey, the biographer, was a member, as was John Maynard Keynes, the influential economist. The group also included the art critics Roger Fry and Clive Bell, who championed the new

VOICES OF THEIR TIMES

Virginia Woolf

In this abridged version of her diary entry for January 15, 1941, Virginia Woolf describes the results of the German bombing of London. Shortly after writing this entry, Virginia Woolf committed suicide.

Then Joyce is dead: Joyce about a fortnight younger than I am. I remember Miss Weaver, in wool gloves, bringing Ulysses in typescript to our teatable at Hogarth House . . . One day Catherine [sic] Mansfield came, and I had it out. She began to read, ridiculing: then suddenly said: But there's something in this: a scene that should figure I suppose in the history of literature . . . Then I remember Tom [T. S. Eliot] saying: how could anyone write again after the immense prodigy of that last chapter?

We were in London on Monday. I went to London Bridge. I looked at the river; very misty; some tufts of smoke, perhaps from burning houses. There was another fire on Saturday. Then I saw a cliff of wall, eaten out, at one corner; a great corner all smashed: a bank; the monument erect; tried to get a bus; but such a block I dismounted; and the second bus advised me to walk. A complete jam of traffic; for streets were being blown up. So by Tube to the Temple; and there wandered in the desolate ruins of my old squares: gashed, dismantled; the old red bricks all white powder, something like a builder's yard. Grey dirt and broken windows. Sightseers; all that completeness ravished and demolished.

art coming from France, and had close contacts with mathematician-philosopher Bertrand Russell and poet T. S. Eliot.

Two small books, written by Woolf as polemical pieces, are of special contemporary interest. *A Room of One's Own* (1929) and *Three Guineas* (1938) were passionate but keenly argued polemics against the discrimination of women in public intellectual life. Woolf argued that English letters had failed to provide the world with a tradition of great women writers not because women lacked talent but because social structures never provided them with a room of their own; that is, the social and economic aid to be free to write and think or the encouragement to find outlets for their work. Woolf, a brilliant and intellectually restless woman, passionately resented the kind of society that had barred her from full access to English university life and entry to the professions. Her books were early salvos in the battle for women's rights. Woolf is rightly seen as one of the keenest thinkers of the modern feminist movement whose authority was enhanced by the position she held as a world-class writer and critic.

THE HARLEM RENAISSANCE IN THE UNITED STATES

Also between the wars, a cultural movement was taking root in a section of New York City known as Harlem. There, a concentration of African American writers,

artists, intellectuals, and musicians produced such a conspicuous body of specifically African American work that the movement became known as the *Harlem Renaissance*. There were explorers of African American culture like Zora Neale Hurston, James Weldon Johnson, and Alain Locke; poets like Countee Cullen, Helene Johnson, Langston Hughes, and Claude McKay; artists like Hale Woodruff, Sargent Johnson, Augusta Savage, Romare Bearden, and the famous muralist and painter, Aaron Douglas [**Fig. 21.2**].

When one reads the poetry and fiction produced during the 1920s and 1930s by the Harlem Renaissance writers, it is easy to detect abiding themes of the African American experience: the ancestral roots of Africa; the quest for dignity in a culture of racism; a debate over the degree to which African American values should be part of—as opposed to distinct from—the majority culture; and the role of the church in life.

Behind most of these questions was the one posed at the beginning of the century by the African American intellectual W. E. B. DuBois (1868–1963): What self-identity does an African American affirm who must hold in balance his identity as being African, his place in American life, and the racism he endures? Those issues burn at the heart of Harlem Renaissance debates.

FUTURISM

Great art always has a thrust to the future. This chapter began with the observation of William Butler Yeats that

◆ **21.2** Aaron Douglas, *Aspects of Negro Life: From Slavery through Reconstruction*, 1934.

Oil on canvas, 60″ x 139″ (1.5 x 3.5 m). Schomburg Center for Research in Black Culture, The New York Public Library, New York, NY, USA//Copyright © Aaron Douglas. Courtesy of the Aaron and Alta Sawyer Douglas Foundation//Digital image © Schomburg Center/Art Resource, NY

"the centre cannot hold"—a prescient observation, as the aftermath of World War I was to show. Not all artists, however, were either so pessimistic or so prophetic as Yeats. A small group of painters, sculptors, architects, and intellectuals in Italy looked to the future with hope and to the past with contempt. Known as the *Futurists*, they exalted the values of industrial civilization and the power of urban accomplishment, and (with equal intensity) despised the artistic culture of the past. The theorist of the movement was a Milanese poet and writer, Filippo Tommaso Marinetti (1876–1944), who issued a long series of Futurist manifestos between 1908 and 1915.

Lewis The Futurist romance with industrial culture and the idea of technological progress was not shared by all artists of the twentieth century. We have already noted that T. S. Eliot pronounced his world a wasteland. The American novelist Sinclair Lewis (1885–1951) viciously satirized American complacency in the post–World War I period. His novel *Babbitt* (1922) was a scathing indictment of the middle-class love for the concept of "a chicken in every pot and a car in every garage" (Herbert Hoover's 1928 presidential campaign slogan). His philistine hero, George Babbitt, became synonymous with a mindless materialism in love with gadgets and comfort.

Huxley By contrast, the English novelist Aldous Leonard Huxley (1894–1963) saw the unrestrained growth of technology as an inevitable tool of totalitarian control over individuals and society. His 1932 novel *Brave New World* is set in the far distant future—600

A.F., the abbreviation for After Ford, referring to Henry Ford, who has been deified as the founder of industrial society. In this society, babies are born and raised in state hatcheries according to the needs of the state. They are produced in five classes (from Alpha to Epsilon) so that the exact numbers of needed intellectuals (Alphas) and menials (Epsilons) are produced. The goal of society is expressed in three words: Community/Identity/Stability. All sensory experience is supplied either by machines or a pleasure drug called *soma*. Individuality, family relationships, creativity, and a host of other "unmanageable" human qualities have been eradicated from society either by coercion or programming.

Toward the end of the novel there is a climactic conversation between John Savage, a boy from the wilds of New Mexico raised outside the control of society, and Mustapha Mond, one of the controllers of the "brave new world" of the future. Patiently, Mustapha Mond explains to the uncivilized young man the reasons why certain repressions are inevitable and necessary in the society of the future. The reader understands Huxley's warning that the great humanistic achievements—literature, art, religion—are threatening forces to any totalitarian society and as such are logical targets for a scientifically constructed society. His explanations now have a prescient and somber reality to us in the light of what we know about the real totalitarian societies of our own time.

Severini In the few years during which Futurism flourished, its followers produced significant paintings, sculptures, and ideas about city planning and urban architecture. World War I was to end their posturing;

◆ **21.3** Gino Severini, *Armored Train in Action*, 1915. The influence of Cubism in the composition of this Futurist painting is obvious.

Oil on canvas, 45⅝" x 34⅞" (115.8 x 88.5 cm). The Museum of Modern Art, New York, NY, USA//Copyright © 2009 Artists Rights Society (ARS), New York/ADAGP, Paris//Digital Image © The Museum of Modern Art/Licensed by Scala/Art Resource, NY

the sculptor Umberto Boccioni and the futurist architect Antonio Sant'Elia both died in 1916, victims of the war. Some of the futurists, including Marinetti, true to their fascination with power, war, destruction, and the exaltation of might, were increasingly used as apologists for the emerging fascist movement in Italy. Thus a painting like Gino Severini's *Armored Train in Action* [**Fig. 21.3**] proved prophetic in ways not quite appreciated in 1915.

THE REVOLUTION IN ART AFTER WORLD WAR I

Between 1908 and 1914, two young artists—Frenchman Georges Braque (1882–1963) and expatriate Spaniard Pablo Ruiz Picasso (1881–1973)—began a series of artistic experiments in Paris that revolutionized the direction of Western painting. For nearly five hundred years, painting in the West had attempted a reconstruction on canvas of a real or ideal world "out

there" by the use of three-dimensional perspective and the rules of geometry. This artistic tradition, rooted in the ideas of the Italian Renaissance, created the expectation that when one looked at a painting one would see the immediate figures more clearly and proportionally larger while the background figures and the background in general would be smaller and less clearly defined. After all, it was reasoned, that is how the eye sees the real world. Braque and Picasso challenged that view as radically as Einstein, a decade before, had challenged all of the Classical assumptions we had made about the physical world around us.

ANALYTICAL CUBISM

To Braque and Picasso, paint on an essentially two dimensional and flat canvas represented a challenge: how could one be faithful to a medium that by its very nature was not three-dimensional while still portraying objects that by their very nature *are* three-dimensional? Part of their answer came from a study of Paul Cézanne's many paintings of Mont Sainte-Victoire (see Figure 18.21) executed the century before. Cézanne saw and emphasized the geometric characteristics of nature; his repre-

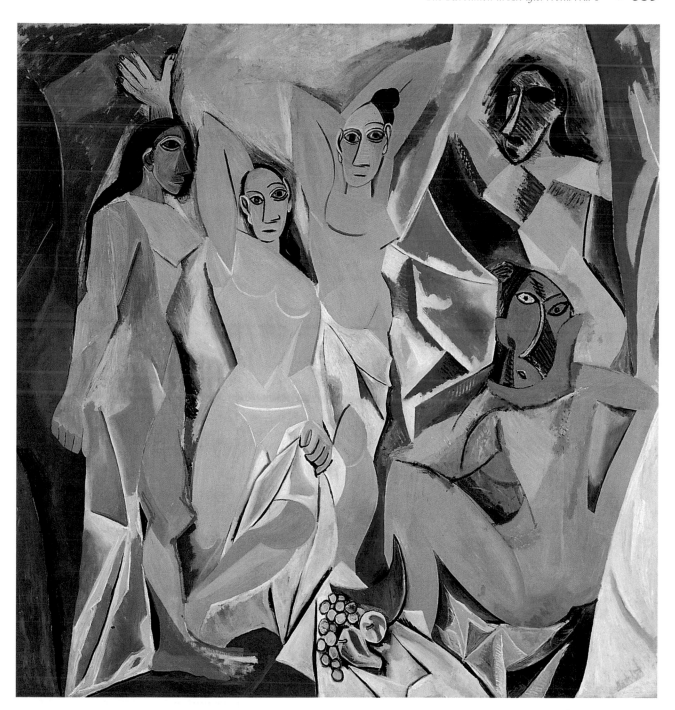

◆ **21.4** Pablo Picasso, *Les Demoiselles d'Avignon*, Paris, 1907. Note the increasing distortion of the faces moving from left to right.

Oil on canvas, 8' x 7'8" (243.9 x 233.7 cm). The Museum of Modern Art, New York, NY, USA//Copyright © 2009 Estate of Pablo Picasso/Artist Rights Society (ARS), New York/Digital Image ©The Museum of Modern Art/Licensed by SCALA/Art Resource, NY

sentations of the mountain broke it down into a series of geometrical planes. With the example of Cézanne and their own native genius, Braque and Picasso began a series of paintings to put this new way of "seeing" into practice. These experiments in painting began an era called *analytical Cubism* because the artists were most concerned with exploring the geometric qualities of objects seen without reference to linear perspective.

Picasso Picasso's *Les Demoiselles d'Avignon* [**Fig. 21.4**], painted in 1907, is regarded as a landmark of twentieth-century painting. Using the traditional motif of a group of bathers (the title of the painting is a sly joke; it alludes to a brothel on Avignon Street in Barcelona), Picasso moves from poses that echo Classical sculpture on the left to increasingly fragmented and distorted figures on the right. His acquaintance with African art

◆ **21.6** Pablo Picasso, *Daniel-Henry Kahnweiler*, 1910. Note the intensely two-dimensional plane of the painting.

Oil on canvas, 40" x 28½ " (101.6 x 73.3 cm). Art Institute of Chicago, USA. Copyright © 2009 Estate of Pablo Picasso/Artists Rights Society (ARS), New York//Digital image © Art Institute of Chicago/AKG, Berlin/SuperStock

◆ **21.5** Georges Braque, *Still Life with a Violin and a Pitcher*, Paris, 1910. By visually attempting to reconstruct the normal shape of the violin, one can see the analytical Cubist strategy of breaking up into planes objects with infinite viewpoints.

Oil on canvas, 46" x 28¾" (117 x 73 cm). Kunstmuseum, Basel, Switzerland. Copyright © 2009 Artists Rights Society (ARS), New York/ADAGP, Paris// Digital image © Giraudon/The Bridgeman Art Library

prompted him to repaint the faces that same year to reflect his delight with the highly angular and "primitive" African masks he had seen at a Paris exhibition. The importance of this work rests in its violently defiant move away from both the Classical perspective of Renaissance art and the experiments of Cézanne in the preceding century. It heralds the Cubism with which both Picasso and Braque became identified the following year.

Braque A look at representative paintings by Braque and Picasso will help clarify the aim of the Cubists. In *Violin and Pitcher* [**Fig. 21.5**], Braque depicts a violin so that the viewer sees at once the front, the sides, and the

bottom of the instrument while they appear simultaneously on a single flat plane. The ordinary depth of the violin has disappeared. The violin is recognizable, but the older notion of the violin as appearing "real" has been replaced by the artist's vision of the violin as a problem to be solved according to his vision and through his analysis.

In Picasso's portrait of Daniel-Henry Kahnweiler [**Fig. 21.6**], the entire picture plane has become a geometric grid in which the traditional portrait form has been broken into separate cube-like shapes and scattered without reference to traditional proportion. The viewer must reconstruct the portrait from the various positions on the cubist grid. Within the picture one detects here a face, there a clasped hand, and a table with a bottle on it. The intense preoccupation with line and form in this work can be noted by a close examination of the tiled surface facets that provide the painting with its artistic unity.

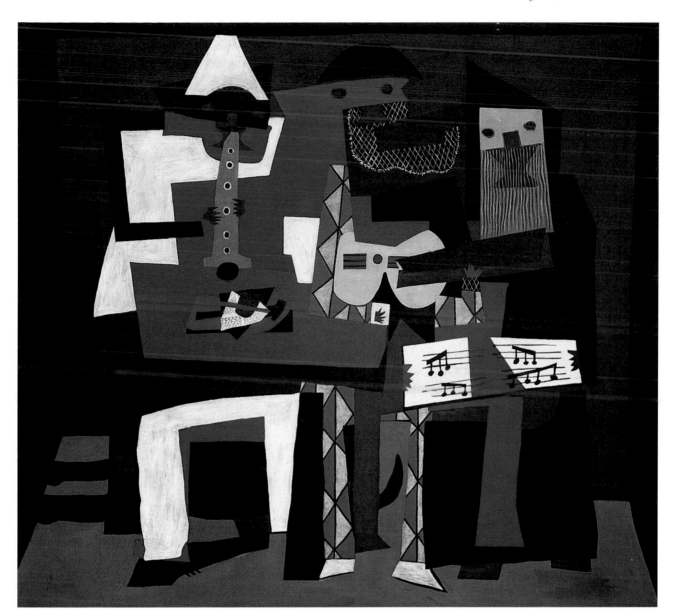

◆ **21.7** Pablo Picasso, *Three Musicians*, Fontainebleau, 1921. Synthetic Cubism added brighter colors to the muted, neutral color palette of analytical Cubism. The playful masks and costumes of traditional harlequin, clown, and monk with tiny hands and reclining dog (partially hidden) add to the playful quality. Another, more decorative, version of this painting done in the same year hangs in The Philadelphia Museum of Art.

Oil on canvas, 6'7" x 7'3¾" (2.7 x 2.23 m). The Museum of Modern Art, New York, NY, USA//Copyright © 2009 Estate of Pablo Picasso/Artists Rights Society (ARS), New York//Digital Image © The Museum of Modern Art/Licensed by SCALA/Art Resource, NY

SYNTHETIC CUBISM

In the postwar period, the impact of Cubism on the artistic imagination was profound and widespread. Picasso moved away from the technically refined yet somewhat abstractly intellectual style of analytic Cubism to what has been called *synthetic Cubism*. In *Three Musicians* [**Fig. 21.7**], he still employs the flat planes and two-dimensional **linearity** of Cubism, as the geometric masks of the three figures and the way they are lined up clearly show, but their color, vivacity, playfulness, and expressiveness somehow make us forget that they are worked out in terms of geometry. These postwar paintings seem more humane, alive, and less intellectually abstract.

Mondrian The visual revolution of Cubism stimulated other artists to use the Cubist insight in various ways. Only a close historical analysis could chart the

◆ **21.8** Marc Chagall, *Green Violinist*, 1918. This highly complex work blends Cubist, primitive, and dreamlike characteristics. Chagall's work blends memories of his Russian past and Jewish mysticism in a highly formal manner.

Study for the mural of the Theater of Jewish Art. Watercolor, pencil, gouache, 9¾″ x 5¼″ (24.7 x 13.3 cm). Musée National d'Art Moderne (AM1988-221), Centre Georges Pompidou, Paris, France//Copyright © 2009 Artists Rights Society (ARS), New York/ADAGP, Paris. Photo by Bertrand Prévost// CNAC/MNAM/Réunion des Musées Nationaux/Art Resource, NY

many ways in which Cubism made its mark on subsequent art, but a sampling shows both the richness and diversity of art in the West after the Great War. The Dutch painter Piet Mondrian (1872–1944), after visits to Paris where he saw Cubist work, abandoned his earlier naturalistic works for paintings like *Composition in Oval with Color Planes I*, a work whose main focus is on line and square highlighted by color.

Chagall The influence of Cubism was not confined to a desire for simplified line and color, even though such a trend has continued to the present in *Minimalist* and Hardedge art. The *Green Violinist* [**Fig. 21.8**] by Marc Chagall (1889–1985) combines Cubist touches (in the figure of the violinist) with the artist's penchant for dreamy scenes evoking memories of Jewish village life in Eastern Europe.

Tamayo The extraordinary Mexican painter Rufino Tamayo (1899–1991), who deeply understood his own culture, came under Cubist influence during his long career. His brilliant *Woman with Guitar*, for example, reflected a subtle Cubist composition in its layered background and foreground and use of planes and shapes of rich colors. The lush colors drawn from Pre-Columbian art frame and shape the Indian woman who sits slightly off center. The poet Octavio Paz said about Tamayo, "If I could express with a single word what it is that distinguishes Tamayo from other painters, I would say without a moment's hesitation: Sun. For the sun is in all his pictures, whether we see it or not."

GUERNICA: ART AS PROTEST

The late Protestant theologian Paul Tillich once called Picasso's *Guernica* [**Fig. 21.9**] the great Protestant painting. He said this not because Picasso was religious (which he was not) but because of the quality and depth of Picasso's protest against inhumanity. The title of the painting comes from the name of a small Basque town that was saturation-bombed by Germany's Condor Legion in the service of Franco's fascist rebel forces during the Spanish Civil War. Picasso completed the huge canvas in two months—May and June 1937—so that he could exhibit it at the Paris World's Fair that year.

The genesis and development of *Guernica* have been intensely studied in order to "unlock" its symbolism, but it would be safe to begin with Picasso's particular images. Many of these images recur repeatedly in his work to convey Picasso's sense of horror at the destruction of war together with his muted affirmation of hope in the face of the horror. His iconography is reinforced by its somber palette: gradations of black, brown, and white.

The complexity of images in *Guernica* at first glance seems chaotic, but prolonged viewing reveals a dense and ordered rhythm. Starting at the left with the bull—Picasso's symbol of brute force, of Spain, and at times of the artist himself—we see beneath the animal a woman with the broken body of a child. The echo of the Pietà theme is obvious. In the lower center and to the right is a dismembered figure, in the Cubist style, over whom rears up a "screaming" horse. At the top right of the work are Picasso's only hints of hope in the face of such evil: a small open window above a supplicant figure and

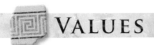

VALUES

Disillusionment

The period between the two world wars has often been characterized as a time of disillusionment. The horrendous slaughter of World War I, the brief spasm of economic prosperity followed by the worldwide Depression, the lack of trust in governments, and the questioning of traditional culture created a culture seeking ways to fill the moral vacancy of the times. Responses ranged from a new hedonism reflected in the excesses of the Jazz Age to a renewed search for some kind of a center for culture in the works of the modernist writers.

The most dangerous reaction to this disillusioned spirit was the rise of the total state. From Lenin's Russia, Hitler's Germany, and Mussolini's Italy arose a totalitarianism that saw the state as the total cen-

ter of power that would guide everything from economics and social policy to the arena of culture, arts, and propaganda. The distinction between public and private life was erased by the total state.

One great lesson that can be learned from the rise of modern totalitarianism is the vigor with which the total state repressed all cultural alternatives to its own vision of reality. The suppression of free speech, independent media, toleration for the arts, the space for independent social groups or churches or civic organizations was total in the Soviet Union, Germany, and Italy. The vigorous antifascist novelist Ignazio Silone once wrote that what the state feared more than anything else was one person scrawling "NO" on a wall in the public square.

◆ **21.9** Pablo Picasso, *Guernica*, 1937. By Picasso's specifications, this monumental painting remained on extended loan in New York until after the death of General Francisco Franco, when it returned to his native Spain.

Oil on canvas, 11′5½″ x 25′5¼″ (3.49 x 7.77 m). Museo Nacional Centro de Arte Reina Sofia, Madrid, Spain. Copyright © 2009 Estate of Pablo Picasso/Artists Rights Society (ARS), New York//Digital image © Erich Lessing/Art Resource, NY

an emerging figure holding a lamp. Over the center is an *oculus* ("eye") in which a lamp burns and casts off light.

As a social document the importance of *Guernica* cannot be overestimated. The German bombing of the little town was an experiment in a new style of warfare, a style that would be refined into a deadly technique

in World War II. In *Guernica*, Picasso innovatively combines various stylistic techniques that were employed on the eve of World War I—Expressionistic distortion and Cubist abstraction—to protest a technological development that became commonplace in the next war. In this sense, *Guernica* is a pivotal document—it

◆ **21.10** Wassily Kandinsky, *Pink accent*, 1926.

Oil on canvas, 39½" x 31½" (100.5 x 80.5 cm). Musée National d'Art Moderne, Centre Georges Pompidou, Paris, France//Copyright © 2009 Artists Rights Society (ARS), New York/ADAGP, Paris//Image © Erich Lessing/Art Resource, NY.

straddles two cataclysmic struggles in the century. *Guernica*'s cry of outrage provides an important observation about human culture. The painting reminds us that at its best the human imagination calls up the most primordial symbols of our collective experience (the woman and child, the horse and bull, the symbol of light) and invests them with new power and expressiveness fit for the demands of the age.

EXPRESSIONISM AND KANDINSKY

Although Cubism was the most radical departure in modern art, it was not the only major art trend that overarched the period of the Great War. German painters continued to paint works in the Expressionist style of the early years of the century. Perhaps the most accomplished exponent of Expressionism was Wassily Kandinsky (1866–1944), who was also one of the few painters of his time who attempted to state his theories

of art in writing. Kandinsky's *Concerning the Spiritual in Art* (1910) argued his conviction that the inner, mystical core of a human being is the truest source of great art. That attitude, together with Kandinsky's conviction that the physical sciences were undermining confidence in the solidity of the world as we see it, led him closer to color abstraction and further away from any form of representation. By 1926, Kandinsky was attempting to express the infinity and formlessness of the world (indeed, the cosmos) in paintings like *Pink accent* [**Fig. 21.10**] without appeal to any representative figures or sense of narration (nonobjective art).

DADA: ART AS ESCAPE

A group of artists, writers, and musicians who gathered around the tables of the Café Voltaire in Zurich in 1915 founded a movement to protest what they considered the madness of the war and its senseless slaughter. They

◆ **21.11** Marcel Duchamp, *L.H.O.O.Q.*, 1919. The French pronunciation of the letters under the picture sounds like an off-color expression.

Pencil on colored reproduction of Leonardo da Vinci's Mona Lisa, 7¾″ x 4⅞″ (20 x 12 cm). Private Collection. Copyright © 2009 Artists Rights Society (ARS), New York/ADAGP, Paris/Succession Marcel Duchamp//Digital Image ©Cameraphoto Arte, Venice/Art Resource, NY

decided to fight the so-called scientific and rational war makers and politicians with nonsense language, ugly dissonant music, and a totally irreverent and iconoclastic attitude toward the great masterpieces of past culture. It was called *Dada*, a nonsense word of disputed origin that could be a diminutive of *father* or the word for *yes* or a child's word for *hobbyhorse*. One of its poets, Tristan Tzara, wrote a Dada manifesto in 1918 that called for, among other things, a destruction of good manners, the abolition of logic, the destruction of memory, forgetfulness with respect to the future, and the elevation of the spontaneous to the highest good.

Duchamp   One of the most representative and creative of the Dada artists was Marcel Duchamp

(1887–1968), who after 1915 was associated with an avant-garde art gallery in New York founded by the American photographers Alfred Stieglitz (1864–1946) and Edward Steichen (1879–1973). Duchamp was a restless innovator who originated two ideas in sculpture that became part of the common vocabulary of modern art: *mobiles* (sculptures with moving parts) and *ready-mades* (sculptures constructed from preexisting fabricated material originally intended for other purposes). Besides these important innovations, Duchamp has also gained notoriety for his whimsically irreverent attitude toward art, illustrated by his gesture of exhibiting a urinal at an art show as well as his humorous but lacerating spoofs of high culture, the most "Dada" of which is *L.H.O.O.Q.*—his famous defacement of the *Mona Lisa* [**Fig. 21.11**].

The Dadaists could not maintain the constant energy of their anarchy, so it was inevitable that they would move individually in other directions. Dada was a movement symptomatic of the crisis of the times, a reaction to war's chaos but no adequate answer to it. It is no small irony that while the Dada theater group performed in Zurich's Voltaire cabaret in 1916, there lived across the street an obscure Russian political activist in exile from his native land. He would also respond to the chaos of the time but in a far different way. His name was V. I. Lenin.

FREUD, THE UNCONSCIOUS, AND SURREALISM

In 1900, on the threshold of the century, Viennese physician Sigmund Freud (1856–1939) published *The Interpretation of Dreams*, one of the most influential works of modern times. In it, Freud argued that deep in the unconscious, which Freud called the *id*, were chaotic emotional forces of life and love (called *libido* or *Eros*) and death and violence (called *Thanatos*). These unconscious forces, often at war with each other, are kept in check by the *ego*, which is the more conscious self, and the *superego*, which is the formally received training of parental control and social reinforcements. Human life is shaped largely by the struggle between the ego and superego to prevent the deeply submerged drives of the *unconscious* from emerging. One way to penetrate the murky realm of the human unconscious, according to Freud, was via dreams. In the life of sleep and dreams, the ego and superego are more vulnerable in their repressive activities. "The dream," Freud wrote, "is the royal road to the unconscious." To put it simply, Freud turned the modern mind inward to explore those hidden depths of the human personality where the most primitive and dynamic forces of life dwell. Freudian **psychoanalysis** is

◆ **21.12** Salvador Dalí, *The Persistence of Memory*, 1931.

Oil on canvas, 9½″ x 13″ (24.1 x 33 cm). The Museum of Modern Art, New York, NY, USA//Copyright © 2009 Salvador Dali, Gala-Salvador Dali Foundation/ Artists Rights Society (ARS), New York//Digital Image © The Museum of Modern Art/Licensed by SCALA /Art Resource, NY

not only a therapeutic technique to help anxious patients but also a descriptive philosophy that proposes to account for both human behavior and culture in general.

FREUD AND SURREALIST LITERATURE

After the Great War, Freud's ideas were readily accessible to large numbers of European intellectuals. His emphasis on nonrational elements in human behavior exercised a wide influence on those who had been horrified by the carnage of the war. One group was particularly anxious to use Freud's theories about the dream world of the unconscious as a basis for a new aesthetics. The result was the movement known as *Surrealism*.

Surrealism was both a literary and an artistic movement, gathered around the journal *Littérature*, edited in Paris by the French critic André Breton. In 1924 Breton published his first *Manifesto of Surrealism*, which paid explicit homage to Freud's ideas on the subjective world of the dream and the unconscious. "Surrealism," Breton

declared, "is based on the belief in the superior reality of certain forms of association hitherto neglected, in the omnipotence of the dream, and in the disinterested play of thought."

Throughout the twentieth century in fiction, poetry, drama, and criticism, other writers explored the implications of Freud and his followers. The great American dramatist Eugene O'Neill (1888–1953) restated basic Freudian themes of love and hate between children and parents (the *Oedipus* and *Electra* complexes) in plays like *Desire under the Elms* and *Mourning Becomes Electra*. Other writers of world repute like Franz Kafka and the American William Harrison Faulkner (1897–1962) may not have directly depended on Freud's writings, but their works are more accessible when we understand that they are dealing with similar issues and problems.

SURREALISM IN ART

Dali The painters first associated with Surrealism are familiar to every museumgoer: Jean Arp, Giorgio

◆ **21.13** René Magritte, *Man with a Newspaper*, 1928. Evident here is Magritte's power to invoke solitude.

Oil on canvas, 45½″ x 32″ (116 x 81 cm). Tate Gallery, London, UK. Copyright © 2009 C. Herscovici, London/Artists Rights Society (ARS), New York//Digital Image © Tate Gallery, London/Art Resource, NY.

de Chirico, Max Ernst, Paul Klee, Joan Miró, Pablo Picasso. The Spanish artist Salvador Dalí (1904–1989), who joined the movement in its latter period, however, was to become almost synonymous with Surrealism. His *The Persistence of Memory* [**Fig. 21.12**] is perhaps the most famous Surrealist painting. Its dreamlike quality comes from the juxtaposition of almost photographic realism with a sense of infinite quiet space and objects that seem unwilling to obey the laws of physics. The soft watches seem to melt in their plasticity. This juxtaposition of solidity and lack of solidity contributes to the "surreal" tone of the painting.

Kahlo Although Frida Kahlo (1907–1954) was not a self-described surrealist, those in that circle claimed her as one of their own. In her 1940 *Self Portrait with a Monkey*, the artist depicts herself in her native Mexican dress framed by lush tropical foliage, with her pet monkey and hair ribbons wound about her neck. Kahlo, who frequently painted her own portrait, made a profound study of the self, so that the viewer is invited to penetrate behind the mask of her persona to grasp the deep meaning of her life behind her direct gaze.

Magritte Another surrealist, René Magritte (1898–1967), was no less a draftsman but was less concerned with the dark side of the unconscious. His work, done with scrupulous attention to realistic detail, calls into question our assumptions about the reality of our world. In his *Man with a Newspaper* [**Fig. 21.13**], even

◆ **21.14** Paul Klee, *Around the Fish,* 1926. The figures in the painting seem to float freely in an indeterminate space.

Oil and tempera on primed muslin on cardboard; original frame, 18¾″ x 25″ (46.7 x 63.8 cm). The Museum of Modern Art, New York, NY, USA//Copyright © 2009 Artists Rights Society (ARS), New York/VG Bild-Kunst, Bonn//Digital Image ©The Museum of Modern Art/Licensed by Scala/Art Resource, NY

the title of the painting misleads because the man, like a figure in a single frame of a motion picture, disappears quickly.

Klee Although Klee's association with the surrealist movement was important, it does not adequately define his originality. The Swiss painter Paul Klee (1879–1940) had been influenced by most of the major art movements of his day. He knew the work of Picasso in Paris; he exhibited for a time with Der Blaue Reiter in Germany; after the war he taught at the famous design school in Germany called the Bauhaus. Finally, Klee showed his work at the first Surrealist exhibition of art in Paris. It was characteristic of Klee's talent that he could absorb elements of Cubist formalism, Expressionist colorism, and the fantasy of the Surrealists without being merely a derivative painter. He was, in fact, one of the most original and imaginative artists of the first half of the twentieth century. A painting like his 1926 *Around the Fish* [**Fig. 21.14**] is typical. The cylin-

drical forms hint at Cubism, but the floating shapes, some enigmatic, and the brilliant coloring evoke the dreamlike world of the surreal.

MUSIC IN THE JAZZ AGE

Born out of the unique experience of Americans of African heritage, jazz is a distinctively American contribution to Western culture. The matrix out of which jazz was born is an imperfectly documented history of a process that combined intonations, rhythmic patterns, especially repetition, and melodic lines that came from the African ancestors of African Americans with the tradition of the black spiritual, Christian hymns sung both in the slave culture of the South and in the free churches of blacks after the Civil War. In addition, jazz drew on the ineffable music of the blues, developed in the Deep

South with its characteristic and instantly recognizable *blue note* (bending a melody's note a half-step down). The blues existed mainly as an oral tradition in the rural Deep South in the nineteenth century, with one singer passing down songs to another, but it became a popular, public entertainment in city life from the 1920s onward. Musicians like W. C. Handy (the "grandfather of the blues") and singers like Mamie Smith, Ethel Waters, Ma Rainey, and Bessie Smith were immensely popular in the 1920s. And finally, jazz adapted certain European songs, especially French quadrilles and polkas, into a slightly different style of music that became known as *ragtime*.

Ragtime and Scott Joplin Although ragtime music has undergone many revivals, and is in fact still composed and performed today, it reached its height in popularity during the approximately twenty-year period stretching from the last decade of the nineteenth century to the second decade of the twentieth. Its single most important feature is rhythmic syncopation: the accentuation of melodic notes not coinciding with the tune's beat. (Indeed, many believe that the designation "ragtime" derives from the longstanding African American tradition of playing music in syncopated or "ragged" time.) In the typical rag, a solo pianist's left hand defines the regular beats of the piece by playing a steady bass line in an upbeat march meter while the right hand plays the melody with opposing beats, creating the rhythmic push-and-pull that gives the genre its distinctive feel.

CD Track 19
Scott Joplin, "Maple Leaf Rag," piano, Scott Joplin

Scott Joplin (1868–1917), the unrivaled "King of Ragtime," scored his biggest success with the "Maple Leaf Rag," composed in 1897 and published as sheet music in 1899. The publication sold over one million copies, making it by many accounts the first platinum hit of all time. Its irresistible appeal still can be felt today in the jaunting, forward-driving rhythms, the effective contrast between the piano's high and low registers, and the remarkable variety: it packs four distinct sections, each repeated at least once, into less than three and a half minutes of music.

The history of the recording presented on this CD collection is itself of some interest. Shortly before his death in 1916, Joplin recorded his ragtime hits onto a piano roll—a perforated roll of paper that, when inserted into a mechanized apparatus, makes it possible for a piano essentially to "play itself." Thus, we are able to hear Joplin's performance of his own song, but in much higher fidelity than would have been possible using the standard audio recording technology of his day.

Louis Armstrong and the Emergence of Jazz Jazz rose to prominence early in the twentieth century in cities throughout the American South and Midwest. Without question, however, the epicenter of the jazz boom was New Orleans, Louisiana. The rich and varied musical culture of the city—including African American, French, Cuban, and other Caribbean idioms—made it the ideal locale to spark a new, progressive musical genre, one that has now become so revered as to be referred to as "America's Classical Music." The musicians, who were all African Americans, performed without written music and were self-taught. They formed bands and played in the streets and in the cabarets of the city. By the end of World War I, many of these musicians had migrated north to Chicago, which, in the early 1920s, was the center of jazz music. From there, jazz spread to St. Louis, Kansas City, Harlem in New York City, and to other urban centers on both coasts.

CD Track 20
Joe "King" Oliver, "West End Blues," Louis Armstrong and His Hot Five (Louis Armstrong, trumpet and vocals; Earl Hines, piano; Zutty Singleton, drums and woodblock; Fred Robinson, trombone; Jimmy Strong, clarinet)

So profound was the influence of the blues on the emergence of the earliest jazz idioms that it is entirely appropriate that the first true jazz selection on this CD compilation carries the word "blues" in its title. In "West End Blues," blues elements are featured prominently throughout the song. The piece begins with an expressive and virtuosic trumpet introduction, performed by Louis Armstrong—not only the most prominent exponent of New Orleans jazz, but also among the most important and revered American musicians of the twentieth century. Armstrong's "Hot Five" then launch into the **twelve-bar-blues form** that will persist throughout the rest of the song. In a twelve-bar blues, a fixed series of chords, twelve bars (or measures) in length, is restated continuously throughout the piece. What maintains the musical interest in such a seemingly repetitive form is the ongoing variation that occurs above the chords; it is as if with each pass through the series the ensemble offers a new perspective on a familiar story.

Armstrong's recording of "West End Blues"—a piece composed originally by Joe "King" Oliver with lyrics by Clarence Williams—features four passes through the twelve-bar form. The first (beginning at 0:15) is something of a communal effort, with Armstrong's solo trumpet accompanied by lively, responsorial interplay between the clarinet and trombone, while the rhythm section provides the beat steadily underneath. The second time through (0:49–1:23), Armstrong's trumpet gives way to a soulful, bluesy trombone solo, featuring repeated bends and slides in pitch, often exploring the spaces *between* the pitches that the Western ear is used to, and in the process passing through countless blue notes. The third statement of the form (1:23–1:57) shifts to a **call-and-response texture**—another hallmark of blues practice—between Armstrong and his clarinetist. Here, the clarinet takes the lead, performing short phrases, and Armstrong, **scatting** (singing improvised syllables with no literal meaning), first imitates and then embellishes them, before the two "voices" perform the last phrase together in parallel harmony. The piano takes over with a lively solo for the fourth statement of the form (1:57–2:30), before the full band returns for the final pass (2:31), with trumpeter Armstrong taking the lead once again, beginning impressively by holding a single pitch fully sixteen beats. Finally, the piano initiates a flashy solo passage that leads to the song's concluding strains, which the full band plays in rich harmony.

JAZZ AS SWING

By the 1930s, the influence of jazz in the United States had moved into the cultural consciousness of the country at large. Jazz was now commonly referred to as *swing*, and swing bands toured the country. By far the most popular jazz ensemble during the 1930s and 1940s, the swing band, or big band, typically consisted of between twelve and twenty-five musicians: sections of trumpets, trombones, and saxophones and clarinets (each section of which featured approximately three to five musicians) as well as a rhythm section made up of drums, bass, piano, and guitar. In contrast to the improvised nature of New Orleans jazz, swing-era jazz pieces were arranged in advance by the band leader and read from sheet music or "charts" by the band members in performance. The genre is characterized by intricate, lush arrangements with a danceable "swing" feel.

CD Track 22
Billy Strayhorn, "Take the A Train," The Duke Ellington Orchestra, piano and conductor, Duke Ellington

The song "Take the A Train," unquestionably holds a place among the most popular, influential, and enduring of all big-band-era jazz standards. Its title and lyrics refer to the "A" subway line running through New York City's Brooklyn, Harlem, and Manhattan. Edward Kennedy "Duke" Ellington (1899–1974), a giant in history of jazz, gained fame at the glamorous Cotton Club in Harlem in the 1920s. This recording showcases his skills as an arranger and bandleader, creating a lively, creative, and varied instrumental showpiece. The piece was to

become the signature number for Duke Ellington and his big band and has been performed and recorded by countless jazz luminaries.

After an introduction by piano (performed by Ellington) and drums, the piece lays out its AABA form. A (0:06–0:17), A (0:17–0:28), B (0:28–0:39), A (0:40–0:50). After this initial iteration of the melody and chord progression (the "head" in jazz parlance), the rhythm section repeats the AABA progression, while a muted trumpet performs an improvisatory solo (0:50–1:35). After the trumpet solo, the AABA pattern is unexpectedly interrupted by a lively call-and-response sequence (the brass "call" and the winds "respond"), which executes a **modulation** (a shift to a new key). After this brief interlude, the AABA form repeats, now in the new key (beginning at 1:41). Here, the winds and solo trumpet alternate and interweave phrases before a brilliant, staggered, "stop-time" passage (2:12–2:14) leads to a coda that repeats the A melody in subdued fashion as the piece draws to a close.

Today Ellington is known not only for his virtuoso orchestral skills, but with such popular works as "Mood Indigo," is considered the most important composer in big-band jazz. But he was also a true original in his attempt to extend the musical idiom of jazz into a larger arena. After World War II, Ellington produced many works for symphonic settings. His symphonic **suite** *Black, Brown, and Beige* had its first hearing at Carnegie Hall in 1943. This work was followed by others—the titles of which alone indicate the ambition of his musical interests: Shakespearean Suite (1957), Nutcracker Suite (1960), Peer Gynt Suite (1962), and his ballet *The River* (1970), which he wrote for the dance company of Alvin Ailey, a notable African American choreographer.

THE INFLUENCE OF JAZZ

Jazz as a musical and cultural phenomenon was not limited to the United States in the period after World War I. Jazz had a tremendous following in Paris in the 1920s, where one of the genuine celebrities was the black American singer and dancer Josephine Baker [**Fig. 21.15**]. Furthermore, just as Pablo Picasso had assimilated African sculptural styles in his painting, so serious musicians on the Continent began to understand the possibilities of this African American music for their own explorations in modern music. As early as 1913, Igor Stravinsky (1882–1971) utilized the syncopated rhythms of jazz in his path-breaking ballet *The Rite of Spring*. His *L'Histoire du soldat* (1918) incorporates a ragtime piece that he composed based only on sheet music copies he had seen of such music. Other avant-garde composers in Europe also came under the influence of jazz. Paul Hindemith's (1895–1963) *Klaviersuite* (1922) shows the clear influence of jazz. Kurt

◆ **21.15** Josephine Baker, Paris, c. 1925. Shown here lying on a tiger rug in a silk evening gown and diamond earrings, Baker was born in St. Louis, Missouri. She first danced for the public on the streets of St. Louis and in the Booker T. Washington Theater, a black vaudeville house in her native town. Her first job in Paris was at the Folies Bergère where, nicknamed Black Venus, she became a tremendously popular jazz entertainer. Just before the onset of World War II, she renounced her American citizenship to become a citizen of France and worked for the French resistance. (© *Getty Images*)

Weill's (1900–1950) *Dreigroschenoper (Threepenny Opera)* (1928), with a libretto by Bertolt Brecht, shows a deep acquaintance with jazz, demonstrated notably in the song "Mack the Knife."

Most music can be placed on one side or the other of the classical/popular divide. Mozart's Symphony No. 40 in G Minor (K. 550) is an unequivocally classical symphony; Usher's "Love in This Club" falls comfortably into the popular genre. But a number of artists have made efforts to straddle or cross over this border—British pop star Sting's *Songs from the Labyrinth* is a collection of Renaissance composer's John Dowland's material; and classical cello virtuoso Yo-Yo Ma collaborates with renowned fiddler Mark O'Connor, bluegrass artist Alison Krauss, and singer/songwriter James Taylor on *Appalachian Journey.*

Many of the extremely talented musicians of the popular swing era were able to cross musical boundaries. The great swing clarinetist Benny Goodman recorded Mozart's Clarinet Quintet with the Budapest String Quartet in 1939. In the same year, the African American jazz pianist Fats Waller wrote his London Suite, an impressionistic tribute to that city. Such crossovers were the exception rather than the rule, but they underscore the rich musical breadth of the jazz movement.

Among the most fascinating crossover musicians in history is George Gershwin (1898–1937) who strove to bring African American idioms into contemporary American classical music. Gershwin's fascination with African American music predated his American opera *Porgy and Bess* (1935); many of his compositions had drawn on ragtime, blues, and jazz (the latter most

famously in his *Rhapsody in Blue* of 1924). Nevertheless, *Porgy and Bess* represents Gershwin's magnum opus, and one of the most ambitious attempts ever to integrate traditional African American cultural and musical characteristics with those of classical music. The opera incorporates jazz rhythms and "shouting" spirituals of the Carolina coastal black churches into a libretto written by the Southern novelist DuBose Heyward and Gershwin's brother, Ira. Some of its most famous songs, such as "Summertime" and "It Ain't Necessarily So," have become standards.

CD Track 21
George and Ira Gershwin, "Summertime," *Porgy and Bess.*
Vocal, Camilla Williams

Porgy and Bess features an all-black cast of characters and is set in the fictional Catfish Row, an African American neighborhood in South Carolina in the 1920s. In the first scene, Clara, a fisherman's wife, sings the opera's most popular song, "Summertime," to her baby as a lullaby. The tension between the supremely optimistic text of the libretto ("the livin' is easy . . . the fish are jumping . . . your daddy's rich and your momma's good looking") and the anxious chromaticism of the minor key foreshadows the profound tension that is to persist throughout this tragic story of poverty, murder, drugs, and betrayal. The longevity of the song, and especially the diverse nature of subsequent renditions, is perhaps a testament to Gershwin's success in integrating popular and traditional African American idioms into the operatic medium. Indeed, most listeners are likely to be more familiar with the variety of jazz recordings of the piece—from Louis Armstrong and Ella Fitzgerald to Billie Holliday, to John Coltrane—than with the full-throttle operatic version performed by Camilla Williams on this CD.

Porgy and Bess was not an immediate success in New York, but later revivals in the 1940s and after World War II established its reputation. In 1952 it had a full week's run at the La Scala opera house in Milan; in 1976 the Houston Opera mounted a full production, with earlier deletions restored, that was seen subsequently at the Metropolitan Opera in New York. It now ranks as a classic.

Ultimately, as Gershwin's opera perhaps foreshadowed, jazz itself would move away from popular music for dancing and toward classical music for the listener. In the post–World War II era, John Birks "Dizzy" Gillespie (1917–1993) and Charlie ("Bird") Parker (1920–1955) would lead the way in the transformation of swing to bebop and modern jazz, and John Coltrane and Miles Davis (1926–1991) would later experiment with *new wave* or cool jazz that further extended the definition and range of jazz.

BALLET: COLLABORATION AMONG THE ARTS

In the period between the world wars, one form of culture where the genius of the various arts most easily fused was the ballet. The most creative experiments took place in Paris, and the driving force was Serge Diaghilev (1872–1929). A Russian-born impresario, Diaghilev founded a dance company called the Ballet Russe, which opened its first artistic season in 1909. Diaghilev brought from Russia two of the most famous dancers of the first half of the century: Vaslav Nijinsky (1890–1950), whom we saw in Figure 18.33, and Anna Pavlova (1881–1931).

Ballet, like opera, is an art form that lends itself to artistic integration. To enjoy ballet, one must see the disciplined dancers in an appropriate setting replete with theatrical sets and costumes, hear the musical score that at once interprets and guides the movements of the dancers, and follow the narrative or "book" of the action. Seeking out and nurturing the efforts of the most creative artists of his era, Diaghilev had a particular genius for recruiting artists to produce works for his ballet. Over the years, the Ballet Russe danced to the commissioned music of Igor Stravinsky, Maurice Ravel, Serge Prokofiev, Claude Debussy, Erik Satie, and Darius Milhaud. In that same period, sets, costumes, and stage curtains were commissioned from such artists as

Pablo Picasso, Georges Rouault, Naum Gabo, Giorgio de Chirico, and Jean Cocteau.

Parade Diaghilev produced a one-act dance called *Parade*, which debuted in Paris in 1917. This short piece (revived in 1981 at the Metropolitan Opera with sets by the English painter David Hockney) is an excellent example of the level of artistic collaboration Diaghilev could obtain. The story of the interaction of street performers and men going off to war was by the poet Jean Cocteau (1891–1963), and the avant-garde composer Erik Satie (1866–1925) contributed a score replete with street sounds, whistles, horns, and other accoutrements of urban life. Pablo Picasso designed the curtain drop, the sets, and the costumes [**Fig. 21.16**]. *Parade* had much to say about musicians, players, and street performers, so the production was ready-made for Picasso's well-known interest in these kinds of people.

The collaborative effort of these important figures was a fertile source of artistic inspiration for Picasso who had a great love for such work and returned to it on several occasions. He designed the sets for the ballets *Pulcinella* (1920), music by Igor Stravinsky, *Mercury*, music by Erik Satie, and *Antigone*, based on Jean Cocteau's French translation of Euripides' Greek tragedy.

FILM

The first motion pictures are attributed to the French Lumière Brothers (1895), and the American Panopticon and Vitascope developed in New York the year after. By the time of World War I, a vast movie industry was already turning out short silent films for an eager audience. Sound technology was added to films in 1927. But already longer films with lavish productions were being produced.

Some of the first artists associated with Surrealism—like the American Man Ray—experimented with both still photography and moving pictures. The motion-picture camera could be used to make images that corresponded closely with surreal intentions. Figures could dissolve, blend into other figures, be elongated, or slowly disappear. Dalí collaborated with his compatriot film director Luis Buñuel to produce two famous Surrealistic films: *Un Chien Andalou* (1929) and *L'Âge d'Or* (1930). The French poet Jean Cocteau also produced a famous Surrealistic film in 1931: *Blood of a Poet*.

PROPAGANDA FILMS AS ART

Propaganda is the presentation of a point of view with the intention to persuade and convince. We usually think of it in political terms. Throughout history, propagandists have used books, art, and music to spread their ideas, but inventions in the early part of the twenti-

◆ **21.16** Pablo Picasso, curtain for the ballet *Parade*, Paris, 1917. Critics agreed that Picasso's brilliant sets and costumes overwhelmed both Satie's music and Léonide Massine's choreography.

Tempera on cloth, 34'9" x 56'¾" (10.6 x 17.3 m). Musée National d'Art Moderne, Centre Georges Pompidou, Paris, France. Copyright © 2009 Estate of Pablo Picasso/Artists Rights Society (ARS), New York/Digital image © CNAC/MNAM/Réunion des Musées Nationaux/Art Resource, NY

eth century added immeasurably to the propagandist's weapons. During the period between the wars, at a time when totalitarian governments rose dependant on a cooperative populations, people began to understand the power of film to educate, persuade, and shape public opinion. Film most successfully blended propaganda with attempts at an artistic vision. Two acknowledged masters of the use of film for propaganda need to be singled out because they set such a standard of excellence that, at least through their finest work, propaganda became high art.

Sergei Eisenstein The greatest filmmaker the Soviet Union has produced, Sergei Eiscnstein (1898–1948) also remains one of the most influential artists in the history of the cinema. A dedicated supporter of the Russian Revolution, Eisenstein fully appreciated Lenin's observation that the cinema would become the foremost cultural weapon in winning over the proletariat to the Revolution. From his early film *Strike!* (1925) to his last work, *Ivan the Terrible, Part I* (1944) and *Part II* (1946), Eisenstein was conscious of the class struggle, the needs of the working class, and the inevi-

table advance of socialism in history—themes dear to the official line of Stalin's USSR. Despite this orthodox line, Eisenstein was never an ideological hack. His films were meticulously thought out, and he brought to bear his own considerable cultivation to make films of high art. His *Alexander Nevsky* (1938) had an impressive musical score by Serge Prokofiev, and the two men worked closely to integrate musical and visual concepts. His vast *Ivan the Terrible* was deeply indebted to a study of El Greco's paintings in which Eisenstein was struck by the cinematic possibilities in that artist's striking canvases.

Eisenstein's most influential film, *Potemkin* (finished at the close of 1925), is the story of the 1905 naval mutiny on the battleship *Potemkin* and the subsequent riot in Odessa that was crushed by the tsarist police. The communists saw in that historical incident a major foreshadowing of the **October Revolution** of 1917, which brought the Bolsheviks to power.

The scene in *Potemkin* of the crowd cheering the mutineers on a broad flight of stairs in Odessa and the subsequent charge of the police is a classic sequence in film history. In that sequence, Eisenstein uses the device

◆ **21.17** Sergei Eisenstein, still image from his film *Potemkin*, 1925. A classic shot in the history of film, this single close-up from the Odessa steps sequence represents the horror of the entire scene. *(Goskino/The Kobal Collection)*

◆ **21.18** Leni Riefenstahl, still image from her film *Olympia*, 1938. This shot from the diving sequence shows the uniquely original camera angles Riefenstahl used. Such angles became a model for documentary filmmakers. *(Olympia-Film/The Kobal Collection)*

of *montage* (the sharp juxtaposition of shots by film cutting and editing) with such power that the scene became a benchmark for subsequent filmmakers.

His close-ups were meant to convey a whole scene quickly: A shot of a wounded woman cuts to a close-up of a clenched hand that slowly opens, telling the story of death in a moment. A crazily moving baby carriage is a macabre metaphor for the entire crowd in panic and flight. Shattered eyeglasses and blood pouring from an eye [**Fig. 21.17**] become a terrible shorthand statement of police violence.

Leni Riefenstahl For sheer explicit propaganda, one must turn to two documentary films made in Nazi Germany in the 1930s by the popular film actress and director Leni Riefenstahl (1902–2003). Her first great film was a documentary of the 1934 Nazi Congress in Nuremberg called *Triumph of the Will* (1936). Designed to glorify the Nazi Party and to impress the rest of the world, the film made ample use of the great masses of party stalwarts who gathered for their rally. That documentary allowed the young filmmaker to show the party congress as a highly stylized and ritualistic celebration of the Nazi virtues of discipline, order, congregated might, and the racial superiority of the Teutonic elite of the party members.

Riefenstahl's other great film, and arguably her masterwork, was a long documentary made at the Berlin Olympics of 1936 and issued in 1938 under the title *Olympia*. Riefenstahl used five camera technicians and thirty-eight assistants as well as footage shot by news agency photographers to make her film. The completed documentary, divided into two parts, pays tribute to the Olympic spirit of ancient Greece, develops a long section on the carrying of the Olympic torch to Berlin, records the homage to Hitler and the Nazi Party, and shows most of the major athletic competitions.

As a film, *Olympia* is matchless in its imaginative use of the camera to catch the beauty of sport [**Fig. 21.18**]. The vexing question is to what degree the film is political beyond the obvious homage paid to the German Third Reich, which sponsored the Olympics in 1936. Many critics note its elitist attitude to justify their contention that it is propaganda, albeit of a very high and subtle quality. Athletes are depicted as superior beings who act beyond the range of ordinary mortals. They give all and seem almost demigods. The film praises the heroic, the conquest, the struggle. It praises the ritualized discipline of the crowds and lovingly seeks out examples of the adoring Berlin masses surrounding the party leaders.

◆ **21.19** Walker Evans, *Floyd and Lucille Burroughs on Porch, Hale County, Alabama*, 1936.

Gelatin silver print, 7⁷⁄₁₆" x 9⁵⁄₁₆" (18.9 x 23.7 cm). The Metropolitan Museum of Art, New York, NY, USA. © Walker Evans Archive, The Metropolitan Museum of Art // Digital Image © The Metropolitan Museum of Art/Art Resource, NY

PHOTOGRAPHY

Photography is a nineteenth-century invention, as we have seen. During the nineteenth century, photography had a complex technological evolution as photographers sought ways to make cameras and photographic equipment more mobile. As this mobility increased, photography developed several specialties: portraiture, landscapes, documentation, and reportage. Most important and more basic, photography gave to the world what no other visual medium could: immediacy. Before the advent of photography, field artists transcribed events in sketches and then transferred those drawings onto etching plates for reproduction in newspapers and magazines. With the photograph, people could "see" events as they were actually happening. The idea that "a picture is worth a thousand words" has become a tired cliché, but it is difficult for us today to comprehend the impact the first photographs of war must have made when traveling photographers sent back to England pictures of dying soldiers in the Crimean War of the 1850s or when the American public first saw the pictures made by Mathew Brady (1823–1896) and his assistants of death and devastation during the Civil War in the 1860s.

Further technical advances, like the small portable Kodak camera invented by the American George Eastman in the late nineteenth century and 35 mm cameras (including the famous Leica) invented in the early twentieth century in Germany, contributed to the advance of photography in the twentieth century. In the period after World War I, there was an intense interest in photography as a new instrument for art. Man Ray (1890–1976), an American artist living in Paris, experimented with darkroom manipulations to produce what he called *rayograms*.

László Moholy-Nagy (1895–1946) taught a wide range of techniques in photography while he was an instructor at the influential Bauhaus school of design in Germany. When the school was closed by the Nazis, Moholy-Nagy came to the United States in 1933, where he continued to be a great influence on the development of American photography. A group of American photographers loosely connected with what was called the "f/64 Group" included pioneer photographers who are now recognized as authentic geniuses of the medium: Edward Weston (1886–1958), Ansel Adams (1902–1984), Imogen Cunningham (1883–1975) and Alfred Stieglitz (1864–1946). These photographers, and others like them, emphasized direct, crisp, and non-manipulative pictures that set the standard for much of modern photography.

In the United States between the world wars, the most powerful pictures produced for social purposes were those photographs made to show the terrible economic deprivations of the Great Depression of the 1930s. In the mid-1930s, the Farm Security Administration of the United States Department of Agriculture commissioned photographers to record the life of America's rural poor. The resulting portfolios of these pictures taken by such photographers as Dorothea Lange, Arthur Rothstein, and Walker Evans have become classics of their kind. In 1941 the Pulitzer Prize–winning writer James Agee wrote a prose commentary on some of the photographs of Walker Evans. Evans' photographs and Agee's text were published together under the title *Let Us Now Praise Famous Men* [**Fig. 21.19**]. Along with John

◆ **21.20** Walter Gropius, Technichal wing, Bauhaus School, 1925–1927, Dessau, Germany. The school consisted of three arms radiating from a center hub. Each arm was bent into an L shape and each served a distinct purpose: studio/dormitories, workshops, classrooms. *(Image © Vanni/Art Resource, NY)*

Steinbeck's novel *The Grapes of Wrath* (turned into an Academy Award–winning film), Agee's book is one of the most moving documents of the Great Depression, as well as a model of how word and picture can be brought together into an artistic whole for both social and aesthetic purposes.

BAUHAUS AND ARCHITECTURE

Some artists discussed previously (Klee and Kandinsky) also had connections to a new and creative center in Germany. In 1919, the year after Germany accepted the Weimar constitution at the conclusion of World War I, Walter Gropius organized the Bauhaus, a school founded on the desire to integrate craft, art, industrial design, and architecture. Its basic principles, in full reaction against romanticism, emphasized simplicity, rationality, and functionality. The Bauhaus was one of the most important artistic influences in the period between the wars—a period that almost exactly coincides with the physical life of the school [**Fig. 21.20**]. Its faculty offered courses in art, graphics, typography, and domestic and industrial design. Paradoxically enough, the school did not teach architecture as such until 1927. Its faculty designed everything from factories and apartment complexes to furniture, typefaces, and household items. Gropius's successor, Ludwig Mies van der Rohe, oversaw the school when it moved from Weimar to Dessau. The interim director, the Swiss Hannes Meyer, was a militant communist whose political views brought unwelcome attention to the Bauhaus by the Nazi authorities in the early 1930s. Meyer fled to the Soviet Union when the school was closed in 1933. The Bauhaus was judged "decadent" and a front for communist activities.

Walter Gropius found refuge in the United States, settling at Harvard University's School of Design. Mies van der Rohe moved to Chicago. Both architects had an enormous influence on the subsequent history of American architecture (as we shall see in the next chapter) where both, in their quite different ways, laid the foundations for what is now known as modernist architecture. Other members of the Bauhaus school like Marcel Breuer were instrumental in the field of design as well as architecture.

The Bauhaus "style" is almost a synonym for "modern" architecture and design—a movement so powerful, especially in the United States, that it was a major voice in American building with its characteristic unity of glass, steel framing, and clean lines. Its influence would persist well into the last quarter of the twentieth century and still lingers today.

SUMMARY

Advanced technologies used in the service of death made World War I catastrophic. The invention of the machine gun made obsolete the old military charge against an enemy just as the use of poison gas (not outlawed until after the war) made a mockery of military exercises of strategy. The result was an appalling slaughter of youth on a scale unparalleled in human history.

◆ **The Great War (1914–1918).** In the period between the wars, the memory of that slaughter shook intellectuals to the core. Their response was predictable enough: protest or pacifism or a total distrust of the powers of rationality to cope with human evil. The reaction to the Great War ranged, in short, from T. S. Eliot's combination of pessimism and faith to the playful nonsense of the Dada artists and the inner retreat of the Surrealists.

◆ **Technology.** The technological advances that had made the war so terrible also gave promise of new forms of communication that would advance the arts radically into new and different fields. The widespread development of radio networks, the transition of the film from the silent screen to the "talkies," the increased mobility brought about by the automobile, and the advances in photography would not only produce new art forms but also provide their availability to larger audiences.

◆ **Social Change.** Coupled with these advances were some profound shifts in social status. People were leaving rural areas in great numbers for the factories of the cities of America and Europe. The old social stratification of the classes was beginning to break down in Europe. The economic dislocations brought on by the war created urban poverty in Europe and, after a giddy decade of prosperity in the 1920s, the Depression years in the United States. In response to these social and economic dislocations, new political movements seemed attractive and compelling. Hitler's National Socialist party rose against the background of Germany's defeat, as did Mussolini's fascists. The period between the wars also saw the consolidation of communist power in Russia and the rise of the totalitarian state under Stalin.

◆ **Ideas.** Finally, we should note other fundamental (and radical) ideas that were beginning to gain notice. Einstein's physics, which contained the seeds of the atomic era, were changing the picture of the world in which we lived. Sigmund Freud's ideas were radically reshaping our notions of the interior landscape of the human soul.

All of these forces—political, technological, scientific, social, and artistic—shaped a culture that in its richness (and sadness) we call the Western world between the two great wars.

EXERCISES

1. Look carefully at a Cubist painting. Can you analyze the precise manner in which a Picasso or a Braque tries to get us to see in a new and unaccustomed way?
2. Some people have called Kafka a Surrealist writer. Is that an apt description of his writing? Why or why not? Is "dreamlike" ("nightmarish") an apt way to think of his writing?
3. Jazz is a much-respected art form today. Describe your understanding of jazz and distinguish it from rock music.
4. Discuss ways in which photography and film are used for propaganda currently.

 Visit the *Culture & Values* Companion website at **www.cengage.com/art/Cunningham/Cultureand Values7E** and the *Humanities Resource Center* for an array of primary source readings, key terms with pronunciations, flash cards, quizzes, and study materials designed especially to help you do well in this course.

CHAPTER 22

THE CONTEMPORARY CONTOUR

In December of 1947 at the Bell Laboratory in New Jersey, scientists John Bardeen, Walter Brattain, and William Shockley invented a device known as the transistor, a point-contact, solid-state semiconductor used to amplify or switch electronic signals. Their breakthrough would change the world. The transistor spelled the death knell for vacuum tubes then used in everything from radios to the first computational machines. In 1951 Shockley invented the bipolar junction transistor, a semiconductor that operated on a different principle, eclipsing the previous invention and setting the stage for modern electronics. By 1954 the first portable transistor radios were on the market. In 1955 Shockley joined Beckman Instruments in California where he headed its semiconductor laboratory division; key members would later disperse to form their own companies (among them Intel) in pursuit of integrating transistors in the first circuit boards.

Today, greatly miniaturized, over 130 quadrillion transistors are produced a year, primarily from silica, for which the region of electronic innovation—Silicon Valley—is named. Because of its low cost, reliability, and universal applicability, the transistor is the key active component in computers, calculators, iPods, cell phones, and all other modern electronic devices.

Shockley, Bardeen, and Brattain won the Nobel Prize for Physics in 1956. Toward the end of the millennium *Time* magazine named Shockley one of the most influential persons of the twentieth century while scholars regularly cite the invention of the transistor as one of the most important inventions of modern time. Ultimately, the transistor has led to the World Wide Web, revolutionizing communications in the way we receive and disperse information and ideas, and changing forever the many different ways we display our creative and imaginative products.

TOWARD A GLOBAL CULTURE

Now that we have entered the twenty-first century and the new millennium has begun, the events that happened after 1945 seem to recede into distant history. It is difficult to remember what has happened to our culture in the three generations since the end of World War II. Events that occurred in the past more than four decades ago are still perhaps too close to know whether they have permanently changed us as a people. Was the moon landing of 1969 really a watershed in our consciousness as humans? Did the "American Century," so proudly forecast by commentators at the end of World War II, end? Has the revolution in communications already radically changed the way we learn things? Is the age of microtechnology, new forms of communication, and the computer age going to bring in a new, wonderful era or an anti-utopia?

The decades following World War II were rightly called The Atomic Age. Developed largely by refugee

◆ Large black transistors on a portable radio circuit board, c. 1959. (© *Andrew Lambert Photography/Photo Researchers, Inc.*)

scientists during that war, atomic weaponry loomed like an ominous shadow over all international tensions and potentially belligerent situations. It is not merely a question of nuclear bombs being bigger or more deadly weapons, although they are surely that. Nuclear weapons can have long-term and little-understood consequences for both nature and the individuals who might survive the first blast. Today, with a precariously balanced peace, the real fear of nuclear weapons is their possible use by rogue nations or terrorist groups.

First, because modern warfare was so far beyond the power of the postwar human intellect to imagine, art-

ists turned to satire as a way of expressing their fear and hatred of it. Novels like Joseph Heller's *Catch-22* (1961) and Thomas Pynchon's *Gravity's Rainbow* (1973) sketched out war in terms of insanity, irrationality, and the blackest of humor, while Stanley Kubrick's brilliant movie *Dr. Strangelove* (1964) mounted a scathing attack on those who speak coolly about "megadeaths" and "mutual assured destruction" (MAD in military jargon). Any attempt at mere realism, these artists seemed to say, pales into triviality.

Second, at the end of World War II, the United States emerged both as a leading economic power in

GENERAL EVENTS	ART
1939	
1939 World War II begins; commercial television becomes viable	**late 1930s** Refugee artists Hoffman, Albers, Grosz bring ideas to North America
1941 Japanese attack Pearl Harbor	**1941** O'Keeffe, *An Orchid*
1945 World War II ends after first atomic bomb dropped on Japan	**1942** Hopper, *Nighthawks*
1946 First meeting of UN General Assembly in London	Peggy Guggenheim exhibits European art at New York Gallery
1947 Shockley, Bardeen, and Brattain invent the transistor	**1942–1953** Cornell, *Object (Roses des Vents)*
1948 Israel becomes independent state; Berlin airlift marks beginning of Cold War	**1943** Pollock's first exhibition
1949 Mao Zedong becomes leader of communist China	**c. 1945** New York becomes international art center; New York School includes abstract expressionism, color-field painting
	1948 Pollock, *Number 1*
	1948 Shahn, *Miners' Wives*
1950	
1950 Korean War begins; FCC approves first commercial transmission of color TV	**1951** Frankenthaler begins stained canvases: *The Bay* (1963)
1952 U.S. explodes first hydrogen bomb	**1950s** Rauschenberg experiments with "combine" paintings and, with Cage, "happenings"
1954 School segregation outlawed by Supreme Court	**c. 1955** Reaction to abstract expressionism results in "Pop" art; Johns, *Flag* (1954–1955); Warhol, *Mick Jagger* (1975)
1955 U.S. Civil Rights Movement starts in the South	**1956** Bergman, film *Wild Strawberries*
1956 Shockley, Bardeen, and Brattain win the Nobel Prize for Physics	Calder, *Eleven Polychrome*
1957 First earth satellite launched by USSR	**1957** Gottlieb, *Blast I*
	1957–1960 Nevelson, *Sky Cathedral*
	1955–1959 Rauschenberg, *Monogram*
1960	
1961 East Germans erect Berlin Wall	**1960s** Rothko panels for Houston Chapel, opened 1971
Soviets put first person in space	**1962** Stella, *Hyena Stomp*
1962 American orbits earth in space	**1963** Segal, *Cinema*
Transatlantic transmission of television signal via earth satellite	**1964–65** Kienholz, *The Wait*
1963 President John F. Kennedy assassinated	**1964** Smith, *Cubi XIX*
1964 Massive buildup of American troops in Vietnam	**1964** Kubrick, film *Dr. Strangelove*
Cultural Revolution in Communist China	**1965–1967** Motherwell, *Elegy to the Spanish Republic #108*
1966 Founding of National Organization for Women in U.S.	**1966–1967** Oldenburg, *Giant Soft Fan*
1968 Martin Luther King Jr. and Robert F. Kennedy assassinated	**1967** Hockney, *A Bigger Splash*
Youth movement at apex	**1970s** Resurgence of realism; incorporation of technology (videotapes, computers, lasers) in art
1969 Astronaut Neil Armstrong takes first walk on moon	**1972–1976** Christo and Jeanne-Claude, *Running Fence*
	1974 Bearden, *Empress of the Blues*
1975	
1975 American withdrawal from Vietnam	**1975** Rothenberg, *Two-Tone*
1977 New Chinese government allows art previously banned	**1978** Pearlstein, *Male and Female Nudes on Carpet*
1981 First space shuttle flight	**1979** Stella, *Katsura*
1989 Berlin Wall falls; soft revolutions in Eastern Europe	**1981** Picasso's *Guernica* returned to Spain on Franco's death
1991 Soviet Union dissolved in favor of independent nations	**1982** Lin, *Vietnam Veterans Memorial*
	1982 Richter, *Clouds*
	1984 Frank, *Chant*
	1985 Bartlett, *Sea Wall*
	1990 Ringgold, *Tar Beach 2*
	1991 Hanson, *Homeless Person*
	1995 Nam June Paik, *Electronic Superhighway*
2000	
2001 Twin Towers Disaster	**2000** Whiteread, *Nameless Library*, Holocaust Memorial
	2004 Plensa, *Crown Fountain*
	2005 Murray, *Do the Dance*
	2005–2006 Abakanowicz, *Agora*

WORLD WAR II AND THE ATOMIC AGE
THE BEAT GENERATION
THE YOUTH MOVEMENT
CONTEMPORARY TRAJECTORIES

the world and as the leader of the "free world" in its struggle against communism. This preeminence explains both the high standard of living in the West and the resentment of those who did not share it. Only recently have we understood that economic supremacy does not permit a nation to live free from outside forces. The energy crises, the need for raw materials, the quest for labor, and the search for new markets today bind many nations together in a delicate economic and social network of political relationships. The United States depends on other countries; the shifting patterns of economic relationships among North America, Europe, the Developing World, China, Japan, and the oil producers of the Middle East are all reminders of how fragile that network really is. That is why we can speak of a global economy. With the collapse of communism in Eastern Europe, new patterns of culture slowly began to emerge, as the vigor of the Pacific Rim nations attest. We do not know exactly how the New World Order will operate. What we do know is that our lives are not insulated: Our stereos are assembled in Malaysia; our vegetables may come from Mexico; our blue jeans are sewn in Bangladesh; and our sneakers manufactured in Romania.

ARCHITECTURE	LITERATURE & PHILOSOPHY	MUSIC
late 1930s Bauhaus architects Gropius and van der Rohe flee Nazi Germany for United States **1943** Wright designs Guggenheim Museum, New York **c. 1947** Buckminster Fuller develops geodesic dome	**1946** Sartre, *Existentialism Is a Humanism* Existentialist philosophy influences writers and dramatists: Camus, *The Stranger* (1942); Beckett, *Waiting for Godot* (1953) **1949** Miller's *Death of a Salesman* wins Pulitzer Prize for Drama Faulkner wins Nobel Prize for Literature	**1945** Britten composes opera *Peter Grimes* **1948** Structuralist Boulez composes Second Piano Sonata LP records become commercially available
1952 Le Corbusier, *L'Unité d'Habitation*, Marseille **1956–1957** Reinforced concrete technology results in building as sculpture Nervi and Vitellozzi, *Palazzetto dello Sport*, Rome **1956–1958** van der Rohe and Johnson, Seagram Building, New York **1959** Guggenheim Museum completed **1957–1972** Utzon, Opera House, Sydney, Australia	**1950** Sociologist Riesman writes *The Lonely Crowd*; Gwendolyn Brooks, first African American poet to win Pulitzer Prize **1951** Langston Hughes, "Harlem," "Theme for English B" **1950s** Alienation and anxiety become major themes of Beat writers Kerouac and Ginsberg	**1950s** Beginnings of electronic music with first use of synthesizer **1952** Boulez, *Structures* Cage experiments with aleatoric music, *4' 33"* **1955–1956** Stockhausen, *Song of the Boys* **1958** Cage, *Concert for Piano and Orchestra*
1962 Saarinen, TWA Flight Center, New York **1977** Piano and Rogers, Pompidou Center, Paris	**1960** Wiesel, *Night*, memoir of Nazi concentration camps **1961** Heller, *Catch-22*, satire on absurdity of war **1963** Flannery O'Connor, "Revelation" **1963** Plath, *The Bell Jar*, first published under a pseudonym **1964** Stoppard, *Rosencrantz and Guildenstern Are Dead* **1970** Solzhenitsyn wins Nobel Prize for Literature Toffler, *Future Shock* **1973** Pynchon, *Gravity's Rainbow* **1974** Rich, "Diving into the Wreck"	**1960** Penderecki, *Threnody for the Victims of Hiroshima* **1962** Britten, *War Requiem* Shostakovich, Symphony No. 13, text from poems by Yevtushenko **1965** Stockhausen, *Mixtur* **c. 1965** Dylan, protest songs; rock music and Beatles; eclectic music of Mothers of Invention **1971** Shostakovich, Symphony No. 15 **1973** Stockhausen, *Stop* Britten, opera *Death in Venice*
1978 Pei, East Wing of National Gallery of Art, Washington, DC **1978** Moore, Perez and Assoc., Plaza d'Italia **1994** Gehry, American Center, Paris **1997** Gehry, Guggenheim Museum Bilbao, Spain **1997** Meier, Getty Center, Los Angeles	**1993** Morrison awarded Nobel Prize for Literature	**1975–1985** Philip Glass, *Einstein on the Beach*, *Satyagraha*, *Akhnaten* **1978** Penderecki, opera *Paradise Lost* **1983** Reich's *The Desert Music* **1992** Philip Glass, *The Voyage*
2000 Herzog and de Meuron, Tate Modern, London		

THE DEMAND FOR RIGHTS

The material satisfactions of Western life spawned other kinds of dissatisfaction. While we may be the best-fed, best-housed, and best-clothed citizens in history, the hunger for individual and social meaning remains a constant in our lives. For instance, many sociopolitical movements in this country are signs of that human restlessness that will not be satisfied by bread alone. These movements are not peculiar to North America, as democratic movements in other parts of the world so readily attest.

The incredible achievements of modern society have exacted their price. Sigmund Freud shrewdly pointed out in *Civilization and Its Discontents* (1929) that the price of advanced culture is a certain repression of the individual together with the need of that individual to conform to the larger will of the community. North Americans have always been sensitive to the constraints of the state, because their history began as a revolt against statist domination.

The Western world tends to view repression in terms more social than political. The complexity of the technological management of modern life has led many to complain that we are becoming mere numbers or ciphers under the indifferent control of databanks and computers. Such warnings began as early as George Orwell's political novel *1984* (1946), written right after World War II; progressed through David Riesman's sociological tract of the 1950s, *The Lonely Crowd*; to the futurist predictions of Alvin Toffler's *Future Shock* in the 1970s. Now, in the new millennium, many more such analyses are sure to appear.

THE ARTIST AND CHANGE

Art, of course, reflects not only the materials of its age but also its hopes and anxieties. The art, literature, and music of contemporary times attempt to diagnose our ills, protest our injustices, and offer alternative visions of what life might become. On exceptional occasions, the voice of the artist can sum up a cultural condition in a way strong enough to produce change. Who would have predicted that an obscure convict, buried in the vast prison complex of the Siberian wasteland, would raise his voice against injustice and repression to change radically the way a whole society is understood? And yet in *The Gulag Archipelago* (1978), Alexander Solzhenitsyn did just that about the ominous character of a now-collapsed Soviet communism. The same may be said of Nelson Mandela, who went from being a political prisoner to becoming the first African president of South Africa.

The true artist can articulate a vision of what humanity can trust. In the midst of alienation, the artist can bring community, and in the midst of ugliness, beauty.

The artist, in short, acts not only as a voice of protest but also as a voice of hope. The American novelist William Harrison Faulkner (1897–1962) spent a lifetime chronicling the violence, decay, injustice, poverty, and lost dreams of the American South. His novels are difficult to read, because they reflect the modernist sense of dislocated place and fragmented time. His most famous novel, *The Sound and the Fury* (1929), was notorious for its depiction of defective children, incestuous relationships, loutish drunkenness, and violence. In that sense it reflects the bleak landscape of the modern literary imagination. Yet Faulkner insisted that beneath the horror of modern life was a strong residue of human hope and goodness. Faulkner reaffirmed it resoundingly in his acceptance speech when he was awarded the Nobel Prize for Literature in 1949: "I believe that man will not merely endure; he will prevail."

Two generations later, in 1993, the African American woman of letters and novelist Toni Morrison would accept that same prize with a ringing act of faith in the power of language to aid our common humanity as well as a powerful description of how much the evil powers of the world fear the depths of true language.

In the rapidly shifting contours of our contemporary world, we might reflect on the ways in which artists have participated in the restructuring of societies. Many of those who struggled for human rights in the former Soviet Union and the Eastern Bloc were poets, novelists, filmmakers, musicians, and playwrights. The subversive quality of popular music is not only a part of our culture but has become a worldwide phenomenon. The role of artists in the changing of society is very much a part of the fabric of this chapter.

PHILOSOPHY: EXISTENTIALISM

The philosophy that most persistently gripped the intellectual imagination of the Western world in the period immediately after World War II was *existentialism*. Existentialism is more an attitude than a single philosophical system. Its direct ancestry can be traced to the nineteenth-century Danish theologian and religious thinker Søren Aabye Kierkegaard (1813–1855), who set out its main emphases. Kierkegaard strongly reacted against the great abstract philosophical systems developed by such philosophers as Georg Wilhelm Hegel (1770–1831) in favor of an intense study of the individual person in his or her actual existing situation in the world. Kierkegaard emphasized the single individual ("the crowd is untruth") who exists in a specific set of circumstances at a particular time in history with a specific consciousness. Philosophers like Hegel, Kierkegaard once noted

Table 22.1 *Writers in the Existentialist Tradition*

Fyodor Dostoyevsky (1821–1881)—Russian
Søren Kierkegaard (1813–1855)—Danish
Friedrich Nietzsche (1844–1900)—German
Miguel de Unamuno (1864–1936)—Spanish
Nicholas Berdyaev (1874–1948)—Russian
Rainer Maria Rilke (1875–1926)—Czech/German
Martin Buber (1878–1965)—Austrian/Israeli
Jacques Maritain (1882–1973)—French
Karl Jaspers (1883–1969)—German
Franz Kafka (1883–1924)—Czech/German
José Ortega y Gasset (1883–1955)—Spanish
Martin Heidegger (1889–1976)—German
Jean-Paul Sartre (1905–1980)—French
Albert Camus (1913–1960)—French

ironically, answer every question about the universe except "Who am I?," "What am I doing here?," and "Where am I going?"

This radically subjective self-examination was carried on throughout the twentieth century by philosophers like Friedrich Nietzsche and novelists like Fyodor Dostoyevsky, who are regarded as forerunners of modern existentialist philosophy (see **Table 22.1**). In the twentieth century writers like Franz Kafka, the German poet Rainer Maria Rilke, the Spanish critic Miguel de Unamuno, and, above all, the German philosopher Martin Heidegger gave sharper focus to the existentialist creed.

Sartre The postwar writer who best articulated existentialism both as a philosophy and a lifestyle, however, was the French writer and philosopher Jean-Paul Sartre (1905–1980). Sartre believed it the task of the modern thinker to take seriously the implications of atheism. If there is no God, Sartre insisted, then there is no blueprint for what a person should be and no ultimate significance to the universe. People are thrown into life, and their very aloneness forces them to make decisions about who they are and what they shall become. "People are condemned to be free," Sartre wrote. Existentialism was an attempt to help people understand their place in an absurd world, their obligation to face up to their freedom, and the kinds of ethics available to individuals in a world bereft of absolutes.

Sartre began his mature career just as Germany was beginning its hostilities in the late 1930s. After being a prisoner of war in Germany, Sartre lived in occupied France, where he was active in the French Resistance, especially as a writer for the newspaper *Combat*. Sartre as well as feminist writer Simone de Beauvoir (1908–1986) were the major voices demanding integrity in the face of the absurdities and horrors of war-torn Europe. Such an attitude might be considered a posture if it were not for the circumstances in which these existentialist writers worked.

The appeal of existentialism was its marriage of thought and action, its analysis of modern anxiety, and

its willingness to express its ideas through the media of plays, novels, films, and newspaper polemics. After the close of the war in 1945, there was a veritable explosion of existentialist theater (Samuel Beckett, Harold Pinter, Jean Gênet, Eugène Ionesco) and existentialist fiction (Camus, Sartre, Beauvoir) in Europe. In the United States, existentialist themes were taken up eagerly by intellectuals and writers who were attracted to its emphasis on anxiety and alienation.

The Beats The so-called Beat writers of the 1950s embraced a rather vulgarized style of existentialism filtered through the mesh of jazz and the black experience. Beat writers such as the late Jack Kerouac, Gregory Corso, and Allan Ginsberg embraced the existentialist idea of alienation even though they rejected the austere tone of their European counterparts. Their sense of alienation was united with the idea of experience heightened by ecstasy either of a musical, sexual, or chemical origin. The Beats, at least in that sense, were the progenitors of the 1960s hippies.

Camus The existentialist ethic remained alive mainly through the novels of Albert Camus (1913–1960). In works like *The Stranger* (1942), *The Plague* (1947), and *The Fall* (1956), Camus, who disliked being called an existentialist, continued to impress his readers with heroes who fought the ultimate **absurdity** of the world with lucidity and dedication and without illusion.

Today, existentialism is mainly a historical moment in the postwar culture of Europe and America. Its importance, however, resides in its capacity to formulate some of the most important ideas of modernity: the absence of religious faith, the continuous search for meaning, the dignity of the individual, the concern for human subjectivity.

PAINTING SINCE 1945

Art critic Barbara Rose wrote that the history of world art in the second half of the twentieth century bore an unmistakable American stamp. It is hard to quarrel with that historical judgment since in the 1940s the United States, and more specifically New York, became the center of new impulses in art, much the way Paris had been in the first half of the twentieth century. At the end of that century, however, it was also clear that American supremacy may well have diminished as art took on an international and transnational character.

Expatriates in the United States Part of this geographical shift from Paris to New York can be explained by the pressures of World War II. Numerous artists and intellectuals fled the **totalitarian** regimes

◆ **22.2** Edward Hopper, *Nighthawks*, 1942

Oil on canvas, 33" x 60" (84.1 x 152.4 cm). The Art Institute of Chicago, Chicago, USA//Photography (Robert Hashimoto) © The Art Institute of Chicago

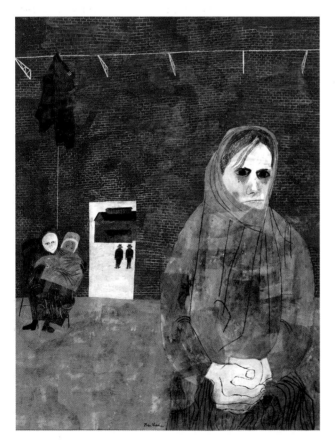

◆ **22.3** Ben Shahn, *Miners' Wives*, 1948.

Tempera on panel, 48" x 36" (121.9 x 91.4 cm). Philadelphia Museum of Art, Philadelphia, PA, USA//Art © Estate of Ben Shahn/Licensed by VAGA, New York, NY//Digital Image © The Philadelphia Museum of Art/Art Resource, NY

of Europe to settle in America. Refugee artist-teachers like Hans Hofmann (1880–1966), Josef Albers (1888–1976), and George Grosz (1893–1959) brought European ideas to a new generation of American painters. When war broke out, the American patron and art collector Peggy Guggenheim, who was then married to the surrealist painter Max Ernst, fled their European home to return to New York City. At her gallery Art of This Century, she exhibited such European painters as Braque, Léger, Arp, Brancusi, Picasso, Severini, and Miró. She quickly became a patron of the American painters who eventually led the American avant-garde movement. Peggy Guggenheim's support of this group in New York was crucial to the Americanization of modern art.

Traditional American Styles History nevertheless rarely records total and immediate shifts in artistic styles. Thus, while a revolution was taking place in

◆ **22.4** Georgia O'Keeffe, *An Orchid*, 1941. The artist took the common subject of flowers and, through her profound line and strong sense of color, turned them into mysterious, nearly abstract, shapes of feminine power.

Pastel on board, 21¼" x 27⅛" (55.25 x 69.9 cm.). The Museum of Modern Art, New York, NY, USA. Bequest of Georgia O'Keeffe//Copyright © 2009 Georgia O'Keeffe Museum/Artists Rights Society (ARS), New York//Digital Image © The Museum of Modern Art/Licensed by SCALA/Art Resource, NY

American art and, for that matter, in world art, some excellent artists continued to work in an older tradition relatively untouched by this revolution. Edward Hopper (1882–1967), for instance, continued to produce paintings that explored his interest in light and his sensitivity to the problems of human isolation and loneliness. His *Nighthawks* [**Fig. 22.2**] is an example of Hopper's twin concerns. Ben Shahn (1898–1969) never lost the social passion that had motivated his work all through the 1930s. His *Miners' Wives* [**Fig. 22.3**] is both a tribute to and an outcry against the death of workingmen in a senseless accident as their wives wait and mourn.

Another painter who remained untouched by the postwar American revolution in painting was Georgia O'Keeffe (1887–1986), who had her first show in New York in 1916 at the galleries of Alfred Stieglitz, the photographer she married in 1924. Her paintings, like *An Orchid* [**Fig. 22.4**], show both a masterful sense of color and scale and a precise sense of line. She belonged to the early strain of American modernism but continued in her own style. O'Keeffe has been recognized not only as a major artist in her own right but also as the focus for serious discussion about a feminist **aesthetic** in art contemporaneously.

ABSTRACT EXPRESSIONISM

The artists discussed in the last section have a secure reputation in the history of art, but the Abstract Expressionists gave art in the period after 1945 its "unmistakable American stamp." The term *Abstract Expressionism* is useful because it alludes to two characteristics fundamental to the work of these artists: it was devoid of recognizable content (and thus abstract), and it used color, line, and shape to express interior states of subjective aesthetic experience. *Action painting* and *New York School* are two other terms that further classify these painters.

Jackson Pollock The acknowledged leader of the Abstract Expressionists was the Wyoming-born painter Jackson Pollock (1912–1956), who had his first one-man show at Peggy Guggenheim's gallery in 1943. Pollock's early work was characterized by an interest in primitive symbolism, deriving from the artist's long encounter with the psychology of Carl Jung. By the early 1940s, under the influence of the surrealists and their technique of automatic creation—in which the artist allows the unconscious rather than the conscious will to stimulate the act of creation—Pollock began to depart radically from traditional ways of painting.

At first Pollock discarded brush and palette for sticks, small mops, and sponges to apply paint in coarse, heavy gestures. Then he set aside instruments altogether and poured, dripped, and spattered paint directly on the canvas in nervous gestural lines rather than enclosed shapes. For his colors he mixed the expensive oils of the artists with the utilitarian enamels used by house painters. Perhaps most radically, instead of using an easel he rolled out on the floor of his studio large expanses of canvas and applied paint in his unusual manner as he walked around and on them. The dimensions of the

◆ **22.5** Jackson Pollock, *Number 1, 1948*, 1948. The theoretical basis for such random painting can be traced to the Freudian idea of free association and the surrealist adaptation of that technique for art called *psychic automatism*.

Oil and enamel on unprimed canvas, 6′8″ x 8′8″ (2 x 2.6 m). The Museum of Modern Art, New York, USA. Copyright © 2009 The Pollock-Krasner Foundation/ Artists Rights Society (ARS), New York//Digital Image © The Museum of Modern Art/Licensed by SCALA/Art Resource, NY.

finished painting were fixed when Pollock decided to cut out from this canvas a particular area and then attach it to the traditional wooden support or stretcher. The result of these unorthodox procedures was huge paintings composed of intricate patterns of dribbles, drops, and lines—webs of color vibrant in their complexity [**Fig. 22.5**]. The energy-filled nets of paint extended to the limits of the stretched canvas and by implication beyond, seeming to have no beginning or end and hence attracting the stylistic label *overall painting*. Neither did these colors and lines suggest the illusion of space receding in planes behind the surface of the picture, although they did create a sense of continuous rhythmic movement.

The New York School Other painters in the 1940s and 1950s were more interested in the potentialities of large fields of color and abstract symbol systems, often with obvious psychological meanings. Adolph Gottlieb (1903–1974) painted a series of "bursts" in the 1950s in which a luminous sun-like **color field** hung over a primordial exploding mass. Robert Motherwell

(1915–1991) executed hundreds of paintings in which huge primitive black shapes are in the foreground of subtle, broken color fields [**Fig. 22.6**]. Mark Rothko (1903–1970) experimented restlessly with floating color forms of the most subtle variation and hue. In the 1960s, Rothko painted a series of panels for a chapel in Houston [**Fig. 22.7**] in which he attempted with some success to use color variations alone to evoke a sensibility of mystical awareness of transcendence.

What did these artists have in common? Their energy and originality make it difficult to be categorical, although some generalizations are possible. They all continued the modernist tendency to break with the older conventions of art. As the Cubists turned away from traditional perspective, so the Abstract Expressionists turned away from recognizable content to focus on the implications of color and line. Second, they were expressionists, which is to say that they were concerned with the ability of their paintings to express not what they saw but what they felt and what they hoped to communicate to others. As one critic has put it, in an age when organized religion could no longer

◆ **22.6** Robert Motherwell, *Elegy to the Spanish Republic #108*, 1965–1967. The title of the painting was inspired by the poetry of Federico García Lorca, but no direct literary reference should be seen in the painting. Motherwell insists that the "painter communes with himself."

Oil on canvas, 6′10″ x 11′6¼″ (2.08 x 3.5 m). The Museum of Modern Art, New York, USA//Art copyright © Dedalus Foundation, Inc./Licensed by VAGA, New York, NY//Digital Image © The Museum of Modern Art/Licensed by SCALA//Art Resource, NY

◆ **22.7** The Rothko Chapel, Houston, Texas, consecrated 1971. Chapel design by Philip Johnson. Murals by Mark Rothko. This ecumenical chapel contains fourteen panels finished several years before the artist's death. Rothko intended the panels' brooding simplicity to be a focus for the personal meditations of each viewer. He said he sought to create, between the chapel's entrance and its apse, the tension between doom and promise.

North, northeast, and east wall paintings, oil on canvas, 1965–1966. © 2009 Kate Rothko Prizel & Christopher Rothko/Artists Rights Society (ARS), New York//Digital Image courtesy of the Rothko Chapel.

◆ **22.8** Helen Frankenthaler, *The Bay*, 1963. Frankenthaler's work gains its almost watercolor luminosity by her practice of thinning her paints to the consistency of washes.

Acrylic resin on canvas, 6′8¼″ x 6′9¼″ (2.02 x 2.08 m). Detroit Institute of Arts, MI, USA//Copy right © Helen Frankenthaler//Photograph, The Detroit Institute of Arts Founders Society Purchase, Dr & Mrs Hilbert H. DeLawter Fund/The Bridgeman Art Library

compel people with the power of revelation, these artists wished to express their sense of ultimate meaning and their thirst for the infinite. "Instead of making cathedrals out of Christ, Man, or 'Life,'" painter Barnett Newman wrote, "we are making them out of ourselves, out of our own feeling."

Frankenthaler and Murray The desire to expand the possibilities of pure color detached from any recognizable imagery has been carried on and extended by a second generation of color field painters, the most notable of whom is Helen Frankenthaler (b. 1928). Around 1951, Frankenthaler began to saturate unprimed canvases with poured paint so that the figure (the paint) merged into the ground (the canvas) of the work. By staining the canvas, she carried Pollock's action painting one step further, emphasizing the pure liquidity of paint and the color that derives from it. Frankenthaler uses the thinnest of paints to take advantage of the light contrast between the paint and the unstained canvas (unlike Pollock she does not paint all over her ground). The result has been paintings with the subtlety of watercolors but distinctively and inescapably different [**Fig. 22.8**]. Her younger contemporary, Elizabeth Murray (b. 1940) still finds energy in abstract art. She paints large canvases but experiments with more than one canvas and uses a firmer control over her paint, as is apparent in her work *Do the Dance* [**Fig. 22.9**].

THE RETURN TO REPRESENTATION

Johns It was inevitable that some artists would break with Abstract Expressionism and return to consideration of the object. This reaction began in the mid-1950s with painters like Jasper Johns (b. 1930), whose *Flag* series [**Fig. 22.10**] heralded a new appreciation of objects. Furthermore, Johns's art focused on objects taken from the mundane world. Johns went on to paint and sculpt targets, toothbrushes, beer cans, and even his own artist's brushes. This shift signaled a whimsical and ironic rejection of highly emotive, content-free, and intellectualized abstract art.

Rauschenberg Robert Rauschenberg (1925–2008) was another artist who helped define the sensibility emerging as a counterforce to Abstract Expressionism in the 1950s. Rauschenberg studied at Black Mountain College, an experimental school in North Carolina, under the tutelage of the refugee Bauhaus painter Josef Albers. A more important influence from his Black Mountain days was the avant-garde musician and composer John Cage (1912–1992), who encouraged experiments combining music, drama, dance, art, and other media into coherent artistic wholes, which were called *Happenings*. Rauschenberg began to experiment with what he called **combine paintings** that utilized painting combined with any number of assembled objects in a manner that had deep roots in the avant-garde. By 1959 he was doing

◆ **22.9** Elizabeth Murray, *Do the Dance*, 2005. The title comes from the 1960 Ray Charles/Betty Carter hit Murray listened to while painting this work. Murray describes this painting as "a construction."

Oil on canvas on wood, 9′5″ x 11′3″ x 1½″ (2.9 x 3.4 m). The Museum of Modern Art, New York, USA//© Elizabeth Murray, courtesy PaceWildenstein, New York//Digital Image © The Museum of Modern Art/Licensed by SCALA/Art Resource, NY

◆ **22.10** Jasper Johns, *Flag*, 1954. The rather banal subject should not detract from Johns's phenomenal technique. Encaustic is painting done with molten colored wax.

Encaustic, oil, and collage on fabric mounted on plywood, 3′6¼″ x 5′⅝″ (1.07 x 1.54 m). Museum of Modern Art, New York, USA//Art copyright © Jasper Johns/ Licensed by VAGA, New York, NY//Digital Image © The Museum of Modern Art/ Licensed by SCALA/Art Resource, NY

◆ **22.11** Robert Rauschenberg, *Monogram*, 1955–1959 (side view). Although Rauschenberg's work was once considered a spoof of abstract art—a sort of contemporary Dada—he is now regarded as one of the most inventive of American artists.

Freestanding combine, 5′4½″ x 3′6″ x 5′3¼″ (1.64 x 1.07 x 1.61 m). Moderna Museet, Statens Kunstmuseer, Stockholm, Sweden//Art © Robert Rauschenberg/Licensed by VAGA, New York, NY// Digital Image SuperStock

large-scale works like his *Monogram* [**Fig. 22.11**], which combined an assortment of elements (including a stuffed goat) in an outrageous yet delightful collage.

Warhol The third artist who emerged in the late 1950s, Andy Warhol (1930–1987), became notorious for his paintings of soup cans, soap boxes, cola bottles, and the other throwaway detritus of our society. This made his name synonymous with *Pop Art*, a term first used in England to describe the art of popular culture. The long-range judgment on Warhol as a serious artist may be harsh, but he understood one thing quite well: taste today is largely shaped by the incessant pressure of advertising, mass media, pulp writing, and the transient culture of fads. Warhol, who began his career as a commercial illustrator, exploited that fact relentlessly.

Over the years, Warhol increasingly turned his attention away from painting and toward printmaking, videotapes, movies, and Polaroid® photography. His subjects tended to be the celebrities of film and the social world. Whether his art is a prophetic judgment on our culture or a subtle manipulation of it is difficult to answer because Warhol could be bafflingly indirect. His lightly retouched silkscreen prints of entertainment celebrities [**Fig. 22.12**] seem banal and of little permanent value, but that may be exactly what he wished to express.

Stella Painting from the 1970s is difficult to categorize. Some artists continued to explore color-field painting with great verve. Others, such as Frank Stella [**Fig. 22.13**], explored more formal elements with carefully drawn "hard edges," primary colors, and geometrically precise compositions.

PHOTOREALISTS

Another group of painters went back totally to the recognizable object painted in a manner so realistic that

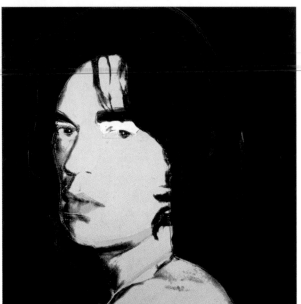

◆ **22.12** Andy Warhol, *Mick Jagger*, 1975. Warhol incorporated into high art the world of the media, money, and fashion. Until his death in 1987, he incarnated the notion of the artist as celebrity figure with his explorations in video, film, photography, magazine publishing, graphics, and painting.

Synthetic polymer paint and silkscreen ink on canvas, 40″ square (102 cm). © 2009 The Andy Warhol Foundation for the Visual Arts/Artists Rights Society (ARS), New York//Image © The Andy Warhol Foundation, Inc./Art Resource, NY

critics called them *Photorealists*. Less glossy than the Photorealists but almost Classical in their fine draftsmanship are the erotically charged nudes of Philip Pearlstein, who takes a position somewhere between the fragmented world of Cubism and the slick glossiness of popular magazines. His *Male and Female Nudes on Carpet* [**Fig. 22.14**] is a serious and unsentimental study of the female and male figures.

◆ **22.13** Frank Stella, *Hyena Stomp*, 1962. The title comes from a song by the American jazz musician Jelly Roll Morton. Stella was thinking about syncopation while working on the painting.

Oil on canvas, 77" square (195.6 cm). Tate Gallery, London, UK//Art © 2009 Frank Stella/Artists Rights Society (ARS), New York//Digital Image © Tate, London/Art Resource, NY

◆ **22.14** Philip Pearlstein, *Male and Female Nudes on Carpet, 1978*. Compare Pearlstein's nudes to those of the Renaissance tradition represented by an artist like Titian (Figure 13.20) to get a feeling for the modern temper.

Oil on canvas, 60" x 72" (152.4 x 182.88 cm). Yale University Art Gallery, New Haven, CT, USA//© Philip Pearlstein//Digital Image © Yale University Art Gallery/Art Resource, NY

◆ **22.15** Alfred Leslie, *Constance West Seated with Rifle*, 1965. Leslie uses the technique of *chiaroscuro* in conscious homage to baroque masters like Caravaggio and Rembrandt.

Oil and acrylic on canvas, 9′ x 6′ (2.7 x 1.8 m). Private Collection//© 2009 Alfred Leslie. All rights reserved//Digital Image SuperStock

◆ **22.16** Romare Bearden, *Empress of the Blues*, 1974. The prominent female singer is Bessie Smith, the legendary blues singer, called the Empress of the Blues.

Collage, acrylic, pencil, printed paper, 36″ x 48″ (91.44 x 122 cm). Smithsonian American Art Museum, Washington, DC, USA//Art © Romare Bearden Foundation/Licensed by VAGA, New York, NY//Digital Image © Smithsonian American Art Museum, Washington, DC/Art Resource, NY

◆ **22.17** Faith Ring-gold, *Tar Beach 2*, 1990. The work celebrates her family's summer evening picnics at the "beach," the tar rooftop of her home in Harlem. It is a story quilt that weaves fiction, autobiography, and African American history and literature.

Silkscreen on silk with quilted silk pieced border, 68" x 64" (172.7 x 162.6 cm). Philadelphia Museum of Art, Philadelphia, PA, USA// Faith Ringgold © 1990//Digital Image from The Philadelphia Museum of Art/Art Resource, NY

For Alfred Leslie (b. 1927) the past can still be a teacher for the modern painter. In a work like *Constance West Seated with Rifle* [**Fig. 22.15**], Leslie combines an eye for contemporary reality and the use of *chiaroscuro*, a technique he consciously borrows directly from the seventeenth-century painter Caravaggio (see Figures 15.3–15.5). With Leslie we have come, as it were, full circle from the Abstract Expressionist break with tradition to a contemporary painter who consciously looks back to seventeenth-century masters for formal inspiration.

One can say that two intellectual trends seem to have emerged in American painting in this period. One strain, Abstract Expressionism and its various offspring, is heavily indebted to the modernist intellectual tradition, with its many roots in psychological theories of Jung and Freud and the existentialist vocabulary of anxiety and alienation. By contrast, the work of painters like Johns, Warhol, Rauschenberg, and others is far more closely linked to the vast world of popular culture in postindustrial America. Its material, its symbols, and its intentions reflect the values of consumer culture more than the 1940s work of the New York School. Pop art, largely free from the brooding metaphysics of the Abstract Expressionists, can be seen—perhaps simultaneously—as a celebration and a challenge to middle-class values.

OTHER TRENDS

One sees that same blend of "isms" and references to popular culture in the work of African American artists. Romare Bearden (1914–1988) produced work that absorbed collage, Cubism, and tendencies to abstraction in order to make a body of art that was distinctively his own. His painting *Empress of the Blues* [**Fig. 22.16**] celebrates traditional blues with references to Africa done in a Synthetic Cubist style. By contrast, the painter Faith Ringgold (b. 1930) utilizes mixed media in the work *Tar Beach 2* to celebrate her racial heritage, her family, storytelling and, at the same time, rejoice in the energy of city life [**Fig. 22.17**].

◆ **22.18** Frank Stella, *Katsura*, 1979. Stella has been the foremost and most persistent defender of abstract art on the American scene today. See Figure 22.13 for the radical change in Stella's work.

Oil and epoxy on aluminum, and wire mesh, 9'7" x 7'8" x 30" (292 x 233.6 x 76.2 cm). The Museum of Modern Art, New York, USA//© 2009 Frank Stella/Artists Rights Society (ARS), New York//Digital Image © The Museum of Modern Art/Licensed by SCALA/ Art Resource, NY

◆ **22.19** Susan Rothenberg, *Two-Tone*, 1975. A life-sized image of a horse is reduced to essential elements in which the artist explores the meaning, mechanics, and essence of painting.

Acrylic and tempera on canvas, 69" x 113" (175.26 x 287 cm). Albright-Knox Art Gallery, Buffalo, NY, USA//Copyright © 2009 Susan Rothenberg/Artists Rights Society (ARS), New York//Digital image © Albright-Knox Art Gallery/CORBIS

◆ **22.20** David Hockney, *A Bigger Splash*, 1967.

Acrylic on canvas, 95½" x 96" (242.6 x 243.8 cm). Tate Gallery, London, UK//Copyright © David Hockney//Digital Image © Tate Gallery, London/ Art Resource, NY

◆ **22.21** Gerhard Richter, *Clouds (Wolken)*, 1982. The artist has said that he believes in nothing and that his work forms from structures and ideas that surround him, nothing more profound than that.

Oil on canvas; two parts, overall, 6'7" x 8'6½" (200.7 x 260.7 cm). The Museum of Modern Art, New York, USA//© Gerhard Richter// Digital Image © The Museum of Modern Art/ Licensed by SCALA/Art Resource, NY

Painting in the late 1970s and 1980s went in many directions. Critics are agreed on one point: no dominant "ism" defines contemporary art. The profusion of styles apparent on that day's art scene testifies to either a vigorous eclecticism or a sense of confusion. Older painters like Frank Stella still pushed the limits of abstract art [**Fig. 22.18**], whereas Susan Rothenberg's canvases reflected a concern with the texture of painting, in which recognizable figures emerged like risen ghosts [**Fig. 22.19**]. The same polarity of styles can be seen by contrasting the sunny optimism of the English-born David Hockney (now living in California) [**Fig. 22.20**] with the brooding work of the German painter Gerhard Richter (b. 1932) [**Fig. 22.21**]. These artists worked

◆ **22.22** David Smith, *Cubi XIX*, 1964. Critics recognize Smith as one of the most important sculptors of the twentieth century.

Stainless steel, 112 ¾″ x 58¼″ x 40″ (286.4 x 148 x 101.6 cm). Tate Gallery, London, UK//Art © Estate of David Smith/Licensed by VAGA, New York, NY//Digital Image © Tate, London/Art Resource, NY

in a time when "older masters" like Johns, Rauschenberg, and others still pushed the limits of their original insights and flights of imagination.

A new generation of artists like the Native American painter Jaune Quick-to-See Smith (b. 1940) incorporates images, words, scribbles, and drips in works such as *Indian, Indio, Indigenous* to affirm both her own identity and her protest against racism in general and the mistreatment of Native Americans specifically.

CONTEMPORARY SCULPTURE

Much of contemporary sculpture has utilized newer metals (stainless steel or rolled steel, for instance) and welding techniques to allow some freedom from the inherent density of cast bronze, the traditional metal of the sculptor. David Smith (1906–1965) used his skills

VOICES OF THEIR TIMES

Magdalena Abakanowicz

In 2005 the International Sculpture Center conferred on Magdalena Abakanowicz a Life Achievements award. These remarks are from her acceptance speech.

What is sculpture? With impressive continuity it testifies to man's evolving sense of reality, and fulfils the necessity to express what cannot be verbalized.

Banished from Paradise, man found himself confronted by the space of the world. It was a territory unknown and inconceivable, as inconceivable as are overabundance or emptiness. He tried to reach unknown powers, raising stones, building areas of special meaning. . . . With the development of society, sculpture began to visualize gods, to glorify leaders, to commemorate history, finally to decorate life.

Today we are confronted with the inconceivable world we ourselves created. Its reality is reflected in art.

◆ **22.23** Alexander Calder, *Big Red*, 1959. By bending and twisting wire and attaching shapes, Calder created three-dimensional figures in space. The suspended, abstract shapes are based on an ascending scale of weights and counter weights that move and balance in harmony.

Painted sheet metal and steel wire, 6'22" x 9'6" (1.9 x 2.9 m). Whitney Museum of American Art, New York. Copyright © 2009 Calder Foundation, New York/ Artists Rights Society (ARS), New York//Digital image © 2001 Whitney Museum of American Art, New York.

as a one-time auto-body assembler to produce simple and elegant metal sculptures that reflected his not-inconsiderable technical skills with metal as well as his refined sense of aesthetic balance. In works such as *Cubi XIX* [**Fig. 22.22**], Smith used stainless steel to produce a geometrically balanced work of solidity that conveys a sense of airy lightness.

Calder Alexander Calder (1898–1976) used his early training as a mechanical engineer to combine the weightiness of metal with the grace of movement. Mobiles such as *Big Red* [**Fig. 22.23**] are constructed of painted sheet metal and wire; these constructions move because they are so delicately balanced that they respond to even the slightest currents of air. Calder once said that people think monuments "come out of the ground, never out of the ceiling"; his mobiles were meant to demonstrate just the opposite.

Cornell Other contemporary sculptors expanded the notion of assembling disparate materials into a coherent artistic whole. Employing far-from-traditional materials, these artists utilized various found and manufactured articles of the most amazing variety to create organic artistic wholes. Louise Nevelson (1900–1988), for example, used pieces of wood, many of which had been lathed or turned for commercial uses, to assemble large-scale structures that seemed at the same time to func-

◆ **22.24** Louise Nevelson, *Sky Cathedral*, 1958. This work shows the intricate and complex nature of Nevelson's art. At her death in 1988, she was considered one of the most accomplished sculptors in the world.

Assemblage. wood construction painted black, 11'3½" x 10'¼" x 18" (313.7 x 305.5 x 45.7 cm). The Museum of Modern Art, New York, USA//© 2009 Estate of Louise Nevelson/Artists Rights Society (ARS), New York//Digital Image © The Museum of Modern Art/ Licensed by SCALA/Art Resource, NY

tion as walls closing off space and as containers to hold the items that made up her compositions [**Fig. 22.24**]. Joseph Cornell (1903–1972), early influenced by both surrealism and Dada, constructed small boxes that he filled with inexpensive trinkets, maps, bottles, tops, stones, and other trivia. In contrast to the larger brooding, almost totemic spirit of Nevelson, Cornell's painstakingly organized boxes [**Fig. 22.25**] allude to a private world of fantasy.

Segal and Kienholz The sculptural interest in *assemblage* has been carried a step further by such artists as George Segal (1924–2000) and Edward Kienholz (1927–1994). Their works re-create entire tableaux into which realistically sculptured figures are placed. Segal, once a painting student of Hans Hofmann in New York, liked to cast human figures in plaster of Paris and then set them in particular but familiar settings [**Fig. 22.26**]. The starkness of the lone white figure evokes a mood of isolation and loneliness not unlike that of the paintings of Edward Hopper (see Figure 22.2). Kienholz was far better prepared to invest his works with strong social comment. His *The Wait* [**Fig. 22.27**] obviously refers to death; this is a refashioning of the traditional *memento mori* (remember death) theme. Surrounded by portraits of family, the central skeletal figure waits for her own death.

◆ **22.25** Joseph Cornell, *Object (Roses des Vents)*, 1942–1953.

Wooden box, 2⅝" x 21¼" x 10⅜ (6.7 x 53.9 x 26.4 cm), with twenty-one compass roses set in a wooden tray resting on Plexiglas-topped-and-partitioned section divided into seventeen compartments containing small miscellaneous objects (not seen), and three-part hinged lid covered inside with parts of maps of New Guinea and Australia. The Museum of Modern Art, New York, USA//Art © The Joseph and Robert Cornell Memorial Foundation/ Licensed by VAGA, New York, NY//Digital Image © The Museum of Modern Art/Licensed by SCALA/Art Resource, NY

◆ **22.26** George Segal, *Cinema*, 1963. In the late 1990s, Segal experimented with colored plasters and large cast bronze outdoor pieces.

Plaster, illuminated Plexiglas and metal, 118″ x 96″ x 96″ (299.72 x 243.84 x 99.06 cm). Albright-Knox Art Gallery, Buffalo, NY, USA//Art copyright © George and Helen Segal Foundation/Licensed by VAGA, New York, NY// © Digital Image © Albright-Knox Art Gallery/CORBIS

◆ **22.27** Edward Kienholz, *The Wait*, 1964–1965. Kienholz's work provokes such violent reactions that in 1966 some works were threatened with removal from a one-person show he had in Los Angeles.

Mixed media. 80″ x 248″ x 78″ (203.2 x 630 x 198 cm). The Whitney Museum of American Art, New York, USA//Copyright © Edward Kienholz courtesy of LA Louver, Venice, CA//Digital Image © Burstein Collection (Barney Burstein)/CORBIS

◆ **22.28** Claes Oldenburg, *Giant Soft Fan*, 1966–1967. Oldenburg's humor derives from the well-known device of taking the expected and rendering it in an unexpected self-parodying form.

Vinyl filled with polyurethane foam, canvas, wood, metal, and plastic tubing; 10' h x 4'10⅞" w x 5'1⅛" d (3.05 x 1.50 x 1.57 m) plus cord and plug, 24'2" (7.37 m) long. The Museum of Modern Art, New York, USA//Copyright © 2008 Claes Oldenburg//Digital Image © The Museum of Modern Art/ Licensed by SCALA/Art Resource, NY

◆ **22.29** Henry Moore, *Reclining Figure. Wing*, 1978. Moore was influenced early in his career by Pre-Columbian sculptures of recumbent figures he had seen in museums.

Travertine Marble, 54" (137 cm) long. Private Collection//© Reproduced by permission of the Henry Moore Foundation (www.henry-moore-fdn.co.uk)// Digital Image © Visual Arts Library/Art Resource, NY

◆ **22.30** Maya Ying Lin, *The Vietnam Veterans Memorial* known as *The Wall*, Washington, DC, 1982. Over 25 million people a year visit the memorial.

Black granite, 492' (150 m) long. The Mall, Washington, DC, USA. Image © Kokyat Choong/Alamy

◆ **22.31** Rachel Whiteread, *Nameless Library*, Holocaust Memorial, Vienna, 2000. Representing the interior of a library with shelves of closed books facing inward and having impressions of pages of the books, the doors in relief have no handles. The inscription on the base reads "In commemoration of the more than 65,000 Austrian Jews who were killed by the Nazis between 1938 and 1945."

Cast concrete, 12' h x 24' w x 33' l (36.6 x 73.2 x 100.6 m). The Judenplatz in Vienna, Austria. Image © Reuters (Herwig Prammer)/CORBIS

Oldenburg Both Segal and Kienholz have certain ties to Pop Art, but neither artist worked within its whimsical or humorous vein. Claes Oldenburg (b. 1929), however, is one of the more humorously outrageous and inventively intelligent artists working today. He has proposed (and, in many cases, executed) monumental outdoor sculptures depicting teddy bears, ice-cream bars, lipsticks, and baseball bats. From the 1960s on, Oldenburg experimented with sculptures that turn normally rigid objects into "soft" or "collapsing" versions made from vinyl or canvas and stuffed with kapok. A piece like his *Giant Soft Fan* [**Fig. 22.28**] is simultaneously humorous and mocking. It echoes Pop art and recalls the oozing edges so characteristic of surrealism.

Henry Moore Overarching these decades of sculptural development is the work of the British sculptor Henry Moore (1898–1986). Moore's work, which extends back into the 1920s, is a powerful amalgam of the monumental tradition of Western sculpture deriving from Renaissance masters like Michelangelo and his love for the forms coming from the early cultures of Africa, Mexico, and pre-Colombian Latin America. From these two sources, Moore worked out hauntingly beautiful works some on a massive scale—that speak of the most primordial realities of art.

Moore's *Reclining Figure: Wing* [**Fig. 22.29**] is a complex work that illustrates many of the sculptor's mature interests. The outline is obviously that of a person in a rather abstract form. There is also the hint of bonelike structure, a favorite motif in Moore's abstract sculpture, and holes or voids that pierce the figure. The holes, Moore once said, reminded him of caves and openings in hillsides with their hint of mystery, and critics have also noted their obvious sexual connotations. The figure reclines after the fashion of Etruscan and Pre-Columbian burial figures. In a single work, Moore hints at three primordial forces in the universal human experience: life (the human figure), death (the bonelike configurations), and sexuality (the holes). It is a sculpture contemporary in style but timeless in its message.

OTHER DIRECTIONS

Outdoor Sculpture Most of the sculpture just discussed was made for a gallery or a collector. Thanks to increased government and corporate patronage in recent decades, it is possible for an average citizen to view outdoor sculpture as part of the urban environment. A walk in the downtown area of Chicago, for example, provides a chance to see monumental works of Picasso, Chagall, Bertoia, Calder, Oldenburg, Abakanowicz, Plensa, and Gehry. The fact that the federal government set aside a certain percentage of its building budget for works of art to enhance public buildings has been an impetus for wider diffusion of modern art and sculpture. In one sense the government, the large foundations, and the corporations have supplanted the church and the aristocracy as patrons for monumental art in our time.

One of the most moving public outdoor works is the Vietnam Veterans Memorial [**Fig. 22.30**] in Washington, DC. The work's designer was a young architecture student at Yale University, Maya Ying Lin. Two polished black granite walls, each more than two hundred feet in length, converge in a V-shape. Inscribed on the walls are the names of 58,245 service personnel killed in Vietnam; the polished surface acts as a mirror for those who visit what has become one of the most popular pilgrimage spots in the nation's capital.

The British artist Rachel Whiteread (b. 1963) created a large concrete sculpture of the interior of a library that once was in the Judenplatz in Vienna as part of a larger Holocaust memorial. The spare façade with its striated panels represents the lost books destroyed by the Nazis and, by extension, the attempted destruction of Jewry itself [**Fig. 22.31**].

In the 1980s, sculpture demonstrated a variety not unlike that of contemporary painting. The Bulgarian-born Christo and his wife, Jeanne-Claude, sought out large natural sites to drape and wrap with various fabrics for temporary alteration of our perception of familiar

◆ **22.32** Christo and Jeanne-Claude, *The Gates, Central Park, New York, New York, 1979-2005.* Seen from afar, as in this photo, the fabric panels of the gates created a ribbon of color among the leafless branches of the park's trees. On the meandering walkways people passing through the gates sensed the fabric forming a ceiling in the open air. The artwork stood from February 12 through the 27th in 2005 when it was removed and the materials industrially recycled.

An installation of 7,503 gates, 16′ (4.87 m) tall, ranging in width from 5′6″ to 18′ (1.68 to 5.48 m) according to the 25 different widths of walkways, on 23 miles (37 k) of paths through Central Park. Gates installed at 12′ (3.65 m) intervals, except where low branches extended above the walkways; free-hanging, saffron-colored fabric panels, suspended from the horizontal top beams of the gates, hung approximately 7′ (2.13 m) above the ground to allow people to walk under them. Image © Spencer Platt/Getty Images

◆ **22.33** Magdalena Abakanowicz, *Agora,* 2005–2006.

Iron installation of 106 figures, c. 9 1/3′ x 3 1/8′ x 4 1/2″ (285 x 95 x 135 cm) on 3 acres. Grant Park, Chicago, IL, USA//Copyright © Magdalena Abakanowicz, courtesy, Marlborough Gallery, New York/Digital Image © Cecilia Cunningham

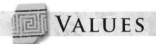

VALUES

Liberation

If we understand *liberation* in the deep social sense as freedom *to* realize one's full human potential as well as freedom *from* oppressive structures, we would then have to say that the desire for, and realization of, liberating freedom is one of the hallmarks of modern world culture. This was especially true in the second half of the twentieth century.

Liberation has come both for millions from the totalitarian regimes of fascism, Nazism, and Marxism as well as freedom from the colonial powers in areas as diverse as India and Africa. These liberation movements have their mirror image in the struggle for civil rights for people of color, for women, for exploited social minorities, as well as struggles to end poverty, hunger, and the exploitation of children.

What energizes these quite different movements for freedom and liberation? A partial answer is to be found in the power of mass communication to let people know that they are victims of oppression. There is also the power of certain fundamental ideas derived, in the West, from Greek philosophical thought and biblical prophetism, which crystallized in the Enlightenment that held forth the promise of the right to "life, liberty, and the pursuit of happiness."

The struggle for social and political liberation has involved many communities, with some spokespersons standing out both because of their personal bravery and the power of their convictions. We think immediately of Mohandas Gandhi in India; Martin Luther King Jr. in the United States; Desmond Tutu and Nelson Mandela in Africa; Lech Walesa and Vaclav Havel in Eastern Europe, as well as the many unnamed people who put their lives on the line to live free.

◆ **22.34** Duane Hanson, *Homeless Person*, 1991. Compare this work to George Segal's casts in Figure 22.26.

Mixed media, polyester resin and fiberglass polychromed in oil with accessories, 66″ (168 cm) high. On Loan to the Hamburg Kunsthalle, Hamburg, Germany//Art © Estate of Duane Hanson/Licensed by VAGA, New York, NY//Digital Image © The Bridgeman Art Library

places [**Fig. 22.32**]. According to the artists, their intent is to create works of art, of joy, and of beauty—artwork that has absolutely no purpose, conveys no message or symbol. Never static, all of their projects are living objects with an aesthetic that explores inner space. Part of Christo's strategy is to mobilize large numbers of volunteers to create the actual work he has so carefully planned. In addition to *Gates*, Christo and Jeanne-Claude's realized projects include the 24½-mile *Running Fence, Sonoma and Marin Counties, California, 1972–1976; Surrounded Islands, Biscayne Bay, Greater Miami, Florida, 1980–1983; The Pont Neuf Wrapped, Paris, 1975–1985; The Umbrellas, Japan-USA, 1984–1991; Wrapped Reichstag, Berlin, 1971–1995;* and *Wrapped Trees, Fondation Beyeler and Berower Park, Riehen, Switzerland, 1997–1998.* By contrast, the haunting work of Magdalena Abakanowicz (b. 1930) uses basic fibers to make pieces that have fearful references to twentieth-century human disasters [**Fig. 22.33**].

New Materials All of these sculptors have drawn on the most advanced contributions of material science and technology while meditating on problems of the human condition as old as art itself. The American sculptor Duane Hanson (d. 1996) took advantage of new materials like polyvinyl to create hyper-realistic visions of ordinary people in ordinary experiences [**Fig. 22.34**].

The American painter Jennifer Bartlett (b. 1941) has more recently moved into sculpture, taking some of the iconic symbols from her painting and turning them into

◆ **22.35** Jennifer Bartlett, *Sea Wall*, 1985.

Oil on three canvases, each 84″ x 123″ (213.4 x 312.4 cm) with pastel colored, sculpted boats and small beach shacks. Installation at Brooklyn Museum of Art, New York//Image © Adam Bartos/Time Life Pictures/Getty Images

◆ **22.36** Mary Frank, *Chant*, 1984.

Ceramic, 40″ x 60″ x 38″ (102 x 152.4 x 96.5 cm). Virginia Museum of Fine Arts, Richmond, VA, USA//Art copyright © Mary Frank//Digital Image © Virginia Museum of Fine Arts/Ron Jennings

sculptures like her installation *Sea Wall 1985* [**Fig. 22.35**], at the Brooklyn Museum. By contrast, Mary Frank (b. 1932) has stepped into the world of ceramics to use terra-cotta to create large-scale sculptures of women that reflect a haunting beauty and an almost primitive power [**Fig. 22.36**]. One sculptor (if that is the word) who has fully explored the potentialities of our media culture is the Korean-born Nam June Paik, whose assemblage titled *Electronic Superhighway* pays homage to what is surely one of the most revolutionary elements of contemporary culture [**Fig. 22.37**].

ARCHITECTURE

Wright The most influential American architect of the twentieth century was Frank Lloyd Wright (1869–1959), who was a disciple of Louis Sullivan (1856–1924). Sullivan had built the first skyscrapers in the United States in the last decade of the nineteenth century. Like Sullivan, Wright championed an architecture that produced buildings designed for their specific function with an eye focused on the natural environment in which the building was to be placed and with a sensitivity to what the building should "say." "Form follows function" was Sullivan's famous aphorism for this belief. For Wright and his disciples, there was something ludicrous about designing a post office to look like a Greek temple and then building it in the center of a Midwestern American city. Wright wanted an *organic* architecture—an architecture that grows out of its location rather than being superimposed on it.

For decades Wright designed private homes, college campuses, industrial buildings, and churches that reflected this basic philosophy. In the postwar period, Wright finished his celebrated Solomon R. Guggenheim Museum [**Fig. 22.38**] in New York City from plans he had made in 1943.

This building, one of Wright's true masterpieces, is a capsule summary of his architectural ideals. Wright was interested in the flow of space rather than its obstruction ("Democracy needs something basically better than a box"), so the Guggenheim Museum's interior

◆ **22.37** Nam June Paik, *Electronic Superhighway: Continental U.S., Alaska, Hawaii*, 1995. Detail of Continental U.S. section.

49-channel closed circuit video installation, c 15′ x 32′ x 4′ (4.6 x 9.8 x 1.2 m) using multiple television monitors (313 for continental U.S., 24 for Alaska, 1 for Hawaii), audio, laser disk images, neon, steel and electronic components. Smithsonian American Art Museum, Washington, DC, USA//Art Copyright © Nam June Paik//Digital Image © Smithsonian American Art Museum, Washington, DC/Art Resource, NY

◆ **22.38** Frank Lloyd Wright, Solomon R. Guggenheim Museum, 1957–1959. One of the most discussed American buildings of the twentieth century, it is hard to realize that it sits in the midst of New York's Fifth Avenue buildings. A new rectangular addition now stands behind the museum.

Reinforced concrete, diameter at ground level c. 100′ (30.48 m), at roof level 128′ (39 m), height of dome 92″ (28 m). © 2009 Frank Lloyd Wright Foundation, Scottsdale, AZ/Artists Rights Society (ARS), New York//Digital Image © Timothy McCarthy/Art Resource, NY

◆ **22.39** Pier Luigi Nervi, Palazzetto dello Sport (Olympic Games Stadium) Rome, Italy, 1956–1957. The walls beneath the dome are of glass. The Y-shaped ferroconcrete columns are reminiscent of caryatids who support the dome with their outstretched "arms." *(Image © David Lees/CORBIS)*

◆ **22.40** Eero Saarinen, Trans World Flight Center, Kennedy International Airport, New York, New York, 1962. The TWA Terminal building brilliantly shows the sculptural possibilities of concrete. With the demise of TWA, the flight center is temporarily closed after a short period as an exhibit space. *(Image © Arcaid (Ezra Stoller/ESTO)/Alamy)*

is designed to eliminate as many corners and angles as possible. The interior is essentially one very large room with an immensely airy central space. Rising from the floor in a continuous flow for six stories is a long, simple spiraling ramp cantilevered off the supporting walls. A museumgoer can walk down the ramp and view an exhibition without ever encountering a wall or parti-

tion. The viewing of the art is a continuous unwinding experience. Thus the *function* of the museum (to show art) is accomplished by the *form* of the building.

The exterior of the Guggenheim Museum vividly demonstrates the possibilities inherent in the new building materials that became available in that century. By the use of reinforced or ferroconcrete, one could model

◆ **22.41** Jörn Utzon, Opera House, Sydney, Australia, 1957–1972. The building juts dramatically into Sydney's harbor. Structural technology was pushed to the limit by the construction of the shells, which are both roof and walls. The openings between the shells are closed with two layers of amber-tinted glass to reduce outside noise and to open up views to people in the lobbies of the buildings. The building received World Heritage recognition in 2007.

Reinforced concrete and tile-clad concrete, tallest shell 200′ (60.96 m) high, 607′ (185 m) long x 394′ (120 m) wide; 67,000 square feet (6,225 square meters) of glass; and 387 miles (645 km) of electric cable. Image © R. Wallace / Stock Photos / zefa / CORBIS

or sculpt a building easily. The Guggenheim Museum, with its soft curves and cylindrical forms, seems to rise up from its base. The undulating lines stand in sharp contrast to the boxy angles and corners of most of the buildings found in New York City. By using such a design, made to fit a rather restricted urban space, the Guggenheim almost takes on the quality of sculpture.

CONCRETE AND ARCHITECTURE

The sculptural possibilities of reinforced and pre-stressed concrete gave other architects the means to "model" buildings in dramatically attractive ways. The Italian engineer and architect Pier Luigi Nervi (1891–1979) demonstrated the creative use of concrete in a series of buildings he designed with Annibale Vitellozi for the 1960 Olympic Games in Rome [**Fig. 22.39**]. Eero Saarinen (1910–1961) showed in the TWA Flight

Center at Kennedy International Airport in New York City [**Fig. 22.40**] that a building can become almost pure sculpture; Saarinen's wing motif is peculiarly appropriate for an airport terminal. That architects have not exhausted the potentialities of this modeled architecture seems clear from the Opera House complex in Sydney, Australia [**Fig. 22.41**]. Here the Danish architect Jörn Utzon utilized Saarinen's wing motif, but it is no slavish copy because Utzon gives it a new and dramatic emphasis.

Le Corbusier The influential French architect Le Corbusier (1887–1965; born Charles Édouard Jeanneret-Gris) did not share Wright's enthusiasm for "organic" architecture. Le Corbusier saw architecture as a human achievement that should stand in counterpoint to the world of nature. During his long career, Le Corbusier designed and oversaw the construction of

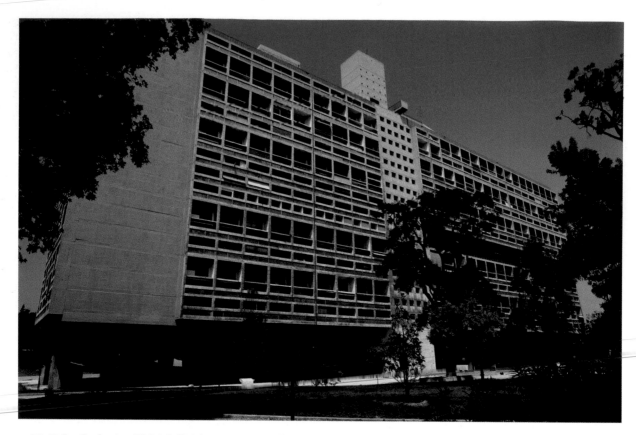

◆ **22.42** Le Corbusier, L'Unité d'Habitation, Marseille, France, 1947–1952. The individual balconies have colored panels to break up the stark, rough concrete exterior. Imitation of this style resulted in much soulless public housing in the large cities of the world.

Rough concrete, 550′ l (167.64 m), 184′ h (56.08 m), 79′ d (24.08 m). Image © Thomas A. Heinz/CORBIS

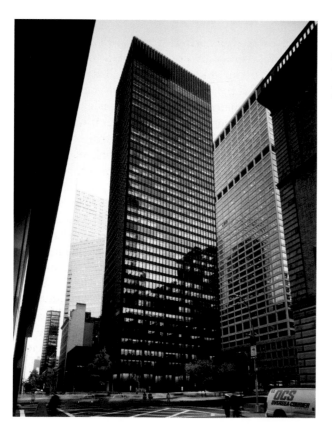

◆ **22.43** Ludwig Miës van der Rohe and Philip Johnson, Seagram Building, New York, 1956–1958. Compare the cleanly severe lines of this building (512′/156.2 m tall) to those of the more ornate buildings in the background. *(Image © Angelo Hornak/CORBIS)*

both individual buildings and more ambitious habitations ranging from apartment complexes to an entire city. One of his most important contributions to architecture is his series of L'Unité d'Habitation in Marseille (1952) and Nantes [**Fig. 22.42**]. These complexes were attempts to make large housing units into livable modules that would not only provide living space but would also be sufficiently self-contained to incorporate shopping, recreation, and walking areas.

Le Corbusier used basic forms (simple squares, rectangles) for the complexes and set them on pylons to both give more space beneath the buildings and break up their rather blocky look. Many of these buildings would be set in green park areas situated to capture something of the natural world and the sun. The basic building material is concrete and steel (often the concrete was

◆ **22.44** I. M. Pei, East Wing of the National Gallery of Art, Washington, DC, opened 1978. Pei combined a modernist look with a classical one that prevents the edifice from clashing with the older buildings on the mall leading to the Capitol. *(Image © Sean Gallup/Getty Images)*

not finished or polished because Le Corbusier liked the rough texture of the material). Less inspired architects have utilized these same concepts for public housing with indifferent success—as visits to the peripheries of most urban centers will attest. Time has been a harsh judge of Le Corbusier's vision of human living space, which is now judged to be soulless and deadening.

BAUHAUS IN AMERICA

Le Corbusier's influence in North America has been mainly derivative. Two other European architects, however, have had an immense impact on American architecture. Walter Gropius (1883–1969) and Ludwig Miës van der Rohe (1896–1969) came to this country in the late 1930s, refugees from Nazi Germany. Both men had long been associated with the German school of design, the Bauhaus.

van der Rohe Miës Van der Rohe's Seagram Building [**Fig. 22.43**] in New York City, designed with Philip Johnson (1906–1991), beautifully illustrates the intent of Bauhaus design. It is a severely chaste building of glass and anodized bronze set on stainless steel pylons placed on a wide granite platform. The uncluttered plaza (broken only by pools) contrasts nicely with the essentially monolithic glass building that rises up from it. The lines of the building are austere in their simplicity, while the materials are few and well chosen, which results in an integration of the whole. It illustrates the "modern" principle of the Bauhaus that simplicity of design results in an aesthetically harmonic whole—"less is more" according to the slogan of this art.

Pei The Seagram Building now seems rather ordinary to us, given the unending procession of glass-and-steel buildings found in most large city centers. That many of these buildings are derivative cannot be denied; that they may result in sterile jungles of glass and metal is likewise a fact. Imitation does not always flatter the vision of the artist, but excesses do not invalidate the original goal of the Bauhaus designers. They were committed to crispness of design and the imaginative use of material. In the hands of a master architect that idea is still valid, as the stunning East Wing addition to the National Gallery of Art in Washington, DC clearly demonstrates [**Fig. 22.44**]. This building, designed by I. M. Pei (b. 1917), utilizes pink granite and glass within

◆ **22.45** Renzo Piano and Richard Rogers, Georges Pompidou National Center for Arts and Culture, Paris, France, 1977. In the recent past this center has taken on a lively bohemian air; nearby streets are lined with galleries, and adjoining squares are dotted with street performers and musicians. *(Image © Patrick Ingrand/Getty Images)*

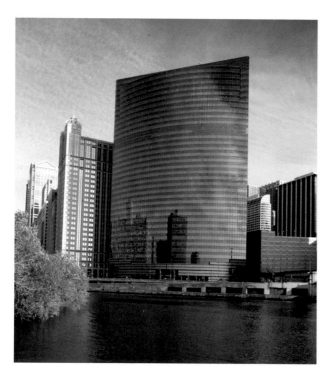

◆ **22.46** Kohn, Pedersen, Fox, 333 West Wacker Drive, Chicago, Illinois, 1983.

Skyscraper, 487' (149 m) high x, 301' (92 m) wide, steel, blue-green glass façade, Vermont marble and granite base. Image © Angelo Hornak/CORBIS

the limits of a rather rigid geometric design to create a building that is monumental in scale without loss of lightness or crispness of design.

Piano and Rogers One can profitably contrast the chaste exterior East Wing of Washington's National Gallery with the Georges Pompidou National Center for Arts and Culture in Paris [**Fig. 22.45**], designed by Renzo Piano and Richard Rogers. The Pompidou Center was opened in 1977 as a complex of art, musical research, industrial design, and public archives. The architects eschewed the clean lines of Classical sculpture, covering the exterior with brightly colored heating ducts, elevators, escalators, and building supports. It has been a highly controversial building since its inception, but Parisians (and visitors) have found it a beautiful and intriguing place. Whether its industrial style will endure is open to question, but for now its garishness and nervous energy have made it a cultural mecca for visitors to Paris. It may in time even rival that other monument once despised by Parisians and now practically a symbol for the city: the Eiffel Tower.

NEW DIRECTIONS

Since the 1970s, several architects, including Philip Johnson and Robert Venturi, have moved beyond the

◆ **22.47** Charles Moore, Perez and Associates, Plaza d'Italia, New Orleans, Louisiana, 1978. The architect combined elements from Italy's rich cultural past with the materials of neon and stainless steel to create an eclectic postmodern plaza. Note the loud color combinations and stylistic collisions playfully arranged. *(Image © Robert Holmes/CORBIS)*

standard modern design of large buildings to reshape them with decorative elements and more broken lines; this break from the severe lines of modernist taste has come to be called *postmodernism* in architecture. The country now has many such buildings, but one, a skyscraper facing the Chicago River in Chicago, Illinois, well illustrates the postmodern sensibility [**Fig. 22.46**]. The designer, William Pedersen, retains the severe lines and the ample use of glass characteristic of most modern business buildings, but the curved facade follows the bends in the river, and the rear forms a parallelogram (to fit the street grid) broken by a vertical V creating more angles. The stone base forms a long X with the main entrance placed at the shape's vacant space.

Charles Moore The Plaza d'Italia in New Orleans, Louisiana, reflects a wild combination of ancient and Baroque architecture. Designed by the architect Charles Moore (1925–1993), it ignores the traditional rules of

architecture and plays with the vocabulary of Classical Roman and Baroque architecture and modern materials. It is a city space dedicated to Italian-Americans and their contribution to the city of New Orleans. The Plaza d'Italia includes a map of Italy with the Adriatic and Tyrrhenian seas represented by flowing water surrounded by concentric colonnades painted bright yellow, red, and ochre. Moore used modern construction materials and techniques, such as ferroconcrete, neon, and polished stainless steel disregarding principles of proportion and scale. He invented a sixth order of architecture called the Delicatessen Order, seen on the red stylized colonnade [**Fig. 22.47**]. Moore believed architecture was to elicit responses from all the senses. His works engage history, myth, and creativity.

Gehry A far more radical and "destabilizing" example of postmodern architecture is the innovative work of the Los Angeles–based architect, Frank O. Gehry (b. 1929),

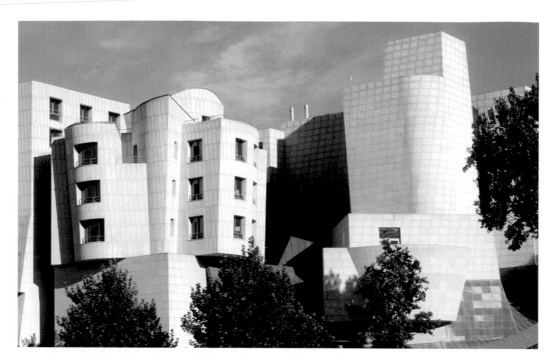

◆ **22.48** Frank Gehry, American Center at Park de Bercy, Paris, France, 1994. Originally housing galleries, a theatre, and a cinema plus lobby and balconied area for receptions, a café, and apartments for visiting artists, the Center eventually closed because of lack of funding. The building now houses the Cinematheque Francaise, a cinema museum and film library. *(Image © age fotostock/SuperStock)*

◆ **22.49** Frank Gehry, Guggenheim Museum, Bilbao, Spain, 1997. Against the city fathers' wishes for a museum set high on a hill overlooking the city, Gehry decided to place the museum on the estuary in the city.

Steel framing with titanium sheathing and glass curtain walls. Image © Steve Vidler/SuperStock

◆ **22.50** Herzog and de Meuron, The Tate Modern, London, Great Britain, 1906–2000. Exterior view of the Tate Modern and gardens on the south bank of River Thames. A former power station, the building now houses the collection of international modern art (defined as art since 1900). *(Image © Tate Gallery, London/Art Resource, NY)*

whose 1994 American Center in Paris [**Fig. 22.48**], done in Parisian limestone and zinc, is an energetically eccentric work of angles and sweeping lines. Gehry's more recent Guggenheim Museum Bilbao in Spain has been such a success that it is a premier visitor's destination, changing a once industrial city in decline into a much-appreciated place for tourists and artists to see [**Fig. 22.49**].

Creative Uses of Space We should take note of two other museums opened in the 1990s as examples of creative architectural thinking. The Tate Modern, across the river Thames from Saint Paul's Cathedral in London, is a fine example of how to engage in urban renewal creatively. The museum, housed in what was once a power station, was designed by two Swiss architects—Jacques Herzog and Pierre de Meuron—who turned a massive industrial plant into a severe museum with spacious galleries, including the stunning room where the main dynamo was once housed [**Fig. 22.50**]. By contrast, the Getty Center in the Santa Monica Mountains outside Los Angeles is a stunning complex of six buildings faced with sixteen thousand tons of travertine stone quarried in Italy. The architect, Richard Meier, joined forces with the noted environmental artist Robert Irwin to create a multileveled building complex with Irwin's central garden as a unifying centerpiece [**Fig. 22.51**].

Finally, the new Millennium Park in Chicago is a complex of open spaces, monuments, and artistic venues, which include the Crown Fountain designed by

◆ **22.51** Richard Meier, Getty Center, Los Angeles, California, 1997. Overview of the Center complex showing galleries, auditorium, gardens, research center, and circular fountain built into the Santa Monica Mountains. Lower center is the garden designed by installation artist Robert Irwin. *(Image © David Frazier/Photo Edit)*

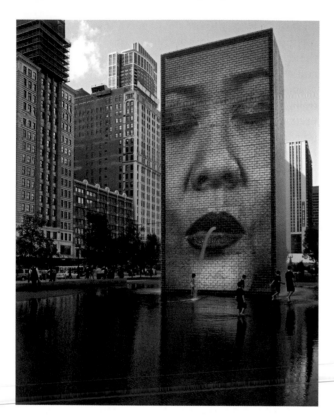

◆ **22.52** Jaume Plensa, Crown Fountain, Millennium Park, Chicago, Illinois, 2004. *(Image © Art on File/CORBIS)*

the Barcelona-born (1955) Spanish artist, Jaume Plensa. It features a reflecting pool with various patterns of cascading waterfalls from a pair of fifty-foot tall glass block towers that project, thanks to embedded video screens, the faces of one thousand Chicagoans [**Fig. 22.52**].

SOME TRENDS IN CONTEMPORARY LITERATURE

By the end of World War II, literary figures who had defined the modernist temperament—T. S. Eliot, James Joyce, Thomas Mann, Ezra Pound—had died or had already published their best work. Their passionate search for meaning in an alienated world, however, still inspired the work of others. The great modernist themes received attention by other voices in other media. The Swedish filmmaker Ingmar Bergman (b. 1918) began a series of classic films starting with his black-and-white *Wild Strawberries* in 1956, which explored the loss of religious faith and the demands of modern despair. The enigmatic Irish playwright (who lived in France and wrote in French and English) Samuel Beckett produced

plays like *Waiting for Godot* (1952), absurdist literature that explores a world beyond logic, decency, and the certainty of language.

Beckett *Waiting for Godot*, for all its apparent simplicity, is maddeningly difficult to interpret. Two characters, Vladimir and Estragon, wait at an unnamed and barren crossroads for Godot. Their patient wait is interrupted by antic encounters with two other characters. In the two acts, each representing one day, a young boy announces that Godot will arrive the next day. At the end of the play, Vladimir and Estragon decide to wait for Godot, although they toy momentarily with the idea of splitting up or committing suicide if Godot does not come to save them.

The language of *Godot* is laced with biblical allusions and religious puns. Is Godot God? And does the play illuminate the nature of an absurd world without final significance? Beckett does not say and critics do not agree, although they are in accord with the judgment that *Waiting for Godot* is a classic—if cryptic—statement about language, human relations, and the ultimate significance of the world.

Wiesel Gradually, as the war receded in time, other voices relating the horrors of the war experience began to be heard. The most compelling atrocity of the war period, the extermination in the Nazi concentration camps of six million Jews and countless other dissidents or enemies, has resulted in many attempts to tell the world that story. The most significant voice of the survivors of the event is the European-born Elie Wiesel (b. 1928), a survivor of the camps. Wiesel describes himself as a "teller of tales." He feels a duty, beyond the normal duty of art, to keep alive the memory of the near-extermination of his people. Wiesel's autobiographical memoir and arguably his greatest work, *Night* (1960), recounts his own years in the camps. It is a terribly moving book with its juxtaposition of a young boy's fervent faith with the demonic powers of the camp.

American Literature In the United States an entirely new generation of writers defined the nature of the American experience. Arthur Miller's play *Death of a Salesman* (1949) explored the failure of the American Dream in the person of its tragic hero, Willie Loman, an ordinary man defeated by life. J. D. Salinger's *The Catcher in the Rye* (1951) documented the bewildering coming of age of an American adolescent in so compelling a manner that it was, for a time, a cult book for the young. Southern writers like Eudora Welty, William Styron, Walker Percy, and Flannery O'Connor continued the meditations of William Faulkner about an area of the United States that has tasted defeat in a way no other region has. Poets like Wallace Stevens, Theodore Roethke, William Carlos Williams, and Marianne

Moore continued to celebrate the beauties and terrors of both nature and people.

We have already noted that existentialism was well suited to the postwar mood. One aspect of existentialism's ethos was its insistence on protest and human dissatisfaction. That element of existential protest has been very much a part of the postwar scene. The civil rights movement of the late 1950s and early 1960s became a paradigm for other protests, such as those against the Vietnam War; in favor of the rights of women; and for the rights of the dispossessed, underprivileged, or the victims of discrimination. The literature of protest has been an integral part of this cry for human rights.

African American Literature First and foremost, one can trace the African Americans' struggle for dignity and full equality through the literature they produced, especially in the period after World War I. The great pioneers were those writers who are grouped loosely under the name Harlem Renaissance (discussed in Chapter 21). By refusing the stereotype of Negro, they crafted an eloquent literature demanding humanity and unqualified justice. The work of these writers presaged the powerful torrent of African American fiction chronicling racial injustice in America. Two novels in particular, Richard Wright's *Native Son* (1940) and Ralph Ellison's *Invisible Man* (1952), have taken on the character of American classics. Younger writers followed, most notably James Baldwin, whose *Go Tell It on the Mountain* (1953) fused vivid memories of black Harlem, jazz, and the intense religion of the black church into a searing portrait of growing up black in America. Alice Walker explored her Southern roots in the explosively powerful *The Color Purple* (1982).

For many of the younger black writers in America, the theme of black pride has been linked with the consciousness of being a woman. Nikki Giovanni (b. 1936) produced a body of poetry celebrating both her sense of "blackness" and her pride in her femininity. Her poetry has been a poetic blend of black history and female consciousness done in an American mode. Similarly, Maya Angelou has become an enormously important voice for the African American community, as has Gwendolyn Brooks, whose ties go back to the writers of the Harlem Renaissance.

The Feminist Perspective The rightful claims of women have been advanced currently by an activist spirit that seeks equality of women and men, free from gender discrimination. The battle for women's rights and suffrage begun in the nineteenth century continues today in the feminist movement opposing cultural oppression around the globe. Writers like Doris Lessing, Margaret Atwood, Adrienne Rich, Maxine Kumin, and others continue to explore feminine consciousness from differing angles of vision.

Two twentieth-century poets deserve particular mention, because both of them dealt so clearly with the dissatisfaction of women. Sylvia Plath (1932–1963) and Anne Sexton (1928–1974) used the imagery of traditional gender roles to examine the restraints of their positions. They knew each other, and while the precociously talented Sylvia Plath produced an important body of poetry as well as a largely autobiographical novel, *The Bell Jar* (1963), describing most of her short and unhappy life, Anne Sexton wrote only poetry. Both, alas, died by their own hands after tortured lives of emotional upheavals.

MUSIC SINCE 1945

Avant-Garde Developments

Since World War II, many avant-garde composers have been moving toward greater and greater complexity of musical organization, coupled with an increasing use of new kinds of sound. At the same time, other musicians, disturbed by their colleagues' obsessive concern for order, have tried to introduce an element of chance—even chaos—into the creation of a work of music. Both the structuralists and the advocates of random music have attracted followers, and only time will tell which approach will prove more fruitful.

Before considering the nature of these two schools in detail, some general observations are in order. It must be admitted that advanced contemporary music presents a tough challenge to the patience, sympathy, and ears of many sincere music lovers. Unlike the visual arts and literature, modern music seems, at least superficially, to have made virtually a complete break with past traditions. Furthermore, much of it seems remote from our actual experience. Developments in painting or architecture are visible around us in one form or another on a daily basis, and modern writers deal with problems that affect us in our own lives. Many creative musicians, however, have withdrawn to the scientific laboratory, where they construct their pieces with the aid of machines and in accordance with mathematical principles. It is hardly surprising that the results may at first seem sterile.

Yet it is well worth making an effort to understand and enjoy the latest developments in music. Concentration and an open mind will remove many of the barriers. So will persistence. Music lovers who listen twenty times to a recording of a Chopin waltz or a Mahler symphony for every one time they listen to a work by Boulez or Stockhausen can hardly expect to make much progress in understanding a new and admittedly difficult idiom. Much of today's music may well not survive the test of time, but it is equally probable that some pieces will become classics in this twenty-first century.

By discriminative listening we can play our own part in judging which music is worthless and which will be of permanent value.

Structuralism The principle of precise musical organization had already become important in twentieth century music with the serialism of Arnold Schönberg. Schönberg's ordering of pitch (the melodic and harmonic element of music) in rigidly maintained twelve-tone rows has been extended by recent composers to other elements. Pierre Boulez (b. 1925), for example, constructed rows of twelve-note durations (the length of time each note sounds), twelve levels of volume, and twelve ways of striking the keys for works like his Second Piano Sonata (1948) and Structures for two pianos (1952). In this music, every element (pitch, length of notes, volume, and attack) is totally ordered and controlled by the composer in accordance with his predetermined rows, because none of the twelve components of each row can be repeated until after the other eleven.

The effect of this total control is to eliminate any sense of traditional melody, harmony, or counterpoint along with the emotions they evoke. Instead the composer aims to create a pure and abstract musical structure that deliberately avoids any kind of subjective emotional expression.

There remains, however, one element in these piano works that even Boulez cannot totally control: the human element. All of the composer's instructions, however precise, have to be interpreted and executed by a performer, and as long as composers depend on performers to interpret their works, they cannot avoid a measure of subjectivity. Different pianists will inevitably produce different results, and even the same pianist will not produce an identical performance on every occasion.

Electronic Music In order to solve this problem, some composers in the 1950s began to turn to *electronic music*, the sounds of which are produced not by conventional musical instruments but by an electronic oscillator, a machine that produces pure sound waves. A composer can order the sounds by means of a computer and then transfer these to recording tape for playback. In the past few years, the process of manipulating electronic sound has been simplified by the invention of the *synthesizer* (an electronic instrument that can produce just about any kind of sound effect). In combination with a computer, machines like the Moog synthesizer can be used for either original electronic works or creating electronic versions of traditional music, as in the popular *Switched-on Bach* recordings of the 1960s.

From its earliest days, electronic music has alarmed many listeners by its apparent lack of humanity. The whistles, clicks, and hisses that characterize it may be eerily appropriate to the mysteries of the Space Age but have little to do with traditional musical expression. Composers of electronic music have had considerable difficulty inventing formal structures for organizing the vast range of sounds available to them. In addition, there still exists no universally agreed-on system of writing down electronic compositions, most of which exist only on tape. It is probably significant that even Karlheinz Stockhausen (b. 1928), one of the leading figures in electronic music, has tended to combine electronic sounds with conventional musical instruments. His *Mixtur* (1965), for example, is written for five orchestras, electronic equipment, and loudspeakers. During performance, the sounds produced by the orchestral instruments are electronically altered and simultaneously mixed with the instrumental sound and prerecorded tape. In this way an element of live participation has been reintroduced.

For all its radical innovations, however, *Mixtur* at least maintains the basic premise of music in the Western tradition: that composers can communicate with their listeners by predetermining (composing) their works according to an intellectual set of rules. The laws of baroque counterpoint, classical sonata form, or Stockhausen's ordering and altering of sound patterns all represent systems that have enabled composers to plan and create musical works. One of the most revolutionary of all recent developments, however, has been the invention of *aleatoric* music. The name is derived from the Latin word *alea* (a dice game) and is applied to music in which an important role is played by the element of chance.

John Cage and Aleatoric Music One of the leading exponents of this genre of music is the American composer John Cage (1912–1992), who had been much influenced by Zen philosophy. Adopting the Zen attitude that one must go beyond logic in life, Cage argued that music should reflect the random chaos of the world around us and not seek to impose order on it. His *Concert for Piano and Orchestra* (1958) has a piano part consisting of eighty-four different "sound events," some, all, or none of which are to be played in any random order. The orchestral accompaniment consists of separate pages of music, some, all, or none of which can be played by any (or no) instrument, in any order and combination. Clearly, every performance of the *Concert* is going to be a unique event, largely dependent on pure chance for its actual sound. In other pieces, Cage instructed the performers to determine the sequence of events by even more random methods, including the tossing of coins.

Works like these are more interesting for the questions they ask about the nature of music than for any intrinsic value of their own. Cage partly reacted against what he regarded as the excessive organization and rigidity of composers like Boulez and Stockhausen, but at the same time he also raised some important considerations. What is the function of the artist in the modern world? What is the relationship between creator and performer? And what part, if any, should the listeners play in the creation of a piece of music? Need it always be a passive part? If Cage's own answers to questions such as these may not satisfy everyone, he had at least posed the problems in an intriguing form.

THE NEW MINIMALISTS

Reich A very different solution to the search for a musical style has been proposed by a younger generation of American composers. Steve Reich (b. 1936) is one of the first musicians to build lengthy pieces out of the multiple repetitions of simple chords and rhythms. Critics sometimes assume that the purpose of these repetitions is to achieve a hypnotic effect by inducing a kind of state of trance. Reich stated that his aim is, in fact, the reverse: a state of heightened concentration.

In *The Desert Music*, a composition for chorus and instruments completed in 1983, Reich's choice of texts is helpful to an understanding of his music. The work's central section consists of a setting of words by the American poet William Carlos Williams (1883–1963):

> It is a principle of music
> to repeat the theme. Repeat
> and repeat again,
> as the pace mounts. The
> theme is difficult
> but no more difficult
> than the facts to be
> resolved.

William Carlos Williams from *Collected Poems 1939–1962*, Volume II, copyright 1953 by William Carlos Williams. Reprinted by permission of New Directions Publishing Corp.

The piece begins with the pulsing of a series of broken chords, which is sustained in various ways, chiefly by tuned mallets. This pulsation, together with a wordless choral vocalization, gives the work a rhythmical complexity and richness of sound that is at times reminiscent of some African or Balinese music.

Glass The works of Philip Glass (b. 1937) are even more openly influenced by non-Western music. Glass studied the Indian tabla drums for a time; he is also interested in West African music and has worked with Ravi Shankar, the great Indian sitar virtuoso. Many of Glass's compositions are based on combinations of rhythmical structures derived from classical Indian music. They are built up into repeating modules, the effect of which has been likened by unsympathetic listeners to a needle stuck in a record groove.

Length plays an important part in Glass's operas, for which he has collaborated with the American dramatist Robert Wilson. Wilson, like Glass, is interested in "apparent motionlessness and endless durations during which dreams are dreamed and significant matters are understood." Together they have produced three massive stage works in the years between 1975 and 1985: *Einstein on the Beach, Satyagraha,* and *Akhnaten.* The performances involve a team of collaborators that includes directors, designers, and choreographers; the results have the quality of a theatrical "happening." Although a description of the works makes them sound remote and difficult, performances of them have been extremely successful. Even New York's Metropolitan Opera House, not famous for an adventurous nature in selecting repertory, was sold out for two performances of *Einstein on the Beach.* Clearly, whatever its theoretical origins, the music of Glass reaches a wide public.

TRADITIONAL APPROACHES TO MODERN MUSIC

Not all composers have abandoned the traditional means of musical expression. Musicians like Benjamin Britten (1913–1976) and Dmitri Shostakovich (1906–1975) demonstrated that an innovative approach to the traditional elements of melody, harmony, and rhythm can still produce exciting and moving results, and neither can be accused of losing touch with the modern world. Britten's *War Requiem* (1962) is an eloquent plea for an end to the violence of contemporary life, whereas Shostakovich's entire musical output reflects his uneasy relationship with Soviet authority. His Symphony No. 13 (1962) includes settings of poems by the Russian poet Yevtushenko on anti-Semitism in Russia and earned him unpopularity in Soviet artistic and political circles.

Both Britten and Shostakovich did not hesitate to write recognizable "tunes" in their music. In Symphony No. 15 (1971), his last symphony, Shostakovich even quoted themes from Rossini's *William Tell Overture* (the familiar "Lone Ranger" theme) and from Wagner. The work is at the same time easy to listen to and deeply serious. Like much of Shostakovich's music, it is concerned with the nature of death (a subject also explored in his Symphony No. 14). Throughout its four movements, Shostakovich's sense of rhythm is much in evidence, as is his feeling for orchestral color, in which he demonstrates that the resources of a traditional symphony orchestra are far from exhausted. The final mysterious dying close of Symphony No. 15 is especially striking in its use of familiar ingredients—repeating rhythmic patterns, simple melodic phrases—to achieve an unusual effect.

If Shostakovich demonstrated that a musical form as old-fashioned as the symphony can still be used to create masterpieces, Britten did the same for opera. His first great success, *Peter Grimes* (1945), employed traditional operatic devices like arias, trios, and choruses to depict the tragic fate of its hero, a man whose alienation from society leads to his persecution at the hands of his fellow citizens. In other works, Britten followed the example of many of his illustrious predecessors in turning to earlier literary masterpieces for inspiration. *A Midsummer Night's Dream* (1960) is a setting of Shakespeare's play, while *Death in Venice* (1973) is based on the story by Thomas Mann. In all of his operas, Britten writes music that is easy to listen to (and, equally important, not impossible to sing), but he never condescends to his audience. Each work deals with a recognizable area of human experience and presents it in a valid musical and dramatic form. It is always dangerous to predict the verdict of posterity, but from today's vantage point the music of Britten seems to have as good a chance as any of surviving in this new century.

A NOTE ON THE POSTMODERN SENSIBILITY

In the past generation some critics have been insisting, with varying degrees of acceptance, that much of contemporary art has moved beyond the modernist preoccupation with alienation, myth, fragmentation of time, and the interior states of the self. The most debated questions now are: What exactly followed modernism that makes it distinctively postmodern? Does it have a shaping spirit? What do the artists in all media hold in common that permits them to be considered representative postmodernists?

Some critics see the postmodernists as those who push the modernist worldview to its extreme limit. This is hardly a satisfactory definition because rather than define a new sensibility, it merely elasticizes the definition of modern to include more of the same. While postmodernism must build on what modernism has accomplished, it must also find its own voice.

It is impossible to create art today as if Cubism or Abstract Expressionism had never existed, just as it is impossible to compose music as if Stravinsky had never lived. Furthermore, we cannot live life (or even look at it) as if relativity, atomic weapons, T. S. Eliot's poetry, and Freudian explorations of the unconscious were not part of our intellectual and social climate. If art is to be a genuine part of the human enterprise, it must surely incorporate its past without being a prisoner of it, reflect its present, and point to the future. In fact, most of the great achievements in the arts have done precisely that; they have mastered the tradition and then extended it.

It may well be that the key word to describe the contemporary situation in the arts is *pluralism*: a diversity of influences, ideas, and movements spawned by an age of instant communication and ever-growing technology. In an age when more people than ever before buy books, see films, watch television, go to plays and concerts, use the Internet, and listen to radios, iPods, and CDs, what we seem to be seeing is the curious puzzle the Greek philosophers wrote about millennia ago—the relationship of unity and diversity in the observable world: we are one, but we are also many.

SUMMARY

This chapter deals with Western culture after the time of World War II. In the postwar period, with Europe in shambles and the Far East still asleep, we confidently felt that the twentieth was the American century; many people, not always admiringly, spoke of the "Coca-Colazation" of the world. From the vantage point of the beginning of the twenty-first century, we see that, however powerful the United States may be, there now exist other countervailing powers, as the economic power of the European Union, Japan, and China readily demonstrate.

◆ **The Rise of the Postmodern in the Arts.** This postwar period saw dramatic shifts in the arts. The modernist temper that prevailed both in literature and in the arts had its inevitable reaction. The power of the New York School of painting (Abstract Expressionism/color-field painting/minimalism) has been challenged by new art forces, mainly from Europe, that emphasize once again the picture plane and the expressive power of emotion. In literature, the modernist temper exemplified in writers like Eliot, Woolf, and others gave way to a postmodern sensibility represented in writers from Latin America, Japan, and Europe. Increasing attention is being paid to the writers from both Eastern Europe and Africa.

Out of the human rights movement of the past decades has arisen a determined effort to democratize the arts, to bring to the attention of large audiences the artistic contributions of women and nonwhites both by retrieving their overlooked work from the past and by careful attention to those at work today. Contemporary debates over the core humanities requirements in universities—should they restrict themselves to the classics or should they represent many voices and many cultures—simply reflect the pressures of the culture, which is no longer sure of its older assumptions.

◆ **From Existentialism to Pluralism.** No consensus exists on a humanistic worldview. The postwar power of existentialism sprang both from its philosophical ideas and from its adaptability to the arts, especially the literary arts. Although the writings of Albert Camus are still read and the plays of Beckett and Ionesco are still performed, they now reflect a settled place in the literary canon, with no new single idea providing the power to energize the arts as a whole. The notion of a global culture argues for a common culture growing out of mutual links. But while there is some evidence of commonality, regional differences and even antagonisms remain. Pluralism, a term that allows us to include the many different directions in artistic expression throughout all the media, may be the term that most accurately describes our contemporary culture.

EXERCISES

1. When we look at Abstract Expressionist art, it is tempting to believe that "anyone could do that." But *can* anyone do it? How does one go about describing in writing the character of abstract art?

2. Look closely at a work by Alexander Calder. Would a Classical sculptor (Rodin, Michelangelo) have recognized Calder's work as sculpture? What makes it different? Why is it called *sculpture*?

3. After reading Sartre's essay on existentialism, ask yourself: is this a philosophy that could serve as a guide to my life? Give the reasons for your answer.

4. Look carefully at your campus buildings. Does "form follow function"? Is "less more"? Can you detect the styles that influenced the campus architect?

5. A classic is said to have a "surplus of meaning"—it is so good that one can always go back and learn more from it. Are there compositions in popular music that are now "classics" in that sense? List five songs that still inspire musicians today.

6. Have the twentieth-century forms of entertainment (especially television) made you less of a reader? How does reading differ from watching television? How does looking at art differ from looking at television? Listening to music? How do the computer, especially its access to the Internet, and the cell phone affect how you communicate? Explain.

 Visit the *Culture & Values* Companion website at **www.cengage.com/art/Cunningham/Cultureand Values7E** and the *Humanities Resource Center* for an array of primary source readings, key terms with pronunciations, flash cards, quizzes, and study materials designed especially to help you do well in this course.

PRONUNCIATION GLOSSARY

Key Terms, Places, and People

Note: A hyphen separates the syllables of a word; the syllable in capital letters receives greater emphasis.

a capella (ah cuh-PELL-uh) from Italian *alla capella* or "in the manner of the chapel." Unaccompanied singing.

Aachen (AW-kuhn) City in western Germany; location of Charlemagne's palace school and the center of scholarship in the Carolingian period. Known as **Aix-la-Chapelle** (AY-lah-shah-PELL) in French.

abacus (AB-uh-kuss) Square block forming part of a Doric capital.

Abdullah, Saiyid (sigh-YEED ab-DOO-luh) c. 1720–1810 African poet born on the island of Lamu, in present day Kenya. Author of *Self-Examination*.

Abelard (Peter) (A-buh-lard) 1079–1142 CE French priest and philosopher who studied under William of Champeaux. He became canon and chair of Notre Dame in 1115 CE and his fame as a teacher attracted scholars from throughout Europe. His major contribution to philosophy was his emphasis on the scholastic manner, giving formal rational expression to received ecclesiastical doctrine.

absurdity Term adopted by existentialists to describe the ultimate meaninglessness of human existence.

Académie des Beaux Arts (BOHZ ARR) French for "Academy of the Fine Arts." French learned society founded by King Louis XIV in 1667. Members of this academy defended traditional standards and values within the arts.

Achebe, Chinua (CHIN-wah ah-CHAY-bay) b. 1930 Nigerian writer. His most widely read novels *Things Fall Apart* and *No Longer at Ease* deal with the intersection of Western and traditional African culture and the conflicts and confusion which arise within the characters.

Achilles (uh-KILL-eez) The mythical hero of Homer's epic poem, *Iliad*, and Greece's greatest warrior.

Acropolis (uh-KROP-uh-liss) The fortified highest point of the ancient city of Athens and site of the Parthenon.

adagio (ah-DAH-jee-oe) The Italian word for "slow." Used by composers to indicate the speed at which music should be played.

adobe (uh-DOE-bee) Building material composed of sand, mud, dung or clay mixed with straw or other fibers and then dried into bricks.

Aegisthus (ee-JISS-thuss) Cousin and murderer of Agamemnon. Killed by Orestes for seducing Clytemnestra, Orestes' mother.

Aeneid (uh-NEE-ihd) A Latin epic poem by Virgil divided into twelve books recounting the adventures of the Trojan prince, Aeneas.

Aeschylus (ESS-kuh-luss) 525–456 BCE Greek poet and playwright; author of the *Oresteia* trilogy.

aesthetic (ess-THEH-tick) Descriptive adjective used (sometimes negatively) to characterize certain artworks as more interested in beauty than content. Also used as a shorthand way of speaking about a certain philosophical standard for the making of art (e.g., the Surrealist aesthetic).

Agamemnon (agg-uh-MEM-non) In Homer's poem, *Iliad*, he is king of Mycenae and leader of the Greeks in the Trojan War.

Agamemnon (agg-uh-MEM-non) The first play of Aeschylus' trilogy, the *Oresteia*, in which Agamemnon, king of Mycenae, sacrifices his daughter, Iphigenia, and is later killed by his wife, Clytemnestra.

ahimsa (uh-HIM-zuh) The Buddhist teaching of nonviolence.

Akhenaton (ahk-NAH-tuhn) 1379–1362 BCE Pharaoh of the New Kingdom, Egypt. He attempted a total reform of Egyptian religious and political life. Spouse of Queen Nefertiti.

Akkadian (uh-KAY-dee-uhn) 2350–2150 BCE Sumerian culture named for the capital city, Akkad, under King Sargon and his descendants.

Albrecht, Altdorfer (ALL-brekt ALT-dor-fuhr) 1480–1538 German painter and engraver. One of first artists to develop landscape painting, see *Danube Landscape Near Regensburg*.

Alcuin of York (AL-kwin) 735–804 BCE English theologian and scholar, brought by Charlemagne to develop a curriculum for schools to improve the literacy of his subjects. The letter *On the Cultivation of Learning* is attributed to Alcuin.

Alexander of Macedon (MASS-ih-don) 356–323 BCE King of Macedonia and conqueror of the Persian Empire. Also known as Alexander the Great.

Alexandria (al-ihg-ZAN-dree-uh) City in northern Egypt founded by Alexander the Great in 332 BCE.

Al-Ghazali (al-gha-ZAH-lee) 1058–1111 CE Sufi scholar who criticized the influence of Greek philosophy on Islamic thought. Author of *The Incoherence of the Philosophers*.

Alhambra (al-HAM-bruh) Moorish palace in Granada, Spain, built between the 12th and 13th centuries. It is composed of two adjoining palaces: the Palace of the Myrtles and the Court of the Lions.

Al-Hazen (al-HA-zihn) 965–1039 CE Persian-Arab scientist who developed the field of optics and the technology of making lenses. Considered to be a pioneer in the modern scientific method.

Alighieri, Dante (DAWN-tay ahl-ee-GYAIR-ee) 1265–1321 CE Exiled Florentine poet. His masterpiece *The Divine Comedy* relates the symbolic journey of the poet through hell, purgatory, and heaven and encompasses in its description major political, literary, and church officials of both his and ancient times. In addition, Dante wrote treatises on language, general knowledge, and poetry.

Al-Khwarizmi (al KWAR-iz-mee) 780–850 CE Arab mathematician who invented algebra and developed our current nine number systems and the place holder, zero.

allegory In art, a genre where fictional characters symbolically represent another level of truth.

allegro (uh-LEH-grow) The Italian word for "happy." Used to indicate the fast speed at which a piece of music should be played.

Altamira (al-tuh-MEE-ruh) A group of caverns in northern Spain, near Santander noted for Paleolithic paintings of bison, deer, and pigs.

Amarna (uh-MAR-nuh) Egyptian city (known today as Tel el-Amarna) to which Akhenaton moved his capital to create his reforms.

Ambrosian chant (am-BROE-shin) Liturgical singing established by Saint Ambrose of Milan 340?–397 CE .

ambulatory (AM-byoo-luh-tore-ee) Covered walkway around the apse of a church.

amphora (AM-fuh-ruh) A two-handled jar with a narrow neck used to store wine or oil.

Anabaptists (ann-uh-BAP-tists) Members of a radical branch of the Reformation movement who insisted on adult baptism even for those who had been baptized in infancy. The word means "those baptized again."

Anchises (an-KIGH-seez) In Vergil's *Aeneid*, father of Aeneis, who is rescued by his son during the sack of Troy.

Anglo culture Common description of the majority culture of native English speakers in the United States, Canada, and the United Kingdom.

Animism (AN-uh-mizm) Belief that the world is governed by the workings of nature.

anthem A musical composition written for choir (sometimes with solo voices added), the text of which is in English.

Anthemius of Tralles (an-THEE-mee-us, TRA-leez) 6th century CE Greek architect, engineer, and mathematician. Under Emperor Justinian, he designed and built the church of Hagia Sophia in Constantinople.

Antigone **(an-TIGG-uh-nee)** c. 440 BCE A tragedy by Sophocles in which King Creon of Thebes condemns his niece, Antigone, for performing funeral rites for her brother, Polynices.

Antioch (AN-tee-awk) City in southern Turkey; founded in c. 300 BCE by Seleuces I as part of the Roman Empire.

antiphonal (an-TIFF-uh-nuhl) Sung chant with the cantor and the congregation, or separate sections of the congregation, alternating verses of a psalm.

antithesis (an-TITH-uh-siss) An opposing or contrasting element or proposition. In Hegelian philosophy, a term used to designate Nature. Compare *synthesis*.

Aphrodite (af-ruh-DIE-tee) Greek goddess of love and beauty.

apocalypse From the Book of Revelation in the Bible, the period of catastrophic upheaval expected to occur just before the end of the world when God will sit in judgment on humankind.

Apollo (uh-PAWL-oh) Greek and Roman god of music, poetry, medicine, and prophecy. Brother of Artemis.

apologists Christian writers who wrote about the moral code of Christianity in defense of the Roman charge of treason against the state.

Aquinas, Thomas (Saint) (uh-KWINE-uss) 1225?–1274 CE The most famous theological thinker of the 13th century. His prodigious writing culminated in *Summa Theologica*, a masterful attempt to harmonize human reason and religious revelation. His writings made use of ancient Greek philosophy and Hebrew scripture.

Ara Pacis (ah-ruh-PAH-kiss) The Altar of Peace, chief monument of Augustan sculpture.

arabesque (air-uh-BESK) Decorative feature using highly complex interlaced lines (sometimes of fruits or foliage). The word derives from Islamic decorative arts.

architrave (AHR-kuh-trayv) The lowest division of an entablature, or the lowest of three bands forming the upper part of a Greek temple.

archivolt (AR-kuh-volt) Ornamented molding on an arch.

Ares (AIR-eez) Ancient Greek god of war; son of Zeus and Hera.

aria (AR-ee-uh) A solo song in an opera, oratorio, or cantata, which often gives the singer a chance to display technical skill.

Arians (AIR-ee-uhns) A dissident branch of early Christianity that did not accept Jesus Christ as equal to the Father. Named for the Alexandrian priest Arius.

Aristophanes (air-uh-STOFF-uh-neez) c. 450–385 BCE Athenian satirical playwright whose comical works include *The Birds* and *Lysistrata*.

Aristotle (air-uh-STOT-uhl) 384–322 BCE Greek philosopher and pupil of Plato. Author of the classic philosophical works *Metaphysics, Physics, Rhetoric,* and *Poetics*. Founder of the Lyceum.

ars nova **(ARZ NO-vuh)** A new musical style that developed in the early 14th century characterized by greater richness and complexity of sound. The term was taken from a treatise by the composer Philippi de Vitry called *Ars Nova Musicae* or "The New Art of Music."

Artemis (AHR-tuh-mis) Virgin goddess and huntress. Sister of Apollo. Often associated with the moon.

Aryans (AIR-ee-uhns) Derived from the Sanskrit word "Arya," meaning noble or honorable. An ancient people who spoke the Indo-European language, they invaded India c. 1500 BCE.

Ashoka (uh-SHOW-kuh) 304–232 BCE Indian emperor who expanded and unified India. In 261 BCE he converted to Buddhism, which he established as the religion of the state and then devoted himself to the spread of Buddhism throughout Asia. He founded several monasteries, erected monuments, and ordered the creation of a canon of sacred Buddhist texts.

Assurbanipal (ah-suhr-BAH-nee-pawl) 668–626 BCE Assyrian king overseeing achievements that marked the culmination of the culture of ancient Mesopotamia.

Athena (uh-THEE-nuh) Greek goddess of warfare, wisdom, and fertility; born fully grown from the head of Zeus. Protector of cities.

atman (AWT-muhn) The personal manifestation within each individual of Brahman.

atomists (AT-uh-mists) Pre-socratic philosophers who believed that reality consisted of atoms (small "indivisible" particles) and the void (nothingness). Foremost philosophers were Leucippus and Democritus.

Aton (AHT-n) Egyptian deity of the sun declared by Akhenaton to be the only god.

atonal (ay-TOH-nuhl) Term used to describe music that lacks a "home" key or pitch; music with no tonal center.

atonality Music that lacks a traditional harmonic (or tonal) center.

atrium (AY-tree-um) Courtyard entrance of an early or Medieval Christian church.

Attica (AT-uh-kuh) Region in southeastern Greece surrounding Athens that was under Athenian control during ancient times.

Augustans (aw-GUSS-tuhns) 18th century A group of poets and writers whose work was influenced by the emergence of interest in Classical and Roman authors. Members included Dryden and Pope.

Augustine of Hippo (AW-guh-steen) 354–430 CE Christian philosopher and theologian. Born in present day Algeria and educated in North Africa; his teachings greatly influenced the development of Western Christianity. Author of *The City of God* and *Confessions*.

aulos (AW-loss) Greek double-reed musical instrument similar to the modern oboe.

Aurangzeb (AW-rung-zeb) 1618–1707 Last of the great Mughal emperors. A devout Muslim, his reign was marked by the persecution of Hindus.

avant-garde (uh-vont-GUARD) Referring to creative expressions that push the boundaries of what is considered normal and acceptable. Applied to experimental art, music, and literature forms of the mid to late 20th century.

avatar (AV-uh-tahr) The incarnation of Hindu deity on earth.

Averröes (uh-VER-u-weez) 1126–1198 CE Arab philosopher, physician, and mathematician. Author of the treatise *The Incoherence of Incoherence*, which argued that Greek philosophy could be reconciled with Islamic thought.

Avignon (a-vee-NYAWN) A city in the southeast of France and the location of the papacy from 1309 to 1378 during the Great Schism.

ayres (AIRZ) Simple English songs written for one singer and accompaniment.

Babur (BAH-buhr) 1483–1503 Founder of the Mughal Empire in India. Author of the autobiography *Babur-nama*, considered a classic in Turkish literature.

Bach, Johan Sebastian (YO-hahn suh-BASS-chin BAHK) 1685–1750 German composer. Considered to be one of the greatest and most prolific composers in the Western musical canon. His work reflected his deep religious faith, as in his magnificent *St. Matthew's Passion*, which was written in German and included several Lutheran chorales. His secular works include *The Brandenburg Concertos*, written in the **concerto grosso** form.

Baghavad-Gita (BAHG-uh-vahd GEE-tuh) c. 5th–2nd century BCE The second text in the Mahabharata, this epic poem presents a conversation between Krishna (the divine one) and Prince Arjuna. Through Krishna's response to Arjuna's dilemma about going to war, the god explains the core teachings of Hindu philosophy.

ballades (bah-LAHDZ) Songs or ballads, often written for a single voice with accompanying instruments.

Balzac, Honoré de (aw-naw-REY duh BALL-zak) 1799–1850 Recognized as one of France's preeminent novelists. Prolific author who dealt with social and political themes in a realistic style. His stories and novels are included in his anthology *The Human Comedy*.

baptistery (BAP-tuh-stree) (pl. baptisteries) A part of a church, either a separate structure or attached to the main body of the church, where the sacrament of baptism is performed.

Baroque (buh-ROHK) A period marked by a widening spectrum of individual expression and a shift toward secular themes within the arts. In an effort to reestablish authority after the Reformation, the Catholic Church invested heavily in the arts. However, the Reformation and several scientific discoveries contributed to a pervasive skepticism and questioning of reality.

barrel vault A series of arches forming a tunnel, or "barrel."

Basho, Matsuo (mat-soo-oh bah-show) 1644–1694 Japanese poet and essayist. He developed the haiku form of verse. His work explores nature, beauty, and human suffering.

Basilica (buh-SILL-uh-cuh) Early Christian church modeled on secular Roman buildings, generally having a central nave, a semicircular apse, two- to four-sided columned aisles, a clerestory, and a narthex. The most famous were founded by Emperor Constantine.

Basilica at Paestum (buh-SILL-ih-kuh, PESS-tuhm) c. 550 BCE Temple to Hera located near the coast of southern Italy. One of the earliest Greek temples.

Battle of Actium (ACK-tee-uhm) 31 BCE Battle in which Octavian decisively defeated Mark Antony and Cleopatra.

Battle of Pharsalus (fahr-SAY-luhs) 48 BCE Ceasar's final victory over Pompey.

Bauhaus (BOW-house) German school of architecture and design founded in 1918 by Walter Gropius. The school became an important nexus of German creativity and thought in the 20th century.

Beaumarchais, Pierre-Augustin (PYER ogg-y-STAN bow-mar-SHAY) 1732–1799 French playwright. Author of social comedies *The Barber of Seville* and the *Marriage of Figaro*, which became the basis for operas by *Rossini* and *Mozart*. He founded the Société des Auteurs to enable playwrights to obtain royalty payments.

Bede (BEED) 763?–735 CE English monk and historian; author of the *Ecclesiastical History of the English Nation*. Also called "the Venerable Bede."

Beethoven, Ludwig van (LOOD-vig fan BAY-toe-ven) 1770–1827 German composer. Emerging from a strong classical tradition, his works became the beacon of musical Romanticism, representative of the Age of Enlightenment, and the revolutionary mood of the times, as seen in his Symphony No. 3 in E Flat, Op. 55 subtitled *Eroica*, originally a tribute to Napoleon. In addition to his symphonies, he wrote the opera *Fidelio* and several piano sonatas, including The Piano Sonata No. 21 in C major, Op.53, nicknamed *Waldstein* dedicated to Count von Waldstein, Beethoven's patron and personal friend.

Beijing (BAY-JEENG) Capital city of the People's Republic of China located in northeastern China. Cultural, commercial, and political center since the 14th century.

bel canto (bell KAHN-toe) Italian for "beautiful singing." A term applied to a school of early 19th century opera, which emphasized the aesthetic of a song over realism in plot or action.

belle époque (bel eh-POCK) French for "beautiful age." Used to describe the growing prosperity of the late 19th century.

Benedict of Nursia (NUHR-shee-uh) 480–547? BCE Italian monk who founded the Benedictine order; author of the *Rule of Saint Benedict*, which outlines the precepts of living a monastic life.

Berbers (BUHR-buhr) North African tribes who, although culturally distinct, share the Berber language. Predominantly Muslim.

Berlioz, Hector (HEK-tuhr BAIR-lee-owze) 1803–1869 French Romantic composer. One of founders of 19th century program music. His *Fantastic Symphony*, a piece often cited as representative of the Romantic period, supposedly depicts opium induced hallucinations. *The Damnation of Faust* is a musical setting of Part One of Goethe's novel.

Bernini, Gian Lorenzo (ber-NEE-nee) 1598–1680 Italian sculptor and major Baroque architect. His designs are prevalent throughout Rome, the most spectacular being the colonnade around the square of Saint Peter's. His sculptures are masterfully rendered studies in the human form, having both great energy and expressiveness, as seen in his *David*, his bust for *Cardinal Scipione Borghese*, and *Saint Teresa in Ecstasy*.

bhakti (BAHK-tee) Act of devotion to a god or the gods in general.

Biafra (Republic of) (bee-AH-fruh) Briefly an independent state between 1967–1970, founded by the Igbo people of eastern Nigeria.

black-figure Athenian vase-painting technique in which the outline of a figure was painted in solid black and the details were produced by cutting away the paint with a fine point.

Blaue Reiter (BLAU-uh RYE-ter) German for "blue rider." An early 20th century school of German Expressionist painting.

Boccaccio, Giovanni (joe-VAHN-ni bow-CAH-chee-yo) 1313–1375 Italian poet and writer. Author of the *Decameron*, a collection of 100 tales, recounted by a fictional group of people fleeing the bubonic plague of the 1340s.

Bodhisattva (bow-dee-SAHT-vuh) A Buddhist saint.

Boethius (bow-EE-thee-uss) 475?–525? CE Roman philosopher. Author of *The Consolation of Philosophy*, a work that had profound influence on subsequent Christian thinkers. Through his translations and commentaries on the works of Aristotle, he brought Greek philosophy to the Middle Ages. Also the author of several treatises on music.

Boke of Common Praier Noted One of the first Protestant hymnals, published by John Merbeke in 1549, it used a simplified traditional Gregorian chant that highlighted the text.

Book of the Dead Sacred Egyptian funerary texts that served as a guide for the soul in the journey into the afterlife.

Borges, Jorge Luis (HOAR-heh loo-EES BOR-hez) 1899–1986 Argentine writer. While in Spain, he was member of the avant-garde Ultraist literary group. His first book of poems, *Fervor de Buenos Aires*, was published in 1923.

Borromini Francesco (Frahn-CHESS-coh boh-roh-MEE-nee) 1599–1667 Influential Italian Baroque architect. He designed the church of San Carlo alle Quattro Fontane, Rome. Unique at the time for the highly ornamented and sinuous curves of its façade, the style would be replicated throughout the Baroque period.

Bosch, Hieronymus (hy-uh-RONN-ih-muss BOSH) c. 1450–1516 Flemish painter. Noted for his allegorical pictures displaying sinister scenes. Among his best-known works is the triptych *The Garden of Earthly Delights* in which he vividly portrays the fall of man from grace, his existence in a world replete with sin, and finally his damnation in hell.

Botticelli, Sandro (sahn-droh bott-ee-CHELL-ee) c. 1444–1510 Florentine painter. His early paintings depicted biblical subjects, but later he turned to classical themes, producing such masterpieces as *The Birth of Venus* and *La Primavera*. His works characterize the intersection of the Classical ideal of the female figure, Platonism, a harkening back to Greek paganism and Christian mysticism of the Virgin prevalent in Renaissance Italy.

Boucher, François (fran-SWAH boo-SHAY) 1703–1770 French rococo painter. He depicted lighthearted scenes of voluptuous beauty, as seen in *Cupid a Captive*.

boule (BOO-lee) Directing council of the Athenian Assembly.

Boulez, Pierre (PYAIR boo-LEZZ) b. 1925 French composer and conductor. He developed a highly controlled compositional style devoid of subjective emotional expression that underscored the abstract elements of music by eliminating melody, harmony, and counterpoint. See his Second Piano Sonata and *Structures*.

Brahman (BRAH-min) According to Hindu belief, the underlying reality of the world.

Brahms, Johannes (yo-HAH-ness BRAHMZ) 1833–1897 German composer. His works include concertos, four symphonies, choral compositions, songs, and chamber music. His compositions blend the structure of classical forms with the Romantic expressiveness characteristic of the period, see Symphony No. 1 in C minor, Op. 68.

Bramante, Donato (bruh-MAHN-tay) c. 1444–1514 High Renaissance architect. He began the designs for the Basilica of St. Peter's, which was not completed until after his death. Designer of the Church of San Pietro in Montorio, Rome.

Braque, Georges (JORJ BRAWK) 1882–1963 French painter. One of the founders of Cubism. Many of his paintings are abstract still-lives depicting composite images of how the mind approaches the visual problem of perception. Outstanding paintings include *Violin and Palette*.

Breton, André (ahn-DRAY bre-TONG) 1896–1966 French poet, essayist, and critic. In 1916 he joined the Dadaist group, and in 1922 turned to Surrealism. He published his first Surrealist manifesto in 1924 and became editor of *La Révolution surréaliste*. His major novel, *Nadja*, was published in 1928, and his collected poems in 1948.

Bronze Age 3000–1000 BCE Period marked by the use of bronze for tools and weapons, and ending with the introduction of iron.

Bruckner, Anton (AHN-ton BROOK-ner) 1824–1896 Austrian composer and organist. He wrote nine symphonies (the last unfinished), four Masses, several smaller sacred works, and choral works. His music, influenced by Wagner and Schubert, was unique for its modulations and dissonance, see Symphony No. 8 in C minor.

Bruegel, Pieter (The Elder) (Pee-tuhr BROY-gull) 1525–1569 Flemish painter. His works portray the full range of human existence, from the grotesque, as in *The Triumph of Death*, to the sublime. Often he depicted peasant life, as in his *Peasant Wedding Feast*, and placed his humble subjects in carefully rendered landscapes, see *Hunters in the Snow*.

Brunelleschi, Filippo (fih-LEE-poe broo-nuh-LESS-kee) 1377–1446 Renowned Florentine architect and sculptor; designer of the duomo for the Cathedral of Florence. He introduced a style of gallery called *loggias*, which was imitated throughout Europe. Other works include the Pazzi Chapel and Foundling Hospital, examples of the grace, simplicity, and precision of Renaissance architecture.

bubonic plague or the Black Death. A pandemic that spread throughout Europe in the 1340s. Estimated to have killed between thirty to sixty percent of Europe's population depending on the area.

Buddha (BOO-duh) c. 563–483 BCE Title meaning "the enlightened one." Also called Siddhartha Gautama (si-DAHR-tuh GAW-tuh-muh). He is the founder of Buddhism, in which he calls his disciples to take the "Middle Way" by following the Four Noble Truths.

Buñuel, Luis (loo-EES boon-WELL) 1900–1983 Spanish filmmaker. Considered Spanish cinema's finest director, his works include the surrealist films *Un Chien Andalou* and *L'Âge D'Or*.

Buonarroti, Michelangelo (bwo-nuh-ROW-tee) 1475–1564 Italian sculptor and painter. Favorite of Lorenzo de' Medici for whom he designed the Medici Chapel. His most well-known sculptures include the *David*, *La Pieta*, and *Moses*. These works show his precise attention to the musculature and grace of the human (especially male) form. Painter of the frescos on the ceiling of the Sistine Chapel, which depict major events from the Old and New Testaments.

burin (BYUHR-in) Sharp-pointed steel instrument used for incising the lines for an engraving.

Bushmen A people of South Africa, living around the Kalahari Desert, noted for their vivid painting.

Byrd, William c. 1540–1623 Foremost English composer of the Elizabethan age. He wrote music for the virginal, several secular instrumental and vocal pieces, such as his elegy *Ye Sacred Muses*, as well as music for the Catholic and Protestant church, including three Latin masses.

Byron, Lord 1788–1824 Considered one of the greatest and most influential English Romantic poets, his language and themes are reflective of his passionate life. Among his most famous works are *Childe Harold's Pilgrimage* and *Don Juan*.

cadence (KAYD-enss) A passage that brings a musical sequence to a close; can serve either as a momentary musical "resting point" or as the conclusion of a section, movement, or piece.

caliph (KAY-lif) From the word *kalifa* meaning "successor" in Arabic. The spiritual and civil leader of the Islamic state and believed to be a successor to Muhammad.

call-and-response A back-and-forth interplay of melodic phrases between musicians that mimics the quality of dialogue.

calligraphy Literally, fine handwriting; the cultivating of writing as an art form.

Calvin, John 1509–1564 French theologian. He was a leader in the Protestant Reformation.

cameo carving Small engraved sculptures on shell or stone in which figures in relief are set off from the background of the shell or stone.

Camus, Albert (ka-MOO) 1913–1960 Algerian-born French existentialist writer. Coeditor of the left-wing newspaper *Combat*. Earned an international reputation with his nihilistic novel, *The Stranger*. Winner of the Nobel Prize for Literature in 1957.

Candide (kan-DEED) 1759 Classic novel by Voltaire aimed at ridiculing the German philosopher Leibnitz for his unreserved optimism.

canon Authoritative list of books accepted in the Bible. In general, the body of work considered fundamental to a particular field of knowledge.

cantata (kahn-TAH-tah) Short oratorios, alternating arias and recitative.

canto (pl. cantos) (KAHN-towz) Italian for "songs." Used to describe the sections of Dante Alighieri's *Commedia*.

cantor Musical director who leads singing in synagogue or church services. In the Christian church, this position was officially established in 361 CE in order to discourage professionalization of musical performances intended as worship.

cantus (KAHN-toose) Early term for singing as opposed to *musica*, which meant the ordering of tones and intervals.

cantus planus (CAHN-toose PLAH-noose) Latin for "plain song." The traditional songs used in the liturgy of the Catholic Church.

canzone (pl. canzoni) (kahn-TSOH-nee) Italian for "songs"; generally offer more literary texts than ballads.

canzoniere (kahn-tsoh-NYEH-reh) Italian word for song book.

capital The head, or crowning part, of a column, supporting the weight of the entablature.

capitularies (kuh-PICH-uh-lair-ee) Official letters with legal and administrative stipulations sent out under the imperial seal.

Caravaggio (kar-uh-VAH-joe) 1573–1610 Italian Baroque painter. His works used dramatic contrasts of light and shade, a technique called *chiaroscuro*, which was imitated by many subsequent artists. His emotion-

ally powerful and honest depiction of the humanity in religious subjects is exemplified in *The Calling of Saint Matthew*, *The Martyrdom of Saint Matthew*, and *Madonna di Loreto*.

Caravan routes Trade routes, often through rough terrain (e.g., the Sahara Desert), used by groups of merchants traveling together for reasons of safety.

Carmina Burana (car-MEE-nuh buh-RAH-nuh) 1935–1936 CE A modern choral composition by Carl Orff of Goliardic verse (medieval student's verse).

Carracci, Annibale (kuh-RAH-chee) 1560–1609 Italian Baroque painter. Decorated the galleria of the Palazzo Farnese with light-hearted frescos depicting the loves of gods and goddesses as in *The Triumph of Bacchus and Ariadne*. His works also emphasized the natural landscape as seen in *The Flight into Egypt*.

Carter, Howard 1874–1939 CE English archaeologist who discovered the sealed tomb of Tutankhamen.

Carthage (KAR-thihj) Ancient city in northern Africa originally founded by the Pheonicians in the 9th century BCE. It was destroyed in 146 BCE in the Punic Wars.

caryatids (kair-ee-AT-idz) Female statues used instead of columns to support a roof, as on the South Porch of the Erechtheum (eh-REK-thee-uhm).

caste system Hindu system of organizing class distinctions. Each caste has its unique position within Indian society and accompanying privileges and sanctions. Caste is transferred from one generation to the next within a family.

Castiglione, Baldassare (bal-dal-SAR-ay koss-tee-lee-OW-nay) 1478–1529 Italian writer and diplomat. Studied in Milan and began a career at court of Urbino. His chief work, *Il cortegiano* or "The Courtier" is a manual of etiquette in which he describes the virtues of an ideal courtier, including being a *uomo universale* or "well-rounded person" and exhibiting *sprezzatura* or "effortless mastery."

catacomb (KAT-uh-cohm) An underground cemetery.

catharsis (kuh-THAHR-siss) According to Aristotle, the "cleansing of the soul" experienced by a person who has undergone a tragic series of events.

cathedral The church of the bishop named for the seat or chair (*cathedra*) from which he preached and taught.

Catullus (kuh-TULL-uss) c. 80–54 BCE Roman lyric poet.

Cellini, Benvenuto (ben-ve-NOO-toe che-LEE-nee) 1500–1571 Florentine goldsmith, sculptor, engraver, and writer. His famed *Autobiography* describes his life as an artist and adventurer. His artistic works include a bronze statue of *Perseus* in Florence.

Ceres (SEER-eez) Goddess of agriculture.

Cervantes (Saavedra), Miguel de (mee-GELL de ser-VAHN-tess) 1547–1616 Spanish writer and playwright. His best-known work, *Don Quixote*, is considered the greatest novel in the Spanish language. In it he follows the humorous and ultimately tragic misadventures of a man who imagines that he is a medieval knight in the age of chivalry.

Cerveteri (ser-vuh-TER-ee) Site of an Etruscan city.

Cézanne, Paul (shey-ZANN) 1839–1906 French Post-impressionist painter. He greatly influenced the development of 20th century art, especially Cubism. Cézanne challenged conventional values by insisting on the communication of his personal vision and the expressive integrity of the painting itself as an entity, regardless of the literal appearance of the subject matter. See *Still Life with Commode* and *Mont Sainte-Victoire*.

Chaeronea (ker-uh-NEE-uh) Ancient city in eastern Greece. Site of the victory of Philip of Macedon over the Athenians and Thebans.

Chagall, Marc (shuh-GALL) 1887–1985 Russian Expressionist artist and forerunner of Surrealism. His paintings are characterized by a dream-like quality and include animals, objects, and images from Russian folklore, as seen in his *Green Violinist*.

Chandra Gupta II (SHAHN-druh GOOP-tuh) ruled c. 380–c. 415 CE Also known as "The Sun of Power," he was the most powerful of the Gupta emperors under whose reign India achieved its zenith in cultural achievements, economic stability, and religious tolerance. This period is also referred to as The Golden Age of India.

chanson (shan-SAHN) Popular French song.

Chansons de geste (shan-SAHN, JEST) From medieval French literature, "songs of deeds." Epic poems composed about prominent figures or legendary events. Also called *chansons d'histoire* or "songs of history."

chapel A small worship space either free standing or part of a larger church.

Chartres (Cathedral of) (SHAR-truh) Rebuilt after a fire in 1194 CE. Considered the finest example of French Gothic architecture. As early as the 9th century, Chartres was a major pilgrimage site for Christians who believed it held a relic of the Virgin Mary.

Châteaux de Chambord (SHAH-tow duh SHAM-bor) Built along the Loire River. Begun in 1519 by King Louis I in central France, it combines the French Gothic style with the decorative motifs typical of Italian Renaissance architecture.

Chaucer, Geoffrey 1340–1400 Considered the greatest English writer of his century, his most renowned literary work is *The Canterbury Tales*, twenty-three stories told by a group of pilgrims on their journey from London to the shrine of Saint Becket of Canterbury. Through these tales, Chaucer represents medieval culture, the concerns, values, and weaknesses of the average person. His vivid characters have become standard types in English literature.

Chefren (KEFF-ruhn) 2575–2525 BCE Egyptian pharaoh who built the second of the three great pyramids at Giza and the colossal Great Sphinx.

Cherubino (kair-oo-BEE-noh) Pageboy in Mozart's opera *The Marriage of Figaro*, remembered best for his aria "Non so più."

Chi Rho (kee row) First two letters of the Greek word for Christ, prominent in early Christian art.

Chiang Kai-shek (JANG kigh-SHEK) 1887–1975 Leader of the Kuomintang and later president of Nationalist China.

chiaroscuro (kya-row-SKOO-row) A painting technique that employs extreme contrasts between light and darkness.

Chikamatsu, Monzaemon (MAWN-zigh-uh-MAWN CHEE-kuh-MAHT-soo) 1653–1723 Japanese dramatist. Author of tragedies, historical romances, and kabuki plays. He influenced the development of modern Japanese theater. Among his most famous plays is *The Love Suicide at Amijima*.

china Porcelain pottery of high quality.

Chopin, Frédéric (FREH-der-ik SHOW-pan) 1810–1849 Polish Romantic composer and pianist. Chopin wrote predominantly for piano, including nocturnes and etudes, and incorporated folk dances and songs into the melodies of his mazurkas and polonaises. His work reflects desire for personal expression over concern for formal structure, as heard in his twenty-four Preludes, Op. 28.

chorale prelude Instrumental music that uses a familiar hymn or sacred song as the basis of an improvisation.

chorale variation Instrumental music consisting of a set of variations upon melodies taken from a familiar hymn or sacred song.

chorus The collective body that interacts with the individual actors in a Greek tragedy (for example, the People of Thebes). Singers and performers of the dithyrambic hymn.

Chou Dynasty (SHOO) c. 1110–c. 221 BCE Under this dynasty, China was divided into separate kingdoms or feudal states. The last 200 years were known as the Period of the Warring States.

Christ Greek translation of Hebrew *messiah* meaning "anointed one."

Chrysostom (John) (KRISS-uss-tumm) 347?–407 CE Greek prelate. Commonly known as Saint John, his eloquent preaching earned him the title "Golden Mouth."

Cicero (SISS-uh-roe) 106–43 BCE Roman statesman, orator, and philosopher whose works introduced Greek philosophy to Rome.

Cimabue (chee-muh-BOO-ay) 1240?–1302? Italian painter merited for introducing naturalistic elements into the Italo-Byzantine style. Considered the first master of the Florentine school of painting; his works include the *Crucifixion* and *Madonna Enthroned*.

cithara (SITH-uh-ruh) Greek musical instrument. A seven-stringed lyre.

civilization Society characterized by settlement in urban environs with a system of government, shared religious beliefs, a system of writing, distinct social classes set apart by wealth and occupation, and specialized skills and tools for the production, manufacture, and trade of goods.

Cleopatra (klee-uh-PA-truh) 69–30 BCE Queen of Egypt. First the lover of Julius Caesar and later wife to Mark Antony. She was defeated and captured by Octavian (Augustus), after which she committed suicide.

clerestory (KLEER-stoe-ree) Windows set above the arches and below the roof of a building.

cloister (KLOY-stuhr) Technically, the covered interior walkways in a monastery, but more broadly, the interior of a monastery that was generally off-limits to laypeople.

Clytemnestra (kly-tuhm-NESS-truh) According to Greek mythology, the wife of Agamemnon who murders her husband and is later killed by her son Orestes.

coda The Italian word for "tail"; the concluding section of a sonata form movement

Codex (KOE-decks) Book with bound pages of parchment used instead of scrolls.

Codex Sinaiticus (Koe-decks sin-ay-IT-ick-uss) The earliest known Greek codex of the New

Testament, found in the monastery of Saint Catherine at the foot of Mount Sinai.

color field That form of painting characterized by its focus on color as the very description of a painting.

combine paintings Term used to describe works of art that add actual objects to the paintings, which frequently jut out from the canvas, as in Rauschenberg's collages.

conceptual style The depiction of an ideal form rather than its actual appearance.

Concerto grosso (kun-SHER-tow GROW-soe) A composition that alternates between the full orchestra and a small group of soloists, generally in three movements: fast-slow-fast.

Confucius (kuhn-FYOO-shuss) c. 551–479 BCE Chinese philosopher and teacher whose sayings and works, collected after his death, became the canon of Confucianism. During his life, he traveled throughout China teaching his pupils to be virtuous, educated, and to have a proper sense of duty and decorum.

Constable, John 1776–1837 English painter. Known for depicting the physical beauty of the natural world, as in his landscape *Hay Wain*.

Constantine I (CAWN-stun-teen) 288?–337 CE First Christian emperor. During his reign he rebuilt Byzantium, calling it Nova Roma, establishing it as the new capital of the Roman Empire. After his death, the city was renamed Constantinople in his honor. Constantine I put an end to the official policy of persecuting Christians. Also referred to as "Constantine the Great."

Copernicus, Nicolas (kuh-PURR-nih-kuss) 1473–1543 Polish founder of modern astronomy. His treatise, published in 1543, *De revolutionibus orbium coelestium* (On the Revolutions of the Celestial Spheres) asserts the theory of the solar-centered system.

Corinth (KOR-inth) An ancient city in the northeast Peloponnesus.

Corneille, Pierre (PYAIR kor-NEY) 1606–1684 Prolific French poet and playwright. His plays *Médée* and *Le Cid* established him as the creator of French classical tragedy. He also wrote several comedies, such as *The Liar*.

cornice (KOR-niss) Top part of a Greek temple that projects over the rest of the building.

Cosimo de' Medici (KOE-sih-maw deh MEH-duh-chee)1389–1464 Often called Cosimo the Elder. First member of the Medici family to rule Florence. Patron of the arts, successful banker, and shrewd political manipulator. Founder of the Medici Library and an academy for Greek studies.

counterpoint From the Latin word *contrapunctum* or "against the note." A musical form that developed in the late medieval period involving multiple melodies moving in opposition to one another to create a rich musical texture.

Counter-Reformation In response to the success of Protestantism, the Catholic Church reaffirmed its authority and doctrines, as outlined in the Councils of Trent, and began campaigns both within the priesthood and the artistic community to amplify the religious authority, splendor, and power of the church.

couplet (CUP-let) Two lines of a poem in which the last words of each line typically rhyme.

Courbet, Gustave (gooss-TAHV coor-BEH) 1819–1877 French painter. A proponent of the working classes and a founder of Realism, his pictures depict everyday scenes absent of idealism, such as *Burial at Ornans*. His best-known work is the large *Studio of the Painter: An Allegory of Realism*.

courtier (CORE-tee-uhr) A person who is attached to a royal court and who is trained to act appropriately.

covenant (KUV-uh-nuhnt) In biblical terms, the agreement between God and humanity (originally the ancient Israelites) that he would protect them in

exchange for their faith and obedience as set down in the Scriptures.

Crécy, Battle of 1346 (cray-SEE) Battle in The Hundred Years War in which the French suffered enormous casualties at the hands of the better armed English, estimated to include over thirty thousand fatalities.

Creon (KREE-on) Legendary king of Thebes and successor to Oedipus.

cuneiform (kyoo-NEE-uh-form) A system of writing, common in the ancient Near East, using characters made up of wedge shapes.

curia (KYOO-ree-uh) The body of tribunals and assemblies through which the pope governed the church.

Cybele (SIB-uh-lee) Mother goddess of ancient Anatolia.

Cyclades (SICK-luh-deez) A group of islands southeast of mainland Greece in the Aegean Sea.

Dadaism (DAH-dah-izm) A cultural movement that emerged in Zurich after World War I. Its proponents reacted to the destruction of the war by rejecting prevailing social and artistic standards and embracing chaos and spontaneity. Predecessor to the Avant Garde and Absurdist movements.

Dagulf Psalter late 8th century CE A book of psalms made as a gift for Pope Hadrian I; an example of elaborate ivory work and illumination (decoration of a manuscript).

Daimyo (DAYM-yo) Feudal Japanese warlords.

Dali, Salvador (SAL-vah-dor DAH-lee) 1904–1989 Spanish painter. Master among surrealists, his graphic realism depicts dreamlike, sometimes disquieting images as in his most famous *The Persistence of Memory*.

Darius (duh-RYE-uss) r. 521–486 BCE King of Persia who attacked mainland Greece and was defeated by the Athenians at the Battle of Marathon in 490 BCE.

Daumier, Honoré (on-oh-REY doe-MYAY) 1808–1879 French painter and caricaturist. Won contemporary fame for satirical cartoons about government corruption and was imprisoned for caricaturing the king. An opponent of Classicism, he painted strongly realistic pictures, such as *The Third Class Carriage, Three Lawyers in Conversation,* and *The Refugees.*

David, Jacques-Louis (JAHK-LWEE dah-VEED) 1748–1825 French painter. An influential figure of the Neoclassical movement, his work demonstrates a revived interest in Classical ideas and forms as well as the revolutionary political and social climate of the new French Republic, as seen in *Oath of the Horatii* and *Napoleon Crossing the Alps.*

De Pisan, Christine (kree-STEEN deh pee-ZAH) 1365–1428? One of Europe's first female professional writers. Author of fifteen books, including *A letter to the God of Love* and *The Book of the City of Ladies,* in which she responds to Jean de Meung's criticism of women.

Debussy, Claude (DEBB-you-see) 1862–1918 French composer. Influenced by the Impressionist movement in painting, his music is characterized by shifting tone colors and mood, as heard in his orchestral work *La Mer.* Some of his finest compositions include music composed for the piano.

Decius (DEE-shuss) 201–250 CE Roman emperor under whom there was widespread persecution of Christians.

deduction A process of reasoning that begins with a general assertion and then seeks instances that confirm it.

Degas, Edgar (dey-GAH) 1834–1917 French painter during the Impressionist movement. His paintings portrayed intimate moments in people's everyday lives, showing spontaneity of action often at unusual angles, see *The Tub.* One of his favorite subjects was ballet dancers, as in *The Rehearsal.*

dies irae (DEE-ess EE-ray) Latin for "day of wrath."

Delacroix, Eugène (oo-JEHN de-lah-KWAH) 1798–1863 French painter and leader of the Romantic Movement. His

historical and dramatic works often portrayed violent events or macabre subjects causing an uproar in the artistic community, as in his *The Massacre at Chios* (KIGH-oss) and *The Death of Sardanapalus* (sar-dun-AH-polus), based on the 1821 play by Byron. His painting signifies a shift toward the use of bold fields of color.

Delian League (DEE-lee-uhn) 5th century BCE Association of Greek city-states.

Demeter (duh-MEE-ter) Greek goddess of agriculture, marriage, and social order.

Demosthenes (di-MOSS-thuh-neez) 384?–322 BCE Athenian statesman and orator who led the resistance against Philip of Macedon.

Der Blaue Reiter German for "The Blue Rider." A group of German artists whose works were fundamental to the continuation of the German Expressionist movement.

Descartes, René (ruh-NAY day-CART) 1596–1650 French philosopher and mathematician. Called the father of modern science, he rejected ideas founded on assumptions or beliefs and accepted only those ideas that could be proven by or induced from direct observation.

descriptive style The depiction of a form striving for natural, realistic representation of physical characteristics.

deuterocanonical books (doo-tuhr-oh-kuh-NON-uh-kuhl) Certain books, other than those contained in the New and Old Testaments, that are accepted by Roman Catholics and Orthodox Christians as canonical. These texts were part of the Greek Old Testament called the *Septuagint* version.

development The central section of a sonata form movement in which a composer changes and combines the themes stated in the opening **exposition**.

Diaghilev, Sergei (SER-gay dee-AH-gul-eff) 1872–1929 Russian ballet impresario. His company, *the Ballets Russes,* was founded in Paris in 1909 and revolutionized the world of dance. In

Diaghilev's ballets, music and scenery were integral parts of the performance. His productions were based on the principles of asymmetry and perpetual motion.

dialectics (die-uh-LECK-ticks) Originally from the Greek word *dialectics* or "the art of conversation." The study and development of logical theories and arguments.

Dickens, Charles 1812–1865 English writer. One of the most popular and widely read novelists, his work centers on themes of poverty, industrialization, human hypocrisy, and injustice, as in *Hard Times* and *Oliver Twist.* Known for his vivid portrayals of characters and intense development of plot.

Dickenson, Emily 1830–1886 American poet. Many of her poems reflect a struggle between her private spiritual life and traditional religious faith. Although most of her work was published posthumously, she is now considered one of the greatest and most influential American poets.

Diderot, Denis (du-NEE DEE-duh-row) 1713–1784 French philosopher and writer. A towering figure of the 18th century, he influenced the intellectual and political developments in prerevolutionary France. Creator and editor of the *Encyclopédie,* a catalogue of contemporary knowledge in which he argues that humans are rational beings whose minds should be free of any political or religious control.

Dido (DIE-doe) Mythological queen of Carthage who committed suicide after being abandoned by Aeneas.

Die Brücke German for "The Bridge." A group of German artists whose works initiated the German Expressionist movement.

Diocletian (die-uh-KLEE-shun) 245–313 CE Roman emperor under whom the last major persecution of Christians occurred. In 286 CE he divided the Roman Empire into two territories, east and west, in order to rule more effectively.

Dionysius the Areopagite (die-uh-NISH-ee-uss, a-ree-OP-uh-gight) 5th century CE A monk whose work on mystical theology was strongly influenced by Neoplatonic philosophers. In the early medieval period, a doctrine developed called Pseudo-Dionysius, which maintained that everything contains the essence of God.

Dionysus (die-uh-NIGH-suss) Ancient Greek god of wine and emotions (drama).

diptych (DIP-tick) Painting made up of two panels.

dithyramb (DITH-uh-ram) Choral hymn sung in honor of the god Dionysus, often wild and violent in character.

dome Circular vault made up of a series of arches intersecting each other around a central axis.

Dome of the Rock (The) later 7th century A major Islamic landmark in Jerusalem built by the Caliph Abd al Malik. It is one of the earliest Islamic buildings in the world and exhibits the influence of Roman and Byzantine architectural design.

Don Quixote (don kee-HOE-tay) See *Cervantes*.

Donatello (daw-nuh-TELL-oh) 1386–1466 Florentine sculptor. Noted for his highly individual interpretation of biblical subjects. His most renowned pieces include *David*, the first free-standing statue of a nude sculpted since Roman antiquity, and the emotionally powerful, *Saint Mary Magdalene*.

Donne John (DUNN) 1572–1631. English poet and cleric. An eloquent Anglican preacher and dean of St. Paul's Cathedral, he is known as one of the greatest English metaphysical poets for his passionate and spiritual verse, particularly his Holy Sonnets. His lyric poems show a renewed interest in self-analysis.

Dorian (DOR-ce-uhn) Mode of Greek music expressing powerful and at times warlike sentiments.

Doric (DOR-ick) One of the Greek orders of architecture, simple and austere in style. *Compare Ionic*. The major differences between the Doric and Ionic orders are the form of the capitals and the treatment of the frieze. The Doric frieze is divided into triglyphs and metopes.

Doryphoros (dor-IFF-or-uss) or *Spear bearer* A bronze statue by Polykleitos that illustrates his theory of ideal beauty.

Dostoevsky, Fyodor (dah-stuh-YEFF-skee) 1821–1881 Russian novelist. His masterpiece *Crime and Punishment* is a pointed exploration of human psychology and morality. His works show the influence of the ideas of Sigmund Freud and his own Russian Orthodox Christian faith. His other novels include *The Idiot*, *Notes from the Underground*, and *The Brothers Karamazov*.

drum Supporting structure for a dome or *duomo*.

Dryden, John 1631–1700 English poet, writer, and critic. Many of his works reflect his admiration for the ancient Roman poets, drawing parallels between English achievements and the glory of the Augustan age.

dualists Presocratic philosophers who believed in the existence of two worlds: one real, the other ideal. Chief proponents of this school of philosophy were Heraclitus (her-uh-KLIE-tuss) of Ephesus and Parmenides (pahr-MIN-i-deez) of Elea.

Duccio di Buoninsegna (DOO-choh dee bwon-ihn-SEN-ya) c. 1255–1318 Italian painter whose work exemplifies the Byzantine aesthetic tradition to which he brought greater detail and emotional depth. Among his most revered works is the *Maestá* for the altar of Siena Cathedral.

Duchamp, Marcel (mar-SELL doo-SHAWN) 1887–1968 French artist. He led the American Dada movement and was among the first to construct *mobiles* (sculptures with moving parts) and *ready-mades* (works made of found objects). His most famous piece is *L.H.O.O.Q*, a reproduction of Leonardo's *Mona Lisa* to which he added a moustache and goatee.

Dufay, Guillaume (gee-YOME doo-FAHY) c. 1400–1474 French composer. He composed several *chansons* and secular motets. He introduced the folk song into the music of the Mass, as seen in *L'homme armé* (The Man in Armor).

duomo (DWOH-mo) Italian for "dome." Used generally to refer to an Italian cathedral; more specifically, "Il Duomo" refers to the Cathedral in Florence.

Dura-Europos A small town in Syria on the Euphrates river. Site of a 1930s archeological discovery that revealed evidence of early Christian, Jewish, and pagan (Roman) communities coexisting. Destroyed by the Persian army in 265 CE.

Dürer, Albrecht (ALL-brekt DOOHR-er) 1471–1528 German painter, printmaker, and theoretician. Influenced by his contact with Italian art, his work reflected a strong sense of the artist as genius as well as a focus on linear perspective. His works include the *Knight, Death, and the Devil*, *The Fall of Adam* and his *Self-Portrait*. Author of the *Libri IV de Humani Corporis Proportionibus* (Four Books on Human Proportions), a series of theoretical treatises examining principles of mathematics, perspective, and ideal proportions.

Eakins, Thomas 1844–1916 American painter, photographer, and sculptor. His painting *The Swimming Hole* shows a concern for accurate representation indicative of the general movement toward Realism within the arts of the period.

ecclesia (uh-KLEE-zee-uh) The Athenian General Assembly.

echinus (ih-KIGH-nuss) Convex disc forming part of a Doric capital.

Eisenstein, Sergei (SER-gay EYES-uhn-stine) 1898–1948 Soviet filmmaker. Considered one of the most influential artists in cinema, his powerful films portray his vision of class struggle and support for the socialist revolution. He developed the editing technique *montage* (the sharp juxtaposition of shots), which uses a quick series of images for dramatic effect. Most famous films include *Potemkin* and *Alexander Nevsky*.

El Greco (Theotokopoulos) **(thay-ah-tah-KAW-poo-loss)** 1541–1614 Greek born Spanish painter. His works exhibit sharp contrast of colors and unusual proportions characteristic of Mannerism. His masterpiece is *The Burial of the Count de Orgaz*.

Electra (uh-LEK-truh) Legendary daughter of Agamemnon, who incites her brother Orestes to kill their mother Clytemnestra.

Elgin, Lord (ELL-jin) British ambassador to Constantinople who removed several sculptures from the Parthenon in the early 19th century.

Empfindsamkeit (emp-FEEHND-zam-kite) The German word for "sensitiveness." In music, the term was used to describe the emotional music popular in the mid-18th century.

Encaustic method of painting (enn-KOSS-tik) A technique common in Roman funerary portraits in which pigment is mixed with wax and then fixed to a surface with heat.

engraving Process of incising lines on a copper plate, which is then printed to produce an impression (itself also known as an engraving).

Enlightened despots Eighteenth century rulers who, while retaining full powers, sought the improved welfare of their subjects.

Ennius (EN-ee-uss) 239–169 BCE Roman poet and playwright. Known as the father of Roman poetry. Author of the *Annals*, an epic poem chronicling the history of Rome.

ensemble In opera, a scene in which several characters sing simultaneously.

entablature (en-TAB-lauh-chuhr) The part of a Greek or Roman temple above the columns, normally consisting of architrave, frieze, and cornice. In architecture more generally, the upper part of a wall supported by a column or pillar.

entasis (EN-tuh-siss) A slight convexity given to a column or tower as seen in the architectural design of the *Doric* column, which is thickest at a point one-third from the base and then tapers to the top.

epic poem A long poetic composition that recounts events and achievements in the life of a hero.

Epictetus (ep-ick-TEE-tuss) c. 50–134 CE Stoic writer and philosopher who established schools in both Rome and Greece. Author of *Enchiridion* (*Handbook*), a guide to daily life.

Epicureanism (ep-uh-kyoo-REE-uhn-ism) A philosophy, originally Greek, holding that the correct goal and principle of human actions should be pleasure.

Epicurus (ep-i-KYOO-russ) 341–271 BCE Greek philosopher.

epiphany Literally: a "showing forth." Frequently used as a term for a sudden illumination, intuition, or insight.

episcopal (uh-PISK-uh-puhl) Pertaining to the governing authority of bishops. Compare to **Episcopal**, a term referring to the Anglican Church or a branch of it.

Erasmus, Desiderius (dess-uh-DEE-ree-uss i-RAZZ-muss) 1466–1536 Christian humanist. Author of *Enchiridion Militis Chrtiani*, a practical handbook on Christian humanism, and *The Praise of Folly*, in which he reveals the immorality and vice prevalent in European society.

Erechtheum (uh-REK-thee-uhm) began c. 420. BCE Athenian temple distinguished by its porch of caryatids, or *Porch of the Maidens*.

essay A short literary work, generally in prose, dealing with a specific topic.

ethos (EE-thohs) Term used by Plato to describe a person's moral character.

Etruscans (ih-TRUSS-kuhns) 800–500 BCE An ancient people who inhabited the region now known as Tuscany in north central Italy. They had a sophisticated and technologically advanced civilization that contributed to the subsequent rise of Roman culture and power.

Eumenides **(yoo-MEN-uh-deez)** The last play in Aeschylus' Oresteia trilogy, literally translates as "the kindly ones," referring to the Furies in his second play, *The Libation Bearers*.

Euphrates (yoo-FRAY-teez) One of the two rivers (the other being the Tigris) bordering the fertile crescent of ancient Mesopotamia.

Euripides (yoo-RIP-uh-deez) One of the best-known Greek tragic dramatists, his works include the *Suppliant Women, Helen, Iphigenia in Taunus* and *Bacchae*.

Evans, Arthur 1851–1941 CE English archeologist who discovered the ruins of the ancient Minoan civilization at Knossos.

exempla (pl. exemplum) Story or work of art used to illustrate a moral point.

Existentialism A 20th century philosophical movement that emphasizes an individual's existence, freedom, and choice to define oneself and the world subjectively. The first philosopher to use the term was Kierkegaard. Other proponents include writers Jean Paul Sartre and Albert Camus.

exodus Greek for "a going out." Term used for the Israelites' flight from Egypt and the name of the biblical book describing the event.

expatriate Literally "out of one's country." Used for those individuals or communities who live outside of their homeland for extended periods.

exposition The opening section of a sonata form movement, setting out its main themes.

Expressionism Early 20th century style of painting, popular in Germany, which aimed to use color and theme to express the growing social and political tensions of the times.

fabliaux (FA-blee-ohz) Fables, often obscene.

Fauvism (FOE-vizm) From French *les fauves* or "the wild beasts." Early 20th century style of painting characterized by extremes of color and form. See *Henri Matisse*.

Fetes galantes (FETT gal-OHNT) In the 18th century, elegant festivals or parties, held outdoors.

feudal (FYOO-duhl) Describes the highly structured social organization typical of the early Middle Ages based on a pyramidal model with the lord at the top and gradations down to the serfs, who were bound to the land.

Ficino, Marsilio (mar-SEE-lee-oh fee-CHEE-noh) 1433–1499 Italian philosopher. Friend and tutor to the Medicis, he translated numerous Greek classics into Latin and wrote a compendium of Platonism, the *Theologia Platonica*. He contributed significantly to the development of humanism during the Renaissance.

Flaubert, Gustave (goos-TAHV flow-BEAR) 1821–1880 French novelist. In a realistic style, he displays the social problems of his day while making a critique of bourgeois society, as in his most famous novel *Madame Bovary*.

flying buttresses External curved buttresses of medieval churches characteristic of the Gothic style.

forum Originally any open space available for public use. The Forum Romanum (Roman Forum), at the foot of the Capitoline and Palatine Hills, became the center of Roman political, economic, social, and religious life for more than a thousand years.

fourth A musical interval important in the construction of the Greek modes.

Fragonard, Jean-Honoré (JON aw-no-RAY fra-go-NAR) 1732–1806 French rococo painter. Portrayed sumptuous landscapes and subjects in decorative, lightly erotic scenes, such as *Love Letters*.

Frances of Assisi (Saint) (FRAN-siss, uh-SEE-zee) 1181–1226 CE Born Giovanni Bernadone. A religious experience in early manhood led him to turn his back on a life of privilege and become a poor wandering preacher. He was a favorite subject of medieval and Renaissance artists. He was the inspiration for the creation of the Franciscan order of monks, first called "Little Brothers," that stressed poverty, humility, and reverence for the natural world.

fresco Wall painting on moist plaster.

Freud, Sigmund (SIG-moond FROYD) 1856–1939 Viennese physician and pioneer of modern psychology. His book *The Interpretation of Dreams* is considered one of the most influential books on modern thought. In it, he posited the basic elements of the human psyche; the unconscious *id*, which is controlled by the *ego*, or the conscious *self*, and the *superego*, the socially educated self.

frieze (FREEZ) Middle band of the upper part of a Greek or Roman temple.

fugue (FYOOG) Piece of music in which the same themes are repeated and combined in counterpoint.

Furies Goddesses of vengeance who drive Orestes mad in Aeschylus' *Libation Bearers*.

Galileo Galilei (gal-uh-LAY-oh gal-uh-LAY-ee) 1564–1642 Italian astronomer and physicist. Through his invention of the telescope, he empirically confirmed Copernicas' theory of a solar centered system. His discoveries brought ecclesiastical censure, and he was forced to recant before the Inquisition. Author of *Dialogues Concerning Two New Sciences*, which outlined many areas of modern physics.

Galla Placidia built 425–430 CE Roman Mausoleum in Ravenna, Italy. Containing some of the most magnificent and well preserved examples of early mosaic art.

Galleria (gall-uh-REE-uh) (in a Baroque palace) Formal reception hall.

Gandharan (guhn-DAHR-uhn) Indian Buddhist sculpture influenced by Greek models.

gargoyle (GAR-goyl) Extravagant animal carving, symbolizing the flight of demons, used on gothic churches to serve as drains.

Gauguin, Paul (go-GAN) 1848–1903 French Postimpressionist painter. From 1891 he lived in Tahiti and the Marquesas Islands, using local people for subjects. His style, *Synthétisme*, reflected his disdain for civilization and the inspiration he found in primitive peoples. Among his best-known works are *Ia Orana Maria* and *The Vision After the Sermon*.

Genji (jen-jee) Hero in Murasaki's *The Tale of Genji*, which chronicles the adventures of a prince in the aristocratic courts of Japan.

Gentileschi, Artemesia (ar-tuh-MISS-ee-uh jen-tee-LESS-kee) c. 1597–c. 1652 Italian painter. One of the first women to significantly contribute to the art of her time, her work reflects the influence of Caravaggio, as seen in her most well-known painting *Judith and Holofernes*.

geometric style 900–700 BCE An artistic style employed by the Greeks, emphasizing linear designs and precise mathematical relationships.

geranos (jair-uh-noss) An ancient Greek dance in which performers executed intricate steps resembling the movements of a crane.

Géricault, Théodore (teh-oh-DOOR jeh-ree-KOWE) 1791–1824 French painter and pioneer of the Romantic Movement. In Paris, his huge *Raft of the Medusa* aroused controversy due to the macabre subject matter and political overtones. His work influenced later artists, most notably Delacroix.

Gesamtkunstwerk (geh-ZAHMT-KOONST-verk) German term invented by Wagner meaning "complete art work" to describe his combination of music, poetry, the visual arts, and movement in a single work.

Ghiberti, Lorenzo (ghee-BAIR-tee) 1378–1455 Italian sculptor and goldsmith. Best known for his paneled North and East Doors of the Baptistry of the Cathedral of Florence. The East Doors are also called the "Gates of Paradise."

Gilgamesh (GILL-guh-mesh) c. 2700 BCE Sumerian ruler of Uruk around whose name developed a series of legends leading to one of the first great masterpieces of poetic expression, *The Epic of Gilgamesh*.

Giorgione, Giorgio di (jor-JOAN-nee) c. 1478–1510 Italian painter who studied and worked in Venice under Giovanni Bellini. His early paintings exhibit a precise arrangement of subjects and a unique attention to light, as seen in the *Enthroned Madonna with Saints Liberalis and Francis of Assisi*. Later his work increasingly treated secular subjects, as in *Le Concert Champêtre*.

Giotto (JAH-toe) 1266–1337 Florentine painter, architect, and sculptor whose work moved away from the highly stylized Byzantine aesthetic sensibility to a more natural and personally expressive representation of the human form. His paintings include *Madonna Enthroned*, *The Meeting of Joachim and Anna* and *The Lamentation over the Dead Christ*.

Gnadenaltar (GNAH-duhn-ahl-tuhr) The German word for "Mercy Altar." Generally found in pilgrimage churches in southern Germany and Austria.

Godot (guh-DOE) *Waiting for Godot* (1954) An influential play by Samuel Beckett.

Goethe, Johann Wolfgang von (YO-hahn VOLFF-gahng fon GUHR-tuh) 1749–1832 German poet, dramatist, novelist, and scientist. Leader of the literary movement known as *Sturm und Drang* or "Storm and Stress," which rejected Neoclassicism in favor of the expression of raw and original feeling. His novel, *The Sorrows of Young Werther*, in which he recounts the tragic story of an idealist, was enormously popular and appealed to Romantic sensibilities.

Goliardic verse (goal-YAR-dik) Term used to describe medieval student poetry and songs.

gospel From Medieval English "good news." The Anglo-Saxon word for both Christian preaching and the four books named in the New Testament: Matthew, Mark, Luke, and John.

Gothic Originally a derogatory term, meaning "rude" or "barbaric." Commonly used to describe medieval architecture.

Goya, Francisco (fran-SISS-kow GOY-uh) 1746–1828 Spanish painter. He depicted scenes of violence and injustice, with sometimes brutal realism, as in his *Execution of the Madrilenos* or *Satan Devouring his Sons*, as well as unveiling the hypocrisy of society, as in his portrait *The Family of Charles IV*.

Great Schism (SKIZ-uhm) 1378–1417 Division within the Catholic Church, which led to various groups claiming to be entitled to the papacy (**schism**: a split or division of a group into opposing parties).

Gregorian chant The plain unaccompanied song of church liturgy in which the notes of the chant correlate with the syllables of the liturgical text. Named after Pope Gregory the Great.

ground, groundlings The part of an Elizabethan theater where the spectators stood. These poorer members of the audience became known as the *groundlings*. The ground was sometimes called the *pit*.

Grünewald, Matthias (muh-TAY-uss GROON-uh-valt) c. 1480–1528. German painter. Favorite of the Archbishop of Mainz, his work dealt with religious themes, which he rendered with powerful emotion and unique style, as in his masterpieces for the Isenheim Altarpiece, *Crucifixion* and *Resurrection*.

Guernica (GWER-nee-cah) 1937 Pablo Picasso's surrealistic, allegorical painting, which captures the horror of the bombing of the Basque town of Guernica, which killed many innocent civilians during the Spanish Civil War.

Guido di Arezzo (GWEE-doe dee uh-RET-soe) 11th century Italian musician and philosopher who worked out a system of musical notation that is the basis for modern musical notation.

Guilds Various fraternal associations of craftsmen or merchants organized to maintain standards and protect the interests of its members; a prominent political, social, and economic entity during the medieval period.

Gutenberg, Johan (GOOT-n-berg) c. 1395–1468 Originator of the movable type method of printing. Printed the first Bible in Mainz in 1455.

Hades (HEY-deez) The underworld in classical Greek mythology.

Hadith (huh-DEETH) A body of literature based upon the teachings and practices of Muhammad.

Hagia Sophia (HA-ghee-uh so-PHEE-uh) Principal church of Constantinople, destroyed twice and finally rebuilt in 532 CE under Roman emperor Justinian. Architects Isidore of Miletus and Anthemius of Tralles collaborated in the design of this masterpiece of Byzantine architecture. After the Turks seized Constantinople in 1453, it was converted into a mosque.

haiku (HIGH-koo) Japanese verse form consisting of three lines of five, seven, and five syllables.

Haj (HAJ) The Arabic term for the pilgrimage to Mecca that a Muslim is required to make within a lifetime.

hamartia (hah-mar-TEE-uh) In Greek tragedy, the character flaw in otherwise noble people that causes their tragic fate.

Handel, George Frederick 1685–1759 Leading Baroque composer. German born, yet built his career in England. He wrote several oratorios, the *Messiah* being most well known, and orchestral music, such as *The Water Music* and *The Music for the Royal Fireworks*. He also wrote a series of operas in Italian, which include the famous aria "Ombra mai fu" from *Xerxes*.

Harappa (huh-RAP-uh) Village in Pakistan and site of an ancient Harrapan city in the Indus Valley c. 3300–1600 BCE.

harmony Used by the Greeks to describe certain musical scales; in modern usage, the sounding together of consonant musical pitches.

harpsichord Keyboard instrument, the forerunner of the modern piano.

Harun ar-Rashid (huh-ROON ar-ruh-SHEED) c. 764–809 CE One of the most revered caliphs of Baghdad and subject of several tales in *A Thousand and One Nights*. Patron of the arts and letters. He maintained diplomatic relations with Charlemagne.

Haydn, Franz Joseph 1732–1809 (FRAHNS YO-sef HIDE-n) Austrian composer. He spent most of his career in the employ of Prince Esterhazy. Nicknamed "the Father of the Symphony," he composed over one hundred, his most famous being the London symphonies. He also wrote operas, string quartets, and concertos.

Healer A person with special spiritual powers, often related to fertility.

Hector (HEK-tuhr) A great Trojan hero. Son of Priam who was killed by Achilles.

Hegira (heh-JAHY-ruh) Originally meaning the flight of Muhammad from Mecca to Medina July 16, 622 CE. Now it refers to first day of the Islamic New Year.

Heian (HAY-ON) Japanese commercial and cultural center between 8th–12th centuries (present day Kyoto).

henotheism (HEN-uh-thee-ism) The belief that other gods may exist, but one in particular is chosen to be worshipped.

Henry VIII 1491–1547 King of England who broke from the Catholic Church and thereafter declared himself, in the Act of Supremacy, the English sovereign and the head of the Protestant church in England (later known as the Anglican Church).

Hera (HAIR-uh) Greek goddess, wife of Zeus and patron of women, marriage, and childbirth.

Herodotus (huh-RODD-uh-tuss) 484–420 BCE Greek historian called the Father of History. Considered one of the first writers in the Western tradition of historical prose. Author of the *History of the Persian Wars* and *Rhampsinitus and the thief*.

hieroglyphics (high-ruh-GLIFF-icks) A system of writing in which the characters consist of realistic or stylized pictures of actual objects, animals, or human beings (in whole or part).

high relief See *relief, high*.

Hilda 614–680 CE Abbess of Whitby, a center of learning and meeting place of the church synod, or council, which determined issues of doctrine and administration.

Hildegard of Bingen 1098–1179 CE German abbess, musician, philosopher, and scholar; distinguished for her florid compositions of Gregorian chant, most notably in the song sequence *Symphonia*. Her philosophical works include *Scivias* (The Way to Knowledge). She wrote treatises on medicine, including *Physica* and *Causae et Curae*.

Hillard, Nicolas 1547–1619 English painter. His works include *Ermine Portrait of Queen Elizabeth I* and a number of small portraits, watercolors, and miniatures.

Hinayana (hee-nuh-YAH-nuh) translates to "Lesser Vehicle." One of the two main branches of Chinese Buddhism, more ascetic than the other, Mahayana.

Hokusai Katsushika (HOE-kuh-sigh) 1760–1849 Japanese painter, wood engraver, and printer. Considered a master of polychrome printing, he produced hundreds of images, including the series *Thirty-Six Views of Fuji*.

Holbein, Frances (the Younger) (HOLE-bine) c. 1497–1543 English painter. Served as chief portraitist for Henry VIII. He was charged with painting several portraits of prospective wives for the king, see *Anne of Cleves*.

Homer (HOE-muhr) Between 12th and 9th centuries BCE Greek poet. Reputed author of the great classics the *Iliad* and the *Odyssey*.

Homo erectus (hoe-moe-ee-RECK-tuss) First direct ancestors of modern humans.

Homo sapiens (hoe-moe-SAY-pee-uhnz) Evolved form of *Homo erectus*. First humans.

Honorius (huh-NOR-ee-uss) 395–423 CE Roman emperor of the west.

Horace (HOR-uss) 65–8 BCE Roman lyric poet and satirist whose work was later to influence English poetry.

horarium The daily schedule in a monastery or a church community; a term derived from the Latin word *hora* or "hour."

Hortensian Law Passed in 287 BCE This code made the decisions of plebian assembly binding upon the Senate and all Romans.

Horus (HOR-uhs) Egyptian deity. Morning or sun god, son of Osiris and Isis. Depicted as a man with the head of a falcon.

House of Wisdom (*Bait al-hikma*) completed in 833 CE A library and study center built by Caliph Al-Mamun. It became a center of scholarship where the works of the foremost Greek philosophers were translated and preserved by Arab scholars.

Hroswitha (Roswitha) (rose-VEE-tah) c. 935–c. 1002 CE German nun and poet. Author of several legends and plays modeled after the Roman dramatist Terence. Her literary works aspired to edify and convert, as exemplified in the play *The Conversion of the Harlot Thais*.

Hua-Pen (hoo pen) Chinese short stories based upon the oral tales of travelling storytellers.

hubris (HYOO-briss) Excessive pride and ambition leading to self-destruction.

Hugo, Victor 1802–1885 French Romantic novelist. Author of *Les Miserables*, in which he treats themes of crime, responsibility, and redemption, as well as portraying the injustice and suffering of the poor.

humanism A cultural and intellectual movement which emerged in the Renaissance that embraced the belief in human perfectibility. It inspired a renewed study of the literature and philosophy of ancient Rome and Greece.

Hundred (The) Years War 1337–1453 A devastating war between England and France motivated by commercial rivalry for the wool-manufacturing region of Flanders. Battle of Poitiers in 1356 marked the apex in a series of English victories; however, the war ultimately resulted in a stalemate between the two powers.

hymnody (HIM-nuh-dee) A musical tradition which emerged in Germany as part of the Reformation that stressed vernacular hymns as a means of praise and religious instruction.

Ibsen, Henrik (HEN-rick IB-suhn) 1828–1906 Norwegian playwright and poet. His first major play was *The Pretenders*. Many of his plays explored women's changing roles in society, see *A Doll's House* and *Hedda Gabler*.

Iconoclasm (eye-KAWN-oh-klasm) Literally "image breaking." A movement in the Christian East that militated against the use of icons in worship and devotion.

Ictinus (ick-TIE-nuhs) mid-5th century BCE Greek architect. One of the designers of the Parthenon.

ikegobo Royal altar used by the **Oba** (ruler) of Benin.

Ile de France (eel duh FRAHNS) Literally "the Island of France." Referring to Paris and its surrounding suburbs and towns.

Iliad (ILL-ee-uhd) A Greek epic poem attributed to Homer about the hero Achilles and the Greek siege of Troy.

Ilium (ILL-ee-uhm) Latin name of the ancient city of Troy.

Imam (ih-MOM) The title for a Muslim religious leader.

Imhotep (im-HOE-tep) Egyptian architect who designed the first pyramid for King Zoser c. 2650 BCE.

Impressionism An artistic movement during the late 19th century that radically shifted emphasis away from realism of form and toward capturing light and color as perceived by the eye.

Index A list of forbidden books that was issued by the Catholic Church in the mid-16th century.

induction A system of reasoning that starts from the observation of specific instances and from this proposes a general explanatory theory. *Compare deduction.*

Indulgences Forgiveness of sins in return for prayer, good works, and/or money.

Ingres, Jean Auguste (JON oh-GYOOS AN-gruh) 1780–1867 French painter. Leading proponent of Neoclassical painting in the face of Romanticism, his work harkens back to classical themes of classical painters while reflecting a unique personal vision and masterful control of line and composition.

Inquisition A court created by the Catholic Church to try cases of heresy or other offenses against the church.

intermezzo (in-ter-MET-so) The Italian word for "interlude." Originally used to describe a short musical piece between two longer ones, or between two acts of an opera, it became used by some Romantic composers to describe a short independent composition.

Inversion See *serialism.*

Ionic (EYE-ON-ick) One of the Greek orders of architecture characterized by an elaborate and graceful style with capitals ornamented by volutes and a running frieze of sculpture. *Compare Doric.*

Iphigenia (if-uh-juh-NIGH-uh) Daughter of Agamemnon who is rescued by Artemis from being sacrificed by her father.

Isidore of Miletus (my-LEE-tuss) Greek architect and mathematician who worked with Anthemius of Tralles to build the Hagia Sophia in 532 CE.

Isis (AHY-siss) Egyptian goddess of fertility. Sister and wife of Osiris. Mother of Horus; depicted as a woman with cow's horns.

Isorhythm (EYE-so-rih-thuhm) System of musical composition whereby one voice in a polyphonic work is given a single, repeating rhythm.

Ius Civile **(yoos kuh-WILL-uh)** Rome's Code of Civil Law, first organized under Julius Caesar and later published by Byzantine Emperor Justinian 527-565 BCE. *Ius Civile* made a significant contribution to the development of modern legal systems.

Jannequin, Clement (Cluh-MONT jonn-uh-KANN) c. 1485–1558 French composer of narrative chansons. Enhanced the genre by using real world elements, such as the sounds of birds. His 286 chansons include the well-known, *La Guerre* or "The War."

jongleurs **(jahn-gluhrs)** Itinerant entertainers (musicians, actors, storytellers, and dancers) during the Middle Ages.

Joyce, James 1882–1941 Irish writer. A revolutionary literary innovator, his multifaceted prose combines myth, puns, autobiographical segments, and literary allusions and employs the technique **stream of consciousness**. His most famous novels include *Dubliners* and *Portrait of an Artist as a Young Man.*

Julius Caesar (SEE-zuhr) 100–44 BCE Roman general, statesman, and historian who described his military campaigns in his *Commentaries.* After his triumph over Pompey at the Battle of Pharsalus, he was named dictator of Rome. He was later assassinated by a group of republicans led by Cassius and Brutus.

Justinian (juss-TIN-ee-uhn) 482?–565 CE Roman Emperor who attempted to restore the empire to its former glory. An ardent Christian, he implemented building projects throughout Byzantium including the church of Hagia Sophia, considered a masterpiece of Byzantine architecture. Under his reign, Roman law was revised and codified.

Juvenal (JOO-ven-all) 527–565 CE Roman satirist who sharply criticized the decadence and corruption of Roman society.

Kabuki (kah-BOO-kee) Began 17th century. Japanese drama incorporating dance, highly decorative costumes, music, and dialogue. All roles played by males.

Kafka, Franz (FRAHNS KAHF-kuh) 1883–1924 Czech novelist of German Jewish parents. His short stories and essays, such as The *Metamorphosis*, appeared during his lifetime, but three unfinished novels were published posthumously: *The Trial, The Castle,* and *Amerika.* His vision (often called 'Kafkaesque') depicts society as an indifferent or tortuous bureaucracy in which bewildered individuals search for meaning.

Kahlo, Frieda (KA-low) 1907–1954 Mexican painter. Creator of numerous self-portraits, including the *Self-Portrait Dedicated to Leon Trotsky.* Her works incorporate surreal, symbolic, and Mexican folk elements.

Kalidasa (kah-lee-DAH-suh) c. 400 CE Dramatist and lyric poet, regarded as the greatest in Indian Classical literature, his work often deals with intense romantic love. Some of his most famous works include *Sakuntala, Vikramorvasi,* and *Malavikagnimitra.*

Kandinsky, Wassily (VAS-uh-lee kan-DIN-skee) 1866–1944 German expressionist painter. Author of *Concerning the Spiritual in Art,* in which he claimed that the source of true art was the human soul. His paintings include *Several Circles,* an example of nonobjective art or nonrepresentational art.

Kant, Immanuel (im-MAN-yoo-uhl KAHNT) 1724–1804 Prussian philosopher. His major works include *Critique of Judgment*, in which he defines pleasure form art as "disinterested satisfaction." His views on ethics are set out in *Foundations of the Metaphysics of Morals*. He influenced later thinkers, in particular Fichte, Hegel, and Schelling.

kantor The singer and musical leader of a church.

karma (CAR-muh) For Hindus and Buddhists, the belief that each action in this life brings an inevitable result, good or bad, in either one's current life or in a later reincarnation.

kettle drums A kind of drum that can be tuned to a specific pitch (note). Known in Italian as *timpani*.

Kierkegaard, Søren (SEE-ren KEER-kuh-gahrd) 1813–1955 Danish existential philosopher. He condemned speculative philosophical systems and formulated the thesis that subjectivity is the only truth.

King Minos (MY-noss) Legendary ruler of Crete. Son of Zeus.

Knossos, Crete (NOSS-uss, KREET) Center of the Minoan civilization on the island of Crete and site of the Palace of Minos.

koine (koi-NAY) A common form of Greek used throughout the Roman empire; also the language of the New Testament.

kore (KOHR-ee) (pl. kouroi, KOOR-oy) Draped, standing, female figure common in Archaic sculpture.

kouros (KOOR-ohs) Nude, standing, male figure common in Archaic sculpture.

Kublai Khan (KOO-blay KAHN) c. 1210–1294 Mongol King who established Beijing as China's capital. Grandson of Genghis Khan.

Kufic (KOO-fik) A sophisticated form of Arabic script.

Kurosawa, Akira (ah-KEE-rah koor-uh-SAW-wah) 1910–1998 Japanese film director. Creator of the cinematic masterpieces *Rashomon*, *Seven Samurai*, and *Kagemusha*.

Laertes (lay-AIR-teez) Father of Odysseus in Homer's *Odyssey*.

Landini, Francesco (lan-DEE-nee) 1325–1397 CE Italian composer and virtuoso. He composed several madrigals and ballads.

Laocoön **(lay-OCK-oh-awn)** late 2nd century BCE A marble sculpture depicting the Trojan priest Laocoön and his sons entangled by two sea serpents sent by Apollo.

Laodicea (lay-odd-uh-SEE-uh) Ancient city in Asia Minor. Built in the 3rd century BCE, it was the Roman center of trade and commerce and an early center of Christianity.

Lao-tzu (LAO-dzoo) active c. 570 BCE Chinese philosopher and reputed founder of Taoism, his teachings were recorded in *The Classic of the Way and Its Power (Tao te ching)*, written sometime between the 6th and 3rd centuries BCE.

Lascaux (la-SKOE) Cave site of important Paleolithic paintings, primarily of animals, in southwest France.

Laurentian (law-REN-shun) Term pertaining to works commissioned by or under patronage of Lorenzo de' Medici, especially the Laurentian Library in Florence.

Law Code of Hammurabi (hah-moo-RAH-bee) Authored by the most famous king of Babylonia (1792–1750 BCE), one of the earliest attempts to achieve social justice by legislation heralding a major development in the growth of civilization.

Law of the Twelve Tables 451–450 BCE Earliest legal code of the Roman Republic.

Le Corbusier (luh kor-boo-ZYAY) 1887–1965 Swiss architect. He developed a theory of the interrelation between machine forms and architectural techniques. Designer of the Unités D'Habitation in Marseille and Nantes, living complexes that incorporated shopping areas, walkways, and recreational spaces.

Le Lorrain, Claude (lo-RAIN) 1600–1682 French landscape painter during the Baroque period.

lectio divina **(leck-TEE-oh duh-VEE-nuh)** Latin for "divine reading." Originated by Origen in 220 CE. It was considered to be a cornerstone of monastic life.

legend Stories meant to be read aloud. Often used for stories about the saints in medieval literature.

Leitmotiv (LIGHT-moe-teef) German for "leading motif." A recurring musical theme, associated with a particular person, place, or idea. Although usually a short melody, it can also be a chord progression or simple rhythm. Also used to mean any sort of recurring theme, whether in music, literature, or the life of a fictional character or a real person.

Lendit (lawn-DEE) 12th century CE A trade fair held at the Abbey of Saint Denis in Paris; popular destination of tourists and pilgrims.

Leonardo da Vinci (lee-oh-NAR-doh dah VIN-chee) 1452–1519 Florentine painter and inventor; considered the genius of the Renaissance. His most renowned paintings include *The Last Supper*, *The Virgin of the Rocks*, and *The Mona Lisa*. The scope and breadth of his intellect is captured in his *Notebooks*, a compilation of sketches and writings that investigate the fields of anatomy, mathematics, natural sciences, urban planning, and engineering.

Léonin (lay-oh-NEEN) 1150–1201 CE Composer and music theoretician who wrote several pieces for the organum and introduced a rational system of rhythmic notation into polyphonic music. He was one of the first students at the school of Notre Dame. Author of *Magnus Liver Organi* in 1160 CE.

Lesotho (luh-SOE-toe) A kingdom located within South Africa inhabited by speakers of the Sotho language.

Li Po (LEE POE) 701–762 BCE Chinese poet of the T'ang dynasty. His verse challenged classical Chinese norms of style, treating themes of nature and human emotion with a playful and unique sense of rhyme and diction.

Lieder (LEE-der) The German word for "songs," generally used to describe songs set to a German text.

light-wells Vertical shafts running down through Minoan palace complexes to light the lower stories.

Limbourg, Brothers (Pol, Hennequin, and Herman) (lan-BOOR) 1380–1416 Flemish painters. They illustrated the illuminated prayer book, entitled *Trés Riches Heures du Duc de Berry* or "Book of Hours," for Philip the Bold's brother in 1416. The twelve illustrations depict the lives of the peasants and aristocracy in vivid detail. Forerunners of the great Flemish tradition of scenic painting.

linear perspective A system of perspective in which all parallel lines converge at a single vanishing point.

linearity Used as a description for art that emphasizes the geometrical quality of drawing as opposed to melding, blurring, or otherwise lessening the division of descriptive spaces within an artwork.

Liszt, Franz (FRAHNS LIST) 1811–1886 Hungarian Romantic composer and virtuosic pianist. His works include symphonic poems, masses, two symphonies, and a large number of piano pieces, some of which are extremely challenging technically.

Liturgy (LITT-uhr-jee) The official public worship of the Christian church.

Locke, John 1632–1704 Leading English philosopher during the Baroque period. In *An Essay Concerning Human Understanding*, published in 1690, he argued against the theory of innate ideas and proposed that ideas are derived from perceptions. His *Two Treatises on Government* influenced the writers of *The Declaration of Independence*.

logarithm Table of numbers that simplifies mathematical calculation by substituting addition and subtraction for multiplication and division.

loggia (pl. loggias) (LAW juh) A roofed gallery of a building.

Loire (LWAR) The longest river in France flowing northwest into the Atlantic Ocean. The Loire valley is renowned for its fertility, beautiful landscape, historical landmarks, and chateaux.

Lorenzetti, Pietro and Ambrogio (pee-ay-troh, ahm-BRO-jyoh, loh-ren-ZETT-ee) 1280/1285–1338 Italian painters from Siena influenced by Giotto's realistic style. Ambrogio Lorenzetti's paintings are particularly innovative, such as the *Peaceful City* and *Peaceful Country*, both which demonstrate a heightened sense of perspective and detail depiction of contemporary society.

Lorenzo de' Medici (low-REN-zoe deh MEH-duh-chee) 1449–1492 Called Lorenzo il Magnifico or "the magnificent." Florentine political and social leader, poet, and patron of the arts. He supported the University of Pisa and the *Stadium* of Florence. Author of *Comento ad alcuni sonetti* (*A Commentary on Some Sonnets*) and "The Song of Bacchus."

low relief See *relief, low*.

Lucifer Derived from the Latin words *lux* and *ferre* or "light-bearing." In the Christian tradition, another name for Satan.

Lucretius (loo-KREE-shuss) 99–55 BCE Roman poet and philosopher who composed *On the Nature of Things (De Rerum Natura)*, a long poem expounding the teachings of Epicureanism.

Luminism Mid-19th century A school of landscape painting that grew out of the Hudson River School, a group of American artists. Distinctive for effects of light in landscapes, luminist landscapes express tranquility and often depict calm, reflective water and a soft, hazy sky.

Luther, Martin 1483–1546 German religious reformer. Leading figure in the Protestant Reformation who protested against corruption in the Roman Catholic Church. In his pamphlet, *De Servo Arbitrio* (On the Bondage of the Will), he argued that faith alone was the means to salvation. Luther wrote his own translation of the Bible as well as several religious hymns.

lyre (LIAR) A stringed musical instrument used to accompany songs or recitations in ancient Greece.

lyric poetry (LEER-ick) Verse in which the author expresses his or her own emotions and opinions.

Lysippus (lie-SIPP-uss) 4th century BCE Prominent Greek sculptor who had a great influence on Hellenistic art. His figures were realistic and large in scale.

Macao (muh-COW) City in southeastern China established as a Portuguese trading post in the 16th century.

Machaut, Guillaume (gee-YOME duh mah-SHOH) c. 1304?–1377 French poet and composer who influenced the work of Geoffrey Chaucer. His most famous composition is the *Messe de Notre Dame*, a four-part setting of the Ordinary Mass.

Machiavelli, Niccolò (nee-koh-LOW mah-kyah-VEH-lee) 1469–1527 Italian political theorist; author of *The Prince*, a treatise on the pragmatic use of power to maintain the authority of the state. His rejection of religion and morality as the foundation of the code of law caused his work to be censored by the Catholic Church. Referent of the epithets "Old Nick" and "Machiavellian."

Madrigal (MAD-ruh-guhl) Song for two or more unaccompanied voices developed in the late 13th and early 14th centuries. Two verses would be set to the same melody separated by a refrain set to a different melody and rhythm.

Mahabharata **(muh-HAH-BAHR-uh-tuh)** A sacred epic poem of India recounting the struggle of two families over the dynasty. The *Baghavad-Gita* is the central section of this work. See also, *Ramayana*.

Mahayana (mah-huh-YAH-nuh) meaning the "Greater Vehicle." The other main strain of Chinese Buddhism, more worldly (and therefore more acceptable to Confucians) than Hinayana.

Mahler, Gustave (GOOS-tahf MAW-ler) 1860–1911 Autrian composer and conductor. His works include nine symphonies and *Das Lied von der Erde* or "The Song of the Earth." He broke with conventional forms, incorporating lied, folksong, symphonic poems, and other elements within his symphonies to create an immersive musical experience.

Maimonides (my-MAWN-uh-deez) 1135–1204 CE Jewish philosopher and physician as well as personal physician to the Sultan of Baghdad. Author of the *Guide for the Perplexed*, which reconciles Hebrew scripture and Aristotelian philosophy.

mandorla An almond shaped aureola (golden outline) used to frame the figures of Christ or Mary in Romanesque art.

Manet, Edouard (ed-WAHR ma-NEY) 1832–1883 French painter. His innovative use of color and space laid the philosophical foundations of Impressionism. His works *Luncheon on the Grass* and *The Bar at the Folies-Bergère* demonstrate the developing shift in artistic vision of the period.

Manetho (MAN-uh-thoe) Egyptian priest and author of the *History of Egypt* (280 BCE).

mannerism c. 1520–1600 A style of art and architecture that shifted away from the balanced aesthetics of the High Renaissance. It favored unexpected arrangement and treatments of subjects and use of space, highly contrasted color schemes, and complex allegories.

manuscript Literally (from the Latin) a text written by hand. The way of book production before the invention of printing.

Manutius, Aldus (AHL-duss muh-NOO-shee-uss) 1449–1515 Italian printer and publisher. His Aldine Press, located in Venice, printed several Classical works. His technical innovations to the field of printing contributed significantly to the spread of humanism throughout Europe.

Marcus Aurelius (aw-REE-lee-uss) 121–180 CE Roman emperor and stoic. Author of *Meditations*, an account of his trials as a stoic.

Martyr, Justin c. 100–165 CE Christian apologist who sought to persuade the Roman emperors to understand and tolerate Christianity.

Masaccio, Tommaso (toe-MAH-soe mah-SAH-choh) 1401–1428 A master Italian Renaissance painter, his work exemplifies a shift toward precise mathematical perspective, clarity of line, realistic portrayal of people, and open arrangement. His most renowned works include *The Holy Trinity*, the *Tribute Money*, and the *Expulsion of Adam and Eve from Eden*.

materialism Belief that nothing exists except material things.

materialists A presocratic school of philosophy that sought to explain all phenomena in terms of one or more elements.

maternity figure Small statue representing a female ancestor of a pregnant woman, to watch over the birth, prevent miscarriage, and protect the newborn child.

Matisse, Henri (ahn-REE ma-TEESS) 1869–1954 French painter. Leader among the Fauves, his work embraced the abstract over realistic through emphasizing form and color in space to achieve his artistic vision, as in *The Joy of Life* or *The Red Studio*.

Matteo Ricci (mah-TEH-oh REE-kee) 1552–1610 Italian Jesuit missionary who served under Kang His, a Qing emperor in China.

Maximian (mack-SIMM-ee-an) Roman Emperor who ruled the western part of the empire between 286 and 305 CE He abdicated in 308 CE and was forced to commit suicide two years later.

mazurka (muh-ZUHR-kuh) A Polish folk-dance in fast triple time.

mbari house An adobe shrine made by the Igbo people of eastern Nigeria.

meander (mee-ANN-duhr) Maze pattern, used frequently in Geometric pottery decoration.

Medea (mih-DEE-uh) Legendary sorceress who helped Jason obtain the Golden Fleece; also the main character in Euripides' play *Medea* written in 431 BCE.

Meiji (MAY-JEE) Japanese for "enlightened government." The period beginning in 1868 during which feudalism in Japan was abolished and a strong central government established.

melisma (muh-LIZ-muh) An intricate series of notes used to embellish the final syllable of a chanted phrase.

mendicant (MEN-dih-kuhnt) A member of an order of friars who rejected ownership of property and begged for daily necessities.

Mesopotamia (mes-uh-puh-TAY-mee-uh) Settled by a succession of cultures, the so-called "fertile crescent" region in the Middle East between the Tigris and Euphrates rivers.

Messiah From the Hebrew word for "anointed one," he is the anticipated deliverer and king of the Jewish nation. In the Christian religion that promise is fulfilled in the form of Jesus Christ.

Metaphysical A term used (confusingly) to describe a group of 17th century English poets.

metope (METT-uh-pee) Rectangular panels alternating with triglyphs in a Doric frieze.

Miës van der Rohe, Ludwig (LOOD-vig MEEZ fahn der ROE-wuh) 1896–1969 German-American architect. Following his credo, "less is more," his buildings are characterized by accessible, simple designs devoid of applied ornament, see the Seagram Building in New York and the Museum of Fine Arts in Houston.

Milton, John 1608–1674 English poet. Author of *Paradise Lost*, a Christian-based epic describing Satan's temptation of Adam and Eve and their expulsion from paradise. Through the main protagonist, the fallen angel Satan, we learn of his thwarted attempt to wage war against his creator.

minaret (min-uh-RETT) Tower of a mosque, from where the call to prayer is chanted.

minbar (MIN-bar) The pulpit in an Islamic mosque where the Imam stands to deliver sermons.

miniscule (mee-nee-SKYOOL) French for "lower case letter." A script developed by Carolingian scribes between 800 and 1200 CE that became the standard form of lettering in manuscripts. Compare to majuscule (capital lettering).

Minoan (mih-NOE-uhn) The first urban culture in the West arising on the island of Crete and marked by sophisticated technical, artistic, and architectural achievements.

Minotaur (MIN-uh-tahr) A Greek mythological creature with the body of a man and head of a bull. Killed by the Athenian hero, Theseus.

minuet (minn-you-ETT) A French 17th century dance, the rhythm of which came to be used in the third movement of 18th century sonatas and symphonies.

Mithraism (MITH-ruh-ism) Ancient Persian religion and rival of Christianity within the Roman Empire during the 2nd and 3rd centuries CE.

Mnesikles (NESS-uh-kleez) 5th century BCE Athenian architect who designed the Athenian Acropolis.

mode (MOED) In music, a variety tones within an octave, distinguished by the arrangement of half tones and whole tones.

Modernist Temper 1919–1920 A literary movement that turned away from traditional forms and values. Characterized by fragmentation of line and image and discontinuity of time. Authors writing in this vein include James Joyce, Virginia Woolf, and T.S. Eliot.

modes The scales that formed the basis of the Greek system of music.

modulation In music, the process of movement from one tonal center or key to another.

Mofolo, Thomas 1875?–1948 First African novelist. His *Traveler of the East* is also the first novel written in an African language. His subsequent novel, *Chaka*, gained worldwide fame.

Mohandas Gandhi (moe-hun-DAHS GAHN-dee) 1869–1948 Indian political and spiritual leader. He led the movement for independence of India from British rule. He introduced the idea of nonviolent resistance, or *satyagraha*, as a tool for political leverage.

Mohenjo-daro (moh-HEN-juh-DAR-owe) c. 3000 BCE Site of an ancient city in the Indus Valley.

Molière (mol-YAIR) (stage name of Jean Baptiste Poquelin) 1622–1673 French actor, playwright, and ballet librettist. Creator of a new form of French Baroque comedy that candidly revealed his character's faults and delusions, as in *Le Bourgeois Gentilhomme*.

Monet, Claude (mow-NEY) 1840–1926 French painter. Recognized as one of the creators of Impressionism, his paintings capture subtle nuances of color, atmosphere, and light in landscape and water, as in *Impression: Sunrise*, *Red Boats at Argenteuil*, and *Water Lilies*.

monody Taken from the Greek term *monoidia*, meaning ode for one voice or actor. In early opera, it referred to a single declamatory vocal line with accompaniment. See *recitative*.

monophonic (mawn-uh-FAWN-ick) One or more voices singing a single melodic line.

Monotheism (MAWN-uh-thee-ism) Religious belief affirming that there is only one God, as opposed to polytheism, which accepts many gods, or henotheism, which admits that there are many gods but only one is to be worshiped.

Montaigne Michel (mee-SHELL mon-TAYNE) 1533–1593 French writer. Influence by his studies of the classics, his *Essais*, short introspective prose in which he reflected on many subjects of his day, began the tradition of essay writing.

Montesquieu, Charles Louis (SHAHRL LWEE MON-tuh-skyoo) 1689–1755 French philosopher. Contributor to Diderot's *Encyclopédie*, Montesquieu advocated the sharing of political power among the monarchy and other social institutions. Author of *De l'esprit des lois* (The Spirit of Laws), a major influence on 18th century Europe and inspiration for American Constitution and the Declaration of the Rights of Man. Best remembered for his theory of the separation of governmental authority into legislative, executive, and judicial powers.

Monteverdi, Claudio (mon-tuh-VAIR-dee) 1567–1643 Italian composer. Considered one of the first great composers of opera, his first work, *Orfeo*, was revolutionary for its dramatic power and expressive orchestral accompaniment.

morality play A theatrical allegory in which the main character encounters personifications of moral virtues; exemplified in *Everyman*, a popular play in the Middle Ages that aimed to motivate the audience to lead a Christian life.

Morisot, Berthe (BAIRT maw-ree-ZOW) 1841–1895 French painter. The leading female exponent in the Impressionist circle, her works include *View of Paris from the Trocadero*.

Mosque of Damascus built between 706–715 CE under the direction of the caliph Al-Walid. The mosque was erected over the ruins of a Roman temple and a Byzantine church and contains elaborate mosaics and geometric decoration. Also referred to as the Great or Grand Mosque of Damascus.

motet (moe-TET) 13th–14th centuries CE A polyphonic form of music comprised of three to four voices that developed out of Gregorian chant. The form evolved to include unique melodies assigned to the upper voices as well as the addition of lines in French.

Mount Olympus A mountain in northeastern Greece. Mythical home of the gods.

Moussorgsky, Modest (moe-DEST moo-SORG-skee) 1839–1881 Russian composer. His masterpiece, the historical opera *Boris Godunov*, recounts Tsar Godunov's rise to power. The opera highlights Russian folksongs and religious music.

movement In music, a self-contained section of a work; the Classical symphony, for example, had four distinct movements.

Mozarabic chant (moe-ZAHR-uh-bick) From *Mozarab*, the term used for Christians living under Muslim rule, the liturgical song used in the churches of the Iberian Peninsula around the 7th century.

Mozart, Wolfgang Amadeus (VOLF-gahng a-ma-DEH-yoos MOAT-sart) 1756–1791 Austrian Composer. Considered one of the greatest and most prolific composers in history, his works include symphonies, sonatas, chamber works, and piano concertos, see Piano Concerto No. 27 in B Flat, K. 595. He also wrote several operas, including *The Marriage of Figaro*, based upon a play by Beaumarchais. His compositions demonstrate a mastery of form and melody, as well as profound emotional depth.

Muezzin (myoo-EZ-in) The person who calls Muslim worshipers to services and daily prayers.

Mughal The Persian word for "Mongol." It is used to describe the period of Muslim rule in India.

Mughals (MOE-gul) 1526–1858 CE Also spelled Mogal. A member of the Muslim dynasty founded by Babel in India.

mullion (MULL-yuhn) A slender divider of light panels on a window.

Munch, Edvard (ED-vahrd MOONK) 1863–1944 Norwegian Expressionist painter. He explored social and psychological problems employing bright colors and tortuously curved designs, as in his most famous painting *The Scream*. His work influenced the course of modern German painting.

Murasaki Shikibu (moo-rah-sah-kee shee-kee-boo) c. 980–1030 Japanese writer. Author of *The Tale of Genji*, considered to be the first Japanese novel, in which she portrays the complexities of Japanese society.

musica ficta (MOO-si-kuh FICK-tuh) The art of performing music by departing from the written notes and introducing embellishments.

Mustapha Mond (MOOS-tuh-fah MOND) Main character in *Brave New World*, a novel by Aldus Huxley. Set in London in AD 2540, the novel anticipates developments in reproductive technology, biological engineering, and sleep-learning that combine to change society.

Mycenae (my-SEE-nee) 1600–1100 BCE City on mainland Greece that flourished during the late Bronze Age as the center of a culture of traders and warriors who were to exert an influence on later Greek civilization; the **Mycenaeans (my-suh-NEE-uhns)**.

Myron (MY-ron) 5th century BCE Famous Greek sculptor whose works portray the human body in motion, see the *Discus Thrower*.

narthex (NAR-theks) A passageway joining the main entrance to the nave (principle area) of a church.

Nationalism The identification of individuals with a nation-state, with its own culture and history. A phenomenon linked to the rise of urbanization and political consciousness.

natural selection According to Charles Darwin, the process of evolution by which some variations of each species die out, while others survive.

nave (NAYV) Central, long aisle of a basilica, with two parallel side aisles.

Neanderthal (nee-ANN-der-thawl) Ancestors of Homo sapiens and the first species to bury their dead with offerings in graves.

Nefertiti (neff-er-TEE-tee) Egyptian queen. Wife of Amenhotep IV.

Negritude Term created by Leopold Senghor to summarize the African contribution to world culture.

Neolithic (nee-oh-LITH-ick) 8000–3000 BCE The Late Stone Age, marked by the development of agriculture, domestication of animals, invention of pottery and bronze tools, and first large-scale architecture.

Neoplatonism Philosophical movement derived from the work of Plato and his followers, which emphasizes the drive toward the ideal as the goal of transcending mere material reality.

neum (NOOM) The name of the sign that stood for a musical note in Gregorian chant.

Neumann, Johann Balthazar (YO-hann BAL-ta-zar NOY-mann) 1687–1753 German architect. His designs include the pilgrimage church of Vierzehnheiligen (feer-tsen-HIGH-luh-ghen) or "fourteen saints," an example of the rococo decorative style prevalent in late southern German and Austrian architecture.

Nietzsche, Friedrich (FREED-rick NEE-chuh) 1844–1900 German philosopher and critic. His major work, *Thus Spake Zarathustra*, is a repudiation of Christian and liberal ethics and a denigration of democratic ideals. He proposed the idea of *übermensh* or "overperson" as the true manifestation of human greatness, one who asserts his individuality without concern for moral constraints. Some elements of his doctrine appealed to Nazis, and he was a major influence on the development of existentialism.

Nijinsky, Vaslav (VASS-lev nih-JINN-skee) 1890–1950 Russian ballet dancer. Considered one of the most innovative male dancers of the 20th century, he became the leading dancer in Diaghilev's Ballets Russe. Known for his riveting performances in Stravinsky's ballets *Petrouchka* and *Afternoon of a Faun*.

nirvana (nuhr-VAH-nuh) Freedom from individual suffering and ultimate union with the supreme spirit.

Noh (or No) Traditional Japanese drama, generally based on stories passed down from generation to generation, involving acting, song, dance, and mime.

nocturne (NOCK-turn) Short, dreamy piece of music, generally for solo piano. Invented by the Irish composer John Field, it was popularized by Chopin.

***Notre Dame de Belle Verriere* (bell vehr-YEHR)** 12th century CE In French "Our Lady of the Beautiful Window." A famous stained glass window located in the Chartes Cathedral.

Notre Dame French for "our lady." Begun in 1163 CE. A famous cathedral in Paris and an example of the early gothic style in architecture. One of the first cathedrals in which flying buttresses were used.

Oba (AW-buh) The hereditary male absolute ruler of the ancient kingdom of Benin.

octave (OK-tiv) Modern musical scale consisting of eight tones that originated from Pythagorean ideas about harmony.

Octavius (ock-TAY-vee-uss) 63 BCE–14 CE Known as Gaius Julias Caesar Octavius and later, in 27 CE, as Augustus. Heir and successor to Julius Ceasar, he defeated Mark Antony and Cleopatra in the Battle of Actium. The first emperor of Rome under whom the empire achieved stability, prosperity, and great cultural achievement.

October Revolution Common way of designating the overthrow of the Tsars and the emergence of Marxist government in Russia in 1917.

Oculus (OCK-yuh-luss) Regular Latin word for "eye." Used to describe the empty round hole at the top of the dome of the Pantheon.

Odysseus (oh-DISS-ee-uss) Hero of the epic poem the *Odyssey*. King of Ithica. Son of Laertes.

Odyssey (ODD-uh-see) Epic poem attributed to Homer recounting the adventures of the hero Odysseus on his travels homeward after the Trojan War.

Oedipus (ED-uh-puss) In Greek legend, the king of Thebes, who kills his father and marries his mother as ordained by the gods. Central character in the play *Oedipus Rex* by Sophocles.

opera A dramatic performance in which the text is sung rather than spoken.

oratorio Sacred drama performed without action, scenery, or costume, generally in a church or concert hall.

Ordinary (The) of the Mass Parts of the Catholic liturgy that do not change from day to day. These include the *Kyrie*, the *Gloria*, the *Credo*, the *Sanctus* and *Benedictus*, and the *Agnus Dei*. This mass has been and continues to be the framework and subject of a long tradition of musical compositions, including the works of Machaut, Palestrina, Bach, and Leonard Bernstein.

Orestes (oh-RESS-teez) According to Greek legend, son of Agamemnon who kills his mother and her lover in order to avenge the murder of his father. Main character in Aeschylus' *The Libation Bearers*, the second play in the *Oresteia* trilogy.

Orfeo (or-FAY-oh) See *Monteverdi*.

organum (OR-guh-nuhm) A musical form originating from Gregorian chant; the simultaneous singing of musical lines within a composition, based around the *cantus firmus* (the primary chanted melody) and then harmonized with a second, third, or fourth melodic line. Precursor to counterpoint.

Orientalizing An artistic style that emerged in Greece between 700 and 600 BCE showing the influence of Near Eastern ideas of aesthetics.

Orpheus (OR-fee-uss) Poet and musician in Greek legend who sought to free his wife, Eurydice, from the underworld.

Orthodoxy (OR-thuh-dock-see) Greek term meaning both correct belief and correct worship. It later became the generic name for Eastern Christianity, which broke from Rome.

Osiris (oh-SIGH-riss) Egyptian god whose death and resurrection were symbolic of annual death and rebirth of the land surrounding the Nile; husband to Isis. Judge of the dead and king of the underworld.

outcasts The lowest category of the Hindu caste system. Also called "untouchables."

paean (PEE-uhn) Song of solemn invocation to the gods. *Compare dithyramb.*

Paganini, Nicolò (NIH-kuh-low pah-guh-NEE-nee) 1782–1840 Italian violinist and composer. Extremely accomplished and successful virtuoso performer known for cultivating a diabolical appearance.

Palazzo Vecchio (pah-LAHT-soe VECK-yoe) Italian for "Old Palace" begun in 1298; the town hall of Florence noted for its massive, fortified walls and bell tower.

Paleolithic (pay-lee-oh-LITH-ick) 8,000 BCE and earlier. The Old Stone Age marked by the first appearance of *Homo erectus*, stone tools, first cave art, artifacts, and ritual burials.

Palestrina, Giovanni Pierluigi da (pal-uh-STREE-nuh) c. 1525–1594 Distinguished Italian composer. He was the organist and *maestro di canto* at the cathedral of St Agapit, Palestrina, and later master of the Julian choir at St Peter's in Rome. He composed over 100 Masses, as well as motets, madrigals, and hymns.

Palio (pahl-yo) Bareback horse race held in Siena twice a year.

Panathenaic (pan-ath-uh-NAY-ick) Pertaining to the ancient Greek festival in honor of Athena, which was celebrated yearly with music and athletic games.

Pantheon (PAN-thee-on) at Rome A domed circular temple, first built by Agrippa in 27 BCE and rebuilt again in c. 126 BCE under Emperor Hadrian.

Parmigianino (par-mee-ja-NEE-no) 1503–1540 Italian painter. His work masterly exemplifies the characteristics of Mannerism in art following the High Renaissance, particularly in the graceful, elongated, and sensual figures, as seen in the unusually proportioned *Madonna of the Long Neck*.

Parthenon (PAR-thuh-non) Main temple to Athena on the Acropolis. Built between 447 and 438 BCE under the direction of the sculptor Phidias.

Parthenos (par-THEN-uss) Literally "virgin." The attribute of Athena used to name her temple, the Parthenon.

pastel Dry sticks of colored chalk that leave a soft, powdery hue when rubbed on paper.

patricians (puh-TRISH-uhnz) The upper classes of the Roman Republic. Before 287 BCE, they had exclusive rights to the Roman Senate and magistracies.

Patroclus (puh-TROE-kluhs)
Friend to Achilles in Homer's
epic poem the *Iliad*. Killed by
the Trojan king Hector.

patronage Financial backing and
other support provided by a person or institution—the patron—
for artistic or literary projects.

pediment Long extended triangle
at the top of each end of a
Greek or Roman temple, often
filled with sculpture.

**Peloponnesian War (PELL-uh-
puh-NEE-shuhn)** Greek con-
flict that lasted from 431–404
BCE between the Delian
League, led by Athens, and the
Peloponnesian League, led by
Sparta and Corinth.

**Peloponnesus (PELL-uh-puh-
NEE-suss)** The southern
peninsula of Greece. Site of
Mycenaean civilization and, later,
namesake of the war that weakened the city-states of Greece
and made them vulnerable to
Macedonian conquest.

Penelope (puh-NELL-uh-pee)
Wife to Odysseus in Homer's
epic poem the *Odyssey*.

Pericles (PAIR-uh-kleez) c. 495–
429 BCE Statesman who assumed
leadership of the Athenian
democracy in 443 BCE.

peristyle (PAIR-uh-style) An open
space surrounded by a series of
columns.

Pérotin (PAIR-oh-teen) 12th–13th
century CE Composer for the
organum. He became the director of the music school of Notre
Dame in 1181 CE.

Perpendicular In architecture,
English style that emphasized the
vertical lines of the inside of a
building.

Persepolis (per-SEPP-uh-liss)
Ancient capital of Persia located
in southwestern Iran.

Petrarch (PEE-trahrk) 1304–1374
Italian poet and author; best
known for his book of sonnets
composed about his beloved
Laura. He is also the author
of *Secretum* or "My Secret" in
which he describes an imaginary conversation between St.
Augustin and himself, and *Letter
to Posterity*, an autobiographical work that paints a portrait
of both himself and the age in
which he lived.

Phaedo (FEE-doh) The last of three
works in which Plato represents
the teachings of Socrates (see
also *Apology* and *Crito*).

Phaedra (FED-ruh) In Greek
mythology, the daughter of
Minos and wife of Theseus who
falls in love with her stepson and
then commits suicide.

pharaoh (FAIR-oh) The title of an
ancient Egyptian king.

Phidias (FIDD-ee-uss) c. 500–432?
BCE Greek sculptor who contributed to the design of the
Parthenon; creator of the famous
statue *Zeus at Olympia*.

Philip of Macedon II 382–336
BCE King of Macedonia who
unified most of Greece under
the League of Corinth. Father of
Alexander the Great.

philosophy The study of the nature
and ultimate significance of the
human experience.

Phrygian (FRIJ-ee-uhn) A mode
of Greek music expressing passion and sensuality.

piazza (pee-AHT-suh) The Italian
word for a city square or
marketplace.

Picaresque novel (pik-uh-RESK)
Novel telling a story involving a
rogue or adventurer.

Picasso, Pablo 1881–1973 Spanish
painter and sculptor. His works
revolutionized 20th century art.
He founded cubism and incorporated African imagery into his
works. His masterpieces include
Les Desmoiselle D'Avignon and
Guernica.

**Pico della Mirandola (PEE-koh
deh-lah mee-RAHN-doe-
lah)** 1463–1494 Italian philosopher and humanist; member of the Platonic Academy
and chief exponent of Italian
Neoplatonism. Author of *Oration
on the Dignity of Man*.

Pietá (pee-ay-TAH) Term used to
describe depictions of Mary holding the dead Christ in her arms.

pietás (pee-ay-TOSS) A Roman
virtue expressed in a combination of love and reverential fear
that bound the individual to the
family, the family to the state, and
the state to the gods to produce a
harmonious, flourishing society.

pilgrimage church A church
designated as a pilgrimage
destination as opposed to a
church (e.g., Chartres) that was
a pilgrimage destination but was
also a cathedral.

pillow-book Japanese literary form
consisting of a diary describing the day's events often of an
erotic nature.

Pisano, Nicola 1220–1284 and
Giovanni c. 1270–1314 **(pee-
SAH-noh)** Italian sculptors,
father and son, respectively. Their
work joined the classical elements of realism characteristic
of Roman sculpture with the
naturalism and emotional power
of Gothic sensibilities.

pit See *ground*.

Plato (PLAY-toe) 427–347 BCE
Greek philosopher, disciple of
Socrates, and author of *Dialogues*,
Republic, *Phaedo*, and *Theory of
Forms*. Founder of the Academy,
an institution of education and
research, and the precursor of
our present day university.

plebeians (pluh-BEE-uhnz) The
Roman lower classes.

Pliny (PLY-nee) the Elder 23–79
CE Roman naturalist and writer
who died in the eruption of
Vesuvius. Uncle to **Pliny the
Younger** 62?–c. 113 CE whose
letters provide an insight into the
events of the eruption and subsequent destruction.

Poitiers (pwah-TYAY) City in
west central France and the location of the court of Charles the
VII in 1432.

polis (POE-liss) Greek self-
governing city-state.

polonaise (pawl-uh-NAYZ) A
stately Polish processional dance,
frequently performed at weddings and public ceremonies.

Polychrome (PAWL-ee-krowm)
Literally "many colors." Used to
describe sculpture or ceramics
that are painted.

Polykleitos (pol-uh-KLIGH-tuss)
Greek sculptor. Creator of the
Doryhporos (Spear Bearer). His
Cannon, devised in 440 BCE, is a
mathematical system for portray-
ing the perfect male figure.

Polynices (pol-uh-NIGH-seez)
Legendary son of Oedipus.

polyphonic (paw-luh-FAWN-ick)
From the Greek word polypho-
nia or "variety of sounds." Music
comprised of many voices or
instruments.

polytheism (paw-lee-THEE-ism) The belief that there are many gods.

Pompeii (POM-pee) Ancient city in southwestern Italy, on the Bay of Naples. It was destroyed 79 CE by the eruption of Mount Vesuvius (vuh-SOO-vee-uhs). Site of well-preserved ruins that have provided archeologists and historians with valuable information about the everyday lives of Romans.

Pontormo, Jacopo da (yah-KOE-poe pon-TOR-moe) 1494–1556 Italian painter, born in Pontormo. His works include several frescoes, notably the *Passion* in the Certosa near Florence. His masterpiece is *The Deposition*, a chapel altarpiece in Santa Felicità, Florence.

Pop Art A 20th century art movement characterized by incorporation of elements from mass media and fad culture.

Pope, Alexander 1688–1744 Considered the greatest English poet of the 18th century, his satirical writing unveiled human absurdity and moral decay, see *The Rape of the Lock*. This censure was contrasted by his belief in human potential as seen in his long poem *Essay on Man*.

Postmodernist A term applied to late 20th century art and culture designating it as following the modernist period. It delineates a contemporary point of view from which there is no central organizing principle, aesthetic or hierarchy.

Postimpressionism General term for varying styles of painting, mainly in France, that developed after the Impressionist movement.

Praeneste (pree-NESS-tee) Ancient city to the east of Rome, known today as Palestrina. Site of impressive sanctuary constructed by the Sulla in 82 BCE.

Praxiteles (prak-SIT-leez) c. 350 BCE Greek sculptor whose works include the *Hermes* and *Aphrodite* statues.

prelude (PREY-lood) Originally a short opening section of a longer piece (it was used in this way by Bach). Composers in the Romantic era also used it to describe a short independent piece.

Presocratics (pree-suh-KRAT-iks) Greek philosophers before the time of Socrates.

Priam (PRY-uhm) King of Troy in Homer's epic poem, the *Iliad*, about the Trojan War.

Program music Music that illustrates a story or program.

prophet One who speaks authoritatively for a deity or God.

propylaea (prop-uh-LEE-uh) Entrance to a temple or enclosure of architectural importance.

Protogeometric style A decorative style, mainly found in ancient Greek pottery, that emphasizes simple, bold designs of concentric circles and semicircles.

Proust, Marcel (mar-SELL PROOST) 1871–1922 French novelist of Jewish descent. In 1912 he published the first part of his thirteen-volume masterpiece *Remembrance of Things Past*. The following volume of this work won the Prix Goncourt in 1919. His massive novel explores the power of the memory and the unconscious, as well as the nature of writing itself.

Psychoanalysis A method of psychological investigation derived from the ideas of Sigmund Freud that explores the patient's unconscious and personality for the purposes of therapeutic benefit or research.

Ptolemy (TOLL-uh-mee) King of Egypt at Alexandria who established the Temple of the Muses (museum) that contained the most extensive collection of Greek literature (destroyed in 47 BCE).

puja (POO-jah) An act of prayer in the home, generally in front of a small altar.

Punic Wars (PYOO-nik) Three wars waged by Rome against Carthage between 264 and 146 BCE; named after the Roman word for Phoenicians (*Poeni*). After achieving victory, Rome annexed its territories.

pyramid (PEER-uh-mid) A four-sided form of Egyptian architecture, generally (although not exclusively) used for the tombs of royalty and aristocracy.

pyramidal configuration (puh-RAM-uh-duhl) The manner of articulating artworks, common in the Renaissance, in which minor figures form the base and the central figure the apex of the artwork.

Pythagoreanism (puh-thag-uh-REE-uhn-izm) The moral and intellectual teachings of Pythagoras.

Qa´aba (kuh-AH-buh) Arabic for *cube*. The draped sacred stone located in the Sanctuary at Mecca, which is believed to bear the footprints of Abraham.

Qing (CHEENG) 1644–1911 Powerful Chinese dynasty with origins in Manchuria.

Quem Quæritis (kwem KWAIR-uh-tiss) Latin for, "Whom do you seek?" A trope added to the music of the Easter vigil in the 10th century; sung by two choirs or two singers to form a short dialogue.

Qur'an (kuh-RON) from the Arabic term for "recitation." The sacred text of Islam that records the divine revelations of God to Muhammad. Also spelled Koran.

Rabia (ruh-BEE-uh) d. 801 CE Sufi writer also known as "the flute player." Author of a series of poems, aphorisms, and meditations that expressed her profound faith in and love for God.

Rabindranath Tagore (ruh-BEEN-druh-not tuh-GOR) 1861–1941 Indian poet. In 1913 he won the Nobel Prize for literature for *Gitanjali*, a collection of poems based upon traditional Hindu themes.

Racine, Jean-Baptiste (jon ba-TEEST rah-SEEN) 1639–1699 French playwright. Much of his work treated Classical or mythological events and dealt with universal themes such as patriotism, as in *Horace*, martyrdom, seen in *Polyeucte*, or in the psychological state of his characters, *Phèdre*.

rajput (RAHJ-poot) Rulers of local Indian kingdoms following the fall of the Gupta Empire.

Ramadan (ra-muh-DAWN) The month in the Muslim (lunar) calendar in which fasting from before dawn to sundown is stipulated.

Ramapithecus (rah-muh-PITH-i-kuss) Earliest known form of hominid (human-like creature).

Ramayana (rah-MAH-yuh-nuh) Indian epic poem that recounts the banishment of the Hindu god Rama, the abduction of his wife Sita, and his subsequent return to the throne. See also *Mahabharata*.

Ramayana (rah-MAH-yuh-nuh) c. 3rd century BCE Classical Sanskrit epic poem based upon a number of legends about the god Rama.

Rameau, Jean Philippe (jon fee-LEEP rah-MOW) 1683–1764 French composer and music theorist. His harpsichord works and chamber music exemplify the mid-18th century rococo style.

Rauschenberg, Robert (RAHW-shin-berg) b.1925 North American painter. Used mix of sculpture and paint in works he called "combines," as in *Monogram*. He incorporated sound and motors in some work, such as *Broadcast* and silkscreen transfers as in *Flush*.

Ravenna (ruh-VENN-uh) A city in north central Italy. The capital of the Western Empire in the 5th and 6th centuries and later the seat of the Ostrogothic kingdom. Site of numerous Christian relics including the Mausoleum of Galla Placidia, the Church of Sant'Apollinair, and two Orthodox baptisteries.

Ray, Katyajit (kaht-yah-JEET RAY) b. 1921 Indian filmmaker. Best known for *The Apu* Trilogy, which depicts a Bengali boy's childhood into maturity.

Realism A mid-19th century artistic movement that turned away from idealized portrayals of subjects in preference for more commonplace, real-world scenes and topics.

recapitulation The third section of a sonata form movement, which restates the themes heard in the first section, the *exposition*.

recitative (res-uh-tuh-TEEV) The free declaration of a vocal line, with only a simple instrumental accompaniment for support.

red-figure 6th–3rd century BCE A style of Athenian vase-painting in which the figures are painted in red on a black background.

Reformation A 16th century movement originating in northern Europe against the corruption in the Catholic Church, in particular that of conferring indulgences, the authority given to theologians to interpret the Bible, and the low standard of education of the parishes. This ultimately led to the formation of the Protestant Church, which rejected the idolatry of icons and placed emphasis on the Word, and in turn resulted in a strong focus on literacy throughout the Protestant world.

relics Parts of body or material (clothing, personal objects) associated with a saint.

relief, high Sculptures carved out of a block of stone so deeply that they appear to stand independently.

relief, low Sculptures carved out of the surface of a block of stone.

reliquary (RELL-uh-kwair-ee) A repository for sacred relics, such as the clothes, body, or personal objects of an important religious or historical figure.

Rembrandt van Rijn (REM-brant) 1606–1669 Dutch Painter. Considered one of the great painters in history, his works show striking contrasts in light and shadow as well as richness in color and texture. His subjects are rendered with a tender, honest humanity, as in *The Night Watch* and *Jacob Blessing the Sons of Joseph*. He painted numerous portraits, including *Old Self-portrait*.

Renaissance (REH-nuh-zawnss) Derived from the Latin word for "rebirth." A revival of learning and artistic creativity in Europe between the 14th and 17th centuries.

Renoir, Pierre Auguste (PYER aw-GOOST ren-WARR) 1841–1919 French Impressionist painter. His paintings, such as *Le Moulin de la Galette*, epitomize his colorful, sensual style and his love of women as symbols of life.

responsorial (ree-spon-SOR-ee-uhl) Call-and-response vocal style of music common to early Christian church services.

Retrograde inversion See *serialism*.

Rhazes (RAHZ-iss) 860–932 CE Persian physician and head of the hospital in Baghdad who formulated the first description of measles and smallpox. Also the author of several papers and treatises in various fields of science.

Riefenstahl, Leni (REEF-en-shtall) 1902–2003 German filmmaker. Her first major film *Triumph of the Will* in 1935 is a compelling record of a Nazi rally at Nuremberg. Her epic documentary of the 1936 Berlin Olympic Games, *Olympiad* (1938) is considered a cinematic masterpiece, noted for the innovative use of camera work to capture the human body in motion.

Robespierre, Maximilien (MAHX-ee-MEE-yon ROWBZ-pee-air) 1758–1794 French revolutionary leader. Influenced by Rousseau, Robespierre wanted to build a "republic of virtue." His extreme and violent response to opposition was dubbed The Reign of Terror.

Rococo (roe-coe-COE) Derived from the French word *rocaille* or "shell." A Baroque art style characterized by charm and decoration, in which subjects were treated with light heartedness, intended to entertain the eye.

Rodin, Auguste (aw-GOOST row-DAN) 1840–1917 French sculptor. Like the Impressionist painters of the day, his sculptures depict the concept of the subject rather than strict physical appearance. The textured surfaces and blurring contours of his sculptures resemble the Impressionist interest in shifting light and shade. Among his works are *The Kiss* and *Monument to Balzac*.

Roland (Song of) 11th or 12th centuries CE Medieval epic poem, traditionally delivered orally, that recounted the fall of the French hero Roland. Based upon a battle in which the Spanish attacked Charlemagne's forces.

Romanesque (row-muh-NESK) c. 1000–1200 An architectural style that emerged in the later medieval period that borrowed from Roman architectural aesthetics; most characteristic for the use of massive walls, heavy stone arches, and profuse exterior ornamentation, particularly sculpture.

Romanticism An 18th century artistic movement that placed emphasis on personal expression over reason, revered mysticism in nature, gave greater reign to the imagination and, in some cases, incorporated regional folk traditions into creative works as a part of growing national consciousness.

Roncesvalles (RAWN-suh-vals) A village in northern Spain. Site of 788 CE battle in which the legendary hero Roland died.

Rousseau, Jean Jacques (JAHN JAHK roo-SOH) 1712–1778 Philosopher and composer. He believed that the natural goodness of man was destroyed by civilization. Author of *The Social Contract*, in which he attempted to describe an ideal state based upon the General Will of the people.

Row See *serialism*.

Rubens, Peter Paul (ROO-bins) 1577–1640 Flemish painter and diplomat. He produced large-scale works on a wide range of subjects, often conveying intense energy, as seen in *The Rape of the Daughters of Leucippus*. His prodigious output included canvases of the life of Marie de' Medici, see *Journey of Marie de' Medici*. In his last years, he turned to themes of intimate married love, as in *Hélène Fourment and her Children*.

Rumi (ROOM-ee) 1207–1273 CE Sufi mystic and poet. Author of over three thousand poems and seventy discourses on his spiritual experiences and insights. His practice of dancing while reciting his poetry developed into a tradition of devotional dance practiced by the *dervishes*.

Saikaku Ihara (ee-hah-ruh sigh-kah-koo) 1642–1693 Japanese poet and novelist. His works depict the loves and adventures of the Japanese middle class; see *Life of an Amorous Woman*.

Samurai (SAM-uh-righ) Japanese professional warrior.

Samurai-dokoro (SAM-uh-righ DOE-koe-roe) Office held by Japanese emperor, giving him command over all Japan's professional warriors.

San Vitale (sahn-vee-TAH-lay) c. 530–548 CE An elaborate and unusually designed church located in Ravenna. Constructed in two octagons, one within the other. It is renowned for its mosaics.

sangha (SUNG-guh) A Buddhist monastery.

Sanskrit (SAN-skrit) Language spoken by the Aryans.

Sant' Apollinare Nuovo (sant a-pole-ee-NAH-ray nwoh-voh) Also called Church of the Redeemer. Constructed under the king Theodoric in the early 6th century, the mosaics decorating the interior reflect both the Roman and Byzantine artistic styles.

Santa Croce (sahn-tah KROH-chay) Basilica in Florence, Italy, begun in the late 13th century, that contains several frescos by Giotto and his students. According to legend, it was originally founded by St. Francis of Assisi.

Sanzio, Raphael (SAHN-zee-ow) 1483–1520 Italian painter. Painted numerous biblical figures, such as *Madonna of the Meadow*, noted for revealing humanity in the divine form. His most revered work is *Philosophy*, or *School of Athens*, which depicts the great philosophers of antiquity.

Sappho (SAFF-oh) b. 612 BCE Greek lyric poetess.

sarcophagus (sar-COFF-uh-guss) A burial container for a human body typically made from some form of stone and often ornamented both on the lid and the side panels. From the Greek words for flesh (*sarx*) and to consume (*phagein*).

Sartre, Jean-Paul (SAWR-truh) 1905–1980 French writer and philosopher. Leading existentialist thinker, he argued that each individual is responsible for creating meaning out of subjective existence.

satire The use of ridicule and sarcasm to expose and discourage what the author considers folly or even more serious shortcomings; popular in 18th century literature.

Satyagraha (SAHT-yah-grah-hah) From Sanskrit *satya* "truth" and *agraha* "to persist." Nonviolent civil disobedience; a form of protest against British rule in India developed by Gandhi.

satyr play (SAY-ter) The light-hearted play that followed the trilogy of tragedies in performances at the Festival of Dionysus at Athens.

Saul of Tarsus (SOLL) The name of the apostle Paul before his conversion to Christianity c. 35 CE. Apostle and founder of the early Christian church. Author of several Epistles in the New Testament.

Savonarola, Girolamo (jee-RAW-luh-moe sav-uh-nuh-ROW-luh) 1452–1498 Dominican preacher and reformer who decried the moral decline of Florentine arts and culture.

scatting The singing of improvised "nonsense" syllables with no literal meaning, common in jazz.

scherzo (SCAIRT-soe) The Italian word for "joke." A light or playful musical segment, often in the second or third movements of a symphony or sonata.

Schliemann (SHLEE-mahn) Heinrich 1822–1890 CE German archaeologist who excavated the Bronze Age site of Mycenae.

Schönberg (Schoenberg), Arnold (SHUHRN-berg) 1874–1951 Austrian/later American composer, associated with German expressionist movement. Known for his pioneering innovations in atonality. He developed twelve-tone technique, a compositional method of manipulating an ordered series of all twelve notes in the chromatic scale. To vocal music he introduced the device *Sprechstimme* or "voiced speech."

Schopenhauer, Arthur (SHOW-pun-how-uhr) 1788–1860 German philosopher. He reacted against the idealism of Kant and Hegel. In *The World as Will and Representation* he argues that the dominating power in the world is evil, which is caused by the incessant conflicts arising between individual wills. His writings on psychology, aesthetics, ethics, and politics influenced Nietzsche, Wagner, and Sigmund Freud.

Schubert, Franz (FRAHNS SHOO-bert) 1797–1828 German composer. Composed over six hundred Lieder or "songs," exhibiting an astounding melodic ingenuity as well as the ability to communicate strong emotional depth within a short piece. Some of his finest music was written for small ensembles, *Trios for Piano, Violin and Cello, Op. 99*. Also of note is his two-movement Unfinished Symphony or Symphony No. 8 in B Minor.

Schütz, Heinrich (HINE-rick SHOOTS) 1584–1672 German composer. Composed a wide variety of oratorios and other sacred works, including *The Judgment of Solomon and Job*, *Psalms of David*, and *The Seven Last Words of Christ*.

Scopas (SKOE-puss) Greek sculptor. Creator of *Pothos* c. 350, his art emphasized emotion and intensity.

scriptorium (skrip-TOHR-ee-uhm) The monastic room used by monks for the copying of manuscripts and their study.

seal-stones Image cut into soft stone and used to authenticate a document or bundle of trade goods.

Sei Shonagon (say show-nah-gon) c. 1000 Japanese writer. Her journal or "pillow-book" recounts her observations of court society while serving Empress Teishi.

Seleucids (si-LOO-sids) 312–64 BCE Macedonian dynasty that controlled much of Asia Minor. Founded by Seleuces after the death of Alexander the Great.

Semites (adj. Semitic) A group of early Mesopotamian peoples, including the Akkadians, Babylonians, Assyrians, Phoenicians, and Hebrews, who spoke variations of the same language.

Seneca (SEN-uh-kuh) 8 BCE–65 CE Roman philosopher, tragic playwright, and stoic. Author of several essays on stoicism. He was ordered to commit suicide by his former pupil, Emperor Nero.

Senghor, Leopold (san-GORE) 1906–1989 African writer and statesman. He created the literary movement negritude. From 1960 to 1980 he was the president of Senegal.

Septuagint **(SEP-too-uh-jint)** Greek translation of the Old Testament made two centuries before Common Era.

Serialism, Twelve-tone technique A system of music based on an arrangement of the twelve notes of the chromatic scale, which remains fixed during a piece of music. In strict serialism, the only variations of this *row* or *series* permitted are *inversion* (the row turned upside down), *retrograde* (the row turned backward), and *retrograde inversion* (the backwards version of the row turned upside down).

Series See *serialism*.

Sermon on the Mount First major sermon delivered by Jesus. Also referred to as the Beatitudes.

Seven Liberal Arts The basic classic set of courses typically constituting education up to the university level made up of grammar, rhetoric, and dialects (the *trivium*) and arithmetic, geometry, music, and astronomy (the *quadrivium*).

Shang Dynasty (SHUNG) c. 1600–1100 BCE Ancient dynasty centered on eastern China. Earliest urban center in China with evidence of sophisticated bronze craftsmanship and a system of writing.

Shari'a (shah-REE-uh) The code of law that covers religious, civil, and criminal law. It is the law of the land in several Muslim countries.

shawabtis (shuh-WAB-teez) Small figurines representing servants, buried with the mummified body of their masters in ancient Egypt.

Shen Zhou (SHEN JOE) 1427–1509 Chinese painter and scholar. He painted landscapes, see *Poet on a Mountaintop*.

sheyk (SHEEK) from the Arabic word *shaykh* meaning "old man." The head of an Islamic religious order or head of an Arab family. Also a polite form of address for males.

Shih Huang-ti (shee wong tee) ruled 221–202 BCE Shih Huang-ti, a title meaning First Emperor, unified the Chinese states and established a centralized government. He ordered the building of the Great Wall, a defensive wall approximately 1,400 miles long. To quell dissent, he instigated the Burning of the Books, in which several philosophical writings were destroyed.

Shiite (SHEE-ite) One of the two main branches of Islam that recognizes Ali, son-in-law to Muhammad, as the prophet's lawful successor. *Compare Sunni*.

Shintoism (SHIN-toe-izm) Native Japanese religion, combining reverence for nature spirits, worship of the emperor, and reverence for one's ancestors.

Shogun (SHOW-gun) Official title of the Japanese emperor.

Shona (SHOW-nuh) One of the peoples now living in modern Zimbabwe, who may be the descendants of the inhabitants of the ancient kingdom of Zimbabwe.

Shostakovich, Dmitri (duh-MEE-tree SHAH-stuh-KOE-vitch) 1906–1976 Russian composer. He wrote fifteen symphonies, as well as violin, piano, and cello concertos, chamber music, and choral works.

sibyl (SIB-uhl) A woman of ancient times said to possess prophetic or divine powers.

Sikhism (SEEK-ism) Monotheistic religion founded in the 15th century in present northern western India and the Pakistani province of Punjab.

Sluter, Claus 14th century Flemish sculptor; one of his most impressive works, *The Well of Moses*, reveals a heightened realism and attention to the human form not common in Gothic statues of his time.

Socrates (SOK-ruh-teez) 469–399 BCE The most revered Greek philosopher who is best known for his question-and-answer method of philosophical investigation. He was executed in 399 BCE on charges of impiety and leading youth to question authority. Among his followers was Plato, whose *Dialogues* represent the only written record of Socrates' teachings.

Soliloquy (suh-LILL-uh-kwee) Speech made by characters in a play who utter their thoughts aloud, without addressing them to any other character.

Solon (SOE-luhn) c. 639–559 BCE Athenian legislator and poet who reformed the legal system.

sonata form, sonata allegro form A musical form evolved during the 18th century that became the basis of the first movement (and sometimes also the last) of a *sonata*.

sonata In the 17th century, a short instrumental piece. From the 18th century on, a piece of music for one or two instruments (piano sonata for solo piano, violin sonata for violin and piano, etc.) in several self-contained movements.

sonnet Short poem of fourteen lines.

Sophists (SOFF-ists) Traveling professional "philosophers" who taught their pupils, among other things, how to win arguments and debates.

Sophocles (SOFF-uh-kleez) 496–406 BCE Tragic poet whose plays include *Antigone* and *Oedipus the King*. In his *Poetics*, he explores the nature of tragedy.

Sorbon (soar-BUNN) 1258 CE Founded by Robert de Sorbon, it was originally a theological college, and later became the famous *La Sorbonne* or University of Paris.

Soyinka, Wole (WOE-lay sho-YEENG-kuh) b. 1934 Nigerian playwright, novelist, and poet. Winner of the Nobel Prize for literature in 1986 for *The Man Died*.

Sparta (SPAR-tuh) Ancient city in southern Greece that controlled the region of Laconia (luh-KOE-nee-uh).

Sprechstimme (SHPREKT-shtim-uh) A device invented by Schoenberg whereby a singer "speaks" musical notes rather than singing them in traditional style.

stele (STEE-lee) An upright stone slab decorated with relief carvings and frequently used as a grave marker.

Stigmata (stig-MAH-tuh) Marks on the body resembling the wounds of Christ during the crucifixion; said to occur during states of spiritual ecstasy.

Stoicism (STOE-uh-sizz-uhm) A philosophy, originally Greek, which held that the world was governed by Reason, and that Divine Providence watched over the virtuous.

Strauss, Richard (REE-kard STRAUSS) 1864–1949 German composer. His rich and innovative use of orchestration redefined conventional forms, conveying both the tragic and comedic through his symphonic poems, such as *Don Juan*, *Till Eulenspiegel*, and the *Alpine Symphony*. Also a leading 20th century opera composer, his highly dramatic operas delve into human psychology, as in the erotic and disturbing *Salomé*.

Stravinsky, Igor (EE-gor struh-VIN-skee) 1882–1971 Russian-born composer. Considered one of the innovators of modern music, his compositions are noted for extreme variations in dynamics and rhythm, alternating between intense excitement and release, as in his most famous ballets *The Rite of Spring* and *The Firebird*.

Stream of consciousness A literary technique that attempts to describe a character's or the author's thought processes, either of memory or perception of the outside world, without imposing structure.

Strozzi (STROT-see) A powerful banking family in Florence during the Renaissance with branches spread throughout Europe. Known for the famous Strozzi Palace in Florence.

studia (STOO dee ah) Latin for "schools." Fifteenth-century institutions throughout Italy where scholars taught and wrote.

***Studium* of Florence (STOO dee uhm)** A university in Renaissance Florence supported by Cosimo de' Meidici.

stupa (STOO-puh) A large Buddhist shrine, often in the form of a tower or mound.

Sturm und Drang (SHTOORM oont DRAHNG) German for "Storm and Stress." A late-18th century German literary school that rejected Neoclassicism and emphasized emotions and protest against established authority.

Style galant (guh-LAHNT) A style of elegant, lighthearted music popular in France in the early 18th century.

Sudraka c. 300–500 CE Indian king and playwright. Author of the play *The Little Clay Cart*.

Sufism (SOOF-izm) A mystical line of Islam that aims to lead its practitioners to a direct experience of God.

Suger Historian and patron of Gothic architecture. Abbot of Saint Denis between 1080 and 1152 CE.

suite In music, an instrumental composition of several parts (originally dances) in the same or a related key but of a different rhythm and mood. In ballet, an adaptation of a longer orchestral work for purposes of dance.

Sumerians (soo-MEER-ee-uhns) c. 3000 BCE Source of the oldest written texts and creators of Mesopotamian civilization centered in city-states.

Sunni (SOO-nee) A member of one of the two main branches of Islam that regards the first four caliphs as legitimate successors to Muhammad. Considered the more orthodox line of Islam, Sunnis follow the laws of the Sunna, based upon the words and actions of Muhammad. *Compare Shiite.*

sûra (pl. sûras) (SUR ah; SUR ahz) Arabic for "things enclosed"; used to denote the chapters in the *Qur'an*.

Swahili (swah-HEE-lee) An African language strongly influenced by Arabic, spoken by many of the inhabitants of East Africa.

Sweelinck, Jan Pieterszoon (jahn PEE-tuhrs SVAY-link) 1562–1621 Flemish composer. Wrote several vocal works, including a complete French psalter, motets, *chansons*, and Italian madrigals. Best known for his compositions for keyboard.

Swift, Jonathan 1667–1745 Irish satirical writer and political activist. His work exhibits a deep pessimism in man's ability to behave morally and rationally. His best-known work is *Gulliver's Travels*. In his shocking satirical essay, *A Modest Proposal*, he lays out a grim "solution" to the problem of the Irish poor.

symphonic poem, tone poem A piece of *program music* that tells a story in sound.

symphony A musical work in several self-contained movements, written for full orchestra; essentially a *sonata* for orchestra.

synthesis (SIN-thuh-siss) A philosophical theory developed by Hegel that aimed to achieve a balance between *thesis*, the world of humans, which he called "pure, infinite being," and *antithesis*, the world of nature.

T'ang Dynasty (TAHNG) 618–906 CE Known as China's Golden Age, this dynasty established a period of economic and political progress and stability, thus enabling fertile growth in Chinese arts and culture.

Taj Mahal (TAWJ muh-HALL) c. 1640 A mausoleum constructed from white marble located in Agra, India. Built by Shah Jahan for his deceased wife, Mumtaz.

Talmud (TAHL-muhd) The authoritative collection of ancient Jewish learning.

Tao (DOE) Translates from Chinese into "the way" or "the path."

Taoism (DOE-ism) A Chinese philosophical system furthered by the teachings of the philosopher Lao-tzu, which emphasizes the limitation of human perception and encourages simplicity, mystical contemplation, passivity, and freedom from desire.

tariqa (tah-REE-kuh) Persian word for "path." Used to describe the various Sufi orders.

Tarquinia (tar-KWIN-ee-uh) Ancient Etruscan city located in the province of Viterbo, Italy.

Telemachus (tuh-LEM-uh-kuss) Son of the legendary hero Odysseus.

tempera (TEM-puhr-uh) From Latin *tempere* or "to mix." A painting technique in which pigment is mixed with egg water.

Tempietto (tem-PYET-tow) "little chapel" in Italian. A building designed in 1502 by the Renaissance architect Donato Bramante. The Tempietto, inspired by classical temples, is in the courtyard of San Pietro in Montorio in Rome.

tempo The Italian word for "time." The speed, indicated by the composer, at which a piece of music should be performed.

tercet (tur-sit) A three-line stanza of a poem.

tesserae (TESS-er-ray) The small colored cubes that make up a mosaic.

testament Another word for covenant (see *covenant*).

tetrachord A unit of four musical tones, the first and last of which are a perfect fourth apart. (A combination of two tetrachords, eight consecutive notes, formed a musical mode.)

The British East India Trading Company 1600–1873 A commercial trading company chartered by Queen Elizabeth and given exclusive rights of trade between Britain and the Far East. In the 18th century it governed most of India.

The Enlightenment An 18th century philosophical movement founded upon the power of human reason, as opposed to divine will or faith. The period was marked by an assertion of individual rights, the emergence of democracy, and scientific innovation. Some influential thinkers during this period were Immanuel Kant, John Locke, and Voltaire.

The Left Bank A district renowned for being a student haunt located on the left bank of the Seine river in Paris. The location to which the arts branch of the University of Paris moved in 1210 CE.

Thebes (THEEBZ) Ancient city located in east-central Greece that controlled the region of Boeotia (bee-OH-shuh).

theme A short musical idea, or tune, that a composer can then vary and develop.

Theodora (thee-uh-DOR-uh) c. 547 CE Former dancer and prostitute, she became the wife of Emperor Justinian and alongside him, a devout and active Christian. Her image is represented in the mosaics of the church of San Vitale in Ravenna.

Theodoric (thee-AW-duh-rick) 424–526 CE Ruler of the Ostrogoths, Italy, and Visigoths; also known as "Theodoric the Great." He was an Arian Christian and ordered the execution of Boethius. He is interred in a mausoleum in Ravenna.

Thermopylae (ther-MOP-uh-lee) Site of heroic Spartan defense of the Greek mainland against a Persian attack.

theses (THEE-seez) Academic propositions that seek to establish the truth of statements.

thesis (THEE-siss) See *synthesis*.

tholos (THOE-loss) A circular building style that emerged in 4th century Greek architecture.

Thoreau, Henry David (thuh-ROW) 1817–1862 American writer. Model of Transcendentalism as recorded in his masterwork, *Walden*, and advocate of civil liberties, as evidenced in his essay *Civil Disobedience*.

Thucydides (thoo-SIDD-uh-deez) c. 460–400 BCE Greek historian; author of the *History of the Peloponnesian War*.

timpani See *kettle drums*.

Titian (TISH-uhn) c. 1477–1576 Italian painter. Trained and influenced by Giovanni Bellini. Like many Venetian painters of his day, his works depict the intense emotions of the subjects, vivid use of color, and a carefully balanced arrangement of figures to create energy and focus, see *Assumption of the Virgin*. His later paintings show a shift to secular themes, as in his sensual *Venus of Urbino*.

toccata (tow-KAH-tuh) A musical composition developed in the 16th century. Originally used to demonstrate the performer's technical accomplishments, these compositions often combined extreme technical complexity and dramatic expression.

toga (TOE-guh) Civil dress of male Roman citizens, made of a single piece of material draped to cover the whole person except for the head and right arm.

Togu na "Men's House of Words," used by the Dogon people for meetings of the male community assembly.

Tokugawa (tock-oo-gah-wah) 1603–1867 Japanese ruling family who consolidated power, creating the capital city Edo (present day Tokyo).

tonality The characteristic of most music written between the 17th and 20th centuries to be anchored around a fixed key and mode (i.e., major or minor), from which it can move but to which it eventually returns.

Torah (TOHR-uh) Hebrew word meaning "instruction" or "law." Also the name of the first five books of the Old Testament: Genesis, Exodus, Leviticus, Numbers, Deuteronomy.

Totalitarian Any political system that asserts total control over all aspects of public life and thought while disallowing any independent ideas to intervene.

trade fairs Periodic gatherings of merchants for buying, trading, and selling. In the Middle Ages, these fairs coincided with major religious holidays and were held roughly four times a year.

Transcendentalists An American literary school of the 19th century that emphasized the transcendental unity of humans and nature.

transept (TRAN-sept) Aisle intersecting the nave at one end of the basilica and covered by a pitched roof.

trecento (tray-CHEN-toe) Italian for three hundred. Generally used to refer to the 1300s, that is, the 14th century.

Tribonian (tri-BONE-ee-an) d. 454 ? Roman jurist who directed the compilation of Roman civil law, (*Corpus Juris Civilis*) under Justinian I.

tribune (tri-BYOON) Representative of the plebeians who could intervene with state officials on their behalf.

triglyph (TRY-gliff) Panel carved into three vertical bands, alternating with metopes on a Doric frieze.

trilogy A series of three tragic plays, either related or on separate themes, performed at the Athenian Festival of Dionysus.

Tripitaka (truh-PIT-ih-kuh) Buddhist priest and leading character in the 16th century Chinese novel *Monkey* by Wu Ch'eng-en.

triptych (TRIP-tik) Painting consisting of three separate panels.

Trojan War The legendary war between a confederation of Greeks and the city of Troy.

trope (TROHP) A word, phrase, or verse used as embellishment in medieval liturgical chant.

troubadours (TROO-buh-dohrs) Aristocratic southern French musicians of the Middle Ages, specialized in secular songs on themes of love and chivalry. Called *trouveres* in northern France. *Compare Minnesingers.*

trumeau (troo-MOE) The central supporting post of a portal.

tuba (TOO-buh) Long bronze trumpet used on public occasions and in battle.

Tulsi Das (tool-see DAHS) 1543–1623 Hindi poet, Sanskrit scholar, and philosopher. Considered the greatest Hindi poet, he wrote the epic poem *Ramcaritmanas* or "The Holy Lake of the Acts of Rama." His teachings influenced the development of Hinduism.

Tutankhamen (toot-ong-KAH-muhn) 1361–1352 BCE Egyptian pharaoh. Discovery of his tomb and its contents led to archheologists' revised and expanded knowledge of Egyptian culture.

twelve-bar blues The standard form of a traditional blues song. Textually, the sung lyric is a rhymed couplet, with the first line repeated. Musically, the first phrase establishes a melody, the second repeats it over a changing harmony, and the third presents both new melody and harmony.

Twelve-tone technique See *serialism.*

tympanum (TIM-puh-nuhm) The space above a portal, triangular or moon-shaped, often ornamented with sculpture.

typeface The carved pieces of letters used by printers to assemble a page for printing. The type varied according to design (e.g., italic or Roman).

tyrants A class of rich merchant traders who came into power in 5th century Greece.

Übermensch (OO-ber-mensh) Term invented by Nietzsche to describe a "superior human."

uncanonical Any form or idea that violates the agreed-on rule (canon) of the authentic or the generally accepted.

Universitas A guild or cooperative body. The academic *universitas* is the ancestor of the present-day university.

university Originally from the Latin word *universitas* meaning "whole or entire." An institution of higher learning that developed throughout Europe during the Middle Ages.

Upanishads (oo-PAH-ni-shahdz) before the 7th century c. 3300–1600 BCE Considered part of Vedas, these texts form the core of Vedantic Hinduism. They deal with philosophy, meditation, and the nature of God.

Urdu (OOR-doo) Official language of Pakistan, based on Hindi, Arabic, and Persian, created during the reign of Akbar.

Uruk (OO-rook) An ancient Sumerian city in southern Iraq.

usury (YOO-suh-ree) The practice of lending money and charging excessive interest rates.

Utrecht (YOO-trekt) City in the central Netherlands; a commercial and cultural center in the Middle Ages.

Utrecht Psalter **(YOO-trekt SAHL-tuhr)** c. 820–840 CE A lavishly illustrated psalm book that exemplifies the style common to early Christian art, in this case borrowing from the Byzantine and Celtic traditions.

van Gogh, Vincent (van GO) 1853–1890 Dutch painter. His early work reflected a concern for social problems, see *The Potato Eaters.* In later paintings, he used intense color, contrast, and bold strokes to create scenes of heightened intensity, see *The Night Café* and *Starry Night.* He painted numerous self-portraits and flowers.

Vasari, Giorgio (jor-joe vuh-ZARR-ee) 1511–1574 Italian writer, architect, and painter. Author of *Vite de' più eccellenti* *architetti, pittori e sculturi italiani*, later translated into English as Lives of the Artist. These biographies have served as a foundation for research on the Renaissance artists.

Vedas (VEY-duz) The corpus of Hindu sacred writings written in Sanskrit and gathered in four collections.

Velázquez Diego (DYAY-go vel-AHS-kez) 1599–1660 Spanish painter. He produced several portraits of Philip IV and his family. His masterpiece *Las Meninas* or "The Maids of Honor" depicts princess Margarita and her attendants. His portraiture shows attention to minute detail as well as an overall sense of unity and color.

vendetta (ven-DETT-uh) A feud in which revenge is taken for the murder of a family member or the member of one's clan. In English "blood for blood."

Verbiest, Ferdinand (fer-BEAST) 1623–1688 Flemish Jesuit missionary and astronomer in China. Head of Beijing's Astronomical Bureau.

Verdi, Giuseppe (joo-ZEP-pee VAIR-dee) 1813–1901 Preeminent opera composer. His three major masterpieces *Rigoletto*, *Il Trovatore*, and *La Traviata*, continue to be the most frequently performed operas. His early opera, *Nabucco*, which depicts the captivity of the Jews in Babylon, became associated with rising Italian nationalism. In 1887 he produced the opera *Othello*, based upon Shakespeare's play, now considered one of the supreme works in Italian opera.

Vermeer, Johannes (yo-HANN-iss ver-MEER) 1632–1675 Dutch painter. Later recognized as one of the principal artists of the Baroque period, his paintings show a unique vision and sensitivity through the depiction of his subjects in private repose and contemplation, as in *Woman Reading a Letter*.

Versailles (ver-SIGH) City just southwest of Paris. Location of the resplendent palace built in the mid-17th century under Louis XIV.

Villard de Honnecourt (vill-AR duh onn-eh-COOR) 13th century CE Architect and master builder whose portfolio of records, notes, and sketches provide insight into the concerns and techniques involved in cathedral building in his day.

Virgil (VUHR-juhl) 670–19 BCE (Full name: Publius Vergilius Maro) Roman poet. Author of the epic poem the *Aeneid*, an account of the travels and life of the hero, Aeneas. This work was considered an allegorical account of the origins of Rome. Lauded among the master poets, Virgil influenced later writers including Dante, Tasso, Milton, and T.S. Eliot.

virginal (VURH-juh-nuhl) Early keyboard instrument small enough to be placed on a table or the player's lap.

Vivaldi, Antonio (ahn-TOE-nee-oh vuh-VALL-dee) c. 1676–1741 Venetian composer of the Baroque period. Best known for his orchestral works, which are distinct for their strong contrasts between orchestra and solo instruments, *The Four Seasons*.

Voltaire (vol-TAIR) born **François Marie-Arouet** 1694–1778 French writer and philosopher. A zealous defender of religious and political freedom, the publication of his *Lettres philosophiques*, in which he criticized French religious and political systems, caused such an outrage that he was forced to flee Paris. He also wrote poems, plays, historical works, and novels. Best known is his novel, *Candide*, a satire on philosophical optimism.

volute (vuh-LOOT) Spiral design of an Ionic capital.

votive chapel (VOE-tiv) A small church built as fulfillment of a vow or a promise most usually dedicated to the Virgin Mary or one of the saints.

Vulgate Bible (VULL-gate) The Latin Bible translated by Saint Jerome in the 4th century, which was the normative text for the Western (Catholic) Church until modern times.

Wagner, Richard (REE-kard VAHG-nuhr) 1813–1883 German composer. Influential, revolutionary artist and thinker, he strived for a unified artistic expression called *Gesamtkunstwerk* or "complete work," which synthesized drama, philosophy, music, poetry, and movement. In his operas, he broke away from traditional structures of form and focus on the singers, emphasizing the orchestra. He introduced the *leitmotiv* or "leading motif." Some of his most acclaimed works include *The Ring*, a cycle of four separate music dramas.

Watteau, Jean-Antoine (jahn ahn-TWAN wah-TOE) 1684–1721 Greatest French rococo painter. Best known for his paintings of *fêtes galantes* or "elegant outdoor festivals." His works reveal a graceful nostalgia rendered in the rococo style, such as his *Pilgrimage to Cythera*.

Whitman, Walt 1819–1892 American Romantic poet. His *Leaves of Grass*, a collection of poems written throughout his life, expresses his deep personal impressions as well as his belief in the universality of human experience.

Wiesel, Elie (ELL-ee wih-ZELL) b. 1928 Jewish Romanian writer. His first novel, *Night*, was based on his life in a Nazi concentration camp. Other novels include *Dawn* and *Jews of Silence*. A principal force behind establishing the Holocaust Memorial Museum in Washington, DC. In 1986, he received the Nobel Peace Prize.

Winckelmann, Johann Joachim (YO-hann YO-ah-keem VING-kell-mahn) 1717–1768 German scholar. Called the Father of Archeology, his writings about discoveries made at Pompei and Hurculaneum reawakened interest in Classical art and antiquities.

woodcut A work produced by cutting away parts of a wooden block, which is then inked and printed.

Wordsworth, William 1770–1850 English poet. Coauthor (with Coleridge) of a collection of poems titled *Lyrical Ballads*, which contributed to the establishment of the Romantic Movement in English poetry. His writing reflected both his interest in humanity and love of the nature.

Xerxes (ZUHRK-seez) King of Persia who led the second attack against Greece and was ultimately defeated at the naval battle of Salamis (SALL-eh-mihs) in 480 BCE.

Yoruba (YORE-uh-buh) Members of a West African coastal people.

Zeus (zoos) The supreme ancient Greek deity. God of heaven.

ziggurat (ZIGG-oo-rat) Sumerian religious structure made of bricks built to form terraces.

Zimbabwe (Great) (zim-BAHB-way) c. 14th century stone ruins of a large palace or royal residence and court. Believed to be part of the kingdom of Monomotapa.

Zulu (ZOO-loo) Inhabitants of the northeast region of Natal Province, South Africa. Most are traditionally farmers and cattle raisers.

INDEX

Page numbers in italics refer to illustrations, photos illustrations, or tables.

CHAPTER 1—Photo 1.1: British Museum, London, UK//© Werner Forman/Art Resource, NY **1.2**: © Caves of Lascaux, Dordogne, France/ The Bridgeman Art Library **1.3**: Naturhistorisches Museum, Vienna, Austria//© Erich Lessing/Art Resource, NY **1.4 left**: Musée du Louvre, Paris, France//© Réunion des Musées Nationaux (J. Schorman)/Art Resource, NY **1.4 center**: Karnak, Thebes, Egypt//© Erich Lessing/Art Resource, NY **1.4 right**: Musée du Louvre (AO 3766), Paris, France//© Erich Lessing/Art Resource, NY **1.5**: Iraq Museum, Baghdad, Iraq//© Aladin Abdel Naby/Reuters/CORBIS **1.6**: Iraq Museum, Baghdad, Iraq//© Scala/Art Resource, NY **1.7**: Musée du Louvre, Paris, France//© Réunion des Musées Nationaux (Inv. SB 4)/Art Resource, NY **1.8 top**: © Topham/ The Image Works **1.9**: Image copyright © The Metropolitan Museum of Art/Art Resource, NY **1.10**: © Réunion des Musées Nationaux (Hervé Lewandowki)/Art Resource, NY **1.11**: © Werner Forman/Art Resource, NY **1.12**: © Valley of the Kings, Thebes, Egypt//Giraudon/The Bridgeman Art Library **1.13**: © Steve Vidler/SuperStock **1.14**: © The Art Archive/Egyptian Museum, Cairo, Egypt/Gianni Dagli Orti **1.15**: © British Museum, London, UK/The Bridgeman Art Library **1.16**: Aegyptisches Museum, Staatliche Museen zu Berlin, Berlin, Germany//© Bildarchiv Preussischer Kulturbesitz/Art Resource, NY **1.17**: Ägyptisches Museum, Staatliche Museen zu Berlin, Berlin, Germany//© Bildarchiv Preussischer Kulturbesitz (Margarete Büsing)/Art Resource, NY **1.18**: © François Guenet/Art Resource, NY **1.19**: Egyptian Museum, Cairo, Egypt//© François Guenet/Art Resource, NY **1.20**: ©Vanni/Art Resource, NY **1.21**: National Archaeological Museum (Inv. 6167), Athens, Greece//© Erich Lessing/Art Resource, NY **1.22**: British Museum (Inv. 18,630,213.10), London, UK//© British Museum/Art Resource, NY **1.23**: ©Vanni/Art Resource, NY **1.24**: © Gail Mooney/CORBIS **1.25**: Private Collection, Paris, France/© The Art Archive/Gianni Dagli Orti **1.26**: © The Art Archive/Heraklion Museum, Crete, Greece/Gianni Dagli Orti **1.27**: National Archaeological Museum, Athens, Greece//© The Art Archive/Gianni Dagli Orti **1.28**: Archaeological Museum, Heraklion, Greece//© Leonard Von Matt/Photo Researchers, Inc. **1.29**: National Archaeological Museum, Athens, Greece//© Nimatallah/Art Resource, NY **1.30**: © Kevin Fleming/CORBIS

CHAPTER 2—Photo 2.1: Antikensammlung, Staatliche Museen zu Berlin (Inv F1855), Berlin, Germany//© Bildarchiv Preussischer Kulturbesitz (Johannes Laurentius)/Art Resource, NY **2.2**: National Archaeological Museum, Athens, Greece//© Nimatallah/Art Resource, NY **2.3**: National Archaeological Museum, Athens, Greece//© Nimatallah/Art Resource, NY **2.4**: © Benaki Museum, Athens, Greece, Gift of Georgios and Athanasia Pappas/The Bridgeman Art Library **2.5**: Museo Archeologico, Florence, Italy//© Scala/Art Resource, NY **2.6**: © The Art Archive/Archaeological Museum, Gela, Sicily, Italy/ Gianni Dagli Orti **2.7**: The Metropolitan Museum of Art, New York, NY, USA//Image copyright © The Metropolitan Museum of Art/Art Resource, NY **2.8**: National Archaeological Museum, Athens, Greece//© Scala/Art Resource, NY **2.9**: Acropolis Museum (Inv. 624), Athens, Greece//© Nimatallah/Art Resource, NY **2.10**: Acropolis Museum (Inv. 679), Athens, Greece//© Nimatallah/Art Resource, NY **2.11**: © The Art Archive/National Museum, Palermo, Italy/Gianni Dagli Orti

2.12: National Archaeological Museum, Athens, Greece//© Scala/Art Resource, NY **2.13**: Acropolis Museum, Athens, Greece//© Nimatallah/Art Resource, NY **2.14**: © Musée des Beaux-Arts et D'Archeologie, Boulogne, France//Giraudon/The Bridgeman Art Library **2.15**: Musée du Louvre (Inv: C 103), Paris, France//© Erich Lessing/Art Resource, NY **2.16**: ©Vanni/Art Resource, NY **2.17**: Artwork by John Burge **2.18**: Musée du Louvre, Paris, France//© Erich Lessing/Art Resource, NY **2.19**: Antikensammlung (Inv. F2285 B), Staatliche Museen zu Berlin, Berlin, Germany// © Bildarchiv Preussischer Kulturbesitz (Johannes Laurentius)/Art Resource, NY **2.20**: Musée du Louvre (Inv. G 136), Paris, France//© Erich Lessing/Art Resource, NY

CHAPTER 3—Photo 3.1: Musée du Louvre (G 372), Paris, France//© Réunion des Musées Nationaux (Hervé Lewandowski)/Art Resource, NY **3.2**:Vatican Museums,Vatican State//© Bildarchiv Preussischer Kulturbesitz (Alfredo Dagli Orti)/Art Resource, NY **3.3**: © Erich Lessing/Art Resource, NY **3.4**: Kunsthistorisches Museum (Inv. IV 3725),Vienna, Austria//© Erich Lessing/Art Resource, NY **3.5**: Museo Nazionale Romano (Terme di Diocleziano), Rome, Italy//© Scala/Art Resource, NY **3.6**: Museo Archeologico Nazionale, Reggio Calabria, Italy//© Scala/Art Resource, NY **3.7**: Museo Archeologico Nazionale, Naples, Italy// © Scala/Art Resource, NY **3.8**: National Archaeological Museum, Athens, Greece//© Nimatallah/Art Resource, NY **3.9**: Archaeological Museum of Rhodes, Greece//© Wolfgang Kaehler/CORBIS **3.10**: © Interfoto Pressebildagentur/Alamy **3.11**: Archaeological Museum, Olympia, Greece//© Joan Swinnerton/Alamy **3.12 left**: © The Art Archive/ Agora Museum, Athens, Greece/Gianni Dagli Orti **3.12 right**: ©Yann Arthus-Bertrand/CORBIS **3.13** Photograph © William Katz/Photo Researchers, Inc. **3.14**: British Museum, London, UK// © Grant Rooney/Alamy **3.15**: © British Museum, London, UK/The Bridgeman Art Library **3.16**: © British Museum, London, UK/The Bridgeman Art Library **3.17**: © Scala/Art Resource, NY **3.18**: © Altrendo Travel/Getty Images **3.19**: ©Vergina, Macedonia, Greece/The Bridgeman Art Library **3.20**: Archaeological Museum, Olympia, Greece// © Scala/ Art Resource, NY **3.21**: Museo Nazionale Romano (Terme di Diocleziano), Rome, Italy//© Alinari/Art Resource, NY **3.22**:Vatican Museums,Vatican State (Rome, Italy)//© Canali Photobank, Milan/SuperStock **3.23**: © Robert Everts/Getty Images **3.24**: Archaeological Museum, Istanbul, Turkey//© Erich Lessing/Art Resource, NY **3.25**: © Mary Evans Picture Library/Everett Collection **3.26**: Antikensammlung, Staatliche Museen zu Berlin, Berlin, Germany//© Bildarchiv Preussischer Kulturbesitz/Art Resource, NY **3.27**: Antikensammlung, Staatliche Museen zu Berlin, Berlin, Germany//© Erich Lessing/Art Resource, NY **3.28**: Museo Pio Clementino,Vatican Museums,Vatican State//© Scala/Art Resource, NY

CHAPTER 4—Photo 4.1: Museo Nazionale Romano (Terme di Diocleziano), Rome, Italy// © Scala/Art Resource, NY **4.2**: © The Art Archive/Gianni Dagli Orti **4.3**: Musei Capitolini, Rome, Italy//© Scala/Art Resource, NY **4.4**: Museo Nazionale di Villa Giulia, Rome, Italy// © Araldo de Luca/CORBIS **4.5**:Tomb of Hunting and Fishing, Tarquinia, Italy//© SEF/Art Resource, NY **4.6**: Museo Etrusco Guarnacci, Volterra, Italy//© Scala/Art Resource, NY **4.7**: © 1994 Richard T. Nowitz/Photo Researchers, Inc. **4.8**: Galleria degli Uffizi, Florence, Italy//

© Alinari/Art Resource, NY **4.9** Artwork by John Burge **4.10**: Museo Nazionale Romano (Terme di Diocleziano), Rome, Italy//© Scala/Art Resource, NY **4.11**: © Ara Pacis (Altar of Peace), Rome, Italy/The Bridgeman Art Library **4.12**: Museum of the Ara Pacis, Rome, Italy//© Scala/Art Resource, NY **4.13**: Braccio Nuovo,Vatican Museums,Vatican State//© Scala/Art Resource, NY **4.14**: © O. Louis Mazzatenta/National Geographic/Getty Images **4.15**: © G. R. Richardson/ Getty Images **4.16**: © Leonard Von Matt/Photo Researchers, Inc. **4.17**: Museo Archeologico Nazionale, Naples, Italy//© Erich Lessing/Art Resource, NY **4.18**:Villa of the Mysteries, Pompeii, Italy//© Scala/ArtResource, NY **4.19**: © Scala/Art Resource, NY **4.20**: Museo della Civilta Romana, Rome, Italy//© Scala/Art Resource, NY **4.21**: © Erich Lessing/Art Resource, NY **4.23 left** © PictureNet/CORBIS **4.23 right**: © Scala/Ministero per i Beni e le Attività Culturali/Art Resource, NY **4.26**: © DeA Picture Library (S.Vannini)/Art Resource, NY **4.27**: Museo della Civilta Romana, Rome, Italy//© Scala/Art Resource, NY **4.28**: Forum Romanum, Rome, Italy//© Scala/Art Resource, NY **4.29**: Palazzo dei Conservatori, Rome, Italy//© Scala/Art Resource, NY **4.31**: © Alinari/Art Resource, NY

CHAPTER 5—Photo 5.1: © The Art Archive/ Musée Guimet, Paris, France/Gianni Dagli Orti **5.2**: National Museum, New Delhi, India//© Borromeo/Art Resource, NY **5.3**: © Archaeological Museum, Sarnath, Uttar Pradesh, India//Dinodia/ The Bridgeman Art Library **5.4**: Parsvanath Temple, Khajuraho, Madhya Pradesh, India//© Adam Woolfitt/CORBIS **5.5**: © Horniman Museum, London, UK//The Bridgeman Art Library **5.6**: Musée des Arts Asiatiques-Guimet, Paris, France//© Réunion des Musées Nationaux (Arnaudet)/Art Resource, NY **5.7**: Museum fuer Asiatische Kunst (Inv. MIK I 72), Staatliche Museen zu Berlin, Berlin, Germany//© Bildarchiv Preussischer Kulturbesitz (Jürgen Liepe)/Art Resource, NY **5.8**: Lahore Museum, Lahore, Pakistan//© Scala/Art Resource, NY **5.9**: © The Art Archive/Hunan Provincial Museum, Changsha, China/Laurie Platt Winfrey **5.10**: © Mary Evans Picture Library/Alamy **5.11**: © Steve Vidler/SuperStock **5.12**: Xian, Shaanxi Province, China//© Gavin Hellier/Getty Images **5.13**: Musée des Arts Asiatiques-Guimet (Inv. MG 18435), Paris, France//© Réunion des Musées Nationaux (Thierry Ollivier)/Art Resource, NY **5.14**: Gansu Provincial Museum, Lanzhou, Peoples Republic of China//© Lauros-Giraudon, Paris/ SuperStock **5.15**: © Werner Forman Archive/ Topham/The Image Works **5.16**: National Palace Museum, Taipei, Taiwan//© Werner Forman/Art Resource, NY **5.17**: © Liu Xiaoyang/Alamy **5.18**: National Palace Museum, Taipei, Taiwan//© Werner Forman/Art Resource, NY

CHAPTER 6—Photo 6.1: S. Marco,Venice, Italy//© Cameraphoto Arte,Venice/Art Resource, NY **6.3**: © Werner Forman/Art Resource, NY **6.4**: Catacombs of Domitilla, Rome, Italy//Photo © Held Collection/The Bridgeman Art Library **6.5**: Catacomb of Priscilla, Rome, Italy//© Scala/Art Resource, NY **6.6**: Museo Pio Cristiano,Vatican Museums,Vatican State//© Scala/Art Resource, NY **6.7**: Museo Lateranense,Vatican Museums, Vatican State//© Alinari/Art Resource, NY **6.8**: © British Museum, London, Great Britain// HIP/Art Resource, NY **6.9**: © The Art Archive/ Archaeological Museum, Sousse, Tunisia/Gianni Dagli Orti **6.10**: © Princeton University Press/Art Resource, NY **6.11**: Artwork by John Burge **6.12**:

Resource, NY **18.22**: The Museum of Modern Art (472.1941), New York, NY, USA//Digital Image © The Museum of Modern Art/Licensed by Scala/Art Resource, NY **18.23**: Yale University Art Gallery (1961.18.34), New Haven, Connecticut, USA//© Yale University Art Gallery/Art Resource, NY **18.24**: Musée d'Orsay, Paris, France//© Réunion des Musées Nationaux (Gérard Blot)/Art Resource, NY **18.25**: © 2009 Succession H, Matisse, Paris/Artists Rights Society (ARS), New York. Digital image © The Barnes Foundation, Merion, Pennsylvania, USA/The Bridgeman Art Library **18.26**: © 2009 Succession H. Matisse, Paris/Artists Rights Society (ARS), New York. The Museum of Modern Art (8.1949), New York, NY, USA//Digital Image © The Museum of Modern Art/Licensed by Scala/Art Resource, NY **18.27**: National Gallery, Oslo, Norway/Copyright © 2009 The Munch Museum/The Munch-Ellingsen Group/Artists Rights Society (ARS), New York//Digital image ©Scala/Art Resource, NY **18.28**: © Stephanie Colasanti/CORBIS **18.29**: Hamburger Kunsthalle (Inv. 2948), Hamburg, Germany. © 2009 Artists Rights Society (ARS), New York/VG Bild-Kunst, Bonn//Digital image © Bildarchiv Preussischer Kulturbesitz (Elke Walford)/Art Resource, NY **18.30**: © Nolde-Stiftung Seebuell, Neukirchen, Germany//Private Collection/The Bridgeman Art Library **18.31**: Museum der Bildenden Kuenste, Leipzig, Germany//© Erich Lessing/Art Resource, NY **18.32**: Vienna State Opera, Vienna, Austria//© Erich Lessing/Art Resource, NY **18.33**: Performing Arts Dance Division The New York Public Library, New York, NY, USA//© The New York Public Library/Art Resource, NY

CHAPTER 19—Photo 19.1: © Private Collection//Dinodia/The Bridgeman Art Library **19.2**: © Brian A. Vikander/CORBIS **19.3**: Musée des Arts Asiatiques-Guimet (Inv. 3676B), Paris, France//© Réunion des Musées Nationaux (D. Arnaudet)/Art Resource, NY **19.4**: Victoria and Albert Museum (Inv. IS.2-1896 22-117), London, UK//© Victoria & Albert Museum, London/Art Resource, NY **19.5**: © British Library, London, UK/The Art Archive **19.6**: Bibliothèque Nationale, Paris, France//© Giraudon/Art Resource, NY **19.7**: © Indianapolis Museum of Art, USA, Bequest of Mrs Enid Goodrich/The Bridgeman Art Library **19.8**: Museum of Fine Arts, Boston, MA, USA//Image © Burstein Collection/CORBIS **19.9**: Victoria and Albert Museum (Inv. FE.4-1974), London, UK//© Victoria & Albert Museum, London/Art Resource, NY **19.10**: © age fotostock/SuperStock **19.11**: Victoria and Albert Museum (Inv. D.90-1898), London, UK//© Victoria & Albert Museum, London/Art Resource, NY **19.12**: Musée des Arts Asiatiques-Guimet, Paris, France//© Réunion des Musées Nationaux (Richard Lambert)/Art Resource, NY **19.13**: Musée des Arts Asiatiques-Guimet (Inv. MA 887), Paris, France//© Réunion des Musées Nationaux (Daniel Arnaudet)/Art Resource, NY **19.14**: © Panorama Media (Beijing/Chai Zhirong) Ltd./Alamy **19.15**: © Private Collection/The Bridgeman Art Library **19.16**: © Scala/Art Resource, NY **19.17**: © The Art Archive/Private Collection Paris/Gianni Dagli Orti **19.18**: Kawabata Yusanari of Kanagawa prefecture, Japan//© Sakamoto Photo Research Laboratory/CORBIS **19.19**: © The Detroit Institute of Arts, USA, Founders Society Purchase/The Bridgeman Art Library **19.20**: Private Collection//© Art Resource, NY **19.21**: Mingei International Museum, San Diego, California, USA//© Mingei International Museum/Art Resource, NY

CHAPTER 20—Photo 20.1: © Raveendran/AFP/Getty Images **20.2**: © British Museum, London, UK/The Bridgeman Art Library **20.3**: National Museum, Lagos, Nigeria//Photo © Held Collection/The Bridgeman Art Library **20.4**: © British Museum, London, UK/The Bridgeman Art Library **20.5**: © SuperStock, Inc./SuperStock **20.6**: Private Collection, New York, NY, USA//© Werner Forman/Art Resource, NY **20.7**: Ameri-

can Museum of Natural History, New York, NY, USA//© Werner Forman/Art Resource, NY **20.8 left & right**: © Charles & Josette Lenars/CORBIS **20.9**: © Wendy Stone/CORBIS **20.10**: © Indianapolis Museum of Art, USA, Gift of the Alliance of the Indianapolis Museum of Art/The Bridgeman Art Library **20.11**: © Torlett Svensson/CORBIS **20.12**: Copyright © 2009 Estate of Pablo Picasso/Artists Rights Society (ARS), New York/Digital image © Art Resource, NY

CHAPTER 21—Photo 21.1: © Biophoto Associates/Photo Researchers, Inc. **21.2**: Schomburg Center for Research in Black Culture, The New York Public Library, New York, NY, USA//Copyright © Aaron Douglas. Courtesy of the Aaron and Alta Sawyer Douglas Foundation/Digital image © Schomburg Center/Art Resource, NY **21.3**: The Museum of Modern Art, Gift of Richard S. Zeisler. (287.1986), New York, NY, USA//Copyright © 2009 Artists Rights Society (ARS), New York/ADAGP, Paris//Digital image © The Museum of Modern Art/Licensed by Scala/Art Resource, NY **21.4**: The Museum of Modern Art, New York, NY, USA//Copyright ©2009 Estate of Pablo Picasso/Artist Rights Society (ARS), New York/Digital image ©The Museum of Modern Art/Licensed by SCALA/Art Resource, NY **21.5**: Copyright © 2009 Artists Rights Society (ARS), New York/ADAGP, Paris//Digital image © Kunstmuseum, Basel, Switzerland//Giraudon/The Bridgeman Art Library **21.6**: Art Institute of Chicago, IL, USA//Copyright © 2009 Estate of Pablo Picasso/ Artists Rights Society (ARS), New York//Digital image © Art Institute of Chicago, IL/AKG, Berlin/SuperStock **21.7**: The Museum of Modern Art, New York, NY, USA//Copyright © 2009 Estate of Pablo Picasso/Artists Society (ARS), New York//Digital image © The Museum of Modern Art/Licensed by SCALA/Art Resource, NY **21.8**: Musée National d'Art Moderne (AM1988-221), Centre Georges Pompidou, Paris, France//Copyright © 2009 Artists Rights Society (ARS), New York/ADAGP, Paris//Digital image © Bertrand Prévost//CNAC/MNAM//Réunion des Musées Nationaux/Art Resource, NY **21.9**: Museo Nacional Centro de Arte Reina Sofia, Madrid, Spain//Copyright © 2009 Estate of Pablo Picasso/Artists Rights Society (ARS), New York//Digital image © Erich Lessing/Art Resource, NY **21.10**: Musée National d'Art Moderne, Centre Georges Pompidou, Paris, France//Copyright © 2009 Artists Rights Society (ARS), New York/ADAGP, Paris//Digital image © Erich Lessing/Art Resource, NY **21.11**: Private Collection//Copyright © 2009 Artists Rights Society (ARS), New York/ADAGP, Paris/Succession Marcel Duchamp//Digital Image © Cameraphoto Arte, Venice/Art Resource, NY **21.12**: The Museum of Modern Art, New York, NY, USA//Copyright © 2009 Salvador Dali, Gala-Salvador Dali Foundation/Artists Rights Society (ARS), New York//Digital Image © The Museum of Modern Art/Licensed by SCALA /Art Resource, NY **21.13**: Tate Gallery, London, UK//Copyright © C. Herscovici, London/Artists Rights Society (ARS), New York//Digital image © Tate Gallery, London/Art Resource, NY **21.14**: The Museum of Modern Art, New York, NY, USA//Copyright © 2009 Artists Rights Society (ARS), New York/VG Bild-Kunst, Bonn//Digital image © The Museum of Modern Art/Licensed by SCALA/Art Resource, NY **21.15**: © Getty Images **21.16**: Musée National d'Art Moderne, Centre Georges Pompidou, Paris, France//Copyright © 2009 Estate of Pablo Picasso/Artists Rights Society (ARS), New York/Digital image © CNAC/MNAM/Réunion des Musées Nationaux/Art Resource, NY **21.17**: Goskino/The Kobal Collection **21.18**: Olympia-Film/The Kobal Collection **21.19**: The Metropolitan Museum of Art, New York, NY, USA. Purchase, Marlene Nathan Meyerson Family Foundation Gift, in memory of David Nathan Meyerson; and Pat and John Rosenwald and Lila Acheson Wallace Gifts, 1999

(1999.237.4)//© Walker Evans Archive, The Metropolitan Museum of Art//Image copyright © The Metropolitan Museum of Art/Art Resource, NY **21.20**: © Vanni/Art Resource, NY

CHAPTER 22—Photo 22.1: © Andrew Lambert Photography/SPL./Photo Researchers, Inc. **22.2**: Art Institute of Chicago, IL, USA//Friends of American Art Collection (1942.51). Photography (Robert Hashimoto) © The Art Institute of Chicago. **22.3**: Philadelphia Museum of Art (Gift of Wright S. Ludington, 1951), Philadelphia, Pennsylvania, USA//Art copyright © Estate of Ben Shahn/Licensed by VAGA, New York, NY//Digital image © The Philadelphia Museum of Art/Art Resource, NY **22.4**: The Museum of Modern Art (556.1990), New York, NY, USA. Bequest of Georgia O'Keeffe//Copyright © 2009 Georgia O'Keeffe Museum/Artists Rights Society (ARS), New York//Digital Image © The Museum of Modern Art/Licensed by SCALA/Art Resource, NY **22.5**: The Museum of Modern Art (77.1950), New York, NY, USA//Copyright © 2009 The Pollock-Krasner Foundation/Artists Rights Society (ARS), New York//Digital Image © The Museum of Modern Art/Licensed by SCALA/Art Resource, NY **22.6**: The Museum of Modern Art (Charles Mergentime Fund 155.1970), New York, NY, USA//Art copyright © Dedalus Foundation, Inc./Licensed by VAGA, New York, NY//Digital image © The Museum of Modern Art/Licensed by SCALA/Art Resource, NY **22.7**: Copyright © 2009 Kate Rothko Prizel & Christopher Rothko/Artists Rights Society (ARS), New York. Digital image courtesy of the Rothko Chapel. **22.8**: The Detroit Institute of Arts, USA//Copyright © 2008 Helen Frankenthaler//Photograph, The Detroit Institute of Arts Founders Purchase, Dr & Mrs Hilbert H. DeLawter Fund/ The Bridgeman Art Library **22.9** The Museum of Modern Art (Gift of Jo Carole and Ronald S. Lauder, Agnes Gund, and Arne Glimcher 212.2006.a-e), New York, NY, USA//Copyright © Elizabeth Murray, Courtesy PaceWildenstein, New York//Digital Image © The Museum of Modern Art/Licensed by SCALA/Art Resource, NY **22.10**: The Museum of Modern Art, New York, NY, USA (Gift of Philip Johnson in honor of Alfred H. Barr, Jr. 106.1973)//Art © Jasper Johns/Licensed by VAGA, New York, NY//Digital image © The Museum of Modern Art/Licensed by SCALA/Art Resource, NY **22.11**: Moderna Museet, Statens Kunstmuseer, Stockholm, Sweden//Art copyright © Robert Rauschenberg/Licensed by VAGA, New York, NY//Digital image SuperStock **22.12**: Copyright © 2009 The Andy Warhol Foundation for the Visual Arts/Artists Rights Society (ARS), New York//Image © The Andy Warhol Foundation, Inc./Art Resource, NY **22.13**: Tate Gallery, London, UK//Copyright © 2009 Frank Stella/Artists Rights Society (ARS), New York//Digital image © Tate, London/Art Resource, NY **22.14**: Yale University Art Gallery (Charles B. Benenson, B.A. 1933, Collection 2006.52.45), New Haven, Connecticut, USA//Copyright © Philip Pearlstein//Digital image © Yale University Art Gallery/Art Resource, NY **22.15**: © 2009 Alfred Leslie. All rights reserved. Digital Image SuperStock **22.16**: Smithsonian American Art Museum, Washington, DC, USA//Art copyright © Romare Bearden Foundation/Licensed by VAGA, New York, NY//Digital Image © Smithsonian American Art Museum, Washington, DC/Art Resource, NY **22.17**: hiladelphia Museum of Art (Fund W. B. Dixon Stroud, 1992), Philadelphia, PA, USA//Copyright © 1990 Faith Ringgold//Digital image The Philadelphia Museum of Art/Art Resource, NY **22.18**: The Museum of Modern Art (acquired through the Mr. and Mrs. Victor Ganz, Mr. and Mrs. Donald H. Peters, and Mr. and Mrs. Charles Zadok Funds 361.1980), New York, NY, USA//Copyright © 2009 Frank Stella/Artists Rights Society (ARS), New York//Digital Image © The Museum of Modern Art/Licensed by SCALA/Art Resource, NY **22.19**: Albright-Knox Art Gallery,

LITERARY CREDITS

CHAPTER 1—Page 10: From *The Law Code of Hammurabi*. Copyright University of Chicago Press. Reprinted by permission. **Page 18**: Cottrell, Leonard. From *Life Under the Pharaohs*. Henry Holt and Company, 1960. Copyright © 1960 by Leonard Cottrell. All rights reserved. Reproduced by permission of Henry Holt and Company, LLC, and the author. **Page 18**: Cottrell, Leonard. From *Life Under the Pharaohs*. Henry Holt and Company, 1960. Copyright © 1960 by Leonard Cottrell. All rights reserved. Reproduced by permission of Henry Holt and Company, LLC, and the author. **Page 18**: Mertz, Barbara. From *Temples, Tombs, and Hieroglyphs*. William Morrow, 1978. © 1964, 1978. Reproduced by permission of HarperCollins Publishers Inc, and MPM Manor Inc.

CHAPTER 2—Page 36: Excerpt from *The Iliad* by Homer, translated by Richard Lattimore, copyright 1951 from books XVIII, XXIII, XV, XXIV. Copyright © 1951 by The University of Chicago. All rights reserved.

CHAPTER 3—Page 78: Herondas. From *Greek Literature in Translation*, translated by George Howe & Gustave Adolphus Harrer. HarperCollins, 1924. Reprinted by permission of Marcella Harrer.

CHAPTER 7—Page 156: Reprinted by permission of the publishers and the Trustees of the Loeb Classical Library from *Procopius: Volume I*, Loeb Classical Library®, Volume 48, translated by H. B. Dewing, Cambridge, Mass.: Harvard University Press, 1914. The Loeb Classical Library® is a registered trademark of the President and Fellows of Harvard College.

CHAPTER 10—Page 227: Extracts from the modern-verse translation of *The Canterbury Tales* by David Wright (copyright © Estate of David Wright 1985) are reproduced by permission of PFD (www.pfd.co.uk) on behalf of the Estate of David Wright.

CHAPTER 14—Page 328: From *Women of the Reformation in Germany and Italy* by Roland H. Bainton, copyright © 1971 Augsburg Fortress Press. Used by permission of Augsburg Fortress Press.

CHAPTER 15—Page 366: From *Born Under Saturn* by Giambattista Passeri, translated by Rudolf & Margot Wittkower, © 1963 by Rudolf & Margot Wittkower. Used by permission of Random House, Inc.

CHAPTER 18—Page 487: Letter of Gustav Mahler to his wife from *Letters of Composers* by G. Norman and M. L. Shrifte. A. A. Knopf, 1946. Copyright © 1946 by A. A Knopf. All rights reserved. Reproduced by permission.

CHAPTER 19—Page 507: From *Emperor of China* by Jonathan D. Spence. Copyright © 1974 by Jonathan D. Spence. Used by permission of Alfred A. Knopf, a division of Random House, Inc.

CHAPTER 21—Page 534: Reprinted with the permission of Scribner, a Division of Simon & Schuster Adult Publishing Group, from *The Collected Poems of W. B. Yeats, Volume I, The Poems*, Revised, edited by Richard J. Finneran. Copyright © 1924 by Macmillan Publishing Company; copyright renewed © 1952 by Bertha Georgie Yeats. Reproduced by permission of Simon & Schuster and A P Watt Ltd on behalf of Grainne Yeats.

CHAPTER 22—Page 597: By William Carlos Williams from *Collected Poems 1939–1962*, Volume II, copyright 1953 by William Carlos Williams. Reprinted by permission of New Directions Publishing Corp. and Carcanet Press Limited.